Encyclopedia of Democratic Thought

Encyclopedia of Democratic Thought

Edited by Paul Barry Clarke
and Joe Foweraker

London and New York

First published 2001
by Routledge
11 New Fetter Lane, London EC4P 4EE

Simultaneously published in the USA and Canada
by Routledge
29 West 35th Street, New York, NY 10001

Routledge is an imprint of the Taylor & Francis Group
©2001 Routledge

Typeset in Times by Taylor & Francis Books Ltd
Printed and bound in Great Britain by TJ International, Padstow, Cornwall

British Library Cataloguing in Publication Data
A catalogue record for this book is available from the British Library

Library of Congress Cataloging in Publication Data
Encyclopedia of democratic thought/edited by Paul Barry Clarke and Joe Foweraker.
Includes bibliographical references and index.
1. Democracy–Encyclopedias. I. Clarke, Paul A. B. II. Foweraker, Joe.
JC423 .E54 2001
321.8'03–dc21 00-045740

ISBN 0–415–19396–6

Contents

Consultant editors

List of contributors

Richard Alba
Department of Sociology, State University of New York, Albany, USA

Carol Lee Bacchi
Department of Politics, University of Adelaide, Australia

Benjamin Barber
Walt Whitman Center for the Culture and Politics of Democracy, Rutgers University, USA

Norman Barry
Department of Politics, University of Buckingham, UK

Frank R. Baumgartner
Political Science Department, Pennsylvania State University, USA

Kathleen Bawn
Department of Political Science, University of California, Los Angeles, USA

David Beetham
Institute for Politics and International Studies, University of Leeds, UK

Ronald Beiner
Department of Political Science, University of Toronto, Canada

Richard Bellamy
Department of Politics, University of Reading, UK

Ted Benton
Department of Sociology, University of Essex, UK

Hugh Berrington
Politics Department, Newcastle University, UK

Sarah Birch
Department of Government, University of Essex, UK

Jean Blondel
Robert Schuman Centre, European University Institute, Italy

Joan Price Boase
Department of Political Science, University of Toronto, Canada

John Brigham
Department of Political Science, University of Massachusetts at Amherst, USA

Ian Budge
Department of Government, University of Essex, UK

Simon Caney
Department of Politics, University of Newcastle, UK

Margaret Canovan
Department of Politics, University of Keele, UK

Ann Capling
Department of Political Science, University of Melbourne, Australia

Hiram Caton
Emeritus Professor of Humanities, Griffith University, Australia

Helena Catt
Department of Political Studies, University of Auckland, New Zealand

Joseph Chan
Department of Politics and Public Administration, The University of Hong Kong, Hong Kong

Paul Barry Clarke
Department of Government, University of Essex, UK

Susan E. Clarke
Center for Public Policy Research, University of Colorado, Boulder, USA

Anthony M. Clohesy
Department of Government, University of Essex, UK

Jean Louise Cohen
Department of Political Science, Columbia University, USA

List of contributors

Ruth B. Collier
Department of Political Science, University of California, Berkeley, USA

Ivor Crewe
Department of Government, University of Essex, UK

Robert Dahl
Department of Political Science, Yale University, USA

Alastair Davidson
Politics Department, Monash University, Australia

Malcolm Deas
St Antony's College, Oxford University, UK

Peter deLeon
Graduate School of Public Affairs, University of Colorado at Denver, USA

Larry Diamond
Hoover Institution, Stanford University, USA

Andrew Dobson
Department of Politics, University of Keele, UK

Lynn Dobson
Department of Government, University of Essex, UK

Peter Dorey
School of European Studies, University of Cardiff, Wales, UK

Keith Dowding
Department of Government, London School of Economics and Political Science, UK

James Dunkerley
Institute of Latin American Studies, London, UK

Mark A. Evans
Department of Politics, University of Wales, Swansea, UK

Joe Foweraker
Department of Government, University of Essex, UK and Executive Director of the European Consortium for Political Research

Michael Freeman
Department of Government, University of Essex, UK

Michael Gallagher
Department of Political Science, Trinity College, Dublin, Ireland

Paul Gilbert
Department of Philosophy, University of Hull, UK

Amy Gutmann
Department of Politics, Princeton University, USA

Axel Hadenius
Department of Government, Uppsala University, Sweden

Vinit Haksar
Department of Philosophy, University of Edinburgh, UK

Russell Hardin
Department of Politics, University of New York, USA

Roderick P. Hart
Department of Communication Studies, University of Texas, Austin, USA

Neil Harvey
Department of Government, New Mexico State University, USA

David Held
Department of Government, London School of Economics and Political Science, UK

Barry Hindess
Political Science Program, The Research School of Social Sciences, Australian National University, Australia

Jane Hindley
Department of Sociology, University of Essex, UK

Paul Hirst
School of Politics and Sociology, Birkbeck College, UK

Christopher C. Hood
All Souls College, Oxford, UK

John Horton
School of Politics, International Relations and the Environment, University of Keele, UK

David Howarth
Department of Government, University of Essex, UK

Ronald F. Inglehart
Institute for Social Research, University of Michigan, USA

Vivienne Jabri
London Centre of International Relations, University of Kent, UK

Sharon E. Jarvis
Department of Communication Studies, University of Texas, Austin, USA

Bob Jessop
Department of Sociology, Cartmel College, Lancaster University, UK

Ron Johnston
Geography Department, University of Bristol, UK

Bryan D. Jones
Department of Political Science, University of Washington, USA

David M. Jones
Government Department, University of Tasmania, Australia

Peter Jones
Department of Politics, University of Newcastle, UK

Emil Kirchner
Department of Government, University of Essex, UK

Hans-Dieter Klingemann
Wissenschaftszentrum Berlin für Sozialfurschung (WZB), Germany

Roman Krznaric
Department of Government, University of Essex, UK

Rowena Kwok
Department of Politics and Public Administration, The University of Hong Kong, Hong Kong

Ernesto Laclau
Department of Government, University of Essex, UK

Todd Landman
Department of Government, University of Essex, UK

Susan E. Lawrence
Department of Political Science, Rutgers University, USA

David Lehmann
Centre of Latin American Studies and Faculty of Social and Political Sciences, University of Cambridge, UK

Arend Lijphart
Department of Political Science, University of California, San Diego, USA

Juan J. Linz
Department of Sociology, Yale University, USA

Brian E. Loveman
Department of Political Science, San Diego State University, USA

Kurt Richard Luther
Department of Politics, University of Keele, UK

Mathew D. McCubbins
Department of Political Science, University of California, San Diego, USA

David H. McKay
Department of Government, University of Essex, USA

Denis McQuail
Politics Department, University of Southampton, UK

Kenneth Medhurst
University of Bradford, Bradford, UK

Roland Meighan
Formerly Professor of Education, University of Nottingham, UK

Susan Mendus
Department of Politics, University of York, UK

David S. Meyer
Department of Political Science, CUNY/City College, New York, USA

Frances Millard
Department of Government, University of Essex, UK

List of contributors

Nicholas R. Miller
Department of Political Science, University of Maryland, USA

Juli Minoves-Triquell
Ambassador of Andorra to the United States of America , New York, USA

Christopher Morris
Department of Philosophy, Bowling Green State University, USA

Peter Morriss
Department of Political Science and Sociology, National University of Ireland, Galway

Gerardo L. Munck
Department of Political Science, University of Illinois, USA

Philomena Murray
Department of Political Science, University of Melbourne, Australia

Klaus-Jürgen Nagel
Political and Social Sciences Department, Universitat Pompeu Fabra (UPF), Barcelona, Spain

Kate Nash
Department of Sociology, Goldsmiths College, University of London, UK

Ken Newton
Politics Department, University of Southampton, UK

The Rt. Hon. The Lord Nolan, PC, QC, DU Essex
Chancellor of the University of Essex, UK

Emma R. Norman
Department of Government, University of Essex, UK

Aletta Norval
Department of Government, University of Essex, UK

Claus Offe
Humboldt-Universität zu Berlin, Institüt fur Sozialwissenschaften, Berlin, Germany

Nikos Papastergiadis
Department of Economics and Social Studies, University of Manchester, UK

Mogens N. Pedersen
Department of Commercial Law and Political Science, Odense Universitet, Denmark

B. Guy Peters
Department of Political Science, University of Pittsburgh, USA

Philip Pettit
Research School of Social Sciences, Australian National University, Australia

Mark Philp
Department of Politics and International Relations, University of Oxford, UK

Michael Pinto-Duschinsky
Senior Research Fellow in Politics, Brunel University, UK

Lawrence Quill
Department of Government, University of Essex, UK

Richard S. Randall
Department of Politics, New York University, USA

Vicky Randall
Department of Government, University of Essex, UK

Andrew Reeve
Department of Politics, University of Warwick, Coventry, UK

William Rehg
Department of Philosophy, Saint Louis University, USA

Ferran Requejo
Political and Social Sciences Department, Universitat Pompeu Fabra (UPF), Barcelona, Spain

R.A.W. Rhodes
Department of Politics, University of Newcastle, UK

David Robertson
St Hugh's College, Oxford University, UK

Neil Robinson
Department of Government and Society, University of Limerick, Ireland

Christopher A. Rootes
Centre for the Study of Social & Political Movements, University of Kent at Canterbury, UK

Dietrich Rueschemeyer
Department of Sociology, Brown University, USA

Bruce M. Russett
Political Science Department, Yale University, USA

Thomas Saalfeld
Department of Politics and International Relations, University of Kent at Canterbury, UK

Arlene W. Saxonhouse
Department of Political Science, University of Michigan, Ann Arbor, USA

Elinor Scarbrough
Department of Government, University of Essex, UK

Norman Schofield
Center in Political Economy, Washington University in St Louis, USA

Itai Sened
Center in Political Economy, Washington University in St Louis, USA

Matthew S. Shugart
School of International Relations, University of California, San Diego, USA

Richard Sinnott
Department of Politics, University College, Dublin, Ireland

Metta Spencer
Emeritus Professor of Sociology, University of Toronto, Canada

Judith Squires
Department of Politics, University of Bristol, UK

Yannis Stavrakakis
School of Politics, University of Nottingham, UK

Jürg Steiner
University of Bern, Switzerland and University of North Carolina at Chapel Hill, USA

Sven Steinmo
Department of Political Science, University of Colorado, USA

John Stone
Department of Sociology and Anthropology, George Mason University, USA

Tracy B. Strong
Department of Political Science, University of California, San Diego, USA

Göran Therborn
Swedish Collegium for Advanced Study in the Social Sciences, University of Uppsala, Sweden

Dennis Thompson
Department of Government, Harvard University, USA

Kees van Kersbergen
Faculty of Policy Studies, University of Nijmegen, The Netherlands

Andrew Vincent
School of European Studies, University of Wales, Cardiff, UK

Rachel Walker
Department of Government, University of Essex, UK

Hugh Ward
Department of Government, University of Essex, UK

R.A. Watt
Department of Law, University of Essex, UK

Albert Weale
Department of Government, University of Essex, UK

Christian Welzel
Wissenschaftszentrum Berlin für Sozialforschung (WZB), Germany

Mark Wickham-Jones
Department of Politics, University of Bristol, UK

Marcel Wissenburg
Department of Political Science, Nijmegen School of Management, University of Nijmegan, The Netherlands

Steven B. Wolinetz
Department of Political Science, Memorial University, Newfoundland, Canada

Andrew J. Wroe
Department of Government, University of Essex, UK

Sven Wynants
Political and Social Sciences Department, Universitat Pompeu Fabra (UPF), Barcelona, Spain

Preface

The *Encyclopedia of Democratic Thought* is designed to bring together all the ideas that matter to democracy, past, present and future. It does not address these ideas piecemeal, but explores them through a co-ordinated collection of essays on key concepts and issues. Nearly every essay is written by a recognised authority on its topic. The result is a unique encounter of many of the world's leading political scientists, political sociologists and political philosophers.

The design of the *Encyclopedia* is driven by ideas, and so the content is both analytical and reflective. Indeed, the essays draw on every tradition of democratic thought as well as developing new thinking. But the essays also consider the practical implications of the ideas for the conduct of democratic politics in the world today. Without seeking to compose any kind of recipe for democratic success, the essays taken together do offer guidelines for good democratic practice.

The *Encyclopedia* is a work of reference that is designed to be the first port of call for everyone interested in democratic ideas, democratic practice and the quality of democratic governance. Each essay is crafted to achieve a concise but comprehensive account of the topic, and so each essay can stand alone. But all the essays are cross-referenced, so offering the reader different lines of inquiry whatever the topic of entry. In addition, each essay carries summary references and/or suggestions for further reading. The content of the *Encyclopedia* is therefore clear and accessible, but not necessarily simple.

The *Encyclopedia* is therefore a work of reference with a difference. It may certainly be consulted topic by topic. But it is designed to provide a place for browsing, reflecting, discovering and enjoying the delights of serendipity. At the same time, it is full of argument, sometimes on difficult and demanding issues, that invites critical responses. In sum, the *Encyclopedia of Democratic Thought* aspires to stimulate critical thinking.

The *Encyclopedia* is global in scope and responds to the democratic revolution of recent decades. It therefore refers both to the long-established democracies of Western Europe, North America and Australasia, and to the more recent democracies of Latin America, Eastern and Central Europe, Africa and Asia. Classical democratic concerns are related to new democracies, and to important changes in old democracies. Democratic thought, new and old, is brought to bear on the challenges facing contemporary democracies, and to the possibilities of the democratic future.

* * *

The idea of making the *Encyclopedia* was first mooted some five years ago. Its present title emerged a little later. The first months were spent on designing the blueprint. This print was shaped by the key decision to develop a substantial argument on a relatively limited number of topics. The composition of the list of topics involved consultation, debate, and imagination. The original list of some 200 topics certainly went through some changes, but the basic architecture remained firm. There are now 188 topics.

The next step was to recruit authors for every topic and invite them to write. The main criterion for selection was simple: choose the very best! And there was no hesitation about setting out to recruit the foremost scholars in each and every case. At the same time, it is true that this aim was tempered in some degree by considerations of balance, both gender and geographical, and there was some modest success in marrying these distinct principles. But the main emphasis remained throughout on the quality of the entries to the *Encyclopedia*.

Yet, it will be apparent that a good number of contributions come from colleagues at the University of Essex, most of them in the Department of Government. It was part of our original plan to draw in this way on the research capability of the leading department of political science in the United Kingdom. Furthermore, on the infrequent occasions when contributions failed to appear, we tended to turn to our Essex colleagues to supply the lack and maintain the integrity of the enterprise. For this reason, all of the younger scholars present in the *Encyclopedia* either come from Essex or have an Essex connection.

Happily, the topics that eventually had to be re-allocated were few and far between. Overall, the commitment of our colleagues world wide to the enterprise has been outstanding. Despite the professional pressures, and even health problems in some cases, they have all risen bravely to the considerable challenge of making the *Encyclopedia*. In large degree, this simply reflects their professionalism and intellectual engagement, even if a small minority did have some trouble in grappling with the concept of 'the deadline'. But it may not be too far-fetched to suggest that enthusiasm for the project itself had something to do with it.

Whatever the effort invested in designing the *Encyclopedia*, it inevitably took on a life of its own. We tried to make a virtue of this necessity, and anticipate it. While we were certainly willing to sketch an appropriate approach for individual essays, and to respond with criticism and guidance where requested, there was never any attempt to impose any kind of editorial line. On the contrary, each contributor was encouraged to blend objective enquiry with personal judgement, to use and develop their own voice. We count this variety of voices as one of the chief virtues of the *Encyclopedia*.

In our view, the result is neither discord nor harmony, but a wide range of ideas that resonate with tested truths and new meanings. Indeed, a review of these essays can leave little doubt that 'democratic thought' constitutes a coherent field of intellectual inquiry and reflection. In small part, this may be attributed to the architecture of the *Encyclopedia* and the watching brief of its editors. The much greater part is owing to the powerful polar attraction still exercised by democratic ideas themselves.

* * *

No project of this scope can be completed without considerable help. It is impossible to mention everyone who helped us. But, we wish to acknowledge the good offices of the distinguished members of our International Advisory Board, and to thank our colleagues in the Department of Government at the University of Essex for their unstinting support and good humour. It is hard to imagine a better academic context for carrying out the work of the *Encyclopedia*.

We give special thanks to two gentle and generous people who have seconded our efforts throughout. Ildi Clarke maintained an effective administrative grip on the project, despite its many stresses and strains, and played a key role in delivering it in good order. Clare Dekker provided logistical support, as well as constant encouragement and good cheer. We gladly recognise that we could not have done the job without them.

Paul Barry Clarke
Joe Foweraker
University of Essex
September 2000

List of entries

List of entries

A

accountability

Democracy is about elections, but after elections are concluded there must be other mechanisms for holding the government of the day accountable for its actions on a regular basis. Accountability is often used synonymously with other concepts, such as responsibility and responsiveness, but in a strict sense the term refers to requirements for an individual or public organisation (usually an executive) to render an account to parliament or some other source of legitimate authority (Thomas 1998). This conception of accountability implies that some powers have been delegated and that the 'agent' must later justify its actions to the source of those delegated powers. Most accountability systems are retrospective, have been devised to detect and expose error by the agent, and emphasise imposing some form of punishment on wrongdoers when found. This conception is in contrast to accountability being conceptualised as generalised systems for evaluating and improving performance in the public sector, or as a prospective means of specifying responsibility.

Conceptually, accountability is defined by formalised requirements to render an account, but in practice a number of issues arise when attempting to make accountability function. The most important distinctions arise among methods for holding the political executive accountable as a collectivity, as against mechanisms for enforcing accountability over individual ministers, public organisations and even individual public employees. The same term is used in reference to controlling all these actors, but the mechanisms used and the remedies for any malfeasance detected are markedly different.

In Westminster political systems, the conception of rendering the account has been clearly defined (Woodhouse 1994). The theory of accountability in these systems remains focused largely on the relationship between the government and parliament, with the constitutional principle being that the government is the agent to whom powers have been delegated by parliament, those powers in turn having been granted by the people. The government of the day must respond to questions on the floor of parliament, it may have to respond to motions of no confidence, and committees are increasingly empowered to investigate and evaluate the programs of the government (see WESTMINSTER MODEL).

In other democratic systems, even other parliamentary systems, the conception of accountability has been more diffuse, although many of the same mechanisms for enforcing it are in place as in Westminster systems. For example, in presidential regimes such as the United States, the legislature may not be able to call the chief executive to account in quite the way of a Westminster system (except in impeachment proceedings), but individual agencies and departments certainly are forced to appear before the legislature, or one of its committees, and to render an account (see PRESIDENTIALISM). Public organisations are also forced to account for their actions through the budgetary process, as well as in a variety of substantive investigations and policy discussions. Other specialised institutions, such as the ombudsman, which originated in the Scandinavian countries but is now widely diffused, are used to enforce accountability.

Of course, the convention in Westminster systems (followed more in rhetoric than in practice) is that ministers are accountable for all actions taken in their ministry, although in fact few if any ministers are now forced to resign over the actions of lower-echelon officials. In this conception, individual civil servants are not only not directly accountable, they are also anonymous; the minister must accept the responsibility for the actions of his or her civil servants. The actual practice has evolved far from the theory. Not only do ministers no longer resign, they have in some Westminster systems begun to identify the career officials responsible for failures of policy or administration, and those officials increasingly are being held to account personally. As the security of civil service systems is lost, then that personal accountability may mean loss of the government position, or certainly other sanctions.

In political systems in which ministerial responsibility does not purport to cloak the individual public employee from culpability, and in Westminster systems faced with overt malfeasance by a public servant, there are a host of mechanisms that require some accounting. There is hardly space here to discuss them all, but mentioning a few points to the multiple meanings of the term 'accountability'. For example, administrative law will define the nature of the responsibilities of public servants and provide appropriate sanctions when they fail to meet those responsibilities, or when they exercise their powers in an 'arbitrary and capricious' manner. The remedies generally are to declare their actions void, but the individual public servant may also be held personally liable in some settings.

Accounting is one of the important means for defining accountability. That is, a major question about the actions of government organisations is whether they have used public money appropriately, and legislatures have invested a great deal of time and effort in monitoring the probity of public expenditures. As the accounting organisations, such as the General Accounting Office in the United States or the National Audit Office in the United Kingdom, have been more skilful they have moved from strict financial accounting to a concern with the efficiency and effectiveness of expenditures. It is no longer sufficient to demonstrate that money has been spent legally; public organisations must also demonstrate that they money was put to the best possible use.

Although accountability has been well established normatively and empirically, the last two decades of public sector reform are beginning to require some reconceptualisation. Just as was noted for accounting offices, the more general emphasis in accountability is shifting from judging procedures to evaluating outcomes, and especially to developing outcome measures that can be used to evaluate performance. Thus, to some extent, ideas concerning accountability are coalescing even more closely with mechanisms for evaluation and policy analysis.

Especially for public servants, the general conception had been that if they followed the correct procedures then they were not culpable for any failures. As governing has become more informed by market principles than in the past, there is a greater concern with being able to demonstrate that programmes are indeed producing results, and that they are efficient (see MARKET FORCES). Further, as managers come to be placed on performance contracts, rather than taking positions as part of a career in government, then accountability becomes in large part measuring that performance. As well as shifting the idea of accountability from detecting error and punishing the malefactor, this version of accountability emphasises results, and perhaps positive rewards.

Obviously, the principles of accountability for performance apply more directly to public organisations, and even individual administrators, than they do to the political executive. In some ways the executive has also been held accountable for poor policy choices, and may lose office (by parliamentary or electoral action) because of those choices. The more recent changes in accountability begin to make organisations and individual administrators more directly liable for their actions. These changes in accountability regimens also imply a shift away from punishment toward management as the general principle governing the arrangements.

Another important development in thinking about accountability is to remove intermediate organisations and to attempt to make public organisations more directly accountable to the people. In this case, the people involved generally are only the immediate 'customers' of the programme. This is an attempt to ensure direct popular, and hence to some extent democratic, control over the operation of those organisations. It may, however, become undemocratic through ignoring the wants and needs of the larger political community; a programme that serves its clients well may impose additional costs on taxpayers or on competing groups in the society.

Some recent reforms undertaken in the public sector run exactly counter to the conventional approaches to accountability, and perhaps also to the performance-based systems being implemented. For example, there is a strong impetus to encourage more administrative entrepreneurship and risk-taking, especially in newly created quasi-autonomous agencies. The latitude for action for public servants implied here prevents enforcing conventional conceptions of accountability, and may effectively create a sphere of activities over which elected officials have little or no control. The ultimate form of control, dismissing the leadership of the organisation, may be perhaps the only real means of control, but that may only punish rather than create greater compliance.

Government will always have to be concerned with procedures and with ensuring equality of treatment for citizens, as well as the appropriate use of public money. That having been said, those procedural concerns are being augmented, and to some extent supplanted in importance, by more substantive approaches to accountability; as Day and Klein (1987) have pointed out, there are now multiple accountabilities, rather than any single form. Public organisations are now being held accountable upward to the sources of delegated powers, down to the public, and also to objective performance standards. All these measures are designed to be means of ensuring that there is democracy (meaning here adherence to the laws adopted through democratic means) after elections have been completed. Even all these mechanisms taken together will not be a perfect check on malfeasance and nonfeasance, but they do provide a check on the excessive or inappropriate use of power. Indeed, there may be so many competing forms of accountability that overall control over public organisations has been lessened rather than enhanced.

See also:

civil service; democratic executives; democratic performance; parliamentary models; presidentialism; Westminster model

Further reading

Bouckaert, G. and Pollitt, C. (1996) *Quality in European Public Services*, London: Sage.

Bovens, M.A.P. (1997) *The Responsible Organisation*, Cambridge: Cambridge University Press.

Day, P. and Klein, R. (1987) *Accountabilities: Five Public Services*, London: Tavistock.

Light, P.C. (1995) *Thickening Government: Federal Hierarchy and the Diffusion of Accountability*, Washington, DC: The Brookings Institution.

Thomas, P.G. (1998) 'The Changing Nature of Accountability', in B.G. Peters and D.J. Savoie (eds), *Taking Stock: Assessing Public Sector Reforms*, Montreal: McGill/Queens University Press.

Woodhouse, D. (1994) *Ministers and Parliament: Accountability in Theory and Practice*, Oxford: Clarendon Press.

B. GUY PETERS

affirmative action

Affirmative action describes pro-active efforts to redress social inequalities. The term 'pro-active' distinguishes affirmative action from 'reactive' anti-discrimination policies which are complaint-based. Where anti-discrimination policies respond to individual complaints, affirmative action produces structural change which should, ideally, obviate complaints of discrimination. John F. Kennedy's Executive Order 10925 (16 March 1961) invoked the term 'affirmative action' for the first time, though the idea of active state intervention to reduce social inequalities had precursors (Curry 1996: xiv).

Affirmative action can be introduced in a number of domains: in the labour market, in systems of political representation, in higher education, in other kinds of associations such as trades unions and political parties. The reform efforts characterised as 'affirmative action' (or 'positive action' in Europe) span a spectrum, from training courses for members of targeted groups to attempts to tie job offers, promotions or higher education places to membership of such groups. Designated groups are not the same in every country and can change over time. North American blacks and women are the primary focus in the United States. Canada's employment equity legislation (1986) targets four groups: women, Aboriginal peoples, the disabled and visible MINORITIES.

When affirmative action is introduced to increase the political representation of targeted groups, either through quotas in political parties or set-aside seats in legislative institutions, the connection with democratic theory is clear. Demanding that blacks need to represent blacks, and that women need women representatives, follows logically from the view that the make-up of a legislature should reflect the composition of the community. This position is contested by those who believe that representative government relies upon candidates who put aside commitments to particular groups. For those who support some notion of group representation (see REPRESENTATION, CONCEPT OF), there remain debates about just which groups deserve separate representation, whether or not those representatives are beholden in some way to their communities

(see Phillips 1991), and what to do about the fact that people cross over identity categories.

Labour market affirmative action is linked to democratic debates through two sorts of claims. First, the argument is that a true democrat should be concerned to address social inequalities which mean that only some privileged voices get heard in political debate. Second, there is the claim that democracy has, as a *raison d'être*, empowering members of the polity in every area of their lives, including the workplace and the home. Affirmative action in the distribution of places in universities builds upon this principle. Conceptions of democracy, which focus upon electoral processes and which consider social inequalities irrelevant to representative government, dispute these claims. There are debates about the extent to which affirmative action actually reduces social inequalities, and about whether it encourages assimilation to capitalist norms; however, the suggestion that affirmative action produces more democratic practice hinges upon the claim that, to some extent, it reduces social inequalities and consequently strengthens the political influence of those previously marginalised.

The relevance of social status to political influence cuts across debates about the meaning of EQUALITY in liberal democracies. Typically, the argument is put that affirmative action produces equal outcomes, while liberal democracies guarantee only equality of opportunity. Some admit that a degree of equality of outcome is necessary to make equal opportunity meaningful. In fact, this was just the argument advanced by Lyndon Johnson in 1965 (in Curry 1996: 17) in defence of affirmative action:

> You do not take a person who, for years, has been hobbled by chains and liberate him [sic], bring him [sic] up to the starting line of a race and then say, 'You are free to compete with all the others', and still justly believe that you have been completely fair.

In this scenario, affirmative action becomes a form of beneficence handed to 'disadvantaged' groups to help them 'catch up'. The disadvantaged become the problem (Eveline 1994), and the 'benefactors' remain invisible and unchallenged because of their invisibility (Bacchi 1996). In the process, affirmative action is produced as 'preferential treatment'.

As 'preference', affirmative action is said to contravene procedural justice, raising questions about the desirable shape of a democratic polity. In a period commonly characterised as one of diminishing public interest in politics, models of democracy are put forward which attempt to smooth over differences, either to (re?)generate a kind of community commitment to something called the 'common good' (the republican model), or to insist that value differences can be resolved procedurally (the liberal democratic model), that the right takes precedence over the good (Rawls 1971). Opponents of affirmative action contend that the reform, by emphasising the irrelevant factors of gender and race, undermines the kind of social cohesion which democratic politics requires. A model of society as gender-blind and/or race-blind is put forward as the ideal. Defenders of affirmative action argue that the polity is already deeply divided by power differentials, and that these make a farce of procedural justice. By challenging procedural justice, affirmative action raises the possibility that consensus about JUSTICE may not be possible, a devastating prospect to some defenders of PROCEDURAL DEMOCRACY. For others, the kind of fundamental clash over values evinced in affirmative action debates illustrates the need for a democratic vision which invites agonistic debate and which refuses to displace 'difference' onto those who consider themselves, to varying extents, unrepresented in democratic processes.

Because affirmative action is held responsible by its opponents for creating dissent where harmony once existed or where harmony is needed, the members of the targeted groups are described as the destabilisers. As in the construction of affirmative action as 'preferential treatment' (see above; attention is focussed upon those who consider themselves, to varying extents, unrepresented in democratic processes), those who set the norms for democratic behaviour remain invisible and unscrutinised.

See also:

agonism; capitalism; citizenship; education; empowerment; equality; gendering democracy; liberalism; procedural democracy; representation, concept of; republicanism

Further reading

Bacchi, C.L. (1996) *The Politics of Affirmative Action: 'Women', Equality and Category Politics*, London: Sage.

Curry, G.E. (ed.) (1996) *The Affirmative Action Debate*, Reading, MA: Addison-Wesley.

Eveline, J. (1994) 'The Politics of Advantage', *Australian Feminist Studies*, special issue, *Women and Citizenship*, 19 (Autumn): 129–54.

Johnson, L.B. (1965) 'To Fulfill These Rights', in G.E. Curry (ed.), *The Affirmative Action Debate*, Reading, MA: Addison-Wesley, 1996, 16–24.

Phillips, A. (1991) *Engendering Democracy*, Cambridge: Polity Press.

Rawls, J. (1971) *A Theory of Justice*, Cambridge, MA: Belknap Press of Harvard University Press.

CAROL LEE BACCHI

agonism

The concept of agonism is commonly identified with democracy in its purest form and emphasises popular CONTESTATION and debate as the principal aspects of political activity. Many of the principles associated with agonism are deeply rooted in the socio-political world of ancient Greece. This is often taken as a limitation to the practical applicability, theoretical scope and contemporary relevance of this model of politics. Yet the possibilities of agonism radiate far beyond the walls of the *polis*. Indeed, the conceptual contestation that currently underpins contemporary political debates places agonistic principles at the very core of the postmodern democratic enterprise.

The term 'agonism' is derived from the scene of the *agon* in Ancient Greek drama, where the primary prot*agon*ists of the play appear, centre stage, to confront each other in verbal contest (Clarke 1996: 56). In this part of the play, the chorus, who otherwise provide an 'outsider's' perspective explaining the development of the plot and the inner motives of the characters through pure and formal poetry, recede into the background. In consequence, the dialogue and actions of the main characters dominate the scene unaided and unexplained to the audience from a narrator's point of view. In the *agon*, the main characters are given the chance to appear with only their actions and speech to account for themselves. The plays of Aristophanes provide noteworthy examples of the dramatic exploration of the *agon*.

In its most basic political form, the notion of agonism represents the activity of popular confrontation, contestation, conflict and debate on public matters and the arena(s) in which such contestation takes place. Traditionally, this concept applied to radically participatory conceptions of democracy that have their roots in the Athenian *polis*. Pericles's stirring funeral oration in Thucydides's *History of the Peloponnesian War* illustrates the virtues peculiar to the Athenian understanding of agonistic political participation. This is particularly salient in his proud passage declaiming that, 'we Athenians, in our own persons' do not make policy decisions until they have been thoroughly debated (Thucydides 1954: 147). As Pericles averred, in the polity words and deeds were complimentary rather than incompatible, and even those most engaged in their own affairs were 'extremely well-informed on general politics'. In fact, he made it quite clear that the common perception of those who failed to take any interest in politics was not that they were simply 'minding their own business'; they had no business in Athens at all! (Thucydides 1954: 147).

From this perspective, the major components of classical agonism can be identified as first, genuine public interest in political concerns; second, personal participation in political matters; and third, the ineluctable connection between action and speech in politics; all of which lead to the idea of democratic deliberation through personal engagement in contestative political debate. These basic agonistic tenets were extended in Aristotle's forms of government. However, after the decline of the *polis*, agonistic forms of politics resurfaced only briefly in the medieval Italian city-republics, and were not significantly revitalised until Rousseau's radically participatory conception of democracy appeared in the eighteenth century. More recently, the agonistic principles of conflict and contestation were revived in the 1920s and 1930s as a central element of Carl Schmitt's concept of 'the political' (*The Concept of the Political* and *The Crisis of Parliamentary Democracy*). The deeper facets of political agonism have been explored most extensively in the work of Hannah Arendt, particularly in *The Human Condition* (1958).

Arendt attempted to describe agonism as an intrinsically valuable conception of politics through a comprehensive reading of the classical *agon*. The most fundamental agonistic component of her thought lies in her assertion that politics, like its theatrical counterpart, is an essentially and radically *active* enterprise. For Arendt, the unconditioned action and speech found in the *agon* and the human values formed within them could be translated into the purest form of political activity. To do so, however, would require an absence of formal/structural constraints on political actions and speech. Hence, agonistic political activity in the Arendtian sense calls for an otherwise unconditioned space in which the substance of politics can be freely enacted and spoken and the individuality of the political actor can be authentically revealed. The argument displays several links with Rousseau's contention that the road to sincerity and authenticity lies in direct political PARTICIPATION and debate.

It is clear that this interpretation of agonism embodies an extreme departure from politics in its currently accepted (statist) sense. Pure agonistic politics is concerned not with structures, places, institutions, or with activities of fabrication (*poesis*) such as law-making as in modern state politics. It is rather concerned with action in its deepest sense (*praxis*) and, in particular, with the activities of appearing, contesting, persuading and deciding that can be valued intrinsically because they leave no tangible products behind. Politics, according to Arendt, belongs not to the world of things but to the world of human beings and the relations between them. Agonistic activity is also perceived as constitutive of human freedom and togetherness, rather than instrumentally facilitative of it.

These agonistic ideas require a notion of political participation that is far more extended and extensive than modern representative democracy has hitherto offered. Indeed, the importance of active and sustained personal political engagement in agonistic political participation is fundamentally antagonistic to ideas of democratic representation, party politics and politics-as-statecraft. In consequence, the most obvious, and most serious, criticism of this understanding of agonism is that it is currently unrealisable in practical terms.

Pure agonism might, perhaps, have been possible within the small polities of the *polis* or even the free city-states of Switzerland that so enamoured Rousseau. Yet, contemporary social, political, demographic and economic circumstances and the entrenched nature of existing conceptions of the state render a complete application of agonistic modes of political being and political relations impossible. Moreover, as Arendt's conception of politics is so ineluctably tied to unconditioned *praxis*-action and speech within a distinct 'space of appearances,' her arguments suggest that there can be no politics where agonistic conditions do not hold (Clarke 1996: 113). If Arendt's position here is accepted and agonism is impossible to implement practically in its pure form(s) within the conditions of modern life, then politics itself appears to be impossible.

Even if the contrary position is assumed, and this kind of agonism was possible, it is not entirely clear that the consequences would be as empowering or as beneficial as Arendt implies. While the dark side of extreme state power is

totalitarianism, the dark side of radically participatory democratic power invokes the spectre of ochlocracy. If the conditions for agonistic politics are provided by the absence of formal political structures, then the substance of agonism solely concerns people acting, speaking, persuading and making decisions on this basis. While in theory these conditions are intended to foster clear political judgements that are as formally unconditioned as possible, in practice they could promote the possibility of mob rule. If political actions and decisions are not structurally limited internally in some way, it is difficult to see how agonism could be prevented from descending into the proverbially fickle 'to-ing and fro-ing' of the whims of the mob.

Despite these criticisms, pure models of agonism are important in that they illuminate how far modern forms of statism have strayed from politics and democracy as they were originally conceived. The point is significant since disturbing existing patterns of political theory and practice generates the potential for extending their frontiers of possibility. Pure agonism offers a clear conceptual vantage from which existing conceptions of politics may be reflected upon, critically assessed and modified from a position outside their own confines. Its legacy has been to emphasise not merely radical action in politics, but that political activities require a highly reflective corollary if they are to be ethically sustainable, self-empowering and historically durable.

If agonistic conceptions of participatory democracy are taken as important for their implications concerning our conceptions of the world, their contemporary practical unsustainability is not so relevant. Those implications suggest that, in addition to engaging in the socio-political processes of the world, we should also take the time to disengage: to reflect upon those processes and their consequences. What matters is that we reflect upon notions of politics and democracy and that we construct arguments, debate with others and make decisions concerning what we should do about our current political institutions and practices. The effects of this critical perspective on contemporary political theory and political practice have been momentous, for it has called into question the very notions that constitute our political enterprises. In doing so, the concept of agonism has re-entered contemporary politics at its core, in a new and ineluctably dynamic form.

Agonism *is* present at the centre of current conceptions of politics, but not in the classical or Arendtian sense of face-to-face contestation within a true political *agora*. The agonistic components of postmodern democracy are found in the political contestation of *concepts*. This has been at least partially a result of the epistemological challenges that the death of universalism has presented to traditional LIBERALISM and to democratic modes of politics. A most crucial consequence of the postmodern recognition of value-pluralism, contingency, anti-foundationalism and incommensurability has been the shift away from the Enlightenment search for single, rational, systematic and foundational principles upon which human action could be based and justified. Acknowledging diversity and incommensurability has simultaneously required the acknowledgement of a plurality of competing values, and ways of life that are inconsonant or even incommensurable with each other (Gray 1995). In consequence, it is now recognised that a variety of irresolvable tensions and contradictions exist in postmodern life that are often incapable of formal, rational, algorithmic or intellectual resolution.

Contemporary democracy appears to have supplied an alternative that attempts to resolve such intellectually and rationally incommensurable models of being in the world in a practical manner. As democracy thrives on acknowledging rather than repressing diversity, so it might also provide a way in which people can live together in spite of their differences. In the face of incommensurable values and 'essentially contestable concepts' (Gallie 1964: 157–91) it appears that agonistic contestation rather than consensus provides the more appealing democratic solution. However, that democratic solution does not necessarily require face-to-face participation in the political process. Instead, it embraces contestation between irreducible values and endless essentially contestable political concepts such as 'democracy', 'the state', 'power', 'social justice' and 'FREEDOM' at its core.

In short, postmodern democracy embodies an understanding of political agonism modified in such a way that it is no longer an anachronistic, impractical political ideal. On the contrary, the agonistic contestation of concepts, values and ideas appears most eminently and pragmatically suited to the postmodern condition and to postmodern democracy. The 'rush to democracy' that has characterised the plethora of global political transformations since 1989 indicates that this agonistic solution has, so far, enjoyed some measure of success.

At the centre of contemporary democracy lie debate, discussion and contest. But that debate, discussion and contest occur not merely within the established and institutionalised conceptual frameworks of developed democracies. They also, and often more significantly, concern the framework itself. This implies that established democracies may have difficult questions to deal with about how they both manage their broadly agreed framework and how they resolve difficulties within that framework. It also suggests that emerging democracies have even more crucial contests in attempting to agree upon possible frameworks themselves. Indeed, developing democracies are perhaps the arenas in which agonistic contestation over concepts becomes most salient precisely because their old systems of values, beliefs and institutions have disintegrated. The resulting 'conceptual confusion' (Geertz 1964: 64) provides what could be termed as a conceptual *agora*; a space in which fresh ideas and rival concepts can appear to compete for ascendancy in the new socio-political order.

While agonistic disputes rage over many concepts related to contemporary social and political life, the most prevalent and most heated often concern the exchange of opinions as to what counts as democracy itself. Post-Soviet Russia offers an interesting example of the essentially contestable nature of 'democracy' and the ways in which agonistic disputes over the 'proper use' (Gallie 1964: 158) of this concept occurs. Two terms for 'democracy' are widespread in current Russian political discourse, *demokratsiia* and *narodovlastiye* (Urban 1994). However, while both terms are etymologically reducible to People's (*demos, narod*) Power (*kratia, vlastiye*) each signifies a very different idea of democracy and a very different approach to Russian politics. *Demokratsiia* was invoked by the Yeltsin camp and betokens an acceptance of some elements of Western models of representative democracy. The concept denoted by *demokratsiia* relates democratic accountability to ideas of the minimalist state, deregulation of the market, parliamentarist elections, SEPARATION OF POWERS and policies of PRIVATISATION.

The contesting notion of *narodovlastiye* appears in Communist Party and Russian nationalist discourse in stark contrast to the 'Westernist,' *demokratsiia. Narodovlastiye* reflects a more traditional concept of the people's power recalling popular representation of the kind found in the pre-Parliamentary soviets. Following the Marxist–Leninist critique of parliamentary democracy, *narodovlastiye* is often invoked to imply 'DIRECT DEMOCRACY' (see Held 1996: 105–39) and to criticise the undemocratic, corrupt, paternalistic and exploitative nature and practices of the presidential system. However, after 1993 the institution of democratic elections in Russia has required the communists to make certain compromises in spite of their ideological differences in order to maintain popular appeal, most notably in their acceptance of the parliament.

Traditional political elites and the intelligentsia remain crucial to conceptual contestation and debate in Russia (Kullberg 1994). Yet contestation over the 'proper use' of essentially contestable concepts is often carried well into the realms of the *demos*. Discussions take place in both journals and more accessible newspaper publications, where popular debates are encouraged through the exchange of views in 'letter pages'. This is a particularly important agonistic arena for contests concerning what is to constitute Russian identity. It has also

increasingly become a testing site for ideas concerning how to deal with the breakup of the former Soviet state, the way in which Russians must now relate to former member states of the Soviet Union such as the Ukraine, and how the Russian identity can be constituted in the post-communist era (Urban 1994).

The agonistic contestation of concepts is also very salient in the experience of established democracies. This is visible in the extent their conceptual foundations continue to provoke challenge. The contestations themselves, however, remain largely focused on the ways in which democracy can and ought to be construed. In the United States, for example, one of the most disturbing problems revolves around how democracy should be construed, given that less than half the population feel represented enough to turn out to vote at presidential elections. This constitutes a major challenge for the USA to reconstruct its political system, its institutions and its popular appeal in such a way that they not only function in a more acceptable democratic sense, but that such functioning appears as visibly democratic to the public.

In the established democracies of Europe, a principal arena of agonistic contestation concerns whether European institutions are truly 'democratic' or whether there exists a 'DEMOCRATIC DEFICIT' that demands replenishing in some way. The ensuing series of heated debates over how future European democracy should be constituted are compounded by inter-state differences of interests, values and opinions in addition to intra-statist economic, social, demographic and political diversity. One of the clearest areas provoking British debate over the European Union (EU) was Prime Minister John Major's refusal to hold a referendum in the UK over some central conditions of Britain's membership of the EU, on the grounds that the issue pertained to questions of parliamentary rather than popular SOVEREIGNTY.

Rivalry between 'open' or 'underdetermined' concepts and the political contestations over how they ought to be construed and applied turns out to be absolutely central in all these issues. That conceptual contest itself lies at the very basis of postmodern democratic politics, for concepts define how we understand ourselves, others and the world in which we live, and concepts shape how we are to interact with that world in a way that is meaningful to ourselves and fair to others. In the absence of rational methods to determine the proper use of significant concepts, the democratic projects of the postmodern era are grounded not in intellectually derived foundations, but in the practical process of political contestation and debate. And that is ineluctably agonistic.

Agonism has indeed extended far beyond the walls of the *polis*. To meet the changing circumstances of a global system that bears little resemblance to the classical world, ideas of agonism have progressed from personal contestation to conceptual contestation. Yet, through this resilient concept, some continuity with the past, and thus a measure of stability and identity, has been preserved. The agonistic contestation of concepts has provided many new resources that can enable coping with the tensions, dislocations and pluralisms of the present. At most, it might well inspire democratic practices that encourage postmodern individuals and groups to discover a satisfactory way of living together in spite of their differences. At the very least, agonism can illuminate a conception of democracy that stands firm at the entrance to an uncertain future, without losing sight of the enduring wisdoms of the past.

See also:

autonomy; citizenship; civic virtue; contestation; deliberative democracy; democratic deficit; democratic origins; demos; direct democracy; empowerment; liberalism; participation; pluralism; public–private distinction; radical democracy; republicanism; toleration

Further reading

Arendt, H. (1958) *The Human Condition*, Chicago: University of Chicago Press.

Clarke, P.B. (1996) *Deep Citizenship*, London: Pluto Press.

Gallie, W.B. (1964) 'Essentially Contested Concepts', in W.B. Gallie, *Philosophy and Historical Understanding*, London: Chatto & Windus, 157–91.

Geertz, C. (1964) 'Ideology as a Cultural System', in D.E. Apter (ed.), *Ideology and Discontent*, New York: The Free Press.

Gray, J. (1995) 'Agonistic Liberalism', in J. Gray, *Isaiah Berlin*, London: HarperCollins.

Held, D. (1996) *Models of Democracy*, 2nd edn, Cambridge: Polity Press.

Hornblower, S. (1992) 'Creation and Development of Democratic Institutions in Ancient Greece', in J. Dunn (ed.), *Democracy: The Unfinished Journey, 508 BC to AD 1993*, Oxford: Oxford University Press.

Kullberg, J.S. (1994) 'The Ideological Roots of Elite Political Conflict in Post-Soviet Russia', *European Studies* 46(6): 929–53.

Thucydides (1954) *History of the Peloponnesian War*, trans. R. Warner, London: Penguin.

Urban, M. (1994) 'The Politics of Identity in Russia's Postcommunist Transitions: The Nation Against Itself', *Slavic Review* 53(3): 733–65.

EMMA R. NORMAN

apathy

'Apathy' is derived from the Greek *apathia*, a basic tenet of the philosophy of the Stoics led by Zeno. It was developed further in the philosophy of the Roman Marcus Aurelius and was popularised by Seneca. The word passed into French as *apathie* and thence to English.

In politics, the term was increasingly used to indicate a disinclination to be actively involved in the political process. In regimes of liberal democracy, this disinclination can be expressed in various ways. The most common and widely discussed expression is a refusal to exercise the vote in ELECTIONS for representatives in parliament, although the vote is regarded as the basic duty of the democratic system. Where a significant proportion of citizens do not vote the power 'from below', which is the marker of democracy, disappears.

In Athenian democracy, *apathy* was regarded as antithetical to the notion of democracy and the democratic citizen (see CITIZENSHIP). Pericles made clear in his Funeral Oration that the essential virtue of a citizen was his attachment to and active involvement in democratic polity to the degree that he was prepared to die in its defence. Such feeling and commitment arose from belonging to the polity and was necessary to its survival. A passive attachment was not enough. People who were apathetic should be excluded from the polity: 'we do not say that a man who takes no interest in politics is a man who minds his business; we say that he has no business here at all' (Thucydides 1956: 119).

When the nation-state based on the 'people' first emerged, the view continued that apathy was incompatible with democracy. Following Rousseau, who, like Pericles, demanded an emotional commitment to democracy, Benjamin Constant (1806–10) argued that anyone who was too independent to take sides was a coward who in fact was siding with the existing power system. Fifty years later, Mill in 'Utilitarianism' was adamant that liberal representative institutions were of little value and might be used tyrannically if electors were not sufficiently interested to vote on public grounds rather than for private interests. Again, after the introduction of adult suffrage, James Bryce made clear that democratic citizenship required an active participation which went well beyond the obligation to vote (Bryce 1909). In the *Future of Democracy* (1984: 20ff) Norberto Bobbio lamented apathy as destructive of democracy.

When regional democracies like the European Union emerged, the criticism of apathy took on new form as the DEMOCRATIC DEFICIT which endangered the further development of the Union. To it were added the fears of proponents of global democracy that a global citizen could not feel sufficiently about a global community to play an active role in its government (see GLOBALISATION).

These concerns show that apathy is regarded as inimical no matter what the democratic procedures because it disempowers the popular sovereign. As the main civic duty in representative democracies is the exercise of the vote, it is failure to vote by large numbers of citizens which provokes anxiety. In the later nineteenth and early twentieth century, it was clear that many who were entitled to vote abstained. By the middle of the twentieth century in the USA, only about one-third of eligible voters voted for the Congress, and the highest proportion to vote in a presidential election was 63 per cent. In Great Britain 75 per cent voted; in Canada 70 per cent and in Australia, before compulsory elections, 59 per cent. Significantly, even in West Germany, Italy and France, where once 90 per cent voted, in the mid-1990s as few as half are voting in some elections. This follows the trend first manifest in the United States (Dalton 1988: 38–41). In European Union elections from 1979–94, between 58.5 and 62.4 per cent voted.

Alexis de Tocqueville had identified this trend and explained it as due to a lack of CIVIC VIRTUE, a concern for private interest. The solution was sought in civic EDUCATION, both practical and in school, about the benefits of voting (Mill 1964; Eckstein 1984). In the 1990s, many states are again promoting civic education to develop an active citizen. When this fails to stop abstention, it is argued that in the absence of economic, social and health rights it is difficult to be an active citizen (Marshall 1950). Yet the welfare state saw a worsening of the trend. It was then argued that WELFARE benefits rendered individuals passive. Finally, it is often asserted that the citizen's vote has no influence on the state and therefore citizens have no incentive to participate (Rosenberg 1954–5). In the United States this was even turned into a virtue on the grounds that it allowed competent elites to govern between elections (Berelson *et al.* 1954; Campbell *et al.* 1960).

Focus on the impotence of the voter to influence political decisions as an explanation for apathy led to many procedural changes to create more democracy in more places in the 1980s and 1990s. The object of bringing voter and representative institution closer together did not have the effect of raising voter participation. Experiments with electronic democracy are much contested (Dagger 1997: 135–9).

Compulsory voting and compulsory registration with sanctions for failure to do so do increase participation. The first exists in Australia, Belgium and Venezuela, and the second in New Zealand and Italy. Both are supposed to have an educatory function. It is also criticised as interference with the right not to vote for any candidate. No real evidence exists that it fosters the active citizen.

Apathy has usually been decried as inimical to democracy, and the passivity it breeds as likely to lead to despotism. When it is argued that apathy is functional to a complex democracy with its need for experts or is accepted as a sign of health in the polity, this provokes the criticism that, if accepted, it would undermine power from below and popular sovereignty. It makes the people, the mass or crowd, apathetic and alienated and suggests, like Marx, that there are only revolutionary solutions.

Yet in a postmodern future, personal fortitude in the face of risk and chaos may become an everyday mechanism for coping, which requires a distancing from affective politics. Such stoicism would not deny the possibility of popular irruption into the public place when the democratic stoics decided that the elite's decisions had left them out. This would remind the political experts that in the last analysis the people are sovereign, be they ever so absent on the day-to-day level (Brossat 1996: 9–22).

See also:

citizenship; civic virtue; democratic origins; education; elections

Further reading

Berelson, B., Lazarsfeld, B. and McPhee, W. (1954) *Voting*, Chicago: University of Chicago Press.
Bobbio, N. (1984) *Il futuro della democrazia*, Turin: Einaudi.
Brossat, A. (1996) *Fêtes sauvages de la démocratie*, Paris: Austral.
Bryce, J. (1909) *Promoting Good Citizenship*, Chicago: Houghton Mifflin.
Campbell, A., Converse, P., Miller, W. and Stokes, D. (1960) *The American Voter*, New York: John Wiley.
Constant, B. (1806–10) *Principes de politique applicables a tous les gouvernements*, Paris: Hachette.
Dagger, R. (1997) *Civic Virtues: Rights Citizenship and Republican Liberalism*, New York: Oxford University Press.
Dalton, R. (1988) *Citizen Politics in Western Democracies*, Chatham, NJ: Chatham House Publishers.
Eckstein, H. (1984) 'Civic Inclusion and its Discontents', *Daedalus* 113: 107–43.
Marshall, T. (1950) *Citizenship and Social Class and Other Essays*, Cambridge: Cambridge University Press.
Mill, J. (1964) *Utilitarianism, Liberty and Representative Government*, London: Everyman.
Rosenberg, M. (1954–5) 'Some Determinants of Political Apathy', *The Public Opinion Quarterly* Winter.
Thucydides (1956) *The Peloponnesian War*, Harmondsworth: Penguin.

ALASTAIR DAVIDSON

Asian models of democracy

The emergence of Asian developmental states in the course of the 1980s has caused much debate concerning their democratic character. Central to this debate is the role that cultures of an illiberal character play in promoting democratic legitimacy, effectiveness and institutionalisation. Asian democratisation has reflected a historically contingent and distinctive late developmental path.

Interestingly, democratic ideals constituted the most effective argument against colonial rule in the first half of the twentieth century. Decolonisation movements organised themselves around a democratic principle, of either a Marxist or a nationalist provenance. However, this principle viewed the people not as autonomous, rational individuals, but instead as a mass, organised collectively to release the inchoate people from colonial oppression. Asian development subsequently recognised the necessity for guidance by a nation building elite characterised by strong leadership. Modified to the needs of development, the Asian way came to emphasise superior men rather than good laws. Cultural understandings of a Buddhist, Islamic or Confucian provenance, modified for developmental purposes, reinforced a trend that devalued the role of the liberal individualism of the free market, which in any case evoked unsavoury associations with the colonial era.

While modernisation theory maintained that economic development created the preconditions for transition to democracy (Lipsett 1959), this transition acquired distinctive features in industrialising East Asia. Asian democracy emphasises society before self and processes of consensus and co-operation reached through face giving and face saving rituals that resist the institutionalisation of adversarial opposition. The consequences of this legacy has been a predilection in Asia for a one party dominant model of democracy, facilitating an autonomous BUREAUCRACY that promoted close links between party, bureaucracy and business conglomerates in an interventionist, developmental coalition (Quah 1993; Chan 1993).

In procedural terms these illiberal understandings by no means disqualify Asian states for purposes of democratic comparison. Asian models may be evaluated in terms of the extent to which they have established a democratic method that offers stable 'arrangements for arriving at popular decisions in which individuals acquire the power to decide by means of a competitive struggle for the people's vote' (Schumpeter 1946: 269, Huntington 1993: 6).

From this perspective, Asia has spawned a variety of electoral practices that have broadly promoted two models with distinctive Asian characteristics: a single party-dominant system, and multiparty democratic systems lead-

ing to unstable coalition governments with limited political effectiveness and uncertain legitimacy. India, the longest standing and most populous democracy in Asia, has been distinctive in that it democratised before it developed economically. Its federal constitution was most effective in the period before 1967 when the Congress Party operated as the vehicle of a secular national consensus at both federal and state level in a single party-dominant system. In the 1970s and 1980s the legitimacy of the Congress Party declined with the erosion of consensus and the failure of democracy to deliver economic growth or avoid bureaucratic corruption. Separatist movements in the Punjab, Kashmir and Tamil Nadu injected the potential for terror into the body politic. After 1986 the emergence of a militant Hindu caste-based nationalism under the auspices of the Bharatiya Janata Party (BJP) has introduced a new communalist element into an increasingly divided polity, characterised by unstable coalition governments. Between 1996–9, India witnessed four governments and a growing dissensus between an increasingly militant Hinduism and India's numerous religious and political minorities (Thakur 1995).

In Southeast Asia, single party-dominant systems have entrenched themselves in Singapore and Malaysia, while in the Philippines and Thailand, military-sponsored regimes have been replaced by uncertain but democratically legitimated civilian rule. In Malaysia the National Front, dominated by the United Malay National Organisation (UMNO) which rules in the Malay interest, has exploited its electoral dominance at both federal and state level since 1969 to extend its control over press and judiciary within a formally parliamentary system. In Singapore, the PAP has won successive elections since independence and has proved notably intolerant of political opposition. Here too, government control of the media and the absence of judicial independence, together with modifications to electoral BOUNDARIES through the shift from single-member to group representation constituencies has ensured the PAP retains absolute dominance over a unicameral parliament and over the hearts and minds of the population despite a declining share of the popular vote. In both Singapore and Malaysia, a procedurally democratic electoralism legitimates single-party rule and the attenuation of civil space.

Perhaps the most dubious electoralist politics in Southeast Asia sustained the *pancasila* democracy of Indonesia's New Order from 1966–98. New Order CORPORATISM legitimated itself through an electoral process which permitted only three state-licensed parties and ensured that the government party Golongkan Karya (Golkar) dominated the People's Consultative Assembly (MPR). The inability of the New Order to sustain its legitimacy in the wake of the Asian financial meltdown (1997) led to Indonesia holding its first multiparty elections since 1956 in conditions of economic and political turmoil.

In Thailand, by contrast, as in South Korea, government since 1945 has oscillated between long periods of military rule and brief and uncertain periods of democratisation. Since the failure of the last military coup in Thailand in 1992, government has been characterised by highly factionalised, weak coalitions composed of five or more parties, which have rendered decision-making difficult and meant that governments have been short-lived. Thailand has witnessed three general elections and four coalition governments between 1993–9. In South Korea, the transition from military rule to democracy has been accompanied by growing political uncertainty. After the 1992 election of the first civilian president for forty years, there has been a notable tendency to factionalism and vote-buying. As a consequence of the meltdown, successive leaders have failed to establish a grand factional alliance, common elsewhere in Northeast Asia, in order to sustain one-party rule. Little progress has been made in institutionalising constitutional safeguards on governmental control over media, judiciary and bureaucracy.

Elsewhere in Northeast Asia, the Nationalist Kuomintang (KMT) has ruled Taiwan uninterruptedly since independence. Significantly, it was the KMT that sponsored the transition

from authoritarianism. This elite-driven democratisation enabled the party to consolidate its mandate to rule when the Taiwanese 'entity' held its first democratic elections for the presidency in 1996. The consolidation of single-party dominance was further facilitated by the fact that the KMT has extensive business links and is the richest political party in the world. Similar links have enabled the Japanese Liberal Party to remain in effective political power since 1955. Apart from one brief spell out of office (1993–4) the Liberal Party has reigned but the bureaucracy has ruled in an iron triangle of business, party and bureaucracy. This governmental machine proved notably successful in securing postwar growth, but its resilience to change has demonstrated a structural incapacity to deal with the consequences of the Asian financial meltdown (1997–9).

In this context of electoral democracy the most efficient Asian models, whose legitimacy and effectiveness (Lipsett 1959: 86) reflected the ability to deliver growth with equity while maintaining political stability, have all possessed single party-dominant systems. Thus rule in Singapore, Malaysia, Japan and Taiwan has involved competition for power, but rarely entails alternation in power. It involves PARTICIPATION in ELECTIONS for all, but participation in office only for those of the dominant party.

The central problem encountered by both the single party-dominant and the less stable coalitional Asian model has been drawing boundaries between the domain of the dominant party and the degree of tolerance of an opposition. Thus although a number of East Asian states have made an uncertain transition from praetorianism or authoritarianism to a form of electoral democracy, constitutional constraints on government have been notable only for their absence, while cronyist relationships between government bureaucracy and business have tended, over time, to prevail. Even those states that have developed some elements of ELECTORAL COMPETITION, such as Thailand, South Korea, India and Taiwan, are notable for an intolerant factionalism and recourse to electoral bribery or 'money politics'. In all Asian states, constitutional safeguards on government intervention have been ineffectual. Long-established party rule tends to draw the judiciary and bureaucracy into a clientelist (see CLIENTELISM) arrangement that undermines the constitutional capacity for checks and balances. South Korea, which has uncertainly moved from praetorianism to electoralism, is currently enjoying its sixth constitution since 1950. Consequently, Asian models have encountered difficulty in securing leadership transition without undue economic or political chaos. Ultimately, Asian models reflect cultural understandings that emphasise hierarchy and deference and the value of co-operation and non-binding consensus rather than the face-losing consequences of rule-governed relationships, and the polymorphous joys of an autonomous CIVIL SOCIETY. The Asian model presents itself as a form of incorporated enterprise association rather than a civil association constrained by rule of law (see Oakeshott 1985).

See also:

associational democracy; democratic transition; representation, models of

Further reading

Bartley, R., Chan, H.C., Huntington, S.P. and Ogata, S. (1993) *Democracy and Capitalism: Asian and American Perspectives*, Singapore: Institute of South East Asian Studies.

Chan, H.C. (1993) 'Democracy, Evolution and Implementation', in R. Bartley, H.C. Chan, S. Huntingdon and S. Ogata (eds), *Democracy and Capitalism: Asian and American Perspectives*, Singapore: Institute of South East Asian Studies.

Huntington, S.P. (1993) *The Third Wave Democratisation in the Late Twentieth Century*, Norman, OK: University of Oklahoma Press.

Lipsett, S.M. (1959) 'Some Social Requisites of Democracy: Economic Development and Political Legitimacy', *The American Political Science Review* 53: 69–106.

Oakeshott, M. (1985) *Human Conduct*, Oxford: Clarendon Press.

Quah, J. (1993) *Shared Values*, Singapore: Centre for Policy Studies.

Schumpeter, J.A. (1942) *Capitalism, Socialism and Democracy*, London: Allen and Unwin.

Thakur, R. (1995) *The Government and Politics of India*, London: Macmillan.

DAVID M. JONES

assimilation

Assimilation occupies an ambiguous place in democratic thought, one that has shifted greatly over the course of the twentieth century. In the earlier part of the century, assimilation was the crowning concept in social thought about race and ethnicity. It emerged most prominently in the study of ethnic groups arising from immigration, which was assumed to be a movement from less to more developed societies. Assimilation was seen then as a form of liberation from the confines of an ascriptively assigned ethnic (or racial) group, thus opening up to the individual the wider possibilities of the mainstream society. At the close of the century, by contrast, the role of assimilation has generally been demeaned as a form of compulsion, requiring the individual to surrender ethnic cultures and loyalties for a possibly subordinate status in the mainstream. In an era of GLOBALISATION, when relationships across borders are relatively easily maintained, the preservation of ethnic memberships is seen as more possible than before and connected with economic, social and psychological benefits. Both of these contrasting views deserve to be handled sceptically.

One must recognise from the start that the concept of assimilation is multifaceted and mutable to a degree; it has been shaped by the reigning assumptions of an era. The concept nevertheless has deep roots in classical social theory as well as in North American social science, where it is often traced to Robert E.

Park's 1926 formulation of a race-relations cycle of 'contacts, competition, accommodation, and eventual assimilation' (Park 1950: 150). But the canonical statement of assimilation is due to Milton Gordon (1964). Although Gordon was addressing the role of ethnicity in the United States, his formulation is so general that it has been applied without much modification to other societies. At the heart of his contribution is the recognition that assimilation is a multidimensional concept. He distinguished, in fact, among seven types of assimilation, but the critical distinction lay between two: acculturation and structural (or social) assimilation. Acculturation means the adaptation by an ethnic group of the cultural patterns of the dominant, or majority, group. Such acculturation encompasses not only external cultural traits, such as dress and language, but also internal ones, such as beliefs and values. Gordon (1964: 77) theorised that acculturation is typically the first of the types of assimilation to occur, and that the stage of '"acculturation only" may continue indefinitely'; hence the importance of the second assimilation type, structural assimilation. Structural assimilation is defined by Gordon to mean the entry of an ethnic group's members into close, or primary, relationships with members of the dominant group (or, at least, with ethnic outsiders). The cardinal hypothesis in Gordon's scheme is that structural assimilation is the key that unlocks all other types: 'Once structural assimilation has occurred . . . all of the other types of assimilation will naturally follow' (Gordon 1964: 81). Once structural assimilation occurs, the way is open to widespread intermarriage, an abating of prejudice and discrimination and the full participation of ethnic group members in the life of a society.

One flashpoint for debate in the canonical statement concerns the apparent one-sidedness of assimilation. Indeed, Gordon characterised it as a largely one-way process, whereby the minority changes in order to become like the majority, which changes only marginally. Many subsequent commentators have found this feature objectionable and inherently undemo-

cratic. But, in truth, it is hard to see it as essential, and it appears to confuse the experience of assimilation by individuals, who surely do experience it as a one-way process of adjustment, with the changes that that take place at the group level. From this standpoint, the most suitable definition of assimilation is as the decline, and only at some ultimate endpoint the disappearance, of an ethnic distinction and the social and cultural differences that represent and reinforce it in everyday reality (Alba and Nee 1997). This definition is agnostic as to whether assimilation is one-sided or takes place as a result of changes in two (or more) groups that progressively narrow the cultural and social distance between them. In light of the North American experience, the fertile soil for assimilationist thought, the latter may be more common. Indeed, the melting-pot metaphor that so long stood for assimilation in the USA envisioned a society would become a cultural and social *mélange* through the fusion of its various racial and ethnic groups. In the famous formulation of Emerson (1921: xxxiv), for instance, it was patent that all groups would contribute to the resulting culture and that all would change as well. In America 'the energy of Irish, Germans, Swedes, Poles, and Cossacks, and all the European tribes, – of the Africans, and of the Polynesians – will construct a new race, a new religion, a new state, a new literature, which will be as vigorous as the New Europe which came out of the smelting-pot of the Dark Ages . . . La Nature aime les croissements'.

From the standpoint of democratic thought, another problematic aspect of assimilation has been the compulsion that many critics see in it. To be sure, there is an historical basis for the criticism, because in the USA assimilation was promoted during and shortly after the First World War by a crusade for '100 percent Americanisation', which aimed to remake the immigrants and their children into carbon-copy Americans in the shortest time possible. It is unclear how successful this campaign was, but in any event it seems evident in retrospect that assimilation in the USA occurred for the most part as a result of choices made by immigrants and their descendants. In fact, it is almost impossible to imagine that compulsion can be the means to successful assimilation on a broad scale, and much in the US experience suggests that compulsion produces defensive reactions that lead to a rejection of the mainstream society. Nevertheless, the immigrants and their descendants did not always intend to assimilate *per se*. They sought instead to take advantage of opportunities to improve their social and material situations, but the choices they made in doing so contributed to a gradual assimilation, which thus occurred as a by-product. This sort of assimilation was exemplified when socially mobile European ethnics departed from urban, working-class, ethnic neighbourhoods for middle-class and more ethnically mixed suburbs, with obvious ramifications for the environments in which their children would be raised.

Other criticisms of assimilation and its role in a democratic society strike closer to home and are therefore harder to counter. An especially strong challenge has been mounted by criticisms that are embedded in a multicultural framework. Multiculturalism here does not mean merely the factual existence of plural cultures sharing the same territory and state, for that has probably been true of most nation-states since this form of statehood was founded. Rather, it entails what the Canadian philosopher Charles Taylor (1992) has described, in his influential formulation of the concept, as the 'politics of recognition', in particular, a recognition by the cultural majority of the equal worth of minority cultures. Involved is more than the Enlightenment concept of tolerance (or 'negative liberty', in the terminology of Isaiah Berlin), allowing the minority to live as it chooses (with the usual qualifier: so long as this does not interfere with the right of others to live as they choose). According to Taylor, multiculturalism implies that the majority is willing, at least in some circumstances, to adopt measures that assure the survival of a minority culture. This could, for instance, require the state to provide schooling in a minority language, a policy that runs very much against the grain of assimilationist thinking.

At this juncture, whether the respective advantages associated with the multicultural and assimilationist positions can be joined in a synthesis of the best aspects of the two is a challenge of unclear resolution (for one attempt, see Hollinger (1995)). What is most attractive in the assimilationist position is its voluntarism with respect to ethnic membership, which thereby loses its originally ascriptive character. Moreover, unless one is willing to assume that the dissolution of minority–majority boundaries (an outcome that is envisioned in more utopian statements of multiculturalism), it is difficult to imagine how members of minorities can gain access to the full range of societal possibilities (for example, socioeconomic opportunities) without assimilation (see MINORITIES). But the cost of that access, according to the assimilation perspective, is the loss of at least some ethnic qualities and ultimately of full ethnic membership. These are the very assets that multiculturalism seeks to preserve for the individual; however, this can only be done by maintaining group-level structures, such as ethnic communities, and this requires that most individuals remain loyal to their groups (otherwise, the group structures will dissolve through depopulation, as an assimilation perspective predicts). This implies less FREEDOM for the individual in choosing group affiliations, and insofar as ethnic lines of division correlate with significant inequalities of wealth, power or prestige (which, of course, they do virtually everywhere), this loyalty constrains the opportunities available to the members of many ethnic groups. This dilemma is one that, at the beginning of the new millennium, is being confronted in the large number of societies that have become immigration nations since the end of the Second World War.

See also:

citizenship; civic virtue; ethnicity; minorities; rights, minority and indigenous; statelessness

Further reading

Alba, R. and Nee, V. (1997) 'Rethinking Assimilation Theory for a New Era of Immigration', *International Migration Review* 31: 826–74.

Emerson, R.W. (1921) *Essays and Poems of Emerson*, New York: Harcourt Brace.

Gordon, M. (1964) *Assimilation in American Life*, New York: Oxford University Press.

Hollinger, D. (1995) *Post-Ethnic America*, New York: Basic Books.

Park, R.E. (1950) *Race and Culture*, Glencoe, NY: The Free Press.

Taylor, C. (1992) *Multiculturalism and 'The Politics of Recognition'*, Princeton, NJ: Princeton University Press.

RICHARD ALBA

associational democracy

Voluntary associations are organisations formed by private citizens in order to pursue a common interest. Such associations are a typical feature of market societies in which governments exercise limited powers. Associations have played two main roles in modern democratic political theory. Pluralist theorists of liberal democracy from Alexis de Tocqueville to Robert A. Dahl (see POLYARCHY) have stressed the vital role of 'secondary associations' in mediating between the individual and the state. The FREEDOM of individuals to organise in civil society provides the foundation for that plurality of interests that makes it possible to have democracy without the tyranny of majority. Associational democrats have seen the function of such organisations very differently. For them, associations are not secondary, rather it is the state and market (see MARKET FORCES) that are subsidiary to the governing activities of freely associating individuals.

Associationalism was the original 'third way' between free-market INDIVIDUALISM and state socialism. Associationalists contended that, on the one hand, extreme LIBERALISM left large areas of social life ungoverned and that most citizens could actually only achieve their goal by banding together with their fellows, and on the other hand, socialism would lead to an excessive power of the centralised state over society. Voluntary associations could and should, therefore, take over the running of most social affairs. Such organisations should be democratically self-governing. Authority should be as decentralised and pluralised as possible. The state should be confined to only those roles for which it is absolutely inescapable and subject to the greatest possible bottom-up control.

There were three main traditions of associationalist thought that developed in the period from the mid-nineteenth century until the later 1920s. The first was the British Co-Operative Movement. Co-operators sought to organise production and distribution by mutually owned and democratically controlled institutions. They sought to build communities based on common ownership in civil society, relying on working-class self-action to challenge capitalism. The leading thinkers and organisers were Robert Owen and George Jacob Holyoake.

The second tradition was French mutualist socialism, of which the inspiration was Pierre-Joseph Proudhon. Proudhon advocated an economy decentralised to meet local needs and organised on non-profit principles. Production was to be controlled by self-regulating groups of workers. The economic system was designed to facilitate production and exchange, giving fair returns to labourers and consumers. It was designed to exclude unproductive incomes from land and financial assets, the true meaning of his misunderstood proposition, 'property is theft'. In *The Principle of Federation* (1863) he argued for a decentralised political system in which SOVEREIGNTY was to be vested in local communes, who made specific delegations of power upwards. Political authority above the local level was to have strictly limited purposes and powers, and the taxation to support it required the consent of the communes. Proudhon thought omnicompetent centralised states a threat to liberty and, for example, opposed the unification of Italy (Proudhon 1979).

The third tradition was English political pluralism and guild socialism. This had a German inspiration in Otto von Gierke's history of the law of associations, translated by the eminent legal historian F.W. Maitland. He and the theologian and political thinker John Neville Figgis developed a distinct pluralist critique of state sovereignty (Hirst 1989). Figgis's main work was *Churches in the Modern State* (1913). He argued that the modern sovereign state concentrated too much power in too few hands. Demagogic forces could easily capture this state, and there were too few countervailing powers to check it. He saw in Bismarck's campaign against the Catholic Church and French anti-clericalism a tendency toward the authoritarian use of state power that would culminate in fascist and communist totalitarianism. Figgis held that voluntary societies like churches and trades unions were no less real than the state; they should be free to govern themselves as they chose (provided they did not harm others). The concessionist theory of associations, then dominant in Britain and France, held on the contrary that associations were creations of state law and enjoyed only such powers as they were explicitly given. Figgis accepted the need for a public power, but saw it as the association of associations, facilitating their activities (see STATE, RELATIONS OF CHURCH TO).

The principal associationalist thinkers, G.H.D. Cole and H.J. Laski, drew on this pluralist theory (Hirst 1989). Cole was the leading theorist of guild socialism, rescuing it from neo-medievalist irrelevance. In *Guild Socialism Re-Stated* (1920) and *The Social Theory* (1920) he advocated the reorganisation of industry by national producer's guilds. Each guild was to have a representative structure. The national guilds were to join in an economic forum to co-ordinate industry. Consumer interests and individual rights were to be protected by a democratic parliament parallel to the guilds. Cole thus combined common ownership and the pluralisation of power with a degree of pragmatism. His guilds were intended to be capable of organising large-scale industry and to be compatible with professional management.

Laski argued equally cogently for both the decentralisation of government and democratic control in industry. He saw the danger of the political dominance of society by any one institution or interest, including organised labour. In his major work *A Grammar of Politics* (1925), he argued that all power in complex societies is inherently federative and that excessive centralisation simply distorts and masks the real need to make effective decisions at local level. Both state and industry needed decentralised political control.

Associationalism differed from other theories that advocated corporatist or FUNCTIONAL REPRESENTATION as an alternative to liberal democracy in its emphasis on voluntarism and individual liberty. CORPORATISM was often anti-liberal, seeing corporate representation as a vehicle for objective social interests and a check on the anarchy of INDIVIDUALISM. The only advocates of corporate representation compatible with associationalism were the French sociologist Émile Durkheim and his disciple, the legal theorist Léon Duguit. Durkheim saw organised occupational groups as a way of bringing the state and civil society together to co-ordinate economic and social life. Such corporatism was a supplement to representative democracy, not a replacement, and was designed to promote economic efficiency without the domination of state over society that Durkheim saw as inevitable in socialism.

Associationalism was influential in the period immediately before and after the First World War. It was widely seen as an alternative to communism after 1917. It declined when international conflicts and authoritarian social movements gave greater saliency to the central state. The Great Crash of 1929 also increased the credibility of state intervention and planning. Guild socialism also failed because it neglected the need to ensure state legislation favourable to the acquisition of economic power by the guilds.

Thus associationalism seemed an obsolete

doctrine, until the 1980s produced social and economic changes that gave it a new relevance. After the turbulence of the 1970s, large-scale hierarchically managed industries began to give way to new technologies and competitive pressures that favoured more flexible production methods and more decentralised authority structures in the firm. Increased economic internationalisation has weakened the perceived capacity of the central state to practice macroeconomic management. Welfare states are under increasing pressure from the contradictory trends of rising expectations about services and tax aversion. States have become providers of an increasingly diverse bundle of public services and, as such, difficult to control by traditional representative democratic means. Hence the new pressure for decentralisation and the devolving of state functions to publicly funded self-governing voluntary associations. The collapse of communism has also reinforced the attractiveness for radicals of a doctrine that advocates the control of firms by their stakeholders. Associationalist ideas are thus being explored and developed anew.

See also:

capitalism; civil society; corporatism; functional representation; trades unions; welfare

Further reading

Cohen, J. and Rogers, J. (1995) *Associations and Democracy*, ed. E.O. Wright, London: Verso.

Hirst, P. (ed.) (1989) *The Pluralist Theory of the State: Selected Writings of G.D.H. Cole, J.N. Figgis and H.J. Laski*, London: Routledge.

——(1994) *Associative Democracy*, Cambridge: Polity Press.

Nicholas, D. (1994) *The Pluralist State*, 2nd edn, London: Macmillan.

Proudhon, P.-J. (1979) *The Principle of Federation*, trans. R. Vernon, Toronto: University of Toronto Press.

PAUL HIRST

authority

Authority is a central concept in legal and political philosophy. 'Authority' may sometimes mean theoretical authority, which refers to an expert whose opinion on certain matters is superior to those of others and therefore entitled to be believed. But more often the word means practical authority, which refers to people who occupy some office or social role that entitles them to make decisions that are binding on the conduct of other people. Political authority is one kind of practical authority. To bring out more clearly the sense of practical authority, and political authority in particular, let us see what authority (as practical authority) is not. There are many ways to influence or change people's behaviour, authority being only one of them. COERCION can change behaviour, but it does not give the coercer an authority over the coerced. Authority is not even the legitimate use of coercive force. Sometimes it may be morally justified for X to coerce Y, as in the case of self-defence or humanitarian intervention, but it does not imply that X has authority over Y. Max Weber sometimes defines the state as an organisation which monopolises the legitimate use of force. The modern state claims more than this. What is claimed to be monopolised by the modern state is not only the legitimate use of force, but the authority to command people's behaviour through law. Authority is exercised through making commands or decisions that are regarded as binding. The more a state relies on coercion to secure compliance, the less authority it has over its subjects. The characteristic activity of authority is command, not threat or force.

The characteristic activity of authority is not the act of persuasion or of giving advice. As Hannah Arendt famously puts it, 'If authority is to be defined at all, it must be in contradistinction to both coercion by force and persuasion by argument' (1961: 93). If my superior asks me to do something simply by persuading me that that is the best available option, then he is exercising his persuasive reasoning skills, not authority. The distinctive feature of authority, as opposed to advice or persuasion, is that the command of an authority is itself the reason for action; I am not asked to judge whether the content of the command is reasonable, rather I am asked to act on the very command and not on my own personal evaluation of its merit. Following some legal theorists, we may say that that the command of an authority gives a 'content-independent reason' for the subject to act in the way required (Raz 1986: ch. 2; Green 1988: ch. 2). On the contrary, a piece of advice gives a 'content-dependent reason' for action. If I act on my friend's advice, I do so because I think the content of the advice is sensible or right.

Furthermore, authoritative commands are content-independent reasons that are also binding. They are binding, in the sense that they exclude the subject's own reasons for not doing what is commanded. This is why it is often said that authority requires 'surrender of private judgement' (Green 1988: 37; Friedman 1990) on the part of the subject. As Hobbes writes in his *Leviathan*, Part II, Chapter 25, 'Command is, where a man saith, Does this, or Does not this, without expecting other reason than the Will of him that sayes it.' In the *Second Treatise* (S.87), Locke is even more explicit about the necessity of surrendering private judgement in political society: 'All private judgement of every particular member being excluded, the community comes to be Umpire, by settled standing rules, indifferent, and the same to all parties.' The notion of 'surrender of private judgement' does not mean that we should not make any personal JUDGE-MENT on the merit of a command. What it means, rather, is that whatever personal judgement we may have, it should not be the reason for our obedience.

Authority thus puts a stringent demand on the subject. The one in authority can end a dispute with his subject simply by uttering: 'This is an order!' The subject in turn has to put aside his opinion and follow the order. The demanding nature of authority raises a question of its justifiability. Why should anyone put himself in such a dangerous position as being a subject of some authority? Why should we be morally obliged to recognise the authority of anyone? This problem is even more acute when political authority is in question, for political communities typically claim that their authority over the lives of citizens has a very wide, if not unlimited, scope. Perhaps it might be easier to show why it was readily accepted in pre-modern society, which is marked by value or religious homogeneity. Traditional political authority was typically supported by an authority supposedly higher than human will or reason, be it God's command, the Mandate of Heaven or the Natural Law. Obedience to political authority was seen as part and parcel of a general obedience to a divine form of authority. In this age of secularisation, however, human society and its institutions are primarily seen as human artefacts, which are the results of human choice, and hence ought to be answerable to the tribunal of human reason. Is there any reason, intelligible to the human faculty, that can justify the wide scope of authority of the modern state? This is a difficult question, especially for modern liberal society. Liberal society gives pride of place to individual AUTONOMY and RIGHTS. It allows a wide range of diverse ethical and religious beliefs and ways of life. There is an increasing number of theorists who argue that the authority of the modern state cannot possibly be justified, given the values and conditions of liberal society. One such argument is put forward powerfully by Robert Wolff.

Wolff's argument begins with the view that authority means 'the right to command', which entails the correlative obligation of obedience. The state claims to have authority precisely in this sense that citizens have a duty to 'obey the laws of the state simply because they are the laws' (Wolff 1970: 18). However, there is a fundamental conflict between this moral duty to obey state authority and our moral autonomy. Wolff adopts the Kantian view that we are not morally free to relinquish our moral autonomy. Every person has the duty to exercise his rational faculty in deliberating and judging whatever moral principles or commands that are to fall upon him. Morally autonomous agents may submit only to laws that they have made for themselves. To obey a command, to do something simply because we have been ordered to do, is to surrender our moral autonomy. So Wolff concludes that the 'defining mark of the state is authority, the right to rule. The primary obligation of man is autonomy, the refusal to be ruled. It would seem, then, that there can be no resolution of the conflict between the autonomy of the individual and the putative authority of the state' (Wolff 1970: 18).

This argument, though simple and powerful, depends on a crucial assumption that not everyone would accept. The assumption is that each person has a moral duty not to surrender his or her autonomy in any circumstances. However, one might argue that if, in the long run, it is in each individual's self-interest to obey the authority of the state, then why should we not surrender part of our autonomy and accept the authority of the state? Do we not often forfeit part of our autonomy in many different contexts of personal relationships and social organisations (for example, such autonomy-surrendering activities as making promises and commitments, consenting and so on)?

These questions lead us to consider whether there are any weighty reasons for anyone to submit to political authority, whether or not the latter restricts people's moral autonomy. Joseph Raz gives a set of conditions the fulfilment of which may show that there are such reasons for submitting to state authority. Raz holds what he calls 'the service conception of authority', that is, the view that authority's 'role and primary normal function is to serve the governed' (Raz 1986: 56). We have goals to pursue, and there are things that we ought to do as fellow members of a community, such as respect the rights of others and promote JUSTICE and the common good. All these are reasons for action whether or not there is an authority that tells us to do so. But sometimes we might better comply with these reasons if we collectively submit to an agent's authoritative commands and not act separately on our own. In this situation, we may have a good reason to accept the agent as having authority

(Raz 1986: chaps 3–4). Raz points out that this reason is normally sufficient to justify authority, unless there are counter reasons that defeat it. One important counter reason is the value of personal autonomy, namely, the 'intrinsic desirability of people conducting their own life by their own lights' (Raz 1986: 57). If we care about our autonomous choice of marriage partners as well as the rightness of our choices, then even the most effective marriage matching agency cannot claim authority over our choices of marriage partners.

Raz makes this argument only to show that the authority of the modern state can seldom satisfy these conditions. There are people who do not need authoritative guidance from any collective agency and still can effectively pursue personal goals and comply with moral reasons that apply to them. That they can do so may be due to their superior knowledge, skills or strength of character. In addition, there are also people who care as much about making decisions and pursuing goals by themselves as about doing them right. To the extent that this is the case, the state has no authority over the lives of these people. Raz concludes that his approach 'invites a piecemeal approach to the question of the authority of governments, which yields the conclusion that the extent of governmental authority varies from individual to individual, and is more limited than the authority governments claim for themselves in the case of most people' (1986: 80).

Does democracy provide any strong support to the justification of state authority? Maybe this is not the right question, for democracy offers an answer to the question 'Who should rule?', rather than 'Should anyone rule?' Many democratic theorists seem to have presupposed the legitimate existence of the state, and then to proceed to argue that the best form of the state is one of democracy. However, we may still ask whether democracy can offer us any help, however indirectly, in justifying state authority. One common answer is that it can, because people express consent to the state and its authority through taking part in democratic elections. Unfortunately, the connection between voting and consent seems at best uncertain. In some countries such as Australia, people are required to vote, and so voting of this kind cannot be taken as signifying voluntary consent to the state. On the other hand, in countries which do allow abstinence, there is always a large proportion of eligible voters and non-eligible residents who do not take part in voting, hence failing to indicate consent. More important, voluntary voting does not necessarily imply consent to the authority of the state. Even if voluntary voting confers some LEGITIMACY on the government elected, it does not imply that the voters have thereby promised to obey all the laws or policies made by the government. There is simply no clear and publicly known social convention from which we can draw this conclusion about the mental attitude of voters. Furthermore, any stipulation that such a convention should exist is highly unreasonable.

Nonetheless, while democracy may never justify state authority in its entirety, it might help to justify it to some extent. It does so in a negative and a positive way. Consider for example liberal democracy, which is the dominate form of democracy in Western countries today. First, notice that the self-image of a liberal democratic state does not claim, at least morally, that it has unrestricted scope of authority. No citizens have moral obligation to obey any state command or law that fundamentally violates the principles of individual rights and political EQUALITY. Therefore, liberal democracy makes state authority more legitimate (or less illegitimate) by re-defining the self-image of the state and delimiting the scope of its authority. Second, within the bounds of individual rights and political equality, the authority of the state may be made less problematic by the presence of democratic mechanisms and channels for public deliberation. Recall Raz's argument that authority is normally justified when it can help us better comply with reasons or pursue goals that we are already pursuing. However, a lot of controversies would arise on issues like what reasons we ought to comply with, what goals we want to pursue, whether the state has the capacity to help us do so and how much weight

we attach to individual FREEDOM. Now the crux is that neither state officials nor private individuals have clear and certain access to answers on these questions. Right reasons that justify or disqualify state authority are not easily available to everyone, let alone command agreement, prior to public deliberation. DELIBERATIVE DEMOCRACY, an ideal that emphasises the importance of reasoned discussion and deliberation in the public sphere, precisely aims to find out as best as we can the right reasons for the necessity of state action or otherwise. Reasoned public deliberation promotes the accessibility and TRANSPARENCY of the relevant reasons for or against state action. If the decisions coming out from reasoned public deliberation favour state action, then it improves the public acceptability of state decision and action. Liberal democracy may not justify state authority in the sense of justifying authoritative commands and the correlative moral obligation to obey. But in exposing the reasons behind state laws and decisions through democratic deliberative processes, it might achieve a similar practical effect in bringing about civil compliance if not obedience.

See also:

autonomy; civic virtue; deliberative democracy; equality; freedom; law, rule of; liberalism; rights; security

Further reading

Arendt, H. (1961) 'What is Authority?' in H. Arendt, *Between Past and Future*, New York: Viking.

Flathman, R.E. (1980) *The Practice of Political Authority*, Chicago: University of Chicago Press.

Friedman, R.B. (1990) 'On the Concept of Authority in Political Philosophy', in J. Raz (ed.), *Authority*, Oxford: Basil Blackwell.

Green, L. (1988) *The Authority of the State*, Oxford: Clarendon Press.

Hampton, J. (1997) *Political Philosophy*, Colorado: Westview Press.

McMahon, C. (1994) *Authority and Democracy*, Princeton, NJ: Princeton University Press.

Raz, J. (1986) *The Morality of Freedom*, Oxford: Clarendon Press.

Warren, M. (1996) 'Deliberative Democracy and Authority', *American Political Science Review* 90(1): 46–60.

Wolff, R.P. (1970) *In Defense of Anarchism*, New York: Harper & Row.

JOSEPH CHAN

autonomy

The term autonomy is derived from the Greek *auto nomous* and means literally, to give the law to oneself or to be self governing. In one sense it cannot be separated from the idea and institution of the state for its origin applied to institutions, primarily the polities of ancient Greece. It may also have been applied in a practical, if not theoretical, form to the ancient Mediterranean city-states (Weber 1960). Extant literature from the Greek and Roman periods contains numerous examples of the autonomy of polities. For instance, Dioderus Siculus, the first-century BC historian, when writing of the peace of the fourth-century BC, tells us that, 'The Greeks were enjoying the general peace of Antaclidas, in accordance with which all the cities had got rid of their garrisons and recovered by agreement their autonomy' (*Library*, Bk. 15, 5: 1 Perseus). He probably exaggerated both the peace and the autonomy, but the general point survives. The idea of a people having political autonomy continued through to Roman times. Marcus Tullius Cicero wrote that, 'A great number of states have been entirely released from debt, and many very sensibly relieved: all have enjoyed their own laws, and with this attainment of autonomy have quite revived' (*Letters*, Text A, 6: 2 Perseus).

In another, later, sense 'autonomy' applies not merely to states but also to individuals. Individuals were not present in any modern sense in ancient Greek communities. While Plato, and even before that Solon (594 BC)

writes often in what appears to be the first person singular, this is misleading, for the meaning and significance of the first person singular were quite different from meanings in more recent times. The ancient mind was more disparate than the modern mind. Comparisons must be made with the greatest caution. To take an extreme example Pritchard recounts the story of a young man who in contemplating suicide has a dialogue with his soul who threatens to leave him. Only the translation can enable us to make sense of this experience and it is clear that we are missing something of the directness of that kind of experience (Pritchard 1955: 405–07).

The rise of INDIVIDUALISM in the seventeenth century gave a new meaning to the term autonomy, indeed it is at this point that it came to the fore and came to be applied to human individuals. Its first formal occurrence in the modern individual sense seems to have been given by Cockerham in 1623, in the legal and proprietal dictum that a man may exchange something for something else (OED). The term was also applied to the newly emerging states of Europe. In 1793 Taylor alluded to the independence of all European states (OED). Concomitant with this development was the idea of personal autonomy developed most significantly by the philosopher Immanuel Kant. After Darwin, and as the biological sciences increased in significance, so the term autonomy was applied to biological entities capable of self-sustenance.

From the point of view of democracy, autonomy presents a necessary but problematic function. On the one hand, autonomy of states is required to provide the BOUNDARIES within which personal autonomy is possible, on the other hand personal autonomy is a threat to the autonomy of the state. Theologians have debated whether unbounded autonomy is possible for God, but be that as it may, it is clear that for humans autonomy is always bounded (Clarke 1999), that is to say, that humans require structures within which to act. Some structures prevent or inhibit autonomy, totalitarianism for instance, whereas other structures may possibly enhance autononomy. An example of the latter is a major claim that democracy enhances and even advances autonomy. To the extent that it continues to advance autonomy democracy is always an unfinished project. In this model the challenge for democracy is to continue to open its institutions while never losing control of the body politic.

This challenge to be both open in government and to retain control is almost insurmountable given the origin and nature of the modern European state and its offshoots; for other non-European forms of political life the challenge is even more difficult and different models of government may be necessary.

Schmitt (1985) argued that all political theory is founded in theology. This is no less true of the state than of any other political concept. Consequently it is not surprising to find that the absolutist and autonomous political state has its precursors in the early Middle Ages and in ecclesiastical theory and discussion. Its secular turn occurred as a consequence of the writings of Dante (see especially *De Monarchia*) and others who argued that the state and the church should be separate from each other (see STATE, RELATIONS OF CHURCH TO). The turning point in the development of the state and the autonomy of the prince is often placed with Machiavelli's *The Prince* published in 1513.

Hitherto the term 'state', as referring to the trappings of the great, was used frequently. The term 'state' has many uses dating back to Roman times but by the sixteenth century it was increasingly being used of the body politic. Thus Machiavelli refers to the state of the prince as partly his estate and person, but also partly and increasingly as a condition independent of the man and his possessions, and in any significant extent also of the Church. In every significant sense Machiavelli's writings, and those of his contemporaries, represented the development of the secular sovereign as autonomous and self-governing.

By 1538 the term 'state' was clearly established in early English political thought. Starkey writes in *England* that, 'The king, prince and ruler of the state...The governance

of the community and politic state...He or they which have authority upon the whole state' (*Oxford English Dictionary*, recension modified by author). But he goes onto suggest that while rule might be by a prince it could be by a group of wise men or even by the 'whole multitude' itself. This suggests that the people as a whole could be an autonomous political body.

By 1593, Shakespeare had incorporated the political sense of the term 'state' into many of his plays. For instance, in *Henry VI* III, 1 50–3, Henry enters the Parliament House and finds the Duke of York sat upon the throne. Henry speaks to those assembled:

> My lords, look where the sturdy rebel sits,
> Even in the chair of state! Belike he means
> Back'd by the power of Warwick, that false Peer –
> To aspire unto the crown and reign as king

The evidence is that the idea of, if not the word, autonomy was used in early modern times of states rather than of individuals and it was frequently held that obligation to the state was complete and absolute (Hobbes, Bodin). This absolutism undercuts autonomy, but the inverse is also the case, for personal autonomy, if complete, undercuts the authority of the state. This is an additional problem associated with autonomy and the state.

In the conditions of an absolutist state personal and moral autonomy are weakened or even eliminated. It follows, therefore, that obligation to the state may, in such conditions, be absolute. In such a case all orders given by the state should be obeyed. If state law was absolute and the state was also autonomous then it would seem that an absolute defense for committing heinous crimes could be given if it were shown that the defendant was following orders of the state. Since 1945 and the Nuremberg Tribunals this situation has formally shifted. After General Jodl's defense at Nuremberg, that he was only obeying orders, it is held now that there is a difference between legitimate and illegitimate orders. Nuremberg showed that the claim that one is merely obeying orders is an insufficient defense to an action taken under municipal law. It remains to be seen whether the same principle will apply to actions taken under international law. Would it for instance be a defense to claim that one was acting under international law sanctioned by the Security Council? The tentative answer would appear to lie in the negative, for even the Security Council is bound by its own rules, the Charter of the United Nations and the Declaration of Human Rights and other rules and codes of law and practice.

The underlying moral claim to these limitations are manifold but are, perhaps, nowhere better expressed than in Adolf Eichmann's trial in Jerusalem, when Kant's philosophy of moral autonomy was given its ultimate distortion by Eichmann. Eichmann was the overseer of the death of six million Jews. He said in his trial that he just sat at his desk and did his business and that he obeyed the Categorical Imperative, the supreme moral command given by Kant (Clarke 1980). Understanding this moral distortion requires understanding the moral philosophy of Immanuel Kant who above all brought autonomy and individualism to the forefront of modern moral philosophy and into the heart of democracy.

In the *Groundwork to a Metaphysics of Morals* (1785), Kant argued that morality required a good will. This was the only condition of being that was unconditional and unconditionality was required for pure morality. Kant argued that all other causes of action were motived by some external source such as desire. Kant thus set autonomous or unconditional action against empirical or motivated action, so called heteronomous action. A moral action included, among other features, autonomy, whereas an immoral or amoral action included heteronomy. Central to Kant's formulation of morality was the Categorical Imperative, the basic principle of which was that one should always act on a maxim that one could will to become a universal law.

Kant's basic principle came under considerable attack. Hegel charged it as a generator of moral action and therefore not a moral principle at all. Numerous readings have followed Hegel and, therefore, underestimi-

tated Kant's freedom from social formations and his contribution to the idea of individual autonomy and responsibility for one's own actions. This seems to be a basic misreading of Kant. The Categorical Imperative is not a generator of moral actions but a test of a proposed moral action: it is a maxim, not a rule.

In *The Second Critique, The Critique of Practical Reason* (1788), Kant drew a distinction between the principles of the right and the good. In drawing this distinction he broke with an ancient tradition, going back at least to Plato, that one could specify the good polity. In *The Republic*, Plato had specified a perfect polity. He admitted that it was unlikely that this would ever come into being but that it was a reality residing in eternity. In drawing a distinction between the right and the good Kant dispensed entirely with this powerful tradition. He placed the right before the good, the consequence of which led to diversity rather than unification. The good specified a particular way to live and brooked no contrary actions whereas the right permitted diversity provided the moral law was kept. Again we see the effect of the Categorical Imperative as a test of action rather than a generator of action. The effect of this intellectual revolution was profound, if delayed in its effects.

Concomitant with Kant's intellectual revolution was a revolution in the European states. No sooner had the nation state reached its condition of autonomy than its autonomy began to be eroded. The major example was the French Revolution, which heralded the Sacred Rights of Men. There is no suggestion that Kant was responsible for this revolution – far from it – but the historical closeness of the two events and Rousseau's own use of the term autonomy tend to indicate an era of massive change. As it happens, the autonomy of the state grew until the nineteenth century when it reached its autocratic, warlike and imperialist height (see IMPERIALISM). In places, for example in Great Britain, a modicum of democracy was evident in a limited voting system but the state, for all that, retained its effective autocracy and autonomy.

Nonetheless, several things were occurring: treaties, human rights talk, ineffective wars and the idea of individual autonomy. Treaties made alliances between countries and limited their actions in and of war. The idea of human rights, the term which was introduced by Thomas Paine, gave a language to what could be done by one person or institution to another person. Ineffective wars led both to peace treaties and agreements on the limits of war, for instance it was agreed after the First World War that it would be a war crime to wage an aggressive war. The idea of individual autonomy made the individual responsible for their actions; the *locus classicus* of which is General Jodl's defense, struck down by the Nuremberg court on the grounds that he was responsible to a higher law than municipal law.

'Autonomy' applies to both persons and institutions although in different ways and these, as indicated, come into conflict at numerous points. The autonomy of institutions, or things, is certainly sortal (Clarke 1988: Pt. II) but there is no evidence that they are conscious. While it is often disputed that individuals are conscious the Kantian model, which takes individuals as rational beings, as persons, does assume consciousness and reflexivity. Indeed Kant in *The Third Critique, The Critique of Judgment* (1790) takes it that an autonomous person is able to take the point of view of someone else. This assumes that an autonomous person is reflexive and capable of judgment. To some extent, advanced institutions exhibit these characteristics but they do not demonstrate the independence of action, reflexivity and project making that such abilities show of Kant's rational beings. They are constructs, not persons.

The Nuremberg Tribunals, the trial of Eichmann in Jerusalem and the recent, if weak, trials in The Hague settled in international law the principle that a state was not autonomous: it was responsible to the international community for its actions. In practice this was rather weak, but it established a firm principle: that states were not fully autonomous, they were accountable to the newly established international community. This newly established international community is delicate and vulnerable in practice but it establishes an important principle: namely, that no state could be wholly responsible for its own actions. It was responsible, in principle, to forces outside as well as inside itself. Machiavelli's realism was ameliorated, if not ended.

Kant's principle of placing the right before the good resurged in the 1980s in the debate between COMMUNITARIANISM and LIBERALISM. The essence of this debate was whether the self preceded or succeeded society. The issue was significant: the Kantian position required that there was autonomy prior to society, whereas the minimal liberal position posited that the self was successant to society.

This brings the variety of conflicts between autonomy, democracy and political obligation to a head. On the one hand, democracy demands the capacity to act according to its own constitutional imperatives including the imperative to act according to its own interests (Machiavellian and post-Machiavelli realism). Yet personal autononomy requires the ability and practice of the individual person to act according to self-governing principles. There may well be cases where the demands of the state conflict with the autonomy of the individual. In such a case there is a conflict of POLITICAL OBLIGATION.

While there is no exact source of the modern individual, it is generally accepted that the principal roots were laid in 394 with Augustine's *Confessions*, a tract written for the first time in the modern sense of the first person singular. Augustine introduced into discourse the use of the word and concept 'I' as it is broadly understood in its present sense. In modern times that 'I' became central and was centered on the individual by Descartes who in his famous phrase, *Cogito ergo sum*, 'I think, therefore I am', placed the thinking subject at the center of life. The individualism that resulted from this became the modern source of the philosophical idea of autonomy. This idea of the individual as centered persists even now: it is the apotheosis of basic autonomy. Similarly the idea of the state as autocratic and absolute is the apotheosis of the nation state:

the one reflects the other. That they reflect each other is not surprising, they came into being together, grew together and mirrored each other in their development and aspirations. A *problematique* of obligation and a conflict was inevitable, the center of which is to be found in political obligation: this is the issue for democracies.

However, a series of intellectual and practical events came to challenge Descartes's powerful formula. Descartes's maxim rested on the view that the mind was transparent and could examine itself. Kant argued in his First Critique, *The Critique of Pure Reason*, that the mind had only its own faculties, reason, with which to examine itself. The implication of this was that the mind was not transparent to itself; a view he incorporated into some of his moral philosophy. Later philosophers Freud, Saussure, Wittgenstein, Schutz, for example, demonstrated in various ways that the mind was not so much transparent as opaque. The implication of this, if correct, was that the individual was decentered, not existing at a single point but composed of a locus of separate traces. If correct, this has considerable consequences for the issue of autonomy for it is not clear *who* it is that could be autonomous. Similarly, it is not clear whom it is that could owe obligation to the state.

Fortunately for this otherwise insoluble conundrum, a similar deconstruction was occurring to advanced western democratic states. Many treaties, often led by CIVIL SOCIETY, combined the ideal of human rights with the actions of multilateral forces under either the mandate of the United Nations or NATO. This has led to a moderation in the autonomy of the state. This process of a weakening of the autonomy of the state is far from complete but it is at its beginning. What one can say is that the autonomy of the nation state is in the process of being undercut.

How far this twin undercutting of the hitherto strict boundaries that have surrounded the state and the individual will go is impossible to say. What it is possible to say is that a complete deconstruction of either the individual or the state or both would undercut

autonomy. Autonomy requires boundaries as well as the idea of the individual, the person and cognate notions. The state and cognate notions gave those boundaries within which autonomy could be exercised. Relatedly moral codes and cognate ideas, such as mores and folkways, provide structures within which autonomy can be exercised. Whether it is in practice exercised depends on the codes, mores, folkways and communal and political structures that exist at the time. No political structure has to have autonomous arrangements and it is a moot point whether such arrangements suit all cultures at all times. It is also a moot point as to whether autonomy requires individualism or not. Western autonomy is built on Christian values but it is far from clear whether that is necessary or not. As it happens the answer to all these questions is far more a posteriori than it is a priori. Indeed, one could go further and assert that any claim that Western values are required for autonomy is asserting a prejudice rather than a study.

One more claim needs to be dealt with; this is the view that autonomy is impossible because all our actions are determined. In one sense this is easy to deal with. If by determinism is meant some kind of Laplacian universe, then that is clearly untrue. Quantum physics and other domains of science deal with that kind of determinism and its successors quite nicely and no more need be said about that. If by determinism is meant, however, biological, genetic, chemical, molecular, psychological, social, political or similar forms of determinism the dance between autonomy and determinism would become far more interesting. Which if any of these alone could defeat, say, a strong Kantian autonomy would be difficult to determine but the unusual conclusion implied by Weber, Schutz, Wittgenstein and others is that even taken together they could not defeat the ability of the human mind to write part of its own hermeneutic, to play its own poetry and dance its own dance in the circumstances given to it. But that kind of autonomy, as with every autonomy, has also to be tempered by the wisdom of a very wise man who wrote of princes and states many years ago: 'All those autonomies wherewith the world was…one-after another stop and many years ago' (Rankes Popes 1849).

See also:

democratic origins; identity, political; individualism; political obligation

Further reading

Clarke, P.B. (1980) 'Beyond "The Banality of Evil"', *British Journal of Political Science* 10: 417–39.

—— (1988) *The Autonomy of Politics*, Aldershot and Brookfield, USA: Avebury.

—— (1999) *Autonomy Unbound*, Aldershot and Brookfield, USA: Avebury.

Pritchard, J.B. (ed.) (1955) *Ancient Near Eastern Texts Relating to the Old Testament*, Princeton, NJ: Princeton University Press.

Schmitt, C. (1985) *Political Theology: Four Chapters on the Concept of Sovereignty*, trans. G. Schwab, Cambridge, MA: MIT Press.

Weber, M. (1960) *The City*, ed. and trans. D. Martindale and G. Neuwirth, London: Heinemann.

PAUL BARRY CLARKE

B

boundaries

Boundaries are the outer perimeter of a defined area, especially one established for political purposes. Although the terms 'boundary' and 'frontier' are often used as synonyms, formally a frontier is a zone of varying width dividing two areas, whereas a boundary is a fixed line between them. In the study of politics, the term 'boundary' refers not only to the circumference of a state's defined territory, but also more widely to other spatially-defined circumferences (such as those of sub-state units and tracts of private property): more abstractly and generally, it is also used as a metaphor for a variety of demarcation limits, such as those of a discipline within the academic division of labour.

Boundaries have become increasingly important in recent centuries as competition for land has increased and the nation-state has become a dominant player in the world-economy. The emergence of the modern state system since the seventeenth century has involved increased conflict over territory, and acceptance of a state's right to exist within the world-system has involved recognition and respect for its sovereignty over a defined territory.

Boundaries are intrinsically involved with the nature of the state and its power base: the state is necessarily a territorially defined unit in modern theory and practice, and as the modern world-system emerged, along with a structure of international relations between territorial states, so the importance of boundaries grew. Boundaries are the spatial expression of the limits of state power and the lines across which international relationships are conducted: states are the containers within which the modern world is organised and power is structured (Taylor 1994). As Anderson (1996: 1) puts it, 'All political authorities and jurisdictions have physical limits – a characteristic often regarded as so obvious that it does not warrant further comment.'

The importance of boundaries to the modern state reflects the nature of the power that it exercises, and its chosen mode of doing so. Power is multivariate, as Mann (1984) and others have stressed: its two main dimensions are the degree to which it is *despotic*, whereby those in control of the state apparatus make demands on the population without regular consultation on the nature of those demands and how they are operationalised; and the extent to which it is *infrastructural*, infiltrating most (all?) components of CIVIL SOCIETY (of economic, social and cultural life). With a binary classification on each dimension, this gives four types of power, as indicated in the table below:

		infrastructural power	
		low	*high*
	low	feudal	bureaucratic
despotic power			
	high	imperial	authoritarian

Despotic power at low levels of infrastructural infiltration can be exercised without clearly demarcated boundaries: it is imposed on those subject to it simply because of their proximity to its source, as in feudal situations where serfs lived on a lord's lands, and in imperial situations, where control by the outside body depended on the spatial span of its power and ability to sustain it. Where the infrastructural demands are high, however, bounded containers are needed to sustain its practice.

Bounded containers (state spaces) are crucial (necessary?) to the exercise of infrastructural power in a modern state because they provide the context within which territoriality strategies can be exercised. *Territoriality* has been presented as 'a powerful geographic strategy to control people and things by controlling area... It is used in everyday relationships and in complex organisations. Territoriality is a primary geographical expression of social power. It is the means by which space and society are interrelated' (Sack 1986: 5). Sack (1986: 19) defines it as 'the attempt by an individual or group to affect, influence, or control people, phenomena and relationships, by delimiting and asserting control over a geographic area'.

Territoriality involves classifications by area, which can be communicated through territorial markers (on the ground and in representations such as atlases and cadastral plans), and it involves the exercise of power through both controlling access to the defined area (external or international relations) and restraining the behaviour of those within it (internal relations). These characteristics make territoriality an excellent strategy for controlling people, because it identifies the limits within which the power being exercised apply, makes the relationships between the powerful and the controlled impersonal ('it is the law of the land' rather than 'I say you must do this'), and reifies power and its exercise through its association with a thing: territory. As states increased their exercise of infrastructural power through the modern period, and increasingly favoured territoriality as a strategy for controlling

people and interactions, so boundaries became increasingly important elements in the definition of the state apparatus.

Territoriality strategies and the associated boundary definition have played a further crucial function in the creation and operation of the modern state system. The bounded states became the containers within which identities were produced and reproduced: the state became the nation-state, a concept (and associated territory) with which, through a variety of ideological and other means, people associated themselves. Part of the definition of 'self' involved identifying with one's national territory, and the definition of 'others' involved identifying those associated with states apart from one's own. Identities within the world system were thus forged within the system of bounded state territories, forming the basis for much of the patriotism and nationalism that has pervaded nineteenth and twentieth-century life.

Boundary definition and boundary drawing were therefore crucial components of nineteenth and twentieth century geopolitics. Some geographers suggested that states should be delimited by their natural boundaries, elements of the physical landscape which were clearly identifiable and formed limits to human activities and occupance. But even the delimitation of a 'natural boundary' – whether a river course or the watershed of a range of mountains – involves an arbitrary selection, of a line which may not be very stable (as shown by the shifting course of the Rio Grande selected as the boundary between Mexico and the United States of America: Prescott (1985a: 81–90)).

One of the important functions of container definition is delimiting areas with which people identify, and since most societies' territories predate the modern state-system in their broad outline – i.e. the core areas with which they associate are defined, even if the exact boundaries are not – it is these which have influenced most boundary definition rather than lines in the physical landscape that may have no relationship to the territory a group has settled and claimed. (The major exception to this was the imperial claims for already settled lands, notably in Africa, where boundaries delimited by the colonial powers frequently bore little or no resemblance to the lands of the tribes already settled there.) Thus boundary drawing has involved identifying the areas associated with particular groups (tribes, nations and so on). In some cases these were clearly delimited but in many cases they were not, because of the intermixture of various groups over long periods of settlement and the occasional 'leaping' of one group's territories by another to create exclaves/enclaves (as with some Swiss cantons).

Many contemporary state boundaries evolved within frontier regions, some relatively thinly settled. As populations grew and the demand for land intensified, states expanded into those frontier zones, eventually coming into contact and, potentially, conflict. This required boundary definition and demarcation, based on either pre-existing lines or negotiated alignments, with the latter based on a variety of criteria: some in the physical landscape, some on human-made features (including individual property holdings), and some on trigonometric criteria (such as the Canada–USA boundary across much of the Great Plains). Once delimited and demarcated, they became significant elements of the landscape. The boundary may be only vaguely delimited and there may have been no original demarcation, however, providing the potential for later dispute over contested territory, which was especially important if the ownership of valuable resources was involved.

Whereas many boundaries were created through a process of negotiation between representatives of the adjacent states, others were imposed by external bodies such as imperial powers and victorious allies after a war (as with the Treaty of Versailles in 1919). Such imposed boundaries are quite likely to be sources of future conflict, especially if they pay scant regard to pre-existing boundaries/frontiers, as occurred in the Balkans in 1919; attempts were made to create states associated with separate ethnic groups, but the complex settlement mosaic prevented the identification of clear divisions between such groups (exacerbated by the competing claims over territory by representatives of the competing groups: Wilkinson (1951)). The potential for conflict sown then has been reaped during the 1990s with the collapse of the former state of Yugoslavia and the 'ethnic cleansing' that has accompanied the territorial claims of competing groups.

Whereas boundary delimitation and demarcation on land presents many difficulties in a large number of cases, the problems of boundary drawing and marking in what Kish (1973) terms international spaces – basically the high seas and the atmosphere, plus Antarctica – are much greater. Until relatively recently, such spaces were classified as *res communis humanitatis* (*rch*), territory not only beyond state claims but recognised as the common property of all humanity. The right of passage in international waters was generally accepted, for example, but as the demands for movement through them increased and the ability to harvest their resources developed, so states made claims on maritime territory. Until that time, states claimed SOVEREIGNTY over narrow bands of water adjacent to their coasts only, which may have generated conflict where two states were competing for the same waters. These territorial seas became recognised as zones twelve miles wide, but under the various United Nations Conferences on the Law of the Sea convened from 1958 on (Churchill and Lowe 1985), an additional zone was defined over which adjacent states could make sovereignty claims: the continental shelf (later renamed as the *Exclusive Economic Zone*), a zone 200 miles wide within which states could claim near-exclusive rights over seabed resources. Only the high seas beyond that zone remained as *rch*, but even there conflicts have arisen over the exploitation of mineral and other resources on the seabed.

This growing interest in and claims over marine resources has stimulated a need to delimit inter-state maritime boundaries, even if they cannot be precisely demarcated. Conflict has focused in recent decades over the exact delimitation methods for this using trigonometric procedures, as illustrated in Prescott (1985b) and Blake (1994).

Boundaries between states attract most public attention, because of their role as stimuli to major international conflicts. But there are many other political boundaries within individual states that are much more important in most people's daily lives, because they are related to issues of taxation levels, political representation and so forth: many aspects of intra-state economic, social, cultural and political life are organised within political containers, and the state also recognises and defends others, notably the containers that are the basis of individual personal property. Boundary delimitation by the state is also the focus of much conflict and debate – over local government territories, for example, and the definition of constituencies for electoral purposes – as is the role of the state apparatus in adjudicating claims over private property. In a number of states recently, demands for limited autonomy by sub-national groups (if not outright succession) has brought these boundaries into sharper focus: devolution and decentralisation involve not only cartographic exercises, however, but also the creation (or re-creation) of containers within which new identities are forged and new territoriality exercises are played out, as in the ethnic cleansing processes that have characterised several post-socialist countries since 1989.

Territoriality, power and spatial boundaries are also components of many aspects of everyday life which may be only weakly linked to the established political processes, if at all. At the smallest scale, many individuals define their own territories as restricted spaces over which they have power (such as a child's bedroom or a pupil's roughly-bounded area within a dormitory): within those limits, their constrained power is exercised. Most property-owners define the limits of their small tracts of land with fences, hedges or other boundary markers, and claim the right to determine what is done within those containers. Community groups define the territories that they 'control' (as with 'neighbourhood watch' and similar voluntary organisations), and other less formal groups, such as street gangs, may delimit their 'turfs' by markers (such as graffiti) as well as defending them from incursions by opponents. Space is a crucial resource for individuals and groups, for defining themselves and for separating themselves from others, who may be threatening (as in the creation of inner-city defensive ghettos). The boundaries of such containers may lack the legal force of those defined by the state (although most states register property boundaries and provide a range of police functions to sustain them), but they are nonetheless highly significant in the structuration of social and cultural, if not economic and political, life.

Whereas territoriality and associated boundaries have dominated the political landscape of the modern era, there is increasing recognition that with GLOBALISATION and a postmodern world we are at least partially moving beyond containers (Taylor 1995). Just as small-scale containers such as walled cities became obsolescent with the development of modern warfare, bounded states are now going the same way with the development of atomic weapons, intercontinental missiles and 'star wars' technologies (Herz 1957). Similarly, economic life is no longer as constrained by state boundaries as previously and the main non-state actors in the global economy frequently pay them scant regard. Nevertheless, despite the greater porosity if not irrelevance of state boundaries for many aspects of international economic life, states remain important regulators of the world economy and continue to use containers as major elements of their territoriality strategies (Dicken 1997). In the social and cultural spheres, containers and territoriality remain crucial to so many aspects of life, and states police their boundaries as strictly as ever (Johnston 1997), whereas within their territories a variety of groups operate similar strategies as means of promoting their own exclusive ends (McKenzie 1994). Governments, too, continue to use territoriality strategies as administrative conveniences, even though some also make claims to represent people who identify with the state wherever they may live. Boundaries remain very significant features of all landscapes.

See also:

globalisation; imperialism; inclusion/exclusion; political frontiers

Further reading

Anderson, M. (1996) *Frontiers: Territory and State Formation in the Modern World*, Cambridge: Polity Press.

Blake, G.H. (ed.) (1994) *Maritime Boundaries*, London: Routledge.

Churchill, R.R. and Lowe, A.V. (1985) *The Law of the Sea*, Manchester: Manchester University Press.

Dicken, P. (1997) *Global Shift*, London: Sage.

Herz, J.J. (1957) 'Rise and Demise of the Territorial State', *World Politics* 9: 473–93.

Johnston, R.J. (1997) 'Geography in a Restructuring World', *GeoJournal* 42(1): 9–16.

Kish, J. (1973) *The Law of International Spaces*, Leiden: A W Sijthoff.

McKenzie, E. (1994) *Privatopia: Homeowner Associations and the Rise of Residential Private Government*, New Haven, CN: Yale University Press.

Mann, M. (1984) 'The Autonomous Power of the State: Its Origins, Mechanisms and Results', *European Journal of Sociology* 25(1): 185–213.

Prescott, J.R.V. (1985a) *Political Frontiers and Boundaries*, London: Allen & Unwin.

—— (1985b) *The Maritime Political Boundaries of the World*, London: Methuen.

Sack, R.D. (1986) *Human Territoriality: Its Theory and History*, Cambridge: Cambridge University Press.

Taylor, P.J. (1994) 'The State as Container: Territoriality in the Modern World-System', *Progress in Human Geography* 18(2): 151–62.

—— (1995) 'Beyond Containers: Internationality, Interstateness, Interterritoriality', *Progress in Human Geography* 19(1): 1–15.

Wilkinson, H.R. (1951) *Maps and Politics: A Review of the Ethnographic Cartography of Macedonia*, Liverpool: University of Liverpool Press.

RON JOHNSTON

bureaucracy

As a hierarchical organisation of officials appointed to fulfil tasks delegated to them by elected politicians, bureaucracy is historically a component of all modern democratic systems, and a necessary one since democratic systems require agents to implement the tasks that voters charge governments to fulfil. Yet bureaucracy, perhaps more than any other component of democratic systems, is popularly and almost universally regarded as a danger to democracy. As Reinhard Bendix (1945: 195) pointed out many years ago, 'it is part of our folklore to identify the development of bureaucracy with the diminution of individual freedom'. Like most folkloric wisdom, this view of bureaucracy expresses only a partial truth. The problem is not that bureaucracy is necessarily anti-democratic, but that it has a capacity to become so when uncontrolled by other forces. This capacity derives from two main sources.

First, bureaucracy is partially exempt from a basic rule of democracy, namely that accountability and continuity in office are determined through elections. Bureaucrats do, of course, change when governments change because of shifts in electoral fortune, but there is usually a high degree of continuity between administrations because post-electoral changes to a bureaucracy generally only affect a few senior bureaucrats. Moreover, in most political systems it is common for incoming senior bureaucrats to be drawn from the same corpus of bureaucrats that provided their predecessors. The degree to which elections lead to bureaucratic renewal is thus suspect, and rightly so. Changes of personnel do not by themselves lead to changes in bureaucratic 'culture', to changes in how bureaucrats view their responsibilities and work, and most importantly to how they view their relationship to the democratic process and the wishes of electorates.

Bureaucracy is thus beyond democratic – if by this we mean electorally enforced ACCOUNT-ABILITY and tenure of office – control for the most part. As a result, it is seen as able to bring its own preferences to bear on policy, no matter what the wishes of the electorate might be.

Bureaucratic 'culture' is the second source of bureaucracy's anti-democratic capacity, and is inextricably linked to the tasks that bureaucrats undertake. Consequently, all bureaucracies have a latent anti-democratic managerial tendency by virtue of the fact that they are bureaucracies. The function of bureaucracies is to fulfil tasks delegated to them by popularly elected politicians as they create policy. Although they might seek to fulfil electoral promises, politicians' choice of policy and the methods for its implementation are shaped by their interaction with bureaucrats. Bureaucrats not only shape policy in this interaction through their personnel political beliefs and career aspirations, but also because their task of policy implementation requires them to be managers of society and social conflict. As a result, they tend to treat democratic citizens, their supposed masters, 'as an object of management . . . rather than as the autonomous subjects of social and political activity' (Beetham 1996: 99). This managerial view of society creates a bureaucratic ethos of secrecy, a belief that the management of society requires bureaucratic activity to be hidden from public scrutiny in order that it might be more managerially effective, and a bureaucratic imperative towards AUTONOMY, that is, a desire to be as free as possible from interference from social forces that might impair management. It is thus not surprising that there is a tendency in both popular belief and modern political theory (in all its variations) to perceive bureaucracy as anti-democratic. It is important to note, however, that although bureaucracy has the potential to be anti-democratic, it is the actions of politicians rather than bureaucrats that enable a bureaucracy to fulfil its potential. Where bureaucratic power increases without concomitant commitments from politicians to open up both the policy formulation and implementation processes to public scrutiny,

and to prevent the partisan politicisation of the bureaucracy, then the anti-democratic nature of bureaucracy will develop thanks to its own managerial logic.

Such commitments were rare in the twentieth century, even though there was a vast expansion of bureaucratic activity. As a result, the perception of bureaucracy as an anti-democratic force spread. The rise of communist and fascist totalitarian states from the 1920s onwards created bureaucracies that sought to manage all aspects of human activity. Formed by utopian ideologies, the totalitarian state took the basic function of bureaucracy, the pursuit of politically defined goals, to extremes. In such states, bureaucracies claimed not only to strive for the rational implementation of political objectives, but came to define what those objectives might be. The result was a 'dictatorship over needs' in which individuals were turned into dependent supplicants to bureaucrats who determined both access to public goods and the right to, and supply of, private goods as well. Secrecy and bureaucratic autonomy were total and proved inimical to reform. Only systemic collapse via war or total economic failure broke the total hold of totalitarian bureaucracies on public life, and even then systemic collapse has not always led to democracy.

An analogous process to the expansion of bureaucratic power under totalitarianism appeared to occur in advanced capitalist democracies. The postwar expansion of welfare states required a vastly expanded bureaucratic apparatus. This created the impression that bureaucracies were increasingly gaining autonomy, the capacity to define policy independently of elected representatives and at the cost of individuals' ability to decide themselves how to use their wealth. Criticism of the expansion of bureaucratic power came from across the political spectrum (for a fuller summary see Etzioni-Halvey (1985)). Marxist critics viewed the development of welfare states as increasing the bureaucracy's role in mediating the excesses of capitalism. Increases in bureaucratic power to achieve this mediation might be at the expense of the bourgeoisie, so the state was not a simple 'executive of the bourgeoisie' as Marx had originally charged. But in mediating social conflict the role of bureaucracy was detrimental to democracy and acted as a powerful block on the building of a more just, non-capitalist order. As the postwar boom faded, governments and their bureaucracies were deemed by pluralists to be 'overloaded'. The wide range of tasks that welfare provision demanded of bureaucracies was seen as diminishing their effectiveness as both formulators (with politicians) and implementers of policy; the increasing number of competing interests that they were supposed to respond to made it impossible for bureaucracies to operate efficiently and according to a single organisational culture. Overload, it was argued, produced fragmentation between agencies of the bureaucracy so that there was a danger that they – and government more generally – had become increasingly inept at policy formulation and unable to deal with social, political and economic change. Bureaucracies, in short, could not manage the tasks asked of them without resort to compulsion and the suppression of popular initiative and individual freedom of choice in the name of managerialism. Bureaucracies had thus become more powerful to the detriment of democracy and at the same time less efficient in the use of that power. This latter argument was mirrored in 'New Right' economic critiques of the WELFARE state, which posited the impossibility of welfare provision being economically efficient if the resources dedicated to it were allocated by the state rather than the market. Finally, as mass democracy developed and calls were made for the empowerment of previously disenfranchised groups such as women and ethnic and other minorities, bureaucracies in developed capitalist democracies came to be seen as increasingly unrepresentative of the societies that they 'managed'.

The dominant political response to these problems in the 1980s in many advanced democracies was based on the New Right's economic critique of bureaucracy. With the election of New Right governments came attempts to 'roll back the state' and create a 'new public management' that was more responsive to public demands and more efficient in the use of public resources. The policy mix designed to achieve this varied from country to country but commonly included PRIVATISATION and the deregulation of markets, the diminution of public welfare services in favour of individual provision, and the replacement of the bureaucratic provision of public goods by more 'efficient' private agencies. The intention was to create a 'hollowed out' state in which bureaucracy would be reduced to servicing elected politicians' efforts at policy formulation. These moves were legitimated not only by appeal to economic efficiency and anti-bureaucratic sentiment, but also by the obvious failure of the extreme bureaucratic state-socialist systems of the Soviet bloc in the late 1980s, and subsequently by discourses claiming that the GLOBALISATION of economic activity requires the state to scale down welfare provision and economic regulation to insure competitiveness.

The merits of these changes in terms of increased economic efficiency are not something that can be considered here. What is more pertinent is the question of whether or not they actually resolve, or even address, the question of the problematic relationship of bureaucracy to democracy. Arguably they do not. The problem of bureaucracy's relationship to democracy is not who works to implement objectives set by elected politicians, but how and under what political conditions that work is carried out. In and of themselves, there is no reason that the changes made to bureaucracy over the last few years should be democratic because they tend to change who acts as a bureaucrat more than how they act. The capacity for anti-democratic action that is latent in bureaucratic managerialism can remain even as a bureaucracy is reduced in size to be more efficient. The only way that bureaucracy's anti-democratic capacity can be subverted is through the extension of democracy through measures to increase transparency and public input into the policy process, through the empowerment of society in the face of bureaucratic power.

bureaucracy

See also:

civil service; policy-making; privatisation; welfare

Further reading

Beetham, D. (1996) *Bureaucracy*, 2nd edn, Buckingham: Open University Press.

Bendix, R. (1945) 'Bureaucracy and the Problem of Power', *Public Administration Review* 5: 194–209.

Dunleavy, P. (1991) *Democracy, Bureaucracy and Public Choice*, London: Harvester Wheatsheaf.

Etzioni-Halvey, E. (1985) *Bureaucracy and Democracy: A Political Dilemma*, revised edn, London: Routledge & Kegan Paul.

Pollitt, C. (1986) 'Democracy and Bureaucracy', in D. Held and C. Pollitt (eds), *New Forms of Democracy*, London: Sage.

NEIL ROBINSON

C

capitalism

Capitalism and democracy refer to the inter-relations of an economic and a political system, their systemic (in)compatibility, their historical imbrication, and their mutual effects on each other. In the history of ideas, democracy has, since Aristotle, been held to be incompatible with any economic regime of exclusive PRIVATE PROPERTY. This was mainstream political and economic thought that lasted well into the twentieth century. Democracy was assumed to presuppose and/or to lead to socioeconomic EQUALITY, and therefore possible only under the conditions of overriding political equality of citizens, as in the most radical phase of the French Revolution, under conditions of universal property ownership, in Thomas Jefferson's vision of American democracy, or under socialism, envisaged by Karl Marx.

It was among the non-capitalists that modern democracy took root and was raised as a political demand, indeed as *the* demand, of the people, because of democracy's promise as a way out of misery. The new industrial working-class led the battle for democracy, through the British Chartists, the New York craftsmen, the Belgian miners and other industrial workers, and the international Marxist labour movement built up from 1889.

Orchestrations of popular SUFFRAGE from above by authoritarian governments started successfully in France in the 1850s under Louis Napoleon Bonaparte (Napoleon III). It was imitated in many other countries, most forcefully in the new German Reich. In the USA, another form of managed voting emerged in the course of the second half of the nineteenth century, the urban 'political machine', a new pattern of patron–client relations wedded to the capitalist economy by graft and corruption.

From the late nineteenth century, the capitalist enterprise mass circulation newspaper became a major means of public opinion formation. By the end of the First World War, with its dependence on an unprecedented popular mobilisation, the defeat of authoritarian dynastic regimes and the threat of violent socialist revolutions, the possible coexistence of capitalism and democracy became more generally recognised.

Capitalism's fundamental institutions are, point for point, the opposite of those of democracy. The principle of private property with its divisions and exclusions stands along one dimension, opposite to that of a community of citizens. The capitalist principle of inequality of rewards may be seen as the opposite of the equality of CITIZENSHIP. The fundamental principle of allocation, according to monetary resources, and the decision criterion of monetary benefit are in conflict with a conception of collective decision among equal citizens and of allocation by rights, citizens' rights or human RIGHTS.

While democracy makes social change through collective voice formation, capitalism operates primarily by exit, by pulling out of a relationship, and buying, selling, employing or investing somewhere else. A capitalist enterprise is ideal typically run as a one-way hierarchy from a command post of ownership or delegated management. Democracy, by contrast, typically involves leadership with consultations and negotiations, with checks and balances of power, sometimes even with citizens' PARTICIPATION and institutions of elective co-determination.

Oppositeness means normal tension and conflict, but not necessarily incompatibility. Ideal types tend to appear more blurred in empirical light and actual politics are, more often than not, arenas of compromise. Democratic politics tends to be more so than other kinds of politics. Actually, existing capitalist democracies have sprung from compromises between capital and labour and between capital and citizens. Private property, profits and executive command get recognised on one side, employee rights of fair employment, of freedom of association and, more controversially, of collective bargaining, and citizens' rights of voting policies of social security and redistribution are on the other. The terms of these class and capital-citizenry compromises differ from one period to another, and among countries.

As well as the fundamental ideal typical opposition between capitalism and democracy, there are, however, also affinities and routes of accommodation. To capitalism as a system, if not necessarily to individual capitalists, a state of law is functional as a guarantee of property and contracts. Such a state need not be a democracy, but a modern democracy is a state of law.

Because of its inherent competitiveness, capitalism is polycephalous, having neither one single centre nor any stable hierarchy. The modern elective principle of democracy does not come from capitalism, but from canonical and Germanic law. The two highest offices of the European Middle Ages, those of Pope of Emperor (of the Holy Roman Empire), were both elective. But benign observers and participants might also see an isomorphism between competitive politics and competitive economics.

A patterning of social relations according to contract and money implies a certain amount of personal freedom, which may facilitate civic freedom, and the struggle for civic rights. Free industrial labour was in a sense a product of capitalist development, and this free labour created the first sustained popular mass movement in history, as an anti-capitalist, democratic movement.

Marxist social democracy and Anglo-Saxon labourism were the major social forces fighting for universal suffrage and for governments responsible to an electorate of universal adult suffrage. One might, then, say that capitalism has generated democracy through its own internal contradictions. In that dialectical sense, the relation between capitalism and democracy is more than just contingent.

Finally, the dynamics and flexibility of capitalism make it adaptable to very different political regimes, as long as basic property rights are maintained and possibilities of profits remain open. While this makes capitalism perfectly compatible with genocide, as in Nazi Germany, with military dictatorships as well as with dynastic empires, it also means adaptability to democracy, even to SOCIAL DEMOCRACY.

But the fundamental opposition between the most basic principles of capitalism and democracy means that the tension and the conflicts between the two are most unlikely to disappear. Large-scale socioeconomic changes tend to exacerbate them. In the 1960s and 1970s, institutionalised growth expectations, full employment, and the drying up of rural and religious pools of deference through industrialisation, urbanisation and secularisation raised the voice and the demands of workers and citizens. Participatory democracy, economic democracy and more EQUALITY were central demands. Conservative political scientists and ideologues regarded these popular demands with grave concern, as posing problems of government 'overload' and even of 'ungovernability', and therefore requiring more insulation of governments from citizen pressure.

After the oil crises, and with de-industrialisation and the rise of large scale transnational financial markets in the 1980s and the 1990s, the pendulum has swung in the other direction. Weakening, sometimes crushing, the trades unions, 'flexible labour markets' and privatisations replaced 'industrial' or 'economic democracy' on the political agenda. Voices, in particular collective voices, were to be muted, and individual and corporate exit possibilities to be increased. A slimming of democracy was called for in the name of a 'lean' state.

The mobility of capital became a major constraint on democratic DECISION-MAKING, the fear of losing investment and employment, the need to attract them. The 'confidence of the market', of financial investors, became a major point of orientation of elected politicians. In order to lessen the tension between confidence of the market and confidence of the people, new institutions have developed and spread with a view to taking economic and social policy decisions out of the realm of democracy. Central bank independence of democracy has now become official policy of the European Union. Some countries have even abolished their central bank and any possibility of a monetary policy. Another interesting recent development, first systematically undertaken by the military dictatorship in Chile but then vigorously propagated throughout the world by the World Bank, is the virtual abolition of pensions as a right of citizens or employees, and as a responsibility of politics. Instead, there is being instituted a norm to save in private pensions firms. A former social entitlement is thus turned into a means of capital accumulation.

How far the exit power of capital actually goes, and how limited the reach of the voice of the citizenry have become, remains unclear and controversial. Protagonists have an interest in intimidation, and critics have an interest in denunciation. But, other things being equal, the larger the market, in space and in capital, in relation to states, the less is the scope of democracy.

See also:

economic requirements of democracy; globalisation; market forces; social democracy; state, models of

Further reading

Bowles, S. and Gintis, H. (1986) *Democrcacy and Capitalism*, London: Routledge & Kegan Paul.

Crozier, M. *et al.* (1975) *The Crisis of Democracy*, New York: New York University Press.

Hirschman, A. (1970) *Exit, Voice, and Loyalty*, Cambridge, MA: Harvard University Press.

Przeworski, A. (1990)*The State and the Economy under Capitalism*, Chur: Harwood Academic Publishers.

Rueschmeyer, D. *et al.* (1992) *Democracy and Capitalist Development*, Chicago: Chicago University Press.

Schumpeter, J. (l943) *Capitalism, Socialism, and Democracy*, London: George Allen & Unwin.

Therborn, G. (1977) 'The Rule of Capital and the Rise of Democracy', *New Left Review* 103: 3–41.

—— (1992) 'The Right to Vote and the Four World Routes to/through Modernity', in R. Torstendahl (ed.), *State Theory and State History*, London: Sage.

GÖRAN THERBORN

censorship

Politically, censorship is the reciprocal of freedom to communicate and is thus as protean as expression itself. It aims to restrict or suppress information or meaning transmitted through symbol. Though censorship is usually associated with governmental interdiction of speech or press, any symbolic representation – textual, graphic, electronic, or simply embodied in behaviour – may be subject to restraint or regulation because of what it is seen to mean.

In a narrow sense, and one that has currency in Anglo-American law, censorship is 'prior restraint', the authoritative attempt to prevent or alter a communication *before* it reaches an audience. The now defunct American state film censorship boards were institutionalised prior restraints; the American government's attempt to prevent publication of stolen classified documents known as the 'Pentagon Papers' during the Vietnam War was an *ad hoc* instance of such restriction. More broadly, censorship refers to any authoritative or quasi-authoritative action that penalises or otherwise inhibits COMMUNICATION. Prosecutions for obscene publication or civil actions for defamation or invasion of privacy, for example, may impose 'subsequent punishment' through fine, imprisonment or money damages, besides having a generally 'chilling' effect on expression.

Not much is known of censorship in primitive times, but one may imagine those with greater power punishing the threatening expression of those with less. From the ancient world to the present, AUTHORITY has dealt censoriously with communication believed to compromise the SECURITY of the regime or state, invite disorder or simply offer criticism of leaders. During its short life, the American Sedition Act of 1798, a classic of thin-skinned political censorship, made it a crime to speak or write about the President or Congress with 'intent to defame' or to bring them 'into contempt or disrepute'. Totalitarian states have regularly exercised a near-complete prior censorship of communications MEDIA as well as punishing dissenting speech. Modern non-democratic states, such as the Communist People's Republic of China, have often acted strongly against advocates of greater democracy, less for reasons of national security than to protect hegemony of a ruling party or elite.

Where secular and ecclesiastical authority are closely tied, as they were in the European Middle Ages and are in some Moslem countries today, governmental power has been used to punish blasphemy and religious heresy. In the case of Galileo's solar observations in seventeenth-century Italy, this extended to scientific findings. With the Reformation and rise of the nation-state, government became more fully separated from church and the restrictive interests of the two most powerful institutions of the medieval world no longer coincided. Except for such isolated and benighted efforts as barring the teaching of evolution or fixing curricular standing for 'creation science', restricting either unorthodox religious expression or secular ideas that challenge established beliefs is unusual in modern democratic states (see STATE, RELATIONS OF CHURCH TO).

When not in defence of government itself, censorship in modern democracies is usually undertaken to protect public morality, particularly against sexual representation thought offensive or 'indecent'. In an age of universal literacy and a mass audience for media communication, governments controlled by, or at least responsible to, majorities have tended to support conventional morality and give effect to established cultural values. This censorship is, nonetheless, vulnerable to the writ of an expansive free speech doctrine, ramified communications technology and changes in public attitudes. Today in Great Britain and the United States it is largely limited to obscenity, itself now more narrowly defined than in the past.

Many democratic governments, recognising the diversity of their populations and responding to interest group pressures, have enacted laws barring 'hate speech' and other communication thought to encourage racial, ethnic or gender discrimination or simply to be insulting or harmful to self-esteem. In the United States such measures, often defended in the name of CIVIC VIRTUE or 'political correctness', are exceptions to a steadily expanding constitutional doctrine supporting free expression based on liberal INDIVIDUALISM and reveal the tension between the two principles upon which liberal democracy rests: liberty and EQUALITY.

As a negative on free speech, censorship finds its justification today in practical instrumentation rather than high theory. Protecting against threats to national security, incitement to violence, racial insult, child pornography, prejudicial trial publicity, commercial fraud, damage to reputation through falsehood and media intrusion on privacy are all ends that have supported laws or policies imposing some restriction on communication.

Censorship finds it chief theoretical obstacle in the compelling vision of a 'free marketplace of ideas', given eloquent statement by John Stuart Mill in *On Liberty* as an antidote to human fallibility. In it, truth, wisdom or simply 'best choices' are held most likely to emerge where information and competition among views and opinion are left unimpeded. In effect, good expression drives out bad, like an inverse of Gresham's Law of currency dynamics. Hyde Park then becomes not merely a corner of the city but a model for the entire society. The ideal finds reference in scores of American First Amendment decisions of the last sixty years, though in actual application the Supreme Court has held back from embracing its implicit absolutism.

Censorship receives a theoretical reprieve because of questionable assumptions that underlie the free marketplace ideal. Four are of particular consequence: that the marketplace is free, that 'truth' can be recognised and agreed upon when it appears, that embracing it is desirable, and that it will reliably prevail over error and falsehood. In an age of big media, the vaunted marketplace, though enlarged by developments such as the computer modem, satellite transmission and the Internet, is still likely to be an arena dominated by the few and powerful because of the cost of entering and participating in it effectively. Even were the marketplace truly free, truth or the wisest choices might not always be self-evident in the face of INFORMATION bound to be incomplete and perceptions bound to be impaired. And even if truth could reliably be identified, it may sometimes be so stark as to harm other desirable ends, such as belief in an essential human goodness or equality or the need for consolation, both of which might better be served at times by modest fictions.

The assumption that truth or good ideas will prevail in competition with bad is the heaviest of all, carrying an implicit risk. The US Supreme Court Justice Oliver Wendell Holmes recognised the difficulty when observing, 'If in the long run the beliefs expressed in a proletarian dictatorship are destined to be accepted . . . the only meaning of free speech is that they should be given their chance and have their way'. Though Holmes faced this possibility with a certain fatalistic equanimity, the matter is more formidably put where an advocate in the marketplace would, if successful, close the marketplace or do worse. The appeals of Hitler, which succeeded, or those of the American Communist Party, which did not, are but two examples. The danger led the American Justice Robert Jackson to warn: 'The Bill of Rights is not a suicide pact'.

The human being is a communicating animal and thus inevitably a censoring one. Restrictions may rest on well-intentioned pursuit of high-minded ends, rational self-interest or irrational grounds which are partly or wholly unconscious. A capacity for internal censorship, which Freud and others speculated might be necessary for civilisation, provides a psychological base for limiting the expression of others. Thus censorship rather than tolerance may have the better claim to be called 'natural'. Two leading students of freedom of speech reluctantly concluded as much. McClosky and Brill (1983: 13) wonder if 'the impulse to strike out against opponents or ideas that one finds frightening or hateful is a survival mechanism', one produced through evolution. 'Creatures' survive mostly because they learn to recognise their enemies and how to deal with them. 'If one has sufficient strength and cunning to repel the enemy, one is inclined to do so unless one has discovered that, for some reason, another type of response is legally or socially required or preferred.'

If words and other representation of meaning had no capacity to threaten interests, wound sensitivities or challenge certainties, very likely there would be no censorship. That they do makes realisation of a free speech society, which seeks, expects, even demands that 'other type of response', a remarkable political and psychological achievement. In it, censorship remains a sometimes desirable, often short-sighted but all too human counterpoint.

See also:

communication; constitutionalism; freedom; information; media; rights; security; toleration

Further reading

Baker, C.E. (1989) *Human Liberty and Freedom*

of Speech, New York: Oxford University Press.

Clor, H. (1969) *Obscenity and Public Morality*, Chicago: University of Chicago Press.

Emerson, T.I. (1970) *The System of Freedom of Expression*, New York: Random House.

McClosky, H. and Brill, A. (1983) *Dimensions of Tolerance: What Americans Believe About Civil Liberties*, New York: Russell Sage Foundation.

McCormick, J. and MacInnes, M. (eds) (1962) *Versions of Censorship*, New York: Doubleday.

Murphy, P.L. (1992) *The Shaping of the First Amendment: 1791 to the Present*, New York: Oxford University Press.

Randall, R.S. (1970) *Censorship of the Movies: The Social and Political Control of a Mass Medium*, Madison, WI: University of Wisconsin Press.

—— (1989) *Freedom and Taboo: Pornography and Politics of a Self Divided*, Berkeley, CA: University of California Press.

Sullivan, J.L., Piereson, J. and Marcus, G.E. (1982) *Political Tolerance and American Democracy*, Chicago: University of Chicago Press.

RICHARD S. RANDALL

chaos and coalitions

> Political decisions are almost invariably made by winning coalitions.
> (Riker 1986: xvi)

In representative democracies, DECISION-MAKING is typically carried out by legislators who have been selected by coalitions of voters. The legislators themselves are often grouped together into coalitions, called parties. In multiparty systems based on proportional representation, parties themselves usually have to form COALITIONS to govern with a majority (see REPRESENTATION, CONCEPT OF).

It has been a quandary for social choice theory ever since the time of Condorcet in the late eighteenth century as to whether coalition formation can lead to stable choice. Condorcet

himself did not believe in Rousseau's general will, but rather in the fundamental rationality of individual and collective choice. However, he also discovered the possibility of irrational collective choice, in *Essai sur Application* (1785). As a leader of the Girondin faction in the National Assembly, and as a supporter of a constitutional monarchy with Louis XVI at its head, Condorcet must have wondered whether the onset of the Terror in 1793 was simply an aspect of the deeper phenomenon of collective or coalitional irrationality.

Condorcet's insight was essentially forgotten until Kenneth Arrow's astonishing thesis *Social Choice and Individual Values* (1951). Arrow showed that any social decision process is characterised by a family of decisive coalitions (which we can label as D). If the process is to be rational, then D must define a dictator (one who belongs to every single decisive coalition).

In later work by McKelvey (1976) and Schofield (1978), it was essentially shown that any decision process characterised by voting could be *chaotic*. In other words, any voting system which did not depend on a dictator (or some kind of veto group) could potentially give rise to any outcome. This fundamental theoretic problem was initially seen to be associated only with democratic processes, and numerous objections to its validity were raised (Shepsle 1979). In particular, 'neo-institutionalists' argued that coalitional decision-making typically takes place in a restricted domain or game, the 'institution' that forbids or restricts chaos. Game theorists have in recent years used this insight to model almost all aspects of political choice. William Riker's (1980) response to this neo-institutional argument was that those agents who are neglected by the political institution may rise up and destroy the conventions that define the institution. In precisely this fashion during Condorcet's lifetime did a coalition destroy the Bastille, and then the institutions of the *ancien regime*. Riker (1986) also suggested that the initial move to destroy an institution often takes the form of an 'heresthetic' manoeuvre to transform the beliefs of a new political coalition. For example, Lincoln's interpretation in 1860 of the significance for free labour of the Dred Scott decision of the US Supreme Court contributed to the collapse of the Democratic political coalition in 1860. Lincoln's election (by a plurality of the popular vote, not a majority) brought on the secession of the Southern states, and then the Civil War (Schofield 1999a). Although the Democratic Party coalition had been threatened in the past, the apparently insignificant event of the Dred Scott decision catalysed a total transformation in the political institutions of the USA.

It is the belief of this writer that the chaos generated by coalition instability is a fundamental feature of political life. This is not to say that stability is impossible. To pursue Riker's argument, it is probable that the following sequence characterises *all* social evolution:

(a) During a period of chaos a dictator, or Architect of Order, arises, who through some form of institutional innovation is able to put in place certain rules or conventions.

(b) Co-operation is possible within such a framework, and slow evolution (possibly associated with economic growth) occurs. Periods with such stable characteristics are often studied by economic historians in order to determine the determinants of growth.

(c) A quandary, or element of dissatisfaction, makes itself apparent, and prophets of chaos make themselves heard.

(d) Various coalitions with the power to destroy or change the institution come into being. The rationality of the institution is then threatened, precisely because the coalitions are mutually antagonistic. Behaviour becomes chaotic, in the sense that it becomes impossible to predict what will happen.

(e) Who will become the 'new' Architect of Order cannot be determined during the period of coalitional chaos. The rules or conventions that are put in place to re-establish the institution will also be impossible to predict.

In what follows, I shall attempt to illustrate the above sequence of events both from the historical record and from the recent political past. In some cases it will be possible to ascribe the success of the Architect of Order to what has been termed a 'belief cascade' (Denzau and North 1994). The driving force behind a belief cascade will often consist of two parts: (i) exhaustion on the part of coalitions as they see the impossibility of attaining their ends, and (ii) a new belief or convention that makes sense with respect to the recent past, and holds out the prospect of co-operation, or at least stability for the future.

As a first illustration, consider again the lead-up to the American Civil War. In my view, period (a) is 1784–7, when it became obvious that the Articles of Confederation were inadequate. The *Federalist Papers* (1787) by Hamilton, Jay and Madison presented a case for a Federal Union. Those disagreements among the members of the Constitutional Congress were eventually overcome (see Riker (1995) for an excellent discussion) partly because of the fear of foreign aggression by France and Spain (Schofield 2001). Economic growth and expansion continued apace after 1787 but the quandary created by the compromise over slavery became more pronounced. I would identify John Quincy Adams as the predominant prophet of chaos in the period 1840–4, in his efforts to overcome the gag rule. As mentioned above, Lincoln's speeches created a belief cascade. His election in 1860 induced the chaos of the Civil War. I believe it would be impossible to predict from the vantage point of 1840 the future sequence of events.

As a second illustration, consider again Condorcet and the French Revolution. Economists have shown that the French fiscal institutions were much less efficient than those of Britain. The Seven Years War (1756–1762) with Britain had almost induced bankruptcy in France, and Turgot, the French Finance Minister, had attempted to act as Architect of Order in the mid-1770s to reform French finances. The choice by the French King, Louis XVI, in 1776 to aid the American colonies led directly to the French bankruptcy of 1789, and the need for calling the Estates General. In the middle of the Revolution, Condorcet had also attempted to act as Architect of Order, to construct a constitutional monarchy. This was swept away by the coalitional chaos of the Terror. Finally Napoleon came to power; new fiscal institutions were rapidly put in place, and the French army overran most of Europe.

In my view, the reason Napoleon was eventually defeated was because the British had a longer period to develop an efficient fiscal state. As North and Weingast (1989) have noted, the Glorious Revolution of 1688 brought into being a new constitutional convention between Parliament and the Crown. Brewer (1988) has shown how the taxing and borrowing ability of Britain developed rapidly from 1688 to 1783. I suggest that 1688 was causally preceded by a major chaotic event, namely the Civil War of 1641–9. Clearly this war was the consequence of a belief cascade over the proper relationship between the crown and the people. Moreover, this cascade created the context within which Oliver Cromwell became Lord Protector of the Common Wealth. I would see Cromwell as both prophet of chaos and Architect of Order. It is hardly surprising that Hobbes (1651) wrote *Leviathan* at this time.

For a more recent example, consider events from 1918 to 1949. Surely the chaos in Weimar Germany and in Russia in 1918 was due to coalition instability. The dictators of the interwar years came to power through 'belief cascades' that threatened the fundamental liberal belief in the compatibility of economic efficiency and democracy. In 1936, John Maynard Keynes clearly saw that new institutions were needed to reduce coalitional instability at the international level. Though his precise recommendations were not followed, his warnings as a prophet of chaos were heeded. The Marshall Plan, and then the institutions of the World Bank and the International Monetary Fund, did maintain stability until about 1972. In the 1970s, coalitional instability of lesser or greater intensity occurred in most developed countries. Prophets of chaos such as Beer (1982) and Olson (1982) again

speculated that democracy and efficiency could not both be maintained. In fact, new market institutions were put in place after 1980 and chaos in the West was avoided (Schofield 1999b). The success of these institutions in turn generated an unstoppable belief cascade in the Soviet Union and Eastern Europe in 1989. The asset crash in Russia in 1998 was just one delayed manifestation of this belief cascade. Although there have been Architects of Order aplenty in Russia over the last ten years, no one has had any idea about how to impose efficient fiscal institutions in the absence of stable political institutions. It would also seem plausible that the breakdown of Soviet hegemony in Eastern Europe has led, indirectly, to the devastating coalition chaos of the Balkans.

I have written very little here about the role of political coalitions in maintaining democratic stability. The early work by Riker (1962) suggested that minimal winning coalition governments would be stable. It is true that some countries (such as Austria) have experienced fairly stable minimal winning coalition governments. On the other hand, it was noted over twenty years ago that surplus (or supra majority) as well as minority governments are very common in Europe. Trying to ascertain the determinants of parliamentary coalition formation and duration has proved to be a difficult theoretical and empirical problem. While it is plausible that certain types of political institutions can maintain stability, it is as well to remember the events in Italy in 1992 before making pronouncements on this topic. Prior to 1992, scholars were divided over whether Italy was unstable (government lasted on average less than twelve months) or stable (since the Christian Democrat Party (DC) was always in power). It was not realised generally prior to 1992 that the DC was essentially involved in a power-sharing arrangement with the Mafia. Key elements of the DC, with their Mafia allies, engaged in vigorous predatory activities. Indeed, the DC appears to have maintained power by bribery. This system collapsed in 1992 thanks to the extraordinary bravery of a small number of magistrates.

It is not impossible that the current financial

shambles in Asia is due to a political economic institution in Japan, which is similar to the one just described in Italy. The dominant Liberal Democratic Party (LDP) is factionalised (just like the DC was in Italy). These factions compete politically in a fashion that requires large infusions of money. The natural source comprises major banks, other financial institutions and corporations. Since the post office functions as a mechanism to borrow money at zero interest from the people, the LDP dominant faction is able to loan money freely, and be paid privately for so doing. It is hardly surprising that the property market boomed and then eventually crashed. Such bubbles are examples of economic rather than political coalitional instability. In this case, economic chaos was induced by what appeared to be a stable political institution.

While this essay has been very speculative, its intention has been to suggest just how important was Kenneth Arrow's insight. Contrary to the attitudes of some economic historians, and of game-theoretically inclined institutional modellers, it would appear that chaos is a fundamental aspect of the evolution of the system of general rules, the 'constitution', that defines both political and economic institutions.

See also:

coalitions; decision-making; decision-rules; democratic stability; parties

Further reading

Arrow, K. (1951) *Social Choice and Individual Values*, New York: John Wiley.

Beer, S. (1982) *Britain Against Itself*, London: Heinemann.

Brewer, J. (1988) *The Sinews of Power: War, Money and the English State, 1688–1783*, Cambridge, MA: Harvard University Press.

Denzau, A.T. and North, D.C. (1994) 'Shared Mutual Models: Ideologies and Institutions', *Kyklos* 47: 3–31.

McKelvey, R. (1976) 'Intransitives in Multidimensional Voting Models and Some Implications for Agenda Control', *Journal of Economic Theory* 12: 472–82.

North, D.C. and Weingast, B.W. (1989) 'Constitutions and Commitment: The Evolution of Institutions Governing Public Choice in 17th Century England', *Journal of Economic History* 49: 803–32.

Olson, M. (1982) *The Rise and Decline of Nations*, New Haven, CT: Yale University Press.

Riker, W. (1962) *The Theory of Political Coalitions*, New Haven, CT: Yale University Press.

—— (1980) 'Implications from the Disequilibrium of Majority Rule for the Study of Institutions', *American Political Science Review* 74: 432–46.

—— (1986) *The Art of Political Manipulation*, New Haven, CT: Yale University Press.

—— (1995) *The Strategy of Rhetoric: Campaigning for the American Constitution*, ed. R. Calvert, J. Mueller and R. Wilson, New Haven, CT: Yale University Press.

Schofield, N. (1978) 'Instability of Simple Dynamic Games', *Review of Economic Studies* 45: 575–94.

—— (1999a) 'The Amistad and Dred Scott Affairs: Beliefs and Heresthetics in Antebellum America, 1830–1860', *Homo Oeconomicus* 16: 49–67.

—— (1999b) 'The Heart of the Atlantic Constitution, 1919–1998', *Politics and Society* 27: 173–215.

—— (2001) 'Evolution of the Constitution', *The British Journal of Political Science* 31: 127–49.

Shepsle, K. (1979) 'Institutional Arrangements and Equilibrium in Multidimensional Voting Models', *American Journal of Political Science* 23: 27–59.

NORMAN SCHOFIELD

Christian democracy

Christian democracy is a political movement that is distinct from its main competitors by virtue of its specific model of social and economic policy and because it has electorally profited from the salient religious cleavage (see CLEAVAGES) in Western Europe. The contemporary Christian democratic PARTIES are the heirs of the Catholic parties that mobilised roughly between 1870 and 1914 and assumed important political positions in the inter-war period in Austria, Belgium, Germany, the Netherlands and, to a lesser extent, in Italy and France.

Catholic political mobilisation was both a response to the threat of LIBERALISM and socialism, and a project to combine these two. It was also an attempt to distance political Catholicism from the disadvantageous alliances with monarchists and extreme conservatives. At first, these parties were the political representatives of what Whyte (1981) has called 'closed Catholicism', which was characterised by explicit clerical involvement in the political and social organisation of the Catholic population and the existence of an exclusively Catholic party with strong links to Catholic SOCIAL MOVEMENTS, particularly the TRADES UNIONS. These parties were to varying degrees confessional parties, explicitly established in defence of the Catholic interest, with a direct link to the church, and primarily aimed at building and preserving the political unity of all Catholics. Between the late nineteenth century and the Second World War, Catholic parties matured from essentially CLASS-distinctive (middle-class and upper-class) confessional movements, with little interest in social policy, to cross-class, a-confessional people's parties with an articulate social concern (Fogarty 1957).

The contrast between modern Christian democracy on the one hand and political Catholicism, denominational political parties or confessional politics on the other is highlighted by the former's emphasis on the independent lay responsibility for applying Christian principles to the realm of politics. Christian democracy has been open both to different denominations and to secular influences, and has explicitly dissociated itself from too direct an attachment to the churches (Van Kersbergen 1995) (see STATE, RELATIONS OF CHURCH TO).

The religious inspiration of Christian democratic parties has distinguished them from conservative or secular centre parties, but also from liberalism and SOCIAL DEMOCRACY in a number of respects. First, typical were distinctive beliefs with respect to issues that concern private morality, such as divorce, abortion and euthanasia. Second, Christian democratic parties differed from conservative parties in their social concern. Third, the consistently pro-European integration point of view has diverged considerably from other political movements, and from British conservatism in particular.

The key concept of Christian democratic social and political theory has been 'SUBSIDIARITY', which derives its specific and current meaning in relation to other concepts such as 'personalism', 'SOLIDARITY', 'PLURALISM' and 'distributive justice'. As is well known, subsidiarity was first introduced in the social encyclical *Quadragesimo Anno* (1931). Christian democrats subsequently developed this concept into an elaborate political theory of modern democratic government. Contemporary Christian democrats share the conviction that each private, semi-private or semi-public association or institution of society performs indispensable moral, social and economic tasks. In principle, a government should be disinclined to take over the responsibility for these tasks. However, the principle of subsidiarity prescribed that political action was mandatory whenever 'lower social organs' failed to perform their duties. Under such conditions, the state had the obligation to intervene in moral, social and economic relations by offering temporary support with a view to restoring the SOVEREIGNTY of social associations and their capacity to perform adequately in accordance with their natural and organic function.

With respect to social and economic policy, subsidiarity functioned historically both as an encouragement of public intervention and as a justification of non-intervention or even of discontinuing previously initiated policies. In this specific sense, Christian democratic parties tended to be dynamic and historically sensitive, yet open-ended in their moral, social and economic policies.

On the Christian democratic account, 'solidarity' was primarily defined as the attempt to realise harmony between various social groups and organisations with opposed interests. The search for societal 'INTEGRATION' and accommodation in a plural society has characterised the social and political practice of Christian democratic parties to a large extent. The social Catholic notion of 'personalism' constituted a distinctive theory of social justice, that – rather than balancing rights and duties – fundamentally underscored a moral obligation to help the 'weak', 'poor', 'lower strata' or whoever might have been in need for help. This helps to explain the Christian democratic attachment to the transfer-oriented, relatively generous WELFARE state.

It has been the ceaseless attempt of integration and reconciling a plurality of societal groups with possibly opposed interests that has made Christian democracy distinctive. Even within its own ranks, the Christian democratic movements included various social organisations that had opposed social and political interests. As a result, the movements always needed to be flexible and, therefore, continuously attempted to retain or increase their capacity to adapt to changing circumstances and to new wishes and demands in their venture of formulating a compromise of antagonistic interests. Christian democracy was in this sense the embodiment of societal accommodation, or at least aspired to become so. It has been the 'politics of mediation' – that is, the religiously inspired, ideologically condensed, institutionally rooted, and politically practised conviction that conflicts of interests can and must be reconciled politically in order to restore the natural and organic harmony of society – that has governed the social and economic practice of Christian democracy in the postwar era and that has been one of the movement's main electoral assets.

At the end of the twentieth century – a century in which Christian democracy emerged, matured, flourished and helped establish the welfare state – the movement appears in trouble. The decline of power of the movement in Western Europe has a structural and a contingent component. The cause of the structural downfall is not only found in the process of secularisation, but also in the demise of the politics of mediation. Under favourable economic conditions, the Christian democratic parties pursued a strategy of social policy that was capable of generating a payoff between opposed interests and that reinforced their social and economic power. However, the beneficial conditions for such a politics of mediation were disappearing in the 1980s and 1990s as the financial sources that facilitated the accommodation of interests were becoming scarce. The effects of these developments became clear in the 1990s when the embedding of the politics of mediation in political institutions and social coalitions started to erode. This generated a context in which it became increasingly difficult to appeal to religious and non-religious voters alike, as a result of which electoral support is steadily declining.

See also:

class; cleavages; justice; liberalism; parties; pluralism; social democracy; social movements; solidarity; sovereignty; state, relations of church to; trades unions; welfare

Further reading

Fogarty, M.P. (1957) *Christian Democracy in Western Europe, 1820–1953*, London: Routledge and Kegan Paul.

Hanley, D. (ed.) (1994) *Christian Democracy in Europe: A Comparative Perspective*, London: Pinter.

Irving, R.E.M. (1979) *The Christian Democratic Parties of Western Europe*, London: Allen and Unwin.

Lamberts, E. (ed.) (1997) *Christian Democracy in the European Union, 1945–1995*, Leuven: Leuven University Press.

Van Kersbergen, K. (1995) *Social Capitalism. A Study of Christian Democracy and the Welfare State*, London: Routledge.

Whyte, J.H. (1981) *Catholics in Western Democracies: A Study in Political Behaviour*, Dublin: Gill and Macmillan.

KEES VAN KERSBERGEN

citizens' juries

Citizens' juries are a response to generally low levels of public participation and the perception that a passive and ill-informed citizenry fails to consider issues in any depth (Coote and Lenaghan 1997; Stewart *et al.* 1994; Crosby 1995). They comprise a small group of citizens (normally from ten to twenty people), chosen so as to be socially representative, who are asked to take an informed, longer term and impartial view of an issue. They answer a question posed by the organisers, who typically consult the sponsors of the jury and other potential stakeholders when framing it. Jurors are paid to participate in a process that typically lasts from two to three days. During this period they receive written and oral evidence from a range of sources. They can cross-examine witnesses and call for more information. They discuss the issues among themselves. Trained facilitators help jurors through the issues, and proceedings are chaired by a moderator. Typically juries achieve a consensus, although they can resort to majority voting. There are significant variations in practice between the USA and the UK (Crosby *et al.* 1997), and between citizens' juries and German planning cells (Renn 1984).

While citizens' juries could be used to make important decisions, this might generate tensions, because they could override elected bodies that can be held accountable by citizens. For this reason, juries typically make recommendations, to which sponsors should make a formal response. Citizens' juries are usually a form of consultation rather than part of a move to DIRECT DEMOCRACY. Central and local government in Europe make increasing use of them, although concerns are expressed about their relatively high costs compared to other methods of consultation, among other pro-

blems (Armour 1995). They do have distinct advantages, however. Jurors should be well-informed, whereas ordinary citizens may not be; they are socially representative, whereas other forms of consultation may be dominated by special interests; and they have opportunities to debate and deliberate not available to other citizens.

Citizens' juries help overcome the paradox of PARTICIPATION (that it is not worthwhile for rational individuals to participate in democracies when this is likely to have a very low chance of altering the outcome) by paying jurors and making the jury small, thus increasing the potential impact of each member. The danger is that the more citizens' juries carry out the consultation function, the less citizens will be prone to participate in other contexts. To make it compulsory for each citizen to make his- or herself available for citizen jury service would not fully address democratic theorists' concern to see an active and generally well-informed citizenry.

Citizens' juries should operate according to the norms of deliberative conceptions of democracy (see DELIBERATIVE DEMOCRACY). Jurists should be impartial in their final judgements rather than self-interested (although, in jury debates, they may represent the viewpoint of a social group with a stake). They should seek to understand others' points of view, treating their claims as having equal *a priori* validity, rather than evaluating them from a biased baseline. Thus, the jury's judgements should be based impartially upon valid evidence and on whether a compelling ethical case can be made. Second, none should be disadvantaged in group discussion by social stigma associated with gender, CLASS, age and so on. Third, the jury should attempt to resolve differences and come to a consensus on the common good or the right course of action. This conception implies that organisers have to be very careful to ensure that proceedings are not dominated by individual jurors, so that all can have a say. Given the time constraints, it may be very difficult for the jury fully to consider all the evidence they wish to see, to work thoroughly through the arguments and to listen to all points of view. There are deeper problems with the conception of deliberative democracy. First, the rationalistic conception of debate limits the possibilities for using a number of significant forms of political discourse: emotional appeals, personal narratives, claims linked to historical precedent or to identity. Second, the drive to achieve consensus through impartial debate can veil deep-seated social antagonisms that might better be exposed.

Some conceive deliberation as ideally being free from strategising and inequalities in power, approaching the Habermasian ideal speech situation. Arguably the sponsors, and those who organise the jury have too much power for this to be possible. They set the agenda, although juries can sometimes modify the question posed. The jury may not be able to consider aspects of the question they find important, or to call into question structures, institutions and resource inequalities that frame the issues. In practice, juries considering planning issues and resource distribution (the bread and butter of citizens' juries in Europe) are often called on by organisers to choose between sets of options all of which could be regarded as far from ideal (Local Government Management Board 1997; McIver 1998). In effect, their forced choices legitimate framing decisions made by others, providing a veneer of democracy. Second, sponsors and organisers largely control the written information provided and the set of witnesses called, although juries are sometimes allowed to alter things at the margin. Third, there is the possibility that individuals or groups that wish to make representations to the jury cannot do so, either because of resource constraints generated by the time-intensive and rationalistic style of the proceedings or because they are not called.

Less pressure should be applied to juries to achieve consensus. 'Hung' juries, minority judgements and recommendations to reframe the question should be regarded as respectable outcomes. This should go along with giving jurors the time to do the job properly, even if this costs sponsors more. Juries should be made more open to those who wish to bear witness and more power should be given to the jury to explore information in ways that are not tightly controlled by the organisers. As more and more citizens become competent users of the Internet, the use of electronic forums to allow witnesses to air their position at low cost might help. Computer databases with links that can be explored by the jury and other participants would often be a useful way of opening up access to INFORMATION. Although organisers would have to have some responsibility for such databases, concerned groups and individuals should be relatively free to add information and links, and should be able to appeal to a regulatory authority when they are not allowed to do so.

See also:

citizenship; civic virtue; communication; deliberative democracy; information; justice; media

Further reading

Armour, A. (1995) 'The Citizens' Jury Model of Public Participation: A Critical Evaluation', in O. Renn, T. Webler and P. Wiedemann (eds), *Fairness and Competence in Citizen Participation. Evaluating Models for Environmental Discourse*, Dordrecht: Kluwer Academic Publishers.

Coote, A. and Lenaghan, J. (1997) *Citizens' Juries: Theory into Practice*, London: IPPR.

Crosby, N. (1995) 'Citizens Juries: One Solution for Difficult Environmental Questions', in O. Renn, T. Webler and P. Wiedemann (eds), *Fairness and Competence in Citizen Participation. Evaluating Models for Environmental Discourse*, Dordrecht: Kluwer Academic Publishers.

Crosby, N., Romslo, J., Malisone, S. and Manning, B. (1997) 'Citizens' Juries: British Style', internet publication address http://www.auburn.edu/tann/cp/features/juries.htm.

Local Government Management Board (1997) *Citizens' Juries in Local Government: Report for the LGMB on the Pilot Projects*, London: LGMB.

McIver, S. (1998) *Healthy Debate? An Indepen-*

dent Evaluation of Citizens' Juries in Health Settings, London: King's Fund.

Renn, O. (1984) 'An Empirical Investigation of Citizens' Preferences Among Four Energy Scenarios', *Technology Forecasting and Social Change* 26: 11–46.

Stewart, J., Kendall, E. and Coote, A. (1994) *Citizens' Juries*, London: IPPR.

HUGH WARD

citizenship

Citizenship denotes the condition of being a citizen. The concept of citizenship is somewhat more than two and a half thousand years old, and has survived periods of eclipse to endure as a central and resilient component of Western political thought (Clarke 1994). The etymology of citizenship is unclear but the word is Latin in origin, and was settled in its present form by the early Middle Ages when it came to signify the legal status, associated with the granting of economic liberties and capacities, and IMMUNITIES AND PROTECTIONS, of the townsman or burgess.

Human beings describe themselves in various ways, and 'citizen' as a descriptive term is the main political predicate applied to persons. To be a citizen is to be a member of a more or less self-contained political unit such as a modern state; citizenship is the institution which indicates a person's position and status *vis-à-vis* the wider institutional framework of her or his political community. The form of citizenship is always tripartite, comprising a person, the institutional matrix of her or his political community, and the terms of that relationship. The substance of those terms are citizenship's affective, political and legal dimensions, arousing construals of the citizen as, respectively, a member of an affective community (involving important senses of belonging and communal identity); a contributing participant in the collective DECISION-MAKING processes of the polity; and, finally, the holder of legal personality and bearer of publicly enforceable RIGHTS and DUTIES subject to the

jurisdiction of the polity. While the meanings, practices and relative emphases of these aspects of citizenship show subtle shifts over time, it can nonetheless be said that the co-presence of these three is what distinguishes citizenship conceptually from cognate statuses such as subject, denizen and national, where one or more aspect may be absent.

A deeply entrenched strand in the notion of, and expectations surrounding, citizenship is occluded by its etymology: subscription to a common moral or ethical order. That strand probably goes back to the sixth century BC in the Greek *polis* (the first clear example is to be found in Dracon, the Archon of Athens) and to the third or fourth centuries BCE in Roman religious ceremonies, where to be a citizen was to be a familial member of a recognised religion. Along with its historically constant use as a device marking which social discriminations should catalyse political, legal, and economic privileges, citizenship in modern times has become imbued with egalitarian connotations and come to stand as the paradigmatic institutional political expression of the fundamental moral EQUALITY of persons. In this aspirational sense, citizenship is held to embody full membership of a given political community, as evoked by Marshall's 'the right to share to the full in the social heritage and to live the life of a civilised being according to the standards prevailing in the society' (Marshall 1950: 14). It is useful to keep in mind the differences between citizenship's positive (that is, legally established) character and its normative and theoretical character, and also to be alert to the frequent use of the word 'citizenship' to gesture approvingly towards some inchoate sense of full social inclusion.

History

Citizenship's beginnings are located in the shift from 'warrior' societies to agricultural and commercial societies in ancient Greece and the development of the communal decision-making spaces of the *polis* or city state (initially a hilltop citadel). Although citizenship was reserved to a minority of the population (and an exclusively masculine minority), it permitted and expected active and direct PARTICIPATION by that citizenry. Solon, the lawgiver of Athens, is the exemplar: he created citizenship by allowing certain members of tribes and social classes to have some say in Athenian law-making, and also insisted on some duties from all citizens (Socrates, for instance, was tried by the whole citizenry rather than some subset of it). This established for the first time the idea of an active commitment to the common good of the community as the politically dominant form of allegiance, as distinct from the tribal and other restricted affiliations of Homeric Greece or the rule of the great hierarchic bureaucracies in the Near East of antiquity. With the exception of some periods of tyranny, this general model of vibrant participatory political life, suffused with a conflation of CIVIC VIRTUE with moral excellence, applied to ancient Athens for several centuries.

In Rome, by contrast, we have the spectacle of an Empire created on the basis of citizenship deployed as the continuation of politics by other means. Roman citizenship laws differentiated in two ways: first, there were multiple grades of citizenship, bearing different schedules of burdens and capacities, and secondly, there was selective incorporation, or differentiation between people(s) in the distribution of those citizenships. Citizenship was therefore a finely honed policy with which to engender moral and political allegiance and expand fiscal capacity. With the passage of time enfranchisement expanded, later being conditionally offered to all peoples of the Empire, and though its practical import was variable it was not negligible, as illustrated in the Christian tradition of Paul the Apostle, who needed merely to declare his Roman citizenship in order to prevent his scourging by a tribune of the occupying Roman force in Palestine (Acts XXII: 21–9).

With the fall of Rome the concept of citizenship fell largely into disuse, being replaced by a feudal order built upon chains of personal allegiances, serfdom and monastic orders. Its revival began with the revival of the European cities and the rediscovery and dissemination of classical texts, particularly Justinian's *Corpus Iuris Civilis*, from the eleventh century onwards. Early cities flourished in Italy, Germany and the Low Countries and a little later in France and England, and with these arose merchants, guilds and corporations. These burghers were free of bondage, and the function of their elected leaders was primarily to protect and serve, rather than to govern. The principal drive was entrepreneurial and FREEDOM from feudalistic trammels was necessary to that end (a popular maxim of the time, with local equivalents across northwestern parts of Europe, was 'town air makes free'). The protection and safety mounted for the free man, together with the cultural movement re-engaging with classical jurisprudence and political philosophy, gave rise to an early revitalised notion of the citizen. In northwest Europe, where towns and cities were still exceptional and locked in reciprocal (albeit negotiable) relations with the dominant political units, which remained kingdoms, duchies and so on, the notion of the citizen never quite fought free of its economic burgher-like links, but in Italy, whose cities were often truly self-governing and not subordinate to external powers, republican movements arose in the so-called 'civic humanism' or civic REPUBLICANISM of the fifteenth and sixteenth centuries, in which membership of a city was an important and onerous status, usually entailing burdens such as terms in the local militia and other PUBLIC SERVICE.

With the reconfiguration of political AUTHORITY across Europe resulting in the centralised territorial modern state and the rise of monarchical absolutism, citizenship as orienting the imaginary suffered a decline, and political theory and practice focused on what was now taken to be the politically definitive relationship: that between subject(s) and monarch(s). Substantial economic and social changes over the early modern period, and in particular the development of modern CAPITALISM and the shift described as the move from status to contract, meant that the reinvigoration of the citizen in the decades immediately preceding the French Revolution of 1789, with its self-conscious adoption of classical motifs as filtered through Rousseau, had nevertheless to engage with the prevailing temper. This temper was increasingly individualistic and tended to see persons as goal-oriented actors embedded in social and moral frameworks more comprehensive than the comparatively small-scale and self-contained ethical and political worlds of the Athenian or Florentine state. The emphases which have structured citizenship since are evident in this, its second wave: the stress on rights, especially those whose object is freedom or liberty; on the equality of those rights (Paine 1937); and on the role of nationalism or other kinds of communal SOLIDARITY in grounding the justifications and allocations of the rights.

Citizenship's rearticulation with the social stratifications of the modern world was analysed by T.H. Marshall in an influential discussion of the historical relationship between citizenship and social CLASS in England (Marshall 1950). Citizenship, he argued, had been cumulatively enriched in a clear evolutionary trajectory, from the widespread grant of civil rights, won largely in the eighteenth century, through political rights, won largely in the nineteenth, to the socioeconomic rights distinctive of the twentieth century. By these means, citizenship, Marshall claimed, had mitigated the social frictions of modern capitalism by providing an alternative allocative rationale, across some domains of life, to the harsh rigour of the price mechanism. Although this historical excursus is neither a general model nor a general theory of citizenship, it is frequently observed that the account is (a) anglocentric, and of limited comparative applicability: in particular the development of citizenship in some other settings (for example, Third World countries) diverges significantly, in that political INDIVIDUALISM is the last element to arise, if it arises at all, and social citizenship is the primary element; and (b) has a gender bias, since it is the gradual enfranchisement of the males of the population that is taken as the relevant measure to track citizenship's development. The analysis is a lucid expression of the interpretations of, and

aspirations regarding, citizenship that were current in mid-twentieth century Western European WELFARE nation-states.

At the close of the twentieth century, however, the increasing salience of international governmental organisations, the establishment of international retributive justice, increasing economic and environmental interdependence (and externalising of harms), the liberalization of capital markets and accelerating mobility of populations (in short, GLOBALISATION) led to changed understandings of the scope and scale of collective action problems and to a resurgence of interest in citizenship, especially in conceptions of citizenship that move beyond its *locus* in the nation-state. Two broad avenues of thinking are discernible, their differences hinging on the kinds of BOUNDARIES considered most germane. The first avenue continues to assume that citizenship is territorially bounded, relating always to status and practice within a political unit occupying an actual part of the Earth's territory, and here although some interest and attention has been directed to (neo-republican and communitarian (see COMMUNITARIANISM)) notions of citizenship within state and sub-state units, by and large the major intellectual and practical challenges revolve around citizenship of large multipolar and pluralistic political units such as the European Union, the continuing INTEGRATION of which has resulted in the formal creation of citizenship for the nationals of its member-states in Article 8 of The Treaty on European Union in 1992 (the Maastricht Treaty). The second approach stresses citizenship as political practice: of intervention, by non-elites, in the functionally determined competences of international (mostly regulatory) organisations, and the issues raised within this approach relate to the practical possibilities for, and theoretical intelligibility and coherence of, notions such as global or cosmopolitan citizenship and COSMOPOLITAN DEMOCRACY. These emerging explorations of belonging, political action and rights-holding beyond the nation-state are reopening and rejuvenating questions about citizenship.

Distribution

Important questions bearing on any particular positive citizenship are its extent – how inclusive or exclusive it is – and the normative grounds on which the relevant discriminations are made. The most basic boundary is that dividing citizens from non-citizens within a given population. In most historical instances the line has been narrowly circumscribed, making citizenship a very exclusive club. In the Athenian *polis*, for example, the citizen body was generally about 20 per cent of the population and never reached much above that. Its normative grounds of exclusion tend also to affront modern sensibilities: women, aliens, *metics* (resident aliens), male prostitutes and the diverse kinds of slaves were all held to lack the moral AUTONOMY and rationality that were the essential credentials for the playing of an institutional role in the organised politics of the community.

Today, masculinity and substantial property ownership are not in themselves deemed necessary and sufficient justification for the granting of citizenship. The primary determinants for the positive bestowal of citizenship are birth within the polity's territorial precincts, or *jus soli*, and/or birth to an antecedent line of citizens, or *jus sanguinis* (i.e. citizenship on grounds of soil or blood respectively); or, of course, naturalisation. Modern states combine these in citizenship laws, but vary significantly in their manner of doing so. France and Germany provide striking examples: French law has a strong presumption favouring *jus soli*, while German law leans powerfully toward *jus sanguinis*, reflecting different traditions of thought about whether citizenship primarily betokens belonging to a civil association or an ethnos (Brubaker 1992).

Within the body of citizens, citizenship may be a condition establishing formal equality, or a formal recognition of inequality. In recent history, as Marshall indicated, it has ringfenced a zone within which all persons are to be treated as equals not only despite, but precisely on account of, the extraneous social and economic inequalities disfiguring relations between them: so, all citizens equally are under the rule of law and are treated equally by it, and each citizen has one vote and not more than one vote in electoral procedures. 'Second-class citizen' has become a self-evident complaint.

By contrast, classical Greek citizenship had some hierarchical elements, and citizenship both in the Roman Empire and in the early European Renaissance was built on minute gradations of status and accompanying privilege, with an inverse relationship between the desirability of these grades of citizenship and their distributional compass: the better, the fewer. Allocations of citizenship(s) therefore acknowledged, legitimated and consolidated inequalities, though in ways which yoked them partly to the public weal.

Another phenomenon not unusual in classical and medieval times, and re-emerging from obsolescence in the twenty-first century, is multiple citizenship. Dual citizenship (of two nation-states) is a condition known, somewhat reluctantly tolerated, and in the latter half of the twentieth century regulated, by modern states, but the prospect of persons holding two or more citizenships of distinct political communities at different levels of (non-federal) political organisation has begun to be reality with developments in the European Union, whose grant of voting and other rights to EU citizens effective when in a member state other than their 'own' echoes the classical Greek practice of *isopolity* (Riesenberg 1992: 52).

But why should the actual distribution of citizenship matter? Contrary to widespread belief, it is not the qualifying condition for most of the entitlements and duties associated with it. As a result of developments in international law and convention, the developed states by and large accord these rights and benefits either to all persons within their territorial jurisdiction without remainder, or to several categories of person including (but not exclusively) their citizens. Generally, western European states commonly hold only the following rights and duties to require citizenship as a prerequisite: voting in national elections, eligibility to stand as a candidate in national elections, full rights of access to public office, right to a passport, obligation to undertake military service, freedom of entry and right of residence. Access to 'fundamental' or 'human' rights, traditional civil liberties and social and economic rights, and liability to taxation, have either become or are well on the way to being entirely detached from the holding of citizenship status (Gardner 1994). The significance of contemporary citizenship thus lies in (1) citizens' being able to enter and stay in a territory within which the entitlements apply, by right and not, as is the case for non-citizens, by administrative discretion; and (2) citizens having the capacity to determine, by exercising the political rights reserved to them alone, the major decisions of the polity including the contours of that administrative discretion and the responsibilities the polity will undertake to assume with regard to non-citizens within and outside its jurisdiction.

Citizenship therefore remains a powerful mechanism of political control. Persons lacking any citizenship may have difficulty pursuing their fundamental rights for lack of respondents; they will certainly lack effective guarantors, and the plight of the stateless person is far from enviable (see STATELESSNESS). Moreover, the harms occasioned by the stripping of citizenship are not only consequential. Since it is inextricably bound up with possibilities for individual and collective self-determination, and affirmation of persons as full agents in the collective affairs of the polity, to deny or take away citizenship is to deny central aspects of basic humanity.

Quality

Evaluations of citizenship's quality and calibre have been at the heart of political philosophy and can be expected to remain of abiding concern, not least because in the last analysis it is the vigour of citizenship and the openness of its potentialities that decides the difference between polities whose democratic pretensions are well founded and those whose are not (benevolent technocratic despotisms, for example). The cultural and affective preconditions for effective citizenship are also questions that will come increasingly to the fore as political structures of transnational reach continue to proliferate.

Citizenship is the criterion of as well as the precondition for democracy. There are two broad models of contemporary citizenship, founded on what are often thought to be the contrary imperatives with which citizenship is shot through, and which supply a tension between (active) participation in public affairs on the one hand and (passive) enjoyment of rights and entitlements on the other. If citizenship's original Athenian essence is the notion and practice of self-government, the exercise of self-governing has generated its greatest progeny: the establishing of the rights and duties that enable self-government to reproduce itself. So perhaps at root the tension is, rather, a dialectical tangle needing to be teased apart, but it has spawned a variety of reflections on the 'republican' and the 'liberal' ideal types of citizenship. LIBERALISM has, on the whole, had the ascendancy in Western political thought and practice.

Republican conceptions of citizenship (tracing their source ultimately to Aristotelianism) tend to favour a high degree of mobilisation, with active participation in the collective affairs of the political community, a stress on other-regarding behaviour and positive POLITICAL OBLIGATION to fellow citizens, founded on a 'thick' social ontology, an assumption of cultural homogeneity and conflation of 'community' and 'polity', and an ethos which posits citizenship, properly understood, as the highest pinnacle of human flourishing. Liberal conceptions, by contrast, see citizenship (as indeed political life generally) as instrumental to and subordinate to persons' basic moral standing as individual and free members of humanity, give greater weight to negative rights than positive duties, and assume communities inherently heterogeneous internally and in need of a sustainable and so 'thin' ethic of the good and, behaviourally, a public or civic culture of tolerance and civility rather than active concern.

The major objections to be levelled at republican citizenship are (1) that it requires levels of personal motivation and participation from all citizens that are overly burdensome and corrosive of individual freedom; (2) that it assumes and requires degrees of social homogeneity and conformity implausible outside small communities (and perhaps undesirable altogether); (3) worse, that where motivation and conformism are deficient persons should be subject to programmes of motivational and ideological remedial engineering, as with Rousseau's prudential advocacy of a 'civil religion'; and (4) the notion that one's possibilities for moral merit as a person largely or wholly depend on one's performance as a citizen – a view which goes back to Aristotle (Aristotle 1957: 176–83) – strikes many people as not only eccentric but repugnant.

The major objections to liberal conceptions are that (1) its relegation (in some versions, verging on disavowal) of duties and obligations, and positive rights, makes it irresponsibly self-regarding and provides only an arid sense of community; (2) its tendency to identify the exercise of citizenship with infrequent and low-cost activity such as voting in national ELECTIONS constricts citizenship to a puny status increasingly evacuated of any real power and meaning; (3) these taken together render citizenship too threadbare and anodyne to provide the motivational and normative energy required to maintain a flourishing self-governing polity; and (4) the PUBLIC–PRIVATE DISTINCTION on which the liberal conception is founded has theoretical and conceptual shortcomings and undesirable social and political consequences.

A more adequate account of citizenship would fashion a thicker conception, with attention more equally weighted between rights and duties, and with more recognition of the positivity of both. It would veer towards a broad liberalism and a thin republicanism, attempting to capture the best while sacrificing the worst of each tradition (Clarke 1996). The first steps towards a robust and improved conception must involve a re-examination of the 'public–private' divide, greater sophistica-tion in understanding political identity and self-definition and mechanisms of solidarity in pluralistic societies, and a foreswearing of the ideational straitjackets which too often bind us to notions of citizenship which are imprecise, impoverished and hidebound.

See also:

civic virtue; demos; identity, political; inclusion/exclusion; judgement; political frontiers; public–private distinction; statelessness

Further reading

Aristotle (1957) *The Politics*, trans. T.A. Sinclair, Harmondsworth: Penguin.

Brubaker, R. (1992) *Citizenship and Nationhood in France and Germany*, Cambridge, MA: Harvard University Press.

Clarke, P.B. (1994) *Citizenship*, London: Pluto.

—— (1996) *Deep Citizenship*, London: Pluto.

Gardner, J.P. (ed.) (1994) *Hallmarks of Citizenship: A Green Paper*, London: The British Institute of International and Comparative Law and the Institute for Citizenship Studies.

Marshall, T.H. (1950) 'Citizenship and Social Class', in T.H. Marshall, *Citizenship and Social Class and Other Essays*, Cambridge: Cambridge University Press.

Paine, T. (1937) *Rights of Man* ed. H.B. Bonner, London: Watts and Co.

Riesenberg, P. (1992) *Citizenship in the Western Tradition: Plato to Rousseau*, Chapel Hill, NC: University of North Carolina Press.

LYNN DOBSON
PAUL BARRY CLARKE

civic virtue

Civic virtue refers to the quality(ies) of a good citizen. The principal of these, stated Aristotle, is a readiness to participate actively, to ensure the rule of law in any society (see LAW, RULE OF). Its converse is APATHY. The precise nature of the activity required has changed as the context has changed. Four major contexts have required different virtues. These were the Athenian city-state, the Roman Empire, the nation-state and the post-national regional/ global polity. At the end of the twentieth century, the Roman and nation-state emphasis on the citizen as warrior in defence of his community (*virtus* (manly) + *civis* (community)) has become no longer adequate to maintain a stable democratic rule of law. Returning to favour now is the original Athenian notion of efficient excellence in participating in the relevant procedures of ruling (*arete*). 'Civic virtue' is a term that implies 'civility' (Pettit 1997).

History and development

What made a man a good citizen in Athens was participating actively in ruling the polity, particularly through the exercise of an equal vote. Obedience to the law (being ruled) was not essential. Demanding ACCOUNTABILITY from decision makers was paramount. In Pericles, virtue included a readiness to fight and die in defence of those democratic procedures and rules of the polity against any actions or ideas that threatened it. This marked the beginning of an abiding notion of civic virtue in democracies. The highest virtue was a defence of the patrimony of democracy handed down as a heritage by the fathers of the community against anyone who did not accept it either internally or externally. When the polity was defined as the community of kin but excluded foreigners, women and workers because they could not by nature share such values, civic virtue as the defence of democracy became an exclusive rather than an inclusive quality.

Under the Roman Empire, the privilege of citizenship was extended to foreigners because they had fought for Rome. According to Cicero, they were given only passive benefits and not democratic participation. This privilege, accorded to the warrior defenders of the community, continued to be central when the nation-state emerged in the fifteenth century.

Machiavelli insisted on Roman virtue as wilful reason, and Rousseau insisted on a fierce loyalty to the nation and its political arrangements. The refrain of the French revolutionary anthem runs: 'to arms, citizens, form your battalions'. This confusion of virtue and defence of the national patrimony continued in Mill and had become a constant theme by the twentieth century (Cohen 1985).

Equating civic virtue with commitment to the national heritage became increasingly difficult as new states created in the nineteenth century comprised many ethnic MINORITIES and the enemy without became easily confused with the enemy within. Early attempts to exterminate difference and create a homogeneous national citizenry (Renan 1992) provoked opposition to the state and the establishment of rights to different private worlds. Benjamin Constant in 1819 pointed out that ancient virtues were inappropriate in the large nation-state. Rather, the state was called to account by its citizens in a renewed emphasis on liberty and democracy as procedures. Further, to sustain this control from below it was recognised that minimal economic, social, educational and health standards were required for all. Obligation to fight in defence of the national community and to oppose a tyrannical state was complemented with the notion that each citizen had to be his brothers' and then his sisters' keeper (Bobbio 1990). This meant increased subordination to the state and a greater emphasis on the virtue of a mild rather than a warrior-like attitude to those who were different (Dagger 1997).

With the development after 1945 of regional trading blocs and polities like the European Union, the need to accept difference further fostered the replacement of the fierce values of AUTONOMY and strong reason by those of interdependence and weak reason. The notion that virtue meant care for ones' different neighbour, who had rights without belonging to the national community, became law in documents like the Maastricht treaty (ss8) and was promoted by the United Nations (Global Commission 1995). Civic virtue was equated less with attachment to a democratic heritage than with mild virtues of tolerance, trust and brotherly love. A virtuous citizen was expected not only to assert his/her rights against tyranny but to guarantee in different ways to others who lived with them the equal expression of their views about the Good.

Principal ideas

In the modern state system of today, civic virtue requires contradictory qualities which are increasingly difficult to reconcile. Since 1789 the state has been increasingly subject to power 'from below'. This democratic principle has been based on the belief that each individual has inherent rights, the first of which is to make the laws under which he or she lives. Together a community of individuals is the popular sovereign. This requires an assertive stance *vis-à-vis* the state which makes it accountable to the citizen-individual. Strict adhesion to rules of TRANSPARENCY are required. Any relaxation of this assertive presence could allow a tyranny to start to re-emerge.

So, more democracy in more places has been required as the world becomes more complex and difference is increasingly juxtaposed (Bobbio 1984). An exhausting participation in the public realm is an ideal when the original object in the nineteenth century was to secure law making to enlarge private spaces and to restrict public activity.

Moreover, today the creation of the person able to show such virtue requires a minimum of rights in the economic, social, health and educational realm. Without the latter a real participation in the civil and political realm is inconceivable. But to accept an ever-increasing list of rights as each person's due, as has become a reality in ratified UN conventions (Bobbio 1990; Donnelly 1993), means subordinating oneself to a spider's web of laws and regulations which re-empower the state machine which administers the WELFARE state. Civic virtue oscillates between a warrior principle and a caring principle. This creates contradictions for democratic citizens.

It is claimed that welfare creates a 'handout' mentality and a refusal to participate actively in the making of the laws. Proponents of a minimalist state and the market principle argue that civic virtue is harmed by too many laws. These supposedly lead to confusion and the crushing of initiative. In place of the strong individual who thinks for himself or herself increasing dependence on experts is becoming the norm.

The state as authority was once comparatively easily identified, and strong slogans in defence of the democratic community could be maintained against it. Civic virtue was thus easily identified. But who the community is, and what community values are, are no longer given to 'common sense'. Polities like the EU and most states are multi-ethnic. This will be increasingly the pattern as GLOBALISATION promotes massive migration of labour.

The ensuing complexity of a world with a multiplicity of identities is almost impossible to grasp in thought. Today, the local, regional and global compete with the national for each individual's loyalty. To live with others who will remain different in value systems and yet be neighbours in a global market place creates problems for the notion of an individual whose core value is that of thinking for oneself and asserting a fierce subjective autonomy. Such virtues spell conflict when the other lives next door. When citizens are expected to accept culturally vying systems of reason within a political community, the notion of community becomes much less strong and so does confidence in the reasonableness of one's opinions (Bouamama 1992).

Future trends

The complexity of modern society and the distance of DECISION-MAKING from citizens together with the feeling that risk cannot be controlled has led to widespread APATHY, and in some places, notably Africa and the former USSR, chaos. Pessimists argue that democracy is no longer possible in the globalised world (Zolo 1992; Kaplan 1997) and forecast a widespread adoption of the rule of experts, known as the Singapore solution. Optimists admit that civic virtue is very 'thin' when loyalty is demanded to a global polity (Falk 1996), but others point out the widespread commitment to local politics and to SOCIAL MOVEMENTS. The United Nations and other regional authorities like the EU promote civics campaigns designed to foster commitment to democracy and human rights even in the global neighbourhood (Global Commission 1995).

What is ever more widely recognised is that more democracy in more places, while necessary, is not sufficient to build civic virtue. Such commitment rests on centuries of 'social capital' (Putman 1992). This is developed by interaction in the public space without any expectation of an immediate or even distant recompense: say in clubs, co-operatives, church and other groups. It builds attitudes that are not 'interested' and therefore not deterred by setbacks. They are mild, tolerant, trusting and based on brotherly love, categories which have not had much press in the lexicon of civic virtues. Such virtue is learnt and cannot be legislated. The Council of Europe recognised this in recent discussions about a Bill of Obligations, insisting that these were not the same as duties, which rest on possession of RIGHTS. Other groups have drawn up such Bills. Civics programmes to foster such attitudes are often mooted but are not well developed.

See also:

citizenship; civil society; direct action; judgement; social movements

Further reading

Bobbio, N. (1984) *Il Futuro della democrazia*, Turin: Einaudi.
—— (1990) *L'Età dei diritti*, Turin: Einaudi.
Bouamama, S. (1992) 'Nationalité et citoyen: le divorce inévitable', in S. Bouamama, A. Cordeiro and M. Roux (eds), *La citoyenneté dans tous ses états de l'immigration à la nouvelle citoyenneté*, Paris: l'Harmattan.
Cohen, E. (1985) *Citizens and Soldiers: the Dilemmas of Military Service*, Ithaca, NY: Cornell University Press.
Dagger, R. (1997) *Civic Virtues Rights, Citizenship and Republican Liberalism*, Oxford: Oxford University Press.
Donnelly, J. (1993) *International Human Rights*, Boulder, CO: Westview.
Falk, R. (1996) 'The Decline of Citizenship in an Era of Globalisation', in *Globalisation and Citizen: An International Conference*, UNRISD, Swinburne University of Technology, Geneva 9–11 December.
Global Commission (1995) *Our Global Neighbourhood. The Report of the Commission on Global Governance*, Oxford: Oxford University Press.
Kaplan, R. (1997) 'Was Democracy Just a Moment?', *The Atlantic Monthly*, December: 55–80.
Pettit, P. (1997) *Republicanism: A Theory of Freedom and Government*, Oxford: Clarendon Press.
Putnam, R. (1992) *Making Democracy Work: Civic Traditions in Modern Italy*, Princeton, NJ: Princeton University Press.
Renan, E. (1992) *Qu'est-ce qu'une nation?*, Paris: Presses Pocket.
Zolo, D. (1992) *Democracy and Complexity: A Realist Approach*, Cambridge: Polity Press.

ALASTAIR DAVIDSON

civil disobedience

Civil disobedience is the purposeful and public defiance of an established law or norm, undertaken with the intent of altering state policy. Among political theorists, legal scholars and activists, however, there is considerable debate about whether civil disobedience necessarily entails acceptance of state AUTHORITY, recognised lack of other means of political influence, acceptance of criminal punishment or avoidance of some degree of violence. The practice of civil disobedience, explicitly labelled as such, has become a routinised part of the repertoire of contention for challenging movements in the United States and throughout the West, and is often employed in the service of democratisation movements elsewhere in the world, often with the same basic legitimating texts. Whereas once civil disobedience was seen to be the domain of relatively powerless groups, now numerous challengers claim powerlessness and alienation from the political system as their justification for civil disobedience, even if their own marginality – for example, as students or fundamentalist Christians in the United States – is less than immediately obvious.

Civil disobedience generally involves immediate instrumental objectives, but the gains of DIRECT ACTION are modest in the context of broader movement goals. Civil rights activists, for example, used direct action to desegregate buses and libraries, but surely hoped that successful efforts in one locality would obviate the need for freedom rides or sit-ins elsewhere. Similarly, anti-nuclear weapons protestors who smash weapons propose to begin unilateral disarmament by damaging United States nuclear weapons; anti-abortion activists claim to take dramatic action to save a single unborn life, but clearly hope to influence policy beyond the scope of a single clinic. Activists attempt to influence the policy process by a symbolic interference with policy implementation.

This entry will sketch an history of civil disobedience and writing on civil disobedience, identifying two distinct forms, one collective and at least partly instrumental, the other individualistic and justified by claims to some kind of 'higher laws'. Most of the analysis is directed to a second, collectivist mode of civil disobedience, in which civil disobedience actions are part of a larger social and political campaign, and justified by claims to community norms in addition to any 'higher laws'. Dissidents claim their authority from below as well as above. Rather than being an *appeal* to outside authority, civil disobedience is often an *assertion* of alternate sources of authority.

Open, principled and often political, defiance of law has a very long history, and it is tempting to term in retrospect all cases of such activity 'civil disobedience'. Greek theatre suggests two distinct models in *Antigone* and *Lysistrata*, each carrying different political implications. Sophocles's Antigone buried her brother in direct defiance of city law and royal edict. Knowing her act would be punished by death, she defiantly and openly buried her brother, justifying her conduct with reference to divine law. In contrast, Aristophanes's *Lysistrata* tells the story of women who seek to end a war by, among other things, refusing to sleep with their husbands until they negotiate a truce with their enemies. By refusing to fulfil their expected roles in Athenian society, the women effectively confront the city-state where it normally confronts them – in the home and in the bedroom – although they harbour no interest in abstaining from sex *per se*. For the women, non-co-operation is a way to begin dialogue; in effect, to enter democratic dialogue and politics.

Comparison of these plays, as archetypes of different models of civil disobedience, is instructive. In both cases, the protagonists are women, people normally without means, standing or access for participation in conventional institutional politics. Lacking institutional routes for influence as well as the physical force to overturn or reshape the system, they attempted to exercise influence by ceasing to provide expected obedience and compliance, and thereby tacitly supported the policies with which they quarrelled. Confrontation with the state was direct, but on terms other than those the state chose. Civil disobedience was politics by other means, a politics that is most attractive to those who perceive little prospect of meaningful political influence within institutional politics.

The differences between these models of civil disobedience are equally important. Antigone justified her act by reference to higher laws – in this case, the laws of the gods – finding moral authority from personal relationships with the divine and her dead brother. She defied precisely the law she found unjust, and the act in itself, burying her brother, completed her political campaign. She acted alone, asking no support or excuse from those around her. In contrast, Lysistrata and her allies acted collectively, and indeed transnationally in concert with women in warring states. Authority and justification for their claims and their action came from their relationships with each other and their created community, and collective abstention itself was part of a larger political campaign.

We thus have two distinct models or ideal types of civil disobedience. In one, the act is individual, expressive, moralist and political only in the most minimal sense. In the second, civil disobedience is one component in a larger campaign featuring numerous other tactics; it is collective and instrumental, and it may involve violation of laws and practices not inherently offensive. Paradoxically, in contemporary practice, the second model is far more common, yet justifications and arguments from the first are prevalent.

Henry David Thoreau's classic essay 'Civil Disobedience' provides a template definition and justification of civil disobedience that actually obfuscates understanding of the practice. Some years after spending a night in jail for failure to pay his poll tax, Thoreau justified his action as an attempt to disengage himself morally and politically from a national government that allowed slavery and conducted an illegal war in Mexico. Like Antigone, Thoreau acted alone and quite apart from the organised abolitionist and anti-war campaigns of which he was surely aware, proclaiming himself as ultimate authority for all actions. The political efficacy of tax resistance as a topic was of far less interest to Thoreau than the moral inconvenience of compliance.

Thoreau's essay, however, far outlived his action, and found its way around the globe and into the hands of, among others, Mohandas Gandhi. Gandhi saw civil disobedience both as political tactic and a moral instrument, and he attempted to use it for political ends, first in a campaign against racial discrimination in South Africa, then with notably more success in the service of a national independence campaign in India. Gandhi spoke of 'truth force' (*satyagraha*) and explicitly emphasised negotiating with and persuading his opponents, rather than coercing them. Despite this individualistic and moralistic overlay, his politics was that of SOCIAL MOVEMENTS: he and

his followers always used civil disobedience as part of a larger collective action campaign with concrete political goals. In selected protests, Gandhi filled the jails with protestors, and urged his followers to begin developing their own political and economic support structures so as to be able to manage ultimate independence. Through reports of Gandhi's campaigns, civil disobedience returned to the United States through religiously inspired peace and civil rights activists, carried initially by the transnational pacifist group, the Fellowship of Reconciliation.

Rosa Parks learned of Thoreau's essay in 1955 while attending a week-long leadership training course at the Highlander School, where she also read the US Supreme Court's *Brown* decision which banned racial segregation in public schools. Later that year, Parks violated a Montgomery law requiring blacks to sit behind whites on public buses. Her arrest served as a rallying point for a massive bus boycott, as well as a legal and political challenge to laws supporting segregation in the South. The campaign also marked the entry into political action for a young minister, Martin Luther King.

Like Gandhi, whose work he encountered in graduate school, Martin Luther King spoke and wrote of the moral necessity of civil disobedience. He also used the tactic as part of a larger legal, social, and political strategy for change. Success in Montgomery, however, came not solely through the boycott, but through vindication by the United States Supreme Court, which ruled Alabama's bus segregation laws unconstitutional. While King wrote appealingly about 'higher laws', this meant not simply divine laws of God or nature, but also federal and constitutional laws. His civil disobedience efforts here and elsewhere appealed to both moral and higher political authority. Importantly, civil disobedience was never more than one tactic in a broad and integrated campaign for civil rights and social justice.

The early civil rights movement appropriated symbols of liberal JUSTICE and mainstream political culture, invigorating or redefining them by juxtaposition of context. Integrated groups of activists asked to see the Declaration of Independence in segregated libraries; men wore coats and ties and women dressed in church attire when conducting civil disobedience; demonstrators carried American flags in civil rights marches; disobedients prayed, sang spirituals or recited the pledge of allegiance when awaiting arrest, quoting the Gospels or the Founding Fathers whenever possible. No doubt this aided the movement in gaining some element of public sympathy and winning important support from outsiders, by defining integration as a self-evident consensual value, endorsed by both God and the United States Constitution.

This approach effectively skirted difficult questions of political/moral authority for disobedience, and left open to contest for subsequent civil rights campaigns and for later movements that used civil disobedience. It was the civil rights movement's perceived successes with civil disobedience, however, that firmly established this form of collective action for challenging movements in contemporary American politics. Activists for diverse causes, including opponents of taxes, nuclear power, nuclear weapons, abortion and pollution, employed a variety of dramatic and confrontational tactics that they called civil disobedience, although all enjoyed less success than the civil rights movement in reaching the public and the MEDIA and influencing elected officials.

One reason for this is that the civil rights movement, unlike later civil disobedients, always justified its efforts in terms of national law. But activists who claim the legitimacy of their positions, be they against war, discrimination or abortion, feel no compunction to recognise the authority of the state, only its power. Thus, civil disobedients often describe their actions as examples of true obedience, suggesting that the commitments to community values take precedence over those to the state. As Jean Gump, currently in Alderson federal prison for beating on a missile silo with a hammer, explained, 'laws that protect weapons are immoral, against international law, and

simply must be broken' (quoted in Wilcox 1991: 52–3).

Short-term policy changes or vindication from the legal system are only a small part of what a civil disobedience action can achieve. Even failing legitimation from the state, a civil disobedient may effectively contribute to a process of *eroding* state authority and *accreting* support for alternate sources of authority. For example, local action groups opposing nuclear power and nuclear weapons use civil disobedience not only as a political tactic, but also to assert and build new community values. Although the activists in what Barbara Epstein (1991) terms the 'non-violent direct action movement' certainly hope to influence government policy, this is a long-term and indirect objective. More immediately, they work to create a new culture, including ways to organise society. Denying any separation between ends and means, their politics is based in directly creating the kind of society in which they want to live, establishing in effect a 'community of protest', and juxtaposing it with the larger political world.

Groups without the power to win unambiguous victories by military force or within the political system, those likely to choose civil disobedience, derive their greatest potential influence by demonstrating their capacity to disrupt the practice of politics as usual. It is not necessarily the disruptiveness of an action itself that is powerful and threatening; it is challenging opponents in unexpected ways, and creating uncertainty about what challengers might do in the future. This surprise and uncertainty is necessarily limited in time, as the repetition of an action over time invariably creates some degree of routinisation and predictability.

The increased use of civil disobedience raises important questions about the nature of democracy. As more diverse constituencies lose faith in conventional means of political participation as an exclusive means of protecting their interests, non-institutional participation will increase. The history of social protest in American politics is cumulative, and the safe and successful employment of civil disobedience will encourage new challengers to adopt and adapt the tactic, making effective governance and policy reform more difficult. Paradoxically, even as increased tolerance and ritualisation of civil disobedience practices makes protest safer, easier and more prevalent, it also makes it less effective.

See also:

authority; citizenship; civic virtue; democratic debate; legitimacy; social movements

Further reading

Bedau, H.A. (1969) 'Introduction', in H.A. Bedau (ed.), *Civil Disobedience: Theory and Practice*, Indianapolis: Pegasus, 15–26.

Bondurant, J.V. (1965) *Conquest of Violence*, Berkeley, CA: University of California Press.

Epstein, B. (1991) *Political Protest and Cultural Revolution*, Berkeley, CA: University of California Press.

King, M.L. (1969) 'Letter from Birmingham Jail', in H.A. Bedau (ed.), *Civil Disobedience: Theory and Practice*, Indianapolis: Pegasus, 73–90.

Muste, A.J. (1969) 'Of Holy Disobedience', in H.A. Bedau (ed.), *Civil Disobedience: Theory and Practice*, Indianapolis: Pegasus, 133–45.

Shridharani, K.J. (1962) *War without Violence*, Bombay: Bharatiya Vidyha Bhavan.

Thoreau, H.D. (1969) 'Civil Disobedience', in H.A. Bedau (ed.), *Civil Disobedience: Theory and Practice*, Indianapolis: Pegasus, 27–48.

Walzer, M. (1970) *Obligations: Essays on Disobedience, War, and Citizenship*, Cambridge, MA: Harvard University Press.

Wilcox, F.A. (1991) *Uncommon Martyrs: The Plowshares Movement and the Catholic Left*, Reading, MA: Addison-Wesley.

DAVID S. MEYER

civil service

The civil service is the non-military administration of the central state. Civil servants are paid administrators carrying out those functions which central government deems necessary, usually constrained by constitutional law. The functions of the civil service vary dramatically across nations and time. Civil servants are usually organised into hierarchically governed, functionally defined departments, though some departments may be territorially defined. In Britain, only civilian officials in central government are known as civil servants, but in some countries the term applies also to civilians working in the JUDICIARY, employees of local government, public corporations, schools, universities and other agencies. In democracies, most civil servants are permanent officials who do not change with a new government, but they may include some 'political appointees' at the head of agencies or in policy-advising capacities.

In the twentieth century, the functions of the civil service have grown and with them the numbers employed. Exact figures are difficult to provide partly due to the different ways in which civil servants are defined across nations, but also because since the 1980s in many countries, many aspects of civil service duties have been passed on to the private sector through contracting out and PRIVATISATION. Thus gross statistics on the comparative size of the civil service can be a very misleading indicator into the penetration of the state into citizens' lives.

The term 'civil service' came into general use in the UK during the 1850s. It was probably first applied to the East India Company's non-military officials. The earliest known use referring to officials of the state was in a Treasury letter in 1816 (Aylmer 1980: 91). Sir Robert Peel used the term in 1841–2, and it appeared in an Act of Parliament of 1853. The Northcote–Trevelyan Report of 1854 gave the term wide circulation. It was first used in the USA in 1863 and appeared in a statute of 1871, being deliberately borrowed from the UK. However, officials carrying out civil service duties predate the term itself.

Today the term civil service is usually associated with the idea of BUREAUCRACY, which always carries Weberian connotations.

The idea of the civil service still conforms to Weber's conception of a hierarchically organised machine, with individual civil servants cogs of the machine carrying out their functions according to sets of rules laid down by the state. In modern democracies, any suggestion that individuals in such an administrative system would not be appointed on merit as opposed to family connections or funded patronage seems corrupt. In this we have the highest ideals of the civil service. Historically, administrative structures were not so constrained. In Britain, the Northcote–Trevelyan Report set out such principles in order to try to build a civil service that was not suffused with patronage, and where the remuneration of civil servants came through their salary alone and not through payment secured as perks of the job.

Following Weber, we can say a modern bureaucracy is likely to be hierarchical, permanent, specialised, paid and full-time, and rule-governed. Most of these aspects of bureaucracy could be found in ancient Egypt and Sumeria, the later Roman Empire, the Byzantine Empire, the Caliphate and most notably in Imperial China. But we should not be so blinkered by Weberian categories that we fail to recognise a civil service in many other forms of society and government. Under European monarchies, there were sharply distinguished functions between political ministers – lords of the royal household – and clerical assistants. Once the state started to collect taxes, tax collectors were required, though many early civil servants would not be full-time permanent officials. Usually they would take a percentage of fees collected or have a right to charge. They would also have been appointed on a patronage basis rather than through competitive examination (a system invented in Imperial China).

When did public administration first start? It is not possible for ancient monuments such as Stonehenge or regional defence systems to have emerged without some form of administrative structure. Public administration has one of the claims to be the oldest profession. But distinguishing political rule from administration is difficult when the administrative structures are not routinised. From what we know from archaeology and anthropology, the role of middlemen (the male noun being appropriate) often, though not exclusively, a birthright is secured through ritual, and each person's place in the organisational structure of society recognised through the transmission of ritual behaviour. Ritual behaviour forms a COMMUNICATION system both between people and through time.

Despite lacking writing, the Incas centralised power over a large geographic area, with a hierarchy based on a span of control of ten for each level of supervision, from the lowest worker to Lord Inca at the apex. They recorded statistical information on the *quipu*, a cord of threads of different colours, which could be knotted. Their whole economic system of agriculture and trade was under state direction and control. INFORMATION is important to administrative systems, and the most successful are those that are able to handle large quantities of information. Functional division of labour aids this information process or one has departments with overlapping duties not aware of the policies of other parts of the system. It is worth illustrating the importance of information storage and retrieval.

In 1677, the British Treasury was commissioned and its secretary kept minutes for future action. A number of books – the Customs Book, the Letterbook and so on – were kept for these minutes. At that time all Treasury papers were folded twice, docketed and numbered on backs and sides. As more information was collected, other papers would be attached to a docket folded up within the letter. It was not until 1868 that it was decided not to fold papers but keep them flat, filed to a tag and put into a jacket. These files then developed with information on the front of the file containing cross-references to other files. The system was cumbersome, and during the First World War it was radically overhauled. Then it was decided 'one subject, one jacket', so all letters on a given subject would be kept in fat files. These information systems require large buildings and many workers to retrieve them. Here filing clerks were important members of an efficient bureaucracy.

Today's technology is revolutionising the handling of complex information. The Inland Revenue has been organised so that each person has a given tax office which handles their file, and it is to that office one must apply for tax information. Today, networked computer systems mean that large offices with workers in one place are no longer required. Information can be called up from anywhere in the world; so for example, British car registration details can be 'stored' in Texas, while the Inland Revenue can develop 'call centres' for citizens to phone up for information on their taxes run by people who may have no dealings with one's tax assessment but simply specialise in answering telephone enquiries. For other non-private information, websites can provide citizens with information.

These changes in information technology are transforming the nature of public administration and civil service structures. It is no longer necessary to have the hierarchically organised structures on single sites. Specialist centres, contracted-out to private firms can hold information. Monetary transfers can be made automatically to and from personal accounts and government offices. This has heralded a drastic slimming of the numbers of civil servants in many countries, though individuals working in private companies may be working exclusively on government contracts. This blurs the boundaries between public and private employment.

The critics of devolved civil service structures are numerous. Sir Warren Fisher famously claimed for the British civil service (in his evidence to the Tomlin Commission, 1929–31) that it was unified by a spirit and tradition that transcended departmental concerns. This was thought to provide a bulwark in society and keep corruption at bay. Where once all British civil servants were appointed through competitive examination on a service-wide basis, they are now recruited by over 3,000 devolved units overseen in a 'light-handed and economical way' by twenty-two people. Furthermore, the agencies and sub-units are encouraged to develop their own team spirit and loyalties according to the modern 'new managerial' fashions. With more flexible pay structures, and an emphasis on entrepreneurialism rather than rule-governed behaviour, the British civil service changed quite radically toward the end of the twentieth century. Far more employees from the private sector have been enticed into top managerial positions than in the past, partly drawn by the greater rewards that have been made available.

The progress of 'agencifying' and 'privatising' the managerial tasks of the civil service is also affecting the policy advisory role. In the Weberian bureaucratic model of old public administration, senior civil servants should be politically neutral when advising the government of the day. However, increasingly in European and Western administrative systems, policy advice is given by politically appointed advisors from outside government. As committees of experts are formed to help promote increasingly technical legislation the interpenetration of business and commercial concerns, with scientists employed by, for example, pharmaceutical companies also sitting on European Union panels of advisers, is becoming the norm.

Critics will argue that this is more likely to lead to inefficiencies and corruption in the long run. These changes were introduced because the civil service was perceived to be inefficient. How inefficient is open to doubt. In Britain, the Rayner scrutinies of the early 1980s dedicated to finding inefficiencies made only marginal savings. Modern ideology suggests the private sector has much more efficient working practices, and so it is argued these need to be introduced into the civil service. Corruption has certainly surfaced to a greater extent in the agencies in Britain following these changes, but corruption is endemic in many hierarchical civil services around the world, so there is no necessary correlation.

Historically, the size of the civil service and the size of the state's regular army seem to be positively correlated. Where states have had a notables-and-followers type of army, they have had a low level of bureaucratisation; when there is a regular standing army, the civil service is also strong and well-organised. Historically too, the efficiency and honesty of the civil service are a mark of civilisation as we recognise it. While the informational capabilities and powers of the civil service can obviously have a deleterious effect upon liberty and democracy, a well-functioning and penetrative administrative system can also facilitate the WELFARE, liberty and democratic RIGHTS of a people.

The 'penetration' of the civil service into the state has two elements: first, the range of functions it undertakes, and second, how far down it goes. How far down the line of central government, district, city or village the chain of paid professional administrators operates in any state will vary. For example, the Chinese Han Empire had four times as many civil servants per capita as the late Roman Empire, but the paid professional force only reached down as far as the sub-prefecture (districts of regions). Below that, administration was conducted by headmen in the towns and villages. In the Roman Empire, similarly, local administrators were local notables who at first were unpaid. As the tasks became burdensome, many tried to escape this unpaid service, but were compelled to remain in their posts and make up any tax shortfall from their own wealth. We may compare Britain and France in this regard. In England, paid agents of the Crown only penetrated as far as the shire, which has led to the convention of not counting local government officers as civil servants. In France, Philippe-Auguste (1165–1223) planted his agents at the local level to enforce taxation and justice.

In modern states, the penetration of the civil service is great and is likely to increase. While the distinction between public and private sectors continues to be blurred (see PUBLIC–PRIVATE DISTINCTION), this may hold great dangers for liberty and democracy. However, a well-functioning, honest and penetrative civil service is a necessary requirement for both the enjoyment of civil liberties and for a well-functioning democracy.

See also:

bureaucracy; public service; welfare

Further reading

Aylmer, G. (1980) 'From Office-Holding to Civil Service: The Genesis of the Modern Bureaucracy', *Transactions of the Royal Historical Society*, 5th series, 30.
Dowding, K. (1995) *The Civil Service*, London: Routledge.
Finer, S.E. (1997) *The History of Government*, 3 vols, Oxford: Oxford University Press.
Heady, F. (1995) *Public Administration: A Comparative Perspective*, 5th edn, New York: Marcel Dekker.

KEITH DOWDING

civil society

The concept of civil society has been made available to us by such nineteenth-century theorists as Hegel, J.S. Mill, Marx and Tocqueville, and is rich and multi-levelled. Civil society was understood as a separate sphere of social interaction, distinct from both the economy and the state. It was characterised by forms of plurality (voluntary association); civil publics, communicating through the mass media of that century, print; privacy (a domain of personal AUTONOMY) and legality (actionable RIGHTS and the rule of law. Twentieth-century theorists added three crucial components to this understanding.

First, Gramsci (1971: 206–77) pointed to its cultural dimension, which served to generate consent and integrate society (HEGEMONY). Civil society was both a symbolic field and the locus for the formation of action-orienting norms, meanings, values and collective identities. It was thus an arena where competing conceptions of civil society were struggled over either to maintain an existing hegemony or to replace it with a counter-hegemony. Gramsci showed that no conception of civil society could be neutral. The idea of civil society is a political idea. Gramsci's concern was class hegemony, that is, the struggle between classes to control the key institutions, norms, values of civil society to gain cultural hegemony.

Second, the arena of CONTESTATION expanded from Gramsci's focus on class relations to the analysis of more informal networks, initiatives and social movements. Touraine, Melucci and others recognized this dimension and allowed civil society to be seen from two perspectives: civil society as institutionalized civic autonomy and civil society in its dynamic form, where new values, collective identities, new projects and new concerns could be articulated and its implications for democratisation be analysed.

The third addition was Habermas's communicative and deliberative conception of the public sphere. While the category of the public sphere was present in eighteenth and nineteenth-century analyses of civil society, Habermas stressed its normative weight, its role in mediating between the particular and the general. It is in the public sphere that public opinion is discursively generated, where the decisions of rulers and lawmakers are informally controlled without the influence of state CENSORSHIP and manipulation. Civil publics generate influence of public opinion on the political system to which representatives of legislatures are presumed to be receptive and responsive. The core of the normative conception of the public sphere is thus free discursive contestation and debate, openness of access and parity of PARTICIPATION. This can lead to the democratisation of civil society and to the democratisation of political society, i.e. of the party system and of representative institutions. Through processes of deliberation, negotiation and accommodation, citizens who are affected by public policy and laws have the right, with equal voice, to express their views and thus influence deliberation. The normative core of the idea of civil society thus lies at the heart of any conception of democracy. Political legitimacy depends on the principle that action-orienting norms, policies and practices as well as any claim to authority can be contested, expanded or revised by citizens. Claus Offe

(1999) argues that within constitutional democracies it is the provision of unconstrained critical discourse (rights) in the public sphere that forms the LEGITIMACY of that particular democracy. This institutionalised 'distrust' in the public sphere is crucial to maintaining trust or legitimacy.

The relationship between democracy and trust, between responsibility and accountability, has once more become a central concern within political theory in recent years. About twenty-five years ago, the idea of civil society enjoyed a considerable revival within debates of post-Marxist critics of Soviet-type societies in the East (Cohen and Arato 1992). The strategy involved the rebuilding of social ties, organising politically relevant collective action and the forming of independent publics outside state-controlled communication. Correlated to this was the aim to create political publics and institutions that would be electorally responsible and accountable. In short, the revival of the concept of civil society meant the revival of self-organisation. In Western European post-Marxist theory, the emergence of 'new' SOCIAL MOVEMENTS challenged various forms of domination and inequality that differed from CLASS oppression but had systematic bases nevertheless. There the focus was on the need to further liberalise and democratise the institutions of already existing civil societies and to make representative democracies more receptive and responsive to new social issues and groups.

Today, the debate concerning the nature and role of civil society has changed. Now it is the crisis of the WELFARE state, not the totalitarian state that is at stake. Today dissatisfaction with the social and cultural effects of 'normal' rather than 'failed' modernisation motivates the renewal of the discourse of civil society. Models of social integration, associational life and civic engagement which once suited industrial society don't fit post-industrial civil societies which have new forms of social diversity, have been vastly changed by economic, scientific and technological factors and have new institutions. In the context of globalisation, people have lost confidence in the state's ability to implement effective policies or to exercise control over market forces over technological and scientific innovation or social structural change. But belief in the magic of the market as the solution to the problems faced by contemporary civil societies is also fading. Hence the revival of the discourse of civil society and the fears of the 'decline of social trust', and so on.

Civil society is no longer an arcane concept used by a particular group of political theorists. The term has become part of the discourse of politicians, academic theorists and journalists from all sides of the political spectrum. It has become a slogan for the 1990s because it seems to offer another area from which political and economic initiatives can emerge. But instead of widening the way in which the concept is used and understood, the view of civil society that has been revived is one-dimensional, backward looking and idealised. Two prominent and recent debates around the neorepublican position taken by Putnam and his school and the communitarian arguments surrounding the journal *The Responsive Community*, edited by Etzioni, illustrate how the notion of civil society can become so reduced and romanticised that its normative thrust is lost as well as its relevance to contemporary problems (see COMMUNITARIANISM).

Putnam (1993) claims that the basis of a responsive and effective democratic government is a vigorous civil society and he is correct. An important prerequisite for a vital democracy is a civic culture of 'generalised trust' or 'social solidarity', of citizens willing and able to cooperate. Putnam, however, reduces civil society to the dimension of voluntary association, and voluntary association is the only source of social capital that he analyses. The degree of civicness of any given society is measured by the number of voluntary associations, level of newspaper readership, electoral turnout and civic attitudes such as the degree of law-abiding, interpersonal trust and co-operation, and so on. On a descriptive level, Putnam's requirements for civil society seem appropriate. Where his analysis fails is in his reduction of the source of social trust to the

role of voluntary associations. The public sphere, democratic political institutions and law are absent as factors that foster and maintain trust. In reducing the state to a third-party enforcer, seeing law as sanctions that ensure a level of social order and dismissing other institutions as irrelevant to social trust because their very being already presupposes this trust, Putnam offers no mechanism to explain the generalisation of social trust beyond small-scale face to face associations. Thus, his framework prevents him from articulating complex interrelations between law, institutions and associations. Law, however, is two-sided. It is a sanction but it is also institutionalised cultural norms, values, rights and rules. Law substitutes universalistic norms as functional equivalents for personal trust, to engender confidence and a belief of legitimacy in institutions (which are then backed up by sanctions). For example, the norms of fairness, impartiality and justice are believed to limit arbitrariness and favouritism within state and civil institutions. It is expected that institutional actors will live up to and enforce these norms. Rights also reinforce trust in that they ensure that the opportunities for redressing the terrible consequences of unwarranted social trust are available to all.

Putnam (1996) and his associates have pointed to declining membership in traditional voluntary associations as evidence of 'social decapitalisation', that is, of the decline of civil society in America. However Verba *et al.* (1995) point to increases in certain forms of civic activities, some which centre on community problem solving. Contemporary political engagement has shifted into forms that are episodic and increasingly issue-oriented. Yet there are a myriad of small-scale groups and networks, oppositional public spheres, and these may include discussion networks, consciousness-raising groups, self-help groups and so on, all of which show the signs of being able to connect and act in concert. While membership of the traditional voluntary associations such as labour unions and political parties have declined, the conclusion of a decline in civic society thus need not follow. New 'functional equivalents' of traditional forms of voluntary association should not be ruled out. Thus this argument is yet another example showing that old theoretical frameworks cannot accommodate and assess new action repertoires. The thesis of decline is thus unproven and unconvincing.

The Republican right and the neocommunitarian movement also worry about the alleged decline in civil society. The former blames the welfare state for displacing voluntary association with a dependence culture that undermines civic and personal responsibility. Initiative and independence are sought from market incentives, voluntarism and localism, a replacement of interventionist government. It is an argument, however, which does not seek to honor universalistic principles of human JUSTICE but tends to function as a cover for the dismantling of public services and the redistribution of wealth to the top (Cohen 1999: 229).

The communitarians choose a civil society discourse based on the reintroduction of the basic values of responsibility, social solidarity and virtue. They assume that in order to have a strong civil society, there needs to be a 'thick' value consensus on a wide range of public and private issues. The role of the state and law is to encourage discussion about ethics and virtue, foster strong institutions and institutionalise the right values; in effect, an American civil religion. The problem with this view is that it assumes that social INTEGRATION is dependent on value consensus and a strong American identity. While a general acceptance of the principles underlying constitutional democracy is important, it is also possible nevertheless to reach this general consensus with many particular cultural evaluations. Political processes that accommodate diversity yet accept the equal claim of all to participate could encourage social solidarity, trust and inclusion. Thus the communitarian approach also has a political agenda: retraditionalisation and homogenization.

Crises and problems do exist with the welfare state paradigm, with traditional forms of voluntary association, with political partici-

pation and social integration. However, the dichotomous thinking that counterposes civil society to the state, informal to formal associations, duties to rights, culturalist to institutionalist approaches, can lead to a mistaken impression of civic decline, thus prompting a set of false policy choices. It also misidentifies the causes of low voter turnout and general political apathy, especially in the USA.

If we operated with a richer concept of civil society and a more abstract understanding of its cultural presuppositions, the discovery of the erosion of one type of civic institution would not have to lead to a claim of general civic decline. A richer concept of civil society would allow intermediate or functionally equivalent voluntary associations to be assessed and new types of civic engagement to be accounted for, and thus politically relevant policies to be devised. Party and electoral systems could be examined to discover whether they are sufficiently receptive to the new forms of civic engagement, whether they block or channel participation. In turn, this could lead to an evaluation of the role of government in encouraging or discouraging participation with a more direct analysis of institutional design and organisational initiatives and at the deepest level, the constitution. In this way a number of key institutional arenas can be opened up to multiple voices, projects and critical contestation. In short, instead of assuming civil society is in decline because old forms of association, publicity, private autonomy and rights are waning, our focus should be on the new emergent forms of association, communication (new media), personal autonomy and rights. The shape of civil society varies from epoch to epoch. So does its relation to political society (party systems), electoral systems, voting systems and other institutions of government.

There are several areas within which a wider conception of civil society is crucial and can turn the theory of civil society from an attempt at definition and redefinition to a differentiated set of analytical instruments, ones which are more intellectually sound and relevant for the future. Some of these areas are: the globalisation of many of the most important civil society organisations and the effect of this globalisation on local societies and cultures; the impact of various new forms of media and/or of the effect of commodification and commercialisation on the public sphere; and, as raised by the neocommunitarians, the relationship between public virtues, morals, institutional structures and discourses. How can we reconstruct and decentralise the welfare state without compromising personal autonomy, equality and associational solidarity? Most fundamental to democratic theory would be an examination of the problem of legitimacy, a study of the fundamental differences and relation between the narrower formal structures and the more open ones within the civil publics. And finally, one could interrogate the role of civil society in constitutionalism could protect the plurality of forms of life within civil society from intolerant majorities without privatising difference or fostering divisive identity politics.

Civil society as the source of influence and control of representative political institutions is the heart of a liberal democracy. How can we institutionalise the new media of communication to make them more receptive to equal civil imput without allowing the power of money to control debate agendas and to silence those without great wealth? How can civil and political publics play their role in fostering civic engagement, dialogue, legitimacy and social equality on the national and transnational level and what role do courts and legislatures have to play in this new globalised context? How can representative political institutions be made more receptive to the issues, cultural models etc. generated within civil society? How can they be made more accountable to the citizenry? What mediations should exist between the new forms of civil society institutions and the polity? These are the questions civil society theorists must address today.

See also:

civic virtue; institutional design; political culture; social capital; standards of conduct in public life

Further reading

Cohen, J.L. (1982) *Class and Civil Society: the Limits of Marxian Critical Theory*, Amherst, MA: University of Massachusetts Press.
—— (1999) 'Trust, Voluntary Association and Workable Democracy: The Contemporary American Discourse of Civil Society', in M. Warren (ed.), *Democracy and Trust*, Cambridge: Cambridge University Press.
Cohen, J.L. and Arato, A. (1992) *Civil Society and Political Theory*, Cambridge, MA: MIT Press.
Gramsci, A. (1971) 'State and Civil Society', in Q. Hoare and G. Norwell-Smith (ed. and trans.), *Selections from the Prison Notebooks of Antonio Gramsci*, New York: International Publishers, 206–77.
Habermas, J. (1989) *The Structural Transformation of the Public Sphere*, Cambridge, MA: MIT Press.
Offe, C. (1999) in M. Warren (ed.), *Democracy and Trust*, Cambridge: Cambridge University Press.
Putnam, R. (1993) *Making Democracy Work: Civic Traditions in Modern Italy*, Princeton, NJ: Princeton University Press.
—— (1996) 'The Strange Disappearance of Civic America', *The American Prospect* 24: 34–48.
Verba, S. *et al.* (1995) *Voice and Equality: Civic Voluntarism in American Politics*, Cambridge, MA: Harvard University Press.

JEAN LOUISE COHEN

class

Class is a complicated concept, and it has been defined in various ways. Its meaning and use are ideologically contested, because class points to conflicting interests many wish to conceal while others seek to emphasise that antagonism. However defined in detail, class refers to a major dimension of social inequality. One common view distinguishes, following Max Weber, class as economic inequality from social status, which represents differential honour and deference, and from power, the ability to pursue one's goals even against resistance.

Class, status and power are interrelated in many ways. Thus wealth is a major power resource, alongside control over the means of COERCION, strong cultural influence and high status. Status distinctions, which include ethnic, religious and caste membership, can separate or unite people in similar economic class positions, as status boundaries cut across or coincide with lines of economic class division. Many analysts speak of *social* classes when mobility between classes and social interaction across class lines are substantially limited.

Karl Marx considered classes as major actors that, through their antagonisms, shape the course of history. Yet people in similar economic positions, such as the owners of the means of production or workers employed by them, cannot act collectively unless they are organised. Such organisation is of particular importance for subordinate classes, since collective action is the only significant power resource available to them. Different movements and associations claiming to speak for a class may compete for a following with each other as well as with organisations seeking a following on grounds other than class. Their success depends on several factors: on the similarity of conditions the class to be organised finds itself in, on the material and cultural power dominant groups exert over subordinate classes, on the relation of ethnic and other status distinctions to class boundaries, on open clashes of interest that set different classes apart and engage people emotionally, and on the concentration of class members in residential areas and workplaces. The common interests that are pursued once

collective action becomes viable are articulated in the very process of organisation. They are influenced by, but cannot simply be 'read off' from, the objective situation of a class.

Class and, more broadly, structured social inequality stand in tension with the very idea of democracy. This is obvious once democracy is understood as a matter of power. Even formal democracy (or POLYARCHY, defined by a state apparatus that is responsible to elected representatives who were chosen on the basis of universal suffrage and the freedoms of speech and association) is impossible where political AUTHORITY is fused with control over the means of production and other resources of social power. The feudalism of European history illustrates this as well as the East European communist countries of our time. Even formal democracy requires that political DECISION-MAKING be significantly separated from the system of social inequality. More demanding conceptions of democracy look for a substantial equalisation of the influence all citizens have on collective political decisions. That is clearly at odds with large concentrations of economic power, overwhelming cultural hegemony, strong and important status differences, and even substantial income disparities.

If the very conception of democratic rule is at odds with class and related forms of social inequality, what part did classes play in the emergence, stability and quality of democracy? Social theorists of quite different outlook have assigned a major role to class, but they disagree on which classes are most supportive of democracy. Nineteenth-century liberals and later Marxist theorists have given the major role in promoting democracy to the bourgeoisie, the owners of capital. It is of course true that this dominant class of the emerging capitalist order succeeded in claiming for itself a place in political decision-making next to the old landowning aristocracy, and that in the process it created a wide space for the public discussion of political matters. But it is also true that such liberal oligarchies did not automatically open themselves up to full participation of all citizens, that the bourgeoisie not infrequently colluded with the landowners in opposing further democratisation, and that it has been implicated, with or without the collaboration of large landlords, in attempts to roll back democracy. Large landlords who rely on political means (rather than the market) for controlling their labour forces seem to be the class most hostile to democracy, an enemy that often exerts considerable hegemonic influence over other groups.

From Aristotle to such twentieth-century authors as Seymour Martin Lipset, social theorists have claimed that a strong middle class is the major factor in supporting democracy because it moderates conflicts between top and bottom and displays tolerance and reasoned judgement. This hypothesis can point to a good deal of supporting evidence, but it is at odds with the fact that middle classes have not always supported a full extension of universal suffrage and have been among the backers of rollbacks of democracy. Middle classes are – next to peasants and small farmers – among the groups most susceptible to influence from elites with non- or anti-democratic interests.

Marx considered universal SUFFRAGE as a means of empowering the growing industrial working class. Anticipating the effects of democracy before its advent in the major countries of his time, he viewed universal suffrage as a major step toward a dominant role of the proletariat and beyond that toward the 'society of the future'. He overestimated the size, the unity and the organisational strength of the industrial working class, but he was largely correct in his assessment of the working class as a pro-democratic force, capable of organisation and better protected against undemocratic influence than other subordinate classes – small farmers and middle class groups such as craftsmen, shopkeepers, and the emerging white-collar labour force in routine work.

Searching for invariant links between single classes and a clear-cut stance toward democracy seems, however, to be an analytic dead-end. With two near-exceptions at the extremes – large landlords relying on political backing for their economic interests and urban working classes – it seems impossible to identify even

strong tendencies independent of the historical context. This relates to the fact that class interests are socially constructed in the process of organisation (even if the goals actually pursued do not vary at random and thus do not make it impossible to argue with reason about well-understood or 'true' class interests). The most important factor shaping the goals actually pursued by organisations claiming to speak with some justification for one or another class are the relations between classes: alliances and hegemonic co-optations, antagonisms and perceptions of threat. A bourgeoisie facing a fierce threat from subordinate classes is more likely to opt for collaboration with aristocratic landlords than a capitalist class dealing with a moderate coalition of subordinate groups. If dominant groups, whether rural or urban, do not see their interests protected by broad-based parties, they are likely to oppose democracy and to undercut it where it exists. Peasants and farmers are often under the ideological influence of large landlords and their allies. However, where this influence is weak or absent, they are as much a pro-democratic force as urban working-class groups; this is illustrated in the history of the 'agrarian democracies' of Switzerland, Norway and the northern United States. Farmers and urban middle classes that are themselves excluded from full participation and do not feel threatened by the demands of urban and rural workers are more likely to join in a pro-democratic coalition than their counterparts that are already included and/or see some reason to fear working class demands and policies.

The constellation of class interests is important not only for the rise and stability of democracy, but also for its quality. Thus, differences across countries in the extent of political PARTICIPATION are closely associated with class disparities in the rates of participation (the higher the participation, the smaller the differences in participation by social class), and both overall participation and the narrowing of class differences in participation rely on the organisational strength of civil society among the economically disadvantaged strata.

Greater parity in political participation is also related to WELFARE state policies enacted by governments that have a strong backing among subordinate classes. The jury is out on the question of whether democracy tends in the long run to result in such social policies. Even if there is no such overall tendency, it is clear that democracy opens the door to left and left-of-centre policies that move beyond what has been decried as merely formal democracy.

There are those who argue that class may have been an important factor in the past, but that it lost its significance in the twentieth century. Class is clearly not the only factor that shapes the emergence, stability and quality of democracy. The character of the state and of state–society relations as well as power relations in the international scene are of great significance. But class continues to be a major factor, even at the beginning of this new century. Other factors that structure social solidarities and interests along lines of subordination and dominance include ethnicity and race, religion, region, and political factions of a clientelistic character. Often these factors intersect with class issues and take on class-like characteristics. Gender is clearly relevant for the comprehensive character and the quality of democracy. Yet the inclusion of women in no case provoked breakdowns or rollbacks of democracy (see GENDERING DEMOCRACY).

See also:

capitalism; civil society; cleavages; democratic breakdown; democratic development; equality; hegemony; ideological polarisation; minorities; participation; parties; polyarchy; suffrage; welfare

Further reading

Collier, R.B. and Mahoney, J. (1995) *Labor and Democratisation: Comparing the First and Third Waves in Europe and Latin America*, Berkeley, CA: Institute of Industrial Relations, University of California.
Held, D. (1987) *Models of Democracy*, Cambridge: Polity Press.
Katznelson, I. and Zolberg, A. (eds) (1986) *Working-Class Formation: Nineteenth Century Patterns in Western Europe and the United States*, Princeton, NJ: Princeton University Press.
Lipset, S.M. (1980) *Political Man*, expanded edn, Baltimore: Johns Hopkins University Press.
Moore, B., Jr (1966) *The Social Origins of Dictatorship and Democracy*, Boston: Beacon Press.
Muller, E.N. (1988) 'Democracy, Economic Development and Income Inequality', *American Sociological Review* 53 (1 February 1988): 50–68.
Rueschemeyer, D., Stephens, E.H. and Stephens, J.D. (1992) *Capitalist Development and Democracy*, Cambridge: Polity Press, and Chicago: Chicago University Press.
Therborn, G. (1977) 'The Rule of Capital and the Rise of Democracy', *New Left Review* 103 (May–June): 3–41.
Weber, M. (1978) *Economy and Society*, 2 vols, Berkeley, CA: University of California Press.

DIETRICH RUESCHEMEYER

cleavages

The term 'cleavage' is central to understanding democracy as a set of institutions and practices for conflict resolution. With democratic principles rooted in recognising the diversity of – and probable conflict between – interests, outlooks and goals among members of a polity, assessing DEMOCRATIC PERFORMANCE entails, *inter alia*, identifying the sources of conflict, how they are manifest and managed, and with what effects. This perspective is particularly relevant to the performance of political parties, the configuration of PARTY SYSTEMS and the dynamics of ELECTORAL BEHAVIOUR.

In its simplest sense, 'cleavage' denotes a division among members of a community which separates them into definable groups (Rae and Taylor 1970). Here, the term is a synonym for conflict or contest, which, in a democracy, will be several and of varying magnitude. The term is useful in identifying conflicts which, by dividing its members into relatively large collectivities, have structuring effects in a society. The analytic power of 'cleavage' in relation to democratic politics, however, comes from using it to identify a societally structuring conflict which also structures a society's politics. In this sense, the cleavage concept focuses attention on linkages between the social and political orders in a democratic polity, such as the number and nature of the social divisions sustaining PARTIES; the way in which two or more cleavages interact or intersect – or fail to, as in 'reinforcing cleavages' – to shape the 'cleavage structure' underpinning the party system; why some conflicts are mobilised while others are vestigial or latent.

The use of 'cleavage' as an analytic term is derived primarily from Stein Rokkan's work (Lipset and Rokkan 1967) to bring together, within a single model, the affinities and diversities of parties and party systems in Western Europe. Elaborating on his insights, a cleavage can be conceptualised as encompassing three distinct yet empirically entwined phenomena. First, there is a societal conflict engendering groups that attain 'closure', differentiated by class, religion, ethnicity or some other attribute. Second, the members of such groups share a set of values, beliefs, and interests. Third, the conflict is institutionalised in a form of organisation, most often a political party but also other associational groups, such as churches and trades unions (see ASSOCIATIONAL DEMOCRACY). The cleavage concept thus identifies a particularly structured form of political conflict: deeply rooted in the social structure, couched in an ideologically developed frame, and with an institutionally embedded presence in the polity.

Much about the fundamentals of mass politics in West European states can be comprehended in terms of the 'cleavage model'. According to Rokkan, the major parties and the party systems in Western Europe originate in conflicts born out of three revolutions: the Reformation and Counter-Reformation, the French Revolution and the Industrial Revolution. The first ensued in the 'fateful division of Europe' into Catholic states where church power was consolidated, Protestant states where national churches were established and 'mixed' regions harbouring large Catholic or Protestant minorities. The second, in stimulating the 'National Revolution', generated the centre–periphery cleavage engaging resistance to the centralising drive of nation-building elites, and a church–state cleavage – principally in Catholic states – centred on challenging church power (see STATE, RELATIONS OF CHURCH TO). The third revolution pitted landed interests against industrial interests, initiating the urban–rural cleavage and workers against employers, generating a CLASS cleavage. These cleavages supply the roots of the modern party families – conservative, liberal, socialist, agrarian, 'territorial' or 'ethnic' – found across Western Europe.

The transformation of such conflicts into political forces was not spontaneous. It was the work of elites competing for elective office as larger sections of society became incorporated into the polity with the extension of the SUFFRAGE during the nineteenth and early twentieth centuries. Elites fashioned the ideological mobilisation of these conflicts by building a 'common cause' among otherwise inchoate subgroups, and forged their institutional consolidation by creating organisations – parties in particular – to deliver electoral support. How earlier conflicts had been managed, especially which interests were brought into alliance, shaped elite options in confronting later conflicts. Political incorporation was far more fraught in France and Spain than in Scandinavia, for example, as Catholic states had to contend with church–state conflicts at the same time as the land–industry and class conflicts; Protestant states did not, as Catholic privileges had long since been annulled. Although much about the originating conflicts has changed – advancing secularism, for example – their structuring effects persist. This is largely due to the tenacity of the early parties, which had the effect of 'freezing' the party systems as constituted around the time of full adult suffrage, broadly during the 1920s.

The cleavage concept is compelling, but much remains at issue. Conceptually, the distinction between political conflict and cleavage politics is not sharply drawn. Rokkan focused largely on the dislocations underpinning a cleavage, but said less about the ideological and institutional dimensions, suggesting that cleavages spring forth fully formed. Delineating the content and connectedness of the three dimensions is largely the work of later scholars (Lybeck 1985; Mair 1997). Theoretically, the concept is straddled between a sociological perspective, construing politics as a derivative of social conflict, and a conception of politics as an autonomous order, with elites enjoying some independence in determining which conflicts are mobilised. Hence, 'cleavage' is often used descriptively to identify any conflict linking party and electors, without heed to its analytic value in identifying conflicts that have structuring – rather than contingent – effects on a society's politics.

The empirical difficulties are more severe. The three dimensions of a cleavage are not equally quantifiable, particularly not to the same metric; the ideological and the institutional dimensions, for example, enjoin quite different measures (Budge *et al.* 1987). Hence, all three dimensions cannot be incorporated in one model without distortion; and how much change in one, or each, dimension is admissable before a cleavage is exhausted remains indeterminate. The wider relevance of the model is also dubious, sometimes serving as a template for analysing politics in democratising regimes, but more often revealing the particularities of Western European development. Indeed, the model is not equally applicable across Western Europe: it illuminates relatively simple class politics in Britain and complex multi-cleavage politics in Italy, but contributes much less to understanding politics in Greece and Finland.

Two kinds of claims challenge the cleavage model, both construed as inherent in the advent of advanced industrial societies. One proposes that individualisation is freeing citizens from socio-structural constraints; hence,

as 'old' cleavage politics is challenged by new parties, new SOCIAL MOVEMENTS and citizens as rational actors, the stabilities of cleavage politics are being replaced by a more volatile politics (Franklin *et al.* 1992). The second claim is that a new materialism–postmaterialism cleavage has emerged, originating in inter-generational value shifts (Inglehart 1977, 1990) and displacing, in particular, the ubiquitous class cleavage.

Debate about the contemporary relevance of the cleavage model is vigorous, but as yet inconclusive. Whether the cleavage model 'travels' is put to the test in the 'third wave' of democratisation (Huntington 1991) (see WAVES OF DEMOCRACY). Whatever the outcome for the cleavage model, the cleavage concept remains a vital analytic tool for identifying a certain kind of politics. Its looser use to denote any kind of social or political conflict denudes the concept, leaving us unable to distinguish between a particularly structured form, and any other form, of politics.

Further reading:

Budge, I., Robertson, D. and Hearl, D. (eds) (1987) *Ideology, Strategy, and Party Change: Spatial Analyses of Post-War Election Programmes in 19 Democracies*, Cambridge: Cambridge University Press.

Franklin, M., Mackie, T. and Valen, H. (1992) *Electoral Change: Reponses to Evolving Social and Attitudinal Structures in Western Countries*, Cambridge: Cambridge University Press.

Huntington, S. (1991) *The Third Wave: Democratisation in the Late 20th Century*, Norman, OK: University of Oklahoma Press.

Inglehart, R. (1977) *The Silent Revolution: Changing Values and Political Styles among Western Publics*, Princeton, NJ: Princeton University Press.

—— (1990) *Culture Shift in Advanced Industrial Society*, Princeton, NJ: Princeton University Press.

Lipset, S.M. and Rokkan, S. (1967) 'Cleavage Structures, Party Systems, and Voter Alignments: An Introduction', in S.M. Lipset and

S. Rokkan (eds), *Party Systems and Voter Alignments*, New York: The Free Press.

Lybeck, J. (1985) 'Is the Lipset-Rokkan Hypothesis Testable?', *Scandinavian Political Studies* 8(1–2): 105–13.

Mair, P. (1997) *Party System Change: Approaches and Interpretations*, Oxford: Oxford University Press.

Rae, D. and Taylor, M. (1970) *The Analysis of Political Cleavages*, New Haven, CT: Yale University Press.

ELINOR SCARBROUGH

clientelism

Clientelism denotes the practice of distributing jobs, favours and other benefits to a following in return for political support. The word is of ancient derivation: in Rome, *cliens* denoted 'a plebeian under the patronage of a patrician, in this relation called a patron, *patronus*, who was bound, in return for certain services, to protect his client's life and interests' (*Oxford English Dictionary*). The element of exchange, albeit unequal, is already apparent in this early definition of the patron–client relationship.

Elements of clientelism are found in most political systems and in most democracies, and at a national or at a local level a system may be designated clientelistic where such practices are predominant. The ubiquity of some degree of clientelism can make the designation so broad as to be useless, and it is helpful to distinguish the more modern forms from patrimonialism, the private appropriation of power and office, and from systems of aristocratic patronage or ones managed by 'notables', such as prevailed in Britain before the Reform Act of 1832 and its successors. Some recent students of clientelism and the patron–client relationship have been anthropologists who have focused on tribal societies and the peasant societies of the Mediterranean, sometimes with the implied conclusion that clientelistic practices are essentially rural or archaic, and that the clients are chiefly the rural poor.

Others have rightly emphasised that this is not the case: the emergence of the United States 'spoils system', with its origins in the presidency of Andrew Jackson, and the persistence thereafter of clientelistic practices, particularly notorious in urban politics but by no means confined to them, give the lie to the rural and archaic arguments. (The saying, 'To the victor belong the spoils', dates from Jackson's election to the presidency in 1828.) Clientelism, with its essential distortions, favouritism and irrationality, is incompatible with Weberian BUREAUCRACY, but nonetheless can flourish in most ostensibly modern state institutions, and can be nourished with their resources and through the use of the sanctions and regulations they command. All social classes may be thus involved, and the middle and professional classes may well in such cases be more directly involved than the poor.

Clientelism can exist under chiefdoms and monarchies, where it is often considered legitimate, and in authoritarian and totalitarian regimes, but is commonly seen as a feature of imperfect democracies. Various arguments have been used in its defence, or in its extenuation. The clientelist, or patron, at least has some obligations, or at least recognises them in some stages of his career or at some particular junctures, and some downward flow of benefits is usually present, enough to maintain the clientele's expectations. The patron does do some political work, tempers the wind to the shorn lamb, runs a primitive WELFARE system, humanises the impersonal and incomprehensible state for the poor, the ignorant and the immigrant, virtues which were often attributed to the American city boss and his army of precinct captains and ward-heelers. The system may favour a degree of individual social mobility. Some clientelists possess real political talent, and bring about some desirable political changes: Huey Long of Louisiana is one example, one who has been not only the subject of much academic study but also the inspiration of one of the most convincing political novels in English, Robert Penn Warren's, *All the King's Men*. The conceivable alternatives may be worse: clientelistic manipulation is seen as preferable to force and violence. Many states in post-independence Africa, it has been observed, started out as clientelist and became dictatorial, and as they did so the downward flow of resources dried up: the patrons no longer needed the clients.

Such arguments can have more or less plausibility according to each case, as clientelistic systems vary in the balance of bargaining power among those involved, and in the degrees of faction and competition present: some are more all-encompassing, monopolistic, hermetic and static than others. Likewise, they vary in the degree of resources distributed, and may survive better in scarcity than in abundance. Clientelism does not necessarily exclude other forms of political activity, particularly at the national level.

To a greater or lesser degree, all modern clientelist systems entail similar costs. As much clientelist activity revolves around ELECTIONS and voting, representation is distorted and stifled, and parties cease to articulate policies and lines between them are blurred: then 'There is no politics in politics', as an old American saying went. LOG-ROLLING flourishes, fiscalisation and audit are weakened. The degree and scope of PARTICIPATION are controlled and circumscribed. Individual and particular interests prevail over the pursuit of the general good, of nation, community or class: there is always, through the distribution of benefits in such ways, a strong element of old-fashioned divide and rule. Public administration is bloated, inefficient, expensive, unaccountable, wasteful and corrupt. For the many, 'transaction costs' will be high. Control of the JUDICIARY and of all regulating offices has its foreseeable consequences, offering the clientelist what Charles Merriam, author of a classic description of the American spoils system, refers to as 'daily or even hourly opportunities'. LEGITIMACY is weak.

Attempts have been made to develop theories of clientelism which correlate it with emergent states or peripheral regions, with urbanisation and rapid population growth, with immigration, with various political traditions, and with scarce or abundant resources. Clientelism has, however, proved too varied and protean, and too resilient, to be so encompassed.

See also:

authority; class; state, relations of church to

Further reading:

Caciagli, N. (1996) *Clientelismo, corrupción y criminalidad organizada. Evidencias empíricas y propuestas teóricas a partir de los casos italianos*, Madrid: Centro de Estudios Constitucionales.

Chubb, J. (1982) *Patronage, Power and Poverty in Southern Italy: A Tale of Two Cities*, Cambridge: Cambridge University Press.

Clapham, C. (ed.) (1982) *Private Patronage and Public Power: Political Clientelism in the Modern State*, London: Frances Pinter.

Eisenstadt, S.N. and Lemarchand, R. (eds) (1981) *Political Clientelism, Patronage and Development*, Beverly Hills, CA: Sage.

Eisenstadt, S.N., Lemarchand, R. and Roniger, L. (1984) *Patrons, Clients and Friends: Interpersonal Relationships and the Structure of Trust in Society*, Cambridge: Cambridge University Press.

Gellner, E. and Waterbury, J. (eds) (1977) *Patrons and Clients in Mediterranean Societies*, London: Duckworth.

Graziano, L. (1976) 'A Conceptual Framework for the Study of Clientelistic Behaviour', *European Journal of Political Research* 4: 149–74.

Kern, R. (1973) (ed.) *The Caciques: Oligarchical Politics and the System of Caciquismo in the Luso-Hispanic World*, Albuquerque, NM: University of New Mexico Press.

Merriam, C.E. and Gosnell, H.F. (1937) *The American Party System*, New York: Macmillan.

Revista de Occidente (1973) 127 (October), number on *caciquismo* edited by J. Varela Ortega.

Schmidt, S.W., Scott, J.C., Lande, C. and Guasti, L. (eds) (1977) *Friends, Followers and Factions: A Reader in Political Cliente-*

lism, Berkeley, CA: University of California Press.

MALCOLM DEAS

coalitions

The critical role of coalitions in liberal democracies became apparent in Riker's work on *The Theory of Political Coalitions* (1962). His *size principle* states that in n-person constant-sum games, agents would form coalitions just as large as necessary to obtain the prize (Riker 1962: 32–3). Social scientists became fascinated with the study of coalitions, noticing that in such games only minimum winning coalitions (MWC) should form, but any MWC is readily defeated by another MWC.

The concern with coalition instability dates back to Condorcet's (1785) paradox. Three individuals $\{i, j, k\}$ have to choose between three outcomes $\{a, b, c\}$. i prefers a to b to c, j prefers b to c to a, k prefers c to a to b. Using majority rule, a is preferred to b by i and k, b is preferred to c by i and j, but c is preferred to a by j and k. Majority rule leads to *cyclical preferences*. Each outcome has another outcome preferred to it by some coalition of two.

Arrow (1951) generalised this insight, observing that any social choice process is characterised by a set of decisive coalitions. Ruling out dictatorship and imposing some restrictions on social choice mechanisms, Arrow's *Impossibility Theorem* states that any such mechanism may lead to *cyclical preference orders*, given some *preference profiles*. A preference profile specifies the preferences of all individuals in society. A preference order states the preferences of society as a whole, as aggregated by a social choice mechanism such as majority rule. Further research established that majority rule almost always leads to cyclical preference orders (McKelvey and Schofield 1987).

Liberal democracies often rely on majority rule to aggregate preferences of legislators into legislation (see LEGISLATIVE PROCESS). The theoretical prevalence of majority cycles and the generic emptiness of majority core in *constant sum games* suggest that majority rule leads to coalition instability. But in the real world coalitions are often stable, or else no legislation would ever see the light of day. How, then, can we expect coalitions to be stable? What coalitions are likely to form? Finally, what kind of legislation should we expect coalitions to implement?

For Baron and Ferejohn (1989) the key to stability is risk and time constraints. The first legislator who gets to propose an allocation will propose shares to a MWC of legislators. This MWC of legislators – uncertain who will get to propose the next allocation, realising that the value of the 'pie' diminishes with time and that the next legislator to propose an allocation may not include them in the coalition at all – will approve this allocation.

Neo-institutionalism was founded on the observation that institutions mediate between individuals and social choices (Shepsle 1986: 51–5) (see NEW INSTITUTIONALISM). Agenda setting, procedural rules and committee structures reduce the prevalence of cycling. Laver and Shepsle (1996) applied this insight to the study of coalitions. In their model, after each election, parties 'scan' all decisive coalitions to derive the policy that each coalition will implement based on ministries' allocations to coalition members, assuming that each department implements the policy of the party to which it is allocated. Each coalition is associated with a unique multi-dimensional policy point. A MWC associated with a policy point preferred by its members to any policy associated with any other decisive coalition will form.

Duverger's (1954) Law emphasised the importance of electoral rules in this context. It states that plurality rule tends to reduce the set of significant parties to two. Instead of wasting their vote on small parties, voters vote for their preferred party between the two large parties. In the English parliament, one of two parties controls a majority after each election. In this case, the majority party is the 'ruling coalition' (see WESTMINSTER MODEL). Party organisation and common ideology serve as the cohesive forces behind such 'majority party coalitions'.

Schofield (1993) studied parliamentary politics as *weighted voting games*. He found that a large central party endows a parliament with a core if no coalition without it can form. This allowed Schofield to solve the puzzle of dominant parties like the Christian Democrats in Italy between 1948–87. Such parties puzzled researchers in that they were part of each coalition during long periods. Schofield found that dominant parties are simply core parties (see CHAOS AND COALITIONS). Sened (1996) extended Schofield's analysis to predict probable coalitions. PARTIES maximise policy-related payoffs and utility from government perquisites (Laver and Schofield 1998). Schofield's analysis implies that structures of parliaments and not the composition of coalitions determine the set of feasible policies. Parties are concerned about the cost of endorsing these policies that may be distant from their declared policy positions. They bargain for government perquisites to offset this cost. Given the advantage of the core party in this game, it forms a MWC with parties close to it. When the core is empty, coalitions of 'close-by' parties form and implement policies that cycle in the set of feasible outcomes, as determined by the structure of parliament (Sened 1996).

The discussion above focused on theory. But the most exciting current research on coalition is using new tools of statistical analysis that allow, for the first time, careful empirical studies of coalition formation and the incentives of voters, parties and legislators in parliamentary political processes (for example, Schofield *et al.* 1998).

See also:

chaos and coalitions; legislative process; parties; representation, models of

Further reading

Arrow, K. (1951) *Social Choice and Individual Values*, New York: John Wiley.

Baron, D.P. and Ferejohn, J. (1989) 'Bargaining in Legislatures', *American Political Science Review* 83: 1181–1206.

Condorcet, N. de (1785) *Essai sur l'application de l'analyse à la probabilité des dé rendues à la pluralité des voix*, Paris: L'Imprimerie Royale.

Duverger, M. (1954) *Political Parties: Their Organisation and Activity in the Modern State*, New York: Wiley.

Laver, M. and Schofield, N. (1998) *Multiparty Governments*, Ann Arbor, MI: University of Michigan Press.

Laver, M. and Shepsle, K.S. (1996) *Making and Breaking Governments*, New York: Cambridge University Press.

McKelvey, R.D. and Schofield, N. (1987) 'Generalised Symmetry Conditions at a Core Point', *Econometrica* 55: 923–33.

Riker, W.H. (1962) *The Theory of Political Coalitions*, New Haven, CT: Yale University Press.

Schofield, N. (1993) 'Political Competition and Multiparty Coalition Governments', *European Journal of Political Research* 23: 1–33.

Schofield, N., Martin, A., Quinn, K. and Whitford, A. (1998) 'Multiparty Electoral Competition in the Netherlands and Germany: A Model Based on Multinomial Probit', *Public Choice* 97: 257–93.

Sened, I. (1996) 'A Model of Coalition Formation: Theory and Evidence', *Journal of Politics* 58(2): 350–72.

Shepsle, K. (1986) 'Institutional Equilibrium and Equilibrium Institutions', in H.F. Weisberg (ed.), *Political Science: The Science of Politics*, New York: Agathon Press.

ITAI SENED

coercion

The most influential discussion of coercion in social theory is probably Max Weber's definitional claim that a 'state is a human community that (successfully) claims the *monopoly of the legitimate use of physical force* within a given territory' (Weber 1958: 78). This definition has too many open terms – including monopoly, legitimate and physical force – to be taken as very clear and it has, partly therefore, generated an enormous literature in response. In Weber's claim, 'legitimate' seems inescapably to be a normative term to many writers, but others insist, in keeping with the tradition of positive law, on reading it as only a positive term. A striking feature of this enormous literature is that in it there is virtually no disagreement with the supposition that force and coercion are necessary for government. In the most sanguine visions, the threat of physical force is so compelling that the actual use of such force is quite limited, but it is still there.

Weber lived most of his life under a partially democratic but still autocratic government. Yet, virtually all of us have lived only under governments that exercise substantial force, and presumably almost none of us would argue against the claim that at least some force is empirically necessary for maintaining social order. The rise of government might even generally be claimed to have reduced the use of violent force in interpersonal relations, so that at least the more democratic governments have tended to be less coercive and murderous than anarchy might be. The central normative appeal of democracy is that in some degree it gives representation to all and is consensual (see REPRESENTATION, CONCEPT OF). Therefore, while coercion can be a morally significant issue independently of its association with government (Wertheimer 1987), it and its justification are particularly important in democratic theory.

There are several variants of reasoning from consent in political theory, including Lockean natural RIGHTS theories, Hobbesian mutual advantage theory and contractarianism. Natural rights theories require an initial normative assumption about the distribution of resources and goods. With an initial rule in place, subsequent allocations depend on consensual exchange or gift. Hobbesian mutual advantage theories are grounded in a quasi utilitarian or mutual advantage principle that all are better off with coercive government than without, and therefore all should rationally consent to

such government. Contractarianism has gone from the simple model of contract in the law, to claims of merely the rationality of agreement, to certain principles of political order, which might include coercive arrangements.

Superficially, it is hard to see how coercion can be grounded in consent and, apart from Hobbes, consent theorists have not adequately addressed the issue. The simple model of consent to coercion is contract law. We sign a contract agreeing to do various things and submitting to the law to secure each other's compliance. I now default and you take me to court. The judge can now point out that I accepted the terms of my contract and that, in any case, I am far better off in a world in which enforceable contracts are possible. Therefore, it seems right for the law to coerce me, if necessary, to meet the terms of my agreement. There might be special circumstances that weaken this conclusion, but in principle the conclusion is morally compelling. Indeed, it comes very close to being strictly rational or self-interested in this instance. It is rational not merely *ex ante* but continuously just because the institutions of enforceable contracts will continue to be *ex ante* of value for future contexts.

A remarkable feature of such an argument from interest, from mutual advantage, is that it seems to require very little recourse to extra-rational moral considerations. If such an argument succeeds for political order more generally and not merely for contract law, it allows political theory to skate over moral theories with hardly any contact. One might object to a mutual advantage political theory, that it is inadequately attentive to some putative moral principle, but one can hardly object that it makes excessive moral demands on us. Self-interest is almost enough to make it go.

Unfortunately, however, Hobbesian mutual advantage, contemporary contractarian and Lockean natural rights theories, all of which ground the state in rational interests at least in large part, can justify government coercion only in principle. They cannot justify coercion by actual states. In practice, these theories are morally indeterminate. The one possible exception to this claim is Hobbesian mutual advantage theory, *if* we agree with Hobbes that even the slightest effort at reform substantially risks bringing government down and throwing us into violent anarchy. Otherwise, citizens subjected to coercive torture, or even to lesser coercions by governments that they do not honour, cannot be said to have the interest in the maintenance of the government institutions that ordinary citizens might have in the maintenance of the institutions of the law of contract.

In contract law the parties agree, in essence, to make themselves subject to coercion in a very clear sense. Modern society is almost inconceivable without a system of coercive enforcement of contracts because it is the threat of that coercion that makes it possible for us even to get others to contract with us. Similarly, modern society is inconceivable without a system for ordering more general relationships, sometimes coercively. Political contractarianism is about this second issue. It gains its intellectual hold over us in large part because it seems to give us a rationale for coercion that is consensual, as though political order were merely analogous to contract law.

Governments coerce in many contexts that are not overtly, directly consensual in the way that a typical contract is. Hence, if we argue for the consensual basis of political coercion we must somehow argue that people consent to the whole system that authorises officials to decide on coercion (see CONSENSUS DEMOCRACY). This conclusion suggests a problem with the consensual resolution of our problem of social order that Hobbes clearly recognised but that many consent theorists ignore. There might be *many* potential governments that could secure order and even prosperity for us. I might strongly prefer some of these and you might strongly prefer others. We have no way to select from them that does not leave one of us sensibly claiming not to have consented.

Hobbes supposed that this problem is mooted by the fact that, once we have a government in place, it is likely to be better for all of us to honour that government rather than to go through the horrors of civil war to change it to one we might prefer. This claim suggests that, *de facto*, virtually every actual government is presumably consensual. If so, then the assertion of consent to coercion is hollow. Let us reject this view of Hobbes and question what remains of a consensual defence of coercion.

Hobbes's story of the creation of a state and an absolute sovereign from the state of nature is immediately motivated by his supposition that life without government would be grim and unproductive (see SOVEREIGNTY). He thinks everyone stands to be made better off with government than without, no matter which government, so long as it is stable. Even if we agree with his position, however, we do not have a justification for any particular government or any detailed form of government. This is finally the basic question we want to answer: what justifies an instance of coercion by *this particular government*? This is a much more complex issue than the in-principle justification of coercion by *some* government.

If actual coercions, the *sine qua non* of government, cannot be rationally justified by consent, as they can be in contract law, then actual governments cannot be justified by consent either. For whatever reason, those whose moral starting point is consent or mutual advantage have yet to justify political coercion by an actual government in the quasi-rational terms in which they ground their theories. Some kinds of political theorists, such as utilitarians or welfarists, may well be able to justify *actual* instances of coercion by introducing moral arguments rather than relying merely on rational accountings of the interests of those coerced. The often unstated moral vision of a large fraction of social theorists, including Weber, is consequentialist and vaguely utilitarian. Hence, they might be able to justify coercion of some for the benefit of the many. Many democratic theorists, who are commonly contractarian and libertarian rights theorists of mutual advantage, cannot justify major classes of political coercion by actual, as opposed to in-principle, governments.

See also:

authority; civil disobedience; democratic breakdown; revolutions

Further reading:

Hardin, R. (1990) 'Rationally Justifying Political Coercion', *Journal of Philosophical Research* 15(May): 79–91.
—— (1999) *Liberalism, Constitutionalism, and Democracy*, Oxford: Oxford University Press.
Hobbes, T. (1968) *Leviathan*, ed. C.B. Macpherson, London: Penguin.
Pennock, J.R. and Chapman, J.W. (eds) (1972) *Nomos* 14: *Coercion*, Chicago: Aldine.
Weber, M. (1958) 'Politics as a Vocation', in H.H. Gerth and C. Wright Mills (eds), *From Max Weber: Essays in Sociology*, New York: Oxford University Press.
Wertheimer, A. (1972) 'Political Coercion and Political Obligation', in J.R. Pennock and J.W. Chapman (eds), *Nomos* 14: *Coercion*, Chicago: Aldine: 213–42.
—— (1987) *Coercion*, Princeton, NJ: Princeton University Press.

RUSSELL HARDIN

communication

All political systems adopt a distinctive attitude toward communication and those attitudes result in distinct practices. Even oligarchies, for example, sponsor popular rituals, thereby trading bread and circuses for the people's acquiescence. Totalitarians use panoptic modalities to monitor citizens' discourses, and also use a medley of censorships to keep them silent. Monarchists prize traditional narratives; communists sponsor small group collaborations; libertarians lionise the single, unfettered voice; syndicalists trust only the mercantile, populists only the ordinary.

Democracies also regard communication in a special way or, better, in a myriad of special ways. Most fundamentally, a democracy presumes a TRANSPARENCY on the part of its LEADERSHIP (so that laws are not made in the dead of night) and an articulateness on the parts of its citizenry (so that the laws that are made can be contested). Democracy means little without these interdependencies, without a vigorous public dialogue. From such a perspective, the history of democracy becomes a history of its techniques of reproduction. Ten technologies seem especially important.

The ecclesia

The ancient Athenians did not invent democracy, at least not for the women and slaves among them, but they did imagine democracy on a mass scale and they accommodated their imaginations with a special, set-aside place for their religious, commercial, legal and, especially, political, discussions. The Sophists of ancient Greece, the most notable being Isocrates (436–338 BC), were largely itinerant teachers who travelled the countryside providing rhetorical instruction to the young men who would eventually find their ways to the ecclesia, the assembly, to debate the issues of the day. Plato (428–347 BC), true to form, distrusted most such activities, calling his fellow citizens (in the *Phaedrus*) 'a mob' when they adjudicated public matters *en masse*. But Plato's greatest student, Aristotle (384–322 BC), wrote a *Rhetoric* to accompany his *Politics*, knowing that the thoughts a democratic society finds unpersuasive will be thoughts ultimately lost to that society.

The paideia

The Roman Empire stood for nothing if not for communication. It was the Romans' unctuousness that put Western ideas into circulation throughout the then-known world, that made international commerce possible, that made Latin a tongue for non-Romans, and that caused laws to be codified and education made efficient. The *paideia* (from which the term 'encyclopedia' derives) was the humble root of these changes, for it was in these schools that Roman boys learned their gymnastics, grammar, music, mathematics, geography, natural history and philosophy; and their rhetoric, too. One of their teachers, Quintilian (AD 35–96), declared the ideal democrat to be 'a good man speaking well', and personages as grand as Cicero himself (106–43 BC) wrote about the art of persuasion. Rhetorical education in ancient Rome was stultifying by modern standards (repetition and memorisation were the keys to success), but it also opened the door to political ascendancy and effectivity.

De Doctrina

Augustine's *De Doctrina Christiana* was a schoolbook for preachers but it was also a quietly revolutionary document. Augustine adapted the pagan art of rhetoric to a properly Christian world, writing his book to help young priests reach the rabble before whom they preached. Augustine (354–430), himself the Bishop of Hippo, walked a tightrope in *De Doctrina*, endorsing the arts of communication without giving undue regard to human invention or his students too grand a sense of agency. Despite his best efforts to the contrary, however, Augustine became democracy's handmaiden. To learn the art of rhetoric was to learn how to make choices, to distinguish what should be said from what should not be said. Later democrats would find emancipation in that, for thought and speech are natural allies. Democracy is a third ally.

The printing press

Johannes Gutenberg's date of birth is unknown, perhaps because it had never been recorded. By the time of his death in 1468, Gutenberg had presaged changes in all that. Born into a largely oral, largely illiterate society, Gutenberg adapted techniques used in wine-making to create a press that employed movable type. Thus was born a political scandal. The history of democracy would later show that laws that cannot be defended in the light of day, in the light of print, cannot be defended at all (see DEMOCRATIC ORIGINS). To commit a thing to writing is to freeze it, to let others study it on their own. Gutenberg's

invention would also make writing reproducible and shareable, and this enlarged the world of ideas immeasurably. Until Gutenberg, a mass society – a society that had common thoughts, common experiences and common history – could not be envisioned. Because it could not be envisioned, it could not be fashioned into a voluntary political entity.

Ninety-Five Theses

If Gutenberg made mass democracy possible, Martin Luther (1483–1546) made it inevitable. When posting his fabled Theses on the front door of the Castle Church in Wittenberg in 1517, Luther proved audacious in what he said – that the Roman Church was doctrinally in error and secular to the core – but also in how he said it. By posting what amounted to a handbill, Luther also altered the style of ecclesiastical communication. His chosen form had consequences – it aped the promulgations of the Church itself (such as the papal bull), thereby claiming for himself an unseemly AUTHORITY. His Theses were also quite pointed, not circumlocutory in the old, religious tradition. Most important, they were announced in the most public (and sacred) of places. Less than twenty years later, Luther launched a second assault on the old rhetorical genre when publishing a Bible in the language of his people. Thus, Luther's heresies were publicity, contestation and the vernacular, the very heart of what would later become the democratic tradition.

Newspapers

As if willed explicitly by Gutenberg and Luther, the first regularly published newspaper appeared in Germany and Belgium in 1609, thereby making citizens one with their times, a prerequisite in a representative democracy. Glacially but insistently, newspapers allowed PUBLIC OPINION to compete with the old doctrinal realities. True reportorial freedom had to await the development of the free press in England in the 1700s and the decline of government-imposed taxes and restrictions on newspaper content. The dam eventually broke with the advent of the penny press in the 1830s and the professionalisation of journalists. Eventually a space for critique was created, resulting in an assortment of Fleet Street scandals and the resignation of one US president (in 1974) and the attempted impeachment of a second (in 1998). Over the years, newspapers have been accused of crimes ranging from unseemliness to misrepresentation, but rarely have they made democracy dull.

Film

Film made politics indigenous. The first US films, for example, were pitched to blue-collar workers, while early British films concentrated on the classics and Indian films on the mythological. In the 1920s and 1930s, Germany and the Soviet Union maintained state-supported movie industries to promote their interests, with Leni Riefenstahl's *Triumph of the Will* marrying nationalism and aesthetics in memorable fashion. Because film does not demand literacy of its viewers, it becomes a perfect vehicle for the delivery of strong emotion and the easily understood idea. Propaganda – democratic and otherwise – is often the natural result, which is why film censors have found employment in Khomeini's Iran and Franco's Spain, and in more progressive regimes as well. The advent of the videocassette recorder has made film portable, allowing users to consume its images in their own ways on their own time. Film is thus an ideal medium for both indoctrination and critique, and for sundry other political duties.

Radio

Radio added an extraordinary thing to politics – simultaneity – when it reached across region, CLASS, ethnicity and race to broadcast the same event at the same time. Gandhi, Churchill, Hitler, Mussolini and Roosevelt took to the new medium instinctively, refashioning their nations by addressing them. *Pravda* regarded the medium as the most powerful tool of the cultural revolution, perhaps because radio possessed a fidelity, a sense of certainty, which was missing in the disembodied print media. Radio excelled in reporting the breaking story, addicting its audience to newness. The medium was well suited to commercial enterprises (it became a ready purveyor of margarine and war bonds) and it turned all politicians into populists, forcing them to keep their ideas simple and their sentences short. Beginning in the 1950s, radio lost much of its audience to television but the 1990s saw a resurgence when 'talk radio' added a new and feisty adjunct to the democratic conversation. This was a mixed blessing.

Television

At the close of the twentieth century, television holds pride of place in the world of political communication. By mixing the visual qualities of film with the immediacy of radio, television creates in viewers a powerful sense of authority, an arrogance of the eye. By bringing politicians into the very boudoirs of their constituents, television makes citizens feel intimate with their elected officials. These intimacies build over time as television fills voters with IN-FORMATION and affect. Steady viewers have a heightened sense of political PARTICIPATION when, in fact, they are often woefully apathetic and uninformed. By cleverly blurring the boundary between politics and entertainment, that is, television becomes problematic. When featuring the human, the everyday, television democratises its audience, but by emphasising the private sphere television turns voters away from the empirical, injunctive world of public policy that determines who will live and who will die and all else as well. That can be a dangerous emphasis indeed.

The Internet

By one estimate, 21 million Americans obtained political news online during the 1996 presidential election. That experience is being duplicated worldwide even as gaps between cyber-rich and cyber-poor societies also grow. If, as some argue, Gutenberg's press ushered in the modern state, the digital revolution may transform the very concept of nationhood, thereby limiting elites' abilities to control what people know, think and feel. With the emergence of virtual communities, time-shifting, complex search modalities and the digitalisation of all information, the Internet may allow free speech and self-governance to play themselves out unhindered. Nay-sayers, on the other hand, wonder if computers are capable of creating an organic sense of community or producing the heightened passion that civic participation requires. Yet others worry that the forces of capital will soon monopolise cyberspace, driving out alternatives to the status quo. The stakes in this debate are not inconsiderable.

Democracy has been borne on the wings of communication from its often undemocratic beginnings in ancient Greece. Over the years, romantics have overstressed democracy's ideational force, its natural emotional appeal. A bit of reflection shows that democracy also depends on its technologies of reproduction and on people's willingness to use those technologies in new and creative ways. To focus on technique may make democracy seem a pedestrian thing. And so it is.

See also:

censorship; citizenship; democratic debate; direct democracy; education; electoral campaigning; information; media; political culture; public opinion

Further reading

Bizzell, P. and Herzberg, B. (1990) *The Rhetorical Tradition: Readings from Classical Times to the Present*, Boston: Bedford Books.

Davis, R. and Owen, D. (1988) *New Media and American Politics*, New York: Oxford University Press.

Eisenstein, E. (1979) *The Printing Press as an Agent of Change*, New York: Cambridge University Press.

Gronbeck, B., Farrell, T.J. and Soukup, P. (1991) *Media, Consciousness, and Culture: Explorations of Walter Ong's Thought*, Newbury Park, CA: Sage.

Hart, R. (1994) *Seducing America: How Television Charms the Modern Viewer*, Oxford: Oxford University Press.

—— (1997) *Modern Rhetorical Criticism*, Boston: Allyn and Bacon.

Ong, W. (1982) *Orality and Literacy: The Technologizing of the Word*, New York: Methuen.

Pease, E.C., and Dennis, E.E. (1995) *Radio: The Forgotten Medium*, New Brunswick, NJ: Transaction Publishers.

Schudson, M. (1998) *The Good Citizen: A History of American Civic Life*, New York: Free Press.

RODERICK P. HART
SHARON E. JARVIS

communitarianism

Communitarianism derives from the root term community. Community connotes a particular manner of social being implying fellowship, familiarity and intimacy. In a community, individuals purportedly find a deeper sense of identity. Community thus implies a more 'face-to-face' relationship, based upon family, kinship, friendship or neighbourhood. However, there are two points to note. First, community *per se* has no distinctive ideological complexion. It can be found expressed from the mildest of left anarchisms to the most virulent of fascisms. Second, there are stronger and weaker senses of the term community, qua communitarianism. The stronger sense of community is premised on a belief in a more objective value consensus. The kind of society envisaged here is profoundly homogeneous and is difficult to uphold in an advanced industrial scenario with rapid social, political and economic change and mobility. There is, thus, a sense that the stronger use is either foolishly nostalgic or just reactionary. Late nineteenth and early twentieth-century conservative and fascist writers often appealed, with immense enthusiasm, to the values of strong community. Exponents of weak community have limited its application to notions like CITIZENSHIP duties.

History and development

The vision of the natural community, set against the artifice of imposed order, haunts thinkers of all theoretical complexions from the eighteenth century to the present. Edmund Burke's or De Maistre's vision of a traditionalist society based upon natural hierarchy, contrasted to the rootless revolutionary society of cosmopolitans, is typical of conservative communitarianism. G.W.F. Hegel also distinguished the ethical communitarian state from the rootlessness and fragmentation of civil society. The legal theorist Otto von Gierke praised the communal fellowship of *Genossenschaft*, as against the artifice of *Herrschaft*, a distinction partly echoed in Ferdinand Tönnies's famous *Gemeinschaft* and *Gesellschaft* categories. The communitarian perspective is also echoed in the conservative writings of Coleridge and T.S. Eliot, the anarchist theory of Peter Kropotkin and the socialist utopianism of Robert Owen, William Morris and R.H. Tawney. Despite the fact that there was no self-conscious communitarian movement, the theoretical emphases of these diverse writings are clearly recognisable. Communitarian theorising has a long and diverse history over the last two centuries. It is important to realise, however, that some of these modes of communitarian theorising have been profoundly opposed to democracy.

In the 1980s, communitarianism blossomed in a more self-conscious manner, in the writings of thinkers like Charles Taylor, Alisdair MacIntyre, Michael Walzer and Michael Sandel, primarily in reaction to the HEGEMONY of individualistic LIBERALISM. There was a messianic sense that the individualistic rights-based liberal culture damaged communal life. However, each of the above theorists has a distinctly unique manner of approaching the issues. One should not overemphasise their homogeneity. Apart from exceptions, like Charles Taylor's work on Canadian constitutionalism or Amitai

Etzioni's 'Communitarian Network', communitarianism has remained an academic movement and its relation to the world of democratic practices remains unclear. There is, though, a background assumption that contemporary communitarians are basically politically innocuous – unlike fascists and conservative communitarians earlier this century – and that most are considered politically liberal.

Key ideas

The formal tenets of contemporary communitarian thinking are, first, a belief that political and moral goods cannot be determined by abstract reasoning. Such 'goods' arise from particular historical communities. There are no universalist premises, like Kant's 'noumenal self', Hegel's 'Geist', Marx's 'proletarian consciousness', 'cosmopolitan human rights' or John Rawls's 'original position'. We cannot step back to assess communities with a view from nowhere. We always have a view from somewhere. Morality and politics are not invented, but interpreted from within a particular community. Thus, when we argue about democracy, we give an account of the actual existing practices of a particular community. We read off an existing tradition of discourse. Democracy in this sense cannot be used as an external standard of assessment: either a society is democratic or it is not.

Second, the community forms the basis for practical reason. Communitarianism is sceptical about aspects of the Enlightenment (and thus more sympathetic intrinsically to the romantic and expressivist movements of the late eighteenth and early nineteenth century) concerning the ability of abstract universal reasoning to stand apart from social or political traditions. Reason is situated within communities. There is a distinctive ontological claim here. Communitarians assume that there are shared communal resources and traditions that can be drawn upon. In other words, the community is constituted by internal pre-understandings. Democracy, in this reading, must reflect those pre-existing traditions. In this hermeneutic perspective, it is difficult for communitarianism to offer any normative account of democracy.

Third, the self is constituted through a community. There are no 'unencumbered selves' (to use Sandel's term) standing outside a community frame. There is no sense that human nature can be addressed independently of a community. Thus, for Sandel, we cannot adopt the stance of the Rawlsian original position because it makes the unwarranted metaphysical assumption of the unencumbered self (standing outside a communal framework). If we cannot accept this unanchored Rawlsian self, then it follows that we have no grounds for accepting the two principles of JUSTICE which are the outcome of the Rawlsian decision procedures, which are premised, for Sandel, upon the unencumbered self. Rawls thus presupposes an implausible account of the moral subject, which is the logical prerequisite for the impartiality of justice. For Sandel, however, this implausible self creates in turn an implausible theory of justice. Life in the community precedes practices like justice or democracy.

Communitarianism and democracy

Democracy has a complex relation with communitarianism. Three background points should be noted: first, stronger conceptions of communitarianism in the twentieth century (like European fascism) have been largely antagonistic to democracy. Second, even within weaker versions of communitarianism, there is a historically contingent dimension to the appreciation of democracy. Democracy cannot be perceived outside a particular community. This weakens any universalist appeal of democratic theory. Third, communitarianism is distinctly uneasy with certain models of democracy. It is this latter concern which will be the primary focus.

Within recent political theory three basic models of democracy stand out: the liberal, republican and deliberative. The liberal model envisages government as an apparatus of public administration and society as a series of market-oriented contractual interactions among private persons or interest groups. Liberal democratic politics aggregates private preferences. Democracy has the function of transmitting to the political apparatus the atomistic preferences of CIVIL SOCIETY. Individuals, in the liberal model, never leave the domain of their private interests. Democracy is a process of expressing preferences and registering them through a vote. The goal is to decide what leaders or policies will best serve the greatest aggregate of individuals. The whole leitmotif of communitarian theory is antagonistic to this model. The reason for the upsurge of the communitarian movement in the 1980s was a rejection of the individualistic, aggregative conception of social life, implicit within this liberal conception.

The other two models of democracy have found a more receptive audience within communitarianism, with the important proviso that these are still viewed as historically situated. On the civic republican view, individuals consociate under law. Politics is the articulation of the common good of all citizens. REPUBLICANISM embodies, therefore, a more substantive ethical vision of the good life. Democracy is not the mere co-ordination of interests within civil society. It is rather concerned with promoting a SOLIDARITY, INTEGRATION and common good amongst its citizens. Democratic rights embody the right to participate, to perform duties and deliberate over public issues. The republican trust in public discussion stands in marked contrast to the liberal scepticism about public reason.

Theorists like Taylor and Sandel have explicitly linked republicanism with communitarianism. For such theorists, FREEDOM is a crucial value. Taylor's 'civic freedom' is not though negative freedom, but rather 'democratic participatory self-rule', which he calls positive freedom. A direct link is thus made between communitarianism, republicanism, positive freedom and democracy. Positive freedom, for Taylor, is central to establishing a conscientious citizenship, public morality and common good. Some current republican theorists reject this. For example, both Phillip Pettit and Maurizio Viroli see a transformed notion of 'negative liberty' (resilient freedom) as crucial to the republican perspective. Viroli consequently vehemently denies the conceptual link between communitarianism and republican democracy.

The third model is DELIBERATIVE DEMOCRACY. Jürgen Habermas's writings have been a key factor in the formulation of this theory. Like republicanism and communitarianism, deliberative theories are critical of the individualised understanding of interests within liberal democracy. Deliberative democracy is best understood as a model for organising the public exercise of power, in the major institutions of a society, on the basis of the principle that decisions touching the well-being of a collectivity are perceived to be the outcome of a procedure of free deliberation. Democracy is a process of discussion that creates a public. It does not, however, allow the citizen to reason from the standpoint of a private consumer. Democracy is the institutionalisation of a form of public reason, jointly exercised by autonomous citizens. The public sphere of deliberation, about matters of mutual concern, is essential to the legitimacy of democratic institutions. Some communitarian writers have been deeply attracted to this conception of democracy. However, key deliberative theorists, like Habermas, identify both republicanism and communitarianism as committing the same error. Both rest on an overly homogenising model of community identity. For Habermas, this homogenising vision overburdens the democratic process by forcing politics into a collective identity. He thus separates out deliberative democracy from communitarianism.

Conclusion

First, despite the subtlety of communitarian thought, it has turned out to be not so much a critique of liberal democracy, as a partial salvation. Recent communitarianism presents another, more perfectionist face, of liberal theory. In fact, this theme becomes much more systematically developed in the perfectionist liberalism of Joseph Raz, which explicitly tries

to link many communitarian and liberal concerns. In practice, most communitarians paradoxically do prefer liberal democracy, but would like citizens to take democratic practices seriously. Thus, the declared opposition between liberalism and communitarianism is largely fictitious. Second, despite the central role played by groups in communitarianism, it often seems oblivious to the complexity and hazards of group life. Apart from Walzer's work, communitarians appear overly relaxed about group difference, especially qua democracy. Part of the reason for this is that communitarianism does not really offer a clear account as to what community is, sociologically or psychologically. It rests its laurels on an assumed beneficial overarching normative consensus. It does not explain how diverse overlapping and often conflicting groups constitute the self. The phenomena of multinationalism, polyethnicity and multiculturalism consequently create huge problems for communitarian visions of democracy. Third, the heavy communitarian reliance on historical contingency inevitably inhibits the development of normative accounts of democracy. Communitarianism is always caught in what is the case, rather than what ought to be.

Further reading

Avineri, S. and De-Shalit, A. (eds) (1992) *Communitarianism and Individualism*, Oxford: Oxford University Press.

Etzioni, A. (1997) *The New Golden Rule: Community and Morality in a Democratic Society*, London: Profile Books.

Frazer, L. and Lacey, N. (1993) *The Politics of Community: A Feminist Critique of the Liberal-Communitarian Debate*, London: Harvester Wheatsheaf.

Habermas, J. (1994) 'Struggles for Recognition in the Democratic Constitutional State', in A. Gutman (ed.), *Multiculturalism: Examining the Politics of Recognition*, Princeton, NJ: Princeton University Press.

Kymlicka, W. (1989) *Liberalism, Community and Culture*, Oxford: Clarendon Press.

Mulhall, S. and Swift, A. (1996) *Liberal and*

Communitarians, 2nd edn, Oxford: Black-well.

Sandel, M. (1982) *Liberalism and the Limits of Justice*, Cambridge: Cambridge University Press.

Tam, H. (1998) *Communitarianism: A New Agenda for Politics and Citizenship*, London: Macmillan.

Taylor, C. (1992) *Source of the Self: The Making of Modern Identity*, Cambridge: Cambridge University Press.

Walzer, M. (1987) *Interpretation and Social Science*, Cambridge, MA: Harvard University Press.

ANDREW VINCENT

consensus democracy

Consensus democracy can be defined as the polar opposite of MAJORITARIANISM. To the question raised by the definition of democracy as government by and for the people – who will do the governing and to whose interests should the government be responsive when the people are in disagreement and have divergent preferences – the majoritarian answer is: the majority of the people. Consensus democracy's answer is: as many people as possible. It does not differ from majoritarianism in preferring majority rule to minority rule, but it accepts majority rule only as a minimum requirement: instead of being satisfied with narrow decision-making majorities, it seeks to maximise the size of these majorities.

Majoritarian democracy concentrates power as much as possible in the hands of a bare majority; consensus democracy tries to share, disperse and limit power in a variety of ways. A closely related difference is that majoritarian democracy is exclusive, competitive and adversarial, whereas consensus democracy is characterised by inclusiveness, bargaining and compromise. Consensus democracy is similar to the concepts of representational democracy (Powell 1982), proportional democracy (Lehmbruch 1967), 'proportional influence' democracy (Huber and Powell 1994), Madisonian democracy (Dahl 1956) and CONSOCIATIONALISM (Lijphart 1977), which are defined in slightly different ways, but always in contrast with majoritarian democracy.

The ten distinctive institutional characteristics of consensus democracy, the opposites of the ten institutional traits of majoritarian democracy, are: (1) power-sharing in the executive branch of the government by means of broad multiparty COALITIONS, (2) executive–legislative relations in which neither branch of the government is predominant, (3) multiparty systems, (4) proportional representation, (5) corporatist interest group systems aimed at compromise and concertation, (6) federal and decentralised government, (7) bicameral legislatures with two houses that have roughly equal strength but are differently constituted, (8) rigid constitutions that can be amended only by extraordinary majorities, (9) JUDICIAL REVIEW of national legislation by supreme or constitutional courts, and (10) strong and independent central banks (Lijphart 1999).

In practice, contemporary democracies may be purely consensual or purely majoritarian with regard to any of these characteristics, but they are more likely to occupy various intermediate positions. All ten characteristics are therefore variables instead of dichotomies. These variables cluster along two separate dimensions. The first dimension groups together the first five variables, which have to do with the arrangement of executive power, the party and ELECTORAL SYSTEMS, and INTEREST GROUPS, and which, for brevity's sake, may be called the executive–parties dimension. Because most of the other five variables are commonly associated with the contrast between FEDERALISM and unitary government, the second dimension may be called the federal–unitary dimension. The most plausible explanation of the two-dimensional pattern is the distinction between shared power and responsibility on the one hand and divided power and responsibility on the other. Both are forms of diffusion of power, but the first dimension of consensus democracy with its multiparty face-to-face interactions within cabinets, legislatures, legislative committees and concertation meetings between governments and interest groups has a close fit with the shared-power form. In contrast, the characteristics of the second dimension fit the format of diffusion by means of institutional separation: division of power between separate federal and state institutions, two separate chambers in the legislature, and separate and independent high courts and central banks.

Which type of democracy, majoritarian or consensus, works better? The conventional wisdom is that there is a trade-off between their democratic quality and their effectiveness in governing: consensus democracy (along the executives–parties dimension) may provide more accurate representation, especially better minority representation, as well as broader participation in DECISION-MAKING, but the one-party majority governments typically produced by first-past-the-post elections are more united and decisive, and hence more effective policy makers. On the other hand, particularly as far as macroeconomic management is concerned, the policy coherence produced by majoritarian governments may be negated by the alternation of these governments in office, producing sharp policy changes that are too frequent and too abrupt. Coalition governments, in contrast, may be slower but can provide steady, centrist policy-making (Finer 1975).

Comparative analysis shows that consensus democracy (on the executives–parties dimension) is slightly better able to stimulate economic growth, control inflation and unemployment, and limit budget deficits, but most of the differences are too small to be statistically significant. Strong and highly significant differences do appear with regard to various democratic desiderata: consensus democracy is strongly related to better women's representation in parliaments and cabinets, less income inequality, higher participation in elections and closer proximity between government policy and voters' preferences. It is also associated with a stronger community orientation and social consciousness: consensus democracies are more likely to be strong welfare states, to have more responsible envir-

onmental policies, to have less punitive criminal justice systems, and to be more generous in providing economic development assistance to the world's poorer countries. Along the federal–unitary dimension, the performance of consensus and majoritarian democracies does not differ significantly, except that the consensus democracies with their stronger central banks have a better record on controlling inflation (Lijphart 1999).

See also:

coalitions; decision-making; majoritarianism; proportionality; representation, models of

Further reading

Dahl, R.A. (1956) *A Preface to Democratic Theory*, Chicago: University of Chicago Press.

Finer, S.E. (1975) *Adversary Politics and Electoral Reform*, London: Anthony Wigram.

Huber, J.D., and Powell, G.B., Jr (1994) 'Congruence Between Citizens and Policymakers in Two Visions of Liberal Democracy', *World Politics* 46(3): 291–326.

Lehmbruch, G. (1967) *Proporzdemokratie: Politische System und Politisches Kultur in der Schweiz und in Österreich*, Tübingen: Mohr.

Lijphart, A. (1977) *Democracy in Plural Societies: A Comparative Exploration*, New Haven, CN: Yale University Press.

—— (1999) *Patterns of Democracy: Government Forms and Performance in Thirty-Six Countries*, New Haven, CN: Yale University Press.

Powell, G.B., Jr (1982) *Contemporary Democracies: Participation, Stability, and Violence*, Cambridge, MA: Harvard University Press.

AREND LIJPHART

consociationalism

The concept of consociationalism is traceable to Johannes Althusius, who in 1603 used the term *consociatio* to denote a form of political union. Its current meaning dates from the late 1960s, when it was utilised by scholars concerned with a number of small democracies that challenged predominant pluralist and social determinist accounts of the relationship between political CLEAVAGES and DEMOCRATIC STABILITY. Using mainly the cases of Austria, Belgium, the Netherlands and Switzerland, this early literature on consociationalism contained three broad approaches (McRae 1974) to explaining the *prima facie* paradoxical combination of a fragmented political subculture and democratic stability. The first (exemplified by Val Lorwin) suggests the immobilistic or destabilising potential of mutually hostile subcultures can be effectively countered by 'segmented pluralism': a degree of vertical subcultural encapsulation and AUTONOMY sufficient to minimise the opportunity for conflict between the subcultures. The second (associated with Hans Daalder, Gerhard Lehmbruch and Jürg Steiner) argues that these countries' capacity to maintain stable democracy is a product of their tradition of DECISION-MAKING, characterised for centuries by the principles of 'amicable agreement' and PRO-PORTIONALITY.

The third approach – and the one with which consociationalism is most widely identified – is contained in the early work of Lijphart (who later abandoned the concept, however, in favour of CONSENSUS DEMOCRACY). Lijphart's (1986a, 1968b) fourfold typology of democracies is based upon whether (a) their political cultures are homogenous or fragmented and (b) their elite behaviour is competitive or coalescent. Lijphart terms those democracies consociational, where a fragmented political culture co-exists with accommodative elite behaviour, which builds a metaphorical bridge (or 'arch') over the gulf separating the subcultures (or 'pillars') and thus ensures democratic stability. Lijphart attributes this to a strategy of 'prudent leadership' by rival subcultural elites facing the potential collapse of a political system and maintains (1968a: 22–30) that consociational democracy is only viable if subcultural leaders have the ability to recognise the dangers inherent in fragmentation; commitment to

system maintenance; the ability to transcend subcultural cleavage at the elite level and the ability to forge appropriate solutions for subcultural demands. Lijphart's six 'favourable conditions' include external threat, popular acceptance of government by elite cartel and low total load on the system. The structures and techniques he associates with consociational democracy are grand coalition; mutual veto; proportionality; high segmental autonomy; intra-subcultural elitism and LOG-ROLLING.

Empirical studies of the countries originally considered archetypal consociational democracies have on the one hand documented significant change since the 1960s in their political sociology and mass behaviour. These include reductions in deference and in positive affect towards the subcultures; electoral de-alignment; and an atrophying of subcultural organisational networks and a concomitant decrease in the size and impermeability of the pillars. On the other hand, those studies show a remarkable resilience in structures and techniques of elite accommodation such as grand coalition (whether in the governmental or the neo-corporatist arena), mutual veto, segmental autonomy and proportionality. The 'pillar parties' (Luther and Deschouwer 1999) have been the prime linkage mechanisms between the mass and the elite of the encapsulated subcultures, mobilising the rival subcultures, aggregating their interests and recruiting subcultural political elites. They also provided the central political actors for the processes of binding elite accommodation. Indeed, in the highly segmented world of consociational democracy, the party political writ of one or other of the main subcultures ran not only in the key socioeconomic interest groups, but also within many of the formal policy implementation structures. Given that the now more homogenous consociational democracies have retained elite accommodation, many have moved towards Lijphart's 'depoliticised' or 'cartel' type of democracy.

Initially, the normative literature on consociationalism concerned itself with issues of democratic stability and was broadly complimentary of consociational structures and techniques, which it saw as valuable mechanisms for ensuring the inclusion of otherwise potentially alienated social segments. Indeed, systems of consociational 'power sharing' or consensus democracy were often viewed as welcome alternatives to the adversarial politics and MAJORITARIANISM of the WESTMINSTER MODEL and thus frequently prescribed for countries with acute subcultural diversity (for example, South Africa and Northern Ireland). Since at least the 1980s, however, the normative debate has shifted to issues of democratic quality (for example, ACCOUNTABILITY, CONSTITUTIONALISM, CLIENTELISM, SEPARATION OF POWERS and the PUBLIC–PRIVATE DISTINCTION) and become more critical.

Though part of a much wider academic trend, this change reflects growing tensions within the erstwhile archetypal consociational democracies themselves. As the societal linkages of consociational party elites have weakened and their use of state resources and state services to defend their role as central political actors have grown, hitherto accepted practices (such as proportionality and extra-constitutional decision-making) have become increasingly regarded as corrupt and undemocratic. The decline in popular acceptance of government by elite cartel and the growing challenges to democratic performance faced by these systems has helped ensure that the vertical cleavages hitherto central to consociational democracy have started to be replaced by a horizontal cleavage between political elites and the masses. Given the legacy of clientelism and a deferential mass political culture, it is perhaps unsurprising that these systems have in the 1990s proved to be vulnerable to populist mobilisation. The future quality of their democracies will depend to a significant extent on whether political elites are willing and able to address the challenges of distribution and participation in ways that have greater popular acceptance than traditional consociational structures and techniques now enjoy.

There have been numerous critics of the analytical utility of the consociational literature. Its theoretical status and explanatory power have been questioned (Barry 1975), the inclusion of Switzerland (which lacks encapsulated subcultures) widely challenged and Lijphart's notion of 'prudent leadership' deemed a self-denying hypothesis. Doubts have also been raised about its causal assumptions, with suggestions that while pre-consociational democracies might well have been characterised by segmentation (i.e. by visible and permanent cleavage lines), 'pillarisation' (the rival organisational networks that share the identity of their respective subcultures) may well have been a consequence rather than a cause of consociational devices such as proportionality and segmental autonomy and introduced (or at least promoted) by political elites seeking to maximise their potential to exercise political control.

Such criticisms notwithstanding, the consociational literature provides a useful reminder of the importance for the genesis and maintenance of democracy of the values and behaviour of political elites. It has exerted a significant influence upon the comparative study of democracy and remains a model with strong heuristic power.

See also:

corruption; democratic consolidation; parties; pluralism; political culture; Westminster model

Further reading

Barry, B. (1975) 'The Consociational Model and Its Dangers', *European Journal for Political Research* 3(4): 393–412.

Lehmbruch, G. (1967) *Proporzdemokratie: Politisches System und Politische Kultur in der Schweiz und in Österreich*, Tübingen: Mohr.

Lijphart, A. (1968a) 'Typologies of Democratic Systems', *Comparative Political Studies* 1(1): 3–44.

—— (1968b) *The Politics of Accommodation*, Berkley, CA: University of California Press.

Lorwin, V.R. (1971) 'Segmented Pluralism: Ideological Cleavages and Political Cohesion in the Smaller European Democracies', *Comparative Politics* 3(2): 141–75.

Luther, K.R. and Deschouwer, K. (eds) (1999) *Party Elites in Divided Societies: Political Parties in Consociational Democracy*, London: Routledge.

McRae, K.D. (ed.) (1974) *Consociational Democracy: Political Accommodation in Segmented Societies*, Toronto: McClelland and Stewart.

Steiner, J. (1969) 'Conflict Resolution and Democratic Stability in Subculturally Segmented Political Systems', *Res Publica* 11: 775–98.

—— (1974) *Amicable Agreement versus Majority Rule. Conflict Resolution in Switzerland*, Chapel Hill, NC: University of North Carolina Press.

KURT RICHARD LUTHER

constitutional design

Liberal democracies are the heirs to two political doctrines. The first is liberal CONSTITUTIONALISM, with its appeal to the idea of limited government. The second is democracy, with its appeal to the idea of popular government. Although these two doctrines have become fused into the idea of constitutional democracy, they are distinct. The theory of constitutional government says that the constitution is sovereign and that political power should only be exercised in accordance with the powers that a constitution bestows on those in AUTHORITY. Thus the powers of government should be limited. The theory of popular government, by contrast, says that the people, or their representatives, are sovereign and that popular opinion should determine public choices. On this view, democratic governments should be free to pursue popularly determined goals. Taken literally, the principle of popular government does not prescribe any limits on what democratic governments can do.

If the principles are distinct, in what ways can they be fused in a political theory? To answer this question, it is useful, following Rawls (1972: 221–43), to define a constitutional democracy as a political system possessing four features: respect for the rule of law (see LAW, RULE OF); protection of certain fundamental personal freedoms, including FREEDOM of speech, freedom of association and freedom of religion; secure, if not constitutionally entrenched, property rights; and the use of the majority principle in the making of public policy. Roughly speaking, the first three of these conditions stipulate the requirements for constitutional government, and the fourth condition stipulates that a constitutional government should also be democratic.

The fusion of these doctrines in the ideals and institutions of constitutional democracy would not be problematic if the theoretical assumptions and practical implications of the two sets of principles were consistent with one another. However, although the two sets of ideas can often happily co-exist, they can also conflict with one another. Thus, in the USA there is a clear SEPARATION OF POWERS between legislature and JUDICIARY. The Supreme Court has the power to challenge legislation on the grounds that it violates constitutional provisions. For example, the first amendment of the US constitution protects freedom of speech with the requirement that 'Congress shall make no law...abridging the freedom of speech, or of the press'. Of course, this prohibition is not self-evident in its scope. Does it protect the publication of pornography? Or the burning of the US flag as an act of protest? Or the encouragement of sedition? These are all questions that the US Supreme Court has had to decide at various times in its history. Yet that is precisely the point. It is up to the Court, not political representatives, to determine the constitutional limits of congressional legislation. In other words, the separation of powers means that the Court takes priority in determining the limits of what the legislature can do.

It may be argued that the constitution itself can be changed by legislative means in the USA and that the sharp separation of powers that constitutional principles imply should be seen in the light of this potential for modification. However, it is a feature of the constitutional entrenchment of RIGHTS and powers that any legislative changes require especially large majorities among those eligible to decide on constitutional questions, majorities that are difficult to achieve. Since 1788 there have only been twenty-seven amendments to the US constitution, ten of them (the so called Bill of Rights) occurring within two years of the original ratification. In other words, the barriers to legislative alteration of the constitutional allocation of rights and powers are considerable; as indeed they should be, according to the principles of constitutional government.

In consequence, the US constitution imposes restrictions on the scope of policies or legislation that popular majorities, or their representatives, can adopt. The first amendment to the US constitution would mean that some forms of legislation intended to prevent 'hate speech', which some political representatives would like to see in place, would be declared unconstitutional. By contrast in the UK, where there is no such separation of powers, it is a legal offence to incite racial hatred through speech or publications. The tension between popular and constitutional government is thus manifest in both principle and practice.

Dworkin (1996) has contested this assertion. He argues that the separation of powers is one way in which popular government can be realised. The essential premise of his argument is that the judiciary is often in a significantly better position than elected representatives to give expression to the democratic principle that all citizens should be treated with equal concern and respect. On this view, then, the power that the separation of powers doctrine gives to the judiciary provides a way in which the value of political EQUALITY, central to democracy, can be advanced.

The difficulty with this view, however, is that it draws too sharp a distinction between the courts as deliberative institutions, guided by an ideal of equal respect, and legislatures as aggregating institutions, responding simply to the weight of votes. Once we see that legislatures are necessarily deliberative institutions in their own right, involved in the weighing of policy and political arguments as well as the counting of votes, the contrast between the two forms of DECISION-MAKING institution fades. Once we also see that certain political rights, such as the right to petition the legislature, are ways in which social groups can participate in the shaping and interpretation of a society's morality, the contrast ceases to exist at all. Although there is a conflict of principle between the ideals of constitutional and democratic government, we cannot assume the moral superiority of one set of principles over the other. We need to find an alternative way of achieving some reconciliation.

A partial reconciliation

Although constitutional and popular government can be contrasted with one another, it is possible to argue that some form of constitutional arrangement is necessary even if one holds to a view that governments should rest on the popular will. The basis for this view is the recognition that some rights are required by democracy in order to assure its smooth functioning (compare Ely 1980).

For example, the principle of the rule of law involves the prohibition on retrospective legislation and the requirement that law should be knowable in advance by citizens. Ensuring the rule of law can be seen as a device by which only the settled will of the majority informs public policy. Such procedural norms of legislation can be thought of as ways to prevent temporary majorities seizing political control contrary to the underlying will of a more permanent majority.

Similarly, rights protecting the personal freedoms of speech or of free assembly can be given a democratic rationale. Protection of such rights forms the conditions under which everyone in the community is allowed to influence and participate in debate. From this point of view part of the justification of freedom of speech is as much the interest that the public might have in hearing what is said as the right of individuals to speak their minds. Thus, although constitutional restrictions on governments are a protection for individuals, they can also be seen as a protection for the people taken as a whole.

By a parallel line of reasoning, some rights are also necessary to give a minority the opportunity to turn itself into a majority. This is particularly so with rights ensuring fair representation, whether in terms of voting rights or rights to organise political action to promote one's own views and interests. Freedom of association thus provides one of the conditions under which DEMOCRATIC DEBATE and competition can take place.

An unreconciled tension

Although it is possible to achieve a partial reconciliation between the principles of constitutionalism and the principles of popular government, the reconciliation is not complete. There are rights that cannot be related to democracy in a straightforward way. Although they may be associated with democracy in practice, they will be logically distinct from any definition of democracy that we can offer.

Examples of rights in this set include civil rights, such as freedom of religion, freedom of conscience, freedom of non-political speech or freedom of sexual behaviour. Unlike politically valuable rights, these civil rights do not seem to be tied essentially to the notion of democratic government. It is not consistent with the principles of democracy for a democratic government to prohibit a group of citizens from organising peacefully to change public policy. It is consistent with the principles of democracy for a government to impose restrictions or grant privileges in respect of civil rights. For example, both Sweden and Norway, which many regard as archetypal egalitarian democracies, have established churches and levy taxes for their upkeep. If freedom of religion means complete separation of church and state, which arguably it does, then it is apparent that this separation is not always respected within functioning democracies (see STATE, RELATIONS OF CHURCH TO).

To understand why this might be so, we need to go back to the crucial point of difference between constitutional and popular govern-ment. Limiting government power is logically distinct from determining the source of that power. To say what someone in authority may or may not do is quite different from identifying the source of the power they hold. If there is a relationship between the two, it is contingent and empirical, rather than definitional. Limited government might not be responsive to the popular will and governments responsive to the popular will might not respect constitutional limitations.

Another set of rights, sometimes connected by theorists with rights to freedom but in fact logically distinct, are property rights. In one form or another property rights are often made a matter of constitutional provision. For example, Article 14 of the German Basic Law secures a right to private property and inheritance for citizens, although it also prescribes that property has duties in respect of the public interest. As Buchanan (1986: 255–6) has noted, the exact constitutional status of PRIVATE PROPERTY is an area that tends to divide libertarians or classical liberals on the one side from social democrats on the other. Both may agree that there should be clear restrictions upon governments interfering with the civil liberties of citizens, but they disagree on the protection that should be afforded to property rights. Social democrats see property rights as institutional devices by which control of productive assets is assigned to individuals, where the assignment is to be judged in terms of the consequences it produces. Libertarians and classical liberals, by contrast, typically wish to assimilate property to the list of 'natural' rights, and to say that a person's entitlement to property depends upon his or her ability justly to acquire property from others.

Although modern libertarians have offered arguments for a natural right to property, it has proved difficult to make those arguments good and so to assimilate property rights to the category of pre-political natural or human rights. Hence, we should not suppose that a right to private property is definitionally tied to the principles of constitutional democracy. However, since Aristotle there has been an empirical conjecture that a large middle CLASS intent on maintaining the security of widespread property ownership is conducive to democracy because it upholds dispersed sources of power independent of government. For this reason, the constitutional protection of private property may contribute to the maintenance and enhancement of democracy, but the connection is empirical rather than conceptual.

Power concentration and power diffusion

How constitutional rights and responsiveness to popular opinion are to be balanced is thus a fundamental problem in the theory of constitutional democracy. In order to formulate an answer to this problem, we need criteria by which we can evaluate the effects of competing institutional designs (see INSTITUTIONAL DESIGN). At this point, then, we need to turn to broader theories of democratic and constitutional government as the basis for such criteria. One relevant contrast in political theory is between power-concentration views and power-diffusion views of the structure of government (see Barry 1965: 237–42).

On the power-concentration view, elected governments ought to be endowed with the constitutional powers to achieve their goals within a context in which they are held clearly to account for their actions. Decision points need to be reduced rather than multiplied, and single-party control of government needs to be assured. On the power-diffusion view, by contrast, governmental capacity ought to be fragmented in a series of checks and balances to prevent power from becoming out of control or it ought to be shared broadly among many political actors in a consensual fashion (for an influential typology along the these lines, see Lijphart (1984)).

In broad terms, it is possible to state the constitutional designs that embody one or the other of these two conceptions of government. Power-diffusion is achieved through an electoral formula that allocates seats in proportion to votes, legislative rules that encourage opposition participation in the making of legisla-tion, the territorial dispersion of power, a constitutionally established bill of rights that the courts can enforce and a POLITICAL CULTURE of compromise and consensus rather than confrontation.

By contrast, power-concentration, as traditionally found in the Westminster system, is secured through an electoral formula that reduces the effective number of political parties in the legislature and enhances the margin of the winning party, legislative rules that sharply distinguish the roles of government and opposition, practices that foster the executive domination of the legislature and a unitary system of government in which there are few sources of extra-parliamentary veto power on what governments can do.

Although it is possible to identify the types of political designs that lead to one sort of government rather than another, this does not by itself settle the question of which is superior in terms of the theory of constitutional democracy. That question can only be answered by reference to a broader political theory, encompassing a view of the role of government in society, and the conditions that need to be met if governments are to perform their tasks in accordance with the particular conception of the political order that is favoured by a political theory. In the end, therefore, the way in which the balance between constitutionalism and democracy is resolved will reflect the broader concerns of a political tradition, culture or set of principles.

See also:

consensus democracy; constitutionalism; legislative process; representation, concept of; representation, models of; state, models of; Westminster model

Further reading

Barry, B. (1965) *Political Argument*, London: Routledge and Kegan Paul.
Buchanan, J.M. (1986) *Liberty, Market and State*, Brighton: Harvester Press.

Dworkin, R. (1996) *Freedom's Law*, Cambridge, MA: Harvard University Press.

Elster, J. and Slagstad, R. (eds) (1993) *Constitutionalism and Democracy*, Cambridge: Cambridge University Press.

Ely, J.H. (1980) *Democracy and Distrust*, Cambridge: Cambridge University Press.

Lijphart, A. (1984) *Democracies*, New Haven, CT: Yale University Press.

Rawls, J. (1972) *A Theory of Justice*, Oxford: Oxford University Press.

ALBERT WEALE

constitutional monarchy

Constitutional monarchy refers to the alliance between democratic institutions and the figure of a traditionally appointed head of state, a position which is usually hereditary through the law of primogeniture, whose functions are regulated by the law of the land. This concept is a result of the survival and adaptation of the figure of the monarch to modern democratic forms of government.

In modern democracies, there is the office of head of state. In parliamentary democracies, the head of the executive, such as the prime minister or chancellor, and the head of state are separate offices, the latter being a monarch or, in republics, a president, generally indirectly elected. In presidential republics, both offices coincide in the same person. The presence of a monarch, such as an emperor, a king, a prince or a grand duke, male or female, holding office for life according to rules of inheritance in a royal family, is a paradox in democracy.

Monarchy, the rule by a single person, generally as a result of inheritance (in the West normally primogeniture, sometimes preferring males over females) and in fewer cases, by election by dignitaries in councils (like the medieval Holy Roman Emperor or the King of Poland) was the basic form of traditional AUTHORITY. The religious legitimisation was expressed in the idea of divine right of kings. That authority was limited by tradition, charters, law and state representative institutions but, with the advent of the modern state, the notion of SOVEREIGNTY *legibus solutus* led to the so-called absolute monarchy. This conception was challenged by the English and French Revolutions, which in the United Kingdom led to modern constitutional monarchy and in France to a republic.

The French Revolution led in all European countries to demands for participation of elected representatives in power and to constitutions. Kings granted charters or were forced to accept constitutions limiting their powers. France became a republic, but with the exception of the USA, Switzerland, and for a short time Hungary and Spain, all countries were monarchies and even the independent Balkan states and Belgium established new dynasties. In the twentieth century, first in Portugal and then, after their defeat in the First World War when the German, Austro-Hungarian and Russian empires were overthrown, new republics were proclaimed. In the interwar years, seven of the European monarchies became stable democracies. In six other monarchies, democratisation was frustrated by dictatorship, in several with the support of the kings. The first seven are still parliamentary democratic monarchies, to which the instauration of the monarchy in Spain was added in 1975, when King Juan Carlos inherited all powers of the state from Franco as a king in a newly created monarchy. By 1978, a political and popular consensus legitimised the king's dynastic rights as head of state while limiting his functions to those of a constitutional monarch. Of the sixteen European republics between 1918 and 1939, only five democracies survived. One could even argue, therefore, that monarchies contributed to democratic stability.

The apparent contradiction between monarchs and democracies is resolved in modern societies through what one calls a constitutional monarchy where the legitimisation of the office comes from the constitutional system chosen by the people and the monarch does not rule. This system is valid as long as the office gathers enough popular support. The performance of each individual monarch influences this popular support, but scholarship tends to attribute more importance in constitutional democracies to the office of the monarch rather than to the individual as 'was unambiguously demonstrated in Britain during the abdication crisis of Edward VIII' (Rose and Kavanagh 1976: 550).

Evolution rather than revolution has made the British system of government, replicated in other countries once part of the British Empire, such as Canada, Australia and New Zealand, a model when describing the workings of a constitutional monarchy. At the end of the nineteenth century, Walter Bagehot characterised it and defined the functions of an archetypal constitutional monarch as the dignified part of the constitution. It is the theory that, as a general rule, in a democratic constitutional monarchy a monarch reigns but does not rule, being the symbol and the embodiment of the historical continuity of the state but limited in its actions to the directives of the government which, as the emanation of the popular will through regular elections, is the one who directs the national and international policy of the state. This is in contrast to the nineteenth-century non-democratic constitutional monarchies, in which the government did not need the confidence of parliament or where there was the principle of the dual confidence of parliament and king. What are then the functions left to the monarch? Bagehot indicates that he possesses the right to be consulted, to encourage and to warn. The function of advice is important. The monarch is the recipient of a vast amount of information that he or she accumulates through time, which, with good judgement, allows him to form opinions that go beyond the political moment. This, as well as his or her position above party politics, not owing any role in elections, allows him or her to give advice to the government as a non-partisan member of the Cabinet, and also to the opposition. Furthermore, he or she is a player that, thanks to deference accorded to monarchy, cannot be ignored. Another function of the monarch is that of mediator in political difficulties, a good example being the beneficial role of King Juan Carlos in Spain during and after the failed coup of 1981.

In constitutional transitions, such as the advent of independence, a monarch can prove useful. When Norway obtained independence from Sweden in 1905, King Haakon was the basis of the new constitution. In reverse, the maintenance of the Queen of England as head of state of many of the former British colonies after independence facilitated a progressive political transition and the continuation of privileged relations through the Commonwealth. The Andorran Co-Princes were instrumental in 1993 in the transformation of Andorra from a personal feudal possession into a sovereign state with the political form of a parliamentary co-principality. In Japan, where the Emperor had been omnipotent in a country ruled by a military regime, the constitutional change after the Second World War took place under the same monarch. From the position of being a god, Hirohito became a constitutional monarch in a new constitutional system conceived by the American occupying power. The Emperor's denunciation of his divine status on New Year's Day 1946 was useful for bridging the gap between the old monarchical dictatorship and a fully constitutional democratic parliamentary democracy: 'The ties between Us and Our people have always stood upon mutual trust and affection. They do not depend upon mere legends and myths. They are not predicated upon the false conception that the emperor is divine...'. It will be interesting to monitor the role to be played by the monarchy in states not yet fully democratic, such as Morocco, Thailand or the Gulf States, should a transition to democracy take place.

In multinational states, the monarch has a symbolic function which is difficult to define. In Belgium, for example, he is king of all communities, a role difficult to assume by an elected president who would necessarily be Flemish or Walloon. In some countries, the monarch's hereditary titles link him or her with different ethnic groups. The monarch also plays a visible ceremonial and representational function, for which he or she is particularly able. Knowledge in protocol and languages, long training for the office which starts in childhood, connection with military and sometimes religious authorities, all allow the monarch to represent the state both in national and international venues. In some countries, a monarch can be a special asset in foreign affairs through long-lasting knowledge of foreign leaders and peoples. Also, in moments of distress or national catastrophe the monarch can symbolise the feelings of the nation. Emotional outbursts of discontent can be controlled by the presence of a monarch who, through the charismatic authority linked to his or her office and blood, if they show courage, can bring people together. Events closely associated with the monarchy, such as the coronation, can also be 'a great act of national communion' (Shils and Young 1953: 80).

See also:

constitutionalism

Further reading

Bagehot, W. (1965) *The English Constitution*, London: The Economist.

Kaltefleiter W. (1970) *Die Funktionen des Staatsoberhauptes in der parlamentarischen Demokratie*, Koln: Westdeutscher Verlag.

Loewenstein, K. (1952) *Die Monarchie im modernen Staat*, Frankfurt am Main.

Papel (1980) *La Monarquia Espanola y el Derecho Consttucional Europeo*, Barcelona.

Rose R. and Kavanagh D. (1976) 'The Monarchy in Contemporary Political Culture', *Comparative Politics*, July: 548–76.

Rostow, E.V. (1988) *President, Prime Minister, or Constitutional Monarch?*, Washington: The Institute for National Strategic Studies.

Shils, E. and Young, M. (1953) 'The Meaning of the Coronation', *The Sociological Review*, December.

JULI MINOVES-TRIQUELL

constitutionalism

Constitutions provide a set of rules and conventions for the exercise of power. They define who can make decisions, how and within what parameters. However, the nature and content of constitutions differ tremendously, both over time and between polities. There are huge variations as to their purposes and scope, the forms they take, the provisions they contain and the mechanisms they employ. Indeed, principles or procedures fundamental to certain constitutional orders can prove antagonistic to others.

The standard purpose of a constitution has been to avoid the arbitrary, wilful and tyrannous use of power, a goal traditionally encapsulated in the phrase, 'the rule of law not men'. Most liberals and some conservatives and socialists associate this purpose with the negative task of limiting what governments may do. A constitution is conceived as a legal framework of procedures and RIGHTS that constrain state action. This negative constitutionalism is motivated by both practical and principled considerations. The chief practical concern arises from fears that politicians or public servants may prove corrupt or incompetent. The principled reason issues from the belief that governments should remain neutral between people's ideals and interests. Behind both considerations lies a view of the state as a regrettable, if necessary, evil. Its chief role is to reduce the mutual interferences attendant upon social life, thereby preserving as much individual FREEDOM as possible. However, since states can intervene in ways that are potentially more oppressive than any individual could be, they too must be checked.

Libertarians counsel limiting the state to providing physical SECURITY via a police force, army and JUSTICE system. They contend more extensive functions, especially those involving the redistribution of resources, increase rather than diminish the amount of interference with individual liberty, and raise the likelihood of CORRUPTION and inefficiency. The constitution's scope is similarly restricted to upholding civil and property rights. Democracy and political rights have a mainly subsidiary function as a brake on government power, largely by allowing the peaceful removal of rulers. Since democracy can prove a channel for rent seeking and tyrannous majorities it also needs curbing, usually by a constitutional court. Social liberals and socialists acknowledge that social and economic factors may be as significant impediments to human freedom as the direct, physical coercion of others. Consequently, they allow a broader role for the state in such spheres as welfare, education and the provision of public goods, and a correspondingly wider scope for the constitution (see SOCIAL DEMOCRACY). For example, they often argue social and economic rights should be assigned constitutional protection to safeguard individual autonomy. Nevertheless, the constitution's rationale remains the same. It consists primarily of a judicially protected legal framework that restricts state power to maximising the natural liberties of individuals. A bill of rights and constitutional court provide the chief provisions and mechanisms.

Republican and recent post-liberal agonistic approaches adopt a more positive view of constitutionalism. They see freedom as a civic achievement rather than a natural attribute. It results from all citizens possessing an equal status when framing the priorities of the polity and enjoying the opportunities and advantages that result from social life. Arbitrary government is prevented by replacing rule by particular men with that of the people, not through legal rules and norms. This account identifies the constitution with the political system, with rights and the rule of law emerging from rather than framing politics. A polity's constitution consists of those political devices needed to foster deliberation and reciprocity between citizens. Examples include voting systems, the SEPARATION OF POWERS, and the dispersal of SOVEREIGNTY through federal and other forms of political organisation. Instead of limiting political power, a constitution of this type seeks to regulate it. It aims not at neutrality between the various interests and ideals of citizens but at reaching an accommodation amongst them.

Mutual engagement promotes equal recognition, social SOLIDARITY and support for those public goods necessary for individuals to fulfil their potential. These same political mechanisms also empower citizens to contest measures that overlook or damage them. Positive constitutionalism thereby satisfies many of the concerns of those favouring the negative position. Because freedom is politically constituted, even in the personal sphere of familial relationships, all of which are instituted and regulated by law, a positive constitutionalism is broad in scope, for it applies to and seeks to democratise all spheres where power is exercised.

REPUBLICANISM and LIBERALISM were the dominant political languages during the seventeenth and eighteenth centuries when modern, state-centred constitutionalism originated with the English, American and French Revolutions. Aspects of positive and negative, political and legal constitutionalism are present in all western democracies, therefore. Article 16 of the French Declaration of the Rights of Man and the Citizen of 1789 explicitly combines the two, declaring that where rights are not secured and the separation of powers not established, no constitution exists. The American Constitution also contains both elements. For the authors of the *Federalist Papers*, political devices, such as the checks and balances operating between Congress, Senate and President, on the one hand, and the federal government and the various state legislatures, on the other, provided the principal mechanisms for reconciling government by men with the rule of law. However, the constitution also made provision for a Supreme Court and was amended to include a Bill of Rights. Though the mix varies between constitutions, with the French, say, being considerably more republican with its emphasis on popular sovereignty and the relatively weak role assigned to the judiciary compared to the German, with its emphasis on judicially protected rights over and above the federal organisation of power, most draw on both traditions. Constitutions that lack political mechanisms for distributing power tend to be merely 'nominal'. Like the former Soviet Union constitution, they simply offer rulers a spurious legitimacy. However, without an independent judiciary to review and apply legislation, laws risk being inconsistently made and implemented.

By and large, legal and negative constitutionalism has come to predominate over the more positive and political kind, with the United States offering the prime example of this development. The resulting juridification of politics has produced a related shift from unwritten to written constitutions. The former, in the guise of time-hallowed conventions, are favoured by many conservatives and some libertarians. They see such traditions as organic. Spontaneous responses to the needs of people, customary rules lie outside the arbitrary control of any single agent or agency. Though supporters see the flexibility and adaptiveness of this sort of constitution as an advantage, critics argue they are too open to change and of too equivocal a status to provide effective constraints. In fact, most constitutions have conventional and written elements, even if the balance varies and the written parts are not always collected together into a single key document. Thus the British constitution, the standard exemplar of the conventional type, contains numerous written statutes and charters that enjoy constitutional status, such as Magna Carta (1215), the Habeas Corpus Act (1641), the Bill of Rights (1689) and successive Representation of the People, Judicature and Local Government Acts. Moreover, it also involves important elements of political constitutionalism, notably the balance and partial separation of powers represented by the division between Commons, Lords and monarchy and the role of opposition parties in challenging governments. Yet as Walter Bagehot observed in the nineteenth century, many of these bodies, such as the monarchy, have ceased to be 'effective'. Now 'dignified' parts of the constitution, their ability to check the power of the executive is negligible. Recent reforms have sought to revive both the legal and political aspects of the British constitution. These have included new legal instruments, notably the Human Rights Act (2000) which incorporates the European Convention on Human Rights into British law, and institutional innovations, such as devolved assemblies in Scotland, Wales and Northern Ireland and reform of the House of Lords. However, Britain has not adopted a single written constitution, though similar changes to Westminster style systems in New Zealand and Canada have led these countries to take this step.

The relationship of constitutionalism to democracy is fraught with paradox. Constitutions are both constituted by and constitute the people or DEMOS of a state. Brought into being by democratic means in conventions and referenda, they usually specify procedures for subsequent democratic amendment or repeal. Normally, they also list the main elements of the political system, including the powers of central, regional and local institutions, the method of voting, the terms of office and responsibilities of the main post holders, and the rights and duties of citizens (see CIVIC VIRTUE). However, constitutions not only define democracy but also, as we have seen, limit it. Some constitutionally guaranteed rights may have an intrinsic connection to democracy, such as the freedoms of speech, assembly and association, but others protect areas that it is deemed should be immune from democratic interference, such as property or privacy rights. Still others seek to guard against myopia or weakness of will by the demos. Giving the power to set interest rates to an autonomous central bank is a typical example. Finally, certain rights or mechanisms seek to facilitate democracy by taking particularly divisive issues off the agenda. Freedom of religion and the separation of Church and state (see STATE, RELATIONS OF CHURCH TO), minority vetoes or power-sharing arrangements are instances of this reasoning. Note too that even those rights and procedures that are intimately connected to democracy may constrain as well as enable. There are many different models of democracy that define the democratic rules in often incompatible ways. Democrats may feel the people should have the right to redefine these rules whenever they wish. Meanwhile, constitutions frequently omit many factors that are vital to the working of democracy: political parties, the media, pressure groups, and business corporations standardly receive little if any explicit constitutional mention, let alone regulation or protection.

There is probably no entirely satisfactory way of resolving the tensions between constitutionalism and democracy. Democracy requires rules to operate; yet 'people rule' implies the capacity to revise these over time. After all, numerous categories of person and spheres of life that have been excluded from politics in the past are now regarded as legitimately included. Legal constitutionalists tend to see political constitution making as an exceptional event at the moment of creating the state or regime in the wake of a revolution or war. They argue that constitutional courts can assume the process of renewal by looking to the norms and principles of democracy and the political culture of the state involved. However both these aspects are deeply contested; witness the debates over whether democratic EQUALITY is satisfied by one-person one-vote, or demands proportional representation, minority quotas or even power sharing. Though the American Supreme Court for one has attempted to adjudicate on such matters, it is hard not to regard them as deeply political questions that cannot be resolved *a priori* but only in relation to the people and the context concerned. As the continuing constitutional crises and debates in Canada or Belgium indicate, this approach can have the drawback of creating instability, can lead to opportunist bargaining by certain elites and, on some analyses, fosters divisiveness rather than mutual recognition and accommodation. As GLOBALISATION weakens state sovereignty and makes societies more plural, such political constitution making may nonetheless become increasingly the norm rather than the exception.

See also:

civic virtue; constitutional monarchy; representation, concept of

Further reading

Alexander, L. (1998) *Constitutionalism: Philosophical Foundations*, Cambridge: Cambridge University Press.

Bellamy, R. (ed.) (1996) *Constitutionalism, Democracy and Sovereignty: American and European Perspectives*, Aldershot: Avebury.

Bellamy, R. and Castiglione D. (eds) (1996) *Constitutionalism in Transformation: European and Theoretical Perspectives*, Oxford: Blackwell.

—— (1997) 'Constitutionalism and Democracy – Political Theory and the American Constitution', *British Journal of Political Science* 27: 595–618.

Dworkin, R. (1996) *Freedom's Law: The Moral Reading of the American Constitution*, Cambridge, MA: Harvard University Press.

Finer, S.E., Bogdanor, V. and Rudden, B. (1995) *Comparing Constitutions*, Oxford: Clarendon Press.

Greenberg, D., Katz, S.N., Olivero, M.B. and Wheatley, S.C. (eds) (1993) *Constitutionalism and Democracy: Transitions in the Contemporary World*, New York and Oxford: Oxford University Press.

Hayek, F.A. (1960) *The Constitution of Liberty*, London: Routledge.

Sunstein, C.R. (1993) *The Partial Constitution*, Cambridge, MA: Harvard University Press.

Tully, J. (1995) *Strange Multiplicity: Constitutionalism in an Age of Diversity*, Cambridge: Cambridge University Press.

RICHARD BELLAMY

constraint

Democratic political systems have been equipped with a wide variety of written and unwritten rules, institutional obstacles and control mechanisms, together referred to as constraints. Their task is to restrain any political actor who might abuse power, abuse being defined in terms of threats posed to the EQUALITY of citizens, their FREEDOM or their share in political influence. As a form of

COERCION, constraints are in no way the monopoly of liberal democracy: every stable political system requires mechanisms to limit the extent to which, first, one citizen or group can constrain another; second, the system as a whole can constrain individuals; and third, individuals and groups can constrain the system (Weale 1999: 45).

Constraints were understood as necessary and desirable features of political systems long before democracy existed. Within the Greek Classics, six types of political systems can be distinguished: those ruled by one, the best and the many in the interest of all (respectively monarchy, aristocracy, and politeia) and those ruled by one, the powerful and the mob (tyranny, oligarchy, democracy) in the ruler(s)'s self-interest. They observed that rule in the interest of all tended to degenerate into self-interested rule and ultimately ended in chaos. Power could apparently corrupt even the most virtuous. For this reason, Aristotle suggested that a *mixed constitution* containing elements of all three good systems might in practice be the best and most stable form of government. The history of constraints as a *desirable* feature of democracies therefore goes back at least to Aristotle.

It is not until the Middle Ages that constraints were also discovered as a *necessary* feature of the political system. Mindful of the danger of tyranny, medieval political theorists appealed to the monarch's better feelings and stressed the rewards awaiting him in the afterlife, all to morally constrain him. What probably added some force to their arguments were the illustrations they used: histories of princes who failed to rule in the interest of all and to bridle their power when necessary, thus bringing ruin upon their empires and death upon themselves.

Constraints can be moral codes or legal regulations. When in the course of history medieval regimes were replaced by increasingly representative civil regimes, moral constraints lost more and more ground to legal constraints. Nevertheless the appeal to morality remains important to this day. On the one hand, popular opinion still insists on people's representatives, civil servants and governing politicians acting in accordance with a code of conduct or professional ethics. On the other, politicians occasionally appeal to the citizens' better selves, asking them to show 'democratic constraint' as opposed to intolerance, protest or rioting, or they call upon them to remember their civic DUTIES and RESPONSIBILITIES (see CIVIC VIRTUE). No matter how elaborate a system of legal constraints may be, moral constraints are here to stay: in the end, legal constraints remain paper tigers.

Legal constraints, products of bad experiences with absolutism or popular SOVEREIGNTY, are again of two types: those based on the creation of *countervailing powers*, that is opposing forces with (possibly) diverging interests, and those based on the *exclusion* of political entities from power in certain areas. The first tradition dates back, at least, to the conciliary movement within the Roman Church, trying to install a kind of parliamentary control on the pope's powers (see STATE, RELATIONS OF CHURCH TO). In worldly affairs, countervailing powers are inseparably linked to Montesquieu, who introduced the notion of the *trias politica*, a division in the powers of government between an executive, legislative and judicial branch. The Federalists' idea that political institutions should serve as *checks and balances* on one another added a further degree of sophistication to this type of constraint. Today, we find countervailing powers in virtually every possible form and shape (see SEPARATION OF POWERS). At the very least, power constraints (when respected) succeed in continually forcing powers to co-operate and share responsibility; at best, in preventing any power from acting on its own, uncontrolled.

Rather than forcing political actors to co-operate in order to act, *exclusionary* constraints directly prohibit action. They mark off areas in which other citizens, groups or the state are not allowed to intervene (see PUBLIC–PRIVATE DISTINCTION). Exclusionary constraints found their first expression in CONSTITUTIONALISM and the call for religious freedom, to be followed by, for example, minority rights in general, CHRISTIAN DEMOCRACY's demand for

SUBSIDIARITY, and defences of a self-governing CIVIL SOCIETY.

Exclusionary constraints and democracy were linked by social contract theorists from Hobbes and Locke to Rawls. Their defence of a state-free, private sphere rested on the assumption that governments can derive legitimacy from their subjects only insofar as they respect their rights and interests. Almost taken to the extreme, this has been interpreted by Robert Nozick (1974) as an argument for the night-watchman state: politics and policy can only be legitimate after individuals have exercised their individual rights (which serve as 'side-constraints' on the state). Since these include rights to PRIVATE PROPERTY, little room is left for social or economic policy, let alone collective decision-making. In less radical versions of philosophical liberalism (Rawls 1971; Barry 1995), exclusionary constraints serve as basic rights or principles of social justice, limiting but not obliterating room for democratic decision-making. However, it is important to note that all exclusionary constraints are, at least in principle, at odds with the formal idea of democracy: democracy, after all, presumes that the enfranchised are sovereign decision makers, hence not constrained in any way (Hyland 1995: 131; Weale 1999: 167). Moreover, exclusionary rights themselves can have two faces. They may in time be experienced as freedoms by some and – think of the freedom of contract or the privacy of the family – as vehicles of oppression by others.

Exclusionary constraints are embodied in constitutions or bills of rights, as well as international treaties and legally binding declarations like the Universal Declaration of Human Rights. Their exact content and interpretation, and the degree to which they are respected, differ from country to country. It is one of the paradoxes of democracy that exclusionary constraints seem to flourish better in democracies, despite the theoretically uneasy relationship between the two.

Legal constraints cannot be effective without moral constraints, and hence cannot be effective without civic and political virtue. Even then, not all legal constraints will be equally effective or efficient. Apart from technical flaws in their design, this problem is intrinsic to democracy. The greater the number of issues on the political agenda of democracies, the more demand there may be for constraints. Exclusionary constraints do not necessarily mean that the state has less to do: they may require the work of (new) institutions to protect them, which calls for countervailing powers, implying more institutions, checks and balances, and with that the danger of an overloaded, paralysed government (see GRIDLOCK).

In normative terms, constraints can be evaluated by their procedural and substantive effects. From the procedural point of view, what matters is that constraints guarantee PROCEDURAL DEMOCRACY: an equal distribution of power in society, keeping government and policy in some way representative. By substantive criteria, what matters is that some points of view seen as morally contradictory to democracy, or the people representing them, cannot dominate society. Unfortunately, every constraint has both procedural and substantive effects, and judgements on the two may not concur. Excluding the issue of the abolition of democracy from the political agenda, for example, implies excluding many of the ideas of anti-democratic parties and limiting the freedom of anti-democrats. The procedural effects may be easy to defend since it is a matter of protecting democracy against itself, yet the substantive effects require a substantive moral defence of what a 'proper' democracy is, a defence which is necessarily open to debate. What is clear, however, is that the idea that popular sovereignty should always overrule constraints, or that constraints always overrule the majority, are incompatible with democracy. The former could lead to the abolition of the public sphere, the latter to that of the private sphere.

Constraints express a widely shared belief that something is true or truly valuable, worthy of protecting and of passing on to the next generation; as such, constraints may also express cultural and temporal prejudice. Good democratic practice then is both conservative for the moment and self-critical towards the future.

See also:

coercion; constitutionalism; good practice; legal regulation; public–private distinction; responsibilities; separation of powers; sovereignty

Further reading

Barry, B. (1995) *Justice as Impartiality*, Oxford: Clarendon Press.

Hayek, F. (1944) *The Road to Serfdom*, London: Routledge and Kegan Paul.

Hyland, J. (1995) *Democratic Theory*, Manchester: Manchester University Press.

Nozick, R. (1974) *Anarchy, State and Utopia*, New York: Basic Books.

Rawls, J. (1971) *A Theory of Justice*, Oxford: Oxford University Press.

Schumpeter, J. (1954) *Capitalism, Socialism and Democracy*, London: Allen & Unwin.

Weale, A. (1999) *Democracy*, London: Macmillan.

MARCEL WISSENBURG

contestation

Contestation can be both physical and conceptual. An early example of physical contestation includes gladiatorial combat, an example referred to in a wider vein by Hobbes who writes about the gladiatorial stance between contesting princes of different realms (Hobbes 1968: 187). Clausewitz referred to war as an extension of politics by other means, a dictum that has impressed subsequent generations of scholars. Strictly speaking these examples are mistaken, for politics breaks down when combat arises. We have only to turn to the earliest examples of politics to find that the meaning of politics depended upon verbal contestation. Thus the polis in its active capacity depended solely upon verbal contestation: a conflict of concepts. This notion that contestation is primarily a contest of concepts is particularly crucial to democratic regimes who attempt to settle their differences by argument, speech, making a point, and contests at the conceptual level.

The tradition of deciding the outcome of conflicts by means of argument is conventionally traced to the Greek polis and to Greek drama. For instance Antigone takes her case in a verbal vein rather than a physical vein. Notwithstanding these examples of early contestation, even earlier examples can be found in the myths of Mesopotamian gods who frequently set up assemblies to settle disputes in a verbal manner (Pritchard 1958). The earliest examples of such myths known to us certainly date back to the third millennium BCE and can therefore be said to be in the order of four to five thousand years old. Contestation, as a verbal and conceptual product, is therefore rooted in the very origins of our society. In contemporary times, it is absolutely critical to democracies that break down when physical force is used. This entry will therefore be concerned primarily with contestation in the conceptual sense rather than in the gladiatorial sense. The claim made here is that politics is not related to war; it neither extends it nor is extended by war. Politics is primarily centred on speech. Arendt in *The Human Condition* (1958) made action the centrepiece of politics. Action was speech-dependant, and elsewhere Arendt argued frequently that speech in the public domain was almost synonymous with politics.

This observation made in 1958 is almost certainly a by product of the experience in the West of the Second World War, when politics between states and significant politics within states disappeared. Arendt was perhaps the first to note that contestation in the conceptual sense broke down in the presence of violence. This opened the way for a serious examination of contestation as the point of *agonia*, the agonistic moment between competing concepts held by different parties (see AGONISM). We can broaden the hypothesis out to argue that, with Nuremberg, everything changed. Nuremberg ended the Machiavellian concept of the state and replaced it with individual responsibility.

That individual responsibility implied that an individual had to argue for his or her own position or actions. In a sense, this was the apotheosis of Kantian individualism. However, that thesis while attractive and juristically correct fails to account for the fact that individuals occupy conceptual positions. This observation makes conceptual positions and concepts themselves significant in the domain of politics. It can be argued that Arendt's speech actor is not an individual completely but an individual occupying and utilising the conceptual equipment available to them. If this be the case then concepts become important components of contestation and the battle for control of concepts and conceptual meaning lies at the very heart of politics itself.

Some concepts in particular seem to be incapable of final definition. W.B. Gallie noted this in an article called 'Essentially Contested Concepts' (1955). Gallic argued that some concepts were essentially contestable, in other words their final meaning could never be settled. Examples he gave included science and democracy. This notion was later taken up by other writers who claimed that almost any number of concepts were essentially contestable. So Steven Lukes (1974), for instance, argued that power was an essentially contested concept, the examples could be multiplied endlessly. There is some confusion about what it is that is *essentially* contestable, a point made by Clarke (1979) who argued that there was a deep confusion in the idea that a concept could be essentially contestable and that it was the principle behind the concept that was contested and that essentialism should not apply to concepts themselves. Subsequently the idea of essentially contested concepts was eliminated in favour of the idea of the contestability of concepts, thus dropping the metaphysical baggage that went with Gallie's original notion. Contestability, therefore, has become once again the centrepiece of politics just as it was in the polis.

The difference between the modern concept of contestability and that which was found in the polis is that the modern concept allows the contestability of concepts to lie outside of, as well as within, the political arena. Therefore the family and CIVIL SOCIETY are potentially domains within which political contests can be fought. The notion can be taken even further to permit contestability to run through the very fabric of society itself. There is a sense in which one might argue that 'everything is up for grabs'. For some this is a happy situation, for it permits a quiet and bloodless revolution to occur. For others, it is an unhappy situation for exactly the same reasons. One solution to 'the everything is up for grabs' scenario is to argue that societies do hold certain things to be static. A prime example of this is in Richard Rorty's claim (1989: 73) that persons and, by extension, societies have a 'final vocabulary', and this 'final vocabulary', while groundless, is not negotiable. Thus LIBERALISM consists of certain precepts that are held without the possibility of further explanation. A 'final vocabulary' is justified merely by the appeal that it is he who argues or it is just the way we do things. Rorty takes this even further in arguing that liberalism is the last political revolution that we shall ever need. Contestability, therefore, within this view is limited not by an externally justified ground but by habit and sentiment.

In contrast to this liberal view, some postmodern Marxists have hijacked the notion of contestability and turned it to their ends. Their position is that if everything is up for grabs, then conceptual contests can be used as part of their armamentarium. On one view of this, individuals are points of linguistic construction and the radical revision of the language can bring about the radical revision in society. There are theoretical justifications to be found in Wittgenstein's *Philosophical Investigations*, where it is argued that the meaning of a word is its use.

An excellent example of this theoretical approach put into practice is the way in which feminists have altered language and through this the use of linguistic thought patterns and habits and practices. There is, perhaps, no more successful example of how the contestation of concepts can bring about real political and social change. Another example, which relies on a similar principle, is that of political correctness where some terms in the language were eliminated in the hope and expectation of changing political and social ideas. To some extent this succeeded, but it also became a victim of its own excesses.

Contestation, therefore, particularly the contestation of concepts, has been a powerful tool within the operation of liberal democracies. It is also open to the proponents of contestation to turn to the very meaning of democracy itself and here one has seen such a varied meaning put to the term democracy that at times the very term has become almost meaningless itself. Clearly this would be an unsatisfactory situation. No term can be subject to such multiple meanings as to be all-inclusive. It is important therefore in any conceptual contest that there be a relatively clear victor. It is also important to the operation of democracy that conceptual contestation across a fairly wide but bounded range of difference occurs in a peaceful manner.

See also:

democratic origins; identity, political; radical democracy

Further reading

Arendt, H. (1958) *The Human Condition*, Chicago: University of Chicago Press.

Clarke, B. (1979) 'Eccentrically Contested Concepts', *British Journal of Political Science* 9: 122–6.

Clarke, P.A.B. (1988) *The Autonomy of Politics*, Aldershot: Avebury, 145–57.

Gallie, W.B. (1955) 'Essentially Contested Concepts', *Proceedings of the Aristotelean Society* 66: 167–98.

Hobbes, T. (1968) *Leviathan*, ed. C.B. Macpherson, Harmondsworth: Penguin.

Lukes, S. (1974) *Power: A Radical View*, London: Macmillan.

Pritchard, J.B. (1958) *The Ancient Near East*, Vol. 1, Princeton, NJ: Princeton University Press.

Rorty, R. (1989) *Contingency, Irony and Solidarity*, Cambridge: Cambridge University Press.

—— (1991) *Objectivity, Relativism and Truth*, Cambridge: Cambridge University Press, 200–1.

Sophocles (1994) *Three Theban Plays*, trans. R. Fagles, New York: Quality Paperback Club.

Wittgenstein, L. (1968) *Philosophical Investigations*, Oxford: Blackwell.

PAUL BARRY CLARKE

contingency

The word 'contingent' is derived from adding the Latin *contingere*, to be contiguous, to the Latin *tangere*, to touch; hence the base meaning is to contiguously touch. The form of the touch can be logical, physical or metaphysical, and is opposed to necessity. Hence that which is contingent is happenstance, accidental or otherwise not necessary. By contrast, that which is necessary must be the case where the force of the must is logical or modal. A contingent statement can then be defined against its opposite as a statement whose falsity is not logically or modally precluded.

This arcane and rather dry formulation hides a deep problem for when applied to the question of existence it raises the issue as whether there must be anything at all or whether what there is is accidental. Basically, the most fundamental question of all is, 'why is there anything at all': the problem of contingency. The second and derivative question which gives rise to the problem of evil and of theodicy is why what there is is the way it is.

The two most fundamental questions, therefore, are the question of contingency and the question of evil. The first addresses the issue as to why there is is anything at all. The second addresses the question of why what there is the way it is. Contingency is the prime question: it is clearly simpler and less demanding that there be nothing rather than something. This abstract principle has fed into political and social thought as a direct opposition to necessity – the principle that things must be the way they are – hence, in the opposition between necessity and contingency, contingency seems to be the more powerful component. This is significant for it indicates that there is nothing fixed about social and political arrangements.

This conclusion is significant and recent. The problem of contingency is a modern/late modern problem; prior to that, contingency was applied to events in the universe but not to the universe as a whole. The implications of this myopia are significant for it implied that the fact of the universe and its course or trajectory could not be denied. If they could not be denied it was because they were necessary and unchallengeable, and if they were unchallengeable it was because they were given. The form of the given varied. In Ancient Greece, it was found in the idea of *oikonomoia* and right order, and the universe was structured in a strict hierarchy; in ancient Egypt, it was structured according to the rules laid down by the 'all Lord'; in ancient Mesopotamia, it was structured according to certain given principles of justice derived from the gods; and in the Christian reading of the Old Testament given by St Augustine, it was determined by the sins of Adam and the fall that followed.

Within the Western tradition of thought, two significant, yet variant, accounts of necessity can be isolated. The first is derived from Aristotle, the second from Augustine. Aristotle developed the teleological view that the outcome of an entity was contained within its origin. Combined with the Hebraic teleological/apocalyptic view of the universe, this led to the view that the first days contained the last days. In other words, the outcome was determined by its origins. St Augustine took the complementary view that the breaking of the prime interdict not to eat from the fruit of the tree of knowledge led to Adam's fall from grace. A consequence of this led to the doctrine of contrasting eternity against time. God therefore had foreknowledge of time, and the last days were contained in eternity. Put another way, the trajectory of the world and actions in the world were foreknown by God. Taken together these views of Aristotelian teleology, the Hebraic apocalyptic tradition and Augustine's doctrinal position led to a generalised view that the course of the world was determined by factors outside of the world.

This sacral doctrine – that the world had a certain course, which it was modally bound to follow – was secularised in the historical determinisms of Kant, Hegel and Marx. Hegel shifted the transcendent God to the immanent Geist whose unfolding would follow a path to absolute knowingness. Marx inverted the doctrine placing the unfolding in the material world.

Nonetheless all these attempts at historicising human existence in secular terms followed the basic pattern given in the Aristotelian, Hebraic and Augustinian model: namely, there was a given historical pattern that stood outside of significant human intervention. Kant, Hegel and Marx, in varying degrees, followed the sacral modal and were necessary rather than contingent. They were, in spite of their protestations, captive rather than free.

The discovery of history and historicism, the view that social facts are historically specific, effectively undercut the view that history had a pattern whose trajectory could be known by scientific analysis. Once social and historical facts are admitted as historically and socially located, an objective history becomes impossible. If an objective history is impossible then historical determinism is impossible. If historical determinism is impossible then the Hebraic–Aristotelian–Augustinian model collapses and the eschatological tradition which drove it also collapses. The upshot of this is that history, society and culture are the outcome of a set of contingencies rather than a set of necessities. History consists of a set of happenstances or accidents and not a set of necessities.

A clear consequence of this perspective is that there is no objectively given right order or hierarchy or set of precepts that exist and no laws or precepts of history that determine actions, or laws or government. The significance of the break from necessity to contingency in history cannot, therefore, be overestimated for it inverts the tradition of right order and given government to a condition in which order and government have to be created and have to be justified in their own internal terms and not in external terms. This is the democratic moment in history, theology, society, culture and eschatology: it is the moment of transition where what is given is replaced with that which has to be created.

The democratic moment replaces the given with the made and is the source of the OLIGARCHIC CRISIS typical of the mid-to-late twentieth century. Oligarchy depends on the claim that AUTHORITY is given and is well-grounded. When that claim collapses, so the foundations of authority collapse. One possible solution is a non-foundational authority. In theory, there are a number of ways in which this claim might be met. In practice, the best claim derives from the view that authority rests with the people. This claim is well argued from Marsilius of Padua, through to John Locke and into contemporary political theory. The argument usually takes the claim that they who are affected by government ought to have a voice in its selection and application of that government. Here we see natural law theorists break with the theory of right order and introduce the embryonic form of the democratic moment.

The democratic moment consists of three stages. First, there is the twelfth-century break with the social and structural given; second, there is the seventeenth-century break with the idea of right order; and finally there is the mid-twentieth-century break with necessity and the embrace of contingency. Each of these breaks, while separate, are of a piece in that they shift the balance of thought away from the idea of a given order – necessity – to the idea that order is to be given – contingency. The large effect of this is to diminish given authority and to produce the requirement for authority without foundations. This is the democratic moment for in democracy there are no external foundations, there is only the authority found in the people of the moment. A clear consequence of that is an identity crisis. If the democratic moment arises from contingency then identity is contingent. Who we are depends, therefore,

on the circumstances that surround us. We are no more than a contingent set of factors that happen to overtake and dominate us (see IDENTITY, POLITICAL). This argument to identity is frequently used and misused. Taken to its conclusion it leads to the mereological effect that every change, even to atomy, leads to a change of identity. In lesser form it leads to the claim that every change of circumstance leads to a change of identity. Thus if 'a' performs action 'x' rather than action 'y' on a specific day, 'a' changes identity and becomes a different person. It is unlikely that such a result is compatible with a stable democracy. A stable democracy most likely requires stable people. A mere mereology is not therefore sufficient to democracy, where some continuity is required.

This raises the second problem of identity. If we take the first problem as arising from mereology and its cognates, then identity will always be, in Hume's words, 'feigned'. On the other hand, if we take identity as given over time – as substantial – rather than feigned, then the situation becomes quite different and 'a' remains 'a' regardless of a change in circumstances.

At this point necessity intervenes, for it is necessarily the case that 'a' remains 'a' regardless of the change in circumstances. Translated into people talk, person 'a' remains as person 'a' regardless of a change in circumstances. In other words, circumstances may be contingent but people remain much the same. This distinguishes two cases of necessity, historical necessity and personal necessity. The former refers to the giveness of history; the latter refers to consistency of identity over time and space. These two cases are often confused. Historical necessity refers to the claim that history has a fixed course. This is the eschatological case found in the eschatological tradition backed up by Aristotelian thought. The first days contain the last days and the end of history can, in principle, be known, for it is necessary and not contingent.

The necessity of personal identity, however, merely refers to the continuation of substance over time. If mereology holds then identity does not hold and it is pointless, or at least mistaken, to talk of the same person existing past the moment. Identity would at best take the continuing form of Ia + Ib + I . . . n, where no I was identical. An alternative view takes it that identity continues through time and Ia and In are identical. This position holds particularly well when Ia and In are strongly connected and not radically different or disparate. It holds less well when a and n are radically different; for example, a baby initially brought up in one culture and then detached from that culture and brought up in another culture. Here we might find a middle ground and say that while I is purely attached, a and n are contiguously connected. The identity is necessarily connected at some deep level. Another way of putting this is to say that the same person is necessarily involved but the psychological identity is distinct but contiguously connected. Yet another way of putting this is to say that identity and necessity and identity and contingency can be connected in the same person.

This observation, together with the structural breakdown evident from the twelfth century and the decline of the eschatological–apocalyptic turn, was a condition of Western democracy. In other words, no contingency, no democracy. The democratic moment hangs most of all on the decline of necessity and the rise of contingency in an historical rather than in a personal sense.

Traditional modes of political order rested on some model of authority external to them: God, Right Order, external giveness, to mention a few examples. Such models are extant in the earliest known text circa 2000 BC and continue though until the seventeenth century when the fixed models broke down. The reasons for the breakdown are manifold, but prime among them is the death of God, the Protestant ethic and the general disbelief in external authority. Authority reached a crisis of credibility – it was not so much challenged, for a challenge requires reasons – as regarded with incredulity: its demise required no reasons to be given. Authority was mocked. And mockery

and laughter are powerful weapons against given authority.

There is another way of expressing this idea. History has been regarded as a given. Whether sacral or secular, it contained its own teleology within it. To say this is to say that history unfolds, or has a given course set down from the outset and that it will have an end. The end of history can be the second coming of Christ, *Moralitat*, *Sikklicheit* or communism, or whatever one will. Nonetheless, a definite and distinct end there will be. At this point while there may well be events, they will not form part of the engine of history. The engine of history will come to a halt and no significant change will take place thereafter. The last days will be the outcome of the first days, and this will be so because of teleology and necessity.

The argument to contingency challenges this in a variety of ways. Most fundamentally, it begins from the query, noted above, as to why there should be anything at all, especially given the energetic observation that it would be simpler for there to be nothing at all. Second, it introduces the claim that if the universe itself is contingent, then that which is in it is also contingent. This is not an overpowering argument, but it is clearly worthy of pause. It is logically possible, if odd, that a contingently produced universe could be necessary in its unfolding, i.e. it was teleologically determined such that its contingently existing first days necessarily produced its determined last days. This argument works quite well in cosmology but is weak in social and cultural history, which seems to be determined not at all, or at least minimally, by cosmology.

In social and cultural history, what is most impressive is the sheer happenstance, accident or contingency of events. That they seem to be so contingent rather than acts of necessity is due to the perspective of the 'death of God' and to postmodernism combined with the dominance of the secular argument over the sacral argument. Put another way, in a teleological argument, event 'b' at the end of history is conceived as being contained in event 'a' at the start of history; 'b' is thus necessarily determined by the characteristics of 'a'. In a non-teleological argument, 'b' is not a consequence of 'a' or any characteristics of 'a'. Since Nietzsche the perception of the death of God, secularisation and cognate arguments detach 'b' from 'a'. Hence, 'b' is self-contained yet open-textured: it is contingent in that it depends on its own merits and not on the contents of 'a', and it is open-textured in that it is not subject to any pre-given closure.

A similar argument applies to political, social and religious structure, all of which turn out to be interconnected. If political structure 'p' is detached from structures 's' and 'r', then 'p' is contingent. In all these examples, the latter may well be 'chained' to what has gone before but is not determined by it. They may also be genealogically related to each other, but the relation is always contingent, never necessary; an initial action 'a' did produce an event 'b', but it might have produced an event b1.

Clearly, this account needs modifying if it is to hold that the connection between some events is necessary. Events close to the laws of mechanics, for instance, carry a necessity within them that events in history do not. That said, some historical events will be more necessarily related than others and some social events will be more necessarily related than others. Each needs to be taken on a case-by-case basis. The fundamental mistake of the past is to relate all historical events necessarily or all social events or actions necessarily. That mistake is grounded theologically, backed up by Aristotelian teleology, Augustinian history and natural law theory. The break with this produces the possibility of democracy.

The break with necessity in history and in social structure, the end of the right order and the end of natural law, combined with the death of God, introduces an exceptional degree of uncertainty into social, political and moral life. The effect of this is to end grand foundations and reduce grand theory in history and in society. It is also to reduce, or even eliminate, foundation in authority. It is not entirely surprising, therefore, that the end of giveness characteristic of the late twentieth century went hand in hand with the crisis of authority in the nation-state. The upshot of that is the complete breakdown of the nation-state, even anarchical and nihilistic behaviour, or placing the LEGITIMACY of the nation-state on a new but foundationless basis. The most successful of these attempts has been democracy. Democracy provides legitimacy without foundations and is a reasoned and reasonable response to a world of contingency. Even the arch-positivist A.J. Ayer had to admit that there was no firm foundation, for 'there is no way of taking conclusively established pure protocol sentences as a starting point of the sciences. No tabula rasa exists'. Ayer likens us to sailors who have to rebuild their ship, not in a dry dock where they can pull it to pieces and use the best new materials to rebuild it, but on the open sea with the existing materials. 'Only the metaphysical elements can be allowed to vanish without trace. Vague linguistic conglomerations always remain in one way or another as components of the ship. If vagueness is diminished at one point it may well be increased at another' (Ayer 1959: 201).

Contingency makes for democracy. In the contingent society there are no foundations, no natural law, no right order, and no *oikonomoia* that precedes existence and gives it structure and meaning. Democracy is therefore its own self-contained legitimacy.

This would be impossible outside of a narrowly defined set of interests and perspectives, what the Greeks called *homonoia* or likemindedness. The conditions of modern democracy tend, however, to be based on *heteronomoia* or difference. Democracy requires, therefore, a set of ground rules and likemindedness about frameworks in order to allow the diversity to operate. The diversity is also limited by the ground rules, EQUALITY, RIGHTS, moderated MAJORITARIANISM, single voting, free elections, an adequate say in the actual operation of the democracy and so on. A set of historical and social conditions must therefore be met before democracy can flourish. Basic SOLIDARITY rules must exist. Given that these cannot be based on necessity or clear foundations, they must be based on worked out conditions contingently obtained.

There is an obverse set of conditions to this formula. If democracy is based on contingency, then contingency may well be the best (anti) foundation for democracy. Given the increase in contingency, it would be likely, therefore, to see a fourth wave of democratisation.

In sum, while it is possible to identify some relations as necessary, historical and social relations are largely contingent. The effect of this is to remove the ground from traditional modes of viewing historical and social relations. Where that ground is maintained or re-maintained, as for example in some theocracies, the argument for democracy is difficult to maintain; where that ground is absent, the argument to contingency, solidarity and democracy is easy to maintain.

See also:

autonomy; radical democracy; waves of democracy

Further reading

Ayer, A.J. (1959) *Logical Positivism*, Glencoe, NY: The Free Press.
Clarke, P.A.B. (1999) *Autonomy Unbound*, Aldershot: Ashgate.
Rorty, R. (1989) *Contingency, Irony and Solidarity*, Cambridge: Cambridge University Press.

PAUL BARRY CLARKE

corporatism

Derived from the Latin *corpus* (body), the term 'corporatism' broadly refers to the organisation and structure of economic interests along functional lines in society. Modern corporatist thought emerged in the mid to late nineteenth century in reaction to industrial CAPITALISM and political LIBERALISM. With antecedents in medieval Catholic social philosophy, corporatist thought depicted pre-industrial society as a harmonious and organic community divided into different functional categories such as serf

and landlord, under divine authority. Nineteenth-century corporatists observed that CLASS conflict and liberal INDIVIDUALISM eroded social harmony, engendered social injustice and created a society of selfish individuals. They advocated the establishment of collectivist and hierarchical institutions whose purpose was to address inequities and to restore social order and common purpose. The state had a central role in establishing these institutions because of its authority to intervene in society; because corporatist groups were unlikely to emerge without encouragement and assistance from the state; and finally because unregulated MARKET FORCES served neither the national interest nor producers under threat such as small business and peasants (Williamson 1989: 28). One of the most famous expressions of nineteenth century corporatist thought was Pope Leo XIII's 1891 encyclical *Rerum Novarum*, which called for the formation of associations of employers and employees, similar to the medieval guild system where artisans or merchants established organisations for mutual aid, the protection of members and the pursuit of common purposes.

This first version of modern corporatism, with its promise of a 'third way' between capitalism and socialism, reached the height of its popularity during the period between the First and Second World Wars. It was especially influential in western Europe, Latin America and Quebec, where strong Catholic traditions ensured that many corporatist ideas were put into practice. During this same period, a form of corporatism was practised in fascist Italy, where government incorporated producer groups as instruments of autocratic control over the economy and society.

Interest in corporatism was revived in the early 1970s, although theorists of 'neo-corporatism' stressed that their focus was the development of voluntary associations in advanced industrial societies and their relations with the state, rather than the 'authoritarian corporatism' of Mussolini's Italy, Petainist France or Salazar's Portugal. Neo-corporatists used terms such as 'societal corporatism' (Schmitter 1974) or 'liberal corporatism'

(Lembruch 1977) to describe a distinctive mode of policy formation where peak associations of business and TRADES UNIONS were closely involved with government in addressing issues such as economic growth, international competitiveness and structural adjustment.

Stemming in part from intellectual dissatisfaction with both PLURALISM and neo-Marxism, neo-corporatism sought a better understanding of INTEREST GROUPS, power and the nature and role of the state. Thus corporatism provides both a theoretical critique and an alternative understanding of POLICY-MAKING in capitalist societies. Its key analytical category is the organised functional group rather than the pluralist interest group or Marxian socioeconomic class. Consequently, corporatist analysis contends that there are fundamental differences in the organisational capacity and structure of different interests, depending on their role and function in the division of labour within the political economy. Corporatists also maintain that an interest group's ability to exercise political power depends on the extent to which it can concentrate, consolidate and regulate its membership. Where organised interests exercise monopoly representation in a particular functional category and are able to discipline and control their members, the state cannot impose policies unilaterally. Instead, the state must negotiate and bargain with these interests because policy implementation depends upon their co-operation. Cawson's useful summary (1986: 38) describes corporatism as 'a specific socio-political process in which organisations representing monopolistic functional interests engage in political exchange with state agencies over public policy outputs which involves those organisations in a role which combines interest representation and policy implementation through delegated self-enforcement'.

As a distinctive mode of policy formation in capitalist democracies, corporatist practices emerged for a variety of different reasons. Austria, Belgium and the Netherlands are often cited as exemplars of corporatist states, where corporatist patterns of co-operation were established to promote the reconstruction of economies destroyed by the Second World War. Corporatist arrangements have also been used by small, open, trade-dependent countries such as Switzerland as a means of facilitating continuous internal adjustment to fluctuations in world markets (Katzenstein 1985). In countries with relatively weak corporatist traditions at the macro-level, corporatist bargaining is often evident at the meso-level of the economy. For instance, in Australia, corporatist arrangements were used to promote structural adjustment in key manufacturing sectors in the 1980s (Capling and Galligan 1992). Finally, in many cases, economic development in East Asian economies has been fostered through the incorporation of peak producer groups, industrial conglomerates, trading companies and business organisations.

Critics argue that corporatism restricts democratic political PARTICIPATION to organisational elites, while marginalising or excluding other points of view and 'non-functional' interests such as the unemployed. In defence, there is evidence that corporatist bargaining improved the 'social wage', enhanced the power of trades unions, offered the possibility of workplace democracy, and generally shifted political power towards organised labour (Grant 1985: 23–6).

In the 1990s, the ascendancy of neo-liberal ideology was accompanied by the demise of organised labour as a social partner, and the replacement of tripartite corporatism with bipartite arrangements between the state and business, as exemplified in new forms of 'contractualism'. Nevertheless, corporatism has a tendency to emerge in response to the tensions created by capitalism and liberal individualism. Thus we are likely to see new forms of corporatism generated as a response to GLOBALISATION.

See also:

Asian models of democracy; Christian democracy; representation, models of; social democracy; state, models of

Further reading

Capling, A. and Galligan, B. (1992) *Beyond the Protective State*, Cambridge: Cambridge University Press.

Cawson, A. (1986) *Corporatism and Political Theory*, Oxford: Basil Blackwell.

Grant, W. (ed.) (1985) *The Political Economy of Corporatism*, New York: St. Martin's Press.

Katzenstein, P.J. (1985) *Small States in World Markets*, Ithaca, NY: Cornell University Press.

Lembruch, G. (1977) 'Liberal Corporatism and Party Government', *Comparative Political Studies* 10: 91–126.

Schmitter, P.C. (1974) 'Still the Century of Corporatism?' *Review of Politics* 36: 85–131.

Williamson, P.J. (1989) *Corporatism in Perspective: An Introductory Guide to Corporatist Theory*, London: Sage Publications.

ANN CAPLING

correlates of democracy

There is a well-known correlation between socioeconomic development and democracy. In studies from the 1950 onwards, various indicators of development – per capita gross national product (GNP), energy consumption, literacy levels and so on – have proved to be positively associated with democracy (see IN-DICATORS OF DEMOCRACY). A common method has been to measure (given some operational criteria) the degree of democracy in various countries at a certain point in time, and match it against said indicators of development. A clear correlation almost always appears in bivariate analyses, and a substantial correlation remains even after other factors of significance have been controlled for (Hadenius 1992; Vanhanen 1997). The mentioned factors also usually stand out in studies of the democratisation process, as well as in studies of democracy's rate of survival once established. Thus, can Huntington (1991) state that, in the transition from autocracy to democracy, the degree of economic development is an impor-

tant factor? At a certain stage – which in the mid-1970s came to a per capita GNP of between 1,000 and 3,000 US dollars – countries enter a 'political transition zone' in which democracy is often instituted. In cases where democratisation has already taken place, the risk is great that, as Adam Przeworski and his colleges (1996) have shown, the effort will fail if economic conditions are unfavourable. In their study of political conditions in 135 countries over forty years, beginning in 1950, the authors note that the probable life span for a democratic regime at a low level of per capita GNP (under 1,000 dollars) is substantially lower than that for a democratic regime at an intermediate level (4,000–6,000 dollars). And if a country's per capita GNP exceeds this intermediate level, experience shows, it is highly unlikely that democracy will fail. At this economic level, the success of democracy seems assured.

The usual reading of these findings is that social and economic development breeds democracy. This is the tenet of the so-called modernisation theory. The general thrust of this theory is that political changes in direction of democracy are the consequences of transformations in social and economic life. Basically, it is seen as a matter of broadening the access to political resources at the mass level. The improvement of the educational standard in society is a key factor in this regard. With economic development and increased national wealth, greater resources are available for raising the general educational level. As many studies of power and democracy have shown, EDUCATION is a very important political resource. This applies both in poor countries – where literacy is a strategic factor – and in rich ones. Studies of political PARTICIPATION in the USA today show that education is the most important variable governing whether or not citizens vote or otherwise engage in political activities (Verba *et al.* 1995; Diamond 1992; Hadenius 1992). By contributing to education and improved INFORMATION, economic development makes citizens politically stronger and more competent. The common people acquire resources with which to take part in political life. Demands are raised for broader participation. The result is a vitalised and more inclusive system of popular rule (see ECONOMIC REQUIREMENTS OF DEMOCRACY).

It should be noted, however, that there are important deviations from the general statistical pattern depicted above. There are relatively poor and undeveloped countries (such as India and Botswana) that have fared fairly well democratically. On the other hand, there are several extremely wealthy countries (like the oil states of the Arab world) which have remained deeply authoritarian. This indicates that the explanatory power of the theory of modernisation is limited. Its focus of explanation is at the individual level: how (through improved education and so on) the average citizen acquires political resources. When it comes to the collective resources needed to make democracy work – capacities of organising pressure from below and of effectively reconciling conflicts in society – the theory is less instructive.

A great body of literature has been devoted to pinpoint the existence of a relationship in the opposite direction: whether or not democracy favours economic development. For a long time, that was believed not to be the case. There is trade-off, a 'cruel choice', it was held, between democracy and economic growth. To uphold high levels of investments and professionalism in the area of economic planning, authoritarian modes of government (isolated from the demands of society) were to be preferred. Later – due to the many failures of authoritarian development model – a contrary theory was advanced. In view of this theory, TRANSPARENCY, ACCOUNTABILITY and the rule of law (see LAW, RULE OF) are essential for economic growth; and such qualities, it was believed, were much more likely to be upheld in democratic states.

Generally, however, only weak statistical links (if any link at all) have been demonstrated in empirical research into these questions (Helliwell 1993; Przeworski et al. 1996). The bottom line, it seems, is not democracy or not, but the quality of key institutions within the state apparatus; especially, I would assume, the professionalism, integrity and rule-governed governance among legal and regulatory administrative bodies, with which economic actors recurrently interfere.

In another field, we are much surer of the positive impact of democracy. This has nothing to do with economic matter, but rather with peace. It is empirically well-established that democracies are less prone to engage themselves in warfare. That concerns in particular the relationships between democracies themselves. In fact, over the last hundred and fifty years there has been no example of two democracies fighting each other. To explain this state of affairs, it has been suggested that in a democracy it is the citizenry, who will pay the price of war, that have the final say. Besides, the process of DECISION-MAKING is more open and transparent. Furthermore, contacts over state borders (especially at the elite level) are normally more developed among democracies (Russett 1993; see Russett's PEACE, DEMOCRATIC). When it comes to war, on the other hand, democracies have normally defeated their authoritarian adversaries. This, it has been maintained, is owed to the fact that democracies tend, as noted above, to be more developed economically, and hence in command of a better resource base. Thanks to a higher degree of LEGITIMACY on the part of the LEADERSHIP, democratic states also have a better capacity for mobilising the resources (both material and human) at hand. In addition, democratic states have proved more effective in striking alliances with other states, thus enhancing their martial potential (Lake 1992).

Finally, it should be noticed that (not surprisingly, perhaps) democracies have a far better record than authoritarian states in the area of human RIGHTS; they are even less prone to apply capital punishment. Overall, democracies treat their citizens more mildly, and they are generally more caring. The introduction of WELFARE policies (involving social security, unemployment schemes, medicare and so on) has historically, in many cases, followed in the train of democratisation (Flora and Heidenheimer 1981).

See also:

civil society; freedom; leadership

Further reading

Diamond, L. (1992) 'Economic Development and Democracy Reconsidered', in G. Marks and L. Diamond (eds), *Reexamining Democracy: Essays in Honour of Seymour Martin Lipset*, Newbury Park, CA: Sage Publications.

Flora, P. and Heidenheimer, A.J. (1981) 'The Historical Core and Changing Boundaries of the Welfare State', in P. Flora and A.J. Heidenheimer (eds), *The Development of Welfare States in Europe and America*, New Brunswick, NJ: Transaction Books.

Hadenius, A. (1992) *Democracy and Development*, Cambridge: Cambridge University Press.

Helliwell, J. (1993) 'Empirical Linkages Between Democracy and Democratic Growth', *British Journal of Political Science* 24: 225–48.

Huntington, S. (1991) *The Third Wave: Democratization in the Late Twentieth Century*, Norman, OK: University of Oklahoma Press.

Lake, D.A. (1992) 'Powerful Pacifists: Democratic States and War', *American Journal of Political Science* 86: 24–37.

Przeworski, A., Alvarez, M., Cheibub, J.A. and Limongi, F. (1996) 'What Makes Democracy Endure?', *Journal of Democracy* 7: 39–55.

Russett, B. (1993) *Grasping the Democratic Peace: Principles for a Post-Cold War World*, Princeton, NJ: Princeton University Press.

Vanhanen, T. (1997) *Prospects of Democracy: A Study of 172 Countries*, London: Routledge.

Verba, S., Lehman Schlozman, K. and Brady, H.E. (1995) *Voice and Equality: Civic Voluntarism in American Politics*, Cambridge, MA: Harvard University Press.

AXEL HADENIUS

corruption

Corruption involves the degeneration, perversion, defiling or tainting of something so that its naturally sound condition is debased. Political corruption involves the corruption of politics from its naturally sound condition. The clarity of this definition is clouded only by the fundamental disagreement over whether it makes sense to talk of politics having a naturally sound condition and, if it does, what that standard might look like. An additional difficulty is that on this understanding corruption is an irreducibly normative concept, which can be rendered scientifically precise only at the cost of cutting it off from its root sense.

The combination of normative and descriptive components dates back to ancient times when the corruption of the state was seen as involving the subversion of the well-ordered state by stasis or faction, leading to the displacement of politics by disorder and tyranny (Dobel 1978). In contrast, Hobbes rejected an Aristotelian view of the nature of politics and insisted on a strict nominalism with respect to corruption, treating it as simply the expression of a speaker's dislike of certain actions or consequences (Euben 1989). However, even on a Hobbesian view we have to find a way of distinguishing the subset of cases we call political corruption from the broader set of cases of conduct of which we disapprove, and to do that we have implicitly to appeal to some account of the nature of public office and the public interests it serves.

Political scientists in the 1960s and 1970s sought to deal with the difficulties involved in reaching an objective definition of political corruption by emphasising different aspects of the political process. Three main definitions emerged: public office, public interest and market accounts (see Heidenheimer 1970; Heidenheimer *et al.* 1989). Public office definitions identify corrupt behaviour with officials acting in ways which deviate from their formal public role, and with the intent to secure certain

private gains. For public interest accounts, corruption exists whenever a responsible official
is induced by the promise of certain rewards
not legally provided for to act in ways which
favour the provider of the rewards, and thereby
to damage the public and its interests. But the
two definitions are inevitably interdependent.
The public office account, in which corruption
involves deviation from the formal duties of the
public role, also insists that this deviation be
for private regarding gains, thereby covertly
introducing the distinction between public and
private interests (see PUBLIC–PRIVATE DISTINC-
TION). Similarly, public interest conceptions
depend on there being an understanding of
public office in which the substitution of
private for public interests can be recognised
as corrupt.

Market definitions of corruption are associated with theorists who draw on the methods
and principles of economics and rational actor
theory. Corruption is seen as an extra-legal way
of gaining influence over DECISION-MAKING, or
as occurring when a public official turns his or
her office into an income-maximising unit.
However, although market-centred approaches
offer one way of understanding corruption,
they are not a way of defining it (Philp 1997).
What defines an act as corrupt is not that it is
income maximising, but that it is income
maximising in a context where prior conceptions of public office and the principles for its
conduct define income-maximising as corrupt.

Although there are clear links between
public office and public interest accounts of
corruption, the stumbling block to further
agreement on a definition of political corruption is the issue of who or what authoritatively
determines norms for the conduct of public
office or for the content of the public interest.
Alternative definitions of corruption, which
use public opinion or legal norms as the
criteria for corruption have been proposed,
but neither provides a secure basis. It is
implausible to think that public opinion is
always (or ever) agreed on such complex issues
as norms of political conduct, or that consensus is the same as correctness. It is also
evident that the supreme case of corruption is

where those in power set up laws and institutions in ways that serve their individual or
group interest. This means that, while we can
recognise the centrality of public office and
public interest, it is not immediately obvious
how we should give content to these concepts.

Despite these difficulties, there are cases
which we can recognise as incontestably
corrupt. Core cases of corruption usually
involve five key components:

1 a public official (A), who acts
2 in violation of the norms of public office
3 and in a manner which harms the interests of
the public (B)
4 in a way which knowingly exploits the office
for clear personal and private gain in a way
which runs contrary to the accepted rules
and standards for the conduct of public
office within the political culture
5 so as to benefit a third party (C) who
rewards A so as to gain access to a good or
service which C would not otherwise obtain.

The difficulties we have identified with the
definition of corruption arise from ambiguities
and opacity in the way that we identify public
officials, their roles, and the rules governing
their official conduct; and from the fact that
each criterion is intelligible only against the
background of a POLITICAL CULTURE in which
there are clear shared norms and rules governing the conduct both of public officials and of
members of the public in their dealings with
these officials. In less ordered contexts, the
identification of political corruption becomes
correspondingly difficult.

We can add to these difficulties if we follow
Dennis F. Thompson in distinguishing between
individual and institutional corruption. Individual corruption broadly meets the five criteria
listed above: it violates rules of office intentionally for personal gain for the office holder
by rendering illicit service to a third party.
'Institutional corruption' benefits the office
holder politically rather than personally. The
service provided is corrupt not because it is, in
itself, illicit, but because its 'institutional
appearance' or 'institutional tendency' is such

as to suggest that such services can be obtained in ways which are not in keeping with democratic standards. 'We have to show only that a legislator accepted the gain and provided the service under institutional conditions that tend to cause such services to be provided in exchange for gains' (Thompson 1995: 30). The concept of institutional corruption relies on normative judgements as to the essential nature and purposes of democratic political systems, with the result that it extends the scope of the definition of political corruption without automatically increasing its determinacy.

The desire for a universally applicable definition of corruption has encouraged many political scientists to stipulate a definition for the sake of operational utility. This has resulted in complex and sophisticated, but often deeply suspect, cross-national comparisons and indices of corruption, which in turn have fostered a substantial amount of speculation about the causal conditions for corruption. Such endeavours lack sensitivity to different cultural practices and the clear and relatively exacting standards for the conduct of public office found in most advanced democratic states leave most newly developing states faring badly on such indices: less because they are corrupt, and more because they do things differently. This is not an argument against such standards, but it counsels caution as to universalisability. Similarly, standards cannot be imposed wholly by legislation. Indeed, in so far as political standards are treated as hard and fast rules to be enshrined in legal codes prescribing official conduct, they are likely to create perverse incentives and to issue in greater corruption than more 'honour-based' systems which acknowledge that the trust associated with political office is inevitably ethical and informal in kind. Hence the increasing concern in many modern democratic systems with codes of good practice for public officials and politicians, rather than formal statute law (ICAC 1993; Nolan Committee 1995) (see STANDARDS OF CONDUCT IN PUBLIC LIFE).

The problems of definition and comparison are most acute in contrasts between stable Western democracies and societies where strong patrimonial, patron–client, tribal or communal traditions determine access to political power and govern its exercise. Rather than applying the standards of the former to the latter, we should be asking, in the latter case, not so much whether the fragile political system is corrupt, as whether the existing system offers the best prospect for ordering conflict in the society, and whether its attempts to order such conflicts are systematically undermined by the suborning of the political process by individual or group interests which that process is intended to constrain. In such a case it makes sense to talk about the corruption of politics. In contrast, where there is no recognition of a need for a political order, with public offices, formal rules of conduct and a sense of the public interest, the fact that distributions and allocations take place on non-political criteria does not mean there is corruption: allocations within families rely on other principles, but that does not make them corrupt. It is political corruption only where a political order, which expresses the aspirations of some significant part of the culture, and offers a way of reconciling conflicts which alternative modes are acknowledged to exacerbate, is disabled from functioning through its subversion by other orders or systems of exchange. Understanding corruption in such terms draws on the classical tradition, by emphasising the disorder caused by faction, and by insisting that what is distinctive about politics is its attempt to create and sustain a legitimate order of rule for potentially conflicting groups and individuals. It is possible in abstract terms to identify when politics, in this sense, is desirable and possible, and when it is being corrupted. But it is always a more local and culturally relative matter as to what in practice necessitates that order, what threatens it, and what sorts of standards are necessary to preserve it. Few studies of political corruption acknowledge the difficulty of such judgements, but those which do are testimony to the potential richness, both of the subject matter, and of the discipline of politics itself (for example, Chubb 1982).

See also:

accountability; authority; democratic audit; legitimacy; transparency

Further reading

Chubb, J. (1982) *Power, Poverty and Patronage in Southern Italy*, Cambridge: Cambridge University Press.

Dobel, P. (1978) 'The Corruption of a State' *American Political Science Review* 72: 958–73.

Euben, J.P. (1989) 'Corruption', in T. Ball, J. Farrar and R. Hanson (eds), *Political Innovation and Conceptual Change*, Cambridge: Cambridge University Press.

Heidenheimer, A.J. (ed.) (1970) *Political Corruption*, New York: Holt, Rinehart and Winston.

Heidenheimer, A.J., Johnston, M. and LeVine, V.T. (eds) (1989) *Political Corruption: A Handbook*, New Brunswick, NJ: Transaction Publishers.

ICAC (1993) *Defending the Fundamental Political Values of the Commonwealth against Corruption*, New South Wales: Independent Commission Against Corruption.

Nolan Committee (1995) *Standards in Public Life: First Report of the Committee on Standards in Public Life*, London: HMSO, Command 2850.

Philp, M. (1997) 'Defining Political Corruption' *Political Studies* 45(3): 436–62.

Thompson, D.F. (1995) *Ethics in Congress: From Individual to Institutional Corruption*, Washington, DC: Brookings Institute.

MARK PHILP

cosmopolitan democracy

The history of democratic political thought and practice has been marked by two great transi-tions. The first led to the establishment of greater PARTICIPATION and ACCOUNTABILITY in cities during antiquity and, again, in Renaissance Italy; the second led to the entrenchment of democracy over substantial territories and time spans through the invention of representative democracy. From the early modern period to the late nineteenth century, geography could in principle be neatly meshed with sites of political power, AUTHORITY and accountability. Today, this is no longer the case. In the context of intensifying regional and global relations, ques-tions are raised about the limits and efficacy of national democracies. The possibility of a third great transition is put on the agenda: a transition to a multilayered democratic world embracing national, regional and global fora. This possibi-lity can be referred to as 'cosmopolitan democ-racy' (see Archibugi and Held 1995; Held 1995; Archibugi *et al.* 1998).

When city-republics and nation-states were being forged, the idea of democracy could be readily connected to a determinate group of people – a group of citizens – who lived in a bounded social and geographical space. While the notion of who constitutes 'the DEMOS' was always contested, it was rarely considered (and then only by exception, for instance, in the case of travellers and settlers from amongst one's own people) that the demos might include those beyond a delimited set of territories. A self-determining people could rightly set a city's or nation's fate; it was taken for granted that the political good could be deliberated upon and articulated in relation to a particular political community in a delimited terrain. Although the boundaries of such communities often remained quite fluid until the entrench-ment of the modern state system (and still are fragile in some parts of the world), the theory of democracy as it developed assumed that a satisfactory account of democracy could be derived by examining the interplay between 'rulers' and 'ruled' in a delimited political space. There was, and ought to be, democratic theorists argued, a symmetrical and congruent relationship between political decision makers and the recipients of political decisions.

We live now in the age of national democracies, or so it seems. In the mid-1970s, over two-thirds of all states could reasonably be called authoritarian. This percentage has fallen dramatically; less than one-third of all states are authoritarian and the number of national democracies has been growing rapidly. Democracy has become the fundamental standard of political LEGITIMACY in the contemporary era (see Potter *et al*. 1997). But just when the idea of national democracy has gained ground around the world, and when more national communities have began to hold their governments to account, the understanding of political community has become clouded by the increasingly intensive interconnections among communities. While more countries seek to establish national democracies, powerful forces – affecting social, economic, cultural and environmental welfare – now transcend the boundaries of nation-states (see NATIONS AND NATIONALISM).

A more extensive and intensive pattern of interconnectedness among the world's peoples has emerged, a pattern which can be referred to under the heading 'GLOBALISATION'. Globalisation is made up of the accumulation of links across the world's major regions and across many domains of activity (Held *et al*. 1999). It can be related to many factors including the rapid expansion of the world economy. For example, world trade has grown enormously; the world's financial systems are now more integrated than ever before, with over 1.5 trillion dollars changing hands daily in the foreign exchange markets; and multinational companies are centrally involved in national and international economic transactions. In addition, a denser pattern of interconnectedness also prevails as a result of environmental politics, human RIGHTS regimes, international law and many other factors. Although these developments fall far short of creating an integrated world order, they have significant political and democratic consequences.

The theory of cosmopolitan democracy takes as its starting point the increasingly complex interconnections among nation-states. This is no longer a world of relatively 'discrete civilisations' or 'discreet political communities'; rather, it is a world of 'overlapping communities of fate', where the fate of nations is significantly entwined. In the past, nation-states largely dealt with issues which spilled over boundaries by pursuing 'reasons of state', backed ultimately by coercive means. But this power logic is singularly inadequate and inappropriate to resolve the many complex issues, from economic regulation to resource depletion and environmental degradation, which engender an intermeshing of national fortunes.

The notion of cosmopolitan democracy recognises our complex, interconnected world. It views certain policies as appropriate for local governments or national states, others as appropriate for particular regions, and still others – such as the environment, world health and economic regulation – that need new institutions to address them. Democratic, deliberative DECISION-MAKING centres beyond national territories are appropriately situated when those significantly affected by a public matter constitute a cross-border or transnational grouping, when 'lower' levels of decision-making cannot manage and discharge satisfactorily transnational or international policy questions, and when the principle of democratic legitimacy itself can only be properly redeemed in a transnational context.

Put differently, a cosmopolitan democracy describes a world where citizens must come to enjoy multiple citizenships: in their own communities, in the wider regions in which they live and in a form of cosmopolitan global community (see CITIZENSHIP; CIVIC VIRTUE). Institutions need to be developed that reflect the multiplicity of issues, questions and problems which affect and bind people together irrespective of where they were born or reside. Cultural nationalism remains central to people's identity; but political nationalism – the assertion of the exclusive political priority of national identity and national interests – cannot alone deliver many sought-after public goods and values without regional and global collaboration. Only a cosmopolitan political outlook can ultimately accommodate itself to the political challenges of a more global era, marked by overlapping communities of fate and multilayered (local, national, regional and global) politics.

Environmental problems provide an obvious illustration. For example, factories emitting toxic waste must be locally monitored and challenged, nationally regulated and supervised, regionally checked for cross-national standards and risks, and globally evaluated in the light of their impact on the health, WELFARE and economic opportunities of others. Toxic waste disposal and global warming are examples of two pressing issues that require local as well as global responses if their consequences are to be contained and regulated. Democracy can only be adequately developed if such a division of powers and competencies is recognised.

In this conception, the nation-state 'withers away'. But this is not to suggest that states and national democratic polities become redundant. Rather, states can no longer be the sole centres of legitimate power within their own borders, as is already the case in diverse settings. States need to be articulated with, and relocated within, an overarching democratic framework. Within this framework, the laws and rules of the nation-state would be but one focus for legal development, political reflection and democratic mobilisation.

Thus, SOVEREIGNTY would be stripped away from the idea of fixed borders and territories. Sovereignty would become an attribute of democratic principles and arrangements; and it could be entrenched in diverse self-regulating realms, from local associations and cities to states and regions, leading to the recovery of an intensive and participatory democracy at local levels as a complement to the public assemblies of the wider global order.

Accordingly, advocates of cosmopolitan democracy maintain that democracy needs to be thought of as a 'double-sided process'. By a double-sided process – or process of double democratisation – is meant not just the deepening of democracy within a national community, but also the extension of democratic forms and processes across territorial borders. Cosmopolitan democracy proposes a series of short-term and long-term measures in the conviction that, through a process of progressive, incremental change, diverse geopolitical forces can be brought into the sphere of democratic agency and practice (see Held 1995: Part III). Such a policy of democratisation might begin, for example, in key regions by creating greater transparency and accountability in leading decision-making centres. In Europe this would involve enhancing the power of the European Parliament and reducing the DEMOCRATIC DEFICIT across all European Union institutions. Elsewhere it would include restructuring the UN Security Council to give developing countries a significant voice in decision-making; deepening the mechanisms of accountability of the leading international and transnational public agencies; strengthening the enforcement capacity of human rights regimes (socioeconomic as well as political), and creating, in due course, a new democratic UN second chamber.

Objectives such as these point toward the establishment of new forms of accountability at regional and global levels. In short, they define necessary elements of a cosmopolitan democracy. Faced with overlapping communities of fate, citizens in the future must become not just active citizens of their own national communities, but also of the regions in which they live and of the wider global order. Without such developments, democracy risks becoming an anachronistic form of rule progressively out of step with a more intensively regional and global world, in which many central and pressing issues escape the boundaries of the nation-state.

See also:

green democratic thought; nations and nationalism; social democracy

Further reading

Archibugi, D. and Held, D. (eds) (1995) *Cosmopolitan Democracy*, Cambridge: Polity Press.

Archibugi, D., Held, D. and Köhler, M. (eds) (1998) *Re-imagining Political Community: Studies in Cosmopolitan Democracy*, Cambridge: Polity Press.

Held, D. (1995) *Democracy and the Global Order: From the Modern State to Cosmopolitan Governance*, Cambridge: Polity Press.

Held, D., McGrew, A., Goldblatt, D. and Perraton, J. (1999) *Global Transformations: Politics, Economics and Culture*, Cambridge: Polity Press.

Potter, D., Goldblatt, D., Kiloh, M. and Lewis, P. (eds) (1997) *Democratization*, Cambridge: Polity Press.

DAVID HELD

D

decentralisation

Forms of decentralisation

Decentralisation is one of the more emotive terms in politics, almost rivalling democracy and equality in the heat it can produce. Not only is decentralisation 'good', but centralisation is definitely 'bad' (Fesler 1965). It is a romantic term, offering the prospect of the 'good society'. Some care over terms is, therefore, important. Figure 1 illustrates the several uses of decentralisation.

Decentralisation refers to the distribution of power to lower levels in a territorial hierarchy whether the hierarchy is one of governments within a state or offices within a large-scale organisation (Smith 1985: 1). Or, more briefly,

it refers to the areal division of powers. So defined, the term encompasses both political and bureaucratic decentralisation, federal and unitary states, and decentralisation between levels of government and within units of government.

Deconcentration, sometimes referred to as field administration, involves 'the redistribution of administrative responsibilities... within the central government' (Rondinelli and Cheema 1983: 18). A broad distinction can be drawn between prefectoral and functional systems. In the prefectoral system, a representative of the centre – or the prefect – located in the regions supervises both local governments and other field officers of the centre. S/he is the superior officer in the field, embodying 'the authority of all ministers as well as the

x(8)

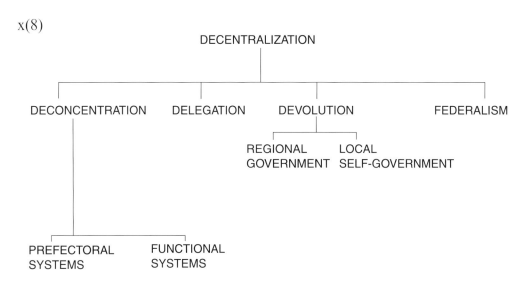

Figure 1 Forms of decentralisation

government generally and is the main channel of communication between technical field officials and the capital' (Smith 1967: 45). The classical examples are the French prefect and the collectors or district commissioners in India. In the functional system, field officers belong to distinct functional hierarchies. The administration of the several policy areas is separate. There is no general, regional co-ordinator; co-ordination occurs at the centre. This system of multifarious functional territories is typified by Britain.

Delegation refers to 'the delegation of DECISION-MAKING and management authority for specific functions to organisations that are not under the direct control of central government ministries (Rondinelli and Cheema 1983: 20). Such organisations are referred to as parastatal organisations, non-departmental public bodies or quangos (quasi-autonomous NON-GOVERNMENTAL ORGANISATIONS). They include public corporations and regional development agencies. This category is also used to cover the transfer of functions to the private sector or voluntary bodies through marketisation, privatisation or contracting-out, cumbersome neologisms which refer to the various ways of delivering 'public' services using markets or quasi-markets. Decentralisation understood as managerial delegation and marketisation has fuelled major reforms of the public sector throughout the world in the 1980s and 1990s.

Devolution refers to the exercise of political authority by lay, mainly elected, institutions within areas defined by community characteristics (Smith 1985: 11). Thus, 'local units are autonomous, independent and clearly perceived as separate levels of government over which central authorities exercise little or no *direct* control' (Rondinelli and Cheema 1983: 22). The *locus classicus* of devolution is said to be British local government. Up to this point, the discussion has focused on the decentralisation of bureaucratic authority, on service-defined areas. With devolution, the discussion turns to the decentralisation of political authority either to local or regional government. As the term 'regional government' is

used to refer to the reform of local government, it is not possible to draw a consistent distinction between these two levels of government. The distinction is necessary because there was a significant spread of regional government in the 1980s in western Europe.

Federal states (see FEDERALISM) are normally seen as more decentralised than unitary states with devolution to local governments. Two notes of caution are in order. First, the formal division of powers in a federal constitution can differ from the practice of federalism. The federal government can exercise great influence and control over the states. Second, the degree of devolution in a unitary state can be large as for Northern Ireland between 1920 and 1973. In other words, it is unwise to assume, as Figure 1 implies, there is a continuum of decentralisation from deconcentration to federalism. It is much more important to question whether 'there is anything about a federal constitution which is important for the way in which intergovernmental relations are conducted' (Smith 1985: 15).

Problems of decentralisation

There are three repeated claims made for decentralisation: that it promotes democracy, improves efficiency and checks central power. Each claim raises important problems.

Doctrine

Liberal democracy assumes that decentralisation promotes democratic participation, especially local self-government. Nationally, decentralisation is said to promote political education, training in political leadership and political stability. In local government, it promotes the values of equality, accountability and responsiveness (Smith 1985: 20). Thus, John Stuart Mill argues in his *Considerations on Representative Government* (1861) that: 'It is but a small portion of the public business of a country, which can be well done, or safely attempted, by the central authorities', and, 'all business purely local...should devolve upon the local authorities' because they are 'most competent in details and executive officers are under popular control'. Most importantly, local representative bodies are also the 'chief instrument' of political education (Mill 1977: Ch. XV).

However, there is no necessary link between decentralisation and democracy. Decentralisation can exist without local democracy and the practice of local democracy often falls short of the theory. Thus, Rallings *et al.* (1996: 64) show how turnout rates in local ELECTIONS range from 80 per cent in Denmark to 40 per cent in Britain and 25 per cent in the USA. One-party rule, local oligarchies and exclusion of the poor are all too common features of local 'democracy'.

In developing countries, local self-government also failed to meet expectations. Thus, Olowu (1987: 5–6) concludes African local governments are in practice only extensions of central state bureaucracy and should be described as local administration systems and Smith's (1985: 188–91) bald and brutal assessment is that experience 'has almost everywhere fallen far short of expectations'.

Management

In developing countries, decentralisation is the fashion for several reasons. First, it is seen as a way or surmounting the limits of national planning by getting closer to problems, cutting through red tape and meeting local needs. Second, it improved central 'penetration' of rural areas, spreading knowledge of and mobilising support for the national plan and bypassing obstructive local elites. Third, it encouraged the involvement of various religious, ethnic and tribal groups, promoting national unity. Fourth, it increased the speed and flexibility of decision-making, encouraging experimentation and reducing central control and direction. Fifth, it increased the efficiency of the centre by freeing top management from routine tasks and reducing the diseconomies of scale caused by congestion at the centre. Sixth, it increased the administrative capacity of the localities and regions and improved the co-ordination or service delivery. Finally, it

institutionalised PARTICIPATION, provided opportunities for many interests to get a 'stake' in the system, trained citizens for democracy and politicians for government and promoted political maturity and democratic stability (paraphrased from Rondinelli and Cheema 1983: 14–16; and Smith 1985: 186–8).

Theory and practice diverged markedly and rapidly. There is a battery of constraints on effective decentralisation. Rondinelli and Cheema (1983: 27–30) conclude the effective implementation of decentralisation policies needs: (1) an understanding of a nation's political structure, its dominant ideology, policy-making processes and local power structures; (2) the interaction and co-ordination of many organisations at several levels of government which depends, in turn, on clear objectives, standardised budgeting, accurate COMMUNICATION and effective linkages; (3) sufficient financial, administrative and technical support with control over such resources and national political support; and (4) agencies with the proper technical, managerial and political skills and the capacity to co-ordinate and control sub-unit decisions. These political factors, organisational factors, financial and human resources, and behavioural conditions necessary to implement decentralisation successfully are conspicuous primarily for their absence. Thus, Mawhood (1983: 7) talks of the 'chaotic inefficiency of decentralised government'.

Old faiths die hard. Decentralisation in its various forms has been a central part of recent attempts to reform the public sector in developed countries. Known as the new public management (NPM), this term refers to a focus on management, not the areal distribution of governmental power. The key elements are performance appraisal and efficiency; disaggregating public bureaucracies into agencies which deal with one another on a user-pay basis; the use of quasi-markets and contracting-out to foster competition; cost-cutting; and a style of management which emphasises output targets, limited-term contracts, monetary incentives and freedom to manage. It is a policy ambition for international organisations like the OECD and the World Bank. It is marketed throughout the world. But there is precious little evidence on the effects of these reforms on the performance of the governments of developed countries, and a growing body of evidence that it has adverse effects on the capacity of the centre to steer. The shift from line bureaucracies to fragmented service delivery increased government dependence on networks of organisations drawn from the public, private and voluntary sectors. Such trends make steering more difficult. Attempts to strengthen central strategic capacity did not match managerial delegation. Decentralisation and NPM lie at the heart of the shift from government to governance or steering networks through indirect management (Rhodes 1997).

Similarly, the fashion for governance in developing countries shows no great changes in either democratic participation or government performance. Crook and Manor (1995: 330) conclude that any claim that democratic decentralisation improves governance in developing countries should be treated with some caution, because the complex, demanding conditions necessary for its success are rarely found. The reasons for this failure are clear; decentralisation cannot be reduced to a set of management techniques because its origins, form and outcomes are powerfully shaped by the political context in which it is put into practice.

Politics

Decentralisation is frequently said to be the counterweight to central power, but the purposes and outcomes of decentralisation vary with its political context. Governmental traditions shape meanings and expectations. The policy can increase participation or help central elites keep control. It can empower local people or sustain local oligarchies. There follow three observations on current trends.

First, managing the balance between centralisation and decentralisation is an endless task. Any change in the distribution of power between levels of government will provoke a response. Local and regional territorial elites will react to any increase in the power of the centre which affects their interests. Centralisation prompts a territorial response. As Sharpe (1979: 20) argues, the trend to decentralisation is a product of an ever greater centralisation: it is 'a *reaction* to centralisation and not a mere epiphenomenon of it'.

Managerial decentralisation clearly sought to get the state out of service delivery; to steer rather than to row. Similarly, the spread of regional government in Western Europe, most notably in France, Italy and Spain but also including devolution to Scotland, can be so interpreted. But greater decentralisation brings with it demands for better co-ordination, improved government regulation and greater capacity to steer. In effect, the centre strikes back.

Second, managerial decentralisation will also provoke a political response, a shift from decentralising to democratising service delivery. Thus, Burns *et al.* (1994) detect a trend away from the market-inspired decentralisation to the customers of public services towards the empowered citizen and neighbourhood decentralisation. Similarly, Bang and Sørensen (1999: 3) describe the 'Everyday Maker' in Danish governance as self-reliant individuals who learn the skills of negotiating, contracting, managing and leading by handling the everyday problems and disputes of low and functional politics. They focus on immediate and concrete policy problems and espouse such political maxims as: 'Do it yourself', 'Do it where you are', 'Do it for fun', 'Do it part time', 'Show responsibility for and trust in yourself', and 'Show responsibility for and trust in others'. As Stoker (1999) points out, the beneficial, unintended consequence of the NPM reforms was not efficient service delivery but the rise of local governance.

Third, developing countries differ markedly from the differentiated polities of advanced industrial democracies, but still we export western management techniques with a monumental insensitivity to the differences in political context. As Smith (1985: 203) argues, we must consider decentralisation in the context of a wider structure of power. So, where centralisation and authoritarian elites coexist with scarce resources, do not expect to see a significant redistribution of power to sub-national territories. If decentralised structures develop a degree of autonomy, they may conflict with existing patterns of domination, provoking repression. Alternatively, decentralised structures can be used to exert more effective local control. Decentralisation is thus a mask covering widely differing objectives, and to look behind the mask we must ask whose interests it serves.

Summary

If this discussion of decentralisation and democracy suggests a maxim, it is 'he who says decentralise says change the distribution of power'; no easy task. But equally, as James Madison argues in *The Federalist* (1887), 'The accumulation of all powers, legislative, executive and judiciary, in the same hands...may justly be pronounced the very definition of tyranny'. So we end where we began – with doctrine – for the heart of the debate about decentralisation does not lie in desiccated analyses of the conditions favouring managerial delegation but in the belief that it a bulwark against central power.

See also:

authority; market forces; state, models of

Further reading

Bang, H.P. and Sørensen, E. (1999) 'The Everyday Maker: a New Challenge to Democratic Governance', *Administrative Theory and Praxis* 21(3): 325–41.

Burns, D., Hambleton, R. and Hoggett, P. (1994) *The Politics of Decentralisation*, London: Macmillan.

Crook, R.C. and Manor, J. (1995) 'Democratic Decentralisation and Institutional Performance: Four Asian and African experiences Compared', *Journal of Commonwealth and Comparative Studies* 33(3): 309–34.

Fesler, J.W. (1965) 'Approaches to the Understanding of Decentralisation', *Journal of Politics* 27: 536–66.

Mawhood, P. (1983) 'Decentralisation: The Concept and the Practice', in P. Mawhood (ed.), *Local Government in the Third World*, Chichester: John Wiley, 1–24.

Mill, J.S. (1977) *Essays on Politics and Society*, London: Routledge and Kegan Paul.

Olowu, D. (1987) 'African Local Government Since Independence' *Planning and Administration* 14(1): 5–7.

Rallings, C., Temple, M. and Thrasher, M. (1996) 'Participation in Local Elections', in L. Pratchett and D. Wilson (eds), *Local Democracy and Local Government*, London: Macmillan, 62–83.

Rhodes, R.A.W. (1992) 'Intergovernmental Relations in Unitary Political Systems', in M. Hawkesworth and M. Kogan (eds), *The Routledge Encyclopaedia of Government and Politics*, London: Routledge and Kegan Paul, 316–5.

—— (1997) *Understanding Governance: Policy Networks, Governance, Reflexivity and Accountability*, Buckingham: Open University Press.

Rondinelli, A. and Cheema, G.S. (1983) 'Implementing Decentralisation Policies: An Introduction', in P.A. Rondinelli and G.S. Cheema (eds), *Decentralisation and Development*, London: Sage, 9–34.

Sharpe, L.J. (1979) 'Decentralist Trends in Western Democracies: A First Appraisal', in L.J. Sharpe (ed.), *Decentralist Trends in Western Democracies*, London: Sage, 9–79.

Slater, D. (1990) 'Debating Decentralisation: A Reply to Rondinelli', *Development and Change* 21: 501–12.

Smith, B.C. (1967) *Field Administration*, London: Routledge and Kegan Paul.

—— (1985) *Decentralisation: The Territorial Dimension of the State*, London: Allen & Unwin.

Stoker, G. (1999) 'Introduction: the Unintended Costs and Benefits of New Management Reform for British Local Government', in G. Stoker (ed.), *The New Management of Local Governance: Audit of an Era of Change in Britain*, London: Macmillan.

R.A.W. RHODES

decision-making

In an ideal typical way, there are two basic motives with which politicians may approach a decision situation. They may take their preferences as fixed, and then they try to use the best strategy to maximise the chances that their preferences prevail. In other words, they pursue their self-interest and try to win by all means (Riker 1962). In the other ideal typical way, participants in political decision-making are discursive rather than strategic actors. They are open to the possibility to change their preferences during the decision process. They are willing to listen to reasoned arguments of other actors. As a consequence, a sustained discourse develops on what is good for all participants (Habermas 1996). In real decision-making situations, these two ideal types are mixed to various degrees. In order to understand political decision-making, one must not only consider the motives of the participants but also the rules governing the decision process. The most important rules are voting, consensus, and interpretation. The two basic motives play out differently depending on what DECISION-RULES are used. This shall be discussed for each decision-rule at a time.

Voting

The decision-rule may require that a formal vote be taken, either by a showing of hands or by ballot. In order to win, it may be sufficient to have the most votes, what is called the plurality of the votes. The requirement may be set higher in the sense that the winning side needs a majority, half of the votes plus one. Sometimes the requirement for winning may even be higher, when a qualified majority must be attained, which means some specified number more than a majority; for example, two-thirds of the votes. In the Belgian parliament, decisions on language issues require a two-thirds majority. When a majority is required, the voting rule must establish how actors are counted who abstain or who are not present at the meeting. In the French National Assembly, the opposition needs a majority of the total membership, present or absent, to win a vote of no confidence. This is a more difficult requirement than in Sweden, where absent and abstaining members are not counted for a vote of no confidence. Such nuances in voting rules may seem trivial, but many empirical examples show they may be of crucial importance for the survival or the downfall of a government (Steiner 1998: 86–87). In most decision-making situations, each vote has the same weight; but there are notable exceptions to this rule. In the Council of Ministers of the European Union, the votes of the individual countries are weighted according to population; Germany as the largest country has ten votes, Luxembourg as the smallest has three. Voting is more complicated when more than two alternatives are under debate. Here, the outcome may very well depend on the specific voting procedures. Assume there are three alternatives: A, B, and C. If a plurality is sufficient to win, there is no problem since the alternative with the most votes wins. But if a majority is required, none of the three alternatives may reach this threshold. Then the two leading alternatives may be pitched against each other in a second vote. Another procedure is to have first a vote between A and B and then the winner against C; the first vote may also be between A and C or between B and C and then the winner against the remaining alternative. Depending on the procedure, a different alternative may win. If the participants disagree on the voting rules, they may first have to vote on these rules. But they may disagree on how to vote on the voting rules, which may make voting impossible as the decision on how to vote is pushed further and further back.

When the participants in a decision situation are strategic actors in the sense that they take their preferences as fixed and try to win by all means, there is the danger that the losers become frustrated by the voting rules. This danger is minimised if the losers have a good chance of being among the winners any time soon. But if the losers lose time and again, their frustration may endanger the stability of the country. This was the case in Northern Ireland, where the Catholics as the minority lost virtually all the votes against the Protestants. By 1968, the frustration of the Catholics had become so great that widespread violence broke out. When the participants in a decision situation are discursive actors who are willing to listen to each other and to change their preferences, the danger of inefficiency comes up since the decision process may become too lengthy. On the other hand, the outcome of the decision may be more readily accepted by the losers since their demands have been considered by the winners. Even if the demands of the losers ultimately have no influence on the decision outcome, the losers may not be too frustrated since they were listened to with respect (Steiner 1996).

Consensus

The decision-rule may require that a consensus be attained before a decision can be enacted. Meetings of the Quakers are governed by this rule. In Poland before its division in the eighteenth century, tax increases required consensus in the responsible decision-making body. In the Council of Ministers of the European Union, issues that are of vital interest to at least one of its member states must be made by consensus. Consensus can be reached by a unanimous vote; it is then a special case of a qualified majority vote in the sense that the majority required to win is 100 per cent. Consensus can also be attained by a verbal expression of consent, nodding, and so on. When the participants in a decision-making situation act strategically, a decision-rule of consensus means that actors supporting the status quo have a veto position. They can refuse consent, and failure to reach a decision means that the status quo remains intact. Discursive actors, on the other hand, are willing to listen and to yield to others, so that the supporters of the status quo have no particular advantage (see CONSENSUS DEMOCRACY).

Interpretation

A decision by interpretation occurs when one of the participants interprets what he or she considers to be the sense of the discussion, and this interpretation is then tacitly accepted by the others. The chairperson may provide the interpretation as part of the final summary of the discussion. Such decisions by interpretation often take place in the British cabinet. Richard Crossman, who was himself a cabinet member, states in his memoir that one of the prime minister's chief jobs in a cabinet meeting is to decide when it is appropriate to come to a decision. The prime minister then provides a two-part summary of the meeting, stating the conclusions reached and the course of action to be taken (Crossman 1972). A decision by interpretation can also be made in the drafting of the minutes. This too is a common pattern in the British cabinet, where minutes often record not what was decided but what should have been decided; what Crossman calls the decision-drafting technique. The most complex and intriguing decision by interpretation occurs when a powerful actor tacitly interprets the group's decision and directs the discussion in such a way that the decision is made implicitly. This author has observed such decision-making in the Swiss Free Democratic Party (Steiner and Dorff 1980). For example, in the party's parliamentary group, actor A proposed that the government issue a bond for highway construction. This proposal was supported in order by actors B, C, D and E. Actor D also introduced a procedural matter, recommending that the parliamentary group submit a corresponding motion in parliament. After these five actors, F spoke, opposing a highway bond. At this point, the process took a decisive turn: B again took the floor, bypassed the question of whether a bond should be issued, limiting himself to the procedural matter; he argued against D that instead of a motion a simple remark in the parliamentary debate would be sufficient. The rest of the discussion concentrated on this procedural matter, while the basic question of whether a bond should be issued was not raised again. This decision of principle had in effect been made when B managed to turn the discussion away from the question of principle to one of procedure. Actor B had interpreted that the group supported the bond. Actor F, the only one who had expressed opposition to the bond, chose to remain silent for the remainder of the discussion.

If interpretations are made by strategic actors, a strongly manipulative element may enter the decision process. Inexperienced actors may fail to realise what is actually happening when decisions by interpretations are made. When they become aware that a decision has been made, they may find it awkward to reopen the discussion. Belatedly contesting a decision by interpretation often runs against the prevailing social norm. As a result, many participants feel pressure to accept a decision by interpretation in a tacit way. In extreme cases, the interpreter may be so powerful that nobody dares contest his or her interpretation; the interpreter can impose his or her preferences. By contrast, if the participants are discursive actors, an interpreter with much wisdom may be able to take account of how well the different arguments are reasoned and with what intensity they are supported. With such wise interpretations, a decision may occasionally also go to an otherwise neglected minority, which may increase the legitimacy of the decision-making process among such minorities.

Critique of research praxis

Empirical research on decision-making is to a large extent based on the assumption that decision-makers have fixed preferences and that they try to maximise their individual utilities in striving for decision outcomes as close as possible to their preferences. Modern political philosophy, by contrast, is dominated by an ethics of the public discourse, where decision-makers are willing to listen to each other and to change their preferences during the decision process. These ethicists, however, hardly ever engage in empirical research to find out to what extent their normative views of decision-making correspond to political reality.

What is needed is an intensive dialogue between these two sub-disciplines of political science. We need empirical studies inspired by the normative questions of modern philosophy. We need to know to what extent, under what circumstances and with what consequences political decision-makers are strategic or discursive actors.

See also:

chaos and coalitions; coalitions; democratic debate; minorities; pluralism

Further reading

Crossman, R. (1972) *Inside View*, London: Jonathan Cape.

Habermas, J. (1996) *Between Facts and Norms: Contributions to a Discourse Theory of Law and Democracy*, Cambridge, MA: MIT Press.

Riker, W. (1962) *The Theory of Political Coalitions*, New Haven, CT: Yale University Press.

Steiner, J. (1996), *Conscience in Politics*, New York: Garland.

—— (1998) *European Democracies*, 4th edn, New York: Longman.

Steiner J. and Dorff, R.H. (1980) *A Theory of Political Decision Modes*, Chapel Hill, NC: University of North Carolina Press.

JÜRG STEINER

decision-rules

A series of tensions have been identified between the arrangements commonly associated with a capitalist market economy and the electoral decision processes taken to be at the heart of liberal democracy. Marxist scholars have long claimed that the inegalitarianism of CAPITALISM, in which reward accrues systematically to the CLASS owning the means of production, cannot be reconciled with any form of majoritarian political system (for a survey, see Przeworski 1991). In the 1970s, with the onset of sustained economic difficulties in many advanced industrial democracies, concerns about whether capitalism could be reconciled with democratic institutions intensified. James O'Connor (1973) argued that the state would face an entrenched fiscal crisis as public expenditures outstripped revenues. In *Politics and Markets*, Charles Lindblom (1977), from a pluralist perspective, outlined the apprehension that the demands of economic efficiency meant that the interests of capitalists must come before those of the electorate. Other writers argued that government was becoming overloaded with a plethora of demands it could never meet. Samuel Brittan (1977) concluded that the direct consequence of unconstrained electoral competition was the development of political PARTIES which offered more and more in terms of material benefits to voters without regard for the provision of such public policies. Some scholars suggested that these difficulties were ingrained and cyclical: a political business cycle had emerged synchronised with the electoral cycle in which booms and busts would come before and after ELECTIONS on a predictable basis. At their darkest, such writers suggested that liberal democracy was unstable and suboptimal: the competition for votes would lead political actors to damage the efficient and free workings of the market economy. Unsurprisingly, such approaches were often associated, in the United Kingdom at any rate, with the political right.

Rules versus discretion

In 1977, Finn Kydland and Edward Prescott, two economists in the United States, published a paper which, arguably at any rate, had as much impact over the next quarter of a century on public policy as the arguments noted above (for surveys, see Blackburn and Christensen 1989; Snowden and Vane 1999). Kydland and Prescott's concern was with 'time inconsistency': what was an optimal decision for a government at one point in time might subsequently cease to be the best and most rational course of action. It appears obvious to state that any administration might reorientate its trajectory away from its original commitments.

The startling insight contained in Kydland and Prescott's argument related to the impact of such realignment on other actors in the economy. For example, a government might enter office promising a tough anti-inflationary stance. As its term of office neared its end and re-election loomed, however, the administration might conclude some relaxation of its commitment to price stability was sensible to ensure re-election. Political actors would have both the incentive and the opportunity to spring an inflationary surprise upon actors in the private sector. Given the assumption of rational expectations (that is, that actors are reasonably well informed and able to process information efficiently), Kydland and Prescott concluded that private agents would quickly anticipate such a surprise. Unsure about the government's true intentions, they would assume the worst from the outset of its election to office. Those responsible for investment decisions would be cautious and risk averse; those seeking wage increases would be likely to maximise money incomes. As a result, investment would be reduced and money wage demands would escalate. The argument need not be restricted to anti-inflationary measures: it can be generalised to cover any government intervention in the economy in which the response of private actors is strategic (that is, depends upon the stance taken by the public authorities). At an extreme, the implication was that an unconstrained government was likely to damage the workings of a free market: the economy's performance would be suboptimal. Government policy statements would not be credible because actors would not trust them. Public promises would not be believed because of the risk that subsequently they would be broken. Though the argument was presented in a politically neutral fashion, the consequences for left-wing parties are intuitively manifest: social democrats are unlikely to be able to manage an economy efficiently because the simple fact of their being in office will depress investment regardless of what they promise to do and regardless of whatever modest commitments they offer.

Kydland and Prescott's argument, presented

here in a simplified (and perhaps politicised) form, rapidly became part of mainstream orthodox economics. Economists came up with two broad forms of solution to the sub-optimality engendered by time inconsistency. The first solution argued that it was mistaken to conceive of the relationship between political actors and those in the private sector as a one-off game. (The relationship is often conceived of as a game between players in which each act strategically, thus allowing analysis using the standard tools of game theory; see Backus and Driffill (1985).) A better approach was to see it as a repeated game in which politicians, voters, capitalists and workers interacted repeatedly over and over again at each and every election. The effect of such repeated interactions was that trust could be built up between politicians and other actors. The politicians would cease to have any incentive to spring a surprise change of policy on the others because it would not be in their long-term interest so to do. It might pay short-term dividends but any administration attempting a surprise would surely be punished at the next opportunity. The problem with this solution is straightforward: it is by no mean obvious how any government can either establish trustworthiness in the first place or sustain a reputation for it over time. In the absence of such a reputation, private actors will continue to assume the worst: unconstrained DECISION-MAKING will persist in fuelling suboptimal economic outcomes.

The case for and against decision-rules

The alternative solution, one favoured by many economists, is to limit the decision-making powers of a government by adopting some form of decision-rule. Essentially such a limitation can be enacted in two ways: either the government can be constrained constitutionally so that explicit limits are placed on its decisions, or decision-making in the relevant area can be delegated to a new body, one that will not be liable to the same incentives as an elected AUTHORITY. In this context, a decision-rule can be defined as a legally binding

regulation which limits the authority of a democratic government (or similar body) either by delineating explicit limits to its capacities or by delegating its powers to other bodies which enjoy considerable AUTONOMY. For example, legal rules might be introduced to direct the state to certain outcomes and close off others. Alternatively, the government might be tied to some form of external constraint such as the gold standard or the European exchange rate mechanism. Public policy would have to be aligned to meet the demands imposed by the constraint. Under the second form of this solution, a central bank might be established charged with the promotion of low inflation. Such a body would be uninterested in manipulation of the economy for electoral purposes and would control important areas of public policy such as the setting of interest rates. The advantage of this form of solution is that, by reducing the government's domain of discretion, it prevents an administration from being tempted. Some empirical studies conclude, for example, that central bank independence is associated with lower rates of inflation (see, for example, Alesina and Sumners 1993). Kydland and Prescott argued directly that: 'By relying on some policy rules, economic performance can be improved' (1977: 473).

An alternative account, from the perspective of political philosophy, of the need for binding rules to guide decisions, is given by Jon Elster in *Ulysses and the Sirens* (1979). He argues that individuals might choose voluntarily to bind themselves to decision-rules in their own interest. He concludes that individuals' preferences are malleable: they are often subject to weakness of the will whereby a change in context will lead to a different ranking of objectives, albeit probably only in the short term. Binding constraints may be needed to secure maximum benefits in the long term: Ulysses must bind himself to the mast of his ship if he is to hear the sirens without dashing the boat onto the rocks as his preferences shift.

There are, however, drawbacks to solutions that seek to limit the discretionary powers of a government. Supporters of the need for decision-rules are concerned by their permanence.

Given the nature and authority of the state, it is hard to bind it irreversibly: constitutions can be amended, gold standards left and independent bodies wound up. Short-term pressures may be alleviated, but credibility concerns about the future intent of any administration may persist. Such apprehension may be particularly germane in cases, such as that of the United Kingdom, where the constitution is neither entrenched nor formally codified. If rules cannot be entrenched, they may not be effective.

The issue of public ACCOUNTABILITY raises a very different and significant concern with decision-rules. Such rules are, of course, designed deliberately to reduce the accountability of a government to the electorate because political actors are perceived to be able to manipulate and distort the processes by which they are held to account. Once a government gives up discretion (either constitutionally or through delegation), it is difficult to blame it alone for policy outcomes in the area under consideration. An administration may even be able to use decision-rules to disguise its own poor performance by blaming outcomes upon either constitutional constraints or other institutional bodies. (There may be alternative routes to accountability; for example, the use of a regulatory processes and the development of parliamentary scrutiny.) A belief in the efficacy of decision-rules presupposes a large degree of consensus as to which public policies should be adopted to deal with which collective goals. In the case of price stability, however, there remains disagreement as to how inflation is best tackled and what level is tolerable for the efficient operation of the economy. Such disagreements make the design and implementation of decision-rules extremely difficult. The delegation of authority to new independent bodies may indicate an unwarranted faith in the ability of experts; for example, economists to manage issues.

Allied to the question of accountability is that of whether such decision-rules can be flexible in the face of the kind of stochastic shocks to which any economy is liable. Exogenous shocks may require atypical policy responses (for example, the suspension of constitutions and the overrule of independent authorities). The initiation of atypical policies may, however, mask unjustified government attempts to break the decision-rule: they need not be a response to the impact of an external shock. In such circumstances, the government will depend upon its policy signals being accurately and rapidly interpreted: private individuals without full information may be unable to discover if changes to announced strategy are either understandable responses to the unforeseeable or unacceptable attempts to distort public policy. A further problem is that the operation of decision-rules may lead to co-ordination problems with other areas of public policy. The government may delegate authority over anti-inflation policy to a central bank while pursuing a permissive fiscal policy. Policy incoherence might result. Overall, such concerns suggest that decision-rules are no guarantee of optimal economic outcomes, and they remain controversial in terms of their impact on democracy.

Decision-rules in practice

The relevance of the rules versus discretion debate that Kydland and Prescott initiated for contemporary politics is immediately apparent. Such ideas have been incorporated into many approaches to public POLICY-MAKING. The Maastricht treaty, under which European Monetary Union was agreed, laid out strict and binding criteria, in an attempt to prevent any state being tempted to pass the costs of high public spending onto other states. For members of the single European currency, monetary policy is determined by an independent European central bank, one that will not be tempted to launch inflationary surprises and can be trusted by all in its anti-inflationary intent.

The significance of these ideas in politics in the United Kingdom is also evident. In the 1980s and early 1990s, given its radical past, the Labour party found it difficult to demonstrate the extent and permanence of its transformation for private agents who doubted its credibility and trustworthiness. It was not enough for Labour simply to adopt a series of modest policies and assume that other actors would adjust their attitudes accordingly. Equally, many did not believe the party's commitment to the rules of the European exchange rate mechanism. Labour needed to convince these actors about the durability of its conversion: it had to establish credibility. What mattered was not just the party's policy statements but its ability to inform, to generate trust with other agents and so foster trustworthiness (Wickham-Jones 1995).

Under Tony Blair's leadership between 1994 and 1997, Labour took considerable trouble to attain credibility. The party laid out a detailed and coherent set of moderate measures, including the proposed adoption of an open system of policy-making under which markets could observe the way that economic decisions were made. Such a transparent system would allow private agents to trust Labour, as there would be no confusion about its true intent from such signals: it could secure a reputation for honesty and probity. This approach emphasised the need to develop the reputation of the party's leaders in repeated interactions. It rejected formal decision-rules. Instead, politicians sought to bind themselves to a modest trajectory in advance of entering office: the cumulative impact, they hoped, of such uncompromising and comprehensive proposals was that any change of direction could not occur without a catastrophic loss in credibility.

In office, however, Tony Blair's New Labour adopted a different approach to demonstrate the probity of its intentions. On 6 May 1997, Gordon Brown, the new Chancellor of the Exchequer, informed the Bank of England that he was handing over operational independence for the conduct of monetary policy to it. A non-elected monetary policy committee made up of five bank officials and four outsiders would take decisions about interest rates. With this approach, the Labour government accepted the imposition of a rules-based approach rather than seeking to build up gradually a trustworthy reputation through repeated interactions. The adoption of rules

was not confined to monetary policy: Labour also adopted a code of fiscal responsibility that laid out a series of guidelines, designed as binding, for the conduct of public spending. Monetary and fiscal policy rules have been in place for a relatively short time in the United Kingdom: press reports have suggested occasional tensions between some members of the government and the newly established monetary policy committee over the latter's decisions to raise interest rates. Whether such a pattern of decision-making and the accompanying reduction in accountability becomes an issue at a future election remains to be seen.

Conclusions

Support for the adoption of decision-rules, especially in the pursuit of price stability, reflects a number of issues. Most notably, of course, many economists doubt the resolution of politicians to sustain anti-inflationary measures in a range of public policies. At another level, the case for decision-rules reflects the difficulty in establishing and sustaining trust between individual actors in a market economy. It is the absence of trust that leads private agents to adopt risk averse and potentially suboptimal strategies. The significance of trust for the efficient operation of the economy has not gone unnoticed by political theorists. Proponents of SOCIAL CAPITAL argue that high levels of trust improve the functioning of the economy by reducing transactions costs between private agents. In such a situation, they claim that the solution to tensions between market economies and liberal democratic arrangements may not be the adoption of rules but the extension of social capital in the form of improved trust.

See also:

market forces; state, models of

Further reading

Alesina, A. and Sumners, L. (1993) 'Central Bank Independence and Macroeconomic

Performance: Some Empirical Results', *Journal of Money, Credit and Banking* 25(2): 151–62.

Backus, D. and Driffill, J. (1985), 'Inflation and Reputation', *American Economic Review* 75(3): 530–8.

Blackburn, K. and Christensen, M. (1989) 'Monetary Policy and Policy Credibility', *Journal of Economic Literature* 28(1): 1–45.

Brittan, S. (1977) *The Economic Consequences of Democracy*, London: Temple Smith.

Elster, J. (1979) *Ulysses and the Sirens*, Cambridge: Cambridge University Press.

Kydland, F. and Prescott, E. (1977), 'Rules Rather than Discretion: the Inconsistency of Optimal Plans', *Journal of Political Economy* 83(3): 473–91.

Lindblom, C. (1977) *Politics and Markets*, New York: Basic Books.

O'Connor, J. (1973) *The Fiscal Crisis of the State*, New York: St. Martin's Press.

Przeworski, A. (1991) *The State and the Economy under Capitalism*, New York: Harwood Academic Press.

Snowden, B. and Vane, H.R. (1999) *Conversations with Leading Economists*, Cheltenham: Edward Elgar.

Wickham-Jones, M. (1995) 'Anticipating Social Democracy, Pre-empting Anticipations: Economic Policy-Making in the British Labour Party, 1987–1992', *Politics and Society* 23(4): 465–94.

MARK WICKHAM-JONES

deliberative democracy

Deliberative democracy is a conception of democratic politics in which citizens or their accountable representatives seek to give one another mutually acceptable reasons to justify the laws they adopt. The reasons are not merely procedural ('because the majority favours it') or purely substantive ('because it is a human right'). They appeal to moral principles (such as basic liberty or equal opportunity) that citizens who are motivated to find fair terms of cooperation can reasonably accept.

A theory of deliberative democracy usually contains both a set of principles to evaluate actual democracies, and a specification of a process to realise the principles. The principles include some familiar ones from theories of JUSTICE, such as liberty and equality, as well as others more common in theories of democracy, such as ACCOUNTABILITY and publicity. In a deliberative theory, the content and interpretation of these principles are subject to the deliberative process, which in turn is evaluated by the principles. Deliberative democracy therefore should not be identified with the process itself: its principles are no less important than its process.

Deliberative democracy is distinguished from theories that rely primarily on procedures that aggregate the preferences of citizens (such as most varieties of procedural, aggregative, pluralist and game theoretic approaches). These theories tend to treat preferences as given, turning them into collective decisions through processes such as voting or bargaining. Without rejecting these processes, deliberative democracy provides critical standards for assessing preferences, and encourages the possibility of changing them through political discussion. Deliberative democracy also differs from theories that take fundamental rights as given, and designate them as constraints on democratic DECISION-MAKING (such as natural law conceptions and many forms of CONSTITUTIONALISM). Deliberative democracy accepts the idea of rights but permits their interpretation and application to be challenged by means of deliberation in the political process. Although at any particular time, some rights are protected from majoritarian decision-making, rights are not always and completely insulated from deliberative democratic processes.

Origins

The roots of deliberative democracy can be found in fifth-century BC Athens, which according to Pericles looked to mutual discussion not as a 'stumbling-block in the way of action' but as an 'indispensable preliminary to any wise action at all' (Thucydides II.40). Aristotle was the first theorist to explain the value of a process in which citizens publicly discuss and justify their laws to one another. In Book III of the *Politics*, he argued that ordinary citizens debating and deciding together can reach a better decision than experts acting alone. Aristotle had in mind a small DIRECT DEMOCRACY acting in assembly, not the large representative democracy that came to characterise democratic practice in modern times.

Yet the idea of deliberation persisted, often contrasted with populist forms of democracy. In England, the term 'deliberative' was used to refer to political discussion as early as 1489. In the eighteenth century, notable moments include Edmund Burke's 'Speech to the Electors of Bristol' (Burke 1959), in which he proclaimed that 'Parliament is a deliberative assembly', and the *Federalist Papers*, which defended a system that 'combined deliberation and democracy' (*The Federalist* 1961). In the nineteenth century, John Stuart Mill (1865) was a leading advocate of 'government by discussion', in part as a means for limiting the dangers of human fallibility.

In the early part of the twentieth century, the core ideas of deliberative democracy can be found in the writings of John Dewey, Alf Ross and A.D. Lindsay, who regarded political discussion as 'the essential of democracy' (Thompson 1970: 86). The theory of deliberative democracy enjoyed a significant revival in the last two decades of the century, stimulated by the work of Jürgen Habermas (1996).

Varieties

Deliberative democrats differ about how to characterise the theory, and these differences yield several different versions of the theory. The first difference is over whether and to what extent ordinary citizens should participate directly in making their laws. Most deliberative democrats defend some kind of *representative* democracy, and therefore do not require ordinary citizens themselves to take part in public deliberations (see REPRESENTATION, MODELS OF). On this view, citizens rely on their representatives to do their deliberating for them, but representatives are expected not only to deliberate among themselves but also to listen to and communicate with their constituents, who hold them accountable. Some deliberative democrats favour a more *participatory* form of government. They argue that more direct PARTICIPATION by ordinary citizens in POLICY-MAKING is an important part of the value of deliberative democracy. James Fishkin's procedure of deliberative polling – which assembles a random sampling of citizens to discuss policy positions of competing candidates – offers a way of partially reconciling the deliberative value of direct participation with the necessities of representative democracy in modern society (Fishkin 1995).

A second difference is whether deliberative democracy requires actual or hypothetical deliberation to justify laws. Theorists who favour *actual* deliberation do not insist that citizens or their representatives deliberate about every decision, but they do require that those decisions that have not resulted from deliberation be subject to challenge in a deliberative process, unless such a process has determined that they should not be so subject. On the *hypothetical* approach, one imagines what citizens or their accountable representatives would decide under ideal conditions, instead of the real conditions of unequal power in existing societies. An advantage of making some room for hypothetical deliberation is that theorists can correct for the results of actual deliberations that unfairly disadvantage certain groups such as minorities and women. A disadvantage is that theorists may substitute their own contestable views of what is just for the views of the people who are to be bound by the decision. These two approaches are reconcilable to the extent that deliberative democracy requires actual deliberation but assesses the conditions under which it takes place according to critical standards of hypothetical deliberation.

A third difference divides deliberative democrats who value deliberation only as a means of arriving at good policies, and those who value deliberation also as an expression of mutual respect among free and equal citizens. On the first view, sometimes called the *epistemic* approach, deliberating about political issues has no value in itself. It is simply the best means of arriving at the most justifiable political ends. On the second view, which emphasises the *intrinsic* value of deliberation, reaching the right result in politics entails the deliberative act of justifying the result to the people who are bound by it. Deliberation is not only instrumental to achieving a desirable outcome, but it also in itself expresses mutual respect among citizens. The epistemic approach is not mistaken in attributing instrumental value to deliberation, but according to the intrinsic approach view neglects its other values.

Criticisms

Critics of deliberative democracy question both its feasibility and desirability. One of the most common objections to deliberative democracy is that it requires too much of citizens. It seems to presuppose that ordinary people value political activity in general, and deliberation in particular, more than they do. To place so much emphasis on the need for more deliberation in democracy is to give political activity an importance that it does not have, except perhaps for a few, primarily people who are drawn to politics or political theory as a vocation. Furthermore, it falsely assumes that nearly everyone is capable of the complex and dispassionate reasoning that deliberation seems to require.

Deliberative democrats reply that deliberative democracy (even in its participatory forms) does not require ordinary people continually to fly to the assemblies, as Jean-Jacques Rousseau once urged, and some civic republicans still advocate. Nor does deliberative democracy require every decision to be discussed by everybody. Accountable representatives are responsible for making most political decisions. It is true that ordinary citizens must be willing and able to hold their representatives accountable, and this accountability requires some substantial understanding of politics. But most

citizens are able to assess at least in general terms the reasons that their representatives give, or fail to give, in justifying laws. To the extent they are not able to do so, any democracy, not only the deliberative forms, is deficient. Furthermore, deliberative democracy makes room, no less than most other forms of democracy, for emotional appeals and passionate rhetoric, as long as they are consistent with its basic principles such as liberty and opportunity.

A second problem raised by critics is that even if deliberative democracy is feasible, it may not be desirable under current social conditions. In many modern societies, citizens who already enjoy the advantages of wealth, power and status are likely to dominate public deliberations. Relying on deliberation under such conditions, critics suggest, is a formula for perpetuating an unjust status quo. To deal with this problem, deliberative democrats specify conditions of basic liberty and opportunity under which all deliberation should ideally take place. But since people reasonably disagree about the content and interpretation of the ideal conditions, deliberative democrats cannot avoid the need to deliberate under non-ideal conditions, which by their own admission are less than fully justifiable. The existence of systematic, institutionalised injustice seems to create a vicious circle of moral reasoning from which deliberative democracy cannot extricate itself.

Deliberative democrats reply that even under non-ideal conditions, deliberation can make a positive contribution to the elimination of injustice, at least compared to feasible alternatives. When prevailing injustices primarily benefit a dominant social group, deliberation can often bring this problem to public attention. Under conditions of inequality, relying on other forms of power is likely to reinforce the existing distribution of benefits and burdens in the society. The power of reason is less directly tied to this distribution, and therefore has the potential to challenge it. Moreover, deliberation seems a more promising way of dealing with injustice than the usually available alternatives, such as decision-making by political elites (who are often the source of the problem) or bargaining among INTEREST GROUPS (which usually reproduce the prevailing inequalities). Under some conditions (when, for example, part of the adult population is excluded from the electorate), the political process may be so contaminated by injustice that the practice of deliberation can have no positive effect. Even so, principles of deliberative democracy – such as public accountability and basic liberty and opportunity – may be invoked to criticise the injustice, without necessarily prescribing the practice of deliberation. The best means of promoting deliberative democracy in the future may sometimes require refraining from deliberation in the present.

A third objection accepts the idea that deliberation is possible and desirable, but complains that deliberative democrats give it too much attention relative to other political activities. Compared to organising, mobilising, demonstrating, bargaining, lobbying, campaigning, fundraising and voting, deliberating does not seem to be a very common or significant form of political action. Why single it out for such special attention? Deliberative democrats reply that deliberating is not just another activity on the list. It provides the means by which the justifiability of the other activities can be determined. Deliberative democracy does not require that all political activities in all places at all times be deliberative. But it does demand that they should be assessed by deliberative principles. Informed by deliberative principles and practices, citizens can modify and improve these other activities, making the routines of bargaining, campaigning, voting and other such activities more public-spirited in both process and outcome.

Institutions

Because deliberative democracy supplements rather than supplants the procedural and constitutional values of more conventional theories of democracy, it endorses familiar institutions that support both fair procedures and individual rights. But deliberative democracy also recognises that important moral questions – including questions about what constitute fair procedures and individual rights – cannot be removed from everyday democratic politics. It therefore supports institutions that enable citizens and public officials to deliberate about their disagreements on these constitutional questions as well as ordinary legislation. Citizens and their representatives, not only judges, should attend to the fundamental values of democratic government.

Deliberative democracy expresses a dynamic conception of politics. As a result of deliberation, the principles and practices that are justified at any particular time may be revised and replaced by different principles and practices over time. Political institutions should therefore allow for the provisional nature of principles (and the decisions they justify) by providing institutional opportunities for regular reconsideration of decisions. Deliberative democrats support reiterative processes in which proposals are modified through a sequence of responses and counter responses. They also tend to favour more flexible procedures for constitutional amendments and more frequent use of devices such as sunset laws that force review of policies. They do not encourage the use of referenda, unless they take place (as they usually do not) under conditions that permit serious deliberation about the issue in question.

Because deliberative democracy assumes that moral disagreement will persist, it seeks institutions that enable citizens to live with it on moral terms. The agenda of democratic theory therefore should give more attention to a wide range of ordinary political phenomena that can facilitate moral accommodation, such as ethical compromise, multi-issue cooperation, coalition building and political civility. Deliberative democracies also would recommend more broad-based political organisations that permit citizens who hold different moral positions to work together on other causes whose goals they share. In this respect, a fluid and open party system would be more desirable than a political structure dominated by single-issue groups.

Many deliberative democrats believe that the practice of deliberation should not be confined to the institutions of government. Unless citizens have the experience of reasoning to-gether outside of governmental institutions, they are not likely to develop either the interests or the skills that would enable them to deliberate effectively in politics. Deliberative democrats take an interest in the whole range of inter-mediary institutions: those that act on citizens (such as the media, health care organisations, professional sports) and those in which they act (interest groups, private clubs, TRADES UNIONS, professional associations), as well as those in which they work (corporations, small busi-nesses, government agencies, military services). From a deliberative perspective, the single most important institution outside government may be the educational system. To prepare their students for CITIZENSHIP in a deliberative democracy, schools should aim to develop the capacities of students to understand different perspectives, communicate their understandings to other people, and engage in the give-and-take of moral argument with a view toward making mutually justifiable decisions.

See also:

accountability; constitutionalism; democratic debate; direct democracy; majoritarianism; procedural democracy

Further reading

Bohman, J. (1996) *Public Deliberation: Plural-ism, Complexity, and Democracy*, Cambridge, MA: MIT Press.

Bohman, J. and Rehg, W. (eds) (1997) *Delib-erative Democracy: Essays on Reason and Politics*, Cambridge, MA: MIT Press.

Burke, E. (1959) *Burke's Politics*, ed. R. Hoff-man and P. Levack, New York: Knopf.

Cohen, J. (1989) 'Deliberation and Democratic Legitimacy,' in A. Hamlin and P. Pettit (eds), *The Good Polity*, London: Blackwell.

Elster, J. (ed.) (1998) *Deliberative Democracy*, Cambridge: Cambridge University Press.

The Federalist (1961) ed. B. Wright, Cam-bridge, MA: Harvard University Press.

Fishkin, J.S. (1995) *The Voice of the People:*
Public Opinion and Democracy, New Haven, CT: Yale University Press.

Gutmann, A. and Thompson, D. (1996) *Demo-cracy and Disagreement*, Cambridge, MA: Harvard University Press.

Habermas, J. (1996) *Between Facts and Norms: Contributions to a Discourse Theory of Law and Democracy*, Cambridge, MA: MIT Press.

Macedo, S. (ed.) (1999) *Deliberative Politics*, New York: Oxford University Press.

Thompson, D. (1970) *The Democratic Citizen: Social Science and Democratic Theory in the 20th Century*, Cambridge: Cambridge Univer-sity Press.

Thucydides (1998) *Peleponnesian Wars*, trans. S. Lattimore, Indianapolis, IN: Hackett.

AMY GUTMANN
DENNIS THOMPSON

democracy and sustainability

Greens typically argue that participatory de-mocracy favours the development of a sustain-able and more ethically balanced relationship between humankind and nature (see GREEN DEMOCRATIC THOUGHT). Here participatory democracy implies: direct citizen participation in decision-making; in forums where debate approximates the norms of deliberative con-ceptions of democracy; with decision-making devolved to the community level, so long as this does not lead to unsustainable results. Their thesis is that participatory democracy helps overcome barriers to the realisation of the green project caused by the atomised self-interest of consumers, the power of big business and the bureaucratic nature of the liberal democratic state.

Not all who prioritise sustainability share this viewpoint. Beside arguing that resource scarcity is a threat to democracy, neo-Hobbe-sians argue that only mutual COERCION mu-tually agreed will ensure that rational, self-interested individuals will co-operate in main-taining the ecosystem (Ophuls and Boyan 1992; Walker 1988). This implies placing consider-able power in the hands of 'environmental guardians' who would ensure that society does not go beyond the limits of sustainability. Among mainstream greens the trend is to argue that liberal democracy should be supplemented with participatory forums, not replaced. Nevertheless, their stress on participatory democracy has heavily influenced the thinking of UN agencies; for instance, in relation to local participatory planning for sustainable development. In some countries undergoing democratic transitions, the indigenous green movement has been a significant force for democratic reform. Greens also press national and international development agencies for policies that favour democratisation. They see democratisation and progress towards sustainability as mutually reinforcing.

It is often argued that a commitment to democracy implies green values. First, there are certain ecological conditions necessary to reproduce a democratic society. Second, certain individual rights standardly associated with democratic citizenship – especially those around health and other basic needs – may be linked to green concerns. Third, there is the argument that democrats recognising individual human rights must, for consistency, recognise animal rights and, perhaps, the right of other living things to flourish. This entry covers arguments that move *from* green concerns *to* democracy. It starts with general arguments that a green perspective implies some form of democracy and then specifically examines participatory democracy.

Are the chances of realising the green project maximised under some form of democracy?

Is democracy the only political form guaranteeing sustainability?

It is logically possible but empirically implausible that the leaders of an authoritarian regime would share green values. The potential instability of authoritarian regimes and their direct, unmediated control of a high fraction of society's resources often encourages them to rape the ecosystem now while the going is good for personal gain, to underinvest in public

goods like environmental quality, retaining the resources for meeting their own priorities, and to ignore the long-term; hence, the interests of future generations. For the vast majority of the world's people who do not live in democracies these are, indeed, pressing concerns.

In democracies, citizens can influence political outcomes through the ballot box, the pressure group/social movements process, the free MEDIA and local political structures. Authoritarian regimes respond to a 'selectorate'; but this is a narrower group, less likely to include those with green concerns. In a democracy there is the possibility of getting rid of an environmentally dysfunctional government without recourse to widespread violence and the ecological damage that typically accompanies it. Authoritarian regimes also fight each other – directly or by proxy – more frequently than do democracies, and such wars can be environmentally devastating.

Arguments such as these have some empirical appeal if we consider the environmental record of communist regimes and military dictatorships in many parts of the world. But it is difficult to disentangle the specific effects of authoritarianism from those of other variables, such as Marxist-Leninist ideology with its emphasis on crash industrialisation. The cases that readily come to mind do not provide uncontaminated evidence, being poorer societies in which demand for environmental cleanup might be weaker. Midlarsky (1998) finds that scores on three standard democracy indexes do correlate significantly with some measures of environmental quality when controlling for other variables, notably gross domestic product (GDP) per capita. However, systems that more closely approach the democratic ideal have lower environmental quality on some measures. Within constraints, democracy allows the will of the majority to prevail. If the majority do not want a clean environment, democratic politics ought not to produce it. One explanation of these results is that high democracy scores will only be associated with high environmental quality when public attitudes favour environmental improvement.

Expertise versus 'partisan mutual adjustment'

Within liberal democracies, many key environmental decisions are made by – or heavily influenced by – experts. Green conservatives might want to take this further, even if this rubs against democrats' concerns for political equality in decision-making over vital issues. Environmental problems are complex, involve difficult scientific and technical issues, and manifest themselves at many different geographical scales. Perhaps poorly educated, ill-informed lay people should have little or no say.

Choosing between different conceptions of sustainability involves ethical trade-offs between the interests of current and future human generations, humankind and other species, and aggregates and individuals. Even if experts know the scientific issues best, there is no reason to suppose that they are any better at making such trade-offs, and good ethical reasons for suggesting that each citizen's views should count. Over many of the most pressing environmental issues there is considerable scientific uncertainty and ambiguity. Similarly scientists cannot claim to be in a position to resolve all the ethical issues around risk, especially as distributive questions about who will bear risks are often central.

When small groups of experts make decisions without recourse to external reporting or criticism, there are few opportunities to question whether the right choice has been made. 'Groupthink', bandwagoning and other small-group processes that lead to bad decisions may be common. Perversions caused by professional ideology are also a possibility. For instance, scientists' caution in rejecting the null-hypotheses that a practice does no environmental harm is often socially inappropriate. While this norm might be functional in relation to internal debates within the scientific community, in policy-making it might be better to assume guilt; a version of the precautionary principle. Elite decision-making gives rise to citizens who are lazy and unquestioning, whereas participation can engage citizens' active concerns. With greater numbers en-

gaged, the chances of finding solutions to knotty problems might be higher.

Environmental agencies often rely on the legitimacy of the natural sciences and tokenistic forms of public participation to ensure that the public acquiesce. However, declining faith in science and the objectivity of decisions made in this way leads to increasing difficulties. Arguably, no elite group is in a position to impose a compromise over key environmental questions. Crucial to sustainability are changes in peoples' mundane behaviour: have fewer children! recycle! consume less! travel less! insulate more and turn down the heating! The problem is that it is difficult to monitor whether people actually are changing their behaviour: to do so in a democracy clashes with individual rights to privacy and property, and even authoritarian regimes find it difficult directly to monitor so much of the private realm, as illustrated by the case of China's population policy. So people's consent has to be engaged. This seems to imply dialogue and social compromise. Through the process of partisan mutual adjustment, liberal democracy may be able gradually to broker such compromises, while simultaneously building legitimacy for them. Political leaders are specialists at brokering such deals, forging relevant alliances and suggesting points of trade-off (see DEMOCRATIC TRADE-OFFS).

Jänicke (1996) argues that progress in relation to environmental problems correlates with a form of environmental CORPORATISM in which an institutionalised dialogue takes place between business, the state and greens. This is facilitated by political input structures relatively open to environmental groups and by an oppositional wing of the green movement that stays partially outside the dialogue, preventing co-optation of the movement. Based on case studies, the claim is that eco-corporatism increases the capacity of the system to solve problems which the state cannot handle, leads to the integration of environmental concerns into a wide range of policy domains, and creates dialogues that change underlying behaviour, allowing policy to go beyond technological fixes and end-of-pipe forms of pollution control.

While there is evidence that one form of partisan mutual adjustment generates progress, it should be recognised that progress can be from a low baseline and need not correlate with measures of quality, such as those discussed above.

The arguments favouring democracy in this section relate more to standard forms of liberal democracy than to participatory democracy. But greens have strong reservations about liberal democracy. It is not difficult to accept that decisions should seldom be left to experts; but it is much more difficult to think through how experts can best serve the citizenry, whether the context is liberal democracy or participatory democracy.

The argument from the primary value of autonomy

Democracy is often favoured because it maximises individual AUTONOMY, within constraints set by social interdependence and the need to regulate harm to others from each individual's actions. Not everyone finds these derivations convincing (for example, Weale 1999: Ch. 4). If individual autonomy means living under laws that are self-chosen, simple majority rule is the voting rule that maximises it. According to the Rae–Taylor Theorem, simple majority rule minimises the a priori probability of being on the losing side of a vote, considering both cases where you prefer to change the status quo and cases where you prefer not to change it.

Green ethics is sometimes founded on the equal right to flourish of all living things, the individual member of a species being conceived of as part of a web of life in which all things are interdependent. As regards humans, green ethics comes close to embodying individual autonomy as a foundational value, because humans flourish when their lives unfold according to some self-chosen plan. If so, democracy and green ethics may derive from the same ethical axiom and might be expected to be consistent with each other.

It is true that some green philosophers problematise the notion of the self in liberal theories of autonomy. This is particularly true of deep ecology with its biocentric ethical approach. Arne Naess's principle of self-realisation superficially seems close to that of individual autonomy; but it actually implies a process whereby the individual increasingly identifies with the totality of living things, through recognising ecological interconnectedness. Nevertheless, this does not prevent Naess arguing for direct, local democracy on the grounds that centrally imposed decisions are coercive (1989: 141–3). The eco-anarchist Murray Bookchin (1982) sees causal links between the historical emergence of social hierarchy – particularly the state – and environmental degradation. He has been centrally concerned to argue that individual autonomy within community-based living promotes green ends.

Democracy is a process, while the green project is an outcome. If outcomes in a democracy should correspond, within certain constraints, to the majority will, there is no normative reason why democratic processes should give rise to the outcomes greens want. True, sustainability of some sort may be a condition for the continued existence for democracy, generating a constraint on the majority will. However, sustainability could take many forms. Some of these go little way towards recognising the intrinsic value of nature or the rights of other species – things definitional of green ethical positions. Greens usually assume that there is potential majority will for green ends, suppressed in industrial societies, to be uncovered or constructed through deliberation (for example, Gunderson 1995). If this is the case, democratically made decisions may well limit the possibilities for members of other species to flourish.

Specific arguments for participatory democracy

The case against liberal democracy

From the perspective of some greens, partisan mutual adjustment is painfully slow to cut compromises on the environment; and these compromises are typically unsustainable. Outcomes are constrained by what is acceptable to big business and tend to reward well-organised special interests opposed to environmental clean up. The lack of power of the poor, who often suffer most from environmental problems, prevents them being cut into deals. The failure of government to divulge INFORMATION is often vital in this respect. The short tenure of political leaders discourages them from articulating the interests of future generations; and the electoral unimportance of the poor prevents politicians compensating for their lack of organisation. Environmental policy problems are often defined and parcelled out within government in ways that favour special interests, for they are devolved to existing policy communities relatively closed to green arguments. In order to break into these policy communities, environmental INTEREST GROUPS limit their demands and form coalitions with business groups around a severely restricted agenda for reform. This agenda may be further circumscribed by GLOBALISATION. In a world economy in which capital is increasingly mobile, there is a temptation to level down environmental regulation, developed democracies being forced to relax regulatory regimes by threats to move jobs and investment to less-regulated regions. Criticisms like these often go with advocacy of participatory democracy.

Against this argument, sympathetic critics claim that liberal democracy will produce green outcomes once green values are widespread, so that the key to change is an ideological shift not an institutional reform (Eckersley 1992: 173–8). Moreover, some greens' refusal, on grounds of ideological purity, to make horse trades disables them from making progress. As those in the reälo wing of the German Green Party have stressed, weak LEADERSHIP and poor organisational structures tie the hands of the green movement. While environmental corporatism is often elitist, it can be bolstered by participatory forums of various sorts and counterposed by the institutions of representative democracy. Ultimately, the green case for participatory democracy cannot rest on the argument against liberal democracy: it must be shown that the participatory alternative is better.

The argument by analogy with nature

For greens, eco-systems consist of mutually interdependent individuals and species. They work without hierarchy or centralised control. Nature flourishes because there is a high degree of local differentiation. Animals that live in groups co-operate in a relatively non-hierarchical way. By analogy, greens – especially those influenced by eco-anarchist thought – argue that human communities will flourish where power is equally spread and where mutual interdependence replaces external imposition. There is no functional need for the concentration of power. Local politics can adapt to local conditions, allowing diversity and ecological stability.

Notoriously, people tend to see in nature a reflection of what they desire for the human world. So conservatives' vision of nature has often emphasised hierarchy, conflict, and the ethical value of strength. Interdependence and co-operation in the ecological sense are not conceptually the same as human co-operation, where intention, identity and symbolisation intervene. The argument by analogy is weak.

The pragmatic argument

In many liberal democracies, greens' best chance of having a political impact is at the local level. Turnout is often lower in local elections. This gives more opportunity to elect representatives of fringe parties, if their support is geographically focused and highly concerned, or if the electoral system is relatively proportional. Voters may be willing to voice interests that conflict with their immediate economic ones, because local political outcomes have a much less significant effect on the macroeconomic picture. Across most democracies, local government has attempted to make itself more open to citizens since the 1960s, often by drawing local environmental groups into a dialogue. So greens have pragmatic reasons to support devolution of power. This is not an argument from ethical principle. In any case, as suggested in the next section, there are potential problems with the devolution of power.

The argument from the ecological functionality of local living

The wave of the green movement that emerged in the 1960s and 1970s stressed DECENTRALI-SATION of economic life, which was seen as implying participatory democracy. As regards economic decentralisation, first, large cities were seen as ecologically damaging. Second, it was argued that local production for local needs in an economically decentralised society is potentially less damaging than current patterns because the ecological effects of transport would be minimised, those benefiting from production would also directly face the ecological consequences, so there would be less tendency to ignore the environment, and production could better be tailored to remain within local ecological constraints. Third, drawing on the historical experience of communities that have avoided significant environmental problems over long periods, some argue that the corrosive environmental effects of free riding are controllable within a community-based society: free-riding can be punished easily when each knows every other and there is a high degree of mutual interdependence. Then, if production were to be locally grounded to meet local needs, it would be best to control it locally and in a maximally democratic way.

Today there is far less emphasis on these arguments (Ward 1996). It is unclear to many authors sympathetic to green principles that cities are more damaging than small communities and that local production for local need is always less harmful than larger scale production. The problems of inequality between communities (breeding environmental problems associated with poverty among others) could not easily be overcome in a highly decentralised society. Even if locally-grounded living makes people more sensitive to their own environment (and the historical evidence for this is highly ambiguous) they might become more parochial and less sensitive

to wider ecological issues and global concerns. Communities might simply externalise their environmental problems on to other communities. They could form loose federations to deal with such problems, maintaining the structure of participatory democracy through strong mandating, recall of representatives and unanimity requirements in making key decisions, along communitarian anarchist lines. However, the sheer numbers and the potential diversity of the communities make it very difficult to see how this would work.

The argument from legitimacy

Legitimating green policies may be more difficult in an authoritarian system than in a democracy and more difficult in a liberal democracy than in a participatory democracy in which people 'own' decisions they have participated in making through face-to-face discussion. Yet it is notoriously difficult actually to get people to participate in time-consuming processes of DIRECT DEMOCRACY. It is almost an axiom for greens that once power is devolved, more people will participate than at present; yet it still will not be rational to participate, because you stand so little chance of changing the outcome.

The belief of many political theorists is that in face-to-face deliberation people are more inclined to see things from the perspective of the general interest rather than some pre-formed notion of their self-interest. Also, norms of democratic deliberation make it hard to articulate a case purely in terms of self-interest (see DELIBERATIVE DEMOCRACY). The critical aspect of democracy for many greens is the discursive construction of consensus around sustainability, so that it becomes the popular will. Gundersen (1995) provides inter-view-based evidence that deliberation unlocks people's latent normative acceptance of green values, making their thinking more collective, holistic and long-term. When farmers participate in the planning and implementation of development projects, the results are more likely to be ecologically sustainable and to be of benefit to the poorest in the community.

There must however be reservations about how much people are willing to sacrifice personal economic interests when the stakes are significant. Existing policy communities in which representatives of special interests and government agencies hammer out bargains that often have considerable environmental significance are deliberative forums. Certainly participants are willing to compromise now in order to preserve forms of reciprocity that will benefit all in the longer term; but it is far from obvious that economic self-interest is submerged. This analogy may be more relevant than it seems, for the problem of getting widespread popular participation is likely to mean that local bargaining would actually be between representatives of 'stakeholder' groups (Ward 1998).

As Saward argues (1993), there is a contradiction between green values and the styles of democracy they advocate. According to greens, there are ecological imperatives, with no real choice between green and other options; yet democracy – and especially deliberative democracy – implies taking others' points of view seriously and making compromises with them, even if they do not buy into the green project. The focus on intrinsic value in nature adds to the problem, for intrinsic value overrides merely instrumental values, and for some greens democracy is just an instrument to get intrinsic value recognised. Deep ecologists often see their ethics as more mature than one based solely on human interests; and this can shade off into the idea that they should lead the unenlightened, immature majority. Thus democracy could be dispensed with if participation was not producing the desired results.

Representing interests

National decisions with environmental implications often affect the interests of those living in other countries and future generations. It may seem morally arbitrary that those interests are not represented. Perhaps this argument carries over to the interests of other species, too. A more egalitarian interchange between humans and nature means humans must become more aware of nature's interests and more receptive to signals coming from her. Dryzek (1996) and Goodin (1996) argue that the chances of the right sort of communication occurring are maximised in a participatory democracy. Dryzek argues for a form of deliberative democracy in which communicative rationality is extended to nature, humans respecting nature and listening to signals emanating from it. Highly centralised, bureaucratised political processes are not well placed to attend to feedback from nature. Often local-level deliberation is better, although some problems are inappropriate for local deliberation. This generates the need for co-ordination between cross-cutting loci of political authority at different levels. Dryzek suggests social movements might do a better job that the state in this regard.

For Goodin, if natural objects have value and those values are akin to interests, then they should be indirectly represented in the political process by humans. Participatory democracy gives the best chances of indirect representation, because more people are involved and so the probability that someone will speak for nature is increased. It may be an analytic truth about communication that it involves putting ourselves in others' position and seeing things from their point of view; so participation may lead us to internalise others' interests and anticipate their positions. This effect might spill over onto nature's interests. If Goodin's arguments apply to other species, they ought also to apply to individuals in other countries or to future generations.

Environmental debates in the scientific community often come closer to the ideal speech situation than those in local deliberative forums, although economic and professional interests intervene often enough. If Dryzek and Goodin's arguments are correct, scientific forums should be relatively well attuned to signals from nature and prone to articulate nature's interests. If this is not the case, these authors' arguments seem questionable. On the other hand, if this is the case, things seem to rest on Goodin's claim that it is statistically more likely that nature's interests will get a hearing if participation is more inclusive. It is certainly true that larger numbers give better odds on representation; but they also 'dilute' the signal by adding a cacophony of other claims. Dobson (1996) shows that liberal-democracy can deal with the need for indirect representation of the interests of foreigners, future generations, and other species. Representatives for these interests could be elected, one possibility being that each citizen would have one vote, to be used either to elect a representative for the current generation, future generations, or other species. Dobson's argument seems especially pertinent in the light of the potential difficulties with pushing up participation levels (see GREEN DEMOCRATIC THOUGHT).

Greening civil society

If the liberal democratic state in a globalised world economy cannot be reformed from within, the alternative may be to try to build a flourishing, 'greened' CIVIL SOCIETY. In many respects, this idea underpins all the other arguments for participatory democracy, for it represents a trajectory along which other developments, such as community-grounded living, increased participation and changes in individual consciousness might flow. Moreover, it might provide an alternative arena for dealing with problems that the state cannot or will not cope with. For example, if the state will not control the use of genetically modified organisms, consumer boycotts organised by social movements might do so. If conventional food systems do not deliver healthy food and 'greened' agriculture, they could be bypassed by linking small-scale local growers with consumers, outside conventional markets, driving a wedge between farmers and agri-business. If a 'greened' civil society could be built, there is no presupposition that it would be completely disengaged from liberal democracy. It would try to influence conventional politics, not only through the insider tactics of mainstream environmental pressure groups, but also through non-violent direct action and by

showing that environmental questions could be resolved without state intervention.

Environmental problems spill over political jurisdictions, and often cannot be adequately dealt with at the national level. The power and secrecy of global institutions pose enormous problems for greens wishing to democratise environmental DECISION-MAKING. To take one example, the trade dispute resolution panels of the WTO, the EU and NAFTA make decisions that have enormous implications for national environmental policy, but citizens have virtually no say in their operation. Greens often favour the development of a global civil society, embodied in NON-GOVERNMENTAL ORGANISATIONS (NGOs) working at regional and global levels, to offset the democratic deficit. Such NGOs cannot be more than part of the solution because they fail to represent many points of view and are weakly responsible to their members.

On a world scale and taking a long time horizon, the green movement has had its share of demagogues and fanatics, and it cannot be presumed that it will be easy to democratise a 'greened' civil society. It is also inescapable that past waves of social movement activity – including earlier waves of the green movement itself – have eventually been incorporated within liberal democratic politics. The horns of the dilemma for advocates of a 'greened' civil society are that if social movements do not become incorporated they have little effect; but without such effects, it is difficult to maintain their momentum.

Conclusion

The outcome of this debate is unclear, partly because green claims rely too much on a-priori reasoning and not enough on evidence. However, certain things emerge. Green advocacy of participatory democracy is on much firmer ground if green values are widely distributed; but this condition will not always hold. Secondly, the arguments for decentralisation of power are not particularly strong ones. This seems to be especially clear, given that we no longer need to tie meaningful direct participation to local-level politics: teledemocracy opens up many possibilities, and participation could be national but take the form of CITIZENS' JURIES, which allow for considerable deliberation. The reasons for greens to picture a patchwork of conventional and unconventional democratic forms are not only practical but principled.

See also:

deliberative democracy; green democratic thought; participation

Further reading

Bookchin, M. (1982) *The Ecology of Freedom: The Emergence and Dissolution of Hierarchy*, Palo Alto, CA: Cheshire.

Dobson, A. (1996) 'Representative Democracy and the Environment', in W.M. Laferty and J. Meadowcroft (eds), *Democracy and the Environment: Problems and Prospects*, Cheltenham: Edward Elgar, 124–39.

Dryzek, J. (1996) 'Political and Ecological Communication', in F. Mathews (ed.), *Ecology and Democracy* (special issue of *Environmental Politics*), Oxford: Frank Cass, 342–63.

Eckersley, R. (1992) *Environmentalism and Political Theory*, London: UCL Press.

Goodin, R.E. (1996) 'Enfranchising the Earth', *Political Studies* 44: 835–49.

Gundersen, A. (1995) *The Environmental Promise of Democratic Deliberation*, Madison, WI: University of Wisconsin Press.

Jänicke, M. (1996) 'Democracy as a Condition for Environmental Policy Success: The Importance of Non-Institutional Factors', in W.M. Laferty and J. Meadowcroft (eds), *Democracy and the Environment: Problems and Prospects*, Edward Elgar: Cheltenham, 71–85.

Midlarsky, M.I. (1998) 'Democracy and the Environment: An Empirical Assessment', *Journal of Peace Research* 35: 341–61.

Naess, A. (1989) *Ecology, Community and Lifestyle*, Cambridge: Cambridge University Press.

Ophuls, W. and Boyan, A., Jr. (1992) *Ecology and the Politics of Scarcity Revisited: The Unravelling of the American Dream*, San Fransisco: Freeman.

Saward, M. (1993) 'Green Democracy', in A. Dobson and P. Lucardie (eds), *The Politics of Nature: Explorations in Green Political Theory*, London: Routledge, 63–80.

Walker, K. (1988) 'The Environmental Crisis. A Critique of Neo-Hobbesian Responses', *Polity* 21: 67–81.

Ward, H. (1996), 'Green Arguments for Local Democracy', in D. King and G. Stoker (eds), *Rethinking Local Democracy*, London: Macmillan.

—— (1998) 'State, Association and Community in a Sustainable, Democratic Polity', in H.J.M. Coenen, D. Huitema and L.J. O'Toole (eds), *Participation and the Quality of Environmental Decision Making*, Dordrecht: Kluwer.

Weale, A. (1999) *Democracy*, Basingstoke: Macmillan.

HUGH WARD

democracy, fat and thin

Democracy has many meanings, and even within the realm of scholarly thought there is no consensus on its usage. Many political thinkers and activists in the past century have insisted on attaching social and economic as well as political meanings to the term. From this perspective, a nation cannot be considered a 'democracy' unless it has some degree of EQUALITY in the distribution of wealth, limitations on the power of large owners of capital, or even substantial public ownership of the means of production. This view has fallen out of favour with the collapse of socialism in the late twentieth century. However, even if we conceive of democracy strictly in political terms – as a distinct form of government or regime – conceptions of democracy range widely from 'thin' to 'fat'. Thin, or 'minimalist,' conceptions are limited to one essential institutional feature of democracy:

ELECTORAL COMPETITION and uncertainty. Fat, or more fully articulated, conceptions identify a wide range of other types of institutions, processes and conditions that must also be present for a regime to be called a democracy. Ranging across this terrain are a profusion of peculiar formulations; by one count, more than 550 subtypes of democracy that have been advanced in the recent literature (Collier and Levitsky 1997).

Democracy stems from the ancient Greek term *demokratia*, meaning 'rule by the people'. While this may seem straightforward, as Robert Dahl (1989: 3) notes, it raises fundamental issues of who constitutes 'the people' and what it means for them to 'rule'. In ancient Greece, political identity was rooted in cities and only a small proportion of the adult population was deemed worthy of the right to participate in collective DECISION-MAKING (see DEMOCRATIC ORIGINS). Today, democracy applies to political systems of much larger scale – nations – but the effort to constitute (or preserve) a nation may confront intense disagreement over BOUNDARIES and identities (see IDENTITY, POLITICAL). In the Greek city states, the number of citizens was small enough to permit their direct participation in and debate over policies. The scale of the modern democracy is such that most citizens can participate in decision-making only indirectly, by choosing leaders and legislators to act on their behalf. Moreover, one point of consensus among all contemporary conceptions of democracy – thin or fat – is that democracy requires inclusive PARTICIPATION, such that all adults (men and women, rich and poor) above a certain age (allowing for numerically minor exclusions of convicted criminals or those declared mentally incompetent) have equal rights of CITIZENSHIP, including the franchise.

Thin conceptions of democracy centre on electoral democracy. Most of them descend or borrow from Joseph Schumpeter (1947: 269), who defined democracy as a system 'for arriving at political decisions in which individuals acquire the power to decide by means of a competitive struggle for the people's vote'. Samuel Huntington (1991), among others,

explicitly embraces Schumpeter's emphasis on competitive ELECTIONS for effective power as the essence of democracy. Adam Przeworski and his colleagues (1996: 51) further clarified this thin conception of democracy by requiring that elections encompass '1) *ex ante* uncertainty, 2) *ex post* irreversibility, and 3) repeatability'. If a system regularly holds elections to fill its chief executive office and the seats in its effective legislative body; if there is some chance that one or more ruling parties can lose office in a particular election; if any winner of a free and fair election can assume office; and if the winners of one election cannot prevent the same competitive uncertainty from prevailing in the next election, then the system is a democracy.

This Schumpeterian or thin conception has the appeal of being lean and concise, but it has required periodic elaboration (what Collier and Levitsky call 'precising') to avoid inclusion of cases that do not fit the implicit meaning. To be meaningful, in this view, the definition of democracy must be fatter. The seminal elaboration is Robert Dahl's (1971) conception of POLYARCHY, which has two overt dimensions: opposition (organised contestation through regular, free and fair elections) and participation (the right of virtually all adults to vote and contest for office). Yet embedded in these two dimensions is a third, without which the first two cannot be truly meaningful: civil liberty. Polyarchy encompasses not only FREEDOM to vote and contest for office but also freedom to speak and publish dissenting views, freedom to form and join organisations, and alternative sources of information.

Thin conceptions of electoral democracy usually also acknowledge the need for minimum levels of freedom (of speech, press, organisation and assembly) in order for competition and participation to be meaningful. But, typically, they do not devote much attention to them, nor do they incorporate them into actual measures of democracy. Thus the thin conceptions commit what Terry Karl (1990) calls the 'fallacy of electoralism': privileging elections over other dimensions of democracy and ignoring the degree to which multiparty elections (even if they are competitive and uncertain in outcome) may exclude significant portions of the population from contesting for power or advancing and defending their interests, or may leave significant arenas of decision-making beyond the control of elected officials.

In recent years, electoral conceptions of democracy have expanded to rule out the latter element of ambiguity or misclassification; many now exclude regimes that suffer substantial reserved domains of military (or bureaucratic, or oligarchical) power that are not accountable to elected officials (Linz and Stepan 1996). But such formulations may still fail to give due weight to political repression and marginalisation, which exclude significant segments of the population – typically the poor or ethnic and regional MINORITIES – from exercising their democratic rights.

Freedom ranges over a continuum of variation. Rights of expression, organisation and assembly vary considerably across countries that do have regular, competitive, multiparty elections in which votes are (more or less) honestly counted and in which the winning candidates exercise (most of the) effective power in the country. A substantial and growing body of democratic theory and analysis insists that democracy is not only about the rule of the majority but also about the rights of minorities. They question whether a regime can be called a democracy when significant minorities – ethnic, regional, religious or class – are brutally repressed, unable to gain meaningful access to the legal system, marginalised in the process of elections and interest competition, or otherwise denied full and equal rights of citizenship.

Liberal (fat) democracy

While the effort to elaborate the 'thin' conception of democracy has been constructive, it has left behind a plethora of what Collier and Levitsky term 'expanded procedural' conceptions, which do not clearly relate to one another and which occupy intermediate locations in the continuum between electoral and liberal democracy. A different approach is to dispense with incremental elaborations and articulate a comprehensive conception of democracy that encompasses not only the classical democratic element of popular rule but also the *liberal* element of protection for individual rights and the *republican* element of harnessing power to the public interest through the rule of law.

This Diamond (1999) has done by advancing a model of *liberal democracy*. In addition to the elements of electoral democracy, it requires first the absence of reserved domains of power for the military or other actors not accountable to the electorate (directly or indirectly). Second, it requires the horizontal accountability of officeholders to one another; this constrains executive power and so helps protect constitutionalism, legality, and the deliberative process (Sklar 1996). Third, it encompasses extensive provisions for political and civic pluralism as well as for individual and group freedoms, so that contending interests and values may be expressed and compete through ongoing processes of articulation and representation, beyond periodic elections. Fourth, it demands a 'rule of law', in which legal rules are applied fairly, consistently and predictably across equivalent cases, irrespective of the class, status or power of those subject to the rules. Under a true rule of law, all citizens have political and legal equality, and the state and its agents are themselves subject to the law. These conditions guard individual and group freedoms of belief, expression, association, demonstration, movement and the like; they also protect citizens from unjustified detention, exile, terror, torture and undue interference in their personal lives not only by the state but also by organised anti-state forces. Among the specific institutional arrangements necessary for this much more ample form of democracy to prevail are institutional provisions in the executive and legislature to enforce civilian supremacy over the military; a politically independent, non-discriminatory and professional judiciary; a parliament with some autonomous capacity and powers to check the executive branch; independent electoral administration; and the absence of provisions severely limiting press freedom or setting up press or broadcast monopolies.

If political AUTHORITY is to be effectively constrained and balanced, individual and minority rights protected and a rule of law assured, liberal democracy also requires a constitution that is supreme. Liberal democracies in particular 'are and have to be constitutional democracies. The lack of a constitutional spirit, of an understanding of the centrality of constitutional stability, is one of the weaknesses of many illiberal third-wave democracies in the postcommunist world, as well as in the Third World' (Linz 1997: 120–21). A constitutional state is a state of justice, a *Rechtsstaat* in German, in which the state acts predictably, in accordance with the laws, and the courts enforce restrictions on popularly elected governments when they violate the laws or the constitutional rules. This in turn requires a legal and judicial system and, more broadly, a state with some capacity. Thus Juan Linz's dictum: 'no state, no *Rechtsstaat*, no democracy' (Linz 1997: 118).

The above elements of liberal democracy compose most of the criteria by which Freedom House annually rates political rights (of CONTESTATION, opposition and PARTICIPATION) and civil liberties for the nations of the world. Political rights and civil liberties are each measured on a seven-point scale, with a rating of 1 indicating the most free and 7 the least free. Countries with an average score on the two scales of 2.5 or lower are considered 'free'; those scoring between 3 and 5.5 are 'partly free'; and those scoring between 5.5 and 7 (as measured by a more discriminating raw point score) are 'not free' (Freedom House 1999).

The 'free' rating in the Freedom House survey is a reasonable empirical indicator of liberal democracy (although some might wish to locate the threshold for liberal democracy higher, at an average score of 2.0, for example). As with any multipoint scale, there is inevitably some arbitrariness in where one draws the line to establish the threshold for a concept. However, there are real differences between a score of 2 and 3 on either scale. Typically, a 3

on political rights indicates significantly more military influence in politics, electoral and political violence, or electoral irregularities: and thus political contestation that is appreciably less free, fair, inclusive and meaningful. The difference between a 2 and a 3 on civil liberties is also significant, as the countries scoring a 3 have at least one area – such as freedom of speech or the press, personal security from terror and arbitrary arrest, or associational freedom and autonomy – in which liberty is significantly constrained.

Mid-range conceptions

Conceptual approaches are not easily dichotomised into electoral and liberal, thin and fat, approaches. Some conceptions of democracy fall somewhere in between, explicitly incorporating basic freedoms of expression and association yet still allowing for constrictions in CITIZENSHIP rights and a porous, insecure rule of law. The crucial distinction turns on whether freedoms are relevant mainly to the extent that they ensure meaningful electoral competition and participation or whether they are, instead, viewed as necessary for a wider range of democratic functions. In one recent, prominent mid-range conception, Guillermo O'Donnell carefully rules out the fallacy of electoralism and the inclusion of reserved domains by adopting Dahl's concept of polyarchy and adding further procedural requirements that elected officials have meaningful power (O'Donnell 1996). On the basis of these criteria, he excludes from his list of polyarchies in Latin America a number of quasi-democracies, such as Haiti, Guatemala and Paraguay. However, the cutting point in his articulation of polyarchy centres on the institutionalisation of elections rather than more broadly on the rule of law.

Indeed, a key point of O'Donnell's essay is that many third-wave democracies are polyarchies, and apparently enduring polyarchies, even though clientelism and particularism undermine horizontal accountability and adherence to formal rules. Thus, all of O'Donnell's cases of polyarchy 'are such because of a simple but crucial fact: elections are institutionalised' (O'Donnell 1996: 53). The institutionalisation of elections requires surrounding conditions of freedom, but the cutting point appears to be their relevance for ensuring democratic electoral competition. O'Donnell concedes that individuals are only citizens in the many new polyarchies 'in relation to the one institution that functions in a manner close to what its formal rules prescribe – elections. "Full" citizenship is only available to a "privileged minority"... Informally institutionalised polyarchies are democratic in the sense just defined... But their liberal and republican components are extremely weak' (1996: 45–46).

The question of how extensive liberty must be before a political system can be termed a liberal democracy is a normative and philosophical one. The key distinction is whether the political process centres on elections or whether it encompasses a much broader and more continuous play of interest articulation, representation and contestation. If we view the latter as an essential component of democracy, then there must be adequate freedoms surrounding that broader process as well, and to use O'Donnell's language, individuals must be able to exercise their rights of citizenship not only in elections but also in obtaining 'fair access to public agencies and courts', which is often denied in 'informally institutionalised' polyarchies.

The distinction between political and civil freedom, on the one hand, and cultural freedom (or license), on the other, is often confused in the debate over whether democracy is inappropriate for Asia (or East Asia, or Confucian Asia, or simply Singapore) because of incompatible values. Liberal democracy does not require the comprehensively exalted status of individual rights that obtains in Western Europe and especially the United States. Thus, one may accept many of the cultural objections of advocates of the 'Asian values' perspective (that Western democracies have shifted the balance too much in favour of individual rights and social entitlements over the rights of the community and the social

obligations of the individual to the community) and still embrace the political and civic fundamentals of liberal democracy as articulated above (Chan 1997) (see ASIAN MODELS OF DEMOCRACY).

The spectrum of conceptions of democracy, from fat to thin, would not be complete without brief mention of those regimes that are not merely thin but so emaciated that they are mere ghosts of democracy. These regimes, which I call 'pseudodemocracies', would like to be considered as democracies, because the status of democracy brings respect internationally and legitimacy at home. Pseudodemocracies have multiple political parties and contested national elections. Those elections may even be fairly spirited, with many candidates from opposition parties elected to parliament. But pseudodemocracies violate one or more of Przeworski's three conditions for electoral democracy. There is not ex ante uncertainty, because it is extremely difficult if not impossible to dislodge the ruling party from power, irrespective of popular preferences. In other words, elections are not free and fair. Second, there is not ex post irreversibility. If by some huge failure of organisation the opposition wins, the results will be fraudulently reported or suppressed, or the opposition will otherwise be prevented from assuming office (otherwise, a transition to democracy may occur). Third, there is no repeatability of a fair and competitive contest. In this instance, an opposition movement may win power, but then it quickly takes on the features of the hegemonic party it has managed to displace.

It is a striking testimony to the lure and legitimacy of democracy in today's world that there remain so few regimes – less than a fifth of all the states in the world – that blatantly eschew even the facade of competitive, multiparty elections (Diamond 1999). But it is one thing to have multiparty elections and another for them to be fair and meaningful. In fact, there is growing evidence that peoples around the world want not just the electoral provisions of 'rule by the people', but the deeper, fatter structures of freedom, constitutionalism, accountability and the rule of law encompassed in the concept of liberal democracy.

See also:

accountability; constitutionalism; freedom; law, rule of; opposition, loyal

Further reading

Chan, J. (1997) 'Hong Kong, Singapore, and Asian Values: An Alternative View', *Journal of Democracy* 8(2): 35–48.

Collier, D. and Levitsky, S. (1997) 'Democracy with Adjectives: Conceptual Innovation in Comparative Research,' *World Politics* 49(3): 430–51.

Dahl, R. (1971) *Polyarchy: Participation and Opposition*, New Haven, CT: Yale University Press.

—— (1989) *Democracy and Its Critics*, New Haven, CT: Yale University Press.

Diamond, L. (1999) *Developing Democracy: Toward Consolidation*, Baltimore: Johns Hopkins University Press.

Freedom House (1999) *Freedom in the World: The Annual Survey of Political Rights and Civil Liberties, 1998–1999*, New York: Freedom House.

Huntington, S. (1991) *The Third Wave: Democratization in the Late Twentieth Century*, Norman, OK: University of Oklahoma Press.

Karl, T. (1990) 'Dilemmas of Democratization in Latin America', *Comparative Politics*, 23(1): 1–23.

Linz, J. (1997) 'Democracy Today: An Agenda for Students of Democracy,' *Scandinavian Political Studies* 20(2).

Linz, J. and Stepan, A. (1996) *Problems of Democratic Transition and Consolidation: Southern Europe, South America, and Post-Communist Europe*, Baltimore: Johns Hopkins University Press.

O'Donnell, G. (1996) 'Illusions About Consolidation', *Journal of Democracy* 7(2): 34–51.

Przeworski, A., Alvarez, M., Cheibub, J.A., and Limongi, F. (1996) 'What Makes Democracies Endure?', *Journal of Democracy* 7(1): 39–55.

Schumpeter, J. (1947) *Capitalism, Socialism, and Democracy*, 2nd edn, New York: Harper.

Sklar, R. (1996) 'Towards a Theory of Developmental Democracy', in A. Leftwich (ed.), *Democracy and Development: Theory and Practice*, Cambridge: Polity Press.

LARRY DIAMOND

democracy, future of

At no time in world history has there been cause for greater optimism about the future of democracy. By the mid-1990s, more countries were democratic than ever before in history, and the percentage of all independent states with democratic forms of government was also the highest in history. This was true, and remained true through the end of the decade, whether one posits a 'thin' (merely electoral) or 'fat' (politically liberal) conception of democracy (see DEMOCRACY, FAT AND THIN). By the beginning of 2000, Freedom House counted 120 electoral democracies in the world, 63 per cent of all states in the world (Karatnycky 2000). This was the highest number and percentage ever recorded, but the figure had consistently topped 60 per cent since 1995 (Diamond 1999: 25). The number and percentage of countries approaching the 'fatter' architecture of liberal democracy, with effective protections for civil liberties and constraints on executive power, was also near a historic high at the close of the century, with 85 countries rated as 'free' by Freedom House.

The progress of democracy in a mere century has been breathtaking. In 1900, most of the current states of the world were part of one or another colonial empire, or at least lacked SOVEREIGNTY in their current form. Few people living under imperial or colonial rule, or within the political system of a protectorate, enjoyed the RIGHTS of CITIZENSHIP that are today widely acknowledged and codified in international covenants and charters. Neither did the more than one-third of the world's population living under absolute monarchical rule. Even more astonishingly, not a single political system in the world 'enjoyed competitive multiparty politics with universal suffrage', the minimum conditions generally acknowledged today for electoral democracy (Karatnycky 2000: 187). Everywhere, women were denied the right to vote, and typically so were racial MINORITIES and the poor.

The fortunes of democracy in the world waxed and waned during this century in two forward and reverse waves before the third period of global democratic expansion began in 1974 (Huntington 1991) (see WAVES OF DEMOCRACY). In contrast to the first two waves, the third wave shows no sign of drowning in a reverse wave of DEMOCRATIC BREAKDOWN. If we conceive of the future of democracy in terms of the extent of its presence globally, one can draw from this recent history both optimistic and pessimistic scenarios for the future. Optimistically, it could be argued that the wave-like pattern of democratic progress and recession has now been transcended. By this logic, democracy is now the only legitimate form of government in the world, with the collapse of communism and the discrediting of virtually every other authoritarian ideology (with rising mass protest even against the Islamic fundamentalist state in Iran). With the established democracies also being the primary centres of military power, cultural influence, financial capital, and economic and technological innovation, there is little sign of challenge to the global ideological and political HEGEMONY of democracy. While democracies will continue to rise and fall at lower levels of economic development, no democracy has ever broken down in a country as wealthy as South Korea was even in 1987, at the time of its democratic transition (Przeworski *et al.* 1996). Furthermore, no member state of the European Union has ever suffered a democratic breakdown, as democracy is a condition for membership. Thus, if economic development and international economic integration can continue, democracy figures to be 'locked' into place in a growing number of countries (see ECONOMIC REQUIREMENTS OF DEMOCRACY)

However, as the new century dawns it is also possible to advance a more worrisome, if not pessimistic, assessment. The majority of the new democracies in the world are not consolidated, in that there does not yet exist a broad and robust consensus, among political elites, organisations and the mass public, that the current democratic constitutional system is the best form of government for the country, and that everyone should be bound to play by its constitutional rules and norms (Diamond 1999: 65; Linz and Stepan 1996: 5–7). Of the more than sixty new democracies that have emerged during the 'third wave', only a few (Spain, Portugal, Greece, Uruguay, possibly a few other Latin American and East European countries) meet an exacting standard of consolidation. Most third wave democracies are still well below the threshold of economic development that has historically rendered them 'impregnable' against democratic breakdown – a per capita income of roughly $6,000 in purchasing power parity (1985 $US) (Przeworski *et al.* 1996: 41).

The vulnerability of the third wave democracies, and of some of older vintage, is underscored by the poor quality of democracy in many countries. Of the 120 democracies at the start of the year 2000, only 85 (71 per cent) were rated by Freedom House as 'free' (what could be taken as a minimum indicator of a liberal political system). When the third wave had spread less far, the percentage was much higher (for example, 85 per cent in 1990). In particular, many of the largest and most influential developing democracies (Brazil, Venezuela, Turkey, Ukraine, Russia and Bangladesh) have very serious problems of democratic functioning that render their democracies illiberal, while others oscillate on the margins between 'free' and 'partly free' status. Even more liberal and stable third wave democracies, such as South Korea, Taiwan, Thailand and Argentina, suffer very serious problems of political corruption and politicisation and abuse of weak judicial systems. The vulnerability of new democracies is underscored by the actual breakdowns that have occurred, for example, by executive coup in Peru in 1992 and by military coup in Pakistan in 1999.

The unique features of the post-Cold War world notwithstanding, history suggests that democracies will continue to fail when they are unable to produce and maintain political order, ACCOUNTABILITY, TRANSPARENCY, a rule of law (see LAW, RULE OF) and LEGITIMACY. If they are to meet the expectations of their people for political performance as well as economic, they must build and strengthen their state structures in order to produce these political goods (Linz and Stepan 1996). Almost universally, the troubled democracies of the third wave have serious problems of political corruption and high levels of crime, and frequently the merger of the two, in the form of organised crime's heavy penetration into electoral and party politics. Much of the future of democracy in these countries will depend on their capacity to control crime and corruption by depoliticising and strengthening the legal system, in particular, the JUDICIARY and the prosecuting authorities. Otherwise, as in Pakistan, some alternative form of government, most likely the military, is likely to supplant democracy, with the enthusiastic support of an exhausted and disgusted public.

The future of democratic transitions

What of the future of democracy in the current authoritarian states? Economic, social, political and global variables all will affect the prospects for durable democratic change in these countries. Statistically, democratic transitions are more likely to last in richer countries. And from the recent history of Spain, Taiwan and South Korea, we know that economic and social development – generating a larger middle CLASS and a more pluralistic, active CIVIL SOCIETY, densely engaged with other democratic societies and networks around the world – generates pressures for transition to democracy. While it has been possible, so far, for a rich city-state like Singapore to resist these pressures even at a very high level of economic development, it is unlikely that this scenario can be reproduced in the typical country, which lacks Singapore's unique features: small size, a charismatic and incorruptible founding leader (Lee Kuan Yew), and a highly disciplined ruling elite, infused with the self-restraint and Confucian benevolent authoritarianism of the founding leader. Even in Singapore, it is likely that pressures for democratisation will grow as a new generation, socialised into an era of affluence and increasingly influenced by global culture, balks at being treated politically like children.

Democratic transitions are also more likely to occur, and to endure, the more democratic the POLITICAL CULTURE of the country, the more vigorous, autonomous and democratically oriented is civil society, and the greater the number of other democracies that are established in the region. However, almost all of the countries favourably disposed on these counts (and in their level of economic development) were already democracies by the year 2000. This included 31 of the 35 countries in the Americas (with Mexico moving toward democracy), and almost every European state (Central and Eastern, as well as Western, with all 24 Western European states being liberal democracies). By contrast, aside from the three Baltic states (which are culturally more a part of Eastern Europe), none of the other twelve states of the former Soviet Union was a liberal democracy; only six of the twelve were democracies, and most of these, such as Russia and Ukraine, were increasingly illiberal and troubled ones. South, East and Southeast Asia were also quite divided between regime types. The two regions with the greatest room for the expansion of democracy are Sub-Saharan Africa, where only 20 of the 48 states were democracies in 2000 (and most of those were quite illiberal and fragile), and the 16 states of the Arab Middle East (including North Africa), which contain not a single democracy. Yet these are the regions with the most formidable obstacles in terms of culture, social structure and levels of development.

The distribution and recent trends of democracy in the world underscore the importance of diffusion and demonstration effects. The prospects for future democratic expansion depend disproportionately on a few, key countries that cast a large political, cultural and economic shadow over their neighbours. In Asia, these prospects rest disproportionately with China and Indonesia. Having made a transition to the barest form of electoral democracy in 1999, Indonesia entered the new millennium facing formidable challenges of institution building and national reconstruction. Its neighbours in Southeast Asia are watching closely to see if an emerging democracy bestriding the archipelago, and one of the largest populations, in the world, can hold itself together and maintain ethnic and religious peace while regenerating economic development and implementing a wide range of urgently needed reforms. If Indonesia can succeed in these respects through the framework of democracy, the political and psychological barriers to democratic change in the region will be lowered. However, if Indonesia fragments into multiple countries, particularly with the kind of horrific ethnic violence that attended the breakup of the former Yugoslavia, authoritarian rulers like Mahathir Mohammed in Malaysia and Lee Kuan Yew in Singapore will cite this as justification for autocratic rule.

Singapore itself figures to exercise influence well out of proportion to its tiny size. As the most economically developed and successful non-democracy in the world, Singapore presents the clearest alternative model of modernisation and GLOBALISATION without democracy. However, if the ruling People's Action Party were to democratise politics some day, perhaps as a result of an internal split or rising civic pressure, this would affect elite calculations and regional politics throughout East and Southeast Asia.

The most important country that looks to Singapore as some kind of model for its own political future is China. There are growing indications that the Chinese Communist Party would like gradually to construct much of the formal architecture of democracy – including competitive ELECTIONS at the township, country, provincial and ultimately national levels –

while remaining the only organised and viable (if not legal) political party. In other words, it would like the internal and external legitimacy that comes from the ability to remove unpopular individual leaders, but without any danger of the party losing control of the state. Yet, it is doubtful that the Singaporean model can work in a country anywhere near the scale of China. China has begun to introduce some reforms that allow for very limited judicial and legislative autonomy, decentralisation and competitive elections at the village level (Pei 1995, 1998; Oksenberg 1998). However, these have made little headway in controlling rampant corruption and refurbishing the waning legitimacy of Communist Party rule. If, as some observers expect, China's economy continues to grow somewhere in the range of 6–8 per cent over the first two decades of the twenty-first century, and if China's entry into the World Trade Organisation is accompanied, as it very likely will be, by the country's rapid integration into other global networks, Chinese society will be transformed in ways that can only be dimly imagined now. In particular, its civil society will become far stronger and more pluralistic, as it gains more resources and much wider access to INFORMATION and ideas, both within China and globally. At some point in the first quarter of the century, modernisation and globalisation will generate increasingly formidable pressures for systemic political change in China, as they did in Taiwan and South Korea (Rowen 1996). The Communist regime will need to adapt rapidly with a strategy for deep political reform or risk a process of tumultuous and possibly convulsive political change.

China is an emerging superpower, with one-sixth of the human population. Outside of the established democracies, especially the United States, no country will have a bigger impact on global patterns of regime change and legitimacy than China. If it eventually does make a peaceful and durable transition to democracy, this will likely ensure that the twenty-first century is truly the democratic century, when other regime types are scattered and ideologically impotent, unable to present themselves as any kind of model. If it fails to evolve a democracy, and either reconstructs a stable one-party autocracy or falls into prolonged political turmoil or state disintegration, the prospects for democracy regionally and globally will be significantly diminished.

Crucial as well will be the political evolution of Russia. Although it is a declining power (and certainly no longer a superpower), Russia still exercises significant political, military and psychological sway over its post-Soviet neighbours. The question is not simply whether Russia can build a stable democracy, but closely related to this, whether it can build an effective state of any kind. If Russia can tame and tax its enormous concentrations of private power, particularly in the incestuous connections between post-communist business empires, organised crime and politics, it can create a context for democracy to develop and grow, as the older generation of die-hard communists fades from the scene. If Russia fails in this challenge, it risks becoming a black hole of criminality, CORRUPTION and crippled institutions, with destabilising effects throughout Eurasia. This would be an extremely difficult context for democracy to advance in the post-Soviet world.

In Sub-Saharan Africa, by far the two most important countries are Nigeria and South Africa. Given its daunting economic and social difficulties – the legacy of apartheid – the new South Africa has achieved in its first six years a remarkable record of liberal democracy. In the long run, South Africa will have to generate more vigorous economic growth, raising EDUCATION, employment and standards of living for the broad bulk of the population, if liberal democracy is to be sustainable. But its commitment to constitutionalism and civic and press FREEDOM, and its growing concern to promote democratic practices and peaceful resolution of conflict throughout Southern and Central Africa, augur well for its neighbours. Democracy in Nigeria, by contrast, will be much more contested and difficult. No country in the world faces a more daunting scale of embedded corruption, affecting every aspect of politics, governance and development. At the same time, the new civilian government that assumed power in May 1999 must confront multiple ethnic and regional fissures more serious than at any time since the Nigerian civil war (1967–70). The future of democracy in West Africa and throughout the continent will be heavily affected by whether Nigeria can build effective institutions to control corruption, mediate conflict, enforce a rule of law and decentralise power and revenue in a way that gives each major ethnic group a sense of SECURITY and a stake in the larger political system.

The weaker the presence of democracy in a region, the more that its future depends on the emergence of at least one or two systems that can provide a model of a functioning and authentic democracy within that type of cultural and social milieu. While the largest and most powerful countries of a region exercise the greatest potential influence, even smaller countries can provide such a model, as Botswana did for some time in Africa. South Korea, Taiwan and Thailand all provide models of democracies that are able to maintain (or revive) economic growth within the cultural and religious traditions of East Asia. Among the most intriguing and important questions for the global future of democracy is whether there are any Arab countries that may forge a viable democratic model for their region. If it were to negotiate a genuine transition, Egypt, as the largest country in the Arab world and the one with the richest history as a civilisation, would have the most impact, but Egypt shows few signs of serious movement in this direction. More scope for democratic change may exist in Morocco and Jordan, the two Arab countries where political PLURALISM and liberalisation has proceeded the furthest, and where much younger and (it is believed) more liberal kings ascended to the throne in 1999. Yet each regime has moved back and forth between liberalisation and repression for some years now, and any breakthrough to electoral democracy would probably require a bold and risky decision by the ruling monarch, in a context of continuing unease about the intentions and international ties of Islamic fundamentalist political forces. More generally, the Islamic world still awaits a successful model of a democratic and relatively liberal state. Any sizeable country with a predominantly Muslim population that constructed such a model – be it Turkey, Pakistan or Indonesia – could have an enormous impact on the other forty countries of the world where Islam is the principal religion.

The future of the established democracies

If democracy is to continue to expand in the twenty-first century, it must remain vibrant, dynamic and worthy of emulation in the oldest, richest and most influential democracies of the world, particularly those of Europe and the United States. The spread of democracy in the last quarter of the twentieth century had much to do with the perception that the established democracies in Europe and North America were more appealing and successful societies in almost every respect than their only ideological competitor, the increasingly decrepit communist systems of the Soviet bloc. Today, there are no foreseeable threats to the stability of the wealthy, established democracies. But there is nagging concern about the role that money, privilege and corporate power play in most of these systems, and questions about the degree to which these constitutional systems will successfully incorporate and adapt to the new information age. For the United States in particular, the invigoration of democracy was seen by many political observers, and by two major presidential candidates in the year 2000 party primaries, to depend on dramatic revision of campaign finance laws to level the electoral playing field and reduce the influence of large corporate and special-interest campaign donors (see POLITICAL FINANCING).

As the electronic MEDIA grow in importance, access to television is becoming an increasingly vital standard by which to judge the fairness of election campaigns, and a growing number of democracies (new as well as old) are experimenting with provisions for free television time for competing parties and candidates. However, most democracies have only begun to address the problem of how to provide fair and meaningful media access to competing PARTIES and candidates, while distinguishing between campaigns that enjoy some significant base of popular support and those that do not. The problem is particularly acute in many new and emerging democracies, where much of the television media is still controlled by a partisan state, or by business interests closely intertwined with the ruling party.

The information age also offers new opportunities for deepening democracy. One opportunity arises from the growing use of the internet by political campaigns to convey their issue positions in depth, recruit financial and volunteer support, and communicate directly with voters. Increasingly, national (and even local) political parties and campaigns will rely on this free medium as an indispensable tool of political competition. And already, some localities in the United States are experimenting with electronic voting over the internet, a practice that will probably become routine in many countries not far into the twenty-first century.

A key question for the future is how new technologies can be harnessed to improve the quality of democracy, not merely its openness but its accountability and deliberative depth. An intriguing possibility in this regard is the 'deliberative poll', which 'takes the two technologies, polling and television, that have given us a superficial form of mass democracy, and harnesses them to a new and constructive purpose – giving voice to the people under conditions where the people can think' (Fishkin 1995: 163). A random sample of the public is given intensive and carefully balanced access to all sides of a political issue or choice, not only through television but through direct, face-to-face encounters with competing experts and politicians, and with their fellow randomly selected citizens in a small group setting. After several days of deliberation (a kind of modern Athenian democracy), the randomly selected citizens are polled about their views, offering the country 'a representation of the considered judgements of the public' – some plausible sense of what the entire electorate might think 'if it had the same experience of behaving more like ideal citizens immersed in the issues for an extended period' (Fishkin 1995: 162). Although such a deliberative poll is expensive, it is well within the means of current technology, and was used to interesting effect during Australia's 1999 referendum on whether to become a republic.

Finally, the future of democracy will also depend on the degree to which, and the effectiveness with which, the established democracies, as well as a growing number of international and regional institutions, promote democracy around the world. One of the most distinctive and remarkable features of the third wave of democratisation is the substantial and growing scope of aid to parties, legislatures, judicial systems, independent think tanks and civil society organisations, the mass media, and a variety of other democratic institutions in emerging democracies from official aid organisations and private foundations in the established democracies. Not all of this aid has been effective, but much of it has not only helped to strengthen and professionalise emerging democratic institutions, it has also drawn their leaders and activists into global networks of unprecedented scope and normative vigour. Together with the growing prominence of political conditions (involving transparency, accountability and other dimensions of 'good governance', if not democracy explicitly) for international development and adjustment assistance, and for membership in such regional organisations as the Organisation of American States, expanded political assistance has created a new global environment with strong incentives for countries to move toward, develop, and maintain democracy. The need for political stability, transparency and an institutionalised rule of law to attract international capital further reinforces this global environment.

If this international assistance and conditionality is sustained, and seeps more and more deeply into the architecture of international institutions and the expectations of national and international actors, it will significantly diminish the prospects of a third 'reverse wave'

of democratic breakdowns. If such a permanent alteration in the global political environment is accompanied by a continued lowering of barriers to international trade and cultural flows, and (partly as a consequence) by more or less sustained economic growth in most of the developing and post-communist worlds, it is likely that democracy will continue its expansion during the first decades of the twenty-first century. Indeed, it is even imaginable that by mid-century most nations of the world will be democratic, and that a great many more of them than today will be solidly and liberally so.

See also:

democratic development; democratic transition

Further reading

Diamond, L. (1999) *Developing Democracy: Toward Consolidation*, Baltimore: Johns Hopkins University Press.

Fishkin, J.S. (1995) *The Voice of the People: Public Opinion and Democracy*, New Haven, CT: Yale University Press.

Huntington, S. (1991) *The Third Wave: Democratization in the Late Twentieth Century*, Norman, OK: University of Oklahoma Press.

Karatnycky, A. (2000) 'The 1999 Freedom House Survey; A Century of Progress', *Journal of Democracy* 11(1): 187–200.

Linz, J. and Stepan, A. (1996) *Problems of Democratic Transition and Consolidation: Southern Europe, South America, and Post-Communist Europe*, Baltimore: Johns Hopkins University Press.

Oksenberg, M. (1998) 'Will China Democratize? Confronting a Classic Dilemma', *Journal of Democracy* 9(1): 27–40.

Pei, M. (1995) '"Creeping Democratization" in China', *Journal of Democracy* 6(4): 65–79.

—— (1998) 'Is China Democratizing?', *Foreign Affairs* 77(1): 68–82.

Przeworski, A., Alvarez, M., Cheibub, J.A. and Limongi, F. (1996) 'What Makes Democracies Endure?', *Journal of Democracy* 7(1): 39–55.

Rowen, H.S. (1996) 'World Wealth Expanding:

Why a Rich, Democratic, and (Perhaps) Peaceful Era is Ahead', in R. Landau, T. Taylor and G. Wright (eds), *The Mosaic of Economic Growth*, Stanford, CA: Stanford University Press.

LARRY DIAMOND

democracy, justifications for

The impulse to justify democracy is born with democracy in fifth-century BC Athens. It needed justification then and needs it now because it often offends philosophers (for whom justification is a way of life), and it offends traditionalist forms of government that are often seen 'natural' and from which every departure demands an explanation. In this sense, the justification of democracy is part of the democratic enterprise itself; that is to say, to practice democracy is in part to argue for its legitimacy, while to debate the meaning and to justify its grounds is much of what democracy is about. To a considerable degree, the history of political thought has been the history of the continuing debate about whether democracy can be justified, and if so, how. All of the major texts of the Western tradition bear on the question of whether the people (the 'demes' or residential tribes of ancient Athens) need to be ruled or have the right and/or capacity to rule themselves. Democracy is one way of justifying political authority itself, and thus always engenders a debate about legitimacy.

Legitimacy is the normative element in governance, and implies good or just or sufficient governance as given by some underlying norm. In classical Greek thought, there were two distinctive ways to ask whether or not democracy is legitimate, or whether or not a people is justified in governing itself. The first concerned itself with issues of capacity, the second concerned itself with issues of right. The relevant question to be asked in the first case is, who rules best? This question requires, in turn, some clear conception of the ends and objects of government: who rules best in terms of which objectives and end? The question in

the second case is who has the *right* to rule? This question entails a discussion of the nature of rulership and the relationship between rulers and ruled. There are to be sure democratic and anti-democratic arguments associated with each of these questions. Nevertheless, arguments from capacity have tended towards aristocratic or meritocratic answers; that is to say, the wisest should rule, or the strongest should rule, or the wealthiest or ablest or most expert should rule. Whereas arguments from right have tended towards democratic answers; the ruled have the right to participate in ruling themselves. Every man has a right *not* to be enslaved by others.

Plato (or, if you like, Socrates) opposed the Athenian demes and denied their LEGITIMACY to rule not only because they lacked the capacity to rule, but because in a republic whose object was justice – a well-ordered commonwealth – only those blessed with the capacity to discern the true and just forms had the right to rule. Thus, Plato concluded, until philosophers (students of true knowledge and hence of justice) became kings or kings became philosophers, human society was doomed to disorder and injustice. The democratic response to Plato has not been that ordinary men can discern the just as clearly as philosophers, although there have been theorists like Machiavelli who have claimed that the people generally know their interests and ends better than individual rulers, whether philosophical or not. Rather, it has been to argue that government is not about what we know but about what we have to do, not about truth but about interests. It is practical rather than a speculative science, and requires debate, political interaction and deliberation, all of which are offered by a democracy. Aristotle understood politics to be a practical science and was more hospitable to democracy, at least as one element in a 'mixed constitution', than his philosophical predecessors.

We can discern in the trial of Socrates the very essence of the quarrel between philosophical aristocrats and practical democrats. To the democrats of ancient Athens, Socrates appeared to be using an appeal to truth to disguise the base interests represented by Athenians of status and wealth who detested democracy. After all, even philosophers have interests, and the cynical Thrasymachus insisted that justice was never much more than the interest of the stronger. To the friends of Socrates, the democrats were trying to impose their prejudices on a noble and just man by brute force, inverting the natural order between reason and passion. The party of philosophy understood government as the rule of reason, which in turn suggested the most reasonable should rule. To the party of the people, the government could never be more than the rule of interests and hence of the interested: since each interest was the equal of the next, the interested (the people themselves) had every right to govern.

The Athenian contest between aristocratic philosophers and ordinary democrats (often supported by the tragedians and poets) also points to the intimate connection between EQUALITY and democracy. Equality finds its way into nearly every justification of democracy. Plato made hierarchical assumptions about human nature: the soul came in several versions, some base, some noble, and the noble were suited by nature to govern the base. In the Greek view, represented by Aristotle, the Greeks were superior to barbarians as men were superior to women; this meant that some men were 'natural' slaves who 'needed' to be ruled by others. Beginning with such assumptions, it is hard to arrive at a position that justifies universal democracy (although equality within a ruling cast, say white propertied males, might ground a partial democracy of the kind established in the new United States in 1789).

From the premise that human nature is defined by equality comes quite a different view of human relations. In Stoic and Christian natural philosophy, a different style of argument emerges rooted in the belief that men are 'born free and equal', or are equal by virtue of common birth from a common parent (the fatherhood of God, the brotherhood of man). Under such circumstances they clearly have an equal right to governance. Among equals, the only suitable form of pre-eminence is numbers:

fifty-one outweighs forty-nine. Majority rule becomes a concomitant of an egalitarian account of human nature.

This is the backdrop for the debate over democratic legitimacy. We can now look to a number of more specific arguments that have been advanced on behalf of democracy, justifying arguments on which democratic legitimacy may be said to depend. These arguments obviously overlap and reinforce one another, and in practice are found mixed together. The debates we have explored here reappear in one form or another in many of them. These arguments include *affirmative* justifications rooted in divine will, liberty and consent, nature and equality, utility, interest, peace and stability, capitalism and markets, and revolutionary will, as well as *scepticist* justifications rooted in scepticism and default.

The argument from divine will: *vox populi, vox dei*

'Democracy is the voice of the people representing the voice of God.' An early democratic argument bent a traditional argument for the divine rule of kings to popular purposes. As Christian monarchists once claimed God spoke to his human subjects through popes and kings – the 'mandate of heaven' – deist democrats like William Godwin could argue that God spoke through the people themselves, who were thus in effect God's deputies in things political: thus, *vox populi, vox dei*. The ultimate legitimacy of the people was thus made to be a matter of divine rather than human will. Often the argument that men were fit by nature to rule themselves concealed the premise that God (as nature's maker) lay behind the natural right.

The argument from liberty and consent: Rousseau

'Democracy is the only form of government for beings who are naturally free and therefore can only be government with their consent.' Although this argument is to a degree built into the argument from equality, it takes a unique form in Jean-Jacques Rousseau's notion of the general will. Rousseau suggests that democracy is the only solution to a natural paradox: how can men, born free, obey government and belong to a community yet still be as free (by nature) as they were before? The answer lies in participatory democracy, where men participate in making the laws to which they owe their obedience. In obeying laws they give to themselves, they are merely obeying themselves, and thus not compromising their liberty. They are willing what they hold in common with others – general will – and thus are at once expressing their liberty and living under a community of laws they create for themselves. Although this solution does not quite make men as 'free as they were before', it endows them with a higher civil and moral FREEDOM. To Rousseau, democracy is the sole form of government that is legitimate, uniting the individual and the community, the will of one and the general will, liberty and legislation. He not only provides a justification for democracy, but an argument that democracy is the only justifiable form of government that is compatible with human liberty.

The argument from nature: equality and right

'Democracy is simply the expression in government of the natural equality of all human beings.' If, as Jean-Jacques Rousseau and Thomas Jefferson argued, human beings are born free and equal, then they have an equal right to participate in government. Endowed naturally (and/or by their creator, see above) with liberty, their consent is required whenever they surrender it to (or comply with) political AUTHORITY. The tradition of social contract reasoning from Hobbes and Locke through Rousseau and the American Founders relies on this instrumental logic: equality and freedom entail right; right entails consent; consent entails a social contract legitimating the exercise of political authority; the social contract entails democracy, the SOVEREIGNTY (original authority) of the people in government.

The argument from utility

'Democracy is rooted in an instrumentalist logic associated with the doctrine of social contract – that men create governments to serve their interests and ends.' Utilitarianism offers contractarian justification for democracy which shares the instrumentalism of the social contract but emphasises the moral worth of the majority. If all humans have comparable needs and desires and they experience commensurate pains and commensurate joys, then the satisfaction of the needs of one can never be privileged over the satisfaction of the needs of another. Each must count for one. In making common decisions, the only just principle is counting, a principle that dictates that the greater number, representing the greater happiness, must prevail over the lesser. Jeremy Bentham and James Mill offer the classical version of this position while John Stuart Mill offers a classic critique (although it is made in the name of utility).

The argument from interest

'Democracy is government by, for and of the interested.' If government is understood as the pursuit of the common interest, it can be argued that only interested selves are fit to govern. Who knows better what the people need or want than the people themselves? Modern social science and pluralist theory have relied on this justification. Since political scientists regard politics as a question of 'who gets what, when and how?', it is necessarily a competition for power by the interested. Joseph Schumpeter's 'neo-elitist' conception of democracy as a competition among elites for the votes of the interested is one version of this argument. David Truman and Robert Dahl offer another focusing on the plurality of interests and on voting as a just system of arbitration. Property as a particularly salient interest has played a special role in this justification. It suggests that to hold property (defined in Locke as the property men hold in those parts of the natural world with which they mix their own labour, which in turn embodies their identity) is to possess a natural right to participate in governance as well as to determine questions of how property is defined, taxed and transferred; it also suggests that those without property do not have such a right, a position some attribute to John Locke and one that has been used to exclude non-property owners from SUFFRAGE, as did many early American states.

The argument from peace and stability

'Democracy is the most stable and pacific form of government and that alone is sufficient justification for it.' Proponents of peace and the international order have argued that democracies are far less likely to engage in warfare with one another than non-democratic states and that democracy therefore offers a recipe for global peace. Others have suggested that democracy produces greater stability over the long run than other forms of government. Both claims are historically contestable, and some have even insisted democracy is a particularly unpredictable and uncertain form of government, particularly in its early developmental phase. Nonetheless, for many the propensity of democracies to breed peace and concord, at least among one another, has served as an important justification.

The argument from capitalism and markets

'Democracy provides capitalism's context and models and undergirds the liberty that CAPITALISM needs and generates.' In its close historical association with the growth of industrial society and the emergence of market economies and in its focus in common with capitalism on liberty, democracy has often been regarded as a concomitant of and thus a justification for capitalism. Friedrich Hayek and Milton Friedman, and more recently Robert Nozick, have all argued that democracy and capitalism are reciprocal entailments of one another; that democratic government is justified by the service it offers to capitalism and the virtues and liberties capitalism putatively secures. This argument, rooted in a

concern with liberty, has had to contend with its contrary: that democracy has a closer kinship to socialism and economic egalitarianism and is naturally at odds with the market. But in recent times the connection to markets has been one of the most widely used justifications for democracy.

The argument from spontaneous revolutionary will

'Democracy embodies the spontaneous will of a revolutionary people, and is justified by the radical engagement and civic PARTICIPATION it engenders.' Jefferson, Hannah Arendt and others have argued that democracy is justified because it maximises spontaneity, revolutionary change and participation: goods in themselves. Jefferson embraced the democratic formula in ward politics because it permitted ongoing participation and the revisiting and revisioning of all dogmas, including constitutional dogmas. Calling for a little revolution every nineteen years, he associated democracy with an activist expression of personal liberty (see REVOLUTIONS). More recently, participatory and 'strong democrats' have suggested that democracy serves common willing understood as common deliberation and common action and that this is itself an argument on democracy's behalf.

The argument from scepticism

'Democracy is how we govern ourselves in the absence of certainty and truth.' John Stuart Mill captured an important sceptical element in justifications for democracy in his insistence that knowledge, being in part a product of social interaction, was secured (if at all) primarily through deliberation, hammered out on the anvil of debate. Since neither truth nor right can be known absolutely or agreed upon universally, uncertainty (or what modern social scientists call contestability) is the human condition and democracy the only prudent system of government. It is, Mill observes, as likely that one man will be right and the whole world wrong as it is that one will be wrong and the whole world right. In the twentieth century, philosophers like Bertrand Russell and Karl Popper have offered similar 'fallibilist' arguments rooted in the idea that such knowledge as we have derives from our capacity to falsify rather than to know with certainty and depends on intersubjective consensus rather than individual discernment.

The default argument from comparison

'Democracy is the least objectionable form of governance.' A version of the sceptical claim for democracy which borders on cynicism can be extracted from Winston Churchill's quip that democracy is the worst form of government in the world except for all the other forms. For all of its failings, democracy can be shown to be far less pernicious than other forms of government, and is thus good government in the default mode. The argument is connected with Jefferson's sharp question asking how those who think men are not able to govern themselves (as critics of democracy insist they are not) can possibly govern others (the aristocratic premise)? The conclusion seems to be that democracy is the only viable way for men incapable of governing others and unwilling to permit others to govern them.

There is a range of justifications by which democracy can be legitimated, then, and those offered here are but a representative selection. While they can be isolated in theory, in practice they are deployed in an overlapping fashion. In this sense, they are not wholly discrete arguments. Moreover, there are three important caveats attending the justificatory enterprise itself: the first a historical point about the secondary role of justification in the founding of democracies; the second a conceptual point about the essentially anti-foundational and thus anti-justificatory character of democracy itself; and the third a vital point about inclusion and democracy.

Justifications for democracy have historically often been post hoc. That is to say, they represent efforts by lawyers and political theorists to legitimise the popular seizing of

government through revolution. It is not as if the rights of the people have been granted to them by elites yielding to rational and sound justificatory arguments. Rather, as a regime form, democracy has most often been established by protest and force. Sovereignty has have been seized, established for the first time by rebels for whom theory and justification come only afterwards. The battle to define democracy and to justify it once it has been established is carried on democratically, but the battle to establish it takes place on the turf of revolution and force. This is not a justification for it, but simply an observation about the secondary role that justification plays in the founding of democratic regimes.

The second caveat grows out of the first: the search for a justification for democracy tends to be foundational, aimed at 'grounding' democracy in some pre-political philosophical or natural or legal or religious footings. But as democracy embraces spontaneity and autonomy, it abhors fixed antecedents. It can be justified externally, but derives its most convincing justification not from its genealogy but from its reflexivity: its self-critical, self-scrutinising practices that continually put its provisional principles to the test of deliberation. It processes itself and produces its own procedural conventions; that is the virtue of its participatory, representative, deliberative and transactional practices. In this sense, paradoxical as it may seem, democracy is its own justification. Its *modus operandi* is justification but for that very reason it does not require prior justification.

Finally, it must be remembered that democracy is a relative construct. As a wag once said, monarchy is a democracy in which there is only one citizen – the king. Athens was a vital participatory democracy, but only for a handful of residents: those who were not females, slaves or resident foreigners. America boasts its democratic origins in an era where slavery was the norm and neither women nor (in many states) unpropertied white males were included in the citizenry. Democracy has felt to many like a sham inasmuch as political and legal rights are not backed up by real recognition or social and economic equality. When the social contract turns out to be merely a sexual contract that assures patriarchy rather than equality, democracy becomes an exercise in hypocrisy.

See also:

capitalism; democratic origins; demos; political obligation

Further reading

Barber, B. (1984) *Strong Democracy*, Berkeley, CA: University of California Press.
—— (1988) *The Conquest of Politics*, Princeton, NJ: Princeton University Press.
Dahl, R. (1961) *Who Governs? Democracy and Power in an American City*, New Haven, CT: Yale University Press.

BENJAMIN BARBER

democratic audit

With the increasing prevalence of democratic forms of government throughout the world, and of attempts to construct and consolidate them, the demand to assess how well a country is doing in its process of democratisation has also become widespread. This demand comes from a number of different quarters: from political scientists keen to develop tools for the comparative analysis of democratic systems, and to explore the socioeconomic conditions which may facilitate or hinder successful democratisation; from Northern governments and NON-GOVERNMENTAL ORGANISATIONS (NGOs) which wish to exercise discrimination in their aid and trade policies; and from concerned citizens, who want to know how well or badly their country is doing in its democratic consolidation. However, this demand is not just directed to recently established democracies. A sense of democratic malaise affecting established democracies over recent decades has also encouraged the demand to assess whether this disquiet is justified and, if

so, in what respects these governmental systems may be judged deficient from a democratic point of view.

In response to these demands, two broadly different methods of democracy assessment can be distinguished. One is quantitative: it uses numerical indicators of performance in the areas of civil and political rights and ELECTORAL COMPETITION and inclusiveness in order to construct an overall league table of democratic attainment, covering all countries. While useful as an impressionistic device, this method suffers from a number of deficiencies. A quantitative index gives a spurious impression of objectivity to what are essentially complex matters of judgement, about the interpretation of evidence and the respective weight to be assigned to different aspects of democracy in an overall aggregative score. Another drawback is that important areas of democratic life are ignored because they do not lend themselves at all readily to quantification, such as the rule of law (see LAW, RULE OF), governmental ACCOUNTABILITY, MEDIA diversity or the vigour of a country's associational life.

A second, qualitative approach to democracy assessment is that of democratic audit. This seeks to take each aspect of a country's democratic life in turn, and subject it to a qualitative assessment of its strengths and weaknesses from a democratic point of view. While not rejecting quantitative or comparative indicators where appropriate, this method aims to produce a systematic discursive survey, or audit report, of the state of a given country's democracy, which can be used to stimulate debate among both government and the public at large, and to identify priorities for possible reform.

Like any other type of audit, conducting a democratic audit entails a number of different components: first, a clear set of questions to guide the investigation, or a checklist of what exactly is to be monitored; second, a clear sense of what evidence is needed to answer the questions, where to look for it, and how to ascertain its accuracy; third, an agreed set of standards as to what counts as a good or acceptable level of attainment, against which the assembled evidence can be assessed; and fourth, some recognition of who is qualified to act as 'auditors'. In the case of a democratic audit, each of these components raises considerable problems, which have to be addressed.

First are the problems of constructing a checklist of what is to be audited. These problems are threefold. There is the disagreement that exists over what constitutes democracy, and what to include within it. There is the complexity which arises from the fact that what is being audited is not a single institution, but an inter-relationship between many different institutions, arrangements and practices. Finally, there is what might be called the problem of 'legitimate variation'; we need to recognise the considerable differences that exist between how democracies work in practice, without abandoning criteria which will enable us to distinguish between more and less democratic arrangements.

These problems are not insuperable, however. There is broad agreement that democratic government is one which is based on free and fair competitive elections for the main public offices, on the basis of equal value votes of the whole adult population; in which government conforms to the rule of law, and is accountable to the people for its performance both directly and through the institutions of parliament, independent media and other organs of PUBLIC OPINION; and in which citizens have guaranteed rights to free expression, assembly and association, and exercise these vigorously but also with TOLERATION towards others. Each of these elements has to be audited, and with some sensitivity to their connectedness and to legitimate variations of practice.

Second is the selection of relevant data or evidence for each of the items on the checklist, and the verification of sources for their accuracy. For the most part, data can be obtained from existing sources, but new primary research may be needed to fill in gaps in the evidence. Among the difficulties to be addressed here is that the legal position, say, in respect of the constitutional guarantee of rights, may not be implemented in practice, or not uniformly throughout the territory of the state. Official sources may be highly misleading, while on the other hand, evidence of undemocratic practice has to be carefully scrutinised to ascertain whether it is typical or aberrant. In principle these problems are no different from those associated with any social scientific investigation, but they may become more sensitive or controversial in view of the explicitly normative character of an audit.

Third is the issue of the appropriate standards against which the assembled evidence is to be assessed. Democracy is not an all-or-nothing affair, but a matter of more or less: of the degree to which democratic principles are realised in institutional practice. But what counts as a good or appropriate standard of attainment? Is it one which shows improvement on a country's past, one which reaches performance levels set domestically by government, one which stands up well in comparison with regional comparators, or one which meets the appropriate international convention standards to which the country has signed up? All of these might be involved, but the balance between them must be a matter of judgement, taking into account the particular context of the country in question. In any case, although in some areas agreed international standards are already well established, as in the jurisprudence on civil and political rights or the criteria employed by election monitoring bodies to assess whether the ballot is 'free and fair', in many other aspects of democratic life standards are only beginning to be developed, or are a matter of considerable disagreement.

Finally there is the question of who is qualified to act as 'auditors', and by what authority they do so. On the one hand the task requires considerable expertise in institutional and political analysis, human rights law and social survey analysis, and an agreement on the normative criteria which are to provide the focus and benchmarks for the audit. At the same time it is now generally recognised, even by governments using audit methodology as a policy tool for focusing overseas aid, that the appropriate people to assess their democratic progress are the citizens of the country concerned; and that wide consultation within the country on both process and outcome is an essential feature of any properly democratic audit. How the tension between the legitimacy of expertise and that which comes from a wider involvement is to be resolved remains a key problem for the undertaking.

In the light of the above difficulties, it is perhaps not surprising that there is as yet no firmly established or generally agreed methodology for democratic audit. In any case, the concept is still at a relatively early stage of evolution. Yet it is likely that the practice and its methodology will become increasingly developed, in view of the demand for it, and that it will also be extended to the assessment of institutions at the regional and international level.

See also:

democratic deficit; legitimacy; transparency

Further reading

Beetham, D. (ed.) (1994) *Defining and Measuring Democracy*, London: Sage.

Freedom House (1999) *Freedom in the World, 1998–9*, New York: Freedom House.

Inkeles, A. (ed.) (1991) *On Measuring Democracy*, New Brunswick, NJ and London: Transaction Publishers.

Klug, F., Starmer, K. and Weir, S. (1996) *The Three Pillars of Liberty* (Vol.1 of the UK Democratic Audit), London: Routledge.

Petersson, O., von Beyme, K., Karvonen, L., Nedelmann, B. and Smith, E. (eds) (1999) *Democracy the Swedish Way* (report from the Democratic Audit of Sweden), Stockholm: SNS Forlag.

Weir, S. and Beetham, D. (1998) *Political Power and Democratic Control in Britain* (Vol.2 of the UK Democratic Audit), London: Routledge.

DAVID BEETHAM

democratic breakdown

In the nineteenth century, the acquisitions of LIBERALISM (constitutional government, the *Rechtsstaat* – a state bound by laws – representative institutions) seemed inalienable signs of progress in most of Europe, Latin America and the white portions of the British Empire, even when SUFFRAGE was often restricted and governments still were appointed by kings or queens and did not require the confidence of a legislature. Only a few countries were democracies based on universal male suffrage and deriving their powers exclusively from the people: they included the USA, New Zealand and Switzerland. At the turn of the century, progress toward democracy appeared as inevitable, and with the First World War, the first great wave of democratisation engulfed a large number of countries and newly independent states became democracies, reaching a maximum of thirty-three states. However, the 1920s and 1930s saw the first reverse wave, reducing this number to eleven. The question of the breakdown of democracies became central, and to it one can add the frustration of processes of democratisation in course in some countries (as in Spain).

The breakdown of democracies in the interwar years has to be placed in the context of competing ideologies, parties or movements and social forces identified with them. The Russian October revolution, led by Lenin, that overthrew the provisional government of Kerensky and closed the elected Constituent Assembly was the first defeat of the democratisers, although the communists had another short-lived success in Hungary. A new, powerful and ideologically attractive alternative to liberal democracy had appeared and would be present in Europe until the fall of the Berlin Wall in 1989 (see REVOLUTIONS). The Italian political and social crisis generated another ideological and political alternative, fascism, which would come to power in 1922 and later serve as a model for anti-democrats. The critique of liberalism and CAPITALISM and the hostility to anti-clerical and even anti-religious policies of democrats would strengthen corporativist–authoritarian tendencies among Catholics in Portugal, Austria and Spain and other Catholic countries. The positive memory of stable monarchies before the war – particularly in Germany and Austria-Hungary (now two states) whose defeat coincided with democratisation – would support anti-democratic tendencies among elites.

In 1929, the world depression, for which countries were not prepared, shattered the optimism of previous years, exacerbated class conflicts, contributed to the doubts or hostility of business elites toward democracy and seemed to require authoritarian responses. Marxist theorists, who prefer structural socioeconomic explanations, found the crisis a sufficient explanation of the breakdown. They argued that capitalism and democracy were incompatible and that capitalism inevitably led to fascism, disregarding other causes of breakdown or that late economic development required developmental dictatorships, particularly in Eastern Europe, the Balkans and Southern Europe. The frustrated or arrested development of democracy in Latin America found other explanations: the cultural tradition of authoritarianism, the Catholic tradition that continued to serve to explain, together with economic and social underdevelopment, the crises of democracy after the Second World War.

Later theoretical efforts, based on a more careful historical analysis of all the cases and the comparison with stable, successful democracies have expanded the variables to be considered as contributing to the breakdown. They questioned some of the more simplistic and mono-causal explanations. Some (Linz and Stepan) have emphasised the responses of different actors, including the democratic leaders and parties, to the crises of efficacy (performance) of democracies, privileging 'agents' over 'structures', questioning socioeconomic overdetermination without denying the constraining effects of socially unfavourable factors.

It is important to note that a number of democracies fell or their transition to democracy was interrupted before the world depression of 1929. Democratic governments survive to this day in the countries that were neutral in the First World War: Switzerland, Denmark, Sweden, Norway, the Netherlands, Belgium and Luxembourg, with the exception of Spain. Among the fifteen European states that existed before the war, democracy survived in nine (counting France, where only the defeat in 1940 by the Germans provided the anti-democratic right with a chance to gain power) while it crumbled or was arrested in six: Italy, Spain, Portugal, Bulgaria, Rumania and Greece. Eight countries gained their independence and democracy after the war but it would survive only in three: Finland, Czechoslovakia and Ireland. In none of the successor states of the defeated empires – Russia (USSR), Turkey, Hungary, Austria, Germany – would democracy persist, although in the last two a consolidation of democratic institutions seemed possible in the 1920s. It might be an accident that of the twelve stable democracies in Europe, seven were parliamentary monarchies and five were republics, while among the seventeen failures, six were monarchies and eleven were republics.

The problems of consolidation of democracy were compounded by defeat, with the loss of territories (like in Hungary), of full sovereignty (Germany and Austria), and the influx of refugees from Asia Minor into Greece after defeat by Turkey. In Italy (the 'frustrated' victory), the conflict between those who favoured intervention in the war and those who opposed it fragmented the party system, exacerbated the semi-revolutionary class conflict and generated the fascist–nationalist extreme anti-democratic right. In Spain, the defeat of the army in Morocco would contribute to the social tensions and political crisis that brought the 1923 dictatorship. The 1920s also witnessed unsuccessful revolutionary uprisings in Hungary (a brief communist rule), Germany, a quasi-revolutionary strike wave in Italy, a civil war in Finland and the Baltic countries, and a border war in the three Baltic republics and Poland with the USSR. The incertitude of borders and irredentist demands also generated conflicts and nationalist militias in Germany, Austria and Italy (the Italian volunteers who followed D'Annunzio in his expedition to Fiume, claimed from Yugoslavia), forces that would later feed anti-democratic violence.

State-building efforts in the new multinational states which also attempted to be nation-states – culturally and linguistically homogeneous – complicated democratic consolidation in new states: Yugoslavia, Poland, the Baltic republics (Estonia, Latvia and Lithuania) and even Czechoslovakia, with a German minority that, by identifying with Hitler's Germany, contributed to the destruction from the outside of the state and with it, of one of the few stable new democracies emerging from the war. In the study of the breakdown of democracies, the fact that the dominant nationality in Czechoslovakia (Czech and Slovaks) were 65 per cent of the population, in Poland 69 per cent, in Lithuania 80 per cent, in Latvia 73 per cent and in Estonia 88 per cent, with the consequent fractionalisation of the party system, should not be forgotten. In Western Europe, only in Spain were peripheral nationalisms a minor contributing factor in the crisis of democracy (see NATIONS AND NATIONALISM). Loyalty to, and a certain identification with, the state of ethnic MINORITIES and, on the other side, a willingness of the dominant nation to respect the rights of cultural and national minorities in a multinational state are requirements for democratic stability.

Communism was weak in the majority of the stable democracies, with the exception of France (where the communists obtained in 1936 15.3 per cent of the vote) and Germany (where, before 1929, they already had 13.1 per cent and in 1932 reached 16.7 per cent). This does not mean that the fear of communism and failed communist revolutionary attempts (in Germany, Finland and Estonia) did not contribute to the anti-democratic response of the right. Fascism in most countries, and particularly in stable democracies, was weak, with the exception of Belgium (with 10.4 per cent of the vote in 1936), and only had significant electoral strength in Italy (19.1 per cent in 1921), Germany (with a maximum of 37.4 per cent in July 1932), Hungary (25 per cent in 1936,

under a semi-authoritarian government that did not allow the fascists to take power) and Romania (15.6 per cent in 1936, although authoritarian governments persecuted the fascists and they attained power only for a short time). It was only in Germany that the added electoral and parliamentary strength of Nazis and communists constituted a majority in free elections making democracy unviable. The failure of anti-democratic mass-movements in a number of countries in which democracy survived despite the deep economic crisis (like Norway and the Netherlands, with unemployment rates higher than Germany) and the fact that democracies failed in countries with weak fascist movements (like Spain) and that fascist movements were suppressed by authoritarian governments (in Romania the Baltic states, Brazil and Japan) suggests the need to turn to explanations other than fascism for the breakdown in most cases (however, without ignoring the contribution of fascist violence and the appeal of fascism to non-democratic governments as a model).

Anti-democrats, those believing in the desirability of one of the four main ideological alternatives to democracy, were a factor of the breakdown, but the failures of democratic leaders and parties that contributed to their success cannot be ignored. The fact that in the Scandinavian countries and Finland democracy not only survived the economic crisis but was strengthened, that in Belgium and the Netherlands democrats united to isolate and defeat significant fascist movements, that even the French Third Republic survived until military defeat, show the resilience of democracy and the importance of democratic political responses. In Scandinavia and Finland, democratic socialist parties were able to form stable coalitions with farmers' parties on the basis of mutual concessions in economic and social policies – the red–green coalitions – that assured stable governments in the crisis years of the thirties. In Belgium, the Christian Democrats, the Social Democrats and the Liberals united to stop the rise of Rex (the fascist party) in crucial elections, even presenting a joint candidate.

Such a cooperation of democrats had been impossible in Italy between a maximalist socialist party, the Christian Democratic Populari and the anti-interventionist Liberals, opposed to each other on a variety of issues, in the early 1920s. The same was true in Austria, where the bitter conflict between socialists – in part ambivalent about the value of democracy – and conservative Christians attracted to corporativist ideology contributed to the cooperation of the latter with a national fascist movement (the Heimwehr) in establishing an authoritarian regime that could not resist the Nazi attack. Only joint defence of democracy, the absence of semi-loyal behaviours and alliances between potentially democratic parties and extremists could save democracies facing crises and avoid polarisation. The basic hostility and distrust of the Spanish socialists of conservatives that led to the failed revolution of October 1934; the ambivalence toward the type of democracy established in 1931 by the less extreme right contributed to the polarisation of two blocs in the 1936 election and the social conflicts that ended in a civil war (1936–9). The semi-loyalty to democracy in the pursuit of other goals, in a society with severe social problems, doomed a hopeful democratic experiment.

This brings us to a basic theoretical model of the breakdown of democracies. Two central dimensions, LEGITIMACY and efficacy, define four situations. Legitimacy is defined as the belief by the majority of the citizens and significant part of key elites (the politicians, military bureaucracy, business and trade union leaders) that a particular regime, in this case democracy, is the best for the particular country (if not for any country). Efficacy refers to the capacity to offer solutions to the most serious problems. Ideally, we would have governments that are legitimate and efficacious. On the other extreme, we have those which are neither and therefore most vulnerable to breakdown. There are, however, regimes supported by a strong belief in their legitimacy – like some of the older democracies, particularly some of the parliamentary monarchies of western and northern Europe – that when

faced with a crisis of efficacy could weather it. The initial rejection of legitimacy of the German democracy, born out of defeat, by many nationalists and conservatives and by frustrated Marxist revolutionaries, combined with the crisis of efficacy in the early 1930s, led to the breakdown. The same is true for Austria, whose independent statehood was questioned by the Pan-Germans. Even in such situations, the anti-democrats offering an alternative model of politics would not always have been successful if those moderates not opposed to democracy in principle would not have considered the extremists justified in their opposition, would not have been ready to make coalitions with them and tolerate their violence, rather than co-operating with the movements on the other side of the political spectrum, forgetting some of the issues separating them. What Linz has called semi-loyal oppositions played a major role in transforming difficult or unsolvable problems into regime crises.

Symptoms of the crisis, that at the same time contribute to it, are growing cabinet instability, the loss of democratic authenticity and the loss of the monopoly of legitimate violence by the state. The loss of authenticity is reflected in the turning of decision-making power to 'neutral' non-partisan institutions: the courts, the presidency rather than parliament in parliamentary democracies, the armed forces by the appointment of military officers to the cabinet. The refusal of party leaders to head the government and the reduction of the DECISION-MAKING arena to small groups often with the participation of those not holding elected office is part of that loss of democratic authenticity.

In last analysis, breakdown is the result of a process initiated by the government's incapacity to solve the problems for which the disloyal oppositions offer themselves as a solution. The communist interpretation of the rise of fascism was that of Georgi Dimitroff (1935), who defined it as 'the openly terrorist dictatorship of the most reactionary, most chauvinistic, most imperialistic elements of finance capital . . . the power of finance capital itself'. Even if one were to accept this interpretation for the rise of Hitler to power, the stability of democracy in the United Kingdom, Switzerland, the Netherlands and Belgium (centres of finance capitalism) alone, leaving aside France and the USA, would make this explanation untenable.

There are more sophisticated Marxist interpretations. Barrington Moore (1966), with his three routes to modernity – the bourgeois-democratic (with a dominant urban industrial bourgeoisie, commercialisation of agriculture, gradual incorporation of the working class), the peasant-based communist route and the authoritarian-fascist route – is more complex and presumably accounts for the failure of democracy on the one side in Russia and China and on the other in Germany and Japan. In the latter, the landed aristocracy continued to be dominant in a centralised system controlled by the bureaucracy and the military, into which the bourgeoisie was integrated (feudalised), at the expense of the working class. The smaller countries are not included in his analysis on account of their economic and political dependency, so that their fate depended on their neighbours, a view that has been highly criticised. Moore's thesis might account for difficulties in the process of democratisation in Germany under the Empire before 1918, but other or additional factors have to be introduced to explain for the rise of Nazism.

The important studies of the social and economic development prerequisites for democracy of S.M. Lipset and Tatu Vanhanen account for the difficulties in consolidating democracies in a number of countries, but neither can account for the dramatic breakdown in Germany, one of the most prosperous, urbanised, literate and industrial countries of Europe.

Rueschemeyer *et al.* (1992) in their important work, *Capitalist Development and Democracy*, develop a complex analysis of the role of different social strata in the emergence, failure and breakdown of democracy in Europe, Latin America, the Caribbean and Central America: these strata include the upper classes, particularly the landed upper class, the middle class and the working class (see CLASS). It is impossible to summarise, even less review critically, their rich contribution which also includes review of the work of other scholars. The patterns of state–class alliances of the nineteenth and early twentieth centuries, together with agrarian class relations, were sufficient but not necessary causes of democratic breakdown in Europe between the wars. The bourgeoisie attained authoritarian options but as the landlord–state–bourgeois alliance affected middle-class and peasant politics, options closed for the working class.

The difficulties of building stable democracies in Latin America since independence early in the nineteenth century, despite the early commitment to constitutional government, liberal values and, first to restricted democracy and in this century to fully democratic institutions, have been the object of considerable theoretical efforts and descriptive historical study (Diamond *et al.* 1989). The conditions for democracy and the causes of the breakdown certainly have not been the same in the Southern Cone – Argentina, Uruguay, Chile and Brazil – as in the Andean republics, or in Central America. Chile has had a democratic development and a party system much more similar to that of Europe, although as Valenzuela (1978) has shown, the crisis that led to the overthrow of Allende and his Unidad Popular government cannot be understood without reference to strain between presidentialism and a polarised multiparty system, and the impact of the Cuban Revolution and Castroism on the whole continent and the US response to the left in the context of the Cold War. The crisis of democracy in Argentina, Uruguay and Brazil led to the formulation of the theory of bureaucratic authoritarianism of Guillermo O'Donnell (1973), although in the case of Brazil, Alfred Stepan (1971) provided a different interpretation giving less weight to structural and economic factors than to specifically political circumstances. Collier and Collier (1981), in their comparative analysis, have focused on the political legacies of the initial incorporation of labour movements. The most complex comparative recent analysis covering all of the Americas is Rueschemeyer *et al.* (1992), which combines structural and conjectural political factors. The history of Latin America does not show a linear progression from oligarchic regimes to full democracy, but a variety of paths involving reversals and skipping of stages. It also presents periods of populist authoritarianism like the Estado Novo of Getulio Vargas (1937–45), who later would be elected president democratically, and of General Juan (Domingo) Peron, who acceded democratically to power to establish an undemocratic rule only to be ousted by a coup establishing a semi-democratic rule. This crisis in turn led to an unstable democratic period which was ended by a military authoritarian regime – the model for O'Donnell's theory of bureaucratic authoritarianism – the democratic return of Peron and the disastrous rule by his wife and vice-president Maria Estela (Isabella) Peron who succeeded him in office. She was in turn ousted by one of the most repressive military regimes. Populist authoritarian or democratic rule contributed to the social modernisation, a distinctive form of economic development that can be seen as favourable to democratisation, but also interrupted the normal development of democratic political institutions. The same can be said about some revolutionary regimes like that of Movimiento Nacional Revolucionario (MNR) in Bolivia and the progressive military dictatorship in Peru.

Uruguay is the country with the most prolonged and stable periods of democratic rule (1919–33, 1942–73), based on a two-party system and a complex electoral system, experiments with a collective presidency and the early development of a welfare state. However, as the result of the anti-democratic wave in the 1960s, between 1973 and 1984 it too was ruled by a military regime.

A major factor in the crises and breakdown of democracy in Latin America has been the military (see MILITARY CONSTITUTIONALISM). Originally the wars of independence, the conflicts between states in the nation-building process, the role of the army in the maintenance of order, but above all the appeal of different political forces for military support either to achieve democratisation or to forestall the consequences of democratisation and in the impasses created by conflicts between presidents and congress and their attempts to impose re-election, led to military intervention. The pattern in some cases became habit-forming. The 1960s witnessed the transition from the military as *poder moderador* (moderating arbiter) to what Stepan (1971) called the new professionalism based on greater political economic and managerial knowledge and the emergence of a 'national security doctrine' as a response to real, potential or imagined subversive revolutionary threats as a result of the Cuban revolution and in the context of the Cold War. Failures of or even support by civilian political and social elites facilitated the military's taking power, although its institutionalisation was not successful. In most cases this did not lead to a personalised dictatorship but to rule by the military as institution.

Guillermo O'Donnell, on the basis of a case study of Argentina, advanced in 1973 a model for the breakdown of democracy linking a higher state of economic and social development with the emergence of bureaucratic authoritarianism. In this influential, though debated, model a new coalition of incumbents of technocratic roles in the public and private sectors, particularly a new type of military elite, with the support of social strata threatened by the mobilisation of popular sectors mainly of the working class and by populist politicians, turned against democracy. Presumably, under certain conditions, continued capitalist development required the exclusion of the demands of the working class and other progressive forces – students, intellectuals – by military intervention and repression. The level of economic development in the specific Latin American international economic dependency relation, the exhaustion of the import substitution-based industrialisation and the economic imbalances it generated, the urbanisation and expansion of the role of the state, the growing popular demands, led to a situation of 'mass praetorianism'. Governments had become unable to respond to these challenges. At that point, these technocratic elites convinced of their ability to respond to them, favoured an authoritarian solution of the crisis.

Other authors have questioned the complex socioeconomic model involved, the need of a repressive authoritarian rule, to assure capitalist development and have emphasised the failures of populist democratic leadership and the impact of the radicalisation of certain sectors as the result of the Cuban revolution, including terrorist activities, that generated the fear and hostility of conservative sectors and the military and also, in the context of the Cold War, a sympathetic response from the United States. This led to the coups that ended for a considerable time democracy in the countries of the Southern Cone. Fortunately, after much suffering, those regimes failed to institutionalise themselves, and in recent decades we have seen successful transitions to democracy in Argentina, Uruguay, Brazil and Chile, despite economic difficulties like the debt crisis and high inflation in some of them.

After the 'third wave' of democratisation (Linz and Stepan 1996), we encounter numerous cases of deterioration of democratic institutions, authoritarian rule with semi-competitive elections, concentration of power in elected presidents, violation of civil liberties, but fewer breakdowns like those in the twentieth-century or classic military dictatorships. Defective or pseudo-democracies (Merkel 1999) are the rule and in some countries 'chaocracies' where the state rather than the regime is in crisis.

See also:

democratic transition; nations and nationalism

Further reading

Berg-Schlosser, D. and DeMeur, G. (1994) 'Conditions of Democracy in Interwar Europe: A Boolean Test of Major Hypotheses', *Comparative Politics* 26(3): 253–79.

Collier, D. (1970) 'The Bureaucratic-Authoritarian Model: Synthesis and Priorities for Future Research', in D. Collier (ed.), *The New Authoritarianism in Latin America*, Princeton, NJ: Princeton University Press.

Collier, D. and Collier, R.B. (1991) *Shaping the Political Arena*, Princeton, NJ: Princeton University Press.

Diamond, L., Lipset, S.M. and Linz, J.J. (1989) *Democracy in Developing Countries*, Boulder, CO: Lynne Rienner.

Huntington, S.P. (1991) *The Third Wave: Democratization in the Late Twentieth Century*, Norman, OK: University of Oklahoma Press.

Linz, J.J. and Stepan, A. (eds) (1978) *The Breakdown of Democratic Regimes*, Baltimore: John Hopkins University Press.

—— (1996) *Problems of Democratic Transition and Consolidation: Southern Europe, South America and post-Communist Europe*, Baltimore, MD: The Johns Hopkins University Press.

Lipset, S.M. (1981) *Political Man: The Social Bases of Politics*, Baltimore, MD: Johns Hopkins University Press.

Maier, C. (1973) *Recasting Bourgeois Europe*, Princeton, NJ: Princeton University Press.

Malefakis, E. (1970) *Agrarian Reform and Peasant Revolution in Spain*, New Haven, CT: Yale University Press.

Merkel, W. (1999) 'Defekte Demokratien', in W. Merkel and A. Busch (eds), *Demokratie in Ost und West: Für Klaus von Beyme*, Frankfurt: Suhrkamp, 361–81.

Moore, B. (1966) *The Social Origins of Dictatorship and Democracy*, Boston: Beacon Press.

O'Donnell, G.A. (1973) *Modernization and Bureaucratic Authoritarianism*, Berkeley, CA: Institute of International Studies.

Rueschemeyer, D., Huber Stephens, E. and Stephens, J.D. (1992) *Capitalist Development and Democracy*, Chicago: University of Chicago Press.

Stepan, A. (1971) *The Military in Politics: Changing Patterns in Brazil*, Princeton, NJ: Princeton University Press.

Valenzuela, A. (1978) *The Breakdown of Democratic Regimes, Chile*, Baltimore, MD: Johns Hopkins University Press.

Vanhanen, T. (1990) *The Process of Democratization*, New York: Crane Russak.

Zimmermann, E. (1983) *Political Violence, Crises and Revolutions*, Cambridge, MA: Schenkman.

—— (1985) 'The 1930 World Economic Crisis in Six European Countries: A First Report on Causes of Political Instability and Reactions to Crisis', in P.M. Johnson and W.R. Thompson (eds), *Rhythms in Politics and Economics*, New York: Praeger.

—— (1986) 'Government Stability in Six European Countries during the World Economic Crisis of 1930: Some Preliminary Considerations', *European Journal of Political Research* 14.

JUAN J. LINZ

democratic consolidation

The concept of democratic consolidation has become one of the most frequently used concepts in comparative politics, being the term of choice for some of the best theory-driven works on the politics of Latin America, Eastern Europe, East Asia and Southern Europe since the 1980s (Mainwaring *et al.* 1992; Higley and Gunther 1992; Gunther *et al.* 1995; Diamond 1999). More recently, the concept has also been used by scholars working on Western Europe. Its significance in current thinking about democracy is beyond dispute.

However, the popularity of this concept has its costs, especially in terms of the lack of clarity and/or agreement about the meaning of democratic consolidation. Responding to these problems, various scholars have begun a reassessment of the concept. Some see the confusion surrounding the concept as an inevitable result of the evolution of a popular concept. Their response has emphasised the need for greater conceptual clarity and order, and to this end they have carried out conceptual analyses that shed light on the structure of the concept and its various uses (Collier and Levitsky 1997; Schedler 1998). If this first approach faces up to the problematic status of

democratic consolidation as a way to ensure its continued value as a analytic concept, other scholars take a more radical approach, arguing that the problems with the concept are so deep that its usefulness has been exhausted. Rather than clarify and thus rescue the concept, they suggest researchers would be better served by simply jettisoning the term (O'Donnell 1996). Though important arguments have been made on either side of the equation, it remains unclear which approach will turn out ultimately to be the most productive. Nevertheless, it is clear that this concept deserves to be closely scrutinised.

The difficulty of establishing a precise meaning for 'democratic consolidation' is apparent in its very origin as a concept used to define a research agenda focused on the politics of countries that had already experienced DEMOCRATIC TRANSITION. The study of democratic transitions – the processes of regime change whereby non-democratic forms of rule are replaced by democratic ones – became a focus of interest after a wave of democratisation got underway in the mid-1970s, and it has continued to be a topic of sustained debate (see WAVES OF DEMOCRACY). Indeed, there are many questions concerning recent democratic transitions that remain unanswered, such as the sources of the initial momentum for a transition, the reason for the failure of many transitions, the role of structural factors and the contingent intervention of actors, the role of elites and masses, and the possible differences between recent transitions and the earlier transitions in Northwestern Europe (Collier 1999). In addition, the continued presence of non-democratic regimes throughout the world gives great relevance to this agenda. Nonetheless, the successful completion of a large number of democratic transitions, first in Southern Europe and then in Latin America in the 1970s and 1980s, gave rise to a new concern. Many of the same scholars who pioneered the study of democratic transitions turned their attention to the question of post-transition politics, that is, to the political processes that began after the holding of 'founding elections', a clear signpost of the end of authoritarian rule (O'Donnell and Schmitter 1986: 61).

To distinguish research on democratic transitions from this new area of inquiry, a new concept – democratic consolidation – was adopted as an umbrella term, and therein lies both the appeal of and the problem with this concept. On the one hand, as a broad term, it helped unify an emerging field of study. Indeed, it gave scholars working on countries as distinct as Spain, Brazil, South Korea, Poland and Russia a vocabulary to engage in a very valuable dialogue. On the other hand, as a term that was used in increasingly different and often unspecified ways, it became an omnibus concept that gradually lost its analytic value. Democratic consolidation became a loose concept attached to the study of virtually any aspect of the politics of countries that had undergone successful democratic transitions. On closer inspection, however, it is possible to go beyond this first and very preliminary approximation to the meaning of the term, which merely differentiates the study of democratic consolidation from the study of democratic transition. Taking this step requires distinguishing between thin and thick versions of the concept of democratic consolidation, a distinction that sheds light on the different meanings of this concept and helps to identify the most valuable uses of the term.

For many authors, democratic consolidation simply meant the institutionalisation of the electoral politics that was inaugurated at the end of democratic transitions. Particular emphasis was put on the durability and effectiveness of the electoral process, that is, on how long ELECTIONS continued to be held and whether these elections allowed for alternation in power (Huntington 1991). Some debate took place over the relevant actors that had to be considered in assessing commitment to the electoral process, a matter framed as a choice between focusing just on elites or, alternatively, on both elites and mass publics. Although this understanding of democratic consolidation, which makes the term practically synonymous with the older concept of DEMOCRATIC STABILITY, was a thin and ultimately unsatisfactory

one, its merits should not be overlooked. The elections that brought about a break with authoritarian rule are a key institutional feature of democracy, and the durability and effectiveness of these elections are obviously key dimensions of the politics of democratic consolidation. Moreover, this thin version of the concept has provided clear and shared criteria for many quantitative studies on the causes of democratic consolidation. But increasingly, scholars have found this meaning of democratic consolidation quite inadequate.

Two fundamental criticisms can be made of the thin version of the concept of democratic consolidation. First, the emphasis on elections alone provides a very restricted understanding of democracy that draws attention to only one of the many 'partial regimes' that a full discussion of democratic regimes requires. As a result, it provides a poor tool for comparative analysis. As more and more countries maintained an effective electoral process, democratic consolidation in this thin sense was achieved. By implication, the politics of the new democracies of Southern Europe, Latin America, Eastern Europe and East Asia could be seen as converging with the politics of older democracies in the North Atlantic. Yet this idea of convergence seemed to run counter to the evidence marshalled by most qualitative scholars, who have sought to capture these differences through discussions of the quality of democracy and types of democracy (O'Donnell 1996). Second, a narrow focus on the maintenance of an effective electoral process deflects attention from the significant institutional changes in other aspects of the regime that frequently take place after a democratic transition. In other words, the emphasis on democratic stability is linked with a static view of politics that overlooks the possibility that regimes are not formed all at once but rather over a fairly long period of time. Furthermore, such a perspective fails to appreciate how democratic regimes might be shaped in significant ways after transitions have been completed.

These criticisms have led to efforts to develop thicker versions of the concept of democratic consolidation. Most of these efforts have focused on the first criticism – the restricted nature of the definition of democracy – by identifying various dimensions that a disaggregated definition of democracy might emphasise. For example, Linz and Stepan (1996) argue that the study of democratic consolidation must pay attention to CIVIL SOCIETY, political society, the rule of law (see LAW, RULE OF), the state apparatus and economic society. Touraine (1997) proposes a concept of democracy formed by three interdependent dimensions: respect for basic RIGHTS, CITIZENSHIP and the role of leaders as agents of representation (see REPRESENTATION, CONCEPT OF). Finally, O'Donnell (1996, 1998) conceptualises polyarchies as consisting of republican, liberal and democratic dimensions.

Although these alternative conceptualisations partially overlap, they have important differences. For example, some do not explicitly use the term democratic consolidation. Thus, there are good reasons to believe that the sort of consensus among scholars who use a thin concept of democratic consolidation might not be as easy to attain among those who employ thick concepts of democratic consolidation. Nonetheless, the advantage of these novel conceptualisations as tools for comparative analysis is readily apparent in the way they avoid the all too common tendency to see countries as converging on a Western model. This point is strongly conveyed in O'Donnell's (1996, 1998) work, which draws a sharp distinction between the formally institutionalised polyarchies of the North Atlantic and the informally institutionalised polyarchies of Latin America, and which stresses the variable extent to which polyarchies have achieved horizontal as opposed to vertical ACCOUNTABILITY (see POLYARCHY). In their different ways, these thick conceptions provide a rich, nuanced understanding of the politics of democratic consolidation and offer a useful starting point for a research agenda that seeks to overcome the limitations of thin concepts of democratic consolidation.

Though less attention has been paid to the second criticism of thin concepts of democratic consolidation – that is, their static view of politics – existing disaggregated notions of democracy lend themselves readily to a dynamic view of politics. The various dimensions that Linz and Stepan, Touraine and O'Donnell identify can be considered partial regimes, which can be transformed at different points in time or, alternatively, which may never develop in some cases. Important questions thus arise about the different sequences that countries may follow in developing the various dimensions of democracy and about the connections among dimensions. A vast and important research agenda that is simply inconceivable with a thin concept of democratic consolidation is opened up.

In sum, there are strong reasons for preferring thicker versions of the concept of democratic consolidation. Though this line of research requires further conceptual clarification, its theoretical fertility is evident. It is central to the study of comparative politics, touching on a concern of relevance to a large number of regions in the world. In addition, this literature stresses the problem associated with efforts to directly extend classical democratic theory to the experience of more recently democratised countries. Thus, it also contributes to theory building by offering a view of democratic theory that breaks with Eurocentric assumptions and that sets classical democratic theory in a new perspective.

Further reading

Collier, R.B. (1999) *Paths Toward Democracy: Working Class and Elites in Western Europe and South America*, New York: Cambridge University Press.

Collier, D. and Levitsky, S. (1997) 'Democracy With Adjectives: Conceptual Innovation in Comparative Research', *World Politics* 49(3): 430–51.

Diamond, L. (1999) *Developing Democracy: Toward Consolidation*, Baltimore: Johns Hopkins University Press.

Gunther, R., Diamandouros, P.N. and Puhle, H.-J. (eds) (1995) *The Politics of Democratic Consolidation; Southern Europe in Compara-*

tive Perspective, Baltimore: Johns Hopkins University Press.

Higley, J. and Gunther, R. (eds) (1992) *Elites and Democratic Consolidation in Latin America and Southern Europe*, New York: Cambridge University Press.

Huntington, S. (1991) *The Third Wave: Democratization in the Late Twentieth Century*, Norman, OK: University of Oklahoma Press.

Linz, J.J. and Stepan, A. (1996) *Problems of Democratic Transition and Consolidation: Southern Europe, South America and Post-Communist Europe*, Baltimore: The Johns Hopkins University Press.

Mainwaring, S., O'Donnell, G. and Valenzuela, J.S. (eds) (1992) *Issues in Democratic Consolidation: The New South American Democracies in Comparative Perspective*, Notre Dame, IN: The Helen Kellogg Institute for International Studies, University of Notre Dame.

O'Donnell, G. (1996) 'Illusions about Consolidation', *Journal of Democracy* 7(2): 34–51.

—— (1998) 'Horizontal Accountability and New Polyarchies', *Journal of Democracy* 9(3): 112–26.

O'Donnell, G. and Schmitter, P. (1986) *Transitions from Authoritarian Rule. Tentative Conclusions about Uncertain Democracies*, Baltimore, MD: The Johns Hopkins University Press.

Schedler, A. (1998) 'What is Democratic Consolidation?', *Journal of Democracy* 9(2): 91–107.

Touraine, A. (1997) *What is Democracy?*, Boulder, CO: Westview Press.

GERARDO L. MUNCK

democratic debate

The central aspects and problems of democratic self-governance in general, and public debate in particular, can be discerned at the origin of democratic theory and practice, the ancient Greek city-states, of which Athens is the prime example. In the classical Greek model of democracy, an enfranchised minority of male citizens, joined together as equals in public assembly, reached their decisions after an open discussion aimed at discovering the stronger arguments on the issue at hand. If consensus could not be reached, then a vote could bring closure on a decision. The actual practice of democracy, however, revealed the problems attending this model: for example, the susceptibility of the assembly to factionalism, rhetorical manipulation and impulsive decisions. Whereas Aristotle's *Rhetoric* spells out the argumentation theory that corresponds to such debates, Plato's *Republic* delineates the various problems which ultimately transform democracies into tyrannies (see DEMOCRATIC ORIGINS).

The tensions between the ideals and realities of democratic debate remain evident in the modern revival of democratic theory. Both civic republicans and liberals are aware of the obstacles to rational public discussion. Nonetheless, up to the late nineteenth century, theorists in both camps, with some exceptions such as Rousseau, tended to be rather optimistic about the cognitive value of open discussion. They assumed that such discussion can uncover the truth of the matter regarding a common good or collective interest; or conversely, that discussion can expose a particular interest posing as general.

In the first half of the twentieth century, however, the rise of national socialism and sobering sociological findings – regarding the irreducible conflicts of values in modern societies, the APATHY and political ignorance of the electorate, the ease with which citizens could be manipulated by advertising techniques – led to more pessimistic views of democratic PARTICIPATION. Rejecting the idea of a common good, theorists conceived democratic politics as a means of regulating the struggle for power among self-interested actors or groups; the role of the citizen was reduced essentially to voting (see CITIZENSHIP). The value of public discussion, if countenanced at all, resided in the exchange of information necessary for each individual or group to make a rational choice among alternatives from the standpoint of self-interest. Aside from some exceptions (such as John Dewey's *The Public and Its Problems*), a general interest in participatory democracy only began to re-emerge in the late 1960s.

Although the new theoretical explorations of participatory democracy drew heavily upon the civic republican tradition, the key to its credibility lay in a readiness to unite civic republican and classical liberal perspectives and, more specifically, the rehabilitation of Kantian notions of public reason. Broadly construed, deliberative democratic theorists take democratic debate seriously without ignoring the problems and obstacles evident since ancient Greece and emphasised by the liberal tradition. On the one hand, thinkers such as Hannah Arendt, Jürgen Habermas and John Rawls could argue that public debate requires – and even fosters, if properly structured – a shift in perspective on the part of citizens that takes them beyond their individual interests and preferences to a civic or public standpoint. Thus they emphasise the transformative character of debate. On the other hand, these theorists typically link their ideals of open debate with the constitutional safeguards and representative institutions championed by classical liberal theory. This move allows their conceptions to avoid some of the problems afflicting conceptions of DIRECT DEMOCRACY and classical REPUBLICANISM, with its over-emphasis on the general will at the expense of individual RIGHTS.

DELIBERATIVE DEMOCRACY raises the questions surrounding the issue of democratic debate to a new level of reflection and analysis. One set of questions concerns the *process* of debate. These touch on the rationality of debate, that is, what makes debate a reasonable process that leads to superior political decisions. For starters, one can ask what exactly defines the civic standpoint and how citizens achieve it. Does the process itself generate this standpoint insofar as deliberating citizens or their representatives must give arguments that appeal to shared interests, or must debate move within the horizon of shared traditions and their retrieval? Habermas's discourse theory of democracy provides an answer that attempts to account for the internal complexity of debate. According to his analysis, political questions involve a spectrum of discursive perspectives, ranging from the universal perspective of justice, through the shared value orientations specific to the particular polity and its traditions, down to the self-interested aims of particular individuals or groups.

A further question is whether reasonable debate requires neutrality toward particular worldviews and conceptions of the good such that certain topics or arguments must, from the very start, be excluded from discussion (for example, appeals to religious convictions). Rawls, among others, has answered this in the affirmative. This view has been challenged by those who would have the process itself sort out the generally convincing arguments. Indeed, as feminists, multiculturalists and other theorists of difference have pointed out, pre-set definitions of what counts as 'publicly reasonable' typically function to exclude from consideration the experiences and perspectives of groups that do not share the majority culture and its assumptions. The consequent failure to consider alternatives and new possibilities presented by MINORITIES would undermine the rational quality of debate. For some theorists (for example, poststructuralists and postmodernists), the universalist and rationalist ideals themselves must be rejected as inherently ideological and exclusionary. These more radical criticisms overshoot their mark, however, insofar as they presuppose notions of inclusion and freedom from COERCION.

Questions of INSTITUTIONAL DESIGN also fall under the umbrella of process. Here, a key issue concerns the relation between the broader public sphere and representative bodies. According to 'two-track' models of democracy, parliamentary debates should channel and reflect a broader, less structured process of communication in the public sphere, the site at which the various SOCIAL MOVEMENTS and informal associations of citizens voice their concerns. However, the relation between the different perspectives and opinions present in the public sphere and legislation raises thorny issues for how one designs representative mechanisms, issues that bear on how one defines the subject who debates. If a reasonable debate aims to account for the perspectives and views of all citizens, are these perspectives defined by individuals or must they also include different group identities? And what does adequate representation require: that the opinions expressed in parliament mirror those found among the electorate, or rather that representatives belong to the same subgroups as their constituencies (see REPRESENTATION, CONCEPT OF)?

A second set of questions concerns the *goal* of democratic debate. For theorists such as Habermas, debate aims at consensus on correct solutions, at least as a regulative ideal: participants in debate must presuppose that questions of justice and the common good admit of right answers on which agreement is, in principle, possible. This 'epistemic' interpretation of deliberation goes beyond Rawls's concept of an 'overlapping consensus', which only extends to the framework of constitutional principles that makes reasonable debate possible (see CONSENSUS DEMOCRACY). In any case, epistemic approaches face a further question: are correct outcomes subject to a process-independent standard of 'political truth', or does the process itself constitute what counts as correct? Habermas attempts to sidestep this opposition by defining the correct outcome in terms of an ideal procedure that real debate can at most approximate, provided it meets certain conditions. Although such ideal procedural models need not assume a metaphysical or realist conception of political truth, they still represent an epistemic approach: debate aims at a right answer to a political question. The conditions specified by the ideal procedure – which typically include publicity, inclusion of all citizens, equality of participation, and freedom from coercion or self-deception, and so on – are those that would allow for the optimal discussion of the question on the merits, given the available information. If debates are procedurally well designed in the light of such criteria, then citizens may reasonably presume that actual outcomes enjoy a presumption of being correct. The conceptual

difficulties with epistemic interpretations are well known. For one, they must disarm certain anti-democratic implications (for example, that experts or the better educated should play a privileged role in debate). They also create problems for the 'minority democrat', that is, the citizen who is not convinced in debate that the actual outcome is correct. Finally, epistemic conceptions have drawn flak for being overly utopian, that is, for underestimating the intractability of conflicts of interests and values, problems of social choice, effects of power and so on. At the very least, a plausible epistemic account must give ample play to bargaining processes and the probability of less than ideal, but still legitimate, outcomes.

One can also ask whether the goal of debate is to legitimate political outcomes, or whether on the contrary LEGITIMACY stems from the procedural fairness or egalitarian features of the DECISION-MAKING mechanisms. On the latter alternative, actual debate could still be useful for improving citizens' satisfaction with outcomes, but it would not define legitimacy or POLITICAL OBLIGATION *per se*. This issue leads into the thorny question of the relation between debate on the one hand and individual rights and constitutional safeguards on the other: if democratic discourse is the sole source of legitimacy, then must not basic liberties, as well as the very rights that structure deliberation, be open to discursive contestation and change?

The foregoing sets of questions reveal the internal tensions and challenges that attend the attempt to link democracy with a robust conception of discourse. But as pessimists have long realised, there are also external challenges arising from the realities of contemporary mass democracies. In other words, a plausible normative account of democratic debate must face the question of *feasibility*: to what extent is the normative model possible, or to what extent can we envision it as an achievable goal, given the social conditions that currently obtain or are likely to obtain? The point is not to make existing social irrationalities into a theoretical virtue, but rather to strive for normative models that are both critical and applicable in particular localities shaped by specific traditions and historical backgrounds. Feasible normative models must in particular address the following questions.

One set of issues concerns the EQUALITY and FREEDOM of participation that normative models of reasonable debate presuppose. Socioeconomic inequalities undercut the capacity of some groups to participate in debate and voice their concerns. This problem has sparked attention to new models of democratic equality that go beyond traditional types of procedural equality (such as one citizen, one vote) to address substantive aspects, such as the capability or resources for participation.

A second set of issues is closely related to the first: the need to recognise and correct for the various forms of power that, even under the best of conditions, are inevitably tangled up both in the interpretation of discursive ideals and their institutional realisation. The ability of powerful interests to steer public media, set agendas, mount massive (and repeated) referenda campaigns and buy off legislators is nothing new. But the effects of such power have been heightened still further by economic GLOBALISATION, deregulation, corporate mergers and so on.

A third set of issues has also long been recognised, at least since the nineteenth century: how debate is possible under conditions of social and technical complexity. Social complexity arises not only from the plurality of interests and diversity of worldviews, but also from the functional differentiation of society, which leads to a variety of perspectives and problem-solving methods that generate competing standards of reasonableness and incompatible solutions for social problems. Social complexity goes hand in hand with an increasing technical complexity of problems. Technically complex problems are multifaceted, and require the expertise of any number of disciplines, which are exploding with new knowledge at a speed that makes it all but impossible for the experts themselves to keep up. How then can one expect a reasonable debate involving ordinary citizens that does not simply fragment into a competition of special interests and single-issue voting?

The last hurdle poses a challenge that goes to the very heart of a normative conception of reasonable debate. That is, in a public sphere conditioned by contemporary modes of COMMUNICATION – the mass MEDIA, telecommunications and the Internet, and soundbite advertising – what norms of debate are still plausible? A number of theories of rational discourse still operate, it seems, with the Enlightenment ideal of face-to-face discourse, an ideal that is becoming increasingly dubious as a general model for democratic debate. The effort to revamp this ideal no doubt requires political theorists to pay closer attention to the roles of rhetoric and the material media of debate. But such attention may require more than superficial modifications to the ideal: if democratic theory is not to slip back into pessimism, theorists may have to rethink the concept of reasonable public discourse from the ground up.

See also:

civic virtue; identity, political; political culture

Further reading

Benhabib, S. (1992) *Situating the Self: Gender, Community and Postmodernism in Contemporary Ethics*, New York: Routledge.

Bohman, J. (1996) *Public Deliberation: Pluralism, Complexity, and Democracy*, Cambridge, MA: MIT Press.

—— (1998) 'The Coming of Age of Deliberative Democracy', *Journal of Political Philosophy* 6(4): 400–25.

Bohman, J. and Rehg, W. (eds) (1997) *Deliberative Democracy: Essays on Reason and Politics*, Cambridge, MA: MIT Press.

Elster, J. (ed.) (1998) *Deliberative Democracy*, Cambridge: Cambridge University Press.

Gutmann, A. and Thompson, D. (1996) *Democracy and Disagreement*, Cambridge, MA: Harvard University Press.

Habermas, J. (1996) *Between Facts and Norms: Contributions to a Discourse Theory of Law and Democracy*, trans. W. Rehg, Cambridge, MA: MIT Press.

Held, D. (1987) *Models of Democracy*, Stanford, CA: Stanford University Press.

Ivie, R.L. (1998) 'Democratic Deliberation in a Rhetorical Republic', *Quarterly Journal of Speech* 84: 491–505.

Pateman, C. (1970) *Participation and Democratic Theory*, Cambridge: Cambridge University Press.

Phillips, A. (1995) *The Politics of Presence*, Oxford: Oxford University Press.

Rawls, J. (1996) *Political Liberalism*, New York: Columbia University Press.

Rosenfeld, M. and Arato, A. (eds) (1998) *Habermas on Law and Democracy: Critical Exchanges*, Berkeley, CA: University of California Press.

Willard, C.A. (1996) *Liberalism and the Problem of Knowledge: A New Rhetoric for Modern Democracy*, Chicago: University of Chicago Press.

WILLIAM REHG

democratic deficit

The concept of democratic deficit resonates in a number of different contexts. Here it is examined in the context of the European Union, the British state and GLOBALISATION. The important question informing this comparison asks whether, across these different fields of analysis, the concept of democratic deficit retains a similar import. Democratic deficit normally refers to the lack of TRANSPARENCY and ACCOUNTABILITY of the central political institutions of the European Union. This has resulted in a legitimacy crisis which has transformed a 'permissive consensus' into a search for new forms of representation and governance capable of restoring the trust of European citizenry in the decision-making bodies of the European Union (see REPRESENTATION, CONCEPT OF). The beginnings of this breakdown of trust were witnessed originally after the signing of the Single European Act in 1986 and, more markedly, after the Maastricht Treaty in 1992. The latter committed the member states to 'even closer social, political and economic union', an extension of areas in which European law prevailed and to a widening of the system of qualified majority voting for decision taking in the Council of Ministers. This development presented serious problems for both intergovernmentalists and federalists. The former were worried by what they saw as a step too far on the road to integration and the subsequent threat posed to the sovereignty of the nation-states. The latter, though supporting the increase in the power of the European parliament, which also resulted from Maastricht, saw this as a wholly inadequate check on the enhanced power of the executive, the unelected Commission and a Council of Ministers remote from parliamentary scrutiny.

It has been noted that the problem of the democratic deficit is not just marginal to the enterprise but central to the entire European project (Norris 1997: 277). This is because the two ways in which the European electorate could influence decision-making and reduce the deficit are fundamentally problematic. Seeking to strengthen *indirect* channels of representation via national governments is unlikely to prove an effective remedy given the low salience of foreign policy on the public agenda. Bolstering *direct* channels of representation, on the other hand, by supplementing the power of the European parliament (by, for example, giving it equal status with the Council in all fields of legislative and budgetary competence), is not promising either given the degree of hostility to federalism in many of the states. In any event, it is not entirely clear how this latter proposal would necessarily restore the link between decision makers and the preferences and interests of the electorate. This is the case for a number of reasons, not least because members of a newly empowered parliament would, under such circumstances, become more subject to the 'disciplinarian instincts' of their respective domestic party leaderships. When the most potent and divisive ingredient of all, the Single European Currency (SEC), is added to the equation, the possibility of conducting a DEMOCRATIC AUDIT of this situation becomes even more remote. The SEC is a particularly apposite area in which the lack of accountability in the policy-making process in Europe can be examined. Dyson *et al.* have commented on how the negotiations leading to agreement on Economic and Monetary Union at Maastricht remain shrouded in secrecy. They also comment on the significant role played by the European banking community in those negotiations and how, in this context, 'the concept of "epistemic community" provides a useful means of understanding important features of that process and its key outcomes' (Dyson *et al.* 1994: 2). What is meant here by 'epistemic community' is a network of professionals from a variety of disciplines sharing a common set of normative beliefs and policy objectives (Haas 1992: 3).

Although the question of the democratic deficit in the European Union is intimately linked to issues such as INSTITUTIONAL DESIGN and political practice, it is important that this concept is not characterised simply as an *objective reality* that can be easily identified or measured. This is important because such a characterisation would overlook the extent to which it is overdetermined by a number of diverse cultural, social and political factors. This can be seen by looking, for example, at the attitudes to Europe from within the two main political parties in Britain. For those both on the right of the Conservative party and the left of the Labour party, the democratic deficit within the European Union is glaring and self-evident. However, for others it is regarded more as a 'contingent deficit' susceptible to democratic reform. This is a significant distinction because it shows how the more ideological positions on this issue are articulated in the context of attitudes towards quite distinct issues such as the integrity of the nation-state or the relationship between the European project and socially progressive politics. The important point about this is that it allows us to see that any purely rational assessment concerning the existence, nature and scale of a democratic deficit is precluded due to the necessarily political nature of any deliberation on it.

It has been noted that it is now impossible to ensure adequate representation in any modern complex state system (Boyce 1993: 466). The debate concerning the alleged democratic deficit in Britain is well rehearsed and, in this context, the political nature of the debate is similarly evident. The present government, for example, is tackling what it regards as the democratic deficit by pursuing a programme of constitutional reform. Three of the important areas of concern in this context are the concentration of executive power, state secrecy and the absence of PROPORTIONALITY in the electoral system (see ELECTORAL SYSTEMS). The important question here is whether the implementation of devolutionary measures, the Freedom of Information Act or the introduction of limited proportional voting have reduced the democratic deficit. As in the context of the European Union, it is clear that answers to these questions are entirely dependent on the existing political/ideological dispositions of those being asked the question. More specifically, in this context it can be seen that answers are dependent on the democratic value attached to the union, an enlightened citizenry and strong undivided government.

This indeterminacy presents problems because of the important need to establish limits beyond which an *absolute* breakdown of trust or confidence that a people has in its political institutions can be identified with certainty. What, for example, can be said of Northern Ireland between 1921 and 1972? It is certainly possible to identify a number of different interpretations of the nature of the northern state during this period. The unionist argument often heard during these years was that any alleged democratic deficit was a construction of the nationalist community, which, for its own political ends, did not support the state. Now, whatever the worth of this argument, it raises a serious theoretical question: is it possible under *any* circumstances to identify conclusively the presence of a democratic deficit? The answer to this is a tentative no. Although it is important that the terms and conditions of the concept are established, at the same time it is important to bear in mind the essential contestability of its content. This entails that the question is ultimately undecideable due to the fact that deliberation on it, as seen in the above examples, is so infused with power relations and contingency.

Despite these theoretical difficulties, it is important to remain sensitive to the fact that democratic deficit entails consideration of issues of real political and ethical significance. This is certainly true in the context of globalisation, in which a similar problematic can be identified. The transfer of power from national governments to the 'forces of global capitalism' implicit within this phenomenon represents what is for many the most serious example of a democratic deficit. The central problem here is the claim that the erosion of national SOVEREIGNTY has broken the lines of accountability between governments and the electorate. In one sense, this is an easily recognised problem. Yet, on further inspection, it becomes clear how assessments of the democratic deficit in this context are similarly structured by other, quite distinct, political or normative issues such as the appropriate role of the state. In contrast to the New Right position, for example, which sees globalisation as part of the solution to the democratic deficit inherent within the state, Hirst and Thompson question the extent to which globalisation will or should lead to a marked and inevitable erosion of state power. Their argument is substantiated by reference to what they see as the 'continued significance of national governments and economies in the regulation and successes of transnational business corporations' (Axford 2000: 246).

What is clear is that political or socioeconomic change on this scale is bound to have significant theoretical implications for democratic theory. This is true because, even if Hirst and Thompson are right in their contention that globalisation has been misunderstood, it has still led to a reappraisal of virtually every variable within the vocabulary of democracy. However, it is important to remember that the concepts we employ to designate such changes are themselves not neutral and that the positions from which assessments are made are highly subjective. This, as we have seen, is true in the three environments in which this category has been examined. What the study of democratic deficit across these different fields also suggests is that, although it is important to acknowledge the specificity of the debate in these and other environments, there is an important theme that transcends them all; that is, that power is exercised by individuals or groups and corporations who remain largely unaccountable to the rest of society. Although there can be no agreement on what constitutes a democratic deficit, at least the parameters of the debate are clear.

See also:

accountability; democratic audit; globalisation; legitimacy; representation, models of

Further reading

Axford, B. (2000) 'Globalisation', in G. Browning, A. Halcli and F. Webster (eds), *Understanding Contemporary Society: Theories of the Present*, London: Sage.

Boyce, B. (1993) 'The Democratic Deficit of the European Community', *Parliamentary Affairs* 46(4): 458–77.

Dyson, K., Featherstone, K. and Michalopoulos, G. (1994) 'The Politics of EMU: the Maastricht Treaty and the Relevance of Bargaining Models', paper presented to the American Political Science Association, New York, 1–4 September.

Haas, P. (1992) 'Introduction: Epistemic Communities and International Policy Co-Ordination', *International Organisation* 46(1): 1–35.

Norris, P. (1997) 'Representation and the Democratic Deficit', *European Journal of Political Research* 32: 273–82.

ANTHONY M. CLOHESY

democratic development

As Samuel Huntington (1991) has shown in detail, democracy advanced over time in three waves. The first began in the USA in the mid-nineteenth century and extended to the years immediately after the First World War. The SUFFRAGE had been extended in that country during the 1840s – as a result of reforms introduced by Andrew Jackson – to include all white men. After the Civil War of the 1860s, black men were included as well. At about the same time, voting rights were being greatly broadened in England. There had long been a vital parliamentary tradition in that country, yet even after the famous Reform Act of 1832, the electorate consisted of no more than 10 per cent of the male population. By the end of the nineteenth century, however, the suffrage was universal, but only for men. The first country to introduce universal and equal suffrage for both men and women was New Zealand in 1889. The process of democratisation then spread in the years after the turn of the century to several countries in Western Europe, as well as to the so-called dominions of the British Empire. Progress could also be noted in certain Latin American countries (Uruguay and Argentina being pioneers in this regard).

The First World War, which was fought to 'make the world safe for democracy' (as US President Woodrow Wilson put it), had an enormous impact. A few years after the Treaty of Versailles, upwards of thirty countries had adopted constitutions that were democratic (at least largely). Above and beyond the geographical areas mentioned, a large number of states in Central and Eastern Europe had also become democratic. Many of these were new nations, which had come into being as a result of Versailles. It was thus natural for them to link up with the prevailing democratic spirit. The trend spread from Estonia in the north to Albania in the south. This was a time of great hopes for the future of democracy.

Soon, however, the tide started to turn. A counter-wave was beginning to take shape, and would gradually gather more and more strength. The 1920s and 1930s were marked by far-reaching democratic setbacks. The new trend was already visible in Petrograd in 1917, with the Bolsheviks' overthrow of the republican regime and their closure of the democratically elected Duma. The same method for gaining power was successfully employed by right-wing nationalist forces in other countries. Benito Mussolini assumed the leadership of a group of Italian fascists and marched on Rome in 1922. He encountered little resistance, and was able to oust the elected government and to make himself dictator. This was, it was later to prove, very much a trend-setting event. The German Nazis were greatly inspired by Mussolini's daring. Democracy now fell victim to usurpers in a great many European lands. By the end of the 1930s, authoritarian governments of various stripes has assumed power in virtually every country of Central and Eastern Europe (Czechoslovakia being the exception). Developments in Southern Europe were similar. Italy we have mentioned already; Spain and Portugal followed. The anti-democratic trend was also powerful in Latin America. In the 1930s, in nearly every state that had introduced a civilian and tolerably democratic regime, a shift to military rule took place. The sole deviating case was Colombia. When Hitler and Stalin concluded a pact in 1939, allowing each to expand within his respective sphere of interest, democracy's prospects undeniably looked bleak. The democratic system in Czechoslovakia had been abolished by armed German assault. The same fate soon befell the Netherlands, Belgium, Luxembourg, France, Denmark and Norway. Meanwhile, the Soviet army attacked Finland. When the outlook was darkest (in the early 1940s), the democracies of Europe could be counted on the fingers of one hand. In the world as a whole, the number of democracies amounted to about ten. Autocracy seemed to sweep all before it.

At the war's end, however, the 'course of history' shifted direction once more. A second wave of democratisation – yet more powerful and far-reaching than the first – now followed.

It stretched roughly from 1945 to the early 1960s. The Western allies established a democratic system, more or less by imposition, in the states that had been defeated in the war: Japan, Italy and Germany (that is, in that part of Germany occupied by the USA, Britain and France). Similar attempts, less successful, were made in South Korea. Democracy was restored in those countries of Northern and Western Europe where it had been destroyed by the German occupiers. Moreover, civic and popular governments were re-established all over Latin America, and democratic institutions were introduced in certain countries of the Middle East, namely Turkey, Lebanon and Israel. These latter cases arose partly as a consequence of the decolonisation process now under way. This process affected Asia as well: for example, democratic institutions were installed at this time in India and Ceylon (Sri Lanka). By the late 1950s and early 1960s, moreover, the principles of popular rule had seemed to advance yet further. Enduring democratic institutions were re-established in Colombia and Venezuela in 1958, following a period of harsh military dictatorship. The new states of Africa, which had been liberated after years of colonial domination, also attracted great attention. Most of these states introduced democratic government upon gaining independence. This was, once again, a time of great hopes regarding democracy's prospects.

Fairly soon, however, a process of unmistakable retrogression set in. In Latin America, military juntas again took the helm of government in the mid-1960s. The formative event was the coup of 1964 in Brazil, which was followed by similar seizures of power throughout the continent. By the early 1970s, military rule had become the dominant pattern. True, such things had happened before. What was new, however, was the naked brutality exhibited by these rulers. The world was shocked by the use – by regimes in such countries as Chile and Argentina – of murder, 'disappearance' and torture. In Africa, the new democratic governments had been toppled over almost the entire continent. In many cases, only a few years had passed before some form of auto-cracy had been introduced, usually in the form of one-party or military rule. These regimes too proved capable, in many cases, of an astonishing degree of repression.

In a short space of time, in other words – a little over a decade – the picture had radically changed. The early 1970s were a time of pessimism as far as democracy is concerned. Dictators seemed to be the men of the hour. This applied particularly outside Europe; yet authoritarian regimes could be found there also. In the years after the Second World War, the Soviet model had been installed throughout Eastern Europe, and there were no signs that this system would change. Autocracy had also long prevailed in Spain and in Portugal, and the overthrow of democracy in the late 1960s by the Greek military attracted great attention. Yet it was here, in Southern Europe, that a new trend would shortly begin.

The third wave of democratisation began with the fall of dictatorships in Portugal, Spain and Greece in the mid and late 1970s. The same thing then happened in Latin America, and with an astonishing speed. Within the course of a single decade, every military regime in the area was replaced by a popularly elected government. A trend toward democracy was also evident in East Asia. A widely noted shift of regime took place in the Philippines, and in such countries as Taiwan and South Korea – long under autocratic rule – distinct changes in a democratic direction took place. Most striking, however – and for the majority of observers most surprising – were the changes that happened in Eastern Europe. The emblematic event here was the fall of the Berlin Wall, which had sealed off communist East Germany, in 1989. The process had started in Poland and Hungary, and it spread quickly throughout Eastern Europe. Within the course of a single year, all of the communist one-party states from the Baltic to the Balkans fell like dominos. Soon it was the turn of the Soviet Union, the state from which autocracy in the Eastern bloc had originated. The old regime in Russia was abolished in 1991. Here, as in other countries of the region, changes in a democratic direction commenced.

The changes in Eastern Europe had immediate repercussions in Africa. This was a continent dominated by authoritarian governments at the end of the 1980s; of the forty-five states south of the Sahara, more than half had some form of one-party rule, and ten were ruled by military regimes. Multiparty systems obtained in the remaining ten or so states (often, however, with restrictions of various kinds). Only four countries – Botswana, Gambia, Mauritius and Senegal – practised forms of government meeting basic democratic criteria. But this picture was shortly to change. When the 'third wave' reached Africa, it penetrated widely. The changes had started by 1990. Francophone West Africa was affected first. Within a short time, however, dictatorships over the entire continent were toppled. Africans could look to examples from afar, especially to Eastern Europe, for the demise of one-party regimes. But there was also an example closer to home: the dismantling of the apartheid system in South Africa in the early 1990s was a great source of inspiration. The one-party regimes were all abolished within a few years, and the majority of military regimes disappeared as well. Across a broad front, multiparty systems were introduced and more or less free and fair ELECTIONS were held.

The states north of the Sahara have been much less affected by this wave of change. The same goes for the rest of the Arab world. There was an opening in Algeria at the beginning of the 1990s. The military regime in that country arranged to hold free elections, but abruptly terminated the experiment when it became clear that a Muslim fundamentalist party was going to win. This set off alarm bells throughout the region. A degree of progress, from a democratic standpoint, has been registered in such countries as Jordan and Kuwait. Viewed as a whole, however, the area is dominated by authoritarian governments.

In the Far East the situation is more varied. Significant progress has taken place in, for example, Thailand and Singapore. Changes have also occurred in Pakistan, Bangladesh and Malaysia, and may be underway in Indonesia. But the tendency in these countries

is quite certain. The same can be said of many of the Central Asian republics which became independent when the Soviet Union dissolved. On the other hand, dictatorship remains firmly ensconced in a good many countries, China being the most prominent example. Such highly autocratic states as North Korea, Burma and Afghanistan should be remembered as well.

As we have seen, the third wave has had a varying impact in different parts of the globe. Its effect has been very limited in certain regions, or even absent altogether. And where its effect has been felt, a subsequent tendency in the opposing direction has in many cases appeared (Diamond 1999; Zakaria 1997). This is especially true in Africa, where dictatorial governments, often of a military type, have reappeared in a number of countries; Gambia and Congo-Brazzaville are examples. In addition, the transition to a multiparty system has in many cases been rather half-hearted. In several countries, the previously dominant one-party system has been replaced by an arrangement that might be called a 'one-and-a-half-party system'. Here, opposition parties are allowed in some measure to operate and to take part in elections (elections in which, however, they have no real chance of challenging the regime). Kenya and Zimbabwe illustrate this pattern. There are also several important countries – Sudan and Congo-Kinshasa (Zaire) among them – in which an old autocratic order has in all essentials been retained. In several of the countries which previously formed part of the Soviet Union, moreover, the movement towards democracy appears to have been halted, and developments have moved in another direction. The Ukraine and Belarus belong to this category, as do several republics in the Caucasus and Central Asia.

Yet we must conclude that, in a longer historical perspective, far-reaching changes in favour of democracy have taken place over the last century. Periods of progress have indeed been succeeded by times in which developments have proceeded in the opposite direction. The long-term trend, however, has been steadily positive. Each new wave of democratisation has embraced a greater number of states, and exhibited a wider geographical scope, than its predecessor. And although the democratic experiment has in some cases been of short duration, it has usually been 'profitable' as an investment for the future even so. For as Huntingdon has pointed out, participation in an earlier wave of democratic advancement has been a good predictor of participation in a later one. Even when the result is a failure, a seed of democratic experience is sown. When new democratic efforts are later undertaken, this seed may take root and grow into a vigorous plant.

At the turn of the new millennium more than half the world's countries may be classified as democratic (Karatnycky 1999). Of course the trend can shift; it has done so before. But if the earlier pattern holds – such that an investment in democracy pays off, if only in the form of delayed returns – then the present high-water mark may be said to constitute support for an optimistic assessment of the prospects of democracy.

See also:

democracy, future of; democratic transition; waves of democracy

Further reading

Bryce, J. (1921) *Modern Democracies*, London: Macmillan.

Diamond, L. (1999) *Developing Democracy: Toward Consolidation*, Baltimore: The John Hopkins University Press.

Huntington, S. (1991) *The Third Wave: Democratization in the Late Twentieth Century*, Norman, OK: University of Oklahoma Press.

Karatnycky, A. (1999) *Freedom in the World. The Annual Survey of Political Rights & Civil Liberties 1997–98*, New Brunswick, NJ: Transaction Publishers.

Zakaria, F. (1997) 'The Rise of Illiberal Democracy', *Foreign Affairs* (November–December): 22–43.

AXEL HADENIUS

democratic executives

Executives are universal. Each country has a national government, as indeed every other social organisation, from the most simple to the most complex. There is always a body, normally relatively small, which has the task of running that organisation. At the national level, since the third quarter of the twentieth century, independent governments have come to rule practically the whole of the planet: the number of national executives has thus more than doubled since the 1940s. There are also local executives in most countries and often regional executives as well.

Among these executives, the most conspicuous are the national governments: they are at the centre of political life. As all other executives, they tend to be compact bodies, whose views and pronouncements are usually well-publicised: PARTIES, legislatures or local councils are more amorphous; their 'will' is less clear. Because executives are relatively small and very visible, it is easier to think of them as groups that have a common goal and even act as teams, although they may be disunited, sometimes openly so.

Yet executives, including national executives, differ markedly from each other in terms of their composition, organisation, selection mechanisms, duration or powers, both formal and informal. They are also sharply divided into autocratic and democratic governments, although the other differences between executives cut across that divide. On the other hand, all have in common a threefold function. First, they elaborate policies, policies which have both to be implementable and to be politically acceptable – this last aspect being particularly important for democratic executives – this function is one of *conception*. Second, executives are concerned with *implementation*: they have to find the means of turning policies into action. The contrast between conception and implementation can create tensions, as those who 'dream' tend to have a different approach from those who 'manage'. Moreover, executives have a third function, that of *coordination*: policies need to develop harmoniously together. Executives must combine all three functions, but this combination poses problems to all governments, democratic and non-democratic alike (Blondel 1982).

The development of two main forms of national democratic executives

Democratic executives are, by and large, creations of the nineteenth century and even of the twentieth century. There were traces of such governments in the ancient world and in the Renaissance, but almost exclusively in city-states: moreover, these executives typically turned oligarchical, their electoral base having gradually shrunk, in Greece, Rome or the Italian cities. The great change occurred from the end of the eighteenth century onwards, when a number of governments in large states ceased to be autocratic and even oligarchical, under pressure for popular PARTICIPATION: but this development took one of two main forms at the national level and a variety of forms at the local level. The two models of democratic national executives have shaped these ever since.

On the one hand, there are parliamentary systems based on *collective cabinets*. This kind of rule originated in England and in Sweden, and spread throughout Europe and many parts of the Commonwealth, as well as Japan, Israel and a number of other countries. It was a consequence of the gradual loss of power of ruling monarchs: the latter had to bow to the demands of elected representatives if they were to keep their thrones. Effective power thus passed to groups of ministers, originally rather small in number, but now usually at least fifteen or even twenty strong, emanating from and responsible to parliament. These ministers, headed by a prime minister, take decisions collectively in cabinet while the large majority of them are individually in charge of particular departments.

In contrast, the *constitutional presidential system* was first established in the United States at the end of the eighteenth century and spread to Latin America, where it had a limited success as it was often interrupted by periods of autocratic rule, primarily of a military character. In the presidential model, the executive is hierarchical and not collective: ministers (officially known as secretaries) are appointed by presidents and responsible only to them (see PRESIDENTIALISM). This formula is therefore closer to old-fashioned monarchical government than to the cabinet system, but, where the president is truly democratically elected, the overall structure is democratic. Many local executives are also organised on such a model.

The basic structure of democratic executives

As parliamentary cabinets emerged in a context in which monarchs gradually lost their power, these systems, unlike presidential governments, were organised on the basis of a distinction between a monarchical head of state performing a ceremonial role and the ministers running the executive. Over time, as some countries became republics – France, Germany or Italy for instance – a parallel distinction was drawn between a ceremonial president elected in some cases by a somewhat enlarged representative body and in some cases by the people, and the cabinet. In all of these cases, the cabinet is parliamentary, as the font of its AUTHORITY is not the head of state, but parliament: to exist and to survive, the cabinet needs the confidence of parliament. Executive and legislature are therefore very close to each other in this system. In presidential government, on the contrary, where the president, elected directly by the people for a specific period, combines the position of head of state and of head of the executive, executive and legislature are formally separated.

It is sometimes suggested that, between these two sharply distinct forms of arrangements, there exists a third intermediate type, referred to as 'semi-presidential', in which the distinction between a head of state and a collective cabinet responsible to parliament does remain but where, because the head of state is elected by universal SUFFRAGE, a number of powers accrue to the president above the ceremonial role which heads of state normally perform in parliamentary cabinet systems. In practice, except in very special circumstances, of which the French Fifth Republic has been almost the only example since 1958, the main features of the cabinet system prevail: as a matter of fact, the characteristics of the French executive have since become increasingly similar to that of other parliamentary cabinets (Lijphart 1992; Mény and Knapp 1998).

The working of national executives

Parliamentary cabinets are formally collective while constitutional presidential governments are formally hierarchical: in practice the distinction is not always as sharp, and the working of these governments may be different from what it is supposed to be in theory. One factor which undermined the collective character of parliamentary cabinets is the number and complexity of the decisions which have to be taken during what are normally short meetings of two or three hours a week. As a result, while the cabinet *ratifies* decisions, many of these are in practice initiated and prepared by individual ministers, by groups of ministers sitting in committees (the number of which has increased markedly in many cabinet governments) or by the prime minister and some of the ministers. Thus many cabinet governments are at most collegial rather than collective (Blondel and Müller-Rommel 1993).

Variations in the nature of the DECISION-MAKING process in parliamentary cabinets are also due to differences in the political structure of these bodies. Some are composed of members of one party only: this is typically the case in Britain and in several Commonwealth countries. Others are coalitions, as tends to occur in Continental Europe. While, on average, single-party governments tend to last longer and seem to be more effective, there are sharp differences among COALITIONS: some are tightly structured

(for instance those which include two parties only); they may be formed after the political differences existing between the parties have been ironed out. Other coalitions are brought into existence in a more haphazard manner. While most are 'small' in the sense that they include only parties which are ideologically close to each other, there are also 'grand' coalitions, to which all the main political parties of the country belong. The Swiss Federal Council is an extreme example of 'grand' coalition: its seven members come from all four main parties that exist in that polity, and it is fully collective, indeed appreciably more collective than any other cabinet (Lijphart 1984).

Meanwhile, presidential governments, which are in principle hierarchical, are sometimes collegial if the presidents and the secretaries depend on each other politically and therefore need each other. This tended to be the case in the United States in the past, but, since the First World War, the move has been in another direction: the executive has been, so to speak, 'atomised' as individual departments have come to have direct relationships with the committees of Congress and with a plethora of lobbies (Heclo 1977).

Democratic executives are primarily a development of the nineteenth and twentieth centuries. They are therefore still developing and, whatever their limitations, they are more responsive and more open than non-democratic executives. This occurred at a time when problems faced by governments were becoming increasingly complex. Further progress may therefore occur among democratic executives, while at least some autocratic governments may come to be replaced by democratic executives.

See also:

coalitions; constitutional monarchy; leadership

Further reading

Blondel, J. (1982) *The Organisation of Governments*, London and Los Angeles: Sage.
Blondel, J. and Müller-Rommel, F. (eds) (1993)

Governing Together, London and Los Angeles: Sage.

Budge, I. and Keman, H. (eds) (1990) *Parties and Democracy*, Oxford: Oxford University Press.

Heclo, H. (1977) *A Government of Strangers*, Washington, DC: Brookings Institution.

Laver, M. and Shepsle, K.A. (eds) (1996) *Making and Breaking Governments*, Cambridge: Cambridge University Press.

Lijphart, A. (1984) *Democracies*, New Haven, CT: Yale University Press.

—— (1992) *Parliamentary versus Presidential Government*, Oxford: Oxford University Press.

Mény, Y. and Knapp, A. (1998) *Government and Politics in Western Europe*, 3rd edn, Oxford: Oxford University Press.

Warwick, P.V. (1994) *Government Survival in Parliamentary Democracies*, Cambridge: Cambridge University Press.

JEAN BLONDEL

democratic ideology

The locution 'democratic ideology' is not commonly used, nor is the word 'democratism', whose very linguistic awkwardness suggests a tension in thinking about democracy as an ideology. Nevertheless, the term is not without interest in exploring and clarifying a range of current phenomena and practices. Contemporary understandings of democracy exceed simplistic ideas about 'the rule of the people', or purely institutional and procedural issues about voting, taking decisions, or translating voter preferences into representative forms and outcomes. Instead, democracy connotes a set of beliefs, norms and values, which alludes to something like an ideology, discourse or even 'form of life'.

Having said this, the term itself is by no means transparent. For a start, it brings together two of the most complex and elusive concepts in social and political thought. Democracy is generally seen as an essentially contested concept, whose meanings range from a system of political rule, to a kind of practice involving popular PARTICIPATION in collective DECISION-MAKING, to a form of self-government in various spheres of social life. The concept of ideology is similarly contested. Not only are there divergent usages, each embedded in a particular theoretical and normative context, but its study in the social sciences divides into two strongly opposed approaches. On the one hand, the concept is used neutrally to refer to a social group's particular set of beliefs or attitudes, and its function is to confer a wider meaning and significance to its actions and mundane practices. In this descriptive sense, a political ideology consists of a system of ideas with which social actors explain and justify their organised social action. On the other hand, ideology is employed as a critical concept to expose the way in which certain ideas and values are a cloak for vested interests, or a mystification of real social relations, or a fantastical construction utterly divorced from social reality. In the latter sense, especially as developed in the Marxist tradition, the concept of ideology is used to reveal exclusions, naturalisations and 'de-politicisations' that follow from ideas and practices which are conventionally accepted or imposed.

The consequence of this complex intersection of usages is that the issue of democratic ideology can be approached from at least five different angles. It can be viewed as a political doctrine; as a system of social and political practice; as a mystification of social relations; as a condition of democratic rule or governance; and as a signifier or ideological element used for political action and mobilisation. Each of these aspects and their attendant focuses of investigation are considered below.

The first angle concentrates on those ideas and values that make up different theories of democratic thought and practice, in which the core elements of such theories would be equal political rights, rule by the people, participation in the public affairs of a state, the promotion of individual AUTONOMY and so on. The point of such an analysis would be to delineate and elucidate different conceptions of democracy, and then to decide which specific

191

combination of ideas best defines democratic institutions, practices and thinking. Naturally, these competing configurations would vary from theorist to theorist and from ideology to ideology. For instance, such a 'morphology' of democratic thinking and practice could involve a comparison and evaluation of libertarian and socialist conceptions of democracy, and would focus on the different combinations of core, adjacent and peripheral concepts in such systems of thought (see Freeden 1996). While socialists would want to extend the scope of democratic values and practices to include their extension to economic and social relations, libertarians would seek to confine democracy to a minimal set of procedures whose main aim is to protect the RIGHTS and liberties of individuals in CIVIL SOCIETY. Indeed, just like Marxist-Leninists, libertarians such as Hayek (1973) and the early Nozick (1974) would go as far as to question the need for democracy at all, seeing in democratic institutions and values a major threat to the rights of individuals. In short, any particular system of democratic thought would seek to combine core ideas of democracy (for example, popular SOVEREIGNTY) with more adjacent or peripheral ideas, such as substantive economic EQUALITY (socialism), or the absolute defence of individual liberty (libertarianism), and then endeavour to justify its particular conceptions against others.

A second usage of the term democratic ideology involves the classification and analysis of different *types* of democratic ideolog*ies*, as they are articulated and function in concrete societies. In this sense, it would include a classification of various democratic forms and institutions, such as 'capitalist democracy', 'social democracy', 'people's democracy', 'green democracy' and 'radical democracy'; not to mention differences within particular types of democracy, such as the contrast between direct and representative forms within liberal capitalist democracy. It would then examine the ways in which concrete democratic ideologies were constructed by linking together available ideological elements in different ways, as well as the conditions for such an articula-

tion. For instance, the emergence and consolidation of European 'social democracy' in the postwar period produced forms of political state in which all citizens enjoyed a basic range of civil, political and social rights, and in which political participation was not restricted by property, birth, race or gender (see SOCIAL DEMOCRACY). The universal inclusion of the citizenry, the representation of important interests in society such as TRADES UNIONS through corporatist arrangements, and the intervention of the state in the economy to secure certain basic goals such as full employment produced a distinctive set of democratic principles, forms and practices. From an analytical point of view, the investigation of concrete democratic ideologies would explore the various ways they were constructed and institutionalised by engineering political frontiers with other projects and systems. It would also examine their political disarticulation in contexts of crisis, dislocation and social change. For instance, it might be argued that the disintegration of social democracy in Europe during the 1970s and 1980s was largely the product of a series of related changes in the global economy, which rendered the existing practices of social democracy untenable, thus opening the way for the production of new ideological configurations such as the New Right, in which the conception and practice of democracy was radically altered.

A third meaning of democratic ideology centres on the way in which the language and rhetoric of democracy functions as a tool of ideological justification and legitimisation by political elites and ruling classes. This meaning originates in Marxist and radical critiques of liberal democratic forms and practices, in which it is argued that the ideology of democracy obfuscates the underlying social inequalities and relations of domination in CLASS-divided societies. Even though what they call 'formal bourgeois democracy' has the potential to treat all citizens as politically and legally equal, it nevertheless conceals fundamental social divisions, thus facilitating the reproduction of exploitative class relations. From this perspective, Marxists such as Lenin demanded the destruction of 'bourgeois democracy' and its replacement by a period of 'proletarian dictatorship' or 'proletarian democracy'. These transitional forms would ultimately be followed by the construction of a fully-fledged communist society in which all political forms would eventually disappear.

Contemporary Marxists and critical theorists have tempered their critique of 'bourgeois democracy' by acknowledging that socialist societies require certain liberal democratic procedures and forms, as well as basic human rights and the rule of law. Nevertheless, they still seek to expose the way in which triumphalist claims about the 'end of ideology' or 'end of history' have naturalised liberal capitalist democracy, thereby excluding more radical forms of democratic thinking and practice. They also criticise the 'emptying out' of the radical charge of democratic demands, as most of the world's political regimes find it in their interests to call themselves functioning democracies. The tasks of analysis in this regard would be to disentangle the rhetoric and ideology of democracy from the actual practices and institutions of the regimes themselves. In its place, post-Marxists and critical theorists such as Claude Lefort (1986) and Jürgen Habermas (1996) call for a radicalisation of democratic forms and processes by extending the democratic imaginary into the economic sphere, or by developing deliberative models of democratic decision-making to supplement existing liberal democratic procedures (see RADICAL DEMOCRACY).

The fourth way of understanding the term democratic ideology focuses on the cultural and ethical conditions for the proper functioning of liberal democratic states and societies. While it is widely held that there are important economic and social conditions that must be met for democracies to take root and flourish, it has also been argued that a belief in, or at least an acceptance of, democracy is a necessary condition for democracy to exist. In recent times, given the belief that democracy involves 'the institutionalisation of uncertainty', writers such as Richard Rorty (1989) and Bill Connolly (1991, 1995) place great stress on the need

to construct a suitable 'democratic ethos' built around an acceptance of concepts such as CONTINGENCY, 'liberal irony' and pluralisation. These ideas are seen as vital ideological underpinnings for the maintenance and extension of democratic forms of life, and they stress the need to cultivate and inculcate an 'ethos of contingency' amongst citizens of democratic societies, as the necessary bulwark to new ideological fundamentalisms, institutional sclerosis, and the exclusion of difference from the public life of existing liberal democratic states.

The final way of thinking about democratic ideology focuses on the way in which different social groups and political forces endeavour to use the signifier 'democracy' to constitute their identities and advance their interests. In this sense, democracy is itself a key ideological element in political mobilisation and struggle, and is used to create POLITICAL FRONTIERS between differently located social groups and agencies (Laclau 1977; Laclau and Mouffe 1985). A concern of this inquiry would be the different political language games that social groups play with 'democracy', and the different forms of ideological articulation that arise from such games. Such formations would be determined by the way in which democratic demands and tropes are articulated by nationalist movements ('national democratic struggles'), socialist parties ('people's democracy'), or by populist forms of politics ('popular democratic struggles').

See also:

democratic debate; hegemony; social democracy

Further reading

Connolly, W.E. (1991) *Identity/Difference: Democratic Negotiations of Political Paradox*, Ithaca, NY: Cornell University Press.
—— (1995) *The Ethos of Pluralization*, Minneapolis, MN: University of Minnesota Press.
Freeden, M. (1996) *Ideologies and Political*

Theory: A Conceptual Approach, Oxford: Oxford University Press.

Habermas, J. (1996) *Between Facts and Norms: Contributions to a Discourse Theory of Law and Democracy*, Cambridge: Polity Press.

Hayek, F. (1973) *Law, Legislation and Liberty. Volume 1: Rules and Order*, London: Routledge.

Laclau, E. (1977) *Politics and Ideology in Marxist Theory*, London: New Left Books.

Laclau, E. and Mouffe, C. (1985) *Hegemony and Socialist Strategy*, London: Verso.

Lefort, C. (1986) *The Political Forms and Modern Society: Bureaucracy, Democracy, Totalitarianism*, Cambridge, MA: MIT Press.

Nozick, R. (1974) *Anarchy, the State and Utopia*, Oxford: Basil Blackwell.

Rorty, R. (1989) *Contingency, Irony and Solidarity*, Cambridge: Cambridge University Press.

DAVID HOWARTH

democratic origins

Athens in the fifth century BC stands as the earliest recognised democratic regime about which we have sufficient historical information to speculate concerning its origins. The story of the rise of democracy in Athens enables us to consider the ways in which those origins define and limit what democracies might achieve as political regimes. To say that ancient Athens offers the model of the democratic regime is not to say that contemporary democracies can trace their own origins back to it; as Finley (1973) among many others shows, there are significant differences between Athenian democracy and contemporary democracies, differences captured most vividly by the degrees of participation both in law making and in office holding. But a democracy that arose out of the social, economic and military transformations that took place during the archaic age of ancient Greece (approximately the seventh and sixth centuries BC) helps us to understand the principles that underlie any democratic regime, ancient or modern.

Ancient Athens was highly participatory on many levels, whether it be attendance at the assemblies, the sharing of offices and magistracies or participation in the law courts. The democratic regime also ensured that those holding offices were held accountable for their actions while in office. Further, Athenian democracy functioned on the principle of EQUALITY, that each citizen shared equally in the life of the city and no citizen could make special claims to AUTHORITY or privilege against other citizens. This equality, though, was practised only within the citizen body itself; democratic Athens excluded many who had not been defined as part of that body.

The emergence of democracy in Athens entails the development of mechanisms that allowed for the transcendence of the ancient aristocratic inequalities, for widespread PARTICIPATION by citizens in all aspects of the political regime, and for magisterial accountability. The development of these practices in turn depended on the breaking away from an aristocratic political regime to one that emphasised independence from the past as the basis for a new ideal of equality among those engaged in self-rule.

The sources concerning this transformation from an aristocratically governed public life to one in which a wide sector of the population engaged in the process of self-rule are limited, and speculation concerning democratic origins depends for the most part on sources, such as the Aristotelian *Constitution of Athens*, that come from a much later time period; fragments of the Solonic poems help us somewhat in this study, as do some brief references in Herodotus and Thucydides, but to a large degree we must look backwards from what existed in the fifth century in order to try to understand how democracy emerged at Athens.

The Archaic Age and the rise of the polis

The emergence of Athenian democracy at the end of the sixth century BC must be understood within the context of the rise of the polis during the Archaic Age, a period during which the scattered communities on the Greek peninsula and the Aegean islands asserted their SOVEREIGNTY over relatively small geographical areas by forming their own armies, minting their own currency, worshipping their own gods and, in particular, turning their inhabitants into citizens who shared in the ownership of the city. The fierce independence of these city-states ensured frequent wars between poleis, but also allowed for a wide range of opportunities for experimentation with forms of political regimes. Aristotle's *Politics* is replete with the varieties of political structure that arose during the formative years of the Archaic period. Yet, there were also some common developments that underlay these varied experiments in self-rule.

Relying on the evidence of Archaic poetry and even more the archaeological remains from grave offerings, Ian Morris (1987) has argued that this early period laid the groundwork for a sense of equality that could be the foundation for claims for self-rule not only at Athens, but in the other poleis across Greece as well. The appearance of 'citizen cemeteries' may be evidence of the breakdown in distinctions between the wealthy, the so-called *agathoi* (the good), and those with fewer resources, the so-called *kakoi* (the bad), throughout Greece of this period. According to Morris, tracing the changes in funerary practices helps to understand the origins of the polis in the movement towards a conception of the political unit as free from class interests (1987: 216).

In the Hesiodic poems, most likely from the eighth or seventh century BC, one finds a worldview that in its focus on the contribution of the average farmer likewise moves towards a potential equality that is distinct from what one sees in Homeric epics of approximately the same period. Hesiod, in the poem *Works and Days*, emphasises that there is no shame in hard work. The energy of the Thracian farmer whose attention to building his plows, to working the fields at the right seasons, to tending his flocks provides for the security and happiness of the community far more than the leadership of any ruler. In the Homeric epics, the hierarchical society relied on the glorious leadership of the noble warrior and kings whom flocks of men followed into battle,

preferably without any questioning. No democratic model appears in Hesiod, but the kings in his poem are no longer arbitrary rulers; they are to be limited by concerns for justice in the community, and this justice is to be enforced by the wrath of Zeus, not by the people.

Along with the emerging sense of equality during the Archaic Age that can be gleaned from some of Hesiod's lines and from the archaeological evidence there were social, military and political changes. 'Tyrants' during the seventh century often overthrew the monarchical and aristocratic rule based on ancestry and introduced a new model for the origins of political power, one which no longer depended on birth as the source of legitimacy. While assessments of the impact of these tyrants vary, the tyrants undermined a political regime based on historical attachment to the land and opened the door to alternative means of access to political power. It is also debated whether the tyrants themselves were the product or the cause of the increased trade and economic development of this period. Whatever the case, the age of the tyrants was accompanied by a wide distribution of wealth within cities such that stature need no longer be based on ancestry but could now follow economic success.

The ideological movement towards equality may also have found further support in the new military formation of the phalanx. The Greek armies changed from ones led by aristocratic warriors in chariots to ones in which heavy armed hoplites stood side by side with each one's shield protecting the warrior standing next to him. Though participation in the phalanx would have required considerable wealth on the part of the warriors in order to cover the expensive armour they used, this military innovation would also have promoted new values that could serve well as a foundation for the democratic political regime. The phalanx required a sense of unity and interdependence; it demanded an acknowledgement of equal participation in military engagement rather than a focus on the glorious exploits of the individual charioteer. The hoplite was part of a whole formation; he did not stand in his chariot literally above the masses of foot soldiers. The phalanx could only succeed insofar as all stood their ground together, insofar as no one stood out from the entire formation, insofar as the warriors practised the virtue of moderation (*sophrosune*) and saw themselves as the same, with each an equal replacement for the other (Forrest 1966: 88, 94; Vernant 1982: 62–3). Heroism no longer entailed standing out from the crowd. The hero was now the equal participant in a military formation. The new 'hero' was the city, seeking precedence among other cities. Ancient democracy began in its support of equality, not, as we will see below, in its support of individuality.

The emergence of democracy at Athens

Democratic regimes were instituted in many other cities besides Athens. Aristotle's *Politics* is in large part a comparative study of political regimes. In it, he records the many types of democracies, from those where offices are filled by elections to ones where they are filled by lot, from those where assemblies rule to ones where laws rule. In describing the many possible forms of democracy, Aristotle cites a multitude of other cities as exemplars. Yet, it is only with reference to Athens that we can attempt to trace some of specific sixth century events that led to the institution of democracy at the end of the century.

At the beginning of the sixth century BC at Athens, the Eupatrids, the 'well-born' or the aristocrats, held the position of archons or rulers in the city. They would meet as an assembly at the Areopagus, a hill in the city, to decide policy. They ruled in Archaic Athens over a city spread across the plain of Attica. In the early part of the sixth century, economic crises, or as Aristotle phrases it in the *Athenian Constitution*, 'strife (*stasis*) between the notables and the many (*to plêthos*)' (12.2), plagued Athens. In 594 BC, in order to resolve these crises, the aristocratic leaders or archons gave unique powers to the archon Solon. Solon instituted a series of reforms intended to reduce the tensions between the wealthy, the *agathoi*,

and the poor, the *kakoi*, and in so doing laid the groundwork for the fundamental principles of the democratic regime that would be put in place at the end of the century (see CITIZEN-SHIP).

Solon's most famous economic reform was the cancellation of the debts of those who worked the land of others and the return of land to others from whom it had been taken, even if poverty had forced them into exile. Ownership of the small farm was now open to Athenians without fear of dispossession, and new laws controlling the transmission of land in families without sons ensured that the small property holder did not disappear. Further, Solon made it illegal for men to sell themselves into bondage by using their own bodies as collateral. Athenians could not become slaves, and those who had become slaves through such agreements were freed. By removing the possibility for dependence on persons, Solon opened the possibility for dependence on the abstract whole of the city. Solon also reorganised the population so that new classes would be defined in terms of productive wealth rather than according to the amount possessed, thus breaking the ancient grounds for distinguishing individuals according to patrimony.

Aristotle, commenting on Solon's reforms in the *Politics*, notes that there are some who say that he dissolved the 'unmixed' oligarchy and instituted the traditional democracy (2.12; 1273b). Aristotle does not accept this claim and disputes whether Solon instituted the popular council or Boulé and election to office as some maintain; he argues instead that Solon's democratic contribution was to make the courts open to all such that anyone, not only the well-born Eupatrids, could bring a civil action to the courts. Thus, Aristotle claims, Solon established the 'ancestral democracy' by mixing the regime so that oligarchy resided in the Council of the Areopagus, aristocracy in the offices, and democracy in the courts. Ostwald (1986: 30ff) speculates that most significant about this opening of the courts was the possibility it may have provided the people of bringing forth cases of *eisaggelai*, the practice by which private citizens could accuse public officials of the misuse of their offices. Those in public office suddenly became accountable; insofar as they did not perform according to law and custom in those offices, they were liable to fines and punishments.

Solon's reforms provided as well that participation in the courts was determined by lot, not by ancestry. For Aristotle, writing in the second book of the *Politics* over two hundred years later, this and Ephialtes's and Pericles's success at limiting the power of the aristocratic Aereopagus while expanding the power of the assembly or *ekklesia* in the fifth century, and later Pericles's institution of pay to members of the court, brought Athens to the 'completion' of the democratic regime that still existed at Aristotle's time in the fourth century (2.12; 1274a).

While the specifics of Solon's reforms may have been overturned when Solon left Athens in order to travel, important legacies remained. From 594 BC onward, eligibility for public office depended not on membership in a certain family, but on membership in one of the census classes, which in turn depended on the measurement of productive wealth, not the possession of wealth. Likewise, magistrates were accountable for actions in office and could be brought to court by anyone of the people. Such participation in the legal system ensured a place for the wider populace in the processes of self-governance before the assembly itself became open to all citizens.

Apart from the direct issues of regime structure, Solon's reforms included the re-affirmation of the publication of laws that had begun with Drakon's code at the end of the seventh century. Knowledge of the laws, no longer resided in a narrow set of elite political rulers, but was shared among the whole population. Solon expanded and reinforced this principle of public access to the laws, to which laws one might appeal, opening the door for criticisms of current laws and allowing for future influence on the formation of law codes.

In no sense can we say that Solon 'originated' Athenian democracy. While some of his reforms expressed fundamental democratic principles such as publicity of laws, participa-

tion in the legal processes of the regime and accountability of public officers, Solon was no egalitarian. He reports that he gave to the demos however much honour or privilege was 'sufficient' so that they might not experience what was unseemly, but he also knows that the best demos follows its leaders and does not display too little restraint or too much strength (fragments 5,6). Yet, the legacy of the Archaic period in general and Athens in particular included increasing equality between the *agathoi* and *kakoi*, legal openness or publicity, accountability and the beginning steps in undermining the political authority of the aristocratic family and increasing dependence on the abstraction of the 'polis'.

The 'founding' of democracy

After admonishing the Athenians to preserve the reforms he had instituted, Solon departed on his journeys to Asia Minor. Shortly after his departure, however, the tyrant Pisistratus took power in the city. It is unclear to what degree the Solonic reforms remained in effect during the rule of Pisistratus, but it was the assassination of Pisistratus's son Hipparchus that the Athenians themselves marked as a crucial moment in bringing about their democracy. The Athenians venerated the tyrannicides, Harmodius and Aristogeiton, acknowledging them as heroes of Athenian democracy, even though the tyrannicides were members of the aristocratic class and most likely were motivated to act against the tyrants for personal and not political reasons (Thucydides 6.53–59, Aristotle *Politics* 5.10, and Plato's little dialogue *Hipparchus*).

Following the assassination, Pisistratus's son Hippias ruled more harshly and aroused considerable discontent among the population. Two aristocrats, Cleisthenes and Isagoras, took advantage of the discontent the Athenians felt under Hippias's tyranny and called in Spartan support in an effort to overthrow Hippias. With the help of the Spartan king they were successful, but shortly thereafter the alliance between them apparently fell apart. Cleisthenes, whom Herodotus describes as establishing the 'tribes and the democracy' for the Athenians and whom the Athenians came to see as the founder of their democratic regime, was the victor in this competition for leadership. Cleisthenes acted most likely not on the basis of principle but, according to Herodotus, 'made an alliance with the demos' (5.66) or, according to the *Athenian Constitution*, 'turned to the demos' and 'handed over the regime to the many' (20.1), because he needed their support in the competition with Isagoras. This 'alliance with the demos' established the central principles that governed the Athenian democracy for its duration over the next century and a half, until the Macedonians invaded Greece and turned Athens into a puppet state.

The descriptions of Cleisthenes's innovations are brief wherever we look in the ancient sources. 'He made the Athenians who had been four tribes ten tribes', writes Herodotus (5.66). The *Athenian Constitution* says that Cleisthenes did this 'wishing to mix them so that more could partake of the regime' (21.2). Cleisthenes also increased the size of the Boulé or executive council, so that fifty members were appointed from each of the ten new tribes making a council of 500 rather than the 400 who had been drawn from the old four kinship-based tribes.

Most significant, though, was Cleisthenes's administrative restructuring of these new tribes or *phylai* comprising newly defined local units called demes. As the *Athenian Constitution* explains: 'And he made all the inhabitants in each of the demes demesmen of one another so that they might call the new citizens not by their patronymic but by their deme' (21.4). He gave each of the demes names with local significance, thereby giving the members a stronger sense of belonging to Athens rather than to a tribal family. Each of the newly created *phylai* included demes from each of the three areas of the city, the coast, the plain and the hills (21.4), removing them thus not only from an association with a particular aristocratic family, but also from attachment to any one geographical area within the city. Identifi-

cation was with the newly created administrative unit rather than with the past.

Significance of Cleisthenes's reforms

The administrative innovations instituted by Cleisthenes lead Aristotle in the *Athenian Constitution* to declare Cleisthenes's regime 'by far more democratic' than Solon's (22.1). Whereas Solon had broken the aristocratic stranglehold on Athens by giving the *kakoi* more of an opportunity to limit the actions of the wealthy, Cleisthenes's reforms completely transformed the people's relationship to each other, to their land and to their ancestors, and brought into institutional political practice the equality and replaceability which had been emerging since the rise of the phalanx. No longer tied to their past, the citizens of Athens now were independent of tribal associations and set into artificially structured units that determined the nature of their participation in the processes of self-rule. They were no longer dependent for such participation on inherited legacies.

The democracy that Cleisthenes was credited with instituting thus asserted the independence of the city from the past. Athenian democratic institutions rested on the denial of the aristocratic family and tribe as the defining characteristic of the individual, and rather related the individual to the political unit of which he was a part. It released the individual from his association with an historically grounded, backward looking regime that characterised Athens at the beginning of the sixth century. Euben (1986) has argued that a break with the land and the past was the defining moment for the emergence of democracy in the Athenian city and was captured vividly in events leading to the battle of Salamis of 479 BC. Prior to that naval battle in which the Athenians defended themselves against the invasion of the Persians, the entire city abandoned the land, left their temples and sacred places and went, in the language of the Athenians in Thucydides's *History*, 'down into their ships' (1.74). That the city could continue to exist independently of the land, that the Athenians still identified themselves as citizens of a city without a locality affirmed their independence from any aristocratic attachment to the land and solidified their interdependence. Their ability to redefine themselves as a community independently of their land attached them to each other rather than to their parental lineage. Liberated from the past, the Athenians could create a new world of equals that served as the foundation for their democratic regime.

During the Peloponnesian War in the latter third of the fifth century, the great democratic leader Pericles in the speeches attributed to him by Thucydides built on this abstraction from the land as an essential quality for the Athenians at war. He asks the citizens of Athens to imagine that they live on an island and urges all those who live outside the city to consider their farms and lands mere baubles (1.143). He arranges for all those living on the land outside the city to abandon their farms and await the invasion of the Spartans from within the city. Removing themselves from an attachment to the land, they define themselves as citizens attached to and dependent on the city, 'feasting [their] eyes on the beauty of the city and becoming lovers of the city', as Pericles urges them to do in the funeral oration as reported by Thucydides (2.43). The democratic regime according to Pericles has created a city in which one is judged not by his wealth or poverty, but by the good one is able to perform on behalf of the city, most especially in time of war. The inequalities that arise have nothing to do with the past and one's birth, but with the actions expended for the sake of the communal world of the city. The connections with the past disappeared when Cleisthenes took the 'four-tribed' city and turned it into a 'ten-tribed' one. For Pericles, this does not lead to an absolute equality; rather, the old inequality based on birth and wealth is replaced by a new inequality based on merit, but the break from history is necessary in order for this meritocratic democracy to replace the aristocratic oligarchy.

A somewhat different view of equality at the foundation of Athenian democracy appears in the practice of ostracism. When Aristotle in the *Athenian Constitution* credits Cleisthenes with establishing a more democratic regime than Solon, he follows that claim with reference to the new laws aimed at getting the support of the many, especially the law of ostracism (22.1) that ensured that the city did not honour the exceptional, but rather saw the exceptional as a threat. Uncertainty about the actual frequency and timing of applications of the law of ostracism remains, but this attention to equality – whether in the Aristotelian or Periclean version – and the breaking of the ties with the past, capture the essential themes of democratic origins. Without a break with the past and a suspicion of the exceptional, inequality of parentage, ownership of land, wealth and skills would plague the self-rule principles of the assembly.

While critical to the formation of the democratic regime at Athens, the reforms of Cleisthenes also created for the democratic regime the deep tensions that continue to plague all democratic societies. As part of his attempt to appeal to the people, Cleisthenes had welcomed back as citizens some of the population that had moved beyond Attica, exacerbating the difficulty of defining the boundaries that separate the citizen from the foreigner when the ancient principle of inheritance is, at least at first, put into question. Wanting to break with the aristocratic and familial bonds of the past and to make CITIZENSHIP depend on membership in the demes, the Athenians found themselves again returning to principles of birth for determining citizenship status. Membership in the demes came too from parentage; at first just from the father, but after the citizenship laws passed in 450/51 BC during Pericles's tenure in office, from both fathers and mothers. Citizenship became exclusive again based on birth, only now it was not dependent on land, but on the elaborate procedures by which the demes evaluated each young man's claims to citizenship. The principle of equality at the founding of democracy as an escape from past associations was modified in the practice of the next century when inequalities governed the polity of citizens, slaves and metics (resident aliens).

The democratic principle of equality that lay at the origins of democratic Athens ended by incorporating the aristocratic principle of exclusion and bringing the issue of birthright back to participation. Plato, in Book 8 of the *Republic*, points to this tension when he describes the democratic regime as above all 'free and equal', which then leads democracies, if they follow their foundational principles, to a situation in which there is no distinction between citizen and non-citizen, man and woman, and animal. Aristotle, in Book 3 of the *Politics*, in his search for a definition of the citizen, also recognises the difficulty of finding the origins of citizenship for egalitarian societies and ends up noting that all citizens are 'made' by the political craft, just as pots are made by potters using the craft of pottery. In democracies, contradictions arise because the art of creating citizens is also the art of exclusion. The democratic citizen who is an expression of egalitarian principles becomes a source of inequality within and outside the regime.

Isonomia versus demokratia

Pericles in the funeral oration recorded by Thucydides refers to Athens as a democracy because, he says, it is a regime that 'cares for the many rather than the few' (2.37). Debate exists about when the term *demokratia* first appears as a description of Athens or any other regime. Some find allusions to the term in the tragedies of the first half of the century in language that describes power as belonging to the many, while others note the relative absence of the word from the literature until near the end of the century.

The word *demokratia* itself first appears in Herodotus, who writes in second half of the fifth century BC. He uses the term three times, while in the plays of Euripides, for example, written shortly afterwards, pride is expressed that decisions are made 'in the middle' or by the many and Sophocles in the *Antigone* emphasises the tyrannical rule of Creon by having Creon's son complain that Creon does not listen to comments of the people who wish

that Antigone not be punished. Nevertheless, there is no use of the word *demokratia* in the plays of the major playwrights of the fifth century.

The word most frequently used to characterise the Athenian regime from Cleisthenes through at least the first half of the fifth century was *isonomia*, an equality before and within the law, or as Vlastos (1953) argues, the principle that all have an equal share in the control of the city, that the city does not belong to one or an elite group, but that all citizens can engage in the self-governance of the city through participation in its laws. *Isonomia* refers to a political equality and not an economic equality. It is equal participation in the life of the city, the role of the many in defining policy and hearing the cases in court, and in holding officers accountable for their actions while in office that marks the first democracy, not a concern with economic equality.

Missing from the language of *isonomia* and *demokratia* is any concept of 'RIGHTS' as they have come to be understood in liberal democracies of the modern period. While Pericles claims in the funeral oration that the Athenians lived 'freely', without fearing the anger or disapproval of one's neighbour when one did what pleased him, Pericles also suggests that the highest activity is service to the city and that while the a-political man is not condemned, he is considered useless (2.37–40). Human fulfilment comes from service to the political regime, not from attention to private life. Indeed, the private individual was, in Greek, the *idios*. The founders of Athenian democracy did not worry as, for example, the authors of the *Federalist Papers* did, about creating a government strong enough to rule, but not so strong as to threaten the liberty of the individual. The role of the ancient democratic regime was not to protect the liberty of the individual; it was to protect the liberty of the city and raise it to a heroic superiority over its neighbours.

The Athenians enjoyed their liberty not in opposition to governmental rule, but by living in a city that was not subject to another city or empire and by not being subject themselves to the rule of another person; that is, living as a slave. Rights against governmental intrusion into one's private life had no place in Athenian democracy. No natural rights sanctioned by higher authority protected the individual (Finley 1981: 27). The political system invaded the lives of individuals in all sorts of ways, from determining whom one could marry, to when one could conduct business, to when and how one worshipped the gods of the city, to whether one could corrupt the young by asking them questions.

One phrase associated with Athenian democracy from quite early on is freedom of speech, a free translation of the word *parrhesia*. *Parrhesia* did not entail the protection of all forms of speech from political control (as the execution of Socrates vividly illustrates), but rather meant the opportunity to speak openly about political affairs in the assembly and elsewhere. Almost a synonym for *parrhesia* was *isegoria*, which is composed of the terms 'equality' and agora or 'marketplace' where conversations were carried on. The equality was to engage in those conversations. When Herodotus writes of the increasing greatness of Athens after the expulsion of the Hippias, he attributes it to equality and *isegoria* (5.78).

At its origins, democracy did not play the role that it does in modern political life. It was not characterised by constitutions that assured protections to its citizens as individuals. Rather, it expressed a sharing of power by the many, even the *kakoi*, a breaking from the ancestral bond, accountability of magistrates, and most especially an assertion of equality among those who were included in the citizen body. The definitions of who was to be included in this shared power, however, posed a constant challenge to the definitions of equality. It was a contradiction that the political theorists of the fourth century such as Plato and Aristotle recognised, and it is a tension that remains for democratic regimes despite the assorted accretions such as constitutionalism and individual rights that have attached to the term democracy since its beginnings in the ancient Greek world.

See also:

agonism; citizenship; civic virtue; demos; republicanism

Further reading

Euben, J.P. (1986) 'The Battle of Salamis and the Origin of Political Theory,' *Political Theory* 14(3): 359–90.

Finley, M.I. (1973) *Democracy: Ancient and Modern*, New Brunswick, NJ and London: Rutgers University Press.

—— (1981) 'Politics', in M.I. Finley (ed.) *The Legacy of Greece*, Oxford: Clarendon Press.

—— (1983) *Politics in the Ancient World*, Cambridge: Cambridge University Press.

Forrest, W.G. (1966) *The Emergence of Greek Democracy: 800–400 BC*, New York: McGraw-Hill.

Hansen, M.H. (1991) *The Athenian Democracy in the Age of Demosthenes*, trans. J.A. Crook, Oxford: Basil Blackwell.

Hanson, V. (1995) *The Other Greeks*, New York: The Free Press.

Hornblower, S. (1992) 'Creation and Development of Democratic Institutions in Ancient Greece', in J. Dunn (ed.), *Democracy: The Unfinished Journey 508 BC to AD 1993*, Oxford: Oxford University Press.

Loraux, N. (1986) *The Invention of Athens*, Cambridge, MA: Harvard University Press.

Manville, P. (1990) *The Origins of Athenian Citizenship*, Princeton, NJ: Princeton University Press.

Morris, I. (1987) *Burial and Ancient Society*, Cambridge: Cambridge University Press.

Ober, J. (1989) *Mass and Elite in Democratic Athens*, Princeton, NJ: Princeton University Press.

Ostwald, M. (1986) *From Popular Sovereignty to the Sovereignty of Law*, Berkeley, CA: University of California Press.

Saxonhouse, A. (1996) *Athenian Democracy: Modern Mythmakers and Ancient Theorists*, Notre Dame, IN: University of Notre Dame Press.

Vernant, J.-P. (1982) *The Origins of Greek*

Thought, Ithaca, NY: Cornell University Press.

Vlastos, G. (1953) '*Isonomia*', *American Journal of Philology* 74: 337–66.

ARLENE W. SAXONHOUSE

DEMOCRATIC PEACE *see peace, democratic*

democratic performance

A focus on democratic performance marks a significant departure from traditional approaches to democracy. Until recently, the predominant concern was to explain democracy, either by revealing its historical determinants or by examining the process of DEMOCRATIC TRANSITION and DEMOCRATIC CONSOLIDATION. In behavioural terms, democracy was the dependent variable. Democratic performance makes democracy the independent variable, and seeks to measure what democratic government does, and, in particular, to assess the degree to which democratic regimes achieve in practice the values to which they subscribe in principle.

Past attempts to explain democracy, and especially MODERNISATION theory, tended to focus on the relationship between democracy and development (see DEMOCRATIC DEVELOPMENT). Quantitative inquiries sought to correlate either democracy itself, or INDICATORS OF DEMOCRACY such as civil and political liberties, with economic growth. What emerged was a 'stable positive relationship between socioeconomic development and democracy' (Rueschemeyer *et al.* 1992: 26), but subsequent causal tests suggested that it was the economic growth that caused democracy, and not democracy that caused the growth (Helliwell 1994; Burkhart and Lewis-Beck 1994). This understanding was reinforced by historical approaches that focused on structural features like class alliances, top-down versus bottom-up modernisation, the international system, or 'critical junctures' to explain the genesis of democracy.

The contemporary idea of democratic performance therefore differs from past approaches to democracy in two main ways. First, it is broader than the notion of economic performance implicit in the relationship between democracy and development, and emphasises political performance more than economic growth. Second, it requires an explicitly comparative approach that seeks to differentiate democratic governments. Rather than comparing the correlates of, or pathways to, a homogeneous historical result, which is democracy, it takes as its main premise the heterogeneity of democratic government, and examines its consequences.

This new idea of democratic performance was generated by two large changes, one historical, one theoretical. The historical change is the democratic revolution of the end of the twentieth century, conventionally referred to as the 'third wave' of democratisation. The result has been not only many more self-styled democratic governments than at any previous moment in history, but a much greater variety of democratic government, which has tended to raise the question of which of the variants works best. The theoretical change is the rise of the 'NEW INSTITUTIONALISM' (March and Olsen 1984), which insists that institutions matter, and that different institutional arrangements tend to produce different political outcomes. As a consequence, it is now commonly assumed that it is the INSTITUTIONAL DESIGN of democratic government that most closely affects its performance. This assumption is sharpened in studies of democratic transition, where such design may determine the very success of the transition and the subsequent consolidation of democracy.

The question of comparative democratic performance is posed in several ways. One follows directly from the traditional concern with the relationship between democracy and development, and its emphasis on economic performance, since it addresses the differential success of democratic and non-democratic regimes in achieving economic growth and social WELFARE. Following the collapse of the existing socialisms in Europe in recent years, the debate now focuses on the relative performance of the ASIAN MODELS OF DEMOCRACY of Korea, Taiwan, Malaysia or Singapore, and the liberal models of the European Union and the United States. The question then becomes whether there is an economic and social price to pay for individual rights and liberties? The countries of the Asian model have national traditions which are relatively impervious to the Enlightenment tradition, and tend to value community cohesion and public order above individual liberty, often resisting international conventions on human rights. The question is fiercely debated, but the evidence remains inconclusive.

More typical of the contemporary idea of democratic performance, however, is the range of inquiries into the comparative performance of different types of democratic regime, which are defined according to their institutional design. If the electoral system is taken as the primary determinant of this design, majoritarian or 'first-past-the-post' systems, with single-member constituencies and one person one vote, can be contrasted with consensus systems built on forms of proportional representation. A recent study measured the performance of these two designs according to the numerical means of the standard economic indicators, as well as some political indicators such as women's representation, social policy and voting turnout, and concluded that consensus regimes perform better politically, and at least as well economically, so making them superior to majoritarian regimes (Lijphart 1994a).

On the other hand, if the relationship of executive to legislature is made primary, the inquiry tends to focus on the comparative performance of parliamentary versus presidential regimes. Here the majority of studies have focused not on particular policy outputs or performance, but on the relative longevity and stability of the two regime types, and on their overall institutional efficacy as measured by their capacity to legislate effectively, even on contentious issues. Equally, these studies have sought to demonstrate the superiority of

parliamentarianism (see PARLIAMENTARY MODELS) since PRESIDENTIALISM embodies two separate 'agents of the electorate', and the lack of policy agreement between executive and assembly can always cause tensions in the regime and ultimately legislative GRIDLOCK and regime breakdown. There have been various attempts to demonstrate that presidential regimes are indeed more prone to DEMOCRATIC BREAKDOWN than parliamentary ones, but much depends on the timeframe and geographical scope of the inquiry. Presidentialism is overwhelmingly a 'Third World' phenomenon, and it is arguable that in this context it has fared at least as well and possibly better than parliamentarianism.

Since different elements of institutional design can be combined and re-combined in various ways, it is always possible to multiply performance comparisons. Thus, it has been argued that it is not presidentialism *per se* but 'the combination of presidentialism and a fractionalised multiparty system' which is 'especially inimical to stable democracy' (Mainwaring 1990: 168). The presidential democracies which endure (Colombia, Costa Rica, United States and Uruguay) are two-party systems, and there is no current example of a stable democracy that is multiparty presidential (with the possible exception of Chile). Stability in presidential-proportional representation (PR) systems seems to depend on 'presidential' majorities or near majorities in the assembly, which themselves depend on electoral laws, not only, or even especially, for legislative elections but also for presidential elections. In parliamentary-PR regimes, on the other hand, many of the key design features may be informal (conditioning the process of coalition formation, for example), and the differential performance of these regimes may depend on their combination with 'extra-political' factors like social cleavages and ideological polarisation. In effect, polarisation in these cases has come to be seen as 'the best single explanatory variable for stable versus unstable...[or]...successful versus immobile...democracy' (Sani and Sartori 1983: 337).

But the uniform if systematic comparison of

differently designed democratic regimes cannot deliver a comprehensive understanding of democratic performance, since performance itself cannot be understood as a linear function of institutional design. On the contrary, it cannot be assumed that all associated democratic values, or their corresponding policy outputs are mutually compatible, and so any assessment of performance will entail an analysis of the trade-offs between them. The structure and balance of these trade-offs will necessarily vary according to institutional design (and much game-theoretic analysis is dedicated to modelling this variation in conditions of 'bounded rationality'). In illustration, majoritarian parliamentary systems like that of the United Kingdom are said to be highly accountable, since voters rarely have any doubts about which party is responsible for the successes and failures of government at the moment of going to the polls, but they are only poorly representative, with governments often voted in by small pluralities. Consensus-PR systems, on the contrary, are – unsurprisingly – more proportional and hence more representative, both in the relationship between votes and parliamentary seats and in government composition, since they encourage coalition governments that better reflect the profile of public opinion. But such systems reduce accountability since the changing composition of coalition governments blurs the voters' sense of party responsibility for government policy.

In similar fashion, although majoritarian parliamentary systems may produce strong and stable government, there are few effective checks and balances on the executive, especially where party discipline is strong and the legislative majority large. As a result, the British government was once famously characterised by Lord Hailsham as an 'elective dictatorship'. Presidential regimes, on the other hand, and especially that of the United States, are specifically designed to produce effective checks and balances, but, as already noted, this exposes them to executive-legislative conflict, and possible legislative gridlock. Institutions matter, therefore, but the way they matter and the degree to which they matter depends on the structure of the democratic trade-offs they promote and contain.

In its strongest form, this observation may appear to challenge the comparative possibility of measuring democratic performance, since this comparative enterprise requires universal values and truly normative expectations. If there is a 'majoritarian' definition of accountability, for example, then it will be impossible to measure such accountability across different democratic systems. But this problem is more apparent than real, for the comparative method requires that the value is defined prior to the moment of measurement, so that all democratic systems will be more or less accountable, more or less representative. Thus, to switch focus, majoritarian systems lack proportionality – by definition – and are less likely, therefore, to be highly representative. But, as Lijphart has argued, all electoral systems are more or less unproportional, and majoritarian systems are not so much more unproportional than PR systems that they cannot be compared on the same scale (Lijphart 1994b).

But this begs the question of how the values that inform the comparative measurement of democratic performance are established in the first place. If this is not done by normative inquiry, then it requires empirical investigation of public opinion and citizen preferences. But sufficient survey data to support such investigation, or the resources to generate it, only exists in the long-lived democracies of the developed world. Elsewhere is either patchily present (for example, in the Visegrad countries), or absent altogether (as in Latin America, with the partial exceptions of Brazil, Chile and Uruguay). Hence it is mainly normative inquiry that must establish the criteria for evaluating democratic performance. Yet this solution is itself not free of problems, since some confusion persists between values which reflect the idea of democracy or the institutional efficacy of democratic government, on the one hand, and, on the other, values which reflect government effectiveness in general. The former value dimensions can be considered intrinsic, and the latter extrinsic to democratic performance.

To exemplify, the first value dimension can be gauged by the degree to which normative democratic values are realised in practice (civil and political liberties and protections; minority rights and social peace; DUE PROCESS and the system of criminal justice; effective representation); the second by the institutional efficacy of the democratic system (responsiveness and degree of gridlock; political deliberation; PARTICIPATION; accountability and JUDICIAL REVIEW; resistance to patrimonialism and CLIENTELISM); and the third by the outputs required of any effective system of government (legislation; policy implementation; economic growth; social welfare; protection of the environment; LEGITIMACY and system support; control of criminality; national security). It is this third dimension which remains extrinsic to democratic performance.

It is not obvious how this confusion has arisen. Possibly there is some conflation of the measures which distinguish the performance of democratic and non-democratic systems with those which differentiate the performance of differently designed democratic systems. Possibly the ubiquitous and catchall concept of governability is at fault, since it tends to encompass both intrinsic and extrinsic value dimensions. There was certainly no confusion in Dahl's original model of polyarchy, since the two main axes of the model, contestation and participation, clearly belong to the value dimensions which are intrinsic to democratic performance. Subsequent studies tended either to maintain the focus on contestation (ELECTIONS, ELECTORAL SYSTEMS, political PARTY SYSTEMS) and participation (SUFFRAGE, voter turnout and POLITICAL CULTURE), or extend it to CONSTITUTIONALISM (presidential, parliamentary and HYBRID SYSTEMS) and CITIZENSHIP (civil, political and social rights), either taken separately or together but they often lost sight of the goal of comparative measurement, which made Dahl's work on polyarchy a seminal study of performance (see Dahl's POLYARCHY).

Yet self-consciously quantitative attempts to measure democratic performance have tended to remain unfocused, since they have not been informed by a clear consensus on how to measure it. The literature produced in the period 1954–65 contained no fewer than 2,080 separate indices of such performance, only twenty-eight per cent of which were ever used more than once (Barsh 1993). All such indices tended to isolate or combine measures of stability, institutional and party systems, ELECTORAL BEHAVIOUR, or individual and press freedoms. But, with rare exceptions such as Gastil's 'index of political freedom' or partial exceptions such as Humana's 'index of human rights', they are all comparative, statistical snapshots taken at one point in time. The plain disadvantage of all such indices is that they conceal the institutional differences of systems with similar scores, and so fail to capture how institutions enhance or retard performance or, in particular, how the institutional design of different systems structures the trade-offs between different democratic values or value dimensions.

In at least two respects, therefore, the institutional literature did represent a clear advance over the quantitative studies. It could address the complexities of the democratic trade-offs, and it could seek to trace the direction of changes in democratic performance. But the institutional literature itself remains flawed on at least three counts. The categorisation of institutions is crude, and often reduced to a binary coding (for example, presidential, parliamentary). The relationship between institutional design and performance remains opaque. And the tendency persists to confuse the measures of intrinsic and extrinsic performance. Yet, despite all these difficulties, the idea of democratic performance is now central to mainstream thinking on democratic government, and is playing a key analytical role in revealing and resolving the crucial problems of contemporary democratic governance. Some examples follow.

Individual rights are a crucial indicator of democratic performance, being both intrinsically democratic in content and expressive of democracy under the rule of law. But their measurement requires close attention to the institutional conditions of minority representation, since minorities are often excluded, *de jure* or *de facto*, from full citizenship. Political tensions may arise from the difficulties of balancing the general conditions of individual rights with specific provision for minority protections, and it is not at all obvious on a priori grounds what institutional forms – whether FEDERALISM, confederalism, consociational arrangements or constitutional protections – can best achieve this balance. The difficulty of designing an institutional solution to the complex trade-off between rights and representation is relevant to countries of Eastern Europe, where individual rights are everywhere cross-cut by minority status, especially where the ethnic nationals of one state are located within the borders of another state, and are recurrently threatened by resurgent nationalisms. It is relevant to Western Europe, where increased rates of international migration and foreign labour enclaves have raised similar issues; and to Latin America, where a general concern for human rights is complicated by renewed calls for indigenous rights.

Social welfare measures and minority protections can be undermined by gridlock, where government is unable to achieve change by imposing losses on groups which benefit from the status quo. Institutional arrangements can contribute to gridlock by structuring the interests that resist the cost of adaptation, or by facilitating blocking coalitions among them. Political institutions may also be colonised by such interests, or permeated by clientelism. In sum, gridlock is a collective action failure that may be either promoted or prevented by political institutions. Typically, it is thought to be exacerbated by divided government between executive and legislature; by fragmented party systems, giving rise to ruling coalitions where many small parties have veto powers; or by ideological or party divisions between president and prime minister in hybrid systems. Institutional reforms may be required to reduce the gridlock which produces stasis or expensive log-rolling policy solutions in both

the United States and the European Union, while institutional inadequacies in the new democracies of the ex-Soviet Union and Eastern Europe may damage the development of the kind of SOCIAL CAPITAL which can underpin successful co-operation between stakeholders in the economic and political systems.

Institutional developments in the European Union will have a direct bearing on political legitimacy and citizen loyalty. The question of fiscal centralisation and redistribution in response to regional demands is central to the future success of the Union. In principle, this response will vary according to national institutional constraints (such as the degree of central bank independence, the commitment to exchange-rate policies such as the ERM or to EMU convergence criteria, and the auditing of tax policy) and to national elements of institutional design (such as the electoral system, the degree of centralisation of the party system, and the degree of consociationalism). But what will be the impact of the institutional design of the Union itself, and especially the DECISION-RULES of the Council of Ministers? Will it favour more fiscal centralisation and more redistribution to buy support for monetary union? Or will enlargement of the Union inevitably constrain such tendencies? And can the democratic deficit best be corrected at the 'federal' level (representation) or at the 'regional' level (responsiveness), and is there a clear trade-off between these two routes to citizen loyalty?

There is an increasing incidence and scope of judicial review, not only in the countries of the European Union but *pari passu* in new democracies across the globe. How far does such review contribute to system-efficacy, and especially the TRANSPARENCY of political decision-making and POLICY-MAKING, and their consistency with the rule of law? The new orthodoxy suggests that judicial review demands more administrative rationality and fair process of government, so guaranteeing democratic and constitutional protections instead of simply ensuring that legislative intentions are respected. Consequently, it may achieve greater transparency, insofar as higher courts call on public administration to adopt judicialised standards for the clear expression of intentions and justification of decisions. It may also increase democratic accountability, not only through the review process itself, but also by setting the agenda for private litigation against the police, local authorities or public agencies for the abuse of power or negligence of duty. In principle, both tendencies can serve to raise the systemic standards of democratic performance.

All these examples demonstrate how the institutional design of democratic government contributes to structure the value judgements and value trade-offs intrinsic to democratic policy-making and its political outcomes. This is not to suggest that the policy issues raised here are in any way unprecedented. On the contrary, they are simply contemporary manifestations of the traditional political problems of democratic government. But the focus on democratic performance does bring to these problems a new and comparative perspective, which consistently seeks to discover and disseminate best democratic practice and best institutional design. By achieving greater analytical leverage on intractable political problems it may promote democratic solutions, so combining intellectual reflection with political innovation. A focus on democratic performance therefore remains indispensable to bolstering the defence of democracy and improving the quality of democracy in the new millennium.

See also:

accountability; coalitions; consociationalism; democratic consolidation; gridlock; legitimacy; log-rolling; new institutionalism; polyarchy

Further reading

Barsh, R.L. (1993) 'Measuring Human Rights: Problems of Methodology and Purpose', *Human Rights Quarterly* 15(1): 87–121.

Burkhart, R.E. and Lewis-Beck, M. (1994) 'Comparative Democracy: The Economic Development Thesis', *American Political Science Review* 88(4): 903–10.

Helliwell, J.F. (1994) 'Empirical Linkages between Democracy and Economic Growth', *British Journal of Political Science* 24: 225–48.

Lijphart, A. (1994a) 'Democracies: Forms, Performance, Constitutional Engineering', *European Journal of Political Research* 25: 1–17.

—— (1994b) *Electoral Systems and Party Systems: a Study of Twenty-Seven Democracies, 1945–1990*, Oxford: Oxford University Press.

Mainwaring, S. (1990) 'Presidentialism in Latin America', *Latin American Research Review* 25(1): 157–79.

March, J.G. and Olsen, J.P. (1984) 'New Institutionalism: Organizational Factors in Political Life', *American Political Science Review* 78(3): 734–50.

Rueschemeyer, D., Stephens, E.H. and Stephens, J. (1992) *Capitalist Development and Democracy*, Cambridge: Polity Press.

Sani, G. and Sartori, G. (1983) 'Polarisation, Fragmentation and Competition in Western Democracies', in H. Daalder and P. Mair (eds), *Western European Party Systems: Continuity and Change*, Beverly Hills, CA: Sage.

JOE FOWERAKER

democratic stability

The concept of democratic stability was central to comparative politics in the 1960s and has seen a resurgence in the 1980s and 1990s. Most research on democratic stability is decidedly explanatory in aim, seeking to uncover the causes of democratic stability. Most of this literature also uses quantitative methodologies. Finally, most authors link the concept, either implicitly or explicitly, to national political regimes as opposed to national governments. These two levels of analysis are related. But as a case such as post-Second World War Italy shows, these two levels need not move in tandem: a stable regime may coexist with unstable governments. Research on democratic stability, then, has focused on a broader and more basic concern than the related research on issues such as cabinet instability or ELEC-TORAL VOLATILITY.

Two waves of research

A first wave of research on the causes of democratic stability was carried out within the framework of the MODERNISATION school. The single most influential work was that of Lipset (1959), which set the terms for a series of quantitative tests of the basic thesis that higher levels of economic development are associated with higher levels of democratic stability (Diamond 1992) (see DEMOCRACY, FUTURE OF). Lipset's pioneering role notwithstanding, his work suffers from a fundamental conceptual flaw. Lipset formulated his basic explanatory thesis as follows: 'The more well-to-do a nation, the greater the chances that it will sustain democracy'. However, in many parts of his article there is considerable slippage. At some points Lipset's dependent variable appears to be the stability of regimes that are already democratic, which is consistent with the summary statement he gives of his thesis. But at other points his dependent variable appears to be something quite different: the origins of democratic regimes.

Though Lipset's tendency to conflate two distinct issues – the origin and the stability of democracies – has been noticed, this distinction has continued to elude many scholars and the cost of this confusion has been quite high. As Rustow (1970) argued in his critique of the early modernisation literature, making a clear distinction between the origins and stability of democracy is important because these two outcomes entail different types of political processes and hence different causal conditions. This is a fundamental critique of the way modernisation theorists studied democracy and regimes, and it was taken up and developed in a number of significant works by qualitative researchers (Linz and Stepan 1978; O'Donnell and Schmitter 1986). But quantita-

tive scholars for the most part ignored Rustow's call for an analysis of the distinctiveness of political processes. Precisely at the time when the field of comparative politics was taking a big step toward becoming a systematic social science, an unfortunate parting of ways between its quantitative and qualitative wings took place.

After a hiatus of nearly two decades, the concept of democratic stability resurfaced in the 1980s and 1990s in the context of research on democratisation triggered by the wave of democratisation that started in the mid-1970s. In this new context, the concept has not been closely linked to a particular school, as had been the case during the heyday of modernisation theory in the 1960s. However, it continued to be used mainly in quantitative research.

Overall, this new literature moves beyond prior research on democratic stability in three ways. First, these studies use sophisticated statistical techniques that were not available to researchers in the 1960s. Second, they conceptualise the outcome of interest more carefully. Indeed, though the old conceptual problem of conflating the origins of democracy and democratic stability has still not been fully resolved, the literature on DEMOCRATIC TRAN-SITION has clarified this distinction and provided a clear signpost for measuring democratic stability: the 'founding elections' which fairly unambiguously mark the end of democratic transitions and open the question of the duration of democracy (O'Donnell and Schmitter 1986: 61).

Third, this new literature assesses a more complete set of explanatory factors. Virtually all studies concerned with democratic stability still consider the favourite variable of modernisation theorists: levels of socioeconomic modernisation. But a long list of other factors is also studied. These include other facets of economic and social life, such as economic performance or inequality, POLITICAL CULTURE, the international environment and, in what is probably the most significant departure, institutions. In short, this is a more sophisticated body of literature compared to the research produced in the 1960s.

A critical assessment

Despite these advances, research on democratic stability continues to suffer from significant shortcomings. First, the conceptualisation of the dependent variable remains a problem. Many studies seek to avoid conflating the origin and stability of democracy by using a very minimal definition of democracy, understood as a regime based on competitive elections, to establish a cut-off point between democracies and non-democracies. Once this criterion is used to define the set of democratic countries, the key concern is to establish how durable these democracies must be to be considered stable.

This approach has merits. Above all, it provides a fairly uncomplicated way of operationalising the dependent variable. But it also has problems. To begin, this approach has led scholars to debate the precise number of years that a country must remain democratic before it can be categorised as a stable democracy, with some authors proposing a twelve-year rule and others a twenty-five-year rule. Yet it is unclear what is gained by seeking a cut-off point that is used to turn the stability of democracies into a dichotomous variable when the durability of democracy seems to lend itself so readily to a continuous treatment.

More significantly, the minimal definition of democracy employed by recent studies leads to an impoverished analysis. Most scholars would agree that democracies must have competitive elections. But many scholars would argue that an analysis of democracy should also address other dimensions. Specifically, the problem with this minimal definition of democratic stability is that it does not allow researchers to grasp how countries that are democratic may vary in their 'democraticness'. Instead, cases in which democracy is under threat or weakened by coup attempts, riots, restriction of the freedom of the press and so on are lumped together with cases in which such features are absent, simply because in both instances competitive elections continue without interruption.

This point remains to be assimilated in research on democratic stability. Quantitative researchers have sought to grasp the significant variation among democratic countries by constructing indexes of democracy that measure levels or degrees of democracy. But existing indexes face their own problems, lacking clear criteria for establishing when a country has completed a democratic transition, and are used in research on democratic stability only at the risk of conflating the origins and the stability of democracy. Therefore, the problematic status of the concept of democratic stability continues to be a key challenge for this agenda of research. One option, followed by qualitative researchers, has been to shy away from this concept and use instead the concept of DEMOCRATIC CONSOLIDATION, which is broader – considering aspects of the regime beyond the electoral process – and which is more attuned to the dynamic nature of politics, refusing to study all politics in the wake of transitions to democracy as hinging primarily on the maintenance of an electoral process. This option may very well be the most productive one. But regardless of whether or not quantitative researchers choose to follow the lead of qualitative researchers, at the very least quantitative scholars should pay increased attention to the conceptual and methodological issues raised by the choice of conceiving democracy as a continuous variable or, alternatively, as a dichotomous variable (Collier and Adcock 1999).

A second limitation of current research on democratic stability concerns its explanatory variables. The tendency in this literature has been to focus on easily measurable variables and to ignore the role of actors and choices stressed by process-oriented theorists. Some notable but not very successful attempts aside, most researchers proceed as though it were unfeasible to collect data on process-oriented factors stressed by qualitative researchers who have increasingly theorised the more contingent, actor-centred aspects of political processes. Indeed, even one of the strongest proponents of a process-oriented approach, Przeworski, totally ignores these factors in his attempt to test theories of democratic stability quantitatively (Przeworski and Limongi 1997). As a result, this research continues to be biased toward structural factors, as was the case with the earlier modernisation literature, and continues to stand in an awkward relation *vis-à-vis* the work of qualitative researchers on democracy.

Finally, a third limitation of this research involves its failure to generate many robust findings. A quick overview of this literature shows that, even with regard to the central arguments in this literature, significant disagreement is quite pervasive. This is the case with the oldest arguments in the literature about the impact of modernisation. Thus, while Przeworski and Limongi (1997) make a strong case that levels of economic modernisation can explain the stability of democracy but have no explanatory power regarding the origins of democracy, most authors continue to argue that levels of modernisation can explain both the origins and stability of democracy (Diamond 1992). Very diverse positions also have been advanced with regard to some of the more novel arguments about institutions. Thus, while some tests indicate strong support for the argument that parliamentary forms of government promote democratic stability (Stepan and Skach 1993; Przeworski *et al.* 1996), others purport to show equally strong support for the argument that presidential forms of government promote democratic stability (Shugart and Carey 1992; Mainwaring and Shugart 1997). In other words, when it comes to the ultimate test of a line of research – its ability to generate significant findings – the literature on democratic stability leaves much to be desired.

In conclusion, much work remains to be done within this tradition of research. There are many ways in which this research could be advanced and, specifically, as this overview suggests, much progress could be made if researchers on democratic stability, who have worked primarily with quantitative methods, began engaging more consciously and carefully with the research on related topics by qualitative researchers (Coppedge 1999). Such cross-fertilisation would improve the conceptualisation of the outcome of interest and lead to a consideration of more sophisticated explanatory arguments. In turn, these refinements might strengthen the findings this literature can produce. Moreover, such an engagement would do much to re-establish a dialogue between quantitative and qualitative scholars who share a concern with democracy but who for far too long have not undertaken in a concerted effort to pool their strengths and coordinate their research agendas.

See also:

correlates of democracy; democratic breakdown; democratic consolidation; democratic performance; modernisation

Further reading

Collier, D. and Adcock, R. (1999) 'Democracy and Dichotomies: A Pragmatic Approach to Choices About Concepts', *Annual Review of Political Science* 5: 537–65.

Coppedge, M. (1999) 'Thickening Thin Concepts and Theories: Combining Large and Small in Comparative Politics', *Comparative Politics* 31(4): 465–76.

Diamond, L. (1992) 'Economic Development and Democracy Reconsidered', *American Behavioral Scientist* 35(4/5): 450–99.

Linz, J.J. and Stepan, A. (eds) (1978) *The Breakdown of Democratic Regimes*, Baltimore: The Johns Hopkins University Press.

Lipset, S.M. (1959) 'Some Social Requisites of Democracy: Economic Development and Political Legitimacy', *American Political Science Review* 53(1): 69–105.

Mainwaring, S. and Shugart, M. (1997) 'Juan Linz, Presidentialism, and Democracy: A Critical Appraisal', *Comparative Politics* 29(4): 449–71.

O'Donnell, G. and Schmitter, P. (1986) *Transitions from Authoritarian Rule. Tentative Conclusions about Uncertain Democracies*, Baltimore: The Johns Hopkins University Press.

Przeworski, A. and Limongi, F. (1997) 'Modernisation: Theories and Facts', *World Politics* 49(2): 155–83.

Przeworski, A., Alvarez, M., Cheibub, J.A. and Limongi, F. (1996) 'What Makes Democracies Endure?', *Journal of Democracy* 7(1): 39–55.

Remmer, K. (1996) 'The Sustainability of Political Democracy: Lessons from South America', *Comparative Political Studies* 29(6): 611–34.

Rustow, D. (1970) 'Transitions to Democracy: Toward a Dynamic Model', *Comparative Politics* 2(3): 337–63.

Stepan, A. and Skach, C. (1993) 'Constitutional Frameworks and Democratic Consolidation. Parliamentarism versus Presidentialism', *World Politics* 46(1): 1–22.

Shugart, M. and Carey, J.M. (1992) *Presidents and Assemblies: Constitutional Design and Electoral Dynamics*, New York: Cambridge University Press.

GERARDO L. MUNCK

democratic trade-offs

One key finding from the study of DECISION-MAKING in the field and in the laboratory is the difficulties people have in making trade-offs between values they hold (Jones 1994, 1999a, 1999b). These findings challenge current approaches to the analysis of decision-making in political and economic institutions. Difficulties in trade-offs also plague democratic decision-making systems composed of multiple voters.

Individual decision-making

Fundamental to economics and formal political theory is the *indifference curve*. Indifference curves are analytical devices that indicate how a consumer substitutes the worth ('utility') of one good ('apples') for another ('oranges'). Similarly, political scientists have used the notion to study voters or members of a legislative committee. Indifference curves are assumed to be smooth ('twice differentiable'), although the justification is analytical convenience rather than empirical study.

Political scientists use a variant of consumer choice theory in the study of voting choice. In politics, it is assumed that the rational voter wants a particular bundle of issues (similar to the commodity bundle of consumer choice theory). Unlike consumer choice, however, it is typically assumed that on any issue a voter can become *saturated*; they can get too much of the issue. As a consequence of political saturation, political scientists depict indifference curves as closed circles or ovals (Ordeshook 1986).

In both variants of choice theory, the shapes of the indifference curves indicate the marginal preference for a good or issue. The steeper the indifference curves as one moves away from the origin (in consumer theory) or away from the ideal point (in voter theory), the relatively more desirable the commodity. Circular indifference curves indicate that the issues are equally valued by the decision maker; ovals indicate that one is more valued than others. In any case, the notion that smooth trade-offs are the norm is embedded in choice theory.

Empirical study indicates difficulties with the notion. How is one to compare the utility of a political candidate's stand on WELFARE policy versus his partisan identification? These are the kind of *incommensurate attributes* that plague political decision-making. The ability to make consistent trade-offs is in part a consequence of the structure of the decision-making situation, and in part a consequence of the limits on individual cognition. With regard to the first, people do better in making trade-offs when there is a standard to compare each attribute against. Economic choice is facilitated by the price system, which acts as a comparative standard. We do not compare oranges and apples to each other, but compare the price of each. That makes the attributes of choice *commensurate* by measuring them on the same scale. In politics, often such a standard is not available, making choice more difficult.

The cognitive limits that cause people to have trouble making trade-offs is a fundamental tenet of the approach to decision-making termed *bounded rationality*. The idea was introduced by Herbert Simon (1947, 1995) to distinguish it from the comprehensive rationality generally postulated in economics and public choice. Compared to the standard of comprehensive rationality, there were bounds or limits to the choice-making abilities of both consumers and citizens.

Two important mechanisms of bounded rationality are associated with difficulties in trade-offs. One is *attention*. People have trouble comparing alternatives because of limits in their attention spans; they tend to focus on a very limited number of basic values or decisional attributes when they make choices (Jones 1994). The second is *identification with the means* (Simon 1947). People do not invariably focus on outcomes in decision-making; rather, they frequently identify cognitively and emotionally with the means or instrument of decision-making. It is common for rational choice scholars to claim that party identification is but an informational shortcut, a way that the voter has of limiting expensive search effort (Lupia and McCubbins 1998). Generally, however, people invest more emotionally in a partisan identification than the information shortcut approach would suggest. As a consequence, they have trouble abandoning a party position in the face of contradictory information.

Democratic political campaigns do not necessarily make trade-offs easier for the voter. Candidates do not tend to engage in debate on one dimension (Simon 1999). Rather, they follow what William Riker (1986) termed the *dominance and dispersion principles*, and Baumgartner and Jones (1993) call *non-contradictory argumentation*. If a candidate is winning the discussion, he or she keeps talking about that issue. If the candidate is losing, he or she is well advised to raise another issue. As a consequence, voters tend not to hear both sides of a single issue. On the other hand, the full set of important issues tends to be raised for the consideration of the electorate as the candidates cycle through issues in a search for electoral advantage (see ELECTORAL CAMPAIGNING).

Decision-making systems

If voting occurs among a number of participants along a single dimension (say, more or less spending for agriculture subsidies), an equilibrium solution is guaranteed, and it is the position occupied by the median voter. This result is known as the median voter theorem (MVT). Any system of voters that involves trade-offs among two or more attributes or dimensions, however, may not yield an equilibrium outcome. Instead, there may exist *issue cycling* among the various alternatives. In such a situation, the order of presentation of the alternatives affects the outcome, and manipulation by leaders is possible (Fiorina and Shepsle 1989).

To the extent that people attend to a single dimension in a complex situation, cycling will not occur. Indeed, political systems tend to process issues serially; they focus only on one issue at a time. This is a consequence of the manner in which attention, which is often more scarce than information, is allocated. Serial processing works against the manipulation by leaders that can occur in indeterminate, multi-dimensional choice systems.

The allocation of attention in a political system can solve the cycling problem, but it leads to another problem. When policy-making drops off the agenda, and is not the subject of scrutiny by democratically elected politicians, policy is generally set by the interested and attentive. This tends to organise policy-making along a set of single dimensions within *policy sub-systems*. If agriculture policy is under the control of agriculture department bureaucrats, farmers and legislators with farm constituencies, conflict will be organised around how much subsidy is provided, and to whom. There will be no explicit trade-off between agricultural productivity and environmental damage. When explicit structures reinforce this system, we refer to *structure induced equilibria* (Shepsle 1979). Because the structure precludes trade-offs, no issue cycling can occur, and hence an equilibrium among interests would be achieved (Redford 1969).

These equilibria may be undemocratic unless there is some provision for the intervention of macro-political forces (Redford 1969; Baumgartner and Jones 1993). The intervention of broader political forces can have the effect of bringing unrepresented dimensions or attributes into the formerly closed POLICY-MAKING system. This, however, involves the direction of attention toward the policy area and consequent mobilisation of broader PUBLIC OPINION, and is costly and uncertain.

The result is a system of *governance by disruption*. Consistent trade-offs are not possible, given the organisation of political systems and the tendency of individuals to have difficulties with making trade-offs. As a consequence, one alternative is to provide an institutional system that allows stability via structure-induced equilibria and disruption via the intrusion of broader democratic forces. Rather than providing a mechanism for smooth trade-offs among competing values, democracies, especially pluralist democracies, provide opportunities to disrupt the prevailing focus on a single dimension by bringing forward for consideration unappreciated attributes. The ability to focus attention on unattended aspects of policy-making is a key weapon of disadvantaged interests in democracies.

The most desirable systems provide for regular disruption rather than allowing pressures to build to the breaking point. This allows the mobilisation of interests within numerous policy-making venues. Such a system has the advantage of openness, but also the disadvantage of yielding the possibility of uncoordinated policy outputs. It suggests the desirability of decentralised policy-making systems, which sacrifice co-ordinated policy-making for responsiveness.

See also:

decision-making; elections; electoral campaigning; policy-making

Further reading

Baumgartner, F.R. and Jones, B.D. (1993) *Agendas and Instability in American Politics*, Chicago: University of Chicago Press.

Fiorina, M. and Shepsle, K. (1989) 'Formal Theories of Leadership', in B.D. Jones (ed.), *Leadership and Politics*, Lawrence, KS: University Press of Kansas.

Jones, B.D. (1994) *Reconceiving Decision-Making in Democratic Politics*, Chicago: University of Chicago.

—— (1999a) 'Bounded Rationality, Political Institutions, and the Analysis of Outcomes', in J. Alt, M. Levi and E. Ostrom (eds), *Competition and Cooperation: Conversations with Nobelists about Economics and Political Science*, New York: Russell Sage.

—— (1999b) 'Bounded Rationality', in N. Polsby (ed.), *Annual Review of Political Science 2*, Palo Alto, CA: Annual Reviews.

Lupia, A. and McCubbins, M. (1998) *The Democratic Dilemma*, Cambridge: Cambridge University Press.

Ordeshook, P. (1986) *Game Theory and Political Theory*, New York: Cambridge University Press.

Quattrone, G.A. and Tversky, A. (1988) 'Contrasting Rational and Psychological Analyses of Political Choice', *American Political Science Review* 3: 719–36.

Redford, E. (1969) *Democracy in the Administrative State*, New York: Oxford University Press.

Riker, W. (1986) *The Art of Political Manipulation*, New Haven, CT: Yale University Press.

Shepsle, K.A. (1979) 'Institutional Arrangements and Equilibrium in Multidimensional Voting Models', *American Journal of Political Science* 81: 85–104.

Simon, A. (1999) *Dynamics in Processing Everyday Political Messages*, Seattle: Centre for American Politics and Public Policy, University of Washington. Occasional Paper.

Simon, H.A. (1947) *Administrative Behavior*, New York: Macmillan.

—— (1995) 'Rationality in Political Behavior' *Political Psychology* 16: 45–61.

BRYAN D. JONES

democratic transition

The current interest in democratic transition and indeed the widespread use of the term stem from an analytic engagement with what has come to be known as the third wave of democratisation, from the mid-1970s to the opening years of the 1990s (see WAVES OF DEMOCRACY). Democratic transition is seen quite straightforwardly as the movement from a non-democratic regime to the introduction of a democratic regime, with substantial consensus in the literature on defining a democratic regime as a set of institutions (rather than as a type of SOVEREIGNTY, popular sovereignty or rule by the people) and on democratic transitions as the adoption of a set of 'minimum' institutional components, referring to provisions for free and fair ELECTIONS, civil rights and legislative governing authority. As such, a democratic transition is distinct from DEMO-CRATIC CONSOLIDATION.

The democratisation literature of the 1960s and 1970s

Prior to the recent 'transitions literature', the prevailing analytic tradition had focused on earlier episodes, particularly on the historical cases of Western Europe in the nineteenth and early twentieth centuries and on the attempt to introduce democratic regimes as part of the post-Second World War process of decolonisation. Two broad strands can be distinguished: MODERNISATION theory and historical sociological analysis. While the latter was sometimes viewed as inspired by Marxist class analysis and the former as pluralist, both advanced explanations that saw democracy as an outcome of social structure. For analysts like Moore (1966), democracy was an outcome of the balance or weight of different classes (particularly a weak, labour-repressive landed class and a strong bourgeoisie) and hence was rooted in class interest. For modernisation theory, democracy was not an outcome of class interest, but almost precisely the opposite: it was associated with a large middle class, a social group that was unlikely to act as a CLASS but instead formed shifting COALITIONS reflecting multiple interests and affiliations.

Both these analytic strands emphasised the impact of economic change on social structure,

the key causal variable. Agency was primarily implied: actors were read off the structural argument and almost epiphenomenal. Actors were sometimes explicitly analysed in the process-tracing case studies that provided the evidence for the structural arguments, but these were not voluntaristic arguments. The social science goal was to find causal regularities, not contingency.

The transitions literature: phase I

The style of analysis changed quite dramatically in the mid-1980s in response to events in southern Europe and South America. An initial phase emphasised a process-oriented analysis that explored the transition as a specific, delimited step in a sequence that started with splits inside the authoritarian regime and ended with the installation of a new government elected under the rules that defined a democratic 'minimum'. This approach was introduced by scholars who attempted to escape the determinism of structural approaches and who adopted a 'possibilistic' rather than a probabilistic stance.

In the dominant analytic framework, actors were no longer epiphenomenal but central decision-makers, making efficacious, consequential choices. Two kinds of choice models represented somewhat conflicting approaches. Neither was sufficiently elaborated, nor was the tension between them made explicit or resolved. The first emphasised contingency, individual LEADERSHIP, personal qualities and crafting (O'Donnell and Schmitter 1986: 4–5; Di Palma 1990; Burton et al. 1992). The second sought to characterise the strategic situation that conditioned actor choices. It described strategic games, such as 'coup poker' (O'Donnell and Schmitter 1986: 24–5), in which rational courses of action were embedded in the structure of the strategic context. Another departure from the earlier literature was the way actors were defined: no longer by class or social group, but by strategic posture; not by features or interests that would 'cause' them to favour or oppose democracy (with the exception that authoritarian incumbents were seen as opponents), but by their actual position regarding democracy and whether they were willing to compromise to achieve or resist it. The framework thus posited a four-player transition game of incumbents and opponents with standpatters and compromisers among each.

The analysis based on these choice models had certain features. First, it defined 'transition' as a delimited stage and saw authoritarian erosion and democratic consolidation as empirically and conceptually separate, requiring different frameworks of analysis. As such, the dynamics of the antecedent regime were exogenous to the proposed analytical models. Second, the emphasis was less on causal analysis than on the elaboration of a kind of 'natural history' or generalised pattern of transition. Aside from the few cases, among the original set, of authoritarian collapse, the transition was seen as a game of strategic interaction and particularly negotiation between the two compromising groups (among both incumbents and opposition), though two sub-types were often delineated according to their relative weights. Third, the main actors were seen as individual elites who made decisions, not protesting groups or social movements, though it was acknowledged that mass action could affect the relative resources of the 'bargaining' leaders.

Many features of the transition were not problematised, perhaps reflecting the commonalities among the cases in Southern Europe and South America. The shared traits included a certain type of authoritarian regime (fascist or bureaucratic-authoritarian) with anti-labour, demobilisational origins, powerful militaries (indeed most were military regimes), roughly similar social structures (at least compared to subsequent cases) and party infrastructures (even though PARTIES may have been banned). The new cases in East Asia, the Eastern bloc and Africa, however, were quite different.

The transitions literature: phase II

A second phase of the transitions literature began with the task of analysing and account-ing for these subsequent transitions. The greater empirical variation challenged a more generalising approach, as more varied combinations of actors played a role in the transition process, and social movements and protest became more prominent features (see SOCIAL MOVEMENTS). In addition, the problems of the authoritarian regime seemed more integrally connected with the way the transition unfolded, so that it seemed inappropriate to exogenise antecedent regime dynamics. Paralleling these developments were theoretical revisions that stemmed from further analysis of the original cases in South America and Southern Europe. A more diverse contemporary literature came to include broader perspectives, endogenised the antecedent regime in analytical models, and became more structural and explanatory.

In the shift back toward causal analysis and structural variables, explanations have focused on international and/or domestic factors and socio-economic and/or political factors. Crossing these two dimensions yields four sets of explanatory factors: the global economy, international politics, the domestic economy and class, and antecedent regime. The first defines common causes and is a natural place to look in explaining a wave phenomenon characterised by temporal clustering. Yet few studies have sufficiently elaborated this argument that relates global economic transformations to the democratic wave as the two historic macro-social processes occurring simultaneously at the end of the century. Further research should explore these factors empirically on a broadly comparative, inter-regional basis. International political factors, including external opportunities, imposition and political conditionality, have received attention, as has the change from a bipolar to a unipolar world. Nevertheless, many analyses, even of those cases where external effects would seem to be particularly strong, such as the impact of changing Soviet policy toward the Eastern bloc, see them as final triggers and put greater causal weight on internal processes.

Domestic socioeconomic factors include the level of economic development, economic performance and class. The modernisation hypothesis linking development to democratisation has been revisited, with some analysts suggesting a threshold effect (Huntington 1991), and others suggesting that wealth affects democratic consolidation but not attempted transitions (Przeworski and Limongi 1997). Conversely, economic stagnation or crises have been seen as disrupting the bargain, relationships or distributive networks that supported authoritarianism. The (in)capacity of regimes to respond to economic crisis, both to overcome it and to distribute its costs in a way that prevents splits, defections and societal opposition, has been seen as having an important impact on the nature of the transition in terms of its timing, the degree of incumbent control, the key actors, the decisional arenas of institutional design and the nature of those new institutions (Haggard and Kaufman 1995) (see ECONOMIC REQUIREMENTS OF DEMOCRACY)

Many of the arguments about economic factors invoke class as a central intervening variable. The association of middle-class growth and demands for democratic regimes has figured prominently in the East Asian literature. In quite a different way, Africanists have emphasised the role of the urban middle classes and the impact of economic crisis on the declining rent-seeking and patronage opportunities of what was once called the organisational bourgeoisie (Widner 1994). The analysis of Rueschemeyer *et al.* (1992) was one of the first to reinsert more classically defined classes into analysis of transitions. Looking at episodes of democratisation drawn from the advanced industrial world, Latin America and the Caribbean, they suggested the leading role of the working class. Collier (1999) also considered the role of the working class in historical and recent transitions in Western Europe and South America. Viewing transitions as outcomes of both political strategies and class-defined interests, she distinguished multiple patterns, most of which are types of multiclass projects, even those historical Northern European cases which have been most commonly identified with working-class demands or agency.

Antecedent regime has become a particu-

larly important causal factor with the advent of additional cases. It has been analysed to account for the particular kinds of problems or crises that may inaugurate a transition, the dynamics among actors or factions within the regime, and the nature and organisation of potential opposition or interlocutory groups. Antecedent regime affects the nature of 'political' society, whether or how it was organised, its resources, and the political opportunity structure afforded for kinds of collective action, from disciplined organised protest to spontaneous demonstrations of rage. Diverse processes of transition have thereby been distinguished in terms of different patterns of authoritarian erosion and different actors with distinct motivations and interests, undertaking different kinds of action for political change (Fish 1995; Linz and Stepan 1996; Bratton and van de Walle 1997; Bunce 1999). In the second phase, then, a less contextualised analysis has been supplemented by historical institutional analyses with more path-dependent models for explaining difference; the analysis of class interest and political economy has been re-introduced; and the literature has begun to incorporate social movement theory into the analysis of transitions.

Finally, the analysis of choice has been expanded in at least two ways. First, analysts have examined the varied arenas of rule making during the transitions, such as interim governments and constitutional assemblies, and have sought to explain the establishment of the innovative round tables and national conferences, which include broad societal forces, in some (but not other) countries in the Eastern bloc and Africa, respectively. Second, institutional and CONSTITUTIONAL DESIGN has received attention as part of the transition. Earlier analysis had usefully pointed to the capacity of the withdrawing military to obtain prerogatives and guarantees against human rights accusations, and the way particular authoritarian leaders (such as Pinochet) could fashion favourable constitutional provisions. Subsequent analyses have gone further in explaining the design of legislatures, executives and electoral laws.

Conclusion

The study of democratic transitions has thus gone from a rejection of earlier structural accounts and a preference for an actor-based model of choice and process to the beginnings of a more complex, multi-faceted literature that moves toward integrating structural, institutional and choice models, as well as explanatory and processual perspectives. Built primarily on case or regional studies, the more recent literature faces the challenges of parsimony and cumulation. A danger of synthesis or broader comparison is simply compiling a laundry list of factors that contribute to democratic transitions. Another is the proliferation of types of transitions and of parallel stories, in which different causal factors account for different transitional processes or outcomes. An increasingly rich literature on democratic transitions is not yet approaching theoretical closure.

Further reading

Bratton, M. and van de Walle, N. (1997) *Democratic Experiments in Africa*, New York: Cambridge University Press.

Bunce, V. (1999) *Subversive Institutions: The Design and the Destruction of Socialism and the State*, New York: Cambridge University Press.

Burton, M., Gunther, R. and Higley, J. (1992) 'Introduction: Elite Transformations and Democratic Regimes', in J. Higley and R. Gunther (eds), *Elites and Democratic Consolidation in Latin America and Southern Europe*, New York: Cambridge University Press.

Collier, R.B. (1999) *Paths Toward Democracy: The Working Class and Elites in Western Europe and South America*, New York: Cambridge University Press.

Dahl, R. (1971) *Polyarchy: Participation and Opposition*, New Haven, CT: Yale University Press.

Di Palma, G. (1990) *To Craft Democracies*, Berkeley, CA: University of California Press.

Fish, S. (1995) *Democracy from Scratch: Opposition and Regime in the New Russian Revolution*, Princeton, NJ: Princeton University Press.

Haggard, S. and Kaufman, R. (1995) *The Political Economy of Democratic Transitions*, Princeton, NJ: Princeton University Press.

Huntington, S. (1991) *The Third Wave: Democratization in the Late Twentieth Century*, Norman, OK: University of Oklahoma Press.

Linz, J. and Stepan, A. (1996) *Problems of Democratic Transition and Consolidation*, Baltimore: The Johns Hopkins University Press.

Lipset, S.M. (1959) 'Some Social Requisites of Democracy: Economic Development and Political Legitimacy', *American Political Science Review* 53(1): 69–105.

Moore, B. (1966) *The Social Origins of Dictatorship and Democracy*, Boston: Beacon Press.

O'Donnell, G. and Schmitter, P. (1986) *Transitions from Authoritarian Rule: Tentative Conclusions about Uncertain Democracies*, Baltimore: The Johns Hopkins University Press.

Przeworski, A. (1991) *Democracy and the Market: Political and Economic Reforms in Eastern Europe and Latin America*, New York: Cambridge University Press.

Przeworski, A. and Limongi, F. (1997) 'Modernisation: Theories and Facts', *World Politics* 7(1): 39–55.

Rueschemeyer, D. *et al.* (1992) *Capitalist Development and Democracy*, Chicago: University of Chicago Press.

Widner, J. (ed.) (1994) *Economic Change and Political Liberalization in Sub-Saharan Africa*, Baltimore: The Johns Hopkins University Press.

RUTH B. COLLIER

demos

The word democracy, based on the Greek words *demos* and *kratos* and commonly translated as 'people power', did not come into common usage until well into the fifth century

BC. That was at least sixty years after the reforms of Cleisthenes, acknowledged as the founder of the regime that has come to be known as Athenian democracy. Prior to that, *isonomia* (equality before/within the law) and *isegoria* (equal opportunity to speak) described the Athenian regime that Cleisthenes founded in 508/507 BC. Both *isonomia* and *isegoria* emphasised the equality of participation that was at the heart of the Athenian political system. *Demokratia*, in contrast, emphasised that authority rested in the demos itself rather than simply the equality of citizens.

The term 'demos' throughout Greek literature takes on two distinct meanings. It refers, on the one hand, to the location of sovereignty or ultimate authority within the Greek polis or city-state. On the other hand, it is a pejorative term used by the critics of democracy to refer to the poorer classes, the less well-born, the mob, who hold power in a democracy and who may respond readily to the rhetorical displays of their demagogic leaders.

The demos as sovereign

Whenever the Athenian *ekklesia* or assembly (which all Athenian citizens were free to attend and, in the later years of the democracy, were paid to attend) passed a decree, it used the formula *dokei toi demoi*, or 'it seems best to the people'. In the treaties for which there are records, it is *ho demos Athenaion*, 'the demos of the Athenians', who are the signatories. The *ekklesia* was for much of the 150 or so years of Athenian democracy the central institutional actor for the Athenian polis. 'Demos' thus serves as the collective term encompassing all citizens and identifying who it is who acts when the city as a whole acts. Demos and polis became synonyms. The demos may have been manipulated by leaders in the city eager to pursue their own agendas, but those leaders needed to act through the medium of the demos, persuading those seated in the *ekklesia* to accept their proposals. It is the demos that decided what seemed best, not the leaders or elite, though the elite using the art of rhetoric may have helped the demos define what

'seemed best' (Ober 1986). Obviously, the demos attending the assembly was not the whole of the city, or even of its citizens; probably never more than two-fifths of the citizen body attended at one time. But the attendees' decisions stood for the decisions of the whole city, what Ober (1986: 337) has called the 'imagined' demos.

In one of the earliest tragedies of fifth century Athens, Aeschylus's *Suppliant Women*, dating from perhaps the late 460s, a chorus of suppliant women are eager to learn if the city of Argos will grant them asylum. When their father returns from the city, they ask him where the larger number of 'hands' (votes) of the demos lay (603–4). The words *demos* and *kratos* lie next to each other in their question. This is the first time in Greek literature that we find these terms in conjunction with one another. Earlier, the Argive king had affirmed that he would not act without consulting the community of the city, but he does not use the word *demos*. Euripides's *Suppliant Women* from the late 420s introduces similar language when his Athenian Theseus criticises a Theban herald for asking to speak to the city's 'tyrant' or ruler. Theseus responds: 'The city is free. The demos rule in turns' (405–6), though he does not here use the verbal form of *kratos*. In both plays, the demos is the decision-making body, symbolising the whole city and affirming its independence from individual rulers.

Around the same time as Euripides's *Suppliant Women*, Aristophanes's comedy *The Knights* introduced Demos as an actual character. Demos is first described by one of his slaves as a harsh despot, an unpleasant old man, and half deaf (40–4). He sits on the Pnyx, the hill where the *ekklesia* met, waiting to be flattered. Despite his being foolish and quite stupid, he is the owner of the city and the various characters strive to please him. In this comedy, it is the sausage maker who successfully woos Demos away from his previous favourite, the leather-tanner Cleon. Plato's *Republic* recalls this comedy when in the parable of the boat in Book 6, Demos is the boat owner whom the Sophists (portrayed as sailors) try to control by drugging him with mandrake. Demos fails to recognise the wisdom of the star-gazer (the philosopher) who stands at the back of the boat and does not compete for his attention.

In all these representations the demos, whether nobly portrayed as sovereign in the tragedies or mocked as the object of manipulation in the comedies, appears as the embodiment of the city, the collective force in whom the final decisions of the city lie. The demos, standing for the whole, represents the unity of the city, transcending individual leaders and partisan factions.

Demos as the poor

Critics of democracy from ancient times to more contemporary writers have identified the demos not with the noble sovereign in the city, but with a faction within the city, namely, the poor, the *hoi polloi*, the *aporoi* (those without resources), the *kakoi* (the 'bad'), and set them in conflict with the wealthy, those with resources, the well-born, the *agathoi* (the good). In this context, the word 'demos' takes on pejorative connotations and any regime that allows the demos to rule serves the particular interests of the poor, not those of the whole city.

A late fifth or early fourth-century BC pamphleteer commonly called the Old Oligarch, details the ways in which the demos of Athens had with great skill structured the Athenian regime to suit its own interests, not those of the city or of the 'good' (read 'wealthy') men who lived in it too. Throughout his commentary, the Old Oligarch equates the demos with the poor and the 'worst' people. While complaining about the distribution of offices to the demos and their stranglehold on the machinery of government, he also admires the thoroughness with which they have organised themselves so that the poor hold unrivalled and insurmountable control over the city.

A sharper critic of the demos is the Socrates of several of the Platonic dialogues. He does not attack the demos because of its poverty, but rather because of its susceptibility to the rhetorical skills of the Sophists. Recalling the parable of the boat in the *Republic* again, the demos as the boat owner there is slightly deaf, with narrow vision and no knowledge about how to steer his boat. He is easily manipulated by others. In another parable in the same book, Demos appears as a wild animal to be soothed by smooth speakers. In the *Gorgias*, the demos again appears as the object of manipulation, not sufficiently educated to distinguish between flattery and knowledge, preferring the pastries of the pastry chef to the necessary medicines of the doctor. In other dialogues, Socrates regularly urges his interlocutors not to care about the opinions of the demos. It has no access to what is according to reason and therefore its opinion can, indeed should, be disregarded.

Aristotle's typology of regimes in Book 3 of *The Politics* at first identifies democracy as the regime in which the many rule in their own self-interest while in an oligarchy the few rule in their self-interest. Yet, immediately after categorising regimes according to number of rulers and whether they serve their own interests or those of the whole city, Aristotle revises his analysis by noting that economic distinctions are primary; the many will always be those without resources, while the rich will always be few in number. Thus, democracy cannot be called the rule of the many. Rather, it is the rule of the poor. This would be true even if by some strange quirk the poor were to be few in number and the rich were numerous. Democracy for Aristotle is the rule of the poor.

Nevertheless, for Aristotle the demos in democracies are not all the same and he discusses various of forms of democracy depending on who exactly comprises the demos: farmers, those who were born free, those who have modest means or the very poor. Varieties of democracies, according to Aristotle, depend then on who actually is in the demos. Though Aristotle sees a wide variety in the potential composition of the demos, a Marxist tradition drawing explicitly on the Aristotelian distinctions between the wealthy few and many poor sees the demos only as a class of the poor and especially the class of the urban poor that has been used by anti-democrats to attack democracy. Wood (1988) illustrates how 'demos' as a word of opprobrium resounds in the literature through the nineteenth century and has frequently controlled the study of Athenian democracy.

Conclusion

The Athenians exalted Demos as the personification of their city. By the fourth century, there were pictorial representation of Demos alongside Demokratia and Athena (Loraux 1986: 282). Demos in its sovereignty captured the unity of the city and suppressed its divisions. Demos as sovereign was the polis, but as the fifth century Old Oligarch and as the philosophers of the fourth century pointed out, that unity hid the divisions within the city. Athens was not in any sense as unified as a statement such as 'it seems best to the demos' might suggest. These authors would argue that a more accurate phrase would have been: 'It seems best to the many poor in the city, but not to the well-to-do, the well-born, or the good'. The tension between these two uses of the term 'demos' captures the tensions between seeing a democracy as a unitary actor, representative of a whole people, or only as the expression of particular dominant interests in a community of diverse and often competing interests.

See also:

citizenship; civic virtue; democratic origins; identity, political

Further reading

Finley, M.I. (1983) *Politics in the Ancient World*, Cambridge: Cambridge University Press.
Hansen, M.H. (1991) *The Athenian Democracy in the Age of Demosthenes*, Oxford: Blackwell.
Loraux, N. (1986) *The Invention of Athens*, Cambridge, MA: Harvard University Press.
Ober, J. (1986) *Mass and Elite in Democratic Athens*, Princeton, NJ: Princeton University Press.

Wood, E.M. (1988) *Peasant-Citizen and Slave*, London: Verso.

ARLENE W. SAXONHOUSE

direct action

Direct action signifies a repertoire of techniques and strategies used by self-selected publics to voice opinion and influence governments. Demonstrations, marches, sit-ins, boycotts, strikes, vigils and civil disobedience are among the most commonly used techniques. In addition, governments sometimes use direct action as a tool for implementing social change or for achieving short-term political leverage.

It is usual to exclude from the scope of direct action politically directed vandalism, killings, riots and other acts of violence, even though violence often accompanies some types of direct action, and even though groups organised initially for civil protest may split on the violence question, as has happened in the environmental movement. Further, there are types of action, such as *intifada*, that straddle the line between civil and violent. These grey areas notwithstanding, direct action events are overwhelmingly non-violent. The scope of this entry is accordingly restricted to civil actions.

An additional difficulty arises in deciding whether ceremonial events may constitute direct action. The question arises because some such events have, and are meant to have, profound public impact; Pope John Paul II's visit to Poland in 1979 stands out as exemplary. There is no touchstone here; decision must be made on a case-by-case basis.

The incidence of direct action events varies with the level of public feeling. There are times when direct action becomes almost habitual, as in the 1960s and 1970s. In calmer times, direct action is less frequent and less visible. Nevertheless, major metropolitan areas, such as London and New York, host about 400 such events annually.

As a technique, direct action is neutral to the objectives and ideals it may used to promote. This fact is occluded by the tendency to identify direct action with social protest and democratic aspirations. But movements of all stripes – fascist, authoritarian, fundamentalist and revolutionary – from time to time employ direct action. Thus the pro-life movement, in one of its phases, copied the techniques of the civil rights movement, partly to claim a mantle of LEGITIMACY and partly because the efficacy of these techniques was proven. The same is true of government use of direct action. Iranian mullahs used direct action to suppress anti-Islamic thought and practices in much the way that Mao used the youthful Red Guards to shame capitalist 'running dogs' into submission.

The moral neutrality of technique does not imply that a given movement may ignore the implications of its choice of techniques on its evangelising goals. On the contrary, the choice of techniques may be controlled fundamentally by moral intention, as was the case with non-violent CIVIL DISOBEDIENCE (Oppenheimer and Lakey 1964). For Gandhi, non-violence was simultaneously tactics, mass training in democratic participation, strategic opposition to colonial rule, and schooling in an ethics of life. At the other end of this spectrum is revolutionary direct action. Questions of morality and citizen development are subsumed under the single objective of seizure of power. To that end all means are fair and the selection of tactics is pragmatic. Thus, while Lenin preached the legitimacy of violence, this did not mean that violence must always be used. It was not inconsistent for him to encourage the Indian communist party to copy Gandhian technique as opportunity might suggest.

Theory

While direct action is probably as old as political life, theories did not emerge until more recent times. Roman writers equated direct action with mobs, and considered mobbing to be the natural modus operandi of the commons. The proto-theory developed in antiquity was brought to fruition in the writings of Niccolò Machiavelli.

The Florentine accepts from classical historians that a dual character is to be attributed to the masses. For the most part they are diligent, honest, law-abiding, and religious. But they may also be riotous, violent, impulsive, and licentious. Classical historians viewed popular politics as an oscillation between public order and turmoil. They recognised that popular leaders ('demagogues') could stabilise society by combining military dominance with 'bread and circuses'.

Ancient historians viewed such Caesar types with distaste, since for them they signified moral decay, or the replacement of civil integrity (virtue) by appetite for public entertainment (license). In accepting the dual character model, Machiavelli denied that the demagogues' craft was symptom and cause of civic corruption. Instead, he accepted it as a legitimate part of the repertoire of statecraft. Uproars and factional contention are, in turn, integral to republican government.

The arrival of mass democracy in the American and French Revolutions marked an abrupt increase in the share that direct action had in political life. In the United States, popular government settled into stable rhythms punctuated by election fevers, urban riots and rough justice on the frontier. But in France the share was so great that it was a watershed in the evolution of political consciousness. Party government, syndicalist mass action, trade unionism, bolshevism and fascism all have roots in the experience of the French Revolution.

That experience is profoundly positive for some, profoundly negative for others. To be assailed by a crowd clamouring for justice is known from many testimonies to be a terrifying experience. It is so potent that merely observing, or even hearing about it, can induce aversion to 'mob politics'. Yet that very scene may be experienced in the opposite valence, and induce a feeling of social integration, of effective power, and euphoric visions, and permanent attachment (Moscovici 1982).

The powerful positive and negative valences of direct action account for the mystique of crowds. In the negative valence, crowds are seen as the epitome of savage, irrational, imperious lawlessness. In the positive valence the crowd effect is the apotheosis of human SOLIDARITY, self-sacrifice and even rapture. These two valences seem to underlie conservative antipathy to revolution as well as the enduring appeal of direct action as the antechamber to revolution.

Modern theory arose in the closing decades of the last century from experimental work on the neurology and psychology of mental processes (Van Ginneken 1992). The key discovery driving new theory is the unconscious. Contrary to the view of man as a rational animal, the new theory situates mental processes in the Darwinian continuum of animal physiology, behaviour and cognition. The human brain, characterised by an enlarged neo-cortex, evolved on top of the mammalian brain and autonomic nervous system, which constitute the sensory-motor apparatus, motivational centres and reward centres. The subjective experience of self as agent and decision maker is replaced by a view of human action as animal behaviour based on pre-rational, subjectively uncontrollable neural processing that evolved for survival purposes. Crowds are one stimulus type (the fight–flight response is another) that can switch off individual neo-cortical control and place human aggregates on automatic pilot, as happens in the collective behaviour of other species. Paradigmatic of click switch shunting are mobbing (fight) and panic (flight). The adaptive function is to prime selfish individuals to sacrifice individual benefit for a distributed collective benefit (eusocial behaviour), as in warfare. Collective behaviour is characterised by mood contagion, suggestibility, imitation, regression to primitive feelings of love and hate, and the replacement of individual conscious identity with group identity (deindividuation). The rational mind accordingly has a shadow, the group mind which, when aroused, overrides rationality.

The picture of the crowd as an adaptive socially directed animal force has dominated academic investigation for a century (Moscovici 1982). It presides over political psychology, including study of propaganda and indoctrina-tion, the social psychology of group behaviour, the sociology of mass action and analysis of the MEDIA. There is at present no synthesis bringing these disparate strands together under a unified set of principles. However, the preparation of such a synthesis is well advanced, thanks to the renewal of study of co-operative behaviour at all levels of biotic organisation and revival of the concept of the group mind or 'superorganism' at the level human action (Bloom 1995).

Practice

Direct action in this century is characterised by three major developments. The most important in terms of impact is Gandhi's practice of civil disobedience, first in South Africa and then in India (Ackerman and Kreugler 1993). After a two-decade slumber, civil disobedience was revived by the British Campaign for Nuclear Disarmament and the American civil rights movement. It spread from there to many nations. The second development was recognition by fascists that direct action offered the means of constructing what democratic theory held to be impossible: an authoritarian state enjoying mass support. While fascism was short-lived, authoritarian regimes of many shades learned the fascist formula, for example, Peronism in Argentina and fundamentalism in Iran. The third development is the conjugation of direct action with mass communications. To observers at the turn of the century, the connection between the penny press and public feeling was palpable (Hobson 1901). A pronouncement from Berlin on a matter of state in South Africa could make headlines in London and stir Englishmen into a fighting frenzy in a day. The advent of live television news casting in the 1960s prompted activists to design events for optimal living room impact rather than optimal impact at the scene. From this experience, activists developed the dramaturgy model of direct action. That in turn led to events designed specifically for television viewing. Greenpeace, for example, stages dramatic, high-risk, carefully planned raids, which it films and distributes to television news services.

The crowd has been eliminated altogether, yet these 'extreme sport' advertisements are highly effective in rallying public support. With the advent of internet COMMUNICATION, grassroots participation has found avenues of expression in cyberspace. It has been used by environmental groups to jam the websites of businesses whose practices offend environmental principles.

The documentation of direct action is diverse and of variable reliability. The most voluminous but least reliable is media reportage, because journalism strives to impart no more than an impression and an attitude. Another voluminous source is social history and memoirs. This literature provides often-detailed description of direct action events over a long time spectrum and across cultures. The description includes accounts of what happened and how events were experienced by participants, opponents and observers. From it we learn that virtually all direct action is organised and executed by groups with a set purpose. This observation is not incompatible with spontaneity of feeling in response to a happening. It is to assert that the expression given to such feelings occurs largely through established channels.

The most extensive catalogue of direct action techniques and scenarios has been compiled by civil disobedience advocates (Sharp 1973; Ackerman and Kreugler 1993). While some techniques are unique to this school, many are perennial methods used by trade unions and indeed by community protesters from time immemorial. The overlap arises from the circumstance that collective action is civil rather than military and usually includes women and children as participants.

Conclusion

If the practice of direct action is overwhelmingly organised, is this not inconsistent with a theory saying that it overrides rational, individual self-control? This question requires an answer that reconciles at least some measure of cognitive control with the attributes of persons who have shunted to the group mind.

The supposed click switch that shunts individual self-control into the group mind mode invokes a 'digital' concept. Shunting is a reality in mobbing, panic, stampede and bereavement shock. While such events occur in the direct action ambience, they are not what direct action is about. The integration of cognitive control and emotional arousal is best understood on analogy to the performing arts. The dance troupe and theatre company speak to the emotions, but arousal occurs via cognitively generated, sometimes highly refined scripts and scenarios. Direct action as performance is like that. It falls onto a continuum ranging from crude to refined. Moreover, the psychological outcomes of direct action events are highly variable. Absorption into the group mind is by no means the inevitable result of joining in with a crowd. Boredom is equiprobable. But when absorption does occur, it is often an indelible, life-changing experience. From an evolutionary perspective, this is an adaptation for group affiliation. The claim of direct action groups to express 'community' feeling reflects this adaptation.

See also:

civil disobedience; green democratic thought; revolutions; social movements

Further reading

Ackerman, P. and Kruegler, C. (1993) *Strategic Nonviolent Conflict: The Dynamics of People Power in the Twentieth Century*, New York: Praeger.

Bloom, H. (1995) *The Lucifer Principle: A Scientific Expedition into the Forces of History*, New York: The Atlantic Monthly Press.

Hobson, J.A. (1901) *The Psychology of Jingoism*, London: Grant Richards.

Moscovici, S. (1982) *The Age of the Crowd*, Cambridge: Cambridge University Press.

Oppenheimer, M. and Lakey, G. (1964) *A Manual for Direct Action*, Chicago: Quadrangle Books.

Sharp, G. (1973) *The Politics of Nonviolent Action*, Boston: Porter Sargent.

Van Ginneken, J. (1992) *Crowds, Psychology and Politics, 1871–1899*, Cambridge: Cambridge University Press.

HIRAM CATON

direct democracy

Direct democracy exists to the extent that citizens can vote directly on policy alternatives and decide what is to be done on each important issue. This contrasts with political arrangements under representative democracy where electors can only vote for individuals (in practice, alternative party governments) who will then decide on the policy outcomes.

Although most countries hold direct votes on policy (REFERENDUMS) from time to time, these are usually confined to particular topics, often constitutional, territorial and moral issues. Referendums are usually called and framed by governments, often to evade deciding themselves on embarrassing or divisive issues. Thus they are not ideal as instruments of direct democracy.

In contrast popular initiatives, where they are allowed, occur by request of a specified number of individual citizens, and hence are held by popular demand on questions framed by their promoters. Both referendums and initiatives therefore bring the public more directly into decision-making. But the initiative does so more than most referendums. The existence and use of initiatives is a useful indicator of the extent to which direct democracy is practised in the modern world, in half the US states (but not at Federal level), Italy and Switzerland. Only in the latter, however, could one say that all-important issues are put to a popular vote. In the other cases the government takes most important decisions with parliamentary support.

Types of direct democracy

Direct democracy as an ideal is often identified with the continuous popular assemblies of classical Athens where all citizens gathered together to discuss and vote on policy. In the eighteenth century this ideal was popularised by Jean-Jacques Rousseau, who added to it the need for the direct unmediated PARTICIPATION in POLICY-MAKING of each individual citizen. Only if each citizen voted his unique, uninfluenced opinion straightforwardly and sincerely would the 'General Will' emerge rather than the 'Will of All', which might be selfish and motivated by factional interests.

Such stringent requirements have often been used to dismiss the practicability of direct democracy out of hand, as they never can be met. Moreover the elimination of parties, interests and other social groups so that individuals can come to their own pure opinions, is highly undesirable from a pluralist point of view. It smacks of the practices of authoritarian regimes that eliminate all non-supportive groups and then get themselves and their policies approved in mass referendums by an atomised and uninformed citizenry.

It is important to realise, however, that Rousseau and ancient Greece do not supply the only models for direct democracy. Swiss practices provide a counter-example. They clearly meet the requirement of allowing citizens to vote on policy alternatives which elsewhere are decided by parliaments and governments. But they also co-exist with a long tradition of representative government and a pluralist society.

It is important therefore to recognise that there are many possible alternative forms of direct democracy ranged along a continuum from Rousseau's idealised small city-state without any intermediation by social groups, to a highly mediated pluralistic and party-based form as found in Switzerland. Once this is accepted, many valid criticisms of Rousseau-esque direct democracy do not hold for direct democracy in general.

Direct democracy and individual participation

If representative democracies work reasonably well why should there be more direct democracy? There are two reasons. First, representative democracies are deficient in many respects, all of which fundamentally stem from the limited role they allow citizens in government. Most decisions are imposed on those affected without consulting them. If we accept that the only way we can know about a person's interests are through their expressed preferences then the best way we can serve these is to find out about them and meet them, not seek to force some bureaucratic vision upon them. Increased popular voting of citizen preferences might make DECISION-MAKING slower but it would also limit the huge and costly blunders which representative governments often make – vast schemes of urban development which destroy the heart of cities, agricultural policies which destroy the environment, costly military adventures and nuclear experiments. These have often been propelled by secretive and powerful businesses that stood to gain. The ability of citizens to vote on a government every four or five years is not enough to hold decision makers closely accountable to the public.

The second argument is a more general one. Democracy finds its main justification in its unique sensitivity to public opinion, through open debate and voting; in short, popular participation. More participation therefore means more democracy. If we think democracy in general is a good thing we cannot object to having more of it.

Quite apart from its defining relationship with democracy, political participation has also been credited with integrating individuals into the wider community, extending their sympathy and understanding, increasing their political knowledge and reasoning powers. These effects can be controverted, but on the basic point of greater democracy being identical with greater popular participation and involvement there can be little argument.

Criticisms of direct democracy

In view of this why is there such widespread suspicion and rejection of direct democracy, not only by bureaucrats and politicians with a direct stake in the existing set-up but also by political theorists with less of a personal axe to grind? The reason is that the inconveniences of greater popular EMPOWERMENT in terms of lack of feasibility, delays, conflicts, sinister influences and possible tyranny of the majority are seen as outweighing its advantages. In a plural world other values, such as political stability, have to be taken into consideration as well as greater democracy. Once these are considered, extending participation seems so dangerous that it should be rejected (see DEMOCRATIC STABILITY).

These counter-arguments often gain their force from addressing only the unmediated Rousseauesque form of direct democracy rather than a Swiss-type system. Switzerland indeed is usually seen as boringly stable, democratic, peaceful and predictable, rather than chaotic and unstable. We can address the main counter-arguments as follows:

feasibility: having a popular assembly of all citizens continuously in session is clearly impossible in modern states. Popular voting and discussion on matters currently reserved for parliament is possible however not only through postal ballots and newspapers, but even more through the electronic interactive media now available. There can be a 'virtual assembly' even if not a real one.

delays: attempting to consult everyone may take longer (though this is not necessarily the actual experience of referendums and initiatives). Many modern projects have been rushed through too quickly. As a result they have entailed horrific costs, which have only been understood fifteen or twenty years later. Slowing down the pace of development may be no bad thing.

conflict: involving the population without the intervention of parties and legislatures will exacerbate conflict between those who stand to gain by decisions and those who stand to lose. However, Switzerland and Italy demonstrate that both parties and parliaments can coexist with and indeed perform essential mediating roles in direct democracies. Conflict does not seem to be greater where there is more participation.

sinister influences: in the American states, initiatives are often started or opposed by business interests that do not reveal their identity but have a material stake in the outcome. There is a danger therefore that citizens may be manipulated by hidden interests which they are too ignorant to detect or resist. All the evidence, however, points to special interests being defeated as often as they win in popular voting. Parties limit the role of interests in Switzerland and Italy.

the tyranny of the majority: many criticisms of direct democracy stem from distrust of popular capabilities. Citizens are regarded as ill informed, lazy and (in this variant) intolerant and highly conformist. Minorities are thus likely to be steamrollered by the majority without the safeguards available to them in representative democracies. If we regard direct democracy as any system where popular voting substitutes for parliamentary voting on important issues, there seems no reason why as many procedural safeguards could not be built in as under representative democracy. The criticism of tyranny seems more applicable to unmediated Rousseauesque forms of direct democracy than others. Thus, it is not a criticism of direct democracy as such.

Citizen capabilities

Proponants of greater popular participation would in any case challenge the stereotype of citizens being intolerant and ignorant. Any form of democracy rests on faith in the people; otherwise why give them power even to choose representatives? There is considerable evidence, certainly for electors in the mass, that they make reasonable decisions and have the necessary (minimal) information to judge wisely and vote soundly. These qualities would only be improved if they were allowed to participate more.

Political parties in direct democracy

American political parties do not normally participate in state initiatives or referendums as such, sometimes by convention, sometimes as the result of a constitutional prohibition. Coupled with Rousseauesque disapproval of 'factions', this has been taken to indicate that direct democracy is incompatible with political parties. As these perform an essential organising role in modern mass democracy, such presumed incompatibility has often been used to show the inadvisability of shifting to direct democracy. Again, however, there seems no reason why in other forms of direct democracy, parties should not play a central role. Popular voting would need them even more than legislatures to focus issues and organise alternatives.

Reversing the argument, it has been claimed that greater popular participation will hasten political party decline, thus diminishing the quality of decision-making even more. There is little evidence for a general modern decline of parties however and no evidence that they are weaker in systems with more popular participation than in those with less.

Direct democracy as a future mode of government

Many of the arguments currently deployed against direct democracy were used in the past against extensions of parliamentary SUFFRAGE. The dire consequences anticipated from enfranchisement of the 'ignorant' or 'tyrannical' masses did not come about then and it is unlikely that they would come about from an extension of direct democracy now. Seen in historical perspective the extension of popular participation to new political areas seems but the latest manifestation of the continuing struggle for greater democracy and control; and just as likely as preceding movements to succeed.

See also:

citizenship; civic virtue; democracy, justifications for; democratic stability; participation; representation, concept of; representation, models of

Further reading

Barber, B. (1984) *Strong Democracy: Partici-patory Politics for a New Age*, Berkeley, CA: University of California Press.

Budge, I. (1996) *The New Challenge of Direct Democracy*, Cambridge: Polity Press.

Butler, D. and Ranney, A. (1994) *Referendums Round the World*, London: Macmillan.

Cronin, T.E. (1989) *Direct Democracy: The Politics of Initiative, Referendum and Recall*, Cambridge, MA: Harvard University Press.

Fishkin, J.S. (1993) *Democracy and Delibera-tion*, New Haven, CT: Yale University Press.

Saward, M. (1998) *The Terms of Democracy*, Cambridge: Polity Press.

IAN BUDGE

due process

The concept of due process can be traced to section 39 of the English Magna Carta's (1215) declaration that 'No free man shall be captured or imprisoned or disseised or outlawed or exiled or in any way destroyed . . . except by the lawful judgement of his peers and by the law of the land'. In Edward III's 1354 confirmation of the Magna Carta, the final phrase from section 39 became 'by due process of law'. The essence of due process is the rule of law (see LAW, RULE OF). Although the concept of legitimate government power being limited by the rule of law developed alongside the emergence of a belief in popular SOVEREIGNTY as the source of legitimate government power and the British doctrine of Parliamentary supremacy, section 39 has never functioned as a limit on Parliament's legislative power, serving instead only to limit monarchial executive power. The mandate of due process is that the government act reasonably and non-arbitrarily – fairly – irrespective of whether that government is a majoritarian democracy, a republic, an oligarchy or a monarchy. While due process shares with democracy a fundamental respect for the natural RIGHTS and sovereignty of the individual, in a democracy the due process guarantee functions as a limit on the power of the majority.

American colonial charters, beginning with the 1639 Maryland Act for the Liberties of the People, and later state constitutions, frequently included some paraphrase of section 39. The specific phrase 'due process of law' can be traced to the bill of rights proposed by New York's 1788 ratifying convention. Under the United States Constitution, due process is found among the original Bill of Rights guarantees of personal liberty against infringement by the national government adopted in 1789. Later, in 1868, the Fourteenth Amendment repeated the language of the Fifth Amendment's guarantee that 'no person shall be . . . deprived of life, liberty, or property without due process of law' in its limiting of state government power. Armed with a written constitution, the United States courts have used the Fifth and Fourteenth Amendments' due process clauses as textual bases for declaring government actions void. Judicial understandings of due process have developed along two lines – procedural and substantive – but the desire to limit arbitrary government action underlies both.

The requirement that governments act fairly and non-arbitrarily is most easily realised in the procedural guarantees that surround the operation of the judicial process and has its most authoritative historical meaning there. In the US Bill of Rights, the due process clause is found among the various provisions governing the procedures to be followed in criminal trials such as the right to be informed of the charges justifying arrest; the prohibition on double jeopardy; the right to refuse to incriminate oneself through testimony; the right to a speedy impartial jury trial; the right to be informed of the nature and cause of the accusation; the right to be confronted by witnesses; the right to have compulsory process for obtaining witnesses; the right to assistance of counsel; and the prohibitions on excessive bail, excessive fines, and unusually cruel punishment. These guarantees are seen as fundamental to the rule of law, to liberty and to limited government. While judicial interpretations of these provisions, and judicial extension of these guarantees (as limitations on state government action by incorporating them into the meaning of the due process clause of the Fourteenth Amendment) have generated debates over the proper balance between public safety and criminal defendants' rights and over the legitimacy of the US Supreme Court dictating the procedures to be used in the criminal process (an area traditionally reserved to the states as part of their police powers), judicial enforcement of procedural due process has not been seen as a challenge to democratic government. JUDICIAL REVIEW in the area of criminal procedure guarantees generally is not viewed as a 'counter-majoritiarian problem'. Indeed, in the vernacular, such procedural guarantees are often thought of as an essential component of a 'democratic' polity.

The core of procedural due process is the idea that government action that deprives the individual of life, liberty or property must accord with the rule of law. Such action must be non-arbitrary; hence, individuals must be given notice of the reasons for an impending deprivation of life, liberty or property and they must be given a fair opportunity to respond to the allegations made. Today, the requirements of due process are seen as so central to a just regime that not only are they observed in the criminal justice process where they are constitutionally mandated, but modern liberal democracies have chosen to follow their main tenets in their rules governing civil court procedures, though specifics of the requirements (such as size of jury and so on) may vary. In the 1970s, the US Supreme Court began constitutionalising due process notice and hearing requirements in some areas of civil litigation involving government. This process began with Goldberg v. Kelly, 397 US 254 (1970) which held that WELFARE recipients were constitutionally entitled to pre-termination notice and hearings, although subsequent cases have allowed government considerable latitude in designing procedures that satisfy due process requirements in the civil context. Nonetheless, a number of commentators, such as Lawrence Friedman, have noted an increas-

ing American obsession for due process, with adjudicatory procedures being adopted throughout a wide range of public and private institutions.

Much more controversial has been the US Supreme Court's attempt to read the due process clauses of the Fifth and Fourteenth Amendments as a limit on the substantive content of legislation enacted by democratic legislatures. While the Supreme Court has disavowed explicit use of natural law in the exercise of judicial review, the Court's substantive due process jurisprudence bears a striking resemblance to a natural law approach. The heart of the substantive due process claim is that there are some legislative actions that are inherently arbitrary and unreasonable. There are certain legislative actions that are illegitimate because no government (democratic or otherwise) could rightfully engage in them; they violate the inherent rights and liberties of the people which government is meant to secure, not invade. Lacking a textual exposition of those rights and liberties beyond those particularly specified in the Bill of Rights and incorporated against the states through the due process language of the Fourteenth Amendment, the Court has, at times, turned to developing its own definition of the individual's inherent, inviolate, rights and liberties.

At the repeated suggestion of litigants seeking to overturn state economic regulation at the end of the nineteenth century and beginning of the twentieth century, the Supreme Court began developing a definition of the rights and liberties protected by the due process clause. In Allegeyer v. Louisiana, 165 US 578 (1897), the Court sketched the outlines of the definition it would rely on for the next forty years:

> The liberty mentioned in that [Fourteenth] amendment [due process clause] means not only the right of the citizen to be free from the mere physical restraint of his person, as by incarceration, but the term is deemed to embrace the right of the citizen to be free in the enjoyment of all his faculties; to be free to use them in all lawful ways; to live and

work where he will; to earn his livelihood by any lawful calling; to pursue any livelihood or avocation, and for that purpose to enter into all contracts which may be proper, necessary and essential to his carrying out to a successful conclusion the purposes above mentioned.

Most notoriously, this definition of the liberty protected from substantive invasion by the due process clause spawned the Supreme Court's 'liberty to contract' doctrine. The 'liberty to contract' doctrine was used to strike down a number of state and local statutes regulating employment hours and wages during the early twentieth century, running from the famous Lochner *v.* New York, 198 US 45 (1905) bakers' hours case to its final repudiation in West Coast Hotel Co. *v.* Parrish, 300 US 379 (1937). While a majority on the Court described itself as preventing the states from exercising unbounded power by asking whether particular statutes were 'fair, reasonable, and appropriate exercise of the [police power], or is it an unreasonable, unnecessary, and arbitrary interference with the right of the individual to his personal liberty or to enter into those contracts in relation to labour which may seem to him appropriate or necessary for the support of himself and his family?', the critics of this series of cases coined the term 'Lochnerizing' to refer to the Court's substitution of the justices' values for those of the democratic majority as reflected in legislation. The Court's selection of particular 'liberties' to be protected via the due process clause was criticised as being itself subjective and arbitrary.

After the rise of the New Deal and in the wake of President Roosevelt's 1937 Court-Packing Plan, the Supreme Court abandoned its 'liberty to contract' doctrine and turned to using the Bill of Rights to define the liberty protected by the Fourteenth Amendment due process clause. It was through this doctrinal device that the Supreme Court has used the Fourteenth Amendment due process clause to apply various Bill of Rights guarantees to state government action. Over a forty-year period, beginning with Gitlow *v.* New York, 268 US

652 (1925), the Supreme Court engaged in a case-by-case process of selectively incorporating those only those rights 'found to be implicit in the concept of an ordered scheme of liberty' (Palko *v.* Connecticut, 302 US 319, 325 (1937)) rather than incorporating the Bill of Rights in its entirety. Although by the mid-1970s virtually all of the Bill of Rights guarantees had been incorporated, during the preceding forty-year period critics charged that the Court's 'fundamental rights' selective incorporation was itself subjective and arbitrary.

In the modern Court, substantive due process has emerged again under the guise of the 'right to privacy' and provoked extensive debate about the proper role of the Supreme Court in a constitutional democracy. Beginning with Harlan's dissent in Poe *v.* Ullman, 367 US 497 (1961) and Goldberg's and Harlan's concurrences in Griswold *v.* Connecticut, 381 US 479 (1965), the Justices have read the due process clause as protecting 'personal rights that are fundamental' including marital privacy, striking down restrictive contraception laws on substantive grounds. A legacy of fear of the 'Lochnerizing' charge can be seen in Justice Blackmun's oblique and scant textual grounding of the reproductive rights protected in Roe *v.* Wade, 410 US 113 (1973):

This right to privacy, whether it be founded in the 14th Amendment's concept of personal liberty as we feel it is, or, as the District Court determined, in the Ninth Amendment's reservation of rights to the people, is broad enough to encompass a woman's decision whether or not to terminate her pregnancy.

After nearly thirty years of charges that the Court subjectively and arbitrarily conferred constitutional protection on a right not codified in the specific language of the Constitution, the Court itself, in the course of upholding Roe in Planned Parenthood *v.* Casey, 505 US 833 (1992), has forthrightly embraced substantive due process:

'Constitutional protection of the woman's decision to terminate her pregnancy derives from the Due Process Clause of the Fourteenth Amendment'. It declares that no state shall 'deprive any person of life, liberty, or property, without due process of law.' The controlling word in the cases before us is 'liberty'. Although a literal reading of the Clause might suggest that it governs only the procedures by which a State may deprive persons of liberty, for at least 105 years...the Clause has been understood to contain a substantive component as well, one 'barring certain government actions regardless of the fairness of the procedures used to implement them.' ...it is settled that the Clause applies to matters of substantive law as well as to matters of procedure...The guaranties of due process, though having their roots in Magna Carta's *per legum terrae*, and considered as procedural, safeguards 'against executive usurpation and tyranny', [and] have, in this country, 'become bulwarks also against arbitrary legislation'.

Due process is deeply embedded in irony. As the Supreme Court has attempted to fulfil both the due process clause's procedural and substantive promise of objective, non-arbitrary, reasonable governance through the rule of law, the Court itself has found no rule of law to constrain its own potential for subjective, arbitrary, unreasonable DECISION-MAKING as it seeks to define and protect fundamental liberties in a constitutional democracy.

See also:

constitutionalism; freedom; law, rule of

Further reading

Friedman, L. (1985) *Total Justice*, Boston: Beacon Press.
Fuller, L. (1964) *The Morality of Law*, New Haven, CT: Yale University Press.
Gillman, H. (1993) *The Constitution Besieged: The Rise and Demise of Lochner Era Police Powers Jurisprudence*, Durham, NC: Duke University Press.
Schwartz, B. (1992) *The Great Rights of Mankind: A History of the American Bill of Rights*, Madison, WI: Madison House Publishers, Inc.

SUSAN E. LAWRENCE

duties

From its inception, democracy has often stood accused of encouraging a libertarian spirit among its subjects which is at least potentially inimical to the constraints that would be imposed upon them by duties: moral requirements of behaviour which it is legitimate to expect, and sometimes force, people to perform. In Plato's *Republic* Socrates proclaims that, for democratic citizens, eventually 'the least vestige of restraint is resented as intolerable, till finally...in their determination to have no master they disregard all laws, written or unwritten' (Plato 1987: 384). Modern versions of this complaint may not depict such extreme consequences, but the commonly expressed belief that the extension of RIGHTS often associated with democracy's expansion has come at the expense of a sense of duty echoes the same fear that democratic EMPOWERMENT chips away people's recognition of their correlative obligations. Too many, it is said, have become so egoistically obsessed with exercising their individual rights to have their voices heard and their interests respected or satisfied that they forget, or refuse to recognise, that there are also duties on their part which they can be legitimately expected to perform regardless of their wishes. If this moral negligence does not necessarily destroy social order, then it is certainly held to corrupt and degrade it (Selbourne 1994: ch. 5; Etzioni 1993).

However, democracy has no necessary connection with such lop-sided, amoralistic anarchism. Anti-democrats who wish to blame it for such moral decline overlook the fact that there are conceptions of democracy, which tightly interweave democratic liberty with an account of duties borne both by citizens and the democratic state, or the civic order. These conceptions typically ground democratic duties in those conditions that are believed to be necessary in order for a democracy to flourish. Far from being opposed to the notion of duties, then, they argue that democracy is heavily dependent upon it and urge that, even if there is merit in the claim that contemporary society has become 'de-moralised', it is manifestly unfair to blame this on democracy.

The concept of 'duties' has undoubtedly suffered from the widespread scepticism about morality's status and validity in post-Enlightenment culture. Those who link duties and democracy may consequently be faced with the perplexing difficulties of justifying the belief that citizens have specific duties. Democratic theorists might ease this problem by claiming that it is one's commitment to democratic politics that provides the justification for acting according to them. The commitment is hollow without embracing them. So if one can justify democracy (which *might* be simpler insofar as there is less resistance to the democratic ideal in contemporary society than there is to the general idea of duties) then one consequently justifies democratic duties (see DEMOCRACY, JUSTIFICATIONS FOR).

What democratic duties citizens are said to have naturally varies according to the differences between the numerous conceptions of democracy itself. Restricted accounts of democracy, which downplay the extent of citizens' PARTICIPATION, will tend to favour accounts of duty which require individuals to desist from certain types of behaviour, rather than enjoining them positively to act. More participatory models of democracy will support more activist accounts of what it means to be dutiful.

The duties of citizens

The idea of duties owed by citizens is based upon what are deemed to be the requirements of a 'healthy' flourishing democratic politics. The 'good' or 'virtuous' citizen is the one who is disposed to, and capable of, acting dutifully and hence play his or her part in maintaining the democratic order (see CIVIC VIRTUE). All conceptions of democracy which embrace a

notion of duties are likely to insist that citizens have duties of respect of each other: to tolerate, within certain relatively minimal bounds, the opinions of others and to respect their rights to articulate and campaign for them; to speak and act in ways which do not compromise the status of any other citizens as equals; and, centrally, to abide by the democratic process and accept its outcomes. If these duties are not discharged, the democratic order cannot function properly; they are the prerequisites of its successful operation. Insofar as citizens have an interest in reproducing the democratic order for future citizens too, it can also be contended that parents, or those who act *in loco parentis*, have a duty to prepare children for CITIZENSHIP by inculcating in them the skills and dispositions they, too, will need to display in order to be good citizens of a vibrant democracy. A duty to provide a suitable democratic EDUCATION is therefore rightfully levied.

The ultimate purpose of these duties, and the nature of any which might supplement them, will be determined by which of two types of duty-based theory is preferred. 'Instrumentalist' accounts, which can be linked to the tradition of civic REPUBLICANISM, hold that the discharge of certain duties is justifiable primarily on the grounds that it is useful or necessary to the maintenance of the democratic order. They certainly require citizens to desist from behaving in ways that would undermine democracy, but they can also posit proactive duties: one must be an active citizen if one is to help maintain the conditions of democratic citizenship at all (for example, Dagger 1997: ch. 9). Even in what are often regarded as the limited practices of actually existing democracies, some such requirements are familiar enough: the duty of jury service and, more strikingly, in some cases (such as Australia) the duty to vote. Most civic republicans, however, tend to believe that democracy can be secured via relatively light demands upon citizens (Mansbridge 1983). They leave the more strenuously activist notions of duty to those conceptions of democracy which are closer to *civic humanism*, in which being a good citizen is deemed to be intrinsically as well as instrumentally worthwhile. In one particularly extensive version of this argument, which proposes a conception of 'deep citizenship', the duties to respect (or 'care') for other citizens are conceptually bound on the one hand to duties which are more purely self-regarding (to live by high moral standards) and, on the other hand, to duties to care for the world beyond the confines of citizenship, including even the well-being of the natural environment. Together, these elements constitute what it means to lead a good life (Clarke 1996).

One charge against this whole account, which intensifies the more demanding are the postulated duties, is that it is utopian, assuming a degree of moral awareness and motivation that simply does not pertain among most people in today's democracies. If this were true, one would need to consider whether the democratic order really has suffered as a result. Nobody need deny that citizens' actual behaviour falls short of such ideals of dutiful conduct to continue claiming that a well-ordered democracy would still require them to be respected. Only when it is not thought that democracy has suffered from the disrespect of duties does the insistence upon them begin to look misplaced.

However, it is not clear that the picture is all that unrealistic. Many democratic norms are, after all, still highly prized by many citizens. The very fact that so many people continue to vote in ELECTIONS where they are not required to do so and when it is plainly irrational if one votes only to influence an outcome suggests that other factors, among which might be a sense of duty, are needed to explain the phenomenon (Downs 1957: ch. 14). Other political acts and attitudes abound which seem hardly explicable as the type of purely self-interested behaviour which some think to be ubiquitous in society (Inglehart 1990: ch. 2) (see POLITICAL CULTURE). Contra the 'moral malaise' critics, therefore, one should not underestimate the persistence of values such as duties in attitudes to the democratic process and the possibility that this continues to perform a function in maintaining and stabilising democracy.

Duties of the democratic political order

The duties of citizens are typically exacted, where necessary, by the state acting as the embodiment or representative of the community of citizens, sometimes known as the 'civic order' (Selbourne 1994: 17) In some versions of duty-based political theory, this notion is presented as the right of the civic order to certain forms of behaviour from its members. But, conversely, the civic order itself can have duties to them and the state, as the instrument that should discharge them, may not be entitled to full obedience if it fails so to do.

Most versions of the theory which take this line will share the idea that the civic order's primary duty is to provide secure social conditions in which its citizens may flourish. It should act against phenomena which are deemed to threaten the stability or well-being of the civic order. Once more, this may be interpreted in a minimalist way, leading to a limited politics in which the provision of physical security and a protective legal order largely suffices. More expansively, a duty-based theory could propose that the security of the citizens also depends upon the provision of a minimum material standard of living for all. The well-being of citizens and the well-being of the civic order could generate duties on the part of the latter to ensure, as best as possible, that citizens are capable of leading dignified, meaningful lives (Selbourne 1994: ch. 8). Consonant with the shift in Western democracies away from Keynesian social democracy towards a neo-liberal, less generous welfarism, duty-based defences of political welfarism are likely to be unsympathetic to the idea that citizens have dutiless rights to benefits. This was the key fault pinpointed in the 'welfare state' by many of its critics, who believed it contributed to the growth of irresponsible popular attitudes and behaviour.

Democracy against duties

There may, of course, be occasions upon which 'higher' moral duties mandate a disregard for the democratically expressed will of the citizens by individuals or the state, even when they have acted according to the requirements of democratic duty. However, it is plausible to contend that a morally aware democratic theory must be able to acknowledge the possibility of such moral dilemmas and conflicts. It should, therefore, accommodate legitimate disobedience in, for example, a recognition of rights to conscientious objection. Nevertheless, if it is true that the performance of democratic duty helps to secure the democratic order and/or the pursuit of a meaningful, flourishing and moral life, the instances of such exceptions should ideally be rare.

There are many democratic theorists who view democracy's workings purely in terms of the interaction of self-interested individuals who, by the luck of an 'invisible hand', just happen thereby to sustain a political order; duty is entirely incidental. But the possibility of a successful democratic order *without* an operative sense of duty on the part of both the citizens and the civic order must surely be doubted. The violent birth pangs of certain democratic civil societies, in South Africa and many post-communist states, show that 'self-interest' which is not tempered and disciplined by a civic culture that is respectful of morality's demands is far from guaranteed to graduate towards what is demanded by social and political stability. If it is utopian to hope for perfectly just societies, with people's duties perfectly fulfilled, the fact that it is virtually impossible to live any kind of life which is not deeply enmeshed in the public world makes it hard not to conclude that what little might be achieved of a good, moral life in a democracy must contain some notion of duty to the kind of society that makes such lives possible at all.

See also:

citizenship; civic virtue; identity, political; political culture; responsibilities

Further reading

Clarke, P.B. (1996) *Deep Citizenship*, London: Pluto Press.

Dagger, R. (1997) *Civic Virtues*, Oxford: Oxford University Press.

Downs, A. (1957) *An Economic Theory of Democracy*, New York: Harper & Row.

Etzioni, A. (1993) *The Spirit of Community*, New York: Simon and Schuster.

Inglehart, R. (1990) *Culture Shift in Advanced Industrial Society*, Princeton, NJ: Princeton University Press.

Mansbridge, J. (1983) *Beyond Adversary Democracy*, Chicago: Chicago University Press.

Plato (1987) *The Republic* 2nd edn (revised), trans. D. Lee, London: Penguin.

Sandel, M. (1996) *Democracy's Discontent*, Cambridge, MA: Belknap Press of Harvard University Press.

Selbourne, D. (1994), *The Principle of Duty*, London: Sinclair-Stevenson.

MARK A. EVANS

E

economic requirements of democracy

The *emergence* and *maintenance* of democracy in the modern world has received considerable attention from political scientists. Using a variety of comparative and statistical methods, scholars have sought to identify the objective 'preconditions' for democracy (Karl 1990). Among the many factors that have been identified to account for democracy, including cultural, structural and external, economic factors such as overall wealth, the level of development, and sustained economic growth continue to be central features of research in this area. Theoretical accounts of the relationship between the economy and democracy argue that new forms of political rule were made possible by the advent of CAPITALISM. Marxist perspectives argue that the development of capitalism effectively separated the political and economic spheres of society, broke down feudal bases of political power, and provided the conditions for the emergence of democracy. Non-Marxist accounts claim that capitalism contributed to the rise of the middle CLASS, which developed the entrepreneurial drive, individualistic qualities, and POLITICAL CULTURE necessary for the realisation and long-term sustainability of democratic rule. Drawing on either of these two theoretical perspectives, empirical political science seeks to uncover the economic requirements of democracy both for the 'old' democracies in the advanced (post) industrial countries and the 'new' democracies in other parts of the world.

The search for the economic requirements of democracy primarily uses two methods found in the sub-field of comparative politics. The first method collects economic and political indicators on a large sample of countries at one point in time or over time, and then uses various forms of quantitative analysis to test the relationship between key aspects of the economy and different forms of political rule (for example, Lipset 1959; Helliwell 1994; Burkhart and Lewis-Beck 1994). The second method compares a smaller sample of countries over time using qualitative and quantitative techniques, and includes important intervening variables thought to lie between the economic and political variables. These intervening variables include such factors as the nature of the export economy, the timing of industrialisation, the role of the state in the process of development, the emergence of new social classes and the alliances they form, and 'transnational constellations of power' (Moore 1966; Rueschemeyer *et al.* 1992) (see DEMOCRATIC DEVELOPMENT).

The conclusion of the many-country studies is that there is a stable positive relationship between the level of economic development and democracy regardless of how each variable is measured. Moreover, this literature concludes that wealthy democracies tend not to collapse (Przeworski and Limongi 1997). In contrast, the conclusion of the few-country studies is that democracy is the product of discrete historical events that are not likely to be repeated in the future, making it a much more elusive outcome than the many-country studies suggest. A comparison of these two methods in terms of their theoretical assumptions, research designs, comparative measures and model specifications reveals how they reach these different conclusions regarding the economic requirements of democracy. This comparison highlights the importance of the topic and the attention that it has received in the larger comparative literature on democracy.

The first many-country study on the 'social requisites of democracy' compared forty-eight European, English-speaking and Latin American countries, which were further divided into stable democracies, unstable democracies, stable dictatorships and unstable dictatorships (Lipset 1959). The comparison used indicators of wealth, industrialisation, education and urbanisation to capture different aspects of economic development. The comparison of means of each indicator across the groups of countries revealed that the European and English-speaking stable democracies and the Latin American democracies and unstable dictatorships score better than the other regime types. In other words, on average, democracies or those countries more likely to become democracies tend to have higher levels of socio-economic development than non-democracies. This pattern of results led Lipset (1959: 80) to claim that all the factors 'subsumed under economic development carry with it the political correlate of democracy'. While not claiming that economic development actually *causes* democracy, this study is the first to establish a correlation between the two, and thus paved the way for a succession of studies that build on the original comparisons.

The studies that followed Lipset's seminal article use the same comparative method but examine different samples of countries, over different periods of time, using different INDICATORS OF DEMOCRACY and economic development, and different functional forms of the relationship. First, the advent of more advanced quantitative techniques has allowed scholars to compare larger samples of countries and use indicators that span longer periods of time thus providing greater variation and stronger comparative inferences. For example, Helliwell (1994) and Burkhart and Lewis-Beck (1994) both use large samples of countries (between 125 and 131) over time (between ten and twenty years), yielding data sets with many observations ($1,250 < N < 2,096$). Second, indicators of democracy include scales that measure the presence of democratic institutions, the protection of political and civil rights, and electoral turnout and party dominance, as well as dichotomous measures of the presence or absence of democracy. Indicators of economic development typically include the level and growth of per capita gross domestic product and energy consumption, both of which tend to be highly correlated. Finally, the relationship between economic development and democracy assumes different functional forms, including linear, curvilinear and a 'step' function. Linear and curvilinear functions suggest that incremental improvement in the level of economic development is associated with positive improvement in, or advance toward, full democracy. In contrast, a step function suggests that there is a minimum threshold of economic development, above which the probability of democracy is higher.

Whether comparing many countries at one point in time or over a period of time, the main finding of the quantitative studies is that there is a 'stable positive relationship between economic development and democracy' (Rueschemeyer *et al.* 1992: 26). The weak version of this finding claims that increased levels of economic development are *associated* with democracy (Lipset 1959; Cutright 1963), while the strong version argues that economic development actually *causes* democracy (Helliwell 1994; Burkhart and Lewis-Beck 1994). These results have supported the larger MODERNISATION perspective in comparative politics, which assumes that there is a universal process of socio-economic development of which democracy is but the final stage (Przeworski and Limongi 1997: 158). This perspective argues that as countries save and invest at appropriate levels that enhance their infrastructure and social institutions, liberal democratic institutions will flourish as a natural response to the functional imperatives of society and supply the best form of governance. The development of social institutions enhances the level of education of the population, improves its social and spatial mobility, and promotes the political culture that supports liberal democratic institutions. In short, the modernisation perspective assumes that the process of socio-economic development is 'a progressive accumulation of social changes that ready a society for its culmination, democratisation' (Przeworski and Limongi 1997: 158).

Objections and criticisms to the modernisation perspective centre on its deterministic and teleological quality, its omission of the importance of political institutionalisation, its Western ethnocentricity and its 'a-historical' prescription for a developmental trajectory that all countries ought to follow. The perspective assumes that all countries that achieve high levels of economic development necessarily achieve democracy, ignores that fact that without proper political institutionalisation the process of economic development may lead to political instability, prescribes a formula for development based on the advanced industrial countries of the West, and ignores the timing of development and important historical events which may have had an impact on both development and democracy. Moreover, in the years following Lipset's (1959) study, the world experienced a period of DEMOCRATIC BREAK-DOWN in precisely those countries undergoing rapid economic development. These criticisms have led scholars to search for important intervening variables that lie between the process of economic development and democracy. Since these variables emerge from a deep reading of history and are not as susceptible to operationalisation for quantitative analysis, studies that seek to identify them tend to adopt a macro-sociological comparative framework with a smaller sample of countries.

The studies that adopt a macro-sociological approach intentionally select a small sample of countries and fit them into the 'most similar' and 'most different' systems designs of comparative politics (Faure 1994). The most similar systems design compares countries with a similar set of features while isolating differences that account for the dependent variable. The most different systems design compares countries that do not share any features apart from those thought to account for the dependent variable. In this way, both systems designs link the presence of key independent variables to the presence of the dependent variable. With respect to the economic requirements of democracy, both systems designs allow the comparison of a few countries over long periods of history in an effort to identify those features that mediate the relationship between economic development and democracy.

For example, de Schweinitz (1964) compares Britain, the USA, Germany and Russia to uncover the relationship between industrialisation and democracy; Moore (1966) compares Britain, France, the United States, Germany, Japan, Italy and China to examine the 'three routes to modernity'; and Rueschemeyer et al. (1992) compare the developmental paths in advanced capitalist countries, Latin America and the Caribbean. In each study, democracy is the dependent variable which is either present or absent across the selected cases and the process of economic development is examined alongside other key factors from the particular histories of these countries. These studies all conclude that there are multiple economic and political paths followed by different countries that lead to a variety of uncertain outcomes, one of which may be democracy.

From his comparison of four countries, de Schweinitz (1964: 7, 11) argues that industrialisation and economic growth are the 'necessary but not sufficient' conditions for the emergence of democracy, and that the 'Euro-American route to democracy is closed'. For Moore (1966: 431), the democratic route to modern society was achieved in Britain, France and the United States through a series of violent breaks with the past known as 'bourgeois revolutions'. The Puritan Revolution (English Civil War), the French Revolution and the American Civil War were events that dramatically altered the developmental paths of these three countries. The process of economic development was accompanied by a balance of power between the crown and the landed nobility (in England and France), but the development of commercial agriculture weakened the role of the landed upper classes while building the ranks of the bourgeoisie. The rise of the bourgeoisie and the absence of a coalition with the landed upper classes against the interests of peasants and workers was critical for the development of democracy: 'No bourgeois, no democracy' (Moore 1966: 418).

Rueschemeyer *et al.* (1992) expand the comparisons found in both de Schweinitz (1964) and Moore (1966) to include seventeen countries from Europe and North America, twelve countries from Latin America and ten countries from the Caribbean, where the intra-regional comparisons fit into the most similar systems design. The inclusion of a larger number of countries reduces the problem of selection bias and demonstrates that a violent break from the past may not be a necessary condition for the instauration of democracy, and that the working class is the key agent of democratisation across all the countries. While certain elements in the middle class have supported democratic ideals, it has been the push for inclusion through the extension of rights by the working class that has made the key difference to the realisation of liberal democracy (Rueschemeyer *et al.* 1992: 97–8). By extending their comparisons beyond the confines of the advanced industrial world, the authors make an important contribution to our understanding of the economic requirements of democracy in those parts of the world that have undergone processes of development at a later time. The countries face different external constraints and internal processes that affect significantly the ways in which economic development is related to democracy.

This brief examination of these studies from the extant literature demonstrates that that the comparison of few countries offers different analytical opportunities for scholars interested in the economic requirements of democracy. This method of comparison allows the intensive examination of individual countries and more focus on the differences between countries in order to explain the ways in which economic development may or may not foster democracy. A small number of countries allows the comparison to highlight historical sequences, and the importance of specific historical events on the subsequent chances of establishing democracy, including wars, revolutions and economic crises. But is the result of

these studies fundamentally at odds with those that compare many countries? Moreover, is the difference in results somehow related to the difference in comparative method?

In answering both these questions, the difference in results is not contradictory and lies in the choice of countries as well as the different emphasis placed on *similarities* versus *differences*. The global comparison of many countries concentrates its efforts on the regularities that hold across a large sample. Deviant countries are a natural occurrence in large samples (for example, wealthy authoritarian countries or poor democracies), while the goal of the analysis is to account for the variation in democracy with a parsimonious set of factors. In contrast, studies that compare few countries place more emphasis on the differences across the countries. Scholars conducting global comparisons would not disagree; merely that the relationship holds more often than not. These methodological points are not trivial since they explain the apparent differences between various efforts to uncover the economic requirements of democracy.

The different results support different theoretical perspectives on the economic requirements of democracy. The global comparison of many countries provides evidence in favour of the modernisation perspective, while the comparison of few countries supports a more eclectic body of theory that is less optimistic than the modernisation perspective regarding the relationship between economic development and democracy. Despite these differences, however, both approaches are deterministic since they specify larger causal forces that account for the emergence and maintenance of democracy (Przeworski and Limongi 1997: 176). The emphasis on macro-causal factors, such as economic growth, social classes and transnational constellations of power, ignores the equally important role that political actors can have in the making of democracy. Indeed, Przeworski and Limongi (1997: 176) rightly observe that during the third wave of democratisation, 'The protagonists in the struggles for democracy could not and did not believe that the fate of their countries would be determined either by current levels of development or by the distant past'. Old and new democracies have in part been 'crafted' (Di Palma 1990) by those political actors operating in specific times and in specific places, and the long-term viability of democracy as a form of rule depends on the continued adherence of future political actors to the institutions formulated during moments of DEMOCRATIC TRANSITION (Przeworski 1991).

In light of these considerations, economic development, whether measured in terms of market capitalism, high levels of growth, equal distribution of income or low levels of unemployment, merely provides a favourable context in which individuals can construct a brighter democratic future. While the elective affinity between the free market and democracy may be another 'Enlightenment utopia' (Gray 1998: 2–7), high levels of economic development provide the resources and latitude for political actors to reach the types of compromise and consensus necessary for establishment and maintenance of democracy. Sustained economic performance can only ease the many difficult challenges faced by old and new democracies alike. The empirical generalisations and inferences of either method of comparison do not contradict the basic point that enhanced resources cushion the democratic project. Thus, there are economic requirements that favour the establishment and maintenance of democracy, but they certainly do not determine it.

See also:

class; correlates of democracy; indicators of democracy; market forces; waves of democracy

Further reading

Burkhart, R.E. and Lewis-Beck, M. (1994) 'Comparative Democracy, the Economic Development Thesis', *American Political Science Review* 88(4): 903–10.
Cutright, P. (1963) 'National Political Development; Its Measurement and Social Correlates', in N. Polsby, R.A. Denther and P.A. Smith (eds), *Political and Social Life*, Boston: Houghton Mifflin, 569–82.
De Schweinitz, K. (1964) *Industrialization and Democracy: Economic Necessities and Political Possibilities*, New York: Free Press.
Di Palma, G. (1990) *To Craft Democracies*, Los Angeles: University of California Press.
Faure, A.M. (1994) 'Some Methodological Problems in Comparative Politics', *Journal of Theoretical Politics* 6(3): 307–22.
Gray, J. (1998) *False Dawn: Delusions of Global Capitalism*, London: Granta.
Helliwell, J.F. (1994) 'Empirical Linkages between Democracy and Economic Growth', *British Journal of Political Science* 24: 225–48.
Karl, T.L. (1990) 'Dilemmas of Democratization in Latin America', *Comparative Politics* 23: 1–21.
Lipset, S.M. (1959) 'Some Social Requisites from Democracy: Economic Development and Political Legitimacy', *The American Political Science Review* 53: 69–105.
Moore, B. (1966) *The Social Origins of Dictatorship and Democracy: Lord and Peasant in the Making of the Modern World*, Boston: Beacon Press.
Przeworski, A. (1991) *Democracy and the Market: Political and Economic Reforms in Eastern Europe and Latin America*, Cambridge: Cambridge University Press.
Przeworski, A. and Limongi, F. (1997) 'Modernisation: Theories and Facts', *World Politics* 49(January): 155–83.
Rueschemayer, D., Stephens, E.H. and Stephens, D. (1992) *Capitalist Development and Democracy*, Chicago: Chicago University Press.

TODD LANDMAN

education

This entry attempts to do three things: first, to identify some essential principles of democracy and democratic education; second, to work through some of the implications those principles have for the operation of learning systems; and third, to indicate some current practices which are incompatible with a democratic approach to education, and ultimately are destructive of democracy.

A common proposition is that 'power corrupts': those who gain power too often use it to control and manipulate for their own ends. But is has also been proposed that, at the same time, 'powerlessness corrupts', by creating a fatalistic and alienated mentality in the general population. Democracy can be seen as an attempt to deal with both problems, firstly by having laws based on human RIGHTS to control those elected or appointed to positions of power, and secondly by sharing power amongst the people.

A notable feature of democracy is the principle that those who are affected by a decision have the right to take part in the DECISION-MAKING. This is expressed in slogans such as 'No taxation without representation!' If we apply this to education, we get, 'No learning and therefore no curriculum without the learners having a say in the decision-making'. In the traditional approach to schooling, however, there is a chronic fear of trusting students and sharing power with them, and a general fear of opting for the discipline of democracy.

Kelly (1995: xii) declares that 'the basic principles of democratic existence are being put seriously at risk by current educational policies'. It is not difficult to weaken and eventually remove democratic activity by design or by neglect, for as Dewey (1916) has suggested, we can easily take democracy for granted, thinking and acting as if our ancestors had established it once and for all. We forget, at our peril, that democratic discipline must be re-created in every generation, in all social relations and in all our institutions.

Democratic practice, in society or in education, is rarely proposed as an ideal state but, paraphrasing an observation of Winston Churchill, is the worst system of organisation and order available – except for all the alternatives. Thus the shortcomings of democratic practice, such as the consumption of considerable time in debate, dialogue and decision-making, the 'camel is a horse designed by a committee' jibe, are all admitted at the outset while maintaining that democratic practice is still the lesser of evils. Another shortcoming is in its complexity: Held (1987) provides nine different models of democracy that we can consider.

Nevertheless, if you do not have some form of democracy, you are bound to have something worse. This could be any of the standard tyrannies of dictatorship. There is a wide choice of forms of domination: totalitarianism, fascism, theocracy, monarchy, bureaucracy or CAPITALISM. For this reason, Professor Sme Bengu, Nelson Mandela's choice for Education Minister in post-apartheid South Africa, proposed that democracy means 'the absence of domination'.

The point that democracy is a preferable state rather than an ideal is made in a passage in E. M. Forster's (1962) famous essay 'What I Believe'. Forster states: 'Democracy is not a beloved republic really, and never will be. But it is less hateful than other contemporary forms of government, and to that extent deserves our support'. Democracy has the advantage for Forster in that it starts by assuming that 'the individual is important, and that all types are needed to make a civilisation. It does not divide citizens into the bosses and the bossed – as an efficiency regime tends to do'. Forster admires those who are creative and sensitive or who wish to discover something, those who 'do not see life in terms of power'. These people are given more of a 'chance under democracy than elsewhere'. Another 'merit' of democracy is that criticism is allowed, which is why Forster 'believes' in the press, 'despite all its lies and vulgarity'. Forster also 'believes' in Parliament. 'Whether Parliament is either a representative body or an efficient one is questionable, but I value it because it criticises and talks, and because its chatter gets widely reported. So two cheers for Democracy: one because it admits variety and two because it permits criticism. Two cheers are quite enough: there is no occasion to give three'.

It is possible to extract from the above quotations and ideas, some propositions about a democratic education. It will tend to:

1 admit variety rather than uniformity;
2 permit critical thought rather than belief;
3 operate power-sharing rather than author-itarian imposition;
4 promote flexibility rather than rigidity.

There are two more important aspects. One is the difference between moral and immoral democracy, the other is the difference between shallow and deep democracy. Aristotle noted that there could be the rule of the untutored mob voting for any fashion or whim that took its fancy; this is immoral democracy. Moral democracy, on the other hand, is underpinned by the value system of human rights. This is important in answering those who have main-tained that democracy is dangerous because it allows the operation of any values any majority cares to adopt, whether fascist, criminal or barbaric. Democracy, as interpreted here, follows the classic analysis of Tom Paine and others in assuming the base values of equal human rights as articulated in the 'Thirty Articles' and similar declarations. It does not occupy a values vacuum.

The distinction between shallow and deep democracy is important in education. Shallow democracy only allows limited power sharing and restricted participation in decision-making. Shallow forms of democracy only allow a small amount of power to be shared, often under limited license, which those in power can withdraw at will, and often confine to only marginal activities. As an example, many schools organise schools councils. They are usually allowed limited time and limited scope, and if they try to extend their range of tasks, they are reprimanded or shut down. Teachers retain a veto and use it whenever it suits them. Such shallow democracy can degenerate to such a sham as to be counter-productive in leading to cynicism, fatalism and a belief that 'democracy does not work'. Sham democracy certainly does not work.

Deep democracy allows more and more power sharing, and in the end, the setting of the agenda itself. Deep democracy is not simply about the number and range of items where power is shared. It is also about the levels of decision-making. It is not just being involved in more items on a longer agenda, but also having the opportunity to decide the agenda itself. Thus in education, learners may be allowed to make choices from a catalogue curriculum: this is shallow democracy. When they move on to construct the curriculum itself, or devise the catalogue, they are engaging in deeper democracy. Thus A.S. Neill's school, Summerhill in the UK, operates democratically in its organi-sational culture, but the formal curriculum is teacher-directed. In contrast, in D. Green-bergh's Sudbury Valley School in the USA both aspects are democratic; indeed there is no timetable of organised studies until the learners set to and devise one, which they invariably do.

Another approach that indicates levels of democracy in operation in a school is that of Davies (1994) where she develops a series of performance INDICATORS OF DEMOCRACY in education covering such areas as the structure of school management, decision-making are-nas, practice opportunities in democracy and preparation for active CITIZENSHIP. Most secondary schools in the UK score nil or low scores on these performance indicators, sup-porting Rogers (1983) when he points out that schools for the most part despise and scorn democracy. The students do not choose the curriculum, the goals, the methods of work or the teachers, nor do they have any part in educational policy. These areas are decided for them. Similarly, the teachers often have no choice in their administrative officers. For Rogers, 'all this is in striking contrast to all the teaching about the virtues of democracy, the importance of the "free world," and the like. The political practices of the school stand in the most striking contrast to what is taught. While being taught that freedom and responsi-bility are the glorious features of our democracy, students are experiencing powerlessness... hav-ing almost no opportunity to exercise choice or carry responsibility' (1983: 186–7).

Russian educators have also expressed con-cern at this mentality. 'Soviet children normally demonstrate better results in mathematics and science' than their counterparts in the UK and elsewhere, Froumin *et al.* (1995: 206) tell us in

Creating and Managing the Democratic School. Nevertheless, Froumin and his fellow writers want to abandon the authoritarian school, imposed curriculum, whole-class teaching pedagogy (shored up by heavy doses of homework) and testing that is responsible for these results, because they deliver the wrong kind of person. They produce the servile, authority-dependent fatalistic outlook and people good at selected mental tricks, rather than the democratic, lifelong learner with a flexible, positive mentality.

There is a crucial difference between various forms of order, sometimes known as discipline systems or the 'problem of discipline', as it is commonly referred to in discussions about education. One difference is between that of authoritarian order and AUTHORITY on the one hand, and democratic order and authority on the other. There is also the third approach of autonomous order and authority where individuals exercise self-discipline. (For a fuller analysis, see Meighan and Siraj-Blatchford (1999).)

In authoritarian systems, one person, or a group of people, exercises dominance over other people although the form of this dominance varies. This can range from outright coercion through fear, to deference to rank or believed expertise, to persuasion through controlled communication, through to consultation initiated by those in power entirely on their terms. In democratic systems, power is shared to some degree or other. If we apply this distinction to educational practice, the result is as follows.

In authoritarian education in its various forms, one person, or a small group of people, makes and implements the decisions about what to learn, when to learn, how to learn, how to assess learning and the nature of the learning environment. These decisions are taken in course planning committees and accreditation boards often before the learners are recruited as individuals or meet as a group. This kind of thinking leads inevitably to an imposed National Curriculum and other compulsory features. It is the general approach favoured by totalitarian systems, whether right-wing fascist or left-wing communist. The spirit of this approach can be summed up in the slogan: You will do it our way! Visitors from societies that have been totalitarian see it at once. (When I asked Professor Eugenia Potulicka from Poland what she would say in her report about UK schools and our education system, she said, 'Oh, I shall tell them it is totalitarian'. She went on to say: 'The 1988 Education Act is a very dangerous development for it has politicised schooling in the direction of fascist thinking. It is the worst development in Europe at the moment'.)

School, based on the current anti-democratic model of the compulsory day-detention centre, is domination-riddled and is therefore a bully institution. It employs a bully curriculum, the compulsory National Curriculum. This is enforced by the increasingly favoured bully pedagogy of teacher-directed formal teaching. Currently this is reinforced by the bully compulsory assessment system. This system is enforced by a bully inspectorate. The unwritten but powerful message of this nasty package is that 'adults get their way by bullying'.

There are at least three types of outcome. The 'successful' pupils grow up to be officially sanctioned bullies in dominant authority positions as assertive politicians, doctors, teachers, civil servants, journalists and the like. A majority of the 'less successful' learn to accept the mentality of the bullied, the submissive and dependent mind-set of people who need someone to tell them what to think and do. A third outcome is the production of a group of freelance bullies who become troublesome and end up in trouble of varying degree of seriousness.

In contrast, in democratic education the learners work as a co-operative group for they have the power to make some, most, or even all of these decisions since power is shared and not appropriated in advance by a minority of one or more. Ironically, in many countries including our own that sustain the illusion that they are very democratic, such educational practices are rare and indeed meet with sustained, hostile and irrational opposition. Instead, it is sometimes proposed that the conscripted learners should be taught 'democratic citizenship'. As one colleague, Derry Hannam, remarked, 'Learning about democracy and citizenship in school is a bit like reading holiday brochures in prison'.

Some of the consequences of democratic practices that have been found in the research are:

1 that there is likely to develop a sense of community amongst a group of learners;
2 there develops a working partnership between appointed teachers and learners;
3 appointed teachers develop trust in the capability and creative ability of their fellow humans who come to them in the role of students;
4 dialogue becomes an essential activity rather than an optional feature, and unmandated or imposed learning is not seen as legitimate;
5 standards of formal work rise, with bonus skills such as increased personal confidence, higher self-esteem, and enhanced discussion and research skills.

But the present non-democratic approach to schooling has been described by Holt (1977) as regimental: 'School is the Army for kids. Adults make them go there, and when they get there, adults tell them what to do, bribe and threaten them into doing it, and punish them when they don't'.

One growing reaction to this domination-riddled approach has been the rapid growth of home-based education, especially in USA, Canada, New Zealand, Australia and the UK. Democratic practice and its five consequences are more likely to be encountered than in the mass, coercive schooling system, because power is usually shared with the learners who have more and more say in the decision-making. Consequently, they usually develop confidence in managing their own learning in co-operation with members of the family and others. The power-sharing that it is proposed must exist before any learning regime can be classified as democratic and can take various forms and occur in varying degrees:

1 a syndicate approach allows learners power

over the methods of learning but the syllabus or content is dictated;
2 a group project approach allows learners to learn co-operatively in groups for a specific part of a course only and the teacher takes over as instructor for the major part of the time;
3 a learning co-operative approach means that the group of learners takes on the power of decision-making about content and method but it often has to meet an externally imposed assessment, although this can often be made flexible enough to avoid being stifling. This threefold classification does not, of course, exhaust the possibilities.

The stress in democratic learning is on the collective aspect of the learning. In reality, the approach allows the development of both the solo type of learner-managed – autonomous education – and the collective form of learner-managed learning, working in co-operation and interaction with each other. The group may well use the device of allocating tasks to individuals, and sometimes pairs and trios, which require them to go off and research and prepare material, activities and sessions. The results of their solo activities will then be fed back into the group programme. The group may also decide to submit to formal, rather authoritarian-looking sessions if that seems the best way to pursue a particular piece of learning.

Summary: the democratic view of education

Slogan: 'We did it our way'.

Discipline is democratic discipline by working co-operatively to agreed rules and principles, rather than those imposed by the coercive principle of 'you will do it our way'. Knowledge is essentially the skills and information needed by the group to maintain and develop its learning. Learning is activity agreed by the group to gain experience, information or particular skills working either together or reporting-back tasks delegated to individuals. Teaching is any activity, including formal instruction, that the group judges will lead to effective learning.

Parents are seen as part of the resources available and potentially as partners in the learning group. Resources are anything appropriate to the group's research and learning including people, places, and experiences. Location is anywhere that the learning group can meet to pursue effective learning. Organisation is commonly in self-regulated groups where democratic dialogue and co-operative learning can take place. Assessment is by any form of assessment using any tests, devised by the learners or by others, that are seen to be appropriate to the situation.

Aims are essentially, to produce people with the confidence and skills to manage their own life-long learning within a democratic culture. Power is shared in the group who are seen as responsible both individually and collectively for its exercise. Leadership is shared and revolves, rather than resides in one assertive person. It is expressed in the words of the ancient Chinese sage, Laozi: 'Of a good leader, they say, when his work is done, we did this ourselves!' (adapted from Meighan and Siraj-Blatchford (1999)).

See also:

citizenship; civic virtue; civil society; decision-making; empowerment; indicators of democracy; moral improvement; republicanism; responsibilities; self and politics; welfare

Further reading

Chamberlin, R. (1989) *Free Children and Democratic Schools*, London: Falmer.

Davies, L. (1994) *Beyond Authoritarian School Management*, Ticknall: Education Now Books.

Dewey, J. (1916) *Democracy and Education*, New York: Macmillan.

Engle, S. and Ochoa, A. (1989) *Education for Democratic Citizenship*, Columbia, MO: Teachers College Press.

Forster, E.M. (1962) 'What I Believe', in *Two Cheers for Democracy*, New York: Harcourt Brace.

Froumin, I., Chapman, G. and Aspin, D. (eds) (1995) *Creating and Managing the Democratic School*, London: Falmer Press.

Harber, C. (1992) *Democratic Learning and Learning Democracy*, Ticknall: Education Now Books.

—— (ed.) (1995) *Developing Democratic Education*, Ticknall: Education Now Books.

Harber, C. and Meighan, R. (1989) *The Democratic School: Educational Management and the Practice of Democracy*, Ticknall: Education Now Books.

Held, D. (1987) *Models of Democracy*, Cambridge: Polity Press.

Holt, J. (1975) *Escape from Childhood*, Harmondsworth: Penguin.

—— (1977) in *Growing Without Schooling*, Number 17, Boston: Holt Associates.

Kelly, A.V. (1995) *Education and Democracy: Principles and Practice*, London: Paul Chapman.

Meighan, R. (1993) *Theory and Practice of Regressive Education*, Nottingham: Educational Heretics Press.

Meighan, R. and Siraj-Blatchford, I.(1999) *A Sociology of Educating*, 3rd edn, London: Cassell.

Meighan, R. and Toogood, P. (1992) *Anatomy of Choice in Education*, Ticknell: Education Now Books.

Nicholls, J.G. (1989) *The Competitive Ethos and Democratic Education* Cambridge, MA: Harvard Univ. Press.

Rogers, C. (1983) *Freedom to Learn for the Eighties*, Columbus, OH: Merrill.

White, P. (1983) *Beyond Domination,* London: Routledge and Kegan Paul.

ROLAND MEIGHAN

elections

At the most abstract level, elections are mechanisms capable of translating the popular will into institutionally-defined roles. At the concrete level, elections are about the choice of individuals. The word 'election' derives from the Latin verb *eligere*, meaning to pick out, to choose. Elections may be defined as the formal process through which people are chosen by discrete collectivities to fill offices. Elections are held in many contexts and to fill many different types of office, public and private alike. But though the vast majority of elections are held in the private and voluntary sectors, most people tend to associate them with pubic DECISION-MAKING, and hence with state governance. Elections to state bodies will be the main concern of the present discussion.

It is commonly believed that competitive elections are the sine qua non of democracy. This is untrue for two reasons. First, elections are not necessary to democracy; it is possible to conceive of a democracy in which leaders are chosen by lot, for instance, rather than through election, or one in which decision-making is conducted entirely through referendum. Second, elections are not sufficient to democracy. The holding of 'free and fair' elections is not an adequate criterion for a state to be considered democratic. Genuine democracy requires rule of law, a vibrant CIVIL SOCIETY and effective political PARTIES. Indeed, the use of elections as means of selecting leaders precedes the advent of modern democracy by several hundred years. Elections are also a common feature of contemporary non-democratic regimes; though fewer than half the states in the world can be considered democratic, only about one in ten states lacks a functioning elected representative body.

These caveats notwithstanding, the competitive election of officials to important POLICY-MAKING offices is a fundamental component of the political process in the world's representative democracies. The election of representatives is a device that allows states to govern large populations efficiently, while at the same time taking account of public opinion. The democratic process involves two key types of activity: deliberation, the voicing of opinions and the effort to change minds; and aggregation, the pooling of opinions, interests, and preferences so as to come to a single decision. Elections are the main mechanism in most modern democratic polities for aggregating citizen preferences. This is not to say that they play no role in deliberative processes; on the contrary, the electoral campaign (see ELECTORAL CAMPAIGNING) acts as an important stimulus to deliberation. But the election itself is an act of aggregation, and it is the most significant way in which the majority of citizens contribute to political decision-making.

Though elections were used to fill some positions in ancient Greece and Rome, their use in modern Europe can be traced back to the selection of the bishops and popes of the Roman Catholic Church in the Middle Ages. Secular elections date back to the thirteenth century, when members of the English House of Commons first began to be returned by their peers. But the popular right to vote for parliamentary representatives is a product of the American and French Revolutions, and it was not until the nineteenth century that elections to representative bodies had become the norm in Europe and its colonies (Nohlen 1978; Katz 1997).

Before the twentieth century, the majority of developments in the conduct of elections had to do with reforms aimed at reducing corruption and expanding the right to SUFFRAGE. Well into the nineteenth century, it was usual for electoral systems to restrict access to the franchise on the basis of property, literacy, gender and other qualifications, and/or to involve weighted franchises that awarded more electoral power to some groups than to others. Indirect elections – in which citizens elected regional delegates who then went on to elect higher-level legislative bodies, – were also common, as was open voting by voice or show of hands. A wave of electoral reform swept the Western world at the end of the nineteenth and the beginning of the twentieth centuries; it was at this time that most European states extended the franchise and introduced the principle of one person one vote. In the contemporary world, electoral systems differ not so much in who votes but rather in how people vote. Most states – democratic and non-democratic – now have universal adult suffrage among citizens (though CITIZENSHIP regulations vary). For this reason, most of the third wave democratisations have not involved extensive changes to the franchise (South Africa being a notable exception), but rather increased opportunities for electoral CONTESTATION.

In modern states, elections are the nexus between private life and public choice. From the point of view of civic engagement, voting is perhaps the most public act the majority of citizens carry out, but in terms of the conditions under which it is conducted it is one of the most private and isolated. This tension between individual choice and collective outcomes structures the electoral ritual. Elections are inward-looking events; the attention of the MEDIA and other forms of voter information typically focuses as much on the electoral phenomenon as on issues and candidates. At the same time, elections reach out to involve the entire population in a common experience, sometimes uniting people, sometimes intensifying the differences among them. Elections are events that happen at regular intervals (albeit more regularly in some states than in others), and their repetition over time causes a certain electoral culture to accrue. This culture is both part of the POLITICAL CULTURE of a state and distinct from it, in that the tenor of elections is that of exceptional events. Electoral culture periodically takes over from the routine style of politics, engulfing it, refracting it and intertwining it with motifs peculiar to the electoral ritual: campaign programmes, pre-election opinion polls and the inevitable predictions of pundits.

For all involved in them, elections bring with them a rupture in continuity. From the point of view of the civil administration, elections represent a mammoth organisational task. Electoral registration involves in virtually all countries total mobilisation of the adult population. Elections are also disruptive in that they bring with them a potential change of government, and the anticipation of this change will alter the normal rhythms and dynamics of the state apparatus. From the point of view of the contestants, the defining feature of elections is that they dramatically increase the stakes of politics; they involve one

group of rulers offering the opportunity for another group to come to power. This brings with it tension and anxiety, but also the possibility of self-advancement. From the point of view of the voters, elections are concentrated politics. They compress a large amount of INFORMATION and suasive effort into a relatively short period of time in a highly structured format. They urge people to consolidate their opinions, to weigh the evidence for and against different electoral options, and to take sides. They force decisions, often requiring people to make compromises and to choose alternatives that fail wholly to match their ideal.

Understanding of the characteristics of the electoral process allows us to assess the role elections play in the functioning of a state. Elections serve a number of functions, some of which are specific to democratic countries, and others of which are relevant in any electoral context (Harrop and Miller 1987). The first and primary purpose of elections in any polity is to choose rulers. In some states, ELECTORAL SYSTEMS are designed in such a way as to allow direct choice over the composition of the government; in other countries, elections are understood mainly as mechanisms for choosing representatives. In either case, one of the most important functions of elections in a democratic setting, and one which distinguishes it from its non-democratic counterpart, is to maximise the ACCOUNTABILITY of the rulers to the ruled. Accountability may be thought of as the qualitative counterpart to numeric representation; though individuals and groups are often represented in non-democracies according to their weight in society, they have few if any means of holding their representatives responsible for their actions. Competitive electoral contests put pressure on rulers to demonstrate their commitment to the common good.

A second main function of elections is to enhance popular participation in the political process. At a minimum, the citizenry participates by voting. Citizens can choose to participate more actively by standing for election or by campaigning for their chosen candidate/party. But the electoral process also involves political participation in other, more diffuse ways, by providing a range of fora in which the citizenry is educated about politics and about each other. Elections are important schools for politicians and aspiring politicians as well, affording them the chance to experiment with new strategies and to receive feedback from the population about its preferences and perceptions.

A third and related function of democratic elections is to stimulate the development and structuration of civil society. The requirement that successful contestants gather widespread popular support creates a strong incentive for politically interested individuals to come together and organise to achieve common ends. Elections thus encourage the formation of political parties, pressure groups and citizens' groups. The need to agree on common platforms spurs debate about values, policy issues, and common aims.

The fourth main function of elections is that of legitimisation. Legitimisation is one of the primary purposes of elections in non-democratic countries; it is the means by which rulers demonstrate to themselves, to the citizenry, and to foreign powers that they can compel compliance (see LEGITIMACY). When they are no longer able to do this, as happened in the USSR at the end of the 1980s and beginning of the 1990s, it spells the death knell of the regime. But legitimisation is also important in democratic contexts. When conducted democratically, elections can help make people believe in the fairness of the political system, its openness to and tolerance of competing views, and the possibility for change through institutional means.

The extent to which elections are democratic is conventionally measured in terms of how 'free and fair' they are; their probity. There are three aspects to the probity of elections: ground rules, conduct and implementation of the results. A fair electoral law is one that provides equal access to all contestants and to all voters. A properly functioning electoral administration is one that succeeds in registering the eligible population, establishes intra-polity

electoral boundaries that do not favour one group of electoral contestants over others, structures electoral campaigns in such a way as to give all contestants an equal opportunity to get their message across to voters, maintains adequate and effective procedures for polling and vote counting, and announces the results in a timely fashion. There must also be mechanisms for lodging complaints and adjudicating disputes among contestants, and the results of the elections must have a real and determining effect on who performs the functions of the office to which they are held. Violations of these norms involve both outright fraud and more subtle forms of discrimination. Personation, ballot box stuffing and irregularities in the counting of results are instances of fraud. Media bias, electoral rules that favour some contestants over others, vote buying and clientelism, and coercive pressure on voters to influence their vote choice are cases of less formal but equally nefarious violations of electoral norms.

In addition to ensuring the probity of elections, it is also necessary to maintain the autonomy of the electoral process. Elections are designed to select officials, and the democratic selection of officials is compromised if the electoral process is used by the state to perform auxiliary functions. For example, if the electoral register is used as a proxy tax register, citizens may disenfranchise themselves in order to avoid having to pay tax. Or if the state violates the secrecy of the ballot so as to identify those it considers to be political deviants, such people may forfeit their right to vote in order to escape politically motivated investigation.

Since the end of the Cold War, there has been a dramatic increase in the number of countries holding competitive elections, and a commensurate increase in the number of organisations involved in monitoring and in some cases even the administering elections in democratising countries. These include foreign states, NON-GOVERNMENTAL ORGANISATIONS (domestic and international) and international organisations. These efforts have gone a substantial way toward identifying universal standards for electoral practice and assessing the extent to which different states live up to these standards (Goodwin-Gill 1994). But there is still disagreement among different organisations as to the precise definition of 'free and fair' elections and what constitutes breaches of these norms. Considerable progress will be made in establishing universal standards when an international convention on the conduct of elections is adopted, and this is a goal toward which all democracies and aspiring democracies should work.

See also:

citizenship; electoral behaviour; legitimacy; suffrage

Further reading

Carstairs, A.M. (1980) *A Short History of Electoral Systems in Western Europe*, London: George Allen and Unwin.

Goodwin-Gill, G.S. (1994) *Free and Fair Elections: International Law and Practice*, Geneva: Inter-Parliamentary Union.

Harrop, M. and Miller, W.L. (1987) *Elections and Voters: A Comparative Introduction*, Basingstoke: Macmillan.

Hermet, G., Rose, R. and Rouquié, A. (eds) (1978) *Elections Without Choice*, London: Macmillan.

Katz, R. (1997) *Democracy and Elections*, Oxford and New York: Oxford University Press.

LeDuc, L., Niemi, R. and Norris, P. (eds) (1996) *Comparing Democracies: Elections and Voting in Global Perspective*, Thousand Oaks, CA and London: Sage.

Nohlen, D. (1978) *Wahlsysteme der Welt: Daten und Analysen*, (1978) Munich and Zurich: Piper.

Posada-Carbo, E. (ed.) (1996) *Elections before Democracy: The History of Elections in Europe and Latin America*, Basingstoke: Macmillan.

SARAH BIRCH

electoral behaviour

The right of all adults in the polity to participate in regular, free, and fair competitive ELECTIONS is central to the concepts of governance and CITIZENSHIP in modern democratic states. PARTICIPATION in elections is seen to provide popular sanction for appointments to political office, to endow governments with LEGITIMACY and thereby AUTHORITY, and to provide for the popular ACCOUNTABILITY of governments. In the genealogy of the concept of democracy, however, the right to vote as a common political right is a relatively recent development. Moreover, although elections are intrinsic to democratic politics, they are not constitutive: uncompetitive, or 'sham', elections are a familiar feature of authoritarian regimes, as in the former Soviet Union. Citizen participation in elections is but one part of a larger ensemble of practices that, together, constitute democratic politics.

The association between democracy and elections is traceable to the emergence of representative government as the viable form of democratic governance in large and differentiated societies. The genesis of this development lies in two related strands in the evolution of political theory: the expansion of natural rights theory to incorporate the concept of political RIGHTS and, by extension, grounding the legitimacy of government in the consent of the governed. One of the earliest expressions of these claims was voiced by the Levellers in the Putney Debates (1647) following the English Civil War: 'every man that is to live under a government ought first by his own consent to put himself under that government'. Such claims were given a more systematic foundation by Locke (1690) in the *Second Treatise on Government*, and extended to give 'the majority...the right to act and conclude the rest'. That political rights are individual rights and that the legitimacy of governments originates amongst the governed were well-established – albeit not widely practised, and problems with the concept of consent notwithstanding – in the political lexicon by the end of the eighteenth century, evinced in the *American Declaration of Independence* (1776) and the *Declaration of the Rights of Man and of the Citizen* in France (1789).

That democracy enjoins MAJORITARIANISM is widely observed but remains theoretically troublesome. Rousseau argued against representative government as degrading to humanity and as assuming a sovereignty that is not capable of representation (see REPRESENTATION, CONCEPT OF). Nonetheless, the representative version of democratic governance has become the standard form. Two aspects of this development are noteworthy. First, citizens' participation in elections brings into governance a popular element, but little systematic attention has been given to theorising the place of elections in the constitutional order of modern democratic states. In part, this reflects the failure of normative democratic theory to find a place for political PARTIES; in part, it reflects the emergence of full adult SUFFRAGE from the heat of political struggles during the nineteenth and early twentieth centuries rather than developments in democratic theory. The effect has been to detach understandings of elections from theoretical debates about the nature of democracy. Second, and related, while representative government is theoretically well bolstered, what or whom is represented in the outcome of elections, and to what ends, remain ambiguous. Elections and modern democratic politics are empirically and pragmatically, not theoretically, connected: Athenian democracy, for example, not only provided for all citizens to participate in the Popular Assembly but also for the appointment of 'magistrates' by drawing lots among citizens. In this respect, the concept of representation is less well delineated than the concept of representative government.

Elections are the primary mechanism linking citizens and governments in democratic political systems. This link can be examined from two perspectives: as inputs into the political system, or as outputs from the political system. Both perspectives treat individual votes as the dependent variable, but thereafter the agendas diverge. From the input perspective, the most

intensively examined question is: why do voters vote as they do? From the output perspective, voting is set in the context of national POLITICAL CULTURE with attention focusing on the norms, rules and institutions that promote, hinder or distort participation in elections. In this entry the focus is on voting as political input; that is, the electoral behaviour of democratic citizens.

Early scholarly interest in electoral behaviour was stimulated by extensions to the suffrage, the development of mass parties, and the availability of aggregate-level official statistics. The modern study of voting, however, is a post-Second World War development, a product of advances in statistical theory, especially sampling theory, and developments in computer technology; the first providing the theoretical foundations for large-scale data collection and analysis based on individual-level national surveys, the second enabling researchers to manipulate large, often complex, data sets. With national election surveys having become firmly established in most democratic countries, a great deal is known about how certain groups of electors voted in particular elections, how particular parties are viewed amongst different sectors of electorates, and what kinds of things mattered most amongst electors in certain elections. No aspect of the political behaviour of citizens in democratic polities enjoys such a wealth and quality of data.

Even so, explanations of electoral behaviour are elusive. Researchers have roamed across the social sciences in the endeavour to establish models of voting with causal force. At some time or another, why citizens vote as they do has been a research project among not only a substantial proportion of political scientists but also sociologists, psychologists, economists, historians, geographers, statisticians and demographers. Thus, whilst voting might be considered an essentially political activity, understandings of electoral behaviour have a multidisciplinary character in which neither democratic concepts nor strictly political concepts play a major part. This very heterogeneity, however, points up electoral behaviour as the outcome of multifarious processes which combine in complex ways, suggesting that elections may be a more effective public choice mechanism than claimed by critics of representative government.

Three 'schools' of thought have come to dominate studies of electoral behaviour, each with variants around a core mode of explanation. The earliest, the political sociology tradition, originated among sociologists at Columbia University, first appearing in Lazarsfeld *et al.*'s study, *The People's Choice* (1944). In its simplest version, the sociological approach examines electoral behaviour in terms of the individual characteristics of voters, such as age, sex, education, occupation, income, religion and, in the American context, race. In a much extended version developed by Lipset and Rokkan (1967), the personal characteristics of voters are identified in terms of their location in the structure of societal CLEAVAGES originating in the upheavals associated with the Reformation, the French Revolution and the Industrial Revolution. The 'cleavage model' specifically addressed Western European political configurations, bringing to the fore conflicts based on religion, class, urban and rural interests, and resistances by peripheral groups to incorporation in the national state. Nonetheless, the model has obvious resonance with 'defining' events in other democratic countries, such the Civil War, the Depression and the New Deal eras in the United States. The influence of the latter, for example, as Miller and Shanks point out in *The New American Voter* (1996), emerges in the distinctive electoral behaviour of the pre-New Deal, New Deal and post-New Deal generations among American voters.

The strength of the sociological approach lies in rooting the dynamics of electoral behaviour in the economic and social life of citizens. By focusing on voters as social agents, rather than as autonomous political actors, sociological models link political developments with societal developments: political alignments reflect societal alignments; as societies change, so political alignments will change. This gives sociological accounts of electoral behaviour a 'real life' quality that is intuitively plausible; a strictly scientific methodology is not needed to understand why industrial workers tend to vote for a party of the left, or that churchgoers tend to be conservative in political outlook.

The transparency of the sociological approach, however, conceals several problems. One difficulty is identifying the mechanism which serves to translate social attributes into political preference. Parties of the left might be seen to speak for the interests of workers; religiosity may be construed to discourage radicalism. Bringing in concepts of interests or value orientations to explain why workers or churchgoers vote as they do means, however, going beyond sociological constructs to incorporate, for example, institutional or system-level variables identifying the place of parties, churches or trade unions in the relationship between citizens and governments. Another difficulty is accounting for 'deviant' voting. If some substantial proportion of a sociologically defined group does not vote for the 'natural' party, explanation has, again, to look beyond standard sociological variables. The most serious difficulty, however, is that the approach comes too close to representing electoral behaviour as a derivative of social life: 'Social characteristics determine political preference', as Lazarsfeld *et al.* (1944: 27) expressed it. The effect is to denude electoral behaviour of specifically political content.

Studies of electoral behaviour in Western European countries have been influenced more by the 'cleavage model' than the simpler sociological approach. This approach too points up socio-demographic characteristics as major independent variables, but limited to a handful of defined oppositions connecting voters to parties and the developmental trajectory of a polity. Oppositions founded on conflicts over matters of religion or class, for example, are significant less on account of their inherent salience than as the grounds upon which the forerunners of contemporary parties mobilised electoral support as the franchise was successively extended to incorporate entire adult populations. Such early alliances have persisted despite the erosion of, in these instances, overt religious and class conflicts on account of the adaptive capacity of parties. Hence, Christian Democratic parties in Western Europe, although long since forswearing confessionalism, still tend to win the votes of churchgoers. Further, the cleavage approach brings into electoral accounts concepts of interests and value orientations; the relationship between voters and parties rests on the capacity of parties both to articulate and shape the broadly common but otherwise inchoate concerns, instrumental and/or moral, of groups identified by their location in the cleavage structure of the polity.

The cleavage model has proven a powerful tool in understanding electoral behaviour in Western Europe, and has application to the 'new' democracies of Eastern and Central Europe. Even so, there are difficulties. Although applicable to the enduring political alignments supporting the 'old' parties of Western Europe despite widespread social and economic change, the approach has less to offer in understanding electoral support for new parties, such as 'green' or extreme right parties, or how to interpret voting which is not cleavage based. Moreover, the cleavage model is difficult to test, for it entails incorporating into a single model the social, ideological and organisational dimensions of cleavage politics. Further, the resilience of historically founded cleavages is sharply disputed among political scientists: some claim their fading salience (for example, Franklin *et al.* 1992); others claim the emergence of new cleavages based solely on value orientations, notably materialist–postmaterialist oppositions (Inglehart 1977, 1990); yet others note that while the structural foundations of cleavage politics show remarkable – albeit variable – resilience, value orientations are growing in importance (Kriesi 1998). In this sense, the cleavage model has more to offer in explaining the origins and persistence of major political alignments than in accounting for political change and the emergence of new alignments.

The second major school of electoral behaviour is the psychological approach, or more correctly, the socio-psychological model, originating in Campbell *et al.*'s study *The American Voter* (1960). Drawing on field theory, they presented voting as the outcome from a sequence of factors brought together, metaphorically, in the 'funnel of causality'. Located towards the mouth of the funnel, the furthest back in time, are factors such as social background, socialisation experiences and socio-economic characteristics; located towards the tip of the funnel are the more proximate factors of attitudes towards the parties, candidates and issues in a particular election, with especial emphasis on 'party identification' as the mainspring of electoral behaviour. The significance of these factors rests on the assumption that 'most events or conditions that bear directly upon behaviour are perceived in some form or other by the individual prior to the determined behaviour, and that much of that behaviour consists of reactions to these perceptions' (Campbell *et al.* 1960: 27).

Although tremendously influential, the legacy of *The American Voter* is ambivalent. On the one hand, the 'funnel' metaphor is comprehensive in scope and suggests a range of empirical propositions that can be linked together in a temporal causal order. Even so, it has seldom been applied explicitly, partly because few national election studies have time-series or panel data of sufficient length, and partly because applying the model entails some formidable methodological problems. On the other hand, the concept of party identification has become an anchor point in studies of electoral behaviour and is widely used in tracking change in voter-party relationships. At the same time, party identification is a much contested notion. One conceptual difficulty lies in grounding the voter–party relationship in 'the individual's affective orientation to an important group-object in his environment' (Campbell *et al.* 1960: 121); that is, a psychological attachment to a party which is apparently free of specifically political content. Another doubt arises about the conceptual independence of party identification: if electoral decisions are expressions of party identification, they become virtual equivalents.

Empirical difficulties also abound: in the American context, identification with one party does not preclude voting for another party; in the Western European context, partisan preference has often emerged as more stable than party identification. The effect of these difficulties has been to substitute the notion of partisanship for party identification, but with continuing debate about the origins and content of partisanship.

The third 'school' of voting studies centres on the concept of rational action drawn from economic theory, introduced by Downs in *An Economic Theory of Democracy* (1957). Amid the several variants spawned by this approach, the common premise is the capacity of electors to calculate the benefits of voting for one party rather than another. In so far as any 'reason' given for supporting a party might be construed as rational, and rationalisation easily confused with rationality, this premise is neither very controversial nor very useful. With no bounds set as to what kinds of reasons count as non-rational, the approach is non-falsifiable and can rapidly fall into tautology. The even more troublesome aspect of the rational choice approach is to point to the apparent irrationality of casting a vote at all. With each vote counting as only a fraction of the total vote for a winning candidate, the costs of voting, especially the information costs attached to the rational calculus, far exceed any possible benefits. The implications of 'rational abstention' cut two ways: on the one hand, it implies the uncomfortable conclusion that the popular element in representative government is rooted in irrationality; on the other hand, in the face of relatively high electoral turnouts in most countries, it implies that the rational choice approach is deficient as an explanatory form.

Despite such difficulties, the rational choice approach has proved highly fruitful in opening up new avenues to understanding electoral behaviour. Whereas the sociological approach has little to say about strictly political phenomena and the socio-psychological approach emphasises the affective elements in electoral politics, the rational choice approach has

stimulated a systematic search for the instrumental or issue-based grounds of electoral behaviour. Although modelling 'issue voting' is bedevilled by methodological problems, especially how to deal with confounding factors such as partisanship and issue trade-offs, this perspective is contributing to building up the picture of voters as, broadly, reasoning and purposeful citizens. Econometric models focusing on electors' evaluations of the economy, in personal and/or national terms, is a case in point. Second, in emphasising information costs, the rational choice approach suggests a degree of convergence between the three 'schools': in common with the sociological approach, social contexts are relevant as imparting political cues; in common with the socio-psychological approach, parties are represented as cue givers. Further, in contrast to – but not in contradiction of – both those approaches, Downs's model proposes an extensive role for political ideology in linking voters and parties, saving voters from having to be informed on a wide range of issues and saving parties from having to elicit voters' reactions to every policy proposal. Unfortunately, investigating the place of political ideology in electoral behaviour is hobbled by the costs of open-ended survey questions, so restricting most researchers to examining the competence of respondents in locating themselves and parties in terms of a left–right analytic dimension or to the degree of attitudinal constraint demonstrated across several issues. The lesson of Lane's *Political Ideology* (1962), that 'the common man' has an ordered understanding of politics which can be revealed by probing beneath the surface of political attitudes, has yet to be assimilated into the study of electoral behaviour.

Little in evidence in any of these perspectives on electoral behaviour is a sense of what might be expected of citizens in democratic regimes. That elections invest governments with legitimacy lies at the heart of democratic politics; that electors view elections in this light is untested. Again, democratic politics requires a readiness to accept that one's own interests or concerns do not prevail, but how voters view electoral defeat or painful policies is not part of the standard repertoire of national election studies. Instead, the sociological approach has moved on to examine the electoral effects of social context and social networks, while the socio-psychological approach has extended to examine the electoral influence of forms of political communication, especially television and, in countries with a partisan press, newspapers. However, recognition is gradually emerging that national electorates are both internally more heterogeneous and cross-nationally more differentiated than is implied by the common process of legitimating governments and holding them accountable via elections. By 'bringing back in' democratic theory, along with incorporating the behaviour of political elites and the effects of institutional arrangements in shaping electoral environments, electoral behaviour studies might get past the present impasse in which, by and large, despite some fifty years or so of consistent investigation, explanations of electoral behaviour are little more scrutable than hitherto.

See also:

accountability; authority; citizenship; cleavages; legitimacy; majoritarianism; political culture; representation, models of; suffrage

Further reading

Campbell, A., Converse, P., Miller, W. and Stokes, D (1960) *The American Voter*, New York: Wiley.

Franklin, M., Mackie, T., Valen, H. *et al.* (1992) *Electoral Change: Responses to Evolving Social and Attitudinal Structures in Western Countries*, Cambridge: Cambridge University Press.

Inglehart, R. (1977) *The Silent Revolution: Changing Values and Political Styles among Western Publics*, Princeton, NJ: Princeton University Press.

—— (1990) *Culture Shift in Advanced Industrial Societies*, Princeton, NJ: Princeton University Press.

Kriesi, H. (1998) 'The Transformation of Cleavage Politics', *European Journal of Political Research* 33(2): 165–85.

Lane, R.E. (1962) *Political Ideology: Why the American Common Man Believes What he Does*, New York: The Free Press of Glencoe.

Lazarsfeld, P., Berelson, B. and Gaudet, H. (1944) *The People's Choice*, New York: Columbia University Press.

Lipset, S. and Rokkan, S. (1967) 'Cleavage Structures, Party Systems, and Voter Alignments: An Introduction', in S. Lipset and S. Rokkan (eds), *Party Systems and Voter Alignments*, New York: Free Press.

Miller, W.E. and Shanks, J. M. (1966) *The New American Voter*, Cambridge, MA: Harvard University Press.

ELINOR SCARBROUGH

electoral campaigning

'Campaign' was originally a purely military term, deriving from the open country (*campagne*) in which a season's military operations were conducted. It was then applied figuratively to 'any course of action analogous to a military campaign, either in having a distinct period of activity, or in being of the nature of a struggle, or of an organised attempt aiming at a definite result' (*A New English Dictionary*, 1893). The reason for the extension of the term to the political realm is obvious. After all, PARTIES and candidates 'fight' ELECTIONS. Contemporary electoral campaigning is probably the area of political life that is most susceptible to the assumption that all has changed, an assumption that has not been discouraged by the new campaigners. However, the academic literature has always included a cautionary or sceptical note (see Agranoff (1976) for an early caution and Bartels (1992) for some systematic scepticism). In reviewing the issues involved, the military analogy remains useful because campaigns vary between countries and over time depending on the rules of combat, the characteristics of the combatants, the state of the technology and the nature of the terrain. The military analogy is preferable to the frequently used marketing analogy because the latter risks prejudicing the case.

The main rules of combat are constitutional or institutional. A campaign designed to achieve a victory that is defined as placing one individual in a single office (head of state or head of government or both) is not going to be the same as a campaign in which victory is marked by winning a majority of seats in an elected assembly. The elected assembly may go on to elect a single individual as head of government and voters may be more or less preoccupied with this indirect outcome. Nonetheless, the campaign will be essentially different in each case. A presidential system puts an overwhelming emphasis on the candidate; a parliamentary system may veer in this direction but it needs 'party' as a device to span the campaigns in the constituencies and to deliver victory in the assembly when the election is over. Congressional-style elections, being centred on individual representatives in each constituency and having no reference beyond that to the election of a leading office holder, have the greatest potential for individualisation and fragmentation and the least countervailing party effect. All of this means that no matter how much 'Americanisation' of campaigning is said to be taking place, presidential campaigns and congressional campaigns are, and will always be, different from campaigns in parliamentary systems.

As well as the function assigned to the assembly by the constitution, assembly election campaigns vary depending on the electoral system. This defines the arena within which the voter decides and the nature of the choice he or she confronts. It thus affects the relative weight of candidate versus party in that choice. Integrated campaigns focusing on party appeals in a national arena and directed from central party headquarters are most likely in fixed party-list systems operating in national constituencies. In all other systems assembly campaigns may aspire to this degree of co-ordination and centralisation, but they rarely fully meet it. The other main institutional variation that affects electoral campaigning is the level of governance involved, that is, whether it is national, sub-national or supranational. One analytical approach (the 'second-order election model') would suggest that this distinction is not of great importance because, it is argued, non-national elections tend, on close inspection, to be surrogate, national elections (Reif and Schmitt 1980). While this model has intuitive plausibility, it may underestimate the degree of autonomy of sub-national and supra-national elections and, therefore, underestimate the significance of the campaigns at sub-national and supra-national level (Blondel *et al.* 1998). Finally, in considering different kinds of electoral contests, REFERENDUMS must be included. Though very specific, their consequences for policy are clear-cut and can be highly significant (for example, Norway's repeated rejection of EEC/EU membership and Ireland's repeated referendums on abortion). Campaigning in referendums is fundamentally different from campaigning in elections. Because of this and because of the definitive consequences of referendums, the question of how referendum campaigns are conducted deserves greater attention than it has received.

The final element in the rules of combat is a matter of legislation and regulation rather than part of the institutional structure. Rules governing the raising and spending of campaign funds and public funding to support party activity and electoral campaigns are now a highly salient aspect of the rules of combat. They are important for three reasons. The first is the mounting costs of campaigning; the second is the presumption that different funding regimes will affect campaign behaviour; the third is the startling extent to which major political figures in several established democracies have been tarnished by their failure to adhere to the regulations, with the result that the process of electioneering becomes an election issue as well as a challenge to those concerned with good electoral practice.

Who the combatants are is partly determined by the rules of combat. It is also affected by more political factors such as the nature of the party system. Campaigns take on a different hue depending on whether the battle is fought between two or three main parties or between explicit or implicit alliances of smaller parties and depending on whether the style of political DECISION-MAKING is adversarial or consensual. In fact, electoral alliances may be only potential, in which case the range of lines of attack is curtailed by the need not to offend possible future partners in government (Farrell 1996). But the combatants are not just the commanders-in-chief (leaders of major parties) or the lieutenant-generals (leaders of smaller parties) who decide such things; nor are they just these plus the colonels (individual candidates). Others are needed to make it all work. Traditionally these others were the foot soldiers (party members) who stuffed the envelopes, who knocked on the doors, who put up the posters and who provided the sense of PARTICIPATION by (at least some of) the citizens. The challenge to the role of the foot soldiers comes from the technicians who control and direct the additional firepower that derives from the new campaign technologies.

It is a truism of studies of military campaigns that technology can determine the nature of the campaign and the outcome of the war. In war and politics, technology is mainly an exogenous factor. The greatest exogenous shock to traditional campaigning was the advent of television. This has made very substantial inroads on the old means of communicating with voters. While the medium is not yet the message, it certainly moulds it. Television news requires striking visual images and very few words. Hence the phenomena of the photo opportunity and the sound bite and hence the accusation of dumbing down. Here it is vital to distinguish between indirect and direct COMMUNICATION. Indirect communication is 'coverage' and, from the point of view of the campaigner, is particularly important. Coverage is free: equally importantly, it has the appearance of objectivity; it is the reporting of what has happened rather than the direct transmission of partisan appeals. The disadvantage is that coverage can be positive or negative. A fundamental objective of campaigning, therefore, is public relations and news management, that is, the creation of events or stories that project a favourable

image of the party or candidate. The instinct of the MEDIA is, naturally, to resist such manipulation and to look for the 'real' story behind the scenes. This points to a wider dilemma that confronts the media: should they focus on the substance or on the process? Is it more interesting for the viewer/reader to learn about the policies and records of the parties and candidates or about the battle itself, about strategy and tactics, about prospective winners and losers and, in the case of the latter, about the ensuing internecine power struggles? Opinion polls, which give hard evidence of who is ahead, reinforce the tendency to focus on process rather than substance.

Whereas campaigners can only strive to turn indirect communication (coverage) to their advantage, direct communication is more under their control. This kind of communication may still rely on the mass media in the form of potentially very expensive newspaper, radio and television advertising (where the latter is permitted) or free political party broadcasts (where they are provided). It also involves the appearance of the parties' candidates or spokespersons in radio and television debates. The summit of this is the debate between the prime ministerial or presidential candidates. As Bartels notes, in the American case 'these debates have probably focused more unmediated public attention on the candidates, their policies, and their political priorities than in any previous electoral era' (Bartels 1992: 269). From a partisan point of view this unmediated attention can be a problem. Debates are not fully controllable or predictable. This often leads strategists to seek to avoid in particular the potentially definitive clash between the candidates for the top job. And debate, like all direct party-originated communication, is subject to the problem of credibility. Confronted with glowing accounts of the achievements of the party or glittering promises of future action and knowing that the source of the communication is partisan, the potential voter may substantially discount the message. This reaction may be less powerful if the message concentrates on the bad points of the other side, since saying bad things rather than good things about politicians carries a higher initial credibility rating; hence the tendency to negative campaigning.

Technological change has also affected the more traditional forms of direct campaign communication. Electronic data banks have taken some of the drudge and guesswork out of mail shots. Telephone canvassing supplements or even replaces door-to-door canvassing, which in any event has always shown an uneven spread across countries. And television has an effect here too: there is no point in knocking at the door when the main evening news or current affairs programme is being beamed into the living room inside. In fact, it is likely to irritate the interested elector and may deprive him or her of sight of the party's leading candidate(s) or spokespersons. One should not, however, conclude that the contribution of party or candidate volunteers can be dispensed with; telephone calls do not happen automatically and hands are still needed to stuff the data banks.

Fundamental changes in campaign technology have not been confined to the technology of communication. The military analogy remains useful; battles are frequently won or lost on the quality of intelligence gathering. In this respect, the second half of the twentieth century witnessed major technical advances. One-shot national opinion polls, tracking polls, polls in marginal constituencies and focus groups have transformed the intelligence that underpins the campaign. Here again, the tendency is for technological change to put a premium on technical skills over traditional political judgement and experience. At the extreme, this tendency raises the issue of who makes the policy that is offered to the elector; the polling consultants or the politicians. On the other hand, one should be wary of attributing omniscience and omnipotence to the campaign professionals and consultants. This is because the terrain on which the electoral battle is fought has yet to be fully mapped, by either the consultants or the political scientists (see PSEPHOLOGY).

The terrain on which the electoral campaign is conducted is the POLITICAL CULTURE of electoral competition. This comprises the elec-

torate's knowledge, perceptions, issue preferences, attitudes, interest, attention span, resources, habits, prejudices, loyalties and behavioural propensities. That this terrain has changed cannot be gainsaid. Traditional CLEAVAGES have become less salient. For many voters, fixed reference points such as party attachment have worn away, leaving the field open to the incursion of issues and to struggles by parties or candidates to establish the salience of those issues on which they are ahead. A further consequence of the changed terrain is the increasing difficulty of mobilising the vote, another fall in turnout often being the most striking outcome of a campaign. These changes have razed the potential gains from campaigning. However, a good deal of uncertainty still attaches to the question of how to ensure these gains. Despite all the consultancy and despite the fact that full-scale election studies, where they exist, now give greater priority to the study of campaign and media effects, Bartel's judgement remains valid, namely that 'much less is known in general about the impact of modern election campaigns on voters than one might gather from a superficial reading of the literature' (Bartels 1992: 263).

The evaluative issues that are said to arise from the new, or perhaps not so new campaigning can be summarised under three headings: cost, content and control. The cost dilemma and its implications are the most clear-cut and far-reaching. Campaign costs rise inexorably; meeting those costs risks undermining the integrity of the process. As noted above, the public funding of referendum campaigns raises in a particularly stark form the issue of who should receive such funding and in what proportions? The dilemma of content confronts both the parties and the media: is the content of campaign communication to be mainly about substance or about process? The more the latter predominates, the more the electors become spectators rather than actors or, at least, the more they are likely to become actors who fail to turn out for their chorus part in the final act. However, one should be wary of exaggerating this point. Even allowing for all the space or time devoted to the process or the battle, campaign coverage still tends to present the potential voter with large amounts of political substance; and the substance might be even more forbidding if interest were not whipped up by reports from the front. The control dilemma is acute in theory but less so in practice. Given that campaign strategy is an inexact science, Kavanagh's contention that there is 'little support [for] the notion that a group of media and public relations maestros manipulates voters and politicians' is probably widely applicable (Kavanagh 1995: 250). The main lesson from campaign studies for both political actors and political scientists is that, ultimately, the voters decide.

See also:

communication; elections; electoral volatility; media; public opinion; psephology; referendums

Further reading

Agranoff, R. (1976) 'The New Style of Campaigning: The Decline of Party and the Rise of Candidate-Centred Technology', in R. Agranoff (ed.), *The New Style in Election Campaigns*, 2nd edn, Boston: Holbrook Press, 3–48.

Bartels, L.M. (1992) 'The Impact of Electioneering in the United States', in D. Butler and A. Ranney (eds), *Electioneering: A Comparative Study of Continuity and Change*, Oxford: Clarendon, 244–77.

Blondell, J., Sinnott, R. and Svensson, P. (1998) *People and Parliament in the European Union: Participation, Democracy and Legitimacy*, Oxford: Oxford University Press.

Buchanan, B. (1996) *Renewing Presidential Politics: Campaigns, Media and the Public Interest*, Lanham, MD: Rowman and Littlefield.

Denver, D. and Hands, G. (1997) *Modern Constituency Electioneering: Local Campaigns in the 1992 General Election*, London: Frank Cass.

Farrell, D.M. (1996) 'Campaign Strategies and Tactics', in L. LeDuc, R.G. Niemi and P. Norris (eds), *Comparing Democracies: Elec-tions and Voting in Comparative Perspective*, London: Sage, 160–83.

Johnson-Carter, K.S. and Copeland, G.A. (1997) *Inside Political Campaigns: Theory and Practice*, Westport, CT: Praeger.

Kaid, L.L., Gerstle, J. and Sanders, K.R. (1991) *Mediated Politics in Two Cultures: Presidential Campaigning in the United States and France*, Westport, CT: Praeger.

Kavanagh, D. (1995) *Election Campaigning: The New Marketing of Politics*, Oxford: Blackwell.

Reif, K.-H. and Schmitt, H. (1980) 'Nine Second-Order Elections: A Conceptual Framework for the Analysis of European Election Results', *European Journal of Political Research* 8: 3–44.

RICHARD SINNOTT

electoral competition

ELECTIONS are the key defining democratic institution in the sense that they are crucial in bringing government policy into line with popular preferences. Some countries hold popular votes directly on whether or not to adopt particular policies (see DIRECT DEMOCRACY). In most, however, the main decision electors make is whether to continue with the existing government (retrospective voting) or to choose an alternative government better able to handle problems in the immediate future (prospective voting).

Combining these two is not easy: what if the most likely party to handle a pressing problem is currently in government? In general it seems that the electorate reward incumbents with slightly more votes if everything is going well, punish them with a moderate withdrawal of support if 'opposition' problems are not being solved, and with a major withdrawal of support if they have not solved problems for which they claim particular competence (above all, unemployment for left-wing parties and inflation for right-wing parties).

All this assumes that there *is* an alternative party government to vote for. In 'grand coalitions' grouping all significant parties (for example, in Switzerland and Austria) there clearly is not, so electors cannot register a policy choice in general elections. Where post-election coalition negotiations, rather than election results, determine which PARTIES form the government, voters are also largely deprived of an election choice (see CHAOS AND COALITIONS; COALITIONS). Only where there are two different, clearly defined alternatives (parties or electoral alliances of parties competing with each other to form a government) can electors make definite policy-based choices between them.

Party choices

These considerations point up the central organising role of parties in elections. It is no exaggeration to say that parties are as important to elections as voters. Without clear party alternatives, election results cannot determine what government will form or what policy it will pursue. It is no coincidence therefore that the spread of democracy over the last 150 years has been closely bound up with the development of parties, and electoral competition between them to control the government.

Competition and division of the national forces was originally regarded as subversive and debilitating. Even democrats regarded parties with suspicion and wanted the best men elected, not those under suspicion of putting party interests above those of the nation. The public interest would be best served by the best individuals debating and voting according to their conscience, not party dictates.

A growing awareness of deficiencies in this argument gradually legitimised parties:

1   What is in the 'public interest' depends on where you are in the society. There are legitimate differences between various social groups, represented by their parties. It is best to let policy compromises emerge from free debate and competition between them, if the happiness of the greatest number is to be secured.
2   Without party labels, electors are unlikely to

know what policies individual representatives have supported in the past, or what they will do in the future, and thus cannot make an informed voting choice. When grouped in a party, however, representatives have a collective government record and alternative policies for the future which they put before electors to attract their votes. Such policies, usually summarised in a single document issued at the beginning of the election (the 'manifesto', 'platform' or 'election programme') constitute the focus of party competition in most elections.

Party objectives

How parties compete depends on *what* they are. Are they tools of self-aggrandising leaders who will offer anything in order to get office? Or are they social organisations firmly rooted in particular sectors and groups, whose ideology and interests they cannot abandon without alienating core supporters essential to winning? This sharp contrast between office seeking and policy pursuit is probably overdrawn, if only because effecting policy requires parties to be in government, while office seeking requires parties to offer voters something that *they* want. Policy and office goals are thus compatible with each other, up to a point. They define the ends of a continuum rather than constituting an exclusive dichotomy. However, individual parties may be located closer to one end than to the other. Some parties, notably in Ireland, Italy (1945–92) and Japan seem more oriented to office. Most, however, including the American Democrats and Republicans, take policy seriously.

Modes of electoral competition

A party whose sole concern was office might seek to win it by offering electors what the majority wanted. It could do this because it would not have fixed policy goals and could therefore adapt itself to whatever policy package seemed most likely to attract votes. In practice this would mean that it adopted the policy preference of the median voter, as that would maximise its votes. As all other (office seeking) parties would do the same they would all converge on the preference of the median voter, thus ensuring a stable and predictable government outcome if the policy-space was one-dimensional (such as left–right).

There is considerable evidence from analysis of party manifestos that the space in which electoral competition takes place is left–right and one-dimensional. Given office-seeking parties, this guarantees that government policy will be as close as it can be to the preferences of the majority. The thesis that parties are becoming increasingly office seeking and 'catch-all' in nature, pursuing votes wherever they can be got, has been quite influential over the last forty years. It is possible therefore that this view of party competition is broadly correct. According to 'catch-all' ideas, office-seeking parties would be so much more electorally successful than policy-pursuing ones that the latter will have to adapt or be driven out of business.

While the idea of parties and governments perfectly duplicating majority preferences seems very democratic (the majority will always becomes government policy), it does present some difficulties. If all parties offer the same policy to electors and therefore have no distinguishable records what is the point of having parties at all, in policy terms? Electors might as well vote directly on policy alternatives, as the parties offer none. In light of the importance of parties in presenting the electorate with clear-cut choices and alternative policies, emphasised above, a failure to do so would deprive electors of occasions to discuss and debate policy. Debate is almost as central to democratic practices as having elections in the first place, so its suppression by party collusion on policy is serious (see DEMOCRATIC DEBATE). This is all the more true as (a) what the median electoral preference is, is often unclear and (b) it may shift in response to discussion; not a possibility envisaged in the 'office seeking' view of election competition, where electors' preferences stay fixed.

Under a policy-pursuing interpretation parties maintain internally consistent but recogni-

sably different policy positions. There is little point in changing well-established positions much since (a) parties cannot, because of uncertainty about the 'real' median position, easily find it; (b) their most reliable 'core' supporters would be put off by shifting policy around, and; (c) to link with such supporters and to provide leaders with a means of interpreting an uncertain world, parties rely on an ideology (socialism, liberalism and so on), which focuses their attention on key developments and instructs them how to respond to them. Reliance on a relatively unchanging ideology limits policy movement and imposes policy consistency on parties. Such policy constraints show up very clearly under empirical analysis of party issue positions, and go against the idea of unrestricted party flexibility. One effect is to make individual parties unresponsive to external developments and to PUBLIC OPINION. Over the party system as a whole, however, electors can shop around for the party with the best policy for current problems. If unemployment is high a left-wing choice can be made or if inflation is bad, a right-wing one. As always, this assumes that parties will form distinct and separate governments and thus offer a clear choice to the electorate.

The saliency theory of electoral competition

Party policies are thus fixed and known, while electoral preferences are uncertain and volatile. This imposes a particular logic on party competition. Parties cannot change their policy position easily but they can try to upgrade or downgrade the importance of particular issues in an election. In particular, they can try to emphasise those issues on which they feel they have an advantage through election rhetoric and debate, and de-emphasise those which 'belong' to rivals by not mentioning them. If they win the argument about which issues are important and put 'their' issues at the centre, they can reasonably hope to gain votes.

Election debate typically consists therefore not of parties putting alternatives forward on the same issue but of parties talking past each other about different priorities: the right's emphasis on (cutting) taxes will be countered by the left's stress on (expanding) services. One election is distinguished from another by the issues prominent in it. Even in the same election however the different party manifestos often seem to refer to totally different situations, one painting a glowing picture of free enterprise surging ahead amid general prosperity, another pointing to growing social disparity and the need for government to intervene.

These are consistent themes of the political debate advanced by the competing parties. They enable the electorate to choose a suitable government by offering a range of alternative policies, from which the appropriate one for a particular situation can be selected. The medicine appropriate for coughs last month may not be appropriate for indigestion today. But another one, which is suitable, is available on the shelves. In this way relatively rigid parties guarantee real electoral competition and a binding popular choice between relatively clear alternatives.

See also:

decision-making; democratic debate; electoral behaviour; parties; public opinion

Further reading

Arrow, K.J. (1951) *Social Choice and Individual Values*, New York: Wiley.

Budge, I. (1994) 'A New Spatial Theory of Party Competition', *British Journal of Political Science* 24: 443–67.

Downs, A. (1957) *An Economic Theory of Democracy*, New York: Harper.

Riker, W. (ed.) (1993) *Agenda Formation*, Ann Arbor, MI: University of Michigan Press.

Robertson, D. (1976) *A Theory of Party Competition*, London: Wiley.

IAN BUDGE

electoral systems

The term 'electoral system' refers in theory to the entire set of the rules relevant to the conduct of an election. In practice, the term is generally used by political scientists in the more narrow sense, to designate procedures for delineating constituencies, formatting ballots and allocating elected offices among contestants. Though systems must be established for ELECTIONS to fill any office, the procedures to which most academic attention has been devoted are those for the election of representative assemblies. Accordingly, most of the present discussion will focus on parliamentary electoral systems, though some attention will be given also to the election of single posts such as presidents.

Until the twentieth century, the norm in most states that held elections was to elect one or possibly two representatives from each constituency by plurality (simple majority) or absolute majority vote. In an era when communications and transport networks were poorly developed, parliamentary representatives provided a vital link between the capital and territorially disparate regions. In most European states, the period of mass enfranchisement at the end of the nineteenth and the beginning of the twentieth centuries brought with it a switch to electoral systems whereby PARTIES receive seats in proportion to the number of votes they win. There are three main reasons for this change. First, the territorial dimension of politics became less important when industry overtook agriculture as the mainstay of the economy and communications links improved. Occupation-based divisions in the electorate gained in political importance as increasingly diverse groups entered the electorate. Second, old elites sought to use proportional representation to maintain their grip on power in anticipation of the newly enfranchised masses dominating politics. Finally, the change was an effort to reduce the high degree of uncertainly surrounding elections in single-member constituencies, where small shifts in party support could generate large changes in outcome (Carstairs 1980). Most democracies in the world today have electoral systems that incorporate some form of proportional representation (Reynolds and Reilly 1997) (see REPRESENTATION, MODELS OF).

Types of electoral system

No two electoral systems are exactly alike, because abstract principles of electoral design must always be adapted to the needs of concrete situations, which vary from country to country and period to period. It is useful, therefore, to identify the most important distinguishing characteristics of electoral systems, which are district magnitude, aggregative mechanism, object of vote choice and ballot structure. In each case, the choice among components of INSTITUTIONAL DESIGN can be linked to particular understandings of the democratic process.

District magnitude is a matter of how many legislators are elected from each electoral district (constituency). In theory, constituencies could be defined according to any criterion on which members of the electorate differ; in practice, they are virtually always defined in terms of geography of residence. As suggested above, small district magnitudes emphasise the link between territory and representation, whereas larger constituency sizes focus attention more squarely on non-geographical political CLEAVAGES.

The *aggregative mechanism* is the formula governing the translation of votes into seats, or, more simply put, the rule for determining who the winners are. Aggregative mechanisms can be classified into three general families on the basis of district magnitude: single-member, multi-member and hybrid systems. One device often incorporated into the aggregative mechanism is a 'threshold' of representation, which excludes from the distribution process all parties, and/or candidates that have not achieved a certain percentage of the popular vote. Thresholds are generally considered a means of filtering out small extremist parties and reducing the size of parliamentary party systems to manageable proportions.

Object of vote choice refers to whether people vote for people or for parties, whether elections are seen as being about selecting individual rulers or selecting teams brought together by a common ideology. Systems in which people vote for individuals are said to have the benefit that they are more 'direct' and that they strengthen the link between representatives and represented. They also tend to weaken parties, as politicians can gain support on the basis of their personal popularity, without the party as an intermediary.

Ballot structure is a question of whether 'what people want' is understood in terms of absolute or relative preferences. Most electoral systems require voters to make a choice for one option among others. Ballots designed on this principle are known as categorical ballots. But voters often do not simply have one favoured party; their perception of the political spectrum may well involve evaluations of relative strengths and weaknesses. Some systems allow voters to reflect their relative evaluations of the different candidates/parties in the way they vote by asking them to rank in order their preferences. Such ballots are known as 'ordinal' ballots.

There are many possible permutations of these four categories. Only the most common will be examined here.

Single-member systems

Single-member systems (SM) are defined by the fact that district magnitude is in all cases one. They have the common characteristic that the object of choice is typically a person, not a party. They differ, however, according to the aggregative mechanism and the ballot structure they employ. The most important distinction within this family is between those that require an absolute majority winner and those in which a plurality of the vote suffices.

Single member simple plurality (SMSP). Also known as 'first-past-the-post', the single-member simple plurality system is one in which the candidate to gain the largest number of votes in each constituency is declared the winner, and there is only one winner per constituency. This system is employed in the UK, the USA, Canada and many of Britain's former colonies. It is simple to use and to understand, and it has the benefit of generating a clear line of accountability between each member of the assembly and relatively small groups of voters responsible for that member's success.

The *double ballot* (DB). MAJORITARIANISM – the idea that no decision should be taken if more people oppose than support it – is one of the main principles of democracy. With two options, the choice of a majority winner is not difficult, provided everyone chooses. But with more than two options, problems arise. The most common way of solving the problem is to hold multiple ballots. In the first ballot, or round, everyone votes for their preferred option, and then if no option receives an absolute majority, a second round, or 'run-off' is held between the two candidates who place highest in the first round. This ensures that the eventual winner will have absolute majority support. Furthermore, the need of candidates to appeal in the second round to the supporters of their eliminated first-round rivals is said to encourage moderation. The main disadvantage of this system, and the reason it has been abandoned by most countries, is the cost associated with holding two rounds of voting. The DB system was widely used in Europe into the nineteenth century, and it has lingered on in non-competitive elections held in many communist or former communist states. It is currently used also in France and several former French colonies.

The *alternative vote* (AV). The alternative vote, used at the national level in the Australian lower house and the legislature of Nauru, is a rank-ordering system that achieves an absolute majority outcome with only one round of voting. Voters are asked not only who their first preference is, but who they would choose if their first preference were eliminated. If voters are required to provide a full preference ranking, this gives the vote counters enough information to determine which candidate has absolute majority support by eliminating the weakest candidates in order of strength and transferring second and lower preference votes

to other candidates until one candidate has more than fifty per cent of all the votes cast. AV has the same advantages as DB; it generates an absolute majority outcomes and it encourages parties to make a broad appeal in order to attract second-choice votes.

Multi-member systems

A large number of aggregative mechanisms have historically been used in multi-member constituencies. One of the simplest and oldest methods is to give each voter a certain number of votes, typically ranging from one to the number of seats in his or her constituency, and to award seats to the candidates who win the largest number of votes (single non-transferable vote or limited vote). Another method is to require parties to field lists for each constituency, and in each case to give all the seats in the constituency to the party that wins the greatest number of votes for its list (bloc vote). But most contemporary multi-member systems are designed to reflect the principle of PROPORTIONALITY. The two main types of system in this category – list proportional representation and the single transferable vote – differ in ballot structure, object of choice and aggregative mechanism.

List proportional representation (list PR). Most of Western Europe and Latin America employ list PR, a system in which voters typically select one from a number of parties listed on a nominal ballot, sometimes with the option of choosing and/or ranking candidates within the list of the party selected (known as open lists). In some list PR systems – that of Switzerland, for example – voters are even allowed to select candidates across lists. In all list PR systems, the outcome is calculated in terms of the proportional support for each of the parties that field lists. But given that a perfectly proportional distribution of seats is rarely possible, complex methods must be employed to approximate this ideal, and some methods generate more proportional results than others. The most common formula is the 'highest averages' method in which parties' vote shares are divided by a series of divisors.

At each stage a seat is given to the party with the highest 'average' total, whereupon this party's total is divided again. Another common method is the 'largest remainders' technique whereby a quota for success is calculated, and seats are distributed to parties according to how many quotas each party achieves. The remaining seats are then shared out among the parties that have the greatest number of votes left over from the first stage of allocation.

The *single transferable vote* (STV) is a rank-ordering system with multi-member constituencies. As in AV, voters order candidates, but because there are several seats to distribute the counting procedure is more complex. First, a quota for success is calculated and seats are distributed to candidates according to the number of quotas achieved in first-preference votes. The remaining seats are allocated by alternatively transferring votes in excess of the quota and votes of the lowest ranking candidates to voters' second and subsequent choices until all the seats are filled. This system has the merit that votes are distributed efficiently; all or virtually all votes go to the election of some candidate, and no candidate is elected with more votes than he or she needs. STV is also commonly defended as a system that combines the best of SMSP and list PR: it generates relative proportionality of outcomes while at the same time preserving the link between the voter and the individual legislator. The main perceived disadvantages are the complexity of the counting procedure, and the fact that the competition it encourages among candidates within the same party can give rise to patronage politics. STV is currently used at the national level in Ireland and Malta, as well as the Australian and Nepalese upper chambers.

Hybrid systems

A growing number of electoral systems are based on combinations of the various types listed above. Many combinations are possible, but there are two that are widespread enough to merit detailed attention.

Two-tier PR systems. One of the most common hybrid forms of list-PR system is that involving two tiers, typically a primary tier involving regional constituencies, and a secondary tier through which a smaller number of seats are distributed at a higher level (usually national). The second tier is generally envisaged as a means of giving seats to parties too small to win representation at the regional level but with large enough state-wide support to be important political actors. In systems that use the largest remainders method of seats allocation, such as the Austrian, the votes remaining after the distribution of seats at the regional level are pooled at the national level. When the highest averages method is used at the regional level, as in Denmark, the second tier is typically composed of compensatory seats for small parties.

Mixed PR-SM systems. Another common hybrid system is that in which a proportion of the seats are elected in single member constituencies and the remainder from national lists (sometimes referred to as the additional member system or the mixed member system). In systems of this type, voters typically have two votes, one for the local constituency member and one for the party list of their choice. In some cases (Germany, Hungary, New Zealand), the list seats are allocated in such a way as to compensate for the disproportionalities induced by the distribution of single-member seats. These are known as compensatory mixed systems. In other cases (Japan, Russia, Macedonia), the two parts of the electoral system operate in parallel and are entirely separate (though there is no difference of parliamentary status among representatives elected in the two ways). These are known as parallel mixed systems. Like STV, mixed systems are favoured by many electoral system designers because they are perceived as combining the best of list-PR (proportional outcomes) with the best of SM systems (the link between representative and represented). Notable is the dramatic rise of the number of mixed systems in the world today. A decade after the end of the Second World War, Germany was virtually the only country with a mixed system, whereas a decade after the end of the Cold War there were over two dozen such states.

So far, the focus has mainly been on elections to representative assemblies. But it is also worth considering elections to single-member offices, most especially presidencies. There are two principal mechanisms through which single-member presidencies are elected: plurality and absolute majority. An absolute majority system (AV or, more commonly, DB) is often seen as preferable for use in presidential elections, in that presidential elections aggregate decision-making to the highest level possible. Unlike a member of a collective body such as a legislature, a president is able to generate certain political outcomes directly and unilaterally. There are also more practical reasons why it is an advantage to have a president who commands majority support of popular opinion, as this increases the likelihood that he or she will be associated with a party (or coalition) that holds a majority of seats in the legislature (see PRESIDENTIALISM).

The effects of electoral systems

The effects electoral systems exert on the political life of a polity depend to a great extent on the socio-economic, geographical and constitutional structure of the country, as well as on historical traditions and political culture. Yet certain regularities have been observed in the workings of different system types. Most studies of electoral systems have focused on their effects on the composition of parliament, with particular reference to two measures: proportionality in the vote-to-seat relationship, and the number of parties represented. Empirical research has demonstrated that district magnitude is the single most important factor in determining the extent to which the distribution of seats in parliament corresponds to the distribution of party support among the electorate (Taagepera and Shugart 1989; Lijphart 1994). Systems, such as those of Britain and the Canada, in which one member is elected from each constituency tend to be the least proportionate, all else being equal, whereas those in which the entire

country is one constituency, such as Israel and the Netherlands, tend to generate highly proportionate outcomes. Most states fall somewhere in between these two extremes, in that they have regionally defined multi-member constituencies and moderate levels of disproportionality.

The size of the PARTY SYSTEMS generated by different electoral regimes can be thought of also as the extent to which different systems aggregate preferences. Electoral regimes that typically generate large party systems aggregate preferences less than those that generate parliaments with fewer parties. In the former case, other mechanisms within the parliamentary process must be employed to generate choices; in the latter case, the electoral process is highly aggregative and is often sufficient by itself to produce a legislature in which one party commands a majority sufficient to make decisions. The ideal balance between preference aggregation through the electoral process and preference aggregation through the parliamentary process is a matter of JUDGEMENT, but it is often held that electorally generated preference aggregation gives more power to voters, whereas aggregation accomplished by parliamentary means allows parties to have more control.

In the 1950s, French political scientist Maurice Duverger formulated what has become known as 'Duverger's law' of the effects of electoral system on party system. Duverger's law holds that SMSP electoral laws tend to produce two-party systems, whereas PR laws allow the development of multi-party systems (Duverger 1959). Subsequent empirical research on established democracies has indeed found that, by and large, single-member systems tend to generate smaller party systems than proportional representation (Taagepera and Shugart 1989; Lijphart 1994; Katz 1997). This is because single-member systems require a party to command a large number of votes at the constituency level to get any seats at all. This blocks out small parties and magnifies the seat-winning success of large parties relative to their share of the vote. Proportional systems, on the other hand, give seats even to small parties (provided they can get enough votes to cross the thresholds most such systems include). Yet the typical effects of electoral institutions in established democracies are not always replicated in democratising countries. Single-member systems have been found to encourage localisation and party system fragmentation in many democratising countries, especially those with weak states and recent party system formation. Under such conditions, thresholds are a more reliable means of reducing the number of parties in parliament, while still maintaining relative proportionality in the strengths of those parties that do enter.

Developments in electoral system design

Electoral system design is influenced by polity-specific understandings of democratic principles, by historical tradition and by foreign examples. But conscious efforts by groups and organisations to design electoral systems to achieve specific ends are also common. There has been a wave of electoral reform associated with the third wave of democratisation (see WAVES OF DEMOCRACY). One general lesson that has been learned from these reform efforts is that electoral systems cannot solve all a state's problems, many of which are often social, economic or political, and need to be solved by other means. A corollary to this is that electoral engineering should not be used as a substitute for reforms to the structure and functions of the office filled by the election. If parliament is not functioning properly, the fault most likely lies in the design of parliament, not the design of the electoral system. Similarly, if there are problems with the executive, then the means of forming this body and its relation to other branches of power should be considered before tampering with electoral structures. An electoral system provides a set of incentives that channels political wills; it does not change the substance of those wills. This is perhaps why electoral system designers tend to be most successful when their aims are most modest.

See also:

elections; parliamentary models; parties; party systems; presidentialism; representation, models of

Further reading

Carstairs, A.M. (1980) *A Short History of Electoral Systems in Western Europe*, London: George Allen and Unwin.

Duverger, M. (1959) *Political Parties: Their Organisation and Activity in the Modern State*, 2nd edn, London: John Wiley.

Farrell, D.M. (1997) *Comparing Electoral Systems*, Basingstoke: Macmillan.

Katz, R. (1997) *Democracy and Elections*, Oxford and New York: Oxford University Press.

Lijphart, A. (1994) *Electoral Systems and Party Systems: A Study of Twenty-Seven Democracies, 1945–1990*, Oxford: Oxford University Press.

Lijphart, A. and Grofman, B. (eds) (1984) *Choosing an Electoral System: Issues and Alternatives*, New York: Praeger.

—— (eds) (1986) *Electoral Laws and their Political Consequences*, New York: Agathon Press.

Powell, G.B. (1982) *Contemporary Democracies: Participation, Stability, and Violence*, Cambridge, MA: Harvard University Press.

Reeve, A. and Ware, A. (1992) *Electoral Systems: A Comparative and Theoretical Introduction*, London and New York: Routledge.

Reynolds, A. and Reilly, B. (eds) (1977) *International IDEA Handbook of Electoral System Design*, Stockholm: International IDEA.

Taagepera, R. and Shugart, M.S. (1989) *Seats and Votes: The Effects and Determinants of Electoral Systems*, New Haven, CT and London: Yale University Press.

SARAH BIRCH

electoral volatility

Electoral volatility denotes a dynamic property of any party system in any democratic regime. It refers to the fact that some voters, from one election to the next, will switch their votes among parties, switch from voting to non-voting, or vice versa. As a reflection of these switches in individual behaviour the format of the party system, that is, its distribution of votes among parties and the number of parties operating in the ELECTIONS, will tend to change over time. At the same time the behaviour of individual voters will be affected by the very same party system format and by changes in the format. It is this complex and dynamic characteristic, which is summarised by the concept of electoral volatility, and which is often measured by means of a specially devised index of electoral volatility.

It follows from this encircling introduction that at least two types of electoral volatility are in existence and lend themselves to theoretical as well as operational definition. The first, gross electoral volatility, is the total amount of vote switching in a party system. It is also termed individual level volatility, referring to the level at which it is measured. It will theoretically range from a zero-situation with total identity of the electorate over time and with no voters at all changing their vote, to a situation in which every single voter will behave differently from one election to the next. From panel studies it is known that neither of these polar situations will ever materialise, and that in real elections considerable differences among elections and across party systems are to be expected, even if most of the voters most of the time will tend to behave in such a way that gross volatility will be closer to the low end than to the high end of theoretical variation. The widely used concepts of critical elections, de-alignment, re-alignment, normal vote and so on are used to capture and describe the various situations.

Gross electoral volatility is next reflected in net electoral volatility, also termed aggregate volatility. This concept is basically defined as 'the net change within the electoral party system resulting from individual vote transfers' (Pedersen 1979).

Net electoral volatility can be measured in several ways, but there seems to be a growing consensus about using for its measurement the so-called Pedersen Index, which is defined as half of the sum of the net changes in the relative electoral strength of all competing parties. This index has the attractive property that it is easy to calculate, and it varies between 0 and 100. It can also be interpreted as the cumulated gains for all winning parties in the party system, or the cumulated losses of all losers. Its range of variation thus has a straightforward interpretation, and it can even be expressed in terms of a simple percentage.

For all its simplicity this measure also has its ambiguity, which has led to criticisms and several attempts to improve it (Bartolini and Mair 1990; Crewe and Denver 1985). Changing turnout can be dealt with in the index by including non-voters as if they constituted a party. Distinctions between important and not so important parties can also be introduced. Most interesting, perhaps, has been the introduction of a related concept of 'intra-bloc volatility' and 'inter-bloc volatility', which measures net vote transfers within as well as across blocs of parties, typically 'left' and 'right' blocs, that is, those aggregate groups or COALITIONS within the party system which compete for control over governments. Not unexpectedly, 'inter-bloc volatility' tends on the average to be lower than the uncorrected volatility.

On the other hand, the persistent popularity of net volatility as a measure of electoral change may also stem from its reliability. While most studies of gross volatility encounter grave measurement problems because of the well-known low reliability of recall data, especially when non-voters are included, the net volatility measure is based on easily available and fairly precise data, which are produced by the public electoral process itself.

Gross and net volatility are related phenomena, but they are not identical. To make inferences from one to the other constitutes a well-known logical fallacy. Even very high amounts of individual vote switching may produce low net volatility, if votes are transferred in equal proportions across the party system. Several studies have, however, documented that a strong empirical relationship does exist, by which, at least in multiparty systems, 50–75 per cent of the gross volatility is showing up as net volatility (for example, Lane and Ersson 1997).

In early studies it was found that West European PARTY SYSTEMS differed considerably in terms of levels of electoral volatility. More interesting was, however, the finding that volatility tended to decline in some party systems, and, noteworthy, to grow considerably in some others (Pedersen 1979). This finding led to a prolonged discussion between those, who, in the tradition of the Norwegian scholar Stein Rokkan, believe that European party systems and the underlying CLEAVAGES in the electorates 'froze' in a fairly stable format around 1920, and those who doubt that this generalisation is still valid.

Later studies have cast doubt of the amount of genuine change in party system formats in Western Europe (for example, Bartolini and Mair 1990), but each time such doubts are raised they tend to be contradicted by eruptions of electoral volatility in Italy, the Netherlands or elsewhere. By taking analyses of electoral volatility from the level of national electoral party systems to the much more volatile level of municipal and local levels new dimensions may also be added to the Western European discussion.

If this theoretically important discussion is still an open one in Western Europe, it is beyond doubt that the concept is useful as a summary measure of political change in other parts of the world. Thus the very high levels of electoral volatility in the newly democratising Eastern and Central European nations have been given much attention (for example, Mair 1997). Levels of electoral volatility in Central and South American party systems have also been found to be relatively high and widely differing (Mainwaring and Scully 1995).

The empirical ranges of electoral volatility thus lead to the observation that even if there may, in the short run, exist a 'normal' level of electoral volatility within a given party system, such levels may vary considerably across party systems, and very few party systems are immune against increasing electoral volatility. Even if 'earthquake elections' are still unusual phenomena, they are not as rare as they used to be.

It is one thing to describe and map in a comparative way the variation of electoral volatility. It is quite another task to explain this dynamic phenomenon and to understand its various political effects. Explanations will often take their departure in aspects of the social structure or the values of the electorate. Here the emphasis is on the level of the individual voter, and increasing net volatility is interpreted in terms of increasing gross volatility, which in turn is seen as a result of some kind of partisan dealignment, decrease in party identification and so on. Some authors aptly conceptualise the relationship as one between 'surface stability' and 'deep structural stability' (Lane and Ersson 1997).

Explanations may, however, also take their departure in observations of changes in the party system itself, that is, in the contextual situation in which voters make up their minds and participate in the election. Thus it has been demonstrated that not only an increasing, but also a decreasing, number of competing parties will tend to lead to higher electoral volatility. Thus there is an effect stemming from the party system format as well as from changes in that format.

The effects of changing volatility on other phenomena are also worthwhile studying. Electoral volatility can be conceptually as well as empirically linked to other variables that relate to political phenomena that are subsequent to the election, i.e. first and foremost the composition of the elective assembly and the composition of the government.

The attractiveness of the concept of electoral volatility stems not only from the easiness of its operational measurement, but also from its generic qualities. First, it is one of those relatively rare concepts in the study of politics, in which time is treated as an essential variable, where the values of a variable at a given moment in time is interpreted in terms not only of values at other times, but also in terms of other variables, which are related to and measured at other moments in time.

Second, and perhaps more important, volatility is a very general concept. Conceptually it is probably derived from chemistry, where it refers to a change in the character of a substance from one state to another, i.e. from liquid to gas (Farlie and Budge 1978). The high level of abstraction may be the main reason for the survival of this concept in the, otherwise very volatile, political science vocabulary. Political scientists have not only made distinctions between gross and net volatility. They also distinguish between various types of intra-party system volatility, 'bloc volatility' and so on. Successful attempts have also been made to relate electoral volatility to 'seat volatility' in parliaments (Lane and Ersson 1997). As many electoral systems tend to translate electoral change in a magnifying way, the average level of 'seat volatility' is somewhat higher than electoral volatility. In some cases, as in France and Italy, the amount of 'seat volatility' has reached very high levels in recent elections. The potential of the concept of volatility for studying change over time in recruitment patterns, turnover, seniority and so on is also obvious, as is the potential for using the volatility concept in studies of cabinet compositions, changes in administrative leadership positions and so on. Apparently, a major quality of the concept is its applicability to the study of change in any kind of political system. Therefore the natural science analogy can, and maybe should, take political science scholars in many different exploratory directions. At least it is worthwhile trying to explore the boundaries of utilisation of a very general, albeit also ambiguous, concept.

See also:

cleavages; elections; electoral behaviour; electoral competition; party systems

Further reading

Bartolini, S. and Mair, P. (1990) *Identity, Competition and Electoral Availability: The Stabilization of European Electorates 1885–1985*, Cambridge: Cambridge University Press.

Broughton, D. and Donovan, M. (eds) (1999) *Changing Party Systems in Western Europe*, London and New York: Pinter.

Crewe, I. and Denver, D. (eds) (1985) *Electoral Change in Western Democracies. Patterns and Sources of Electoral Volatility*, London: Croom Helm.

Farlie, D. and Budge, I. (1978) 'Newtonian Mechanics and Predictive Election Theory', *British Journal of Political Science* 7: 413–22.

Katz, R.S., Rattinger, H. and Pedersen, M.N. (1997) three articles on 'The Dynamics of European Party Systems', *European Journal of Political Research* 31: 83–97.

Lane, J.-E. and Ersson, S. (1997) 'Parties and Voters: What Creates the Ties?', *Scandinavian Political Studies* 20(2): 179–96.

Mainwaring, S. and Scully, T.R. (eds) (1995) *Building Democratic Institutions: Party Systems in Latin America*, Stanford, CA: Stanford University Press.

Mair, P. (1997) *Party System Change: Approaches and Interpretations*, Oxford: Clarendon Press.

Pedersen, M.N. (1979) 'The Dynamics of European Party Systems: Changing Patterns of Electoral Volatility', *European Journal of Political Research* 7(1): 1–26.

Pennings, P. and Lane, J.-E. (eds) (1998) *Comparing Party System Change*, London: Routledge.

MOGENS N. PEDERSEN

emancipation

The idea of emancipation has its origins in Roman Law, where it signified the setting free of a wife or child from paternal authority. Distinctively modern uses of the term derive from the European political philosophy of the seventeenth and eighteenth centuries. The notion of release from prior, unwanted forms of CONSTRAINT or control is retained, but extended to include a much wider range of sources of constraint and subjects of potential liberation. As well as wives and children, colonial churches, apprentices, slaves, wage-labourers, non-Christians, Catholics (in England, through the 1829 Catholic Emancipation Act) and colonial subjects could all be deemed in need of emancipation. Likewise, the constraints from which emancipation was required ranged from the internal and psychological, such as superstitious belief, through the social and political, such as tyrannical rule or the power of employers, to the supernatural and diabolical, such as the temptations of the devil.

Although the term 'emancipation' continued to be applied to the demand for liberation from specific constraints, on behalf of specific categories of subject, there emerged a distinctively modern Western sense of universal human emancipation. Diverse constraints or forms of subordination could be seen as objectionable only on the basis of a normative view of humans as equal in their capacity to be autonomous, self-conscious and self-defining. To be denied the opportunity to exercise autonomous judgement and choice, to be in control of one's own beliefs and actions, was to be denied full humanity, and so to be in need of 'emancipation'. However, in actual societies such opportunities were systematically denied in many dimensions of life: a hierarchical priesthood mediated between God and the individual believer, governments imposed obligations and restrictions, workers were subject to a wide variety of unfreedoms, and so on. These ideas were given their fullest expression in the works of the 'philosophes' of the French Enlightenment, and for many the French and American Revolutions were welcomed as bringing about a general emancipation from traditional, 'patriarchal' AUTHORITY. So, for this way of understanding emancipation, its achievement is very closely identified with the modern concept of CITIZENSHIP in the constitutional state: a legal framework which underwrites basic 'natural' and civil rights, protects citizens from abuses of power by both public authorities and fellow citizens, and does so in a universalistic manner.

However, this view of emancipation as realised in the liberal state was subject to limitations which were soon exposed by more radical thinkers. Most clearly, its universality was open to question. Early feminists, most notably Mary Wollstonecraft, argued that half of human kind was unjustly excluded from this proclaimed universality, and later feminists have shown how even the very concept of the emancipated citizen carried an implicit appeal to a masculine ideal (see PATRIARCHY). Other critics pointed to the continuation of social, cultural and economic forms of subordination which coexisted with, in some respects were even reinforced by, and in any case undermined the effectiveness of, legal and political citizenship. Most obviously, property, protected as a universal right, was, under conditions of radical economic inequality, a basis for continuing oppression and undue influence (see PRIVATE PROPERTY).

By the mid-nineteenth century, socialist and communist thinkers, most notably Karl Marx, had elaborated a twofold critique of this liberal, 'bourgeois' notion of emancipation in the modern constitutional state. Marx welcomed and acknowledged the historic achievement of civil and political liberties, but at the same time made a key distinction between political emancipation and all-round human emancipation. On the one hand, the modern state intimated in an ideal form the future human community. On the other, since CIVIL SOCIETY was still riven with competitive and exploitative relationships, the ideal of human emancipation and EQUALITY proclaimed at the level of politics and ideology was necessarily undermined in practice. The liberal state could, in reality, be no more than an expression of the interests and will of the economically dominant CLASS. Full human emancipation could only be achieved on the basis of a thorough-going transformation of social and economic relations.

But the critique went further than this. Human emancipation meant not just making actual and practical the universal RIGHTS proclaimed in liberal law and ideology, but also challenging the very notion of human self-realisation presupposed by them. For Marx and his associates, the Enlightenment ideal of the self-sufficient, self-interested and rationally calculating individual was merely a reflection of the socially regressive and possessive forms of individuality produced by bourgeois society. In its place, Marx proposed a historical developmental view of human selfhood, according to which new, more diverse and richer contents would be given to the notion of human fulfilment once the limitations imposed by bourgeois society had been overcome. On this view, full human emancipation was premised on a collective transformation of human relationships both with one another and with the rest of nature. In Marx's early writings, human emancipation is understood as a historical process in which multiple estrangements, characteristic of capitalist societies, are overcome. Under regimes of capitalist private property, workers cannot identify with their work, or with what they produce. The more wealth they create, the more they augment the power of those set over them. They work only out of necessity, and as a means to ends extrinsic to their work. They are forced into competitive relationships to one another. For Marx, the root of alienation is estrangement from nature, as expressed in PRIVATE PROPERTY relations. Consequently, the overcoming of estrangement must have at its heart the establishment of a qualitatively different relation between humans and their natural environment. This will take the form of a species-wide project of 'humanisation of nature', in which each would realise his or her potential through co-operative and creative engagement with nature in the meeting of need.

There are two key differences between radical views of emancipation such as that of the early Marx, and those associated with the Enlightenment and more recent versions of liberal political thought. The first of these differences is that on the liberal view, personal AUTONOMY tends to be taken as a 'given' attribute, so that emancipation consists in protecting it from the impositions of public authorities or other individuals. On more radical views, autonomy is understood as an acquired capacity, contingent on the provision of enabling social, emotional and material conditions and relationships. The second difference follows from this. The very content of autonomy cannot be specified in advance of the social and historical conditions under which it is acquired. Autonomy is not just a matter of FREEDOM to choose and to act in accordance with one's choices (important as this is), but it also involves the opportunity to explore new senses of self; to become a kind of being for whom new possibilities of choice and self-hood become available. In short, the social relationships and historical transformations within which individuals are located becomes central to the understanding of what it is to be emancipated (see SELF AND POLITICS).

During the twentieth century, the degeneration of the Russian revolution into an oppressive and murderous tyranny led to widespread disillusionment, and a turning away from radical and 'utopian' versions of emancipation. However, something of the early Marx's moral vision was retained and developed by a tradition of thought known as 'critical theory', initially based at Frankfurt University but later transferred, in the wake of the Nazi seizure of power, to the USA. Thinkers in this tradition (Theodor Adorno, Max Horkheimer, Herbert Marcuse and more recently Jürgen Habermas being the best known) gave up on the classical Marxian expectation of working class revolution. However, they retained an implacable hostility to the economic and, especially, cultural forms of late CAPITALISM, and continued to hold open a vision of a qualitatively different mode of human social existence beyond capitalism. In the absence of any human agency destined to bring about such a future state, the critical theorists were faced with a problem of anchoring their critical stance: in a society of happy consumers, who had the right to demand 'emancipation', and from what? For some, authentic art, philosophical reflection or fantasy contained intimations of an unsatisfied utopian impulse.

Such considerations enabled a number of critical theorists to make links with psychoanalysis. Just as the earlier Marxian view had emphasised the conditionality of personal autonomy on external social and economic relationships, the Freudian notion of the internal complexity of the self brought to light the ways in which the development of personal autonomy could be obstructed by unacknowledged inner psychic forces. In a remarkable work of theoretical synthesis, Herbert Marcuse deployed Freud's pessimistic view of the psychological misery inevitably imposed by the requirements of modern civilisation in the service of a new vision of emancipation. For Marcuse, the unhappiness associated with the repression of instinctual desire was mainly an imposition of the competitive, performance-oriented culture of late capitalism. The future society would make possible psychic and aesthetic as well as economic emancipation.

The most prominent of the 'second generation' of critical theorists, Jürgen Habermas, has sought to anchor the emancipatory project in a strikingly original theory of language and COMMUNICATION. His earlier work identified universal human interests in control over nature and in practical co-ordination of human activity. These interests were the basis for a distinction between instrumental rationality, associated with natural science and the manipulation of things, and communicative rationality, aimed at mutual understanding and cooperation. However, power relations and the spread of bureaucratic forms of organisation have led to the extension of instrumental rationality into the sphere of social relations, so that communication has become distorted. We thus have a third general interest in emancipation from distorted communication, and so also in emancipation from the institutional forms and power relations underlying it. The means of emancipation here are critiques of ideology. Distorted communication is identified by contrast with a vision of communication in which the participants have equal opportunity to call into question the utterances of others, introduce new topics, assume different roles and so on. Habermas terms this the 'ideal speech situation'. He acknowledges its utopian character, but it can nevertheless be used as a measure of the extent to which actual forms of social communication and co-ordination of activity depart from it.

These more radical understandings of emancipation initially converged with demands for extensions of political democracy. These demands were of two main kinds. For some, emancipation implied the extension of rights to democratic PARTICIPATION to classes of subjects hitherto excluded, most famously the campaigns to extend the franchise to women in many countries, and to enable the exercise of political rights on the part of black Americans in the southern states. For others, drawing on the arguments of socialist critics of the limitations of liberal democracy, full human emancipation could be realised only by an extension of the scope of democratic public DECISION-MAKING to include institutions and aspects of the life of the individual in society hitherto excluded from the public determination. Central to this line of argument was recognition that the exercise of entrenched private property rights in the economy impinged in important ways on the well-being and liberties of employees, consumers and other members of the community. Not only this, but such unaccountable power also limited and distorted the exercise of formal political rights on the part of those subject to it. A thoroughgoing socialist conclusion to this line of argument was the demand for the extension of democratically accountable public control of key sectors of the economy through some form of public or common ownership. A weaker, but still robust and influential conclusion was that most famously deployed by Marshall. This retains a commitment to private property and market relations in the economy, but adds to legal and political citizenship a third dimension of 'social citizenship', which seeks to compensate for economic disadvantage and risk by the public provision of extensive WELFARE and social security rights.

Both sorts of extension of democracy link emancipatory aspirations with the extension or deepening of citizenship rights, and so are broadly inclusionary in their claims. However, more recent changes, from the mid-twentieth century onwards, have called this general feature of earlier emancipatory movements into question. The shift has been one in which the demand for autonomy has come increasingly to be seen as the opportunity to express one's difference from, rather than to achieve recognition and participation within, the wider political community. Of course, this brings along with it deep questions about what counts as the 'political community'. In some ways this transformation of the emancipatory project is prefigured in the anti-colonial struggles of the twentieth century: the demand on the part of colonised peoples, usually expressed in the form of an 'imagined community' of independent nationhood, for self-government (see POLITICAL CULTURE). But the notion of emancipation as the liberation of difference as it flourished in the more radical reaches of black American politics, in radical feminism and in some expressions of the politics of sexuality was a direct challenge to the capacity of the nation-state itself to represent any general or universal interest. As such, these newer movements revitalised and gave new content to a key tension within democratic politics: that between majoritarian decision-making and the protection of the rights of MINORITIES. However, their challenge has been deeper than this, in that both the identity of the political community and the authority of its nation-state are called into question. This takes a particularly acute form in the more recent mobilisations of indigenous peoples in the face of threats to their traditional ways of life posed by large development projects, and commercial activities such as mining, logging and ecotourism. Here, the national state may well claim a democratic mandate for policies which infringe the rights of aboriginal peoples and their cultural traditions, but the counter-claim is that these communities have their own autonomous political community and forms of legitimate rule rooted in prior occupancy of the disputed territory (see RIGHTS, MINORITY AND INDIGENOUS).

While diversity of collective identities among human groups is the theme underlying many of the newer forms of emancipatory movements, the latter part of the twentieth century has also witnessed a transformation which moves in the opposite direction, towards ever-wider forms of universalism. Greatly increased permeability of national BOUNDARIES to movements of capital, knowledge, symbols, commodities, ideas and, to an extent, people, has arguably begun to bring into being a global civil society and moral/political community. Many of the social and environmental costs of private property and market relations are now associated with transnational actors, and exceed the SOVEREIGNTY of national governments. Increasingly, emancipatory movements address their claims to a global PUBLIC OPINION, and assert universal moral rights, often against the practices of nation-states.

The discourse of human rights has carried much of the burden of these aspirations, but the issues which have come to the fore in the newly emergent transnational public space include a number which promise to extend the boundaries of the moral and legal, if not political, community still further, beyond the human species itself. The claim for universal human moral rights has provided the philosophical basis for a powerful advocacy of the rights of non-human animals, which suffer exploitation and maltreatment in intensive rearing systems, research and development labs and elsewhere. Wider 'ecocentric' political philosophies assign moral standing (intrinsic value) to all living beings, and the diverse ecological interrelationships among them. In such versions of 'emancipation writ large', the central theme is the envisioning of human emancipation under the constraint of its enabling the simultaneous flourishing of non-human life-forms. This is in sharp contrast to earlier forms of emancipatory politics which were often premised on an unquestioned mastery of nature in the service of human needs and desires. Here again, new forms of emancipatory politics expose further problems for settled notions of democracy and their prevailing forms of institutionalisation. In the absence of the relevant capacities for full participation in political life, how can non-human life-forms be included in an expanded democratic process? Without this, how can their supposed emancipatory interests be identified or pursued? One possibility might be to assign specific human actors the role of advocate on their behalf, rather as is already done for mentally incapacitated humans in some legal contexts. Another possibility, more in line with the politics of difference, would be a strategy of progressive withdrawal of human disruptive and destructive impacts on the rest of nature, of 'living lightly on the planet'. Human emancipation would then take the form of a more contemplative, respectful delight in the diversity of nature, as against the prevailing project of ultimately self-destructive mastery.

See also:

autonomy; gendering democracy; hegemony; identity, political; inclusion/exclusion; patriarchy; pluralism; political culture; public–private distinction; radical democracy; revolutions

Further reading

Adorno, T. and Horkheimer, M. (1979) *Dialectic of Enlightenment*, London: Verso.

Dobson, A. (2000) *Green Political Thought*, London and New York: Routledge.

Eckersley, R. (1992) *Environmentalism and Political Theory*, London: University College.

Habermas, J. (1972) *Knowledge and Human Interests*, London: Heinemann.

Held, D. (1980) *Introduction to Critical Theory*, London: Hutchinson.

Marcuse, H. (1969) *Eros and Civilisation*, London: Sphere.

Marx, K. (1978) 'On the Jewish Question' and 'Economic and Philosophical Notebooks (1844)', in R.C. Tucker (ed.), *The Marx-Engels Reader*, 2nd edn, New York: W.W. Norton.

TED BENTON

empowerment

Empowerment is best understood as a process whereby people gain increased control over their lives as a result of greater awareness and improved capacities, leading to greater participation, to greater DECISION-MAKING power and to transformative action. Oppressed or disadvantaged people achieve such control by taking part with others in the development of activities and structures that allow them increased involvement in matters that affect them directly. Given this definition, it has largely been those concerned to theorise and transform the situation of various oppressed groups that have embraced the concept of empowerment. Notably, it is used widely within feminist discourses in development studies, and in social policy studies of community care.

Uses of empowerment in diverse discourses

Within a feminist literature, empowerment is characteristically used in ways that capture a sense of gaining control, of participating, of decision-making. Specifically, it tends to entail four central components: consciousness raising, providing a sense of group identity and the power of working as a group; skills development, generating the capacity to plan, make decisions, organise and manage; participation and decision-making power in all areas of life; and action to bring about greater equality (see Karl 1995).

But it is not only feminists who have adopted the notion of empowerment. Community care theorists and practitioners frequently invoke the notion of empowerment, arguing that empowerment of 'clients' is necessary if they are to at least partly meet their own 'needs' (Servian 1996: 8). Here the concern with enabling individuals to meet their own needs generates debate about whether official intervention is the key to empowerment (via legislation regarding the allocation of resources) or whether one should also consider democratic RIGHTS and PARTICIPATION.

During the 1990s the term entered into the vocabulary of development agencies, including international organisations and the United Nations. When used by development agencies the concept of empowerment is frequently used to refer to entrepreneurial self-reliance. Critics claim that it is closely allied to individualistic values with an emphasis on people 'empowering themselves' by pulling themselves up by their bootstraps (Young 1993: 157). A more radical deployment of the notion of empowerment focuses on participation in POLICY-MAKING and planning processes, demanding support for a range of social movements, INTEREST GROUPS and NON-GOVERNMENTAL ORGANISATIONS (NGOs). The empowerment of women has become a central goal of many development projects. Two approaches to such empowerment emerge amongst development agencies: empowerment through economic interventions to increase women's economic status through employment and income generation; and empowerment through integrated rural development programmes, which include literacy and fertility programmes and WELFARE provision. Building on both the feminist and the development discourses, the United Nations Children's Fund (UNICEF) is currently using a 'Women's Empowerment Framework' as a 'conceptual basis for gender-responsive assessment, evaluation and programming.' (UNICEF 1993: 5) It advocates the empowerment of women in relation to five levels of equality: welfare, access, conscientisation, participation and control.

Other uses of the notion of empowerment are more varied still. Pascale (1990) has reported how the term 'empowerment' is used by Honda in Japan to develop a high-quality workforce, with the over-riding motivation of increasing company profit. Here empowerment represents a different form of organisation in the workplace, adopting a flexible view of the skills of the worker and of their ability to take on a wide number of roles. Moreover, the fact that a right-wing North American television station committed to freeing people from 'big' government calls itself 'National Empowerment Television' indicates that while self-determination is a common aspect of appeals to empowerment, there is no necessary link between the concept of empowerment and radical political projects.

Theorising empowerment

Notwithstanding the diverse uses of the notion of empowerment across many disparate discourses, the term has played a surprisingly minor role within political science (Rai 1999: 84–5). This is perhaps to be understood in the context of the differing conceptions of 'power' adopted within these discrete discourses. Within the discourses surveyed above the term empowerment has usually signalled a commitment to a concept to 'power to' rather than 'power over': it focuses attention on power as enabling and expansive rather than as zero-sum dominance. In contrast, for those political scientists intent on understanding the distribution of political power attention is focused on the power held by the political institutions of government (national and local) and organisations aiming to influence them (interest groups, unions, NGOs). Power is 'of, by and for elites' (Elshtain 1992: 112). Power is conceived as a possession, something that is observable and measurable. In other words empiricist power theorists have confined themselves to one particular locution of power: 'power over' (see Lukes 1978).

In contrast to this approach, the notion of empowerment draws on an alternative conception of power. Hannah Arendt has been a key theorist here, asserting that power 'corresponds to the human ability not just to act but to act in concert'. Power, for Arendt, belongs to a group and is never 'the property of an individual'. Power stays as long as the group stays together. 'When we say of somebody that he is "in power" we actually refer to his being empowered by a certain number of people to act in their name. The moment the group, from which the power originated to begin with disappears, "his power" also vanishes' (Arendt 1969: 44). From this perspective, power is neither zero-sum nor conflictual, as it arises when people work together rather than when they act against others. It can therefore be distinguished from violence, force and AUTHORITY.

Critics of this notion of power argue that this is a prescriptive rather than descriptive account. Such definitions are often represented within the empirical political science literature as revisionary persuasive re-definitions, which obfuscate or downplay the conflictual aspects of power. Yet many theorists nonetheless view the zero-sum, possessional model of power as problematic. For to represent women as simply powerless, some argue, is to work with a narrow conception of power, and to deny the complexity and richness of women's experiences (Elshtain 1992: 110). Many feminists have followed Arendt in emphasising the benefits arising from conceptualising power as empowerment. This conception of power is claimed to be more inclusive than 'power over', comprising both the ability to act and the ability to refrain from action (which is not quantifiable). The distinction is put forward as a means of breaking out of the dualism between being powerless and being powerful, which is thought to be unhelpfully combative and hierarchical.

Influentially within feminist debates, Nancy Hartsock challenges the notion that the exercise of power can best be understood as the ability to compel obedience. She suggests a connection between masculinity and the exercise of power over others, arguing that the repression of *eros* in a masculinist society underlies the definition of both sexuality and power as domination (Hartsock 1996: 31). She contrasts this with the theories of power produced by women, which stress those aspects of power related to energy, capacity and potential. While admitting that this constitutes only suggestive evidence that there is a distinct female or feminist conception of power, she nonetheless wants to argue that, on the basis of the commonality found in these writings, we can speak of systematic difference between the theoretical accounts of power produced by women and men (Hartsock 1996: 32–7).

From this perspective, to assume that demanding more power entails the idea of imposing one's will on others is to work with a masculinist conception of 'power over'. In contrast, the most effective means of challenging male power is to bring into being the theory and practice of feminist 'power to'. The rejection of the competitive and zero-sum notion of power is important, it is argued, for women who want to demand empowerment for themselves, without thereby denying it to others. In recognition of this, feminist theorists have been keen to break the stranglehold of the narrow political science conceptions of power and recuperate the range of everyday uses of the term which include not only power as a property, but also as the ability to do something.

Within this school of thought, there is a marked tendency to consider power negatively and empowerment positively. The former is seen as domination and lack of connection, the latter as enabling and relational. As one commentator puts it, the 'feminist vision of power, as a co-operative non-zero-sum relationship called empowerment, is heralded as better than the masculinist view it opposes. By better than, feminist theorists mean more humane, less destructive, more fully human' (Deutchman 1996: 8).

There is of course disagreement as to whether empowerment can legitimately be claimed as female. Most, seeking to avoid charges of essentialism, claim not a *feminine* conception of power but rather a *feminist* one, arguing that it is not women's nature that gives rise to a specific way of viewing power, but their particular social role and status (usually caring and private). The systematic and significant differences in life activity experienced by men and women lead to differing worldviews and distinctive theoretical commitments (Hartsock 1996: 37). The concept of empowerment is claimed as part of a 'feminist standpoint' based in historically and materially specific circumstances and realised through a consciousness-raising process. The development of a feminist theory of power is not then simply what women currently understand as power, but rather what women might conceptualise once they have worked beyond systematic domination.

However, power and empowerment need not be pitted against one another as incompatible concepts. Jean Bethke Elshtain, for example, offers a clear argument for viewing these two conceptions as complementary. She claims that human societies throughout time have differentiated between maleness and femaleness and located complementary forms of power in the two sexes (Elshtain 1992: 115). Moreover, she claims, the nature of these sexually differentiated forms of power follow a general pattern whereby *formal* male power is balanced or even underlined by *informal* female power (Elshtain 1992: 116). Elshtain suggests that we understand such sexually differentiated forms of power (both historically and currently) as genuinely complementary. Where men hold institutionalised, 'political' and juridical power, female power is exercised in informal, communal spheres of life. *Potestas*, the Latin term for political power, control, supremacy and domination, is contrasted with *potentia*, power as ability, potency and efficacy; or empowerment. The complementarity of these two forms of power is lost, Elshtain suggests, in modern societies where the formal institutions of the state are allotted ever-greater significance (Elshtain 1992: 116). She therefore invites us to search for new forms of power. Women, she tells us, are well placed to discern and develop such a conception of power in the context of their current role as marginalised from the dominant, though delimiting, norms of *potestas* (Elshtain 1992: 119).

In a related argument, Anna Yeatman claims that the apparent need to choose between a conception of power as domination and as capacity (or between power and empowerment) is itself problematic and neither strategy will be productive. It is the very act of taking too simplistic and cohesive a notion of power as domination that creates the perceived need to define and revalue a directly contrasting conception of power. In order to challenge the celebration of powerlessness entailed in the rejection of all forms of 'power over', Yeatman stresses the importance of the distinction between democratic and undemocratic forms of power over. Centrally, she argues that while the conception of power as 'power to' stands in an antagonistic relation to undemocratic domination, it may require as a precondition of its realisation a democratic form of 'power over' or domination.

Distinguishing between these separable aspects of power would have two significant implications: first, to perceive distinct forms of power used by any single government would allow one to critique undemocratic forms of domination whilst recognising and exploring the positive conceptions of power also at play; second, it would allow one to acknowledge that power is not only manifest as domination, but inheres in all relationships (Yeatman 1997: 147). In other words, this stance makes an internal distinction within 'power over' and endorses the democratic form as a necessary prerequisite for the pursuit of empowerment.

In this context, it is worth noting that whilst the feminist concern with transformative action generally encouraged an emphasis on participatory politics, recent literature has increasingly engaged with institutional strategies for empowerment too. It is now suggested that earlier discussions of empowerment tended to occlude the need to reflect upon the machinery of social and state power itself, and so missed the fact that the state needs to be included in debates on empowerment (Rai 1999: 86). This positive engagement with the notion of empowerment within feminist theory has generated important insights regarding the theorisation of power. In light of the slogan that the 'personal is political' and following the extensive exploration of various conceptions of power, it seems ever less possible to imagine an end to all power relationships, and ever more important to develop theories and practices of empowerment that might counteract the dominance of more conflictual, zero-sum conceptions of power.

See also:

affirmative action; authority; gendering democracy; social movements

Further reading

Arendt, H. (1969) *On Violence*, New York: Harcourt, Brace and World.

Bookman, A. and Morgan, S. (eds) (1988) *Women and the Politics of Empowerment*, Philadelphia: Temple University Press.

Deutchman, I.E. (1996) 'Feminist Theory and the Politics of Empowerment', in L.L. Duke (ed.), *Women in Politics: Outsiders or Insiders?*, Englewood Cliffs, NJ: Prentice-Hall, 4–16.

Elshtain, J.B. (1992) 'The Power and Powerlessness of Women', in G. Bock and S. James (eds), *Beyond Equality and Difference: Citizenship, Feminist Politics and Female Subjectivity*, London: Routledge, 110–25.

Friedmann, J. (1997) *Empowerment: A Politics of Alternative Development*, Oxford: Blackwell.

Hartsock, N. (1996) 'Community/Sexuality/Gender: Rethinking Power', in N. Hirschmann and C. Di Stefano (eds), *Revisioning the Political: Feminist Reconstructions of Traditional Concepts in Western Political Theory*, Oxford: Westview Press, 27–50.

Karl, M. (1995) *Women and Empowerment*, London: Zed Books.

Lukes, S. (1978) *Power: A Radical View*, Basingstoke: Macmillan.

Pascale, R. (1990) *Managing on the Edge*, Harmondsworth: Penguin.

Rai, S. (1999) 'Democratic Institutions, Political Representation and Women's Empowerment: The Quota Debate in India', *Democratization* 6(3): 84–99.

Servian, R. (1996) *Theorising Empowerment: Individual Power and Community Care*, Bristol: Policy Press.

UNICEF (1993) 'The Women's Empowerment Framework', *Women and Girls Advance* 1(1).

Yeatman, A. (1997) 'Feminism and Power', in M.L. Shanley and U. Narayan (eds), *Reconstructing Political Theory: Feminist Perspectives*, Cambridge: Polity Press, 144–57.

Young, K. (1993) *Planning Development with Women: Making a World of Difference*, Basingstoke: Macmillan.

JUDITH SQUIRES

equality

One of the very few points upon which the disputants over the meaning of 'democracy' agree is that it refers to a form of rule which enshrines the political equality of citizens: in some sense, democracy allows each citizen an equal say in governance because it subscribes to what Dahl calls the general 'idea of intrinsic equality' of humans (Dahl 1989: 84–8). Although it is possible to interpret the 'idea' as a non-political principle only (people might be conceptualised as, say, morally equal 'in the eyes of God' without this necessitating a political equality on earth) it has become widely linked to political equality, interpreted as an ideal of equal FREEDOM which could hardly be respected properly if freedom's domain fell short of the political realm. Hence the moral case for democracy is invariably constructed upon a commitment to equality and its public recognition. Fittingly, equality arguably found its very first foothold in Western culture through the politics of democracy, having been proclaimed as the core principle of its original Athenian exemplar in Pericles's famous 'Funeral Oration' (Thucydides 1972: 143–51). The shocking radicalism subsequently perceived in democratic movements through the ages has been largely due to the fundamental challenges they have posed to existing social and political inequalities. Unsurprisingly, then, in the history of anti-democratic thought the rejection of the equality ideal has been a paramount motivation, from Plato's *Republic* to twentieth-century fascism. It is significant that, in an age where the ideal has finally become deeply embedded in the moral consciousness of the international community, nearly all regimes – including outright tyrannies – claim the label of 'democracy' for themselves precisely because of a (sometimes cynically) perceived need to pay at least lip service to it.

Equality, though, is notoriously contestable as a political concept and a major reason why there are multiple forms of democracy is because different conceptions of equality have been employed to substantiate the democratic ideal in highly diverse ways. Even where a particular conception of equality is shared, there remains cavernous room for disagreement over how best to respect it. A central task of any democratic theory, therefore, is to explain how it interprets the ideal of equality in theory and how it is to be rendered in practice.

Despite the variety of conceptions produced by equality's open-textured nature, they can be bracketed into two broad categories by dint of certain similarities: 'juridical equality' and 'social' equality.

Juridical equality

Conceptions of democracy in this category believe that the commitment to political equality is essentially fulfilled by guaranteeing in law the citizens' equal rights of access to DECISION-MAKING procedures and institutions. Liberal democracy typifies the juridical approach to equality. Here, 'equal say' is primarily rendered as the equal right of citizens to choose their government through voting. This is coupled with the principle that each vote is worth exactly the same when they are counted: each person's opinion, or interest, is entitled to equal representation (see REPRESENTATION, CONCEPT OF). Supplementing this is an equal opportunity to participate in decision-making in the sense that no legal restrictions exist upon people in their right to run for political office, or organise campaigns and pressure groups to influence the conduct of public policy. Equal freedom of expression is therefore also intrinsic to this package. For juridical egalitarians, facilitating such freedoms is sometimes thought to require only a 'night watchman' role for the state, but it can in certain circumstances require more proactive political intervention: campaigns to encourage voter registration and legislation to limit and control campaign expenditure are common examples.

In conceptualising citizens' roles as producers of decisions, democracy rests upon what Dahl terms a 'strong principle of equality', an empirical assumption that all citizens are adequately (though not, it must be stressed,

equally) qualified to take part in the democratic process (Dahl 1989: 31). For juridical-egalitarian conceptions, this qualification need stretch no further than the abilities required to exercise a vote which competitive-elitist defenders of representative government in particular believe to be vanishingly small. Once again, however, juridical equality can consistently recommend more interventionist state activity to combat inequality, this time supporting civic EDUCATION in which the state undertakes to provide its (future) citizens with appropriately democratic attitudes and skills to help instantiate the strong principle more substantively.

Of course, citizens are consumers of political decisions, too, and juridical-egalitarian democrats disagree over what exactly it means to show equal respect to citizens. Some, for example, contend that the ideal's commitment to an 'equal representation of interests' should be reflected in the outcome as well as the procedure of the decision-making process, for interests cannot be truly represented if they are never satisfied. Hence they argue against a pure MAJORITARIANISM which holds that the ideal is satisfied by 'one person one vote', urging that the adequacy of this arrangement is severely tested in a situation where a permanent majority is yielded by equal voting, which thereafter persistently fails to respect the interests of a permanent minority (Jones 1983). In this instance, they claim that democracy's equality ideal militates in favour of PROPORTIONALITY.

Despite these potential outcomes and granted that there are states (such as Australia) where voting for example is obligatory and one of citizens' equal DUTIES, juridical-egalitarian democracy generally rests content with legally guaranteeing equal opportunities to vote and campaign. That it renders 'equal say' no more expansively in terms of facilitating more extensive and continuously active equal participation need not reflect what its critics would regard as a naive belief that juridical equality fully satisfies the requirements of meaningfully equal say. Its undemanding possibilities for, and expectations of, citizens may be due to an outlook that decentres politics in people's lives, loosening the conditions for democracy's achievement insofar as political participation is simply one option among many from which people may choose to occupy their time. It can also embody a putatively pragmatic compromise between the democratic ideal, when it is thought in principle to demand more to facilitate 'equal say', and the perceived complexities of twenty-first century governance insofar as these might be thought to be incapable of permitting any further equalisation of condition or any more extensive participation by the citizenry. Nevertheless, democratic critics of juridical equality deride it in its optimistic version for being purely 'formal' in its supposed failure to see how legal guarantees alone do not suffice to facilitate the equal say of citizens in governance, and in its pessimistic version for being unduly negative in assessing democratic egalitarianism's prospects.

Social equality

Social equality is substituted for juridical equality by those who criticise the formalism of the latter. They argue that people's ability to participate is profoundly affected by their social and economic position in society, a contention which they support with impressive statistical evidence of disparities between social groups in participation (Verba and Nie (1987) remains a classic example of such evidence). Politics, they believe, can transform such conditions. Hence the quest for social equality is the pursuit of EMPOWERMENT without which, social egalitarians claim, democracy would be a sham.

Some social egalitarians concentrate upon the command of material resources as the key to power in society, contending that democracy requires an equalisation of those resources. Dispute over exactly how this is to be understood and achieved has riven socialism – arguably the main standard-bearer of social-egalitarian democracy – almost from its inception. Those who think existing (juridical-egalitarian) democratic structures need only be reformed, not overthrown, tend to concentrate their efforts upon formulating policies of redistributive justice within the framework of existing institutions and social structures. Against this is the revolutionary view, of which Marxism is a paradigm, which has long attacked CAPITALISM for using formal, juridical democratic institutions and practices as an ideological cloak for the real inequalities of power separating the classes in society. In claiming that political power is predicated upon economic power and derived from ownership of the means of production, Marxists contend that only collective control of the economy in the aftermath of capitalism's overthrow can yield true democracy (Wright 1986: ch. 4).

Other social egalitarians claim that non-material factors also contribute to inequality. Feminists argue that the social construction of gender roles has often effectively disenfranchised women on top of the economic disadvantages they peculiarly suffer (Phillips 1991). For them, the social organisation of time and space that results from juridical equality's typically tacit acceptance of the disjunction between the public and the private spheres neglects the extent to which the gendered division of labour in the private sphere can severely curtail opportunities to participate in politics on equal terms with men. Norms which specify a domesticated, non-public and inferior way of life for women infest the culture from which they draw their identities and expectations (see GENDERING DEMOCRACY). Cultural bars to equal participation can also discriminate against other groups in society (such as homosexuals) who do not conform to mainstream ('normal') modes of behaviour (Kaplan 1997). Such groups are often marginalised and stigmatised by social attitudes which render others so harshly unreceptive to their interests that they fear even to express their identities and campaign for those interests. In all such instances, a redistribution of material resources may not be sufficient – and could even be incidental – to the project of restructuring such cultures of inequality.

Although there is no necessary link between them, social-egalitarian democracy often advocates DIRECT DEMOCRACY, believing that the only means of guaranteeing equal say on top of the redistribution of wealth and social opportunities and the dismantling of cultural barriers to participation is to institutionalise and practice direct citizen participation. Here, 'equal opportunity to have one's say' is transformed into 'equal actual say' and much more generous assumptions about citizens' abilities are consequently made with respect to the strong principle of equality.

Insofar as they also extend the range of institutions and practices over which citizens exercise democratic control, social egalitarians seek not only a democratic state but also a whole democratic society (Macpherson 1972). This ideal is present as far back as Athenian democracy, and was nourished in the Enlightenment tradition by Rousseau's *Social Contract*, which postulates a directly democratic body politic composed of citizens who are roughly equal in their material possessions and share a common interest – the general will – in how the polity is to be governed. What helps to sustain this general will is precisely the predominance of an egalitarian, participatory public commitment in the broader swathe of people's lives (Rousseau 1973). John Rawls also taps into this communitarian tradition by calling the principle that social and economic inequalities are permissible only where they benefit the least advantaged a conception of 'democratic equality' (Rawls 1972: 74–5).

Unfairly or not, the tarnishing of socialism in the wake of communism's collapse has served to reinforce juridical-egalitarian interpretations of 'democracy', particularly in those states undergoing democratisation. Even among those who are sensitive to its limits, the question of how best to render democracy's ideal of equality is more frequently resolved in juridical equality's favour with the pragmatic argument that other considerations, in particular the lack of a superior feasible alternative to the capitalist free market, curtail the possibility of social-egalitarian democracy. However, to the extent that this is a valid judgement, it nevertheless means that democracy is premised upon an ideal of equality whose full import continually harbours the possibility of an immanent critique of its limited practice; and this helps to keep alive an impetus to campaign, in democracy's own name, for whatever egalitarian reforms are viable.

See also:

class; empowerment; gendering democracy; social democracy; suffrage

Further reading

Dahl, R. (1989) *Democracy and its Critics*, New Haven, CT: Yale University Press.

Jones, P. (1983) 'Political Equality and Majority Rule' in D. Miller and L. Siedentop (eds), *The Nature of Political Theory*, Oxford: Blackwell.

Kaplan, M. (1997) *Sexual Justice*, New York: Routledge.

Macpherson, C.B. (1972) *The Real World of Democracy*, New York: Oxford University Press.

Phillips, A. (1991) *Engendering Democracy*, Cambridge: Polity.

Rawls, J. (1972) *A Theory of Justice*, Oxford: Oxford University Press.

Rousseau, J.-J. (1973) 'The Social Contract', in *The Social Contract and Discourses*, trans. G.D.H. Cole, London: Dent.

Thucydides (1972) *The Peloponnesian War* trans. R. Warner, Harmondsworth: Penguin.

Verba, S. and Nie, N. (1987) *Participation in America*, Chicago: University of Chicago Press.

Wright, A. (1986) *Socialisms*, Oxford: Oxford University Press.

MARK A. EVANS

ethnicity

Ethnicity is a complex and much debated term, which usually refers to a sense of belonging to or identification with an ethnic group. An ethnic group is usually defined as a group of people who see themselves and/or are seen by others as a distinct cultural community, who share some of the following: a language, dialect or idiom, religious beliefs, myths of origin, kinship and social ties, traditions, values, symbols and practices, physical characteristics, geographic origins, immigration status, socio-economic status, institutions and political identity.

The term ethnicity was coined in the early 1950s, but its etymological roots are much older and lie in the ancient Greek *ethnos* (n.) and *ethnikos* (adj.). *Ethnos*, which connoted peoples who lived without *politikos*, was not a central concept or object of debate in classical Greek thought, however. The word 'ethnic' appeared in English in the mid-fourteenth century and was used to denote heathen or pagan until the early nineteenth century when this meaning was replaced by associations with changing notions of race and nation. In the late 1940s, in the wake of the Holocaust, the UNESCO Declaration sought to promote the use of ethnic group to refer to national, cultural, religious and linguistic groups, in an attempt to displace the notion of race with its deeply embedded evolutionist and biological connotations. Despite this attempt, the two concepts are still closely interlinked and are sometimes used interchangeably. But most scholars explicitly reject evolutionist foundations, and treat ethnicity and race as historically, socially and politically constituted, sociobiologists being the notable exceptions. These problematic terms are rarely defined, but in usage ethnicity and race are generally distinguished by connotations of shared culture as against shared physical characteristics, such as skin colour. At the same time, there is a broad consensus that ethnicity and race intersect in complex ways with other forms of social division, such as gender and CLASS.

Despite the obsession with race among Enlightenment and nineteenth-century thinkers (see Hannaford 1996), historically, the issues of ethnicity were marginalized from Western liberal and democratic political theory (see Kymlicka *et al.* 1995; Mills 1997). Contractarians, like Hobbes, Locke and Rousseau, stressed that it was individuals (men) who are parties to the social contract and provided no place for intermediate associations between the individual citizen and the state or government. Nor did they attempt to characterise the men in relation to say shared language, culture or religion. If such omissions suggest an implicit presumption that such individuals share a cultural community, J.S. Mill was explicit in arguing that representative government was next to impossible in a country without shared nationality and language, and that the boundaries of government should coin-cide with those of nationalities.

The influence of these legacies on the constitutional and institutional arrangements of many democratic states, as well as subsequent generations of liberal political theorists and political scientists devoted to the empirical study of comparative politics and democratic systems cannot be overstated; historical cases of CONSOCIATIONALISM and power-sharing notwithstanding. Moreover, the individualist liberal legacy also intersected with, and was reinforced by, evolutionist notions of societal development, which predicted that ethnic differences would be subsumed by class (as the organising principle of social stratification and/or political mobilisation) in the transition to modern industrial societies. Such beliefs are evident in both modernisation theory and structural Marxism, the dominant paradigms in the postwar period. They also underpinned the assimilationist policies pursued by most states, within the framework of nation-building development strategies, in the active attempt to suppress and eliminate ethnic differences (viewed as obstacles to achieving modernity) and construct modern, ethnically homogeneous nations (see ASSIMILATION). Furthermore, such policies also implicitly reinforced evolutionist ideologies of ethnic and racial inferiority and superiority, assigning superiority to whiteness, white ethnicities, majority or politically dominant groups.

In sum, as Connor (1972) observed, until the early 1970s, with a few exceptions, political studies had paid little attention to ethnicity and were based on the presumption of ethnic homogeneity within states, despite the fact that

281

the majority of states within the international system were (and are) characterised by ethnic heterogeneity. However, the salience of ethnicity, race and ethnic identities in political mobilisation, conflict and violence since the 1960s has made the withering away of the ethnicity thesis increasingly untenable. Illustrations include the civil rights and Black Power movements in the USA, movements of racial and ethnic minorities in Western Europe, and of indigenous peoples; and, following the end of the Cold War, the resurgence of ethnonationalisms in the former Soviet Union, Europe and model Third World democracies like India, as well as ethnic cleansing in the former Yugoslavia and ethnically targeted genocide in Rwanda. Such mobilisations and conflicts have also called into question the ahistorical, individualist premises of liberal-democratic thinking and the desirability and viability of assimilationist policies and practices pursued by many governments. They have also shown the urgency of devising democratic institutional arrangements that ensure the recognition of difference and the equitable accommodation of diversity, that facilitate conflict resolution, and that foster long-term peace and tolerance.

The political salience of ethnicity has had a significant impact on scholars in different disciplines, and since the 1970s there has been a proliferation of studies addressing this theme from different perspectives. It is generally accepted that three main theoretical approaches have emerged: primordialist, instrumentalist and constructivist. Primordialist approaches view ethnicity as an inherited cultural inventory and the product of *longue durée* historical processes, which although not permanently fixed or naturally given, is difficult to change. Instrumentalists, in contrast, consider ethnicity to be fluid and manipulable, a resource that only becomes politically salient if mobilised by political entrepreneurs to facilitate collective action in the pursuit of shared or individual economic and political interests. Although these two approaches are sometimes considered to be opposites, in practice each answers questions that the other

leaves begging: that is primordialists provide little explanation for why or how ethnicity becomes politically salient at particular historical moments, and instrumentalists pay little attention to the pre-existing cultural specificities and divisions that make the appeals of political leaders successful or not (for example, why assimilationist nation-building strategies failed to eliminate ethnic diversity). Moreover, they share the notion that ethnic identities are constituted internally within groups (albeit 'invented' or 'made' by leaders or 'given' through sustained intra-group interaction). It is on this point that the third approach, social constructivism (which covers a range of perspectives), most obviously differs. Social constructivists view ethnicity as relationally and contextually constituted through the interplay of subjective experiences and ascriptions of difference, and the negotiation of multiple subjects over identity. Ethnic identities are not internally given or made, they are constituted through the crossing of BOUNDARIES or discourses of otherness and difference embedded in specific historically constituted social and political contexts (see INCLUSION/EXCLUSION).

There is still much work to be done in theorising ethnicity *per se*. But this is not incidental. In part, it reflects the difficulties of theorising the complex ways that ethnicity intersects with the socially, economically and politically embedded structures of privilege and disadvantage that are often the historical legacies of imperialism, internal colonialism, slavery and transnational labour migration. It also reflects the priority given by scholars to the urgent tasks of addressing the more direct challenges posed to democratic theory and governance by the complicated range of issues arising from the ethnic diversity that characterises, and the politicisation of ethnic identities occurring within, most contemporary states.

Since the 1980s the question of the most appropriate constitutional and institutional arrangements, and social policies for ensuring equality of opportunity, representation (see REPRESENTATION, CONCEPT OF) and treatment for all citizens in ethnically diverse democracies has become a significant issue of debate in political theory and philosophy and politically salient in many democratic states. Much of this discussion has been framed in terms of minority and indigenous rights (see RIGHTS, MINORITY AND INDIGENOUS) and reconciling the tension between collective group rights and individual rights in relation to groups historically subordinated by internal colonialism (Kymlicka 1995; Tully 1995). In such cases, there is a growing consensus that diverse FEDERALISM or consociational arrangements, which devolve power and administrative responsibilities, provide models of best practice. Such models have underpinned the proposals of indigenous peoples in Canada and Latin America, as well as those put forward to resolve long-standing violent conflict in ethnically divided societies like Northern Ireland.

Rethinking notions of CITIZENSHIP in the context of ethnic, cultural and linguistic diversity has been central to these debates, including the extent to which recognition of difference is a necessary condition for ensuring equality between citizens, the equal treatment of all citizens before the law, equality of opportunity to participate in democratic deliberation and to obtain access to public goods and services (see, Benhabib 1996, for example). These issues are particularly complicated in relation to the multiple identities, dynamic reconfigurations and generational transformations of ethnicities occurring within democratic societies characterised by high levels of immigration. In these contexts, one obvious dilemma is how to provide recognition that is sufficiently flexible to encompass such 'new ethnicities' and thereby avoid the problem of constraining individual freedoms by assigning group membership a priori on the basis of reified ethnic categories. Moreover, there are also important questions to be resolved in relation to the effectiveness of AFFIRMATIVE ACTION, other quota systems, and equal opportunities policies that seek to redress historic political exclusions and socioeconomic disadvantage experienced by some racial and ethnic groups by providing protections and opportunities that benefit individuals.

A further set of important challenges are involved in devising effective policies and strategies for combating racism, ethnic discrimination and prejudice, and authoritarian assertions of ethnic supremacy or particularism. On the one hand, these include the tasks of addressing the racism and ethnic prejudice embedded in the organisational cultures of public organisations, which perpetuate an inequitable distribution of the goods and services provided by the state, and unequal treatment in relation to criminal JUSTICE systems. Such tasks are not confined to consolidated democracies, where they are gaining some public recognition, they are also important issues to be addressed in the new democracies of Eastern Europe and Latin America.

On the other hand, the proliferation and prominence of far-right political organisations and parties promoting white supremacist ideologies in the consolidated democracies of North America and Western Europe, for example, pose serious dilemmas for governments in relation to the limits of tolerance and the principles of freedom of expression, information and association. Such dilemmas also arise in relation to the less well-documented ethnic absolutist movements operating within minority communities, often disguised in postcolonial or anti-imperialist rhetoric, such as Hindu nationalist organisations (see Bhatt 1997). Moreover, combating these movements, organisations and parties is complicated by the fact they have invariably capitalised on the new communications technology to consolidate transnational linkages and increasingly transcend the boundaries of individual states.

There are obviously no simple solutions to these dilemmas of democratic governance. They require democratic deliberation on a case-to-case basis, deliberation that avoids recourse to simplistic, essentialist ethnic reductionisms, and is informed by careful historical and empirical investigation of ethnic and racial formations, as well as by the specificity of democratic institutions, legal traditions, and political cultures within particular states. What is clear, however, is that the recognition of ethnic diversity as the norm of contemporary societies should be the starting point for democratic thinking and practice.

Finally, it is important to stress that there are limits to liberal democratic solutions to the problems of racism and ethnic prejudice as well as the political mobilisations, conflicts and violence that reveal the ethnic divisions in contemporary societies. If, to paraphrase Stuart Hall, race and ethnicity (and gender) are the modalities through which class is lived, then redistributive measures that address the structures of socio-economic disadvantage, which so easily translate into political exclusion, will also be required. In the context of the growing tolerance for the disparities of wealth and privilege within and between societies associated with current processes of GLOBALISATION, such measures seem a distant prospect.

See also:

citizenship; consociationalism; globalisation; identity, political; minorities; nations and nationalism; pluralism; statelessness

Further reading

Back, L. and Solomos, J. (eds) (2000) *Theories of Race and Racism: A Reader*, London: Routledge.

Barth, F. (1969) *Ethnic Groups and Boundaries*, Boston: Little, Brown.

Benhabib, S. (ed.) (1996) *Democracy and Difference: Contesting the Boundaries of the Political*, Princeton, NJ: Princeton University Press.

Bhatt, C. (1997) *Liberation and Purity: Race, New Religious Movements and the Ethics of Post-modernity*, London: UCL Press.

Bulmer, M. and Solomos, J. (eds.) (1999) *Ethnic and Racial Studies Today*, London: Routledge.

Connor, W. (1972) 'Nation-Building or Nation-Destroying', *World Politics* 24: 31–55.

Guibernau, M. and Rex, J. (eds) (1997) *The Ethnicity Reader: Nationalism, Multiculturalism and Migration*, Cambridge: Polity Press.

Hall, S. (2000) 'Old and New Identities, Old and New Ethnicities', in L. Back and J.

Solomos (eds), *Theories of Race and Racism: A Reader*, London: Routledge, 144–53.

Hannaford, I. (1996) *Race: The History of an Idea in the West*, Washington and Baltimore: Woodrow Wilson Center and John Hopkins University Press.

Kymlicka, W. (ed.) (1995) *The Rights of Minority Cultures*, Oxford: Oxford University Press.

Mills, C.W. (1997) *The Racial Contract*, Ithaca, NY: Cornell University Press.

Tully, J. (1995) *Strange Multiplicity: Constitutionalism in an Age of Diversity*, Cambridge: Cambridge University Press.

JANE HINDLEY

extremism

'Extremism' is a vague pejorative label for the holding of extreme opinions or the advocacy of extreme courses of action. The notion of what is extreme here is, literally, that which is at the outermost point of some ranking of opinions or actions. As such, extremism is popularly represented as antagonistic to democracy. The difficulty is to give the term a sufficiently usable sense to enable one to assess this sort of claim and to evaluate the relation between extremist and democratic politics. What muddies the water is the common equation of extremism with, indifferently, radicalism, revolutionism and totalitarianism, either of the left or the right, or with the advocacy of illegality or violence. This leaves it unclear whether the charge against extremism is that it pursues policies without majority support or that it pursues those that actually oppose democratic principles or violate democratic methods. It is also unclear what is the general connection, if any, between extreme opinions and extreme methods. Is it that extreme opinions are those that prescribe extreme methods? Or that political methods are extreme when undertaken in the furtherance of extreme objectives?

The underlying problem is the lack of an explicit principle for ranking political positions in such a way that some can be identified as extreme. One suggestion might be that extremism contrasts with centrism, because extreme positions are those that diverge most widely from the political centre, where this is thought of as the position with maximum popular support. But the assumption underlying this picture is quite unjustified. There is no general reason to think that political positions can be ranked along an axis above which rises a normal distribution curve of support, with the extreme positions those least supported. A majority may hold extreme views, so that their extremism cannot contrast with centrism understood in this way. Another suggestion might be that extremism is to be measured quite differently as distance from acceptance of the *status quo*, as radicalism is. Yet this is also unsatisfactory, for in certain political circumstances a reactionary position can evidently be extremist.

What extremism in fact contrasts with is moderation, as the history of the notion reveals. The key figure here is George Savile, 1st Marquis of Halifax, the author of *The Character of a Trimmer* (Raleigh 1912). Halifax argues that 'a wise Mean, between barborous Extreams, is that which self-Preservation ought to dictate to our Wishes' (Raleigh 1912: 53). He uses as an analogy the trimming of a boat that threatens to capsize if too much weight is placed on one side or the other. In this way he seeks to justify as necessary to preserve the political system a policy of trimming which, on an ordinary understanding, looks unprincipled. His thinking is that the single-minded pursuit of one set of political objectives can upset the stability of the system. This is because it tends to produce a sharp reaction as a result of which normal politics gives way to conflict and even civil strife. Halifax's own principal example of this tendency was the clash between monarchy and 'commonwealth' as principles of government, a clash resolved, he believed, by the Glorious Revolution of 1688.

Democracy, represented by the Commonwealth, is, it should be noted, one of the extremes in this contest, while what came to be thought of as a revolution is the mean, since it introduced a monarchy constitutionally limited

by parliament. Yet it is Halifax's clear criteria for extremism and moderation which are important here. Extremist positions are identified as those that, in particular political circumstances, are likely to come into conflict and subvert normal political life: moderation is what tends to preserve it. It is not so much that extremists embrace violence, then, that causes extremism to lead to violence, but that the circumstances in which extreme positions are pitted against each other without any moderating influences tend to produce a violent reaction.

Halifax's greatest admirer was Lord Macaulay, who shared his view that the principal aim of politics is to preserve political stability. This stability is threatened by fanatics, whether for political change or in defence of some supposed *status quo*. The danger in such contests, Macaulay thought, was not only that of political chaos, but of a countervailing despotism in which important values of liberty would be lost in pursuit of order (Hamburger 1976). Macaulay saw such a contest emerging in his own day around the Reform Bill of 1832. But Macaulay's support for the Bill did not represent advocacy of democracy in principle. He mistrusted the pursuit of general principles as much as Halifax and believed instead that forms of government should be chosen to suit particular circumstances, the overriding objective being the maintenance of the political stability that renders constitutional government possible. Such stability is threatened by the withdrawal of consent to the political system. Extreme positions alienate sections of the population and thus risk loss of their consent. The moderate path is one that seeks to maintain it, so that their common participation in political life is possible. But the requirement of consent is only a pragmatic principle, not a democratically grounded one.

Macaulay's mistrust of theory and his fear of extremism are connected, as they are in Halifax. Macaulay seems to have taken extreme political positions to be derived deductively from *a priori* principles rather than to be based, like moderate ones, upon experience. Thus, like Karl Popper much later (Popper

1945), he castigates Plato's political utopia, contrasting it with Francis Bacon's modest aim 'to supply our vulgar wants' (Hamburger 1976: 60). Furthermore, again like Halifax he connects extremism with enthusiasm, zealotry and fanaticism, seemingly following David Hume's line that the enthusiast is one who takes a principle to its extremes because he does not fall back, as he should do, into the more moderate and practical attitudes that experience inculcates in most of us (Hume 1739–40). Extremism is thus kept alive by violent passions, rather than the calmer ones of ordinary life. It is less clear how these various supposed features of extremism – its speculative and utopian character, and the zeal and passion of its adherents – fit together. What does seem clear, though, is that all these features militate against extremists participating in ordinary political debate in ways that will lead to conciliation and compromise. They are features which tend to provoke conflict, thus satisfying Halifax's and Macaulay's central criterion for political positions counting as extreme.

What we can see from this brief history is that extremism is best thought of as a *style* of politics, one which involves continuing to take up political positions despite the conflict they provoke and the threat to normal politics which this involves. Two questions immediately arise: what is the motivation for political extremism, and is it somehow incompatible with democratic politics? In answer to the first question we should initially dispose of the suggestion that extremism must be due to a pathological psychological state. Following up Adorno's *The Authoritarian Personality* (1950), Edward Shils argued that the personality type Adorno had identified in fascists was also to be found in communists, that is to say was a feature of extremists generally (Shils 1954). What is suggested is that the extremist psychological type is unable to accommodate the contradictory impulses, towards liberty and order for example, which a moderate politics must negotiate. But while some individual extremists are no doubt pathological there is no reason to suppose this is true of them in

general. Rather, extremists may rationally calculate that their political ends justify the disruption of normal politics. Exactly similar considerations apply to the common tendency to view the resort to violence of terrorist groups, for instance, as irrational.

Another suggestion about the motivation towards extremism is that the extremist holds ideals, by contrast with interests, incompatible with those of other political agents, so that he or she has no way of realising them through normal political processes of conciliation and compromise (Hare 1963). Certainly this may seem to cover many cases, but there is no reason to think it need cover all. The clashes described by Halifax and Macaulay look less like conflicts between different ideals than widely divergent relative evaluations of the same political values; liberty and order could again be taken as examples. A related suggestion is that extremism arises from intolerance of opposing views. Again this may sometimes be a factor but is not a necessary one: anarchists are surely extremists by any standard but are not intolerant of other views, only of their imposition upon others. It is not intolerance as such which characterises extremists, but rather a refusal to limit political activity to channels that do demand a degree of TOLERATION of other views, namely channels in which policy emerges through political processes of mutual concession.

Perhaps instead of asking what is the motivation for extremism we should enquire what are the reasons for moderation where this inevitably involves concession and compromise. In particular, is there a *democratic* argument for not adopting the extremist style of politics? We should notice at once that popular democracy *per se* need not confine itself to a moderate style of politics. Mass support for political objectives can take an extremist form and sweep away opposition without attempting to accommodate its concerns. This is the danger that Halifax and Macaulay see in democracy itself: extremists can use democratic processes to gain majority support for policies that threaten the system by, for example, provoking a reaction from powerful sectional interests. But Halifax's and Macaulay's exclusive emphasis on political stability led them to favour moderate policies not for the principled reason that these are likely to do justice to competing aspirations and concerns, but for the tactical one that they establish a *modus vivendi*. Their reasons for moderation can be given a grounding in democratic theory only to the extent that stability can be seen to be necessary for effective democracy as it is for any continuing form of government (see DEMOCRATIC STABILITY).

To ground moderation in democratic theory more specifically requires one to view democracy not, *à la* Schumpeter (1976), as a struggle for majority support in which the views and interests of the minority can be disregarded, but rather more along the lines of the 'classical' model which he rejected and which is given contemporary expression in theories of DELIBERATIVE DEMOCRACY influenced by Jürgen Habermas (Habermas 1996). Two features of the model are important here. First, the equal respect owed to each democratic actor. This proscribes extremist measures that victimise opponents, terrorise minorities or in other ways create circumstances in which they are effectively excluded from the political process. For it is a feature of normal politics, by contrast with conditions of political conflict, that politics can be engaged in without such risks, and in democracy this implies that they can be engaged in by anyone without jeopardy. The second feature of the classical model that militates against extremism is its conception of the outcome of democratic processes as the will of the people as a whole. Again this contrasts with a merely majoritarian conception which an extremist can espouse. But the popular will conception of democratic outcomes constrains the kind of processes which can produce them to those incompatible with the extremist style. For in countenancing conflict within the polity in pursuit of their objectives extremists tacitly deny its unity as a DEMOS with a single will.

By contrast, democratic moderates aim not simply for the best policy between the extremes, but for one which is best calculated to preserve the unity of the demos in view of the dangers to it posed by the determined pursuit of these extremes. The assumption here is that such a mean can be found within a classically democratic polity, so that there is no longer a rational motivation for extremism. That is to say, classical democracy not only militates against extremism, it also offers an antidote to it. Whether, or perhaps rather in what circumstances, this typically unexamined assumption is justified is an unduly neglected question for democratic theory.

See also:

authority; consensus democracy; constitutionalism; democratic stability; majoritarianism

Further reading

Adorno, T. *et al.* (1969) *The Authoritarian Personality*, New York: Norton.

Habermas, J. (1996) *Between Facts and Norms: Contributions to a Discourse Theory Of Law and Democracy*, Cambridge: Polity Press.

Hamburger, J. (1976) *Macaulay and the Whig Tradition*, Chicago: University of Chicago Press.

Hare, R.M. (1963) *Freedom and Reason*, Oxford: Oxford University Press.

Hume, D. (1978) *Treatise of Human Nature*, ed. L.A. Shelby-Bigge, Oxford: Clarendon, 2nd edn.

Popper, K. (1945) *The Open Society and its Enemies*, London: Routledge and Kegan Paul.

Raleigh, W. (1912) *Complete Works of George Savile*, Oxford: Clarendon Press.

Schumpeter, J. (1976) *Capitalism, Socialism and Democracy*, London: Allen & Unwin.

Shils, E. (1954) 'Authoritarianism: "Right" and "Left"', in R. Christie and M. Jahoda (eds), *Studies in the Scope and Method of 'The Authoritarian Personality'*, Glencoe, IL: The Free Press, 24–49.

PAUL GILBERT

F

federalism

Practice and theory

Federalism, in general, refers to a territorial organisation of the political community in which there are two or more spheres of government, which combine self-rule and shared rule. Federalism can be the result of a process by which different political units, through the establishment of a pact, decide to 'come together' (centripetal, such as the USA) or decide to 'hold together' some kind of political unity (centrifugal, such as Belgium) while giving AUTONOMY to the constituent political units. Etymologically, the term federalism derives from the Latin *foedus*, meaning treaty or contract.

Federal *practices* already took place in ancient history. Daniel J. Elazar (Elazar 1987) observed that federalism stems originally from the Israelite biblical tradition. According to this early tradition, it was considered that humankind should be organised by means of a covenant between God and man, whereby the former would protect the latter on condition that the individual showed his or her loyalty to God. The first political forms of federalism can be traced back to the Israelite Federation (thirteenth century BC to 722 BC) and the ancient leagues of Greek city-states (fifth and fourth centuries BC). The Romans also relied upon federal practices to maintain the territorial integrity of their empire.

Despite these early origins, federalism was not a very popular organisational device during the medieval period, neither was there any general *theory* of federalism in ancient and medieval times. Johannes Althusius, heavily influenced by the earlier biblical tradition, was one of the first theoretical defenders of the idea of federalism in his *Politica Methodice Digesta* (1603, 1610), as a device to ensure the unity of the Holy Roman Empire. Immanuel Kant also refers to federalism in the normative sense in his *Perpetual Peace* (1795), in which he argues for a peaceful world which can only be achieved by the establishment of a supranational federal world structure.

It was only with the establishment of the American federation in the eighteenth century that federal *practice* was reborn and the secularisation and the first coherent exposition of a *theory* of contemporary federalism came about from the writings of Alexander Hamilton, John Jay and James Madison. Their articles, written in defence of the American federation, established in 1787, were brought together in *The Federalist* under the pseudonym 'Publius'. These authors no longer defended federalism in religious terms, but, inspired by the Lockean liberal tradition, in terms of individual FREEDOM. The success of the American federation was so influential that it became a major source of inspiration for many of the federations established during the nineteenth century, such as Switzerland, Canada, Germany, Brazil and Argentina.

Federal agreements

In general, 'federal agreements', a broader concept than that of 'federation', are those which combine the principle of self-rule and shared rule (Elazar 1987; Watts 1997). Adapting a commonly used classification within the current study of federalism, one should distinguish between four basic types of federal agreements: regional states, symmetrical federations, asymmetrical federal agreements and confederations.

Regional states. These are states in which the double level of territorial government is the result of a constitutionally guaranteed process of political decentralisation. Regional political decentralisation, which supposes the previous existence of a centralised state, has in practice only really been established by some of the regions of the state. Unlike in federations, political DECENTRALISATION only occurs with regard to the legislative and executive powers, while the judicial powers usually remain exclusively within the sphere of the central power. Regional fiscal and economic powers tend to be very limited or even absent, as do the mechanisms to provide for regional participation in the process of constitutional reform. Italy, from the Second World War onwards, is considered to be the prototype of a regional state.

Symmetrical federations. In general, federations tend to display the following characteristics. First, there is the presence of two spheres of government, each acting directly upon its citizens through its own legislative, executive and judicial powers within territorially demarcated units. These two spheres include a federal government on the one hand, and several federated units (states, provinces, Länder) on the other hand. Unlike the regions in a regional state, the federated units rely mostly upon their own financial and economic resources. Second, the federal units are allowed to influence the federal POLICY-MAKING process through some specific institutional mechanisms. The most frequently used is the second chamber, formed by equal representation of the federal units (United States of America) or by taking into account to some extent the population of the federal unit (Germany). Third, because there are two spheres of government, each exercising legislative and executive powers, an institutional referee is provided in order to resolve possible conflicts of interest and competences. A constitutional or supreme court usually exercises this function. Fourth, the structure and the division of powers of the federation are mostly written down and guaranteed by a constitutional act, which cannot usually be reformed without the consent of the majority of the federal units. Finally, due to the overlap or the sharing of competences, federations are characterised by the presence of inter-governmental relations.

The symmetrical character of the federation lies in the fact that relations between the federal government and the federal units on the one hand, and between the federal units themselves on the other hand, are more or less uniform. Examples of such symmetrical federations are Australia, Austria, Germany and the USA.

Asymmetrical federal agreements. Here we should distinguish between two types of agreement: asymmetrical federations and specific asymmetrical agreements between different types of units (federacies and associated states).

Although asymmetrical federations tend to display the same general characteristics of federations, they differ from symmetrical federations with regard to the asymmetrical character of their relations, especially between the federal government and the federated units, but also regarding relations with each other. Thus, the federal constitution establishes different relations for certain units, reflected, for instance, in a varying degree of self-government, in the varying degree and form of PARTICIPATION in the representation of the state abroad, in the symbolic and institutional framework and so on. Reasons for governing on the basis of legal asymmetries are various, but they are all based on the *de facto* asymmetries (cultural, geographic, historical and so on) which exist between the federated units. A recent example of such an asymmetrical federation is Belgium (since 1993).

Federacies and associated states are another type of asymmetrical federal agreement. Federacies consist of an agreement between a large unit and one or several smaller units, granting a high degree of internal AUTONOMY to the latter but a limited role in the decisions of the larger unit. The agreement cannot be broken unilaterally, but needs mutual consent. The agreement between Puerto Rico and the USA is an example of this type of asymmetrical federal agreement. Associated states, on the other hand, are very similar to federacies, but they differ with regard to dissolution procedures. Unlike federacies, in associated states either the larger or the smaller unit can dissolve the agreement unilaterally, respecting the pre-established guidelines. The agreement between Italy and San Marino is an example of an associated state.

Confederations. These are federal agreements between different independent states which aim to pursue some specific objectives, such as a certain level of economic INTEGRATION, military defence or the enhancement of their international relations. Hence, unlike federations, confederations are the result of an international treaty or agreement (not of a constitutional act) between various states, which do not give up their SOVEREIGNTY. Common government, therefore, depends entirely upon the governments of the confederated states, which may at any time dissolve the agreement following the previously established rules.

From an historical point of view, confederations have not shown great stability and were called the 'most imperfect federal form' by John Stuart Mill. Although in the past confederations tended to transform themselves into federal states, as happened with the United States of America at the Philadelphia Conference in 1787 and in Switzerland in 1847, this was not the case for the confederal Dutch Republic, which became a unitary state. The Commonwealth of Independent States, established after the fall of the USSR, is one of the few contemporary examples of a confederation of states. Established in 1990, it contains most of the former Soviet Republics, with the exception of some countries such as Estonia, Latvia and Lithuania which from the beginning decided not to join the confederation.

As well these four basic types of federal agreements, one can also identify other federal arrangements of a more limited character and implication. This is the case, for example, of unions, leagues, condominiums and shared functional authorities. *Unions* are states in which the constituent units maintain their integrity, principally by means of general institutions such as councillors' double mandate (regional and general level), as was the case in Belgium before 1993. *Leagues* are arrangements among different states, established in order to achieve some specific objectives through a secretariat, and not through the establishment of any government (for example, the League of Arab States). In *condominiums*, the authority over a territory is shared between various states, as was the case of Andorra (France and Spain) until 1993. *Shared functional agencies*, finally, are established by various states to carry out specific policies (such as the International Atomic Energy Agency).

Current analysis of federalism

Analysts of federalism have concentrated upon different aspects of federalism. One can identify three major aspects: those concerning the whole political system and political processes, and those concerning normative issues.

Federalism and the political system

The principal aim of scholars who focus upon the relationship between federalism and the political system is to demonstrate how elements of the political system influence the practical working of federalism and vice versa. There is extensive literature on the influence of different types of government on the working of federalism. While in presidential systems, which are characterised by a strict separation of powers, both executive and legislative powers are involved in intergovernmental relations; in many parliamentary systems, these relations are mainly dominated by the executive power. Another field of investigation is whether federalism promotes centrifugal or centripetal movements on the one hand, or decentralisation or centralisation on the other. The *de jure* and *de facto* asymmetries of federalism constitute another area of study for many scholars. Of special interest here are the possibilities and limits of asymmetrical federalism in the case of plurinational states, such as Belgium, Canada, Spain or the United Kingdom. A further object of study are the rules of constitutional reform. In most of the federal states, these rules are quite rigid. This gives way, however, to other mechanisms of change in relation to federalism, such as the judicial interpretations (JUDICIAL REVIEW) and sentences brought forward by the constitutional courts. It is now widely recognised that constitutional courts play a significant role in the decentralising or centralising nature of federalism. A last focus of academic attention are fiscal relationships and how they might influence the nature of federalism. Within this field of research there have been studies into how financial aid from the federal government (grants in aid) might lead to a more centralising and uniform character of federalism.

Federalism and political processes

One field of study is the consequences of the way federal agreements are reached. Here we should distinguish between processes of non-centralisation and processes of decentralisation. While the former reflect the existence of a dispersed power, the latter presuppose the previous existence of a centralised power. Thus, it is broadly accepted that both processes correspond to different objectives and that both are sometimes related to different conceptions of the DEMOS in the federations. Another object of study is the relationship between federalism and SUBSIDIARITY, the latter being a principle which contains two aspects: first, it argues that decisions should be taken as close to the citizens as possible; and second, it argues that decisions should be taken at the appropriate level from the point of view of the efficiency of the DECISION-MAKING procedure. It is becoming clear by now that federalism and subsidiarity can be quite conflictive. In other words, subsidiarity can be in conflict with the objective of self-government of the federal units. Another issue is the relationship between federalism and political culture. Here it is usually stressed that a federal culture must exist for federalism to be successful. The relationship between federalism and

the processes of supranational integration is another object of interest for analysts of federalism.

Federalism and cultural pluralism

The study of federalism from the perspective of cultural pluralism, specially from the perspective of territorially concentrated national MINORITIES, and the demands the latter make upon the state, is a third and comparatively recent issue in federal studies. The steadily growing importance of this perspective within political science is basically due to a growing awareness by normative political theorists (such as Taylor, Tully, Kymlicka and Walzer) that liberal political theory and the liberal state have not always been as culturally neutral (see NEUTRALITY) as they might have wished to be. For example, as these scholars have argued, in plurinational states, the choice of the official language of the state (such as Castilian in Spain) or the choice of its national holiday, to give only two examples, are not neutral with regard to the national minorities living within its territory. According to these authors, liberal political theory has never been able to recognise appropriately, in liberal democratic terms, the national differences within the public sphere, due to its INDIVIDUALISM, its universalism and its statism (Requejo 1998). Hence, what is at stake for these authors is a changing conception of the demos and the democratic LEGITIMACY of minority rights. While liberal political theory used to conceptualise the demos in homogeneous terms, there are now academics who argue that this is the exception rather than the rule: most states of the world are *pluri*national rather than *nation*-states. As a consequence, the argument continues, federalism might be considered a possible and adequate way to accommodate the demands for self-government stemming from national minorities by providing them with constitutional recognition as well as political institutions, in order to allow them to make their own policies within the cultural, social and economic spheres. If the basis of democratic liberalism is being revised, so should the case of federal structures based on liberal democratic premises.

Although federalism can never be completely symmetrical, as size, wealth and population differ from one federal unit to another, these scholars mostly advocate asymmetrical or plural federalism as an appropriate way to give public expression to the demands of national minorities (Requejo 1999). In the case of Canada and Spain, for example, this would mean that Quebec and Catalonia should receive asymmetrical treatment with regard to the symbolic and linguistic sphere, the institutional sphere (such as special and guaranteed representation in the second chamber and in the constitutional court) and the sphere of competences (such as full autonomy to regulate the educational curriculum). These measures would ensure that national entities like Quebec and Catalonia are not uniformly treated in terms of political recognition and self-government by the Canadian and Spanish states, as is the case with other Canadian provinces and Spanish autonomous communities. Further study into these and related issues promises to be one of the most promising fields of study of federalism in the twenty-first century.

See also:

citizenship; integration; liberalism; nations and nationalism; state, models of

Further reading

Burgess, M. and Gagnon, A. (eds) (1993) *Comparative Federalism and Federation: Competing Traditions and Future Directions*, Hemel Hempstead: Harvester Wheatsheaf.

De Villiers, B. (ed.) *Evaluating Federal Systems*, London: Juta.

Elazar, D.J. (1987) *Exploring Federalism*, Tuscaloosa, AL: The University of Alabama Press.

—— (1991) *Federal Systems of the World*, Essex: Longman.

Forsyth, M. (ed.) (1989) *Federalism and Nationalism*, Leicester: Leicester University Press.

Fossas, E. and Requejo, F. (eds) (1999) *Asimetria federal y Estado plurinacional. El debate sobre la acomodación de la diversidad en Canadá, Bélgica y España*, Madrid: Trotta.

Requejo, F. (1998) *Federalisme per a què? L'acomodació de la diversitat en democràcies plurinacionals*, Barcelona: Edicions 3i4.

—— (1999) 'Cultural Pluralism, Nationalism and Federalism: A Revision of Democratic Citizenship in Plurinational States', *European Journal of Political Research* 35(2): 255–86.

Riker, W.H. (1975) 'Federalism', in F.I. Greenstein and N.W. Polsby (eds.) *Handbook of Political Science, Vol. 5: Governmental Institutions and Processes*, Reading, MA: Addison-Wesley.

Watts, R. (1997) *Comparing Federal Systems in the 1990s*, Kingston and Montreal: Institute of Intergovernmental Relations, Queen's University and McGill-Queen's University Press.

Wheare, K.C. (1946) *Federal Government*, London: Oxford University Press.

FERRAN REQUEJO
SVEN WYNANTS

freedom

Democracy has always been associated with ideas of freedom. Yet the relationship between these two ideals is less than straightforward and is complicated by the different meanings that have been ascribed to 'freedom'. One celebrated way of distinguishing between different ideas of freedom is Isaiah Berlin's simple dichotomy between negative and positive concepts of freedom (Berlin 1969). That distinction has been much criticised and the labels 'negative' and 'positive' are potentially misleading, but they do identify two ways of thinking about freedom that are importantly different and whose difference is particularly relevant for democracy.

Negative liberty describes a concept of being free as being unprevented from doing or being.

One's freedom consists in the area within which one is unprevented from being or doing what one chooses. Quite what should count as being 'unprevented' is much disputed so that different theorists have different conceptions of what should count as negative liberty, but those disputes are contained within a shared view of liberty as the absence of impediments of one sort or another. Positive liberty shifts the focus of being free from an area of unimpeded action to the question of who or what controls my conduct. It asks not, 'over what area of conduct am I left to do or to be what I please?' but, 'who or what possesses control over me?' I am free to the extent that I am master of my own conduct.

Negative freedom is often thought to stand in an entirely contingent relation to democracy. Thus, for example, liberal democracy is frequently conceived as the yoking together of a commitment to liberty and a commitment to democracy that are otherwise unrelated. For the same reason, the idea of liberal democracy is sometimes alleged to betray a half-hearted commitment to democracy: an acceptance of democracy only insofar as it does not encroach upon a privileged set of freedoms. By contrast the true democrat, it might be alleged, would place complete trust in the DEMOS and not fetter it for the sake of freedom or any other value.

Whether a commitment to freedom independently of democracy really amounts to a reprehensible lapse from the pure democratic faith is highly questionable. Firstly, the idea of being committed to democracy and to nothing else makes little sense. If we are committed to nothing but the rightness or goodness of democracy, how do we decide how to cast our votes when we participate in democratic DECISION-MAKING? Secondly, the idea that we should subordinate every aspect of our lives to the decision of a demos is quite bizarre. Why should we wish to place every jot and tittle of our lives at the mercy of absolute political power, be it democratic or undemocratic?

In fact, democracy and negative liberty are related to one another in more than merely contingent ways. For one thing, democracy

itself requires that the members of a demos must enjoy certain freedoms if their political system is to be authentically democratic. Most prosaically, democratic citizens must be genuinely free to cast their votes as they judge fit; if their votes are subject to COERCION or manipulation, democracy becomes a sham. But ordinarily, democracy entails more than just voting; it also entails public discussion and debate. That in turn requires freedom of political expression. If the members of a demos are prevented from either expressing or hearing certain views on public matters, their AUTONOMY as democratic decision makers is impaired. The fundamental idea of democracy is that of a people deciding or controlling its own affairs, and that idea is compromised to the extent that a population is prevented from reaching and implementing its own decisions on public matters.

Several other freedoms are crucial to democracy in its modern indirect forms. Citizens must be free to run for political office. They must be free to associate with one another for political purposes, most obviously as political PARTIES seeking election but also as groups aiming to influence public decision-making even though they do not seek public office. The freedoms to investigate, criticise and oppose a government's conduct are also crucial to the functioning of indirect democracy.

Another important part of the democratic idea is that people should enjoy these freedoms as *equal* freedoms. Democracy requires not merely that people should have the right to participate but that they should have the right to participate equally, so that the freedoms that are essential to the functioning of democracy are freedoms that democratic citizens should enjoy equally (see EQUALITY).

In some respects then, there is a simple logical relation between democracy and freedom. But the logical nature of that relation does not render the idea of 'democratic freedom' entirely uncontroversial, since it remains subject to dispute over what should count as freedom. Disagreements over the nature of negative freedom focus primarily on what should count as an impediment to freedom.

Few would deny that laws and punishments restrict freedom. Even fewer would deny that physical constraints remove freedom. But suppose I lack the material resources to do something; am I therefore unfree to do it? Given the inequalities of wealth and income that characterise modern societies, the way we answer that question will make a radical difference to our assessment of the freedom, and of the distribution of freedom, that people enjoy as members of an allegedly democratic society. A wealthy press baron and an impoverished citizen may be legally at liberty to express the same range of opinions; should that be enough to satisfy us that they are equally free to voice their political opinions and to influence the political process?

Although some freedoms are logically entailed by democracy, others are not. Consider freedom of religious worship. That freedom is in no way essential to the functioning of democracy and its value cannot find a foundation in the prerequisites of democracy. A measure that limits or removes the freedom of worship of a particular group may be wrong, but it is not obviously undemocratic. The same holds true of many other liberties; the freedom to marry a partner of one's choice, to divorce, to choose a career, to dress as one pleases, to associate with others for non-political purposes, to move within and to leave a state, to engage in scientific enquiry, and so on. We might therefore describe these as 'non-democratic' liberties. Even freedom of expression, in its non-political aspects, has value independently of democracy. It follows that, at least in principle, there is a potentiality for conflict between democracy and these non-democratic freedoms. A democratic community could deprive its members of these freedoms without in any way ceasing to be democratic; indeed, it is possible to point to historical approximations to 'totalitarian democracy' (Talmon 1961). The great fear of many nineteenth-century liberal thinkers, such as John Stuart Mill (1910) and Alexis de Toqueville (1994), was that democratic societies would sacrifice individual liberty to equality and impose a stultifying uniformity upon their members. In particular, they feared that majorities would not tolerate MINORITIES whose opinions and ways of life departed from the majoritarian norm so that democracy would bring with it its own peculiar form of tyranny.

As well as viewing democracy as a threat to individual liberty, it is also possible to regard individual liberty as a shackle upon democracy. If we give a privileged status to certain individual liberties, we establish 'no go' areas for democracy. That is precisely the effect of bills of RIGHTS that give a privileged status to liberties such as freedom of religion. In giving these liberties a constitutionally entrenched status, bills of rights place constraints upon the democratic process. Of course, the individuals who make up a democratic society may be only too happy to enjoy these immunities from political power. It remains true nevertheless that, to the extent that they possess constitutionally entrenched rights to personal liberty, they are constrained in what they themselves can do as wielders of democratic political power.

All that said, it is wrong to counterpose democratic government to non-democratic liberty as though there *must* be some sort of conflict or tension between them. Both in the ancient world and in the modern day, democracies have compared very favourably with other forms of government with respect to the range of liberties they have accorded their members. On the whole, the historical record has not confirmed nineteenth-century fears that democracy would develop at the expense of individual liberty. Moreover, there is good reason why a democratic society should cherish non-democratic along with democratic freedoms. Much of the impetus behind democracy comes from a conception of human beings as persons who enjoy equal standing and whose capacity to make decisions about their own lives we should respect. If we share that conception, it follows that individuals should have an equal right to participate in making the collective decisions that are to govern their lives. But that way of justifying democracy (see DEMOCRACY, JUSTIFICATIONS FOR) also provides reason for according individuals a significant domain of personal liberty and for limiting the extent to which their lives should be subordinate to collective decision-making. In other words, this justification for democracy is simultaneously a justification for limiting the extent to which people's freedom should be placed at the mercy of political power, including democratic political power.

That is not quite enough to warrant the inference that democracy *entails* respect for personal liberty. Democracy is a form of government that can be, and has been, justified in a great variety of ways and the appeal to the status of persons and to the value of their autonomy is only one of these. Other forms of justification, for example, that democracy is maximally effective at promoting economic development or that it is the form of government ordained by God, may entail no similarly favourable implications for personal liberty. But, insofar as we are committed to democracy because we are committed to respecting people's capacity to shape their own lives, our commitment to democracy and to a significant domain of individual freedom will share a common foundation.

The possibility of justifying democracy by appealing to ideas of self-determination begins to take us into the realm of Berlin's concept of positive liberty. Imagine two societies with identical sets of laws. The only difference between them is that in one society the laws have been adopted through a democratic process while, in the other, the same laws have been imposed by an autocratic ruler. Does the first society enjoy greater freedom than the second? If we limit ourselves to a negative concept of freedom, it would seem that it does not. People in both societies are subject to the same range of restraints so that the arenas of actions within which they are free to do or to be what they choose are identical. Yet societies that are governed democratically are often thought to enjoy greater freedom merely in virtue of being democratic.

The root idea behind that thought is that of 'self-government' or 'self-determination'. Democracy means the rule of the people and, if a people rules itself, it is self-governing. If it is

ruled by someone else, such as a monarch, a dictator, an oligarchic elite or an external power, it is not. Thus, in a democracy a people determines its own destiny and, in that sense, is 'free'. It is subject to no one above or outside itself; it is governed only by its own will. That is why a democratic society might be said to enjoy greater freedom than a society ruled by an autocrat even though the members of these societies are subject to identical sets of laws. This idea of a 'free people' has figured prominently in republican thought (see REPUBLICANISM).

In consonance with Berlin's concept of 'positive' freedom, the relevant question here is 'by whom are we governed?' rather than 'how much are we governed?'. On the other hand, as critics of Berlin have pointed out, these two concepts of freedom may not be quite as separate as these two questions suggest. The model of a self-governing people draws upon the analogue of a self-governing (or 'autonomous') person, and the idea of a self-governing person is that of a person who is unprevented by others from following his or her self-chosen path. At root, therefore, the ideas of negative and positive liberty are not clearly differentiated. They stem from a conception of the free person as someone who is unsubordinated to, and so unconstrained by, the will of another.

This analogue with the free individual also points to the main difficulty involved in characterising democratic rule as, in and of itself, a condition of freedom. The analogy works best if we conceived the people (the 'demos') as a unified entity characterised by a unified will. We can then think of the people, as we can think of a person, as an 'individual' with a single will and of democratic enactments as unblemished expressions of that single will. A democratic people so conceived will then be no less free than an individual person who finds himself in no way constrained by the will of others. But, of course, the people who are both the wielders and the subjects of democratic authority normally do not exhibit that undifferentiated unity. They are commonly divided by different preferences, interests, beliefs and values and sometimes by differences of culture, ethnicity and religion. Thus, what some members of the demos may 'will', others may not.

In these circumstances, it would seem implausible and disingenuous to equate democratic decision-making with full self-determination. Some members of the demos will get what they want, but others will not. Thus, as Mill remarked, so-called 'self-government' may turn out to be the government not of me by myself but of me by everyone else (1910: 67). For those on the losing side, particularly if they are almost always on the losing side (as sometimes happens in ethnically or religiously divided societies), democracy can be as oppressive as any other form of rule.

Is there then anything to be said in defence of the common notion that democracy is itself a manifestation of liberty? It was Rousseau (1968) who provided the most celebrated attempt to reconcile liberty and authority by way of democracy. He sought a form of authority to which people could subject themselves and yet remain as free as before and he argued that, under the right conditions, DIRECT DEMOCRACY could provide that authority. His fundamental thought is simply stated. A population that constitutes a genuine community will possess a common good; that is, a good common to all members of the community. All members of the community must want, or 'will', what is for their common good and, since they share that will, we can describe that as their 'general will'. When the members of this community meet as a demos, they should enact rules that promote their general will. In doing so, they exercise authority over one another (as a demos they make decisions collectively that bind each of them severally), yet each member of the community remains as free as before since the demos merely enacts what each wishes it to enact. How can an individual be rendered unfree by an arrangement that simply secures what he or she wishes? Such a regime would seem to realise freedom rather than to hinder or remove it.

As Rousseau himself was keen to insist, this argument holds only so long as democratic decision-making is guided by the general will.

If one section of a society uses the democratic process to promote its sectional interest (its 'particular' will), it impairs the freedom of other sections. So a body of citizens must remain conscientiously committed to the general will if their democracy is not to compromise their liberty. What if citizens are so committed but disagree about what *is* their general will (about what is their common good)? Then, Rousseau says, they have to resolve the matter by majority vote. But how can they do that without diminishing the freedom, the 'self-determination', of the losing minority who will then have to live under rules they have not chosen? Rousseau's answer is that, under the right circumstances, we can suppose that the majority discerns the general will *correctly* and, since that is the *general* will, it is also the true will of the minority. The minority has simply mistaken what it really wants. Thus, in complying with measures supported by the majority, it is complying with measures that conform with its own will correctly conceived and its liberty therefore remains undiminished.

The difficulties that confront Rousseau's ambitious argument are as obvious as its logic. If the general will is in dispute, do we have adequate reason to suppose that the majority will judge it correctly? Must there always be a general will to be judged correctly? On some public matters, it may be that citizens simply have different preferences or interests such that the wishes of some must prevail over those of others and there can be no pretence that the resulting decision embodies the 'real will' of the outvoted minority. Moreover, insofar as Rousseau reconciles liberty with authority through the idea of the 'general will', he leaves democracy dangerously exposed. If what matters to my freedom is that authority is used to promote a general will in which I share (even though I myself may mistake that will), why should it matter that I and my fellow citizens should be involved in the expression of that will? Perhaps a wise individual or elite will judge the common good of a populus, and therefore its general will, more successfully than the people themselves. Indeed, in later history the idea that the freedom of a people lies in the realisation of its real will, and that its real will may differ from its expressed will, has sometimes been used to legitimate regimes that have been both undemocratic and illiberal.

If Rousseau's argument is overly ambitious, can we say nothing in defence of the association of democracy with liberty by way of the idea of self-government? At the very least, we might insist that, in a democracy operating by majority vote, a greater proportion of a population will live under rules and policies that it endorses than under any alternative form of decision-making. To that extent, democracy may claim to *maximise* self-determination even though it cannot deliver self-determination for every individual all of the time. But perhaps we can claim more than that. There seems a significant difference between (1) my being subject to a decision that I have had no part in making and (2) my being subject to a decision in whose making I have had an equal voice and an equal vote but in which I have nevertheless been outvoted. Generally we view the second of these quite differently from the first, though it may be that, insofar as we find the second more acceptable than the first, we do so for reasons of fairness rather than freedom.

There are, then, several dimensions to the relation between democracy and freedom. Democracy itself requires that there be certain public freedoms, such as freedom of political inquiry and expression, since these are essential to the very nature of democratic government. Other freedoms, which we may roughly group together as 'personal liberties', are not similarly intrinsic to democracy but may nevertheless be rooted in the same fundamental values as democracy and have generally fared better in democratic than in undemocratic societies. The attempt to equate democratic rule itself with freedom, through the idea of self-determination, is hard to carry through in a comprehensive fashion once we concede that a democratic population will normally consist of individuals or groups with different beliefs and preferences rather than a body that always possesses a single uniform will. Even so, as long as populations possessing different beliefs and preferences have to be governed by collective decisions, it is hard to see how we can translate the ideal of self-determination into anything better than democracy.

See also:

authority; democratic debate; immunities and protections; individualism; liberalism; toleration

Further reading

Berlin, I. (1969) 'Two Concepts of Liberty', in I. Berlin, *Four Essays on Liberty*, Oxford: Oxford University Press.

De Toqueville, A. (1994) *Democracy in America*, ed. J.P. Mayer, London: Fontana.

Graham, K. (1986) *The Battle of Democracy*, Brighton: Wheatsheaf.

Gray, T. (1991) *Freedom*, Basingstoke: Macmillan.

Leader, S. (1996) 'Three Faces of Toleration in a Democracy', *Journal of Political Philosophy* 4(1): 45–67.

Mill, J.S. (1910) *On Liberty*, in *Utilitarianism, Liberty, Representative Government*, ed. A.D. Lindsay, London: Dent.

Miller, D. (ed.) (1991) *Liberty*, Oxford: Oxford University Press.

Rousseau, J.J. (1968) *The Social Contract*, ed. M. Cranston, Harmondsworth: Penguin.

Talmon, J. (1961) *The Origins of Totalitarian Democracy*, London: Mercury.

Weale, A (1999) *Democracy*, Basingstoke: Macmillan.

PETER JONES

functional representation

The notion of functional representation has been used interchangeably with such other concepts as group, interest, sectional, occupational, organic, associational and corporatist representation. Unlike individual-based representation in which citizens are represented as distinct persons and on a territorial basis, the central idea of functional representation is that citizens in a polity are represented in terms of their membership of social groups. Groups in this context may be organisations that admit of voluntary membership, such as civic associations; or more inclusive entities taken to represent particular sectors in society, for example, minority groupings or occupational interests.

In the history of idea and practice, explications on and justifications for a corporatist view of society have not been lacking. Medieval social theory, Burke's theory of representation, Cole's guild socialist theory and CORPORATISM have all in one way or another advocated a scheme of functional representation. In practice, representation of corporate communities such as the great peers, the landed gentry, merchants and manufacturers had existed in medieval England. In the early twentieth century, Germany under the Weimar constitution of 1919 instituted a Federal Economic Council to complement the political assembly. Its members were drawn from the main divisions of economic life like agriculture, industry, commerce and banking. Occupational representation had also existed in the Irish Senate of 1922–30, while Fascist Italy is widely taken as the exemplary corporatist polity. Elsewhere, Austria after 1934 and Portugal after 1933 experimented with economic parliaments based on group constituencies. Closer to our times, many progressive European economies are managed through corporatist arrangements. A system of functional representation in the legislature has also been in existence in Hong Kong since 1985.

However, until the recent decades, there has not been much scholarly interest in furthering the earlier theories or in more systematically formulating the plausible contribution of functional representation to modern democratic governance. The resurrection of functional representation theory is due to multifold dissatisfaction with representative democracy (see REPRESENTATION, CONCEPT OF; REPRESENTATION, MODELS OF). As modern societies become more complex, not all interests are able to find expression under the existing representation system; party politics has become corrupt and trivialised; decision makers are too outpaced by the knowledge and INFORMATION explosion to find effective answers to social problems; and an informal and shadowy system of interest access raises serious doubts about political EQUALITY and ACCOUNTABILITY.

To ameliorate these problems, Cohen and Rogers (1995) suggest a scheme of 'associative democracy' in which they outline the positive contributions of group representation to democracy. First, groups provide expert information, which improves governmental performance and facilitates citizen deliberations on public issues. Second, if associations take on quasi-public functions and figure more as problem solvers rather than interest lobbies, it advances democracy by offering an alternative mode of social governance to that of markets and public hierarchies. Both of these functions help to further popular sovereignty. Third, political representation can be better equalised through the inclusion of hitherto excluded or under-represented interests. Paul Hirst (1994), in this connection, argues for corporatist representation of industry and labour in economic management, and associationalism to 'pluralise' the state by devolving a range of social and public functions to internally democratic voluntary groups and associations (see Hirst's ASSOCIATIONAL DEMOCRACY).

For John Burnheim (1985), the existing system of representative democracy is objectionable because it allows everybody to have a say in everything as entailed in the principles of individual-based representation and political equality. Such a system makes meaningful participation impossible when people exercise authority over others even without substantive material interests in the issues at stake. To Burnheim, the solution lies in replacing the central state with a system of autonomous agencies, each exercising AUTHORITY in a specific functional area but co-ordinated by negotiation among themselves. PARTICIPATION in decision-making in such functional communities will not be open to just anyone, instead, it is confined to those with a morally justifiable substantive interest in the decisions in question. The decision makers of agencies would be chosen by lot and be a statistically representative sample of those affected by the decisions. Under this scheme, depending on their substantive interests, citizens may be members of more or less functional communities.

Despite the various attempts to complement and revitalise representative democracy through group-based representation, a number of challenges appear to be outstanding. At the practical level, there is the obvious difficulty about inclusion and exclusion. Questions arise as to what and which groups or functions deserve representation. If questions in this regard are not adequately dealt with, political inequality will inevitably result. On the other hand, if societal affairs are to be managed by functional agencies as in Burnheim's scheme, or by groups as proposed by Cohen and Rogers and by Hirst, it is not straightforward what authority precisely should be exercised by such agents.

At a more theoretical level, there is the question of the factionalising nature of groups: the emphasis is on particularity, exclusiveness, and sectional rather than common interests. There is also the fear that any scheme of group representation may further entrench the privileged positions of the more articulate and resourceful groups. Lastly, the assumptions that the division of functions and the configuration of legitimate societal interests can somehow be determined a priori and regarded as static may be fallacious. Eugene Bardach (1981) argues that particular interests are created only out of disagreement with specific policy outcomes. Interest constellation is therefore policy contingent rather than pre-existent. This seems to present as yet the most severe challenge to advocations of functional representation.

See also:

associational democracy; democratic deficit; interest groups

Further reading

Bardach, E. (1981) 'On Representing the Public Interest,' *Ethics* 91: 486–90.

Beer, S. (1982) *Modern British Politics*, New York: Norton.

Burnheim, J. (1985) *Is Democracy Possible?*, Cambridge: Polity Press.

Christiano, T. (1996) *The Rule of the Many*, Boulder, CO: Westview Press.

Cohen, J. and Rogers, J. (1995) *Associations and Democracy*, London: Verso.

Cole, G.D.H. (1920) *The Social Theory*, London: Methuen.

Hirst, P. (1994) *Associative Democracy*, Cambridge: Polity Press.

Loewenstein, K. (1937) 'Occupational Representation and the Idea of an Economic Parliament', *Social Science* 12(1): 420–31, 529–30.

Pennock, J.R. (1979) *Democratic Political Theory*, Princeton, NJ: Princeton University Press.

Pitkin, H.F. (1967) *The Concept of Representation*, Berkeley and Los Angeles: University of California Press.

ROWENA KWOK

G

gendering democracy

The mainstay of feminist thought is that the lived experience of the sexes is constituted in systems of thought, social formations and discourses that define the identity of individuals in terms of a male–female dualism, placing the female in an inferior position to the male. This 'gender-sex system' (Benhabib 1992) is deeply rooted in time and space and is manifest across societies and cultures. While its everyday impact on the lived experience of women may differ across the diversity of cultures, classes or states, such differences, according to feminist thought, do not negate a baseline of exploitation and oppression emergent from gendered social practices.

One such practice is democracy, and the historical trajectory of democratic formations in the western world has not fulfilled the equalities in PARTICIPATION and representation (see REPRESENTATION, CONCEPT OF) sought by campaigners who won the vote for women. While feminist thought has sought to uncover the discursive and institutional continuities that form the basis of exclusionary practices based on gender, the challenge to feminist thought itself centres around difference and the diversity of the lived experiences of women situated in radically different social matrices. The experience of democracy itself may not, therefore, be reduced to formulaic redefinitions of representation in legislative assemblies, but rather is recognised to incorporate the manifestations of institutionalised and discursive practices on the daily lives of women and the multiplicity of their locations. The meaning of CITIZENSHIP and the RIGHTS and RESPONSI-BILITIES contained therein come to be as crucial to the project of gendering democracy as questions relating to the construction of the subject of politics within complex relations of power. To gender democracy is therefore to seek not just the transformation of institutions of governance, but to question the location of politics itself, the relationship between the private and the public (see PUBLIC–PRIVATE DISTINCTION) and the place of the individual within a complex array of practices that, in late modern life, span the local as well as the global.

Feminist critiques of democracy, specifically liberal democracy, point to the view that the theoretical underpinnings of liberal democracy have not only been based upon the negation of gender as a social construct, but have over time excluded the voice of women from the public sphere. In seeking to place gender at the heart of democratic thought and practice, feminist discourse has centred around questions relating to the construction of citizenship, the meaning of participation in the public sphere, and the challenge of difference (Phillips 1991). While the two interrelated themes that frame this project are equality and difference, deliberations around these constructs reveal debate around fundamental issues relating to the epistemological and ontological underpinnings of feminist thought.

Gendering equality in democratic thought

Feminism as a political project has always had an ambivalent relationship with the universalising assumptions that underpin liberal democracy as a specifically modern project. Emerging from the modernist tradition, feminism has at one and the same time historically sought to utilise modernity's universalist aspirations while highlighting gender difference as the mainstay of its critique. If the formative elements of democratic thought were premised on a contractual order based on EQUALITY in representative and participative democracy, then free and equal citizenship had, by definition, to be ontologically based on reason and autonomy. The agent of social, economic and political change within this universalising ontology was the individual self, the citizen, unencumbered by group affiliation, and capable of deliberative reasoning on social norms and institutions. The individuality of the modern self as citizen was manifest and came into being within the public sphere of interaction and debate wherein all individuals could participate on the basis of FREEDOM and equality. The social contract itself, the institutionalisation of the rights and obligations that define free citizenship within democratic formations, was in itself only a possibility if based on an ontology, a mode of being, defined on autonomous rationality.

It is precisely this vision of equal citizenship based on the autonomous self that early feminist thought, from Mary Wollstonecraft to the SUFFRAGE movement, adopted as its aspiration. Highlighting the subjugation of women, their confinement to the private sphere and the exploitative and oppressive practices that impeded their individuality as free citizens, these early feminists sought EMANCIPATION through the enactment of practices based on equality between the sexes. However, such equality could not simply be based on the acquisition of the vote, for such a limited conception of equality would in itself deny or indeed negate the deeply permeated inequalities that constrain the lives of women and their full participation within the public sphere (Squires 1999) (see Squires's EMPOWERMENT).

Recent feminist critiques of democratic thought have sought to deconstruct gendered conceptions of citizenship and political participation. Carol Pateman (1988) has argued that the social contract underpinning the rights and obligations of democratic citizenship has, in actuality, been premised on an already existing 'sexual contract'. Placing the social contract under the feminist lens, Pateman well and truly unpicks the universalising pretensions of contract theory and the individual freedom and institutional or governmental LEGITIMACY assumed to derive from contract. The rights assumed in democratic thought are in fact patriarchal rights and the obligations assumed have a differential impact on men and women. While the social contract was assumed to have created the civic freedoms contained within the public sphere, that which occurred in the private sphere was deemed irrelevant to considerations of politics and political practice. For Pateman, the legacy of this powerful heritage has, in effect, been the social and legal exclusion of women from the basic element of freedom, the 'individual'.

Placing democratic thought under a feminist lens, therefore, highlights the exclusionist consequences that stem from a view of citizenship based on free and equal individuality manifest within a public realm deemed to be entirely separate from the private domain. The complete masculine self in this orthodoxy achieves his individuality within the public realm of interaction where interests, rights and obligations come to be defined in a system of enablement and constraint that is citizenship within a sovereign democratic state. The public–private dualism and the constructed boundaries of these domains are so deeply implicated in the constitution of gendered social formations that an awareness of gender as social construct is at one and the same time also an awareness of the separation of the public from the private. As Jean Elshtain has shown, so powerful is the constitutive impact of this dualism that it has historically enabled conceptions of state, sovereignty, and citizenship based on the exclusion of women (Elshtain 1981). The disruption or indeed the subversion of the public–private dualism has formed the baseline from which feminism has contributed to rethinking the location of politics and the relationship of the individual self to the wider polity.

Feminists seeking to transform democratic thought have, therefore, focused on unravelling the ontological and epistemological underpinnings of a discourse built upon a foundational idea of a transcendental and universal self. If the self within this discourse is primarily a masculine self, located within the public sphere, then that which is conceived as universal and liberating is in actuality a situated entity constructed in discourse as the universal, sovereign self of the Enlightenment. Feminism's ambivalence emerges in that it too has historically defined its emancipatory project as having the aspiration to reach the universalist heights denied to women by a masculinist discourse, while seeking to uncover the gender-based differences that have constrained the full development of women into free individuals. This then would be a citizenship free of the public–private dichotomy that has so determined the gendered basis of political philosophy and practice. The transformative agenda envisaged here is one based on the delegitimation of social constructs of femininity and masculinity and their permeation of social practices, coupled with calls for equality between the sexes in all spheres of social life.

Gender equality is the lynchpin of this modernist critique of a highly modern set of ideas that define liberal democracy. Contained in this vision of emancipation is the view that women across the signifying divides of culture and class share a common agenda, irrespective of differences that define the lived experience of women. Conceptions of equality are often framed in terms of state provision for childcare and motherhood, legal protection within marriage, access to and the enhancement of the welfare state, equal pay and increases in the numbers of women in legislative roles and positions of leadership. While calls for gender equality are framed within Western democratic contexts, the ethos is cosmopolitan in orientation, being based on a discourse of universal rights and the ending of women's oppression globally. The implication here is that while gendering democracy may be of relevance to Western liberal democracies, what is essential elsewhere is the gendering of democratisation, so that the concerns of women are already established in deliberations concerning the institutionalisation of democratic practice.

Gendering difference and democratic practice

Equality and difference have come to form the twin formative ideas of the feminist critique of liberal democracy and the basis of its transformation. The equalities deemed necessary for full participative citizenship would in a sense negate difference between the sexes. However, as indicated above, the ambivalence that immediately emerges is that while what is sought is equality between the genders, this is often articulated within a framework which asserts difference, one that claims a particularity to women and their lived experience that is different from the lived experience of men. If women's rights are bound up with reproductive rights, then this is a specific domain that in a sense belongs to women. If care and motherhood are women's concerns, then such concerns may only be understood and articulated by women. If the experience of gender oppression and violence is predominantly one located in women's lives, then it is women who are best placed to represent the concerns of women. Woman is hence a category and, as such, within discourses that seek to gender democracy, must be the authoritative voice in the transformation of democratic practice.

This 'standpoint feminism' (Hartsock 1987) defines emancipation in terms of difference. While seeking equality, it nonetheless asserts difference as the basis of its political project. The form of difference that is the defining mainstay of standpoint feminism is based on gender. Critique of what is seen as the masculinist discourse of Enlightenment rationality is coupled with a celebration of attributes associated with women. The autonomous self of Enlightenment thought is replaced with woman as a relational entity, constructed in her role as nurturer, carer and peace activist (Gilligan 1982). The autonomous self of Kantian reason is here substituted with the relational self of care. This ontology informs feminist standpoint epistemology just as it frames feminist discourses on ethics and politics. Authors such as Nancy Hirschmann have used standpoint feminism in elaborating a gendered view of democratic thought and practice. Building on Pateman's deconstruction of the social contract and the gendered basis of the rights and obligations embedded therein, Hirschmann seeks to unravel the meaning of choice and of obligation in the lives of women. This, however, does not simply mean the 'addition' of women to 'existing categories of thought' (Hirschmann 1992: 163) as these are constructed on not only gender bias or a distortion of women's lives, but also on an active exclusion of women's experiential relationship to the domain of politics and discourse. In seeking to rethink democratic practice in gendered terms, standpoint feminism suggests that liberal/modernist thought is based on a rationalist and empiricist epistemology or theory of knowledge that in itself is inherently masculinist in its pretensions of universalist objectivity. What is deemed universal is, however, specific to one gender and one culture. A feminist standpoint epistemology can, according to this perspective, translate the lived experience of women into a political theory and conceptions of rights, obligations and participation that are inclusive of such experience.

How we view democratic practice is hence related to how we explain and understand human conduct and human institutions. The realm of politics and our capacities for judgement are intricately related to strategies of justification of our knowledge claims and the ontological make-up of the she or he who claims to know. Democratic thought is, therefore, heavily imbued with epistemological and ontological certainties that seek foundations upon which we may be able to claim legitimacy. The predominant feminist view, as seen above, is that the transformation of democratic thought and practice can only be possible if based upon a root and branch rethinking of fundamental assumptions on which western political thought has relied. To gender democracy would, on the one hand, have to claim equality between the sexes, that ontologically both are rational and free, and capable of full participation within a public sphere of free, rational and universal selves. The consensus

here, from Mary Wollstonecraft to Simone de Beauvoir, to contemporary feminists calling for the full participation of women in the military, is that women could only achieve such equality if taken out of their confinement in the private sphere and allowed to participate in the public sphere of interaction, work and discourse.

Feminist transformations of the political have, however, also sought to move away from systems of thought that denigrate the lived experience of women, arguing that to do so, as liberal feminism does, is precisely to reify the public/private dichotomy that informs the exclusion of women. Transformation can hence only be possible and 'complete' if women are accrued the sovereignty of their own lives, a form of epistemological self-determination that confers authority to woman and her experience as the location from which politics and practices of the political may be transformed.

There is a sense in which gendering democracy could be reduced to the replacement of 'universal man' with 'universal woman', the rational subject of enlightenment thought with the relational subject of primordial nurturing and connectivity. Most feminist reworkings of citizenship and participation seek a form of accommodation between these two perspectives, between gender equality and gender difference. There are here fundamental philosophical issues, relating to epistemology and ontology, that have informed the critique of political theory and democratic practice. However, it is precisely such issues of epistemology and ontology that have formed the basis of alternative conceptions of the political by feminists informed by critical theory and poststructuralism. Authors such as Seyla Benhabib (1992) and Nancy Fraser (1997) seek to develop the idea of the public sphere away from its liberal individualist underpinnings towards forms of deliberative democracy based upon intersubjective communicative practices that take account of difference. Where Benhabib's conception of the public sphere concentrates on elaborating the rules of communication that may incorporate diversity in what is still a rationally conceived process, Fraser provides a more radical conception of the public sphere that incorporates a socialist concern with power differentials together with an expanded view of the communicative process itself. There is, in this latter view, a recognition that what is traditionally conceived as a single public sphere is in fact constituted differently within a number of diverse spheres of communication and deliberation. This multiplicity of communicative arenas may not necessarily follow the same rules of conduct, but may bring in a whole diversity of styles reflecting the plurality of individuals and networks that exist in late modern life and the differential practices and concerns of divergent groups of people. To gender democracy in this conception is therefore to move away from the epistemological and ontological certainties that seem to unite the rational and the relational perspectives outlined above.

Diversity itself has different manifestations in different social contexts. One major challenge to a project that seeks to place gender at the core of democratic thought and practice is cultural difference. Developing the liberal-communitarian debate into a feminist direction, a number of authors have sought to unravel the relationship between gender, cultural practices and the institutions of governance in western multicultural societies (Cohen *et al.* 1999). A significant issue for the development of this area of research is that gender as a cultural form is in itself a signifier of cultural difference and comes to be utilised in claims to cultural autonomy in cases where such autonomy conflicts with the individual rights of women in liberal democratic societies. Practices deemed oppressive to women within the wider society may thus constitute the very basis of identity within the cultural sphere. Negotiating multiculturalism and feminist discourse has, therefore, acquired centre stage in writings that seek to place both gender and cultural diversity at the heart of political theory and inclusive practices.

Conclusion

As we have seen above, the twin formative ideas that frame the feminist critique centre on equality and difference, and how these are framed is in turn informed by epistemological and ontological assumptions that seek to undo the exclusions of the universalising discourse of modernist thought. However, to substitute a universalising masculinist discourse with a standpoint feminist one is in itself fraught with difficulties when confronted by the challenge of difference and the diversity of experiences that define the lives of women. To recognise the complexities of subjectivity and the multiple narratives that constitute the self is to immediately reject any singular definition of woman or indeed of what constitutes the 'political'. To recognise the plurality of locations of the political is precisely to recognise that the subject of politics is a complex being, defying easy categorisation within some instrumental formula accessible to the quantification practices of both national and international institutions.

There is, then, an alternative view on the subject of gender and democracy. This view takes difference seriously and refuses its reduction to a singular definition of personhood based variously on rationality, relationality or an unproblematised cultural identity. It furthermore rejects the view that we may account for cultural difference by the addition of culture to gender and in so doing recognise that gendered practices are differentially manifested in different cultural formations. Recognising the complexities of the subject of politics in late modernity immediately implies a recognition of the proximities of the local and the global, that the social, economic and political positionality of the citizen in the West has manifold and immediate implications elsewhere, that the political events of the local and proximate are intimately related to distant happenings. Late modern feminism and calls for a gendering of democratic practice face a deep challenge therefore when confronted by global political and economic structures that differentially impact upon women, enabling some, those primarily located in the West, while constraining the majority of those located in a space named 'non-Western' (Jabri and O'Gorman 1999). There is, therefore, a sense in which we may no longer confine deliberations on gender and democracy to the domestic, internal sphere of Western liberal societies, but must unravel the complex interrelationships that mutually implicate the local and the global.

See also:

affirmative action; empowerment; identity, political; suffrage

Further reading

Benhabib, S. (1992) *Situating the Self: Gender, Community, and Postmodernism in Contemporary Ethics*, Cambridge: Polity Press.

Cohen, J., Howard, M. and Nussbaum, N.C. (eds) (1999) *Is Multiculturalism Bad for Women: Susan Moller Okin with Respondents*, Princeton, NJ: Princeton University Press.

Elshtain, J.B. (1981) *Public Man, Private Woman: Women in Social and Political Thought*, Princeton, NJ: Princeton University Press.

Fraser, N. (1997) *Justice Interruptus: Critical Reflections on the 'Postsocialist' Condition*, London: Routledge.

Gilligan, C. (1982) *In a Different Voice: Psychological Theory and Women's Development*, Cambridge, MA: Harvard University Press.

Hartsock, N. (1987) 'The Feminist Standpoint: Developing the Ground for a Specifically Feminist Historical Materialism', in S. Harding (ed.), *Feminism and Methodology*, Milton Keynes: Open University Press.

Hirschmann, N.J. (1992) *Rethinking Obligation: A Feminist Method for Political Theory*, Ithaca, NY: Cornell University Press.

Jabri, V. and O'Gorman, E. (eds) (1999) *Women, Culture and International Relations*, Boulder, CO: Lynne Rienner Publishers.

Pateman, C. (1988) *The Sexual Contract*, Cambridge: Polity Press.

Phillips, A. (1991) *Engendering Democracy*, Cambridge: Polity Press.

—— (1992) 'Must Feminists Give Up on Liberal Democracy', *Political Studies*, special issue on Prospects for Democracy, edited by D. Held, Vol. 40: 68–82.

Squires, J. (1999) *Gender in Political Theory*, Cambridge: Polity Press.

VIVIENNE JABRI

globalisation

In the contemporary era, democracy has become the fundamental standard of political LEGITIMACY; that is to say, national democracies have been consolidated as the proper form of the modern state. The liberal democratic regime has set the prevailing norms and rules for political regimes throughout the world. Events such as the election of Nelson Mandela as President of South Africa and the consolidation of democracy in Central and Eastern Europe are symbolic of changes indicating that, in an increasing number of countries, citizen voters are in principle able to hold national leaders to account (Potter *et al.* 1997). Yet, at the same time, the democratic political community is increasingly challenged by regional and global pressures and problems, which raise questions about the nature and efficacy of national, territorial democracies.

How can problems such as the spread of the drugs trade, the debt burden of many countries in the 'developing world', the flow of financial resources that escape national jurisdiction, the regulation of genetically modified foods and the management of genetic engineering in general be satisfactorily brought within the sphere of democracy? What kind of accountability and control can citizens of a single nation-state have over powerful transnational forces, international actors and international organisations? In the context of the contemporary trends towards regionalisation, increased European integration, fundamental transformations in the global economy and in mass communications, how can democracy be sustained? Are new democratic institutions necessary to regulate and control the new international forces and processes?

Questions such as these highlight the expanding geographical scale on which economic and political power is frequently exercised.

While democracy remains rooted in a fixed and bounded territorial conception of political community, contemporary regional and global forces disrupt any simple correspondence between national territory, sovereignty, political space and the democratic political community. These forces enable power and resources to flow across, over and around territorial boundaries, and escape mechanisms of national democratic control. At the root of many of these concerns lie issues that can be associated with 'globalisation'.

Globalisation has become the 'big idea' of our times, even though it is frequently employed in such a way that lacks any precise definition. Moreover, it is so often used in political debate and rhetoric that it is in danger of becoming simply a cliché. Nonetheless, although the term is deeply contested, it does capture important elements of change in the contemporary world, which can be usefully specified further.

Globalisation can best be understood if it is conceived as a spatial phenomenon, lying on a continuum with 'the local' at one end and 'the global' at the other. It implies a shift in the spatial form of human organisation and activity to transcontinental or interregional patterns of activity, interaction and the exercise of power (Held *et al.* 1999). Today, globalisation embraces at least four distinct types of change. First, it involves a stretching of social, political and economic activities across political frontiers, regions and continents. Second, it suggests the intensification, or the growing magnitude, of networks and flows of trade, investment, finance, migration, culture and so on. Third, it includes a speeding up of global interactions and processes, as the evolution of worldwide systems of transport and COMMUNICATION increases the velocity of the diffusion of ideas, goods, information, capital and people. And fourth, it involves the deepening impact of global interactions and processes such that the effects of distant events can be highly significant elsewhere and even the most local developments can come to have enormous global consequences. In this particular sense, the boundaries between domestic matters and global affairs can become increasingly fuzzy. In short, globalisation can be thought of as the widening, intensifying, speeding up and growing impact of worldwide interconnectedness.

The contemporary debate about globalisation consists of a clash between three broad accounts of its nature and dynamics, which will be referred to here as the hyperglobalist, the sceptical and the transformationalist views. The hyperglobalists argue that we live in an increasingly global world in which states are being subjected to massive economic and political processes of change. The latter are held to be eroding and fragmenting nation-states and diminishing the power of politicians. In these circumstances, it is concluded, states are increasingly the 'decision takers' and not the 'decision makers' (Ohmae 1990; Gray 1998). The sceptics strongly resist this view, and believe that contemporary global circumstances are not unprecedented. In their account, while there has been an intensification of international activity in recent times, this has reinforced and enhanced state powers in many domains (Hirst and Thompson 1999). In contrast to both the hyperglobalists and the sceptics, the transformationalists argue that globalisation is creating new economic, political and social circumstances, which, however unevenly, are serving to transform state powers and the context in which states operate. They do not predict the outcome – indeed, they believe it is uncertain – but argue that politics is no longer, and can no longer simply be, based on nation-states (Giddens 1990; Mann 1997).

Behind the intensive debate about globalisation and its impact lies the question of how far, and to what extent, national political communities are being transformed by regional and global forces. In a short dictionary entry of this type, it is clearly not possible to provide a detailed account of these developments. However, to advance an account of globalisation it is necessary to specify some of the key domains of activity and interaction in which global processes are evolving. Illustrative material of this kind indicates that it is neither the case that globalisation is sweeping all democratic politics before it, as the hyperglobalisers contend; nor is it the case that globalisation is leaving political life largely unchanged, as the sceptics argue. Rather, it is the case that political power is being reconfigured – as the transformationalists claim – with important implications for democracy and ACCOUNTABILITY.

Since 1945, there have been changes across different social and economic realms which have combined to create forms of regional and global interconnectedness which are more extensive and intensive than before, and which are challenging and reshaping political communities. These changes involve a number of developments which can be thought of as deep, indicative structural transformations. These include the development of such phenomenon as human RIGHTS regimes, which have ensured that SOVEREIGNTY alone is less and less a guarantee of state legitimacy in international law; the internationalisation of SECURITY and the transnationalisation of a great many defence and procurement programmes, which means, for example, that some key weapon systems rely upon components from many countries; environmental shifts, above all ozone depletion and global warming, which highlight the growing limits to a purely state-centric politics; and the revolution in communications and information technology, which has increased massively the stretch and intensity of all manner of socio-political networks within and across the borders of states.

Much has been written about the particular importance of economic globalisation and its political implications (for example, Hirst and Thompson 1999; Held *et al.* 1999: chaps 3–5). Notable developments have occurred in trade, finance and production. Trade has grown substantially in the postwar period, reaching unprecedented levels. Not only has there been an increase in intra-regional trade around the world, but there has also been sustained growth among regions. More countries are involved in global trading arrangements – for instance, India and China – and more people and nations are affected by such arrangements. If there is a further lowering of tariff barriers across the world, these trends are likely to continue. The expansion of global financial flows has, moreover, been staggering in the last fifteen to twenty years. Foreign exchange turnover is now around 1.5 trillion dollars a day. Much of this financial activity is speculative and generates fluctuations in values (in stocks, shares and so on) in excess of those that can be accounted for by changes in the fundamentals underlying asset values. Furthermore, mutinational corporations now account for at least 20 per cent of world production and 70 per cent of world trade. They are essential to the diffusion of technology, and are key players in international money markets.

Among the many significant points to stress about economic globalisation is the tangible growth in the enmeshment of national economies in global economic transactions; that is, a growing proportion of nearly all national economies involves international economic exchange with an increasing number of countries. It is this broad increase in the extent and intensity of economic interconnectedness that has altered the relation between political and economic power. One shift has been especially noteworthy, and this is 'the historic expansion of exit options for capital in financial markets relative to national capital controls, national banking regulations, and national investment strategies, and the sheer volume of privately held capital relative to national reserves' (Goldblatt *et al.* 1997: 281). Corporations that make direct investments have also expanded their exit options so 'the balance of power has shifted in favour of capital, *vis-à-vis* both national governments and national labour movements' (Goldblatt *et al.* 1997: 281). The structural power of capital has increased.

Economic globalisation has not, however, occurred in an empty political space; there has been a shift in the nature and form of political organisation as well. In mapping this shift, it is important to explore the way in which the sovereign state now lies at the intersection of a vast array of international regimes and organisations that have been established to manage whole areas of transnational activity (trade, financial flows, crime and so on) and collective policy problems. The latter has involved a spread of layers of governance both within and across political BOUNDARIES. It has been marked by the deterritorialisation of aspects of political decision-making, the development of regional and global organisations and institutions, and the emergence of regional and global law.

This can be illustrated by a number of developments including the rapid emergence of international agencies and organisations. New forms of multilateral and global politics have been established involving governments, inter-governmental organisations (IGOs) and a wide variety of transnational pressure groups and international non-governmental organisations (INGOs). In 1909 there were 37 IGOs and 176 INGOs, while in 1996 there were nearly 260 IGOs and nearly five and a half thousand INGOs. In addition, there has been an explosive development in the number of inter-national treaties in force, as well as in the number of international regimes.

To this pattern of extensive political inter-connectedness can be added the dense web of activity of the key international policy-making fora, including the UN, G7, International Monetary Fund, World Trade Organisation, European Union, APEC, ARF and Mercosur summits and many other official and unofficial meetings. In the middle of the nineteenth century there were two or three interstate conferences or congresses per annum; today the number totals over four thousand annually. National government is increasingly locked into an array of global, regional and multi-layered systems of governance; and can barely monitor it all, let alone stay in command.

There has, moreover, been an important change in the scope and content of interna-tional law. Twentieth century forms of interna-tional law – from the law governing war, to that concerning crimes against humanity, environ-mental issues and, as noted previously, human rights – have created the basis of what can be thought of as an emerging framework of 'cosmopolitan law', law which circumscribes and delimits the political power of individual states. In principle, states are no longer able to treat their citizens as they think fit. Although

in practice, many states still violate these standards, nearly all now accept general duties of protection and provision in their own practices and procedures (Beetham 1999).

These developments, and others parallel to them, have contributed to the transformation of the nature and prospects of democratic political community in a number of distinct ways. First, it can no longer be presupposed that the locus of effective political power is synonymous with national governments and the national state. National states and national governments are now embedded in complex networks of political power at regional and global levels. In other words, political power is shared and negotiated among diverse forces and agencies at many levels, from the local to the global.

Second, the nurturing and enhancement of the public good increasingly requires co-ordi-nated multilateral action (for example, to prevent global recession). At the same time, the resolution of transboundary issues (for example, responsibility for certain pollutants) may often impose significant domestic adjust-ments. In this respect, politicians are witnessing a shift in the operation and dynamics of state power and political AUTHORITY. This has become most apparent as states have become locked into regional and global regimes and associations. The context of national politics has been transformed by the diffusion of political authority and the growth of multi-layered governance.

Third, the idea of a self-determining na-tional collectivity – which delimits and shapes a community of fate – can no longer be simply located within the borders of a single nation-state. Many of the most fundamental eco-nomic, social, cultural and environmental forces and processes that determine the nature of the political good and political outcomes, now lie, in terms of their origin and dynamics, beyond the reach of individual national po-lities.

Fourth, while significant concentrations of power are found, of course, in many states, these are frequently embedded in, and articu-lated with, new and changing forms of political authority. The power and operations of national government are altering, but not all in one direction. The entitlement of states to rule within circumscribed territories – their sovereignty – is not on the edge of collapse, although the practical nature of this entitlement – the actual capacity of states to rule – is changing its shape. A new regime of government and governance is emerging which is displacing traditional conceptions of state power as an indivisible, territorially exclusive form of public power.

In the context of these complex transformations, the meaning and efficacy of democracy at the national level is being rearticulated. At the turn of the millennium, citizens live in a world of overlapping communities of fate, where the trajectories of each and every country are more tightly entwined than ever before (Held 1995). In circumstances where transnational actors and forces cut across the boundaries of national communities in diverse ways, where powerful international organisations and agencies make decisions for vast groups of people across diverse borders, and where powerful states make policies not just for their peoples but for others as well, the questions of who should be accountable to whom, and on what basis, do not easily resolve themselves.

The idea of a national, territorial conception of democracy was compelling in the era in which the nation-state was being forged and consolidated. Against the background of the transformation of political community today, it is harder to conceive of political power, sovereignty, democracy and CITIZENSHIP as simply and/or appropriately bounded by a delimited territorial space. The mesh between geography, political power and democracy is being challenged by the intensification of regional and global relations. However, while globalisation is altering the democratic political landscape, it is not merely undermining political choices. On the contrary, by inducing changes within and across levels of governance and by altering the boundaries of different forms of power, it is re-illuminating and reinvigorating the political terrain. As political

power is diffused above, below and alongside the nation-state, so debate has intensified about the proper home of democracy and the determination of the political good. The echoes of this discussion can be heard in the corridors of the UN and the World Trade Organisation, in the organisations of the European Union and in the emerging regional associations of Asia-Pacific, and in the transnational human rights, women's and environmental movements.

In the judgement of this author, democracy will have to be remoulded if it is to retain its efficacy and relevance in a more regional and global era. The intensification of democratic politics within the boundaries of national polities and the establishment of new democratic fora at regional and global levels – in other words, the entrenchment of a COSMOPOLITAN DEMOCRACY – provides a vision of one such possibility. Of course, whether democracy can be reconstructed in this way remains to be seen. But one thing is certain: the democratic nation-state was not built in a generation, and one should not expect major and equally significant transformations to take less time.

See also:

boundaries; cosmopolitan democracy; democracy and sustainability; market forces; nations and nationalism

Further reading

Beetham, D. (1999) *Democracy and Human Rights*, Cambridge: Polity Press.

Giddens, A. (1990) *Modernity and its Consequences*, Cambridge: Polity Press.

Goldblatt, D., Held, D., McGrew, A. and Perraton, J. (1997) 'Economic Globalisation and the Nation-State: Shifting Balances of Power', *Alternatives* 22: 269–85.

Gray, J. (1998) *False Dawn*, London: Granta.

Held, D. (1995) *Democracy and the Global Order: From the Modern State to Cosmopolitan Governance*, Cambridge: Polity Press.

Held, D., McGrew, A., Goldblatt, D. and Perraton, J. (1999) *Global Transformations:*

Politics, Economics and Culture, Cambridge: Polity Press.

Hirst, P. and Thompson, G. (1999) *Globalization in Question*, 2nd edn, Cambridge: Polity Press.

Mann, M. (1997) 'Has Globalisation Ended the Rise and Rise of the Nation-State', *Review of Political Economy* 4(3): 472–96.

Ohmae, K. (1990) *The Borderless World*, London: Collins.

Potter, D., Goldblatt, D., Kiloh, M. and Lewis, P. (eds) (1997) *Democratization*, Cambridge: Polity Press.

DAVID HELD

good practice

Good practice can generally be defined as the proper handling of the body of accumulated knowledge in any field of human experience that lends itself to practical application. Good practice presupposes both the existence of experience-based scientific knowledge as well as a part of society to which this knowledge is of relevance. It is not by accident that a systematic discussion of problems of good practice came up first in domains of human services, such as health care, psychological therapy and EDUCATION. Here the yardsticks to evaluate good practice are relatively straightforward. There is a direct link which connects measures in these areas to the well-being of human individuals.

The case is more difficult for achieving the wealth of nations. In this regard good practice requires strategies of social engineering which are difficult to come by. Defined in terms of social engineering, good practice is confronted with two basic problems. First, there are always normative formulas to legitimate different and potentially conflicting social goals. Which set of social goals is preferable? Second, policy strategies to achieve preferred goals are confronted with rather complex societal relationships. Thus, how to choose the proper means to realise social goals? Yet, despite all these difficulties, debates about 'good practice' flour-

ish even in the social sciences and their different sub-fields, such as public administration or management. The growing relevance of criteria of good practice in the social sciences has obviously something to do with the growing body of knowledge generated by theory guided empirical research and the improved technical capabilities to process INFORMATION through increasingly powerful electronic facilities. It does not need much courage to predict that rules of good practice will gain even more attention in the era of global information, which societies now enter.

Two different approaches to good practice dominate the current debate. The first one can be labelled the 'neo-liberal World Bank approach' to 'good governance' (Kieley 1998; Navarro 1998). The second one encompasses the more comprehensive paradigm of 'sustainable development' (Roy and Tisdell 1998). Interestingly, both approaches are directly related to democracy. From the World Bank's economic perspective, good governance entails not only the consolidation of public finance but also the implementation of individual civil and political rights. Therefore, the World Bank supported and recommended liberal and democratic reforms for all those formerly authoritarian regimes applying for loans from the World Bank. The World Bank policy reflects the conventional wisdom of neo-institutionalist economics claiming that economic prosperity is based on constitutionally guaranteed individual rights and responsible and responsive government. This insight represents a major shift in the political understanding of good practice. Until the mid-1980s many economists, following Mancur Olsen's ideas about the origins of the wealth of nations (Olsen 1982), believed that authoritarian regimes are better equipped to trigger economic growth. The argument was that authoritarian elites have a stronger position to restrict rent-seeking interests. In the meantime, however, leading economic historians, such as Douglas North (1981) and David Landes (1998), have shown that non-responsible government tends to be predatory. Hence, good practice (in terms of good governance which gives rise to prosperity) is equated with liberal, responsible and responsive democratic governance (see ECONOMIC REQUIREMENTS OF DEMOCRACY).

The pro-democratic view of the World Bank is compatible with the broader paradigm of sustainable development. From the sustainable development perspective, per capita income is not the only social goal that should be maximised. Physical quality of life in terms of life expectancy, health care, nutrition and education as well as the ecological quality of life are considered as essential goals of developmental policies as well. In this context, Nobel Prize laureate Amartya Sen (1997) contributed the essential theoretical argument stating that freedom rights are a core element of sustainable development. In addition, Sen demonstrated empirically that Third World democracies, such as India, never experienced famine crises, but these occurred regularly in underdeveloped autocracies such as China. Hence, a major dispute between researchers who have argued that democracy is bad for economic development and those who have considered democracy as an essential precondition of economic takeoff seems to be decided by the empirical facts in favour of the latter. Good practice in developmental policy is to support good democratic practice.

These insights raise the question of whether or not there is an applicable theory of good *democratic* practice. Again, theories of good democratic practice are disputed because of normative differences. While the libertarians want to keep the state out, welfare democrats want to bring the state back in. But despite of these differences there is a broad consensus that a constitutional guarantee of liberal and political rights, together with the rule of law (see LAW, RULE OF), constitute the minimal elements of responsible democratic government. Or to put it in another way, guaranteed civil and political liberties are the institutional component of human development (Welzel and Inglehart 1999). Thus, one can identify some matching theoretical elements for good democratic practice – at least if one accepts liberal democracy as the modal type of modern democracy. Viewed in this context, good democratic practice is consistent with any practice that contributes to the legitimacy, performance and persistence of democracy. This relates specifically to (1) INSTITUTIONAL DESIGN, (2) elite behaviour, (3) policy strategies and policy outcomes, and (4) the values and behaviour of citizens.

With respect to institutional design there has been, and currently is, an intense debate on the vices or virtues of parliamentary and presidential systems of government and on representative or majoritarian electoral systems. While the debate on governmental systems seems to be decided in favour of parliamentary systems (Lijphart and Waisman 1996), the question of the most appropriate electoral system is more complex (see ELECTORAL SYSTEMS). However, given a certain cleavage structure, one can recommend some basic institutional rules in order to produce the desired effects.

On the level of elite behaviour, one crucial point is whether or not elites can be trusted. One potential empirical measure is provided by the corruption scores of Transparency International. Corruption is indicative of costs of social transactions. If corruption is high, interaction costs increase since corruption diminishes trust in institutions, trust in elites, and eventually interpersonal trust. High social interaction costs affect citizens' willingness to co-operate, engage in economic initiative and political participation. Corruption raises social interaction costs and reduces SOCIAL CAPITAL and the society's creative potential (Fukuyama 1995). Corruption is also responsible for bad economic performance and other bad policy performances. So, good democratic practice implies that elites make decisions according to the rational rules of law rather than clientelistic rules of corruption.

As far as policy strategies are concerned, there is a rather large body of research on economic performance. Economic performance can be crucial for mass legitimacy of democracy. Hence, any legitimate policy which is appropriate to improve economic performance also contributes to good democratic practice. The human capital approach in economic theory has generated the crucial insights. The NIC's (Newly Industrialised Countries) economic success in Southeast Asia indicates that promotion of export oriented industries and massive investment in human capital are the most promising strategies on the road to economic prosperity. However, as shown by Hofferbert and Klingemann (1999), mass legitimacy of democracy depends not only on economic performance but on human rights performance as well. This is a policy area that can be much easier controlled and improved upon by national elites than economic performance, which is highly dependent on global developments.

Elite behaviour is highly relevant for good democratic practice. Elites design adequate or inadequate institutions, elites behave due to rational-legal standards or clientelistic ones, and elites implement policies with differing degrees of success. However, almost by definition, democracy depends as much – if not more – on the virtues of ordinary citizens. The characteristics of the 'demos' are decisive for the quality of the democratic process (Foweraker and Landman 1997). No democratic regime can persist and flourish unless citizens support its institutions by their attitudes, values and behaviour. From the viewpoint of mass POLITICAL CULTURE, good elite practice can only take roots if citizens have reason to trust in others, if they tolerate each other as free and equal, if they engage in a minimum of social activities, and if they share a set of basic liberal values. At least this is what can be concluded from comparative survey research, and from theories based on that research, such as the theories of 'civic culture' (Almond and Verba 1963), 'social capital' (Putnam 1993), 'postmodernism' (Inglehart 1997) and 'critical democrats' (Klingemann 1999).

An essential and increasingly important element to insure good democratic practice is the cross-national auditing and surveying of democratic practice (Beetham 1994) (see Beetham's DEMOCRATIC AUDIT). Surveys and audits related to democratic practice are currently flourishing in different ways. On the one hand, there is an increasing network of NON-GOVERNMENTAL ORGANISATIONS (NGOs) which implement democratic audits by expert judgement on a global or at least regional scale. Examples are the liberty scores and the corruption scores provided by Freedom House and Transparency International, respectively. Election watch is another case in point. Organisations like the UN, the National Endowment for Democracy and the OSCE (Organization for Security and Cooperation in Europe) are heavily engaged in this field, offering infrastructure and sending observers to ensure free and fair elections. Cross-national representative surveys can also be regarded a special aspect of democratic auditing by monitoring support for democratic institutions. In this respect the World Values Survey, which has grown out of the European Values Study, has proven an invaluable data collection. It has been conducted the first time in 1981 and was repeated for the fourth time in the year 2000, encompassing sixty-five societies from all parts of the world. Democratic audit, assistance to enable good practice and use of social science methodology to observe further developments have become more and more interrelated and now are part of a global network of politicians, journalists, scientists and concerned citizens.

See also:

civic virtue; clientelism; democratic deficit; institutional design; legitimacy; political culture

Further reading

Almond, G.A. and Verba, S. (1963) *The Civic Culture: Political Attitudes in Five Western Democracies*, Princeton, NJ: Princeton University Press.

Beetham, D. (1994) 'Key Principles and Indices for a Democratic Audit', in D. Beetham (ed.), *Defining and Measuring Democracy*, London: Sage, 25–43.

Foweraker, J.W. and Landman, T. (1997) *Citizenship Rights and Social Movements*, Oxford: Oxford University Press.

Fukuyama, F. (1995) *Trust: Social Virtues and the Creation of Prosperity*, New York: The Free Press.

Hofferbert, R.I. and Klingemann, H.D. (1999) 'Remembering the Bad Old Days: Human Rights, Economic Conditions, and Democratic Performance in Transitional Regimes', *European Journal of Political Research* 36(1): 155–74.

Inglehart, R. (1997) *Modernization and Postmodernization: Cultural, Economic and Political Change in 43 Societies*, Princeton, NJ: Princeton University Press.

Kieley, R. (1998) 'Neoliberalism Revised? A Critical Account of World Bank Conceptions of Good Governance and Marked Friendly Interventions', *International Journal of Health Services* 28(4): 683–702.

Klingemann, H.D. (1999) 'Mapping Political Support in the 1990s: A Global Analysis' in P. Norris (ed.), *Critical Citizens: Global Support for Democratic Governance*, New York: Oxford University Press, 31–56.

Landes, D.S. (1998) *The Wealth and Poverty of Nations: Why Some are So Rich and Some So Poor*, New York: W.W. Norton.

Lijphart, A. and Waisman, C.H. (1996) 'Institutional Design and Democratization', in A. Lijphart and C.H. Waisman (eds), *Institutional Design in New Democracies: Eastern Europe and Latin America*, Boulder, CO: Westview Press, 1–12.

Navarro, V. (1998) 'Neoliberalism, Globalisation, Unemployment, Inequalities, and the Welfare State', *International Journal of Health Services* 28(4): 607–82.

North, D.C. (1981) *Structure and Change in Economic History*, New York: Norton.

Olson, M. (1982) *The Rise and the Decline of Nations: Economic Growth, Stagflation, and Social Rigidities*, New Haven, CT: Yale University Press.

Putnam, R.D. (1993) *Making Democracy Work: Civic Traditions in Modern Italy*, Princeton, NJ: Princeton University Press.

Roy, K.C. and Tisdell, C.A. (1998) 'Good Governance in Sustainable Development: The Impact of Institutions', *International Journal of Social Economics* 25(6–8): 1310–25.

Sen, A. (1997) 'Human Capital and Human Capability', *World Development* 25(12): 1959–61.

Welzel, C. and Inglehart, R. (1999) *Analyzing Democratic Change and Stability: A Human Development Theory of Democracy* (WZB-Discussion Papers, FS III 99–202), Berlin: WZB.

HANS-DIETER KLINGEMANN
CHRISTIAN WELZEL

green democratic thought

Green democratic thought has developed in response to the accusations of authoritarianism that are never far from the surface where green social change is concerned. In the early days of the contemporary environmental movement, North American writers such as Heilbroner and Ophuls appeared to argue that the environmental crisis was so dire that no one could reasonably be expected to accept voluntarily the kinds of measures that would be needed to deal with it, and that therefore only strong government – even authoritarian government – would do. More recently, as the influence of the catastrophist tendency in green politics has declined, attention has turned to the kinds of values held by political ecologists, and it has been suggested that the political-ecological belief that there is a right way to live the green 'good life' is incompatible with the value PLURALISM normally associated with (liberal) democracy. There are, then, both pragmatic and ethical roots to the palpable tension between radical green objectives and the democratic process. In recent years a good deal of attention has been paid to this tension, and a number of ways of lessening it have been suggested. Some have wondered why greens have felt so obliged to defend their democratic credentials – 'greens can ask why they should find new grounds for their adherence to democracy different from those advanced by socialists and liberals?' (Barry 1996: 119) – but both the 1970s authoritarian tendency in some environmental political theory and the corrosive association of 'nature politics' with some forms of fascism are enough to put both greens and their opponents continually on their democratic guard.

The underpinning source of the tension between radical green objectives and democracy is the apparently imperative nature of the former: 'To the extent that the realisation of certain green principles – like dealing urgently with over-population – is seen as essential, we are dealing with an imperative that has a no-real-choice quality' (Saward 1993: 64). This sounds incompatible with the democratic resolution of problems: 'ecological value-sets often contain a considerable tension between advocating certain essential policy outcomes and valuing (direct) democratic procedures' (Saward 1993: 64). And indeed some early environmental political theorists, particularly in North America, appeared to eschew democratic processes in favour of the 'right' kind of ecological outcomes.

It needs to be said, though, that even the villains of the piece, such as Heilbroner and Ophuls, were never as clear in their rejection of democratic procedures as their detractors have claimed. Two examples from William Ophuls will make this evident. First, Ophuls does indeed write that: 'As the community and its rights are given increasing social priority, we shall necessarily move from liberty toward authority, for the community will have to be able to enforce its demands on individuals' (Ophuls 1992: 285). But he also says that: 'this authority need not be remote, arbitrary and capricious. In a well-ordered and well-designed state, authority could be made constitutional and limited' (Ophuls 1992: 286). Second, Ophuls does seem to endorse 'a movement away from egalitarian democracy toward political competence and status', but he is careful to say that the values that inform competence should be arrived at by 'common consent' (Ophuls 1992: 286), and he also writes that: 'extreme centralisation and interdependence... should give way to greater decentralisation, local autonomy, and local culture' (Ophuls 1992: 291). Ophuls concludes by saying that, 'The essential political message of this book is that we must learn ecological self-restraint before it is forced upon us by a potentially monolithic and totalitarian regime or by the brute forces of nature' (Ophuls 1992: 297). A few swallows do not make a summer, of course, but these examples serve to illustrate the care with which we need to treat 'green authoritarian' claims. If indeed, as Saward suggests, 'Ophuls represents the clearest credible example of the authoritarian tendency in green political theory' (Saward 1993: 71), then the tendency would appear to be equivocal.

We need to be clear, in any case, not to confuse anti-liberal elements in green thought with anti-democratic ones. It is worth recalling that a large part of Ophuls's prescription for salvation consisted in a sense of social unity that is not a characteristic of liberal societies. The social unity of which they speak is not at all incompatible with democracy, of course, but it may indeed be in tension with the INDIVIDUALISM associated with LIBERALISM.

So one form of the green imperative is pragmatic, as it were. This is to say that drawing on the dire warnings found in texts such as *The Limits to Growth* (Meadows *et al.* 1974), some writers drew the conclusion that ecological catastrophe could only be averted by authoritarian means. The other form of green imperative is more ethical, or value-oriented, in origin. Bob Goodin has argued persuasively that what drives environmental political thought and action is a 'green theory of value'. According to this theory, something is 'especially valuable' if it has 'come about through natural rather than through artificial human processes' (Goodin 1992: 30). The task of the political ecologist, then, is to work for the preservation of this 'natural value' through time. Goodin carefully distinguishes between this theory of value and a putative green 'theory of agency', and the crucial issue for us is the relationship between them. Can a particular theory of agency be derived from the green theory of value? No, says Goodin. As we have seen, he argues that what 'lies at the core of green thinking...is an abiding concern that natural values be promoted, protected and preserved'. So, 'Given that as the logical primitive in their moral system, I think we would have to say...that it is more important that the right things be done than that they be done in any particular way or through any particular agency' (Goodin 1992: 120).

Goodin himself deploys this distinction to argue against greens endorsing only radical lifestyle change as a means of bringing about green objectives. On Goodin's reading of what green politics is about, the sustaining of natural value is more important than '"clean hands", principles of personal rectitude' (Goodin 1992: 123), and if this means doing boring things like voting for green political parties, then so be it. But his radical distinction between a green theory of value and green theories of agency can be read in more equivocal ways, for if it is true that 'it is more important that the right things be done than that they be done in any particular way or through any particular agency', then any form of agency would seem to do as long as it brings about the right results. As it happens, Goodin himself endorses democratic means of bringing about green ends when he states that green theory regards people as potentially, moral, autonomous and self-governing entities. For Goodin, politically this stresses 'the importance of the full, free, active participation by everyone in democratically shaping their personal and social circumstances' which is he admits is the 'central theme of the green political theory of agency' (Goodin 1992: 124).

But if getting the right thing done is more important than how it gets done, why should greens not endorse authoritarian means to green ends? At root, 'the core green concerns are consequentialistic' (Goodin 1992: 120) and this consequentialism is in tension with the proceduralism of democracy.

As well as the nature of the 'green imperative', two further sources of the tension between ecological problems and democratic processes deserve mention: time and space. We are increasingly aware that policies in the present will have an impact on those in the future; even on those yet to be born. From the point of view of the standard democratic four or five-year cycle this is a problem, since governments generally have an eye on short-term policies for short-term gain. Similarly, the dynamics of political ACCOUNTABILITY cannot easily be made to work in the environmental context: 'how can politicians be brought to book for decisions whose consequences will only be fully felt long after the individuals concerned have retired from the political stage?' (Lafferty and Meadowcroft 1996b: 7).

As for 'space', it is well known that many environmental problems are of an international character: global warming, by definition, is an issue that affects many nations rather than just one or two of them (see GLOBALISATION). This raises particular problems for the democratic process because democratic structures are, almost without exception, based on the nation-state. I shall say more about these issues of time and space below.

A number of reactions and responses to the authoritarianism/democracy conundrum have been given in recent years, and, in no special order, seven of them are outlined below. First, there is the possibility that the distinction drawn between green consequentialism and democratic proceduralism is too sharp. This is to say that consequences matter for democracy and procedures are important for greens and for green theory. Consequences matter for democracy because some consequences may be inimical to democracy itself. This is sometimes referred to as democracy's 'self-bindingness', according to which democracy 'restricts itself, or proscribes certain types of outcome, in order to preserve itself' (Saward 1993: 66). The kind of outcome it might proscribe in our context is ecological catastrophe, since that would undermine the conditions for the practice of democracy itself. John Dryzek refers to this as a 'generalisable interest', and remarks that: 'The continuing integrity of the ecological systems on which human life depends could perhaps be a generalisable interest par excellence' (Dryzek 1990: 55). If a democratic procedure resulted in an outcome that threatened the integrity of ecological systems, it could legitimately be proscribed for self-binding reasons.

I have pointed out elsewhere that this is not a conclusive argument in favour of the compatibility of green objectives and democratic procedures since, 'just as democracy is self-bound not to endorse decisions that endanger the practice of democracy, so is authoritarianism – a sustainable society is as much a generalisable interest for authoritarians as it is for democrats' (Dobson 1993: 138). From the other end of the problem, the end according to which procedures must matter for greens, Robyn Eckersley has sought to connect ecologism and democracy in much the same way as liberalism and democracy are connected: through building on the observation that, 'liberal support for democracy flows from the liberal principles of autonomy and justice' (Eckersley 1996: 222). In particular, the liberal principle of autonomy 'respects the rights of individuals to determine their own affairs' (Eckersley 1996: 222) and if we were to read ecologism not in consequentialist terms but in terms of a 'broader defence of autonomy (let us say, for the moment, the freedom of human and non-human beings to unfold in their own ways and live according to their 'species life') [then]...the connection between ecology and democracy would no longer be contingent' (Eckersley 1996: 223). Both the 'preconditional' and the 'principle' approaches, then, call into question the sharp distinction normally drawn between green consequentialism and democratic proceduralism, and show that in this regard, at least, there may be more common ground than is often assumed.

A second argument for bringing ecologism and democracy into line turns on the indeterminacy of green objectives. The 'green theory of value' to which we have had cause to refer takes us some way towards deciding what is important for greens, but calculations of that value in any determinate and final sense are perhaps impossible to make. 'Natural value' and 'sustainability' are both contested ideas, and according to John Barry the achievement of the latter 'makes democracy a core, non-negotiable, value of green political theory' (Barry 1996: 117), since because of the 'essential indeterminateness and normative character of the concept of sustainability...it needs to be understood as a discursively "created" rather than an authoritatively "given" product' (Barry 1996: 116). Michael Jacobs

points out that this creative and open-ended articulation of the meaning of sustainability, 'involves reasoning about other people's interests and values (as well as one's own) and the weight which should be given to them; about the application of and conflict between ethical principles in particular circumstances; and about the nature of the society one wishes to create or sustain' (Jacobs 1997: 219). For Jacobs: 'This suggests that where public [environmental] goods are at issue, the appropriate kind of value-articulating institution is not a private survey, but some kind of public forum in which people are brought together to debate before making their judgements. That is, the institution should be deliberative in character' (Jacobs 1997: 220). It is a very short step from here to the idea that the appropriate sorts of institutions for determining the nature of green objectives and the means for achieving them are democratic ones (see DEMOCRACY AND SUSTAINABILITY).

A third, family-related suggestion for bringing green and democratic thought into alignment relies on an argument from pragmatism regarding the truth: 'democracy can be justified rationally precisely because of the impossibility of incontrovertible proof of anything' (Saward 1993: 76). Given that we can never be certain of anything, the most justifiable means of POLICY-MAKING and DECISION-MAKING is one which takes turns around a problem and makes provision for reassessing the solution on a regular basis. With its public debate, accountability and periodic elections, this is democracy in all but name. In our context Saward points out that, 'Politics without certainty – indeed, politics as a substitute for certainty – has strong echoes in green political thinking' (Saward 1993: 77). The 'precautionary principle' has indeed become a byword in green policy-making circles, and while there is no reason why authoritarian regimes could not adopt the precautionary principle of decision-making, the supposedly provisional nature of decisions taken in democracies makes them a more appropriate context for the 'epistemological pragmatism' of which we are talking.

The fourth argument takes an alternative view of the truth question. Despite the inherent uncertainty of decision-making, particularly in the environmental context, it can still be argued that some decisions are better – more in line with 'the truth' – than others. The question is, what is the best way of producing these better decisions? John Stuart Mill in his *Utilitarianism* wrote that authority suppresses the very opinion which may possibly be true, and that while those who suppress it deny its truth they are not 'infallible'. This is an argument for open decision-making of the type normally associated with democratic consultation, and it should perhaps be endorsed by greens: even those with a determinate view of what the truth is: 'To the degree that there is a determinate answer about the 'right' values and the 'right' kind of society in which to live (and greens, in the round, believe that there is), then greens should be committed to democracy as the only form of decision-making that ... will necessarily produce the answer' (Dobson 1996a: 139).

A fifth argument derives from the putative environmental benefits of a particular sort of decentralised face-to-face democracy. As Doherty and de Geus point out, 'From an ecological standpoint greens view decentralisation as essential because it is less wasteful of resources, giving priority to local production and consumption rather than the production and transport of goods for a global market' (Doherty and de Geus 1996b: 3). In one direction, this train of thought actually leads to bioregionalism, and bioregionalism is not necessarily democratic. But there are connections in democratic theory and practice between DECENTRALISATION and participation, and to this degree there may be quite specific ecological arguments for localised democracy.

Finally, there are two sorts of argument from historical experience. The first of these rests its case on the respective environmental records of 'democratic' and 'authoritarian' societies in the belief that these records count decisively in favour of the former. The empirical strength of this claim cannot be assessed here, and we should certainly enter the caveat that the undoubtedly poor record of those regimes usually referred to

as authoritarian in this context (the Soviet Union and its eastern European neighbours) may have been due to factors other than their authoritarianism. Nevertheless, Lafferty and Meadowcroft speak for many when they write that, 'it may be that acute environmental crises are more readily (or perhaps only) amenable to authoritarian solution. The response here must be that ... neither theory nor practical experience suggest that authoritarian regimes are likely to best democracies at resolving environmental problems over the long term' (Lafferty and Meadowcroft 1996b: 3).

The second of these arguments from historical experience picks up on Bob Paehlke's observation that at precisely the same time as the theoreticians of 'green authoritarianism' such as Heilbroner and Ophuls were peddling their wares, early environmental activists were favouring 'openness and participation in environmental administration' (Paehlke 1988: 292). More recently, Doherty and de Geus point out that greens just turn out mostly to have been participatory democrats: 'In their organisation green parties and many grassroots green groups have tried to counter what they see as the dominance of political organisations by bureaucracies and leaders' (Doherty and de Geus 1996b: 5). This defence of the existence of 'green democracy' is sociological rather than political-theoretical, however; a statement of what is (or has been) rather than what ought to be. On this reading, the relationship between ecologism and democracy is contingent rather than necessary, based on the sociological origins of ecologism rather than its theoretical foundations:

> Historically and sociologically the ideas on democracy of most of the western European green parties developed from the models provided by the New Left in the late 1960s and from the practices of the new social movements in the 1970s and 1980s. The challenge to the bureaucratic character of modern government, and the call for self-management were unifying elements of the discourse of the New Left.
>
> (Doherty and de Geus, 1996b: 5)

All of these remarks on the possible connections between green and democratic thinking should be accompanied by the thought that there are many types of democracy, and the difference this can make to the compatibility question is considerable. For example, Michael Saward points out that the tensions he identifies between green objectives and democratic procedures are most marked in the context of direct democracy where the participatory proceduralism of democracy is at its height. In representative democracy, it is understood that the representative has room for manoeuvre, and is entitled to take decisions on behalf of her or his constituents. Here, says Saward, the 'tensions [between green imperatives and democratic procedures] would be lessened' (Saward 1993: 70). In other words, the more democracy is understood to be government for the people rather than by the people, the more compatible with the objective-driven nature of green thinking it becomes.

Similarly, the empirical record suggests that some types of democracy are more amenable to environmental problem-articulation than others:

> the link between altruism and environmentalism may explain why the smaller social democracies of northern Europe – Norway, Sweden, the Netherlands – have been more active in promulgating policy discussions about environmental issues which involve regulation of market externalities and making the distributional costs of environmental programmes more transparent.
>
> (Witherspoon 1996: 65).

All of this suggests that a full account of the troubled relationship between ecologism and democracy would require a cross-tabulated assessment of compatibility across all possible types of ecologism and all possible types of democracy. Such an assessment is, naturally and fortunately, beyond the scope of this entry, but enough has been said to show that any equating of ecologism with authoritarianism needs to be treated with great caution.

One more type of 'green democracy' problem remains to be considered. Environmental problems have brought 'new constituencies' onto the political agenda, constituencies whose interests are affected by environmental change, but which are not easily represented through traditional democratic structures and their boundaries. Such constituencies include 'away country' nationals (such as Scandinavians affected by British acid rain), future generations and parts of the non-human natural world. The question is: assuming that the interests of these constituencies should be represented democratically (a large assumption which is discussed in detail in Dobson (1996b)), how might institutions be appropriately redesigned? Two broad, and very different, answers have been given to this question. The first, from Bob Goodin, trades on the possibility of the interests of these constituencies (and particularly those of future generations and non-human nature) being 'encapsulated' in those of present human beings (Goodin 1996: 841) in much the same way as the interests of very small children are regarded as encapsulated in those of their parents. Goodin is aware that this model has a disreputable past: 'slaves' and servants' interests were, in just such ways, encapsulated within those of their master', he says. Likewise, 'Pre-Edwardian wives, having no independent legal personality apart from that of their husbands, saw their interests incorporated within those of their husbands' (Goodin 1996: 842). But, he goes on: 'Both in the cases of young children and of future generations, the model of 'incorporated interests' seems legitimate largely because it seems inevitable' (Goodin 1996: 843).

There are three problems with Goodin's suggestion for 'enfranchising the earth'. First, and most damaging, it is not democratic: if it was not democratic for Edwardian wives to have their interests incorporated in those of their husbands, then the same must apply to the case of present and future generations. Second, 'encapsulation' is not the only method of representation available to us, and third, there is no guarantee that present people will 'internalise [the] interests' (Goodin 1996: 844) of future generations and of non-human nature in the required way; and if they do not, then encapsulation will not bring about the benefits it promises. An alternative strategy is to have proxy representatives, elected by proxy constituencies, to represent 'directly' the interests of future generations and non-human nature in national and transnational legislatures. The proxy would function like any democratic electorate and would, firstly 'be' the 'future generation electorate' with candidates who represent the interests of future generations being drawn from it. In campaigning, these candidates would outline their objectives which would further the interests of future generations. 'The proxy electorate would consider the various candidates' merits and then choose its preferred candidate(s) through a democratic election. The successful candidates would then sit in the democratic assembly alongside present generation representatives' (Dobson 1996a: 132).

This form of enfranchisement is not without its difficulties, many of which are discussed elsewhere (Dobson 1996b), but such a system would avoid the non-democratic implications of encapsulation, and while it would not quite guarantee that the interests of future generations and non-human nature were taken into account, the democratic discipline of accountability – provided by elections, and absent in encapsulation – would help to focus minds appropriately.

The oxymoronic tendencies in 'green democratic thought' have therefore generated a lively debate regarding the normative relationship between green objectives and democratic procedures. On balance, this debate has left green thought on the side of the angels, although the minority authoritarian tendency will always serve to keep the movement on its democratic toes.

See also:

corporatism; cosmopolitan democracy; democracy and sustainability; globalisation; social movements

Further reading

Barry, J. (1996) 'Sustainability, Political Judgement and Citizenship: Connecting Green Politics and Democracy', in B. Doherty and M. de Geus (eds), *Democracy and Green Political Thought: Sustainability, Rights and Citizenship*, London: Routledge.

Dobson, A. (1993) 'Critical Theory and Green Politics', in A. Dobson and P. Lucardie (eds), *The Politics of Nature: Explorations in Green Political Theory*, London: Routledge.

—— (1996a) 'Democratising Green Theory: Preconditions and Principles', in B. Doherty and M. de Geus (eds), *Democracy and Green Political Thought: Sustainability, Rights and Citizenship*, London: Routledge.

—— (1996b) 'Representative Democracy and the Environment', in W. Lafferty and J. Meadowcroft (eds), *Democracy and the Environment: Problems and Prospects*, Cheltenham: Edward Elgar.

Doherty, B. and de Geus, M. (eds) (1996a) *Democracy and Green Political Thought: Sustainability, Rights and Citizenship*, London: Routledge.

—— (1996b), 'Introduction', in B. Doherty and M. de Geus (eds), *Democracy and Green Political Thought: Sustainability, Rights and Citizenship*, London: Routledge.

Dryzek, J. (1990) *Discursive Democracy, Politics, Policy and Political Science*, Cambridge: Cambridge University Press.

Eckersley, R. (1996) 'Connecting Ecology and Democracy: The Rights Discourse Revisited', in B. Doherty and M. de Geus (eds), *Democracy and Green Political Thought: Sustainability, Rights and Citizenship*, London: Routledge.

Foster, J. (ed.) (1997) *Valuing Nature? Economics, Ethics and Environment*, London: Routledge.

Goodin, R. (1992) *Green Political Theory* Cambridge: Polity Press.

—— (1996), 'Enfranchising the Earth, and its Alternatives', *Political Studies* 44(5).

Jacobs, M. (1997), 'Environmental Valuation, Deliberative Democracy and Public Decision-Making Institutions', in J. Foster (ed.), *Valuing Nature? Economics, Ethics and Environment*, London: Routledge.

Lafferty, M. and Meadowcroft, J. (eds) (1996a) *Democracy and the Environment: Problems and Prospects*, Cheltenham: Edward Elgar.

—— (1996b) 'Democracy and the Environment: Congruence and Conflict – Preliminary Reflections', in M. Lafferty and J. Meadowcroft (eds), *Democracy and the Environment: Problems and Prospects*, Cheltenham: Edward Elgar.

Mathews, F. (ed.) (1995) 'Ecology and Democracy', *Environmental Politics* Special Issue, 4(4).

Meadows, D., Meadows, D., Randers, J. and Behrens III, W. (1974) *The Limits to Growth*, London: Pan.

Ophuls, W. with Boyan Jr, A. (1992) *Ecology and the Politics of Scarcity Revisited: The Unravelling of the American dream*, New York: W.H. Freeman and Co.

Paehlke, R. (1988) 'Democracy, Bureaucracy and Environmentalism', *Environmental Ethics* 10.

Saward, M. (1993) 'Green Democracy?', in A. Dobson and P. Lucardie (eds), *The Politics of Nature: Explorations in Green Political Theory*, London: Routledge.

ANDREW DOBSON

gridlock

Introduction

The design of democratic institutions presents many trade-offs (see DEMOCRATIC TRADE-OFFS). If the AUTHORITY to make law is invested in a single institution, whether a legislature or executive, then the likelihood that a single purpose, whether expressed by one individual or a faction, may be able to seize control of law making and pervert it to its own purpose is increased. If, by contrast, legislative authority is so thoroughly fragmented and divided that numerous competing factions each must consent to changes in law and policy, then government might be incapable of pursuing the public good; in which case gridlock ensues. At the extreme, the government might be incapable of even sustaining the public order, leading to chaos and anarchy. Every democracy, then, whether parliamentary or presidential, federal or unitary, treads the space between tyranny and anarchy.

To decrease the likelihood of tyranny, even a tyranny of the majority, the framers of many modern constitutions have created systems of checks and balances wherein the ability to change public policy is shared among multiple, competing departments of government. Checks and balances are instituted by separating legislative from executive and judicial power. Further, the central government may make policy in some domains and lower levels of government may control policy on other issues. Both the ability to set the policy agenda and the power to approve changes may be shared, as in a bicameral legislature, or divided, as in presidential systems. At its heart, a SEPARATION OF POWERS requires that more than one branch of government (or one legislative chamber) must consent to a proposed policy change.

But a separation of powers is not sufficient to provide a guarantee against tyranny. A well-known maxim, derived from the writings of Madison and Montesquieu, holds that the institutional checks meant to protect a democracy from tyranny must be balanced, and that balance is achieved by dividing and separating the purposes of the individuals who occupy the separate offices of government. That is, there must be some conflict of interest between those who hold office.

More recently, modern political scholars have recognised new trade-offs induced by checks and balances, and the costs they impose on the legislative process (Buchanan and Tullock 1962). Some have argued that presidential democracies are prone to gridlock, a situation in which the diffusion of vetoes in a political system allows some actors to stymie others' legislative initiatives (Linz 1990; Shugart and Carey 1992). The danger in this situation is that prolonged or pronounced gridlock might lead to the rise of authoritarianism (Linz and Valenzuela 1994). These observations have led some scholars to flip Madison's logic on its head, arguing that unifying powers through parliamentary government, not separating it in presidential government, is the cure to the ills of tyranny (Lijphart 1992; Linz 1994; by contrast, see Shugart and Carey 1992; Loveman 1993).

Gridlock is, however, merely one symptom of the broader class of ailments known as state indecisiveness. Indecisiveness represents one end of a continuum running between a political system's level of decisiveness (the ability to enact and implement policy change) and its level of resoluteness (the ability to maintain and commit to a policy once established). The trade-off between these two is apparent from their definitions: a more decisive polity, possessing a greater ability to make or implement policy changes, must necessarily be less resolute and thus less likely to be able to maintain the status quo.

In what follows, this entry first describes how a polity's institutions interacts with key aspects of its society to cause state indecisiveness. When political institutions facilitate diversity of opinion in the legislative process, and require that either a larger or a more diverse population of opinions must be taken into account in law making, then the decisiveness of a polity is reduced. Both electoral and legislative institutions affect decisiveness in this way, as described in the next section. After discussing the causes of state indecisiveness, the entry addresses its consequences for POLICY-MAKING.

The causes of indecisiveness

Recent work has demonstrated that political institutions are one, although not the only, source of state indecisiveness. In the abstract, where a polity locates along the aforementioned continuum between resoluteness and decisiveness depends upon the 'effective number of vetoes' in a political system. The effective number of vetoes refers both to the number of groups, factions or parties who must consent to a policy change, and the diversity of those actors.

The effective number of veto players in a polity are affected by the institutions in the following way. First, the separation of power divides up authority among various actors within the national and subnational legislative process. By establishing checks and balances, as Madison argues in *Federalists* 47–51, the goal is to reduce the ability of any single faction (let alone a majority faction) from taking advantage of state power to achieve outcomes that they alone prefer. As American history has shown, however, in the cases of the Alien and Sedition Acts in the 1790s, the suspension of the writ of *habeas corpus* in the 1860s and the internment of Japanese-Americans in the 1940s, the separation of powers is not sufficient for ensuring that the interests of one faction would be checked. In addition to separating powers, the institutions must also ensure that different groups are represented by the persons holding the various positions of power established in a polity. That is, the institutions must establish a separation of purpose among the various veto players as well, to ensure that no single purpose holds all the reins of power at the same time. One way of accomplishing this is by establishing electoral rules that ensure that all groups in society are represented or even over-represented in the legislative process. At one extreme case, that of unanimous rule, the separation of power and of purpose are jointly maximised, but enormous transactions costs are encountered in attempting to change policy. In this case, the polity may be resolute but very indecisive. Meanwhile, at the other extreme dictatorships create very small transactions costs, implying that dictatorships are maximally decisive but minimally resolute.

The theory underlying my focus on vetoes has two components. First, an increase in the effective number of vetoes makes it more likely that no policy that makes all veto players unanimously better off relative to the status quo exists. In this situation, at least one group would exercise its veto and halt any policy change. Consequently enacting policy change becomes more difficult, but committing to established policies becomes easier. Second, increasing the effective number of vetoes also increases the transactions costs that must be overcome in order to change policy. These transactions costs may be simply the costs of negotiating with more people, or they may take the form of side payments that must be offered to each person to guarantee their support of a proposed policy change. As a larger population is provided with vetoes, it becomes increasingly difficult to structure LOG-ROLLING negotiations. As more diverse population is provided with vetoes, it becomes increasingly difficult to ensure that every party to the negotiations receives sufficient value to accept the deal. Hence changing policy becomes increasingly costly as either the number of parties to a negotiation, or as the diversity of their preferences, increases. It follows then that, as the effective number of vetoes increases, the polity becomes more resolute, and less decisive, all else constant. The reverse is also true.

Polities located at either extreme along the continuum from indecisive to irresolute suffer negative symptoms. A state that is irresolute is likely to be plagued by chaos and instability (see CHAOS AND COALITIONS). Alternatively, a state that is indecisive is likely to be afflicted with gridlock and stalemate, and thus it may be unable to meet its challenges efficiently.

The consequences of indecisiveness

As stated above, gridlock is one of the potential consequences of state indecisiveness, which results when a polity becomes unable to change policy because of disagreements between pivotal actors over the goals of the policy change. The image of political DECISION-MAKING just presented is one in which policy is made through an ongoing bargaining session among veto players. In some ways, gridlock is a natural consequence of the bargaining situation when there are multiple veto players. Delay is one of the primary bargaining techniques in such situations: by refusing to agree a party shows willingness to incur the costs of delay, hence toughness. Thus public wrangling and interminable delay are natural features of the politics of bargaining under divided government.

Second, when faced with a stalemate among veto players, some of the veto players may attempt to pursue their goals unilaterally. Indeed, one of the primary criticisms levelled at PRESIDENTIALISM is that is leads to gridlock, and that gridlock in turn leads to unilateral action that circumvents, and undermines, normal constitutional processes (Linz 1994).

Third, Cox and McCubbins (1999) note that the absence of agreement among veto players can lead to other types of unilateral action, such as 'institutional warfare' or 'balkanization'. An example of institutional warfare is the sequence of moves and countermoves concerning impoundments taken by President Nixon and the (Democratically-controlled) Congress during the early 1970s. Nixon, in an effort to stall or derail portions of the Great Society programmes enacted under Lyndon Johnson, began to impound funds for certain programs that had been duly authorised and appropriated. In so doing, he greatly expanded the executive power of impoundment, which had previously been used in a different, and non-controversial, fashion. Had he not been challenged, the consequence would have been a substantial shift in power to the executive, by creating something along the lines of a suspensory line item veto. However, he was challenged: Congress passed the Budget and Impoundment Control Act of 1974, which spelled out the limits on the executive's power of impoundment and reasserted congressional primacy in budgetary matters (Kiewiet and McCubbins 1991; Schick 1980).

Balkanization sometimes manifests itself as multiple actors pursuing parallel but different policies. This is illustrated by the pursuit of separate foreign policies regarding Nicaragua by the Reagan Administration and the Wright Speakership. The Administration, knowing that it could not secure the assent of Congress for its hardline policy, pursued this policy anyway via covert action (the financial aspects of which came to light in the Irangate scandal). The Speakership, knowing that it could not secure the assent of the Administration for its conciliatory policy, pursued this policy anyway via shuttle diplomacy centring on the office of the Speaker.

Another kind of balkanization occurs when each veto actor controls some areas of policy, leading to sub-governments. This kind of result is typically thought to lead to each sub-government acting as a champion of particular kinds of subsidies, and is most likely when the policy decisions made in one sub-government have relatively small external impacts (other than budgetary) on political actors controlling other sub-governments (Cox and McCubbins 1993).

Many of the fears expounded about gridlock are based on reasoning along the lines of, 'if there is no agreement on policy, then "the people's business" is not being done'. If, for instance, gridlock results because a veto player prefers the reversionary policy to other options, then gridlock appears to bias policy-making toward actors whose preferences are nearest the reversionary policy (Kiewiet and McCubbins 1988; McCubbins 1991). Similarly, when policy decisions affect every veto holder in a consequential way, a result of the possibility of gridlock is that policy is passed but takes a long time to negotiate and is laden with substantial side payments to the prospective losers (Cox and McCubbins 1999).

The view of gridlock presented here is that it is an equilibrium outcome to a larger political game among factions in a polity. It follows, then, that it is misleading to speak of gridlock as an immutable feature of a political system. Rather, gridlock is an outcome derived from the more basic features of a political system, and can be changed when those more basic features change.

The view of gridlock presented here also suggests that indecisiveness can and does emerge in non-presidential systems. It is entirely possible among members of a coalition government, or among factions within a single ruling party (such as the LDP in Japan) to be so divided that they cannot reach even common and simple decisions. More generally, gridlock can occur any time there are multiple effective veto players with regard to enactment of a policy. So, any time there is a separation of power that creates multiple veto points – such as a bicameral legislature, a federal system of government, an independent judiciary, or between coalition partners in a government – some form of indecisiveness becomes possible.

Conclusion: decisiveness versus resoluteness

Every polity makes a trade-off between decisiveness and resoluteness. At one end of the continuum, a polity may be unable to change the status quo, and gridlock or stalemate might result. At the other extreme, the polity may be unable to commit to a particular policy, and chaos and instability might result. Whether a polity faces these issues is highly dependent on its constitutional choices, which set the stage on which the policy-making process is played out.

Three propositions follow from the above discussion. First, a necessary condition for state indecisiveness is that either the electorate is fragmented, or the polity's purpose is separated by the electoral institutions, or both. A corollary of this statement is that the separation of power is not sufficient to cause indecisiveness. Second, a necessary condition for indecisiveness is that the purpose of the polity must be separated. However, electoral fragmentation is not sufficient for irresoluteness, since if power is separated and each subgroup possesses a veto, then you end up back at the opposite problem of indecisiveness. This fact has long been part of the conventional wisdom, and Madison relied heavily upon the idea that INSTITUTIONAL DESIGN can overcome problems of instability in justifying the American constitutional structure. Thus there is a second necessary condition for irresoluteness, which is that the power to make policy must be unified (or there is unilateralism, which is merely a form of unified power with a different time frame).

See also:

coalitions; decision-making; presidentialism

Further reading

Buchanan, J. and Tullock, G. (1962) *The Calculus of Consent*, Ann Arbor, MI: University of Michigan Press.

Cox, G.W. and McCubbins, M.D. (1993)

Legislative Leviathan: Party Government in the House, Berkeley, CA: University of California Press.

—— (1999) 'Political Structure and Economic Policy: The Institutional Determinants of Policy Outcomes', in S. Haggard and M.D. McCubbins (eds), *Structure and Policy in Presidential Democracies*, Princeton, NJ: Princeton University Press.

Kiewiet, D.R. and McCubbins, M.D. (1988) 'Presidential Influence on Congressional Appropriations Decisions', *American Journal of Political Science* 32: 713–36.

—— (1991) *The Logic of Delegation: Congressional Parties and the Appropriations Process*, Chicago: University of Chicago Press.

Lijphart, A. (1992) *Parliamentary versus Presidential Government*, Oxford: Oxford University Press.

Linz, J. (1990) 'The Perils of Presidentialism', *Journal of Democracy* 1: 51–69.

—— (1994) 'Democracy, Presidential or Parliamentary: Does it Make a Difference?', in J. Linz and A. Valenzuela (eds), *The Failure of Presidential Democracy: The Case of Latin America*, Baltimore: Johns Hopkins University Press.

Linz, J. and Valenzuela, A. (eds) (1994) *The Failure of Presidential Democracy: The Case of Latin America*, Baltimore: Johns Hopkins University Press.

Loveman, B. (1993) *The Constitution of Tyranny: Regimes of Exception in Spanish America*, Pittsburgh: University of Pittsburgh Press.

McCubbins, M.D. (1991) 'Government on Lay-Away: Federal Spending and Deficits under Divided Party Control', in G.W. Cox and S. Kernell (eds), *The Politics of Divided Government*, Boulder, CO: Westview Press.

Schick, A. (1980) *Congress and Money*, Washington, DC: The Urban Institute.

Shugart, M.S. and Carey, J. (1992) *Presidents and Assemblies: Constitutional Design and Electoral Dynamics*, Cambridge: Cambridge University Press.

MATHEW D. MCCUBBINS

H

hegemony

The category of 'hegemony' – mainly developed within the field of Marxist and post-Marxist theorisation – is closely associated with the notion of 'universal CLASS', as originally presented by Hegel and substantially transformed by Marx. Hegel saw CIVIL SOCIETY as divided into an ensemble of purely particularistic interests – what he called the 'system of needs' – and conceived of the 'universal' moment through which society as a whole reached its unity as incarnated in the state as a separate instance. BUREAUCRACY is, for Hegel, the universal class. Marx denied this universal character of the state and saw it as just one more sphere of particularity: it was an instrument of class domination. The actual universality of the community was to be achieved, according to Marx, at the level of civil society through the emergence of the proletariat as the true universal class that represents pure human essence. This centrality of the proletariat would result, in Marx's vision, from the simplification of social structure under CAPITALISM, which would lead to the dissolution of the middle classes and the peasantry and the reduction of the great majority of the population to a vast proletarian mass. This process of proletarianisation would be the prelude to a withering away of the state and the resulting extinction of a separate political sphere.

At the end of the nineteenth century, however, it was clearly perceived that the main trends of capitalist development were not moving in the direction that Marxism had anticipated and that some kind of privileging of a political (non-economistic) link was necessary to formulate an adequate socialist strategy. This was accomplished in orthodox Marxism through the reinforcement of the Communist Party as bearer of class consciousness, in socialist revisionism through an appeal to ethics, and in revolutionary syndicalism through the myth of the general strike.

This re-emergence of the political instance in socialist reflection is the general background explaining Gramsci's intervention, which will be the crucial moment in the constitution of a political analysis centred in the category of 'hegemony'. The immediate genealogy of the latter, however, is to be found in the Leninist tradition. As Anderson (1976–7) has shown, the first conceptualisations of 'hegemony', as understood in the contemporary sense, should be traced back to the work of the Russian social democrats Axelrod and Plekhanov at the turn of the nineteenth century. The crucial question for Russian socialists of that period was the dislocation, in the Russian experience, between historical processes that in Western Europe had been simultaneous. Thus, the democratic REVOLUTIONS in the West had been led by the bourgeoisie, while in Russia the slow development of an autochthonous bourgeoisie meant that the latter was too weak to take up the leadership of a democratic revolution largely seen as inevitable. That LEADERSHIP consequently passed to the working class, which was far more developed than the bourgeoisie and highly concentrated in the industries resulting from foreign investments. This taking up by one sector of tasks, which in a 'normal' development would have not corresponded to it, is what the Russian revolutionists called 'hegemony'.

The conditions for the generalisation of 'hegemony' to the whole field of politics are to be found in this notion of a paradigmatic 'normal' development. The view of the world economy as an 'imperialist chain' meant that crises at one point of the system could generate dislocations at other different points, whose resolutions would not necessarily follow a classical paradigmatic pattern. In the 1930s, for instance, the notion of 'combined and uneven development' – popularised by Trotsky following the experience of the mobilisation in the colonial and semi-colonial world – presented these dislocations and non-orthodox articulations as the condition of *all* social struggles in the contemporary world.

It is this transformed climate, in which the need for political mediation was widely felt, that established the parameters that make Gramsci's intervention understandable. From the very beginning, he tries to displace the area of validity of Marxian and Leninist categories through the introduction of oppositions, which transform the intellectual field. First, there is opposition between corporative and hegemonic class. While the first refers to a group closed around its particularistic interests, the second alludes to the ability of a group to take up the representation of the community as a whole. The notion of 'universal class' re-emerges, but its universality is no longer the result of the structural location of a class in the relations of production but of its ability to agglutinate and represent the demands of a large variety of social sectors. This is the second opposition; political/intellectual and moral leadership. While the first remains anchored in the Leninist notion of class alliances, which is a mere tactical confluence leaving unchanged the identity of the social actors intervening in it, the second changes that identity as a result of their politico-ideological agglutination around a common task. These two oppositions explain why the hegemonic link weakens the pure class identity of social agents through the formation of what Gramsci calls a *collective will*, which is wider than any narrow class belonging.

A third opposition is that between *war of position* and *war of movement*. Leninism, with its emphasis on seizing state power, had privileged the war of manoeuvre. For Gramsci,

the moment of seizure of power becomes entirely subordinated to the process of *becoming* a state of a hegemonic class. That is, that the war of position is privileged, as far as the establishment of a new hegemony is an epochal process, involving the change in the relations of forces in society over a long period of time. The 'universalisation' of the aims of a group depends on those aims being recognised by vast sectors of society as those of society as a whole. This notion of a pragmatic construction of a hegemonic universality makes Gramsci's approach closer to Marx than to Hegel, inasmuch as hegemony is largely constructed at the level of civil society and not in a separate state sphere; but, from a different angle, it could be considered as closer to Hegel than to Marx, as far as the hegemonic rearticulation of relations in civil society is conceived in political terms. It is in the blurring of the line separating civil society from the state, and in the unification of both spheres in what Gramsci calls a 'historical bloc', where the specificity of his view of hegemony lies. For the same reasons, Gramsci can call his conception 'absolute historicism', as far as the configuration of social relations depends entirely on hegemonic rearticulations and not on aprioristic laws of development, as postulated in classical philosophies of history.

The credibility of the Gramscian hegemonic approach largely depends on how social logics are conceived. If society is seen as unified by detectable underlying mechanisms, explaining out of themselves the multiform variety of social life – as in the nineteenth-century image of a self-regulated economic space – it is clear that there is no room for hegemonic rearticulations. If, on the contrary, society is seen as essentially fragmented and only partially stabilised through transient and contingent logics, the area of operation of hegemonic linkages necessarily increases. It is precisely the fragmentation and proliferation of new social identities in the contemporary world, and the whole gamut of phenomena linked to GLOBA-LISATION and postmodernity, that has widened the field of the operation of hegemonic political interventions as the only way of mediating between the particularism of social agents and the globality of the effects and forms of representation (see REPRESENTATION, FORMS OF). Developing the hegemonic approach and applying it to these changing historical circumstances necessarily requires, however, going beyond Gramsci, whose arguments were clearly limited by a social context which is no longer ours.

A reformulation of the theory of hegemony along these lines can be found in Laclau and Mouffe (1985) and Laclau (1996). The starting point of their analysis is the definition of hegemony as the taking up by a *particular* social agent of a *universal* function of representation; particularity and universality being strictly incommensurable and only articulated by the hegemonic link. In this way they differentiate their approach from extreme forms of universalism (Rawls, Habermas) and particularism (Lyotard, Baudrillard). Hegemonic moves, in this approach, can take place as either relations of difference (characteristics of institutionalised discourses which try to blur social divisions) and relations of equivalence (which dichotomise social spaces and create politico-ideological frontiers). Central to the whole argument is the notion of antagonism, seen as the limit of all social objectivity in that it is not the effect of any underlying objective mechanism but is irreducible; that is, based in constitutive exclusions which make possible the emergence of a plurality of hegemonic projects. Hegemony, in this perspective, becomes the ultimate horizon of constitution of social relations which, being grounded in antagonisms and exclusions, have a necessary political dimension.

See also:

democratic debate; identity, political; political culture; radical democracy

Further reading

Anderson, P. (1976–7) 'The Antinomies of Antonio Gramsci', *New Left Review* 100: 5–78.

Bocock, R. (1986) *Hegemony*, London and New York: Tavistock.

Buci-Glucksman, C. (1980) *Gramsci and the State*, London: Lawrence and Wishart.

Femia, J. (1981) *Gramsci's Political Thought; Hegemony, Consciousness and Revolutionary Process*, Oxford: Clarendon Press.

Gramsci, A. (1971) *Selection from the Prison Notebooks*, London: Lawrence and Wishart.

Laclau, E. (1996) *Emancipation(s)*, London: Verso.

Laclau, E. and Mouffe, C. (1985) *Hegemony and Socialist Strategy*, London: Verso.

Mouffe, C. (ed.) (1979) *Gramsci and Marxist Theory*, London: Routledge and Kegan Paul.

Torfing, J. (1999) *New Theories of Discourse. Laclau, Mouffe and Zizek*, Oxford: Blackwell.

ERNESTO LACLAU

hybrid systems

The categories and classification systems created by political scientists inevitably fail to capture the complex variation we see in reality. In the study of political institutions, two dichotomies are routinely used: PRESIDENTIALISM versus PARLIAMENTARY MODELS of government, and proportional versus plurality-based ELECTORAL SYSTEMS. These dichotomies are very useful for drawing clear contrasts, and many countries fit clearly into pure types. But significant hybrids exist in both domains. Indeed, the decade of the 1990s saw a dramatic increase in the number of countries using a hybrid electoral system for their national parliaments. This entry will discuss each type of hybrid in turn, and conclude with a brief discussion of the normative and practical appeal of hybrid systems in general.

In the pure parliamentary model, the cabinet is chosen by the legislature and must maintain its confidence to remain in power. In the textbook model of presidentialism, the chief executive is directly elected by the people and governs for a fixed term, creating separation of legislative and executive powers. Hybrid systems fall somewhere between the two models.

Duverger (1980) coined the term 'semi-presidential' to refer to systems in which executive and governmental powers are given to both a president, who is directly elected for fixed term, and also to a prime minister and cabinet, who govern subject to parliamentary confidence. Duverger's examples of semi-presidential systems are France, Weimar Germany, Finland, Portugal, Austria, Iceland and Ireland.

Shugart and Carey (1992) further divide this group of hybrids into 'premier-presidential' systems, in which the legislature is able to dismiss cabinet members, but the president is not; and 'president-parliamentary' systems, in which either the president or the legislature can dismiss cabinet members. In Shugart and Carey's terms, Weimar Germany and Portugal from 1976 to 1982 are president-parliamentary, as are Sri Lanka, Namibia and Haiti (1987 constitution). The other hybrids identified by Duverger, including post-1982 Portugal, are premier-presidential.

Presidents have little legislative power in most semi-presidential systems. With the exception of Portugal, none give presidents the ability to veto legislation, whereas most pure presidential systems allow for some type of veto (Shugart and Carey 1992: 155). On the other hand, some notable hybrids, including France, the Weimar Republic and Sri Lanka, allow the president to call referenda on matters of public policy, a power absent in many pure presidential systems.

Hybrid electoral systems combine elements of single member district (SMD) elections with proportional representation (PR). The defining feature of a hybrid electoral system is that some legislators receive their mandates by winning a plurality of votes in a single member district, others receive their mandate according to their position on a party list. The Federal Republic of Germany adopted a hybrid system beginning in 1949, and was the only major country to use one for much of the post-Second World War era. During the 1990s, however, a number of old and new democracies adopted some type of hybrid system.

The logic behind hybrid electoral systems is as follows. They capture a clear advantage of a pure SMD system, namely, direct linkages. Each citizen has a specific legislator whose job is to represent the citizen's interest in parliament. But the hybrids mitigate the notable disadvantage of pure SMD, which is that parties whose support base is small or geographically dispersed are completely excluded from the legislature. A party that gains 20 per cent of the vote in every district will (typically) not receive any seats at all under pure SMD. This distortionary effect can be partially or completely offset by the list seats in a hybrid system.

Electoral scholars distinguish between those hybrid systems that give overall proportional results and those that do not (Taagepera and Shugart 1989). 'Compensatory member system' refers to the first type: hybrid systems in which the overall seat share in the legislature is proportional to vote share (often subject to a minimum vote-share threshold). The compensatory type is used in Germany, and was adopted by New Zealand in 1993. As the name implies, these systems compensate completely for the distortions introduced by single member districts. In compensatory systems, PROPORTIONALITY is achieved by counting the single member district seats won by party members toward the party's allocated seat share. That is, if a party is entitled to fifteen seats on the basis of its vote share, and it wins ten district seats, it will receive five more seats to be filled from the party list. In most cases, then, the outcomes of the district races do not affect overall seat shares. The exception to this general rule occurs when the number of district seats won exceeds a party's allocated seats share. When this occurs, the party receives its excess district seats – so that no district is left without a representative – and the overall size of the legislature increases.

The other major electoral hybrid is often referred to as a 'parallel system' or an 'additional member system'. Under this type of system, the single member district and PR seats are allocated separately, so that the overall result is not proportional. In the Japanese lower chamber, for example, there are 300 single member district seats and 200 list seats. A party's share of the 200 list seats will be proportional to its share of the list vote, but its overall seat share will depend on how many of the 300 single member districts it won as well. Italy, Russia, Mexico, Georgia, Hungary and Albania (in addition to Japan) now use some form of additional member system to elect their national parliament. In these systems, the distortionary effect of the single member districts is offset but not eliminated.

Both types of hybrids – mixed PR/plurality electoral rules and semi-presidentialism – are politically appealing as institutional choices. A large part of the appeal is the mere fact that they are hybrids, and as such can be adopted as an explicit compromise between factions that favour the pure types. Moreover, each type of hybrid has a clear success story associated with it – for semi-presidentialism, Fifth Republic France; for mixed PR/plurality, the Federal Republic of Germany. But it is not clear in either case that the successes are due to the features of the hybrid system, or to something else. Huber (1996) argues, for example, that the relative stability of the Fifth Republic France is due at least as much to the institutions that structure the relationship between the government and assembly (the package vote and confidence vote) than to the role of the president. Similarly, the relatively small number of PARTIES competing in the Federal Republic of Germany is more likely due to the high vote threshold (5 per cent, or three seats) than to the hybrid nature of the electoral system.

Although the adoption of a hybrid may be seem to be a compromise, the results are not necessarily 'in between' those we would expect from the pure systems. For example, the president-parliamentary systems, in which both the legislature and the president are able to dismiss the governments, are arguably more prone to instability than either pure type. Similarly, in Russia, the hybrid electoral system has produced parliaments that were possibly more fragmented than they would have been with either pure type, with some fringe parties winning primarily list seats and others capturing only a few district seats.

Hybrid systems by their very nature tend to be more complicated than pure systems. This complexity may damage ACCOUNTABILITY, and is sometimes regarded as a disadvantage in and of itself. Jesse (1987) has argued that Germany's compensatory member system, which allows separate votes for both district and list races, is confusing and systematically misinterpreted by voters. Bawn (1999), however, found that actual voting patterns imply that voters do understand the system and react strategically to the opportunity to separately influence the identity of the local representative and the overall seat share in parliament. Complexity can also lead to instability, when division of power is ambiguous. Shugart and Carey argue that the poor performance of president-parliamentary systems is due to ambiguity in the powers of the president relative to the prime minister.

It is clear from even this brief discussion that the political consequences of either type of hybrid system will depend on a number of fine details; the precise powers of the president in the semi-presidential cases, for example, and the number of votes, the number of each type of seat and the nominating processes in the mixed plurality/PR cases. These details, and their interaction with other aspects of the political environment, are what determine the ultimate impact of a hybrid system in any particular context.

See also:

accountability; elections; electoral systems; parties; presidentialism; proportionality

Further reading

Bawn, K. (1999) 'Voter Responses to Electoral Complexity: Ticket Splitting, Rational Voters and Representation in the Federal Republic of Germany', *British Journal of Political Science* 29: 583–601.

Duverger, M. (1980) 'A New Political System Model: Semi-Presidential Government', *European Journal of Political Research* 8: 165–87.

Huber, J. (1996) *Rationalizing Parliament*, New York: Cambridge University Press.

Jesse, E. (1987) 'The West German Electoral System: The Case for Reform, 1949–87', *Western European Politics* 10: 434–48.

Shugart, M. and Carey, J. (1992) *Presidents and Assemblies*, New York: Cambridge University Press.

Taagepera, R. and Shugart, M. (1989) *Seats and Votes*, New Haven, CT: Yale University Press.

KATHLEEN BAWN

I

identity, political

Our contemporary world is marked throughout by the increasing importance of questions
of identity. During the last thirty or forty years,
for example, 'identity crisis' has become a
fitting subjective description of our psycho-
social *malaise*. Most important, both national
and international politics are now – especially
since the collapse of the discursive imaginary of
the Cold War – primarily concerned with the
attempts of various collectivities to claim or
reclaim their lost, oppressed or threatened
identity, be that of an ethnic, religious, sexual
or any other type. In relation to democracy, a
first wave of theorists celebrating this political
action of new SOCIAL MOVEMENTS and identity
groups as reinvigorating modern democracy
has been followed by a wave of scepticism
highlighting the potential threat to democracy
posed by certain versions of identity politics.

It is impossible to understand what political
identity is and to discuss identity politics and
its relation to democracy without first defining
identity. This in itself is not an easy task. The
genealogy of the concept reveals a tumultuous
history. The category emerges for the first time
with Aristotle where *tautotes* has the meaning
of 'shared identity'. In Latin, *identitas* from
idem means 'the same'. From antiquity onwards the concept acquires a variety of
significations: mathematical (where identity,
as in a≡a, is distinguished from mere equation,
a=b), philosophical (as discussed in Montaigne, Kant, Locke and Hegel through to
contemporary philosophers), anthropological
and sociological (as discussed by, for example,
G.H. Mead and E. Goffman), psychological
and others. The psychological conception of

identity is of some importance here. It is
associated with the work of Erik Erikson in
the period after the end of the Second World
War. It is Erikson's work, which seems to have
prompted the first wave of public interest into
questions of identity. As David Riesman points
out in the foreword to the 1960 edition of his
acclaimed book *The Lonely Crowd*, 'the current
preoccupation with identity in this country'
(the United States) is clearly related to the
'great impact of Erik H. Erikson's work'
(Mackenzie 1978: 35).

From a political point of view, Erikson's
importance is not so much due to his definition
of identity as to the fact that the concept of
'political identity' emerges for the first time
with reference to his work. This birth of
'political identity' appears to occur around
1960, in the work of the American political
scientist Lucian Pye, who deliberately adapted
the concept from Erikson (Mackenzie 1978).
Although Erikson always spoke of individual
identity, Pye transfers it, at first metaphorically,
from the individual to the collective, political
level. For example, it seems that he is the first
to speak of an 'identity crisis' referring not to
individuals but to what he calls the 'first and
most fundamental' stage of political development leading to the formation of a modern
nation-state (Pye 1966: 63). He also refers to
national identity, 'collective identities' and so
on (Pye 1966: 25).

Two crucial questions emerge from this brief
conceptual history. First, does the current
preoccupation with identity mean that identities are a modern or even a twentieth-century
phenomenon? It would be unwise to conclude
anything of the sort. First of all the exploration
of the meaning of identity is not a modern
innovation; as already mentioned, this activity

starts with Greek and Latin antiquity. Nevertheless, it is important to stress that modernity, and especially late modernity, signals a quantitative change *vis-à-vis* premodernity. Identity is no more the subject of detached philosophical analyses or mathematical treatises, a rare and isolated topic of inquiry, but a matter of intense and sustained public discussion, the focus of media attention, a thoroughly politicised issue. However, what underlies this quantitative shift (the proliferation and increasing centrality of issues of identity) is another more qualitative kind of change. In premodern societies, identity issues did not emerge in the same way because identity was usually considered as a given; it was largely taken for granted. It was seen as determined by an immutable social topography guaranteed by mythical or religious forces (the power of a taboo or the will of God). This was an era of a non-reflexive objective reason: identity was something assigned by what the community defined and obeyed as its unifying principle. This does not mean that identity was not an issue. It was simply more likely to surface in a theological discussion about the nature of the Holy Trinity rather than in any other culturally, socially or politically significant form. Modernity, by proclaiming the 'Death of God' and by advancing individualisation and CAPITALISM, radically disrupts this stability. It involves a multitude of dislocations of traditional practices and types of behaviour and initiates a period of constant change. What these quantitative and qualitative shifts reveal and reinforce is the social and political character of identity.

Second, what is the exact relation between identity, the social and the political in the modern age and especially in late modernity? If, as a result of social transformations taking place in modernity, identity is not considered anymore as given, then it can only be the result of social processes of construction and sedimentation; hence the expression 'social identity'. Furthermore, if identity is understood as the result of social construction then this also opens up the possibility of a political contestation and re-articulation of identity. Hence the expression 'political identity'. In our century

and as a result of this transformation, a multitude of groups began to question their traditionally established identities. Women, for example, contested their location within patriarchal representations of the social, which were previously taken as more or less given, and entered the political arena, first in Western democracies and then globally (see GENDERING DEMOCRACY). The same of course applies to other groups, such as homosexuals, indigenous people, ethnic minorities and so on. This process is clearly associated with the emergence of new social movements and the development, during the last twenty years, of a distinct type of 'identity politics'.

It is possible then to discern two movements leading to the current preoccupation with identity and identity politics. First, the social character of identity is recognised. Human identity cannot be but social identity. But this development, although it goes a long way towards shaking determinist assumptions of the naturalist or theological sort, does not preclude an appeal to social determinism. If it were possible for agents to have an always already determined location within the social structure – if, for example, their identities were to be thought as *a priori* given by their location within CLASS structure – the problem of their identity would still be seen as a question of people discovering or recognising their true, essential identity and not of constructing it (Laclau 1994: 2). Under these conditions the second movement, the politicisation of identity, cannot take place. In order for the political character of identity to emerge, the obviousness of social identities has to be put into question. This also explains why, since the early 1980s, it is as an alternative to class politics that 'identity politics' has been increasingly dominating political discussions on the democratic left. This radical questioning of social, and especially class determinism and essentialism, is surely one of the defining characteristics of democratic societies of the end of the twentieth century. 'The more the 'foundation' of the social is put into question, the less the sedimented social practices are able to ensure social reproduction' and the more we recognise that 'a dimension of construction and creation is inherent in all social practice. The latter do not involve only repetition, but also reconstruction' (Laclau 1994: 3–4). In societies which do not rely on any kind of naturalist, theological or essentialist social foundation, the construction and continuous reconstruction of identity can only be a radical institution, an institution *constitutive* of social practices, in other words a truly *political* institution. The political dimension of identity becomes fully visible only when it is recognised that there is no such a thing as a natural, essential or intrinsic social identity.

This is not, however, an unproblematic conclusion. For, if identities are socially and politically constructed; if the outcome of construction is not guaranteed by any essential ground; if the collapse of the essentialist grounding of identities makes possible the radical questioning of any identity, its destructuration and even its destruction; if, in other words, due to the absence of a universal ground, no identity can totally transcend the historical and political conditions of its emergence; does not this mean that identity itself becomes impossible? The answer can only be affirmative in the sense that the continuous political construction of social identities never results in a closed, self-contained and absolute identity. Identity, at both the personal and political levels, is only the name of what we desire but can never fully attain. This might explain a current trend in contemporary theorising of using the term 'identity claim' in addition to that of 'identity', where identity claims are of a normative and not of a descriptive nature. If the full realisation of identity is impossible and cannot correspond to any representable state of biological, social or other existence, then we must attach greater significance to identity claims, claims of always incomplete subjects and collectivities to something – an image of themselves – they aspire to but can never fully attain.

What is the political practice which supports and sustains our attempts to materialise these identity claims, and which, although it always fails to produce a full identity, plays a crucial role in structuring our lives? The practice in question is *identification*, the psychoanalytic category of identification with its explicit assertion of a lack of identity at its root. One needs to identify with something, a political ideology or ethnic group for example, because there is an originary and insurmountable lack of identity (Laclau 1994: 3). It is Freud who singles out identification as constitutive of both subjectivity and politics. This is the unsettling conclusion of psychoanalytic theory that destabilises any identitarian metaphysics: political subjectivity depends on identification but identification never results in the production of full identity. Here 'identification' becomes a term almost synonymous with 'identity claim'. Normative identity claims cannot be fully satisfied because 'identifications are never brought to full closure; identifications are inevitably failed identifications'. In that sense, identification is simultaneously the condition of possibility and impossibility of identity. On the one hand, it 'brings a sense of identity into being [but] it also immediately calls identity into question . . . Identification is a process that keeps identity at a distance, that prevents identity from ever approximating the status of an ontological given, even as it makes possible the formation of an illusion of identity as immediate, secure, and totalizable' (Fuss 1995: 2).

The paradoxical nature of identity revealed in the role of identification is something constitutive of our subjective and political predicament: 'life without the drive to identity is an impossibility but the claim to a natural or true identity is always an exaggeration' (Connolly 1991: 67). This ambiguity is inscribed in any attempt to define identity. Whether one consults the *Oxford English Dictionary*, philosophical dissertations or sociological textbooks, the result will be the same: identity is commonly defined according to two fundamental criteria, sameness and difference. Sameness is usually defined as continuity, which is to say as unity or consistency in and across time. My identity is what guarantees that I am the same person I was yesterday and that I will be the same tomorrow, at least in my essential characteristics. It has become gradually evident, however, that identity cannot be defined without reference to what stands outside its field. What creates my identity, what defines sameness, is that I differ from the identities of others. Identities are relational and differential. It is possible to ground this observation in a variety of ways. Take structural linguistics and semiology for example. Here, we can argue that since identities are meaningful they must abide by the rules governing systems of signification (language and cultural semiosis). We know from Saussure and from the whole structuralist and poststructuralist tradition that the meaning of a particular element within a system of signification can only arise via its differentiation from other elements within the same system. I cannot understand what 'father' is without situating this signifier within the familial significations embodied in signifiers such as 'sister', 'mother', 'brother', etc. It follows then that, as William Connolly has successfully put it, 'difference requires identity and identity difference' (Connolly 1991: ix).

This inherent ambiguity of identity has profound political consequences. First of all, the realisation of the ultimate impossibility of full identity can be detrimental for any version of politics of identity. How is then possible to inscribe the limits of my identity claims, limits which are becoming visible in one or the other form, without committing political suicide, without, in other words, putting in danger the HEGEMONY of my discourse? The most common way in which political ideologies perform this slight of hand is by constructing scapegoats. If identity itself is a slippery, ambiguous and insecure experience then the political creation and maintenance of the ideological appearance of a true identity can only depend on the production of scapegoats (Connolly 1991: 67). Thus I can be persuaded that what is responsible for the impossibility of realising my (universalised) identity, what is limiting my identity, is not the inherent ambiguity and CONTINGENCY of all identity, its reliance on processes of identification, its social and political conditioning, but the existence or the action of a localisable group: the Jews, the immigrants, etc. If, the ideological argument goes, this group, this 'anomalous' particularity,

is silenced or even eliminated, then full identity will be possible. The next step is, of course, Auschwitz and the Gulags. If universalist political identities can lead in such a direction, this does not mean that particularist identity politics fare any better. The particularism of identity politics can also very easily take an anti-democratic direction. This sort of particularism involves the political construction of an identity around an issue or a specific geographical, ethnic, sexual or social location in a way that does not link up with other identities within the public arena. This effectively negates even the minimum common ground necessary for democracy to function (Laclau 1991: 58).

Second, these dangers are always present in identity politics, but they are not the only ones. An identity politics, premised upon an essentialist and simplistic conception of identity, also puts in danger its potential to radically transform the status quo. The politics of homosexuality is an interesting case in point. Homosexual or gay identity politics (at least from the early 1950s to the end of the 1970s) although articulating a different position *vis-à-vis* homosexuality, a position defending the 'normality' and the rights of homosexuals, did not question the existence of a distinct and uniform homosexual human type. In that sense it did not differ much from the essentialism characteristic of discourses opposing and condemning homosexuality (Seidman 1995). Queer theorists (including Diana Fuss and Judith Butler) have questioned the existence of such an essential, unitary identity, as well as the democratic productiveness of an identity politics articulated along essentialist lines. Another example is feminist politics. Today it is increasingly realised that a feminist politics 'understood as realising the equality of a definable empirical group with a common essence and identity, women' can only lead to a particularist politics with limited effectivity. What the radicalisation of plural democracy requires is 'discarding the essentialist idea of an identity of women as well as the attempt to ground a specific feminist politics' (Mouffe 1995: 329).

Given that identity claims are of crucial

importance in politics, how can we minimise the dangers entailed in their exaggeration? Is it possible to mediate between extreme universalism and extreme particularism and what form of political order emerges when we break away from the essentialism of some versions of identity politics? It does not seem likely that we are entering a post-identity era. Identity seems to be the necessary point of reference for the articulation of our ultimately impossible political aspirations. From this point of view, there is no point in negating identity. What is really at stake is the possibility of acknowledging within identity the impossibility of its full realisation, its own ambiguous and always uncertain character. At least two projects in contemporary democratic theory attempt to explore this new terrain: democratic AGONISM as articulated by William Connolly and RADICAL DEMOCRACY as conceptualised by Ernesto Laclau and Chantal Mouffe. This entry will only refer briefly to the first of these two theoretico-political interventions. Connolly's agonistic democracy can be described as a democratic imaginary that disturbs any dogmatisation of identity by being attentive to the ambiguity inherent in its constitution. Democracy requires contingent identities alert to their own political constitution, identities that strive to curtail 'the problem of evil installed in the demand for surety of identity' (Connolly 1991: 120). On the other hand, it is only in a democratic environment that such an attitude towards identity formation can be cultivated. In that sense, 'the experience of democracy and the experience of contingency in identity can sustain each other' (Connolly 1991: 200).

See also:

hegemony; pluralism; social movements

Further reading

Connolly, W. (1991) Identity/Difference: Democratic Negotiations of Political Paradox, Ithaca, NY: Cornell University Press.
Fuss, D. (1995) Identification Papers, New York: Routledge.
Jenkins, R. (1996) Social Identity, London: Routledge.
Laclau, E. (1991) 'God Only Knows', Marxism Today: 56–59.
—— (1994) 'Introduction', in E. Laclau (ed.), The Making of Political Identities, London: Verso.
Mackenzie, W.J.M. (1978) Political Identity, London: Penguin.
Mouffe, C. (1995) 'Feminism, Citizenship, and Radical Democratic Politics', in L. Nicholson and S. Seidman (eds), Social Postmodernism: Beyond Identity Politics, Cambridge: Cambridge University Press.
Pye, L. (1966) Aspects of Political Development, Boston: Little, Brown.
Rajchman, J. (ed.) (1995) The Identity in Question, New York: Routledge.
Seidman, S. (1995) 'Deconstructing Queer Theory or the Under-theorisation of the Social and the Ethical', in L. Nicholson and S. Seidman (eds), Social Postmodernism: Beyond Identity Politics, Cambridge: Cambridge University Press.

YANNIS STAVRAKAKIS

ideological polarisation

When the term was first coined, 'ideology' meant the science of ideas, just as sociology is the science of society (Ball and Dagger 1999a: 5). It has now come to mean a worldview or a broad belief system about how society should be organised. An ideology might have causal implications that could be objectively evaluated or tested, but often core elements of an ideology are not subject to claims of their truth or falsity. An ideology is typically a normative program with a perhaps vague program for the future. If two competing ideologies, such as CAPITALISM and socialism, hold sway at once in a given society, polarisation of the society into radically opposed political camps may result. Polarisation per se can occur between groups as such or over ideas or beliefs.

Ideologies can be quite diverse. There are ideologies of economic theory, of normative or religious organisation, and even of racial superiority. Economic theories can polarise along class lines or even merely along lines of different beliefs. Racist preferences readily polarise along moderately, but seldom genuinely, simple lines. Apart from establishing racial HEGEMONY, a racial movement might have no programme. An ideology commonly includes at least a semblance of a program, such as reorganisation of the economy. A very articulate ideology would include a virtual blueprint for social organisation. Conservatism, liberalism, capitalism, fascism, and the cluster of socialism, communism and Marxism have been the most influential ideologies of modern times. Libertarianism and, most recently, ecological visions have played some role in actual politics.

Nationalism is commonly referred to as an ideology but one might reasonably exclude it (see NATIONS AND NATIONALISM). Nationalist preferences can polarise along lines that might be little more than randomly associated with CLASS or even ethnic divisions, although ethnic and nationalist divisions often coincide to a substantial degree. Indeed, presumed ethnicity is a common ground for nationalist claims. It is not the only ground and, in fact, it has played little role in many nationalisms in the Americas. Even when nationalism is associated with an ethnic group, it can be relatively catholic in its inclusion of all citizens. Nationalism in many contexts has been proselytising, not exclusionary, just as Christianity and Islam have been proselytising religious and sometime political movements. There have been hundreds of nationalisms, virtually every one of which has been a very specific program for a particular people, sometimes combined with one of the standard ideologies or with a religious vision.

A crude model of ideological polarisation is division into two groups, each of which wants privileged access to the goods of the society. The program of a government in the control of one of the groups in such a context is to take as many resources as possible from the other group and to give them to the group that the government represents. For example, Hutus

and Tutsis in Rwanda might readily accept the same economic structure for the society, but they would distribute resources, primarily in land and government jobs, differently. This is significantly different from the programs of governments that represent political extremes, such as communism versus capitalism. Such governments attempt to structure the economy in ways that may have differential distributional effects across groups, although such effects are not necessarily the point of the policies. Rather, it is often the structures themselves over which the two polar positions struggle.

The struggle between Nazis and communists in Germany in the 1930s was a mix of these two kinds of polarisation. The Nazis wanted racial and nationalist military policies more than they wanted any specific organisation of the economy. Indeed, many of their economic policies were relatively socialist and statist and might readily have been supported in principle by the communists. They were hostile to communists in large part because the communists were universalist and anti-nationalist in addition to being in favour of a particular economic organisation of the economy. Communists' obedience to Soviet policy made them inimical to the Nazis. Had they been nationalist, as many communist movements in other nations have been, they might have made common cause with the Nazis over some issues.

In such a polarisation, each group might genuinely hold that all will be better off with its preferred position. The disagreement then is causal or value-theoretic rather than group-based *per se*. Edmund Burke (1999), often called the father of conservatism, supposed that there are some people who are naturally qualified to lead, the 'true natural aristocracy', and that all must benefit from having them lead in all aspects of social and political life. Aristotle held related views. Many people who are not conservatives in Burke's sense would argue for meritocracy in many aspects of social life. For example, virtually all would want the most qualified surgeons to operate on them. But Burke's conservative ideology runs much deeper than this. He supposed that some are naturally better qualified to establish tastes and values that others should simply accept.

LIBERALISM is a largely contrary view that all individuals should have the liberty to live by their own values and that government should be chosen by all, not by some supposedly natural principle. It is virtually impossible to claim meaningfully that one of these views is true and the other false. It is also extremely difficult to believe we can demonstrate that one of these views would, if adopted politically, produce better results in any broadly accepted sense. Hence, belief in these views, while not entirely abstracted from real effects, is not fully grounded in anything demonstrable.

Beliefs in either of these visions might reflect economic or other status interests. Indeed, adherence to such views may often depend less on the content of the views and what these might entail if instantiated than on the benefits of siding with those who espouse the views. The sheer difficulty of motivating group action merely from the content of the goals of the action provokes the creation of other devices for motivating such action, and these devices need not be related to the goals of the action (Hardin 1995). Ideological debates are often therefore dismissed as phoney by those who find it hard to believe in the ideological vision.

Consider Marxism, perhaps the most extensively articulated ideology of the twentieth century. It is grounded in objective claims as well as value claims and, indeed, the two are often related. For example, the claim that workers are exploited is often taken to be a normative claim. For Marx, this followed from an objective assessment of who receives the value from production: workers or capitalists. Unfortunately, his theory of productive value was the implausible labour theory of value. In the labour theory, the value of what I produce is merely the labour time I have put into producing it. This theory or some variant of it was shared by many economists until late in the nineteenth century. It was on its face implausible because one might labour mightily to produce useless junk that no one would want. Economics was salvaged as a science by the introduction of the subjective theory of value, according to which the value of an object is related to the demand for it. In the subjective theory, value is not inherent in objects.

The core of Marxism therefore has a conceptual flaw that is relatively objectively debatable. Other aspects of the theory are also empirically assessable, but only in the very long run. For example, claims that the working class must become immiserated, that capitalism must collapse of its own force, or that class interest will lead to revolutionary class action, are essentially scientific claims that are subject to test. They seem to have failed the test of history. Marxism might therefore most properly be seen as a scientific theory of the economy of a modern state, and this seems to have been Marx's view of his theory. Unfortunately, it became instead an ideology whose appeal did not depend on its scientific merits.

Ideologies and political principles more generally are sometimes said to fight it out in 'the marketplace of ideas'. This phrase is fundamentally misleading. There is no analogous role for bad products in the marketplace of products. My bad product is out of the market as soon as your better product displaces it. Bad ideas, however, seem never to leave us, especially bad political ideas. Indeed, it often seems that particularly bad political ideas get transformed into ideologies, which are no longer subject to rational analysis and assessment but simply float above the world they are supposed to explain or affect. Their content may have no real effect, but their followers might have massive effect. They are fought out politically and even militarily.

Nevertheless, seemingly bad political ideas might eventually be revised or shown to be good ideas. And, at worst, they may be useful as counterpoints to arguments for other ideas. Merely pointing out that certain political moves have tended to lead to fascism, gross inequality, civil war, or other disasters may be a valuable contribution to public debate and eventual understanding.

See also:

contestation; democratic ideology; radical democracy

Further reading

Ball, T. and Dagger, R. (1999a) *Political Ideologies and the Democratic Ideal*, 3rd edn, New York: Addison-Wesley.

—— (1999b) *Ideals and Ideologies: A Reader*, 3rd edn, New York: Addison-Wesley.

Burke, E. (1999) *Reflections on the Revolution in France*, Indianapolis: Liberty Press.

Hardin, R. (1995) *One for All: The Logic of Group Conflict*, Princeton, NJ: Princeton University Press.

RUSSELL HARDIN

immunities and protections

Definition and principal ideas

The terms 'immunities' and 'protections' are employed to refer to a kind of right possessed by individuals. The canonical definition of an immunity is given by the American legal philosopher Wesley Hohfeld in *Fundamental Legal Conceptions as Applied in Judicial Reasoning* (1919). Here, Hohfeld distinguishes between four types of legal RIGHTS: claim-rights, liberties, powers and, finally, immunities (1919: 36–64; for analysis of which see Jones 1994: 12–25). Immunity rights have two features. The first concerns the implications of a person's immunity right on other people. If P has an immunity right to do X, then others do not have the legal power to determine whether or not P in fact does X. P's immunity thus requires that others lack a power. Hohfeld employs the concept of a 'correlative' to describe this relationship, saying that one person's immunity implies that others have a 'correlative' 'disability' or 'no-power' (1919: 60). The second important feature of an immunity right concerns the implications of a person's immunity right for themselves. Hohfeld states that if P has an immunity right to do X, then P can be said not to be liable as to whether he does X. What he means by this is that if someone has an immunity right then he or she is exempt from being required to do X or

abstain from doing X. Hohfeld employs the term 'opposite' to express this point: thus the 'opposite' of P having an immunity is P having a liability (1919: 60). In short, then, when a person has an immunity right others lack power to determine his or her legal situation and he or she lacks a liability (1919: 60–63). Thus defined, it is clear that immunities and protections function as constraints. Their role is to limit what others can do and to act as a check.

Immunities are a familiar feature of much public and political life. Some examples may illustrate Hohfeld's definition and elucidate the closely related concept of protections. We can divide immunities into two types. Some immunity rights are possessed by some, but not all, individuals and can thus be said to be 'special rights' as opposed to 'general rights'. (See Hart 1984: 84–88 for the distinction between special and general rights.) One example of a special immunity right is parliamentary privilege: this refers to the immunity right of members of parliament to make statements without being liable to prosecution and with others not having the power to prosecute. Another example of an immunity right is 'diplomatic immunity', where this refers to the special privileges and protections enjoyed by diplomats of foreign states which are not enjoyed by other residents of a state. There are other examples of immunity right: 'immunity from prosecution', for example, may be enjoyed by former heads of state and it may be granted to those accused of a crime in exchange for further co-operation.

Other immunity rights are possessed by all citizens in a polity. The most common and politically significant form of such immunity rights are constitutional immunities which entrench certain rights and thereby protect some liberties. Such immunities follow the Hohfeldian paradigm. Constitutionally protected rights imply a correlative disability: legislatures lack the ability to affect some of their citizens' legal options. In addition, they imply the absence of a liability: the possessors of these rights lack a specific liability.

Development and evaluation

Although the formal and technical definition given above dates only back to Hohfeld, the ideas captured by the concepts of immunities and protections clearly long predate him. As Richard Flathman observes, historically the concept has been used (and sometimes is still used) by established and privileged political and economic institutions to exempt themselves from ACCOUNTABILITY to the wider public (1976: 60–61). With the rise of democracy, however, the concept has increasingly been employed to protect individuals from oppressive majorities. Those concerned with protecting individuals and MINORITIES from a repressive majority sought to protect individuals by granting them constitutional immunities which deny legislatures and executives the legal power to restrict their FREEDOM.

This controversy continues today. Those who wish to defend constitutional protections and immunity rights adduce a number of considerations. One common line of reasoning, associated with the American legal theorist John Hart Ely, defends constitutional protections on the grounds that certain rights are integral to a democratic system and are essential for a democratic polity to function (Ely 1980). This argument, however, defends, and is only intended to defend, certain constitutional immunities. It might be deployed both to defend certain rights for all citizens and also some immunity rights for politicians (for example, parliamentary privilege).

A second distinct line of reasoning maintains that constitutional immunities are required to protect individual freedom against the majority. Ronald Dworkin, for example, has argued for a Bill of Rights for Britain on the grounds that people's fundamental rights and liberties would only be adequately protected if a bill of rights were entrenched (1996: ch. 18). Constitutional protections can thus be seen both as compatible with democratic procedures and also in conflict with them (see Weale 1999: 167–88) (see CONSTITUTIONAL DESIGN).

In response to these defences of such constitutional protections, some have argued that both of these represent an intolerable restriction on the freedom of legislatures. Jeremy Waldron, for example, mounts a powerful critique of constitutional immunities and protections, which gives expression to the main concerns of those who object to such measures. As he points out, using Hohfeldian analysis, ascribing immunity rights to citizens also thereby denies powers to legislatures and as such denies a certain type of right to citizens, the right to decide fundamental matters democratically (1999: 221). Immunity rights, thus, involve a cost and do not recognise the importance of legislation. Against the case for constitutional protections, he argues that it is mistrustful of people and as such is out of kilter with the picture of persons that underpins the very concept of rights (1999: 221–3). In addition, constitutional rights are inappropriate because there is controversy about rights and, therefore, what is needed is an authoritative resolution of the disagreement which, in turn, requires that such matters are decided democratically by the people (1999: 243–252).

The concepts of immunities and protections have been deployed not simply to express an important moral ideal. They are, as in the case of Hohfeld, also employed to shed light on legal rights. Hohfeld's aim was not a moral one but to provide a clearer understanding of legal rights. There has, nonetheless, been controversy over the conceptual adequacy of Hohfeld's analysis. H.L.A. Hart maintained that Hohfeld is wrong to claim that all immunities are rights. Some immunities are immunities from benefits and are thus not plausibly construed as rights. As Hart puts the point: 'the expression "a right" is not used to refer to the fact that a man is…immune from an advantageous change' (1982: 191). One might then maintain that immunity rights are rights to be immune from disadvantages.

Controversy also surrounds the implications of constitutional immunities for the choice theory of rights. According to the latter, one feature of a person's having a right is that he or she can waive compliance with that right (Hart 1984: 80–3). Constitutional immunities, by contrast, cannot be waived and hence choice theory can not accommodate this type of legal right. Hart, himself once a defender of the choice theory, took this to be a consideration against the universal application of the choice theory (1982: 190). The central point, then, is that the existence of constitutional immunities casts doubt on one common conception of legal rights.

The analysis, thus far, has concentrated on the standard conceptual and normative treatment of immunities and protections prevalent in works of political and legal theory. It is important to note, however, a different, less technical sense of the concept of an immunity. As Richard Flathman observes, the term is sometimes employed to refer simply to exemptions from more general rules (1976: 58–60). This use has increasing relevance given the increased focus on the multicultural nature of most political societies. It is sometimes suggested, for example, that members of minority cultures should enjoy immunities from general requirements where the latter are incompatible with certain cultural practices. It is often argued, for example, that Sikhs should be exempt from motorcycle helmet regulations and Jews should be exempt from Sunday trading legislation: some persons should thus not be liable to these general requirements. Such suggestions have been powerfully criticised by others, like Brian Barry, who argue that rules should be general or abandoned altogether, but even he recognises the legitimacy of immunities in some circumstances (Barry 2000: Pt. 1).

Summation

Immunities and protections both play an important role in our thinking about political theory and political practice. They serve two important roles in particular. First, they provide a helpful tool by which to understand legal rights and legal practice and in particular the nature of constitutional rights. Second, they articulate an important normative ideal which, although challenged by some, represents one way of securing the interests of individuals and minorities.

See also:

constitutionalism; deliberative democracy; democracy, justifications for; freedom; rights

Further reading

Barry, B. (2000) *Culture and Equality: An Egalitarian Critique of Multiculturalism*, Cambridge: Polity.

Dworkin, R. (1996) *Freedom's Law: The Moral Reading of the American Constitution*, Oxford: Oxford University Press.

Ely, J. (1980) *Democracy and Distrust: A Theory of Judicial Review*, Cambridge, MA: Harvard University Press.

Flathman, R. (1976) *The Practice of Rights*, Cambridge: Cambridge University Press.

Hart, H.L.A. (1982) *Essays on Bentham: Studies in Jurisprudence and Political Theory*, Oxford: Clarendon Press.

—— (1984) 'Are There any Natural Rights?', in J. Waldron (ed.), *Theories of Rights*, Oxford: Oxford University Press.

Hohfeld, W. (1919) *Fundamental Legal Conceptions as Applied in Judicial Reasoning*, New Haven, CT: Yale University Press.

Jones, P. (1994) *Rights*, Basingstoke: Macmillan.

Steiner, H. (1994) *An Essay on Rights*, Oxford: Blackwell.

Waldron, J. (1999) *Law and Disagreement*, Oxford: Clarendon Press.

Weale, A. (1999) *Democracy*, New York: St. Martin's Press.

SIMON CANEY

imperialism

The term 'imperialism' is used for so many purposes that a core meaning is difficult to distil from the surfeit of polemical, historical, literary and social science literature. If there is a core, it is political dominance by a metropolitan power of territories and peoples beyond its borders. Empire and imperialism, so understood, are coeval with the rise of civilisation, or nearly so. The long view of empire is important for the diagnosis of trends and causes of cultural evolution, and it places events close to us in perspective (Crosby 1986).

A second core meaning is the European expansion into Africa, Asia and the New World that began in the fifteenth century. The expansion was characterised by an outflow of settlers from the metropolis into the territories, by the transplantation of economic, cultural, legal and political institutions into overseas acquisitions, and by geopolitical rivalry between imperial powers. The colonial system endured until about 1950, when decolonialisation commenced. Within two decades, European powers handed over rule to a multitude of new nations. The semblance of imperial paramountcy was maintained through the British Commonwealth of Nations and the Union Française. Most of the new nations elected to join these alliances.

A third core meaning, neocolonialism, surfaced as new nations struggled to translate formal political independence into autonomous nationhood. Neocolonialism refers to the residues of colonial rule – language, administration, economic dominance – perceived to hinder the progress of new nations toward self-sufficiency. Neocolonialism found its scholarly voice in dependency theory and world system theory. These theories, inspired mainly by Marxism, were meant to explain and describe how capitalist powers maintain imperial dominance after empire has been disbanded, as well as how the United States, which never had colonies, was nevertheless the arch-imperialist power. Policy formation in Western nations, by contrast, was largely based on study of the conditions for economic development in Third World countries, with a view to assisting development by aid and cultural exchange.

When the Soviet Union dissolved, the motivation for highlighting imperialism and its successive embodiments vanished. Marxism equated imperialism with exploitative advanced CAPITALISM, and contrasted it with Soviet style socialism. This theory unravelled from within when the Chinese attacked Soviet dominance as 'social imperialism'. This attack coincided with deterioration of relations between the Soviet Union and the Peoples' Republic (Polychroniou 1991). It also nearly coincided with China's occupation of Tibet, to which it claimed entitlement based on ancient conquests. The dissolution of the Soviet Union returned its East European client states to independence and removed 25 per cent of its territory by granting independence to some former soviets. In the aftermath, imperialism is no longer used as an analytical concept in international relations or development theory. It has become by default largely a historical concept.

The phenomena that Marxists sought to conceptualise as imperialism are today studied under the rubrics of 'GLOBALISATION', 'regionalism' and economic development. Globalisation exponents argue that state SOVEREIGNTY has been undone by processes that cannot be centrally controlled (Weiss 1998; Waters 1995). They include migration, travel, war and insurrection, communications, finance, manufacture and trade, and a long list of internationally agreed policies in the environmental, health, and human RIGHTS fields. Globalism is heir to the idea that society and the state are determined by economic processes, broadened to include cultural exchange as an independent driver. Regionalists hold that the dynamics of economic change are best understood by aggregating national economies into regional pictures, such as Asian Pacific, Latin American, North American, and the European Union. The issue between these rival theories is where to locate the development dynamic. Regionalists maintain that proximity and cultural similarity outweigh global factors.

When imperialism is taken as a historical category, its description is relatively straightforward.

Origin

The word 'imperialism' emerged in France as a reproach to the territorial ambitions of the autocratic Emperor Napoleon III (1852–70). The term gained currency when it was adopted by the Gladstone Liberals in criticism of the

Tory Benjamin Disraeli's policy of colonial expansion during his tenure as prime minister (1874–80). At that time, Britain and France had but modest territorial holdings in West and East Africa, and none in Central Africa. Three decades later, Africa had been divided into 'spheres of influence' and much of it placed under colonial administration. West Africa was French, except for Sierra Leone, Ghana and Nigeria, which were British. Italy occupied Tunisia, Libya, Sudan, Eritrea and Somalia. Germany had a strong presence in East and Central Africa. Belgium occupied the Congo. Portugal held Angola and Mozambique. Britain consolidated South Africa, Botswana, Zimbabwe, Zambia, Malawi and part of Kenya. In Southeast Asia, the pattern was the same: the British engrossed Burma and part of Malaysia, the French entered Laos, Cambodia and Vietnam, and the Dutch increased their presence in Java and occupied East Irian. China was divided into spheres of influence after its defeat by Japan in 1905. At the outbreak of the First World War, then, European powers had vastly extended their influence or rule, to encompass most the inhabited world (Porter 1991). Britain alone had added 3.5 million square miles to its possessions.

Drivers

A pattern of this kind prompts the search for a single underlying cause. Such was proclaimed by the English liberal economist John A. Hobson in his classic study, *Imperialism* (Hobson 1902). He argued that the 'taproot' of imperialism was a glut of capital. Under the pressure of declining profits and diminished domestic markets, financial interests pushed governments into territorial acquisition to open new markets and new investment opportunities. He maintained that the cost of empire exceeded the return, except for profits to a rich few, and therefore should be abandoned. He also argued that imperialism endangered domestic liberty by engendering a spirit of belligerent nationalism.

Britain's massive capital surplus was common knowledge, but did it drive acquisition for the sake of markets and investment opportunities? Hobson produced little data to this effect. Subsequent investigations have ascertained that African and East Asian investment rates, measured as a percentage of the annual total overseas investment, remained at a steady 2–3 per cent during the imperialist period (Etherington 1984). Clearly investors did not view new African and Asian acquisitions as emerging markets.

More credible is the hypothesis of geopolitical competition by rival European powers for the last remaining 'open lands' on a globe that continuously shrank as transportation and COMMUNICATION improved (Langer 1965). This interpretation is encapsulated in one historian's wry sarcasm that 'the scramble for colonies among continental nations had the good effect at least of determining the English not to be left behind in the race for empire'. Once imperial Germany began building its battle fleet to challenge British naval supremacy, rivalry intensified and led eventually to the Great War. In the Far East, Japan entered the fray under the slogan, 'Asia for the Asiatics', and fought wars of territorial acquisition against Russia and China.

The globe was indeed shrinking. The first marine telegraph cable linked Britain and France in 1851. The Persian Gulf and Atlantic lines were laid in 1863. Australia and New Zealand were linked in 1876. The effect was to transform commerce by making up-to-the minute market information available, thereby increasing competition. Railroads were built in China, India, the Middle East and Africa to bring goods to market. Steam-driven merchant ships decreased transport time and increased freight capacity.

While great power competition, supported by popular nationalist feeling, was doubtless the major driver of European expansion, it was not the sole cause. Newly enfranchised voters were a volatile influence on party government, which changed often in France, Belgium, Portugal, Italy and Britain in the period 1880–1914. It was difficult to maintain and resource expansionist policy when successive governments pursued opposite intentions. When the process of expansion is examined, one finds that major decisions, such as the British occupation of Egypt in 1882 and the partition of China in 1905, were improvised responses reluctantly taken rather than the outcome of well-laid plans. The oft-quoted quip that the British 'conquered and peopled half the world in a fit of absence of mind' underscores the improvised, pragmatic character of territorial acquisition, albeit at the cost of denying, absurdly, any imperialist intention at all.

Causes independent of government were migration, commerce and Christianity. About fifty million Europeans migrated to the New World, Africa and Asia between 1820–1930, with the peak coming between 1890–1910. Without this steady buildup of occupancy by planters and merchants, colonial offices could do little to establish dominance. A key cultural element among the new occupiers was missionaries. The Spanish were unique in imposing direct rule and compulsory conversion. The preferred alternative was indirect rule and non-interference in religion (Fieldhouse 1966). Christianisation was left to church initiative, and was sometimes discouraged by the colonial power, lest proselytising stir up antagonisms. Nevertheless, Catholic and Protestant missions had a great impact in Africa after 1850, as Protestants in China after that date. These efforts were durable. They created traditions of schooling, introduced European languages and functioned as a bridge between indigenous and European cultures. The Protestant missionaries in China, mostly Americans, created a marked pro-American sentiment among China's intelligentsia that was extinguished only by the Communist revolution.

Commerce was the primary long-term driver of colonial expansion. The common notion that government was the primary driver is true of Spain, but not other European powers. The instrument of commercial penetration was the chartered trading company, which originated in the late sixteenth century (Kuitenbrouwer 1991). The basic idea is that investors, combined in a joint stock company, assume all the risks of trade. In return, government grants the company broad military, diplomatic and administrative powers in overseas territories, and grants it favourable trading privileges or monopolies at home.

All European powers chartered such companies, and they became the agents of colonial establishment, expansion and administration. That such companies were for profit shaped the pattern of European penetration. Since decisions were answerable to the balance sheet, trading companies sought the least costly methods of maintaining their presence. The preferred method was indirect rule, meaning a system of local semi-autonomous client states that conducted government according to agreed conditions (Fieldhouse 1966; Misra 1959). The profit motive gave rise to the maxim: 'If empire cannot be had on the cheap, it is not worth having at all.' Trading companies enjoyed the authority of the home government and might well have had direct command, as in India, of large armies of indigenous troops.

The doctrine of 'paramountcy' developed from the relations between trading companies and local authority, and between trading companies and the home government (Smith 1982). Paramountcy meant that the home government could override decisions of the trading company (or missionaries), and could intervene in local government as circumstance might suggest. This principle was invoked to annex territories on grounds of misrule or necessity of defence. Its last strategic use was in the Anglo-French alliance to reverse Egypt's nationalisation of the Suez Canal Company (1956). American intervention in the name of decolonialisation mortified the doctrine, yet it has been used on occasions since, for example, in Britain's opposition to Rhodesian independence.

The Versailles Treaty and its aftermath, the League of Nations, marked the end of commercial colonialism. The new standard was the concept of trusteeship, where the colonial power was required to govern in the interest of the indigenous population, with a view to eventual self-rule. This concept arose in India, where the British Raj supported the foundation of the

National Congress Party (1895) and granted Indians limited participation in government (1909–19). This is not to say that commercial colonialism died suddenly, or that geopolitical rivalries ceased to exercise influence on colonial power decisions. It did mean that foreign offices and the popular press became focused on the transition to self-rule, which in turn was the prelude to the decolonialisation of the 1950s. The case of India is illustrative. India was an entity thanks to its colonial consolidation as the Raj. It was divided by religion, by language, by ethnicity and by geographic dispersion. Although nationalists hoped to bring all the territories of the Raj into one new India, antagonisms between Muslims and Hindus forced PARTITION, and even so independence led straight to war between ethnic and religious groups wearing the new emblems of nationhood (Pakistan, India). This pattern has been repeated in many newly independent colonial nations.

The aftermath of imperialism cannot be reduced to a single formula. Former Spanish possessions in Latin America, long since independent, remained economically somewhat stagnant until the boom of recent decades. The indigenous peoples in Latin America continue to form the lowest socio-economic stratum. Southeast Asia is a mosaic of varying economic prosperity punctuated by ethnic and political conflict, especially in Burma, Malaysia and Indonesia. Sub-Saharan Africa presents, with few exceptions, a grim picture of economic decline, chronic violence and despotic government. What can be said with some confidence is that, for better or worse, no village is untouched by the influences set in train by the great European expansion.

See also:

nations and nationalism; rights, minority and indigenous

Further reading

Crosby, A. (1986) *Ecological Imperialism: The Biological Expansion of Europe 900–1900*, Cambridge: Cambridge University Press.

Etherington, N. (1984) *Theories of Imperialism: War, Conquest and Capital*, London: Croom Helm.

Fieldhouse, D.K. (1966) *The Colonial Empires: A Comparative Survey from the Eighteenth Century*, London: Weidenfeld and Nicolson.

Hobson, J.A. (1902) *Imperialism: A Study*, London: Allen & Unwin.

Kuitenbrouwer, J. (1991) *The Netherlands and the Rise of Modern Imperialism: Colonies and and Foreign Policy*, trans. H. Berger, Oxford: Berg.

Langer, W.L. (1965) *The Diplomacy of Imperialism 1890–1902*, New York: Alfred A Knopf.

Misra, B.B. (1959) *The Central Administration of the East India Company, 1773–1834*, Manchester: Manchester University Press.

Polychroniou, C. (1991) *Marxist Perspectives on Imperialism: A Theoretical Analysis*, New York: Praeger.

Porter, A. (ed.) (1991) *Atlas of British Overseas Expansion*, London: Routledge.

Smith, W. (1982) *European Imperialism in the Nineteenth and Twentieth Century*, Chicago: Nelson Hall.

Waters, M. (1995) *Globalization*, London: Routledge.

Weiss, L. (1998) *The Myth of the Powerless State*, Ithaca, NY: Cornell University Press.

HIRAM CATON

inclusion/exclusion

It is generally agreed that any state or society presumes certain forms of exclusion to constitute itself. The issue for democratic thought is where these divisions are drawn, how they are justified, and whether or not they should be redrawn in ways which recognise and accommodate different constituencies and new identities. More specifically, the problem of inclusion and exclusion arises from a number of puzzling dilemmas inscribed into contemporary democratic theory and practice. These include questions about determining the subjects of democratic rule; the fact that liberal democracy combines democratic and liberal principles; the role of the state as the principal set of institutions and locus of democracy in late modern societies; and the need for groups and individuals to form hegemonic coalitions in order to constitute and express their political wills. In short, the issue of inclusion/exclusion raises the pressing question as to whether contemporary liberal democratic institutions and practices are the best, perhaps only, way of including the greatest range of individuals and groups in the DECISION-MAKING processes of a political community, and of enabling the flourishing of a variety of identities and differences in society, while remaining a stable form of rule.

With respect to who or what constitutes 'the people' in a democracy, we may consider the question rather narrowly by examining who has the right to cast votes in meaningful elections. In one sense, it is possible to tell a plausible Whiggish story about the development of democracy in which there has been a gradual inclusion of more groups and greater numbers of people in democratic decision-making. From its birth in classical Athens, and the attendant exclusion of women, slaves and aliens from the citizenry, to struggles for the establishment of representative systems of government during the seventeenth and eighteenth centuries, to demands for the extension of the franchise to all male adults in the nineteenth and twentieth centuries, and finally to the incorporation of women and minority groups, it may be said that the development of democratic government has become successively more inclusive and universal (see SUFFRAGE). As the classic *bon mot* on the evolution of British parliamentary democracy goes, by the middle of the twentieth century – 1968 to be precise – all adults over the age of eighteen in the United Kingdom were entitled to vote apart from criminals, the insane and members of the British nobility. This progressive storyline can, moreover, be given further credence by stressing the rapid spread of democratic institutions and values in the twentieth century, as new waves of democratisation have resulted

in the dissemination of democratic forms and processes to the four corners of the globe.

Two important issues emerge from this particular narrative. First, are categories of people such as children, the insane, criminals, the socially excluded, guest workers, immigrants or non-humans to be enfranchised or excluded from the vote? Or to put it in different terms, are currently accepted lines of inclusion/ exclusion legitimate, and how are they normatively sustained? Second, do the existing boundaries need to be extended further or modified in significant ways?

With respect to the first question, there are strong arguments to the effect that children (below the age of, say, eighteen) and the insane are legitimately disqualified from voting because they lack the competence or responsibility to exercise democratic choice. The cases of the socially excluded, incarcerated criminals or those newly arrived in a democratic state are more difficult to adjudicate. To do so, we need to spell out the underlying principles upon which the granting of political citizenship rights, such as the right to vote, are based, and then to apply these principles to the cases in question. Albert Weale (1999: 151–9) argues persuasively that the general principles of interest, qualification and commitment underpin the allocation of the franchise in modern liberal democracies, although the application of these principles in specific institutional contexts requires interpretation and a sensitivity to the particular circumstances of each case. This is to say that citizens and potential citizens have to demonstrate an interest that would be protected by formal political inclusion, a competence that they would be able to exercise the vote responsibly, and show a serious commitment to the political institutions of the society in question. Underlying these principles is the view that the granting of political rights is 'contingent on already existing practices within a society', such that the accession is consistent with the principles of those practices (Weale 1999: 157) (see CONSTITUTIONAL DESIGN).

However, while these principles help to clarify the underlying grounds of current thinking about the lines of inclusion and exclusion with respect to the franchise, their application to the difficult cases touched upon above is not necessarily definitive. For instance, although they imply a strong *prima facie* case for the inclusion of guest workers (or immigrants) who demonstrate a commitment to a particular society, as this inclusion is consonant with societies that accept the free movement of labour, the situation is not so clear-cut with respect to expatriates, criminals and the socially excluded. While a focus on the commitment principle might lead a democrat to conclude that those expatriates absent from a particular democratic community for a short period of time, and who can demonstrate a clear allegiance to it, ought not to be excluded from democratic participation in their native political community, for those whose commitment can be shown to be wavering – measured, for instance, in terms of the duration of their voluntary absence – the case for withdrawing fundamental political rights seems more compelling.

Similarly, with regard to convicted criminals, it might be argued that their previous actions and behaviour constitute strong grounds for foreclosing their rights to political representation. On the other hand, it might equally be claimed that further participation in democratic processes encourages speedier social and political rehabilitation. It might also be argued that those who have wilfully chosen to exclude themselves from social life foreswear their political rights, whereas those that have been social excluded because of economic marginalisation or racial and cultural discrimination might have strong grounds for continued political inclusion, although the difficult question here is where to draw the line between voluntary and forcible social exclusion.

One final issue in this regard concerns the necessary exclusion of certain individuals and groups from political citizenship rights on purely political grounds. In this respect, the cases of those who publicly express anti-democratic beliefs or engage in anti-democratic practices come to the fore. This question touches on what Popper (1945) has called 'the paradox of democracy', in which a literal interpretation of 'popular sovereignty' makes possible the suppression of democratic practices and institutions in the name of majority rule. The paradox is evident in fascist and religious fundamentalist parties who are prepared to use democratic procedures to achieve anti-democratic outcomes. Although this is a difficult issue to judge in particular cases, as a general rule it seems consonant with democratic theory to argue that in extreme cases where the existence of democracy itself is jeopardised, there is a powerful reason for the forcible exclusion of anti-democratic forces and practices.

Popper's paradox captures the ideological tension in liberal democracy that arises from the contingent articulation of liberal and democratic principles (Macpherson 1966: 5), and brings us to a second paradox of contemporary democratic rule That is to say, while contemporary liberal democratic states embrace both liberal principles of constitutionalism, individual human rights and the rule of law on the one hand, as well as democratic principles such as majority rule and popular sovereignty on the other, the two sets of principles are not necessarily compatible. In the nineteenth century, fears about 'the tyranny of the majority', as expressed by Alexis de Tocqueville (1994) and J.S. Mill (1991), arose from the perceived threats of majoritarianism, 'mob rule' and 'public opinion' putting into question the values of individual liberty, pluralism and different 'experiments in living'. Moreover, while the articulation of democratic and liberal principles has been strongly sedimented in Western societies during the twentieth century, such that the contingent link has often been naturalised, the tension is still evident in discussions about 'in-built majorities', which exclude ethnic and national minorities in a society. Indeed, more radical critics argue that the majoritarianism and self-proclaimed universalism of most functioning liberal democracies naturally favours dominant interests and constituencies in society, such as white male heterosexuals in Western European countries, thereby occluding cultural, sexual or racial particularities (Benhabib 1996).

In order to offset these exclusions, thus dealing with what James Tully has usefully called the 'the politics of cultural diversity' (Tully 1995), democratic theorists and practitioners have advocated particular forms of democratic rule, such as consociationalism, federalism or even partition, which are designed to include and give institutional expression to ethnic and national minorities (Lijphart 1977) (see CONSENSUS DEMOCRACY). Others have argued for a greater judicial role in dealing with and alleviating the problems arising from cultural difference (Dworkin 1978). These proposed solutions range from the provision of Bills of Rights to constitutional settlements that enshrine the rights of minority groups, as well as a greater role for judges in offsetting majoritarian abuses of power, although question marks have been raised about the problem of 'judicialising' the political process (Gray 1995). A further strategy for dealing with the exclusion of certain voices from the democratic process is to introduce new forms of political representation. For instance, Anne Phillips (1995) has called for a 'politics of presence' to complement liberal democratic forms of representation in Western states that systematically favour certain categories of the population, such as men, the better educated, the wealthier, as well as dominant ethnic and cultural groups (Phillips 1995). According to Phillips, the inclusion of greater numbers of women, members of the working class and minority groups in representative chambers sends a powerful symbolic message to those that have been excluded or under-represented in particular societies. She argues that such representatives are more likely to advance the interests of those with shared social characteristics; that such a presence can broaden the horizons of existing political agendas; and that such representatives can add new issues and dimensions to established party political equilibriums (see GENDERING DEMOCRACY).

A final way of dealing with might be called the politics of identity/difference has been proposed by writers such as Bill Connolly (1995), who argue that the current institutions and practices of liberal democracy have to be supplemented by what he calls 'an ethos of pluralisation'. Capturing the dynamic spirit of democratic rule, Connolly argues for a 'politics of becoming' in which democratic institutions and practices ought to foster and cultivate differences within the public sphere, rather than excluding them altogether, or relegating them to the private realm of CIVIL SOCIETY. In this view, the key question arising from the social exclusion of minority groups and identities is how they are to be included within democratic politics without reducing them to the domesticating logics they oppose (see RIGHTS, MINORITY AND INDIGENOUS). In this respect, Connolly, as well as liberal pluralists such as John Gray, have called for the development and cultivation of new virtues such as generosity, agonistic respect and critical responsiveness to differences and new identities (Connolly 1991; Gray 1995) (see IDENTITY, POLITICAL).

A third and related paradox of contemporary democratic rule arises from the special role which the state plays in democratic societies. Apart from anarchistic conceptions of democracy (see Wolff 1970) or principled libertarian positions (Nozick 1974), most theories of democracy concede an important role to the state as the set of institutions and locus within which democratic rule is exercised. In this regard, democratic institutions and practices run up against the state's imperatives to maintain order, secure peace, defend its territoriality in the international sphere, to construct conceptions of the public interest, and to ensure levels of economic growth and development. In executing these imperatives, the state can be powerfully implicated in the exclusion of certain groups and identities, such as ethnic and national minorities, or the targeting and scapegoating of 'internal enemies' of the state. It is also involved in the surveillance and disciplining of the population as a whole, and is subject to the different political logics of hegemonic coalitions and dominant interests in society. In this respect, as Marxists and other radical critics of the state in capitalist democracies argue, not only does the state need to be restricted to certain roles and functions by legal means, which is the classical liberal solution to the problem, but the very apparatuses of the state need to be democratised and made accountable to a variety of interests and identities in society (Poulantzas 1978).

The final dilemma facing democratic theorists dealing with the question of inclusion/exclusion concerns the distinctively political logic of democratic politics. That is to say, the normal practice of democracy in liberal democratic states involves the building of electoral COALITIONS and 'hegemonic projects' in order to advance the interests and identities of particular groups and individuals (see HEGEMONY). In a less extreme way this question is similar to Popper's democratic paradox, as well as Mill and Tocqueville's difficulties with the 'tyranny of the majority', namely, that the construction of winning coalitions necessarily results in the exclusion of certain interests from power and public life. For some theorists, the politics of hegemonic coalition building are logically antithetical to the principles of democracy, as in this view the construction of hegemonic formations necessarily excludes elements external to any coalition, and erases differences within them. The construction of hegemony is also charged with the problem of institutionalising certain interests and forms at the expense of others, which runs counter to the openness, contingency and PLURALISM supposed of liberal democratic governance.

As it is evident that hegemonic politics is an irreducible and necessary component of actually existing democratic practice, the trick for a number of democratic theorists is to ensure that hegemonic coalitions and formations do not become sclerotic and closed. In this respect, Connolly argues for his 'ethos of pluralisation' and 'politics of becoming' as an antidote to the sedimentation of hegemonic identities. In a similar vein, Ernesto Laclau and Chantal Mouffe (1985) put forward the project of what they call RADICAL DEMOCRACY, as the means both to advance certain egalitarian demands, such as the extension of EQUALITY and FREEDOM to oppressed groups in society, while at the same time retaining a commitment to the pluralism of liberal democracy, which they

understand as a 'logic of difference'. That is to say, while democratic politics always involves the construction of equivalential linkages between oppressed groups demanding greater equality and recognition (for instance, women, gays and blacks demanding the same rights and privileges as men, heterosexuals and whites), this logic is checked by the liberal constraints of protecting individual rights and group autonomy. Radical democracy is thus a continuous tension between these two conflicting logics.

Further reading

Benhabib, S. (ed.) (1996) *Democracy and Difference: Contesting the Boundaries of the Political*, Princeton, NJ: Princeton University Press.

Connolly, W.E. (1991) *Identity/Difference: Democratic Negotiations of Political Paradox*, Ithaca, NY: Cornell University Press.

—— (1995) *The Ethos of Pluralization*, Minneapolis, MN: Minnesota University Press.

de Tocqueville, A. (1994) *Democracy in America*, London: David Campbell.

Dworkin, R. (1978) *Taking Rights Seriously*, London: Duckworth.

Gray, J. (1995) *Enlightenment's Wake: Politics and Culture at the Close of the Modern Age*, London: Routledge.

Laclau, E. and Mouffe, C. (1985) *Hegemony and Socialist Strategy: Towards a Radical Democratic Politics*, London: Verso.

Lijphart, A. (1977) *Democracy in Plural Societies: A Comparative Exploration*, New Haven, CT: Yale University Press.

Macpherson, C.B. (1966) *The Real World of Democracy*, Oxford: Oxford University Press.

Mill, J.S. (1991) *On Liberty and Other Essays*, Oxford: Oxford University Press.

Nozick, R. (1974) *Anarchy, State and Utopia*, Oxford: Basil Blackwell.

Phillips, A. (1995) *Politics of Presence*, Oxford: Clarendon.

Popper, K. (1945) *The Open Society and Its Enemies*, London: Routledge.

Poulantzas, N. (1978) *State, Power, Socialism*, London: Verso.

Tully, J. (1995) *Strange Multiplicity: Constitutionalism in an Age of Diversity*, Cambridge: Cambridge University Press.

Weale, A. (1999) *Democracy*, London: Macmillan.

Wolff, R.P. (1970) *In Defense of Anarchism*, New York: Harper.

DAVID HOWARTH

indicators of democracy

The rise of behavioural research in the United States in the 1950s and 1960s encouraged scholars to adopt a 'scientific' approach to 'measuring' democracy. This enterprise took the nation-state as the unit of analysis and Western liberal democracy as the model of democracy. The measures themselves were determined by the procedural definition of democracy of Schumpeter, later refined by Dahl, that focused on the values of vertical ACCOUNTABILITY, in the form of free and fair ELECTIONS contested by political PARTIES, and political RIGHTS, understood as the right to vote in these elections.

The most influential attempt to measure democracy is Dahl's *Polyarchy*. Setting out to gauge the quality of liberal democracy in 114 countries in 1969, Dahl measured the proportion of population eligible to vote (an 'objective' measure), as well as ranking the degree of public contestation for political office (a 'subjective' measure). His work created the template for subsequent democracy indicators that sought to measure procedural democracy by combining scores into one-dimensional indices, so locating different countries on a single continuum (see Dahl's POLYARCHY).

Over the past thirty years, political scientists have developed new democracy indicators that extend Dahl's enterprise, but do not alter it in any fundamental way. A broader definition of democracy can now address different democratic values like civil rights (Freedom House 1999) and the degree of executive constraint within the political system (Jaggers and Gurr 1995). Time-series measures now allow the descriptive analysis of phenomena such as the 'third wave' of democratisation (see WAVES OF DEMOCRACY), so complementing the traditional cross-sectional studies of the causes or consequences of democracy. Disaggregated indicators allow cases to score high on some values and low on others, even if the tendency remains to combine these separate scores into a single index. Furthermore, the measures attempt greater geographical coverage of an increasing number of nation-states across the world.

One challenge to the Dahl approach is genuinely different. Dahl sought to measure the quality of democracy, understood as the achievement of values that are intrinsic to liberal democracy. Some subsequent studies have focused instead on the endurance or longevity of democratic regimes, or aspects of government efficacy such as macroeconomic management or WELFARE provision. The latter studies set out to measure values that are extrinsic to liberal democracy, insofar as they describe aspects of government performance irrespective of the democratic character of the regime. The following conceptual and empirical critiques of indicators of democracy focus uniquely on intrinsic indicators.

A conceptual critique

One virtue of setting out to measure liberal democracy is that most democratic regimes claim to be liberal democracies. Although one can justify theoretically the principles of associational or participatory democracy, and perhaps develop appropriate measures for the same, no national governments are currently built on these principles (see ASSOCIATIONAL DEMOCRACY). But a focus on the values that are intrinsic to liberal democracy will necessarily exclude social and economic goods, and this may be seen to be a weakness, especially in very poor societies. Conditions of extreme poverty, it may be argued, make it impossible to participate in democratic government or even enjoy liberal rights and protections. The focus on institutional and legal values may then be seen as a kind of cultural imperialism that ignores the social and economic circumstances of the majority of humankind.

Even if the intrinsic focus is accepted, this focus – and the definition of liberal democracy that underpins it – may be too narrow. By and large, the focus only includes measures of vertical accountability and formal political rights, and by these measures the industrialised nations of the West all obtain similarly high or perfect scores. A broader focus may take into account the full development of liberal democratic government over the past two or three centuries, and hence a fuller set of values. A more encompassing focus of this kind might include a range of legal values, such as civil rights, property rights, political rights and minority rights, as well as institutional values like accountability, representation (see REPRESENTATION, CONCEPT OF), CONSTRAINT and PARTICIPATION (Foweraker and Krznaric 2000). This is certainly not the only way to expand the conceptual scope of the measures, but it does encourage the use of a greater variety of indicators like degrees of single party domination (representation) or the rights of women and ethnic minorities.

Measures of liberal democracy frequently combine distinct scores into a single index, but this may be too simplistic to capture the reality. After all, liberal democracy is characterised by a range of distinct values that cannot be simply added together. On the contrary, scores for indicators of distinct values might better be presented separately in order to reflect the multidimensionality of liberal democracy. A disaggregated approach of this kind might also discover the potential trade-offs between distinct values. Participation may advance while minority rights recede, or political rights may improve as civil rights deteriorate. Such trade-offs will depend on CONSTITUTIONAL DESIGN, social CLEAVAGES, cultural cues and so forth, and single indices may obscure the ways in which different regimes are differently democratic. Yet some degree of aggregation is perhaps inevitable – all values may be further subdivided – if the measures are to avoid idiosyncrasy and achieve coherent comparisons.

In a spirit of methodological purity it is possible to question the measurement of any value, liberal democratic or other. In this perspective, indicators of democracy can never actually measure accountability or political rights or executive constraint, simply because these values exist at a level of conceptual abstraction that cannot be accurately quantified. At best, the indicators are proxy measures that may approximate some particular expression of, say, accountability, such as 'free and fair elections'. Even then it is no easy task to define terms like 'free' and 'fair'. This intractable gap between values and measures means that indicators of democracy may best be understood as suggestive or 'indicative' of the quality of democratic government, rather than representing an accurate gauge of liberal *democratic performance*.

An empirical critique

Indicators of democracy cannot carry much in-depth information about individual country cases. This is the classic methodological trade-off between large 'N' studies – in this case of broad comparative scope – and small 'N' studies that can delve deeper into particular social and political realities. The indicators cannot reveal, for example, just how far liberal democratic values may be subverted or diluted by traditional clientelist politics (see CLIENTELISM). The indicators are also limited by a simple lack of quantifiable information about important global phenomena. So there are no comparative measures of the influence of corporate media ownership on the freedom of INFORMATION or the constraints that international financial institutions place on government accountability. Furthermore, the measures tend to stop at national government and ignore the quality of democracy at the sub-national levels. Nor can the indicators capture important aspects of the quality of democracy such as the treatment of minors or of the disabled.

In fact, most indicators are constructed from a rather narrow range of sources. Most are based on Western news sources such as the *New York Times* (for example, Banks 1997) and a small number of standard reference works such as *Europa World Yearbook*, *Keesings Contemporary Archives* and the *International Almanac of Electoral History*. These sources may be the most complete, and are certainly the most 'available'. But their almost exclusive use introduces a systematic bias into indicators of democracy. Thus, it cannot be claimed that the *New York Times* provides comprehensive and consistent foreign news coverage, when Reuters covers ten times as much foreign news and countries and issues go in and out of fashion in response to public opinion, journalistic trends and editorial guidelines (see MEDIA).

Most indicators are ordinal level or 'subjective' measures that code countries according to the categories of a scale. These measures may suffer problems of measurement range, intersubjectivity and plain political bias. The restricted range of scales with just three or four categories often proves insensitive to the degree of variation in the real world, and so may introduce measurement errors. The wide variation in the practice of 'free and fair elections', for example, cannot be easily captured by a simple three-point scale. Without more sensitive scales the countries of the so-called First World tend repeatedly to receive the same top or perfect score for the quality of their democracies; a comforting but unrealistic result.

Problems of intersubjectivity refer to the difficulties that coders may have in defining key terms such as 'free and fair elections' or 'civilian control of the military', let alone the 'real power' of legislators or the 'real representation' of minority interests, and in applying them to particular political circumstances. Reliability tests have demonstrated that the degrees of discrepancy between coders can be disconcertingly high. The same problems of intersubjectivity may occur between coders and the 'consumers' who try to make sense of categories like 'unlimited authority' or 'executive parity' in Polity III's Executive Constraint scale (Jaggers and Gurr 1995). The relative vagueness of coding criteria often makes it difficult either to compare different subjective measures of the same phenomenon, or to replicate measures in a different time or context.

The problem of political bias may take a general or a particular form. It is alleged that Freedom House indicators show a general bias towards right-wing regimes, and some of the most common information sources for constructing indicators such as US State Department and Amnesty International reports have also been accused of bias. Freedom House has also showed particular, but avowed, biases towards individual countries like Poland or South Africa. Other examples of political bias seem to derive from ignorance rather than deliberate distortion, such as Banks's mistaken coding of the governments of Guatemala and El Salvador in the 1970s as civilian and not military or 'civilian-military'.

Interval level or 'objective' measures are designed to avoid the evaluative problems inherent in the subjective measures by counting simple 'facts' such as a percentage of votes or a number of parties. Yet the so-called objective indicators are imbued with subjectivity, making the contrast with ordinal measures more one of degree than of kind. The 'facts' can prove intractable, since their definition will often depend on subjective judgement. The sophisticated measures of the number of parties in a political system, such as Rae's Index of Fractionalization or Laakso and Taagepera's Effective Number of Parties, cannot decide if divided parties should count as one or two, or closely allied parties as two or one. It may even be unclear whether a fact as stark as a political execution should be counted, depending on whether the death occurs in government custody or not.

The counting itself can also be a problem, especially for scholars constructing indicators from events data. Since the events themselves cannot be counted, recourse is had to secondary sources such as newspapers that may or may not record all or some of the events in question. This problem is acute in the field of human rights, since CENSORSHIP can restrict or eliminate the information, and governments are not keen to record or admit their own repressive acts. Thus, the evidence is hard to get, and, in the case of the most notorious crimes against humanity, often arrives a long time after the 'fact'. Analogous problems may affect the recording of social protest events. Furthermore, it cannot be safely assumed that an absence of repressive 'events' implies an absence of repression, since the threat of repression may be enough to impose political quiescence.

Both subjective and objective measures impose arbitrary thresholds for the presence of democracy. Thus, countries are 'free' if their aggregate Civil Liberties and Political Rights score is between one and two point five (in the Freedom House Comparative Survey of Freedom); or 'democratic' if they score seven or above on Polity III's eleven-point scale (Jaggers and Gurr 1995). But this common problem does not make it easier to compare them. In particular, it is difficult to compare ordinal and interval level measures, and yet more difficult to compare ordinal measures derived from subjective coding with interval measures based on counting events or 'facts.' When they are subsumed together into an aggregate score, the result may be incoherence.

The weighting of variables that enter the construction of aggregate measures of democracy will closely affect the final score; and, insofar as the weighting emphasises some democratic values at the expense of others, it may also affect the validity of this score. Yet the weightings within aggregate measures are rarely justified, and often appear to be decided for reasons of statistical presentation, or for no reason at all. In this regard, an equal weighting of variables is itself a decision that requires justification: Freedom House appears to assume that it is 'natural' to average the scores of its Political Rights and Civil Liberties scales to create its global map of Free, Partly Free and Not Free countries. It seems that weightings, whether explicit or implicit, often remain unjustified because they are so difficult to justify. At the same time, measurement techniques may themselves influence weighting.

Variables with a greater range of measurement will tend to trump those with a lesser range. In Polity III's Index of Democracy (Jaggers and Gurr 1995), the Executive Constraint variable has double the range of Competitiveness of Executive Recruitment, and so emerges as the single main determinant of both the aggregate democracy and autocracy scores.

Despite the difficulties of constructing democracy indicators, most studies seek to defend their validity by demonstrating their high statistical correlations with other such measures. Jaggers and Gurr (1995: 473–4) find that the Polity III Democracy score correlates at around 0.90 with that of Freedom House and a number of other measures, allowing them to conclude that their measure 'accurately represents democracy'. Yet highly correlated measures may all contain the same errors, all share similar biases, or all be determined by outside influences that may render their close association spurious. The correlations cannot therefore guarantee that the different measures are all equally effective in quantifying the same underlying value or concept, and hence cannot prove their validity.

The statistical basis of these high correlations may also be suspect since they generally assume that the data are normally distributed. But most of the data is not so distributed, and skewed distributions can either inflate or deflate correlation results. Furthermore, most validity tests use interval level data techniques like Pearson product-moment correlations on data that are mainly ordinal. But the coding criteria for many ordinal variables are sufficiently vague to preclude the precision of interval measures. It is impossible to verify whether a move from one to two (ineffective to partially effective) on Banks's three-point scale of Legislative Effectiveness, for example, is exactly equivalent to a move from two to three (partially effective to effective). In addition, the global tests are likely to obscure regional variations, since the high degree of congruence among measures for the established Western democracies tends to inflate the overall correlation coefficients.

Conclusion

The number of indicators of democracy has multiplied over the past twenty years (Foweraker and Krznaric 2000) for various reasons. First, the 'third wave' of democratisation greatly increased the number of democracies in the world, as well as sharpening perceptions of a greater variation in the quality of democratic governments. Second, a surge of interest in the constitutional design of new democracies expanded demand for precise comparative measurement of the outcomes or performance of different designs. Third, indicators of democracy were used as barometers of free markets by international business and finance, especially if they were sensitive to the protection of PRIVATE PROPERTY like those of Freedom House. This tendency was accentuated as liberal democracy and capitalism became ever more closely associated following the collapse of state socialism in Eastern and Central Europe after 1989, stimulating funding and providing public credibility. Finally, new technology and a widening electronic access to datasets facilitated the development, use and comparison of democracy indicators.

Indicators of democracy can play a useful social scientific and political role in providing an empirical platform for assessing and comparing the quality of democratic governments. But they could be improved. On the one hand, they should seek to measure a wider range of liberal democratic values, and present separate scores for these values before making any attempt to aggregate them into a single index. On the other, they should employ a diversity of data sources, ensure that ordinal scales are sufficiently sensitive, avoid unnecessary weightings, keep interval and ordinal variables separate, and demonstrate their validity in terms of a proper purchase on the liberal democratic values in question. To make best use of the indicators they should be taken as the starting point not the end point of comparative inquiry, and as providing guidelines and hypotheses for more closely focused contextual analysis of individual cases or clusters of cases.

See also:

democratic audit; democratic deficit; democratic performance; legitimacy; waves of democracy

Further reading

Banks, A.S. (1997) *Cross-Polity Time-Series Data*, Binghampton, NY: State University of New York.
Dahl, R. (1971) *Polyarchy: Participation and Opposition*, New Haven, CT: Yale University Press.
Foweraker, J. and Krznaric, R. (2000) 'Measuring Liberal Democratic Performance: An Empirical and Conceptual Critique', *Political Studies* 48(4): 759–87.
Freedom House (1999) *Comparative Survey of Freedom*, New York: Freedom House.
Jaggers, K. and Gurr, T.R. (1995) 'Tracking Democracy's Third Wave with the Polity III data' *Journal of Peace Research* 32(4): 469–82.

JOE FOWERAKER
ROMAN KRZNARIC

individualism

An individual is any particular, the criterion of which is that it can be sorted, enumerated and picked out from the background. Individuals may be abstract or actual. Individuals are 'historical occurrences, material objects, peoples and their shadows and all particulars; whereas qualities and properties, numbers and species are not' (Strawson 1959: 15). Individuals, therefore, need not be equal but can be objects. Individualism by contrast refers to people and places a certain value upon them.

Individualism as a term is derived from the Latin *individuus*. It appears to have been first used as a value applying to people by the French philosopher Alexis de Tocqueville and refers to a modest egoism. More widely, individualism can be economic, psychological, religious or ethical. Economic individualism seems to have been at the centrepiece of Adam

Smith's *The Wealth of Nations* (1776), and the economic doctrine of *laissez faire* is founded on a belief that individual wills will act in harmony. In political theory, Jeremy Bentham in his work *On Utilitarianism* (1776) held that each individual was to count equally. The apotheosis of ethical individualism is to be found in Immanuel Kant's view of the 'Categorical Imperative' (1788) that each person must count as an end in himself or herself.

Religious individualism is to be found in the doctrine that all are equal in the eyes of God. The roots of individualism go, therefore, very deeply into Western society, and de Tocqueville seems to have merely labelled the phenomenon, which has considerable historical depth. He did not invent the phenomenon of individualism.

The opposite doctrine to individualism is collectivism, in a social sense, and holism, in a logical sense. Holism is merely the claim that the whole is greater than the sum of its parts or conversely the whole is not reducible to its parts. Collectivism is the social equivalent of this doctrine holding namely that society is not reducible to the sum of its members but has imperatives of its own.

Though individualism has many forms – economic, logical and ethical, for example – it seems to be primarily a doctrine rooted in Western religious practices and beliefs. It is hard to place the exact moment at which the root of individualism were placed, but they are certainly present in the Beatitudes of Jesus when he breaks down the tribal view of the law. Theologically, this was worked out by St Augustine who in 394 wrote the *Confessions* and used, for the first time, the first person singular in an extensive way. This turn into the self, what Taylor calls 'radical reflexivity' (1989: 131), was a step that changed the Western conception of the person. Indeed it almost invented the notion of the person and certainly invented the notion of 'the self'. Collectivism and tribalism were broken in this move and the self as an individual in the eyes of God, was invented. Augustine's major move was to alter the conception of the individual as a hermeneutic notion to an anthropological notion (Dihle 1982: 144). The self, thus formed,

had a power of its own and became, therefore, a being having will and power as well as selfhood. Augustine's radical reflection that, 'I have become a question to myself' is the foundation of the modern individual (*Confessions* X. 33, 50). This invention of the self as an entity having free will and power can be said to be so fundamental to the Western concept of the individual that individualism can be said to have a firmly religious foundation. Its second foundation is ethical in that individualism places a value, an ethical value, on the individual. The economic aspects of individualism are therefore secondary to the religious and ethical dimensions of individualism but the one supports the other in that economic individualism is supported by a religious and ethical foundation.

The development of the idea of the individual having a power of its own was placed in abeyance during the monastic period and began to be revived again only in the twelfth and thirteenth centuries where the idea of the contrast between freeman and serf became clarified. Thus while a serf might have a value to his lord, it was of a secondary nature, whereas a freeman had a value of his own. Such oddities arose, as the ability of the serf to transform himself into a freeman if he could escape the land and live without hindrance in the town for a year and a day. This doctrine, together with the growth of entrepreneurial skills, led to the foundations of economic individualism. Politically, this was also accompanied by the early rise of social contract theory. The surf was under bondage to his master, but his master was bound by a primitive form of contract to keep him and to take care of his safety. In towns, the entrepreneurial relationship was a relationship of contract between economic equals.

There is also some evidence that individualism was developing in the family by the twelfth century. It seems to have been during this period that, while the family was breaking down as an integral unit, it was developing as a contractual unit. Thus the parents would take care of the child until its maturity on the understanding that the child would take care of the parents at the end of their economic life.

Philosophically the most significant change occurred at the beginning of the Enlightenment with Descartes's first-person examination of the self. His famous claim that 'I think therefore I am' centres the individual and makes the mind transparent to itself. Thus Augustine's claim that 'I have become a question to myself' becomes, 'I can answer that question for myself by internal reflection upon myself'. More significantly, perhaps, is that the consequence of this claim is to make the individual a substance; that is, it exists in its own right, and while dependent upon God, is not dependent on any other force or power for its being.

The next major shift in the development of individualism was again religious. The Reformation once again set individuals as equal in the eyes of God and removed the intermediary, the priesthood, from sole contact with God. A principle idea that came out of the Reformation was the conception that 'good works' contributed to salvation. This doctrine fed the Protestant ethic as an ethic devoted to hard work and the individual responsibility for that work and its products. The relationship between this and CAPITALISM was famously written up by Max Weber as a book entitled *The Protestant Ethic and the Spirit of Capitalism* (1902). Weber took a line of idealism, namely that ideas brought about social change, a line contradicted by Marx who held that the growth of capitalism could be placed at the development of material forces. Economically, Adam Smith's *The Wealth of Nations* not only developed the doctrine of *laissez faire* but also argued that individual enterprise and free trade were essential to the development of national wealth. Ethically, Immanuel Kant developed the conception of the Categorical Imperative, which placed the individual at the centre of value. In his well-known formulation, Kant argued that one must always treat others as ends in themselves and not merely as a means. To some extent, there is a tension in all these doctrines. The individual can be seen as equal in the eyes of God as occupying a place in a hierarchical system, a being and a producer of

wealth, or as being and an end in themselves. Various attempts to resolve these tensions have been attempted, but none are entirely satisfactory. The tensions are basic to the idea of the individual and its many facets.

In a complete inversion of the idea of the 'Protestant Ethic' as being the force behind capitalism, Karl Marx argued that material forces were the engine of history and individuals merely playthings. Capitalism was not the product of individual action but individuals were the product of capitalism. There is thus a contrast between this thesis and Weber's claim. In other words there is a distinction between ideality and materiality, a distinction which cannot be entirely resolved on the historical evidence, for the historical evidence is subject to the interpretation placed on it by the basic theory held. What is clear is that individualism is a western product with a long history behind it. What is not clear, are the causes of that individualism. What is also not clear is the extent to which the individual can be said to be at the centre of social forces and the product of social forces.

This argument has been reflected recently in the debate between holism and individualism, where holism is the view that society cannot be broken down into constituent parts without some loss of meaning or substance. This apparently philosophical debate has some considerable force to it, for if the philosophical issues could be solved then substantive issues would fall into place. The arguments have been well rehearsed by John O'Neill (1973). More recently, the argument has been developed primarily in Continental philosophy that individuals cannot be the centre of either their own lives or that of society, but insofar as they exist, if they exist at all, they are decentred; that is to say they are a part of but not central to society. Society insofar as it exists socially forms individuals.

Individualism has a long and complex role to play in the development of capitalism. It has an equally long and complex role to play in the development of democracy. Democracy with its emphasis on the rule of law (see LAW, RULE OF), moral equality, political

EQUALITY, SEPARATION OF POWERS, a strong independent JUDICIARY and its particular notions of JUSTICE seems to rely upon individualism at its very foundations. Democracy developed alongside individualism, and a question arises as to the extent to which democracy is dependent upon some form of individualism.

Historically, individualism and democracy have gone hand in hand but it does not follow from this historical tie that they are logically tied together. Thus, for instance, is it possible for there to be a non-individualistic democracy? On the face of it the answer would seem to be pessimistic and negative. Democracy takes the individual as its core value yet the experience of some other countries that do not take individualism as their sole core seems to show that there is some room for manoeuvre. India, for instance, which in some accounts is the largest democracy in the world, takes groups rather than individuals as central. Nonetheless, it does seem as if a democracy that denied the value of individuals would be a contradiction in terms. One ought to be careful, however, not to take the historical development of democracy as central to democracy. This would be to limit democracy to Western societies and rule out the possibility of democracy ever being found or developed in non-Western societies. Historical CONTINGENCY should not be mistaken for historical necessity, and the evidence is that it is not yet possible to decide whether individualism and democracy are contingent relationships or necessary relationships. The jury is out.

See also:

autonomy; identity, political; radical democracy

Further reading

Dihle, A. (1982) *The Theory of Will in Classical Antiquity*, Berkeley, CA: University of California Press.

O'Neill, J. (ed.) (1973) *Modes of Individualism and Collectivism*, London: Heinemann.

Strawson, P.F. (1959) *Individuals: An Essay in Descriptive Metaphysics*, London: Methuen.

Taylor, C. (1989) *Sources of the Self: The Making of the Modern Identity*, Cambridge: Cambridge University Press.

PAUL BARRY CLARKE

information

When a dictator has to decide whether or not to raise taxes, he or she needs to know who possesses what, what is required for the survival of the regime and that of his/her subjects, which course of action is desirable and which is prudent. Now let the dictator in this example be called 'The People', and we have in a nutshell both the role and dilemma of information in democratic systems: the people gathering information on the people, and the people informing the people. In both directions, parties can have an interest in hiding information and in disclosing it. In the hands of a government, gathering, disclosing and hiding information can serve goals like efficiency and effectiveness, responsibility, responsiveness (see PUBLIC OPINION) and LEGITIMACY. For citizens and CIVIL SOCIETY, access to information is a form of EMPOWERMENT: it enables people to see alternatives, compare them and choose between them (Hyland 1995). In this sense, information contributes to individual AUTONOMY (Dahl 1989; Weale 1999). At the same time, both hiding and giving access to information can contribute to the FREEDOM of individuals: freedom from interference and freedom to act.

Definition

Information is the substance transported though COMMUNICATION, without which any kind of co-operation and individual action would be impossible. It comes in an endless number of forms, from figures and words to pictures and body language. It is communicated by countless MEDIA, from the spoken word and smoke signals to television and the internet. Finally, its sources are numerous. Even information of a merely political nature can originate in the laboratory, in introspection, party political broadcasts, conversations and so forth.

Despite its vital importance, the concept of information itself is relatively young: it is a particular interpretation of the concept of knowledge, dating back to the sixteenth century. Information cannot be conceived of without two modern distinctions: the Cartesian distinction between subject and object, and the Humean distinction between fact and value. Information always concerns the world outside the subject as it is mediated through study, investigation, hearsay or even introspection. Moreover, information is raw data: it has to be interpreted before it can be called knowledge, tested before it can be called truth, and normatively evaluated before it can guide action.

For classic authors like Plato and Aristotle, the distinction between true knowledge and opinion was fundamental. Teaching and practice could enable us to perceive the 'true' shape of things, their true nature and aims. The categories (temperature, colour, how-ness, what-ness, where-ness) that our senses and minds use to automatically order and structure the world were assumed to correspond with the natural order of the universe. When Descartes questioned the certainty of all knowledge and methods, he radically severed the link between the knower and the known. Knowledge came to be understood as the active structuring of raw material (information) according to rationally and empirically testable theories. David Hume subsequently introduced the gap between is and ought: from descriptive statements about the world as it is, nothing prescriptive logically follows, no statements can be made about how the world should be or about how we should act. Finally, due to amongst others Marx's critique of ideology and twentieth-century discourse analysis, theory itself, the instrument we use to perceive and interpret information, became suspect. It can make us see only what we want to see, or rather, what particular environmental conditions (CLASS; EDUCATION) allow us to see.

History and development

Political theory has in general reflected both these developments in philosophy and simultaneous developments in politics. Religious conflicts and scientific revolutions brought an end to the medieval feudal world. Finding a polity's right path now required, according to liberal and contract theorists, an end to the ruler's monopoly on political truth. Fundamental political decisions required the PARTICIPATION and expertise of all people of sound judgement and the recognition of their equality, particularly of the equal worth of their moral and religious convictions. Note that this usually implied participation only for the 'rational' (read: educated, male) and impartial (read: financially independent). The later EMANCIPATION of the working classes and women, resulting in present-day mass democracy, reflects the idea that we all stand equally 'biased' in life.

All this is not to say that democratisation and increased access to information were symmetrical developments. Both governments and citizens had their reasons to limit access to information. Citizens had their privacy and liberty to defend. Governments, in particular, tended to prefer a need-to-know information policy over a right to know. For one, they could (and still do) defend secrecy in terms of 'reasons of state': the defence of the realm and its way of life against its foreign enemies. For another, information is a policy instrument; the better dosed, the more efficiently it will influence people.

Over time, revolutionary changes in the means of communication – from printing press to internet and from horse cart to satellite – turned the freedom of opinion and press into a serious obstacle to standard government secrecy. Yet it is only in this century that next to the now classic freedom to *spread* information, a freedom of *access* to information as a CONSTRAINT on governmental power, came into the picture. At least three factors contribute to this gradual development from 'no information unless', access to information on a need-to-know basis only, to 'free information unless'. It is partly a means of improving political participation and, secondly, a response to the perceived growing interference of welfare-state governments in private life. It is also a democratic reaction to technocratic DECISION-MAKING and POLICY-MAKING. Inspired by the Soviet experience, the radical and moderate left for a long time argued that most political problems are by nature technical, and could therefore be modelled and solved according to plans or blueprints meeting objective scientific standards. In the hands of technocrats, this left little room for DEMOCRATIC DEBATE, even presuming that ordinary citizens had the ability to master specialist knowledge (see Hyland 1995).

The impartiality or objectivity of descriptive information is no longer taken for granted. It is recognised that different interests, different conceptions of the good and of the world of facts all lead to different assessments of the relevancy, value and meaning of information. In short, information is perceived as both a necessary condition for democratic politics and as a suspicious element that should be handled with care. It is a prerequisite for sound decisions and a weapon against exclusion, and at the same time a potential impediment to these aims: a means of influencing and biasing individuals. Moreover, it can perform both functions in the public and private sphere alike.

The positive role of information in a democracy lies partly in its contribution to rational decision-making, the preservation of democratic egalitarian and liberal values, and AUTONOMY. This explains why information plays a key part in modern defences of DELIBERATIVE DEMOCRACY. Information is seen as more than mere input for a political system aimed at satisfying individual preferences or creating the greatest happiness for the greatest number. Democratic debate may also help to realise the Enlightenment ideal of open-minded citizens, critical of their own and others' preferences and willing to improve.

On the negative side, depending on one's point of view, there can be too much information, too little, or of the wrong kind. From the perspective of the citizen on the receiving side of the information flow, it is as rational to ensure maximum access to information as it is to limit the flow. Gathering and processing information is costly. It takes time, energy and resources, success is not guaranteed, and the costs may simply outweigh the benefits (Downs 1957).

Not all information is relevant: some information may in fact be counterproductive. If the distribution of the benefits and burdens of social co-operation is at stake, not knowing which distribution is in one's private interest may well be the best way to guarantee fairness and equality. For this reason, John Rawls argued that fundamental political choices should be taken as if from behind a veil of ignorance, hiding all personal data that might bias us in favour of ourselves yet allowing us access to general information about society (Rawls 1971).

Next, having only reasonable amounts of relevant information is not enough to warrant a reasonable choice. Citizens also need the expertise to handle information and the ability to deal with the 'burdens of judgement' (Rawls 1993), the limits public reason poses to argument: both normative and purely empirical questions cannot always be conclusively solved.

From the perspective of a government informing society, or of individuals communicating information to the public sphere, information can be a threat to efficiency, freedom of action, or the common good. Hence, relevant information is often framed: providing public access to a wilderness park sounds different than endangering a nature resort. Next, relevant information can also be hidden in plain sight, simply by concealing it under a layer of irrelevant information. And finally, there is always the Machiavellian method of straightforward lying.

Alternatively, there can be too little information. The effects of any economic policy tend to be unpredictable, no matter how sophisticated the economic models used to simulate it. Government officials also occasionally leak information to the media, for example, to test reactions to a controversial policy proposal without immediately committing to it or to embarrass opponents. Finally, both from a technocratic perspective and from that of some advocates of deliberative democracy, more information and more explanation are expected not just to improve the quality of democracy, but also to induce learning processes leading to the 'right' decision.

A final negative role that information can play in a democracy relates to the artificiality of the divide between the private and public spheres, creating a double identity. In a democracy, a politician or civil servant is also an individual member of civil society, and the citizen as individual is also a citizen as public official. With information comes responsibility; with these double roles come double and possibly conflicting responsibilities. On the one hand, an individual who is aware of a breach of public rules – a burglary taking place, a neighbour unlawfully claiming social security benefits – is obliged to act as a public official and report the fact. On the other, 'telling on people' is morally controversial behaviour in the private sphere, and if it were a universal practice, it might turn society into a police state. Civil servants may encounter similar problems: they may have access to information they feel the public should be aware of, and thus be forced to choose between loyalty to the organisation or blowing the whistle (Bovens 1998). The status of whistleblowers like Daniel Ellsberg, leaking the Pentagon Papers on the USA's secret operations in Southeast Asia, and the still unidentified Deep Throat, leaking crucial information on the Watergate scandal, has remained controversial to this day.

The most recent revolution in the field of information, the rise of the Internet, illustrates many of the advantages and shortcomings associated with information in a democratic society. What began as a simple network of army and university computers has evolved into a worldwide communication system capable of connecting, in principle, every human being to every other human being. For some, the Internet signals the beginning of a global democracy (Dahl 1989): it can give everyone access to all possible information, it allows participation in scores of political debates and can cope with – one day – billions of voters. Ignoring the borders between states, the Internet would make CENSORSHIP and propaganda on a national scale futile. Hackers can break into any government network, making secrecy impossible. Then again, critics argue, there is already too much information on the net, too much of which is irrelevant. Moreover, participation in a global PC-democracy requires computer literacy, a scarce good, as well as access to computers, a costly good and a market that governments might still be able to control. The internet changes nothing about the fact that information may be counterproductive, and it may even increase the room for framing, hiding and misrepresenting information. For the moment, however, the greatest obstacle to global PC-democracy is the non-existence of a global polity.

Evaluation

The meaning of information for democracy depends on one's conception of democracy. On a communist (people's democracy) conception, one could argue that it is in the best interest of the people, their equality and autonomy, that governments have access to all the information they find relevant, granting the citizen access only when they find it opportune. On a libertarian account, a government would (if allowed to in the first place) be forced to work in the dark to the degree that citizens refuse to co-operate voluntarily, whereas the citizens would have complete access to all government information. Criteria for who in a democracy should be allowed to know what are therefore necessarily abstract.

First, it is possible to establish a presumption in favour of freedom of access 'unless', and against need-to-know secrecy. Both views obviously agree on free access to information necessary to citizen and government. What logically distinguishes them is the grey zone in between: access to politically irrelevant or redundant information. Information in this zone is by definition, on both views, harmless; there is therefore no principal reason to limit access to it. The real question for any democracy then is: when is it legitimate for a government to limit citizens' access to information, and for citizens to limit their government in gathering information?

Next, within conceptions of democracy, there can be only two reasons to limit the freedom of (access to) information: because of a democratic decision, or because of the danger that it might pose to the democratic process. In virtually every conception of democracy, the first is an insufficient reason (defence of democracy) and can only be accepted if the decision is not self-denying; that is, itself a danger to democracy. For all practical purposes, we may assume that freedom of information can only be limited because of the danger it might pose to democracy itself (Dahl 1989; Hyland 1995; Weale 1999).

As to when information actually poses a danger to the survival of democracy, only indeterminate guidelines exist. An example may clarify this. Censors could appeal to the democratic ideal of equality to prevent the media from publishing any material that might identify the social, cultural or racial background of suspected criminals, so as not to create room for prejudice in society. In fact, self-censorship on points like these is quite common among the media in democratic countries. Part of the justification for censorship on these grounds must be the expectation that no valid conclusions, or only conclusions other than prejudicial ones, can be inferred from information on a criminal's background. Hence, the cause of a prejudice is supposed to lie in the potentially prejudiced, for instance in a lack of analytical prowess on their part, a lack of education, limited reading capabilities, limited time, or limited interest. Whether this is sufficient to justify censorship depends on a choice between two perspectives on risks: a 'clear and present danger' doctrine shifting the onus of proof onto the censors, or a precautionary attitude leading to preventive or proactive censorship. However, given the emancipatory aims of many types of democracy, this kind of justification raises another fundamental question: whether there is merely a negative

duty to grant freedom of (access to) information, or also a positive duty to create conditions under which information can and will be handled responsibly. In the latter case, the danger of giving rise to prejudice is insufficient grounds for censorship unless action is undertaken to make censorship redundant in the future.

A similar line of argument can be made with regard to the citizen informing the government, now in terms of concealing information or refusing to co-operate in, for example, a census. And note that the preservation of equality can also be the aim of policies other than censorship. It has, for instance, been argued that the general freedom of the press can legitimately be limited to prevent MARKET FORCES from creating press monopolies, or to allow equal access of political parties to the media (Weale 1999).

Equality may not be the only ideal that can be protected by not allowing access to information. Liberty, for one, may serve the same goal. However, there is a perceptible imbalance here between the power of the individual citizen and that of the state. Whereas the individual's access to public information is a *prima facie* necessary condition for democracy, the state's access to information on individuals is a *prima facie* threat to individual freedom and the private sphere as such (see CONSTRAINT). This of course takes us back to the choice between a clear and present danger attitude and a precautionary attitude towards risks, but more importantly, it shows that there is a presumption in democracy against granting governments free access to information on citizens. In summary, the onus of proof rests on those opposing openness in the public sphere and for the private sphere on those defending it.

Finally, there is always the reason of state, the *raison d'état*, to appeal to in defence of limits to the freedoms of information. However, next to the precaution/clear and present danger question, the protection of the state against its enemies raises an even more controversial question: that of the compatibility of democracy and nationalism (see NATIONS

AND NATIONALISM) in times of GLOBALISATION and cosmopolitanism.

See also:

freedom; identity, political; participation; public opinion; public–private distinction; responsibilities

Further reading

Bovens, M. (1998) *The Quest for Responsibility*, Cambridge: Cambridge University Press.

Dahl, R. (1989) *Democracy and its Critics*, New Haven, CT: Yale University Press.

Downs, A. (1957) *An Economic Theory of Democracy*, New York: Harper and Row.

Gates, S. and Humes, B. (1997) *Games, Information and Politics*, Ann Arbor, MI: The University of Michigan Press.

Hyland, J. (1995) *Democratic Theory*, Manchester: Manchester University Press.

Kraus, S. and Perloff, R. (eds) (1985) *Mass Media and Political Thought*, Beverly Hills, CA: Sage.

Rawls, J. (1971) *A Theory of Justice*, Oxford: Oxford University Press.

—— (1993) *Political Liberalism*, New York: Columbia University Press.

Smith, A. (1978) *The Politics of Information*, London: Macmillan.

Weale, A. (1999) *Democracy*, London: Macmillan.

MARCEL WISSENBURG

institutional design

There are many ways to conceptualise institutions in the social sciences (Lane and Ersson 2000) This entry focuses on two essential features of institutions, one positive and one negative. The positive feature has to do with the general function of institutions. Institutions are indispensable and hence ubiquitous ingredients of social life because they co-ordinate action, limit conflict, facilitate its resolution, and thus make (economic, political and so on) transactions and social interaction (for example, within families or associations) less costly or risky than they would be in the absence of institutions. Institutions help to resolve such fundamental problems of social life as collective action problems, principal–agent problems, cycling majorities and other nightmares that together make up what Hobbes has classically described as the 'state of nature'. Institutions perform this order-enhancing function through providing participants with shared cognitive and normative orientations. Through their socialising function, institutions endow people with a sense of meaning and appropriateness, as well as an awareness of what is expected of them and what is likely to happen to them, for example, if they attend a funeral, participate in ELECTIONS or take out a bank loan (March and Olsen 1989). Institutions regulate the distribution of, and mode of, access to important values such as health, peace, power, knowledge, love, wealth, JUSTICE, salvation, EDUCATION and many others. Through providing convergent orientations to participants and shaping their preferences, they mitigate the potential for conflict that surrounds these values (Offe 1996: 204–5). The rules and behavioural routines that make up the institution are not just contractually agreed upon between the actual participants, but recognised, validated and expected by third parties and outsiders. Some of the most important institutions come with elaborate normative theories, 'charters', 'animating ideas' (Goodin 1996a: 26) or 'idées directrices' (Hauriou 1925) that serve the purpose of their own justification (as is the case with doctrines of constitutionalism, market economics, the church or the nuclear family), while others rely just on tradition, habits, convention and *Sittlichkeit*.

The distinction just alluded to is that between formal and informal institutions. Formal institutions (such as courts) are those based upon written rules (legal procedures) prescribing specialised roles (such as those of judges and lawyers); incumbents of these roles have passed through and graduated from institutions of formal and specialised training, or they have been appointed, elected, delegated, certified and so on to perform the roles they are performing. Informal institutions are rules inherent in a culture which, although often not being written and explicitly prescribed, still standardise what is considered 'appropriate' or 'normal' behaviour. They are not based upon any explicit 'charter', and they often may remain unknown to participants until they are discovered and described by professional anthropologists or novelists. Examples include what, how and when we eat, how we dress, how we symbolise significant differences such as those between male and female, young and old, work and leisure, the sacred and the profane, or private and public. Both formal and informal institutions do not just generate consequences in the external world (such as the resolution of conflict, the production and distribution of economic goods, the assignment of privileges and competencies), but they also generate internal consequences such as the sense of stability, trust, meaning, identity and agreement among those with whom we live within the same institutional setting. Taken together, these two variants of institutional patterns, the formal and the informal or 'non-chartered', provide the answer to the old and basic question of 'how is society possible?'.

In contrast to the positive 'spirit' that originates from institutions and can inspire the participants to actually perform the (supposedly) collectively beneficial functions of institutions, there is also a *negative* aspect of institutions. This side has to do with their structure. Although they are in no way natural, but manmade, they are only exceptionally at the disposition of those involved in them. Institutions are given to the actors involved in them, which means that they impose binding constraints upon actors. They also endow certain categories of actors (such as teachers in schools, managers in business corporations) with AUTHORITY and power resources, while depriving other of these resources. This bindingness is often sociologically theorised by reference to the Durkheimian notion of the 'non-contractual foundation of contracts'.

In both respects, the presence of an inherent meaning and the non-contingent or rigid nature of institutions, these are different from formal organisations which can be built and rebuilt according to the purposive rationality of those who have the authority and other resources to do so. In contrast, the rules and behavioural routines that make up an institution are not just contractually agreed upon between the actual participants, but recognised, validated and expected to be complied with by third parties and outsiders.

To be sure, actors can always deviate from what institutionalised rules prescribe, such as if they steal property, conduct the pursuit of truth outside the institutions of science, or sexuality and family life outside of marriage. Such deviance from what institutions prescribe as the normal or appropriate place and conduct of certain activities will typically come at a price, be it that of negative sanctions or that of the exclusion from privilege and recognition, or be it just the emotional reaction of shame for having acted improperly. An option that is foreclosed, however, as far as typical actors in typical situations are concerned, is the arbitrary or purposive construction of institutions according to their particular tastes, preferences, or desires. Institutions are 'given', even for the deviant.

Yet institutions are in no way permanently given and fixed; they do exhibit vast variations in time and space. What we are interested in are the rules and causal mechanisms governing institutional change across time. More specifically, our task is here to determine the extent to which institutions change in response to, or new institutions emerge as a result of, the activity of 'designing', which presumably means a successful effort based upon both knowledge and evaluative criteria to meet the challenges that result from new perceived needs for institutional patterns of co-ordination, cooperation and prohibitive transaction costs.

To be sure, there is an abundance of such challenges. The situation of post-authoritarian polities and economies is a case in point, as is the need for the political legitimation of supranational regimes such as the European Union. The interaction of GLOBALISATION (for example, of commerce and financial markets) and technological change (such as the Internet), ecological problems that need to be monitored and controlled, problems of providing pensions and other forms of social security in an ageing society with high levels of unemployment and open economies, the spread of ethnic violence and an entirely new world of international conflicts and contingencies (ranging from migration to the trafficking in arms and drugs), the obsolescence of the organising potential of having a vocation and an occupational identity derived from it: these are just a random selection of items on a list of problems, risks and challenges which all seem to call for vigorous efforts of institutional design and institution building.

Classical political theory has mostly conceptualised the relationship of agency and institutions in unambiguously hierarchical terms. Institutions are created by exceptional and heroic founders, whereupon further agents are subsumed under the premises these founder provided (Edington 1975). It is indeed tempting to think of new institutions as the creation of an unmoved mover, or an unruled ruler, or a non-institutionalised designer of institutions from whose founding decisions institutions emerge. Many political theorists have taken recourse to this *tabula rasa* notion of institutionally unconstrained creativity being at the origin of institutions and rules. From Solon of Athens, to Machiavelli's Prince, to Rousseau's *legislateur,* to the charismatic leader in Weber, rules and institutional order are thought to flow from unruled decisions. The same applies to the contractarian theories of the seventeenth and eighteenth centuries, where institutions (such as the absolutist state in Hobbes) are thought to emerge from the convergent rational decisions of its (future) subjects. In all these examples and traditions, rules of social life are considered derivative from a pre-social agency of creative reason.

Such a 'creationist' view of political institutions is difficult to sustain today. Note that the idea of founding, creating, or designing new institutions involves two aspects. One is the retrospective one. We would speak of an act of designing and implementing new institutions only if any predecessor institution is actually abolished and hence any path-dependency broken. If such abolition does not take place, we would more appropriately speak of institutional development or evolution. The other defining feature of the act of designing an institution is prospective. It is not just any new set of actors, rules, substantive domains and so on that results from a 'design' (as opposed to random selection), but one that aims at certain goals or serves some predetermined purpose. A well-designed institution is one that actually achieves what it was designed to achieve. In order to meet both of these criteria, designers of institutions must indeed be endowed with extraordinary capacities. They need *power* in order to uproot the residues of the old regime and its formal as well as informal institutional components. And they need *prudence* (as Montequieu argued at length in chapter 29 of *Spirit of the Law*) in order to design the new institutions in ways which make sure that the intended functions are actually performed.

Machiavelli has famously specified the power conditions of building a new political regime. In his *Discorsi* (1531), he insists on the need for the ruthless and unrestrained use of power the 'new Prince' needs to employ for the sake of securing and maintaining his new regime: 'Should anyone become the ruler either of a city or of a state . . . the best thing he can do in order to retain such a principality . . . is to organise everything in the state afresh.' New governors were to be appointed with new titles and new authority 'to make the rich poor and the poor rich'. New cities were to be built and the old ones destroyed, the people moved far away . . . Machiavelli states that nothing in the province should be left 'intact . . . nothing in it, neither rank, nor institution, nor form of government, nor wealth' (1970: 176–7).

However Machiavelli was fully aware of the difficulties that such an undertaking was bound to encounter. 'There is nothing more difficult to execute, no more dubious of success, nor more dangerous to administer, than to introduce a new system of things' as the one who introduces the new system makes enemies from 'all those who profit from the old system . . . and he has only lukewarm allies in all those who might profit from the new system' (*The Prince*, VI).

This orgy of demolition that the author envisages, and indeed recommends, presupposes not just the 'negative' power to extinguish the old conditions to the point of exercising sheer terror, but also the positive power to mobilise vast support and compliance. The designer of new institutions must be a charismatic leader of exceptional qualities in order to be able to effectively burn the bridges. But even if these demanding conditions are met, the second step is to design and create the new set of institutions. This requires experience and prudence. How can the new ruler design not any new institution, but the particular one that actually best serves its purpose. The answer given by both Machiavelli and Montesquieu is that the Prince (or the Legislator) should consult history in order to determine which institutional rules will best serve the purpose he has in mind (if only the meta-purpose of *mantenere lo stato*). Even if this condition is met, it raises two objections to the possibility of 'designing' institutions. For one thing, consulting history may result in the combination and adoption not of new institutions, but of selected precedents. For another, there is no guarantee that such precedent will actually still serve the intended purpose under present (and essentially unprecedented) conditions. Thomas Pangle summarises the argument well. He states that the legislator 'must depend on experience. Since his own experience is necessarily limited, he is led to turn to the experience of other lawgivers in other times and places'. To aid him he must study political history which Pangle argues has 'been a paramount feature of the *Spirit of the Law* itself. But . . . the prescriptive character of history [is] questionable: no two situations are really alike' (Pangle 1973: 274).

The theoretical alternative to this notion of deriving institutions from non-institutional factors such as intentional design, human reason, the ingenuity of great men, is to conceptually endogenise the creation of new institutions. As all human action is 'embedded'

in institutions, so is the action of creating and innovating institutions. The paradigm case is the institution that provides the essential foundation of modern statehood, namely the constitution. Constitutions are complete only if they specify the procedures by which they can be changed, and alterations can be adopted. Rather than being created *ex nihilo* or on a *tabula rasa*, institution making and the design of institutions is itself institutionally embedded. If all social action is rooted and embedded in institutional patterns, why shouldn't this also apply to the special case of (re)designing institutions?

If we look more closely at how actors respond to the challenge of having to generate new rules and mechanisms of co-ordination due to some perceived insufficiency of existing ones, the creationist hypothesis of classical political theory is certainly not supported. The stress and anxiety that novel challenges induce may even perversely lead to a rigid adherence to given institutional patterns, in spite of the evident futility of this reaction. But even in more open-minded responses, what we see is not the activity of designers, but of actors performing as vandals, prophets, theorists, revolutionaries, utopians, reformers, historians, critics, translators and opportunists.

To begin with, there are institutional 'vandals'. They destroy existing institutional patterns by violent means without being able, however, due to the limitations of both their power and their prudence, to replace them with successor institutions. What remains is anarchy and terror, or the institutional wasteland of a 'genesis environment' (to borrow a phrase from Ken Jowitt). A case in point is Nazi Germany which, as early as the mid-1930s, had lost all qualities of a constitutional statehood (including an institutionalised solution to a potential crisis of succession) and had turned into a unregulated internal power struggle before it eventually turned to total war.

Often the origin of some of political or religious institutions is credited to mythological or charismatic founders, prophets or framers who, however, can hardly be supposed to have been in the possession of knowledge about either the enabling functions nor the constraining structures of institutions as we see them in operation at the present point. Such foundational narratives serve not the purpose of explaining the actual origin of some institutional pattern and its further evolution, but just of invoking the prestige of alleged founders for the sake of winning support and loyalty for the institution. Other actors relate to institutions as Hobbes to the absolutist state, or Adam Smith to the core institutions of capitalism, the market and the enterprise. That is to say, they are 'theorists' who have not 'designed' the institutions in question, but just provided a supportive theory for institutions which were already in existence, with a view to contributing to their LEGITIMACY and durability by spelling out their inherent reason. Still other institutions, such as the nuclear family or patterns of the symbolic organisation of time and space through significant markers (such as holidays and monuments) have neither founders nor supportive theorists. In fact, they do better without any of those, for as long as their origin and *raison d'être* remains anonymous and clouded by the mist of some distant past, it is hard to challenge such 'fatherless' institutions with meaningful arguments.

On the other hand, we often find pseudo-designers, or actors who put to work their constructive ambition and expertise and build models of institutions, without however ever having a chance to actually implement these models, thereby earning themselves the sometimes derogatory epithet of utopianism. Revolutionaries often see themselves as designing institutions as well as implanting them in the life of a new society or a new polity. But the vision they proclaim (see Lenin's *State and Revolution*) is typically not meant as a guideline for what is actually being done after the revolution, but as a device to gather support for the project of overthrowing the old regime and for discrediting its institutions. What makes it so difficult for utopians and revolutionaries to actually implement their blueprints for future institutions is the fact that, in order to do so, they would have to overrule the veto power and entrenched interests of those who

owe their privilege to exactly those institutions that revolutionaries want to replace with their own designs. Moreover, they can not yet rely on the mass preference for a new type of institutional order, which is still at best 'lukewarm' (according to Machiavelli) as the corresponding 'taste' may come proverbially only with 'the eating'. Even if they succeed in overcoming both of these handicaps, they probably will see themselves forced in the process to resort to practises that have in no way been part of the original design.

Strictly speaking, the activity of designing institutions is also different from what reformers do, because they do not create and implement new institutions, but merely use the range of variation and choice that is allowed for and, in fact, institutionalised by existing ones. Thus the market is an institution that permits the reformist activity of creative destruction, parliaments are the institutional locus of legislative innovation, universities and other research institutions the place for the generation of new knowledge. Similarly, all constitutions contain clauses, written or unwritten, which stipulate the methods, procedural requirements and potential objects of constitutional change. The hierarchy of the Roman Catholic church has been the paradigm case of institutionalised variability of dogma. All these innovative activities consist not in the design of new institutions, but in the exploitation of options, choices and contingencies afforded by existing ones. These choices are made possible exactly by the requisite rigidity of the underlying institutional pattern.

Another contrast to the ideal-typical notion of an architect designing and then actually building a house is the critic, who explores inconsistencies between various animating ideas embodied in a given institution. For instance, the activities of public universities are presumably governed by the principles of equality of opportunity *and* academic excellence, as the political life within liberal democracies is supposed to live up to the standards of both liberty *and* equality. Efficiency can often be enhanced in economic institutions through competition *or* the monopolistic concentration and merger of assets. It is often easy to point at fuzzy demarcation lines, contradictions, inconsistencies, tensions and imbalances between such animating ideas and implicit theories which supposedly govern particular institutional domains. Critics are involved in the activity of exploring and calling for the correction or clarification of such muddled or contaminated situations. Moreover, a difference must be highlighted between the ideal rationalist model of intentional design and the activity of historians (recovering models from the repertoire of some idealised past, as in Montesquieu) or translators. Representative of the latter are policy intellectuals busy with copying and appropriately adjusting institutional patterns that they have found in one institutional domain or one country and transferring it to other countries or institutional sectors. For instance, the free choice that money allows for in markets can be emulated by inventing an analogy of money, namely educational vouchers, to allocate the services of what hitherto was the public school system. The self-styled revolutionaries who brought about the demise of state socialist regimes in Central East Europe were actually, at least to a large extent, either what I have called 'critics' (claiming the actual realisation of principles and animating ideas that had been betrayed and forgotten by the old regime) or translators or propagators trying to transplant institutional patterns from Western capitalist democracies to the post-communist systems.

Finally, when we look at actual institutional changes we come across a type of agents I propose to term 'opportunist'. Rather than attaching to the term the usual verdict of poor character and selfishness, I use the term to emphasise the ability of these actors to make use of windows of opportunity and to capture options for winning agreements on new rules as they emerge, often on the basis of *ad hoc* proposals that are mixed, impure and second-best in terms of clear principles and priorities. The entrepreneurial creativity of such opportunity exploiting actors focuses upon local (both in space and in time) configurations of actors and interests which lend themselves to

the making of lasting compromises, of agreements that serve as models and templates for future agreements, and of COALITIONS, alliances and practices which may (or may not) be remembered as a breakthrough and from which it therefore becomes difficult for participants to diverge. This somewhat messy logic of exploiting opportunities for institution-building as they emerge without relying upon the guidance of some master plan; the logic of creating standards and benchmarks according to unforeseen and generally unpredictable chances of compromise; the logic of making all participants constantly aware of the opportunity costs of non-cooperation and their responsibility for avoiding these costs; and the logic of making these standards irreversible (if not legally so, *de facto*, for example, by effectively attaching stigma to defection) once they are agreed upon; these are all elements of what can be observed in both the (successful) cases of post-communist reconstruction as well as in the process of European integration. Such creative opportunism is probably the closest approximation to the notion of institutional design that we find in the real world of politics. Imaginative proposals of self-styled (and arguably hyper-rationalist) designers may well play an important role in a dynamic that has still more in common with the flow of a glacier than it has with the architect's planful erection of a new building.

See also:

bureaucracy; constitutional design; integration; parliamentary models; representation, models of

Further reading

Edington, R.V. (1975) 'The Ancient Idea of Founding and the Contemporary Study of Political Change', *Polity* 7(4): 162–79.

Goodin, R.E. (ed.) (1996a) *The Theory of Institutional Design*, Cambridge: Cambridge University Press.

—— (1996b) 'Institutions and Their Design', in: *idem*, 1996, 1–53.

Hauriou, M. (1925) 'Théorie de l'institution et de la fondation: Essai de vitalisme social', *Cahiers de la Nouvelle Journée* 4: 1–45.

Lane, J.-E. and Ersson, S. (2000) *The New Institutional Politics. Performance and Outcomes*, London: Routledge.

Machavelli, N. (1970) *The Discourses*, ed. B. Crick, Harmondsworth: Penguin

March, J.G. and Olsen, J.P. (1989) *Rediscovering Institutions: The Organisational Basis of Politics*, New York: The Free Press.

Offe, C. (1996) 'Designing Institutions in East European Transitions', in R. Goodin (ed.), *The Theory of Institutional Design*, Cambridge: Cambridge University Press, 199–226.

Pangle, T.L. (1973) *Montesquieu's Philosophy of Liberalism. A Commentary on The Spirit of the Laws*, Chicago: Chicago University Press.

CLAUS OFFE

integration

The contemporary concept of integration comprises both a process of cooperation among states and institutions and a set of theories about that process. Historically, the momentum for institutionalised interstate cooperation in a new European agency, known initially as the European Community (EC) and later the European Union (EU), is the end of the Second World War. This innovative form of PARTICIPATION in a new political and economic DECISION-MAKING area led to the creation of new institutions and to political outcomes which were different from those in either interstate bargaining or nation-states' domestic politics. EU integration has engendered considerable debate among theorists and those involved in the process. It is especially associated with regional integration, the creation of regional blocs and cooperation among nation states on economic and related issues. The North Atlantic Free Trade Association, Asia Pacific Economic Cooperation, Association of South East Asian Nations and Mercosur all have features of regional economic

integration or cooperation. Approaches to regional integration feature in contemporary debates on the role of GLOBALISATION and its effects on regionalism.

Integration refers to the initiative to unite states in a grouping for the benefit of both the organisation and its constituent members. Integration is also a long-term objective and process, and, as such, is defined as closer cooperation among member states in order to achieve a state of union. In addition to economic integration, monetary integration is evident in the EU, the most advanced example of regional integration.

The main theories of integration are functionalism, neofunctionalism, FEDERALISM and intergovernmentalism. Their usefulness is a matter of debate. Democratic structures do not feature prominently in any of these.

The EU was established to create a stable postwar political and economic order within Western Europe within an interdependence of economies. Economic cooperation, seeking solutions to common problems would avoid further war. There was little discussion of democratic elements and little expectation that the nation state would be replaced or transformed. The EU developed collective decision-making, with public power above the state. It is the only regional organisation which involves a consistent transfer of decision-making power to institutions above the state. Increasingly, contemporary thought sees the EU as a distinctively European governance system or even a polity, with some democratic features (Marks *et al.* 1996; Traxler and Schmitter 1995). There are dangers, however, in allocating to the EU the functions and attributes of a state or polity.

Originally, integration proposals were functionalist; states need international cooperation in economic areas, and this would lead to political understanding. Peace is preserved by international trust, constructed around specific common objectives (Mitrany 1946). This sectoral, incrementalist approach did not necessarily require federalist institutions. The European Economic Community is an example of functional integration, with structures and common policies set in place to administer the process of integration. Gradually, however, an *acquis communitaire* developed, consisting of the body of the rights, obligations, treaties, legislation, measures, declarations and international agreements of the EU. This in effect constitutes norms of governance.

Neofunctionalists forecast spillover, whereby functionalist sectoral integration would lead to increased integration in other areas. Neofunctionalism emphasised beliefs, groups and institutions and assumed a successful operation in low politics would lead to a gradual transfer of the loyalties to the EC. Integration is seen as an inevitable progressive process, with eventual delegation of state AUTHORITY to a supranational agency. Political integration is the process whereby national political actors shift their loyalties, expectations and activities towards a new centre, with a jurisdiction over the nation states (Haas 1958:16). The end result is a new political community, superimposed over pre-existing ones. Neofunctionalism emphasises elite interaction. Decision-making is incremental, problem-solving and technical, avoiding ideological divisions. Although later neglected, neofunctionalism re-emerged in the 1980s (Tranholm-Mikkelsen 1991).

Federalism's primary objective is to create a government of the EU with federal governmental bodies. Federalists rejected functionalist approaches as circuitous, in favour of a European federal state. Federalism is associated with the failed European Defence Community and European Political Community in the 1950s, and the Spinelli-led European Parliament initiative for a European Union Treaty in 1984. Early proposals for a federal Europe emanated from Coudenhove Kalergi, Monnet, Spinelli, Lothian and Brugmans (Murray and Rich 1996). In practice, federalism had limited input in the EC, which developed an incrementalist integration. Federalists were criticised for their idealism and failure to understand nationalism's resilience. Federalists offered no agreement on what constitutes a federal system and which polities are the most useful models.

A reorientation of federalism (neofederalism) emerged in the 1980s (Pinder 1996) with Economic and Monetary Union seen as an essential element of constructing a federal EU polity by blocks. Federalism was redefined as common government in crucial areas, resulting in the concentration of political power based on constitutional democracy. Federalism retains relevance as a tool of analysis, featuring in new institutional approaches and in analyses of supranational elements and constitutional aspects of the EU and the role of institutions.

Intergovernmentalism rejects the transfer of SOVEREIGNTY and maintains that cooperation among states is primary. The state is the central unitary actor, with sovereignty being vital. It originally regarded the EC as low policy. However, the integration project involved increasingly a transfer of state powers in both high and low policy to the EC/EU, including a limited Common Foreign and Security Policy under the Maastricht and Amsterdam Treaties.

Intergovernmentalists claim that the nation-state, despite integration, remains intact (Hoffman 1966). National interests remain primary and indivisible. The gains from cooperation are limited. Intergovernmentalists explain the EU policy process as inter-governmental bargaining. The European Commission is, at times, seen as a significant actor allying with governments (Taylor 1983).

Intergovernmentalism's assumption that POLICY-MAKING is a simple zero-sum game has been challenged, as EU bargaining has often been a positive-sum game. Intergovernmentalism's failure to define and differentiate between vital, non-negotiable, and bargainable interests is criticised (Hix 1994). It has been contended that it is a set of assumptions regarding the role of states in multilateral cooperation or, at best, a partial theory of integration that explains only the major bargains. One innovative approach, however, sees integration as favouring the nation state (Milward 1992), with integration occurring only when there is agreement about integration goals and no antagonism between integration and the state.

Problems within each of these different approaches are evident. Further, there are differing concepts of state, statehood, democracy and integration. There have been considerable transformations within the nation state. Researchers continue to debate whether integration has resulted in the nation state being undermined or strengthened.

The EU has been examined as a political entity and a set of states, policies and institutions. Increasingly, there is discussion of the EU as a polity, with characteristics of a government, the result of integration by stealth or as an evolving governance. Some approaches emphasise the primacy of the state. In many, there is a normative or predictive dimension, which fails to marry theory with the reality of a unique and emerging political entity.

The study of integration has expanded to include comparative macro-regional entities, issues of CITIZENSHIP, democratic ACCOUNTABILITY, DEMOCRATIC PERFORMANCE of the institutions and the DEMOCRATIC DEFICIT, supranationality, multiple loyalties, identities, nationalism and concepts of community. Increasingly analysts express concern at the lack of democratic structures and accountability in the EU, taking as their models national systems on the one hand and transnational and COSMOPOLITAN DEMOCRACY and citizenship on the other (Archibugi *et al.* 1998).

See also:

authority; federalism; nations and nationalism; sovereignty; state, models of

Further reading

Archibugi, D., Held, D. and Kohler, M. (eds) (1998) *Re-imagining Political Community*, Oxford: Polity Press.

Haas, E. (1958) *The Uniting of Europe*, London: Stevens.

Hix, S. (1994) 'The Study of the European Community: The Challenge to Comparative Politics', *West European Politics* 17(1).

Hoffmann, S. (1966) 'Obstinate or Obsolete? The Fate of the Nation State and the Case of Western Europe', *Daedalus* 95.

Lodge, J. (1983) 'Integration Theory', in *The European Community: Bibliographical Excursions*, London: Pinter.

Marks, G., Scharpf, F., Schmitter, P. and Streeck, W. (1996) *Governance in the European Union*, London: Sage.

Milward, A. (1992) *The European Rescue of the Nation-State*, London: Routledge.

Mitrany, D. (1966) *A Working Peace System*, Chicago: Quadrangle.

Murray, P. and Rich, P. (eds) (1996) *Visions of European Unity*, Boulder, CO: Westview.

Pinder, J. (1996) 'Economic and Monetary Union: Pillar of a Federal Polity', *Publius* 26(4).

Taylor, P. (1983) *The Limits of European Integration*, New York: Colombia.

Tranholm-Mikkelsen, J. (1991) 'Neo-functionalism: Obstinate or Obsolete? A Reappraisal in the Light of the New Dynamism of the EC', *Millennium* 20(1).

Traxler, F. and Schmitter, P. (1995) 'The Emerging Euro-Polity and Organised Interest', *European Journal of International Relations* 1(1).

PHILOMENA MURRAY

interest groups

Interest groups have been variously defined by scholars in economics, history, political science, sociology and in other fields. Generally speaking, interest groups are relevant to democratic thought and practice when they interact with government. Therefore, political scientists typically distinguish between social or demographic groups, such as women, and organised interest groups such as the National Organisation for Women (NOW). Sociologists often distinguish between SOCIAL MOVEMENTS, which sometimes have no organised character, and social movement organisations (SMOs), which are interest groups. Other terms often used, generally synonymously with interest groups, include 'pressure group', 'organised interest' and 'lobby'. Truman, in his classic work on the topic (1951), distinguished between 'potential groups' and 'manifest groups'.

Almost any conceivable social, professional or demographic category constitutes a potential group in the sense that it could be mobilised for political action. Interest groups, in current usage, are what Truman called 'manifest groups'; those potential groups that have actually become active in political life.

Interest groups have long been central to the academic and to the popular study of politics, as well as to philosophical perspectives on democracy. Montesquieu was leery of any 'intermediary bodies' coming in between the citizen and the state. Rousseau worried that the general will would never be realised through an aggregation of particular wills, and was therefore hostile to the press of particular wills on government through groups. Madison considered the 'mischiefs of faction' to be a fundamental concern, though he argued in *The Federalist Papers* that they were better controlled than eliminated. Groups have long been seen as a threat to democratic practice because their unfettered mobilisation could exacerbate social and economic inequalities. At the same time, they have also been seen as a guarantee of individual rights because any individual sharing concerns with like-minded individuals should be free to organise to demand redress from government. Curing the 'mischiefs of faction' by somehow limiting the freedom to form and support interest groups could be to provide a remedy that is far worse than the disease. Individual rights like free speech, freedom to associate and freedom to petition government lead to a generally understood FREEDOM to organise into interest groups. Groups, then, are central to philosophical perspectives on how citizens relate to government.

Groups have long been central to studies of governmental operation and to political science in general. In the immediate post-Second World War period, especially in the United States, a 'group approach' to politics became especially pronounced. Rather than study only the constitutionally defined powers of various institutions, political scientists turned to the 'real workings' of government through an analysis of interest groups. Here, they were guided by previous studies such as those done by Bentley (1908) and Schattschneider (1935), who had begun studying the informal relations between government officials and communities of technical experts (or 'pressure groups') even earlier. By the 1950s, 'group theorists' dominated American political science: Truman's *The Governmental Process* (1951) reviewed the entire American political system, from voting to the courts and BUREAUCRACY, through the lens of group activities. Dahl's *Who Governs?* (1961) similarly put groups at the centre of the process of governance.

Groups were not only important in American political science, but in the study of comparative politics as well. Whereas the study of individual countries such as Britain, France or Italy was affected by the 'group approach' just as studies of American politics were, most comparativists followed a slightly different track (but one that also put groups near the centre of things). Those studying Scandinavian countries noted the more 'corporatist' nature of the relations between organised interests and the state. Formalised, routine interactions between state officials and representatives of major social categories – interest groups – make a corporatist system especially manageable, but also quite different from a pluralist one (see CORPORATISM; PLURALISM). Pluralist systems were seen to involve more conflict and less control by the state over outside interests. In any case, the study of group-state relations remains a major element of comparative politics; various countries (or sectors within them) are variously described as 'corporatist', 'pluralist', 'consociational' or 'statist' (for reviews of this literature see Richardson 1982). Putnam's recent and influential work on Italian (1993) and American politics (1995) places interest-group participation at the centre of an idea of civic engagement, harking back to the pioneering comparative work of Almond and Verba (1965) in their five-nation study of political PARTICIPATION. Comparativists as well as those interested in single democracies have long focused their attention on the actions of interest groups.

Probably the single most influential book on interest groups since those of Truman and

Dahl is not really about groups, but about why some groups do not form. Olson's argument in *The Logic of Collective Action* (1965) was telling, and it had a dramatic impact on the study of interest groups: because some groups seek private goods, but others seek public goods (which will be provided to all, member of the group or not), certain types of groups are much more likely to mobilise to their full potential than others. Groups that seek public goods, such as clean air, abolition of the death penalty, lower consumer costs, public access to beaches, or any other good that cannot realistically be withheld from those who do not contribute to its achievement, are unlikely ever to mobilise to their full potential. Many people who share the goals of the group will simply be 'free riders', hoping to benefit from whatever success the group may have, but contribute nothing. On the other hand, groups that seek private selective goods that are made available only to their members will mobilise closer to their full potential, since those who do not contribute can be excluded from whatever benefit the group may gain. With this simple argument, Olson delivered a killing blow to any theory that would rely on the mobilisation of citizens through groups to ensure an equitable and pluralistic representation of interests to government. Some types of groups will be chronically undermobilised, he argued, whereas others will suffer from no problems of mobilisation. The resulting group system could not be considered to be fair or democratic. Olson's enunciation of the public goods problem and how it affects group mobilisation has led to an enormous literature in which scholars have noted the various ways by which groups do indeed mobilise their members (see especially Schlozman and Tierney (1986) and Walker (1991); for a review see Baumgartner and Leech (1998: ch. 4)).

Besides a significant focus on how groups mobilise their members, attention has been perhaps more fruitfully spent on assessing how groups go about affecting government decisions. Large numbers of studies have been done detailing the types of relations that groups develop with government officials. Studies of 'issue subsystems' have given way to studies of 'policy networks' as scholars have noted that cosy subsystems with only a few specialised experts involved have often been replaced by more complicated systems where participants come and go, where conflict among participants can be quite common, and where policy influence depends on the actions and views of many other participants. Significant studies of the policy role of groups have included those of Heclo (1978) and Walker (1991) in the United States, Wilson (1987) in France and Richardson and Jordan (1979) in Britain (for a review see Baumgartner and Leech (1998)).

American scholars interested in the roles and impact of groups have been affected by the Federal Election Campaign Act. This requires contributors to election campaigns for federal offices to report their contributions publicly. Further, it limits the amount of money individuals and organisations can give, and requires the formation of POLITICAL ACTION COMMITTEES (PACs) for those organisations wishing to play an active role in campaign contributions. The requirement that these contributions be made public (along with the massive amounts of money spent) has led to a large literature in which scholars have attempted to link PAC (interest group) spending on elections with impacts on election outcomes or on the voting decisions of sitting legislators (see ELECTORAL CAMPAIGNING). To date, this literature has been quite inconclusive (see Baumgartner and Leech (1998: ch. 7) for a more complete review). While it is clear that interest groups affect both ELECTIONS and voting decisions in legislatures through their lobbying and campaign contributions, demonstrating this effect empirically while controlling for the efforts of groups on the opposite side of the conflict has proven extremely difficult. One recent and well-organised study (Berry 1999) noted how public and consumer-oriented interest groups were often able to push their issues onto the political agenda. Increasingly over the past three decades, Berry found that such groups could put wealthy business organisations on the defensive. Of course, measuring influence is difficult, so studies of lobbying have had difficulty determining the impact of various lobbying activities. Still, Berry showed quite conclusively that money is not the only thing that counts (see also Kollman (1998); for a contrary view see West and Loomis (1999)).

Interest groups have played and will continue to play fundamental roles in all democratic systems. While the term is often used with a pejorative connotation, most understand that many unassailably beneficial groups are nonetheless 'interest groups'. Charities fighting for more money to cure heart disease are 'special interest' just as much as auto manufacturers lobbying for increased smog emission allowances. One's view of what is a 'special interest' and what is a 'public interest' group often depends on the groups to which one belongs. All can agree, however, that no understanding of democratic politics can be complete without a full understanding of the roles of interest groups.

See also:

civil society; consociationalism; pluralism; political action committees; social movements

Further reading

Almond, G.A. and Verba, S. (1965) *The Civic Culture*, Boston: Little, Brown.

Baumgartner, F.R. and Leech, B.L. (1998) *Basic Interests: The Importance of Groups in Politics and in Political Science*, Princeton, NJ: Princeton University Press.

Bentley, A.F. (1908) *The Process of Government*, Chicago: University of Chicago Press.

Berry, J.M. (1999) *The New Liberalism*, Washington: Brookings.

Dahl, R.A. (1961) *Who Governs*, New Haven, CT: Yale University Press.

Heclo, H. (1978) 'Issue Networks and the Executive Establishment', in A. King (ed.), *The New American Political System*, Washington, DC: American Enterprise Institute.

Kollman, K. (1998) *Outside Lobbying*, Princeton, NJ: Princeton University Press.

Olson, M. (1965) *The Logic of Collective Action*, Cambridge, MA: Harvard University Press.

Putnam, R.D. (1993) *Making Democracy Work*, Princeton, NJ: Princeton University Press.

—— (1995) 'Tuning In, Tuning Out: The Strange Disappearance of Social Capital in America', *PS* 28: 664–83.

Richardson, J.J. (ed.) (1982) *Policy Styles in Western Europe*, Boston: Allen and Unwin.

Richardson, J.J. and Jordon, A.G. (1979) *Governing Under Pressure*, Oxford: Martin.

Schattschneider, E.E. (1935) *Politics, Pressures, and the Tariff*, New York: Prentice-Hall.

Schlozman, K.L. and Tierney, J.T. (1986) *Organized Interests and American Democracy*, New York: Harper and Row.

Truman, D.B. (1951) *The Governmental Process: Political Interests and Public Opinion*, New York: Knopf.

Walker, J.L., Jr. (1991) *Mobilizing Interest Groups in America*, Ann Arbor, MI: University of Michigan Press.

West, D.M. and Loomis, B.A. (1999) *The Sound of Money: How Political Interests Get What They Want*, New York: Norton.

Wilson, F.L. (1987) *Interest-Group Politics in France*, New York: Cambridge University Press.

FRANK R. BAUMGARTNER

irredentism

The term 'irredentism' originally derived from the Italian concept of 'terra irredenta', meaning 'unredeemed land'. This idea of 'unredeemed', but potentially redeemable, land centrally informs most modern usages of the term. According to the standard definition irredentism is an attempt, or a desire, or a policy which is directed towards the restoration of a territory (or territories) which, it is claimed, are historically related to a given political unit (usually a nation-state) by reason of linguistic, ethnic or cultural belonging or some other national attachment. Put more simply, it refers to any attempt made by an existing nation-state, or group within it, to 'recover' or 'redeem' land and peoples that are considered to belong to it, and not to the state in which they are currently situated (see also NATIONS AND NATIONALISM).

The concept first appeared around 1878 when the Italian nationalist movement began to agitate for the recovery of *Italia irredenta*, territories like the Trentino, Trieste, Istria, Fiume, parts of Dalmatia, that were populated by Italian-speaking majorities but continued to remain under foreign, mostly Austrian, control even after Italian unification, which was largely completed by 1870–1. The demand that these Italian-speaking territories should become part of the new unified Italy was a source of fierce conflict during the latter half of the nineteenth century, and Italian demands were not satisfied until the First World War, when Italian intervention on the Allied side secured it Trieste, the Trentino and South Tirol.

Irredentism emerges therefore as a questioning of, and a challenge to, the established BOUNDARIES between existing nation-states, not as a challenge to the state itself. Consequently, it has to be distinguished from secessionism which generally demands the creation of a new state and, sometimes, the creation of new boundaries as well. From the perspective of democratic thought and practice, irredentism, at the abstract level, presents the type of paradox that democratic systems find extremely difficult to cope with; namely, it advances an absolutist claim that has some democratic credentials as well as some plausible democratic pretensions.

Irredentism emerges with the birth of the modern nation and the modern nation-state. It is in many ways simply a logical extension of nationalism. The modern nation constituted a new collectivity based on the totality of the people, not just the monarchy and aristocracy; on the emerging concept of popular SOVEREIGNTY and the notion, inherited from the French Revolution, that nations could be forged by revolutionary will, but also on the relatively new idea that nations and states were bounded entities with clearly delineated borders. In these circumstances, particularly given

that international boundaries were not just territorial markers but heavily symbolic of nationhood, it was almost inevitable that once clearly delineated frontiers (see POLITICAL FRONTIERS) were established they could be opened to challenge, especially in cases where the titular nationality in whom the new sovereignty resided was not entirely encompassed by such boundaries.

Thus, in its earliest manifestations in Italy, irredentism was simultaneously a populist intervention in the intensely contested and conflictual process of national unification and state boundary setting and an interrogative step in the equally conflictual process of nation-building. Small groups of nationalists had been agitating for the political unification of Italy since 1815, had fought for it unsuccessfully in the revolutionary year of 1848, and continued to fight for it in the 1850s and 1860s. Unification was finally achieved in part through the efforts and ambitions of the House of Savoy, which ruled the largest kingdom on the peninsula, Piedmont-Sardinia, but also through the efforts, amongst others, of Giuseppe Garibaldi and his followers, the Redshirts, who conquered southern Italy in 1860 and thus enabled the unification of north and south in the Kingdom of Italy in 1861. This process was largely completed with the conquest of Rome ten years later. The combined efforts of the House of Savoy and of popular insurrection thus brought most Italian-speaking territories within the same national boundaries, but crucially not all. This inevitably raised the question, 'Why these boundaries?', given that large numbers of Italian speakers remained subject to other powers and therefore existed in an ambiguous relationship to the 'national we' that was in the process of formation. National boundaries, the markers of a nation, that included some of that nation but not others did not make sense and invited challenge. In this respect, irredentism is merely the logical concomitant of nationhood: where there are boundaries there is logically always the possibility of interrogating them and it is quite likely that there is scarcely a country in the world that is not involved in some sort of irredentist quarrel with its neighbour(s) (although very few would admit to this; see below).

The difficulty, however, is that irredentist claims are based on sovereign assertions about entitlement or belonging and, consequently, rarely allow for much compromise once they are allowed to escalate. The most difficult cases to adjudicate seem to be irredentist claims that reflect a popular will towards union. A relatively recent example is the conflict that broke out when Nagorno-Karabakh, a majority Armenian territory in the former Soviet republic of Azerbaijan, sought by popular affirmation to become part of Armenia; a request that Armenia itself was happy to accede to but which was bitterly opposed by the Azeri government (and most of its people). The case of Kosovo, caught between Albania and Serbia, is an even more recent example. In such cases, the result generally is a vicious and bloody conflict, since the popular desire (or sovereign will) of one nation for greater union with the minority beyond its borders and/or for expanded territorial integrity clashes with the popular desire (sovereign will) of the other nation, or nations, in which this minority and its territory are situated. In such circumstances, where sovereign claims are held to be absolute, irredentism becomes a zero-sum game since no side can make its case 'more just' or more legitimate than the other except by asserting its supremacy through war.

Irredentism, when it appears as an instrument of government at the level of interstate relations, is only slightly less problematic. In these cases, irredentism generally (but not always) has less to do with popular will or ethnic affinities and a great deal more to do with territorial expansion or security issues, and boundary maintenance in particular. The long-standing irredentist claims against Russia (which Russia contests) episodically advanced by China (over the location of the Russo-Chinese border) and Japan (over the Kurile Islands) are examples. Irredentist claims of this sort, although they can and do lead to conflict, are less likely to escalate irretrievably, however,

partly because the threat of interstate war always seems more daunting and potentially costly than the risk of civil war, but mostly because international diplomacy and international law have sanctified international boundaries and state sovereignty and have gone some way to regularising interstate negotiations on such issues. Explicit, overt irredentism at the level of international relations therefore tends to attract international opprobrium.

Irredentism has not received much attention in the scholarly literature and is rarely addressed when the discussion turns to democracy and questions of democratic practice. This may well be because it is associated with EXTREMISM and unreasonableness, and because the concept itself has anachronistic implications that bring nineteenth-century IMPERIAL-ISM to mind. Certainly the term itself is now seldom used. This neglect is unfortunate. Irredentism is decidedly on the increase, particularly in the territories of the former Soviet Union and Eastern Europe, and, if for no other reason, therefore merits greater attention. Deeper study of irredentism would also enrich democratic theory and practice, however, precisely because it is a hard case and should not just be left to the students of crisis management and conflict resolution and because one suspects that irredentism can only be overcome and irredentist conflict avoided through genuine democratic respect for minority (and majority) rights (see RIGHTS, MINOR-ITY AND INDIGENOUS), PLURALISM and democratically inspired give-and-take.

See also:

extremism; imperialism; minorities; pluralism; revolutions; rights, minority and indigenous

Further reading

Chazan, N. (ed.) (1991) *Irredentism and International Politics*, Boulder, CO: Lynne Rienner.

RACHEL WALKER

J

judgement

The idea of democracy presupposes an account of political judgement, for without an understanding of how human beings are capable of making reasoned judgements about a shared public world, it would remain mysterious how one could conceive the very notion of a democratic citizen. Judgement has become a notable theme in contemporary political theory largely owing to the efforts of Hannah Arendt, who was inspired by her reading of Immanuel Kant's *Critique of Judgement* and tried to make his account of aesthetic judgement the basis of a political philosophy (Arendt 1982; Beiner 1983; Beiner 1997b). Arendt in her early version of Kant lectures hoped to draw the following from her politically charged reading of the third *Critique*. She states that the *Critique of Judgement* is where Kant's 'point of departure is the World and the senses and capabilities which [make] men (in the plural) fit to be inhabitants of it'. While she wondered if this was to be regarded as political philosophy she felt it was 'its *sine qua non*. If it could be found that in the capacities and regulative traffic and intercourse between men who are bound to each other by the common possession of a world (the earth) there exists an *a priori* principle, then it would be proved that man is essentially a political being' (Arendt 1982: 141–2). Here Arendt more or less announces the programme for a political philosophy of judgement drawn from Kant.

However, the attempt to reflect philosophically on what makes human beings capable of sizing up the 'ultimate particulars' that compose moral and political life and that present themselves for judgement goes all the way back to Aristotle's analysis of *phronesis*, practical wisdom, in Book 6 of the *Nicomachean Ethics*, and among contemporary theorists, a whole generation of neo-Aristotelian philosophers (for instance, McDowell 1979; MacIntyre 1984; Gadamer 1989; Beiner 1997a) have highlighted once again the importance of concretely situated practical judgement as central to the understanding of ethical and political life. The Aristotelian theme of practical wisdom is nicely encapsulated by Alasdair MacIntyre when he defines moral virtue in terms of a capacity for practical reasoning that 'is not manifested so much in the knowledge of a set of generalisations or maxims which may provide our practical inferences with major premises; its presence or absence rather appears in the kind of capacity for judgement' which, he states further, is possessed by the agent when selecting and applying to particular situations 'the relevant stack of maxims' (MacIntyre 1984: 223). In an important sense, reflection on the theme of judgement teaches us the limits of theory, for judgement (whether in ethical or political life) attends to particulars that are beyond the purview of theory as such. As Hans Jonas makes the point: 'there is no science of judgment . . . judgment as concerned with particulars is necessarily outside science and strictly the bridge between the abstractions of the understanding and the concreteness of life'. He goes on (again in reference to Aristotle) to state that the 'knowledge of use' is acquired differently from knowledge acquired from theory which is why Aristotle denied that there was a science of politics and practical ethics: 'the *where, when, to whom* . . . cannot be reduced to general principles. Thus there is theory and use of theory, but no theory of the use of theory' (Jonas 1982: 199). Or as Hans-Georg

Gadamer more succinctly puts it: 'There are no rules governing the reasonable use of rules' (Gadamer 1989: 121).

An account of political judgement that attempted to vindicate the capacities for judging and deliberating on the part of democratic citizens would be founded on the following three claims:

1 We are constantly making political judgements. In saying 'we', what is meant is not any particular group of specialists, or specially qualified persons, but ordinary people, that is, common citizens.
2 In making these judgements, we relate to (and at the same time constitute) an intersubjectively shared public world.
3 The active exercise of a faculty of political judgement is *good* for us as human beings. The corollary of this is that the shrinking of opportunities for active judgement, or the increasingly passive adherence to norms and beliefs within society, indicates a dislocation, or even pathology, within contemporary political life. This places the account of political judgement within the wider context of a theory of the human good. It also characterises reflection on political judgement as a point of departure for a more general political philosophy of CITIZENSHIP. The exercise of active judgement is good for us because citizenship in general is good for us. Citizenship is an important aspect of the human good, and, it follows, so is 'civic judgement', or the judging of public affairs 'as a citizen' (see CIVIC VIRTUE).

These claims, taken together, are both descriptive and normative. They tell us (descriptively) what it is to be a political being, and they tell us (normatively) what is desirable about being a political being. The exercise of judgement characterises both what we *are* and what we *ought to be*. This is the reason for saying that it presupposes (or serves to develop) an account of the human good, of what conduces to a proper or excellent human life.

In pursuing an argument, say between A and B, where the conflicting claims advanced

clearly refer to worldly, and therefore potentially intersubjective, phenomena (as opposed to matters of mere faith), either A's judgement is more comprehensive than B's, or B's judgement is more comprehensive than A's, or both views are one-sided and need to be encompassed within some third perspective that does justice to the truth in each. Moreover, the fact that we actually take up a particular stance in the discussion *already* commits us to the presumption that there is a truth of the matter (binding on all parties), that is, we think our own judgement is comprehensive, until we can be persuaded otherwise. Without the assumption of a practical truth that forms the object of practical reason, political judgement would be impossible *tout court*.

So it is hard to discern any grounds for denying that a resolution of the conflicting claims is *in principle* within reach. Only if our respective beliefs were matters of unshakeable faith would a resolution, in principle, be unavailable. The fact that each of the participants actually assumes that a resolution is, in principle, available is shown by the fact that each, in fact, holds fast to their respective opinions, entailing that the requisite resolution of the conflict is already at hand, viz., their own opinion. The implicit assumption is that if the other party came to a certain insight or overcame a certain blindness, they too would be converted to one's own, more comprehensive, belief. This means that each of the parties, despite their differences, already assumes that these matters are legitimately within the sphere of common judgement and amenable to common reason. Only someone who had no political opinions and offered no political judgements could coherently deny the claims of reason. (This is a variation of Jürgen Habermas's argument for communicative rationality: see Habermas (1980)) (see DEMOCRATIC DEBATE).

To make the argument a little more concrete, consider conflicting judgements about NATO's 1999 bombing campaign against Yugoslavia. On the one side, the view that this was a legitimate intervention on behalf of the victims of genocide rightly intended to compel the

Serbs to halt their ethnic cleansing of Albanian Kosovars; on the other side, the view that it was a misguided folly that, in violation of international law, infringed upon Yugoslav SOVEREIGNTY and only worsened the condition of the Kosovo Albanians. Let us consider what assumptions are shared by the two sides in this debate. Both parties assume that there is a truth of the matter here. Neither would so much as bother to articulate their position, or rather the grounds of their position, unless they thought that they had appreciated truths (or aspects of the truth) that the other side had undervalued or improperly weighted. Also both sides assume that rational argument is an appropriate way to cope with political differences. Both sides address themselves to those with similar political commitments as well as to partisans of the opposing side. The rendering of a judgement proceeds in the context of a *community* based on certain shared assumptions, or rather, the judgement brings into play a whole range of different communities of shared judgement, both universal and particular, embodying wider or narrower sets of shared assumptions. The purpose of communicating the judgement is to attempt to bridge these different communities. There are, of course, those who are not explicitly addressed in this debate (for example, those who actually support genocidal nationalism). But the crucial point is that the immediate contenders each address their political judgements both to those who share most of their political presuppositions, and to those who do not (fully) share these presuppositions. One articulates a set of political opinions not only to consolidate the views of those who already agree, but also to appeal to those who disagree to reconsider.

These are of course mainly truisms. Nonetheless, they run counter to the prevalent view that opposing political judgements are constituted by irreconcilable 'values', and that this opposition at the level of fundamental values cannot (in principle) be bridged by mere reason. Against this liberal ideology, it should be regarded as a matter of some considerable significance that actual participants in political discourse give the lie to this prevailing view, by the very fact of their participation in rational debate.

Political judgement, then, is a capacity whose exercise is ever-present, all around us, because politics is a realm that admits of intersubjectively binding truth claims. We participate in the worldliness of political relationships, and the faculty of political judgement is an unmistakable token of this worldliness. Judgements as such are *about* the world, and only for this reason is it possible for them to possess validity or lack validity (unless one posits a transcendental subjectivity that enables us to make universally binding claims without reference to the objective world, as Kant does in his theory of reflective judgement for aesthetic experience). In ordinary political discourse, moral–political judgements, whether of JUSTICE or of prudence, do not have status limited merely to the expression of privately held 'values', or an evaluative posture towards the world; rather, they will devolve upon factual judgements concerning states of affairs in the world: past, present and future.

It follows from such arguments that political judgement is the quintessential mode of relating to the world, because, as political beings, we *share* a world. If we start from this fact about our situation (namely, the fact that our subjectivity is grounded in intersubjectivity), we can perhaps go on to show the ways in which political identity is essential to our definition of ourselves (see IDENTITY, POLITICAL), and why citizenship is a crucial aspect of the human good. But this is an exceedingly ambitious argument to make, and certainly cannot be derived from formal considerations such as those presented above. If it can be shown (as I believe a full account of political judgement would seek to show) that the quality of our experience atrophies in proportion as we passively yield to the judgements of others and cede greater and greater dimensions of political responsibility (a process that is everywhere at work in modern liberal society), then we would have powerful reasons to believe that active citizenship is a major component of the human good. In actively rendering judgements upon our shared world, we at the same time resolve to comport ourselves *as citizens* (rather than as clients of the state, or as privatised consumers), and thereby affirm our own nature as political beings. To judge human affairs from the standpoint of the citizen is to acknowledge this aspect of the human good. Therefore, to inquire into the nature of political judgement is not a merely formal endeavour, but involves the assertion of substantive claims about the good for human beings.

See also:

communitarianism; decision-making; deliberative democracy; identity, political; responsibilities

Further reading

Arendt, H. (1968) 'The Crisis in Culture', in H. Arendt, *Between Past and Future: Eight Exercises in Political Thought*, New York: Viking Press.
—— (1982) *Lectures on Kant's Political Philosophy*, R. Beiner (ed.), Chicago: University of Chicago Press.
Beiner, R. (1983) *Political Judgment*, London: Methuen.
—— (1997a) 'Do We Need a Philosophical Ethics? Theory, Prudence, and the Primacy of *Ethos*', in R. Beiner, *Philosophy in a Time of Lost Spirit: Essays on Contemporary Theory*, Toronto: University of Toronto Press.
—— (1997b) 'Rereading Hannah Arendt's Kant Lectures', in R. Beiner, *Philosophy in a Time of Lost Spirit: Essays on Contemporary Theory*, Toronto: University of Toronto Press.
Bernstein, R.J. (1983) *Beyond Objectivism and Relativism: Science, Hermeneutics, and Praxis*, Philadelphia: University of Pennsylvania Press.
Cavell, S. (1976) 'Aesthetic Problems of Modern Philosophy', in S. Cavell, *Must We Mean What We Say?*, Cambridge: Cambridge University Press.
Clarke, P.B. (1980) 'Beyond the Banality of Evil', *British Journal of Political Science* 10: 417–39.
Fleischacker, S. (1999) *A Third Concept of Liberty: Judgment and Freedom in Kant and Adam Smith*, Princeton, NJ: Princeton University Press.
Gadamer, H.G. (1989) *Truth and Method*, 2nd rev. edn, trans. revised by J. Weinsheimer and D.G. Marshall, New York: Continuum, First Part: I and Second Part: II.2.
Habermas, J. (1980) 'On the German-Jewish Heritage', *Telos* 44: 127–31.
Jonas, H. (1982) 'The Practical Uses of Theory', in H. Jonas, *The Phenomenon of Life: Toward a Philosophical Biology*, Chicago: University of Chicago Press.
McDowell, J. (1979) 'Virtue and Reason', *The Monist* 62(3): 331–50.
MacIntyre, A. (1984) *After Virtue*, 2nd edn, Notre Dame, IN: University of Notre Dame Press, chaps 12 and 14–16.
Perelman, C. (1979) 'The Rational and the Reasonable', in T.F. Geraets (ed.), *Rationality To-day/La Rationalité aujourd'hui*, Ottawa: University of Ottawa Press.
Steinberger, P.J. (1993) *The Concept of Political Judgment*, Chicago: University of Chicago Press.

RONALD BEINER

judicial review

The use of a court, or an institution with similar characteristics, to check that legislation is compatible with a constitution started in the modern world with the American Revolution. Thus the US Supreme Court has been the model, more or less consciously, for many of the constitutions that include judicial review, mainly in the common law world, but in some cases even in countries following the continental European system of code law. Until the twentieth century, and largely until the postwar period, the US Supreme Court was the only significant example, though the Canadian Supreme Court played a weaker version of the same role after the passing of Canada's first constitution, the British North America Act in 1867. Similarly, the makers of the new constitution for the Commonwealth of Australia in 1900 endowed their High Court with limited powers of judicial review. In most of Europe however – and in this case, unusually, the United Kingdom was at one with its neighbours – constitutional doctrine so strongly supported the supremacy of either the executive or the legislature that the idea of another, unelected, branch of government being entitled to check the constitutionality of their actions was abhorrent. The reason that Britain, in giving Canada and Australia their independent constitutions, allowed limited judicial review when it did not do this, for example with New Zealand, points to a fundamental aspect of the system of constitutional overview by courts. Where a constitution divides AUTHORITY and power between two or more actors, there is an inescapable need for a body to adjudicate between them: conflicts over whose right it is to make some binding decision or launch some policy initiative are virtually inevitable. Thus Canada and Australia, as federal systems, required a constitutional mechanism to police the federal and state or provincial governments to ensure each kept within its constitutional boundaries, even though the doctrine of legislative supremacy originally held as strongly in those countries as in the UK itself. In contrast the unitary and very simple plan of New Zealand's constitution made no such requirement, and its courts have never had the power of judicial review.

In the last few decades constitutional courts have tended to be more visible carrying out other roles, and this has obscured the fundamental fact that they are, before anything else, mechanisms for this form of structural adjudication and development. There are overview courts which also enforce substantive limitations on legislation, usually via some form of bill of rights, but there are few important overview courts which have this duty without having the more fundamental structural role. (The Italian Constitutional Court is sometimes cited as an example of a court with no structural matters to decide, but even it has

to protect the Italian regions against the Rome government.) In contrast, courts with only the structural role have often been powerful and important for the DEMOCRATIC DEVELOPMENT of their systems. Even the slightest degree of regional devolution of legislative competence may require at least an approximation to judicial review. Thus devolution of some legislative power from Westminster to Scotland has meant that the Scotland Act 1998, in Clause 33 empowers the Advocate General, the Lord Advocate or the Attorney General to 'refer the question of whether a Bill or any provision of a Bill would be within the legislative competence of the Parliament to the Judicial Committee for decision'. The Privy Council here means the Judicial Committee of the Privy Council, which is the Law Lords sitting under different hats, and this clause therefore introduces judicial constitutional review of a kind into the British constitution for the first time in history. The UK has also recently given courts the power to impose human RIGHTS standards on public authorities, but although they may declare a statute incompatible with the Human Rights Act, this does not invalidate the act. The nearest the UK comes to orthodox judicial review arises again from a structural point; since 1973, the courts have had to recognise the supremacy of European Union legislation over Westminster statutes.

FEDERALISM is not the only structural aspect of constitutions which can require a review court in the constitution. Any constitutionally mandated distribution of powers to separate bodies requires the equivalent of judicial review. It was such a requirement, for example, which forced the drafters of the French Fifth Republican Constitution to abrogate a traditional ban, dating from the revolution, on courts having any constitutional interpretative powers, let alone the power to declare legislation unconstitutional. The writers of the Fifth Republic's constitution wished to severely limit the powers of parliament, and to allow the executive considerable legislative power via the issuing of decrees. But such a limitation of parliamentary competence could only be assured by the creation of the Conseil Constitu-tionel, with, at first rudimentary but later very extensive, powers of constitutional review.

The first important judicial review case in modern history, and still the most famous, was the US case of Marbury *v.* Madison in 1803, which illustrates at the very beginning much of the political as well as legal nature of judicial review. Traditionally, it has been though worthy of special note that the US Constitution does not actually grant the Supreme Court the right of judicial review, and Chief Justice Marshall's famous opinion in this case, where he announced the court must have such power, is seen as an assertion by the court itself of a power which it might not have made, with enormous impact for how American politics would have developed. In fact it is very difficult to see how the Supreme Court could for long have failed to develop such a power if the courts were to function effectively in a federal political system which also had a written out SEPARATION OF POWERS. As Marshall himself said, in his opinion, 'The question, whether an act, repugnant to the constitution, can become the law of the land, is a question deeply interesting to the United States but, happily, not of an intricacy proportioned to its interest'. Nor did Marshall invent the concept of judicial review for constitutionality; it had been used in a limited way for years by the English Privy Council when it reviewed the validity of colonial legislation *vis-à-vis* the colonial char-ters. At the time the constitution was written the delegates would have been aware of several instances of state court invalidation of state legislation as inconsistent with state constitu-tions. Nonetheless, the court did have to grant itself the power, though it was to be more than half a century before the Supreme Court was again to strike down a piece of federal legislation. Marbury was a restriction on the Federal Congress's right to legislate at all in a particular area, while the other crucial early American cases, all on structural matters, involved in the federal/state conflict, usually with the result of strengthening the central power against state AUTONOMY. It has often been argued that judicial review courts, being themselves part of the central government, are almost inevitably going to favour their own level of government. If this is so, it is an inevitability coming from political ambition or commitment, not from any logic of constitu-tional law. But what is true is the political views of the early members of such a court are crucial. In Australia, for example, it was the strong personal preference for states rights held by the first justices of the High Court that set a tradition in which federal power to this day is severely limited.

Constitutional lawyers have a refined voca-bulary to discuss constitutional review, most of which is unnecessary here. One distinction they make however is crucial because it can significantly affect the politics of the process, as well as the precise nature and effects of a nation's judicial review. The distinction is between 'abstract' or 'concrete' review. Ab-stract review allows some constitutionally identified actors to ask of a bill which has completed its parliamentary process but not yet been signed into law whether it is, in abstract, and without reference to any factual situation, unconstitutional. The Scotland Act mentioned above thus designates three law officers, the UK's Attorney General and Scotland's Lord Advocate and Advocate Gen-eral, to ask the Privy Council for abstract review, in this case whether or not a piece of Scottish legislation is outwith the Scottish Parliament's legitimate area of competence. Where abstract review powers exist, it is unconstitutional to complete the promulgation of any bill which fails the test of judicial review. Usually, once a bill has been legitimately promulgated, even if abstract review has not been sought at the time, it cannot later be questioned in this generalised or abstract manner.

The opposite, concrete review, in contrast, can only apply to a fully promulgated act of a legislature, and furthermore it cannot be triggered by a political actor calling the constitutionality of legislation into question. Instead, concrete review refers to a situation where, during the course of ordinary litigation before a court, the question is raised as to whether or not some piece of legislation which one or other party is relying on is in fact constitutionally valid. This form of constitutional review is the only way, for example, that a question of constitutionality can be raised before an American court. Concrete review for constitutionality is, in principle, just an extension of the general logic of law by which an agent cannot exceed powers granted to him to do his job; to act *ultra vires*, in legal jargon, always invalidates the act, whether it be a trustee's actions in civil law or a public official granted powers under a statute or ordinance. Judicial review in this sense applies in most jurisdictions. In the UK, for example, challenges to administrative action on the grounds that the official is acting *ultra vires* is specifically called 'judicial review'. The difference between judicial review in the UK and the USA is that the former does not regard the parliament as receiving its powers from a logically prior constitution, and thus parliament itself cannot be said to act *ultra vires*.

Although it is possible for a legal system to have both forms of judicial review, it is more common for one or the other to be chosen according to how either fits into the political culture and legal history of the system. Thus while US and Australian courts are restricted to concrete review in the context of actual litigation, in France only abstract review before the Conseil Constitutionel is permitted. In France an act successfully passed cannot again be referred to the Conseil Constitutionel, and all other courts are prohibited, as they have always been, from even entertaining a question of the constitutionality of legislation. One can only assume, though it is not stated in the Scotland Act, that once an act of the Scottish parliament has received the Royal Assent, no court in the UK would regard themselves as having the power to decide a case before them on the grounds that one party to the case was relying on a legislative clause which did exceed the competence of that parliament.

There are, as we have said, systems which allow both forms of judicial review, but as in the most famous case, that of Germany, the political context is usually one where it was of paramount importance to demonstrate that the political system was doing everything conceivable to ensure the rule of law and to limit executive and legislative action strictly to what was envisaged by the constitution makers. Thus the German constitution has abstract review which can be triggered not only by various officers of state but even by opposition parliamentarians, but it also has concrete review triggered by the ordinary courts during litigation, and yet a third form of judicial review, known as a 'constitutional complaint' whereby citizens can directly challenge administrative action before the Constitutional Court.

The problems of judicial review, both theoretical and in terms of daily political conflict, tend to come less from the structural aspect as from the power of review courts to impose substantive values on the political actors. Such powers mainly come about where courts have to apply a Bill of Rights or equivalent whereby fundamental rights are protected from statutory restriction. The problem is that rights-protecting documents by their very nature are imprecise; rights are described very generally and often very briefly. To the extent that a constitution recognises any restrictions on the exercise of rights, and might allow some legislative interference, the terms on which such interference is to be permitted are themselves not spelled out with precision or detail. Thus, at the very best, a judicial review court is faced with a major task of interpretation in deciding whether a detailed clause in some modern statute does or does not abridge a protected right. In some cases there is no Bill of Rights text at all. The French Conseil Constitutionel, for example, has to decide whether legislation abridges the 'fundamental principles recognised by the laws of the Republic'; and used this to protect the FREE-DOM to form citizen organisations by reference to an ordinary law of 1901 which was held to enshrine the relevant right. In Australia, where the constitution contains no Bill of Rights, the High Court has struck down legislative restrictions on political advertising during election campaigns on the grounds that the very structure of the Commonwealth of Australia's constitution, being based on competitive party democracy, requires maximum protection of a 'right to free speech' which is nowhere mentioned in the text.

Constitutional courts vary enormously in how strongly they will protect rights in this way, but their actions are almost always controversial, because they can be seen as essentially counter-majoritarian. Thus probably a majority of American citizens would like to have prayers said in schools, and almost certainly a strong majority think the courts are over protective of criminals caught up in the criminal justice system. The political conflict can be even worse where a court has to intervene, often because elected politicians dare not do so, to protect what they decide is a constitutional right which itself is a source of intense conflict in society. Thus there is probably no ruling the US Supreme Court could give on the issue of abortion which would be acceptable to most Americans. But the American Supreme Court's decision on abortion is a prime example of what extreme interpretative freedom a constitutional court has in exercising judicial review. The US Constitution makes no mention at all of abortion, nor does it anywhere even mention a right to privacy, which is how the court derived its abortion ruling. Instead, the Supreme Court created these rights and then enforced them. It can be argued they had no choice, because they have to modernise an eighteenth-century document if they are to act at all. However, modernisation involves not only huge moral judgements, but often highly detailed technical decisions, which it is often argued by opponents of activist courts, they are nowhere near competent to handle. US courts, in deciding whether prison conditions breach the constitutional ban on 'cruel and unusual punishment', have, for example, even gone so far as to regulate the wattage of electric bulbs in prison cells.

See also:

constitutionalism; justice

DAVID ROBERTSON

judiciary

Most accounts of political systems, whether constitutional or political science in orientation, agree on regarding the judiciary as an identifiably different branch of the government machine. Most democratic systems claim to grant the judiciary some form of separation of power status (see SEPARATION OF POWERS), though what this means is often unclear, and may amount to no more than the idea that the government will not meddle with the activities of courts, nor seek to influence the outcome of trials. In fact, political science treatments of the judiciary in most countries do not grant them much political importance at all. This may be understandable in those countries that do not have a constitutional doctrine of judicial review, but in fact it runs the risk of underestimating the power of courts by misunderstanding the nature of judicial influence. Much of the power of the judiciary, even in countries which do accept judicial review, comes not from exercising that formal power, but through the power of statutory interpretation and through the exercise of public law roles. This latter phrase covers the basic situation where the state is in conflict with a citizen as a party to litigation. To understand either of these sources of judicial power properly requires a basic grasp of the crucial difference between the two 'legal families' of modern democracies, the common law countries and the code law, or 'civil law' states.

Common law countries are those which owe the origins of their legal system to England as a result of English imperial and colonial influence, and include not only obvious examples like North America and the old 'White Commonwealth', but much of Asia and the Caribbean states. In this system, the idea of judge-made law was completely accepted until relatively recently in these countries' legal histories, and still remains acceptable although there is a tendency on the part both of politicians and judges to gloss over it and pretend that judges have become merely automatic appliers of a fixed body of law. To the extent that parliamentary legislation has replaced large areas of common law precedent with broad statutes this gloss has become more nearly true, and the subject matter of the majority of cases before courts in common law countries will be a statute or executive ordinance. There remain major areas of social and economic life however which are primarily governed by precedent based common law rules, openly changed and developed by the judiciary. Where statutes do govern, the ability of courts to interpret the often very vague language of parliamentary draughtsmen, and the need for them to extend legislative coverage to include unthought-of eventualities and generally avoid lacunae in legislative foresight, ensures a real continued importance to the judiciary as creators of binding law. It is sometimes argued that, except on questions of a constitutional interpretation by a judicial review court, it is always open to a country's legislature to undo a judicial interpretation they dislike. While this is theoretically true, overworked modern parliaments with crowded agendas are in practice unlikely to act in such a way, and courts can and do frequently bend the original parliament intent to blunt policy changes they dislike. The Court of Appeal in England, for example, is widely thought to have weakened the protection of TRADES UNIONS in industrial relations law passed by Labour governments throughout the 1970s.

A feature common to most common law jurisdictions has been the absence of a specialised system of public law courts to deal directly with conflicts between the citizen and the state, such as exists almost universally in code law countries. In England, and to a lesser extent in most common law jurisdictions, such conflicts are governed by the ordinary law, frequently common law, and are dealt with in ordinary courts. It is here that the judiciary of the common law world has, perhaps, most clearly been weaker in defence of democratic values than they might have been. Because the restraints on administrative action have followed the general thrust of the common law, and because it has been largely up to the judges themselves to design the legal instruments that

might have restrained government, the relative weakness of civil rights protections in such systems can fairly be blamed on the judiciary. For various reasons, some of them being a recognition of the politically weaker status of an unelected branch compared with an executive controlled by an elected parliament, English courts have for long time been decidedly pro administration in such conflicts. It is, for example, almost impossible for a citizen to win a case alleging negligence by a local authority or police force in the carrying out of their statutory duties. Very few immigration appeals or appeals against prison conditions ever succeed in English courts. It is in part to remedy this tendency of the courts always to support the administration that the Labour government elected in 1997 passed the Human Rights Act, which may result in a much more Continental European judicial orientation.

One fundamental reason for this tendency of English judges to apply common law doctrines in a pro-administration way stems from a structural difference in the legal professions of the common law and code law countries. The judiciary in nearly all common law countries is selected from amongst practising advocates relatively late in a person's legal career. Thus a common law judge deciding a case between a government department and an aggrieved citizen will probably have been a highly successful commercial advocate with no experience at all of government administration, and relatively little experience even of public law cases either as advocate or judge. He or she will, in England at least, have come from a very small elite profession – the 200 or so senior judges are drawn from the more successful ranks of only some 5,000 practising barristers – and may well sympathise with what he or she sees as another hard-pressed elite, the upper levels of the CIVIL SERVICE. Such a judge is neither professionally nor personally attuned to the need for a critical stance against administration. Although other countries are not quite so extreme in the insulation of their judiciary – American judges and even Australian judges may well have political experience, for example – it is still true that 'judging' is something one comes to after establishing oneself as a successful general advocate. This career route has inevitably meant, at least in the past, that the judiciary in common law countries is male, middle-aged and dominated by whatever is the racial or ethnic majority of that country's upper classes. Even without the conservative tendencies that legal training tends to reinforce through socialisation, such a judicial corps will have a pro-order orientation, albeit usually an unconscious one.

As a rough generalisation, therefore, the judiciary in the common law world have used their extensive powers of common law development and statutory interpretation to mould law in a conservative and property regarding manner in private law, and to protect administrative action against citizen complaint in the public law domain. They have tended also to be highly insulated and inwardly directed. University training came late for the common law world, with law being seen much more as something to be learned as an apprentice at the feet of legal masters. Even today, it is relatively rare for legal academics to be cited in judicial argument and they could never be appointed to the bench in England, and only rarely in other common law jurisdictions. Indeed, many of the more successful advocates and senior judges are not law graduates at all.

Code law countries differ in all of these respects. The very idea that law must be codified, that detailed and explicit rules can and should be drafted by legislatures to cover every eventuality and conceived as an organic whole for each area of life, runs directly against any legitimacy of judicial creativity. Indeed the historic origins of the final appeals court in France, whose Napoleonic regime it was which gave continental Europe its code law tradition, demonstrates this. The Cour de Cassation in France was originally conceived of as a committee of the legislature to which issues which the courts continually found difficult could be referred to for a final interpretation, on the grounds that the courts themselves had no right to be making the substantive value judgements such resolution implied. Though

this format did not outlast the revolution by more than thirty years or so, the spirit survives. French courts, and to a large extent other continental courts, are much more clearly forbidden to legislate.

Inevitably, codes have to be interpreted, and interpretation must allow some room for discretion. But new rules are not created by the development of precedents even then. Precedents have no binding force, though they may be cited. Typically in a French court the precedents, described as *la jurisprudence*, will be cited along with academic writings, which count at least equally, as a way of throwing light on the best technical solution to an interpretative problem, but that solution is a solution only to the specific problem facing the court that day. No future court is bound to decide a similar case in the same way. Even when an appeal court overrules a lower court it does not assert what the 'correct answer' is, it simply invalidates the decision in question and sends it back to a different court at the previous level. That second court is not even prevented from deciding as did the first. The whole stress then is on the sanctity of the code, and the role of the judge as a legal technician.

One interesting demonstration of this is in the form of opinion. Common law courts publish lengthy discursive opinions justifying their decisions and canvassing wide ranges of alternate legal theories. Even in a case where the judges of an appeal court have agreed, they may all publish their own reasons for thinking as they do. It is these lengthy and sometimes rival opinions which are the material of the law, allowing creative counsel to help in shape the real meaning even of a statute. In contrast, most code law courts publish short collective opinions, running only to a few paragraphs, which do little more than state the facts and the relevant article of the code. There is thus no material out of which rules of law independent of the legislature can be constructed.

This difference in curial behaviour is in large part a consequence of the professional nature of the judiciary. Continental judges are all graduates of university law departments who opt at the beginning of their careers to be judges rather than advocates. They go on to professional judicial training, and then work their way up a typical administrative career ladder from junior to senior judicial appointments. They are, in many ways, just another branch of the nation's civil service, and thus develop much more of an autonomous but statist outlook. This may be advantageous from the point of view of not distorting the 'will of parliament', but could be extremely dangerous in cases of state–citizen conflict. However the other politically important difference between the common law and code law jurisdictions is the presence in the latter of a quite separate hierarchy of public law (often called administrative law) courts, with their own specialised judiciary. These administrative law courts, again usually modelled on the French Conseil d'Etat and its lower court structure, have historically been far tougher on governments, far more critical of administrative incompetence or misuse of power, than have the ordinary courts in common law countries.

Powerful legal doctrines have been developed in such courts, notably the ideas of PROPORTIONALITY, which have allowed the administrative courts to control illegal action by governments. Proportionality – there is no equivalent doctrine in the common law – means that a state official can be censured for actions which are not illegal, but where he or she has acted unfairly or irrationally in being more heavy-handed than the law is thought really to have intended. In a common law country, such an official will not be stopped unless he or she literally does not have the legal authority to do what was done; on the continent, he or she may be stopped because no sensible or administratively sensitive person would have used the powers in that way. Though only one example, this may give the flavour of how a professionally dedicated judicial hierarchy can protect citizens. It comes at the cost however, of an approach to the judicial role, which in every other way, stymies any legitimate judicial creativity. It is unclear whether one can have some amalgam of the common law and code law judicial systems.

See also:

civil service; law, rule of; legislative process

DAVID ROBERTSON

justice

The concept of justice, accurately characterised by John Rawls (1972: 3) as 'the first virtue of social institutions', is of ancient provenance; it may be traced back to Classical Greece. This entry proposes to examine the concepts of corrective and distributive justice introduced by Aristotle (1934: V.ii. 12ff) in the context of the modern democratic polity. While corrective justice remains within the province of courts and other adjudicators, distributive justice is primarily a matter for polities and is therefore a pressing matter for political philosophers and social theorists. It will be concluded that there is little dispute regarding the conditions necessary for corrective justice to be efficiently delivered; however controversy surrounds the conditions for distributive justice.

John Finnis (1980: 161ff) helpfully points out that the concept of justice embraces three elements. The first of these, 'other-directedness', describes the factual circumstances in which justice may arise. One can only meaningfully speak of justice when one person, or group of persons, acts towards another individual or group. Second, he argues that justice arises in the context of one individual or group having a moral duty towards another. While it is clear that one acts virtuously when one makes, for example, a supererogatory donation to charity, it is by no means clear that such is necessarily an act of justice. Justice implies, as Aristotle pointed out, either an act of 'paying back' (or corrective justice) or delivering up a person's desert, which he termed 'distributive justice'. This, then, is the moral context of justice; the fulfilment of an obligation. Finally, Finnis follows Aristotle in pointing out that to treat justly is to, at least in some respect, treat with EQUALITY. This is the substantive moral content of justice, and it leads to the *prima facie* greatest difficulties in explicating the concept. It is by no means clear what it means to treat persons equally; it would not be said that I had treated my two children equally if I divided a single dose of a life-sustaining medicine between my healthy child and those of my daughters suffering from a fatal disease. This difficulty falls away, however, when one notices that Aristotle observes that to treat equally, or justly, is to treat like cases alike and unlike cases differently, and to treat unlike cases differently in proportion to their degree of dissimilarity. This latter notion is well set out by Ronald Dworkin when he contrasts equal treatment and treatment as an equal (Dworkin 1978: 227). To impose equal treatment is to treat cases, which may well be unlike, as identical; while to treat persons as equals is to pay attention to their differences in situation. One may summarise by saying that one does justice when one treats all relevant people, that is those towards whom one has a duty, with equal concern and respect.

The principle of 'paying back' or corrective justice remains relatively simple in terms of treating the wronged party as an equal; he or she should have their loss, in whatever form it was sustained, paid back. The difficulties with this principle were seen even in Aristotle's day, when it was conceded that a cash pay-back might have to suffice. In terms of distributive justice, the principle is more complex because there is a choice of substantive moral theories upon which one can base desert or entitlement. The conflict between these underlying moral theories deserves further consideration.

Turning first to corrective justice, and examining one of the most minimal theories of justice set out by modern writers, that of Robert Nozick (1974), it can be seen that even his 'minimal state' must have a well-developed system of corrective justice. Nozick argues that people are born with a set of historical entitlements to property and that the only transactions that are morally permissible are those which are voluntarily made. Nozick believes that the state is justified only when it is limited to the narrow function of providing protection against force and theft, and providing remedies for those wrongs, and in acting to enforce contracts or the payment of damages for their breach. His minimal state has no place for the distribution or redistribution of goods. What would be the form of the rules for 'pure' corrective justice? Joseph Raz (1977) gives a lucid account of the rule of law (see LAW, RULE OF), and this account may be adopted and adapted to give a corrective justice code. First, there are a number of rules which should apply to legislative provisions or the binding norms contained in the common law. The provisions of the law should be open to all to inspect, for a secret law cannot bind parties because they cannot know what it is that they are supposed to do. The rules of law should be prospective rather than retrospective, because a law which does not exist at the time of action cannot guide or bind the actors. The law must be clear, unambiguous and easily understood. These formal provisions also include the requirement for relative stability in the law. A law which is too frequently changed is unlikely, for practical reasons, to meet the other formal requirements. Furthermore a constantly shifting legal order or collection of norms is likely to be inefficient because human affairs, especially in modern complex society, require planning, and constant legal revision may negate the best laid plans. Second, a rule of law for pure corrective justice requires that the authoritative lawmaker be unambiguously identified and bound by a set of procedural requirements which conform to the same formal rules that are imposed upon primary, or directly effective, legislation. Third, there must be a set of constitutional arrangements which guarantee that an independent JUDICIARY may review directly effective norms to ensure that they comply with the formal rules and that the process by which the legislation was made is formally correct. Such a process of JUDICIAL REVIEW would perhaps resemble the US model of constitutional review more closely than the English model with its highly developed notion of parliamentary SOVEREIGNTY. However, a fourth principle which grants the judiciary power to review the practical implementation and enforcement of legal norms by administrators and functionaries corresponds very closely to the power of judicial review possessed by both English and US courts. Power, when administered by functionaries, must be exercised lawfully. A simple example seems necessary here to show that these corrective justice rules are not straying into some other realm which, for example, Nozick would consider inappropriate.

Consider the contracts for sale of a relatively dangerous flammable substance such as motor fuel. Millions of such transactions are concluded every day. It is clearly impossible for consumers to check for themselves that they are receiving exactly the amount of fuel for which they have contracted; so to do would be enormously time-consuming and inevitably dangerous. A Nozickian minimal legislature could legitimately provide that fuel should be sold in aliquots of one litre, which should be accurately measured to within plus or minus 1 per cent. The legislature could further provide that there should be trading standards officers paid for by a levy upon buyers and sellers of fuel so as to enforce the norm. This rule would be to the advantage of both buyers and sellers because it would prevent both under- and over-delivery. Both the substantive provisions of the fuel law and its process of promulgation would be subject to judicial review according to the standards set out. Furthermore, according to these rules, trading standards officers would themselves be liable to judicial review if, for example, they sought to impose accuracy limits of half of 1 per cent. The question arises as to why this action for the failure of an errant, overzealous trading standards officer could not be accomplished using the ordinary principles of contract law, which is to say the private law which operates between parties which does not require either legislation nor the intervention of the regulatory agencies of the state. The answer seems to be that the reason why public officials need to be kept under control is that we can never be sure that we have satisfied all those whom they have wronged. Furthermore, the loss of confidence in the fuel-selling system is itself a harm which may be done to consumers.

For corrective justice to be efficient requires, fifthly, that there be ready access to the courts. However, it seems to be the sixth element of the proposed code for corrective justice which is the most important. For any system of adjudication to be considered just, it must be ensured that the parties come to the court on fair and equal terms. The judges must be free from bias, either real or (to ensure that confidence is maintained in the adjudicatory system) perceived. Rules of evidence and discovery must themselves respect the formal requirements of justice as set out above. Parties must have notice of the hearing and must be able to take part in it.

A problem now seems to confront those writers who wish to convince us that a pure system of corrective justice is sufficient or desirable. For a party to engage in a legal or administrative procedure to vindicate their RIGHTS, they must have sufficient knowledge of their rights and competence in the procedure. Nozick might well reply, at least in the sphere of contract law, that if a party is foolish enough to enter the game without being able to comply with the rules, that is their own fault. It is wrong to expect prudent citizens to bail out imprudent ones. The problem is that sometimes citizens 'enter the game' involuntarily. Imagine a situation in which a person recognising him or herself as lacking the higher social competencies agrees with a number of better-endowed citizens to sweep the streets outside their houses in exchange for a fee. One of these citizens reverses a motorcar into our sweeper and causes injury. Suppose then that our sweeper was unaware of the availability of legal services insurance, being unable to read the forms. Our rich citizen, having the benefit of a good EDUCATION, is able to persuade the sweeper to accept inadequate compensation. The sweeper becomes incapable of work. Nozick might pithily suggest that this is simply tough. The problem seems to be that even a basic system of pure corrective justice seems, if left unchecked, could lead into a descending spiral of social decay. If a high proportion of our street-sweepers become maimed and drop out of society, then we shall all be obliged to sweep our own portion of the pavement, taking away our opportunities to engage in higher pursuits. The physician's time is taken up with street-sweeping, drain-clearing, tree-felling and dustbin-emptying, and he or she becomes unable to keep up with the most recent literature on the specialism, he or she earns less money and so is required to spend more time on chores.

One way out of this is to introduce a modest scheme of distributive justice such as that proposed by John Rawls (1972: 60ff). Rawls proposes a scheme which he suggests is one with which all rational people, subject to certain conditions, would agree. Rawls suggests that if a debate could be conducted behind a 'veil of ignorance' where the participants, all being rational people, were unaware of the position they would subsequently hold, two principles of distributive justice would be agreed. Firstly, society should guarantee to all individual citizens the maximum FREEDOM possible consistent with similar freedom being available to all. Secondly, where derogations are made to the principle of equal treatment, these derogations should be to the benefit of the least well-off. Clearly this avoids the iniquities of the 'pure corrective justice'-driven race to the bottom of the spiral, because it allows for the public provision of, at least, legal services to those unable to provide them for themselves. In reality, it is likely to provide very much more, because in order to be able to take advantage of legal services one needs at least a basic level of education, security and health. Certainly such a system would fulfil the requirement that people be treated as equals, because, like the sick child, those who needed help would receive it and those who, like the healthy child, did not need assistance would be denied it. The problem with Rawls's suggestion is that it seems to provide no more than a 'rotating safety net' at the bottom of society to pick up first one group and then another who become successively the least well-off. While it may be that much of the recent political rhetoric about the 'dependency culture' is driven by self-righteousness and a populist desire to reduce taxation and public expenditure, there is no doubt that there is little of justice, fairness or equality in a life spent bumping along the bottom, and it is suggested that a more robust conception of distributive justice is one which provides people with the opportunities and means to forge their own plans of life.

Dispositional AUTONOMY, the capacity to choose one valuable plan of life from amongst a range of valuable and viable alternatives is the foundation of Joseph Raz's theory of distributive justice (1986: 369ff). He argues that the state ought to provide citizens with the wherewithal and the opportunities to choose a mode and a plan of life commensurate with their own values from amongst a number of alternatives. Raz recognises that what seems attractive and valuable to one person is unappealing and worthless to another; certainly democratic polities reflect value plurality. Furthermore, his formulation fulfils the requirement that people should be treated as equals for, if one person wishes to attend law school and another music school, it would not be treating them as equals to oblige both to enter the law faculty. However, it could be argued that even Raz's formulation of distributive justice fails fully to do justice.

There are two ways in which it seems to fall short. Firstly, it requires only that people be given their own existing choice between a range of valuable alternatives. Suppose that their vision is so blinkered by their experiences that they cannot appreciate all the possibilities which might lie before them. Suppose that a ten-year-old boy knows that all the boys who have lived in his street for the past fifteen years have worked in the leather works, the brewery or the car factory; how is he to appreciate the possibility of becoming an architect? Consider the girl who knows that girls become nurses or secretaries or leave school, marry within a short time, have children and abandon paid work as a career. It does not seem that a polity in which these things happen routinely fully respects the ideal of perfect distributive justice. These examples, however, only go halfway towards illustrating the seeming shortcomings of Joseph Raz's conception of distributive justice. Some people are born into positions, or circumstances develop, such that they are able go on to invent or discover whole new sets of possibilities of valuable life-plans for themselves or others. It is beyond doubt that there are many people who have the necessary physical and mental capacities, but these wither through lack of the opportunities to develop them; we have no a priori mechanism for determining which people will have those capacities.

At its most grand or, as a critic might say, grandiose, it could be said that a polity, whether national, regional or global, which fails to grant to each of its citizens the positive right to develop and revise their own plan of life even to the point of novelty, fails fully to implement the ideal of distributive justice. How, then, could the polity approach a more virtuous condition? To remind ourselves, the element of justice which seems to give the space to create the moral virtue is that to be found in the expanded notion of equality; the treatment of others as equals. In the course of this analysis it has been seen, but not hitherto expressed, that corrective justice deals with harms or infringements of negative freedom; a person's right to be free from harm (Berlin 1969). Even a breach of contract can be seen in this light, because when one enters a contract one does so in the expectation that the desired good will be delivered. Distributive justice seems to be fundamentally concerned with positive rights or entitlements. Unless polities establish constitutional arrangements which grant substantive positive rights, enforceable through the courts using the ordinary rules of law, it remains unlikely that justice will in fact be done.

See also:

equality; judiciary; law, rule of

Further reading

Aristotle (1934) *Nichomachean Ethics*, trans. H. Rackham, London: Heinemann.

Berlin, I. (1969) 'Two Concepts of Liberty', in I. Berlin, *Four Essays on Liberty*, Oxford: Oxford University Press.
Dworkin, R.M. (1978) *Taking Rights Seriously*, London: Duckworth.
Finnis, J. (1980) *Natural Law and Natural Rights*, Oxford: Clarendon.
Nozick, R. (1974) *Anarchy, State, and Utopia*, Oxford: Basil Blackwell.
Rawls, J. (1972) *A Theory of Justice*, Oxford: Oxford University Press.
Raz, J. (1977) 'The Rule of Law and its Virtue', *Law Quarterly Review* 93: 195–211.
—— (1986) *The Morality of Freedom*, Oxford: Clarendon.

R.A. WATT

justiciable norms

A norm is simply an ought-statement. 'Xs *ought to* Φ' is a simple general form of an ought-statement, but it is a very long way short of a justiciable norm. It needs further specification. This entry is an attempt to define and specify the conditions under which a norm becomes justiciable. The general norm statement is progressively refined such that it becomes, in the end, justiciable. Finally, a general definition of a justiciable norm is provided.

A justiciable norm must ultimately refer to action rather than to, for example, emotion or belief. 'Husbands' (as a variety of Xs) '*ought to* love their respective wives' (where 'love their respective wives' is a variety of Φ) is not a potentially justiciable norm; neither is 'Christians *ought to* believe the Bible'. Potentially justiciable norms dealing with related subject matters are, 'Husbands *ought to* buy their respective wives chocolates' and; 'Christians *ought to* attend church each Sunday'. For the avoidance of doubt, the action referred to must be either (at least) potentially voluntary human action, or be dependent upon voluntary human action either for its impetus or moderation. 'Waves *ought to* break on the groyne' is not a normative statement for, as King Cnut showed, the sea does not obey human norms. The statement is either positive, it describes what the waves, in fact, do, or it is predictive; it describes what the waves will generally or always do. The related normative statement is of the form 'Statutory Sea Defence Authorities *ought to* build groynes to break the force of the waves'. Thus norms which refer to action are relevant norms. (For a full analysis of the relationship between norms and reasons for action, see Raz (1990).)

Secondly, in order to be justiciable a norm must be recognised by a system which is capable of altering the legal position of either X or the maker of the norm. For example, suppose that the hierarchy of the church recognised the norm, 'Christians (Xs) *ought to* attend church each Sunday' and took the view that denial of the sacraments was an appropriate penalty for failing to comply with the norm, it would then be, at least, a potentially justiciable norm. This feature of a justiciable norm was pointed out by H.L.A. Hart and distinguishes his theory of positive law from other earlier theories (Hart 1961: 77ff). Clearly such a justiciable norm does not have to be unique to a legal system, for example, when dealing with the 'Christians *ought to* attend church each Sunday' norm, Muslims may well have a similar rule *mutatis mutandis*. Furthermore, the identical norm may well be common to a number of overlapping legal systems and apply within them all. One could imagine that the norm, 'Statutory Sea Defence Authorities *ought to* build groynes to break the force of the waves' could apply within both the English domestic legal order and within the legal order of the European Union. Similarly, one can propose norms which are justiciable to apply only in the dominant or subservient parts of a composite legal system. For example, while both the Church of England and the English state recognise the norm 'People *ought (not) to* murder another', it is not regarded as justiciable by the Church, but it is by the state; and conversely 'Christians *ought to* attend church each Sunday' could be regarded by the Church as justiciable and be ignored by the state for reasons set out below.

Thirdly, in order for a norm to be justiciable, there needs to be some practicable means by which a challenge to the norm can be mounted. This means more than the provision of ready access to the appropriate forum for challenging the norm, such as a court, tribunal or other adjudicator. Clearly this is a necessary prerequisite for justiciability, but it is not sufficient. Given that a competent adjudicator is available, there are in principle three forms of challenge to the norm. If the norm is of the general form 'Xs *ought to* Φ', a challenger can mount a subject-based challenge – 'I am not an X, therefore the norm does not apply to me' – or an action-based challenge – 'What I did was not Φ, therefore the norm is not applicable in this situation' – or, thirdly, a challenge to the validity of the norm. Here the author departs from Kelsen's use of the word 'validity' (Kelsen 1965, 1990). The present use of the term will be set out below. Harris comments that validity, for Kelsen, 'denotes both system-membership and bindingness' (Harris 1997: 77). The term 'validity' is used in place of the clumsy 'bindingness'.

In practical, everyday legal disputes over norms, the courts are usually asked to adjudicate upon disputes about applicability. Common examples of such disputes are implied in the following fragments: 'I do not take the money', 'D lacked the *mens rea* for murder'. Applicability tests have, at least in recent years, tended to become much more complex and have included challenges to norms on the basis that they breach other embedded norms of PROPORTIONALITY or DUE PROCESS; these challenges will be discussed in the context of disputes over validity. Disputes about applicability are essentially factual disputes about the norm and contain a clear acceptance on either side of the dispute that the norm is applicable in appropriate circumstances. In this sense, all relevant norms which are recognised by a legal system and which fall to be adjudicated are justiciable norms.

The more complex, and thus more interesting, challenge to a norm is to its validity, and here a number of problems arise. Not all norms that are recognised by a system are justiciable with regard to their validity; some norms may be absolute. The most obvious absolute norm is the fundamental norm of the political constitution. In its most general form, this reads: 'All members of this political community *ought to* obey the subordinate norms made by the authentic political sovereign of this community, provided that they have been promulgated in accordance with the procedural requirements binding upon the sovereign and do not breach the political constraints placed upon it.' To illustrate the point made in this and the two preceding paragraphs, this norm will be analysed with respect to challenge on its applicability and its validity. Firstly, a challenge could arise with regard to whether an illegal immigrant (as a putative X) was subject to the laws regarding matrimony which cover all nationals. If nationals are permitted one spouse, and if they exceed this number are subject to prosecution for bigamy, does the law apply to Q who has three spouses? Secondly, the bigamy law itself could be challenged on the ground that the sovereign legislature failed properly to comply with its own formal or procedural rules and thus breached. What could not be challenged within the courts (or other part of the adjudicatory system) is the power of the sovereign to make laws according to the rules that bind authentic Xs. Thus an absolute norm is a member of the system of norms and, since it is always legally valid, non-justiciable. The supreme political sovereign is, of course, subject in a democratic polity to political challenge by the opposition PARTIES in the legislature, by the press and other public opinion, and ultimately via an election. In other political systems, the challenge could be mounted by way of insurrection and the replacement of the political sovereign.

A related problem arises when governments take controversial political decisions within the formal or procedural rules which form part of the basic norm, but which offend some part of the polity because of the substance of the norm under review. Such instances might well be described as 'political decisions', although a more accurate general description might well be 'expert decisions'. Suppose that a norm subordinate to the basic norm was promulgated to allow the polity to arm itself with nuclear weapons as a means of defence. A body of citizens hostile to nuclear weapons might then challenge the norm, saying that such weapons are ineffective as a deterrent or unusable or just plain inhuman. Courts often declare such challenges non-justiciable because they are matters within the political competence of the state. Typically, then, absolute foundational norms contain an area of discretion within which the state cannot be challenged; however the breadth of this basic norm may itself be subject to challenge. Perhaps the most famous example of such a challenge happened occurred in the 1980s in the United Kingdom when the government used an executive order, which it claimed fell within the penumbra of the foundational norm, to ban TRADES UNIONS at an intelligence-gathering establishment. The courts accepted that the breadth of the norm could be explored, but maintained that the substance of the executive order was non-justiciable because it fell within the confines of national security. The court used the opportunity to draw up a list of subjects where it would deny itself jurisdiction and thus declared the norms non-justiciable. The list included matters of the right of the executive to call a general election before the allotted time, the exercise of the prerogative of mercy, the setting of economic policy and treaty-making power. In this situation, the norm is held to be non-justiciable because it is legally absolute.

Furthermore, courts will often decline jurisdiction over norms which *prima facie* appear justiciable where the subject matter of the challenged norms requires special expertise in interpretation. Lon Fuller (1978: 394ff) described some decisions as polycentric, meaning that they involved the balancing of a number of factors, and such decisions are recognised as going beyond the technical competence of the courts. One could see, for example, that in a consideration of whether one of the Statutory Sea Defence Authorities, used as an example above, had complied with its duty to build groynes, that it would be beyond the competence of any normal court to consider the relative merits of different formulations of concrete or to recalculate the force of the waves. Similarly, courts will decline jurisdiction over norms internal to bodies subject to the ordinary norms of the law, where the challenged norm is one of faith or doctrine beyond the competence of the court. In these two situations, the norm is non-justiciable because it lacks part of the quality of system membership. It is recognised by the courts, but is incapable of interpretation by them.

In conclusion, a justiciable norm is an ought-statement referring to action, recognised by a legal system capable of changing the legal position of the subject or the author of the norm. There needs to be some practicable means whereby the norm can be challenged. Challenges to norms may refer to their applicability to the subject or to the circumstances surrounding the application of the norm or to the validity of the norm itself. Within these formal rules, norms may be absolute in the sense that they are so fundamental to the legal system that they require some form of revolutionary change to reform them. In some cases, this revolutionary change may be no more than a democratic replacement of the government.

Norms may also be non-justiciable in that the courts may decline jurisdiction because they consider that they lack a competence necessary for adjudication.

See also:

due process; law, rule of

Further reading

Fuller, L. (1978) 'The Forms and Limits of Adjudication', *Harvard Law Review* 92: 353–409.

Harris, J. (1997) *Legal Philosophies*, 2nd edn, London: Butterworths.

Hart, H.L.A. (1961) *The Concept of Law*, Oxford: Clarendon Press.

Kelsen, H. (1965) 'Professor Stone and the Pure Theory of Law: A Reply' *Stanford Law Review* 17: 1128–57.

—— (1990) *General Theory of Norms*, trans. M. Hartney, Oxford: Clarendon Press.

Raz, J. (1990) *Practical Reason and Norms*, Princeton, NJ: Princeton University Press.

R.A. WATT

L

law, rule of

The rule of law is a vital but nearly undefinable aspect of the theory of democracy, which in some usages takes on an almost metaphysical quality. No two authors give very closely similar interpretations, though all clearly strive to put into words a value nowadays held as central in political life. References to the importance of the rule of law abound in many contexts, in both domestic and, increasingly, international politics, and at both high theoretical and practical levels of politics. For example, one formulation, 'the rule of laws and not of men' appears in a truncated form, 'the rule of law, not men' on the official badge of the American FBI. That phrase itself gives the essence of one aspect of the concept. It is somehow or other thought better that abstract and general rules, the law, should confine our behaviour and decide our futures, than the mere decision of a person or group deciding in a one-off manner. In one sense, this is held not to be true. A decision made by a wise and impartial judge, taking into account the full details of the situation, will perhaps produce more justice than the application of a general rule can ever do. This is because the Aristotelian prescription for JUSTICE, to treat like cases alike and different cases differently, inevitably involves the use of general and ultimately arbitrary categories if it is to be carried out by rule application.

Some special circumstances will never be capable of being captured in a rule general enough to have any use, with the consequence that apparently like cases may differ in a significant way. The single all-wise, utterly unbiased judge, as long as his or her decision is not then generalised via precedent into a rule, will be able to take account of such details of cases and give complete justice. Thus for centuries, English law recognised the special role of equity, a form of judging carried out in the Lord Chancellor's courts which was supposed to have this one-off non-precedential character, being based on the Lord Chancellor's conscience as a corrective to the inevitably occasionally harsh decisions arising in other courts from the application of the rules of common law. One could categorise the ultimate fusion of equity law and common law in England in the nineteenth century as the final move to a full recognition of the paramount value of the rule of law.

The problem with individual justice is that of corruption and bias. We do not have a ready supply of the wise and genuinely impartial, and prefer therefore to risk marginal injustice by the application of general rules. Rule application is more transparent, and though some degree of discretion cannot be avoided, the ideal involved in the automatic application of a general rule helps guide and control whatever biases a system may contain. Furthermore, the making of rules can be subject to democratic constraints and influences ahead of time. The preference for the rule of law rather than individual human decisions goes deeper still. Most moral philosophy, at least since Kant, has stressed that a norm can only be valid if universalisable: it can only be wrong for X to do Y if it would be wrong for all to do Y. Yet much law is intentionally discriminatory – granting WELFARE relief to some people not others, extracting higher taxes from the rich, not the average income – and thus tightly defined and justified criteria such as can only be guaranteed in a public democratic law making session. That these are then applied without fear or favour to all who fall into the discriminatory categories is a necessary element of democratic morality.

The rule of law is valuable not only because it creates categories which can be seen to be fair and just, but because governance by rule application rather than by individual AUTHORITY changes the nature of office holders. A police officer, welfare adjudicator, magistrate or town planning official who applies rules of law is, in theory, a perfect Weberian bureaucrat. He has no personal interest or involvement, he stands neither to gain nor lose from any decision, he does not own his office, and his right to make the decisions in question comes from external and formal accreditation; he is, in short, only an agent, not a principal. It is no accident that the key doctrine in what English law calls the rules of 'natural justice' is that no one may hear a case in which he has, or may even be thought to have, a personal interest. Thus any partiality in the decision, if it is taken properly, arises from the very basis of the system itself and is unavoidable. The contrast is with any system of personal authority where the decision maker, whether a feudal baron or tax farmer, in entitled to take his own interests into account in constraining others, or where the system, even if it forbids partiality in principal, puts no external constraints on the decisions that can be taken and thus cannot in practise recognise partiality. Again, English public law gives a good example. When courts are asked to judge the LEGITIMACY of a public official's actions, to decide whether he had the power to do what he did, they are expressly charged with ensuring that the official took into consideration all matters that he ought to have considered, and did not take account of any matters he ought not to have considered; that he decided by the rule of law.

The account given above is different from some given by political theorists in one particular respect; it has been written entirely formalistically, taking no account of the substance of laws. There is no law, as long as it has been properly passed by the appropriate constitutional mechanism, which would not count as part of the general idea of the rule of law in this approach. There are approaches, however, to the idea of the rule of law which are much more substantive. Such approaches limit the content of legitimate rules that can make up the rule of law. Those who treat the concept of the rule of law in this manner sometimes suggest its origin is essentially medieval, coming out of the general approach concerning the laws of nature. Thus basic ideas of EQUALITY and of essential human RIGHTS, inalienable entitlements of man qua man, not depending on any particular political or constitutional settlement, can be written into the very idea of the rule of law. It is because of this strand of thought that the rule of law does sometimes take on a metaphysical aura, seeming to imply that political systems are mechanisms for applying the rule of law, rather than the rule of law being a mechanism that can be used by a political system. To a natural law theorist – John Locke, for example – it is probable that a policy like nationalisation of industry would be seen as opposed to the rule of law itself, it being a biased expropriation of property. PRIVATE PROPERTY, being a human right derived from natural law, is not something that law properly could take away. In this perspective, there would be no difference in principle between a feudal baron grabbing some rich peasant's fields simply on the basis of his assertion of a greater need, clearly a breach of the rule of law, and a democratically elected socialist government compulsorily buying up all shares in the national steel industry.

While the right to private property is a controversial, though very old, candidate for a basic human right, others, especially rights relating to the security of the person such as prohibitions on torture, cruel and usual punishments, slave labour and so on might more plausibly be seen as part of the rule of law itself. One reason this approach makes some sense is that is impossible for an individual meaningfully to consent to being treated in this manner. This means it is impossible for a rule which allowed torture properly to be universalised. Such a rule would be incapable of having the very logical form of the rule of law. (In contrast, it is not impossible for a rich person to accept, in principle, that his wealth could be taken for the public good via nationalisation.) It is probably a mistake, however, to inject very much of a substantive nature into the core idea of the rule of law if it is be a widely applicable touchstone of good government. Unless some policy aim is too basic to human needs as to make it unthinkable for the law to ignore it, it is probably not a defining element of the rule of law.

Since early in the twentieth century, especially since the end of the First World War, there has been mounting pressure to include the concept of the rule of law into international relations. This would-be incorporation received a further boost with the internationally spread horror of the barbarities of the 1930s and the Second World War. It has become an article of faith that international peace can best be achieved by introducing the rule of law into relations between states. At its simplest, this doctrine amounts to the claim that international law itself should decide conflicts between states, and that force should never be resorted to, or certainly only with the classic collective defence justification. As such, given the paucity of effective and genuinely recognised international law and the weakness of mechanisms like the International Court of Justice, an appeal to the rule of law in international relations adds very little to a more general cry for decency in world politics, and has relatively little hard content. A major problem here is that the applicability of the rule of law in a domestic content relies heavily on the existence of mechanisms for the creation of generalised rules of behaviour with justified categories and public TRANSPARENCY in rule making. The rule of law secondarily depends on transparent mechanisms of enforcement of a largely bureaucrat manner so that it can be seen as controlling specific decision-making. Both these elements have historically been largely lacking in international law, although it has since 1945 been possible to regard the UN Charter and UN declarations as partially remedying this lack. We do indeed see clear examples of CONSTRAINT in the actions of national powers which come close to the formal requirements of the rule of law. The insistence of the US-led coalition against Iraq in the early 1990s that it was carrying out a UN mandate, including the manner in which the coalition forces stopped their advance at the Iraqi border because they had no authorisation to go further, seems a clear application of rule-of-law thinking.

Nonetheless, international unease about possibilities of bias and undue influence in UN decision-making, as well as the sense that the rule of law may be of largely cosmetic influence, leaves doubt about the viability of the idea in the international context. The rule of law is, essentially, an effective restraint on power which already exists, as in a national context where a country moves from arbitrary rule to the rule of law, and not a replacement for a non-existent authority and power centre, which it largely is in the international context. A more meaningful expansion of the role of the rule of law in international politics may be the recent but increasing sense that the world community has the authority to impose the rule of law inside a nation's territory, to move into conditions of anarchy and naked power and to set up a law-abiding regime, as with Serbia and Kosovo. Even here, though, the essence is of the imposition of substantive norms rather than the formal structure of the rule of law; it required, after all, considerable force to impose a settlement in Kosovo, against the desire of the *de jure* government of Serbia. To use the concept of the rule of law with any analytic power, its precision needs to be retained, and thus it is still more useful to regard it as a formal requirement inside domestic politics.

See also:

bureaucracy; civil service; judicial review; justice; legal regulation; rights

DAVID ROBERTSON

leadership

Executives are fashioned by the action of their leaders. Political leadership is highly visible, much talked about, but complex to assess. The visibility of leadership has been markedly enhanced by the development of the mass MEDIA, in particular television; yet the phenomenon is not new. Great leaders of antiquity, of the Renaissance and of the modern period were well-known to their contemporaries, despite the fact that they could only be seen and heard by relatively few. Their qualities and defects were analysed by scholars and their actions recorded by historians.

Leaders can be judged to be good or bad, heroes or villains; they are also seen as more or less successful. In this respect, the distinction has been made between leaders in the strong sense of the word and mere 'power-holders' (Burns 1978). Many leaders, probably the majority, are not very influential and can affect only marginally the course of events; on the other hand, a few 'stars' seem to shape the destiny of humanity. Some leaders 'transform' society while others merely 'transact' matters by making compromises (Burns 1978). Such a distinction should not be viewed as dichotomous, however: it constitutes the two poles of a continuous dimension dealing with the 'extent of change' which leaders are able to bring about. It is in a somewhat similar context that Weber introduced the notion of 'charisma', a concept which has been devalued by comparison with the rather strict conception of Weber, but which has played a major part in the categorisation of leaders, largely because the personalisation of leadership is obviously very important alongside the two other Weberian categories of 'traditional' and 'bureaucratic-legalistic' rule (Weber 1968).

Democratic leadership and its origins

Democratic leadership has to be seen in the general context of leadership. Leaders are democratic because the institutional framework obliges them to be responsive to the views of their followers and/or because they are personally predisposed to such a behaviour. More is known about the apparent effect of institutional arrangements and practices than about the effect of personality, however (Greenstein 1969). While the case that the role of the personality structure is likely to be large, that role seems to elude measurement and even broader assessment; studies which have begun to examine these matters have remained vague. Intelligence, dominance, self-confidence, achievement, drive, sociability and energy all appear to be positively correlated with leadership, as analyses undertaken by experimental psychologists have suggested (Bass 1981). Above all, two factors, drive or energy (labelled 'activity' or 'passivity') and satisfaction with the job (a 'positive' or 'negative' approach) appear to be essential, as has been shown in the context of American presidents (Barber 1977) (see DEMOCRACY, JUSTIFICATIONS FOR). Much more work is needed before it becomes possible to determine with assurance what qualities are required of democratic leaders.

Democratic presidents and prime ministers compared

The institutional prerequisites for a democratic leadership are somewhat easier to determine, in large part because constitutional arrangements have typically been set up in order to stop or at least reduce the autocratic character of leadership. At the national level, the two sets of institutional arrangements, which foster DEMOCRATIC EXECUTIVES, also foster democratic leadership. These are the parliamentary cabinet and the constitutional presidential government. In the first case, the leader is the prime minister; in the second, it is the constitutional president. Presidents in constitutional presidential systems are the more prestigious since they exercise the functions of heads of state and have the reality of executive power. However, the strength of their leadership depends partly on the constitution: Latin American presidents have sometimes the power to issue decrees without the approval of congress, while the American chief executive cannot do so (Shugart and Carey 1992) (see Shugart's PRESIDENTIALISM). Presidential influence also depends on the character of the party system: where PARTIES are streamlined and disciplined, as was the case in Venezuela for decades up to the mid-1990s, the president could do more on his own than in places such as the USA or Brazil, where parties are highly decentralised (Coppedge 1994). While constitutional presidents tend therefore to play a crucial part in the life of their country, there are substantial variations, both because of personality characteristics and because of the institutional and political context.

Prime ministers in parliamentary cabinets have ostensibly a less elevated position than that of presidents in presidential government. Yet they may in practice have more power, irrespective of personality, because of the character of the political system. It has thus sometimes been argued that the British prime minister is a kind of 'elective dictator'. This is an exaggeration – as a matter of fact, the influence of British prime ministers varies greatly – but all of the holders of the office have benefited from the disciplined nature of the parties, from the fact that the party in power normally has a clear, sometimes a large majority in parliament and, as a consequence, from the longevity of their tenure. Margaret Thatcher held a record since the First World War in having been in office for eleven years, but six years in power have been almost 'normal'. In other parliamentary systems, variations are even greater: in Germany, Austria or Spain, in particular, prime ministers have often been very powerful, but there are also many examples of much weaker heads of parliamentary cabinets, particularly where coalitions are shaky, as has notoriously been the case in Italy and Japan. Variations in the effective power of prime ministers, both within and across countries, are indeed perhaps even larger than among presidents in constitutional presidential systems.

The impact of democratic leaders

The strength of leaders has to be assessed by the impact that these leaders have on the societies they rule. Yet the measurement of impact has remained approximative. Leaders do not act in a vacuum: many others, whether politicians or civil servants, contribute to this impact. The impact of leadership is also difficult to assess because time, often a long time, must elapse between the moment a leader acts and the moment these actions have a real effect. But perhaps the greatest difficulty stems from the fact that leadership is a relationship between the ruler and the ruled. Thus the impact must be measured in terms of the extent to which leaders make people do what they would not otherwise do. Leaders are not leaders if they just follow others: they have to initiate and change the course of events.

This places democratic leaders in an awkward position. These leaders have to convince: they cannot impose their will by COERCION as autocrats can do. Furthermore, they have to do so over a relatively short period, as the electoral cycle gives them only few years to turn opponents and sceptics into supporters. Thus, not surprisingly, many among those whom history remembers as having had a major impact have been non-democratic leaders, even if this impact has often tended to result in catastrophe. The surprise is that, on the contrary, a number of democratic leaders should have succeeded in shaping the destinies of their country.

Admittedly, the impact of democratic leaders has been greatest when a major cataclysm has occurred, either within the country or because of a foreign danger. These leaders are 'saviours', as US President Roosevelt was both in the 1930s, at the time of the Great Depression, and during the Second World War. Winston Churchill had his real impact during that war: his previous career was mixed and his failures seem to have been as numerous as his successes. Charles de Gaulle's authority was also due to his role during the Second World War, although his greatest impact was when he returned to power in 1958 and he succeeded both in ending the French trauma over Algeria and in giving the country a stable institutional structure. Even Margaret Thatcher received a major boost, not just from the fact that Britain was in deep internal difficulty in the late 1970s but also from the Falklands war, without which it is doubtful whether she would have been able to have such a large impact internally and to stay in power for so long. It does therefore seem that, without such events, democratic leaders are rather constrained, even if they exercise substantial influence; their party and the electorate at large limit their scope for action. Perhaps this is indeed for the better: democratic leaders, save in exceptional circumstances, can and indeed should be innovative, but within a general framework of responsiveness.

See also:

authority; coalitions; coercion; parliamentary models

Further reading

Barber, J.D. (1977) *The Presidential Character*, New Haven, CT: Yale University Press.

Bass, B.M. (1981) *Stodgill'sHandbook on Leadership*, New York: The Free Press.

Blondel, J. (1987) *Political Leadership*, London and Los Angeles: Sage.

Burns, J.M. (1978) *Leadership*, New York: Harper and Row.

Coppedge, M. (1995) *Strong Parties and Lame Ducks*, Stanford, CA: Stanford University Press.

Greenstein, F.I. (1969) *Personality and Politics*, Chicago: Markham.

Rose, R. and Suleiman, N. (eds) (1980) *Presidents and Prime Ministers*, Washington, DC: American Enterprise Institute.

Shugart, M.S. and Carey, J.M. (1992) *Presidents and Assemblies*, New York: Cambridge University Press.

Tucker, R.C. (1981) *Politics as Leadership*, Columbia, MO: University of Missouri Press.

Weber, M. (1968) *Economy and Society*, 3 vols, New York: Bedminster Press.

JEAN BLONDEL

legal regulation

When we speak of legal regulation, the emphasis is usually on regulation. That is, the term refers to a form of social control by agents of the executive branch of government. This would include prosecutors, police and regulators from administrative agencies. Courts monitor this type of social control based on rules laid down by legislatures. Three aspects of legal regulation receive attention here.

First, the subject has considerable breadth and encompasses a variety of enforcement strategies. Regulation may be by means of incentives, like tax breaks or car pool lanes, and/or punishments that range from fines to imprisonment. The sometimes polar, sometimes continuous nature of these phenomena is known as 'the carrot and the stick'.

Second, that aspect most characteristic of the regulation we think of as legal is its relative lack of moral condemnation. Really serious social wrongs, like homicide, are governed by the criminal law. Though they are clearly regulated, we do not say this because it is assumed. Legal regulation generally applies to behaviours like filing documents on time, making energy-efficient cars or setting up equal opportunity guidelines for employers. Morality may be involved, but it is not generally the primary subject of regulation. When these behaviours become bad – something that we see with sexual harassment – it may be at least in part because they are regulated.

Finally, regulation has begun to be less attached to the state and to the sovereign authorities. As much as we try to confine legal regulation to that aspect of regulation associated with government, scholars make this increasingly difficult by extending the notion of governance into everything from shopping to sports. By emphasising the reach of regulation into less formal settings, we come to realise that legal regulation may be diminishing as a form of social control.

The carrot and the stick

The two primary forms or tendencies which appear as aspects of legal regulation bear on the distinction between legal and other types of regulation. In some instances, law regulates by sanctioning behaviour. This is the case when failure to perform the required car safety inspection leads to a determination that a car should not be put on the road. At other times, legal regulation provides incentives for people to behave in a way that is presumed beneficial for social policy. An example might be the lanes on highways and bridges that provide free access where passengers are in the car.

Both are legal when they rely on the force of the state, that is, the government. Thus, when the driver of the uninspected car is left to travel on foot because a trooper has taken his or her keys, we know the state is involved. But similarly, when the toll-taker deems the requisite number of human beings is being transported to justify travel in a special lane, the state is involved.

With continued interest in incentives as a legal mechanism, the distinction between the carrot and the stick is another relevant consideration. Here, force as an aspect of regulation is in one sense juxtaposed with incentives, while at another level force might be in the background of the incentive process. This is the case with the diamond lanes on freeways where the penalties for riding in them when one does not have a full car can tend to take over their meaning in the public eye. Such is the power of the legal sanction that it tends to clear everything out of its way. As anyone of us who have been stopped by the police for a traffic violation can attest, it tends to ruin your day.

When speaking of legal regulation, we generally presume to mean an aspect of state law. Under current scholarship, the penetration of law into social consciousness is recognised as being important, and legal regulation, like other forms of regulation, would include the capacity of judges and other legal commentators and interpreters to influence the way we think about things. Thus, when a citizen thinks about reporting income on his tax returns, he or she may think in terms of what is rightfully Uncle Sam's (or Caesar's), or he or she may simply not want to run the risk of getting caught. We know that some aspects of law, the tax code included, are more widely accepted than others.

Morality and law

A puzzling situation is at the centre of the effort to understand the meaning of legal regulation. The traditional presumption in legal theory is that regulation is not a matter of morality. Regulatory offences are generally thought to be morally neutral. We can think of a time not too far gone in which violation of a mere statute, for example, one regulating the maximum amount of electricity to be produced at a given plant, was understood to a matter between the regulated and the regulatory agency and not one that need be brought up at confession.

The traditional elements of moral content are often said by legal theorists to require two things. One is culpability or blameworthiness, which is called *mens rea*; this is the criminal intent. The other is social harmfulness recognised by the society. This means moral wrongfulness, or that the behaviour be viewed as immoral. It is from the latter element that we get the notion of a distinction in the common law between *malum in se*, things bad in themselves, and *malum prohibitum*, things that are bad because they are prohibited. While some things that were once merely prohibited, like dumping toxic wastes or driving while intoxicated, have become social wrongs over time, for the most part, actions that are legally regulated by law are the ones that are not bad at the core. This makes *malum prohibitum* a key to understanding legal regulation.

Some have argued that criminal law should only be used to prohibit conduct to which the community attaches moral outrage. This might exclude some business practices. It would certainly exclude taking the tag off pillows. This is sometimes associated with a claim that such extensions will weaken the criminal law.

For discussion of the ambiguously criminal nature of parking violations, see Judge Richard Posner's decision in *Van Harken v. City of Chicago* (1997).

An issue of legal regulation that bears noting is the magnitude of the available offences or regulations which one might be held accountable for if vigorous enforcement were to ensue. This may be part of the American public's reaction against the impeachment of Bill Clinton and, ultimately, the failure to convict him on impeachment charges. Scholars such as Stuart Green, Susan Silbey and Robert Kagan have written on this subject. In *Going by the Book*, Kagan and Eugene Bardach (1982) demonstrate the latitude that administrative enforcement agencies have due to the surfeit of possible violations that could be imposed on a regulated agency.

Regulation and governance

The following analysis draws heavily from Michel Foucault, and the excellent work on how his insights might be used in the study of law by Alan Hunt and Gary Wickham (1994). By 1994, when their analysis was published, the influence of Foucault on legal scholarship in the United States had peaked, but his contribution remains important. Social scientific scholars across the disciplines spoke of power and government in new ways and treated knowledge self-consciously as a social construction with a history.

The most salient aspect of the analysis of power for legal studies was the argument that the central locations of big power, the state and capital, were no longer the defining characteristics of power. Instead, small power located in dispersed sites had become central to the way power is constituted. The Queen in her carriage, the President and Air Force One were heads of a much-diminished state in Foucault's framework. The governing institutions that had once exercised AUTHORITY at will and displayed their power in the pomp and circumstance surrounding heads of state had been supplanted by new architectures of power, which he called small. These smaller powers are evident in the form of surveillance cameras in stores and sometimes in the street, the clerk behind the counter at Kinko's with the power to determine what you can copy, or at Benetton with his finger at a buzzer who can determine whether you can enter the store, or the uniform product code that can be scanned at the checkout counter to determine what is being purchased, when and along with which other products. These, for Foucault, amount to forms of discipline. This disciplinary authority is more widely distributed and less obvious than the traditional sites of power.

Foucault did not merely add new aspects of social power to our understanding of law. He and his adherents tried to change the entire image of modern law from the pomp and circumstance of a state dinner or the macabre drama of an execution to the mundane but far more pervasive regulation produced by the UPC scanner at the checkout counter or the clerk with power to open a shop door. It was a dramatic contribution. But its success at transforming our conception of social control diminished mechanisms like the police and the authority of heads of state that were still functional. Hunt and Wickham describe the resulting image of law and the state as 'a mechanism that is ineffectual and generally epiphenomenal' (1994: 57). Paradoxically, this development was being recognised just as mainstream social science was bringing the state back in to the picture.

One result of this mode of analysis was to draw attention away from traditional forms of power, such as law. This was a significant weakness in Foucault's perspective, and it often emerged in the work of those following his lead. Jürgen Habermas, for instance, comments, 'Foucault leaves the ungrounded impression that the bourgeois constitutional state is a dysfunctional relic from the period of absolutism' (Hunt and Wickham 1994: 61). Thus, we are in good company when we note that bringing out the importance of little forms of power should not let us ignore the very real forces that emanate from government and leave considerable power in the modern state. Clearly, the appropriate message to be garnered is that both levels must be incorporated in the description of modern mechanisms of power and social control. We need to include high courts and surveillance cameras, armies and clerks, the FBI and the UPC. Each plays a role in maintaining the social order.

Foucault, with the dramatic image of violence to the condemned that opens *Discipline and Punish*, also drew disproportionate attention to the criminal law as the emblematic legal force to be accounted for even while suggesting that the forces of social control had been transformed. For scholars like Hunt and Wickham, it is: 'The other faces of law which, in so far as one can safely quantify law, make up its great bulk of provisions concern the detail of economic and kinship relations and the distribution of social authority' (1994: 60). This observation is particularly significant when one seeks to delineate the forces of power in society. While the popular news in the West covers crime far more fully than commerce and domestic violence more assiduously than inheritance, it is the latter, in each instance, that is more constitutive of law's place in society.

Indeed, this propensity to equate law with legal institutions in general and violent transgressions in particular is part of the contemporary configuration of power, which must be theorised in order to understand power and law. The reception of Foucault reflects the ideology of legal realism, which incorporates a picture of an emasculated legal form in its own articulation of power. Here, politics is played out on the domain of epistemology. A close reading of the prospects for a post-positivist sociology of law lead us to what it means to take the material world seriously while developing the premises of social construction.

See also:

authority; law, rule of; rights

Further reading

Foucault, M. (1977) *Discipline and Punish*, New York: Vintage.
Green, S.P. (1997) 'Why It's a Crime to Tear the Tag off a Mattress: Overcriminalization and the Moral Content of Regulatory Offences', 46 Emory L.J. 1533.
Hunt, A. and Wickham, G. (1994) *Foucault and Law*, London: Pluto Press.
Kagan, R. and Bardach, E. (1982) *Going By the Book: The Problem of Regulatory Unreasonableness*, Cambridge, MA: Harvard University Press.
Piven, F.F. and Cloward, R.D. (1971) *Regulating the Poor: The Functions of Public Welfare*, New York: Vintage Books.
Van Harken v. City of Chicago (1997) 103 F.3d 134

JOHN BRIGHAM

legislative process

Legislatures make law. Law-making involves a collective effort on the part of at least a majority of legislators. This collective effort requires the allocation of scarce resources, the most important of which is plenary time, among numerous legislators who are competing over its use. To overcome the implied problems of collective action, legislatures typically delegate the task of allocating the legislature's scarce resources to the government or to the majority party leadership. This delegation, however, creates the potential for agency losses, whereby the legislature's agents might use their power to allocate resources for their own benefits rather than for the legislature's benefit as a whole.

Legislatures each attempt to strike a balance between solving collective action problems and mitigating potential agency losses by creating institutions that govern the allocation of resources and the flow of proposed legislation through the system. The rules, procedure and INSTITUTIONAL DESIGN of law-making make up the legislative process.

Three elements of procedure are common to all legislatures, and these will be my focus in what follows. First, because each legislature must allocate plenary time, a substantial fraction of each legislature's rules, procedures and structure are devoted to defining and prescribing the means by which the legislature's agenda is controlled. Second, the rules must also prescribe what happens when no new laws are passed; that is, how is it that the 'reversionary policy' is set? Third, once plenary time is allocated and the reversionary policy is set, the legislature must have rules and procedures that dictate how a collective decision on policy change will be reached.

While the above features of the legislative process are ubiquitous, of course, there are many additional elements to the legislative process that vary from one legislature to the next. Many of these involve attempts to mitigate the aforementioned problem of agency loss. These too have important effects on the flow of legislation. These elements of the legislative process will be discussed in the final two sections of this entry.

Controlling the agenda

Controlling the legislative agenda involves the creation and prescription of two types of powers. One type of power is the AUTHORITY to get proposed policy changes onto the legislative agenda; we call this authority positive agenda control. The alternative type of power is the authority to keep proposed policy changes off of the legislative agenda, and thereby protect the status quo – or reversionary policy – from change; we call this authority negative agenda control. Each is discussed below.

Positive agenda control

Positive agenda control is the power to propose new policies. The issues of who has it or controls access to it, and who does not, may affect the decisions that a legislature can make depending on the various policy-makers' preferences. Possessing positive agenda power grants the policy maker the formal right to introduce bills, or at very least, it entails the privilege to bring up for consideration a motion or an amendment before the full legislative body.

In the United States, there are a variety of routes by which bills are considered. While the Constitution grants the President the right to submit proposals to Congress, only the House of Representatives and Senate possess the power to assure that proposals are considered in their own chamber. Within the House, committees of a particular jurisdiction and specialised task forces have the power to initiate policy change in their policy area. But simply proposing legislation hardly implies that it will be considered by the full legislative body, except in cases where some bills are 'privileged'. An example of this is the five committees, such as the Appropriations and Budget committee, that are outlined by the House Standing Rules as having direct access to the floor on select legislation. Most House scheduling, however, is controlled by the Speaker and the Rules Committee. In the United Kingdom, by contrast, the executive dominates the agenda setting process. While members of Parliament are allowed submit bills, the Cabinet initiates most legislative proposals. Because the legislature can choose and remove the executive, these two branches are interdependent; consequently, they are less likely to be at cross-purposes. The Japanese system presents another variation on positive agenda control. The Diet, Japan's legislature, possesses a standing committee system, and the Policy Affairs Research Council (PARC), which operates as a shadow committee system within the Liberal Democratic Party (LDP). It is the PARC system that possesses formal initiation/proposal power.

To untangle who really controls the legislative agenda, it is important to know both who can initiate proposals and who controls the consideration of proposals, and to whom those actors are accountable. The power to initiate policy and the power to schedule policy consideration may be defined by the constitution or such procedural decisions may be delegated to the legislative chamber itself to resolve. In the United States, these determinations were left entirely to the chambers themselves. Over time, something of a dual system has developed, in which the legislature divides positive agenda power between individual committees and the parties. Committees act as a filter, shaping nearly all proposals in their particular policy jurisdiction, but the majority party leadership may be given the power to allocate scarce common resources, including committee assignments. Presumably, each party's committee contingent acts as a representative of the whole party. To the extent that the party exercises control over committee assignments, and to the extent that those assignments are desirable to individual members, the party's representatives should be faithful to the party's collective interests. A similar relationship holds with regard to the leadership's scheduling activities, such that the leadership will pursue the majority party's preferences to the extent that the party can discipline its agents, their leaders.

Negative agenda control

An alternative form of agenda control also exists, which essentially is the veto power. We call the authority to halt or to delay a bill's progress, negative agenda control, and it can be exercised either explicitly through vetoes or implicitly through inaction. Veto power is usually held by the legislature, although when the executive possesses a decree power, for example, policy may be changed without legislative assent.

Any person or faction with the power to block, or significantly delay policy, is often referred to as a veto gate. There exists significant variance across nations in the number of veto gates that inhabit the legislative process. The United States's presidential system with its bicameral, decentralised legislature represents one end of the spectrum, and the United Kingdom occupies the other end of the spectrum with its more centralised parliamentary form of government. In the House of Representatives alone, the substantive committees, Rules Committee, Speaker and the Committee of the Whole each constitute veto gates through which legislation must pass, and the Senate has even more veto gates due to their liberal restrictions on debate. By contrast, in the United Kingdom the legislative process is much more efficient, since the Cabinet and Prime Minister serve as the main veto gates through which new legislation must pass. Apart from its weak negative agenda control, the Swedish committee system resembles the system found in the US House of Representatives, but represents another important variation. In the Swedish Riksdag, members of the Cabinet or backbenchers alike may submit bills for consideration, but every proposal must go the appropriate committee for consideration. That is, there is no discretion over which committee has jurisdiction; it is pre-determined. The committees, however, cannot kill a bill by failing to act on it. As their rules specify, each committee must submit a report, whether positive or negative, on all policy proposals.

Reversion control

Whenever legislatures consider passing a law, they must always consider its effects relative to what would occur if no law were passed. Indeed, in virtually every legislature the final vote taken on a proposal is that for final passage, which forces members to contrast directly the proposed change and the status quo. Reversion control is the power of setting the default policy outcome that will result if no new legislation is enacted. It is important to note that the reversionary policy is not necessarily the extant policy. For example, some laws are crafted with 'sunset provisions', which mandate that a programme be dissolved or an appropriation be terminated by some specified date.

To understand law-making, it may be important to know whether the reversion policy can be manipulated, and if so, who possesses the power to do so. This requires an understanding of the relationship between the reversion policy, any new policy proposal, and the various policy makers' preferences. Reversionary policies can be defined formally by a constitution and/or statutes, or as the result of informal solutions to immediate problems. In Germany and the United States, the constitution defines the reversion for budgetary items, but the reversionary policy for entitlements, such as Social Security, are typically defined by statutes to be adjusted incrementally.

The importance of reversion control can be seen in the following example of the effect of varying the regulatory burden of proof. The US Federal Food, Drug and Cosmetics Act of 1938, as amended, requires that before a pharmaceutical company can market a new drug, it must first prove that the drug is both safe and efficacious. By contrast, in the Toxic Substances Control Act of 1976, Congress required that the Environmental Protection Agency (EPA), before regulating a new chemical, must prove that the chemical is hazardous to human health or the environment. In one case, then, the burden of proof is on the industry that wishes to promote its product; while in the other case the burden of proof is on the regulator that wishes to halt a product's introduction. The results of the differences in the burden of proof are stark: few new drugs are marketed in the United States relative to European democracies, while the EPA has managed to regulate none of the 50,000 chemicals in commerce under these provisions in the Toxic Substance Control Act.

In fact, the effectiveness of agenda control may itself be contingent on the reversionary outcome. Whether or not those who possess positive agenda control will be able to make 'take-it-or-leave-it' offers (also known as ultimatum bargaining) to the legislature depends largely on the attractiveness, or unattractiveness, of the reversionary outcome to the policy makers.

Procedural control

Most legislatures possess rules that structure the handling of proposed legislation. Rules define voting procedures, the types of amendments that will be allowed, if any, how amendments will be considered, provisions for debate, the public's access and so forth. It is possible to draw a distinction between two different forms of procedural rules: standing rules and special rules. Standing rules guide the day-to-day procedure by which the legislature conducts itself and the internal law-making

processes. Standing rules may continue from a previous legislative session, or they may be redrafted each new legislative session.

By contrast, special rules create exceptions for consideration of a bill, which violate the standing rules. In the House of Representatives, floor debate usually takes place under a special rule restricting debate and amendments, and the Rules Committee possesses the power to write special rules. Successful consideration of most non-trivial bills typically entails giving certain members procedural privileges, whether accomplished by a special rule or by a suspension of the rules. Restrictive rules, such as limiting debate or amendments, is one way for the majority party LEADERSHIP to eliminate opportunities for defection by their party members.

Interestingly, although Japan has a parliamentary system, its internal legislative procedure resembles that of the United States. The Diet decentralises its policy-making into the PARC divisions, but the majority party's leadership holds a veto over their actions through a hierarchy of party-dominated veto gates and through its control of the legislative agenda. But, since Japan is parliamentary, the majority party leadership serves at the pleasure of the full membership, and consequently the full membership has a conditional veto over the actions of the committee system.

The procedure structuring debate, and restrictions on debate, is typically encompassed by a legislature's standing and special rules. In addition to the obvious importance of who gets to participate in the deliberative process and how extensively, control of debate may have serious policy implications. For example, in the United States, judicial interpretation of laws often refers to the congressional record to ascertain the lawmakers' intent. As a consequence of the ability to participate in debate is an opportunity to possibly have your preferences or understanding of a law incorporated in its interpretation.

In the House of Representatives, unless proposed legislation is governed by a special rule or there is a suspension of the rules, the House's standing rules and precedents limit each member's speaking time to one hour during debate and five minutes when considering amendments. Upon recognition, a member controls her allotted time to yield or allocate as she desires, but this rule is circumscribed by the fact that the Speaker of the House possesses recognition power. Hence, given their power to suspend the rules, and to write special rules, and given the Speaker's discretion to recognise members, the majority party leadership is able to structure chamber debate quite effectively. Special rules (for example, limiting debate) are recommended by the Rules Committee and approved by simple majority in the full chamber. The Rules Committee is stacked with majority party loyalists selected by the Speaker. Suspension of the rules, however, requires a two-thirds majority and thus typically requires some bipartisan support.

In the Senate, however, the majority party's control over debate is a bit more tenuous. The Senate's standing rules do not limit debate, and the chamber has developed a notorious reputation for members' ability to frustrate a majority through the filibuster. Over time, the rules have been modified, to allow a three-fifths majority to invoke what is called 'cloture', ending a filibuster by either limiting debate to one hour per member or establishing a maximum of thirty hours more for debate.

By comparison, parliamentary debate in the United Kingdom is fairly structured. In the House of Commons, for example, there are two main types of debate: general and adjournment. General debate is to discuss specific government policies. Adjournment debate includes matters for which the government has no explicit position, such as new or bipartisan issues. Another type is emergency debate, which acts as a safety valve for issues needing immediate attention and lacking another avenue to the floor. Regardless of the classification, the actual debate, or recognition, is controlled by the majority party leadership, the Speaker.

Delegation and the legislative process

The delegation of the legislature's agenda setting authority to the government, to ministers, and to the party or committee leaders creates the potential for mischief, or agency loss. At issue is how members assure that the people to whom the agenda-setting authority has been delegated do not take advantage of this authority and use it for their own, personal gain? In general, legislatures use both checks and balances to accomplish these tasks. They provide others with a veto over the actions of agenda setters and give these others an opportunity and incentive to act as checks. These checks and balances may be very subtle. In the US House of Representatives, for example, the front-bench and back-bench may check each other through the committee system. During the Conservative Coalition era, roughly from 1937 to 1974, the Southern Democrats, who had greater seniority and safer seats, held the control committees and especially the Rules Committee, and for decades were able to bottle up civil rights legislation from those perches of power. Meanwhile the northern Democrats held control on the substantive committees, and they used the implicit gate-keeping power that came with that control to pursue a civil rights agenda by creating log-rolls (see LOG-ROLLING) that could survive the control committees and would benefit both northern and southern Democrats.

Similarly, in the House of Commons in the UK, the Prime Minister and Cabinet may control much of the flow of legislation, but they are personally accountable to the back-bench to facilitate the development of a party brand name, and can be removed for failure to take the backbench's preferences into account. Many legislatures have similar mechanisms for checking the independence of a speaker or coalition leader through either a formal vote of no confidence, or with a less formal recall provision.

The legislative process

By way of summary, the following figure demonstrates many of the preceding points regarding control of the agenda, reversionary policy, procedure, and checks on delegated authority. Figure 2 is a graphic representation of the legislative process in the US House of Representatives, demonstrating the path that any piece of legislation must travel in order to become law. It is important to note the numerous places where a proposal may be revised or amended, or halted altogether; negative agenda control. By unravelling who influences the decision at each of these points (control of agenda and procedure) – whether an individual, a faction or a party – it is possible to assess the degree to which interests are balanced in a nation's legislative process.

In the initial stages of the US POLICY-MAKING process, the substantive committees in each chamber possess significant agenda control within their jurisdiction. Given members' attraction to committees that are substantively salient to their constituents, legislators who are most concerned with the policy at hand have asymmetric influence at this early stage. As a proposal approaches the floor, however, the party's influence may be felt more and more. The majority party's members delegate to their leadership to represent their interests on a broad variety of matters. The Rules Committee and the Speaker – as well as the Appropriations Committee, if any funding is required to implement the proposal – check committee members' ability to exploit their agenda control, for these two central co-ordinating bodies control access to plenary time. If a substantive committee's proposal is unrepresentative of the party's collective interests, and it is an issue of importance to the party, then either the Speaker or the Rules Committee are likely to kill the proposal. The shortage of plenary time itself creates incentives for the substantive committees to compete against each other, in something of a tournament, where the reward for satisfying the party's interest is time for floor consideration. Before the proposal leaves the chamber come the floor amendments and votes themselves, which provide ordinary members with the opportunity to form COALITIONS in order to influence and potentially kill a bill. At all of these stages is the importance of procedure and

who controls it. Lastly, while not explicitly captured by this figure is the matter of reversionary policy. All policy is made, un-made, amended, and/or disregarded with the reversionary policy. Certain policies, which happen to command majority support, may be difficult to take up if the reversionary policy is preferred by members who occupy veto gates; negative agenda control. In sum, the three elements discussed – agenda, reversion and procedural control – repeatedly overlap one another throughout the policy-making process to structure the policy-making, provide checks and balances between the various interests, and define the boundaries of which interests will be represented.

See also:

authority; decision-rules; parliamentary models; parties; policy-making

Further reading

McCubbins, M. and Sullivan, T. (1987) *Congress Structure and Policy*, Cambridge: Cambridge University Press.

McCubbins, M. and Cox, G. (1993) *Legislative Leviathan Party Government in the House*, Berkeley, CA: California University Press.

MATHEW D. MCCUBBINS

legitimacy

The question of what makes political power rightful or legitimate has exercised thinkers since the origin of political speculation, and especially so when governmental AUTHORITY has been substantially contested or widely experienced as oppressive. Rulers in turn have sought to demonstrate the legitimacy of their rule, both to pre-empt possible rivals and to convince their subordinates that obedience is not just a question of prudence or advantage, but also a matter of duty. 'The strongest is never strong enough to be master', wrote Rousseau, 'unless he transforms strength into

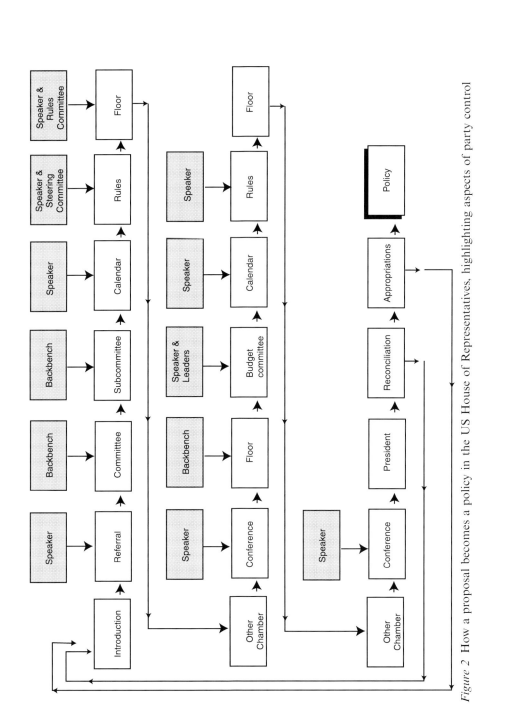

Figure 2 How a proposal becomes a policy in the US House of Representatives, highlighting aspects of party control

right and obedience into duty' (1963: 6). For power to be acknowledged as rightful or legitimate, however, is not merely an advantage for rulers in the consolidation of their rule; the normative assumptions or principles which serve to define what counts as legitimate also typically set limits to what the powerful may do if they are to maintain their moral authority over the governed.

In what, then, does legitimacy consist? A useful starting point is to recognise that legitimacy is a multi-dimensional, rather than mono-dimensional, concept, and that it is constructed at a number of different levels. First is the level of *legality*: power is legitimate insofar as it is acquired and exercised in accordance with established rules, whether these are conventional or legal in form. On its own, however, legality is insufficient, as is shown when the normative principles under-pinning the legal rules of power, its appointment and exercise, are themselves brought into question. Here lies a second dimension of legitimacy, that of *normative justifiability*: power is legitimate to the extent that it can be shown to derive from a valid source of authority, and to fulfil the rightful ends or purposes of government. It is in this dimension of normative justifiability that most philosophical analysis and debate about legitimacy takes place. There is a further dimension still, however, and that is *legitimation*; power is legitimated when it is publicly acknowledged by relevant subordinates through actions which confirm their acceptance of it; and when it is expressly recognised by other legitimate authorities.

These three levels (rules, normative principles and actions) are not alternatives, since all contribute to legitimacy; together they provide the subordinate with moral grounds for compliance or co-operation with authority. The fact that all are required is shown by the different negative words used to express the different ways in which power may lack legitimacy. If there is a breach of the rules, we use the term 'illegitimacy'; if the rules governing the acquisition and exercise of power are only weakly supported by societal beliefs, or

are deeply contested, we can talk of a 'legitimacy deficit'; if consent or recognition is publicly withdrawn or withheld, we speak of 'delegitimation'.

The most extreme example of illegitimacy is usurpation or *coup d'état*, power attained in violation of the rules. Examples of legitimacy deficit are enormously varied: from situations where changing societal beliefs leave existing institutional arrangements unsupported, or those where people have widely diverging beliefs, say, about which state they should belong to; to situations where government is chronically unable to meet the basic purposes, such as WELFARE or SECURITY, which people believe it should. Legitimacy deficits usually only become critical when some performance failure of government exposes a fundamental doubt about its rightful source of authority. Examples of delegitimation include acts of widespread public opposition to a regime, of which revolutionary mobilisation is the most extreme example. REVOLUTIONS follow a typical course from chronic legitimacy deficit of the regime (doubtful or disputed source of authority compounded by performance failure), through its delegitimation by mass oppositional mobilisation which splits the governing apparatus, to an illegitimate seizure of power which heralds its reconstruction under a new set of legitimating principles.

The different dimensions of legitimacy outlined above constitute only the most general or abstract framework, the specific content of which has to be 'filled in' for each historical society or political system. They offer a heuristic tool to guide analysis. In particular, they provide a useful framework for analysing the distinctive components of liberal-democratic legitimacy. Its distinctive mode of legality is the constitutional 'rule of law': the idea that the sphere of competence of government and its officials should be precisely defined and legally regulated, and enforced through an institutional SEPARATION OF POWERS between executive, legislature and JUDICIARY. At the level of normative validity, liberal democracy embodies the principle that all political authority stems from the will of the people, as expressed in their electoral choice of candidates for public office. This principle of popular SOVEREIGNTY as the ultimate source of political authority is complemented by a distinctive articulation of the ends or purposes of government, in the protection of individual rights to FREEDOM, security and welfare. These two key legitimating ideas (source of authority and ends of government) were given classic formulation at the start of the modern democratic era in the US Declaration of Independence and the French Declaration of the Rights of Man, the latter of which asserted that 'the end of all political associations is the preservation of the natural and imprescriptible rights of man... and the source of all sovereignty resides essentially in the people' (Roberts 1966: 172).

To be sure, the precise reference and scope of these two fundamental principles has been subject to contestation and evolution since the eighteenth century. Thus who has counted among 'the people' has been a matter of increasing inclusion, as the exclusions on the propertyless, women, racial and other MINORITIES, have been successively challenged and eroded. And the definition of rights protection has expanded considerably under the pressure of political struggle, to include welfare rights and the general conditions for economic development. The standards in both these respects can be expected to be subject to continuing evolution.

Finally, there is the distinctive liberal democratic mode of legitimation through actions and procedures, which confirm the acknowledgement of authority by subordinates. It is often argued that the 'consent of the governed' is the distinctive feature of liberal democratic legitimacy, and its unique source of obligation to obey political authority. Yet it is a universal feature of all political authority to need to 'bind in' key subordinates through actions and ceremonies which express their consent, their affirmation or their recognition of authority: through swearing an oath of allegiance, concluding agreements, according public acclamation, taking part in mass mobilisation in the regime's cause, and so on. What is distinctive about liberal-democratic legitimation is, first,

that the relevant group qualified to confer such recognition is extended to the whole adult population, to the 'subordinate' as a whole. And, secondly and most importantly, 'consent' is almost wholly subsumed in the authorisation of government through the electoral process, so that the process of appointing the government and the procedure for expressing consent to it become one and the same.

Within this broad framework, theorising about legitimacy, and in particular liberal democratic legitimacy, takes two distinct forms. First there is the age-old tradition of normative political philosophy, which in the early modern period succeeded in establishing the theoretical foundations of liberal politics against the competing legitimating ideas of paternalism, divine right and tradition-derived authority. These foundations were given definitive statement at the end of the seventeenth century in John Locke's *Second Treatise of Government*, which demonstrated that the source of political authority could only lie with the people, and that the rightful end of government lay in the protection of the natural rights of life, liberty and property under the rule of law. Any government which systematically infringed these principles forfeited its right to rule, Locke concluded, and could be legitimately overthrown. Other political philosophers, from Rousseau in the eighteenth century onwards, developed the more specifically democratic principles of political equality, and the right of citizens to a more direct involvement in the legislative process. Within this tradition political philosophy takes on a more critical dimension, postulating an ideal legitimacy of democratic DECISION-MAKING, against which the existing practice of liberal democratic institutions is typically found wanting. Exploring and resolving the tension between the liberal and democratic components of liberal democracy has been an important ongoing task for twentieth-century political philosophy.

A second form of theorising about political legitimacy has taken place within empirical social science. Following Max Weber's pioneering work at the start of the twentieth century, political sociologists have used the different principles of legitimacy as the basis for a comparative analysis of types of political system around the world, both past and present, so as to identify the typical features and characteristic crisis tendencies of each. The assumption of such an analysis is that political institutions and forms of government embody legitimating principles and procedures, which are grounded in the culture and values of the particular society, and in terms of which alone these forms can be rendered intelligible and their points of weakness be identified (see POLITICAL CULTURE). From this perspective, liberal democracy fits into a comparative typology of political systems, and its distinctiveness becomes sharpened by contrast with other legitimated political systems of the twentieth century – traditional, communist, fascist or theocratic – with their respective modes of legality, source of authority and ends of government, and legitimating procedures.

Both these modes of theorising, the philosophical and the social scientific, have their contribution to make to answering a key question: why is it that the liberal democratic mode of legitimacy, and form of political system, has become globally prevalent by the start of the twenty-first century? This is partly for negative reasons, that other forms of legitimate political order have proved ill-adapted to some key aspect of contemporary economic and social conditions, and have lost their internal legitimacy. The hereditary monopoly of political authority characteristic of traditional systems has proved vulnerable to the modern requirement of a career open to talent, and to popular demands for inclusion in the political process. The Marxist-Leninist goal of a communist society came up against the inherent limits of its system of economic planning, and the party's claim to exclusive knowledge of the workers' interests proved increasingly out of step with their own perceptions of them. The fascist pursuit of radical national goals has typically led to self-destructive wars; or, where these have been avoided, an authority vested in the person of an individual leader has proved unable to survive his death. Theocracies have proved vulnerable to funda-

mentalisms that have quickly forfeited popularity, or else they have provoked adherents of other faiths to open disaffection or civil war. Each system has had its own internal crisis tendencies, inherent in its legitimating principles or procedures, which have eventually proved terminal.

Liberal democracy has become prevalent, in contrast, because it has proved the only sustainable legitimate order compatible with the conditions of market CAPITALISM, on the one side, especially in its most advanced form, and with the requirements of multicultural societies on the other. Market capitalism's anti-paternalist principles – individuals are the best judge of their own interests, are responsible for their own fate, and are sovereign in the consumer market – have over time led to the demand for people to be sovereign in the political sphere also, and have undermined all paternalist forms of legitimacy, especially as EDUCATION has become widespread (see MARKET FORCES). At the same time, the increasingly global dimensions of COMMUNICATION have made closed political systems, claiming a monopoly of INFORMATION and ideology, unsustainable. Finally, the potential antagonisms between different communities cohabiting the same state, which are normal for most contemporary states, can only be peacefully resolved through the methods of dialogue and respect for equal rights, such as are intrinsic to liberal democratic procedures.

The long-term superiority and survivability of liberal democracy's legitimating principles and procedures do not mean that they are themselves unproblematic. Indeed, they contain their own inherent crisis tendencies. One stems from the inescapable tension between the economic and social inequalities that are as intrinsic to capitalism as to pre-capitalist economic systems, and the equality of CITIZENSHIP and political voice that democracy promises. This tension requires carefully crafted institutional compromises within the party and political system if it is not to prove unmanageable. The main alternatives are either a pseudo-democracy in which the mass of the people is effectively excluded from power and influence despite the formal exercise of the vote; or else a reversion to dictatorship, when the demands of the masses prove too threatening to the interests of economic and social elites. The second recurrent problem lies in the majoritarian procedure of democracy, which encourages political mobilisation along ethnic lines in divided societies, and threatens the permanent exclusion of minorities from power and influence, with the prospect of consequent degeneration into civil war (see MAJORITAR-IANISM). Again, this requires carefully crafted institutional procedures, such as a form of consociational democracy, for resolution (see CONSOCIATIONALISM).

It is important to stress, however, that liberal democracy's crisis tendencies, where they have not been institutionally resolved, have never proved terminal, in the sense that they have marked a transition to a different legitimate political order. At most they have led to the suspension of legitimacy, in military dictatorship or other forms of exceptional regime, whose rationale is precisely that they are temporary. These have usually ended in turn with attempts to restore the liberal democratic form of legitimacy once more. In this sense the twentieth century, though not history itself, has ended with liberal democracy triumphant.

This dominant position has been reinforced at the international level also. For most of the past few centuries, recognition by the international state system has been an important contributor to the domestic legitimacy of states, particularly for newly established regimes. However, this recognition has simply required that regimes demonstrate a de facto capacity to exercise power within their territory, and especially within the capital city, and has been quite neutral as to the form of regime, which has been regarded as entirely a domestic matter. Increasingly, however, states are now being required to meet externally monitored legitimacy requirements if they are to achieve full international recognition. At first this has been a human rights requirement, according to the standards of the International Covenant on Civil and Political Rights, as it has increasingly become accepted that how a state treats its own citizens is no longer just an internal matter for the state concerned. Since 1989, however, the requirement that a state also meet liberal democratic principles and procedures in its mode of political organisation has started to become generalised as an internationally accepted norm. This norm provides strong external legitimation to domestic political forces engaged in democratisation, and is also given practical effect through positive measures of democracy support and through negative pressure where aid, trade and debt interdependencies are involved.

The liberal democratic principle of legitimacy has become most fully developed as an international norm within the European political space, as applications from the former communist countries to join the economic club of the European Union have been made dependent on prior membership of the Council of Europe, with its democracy and human rights conditions. These norms have also been used to legitimate external military intervention in a sovereign European state, as in the NATO war against Yugoslavia over its treatment of the Albanian population in Kosovo. This war serves to mark the decisive shift in international norms away from the principle of unconstrained sovereignty on the part of states over their own internal affairs, regardless of how they treat their populations. It also underlines the deeply problematic character of external intervention, while states still retain a monopoly of physical force over their own territories. There is a serious disjunction, in other words, between the developing normative framework at the international level, and the means available to enforce it.

The development of a democracy and human rights 'mission' on the part of the European Union has served to focus attention on the legitimacy of its own political arrangements, which is both contested politically and a source of disagreement among analysts. On the one hand are those who model the EU's authority on that of international institutions, whose legitimacy is derived from recognition by member states, and whose audience for legitimacy claims are the states' own bureaucracies.

On the other hand are those who argue that the supranational dimension of the EU's institutions, and the impact its policy and legislation has on the lives of citizens, requires a direct rather than merely indirect form of legitimation; and that this can only be constructed on liberal-democratic principles. At all events, it is clear that political legitimacy in the European political space now involves an interactive, two-level relationship, between the European levels and that of individual states. In this, the EU is simply the most developed example of what can be seen as a more general feature of political legitimacy in the contemporary world: it is no longer determined simply at the domestic level of the individual state, as it has been for the past few centuries, but is increasingly dependent also on the state's conformity to norms defined at the international level.

See also:

authority; decision-making; law, rule of; political culture; rights; state, models of

Further reading

Barker, R. (1990) *Political Legitimacy and the State*, Oxford: Clarendon Press.
Beetham, D. (1991) *The Legitimation of Power*, Basingstoke: Macmillan.
Beetham, D. and Lord, C. (1998) *Legitimacy and the European Union*, London: Longman.
Connolly, W. (ed.) (1984) *Legitimacy and the State*, Oxford: Blackwell.
Locke, J. (1952) *The Second Treatise of Government*, Indianapolis: Bobbs-Merrill.
Roberts, J.M. (ed.) (1966) *French Revolution Documents*, vol. 1, Oxford: Blackwell.
Rousseau, J-J. (1963) *The Social Contract and Discourses*, London: Dent.
Weber, M. (1978) *Economy and Society*, Berkeley, CA: University of California Press.

DAVID BEETHAM

liberalism

The difficulty in explicating the meanings of the two concepts of liberalism and democracy is that both are highly contested (Freeden 1996: ch.2) and it is difficult to arrive at a comprehensive definition without invoking intractable disputes about rivalrous ways of life and irresolvable dilemmas about the concept of the person. Furthermore, both are promiscuous and readily attach themselves to competing social policies and agendas of government. There are minimal state liberals as well as those who believe in extensive WELFARE programmes, which are only a little short of democratic socialism. They are used emotively and seem as much designed to influence attitudes and feelings as to advance understanding. It is probably more correct to describe writers on liberalism (and indeed democracy) as referring to different conceptions rather than elucidating incorrigible conceptual truths. Liberalism cannot even be fully understood by its connection with liberty because this idea is itself the focal point of the contestability.

Yet there are important conceptual similarities between liberalism and democracy in that the competing conceptions of liberalism tend to be allied with certain related conceptions of free government subject to choice. If the latter is preliminarily defined as mechanism for making collective decisions and determining the appropriate range of government activity, then we can almost predict what type of liberalism will generate which solutions to the vexed question of the proper role of government. Those who see democracy as more than a mechanism will cling to a notion of liberalism that recommends a wide social agenda; not one that merely recommends limits on government.

We can cut though some of the verbiage by isolating the major competing types of liberalism (although they are by no means exclusive to the doctrine) which have certain common features. These are economic liberalism and what might be called social liberalism (this term is used for convenience; there is in fact no universally agreed name for the main rival to the economic version). The former refers to that individualistic doctrine that ranks highly the freedom to trade, to own property and recommends an almost unlimited right to contract (Hayek 1960). It limits the role of the state to the enforcement of a rule of law (see LAW, RULE OF) which guarantees these individualistic rights and to the production of genuine public goods, i.e. those which for technical reasons cannot be supplied by the market. Economic liberty then has the same intellectual status as any civil liberty. There is historically much to be said for this view, since the original demands for personal liberty were articulated in the context of the emerging market society in the eighteenth and nineteenth century. The Liberal Party was unequivocally associated with this doctrine. Social liberals, who both historically and in the contemporary world tend to come from America, are not hostile to property and the market, but they do not accord it the same moral value and are prepared to sacrifice economic advancement, in a utilitarian sense, to certain social goals such as free speech, secularism, non-discrimination in relation to sex and race and hindered free movement (Dworkin 1977; Bellamy 2000). But the greatest difference is over EQUALITY and social JUSTICE, for social liberals are always prepared to modify the outcomes of the market should they generate wide disparities in income and wealth. They are as indifferent to the loss of economic efficiency, which that invariably entails, as the economic liberals are to the unequal outcomes of a market process.

Points of agreement

Despite the potential great divergences that exist between the two forms of liberalism on economic matters, their common belief in a version of individual liberty means that they are on the same side in some of the issues that divide contemporary political philosophers. Both would go along with the distinction articulated by John Rawls (1972) between the right and the good. There are certain rules and practices that ought to be enforced by the state,

or at least some version of positive law, but other ideals can be left to personal choice. Justice is the obvious example of an enforceable rule, and although economic liberals have a somewhat narrow version of the ideal, restricting it to the enforcement of property and contract, it is not a matter of subjective preference. And although the social liberals are in favour of redistributive principles of social justice they are supposed to be achieved by hypothetical unanimous agreement (behind Rawls's 'veil of ignorance') and applied impartially. However, how we ought to live, what good life we ought to pursue and the religion we should practice, are all matters of subjective choice in which it would be grossly immoral for the state to intervene. It might be the case that Rawls has relaxed the universality of liberal rules in his later work (1993), indeed they look suspiciously like the products of liberal democratic society, but the whole tenor of his work shows a preference for that generality of traditional liberal rules and their detachment from particular ethnic or local affiliations. This priority of the right over the good is a significant departure from that relativism which could easily be read into rival doctrines.

This relativism seems to be true of a doctrine that has come to be the most serious opponent of liberalism in the post-socialist era: COMMUNITARIANISM. At the philosophical level, liberals identify the person through some conception of INDIVIDUALISM: for social liberals, the individual is identified through his or her rational choice of values, capacity to determine one's own life, and critical faculties which are exercised independently of the lure of particular attachments; for the economic liberal the person is a utility maximiser, driven by self-interest and potentially an inhabitant not of a locatable country but of the 'extended order' of the market which recognises no national or communal BOUNDARIES. Both sorts of liberalism differ on the role of the state in economic matters but they agree that institutions should not be used to compel conformity to insular and exclusively local values. There is then an element of NEUTRALITY here, which communitarians reject; indeed they would say that it is conceptually impossible since liberalism itself is a way of life which competes with others and may even have to be enforced.

Indeed, liberals themselves have slightly relaxed the demands of neutrality and some have resisted the priority of the right over the good. They maintain that the doctrine does depend on its being 'nested' in established communal arrangements (Raz 1986). Furthermore, Raz insists that liberty cannot be defined negatively, as the absence of alterable impediments to choice, whatever that choice may be. Certainly he would authorise the state to promote certain socially valuable ends and purposes; that is, it should choose goods worthy of support irrespective of the (quantitative) demand for them. But economic liberals remain rigorously austere on this; if there is no expressed want for a good, as revealed in the market, then it should not be produced by the state. They take this position not only because they resent the economic redistribution that it entails but also through their rejection of any form of politically generated paternalism. And the same goes for AUTONOMY. Although both forms of liberalism value persons who make choices uninfluenced by external pressure, social liberals might well regard economic circumstances as constituting constraints which the state should alleviate; this is not true of economic liberals who regard choice itself, unfettered by alterable restraint, as the only genuine expression of autonomy. Again, the moral value of the chosen act is itself not relevant to its production.

Economic liberalism and collective choice

It would be false to suggest that the excessive individualism that underlies economic liberalism precludes collective provision of goods and services. Leaving aside anarcho-capitalists, most conventional writers do admit a role for the state. But it is important to note the philosophical reasons here. When the collectivity acts it is doing so to advance individual interests; the state is a kind of conduit for the transmission of private desires for collective action in the face of market failure. The exchange mechanism cannot eliminate externalities (socially harmful effects of private action, such as pollution) or provide some collective goods and services. However, there is no intrinsic value in communal action, it is an instrumental device to maximise efficiency. And, furthermore, it is in theory non-redistributive. For although Benthamite utilitarianism permits the gains of the winners to compensate for the losses of those who do not benefit from collective action, under strict economic liberalism everybody must benefit from collective action. This condition, if rigorously interpreted, would narrow the range of collective action considerably.

Public good problems arise out of the presence of prisoner's dilemmas in society, situations in which collective benefit is not forthcoming voluntarily because, under classical liberal social and economic theory each individual has an incentive to free ride on the actions of others (Barry 2000: ch. 3). Closely allied to this is the assurance problem: even if most people were predisposed to act co-operatively no one person can be sure others will be so virtuous. This especially arises over the possibility of altruism; market institutions may well inhibit its effect. Public goods are normally defined as goods the consumption of which does not reduce their availability to others (they are non-rival) and they are non-excludable. Once supplied, those who have not paid can still consume them, such as clean air or national defence. Although things such as health and welfare are often written of as if they were public goods they are not: they clearly can be priced and their consumption invariably involves some redistribution; sometimes it is perverse (Le Grand 1982). Economic liberals maintain that modern technology has reduced the range of public goods. Also, they claim that the familiar externality of pollution could be solved individualistically if property rights were unambiguously defined; harm to the environment would be a tort which could be alleviated by private action.

Economic liberals accept the role of the state in these areas but they are desperately worried about the sorcerer's apprentice problem, in that the device chosen to solve a problem turns out to be the generator of even more difficulties. Thus the size of the public sector increased dramatically in the twentieth century, and shows no sign of diminishing. Despite the end of orthodox collectivism, the state is by no means confined to traditional public goods; it now engages in essentially private actions. This phenomenon has induced economic liberals to seek constitutional solutions to the problem. It is not that they are opposed to democracy, it is that they argue persuasively that unrestrained majority rule does not reflect accurately people's desires for public activity (see Mueller 1996). The legislature has become a venue for rent seeking, the successful attempts by private groups to transfer to themselves the wealth created by others. Restrictions on free trade to protect home industries are the classic example of the phenomenon but it also covers the making of public expenditure that benefits private groups.

Economic liberals try to find a more 'rational' democratic rule than simple MAJOR-ITARIANISM for the supply of public goods. But there is the problem which all democratic theorists face: the possibility of no determinate decision emerging from the voting process (Arrow 1963). Thus if an individual prefers x to y and y to z, then he or she must prefer x to z if their preferences are to be transitive (logically consistent). But it is only under exceptional circumstances that group voting will exhibit the same transitivity, and if these do not hold, cycling will result; if a vote is taken on each issue, no majority will result. The supporters of each issue can defeat the others if the matter is voted on one by one. A decision will then have to be imposed by a 'dictator'. As it happens, no cycling occurs in political systems with two disciplined parties. The voters only get one choice, and they have to accept the whole policy package. But it is easy to see Arrow's problem arising in committees and in parliaments where there are multi-parties which are weak and undisciplined. Under these conditions, perverse redistributions which do not reflect voters' preferences can result.

The economic liberal's answer to Arrow's problem is to narrow the range of public issues and to provide strict constitutional rules to limit the role of government. The favoured rule is unanimity, since this excludes the collective choice problem and gives each person a veto (although economic liberals favouring unanimity would limit it to representatives, for obvious reasons of convenience). However, they are also aware of the costs of unanimity if it is applied to all stages of government; certain groups could demand such a high price for their PARTICIPATION that nothing would ever get done and citizens would be worse off. Thus what tends to happen is that economic liberals demand unanimity at the constitutional stage (like Rawls) but demand much stricter rules than the majority principle for the supply of public goods. James Buchanan and Gordon Tullock (1962) suggest that a two-thirds rule would be chosen by rational contractors at the constitutional stage. Also, any desired redistribution should occur here and not in parliament. (Qualified majority rule is not that unusual. Finland has a two-thirds rule for parliamentary law, and five-sixths for property matters. And for certain issues, the European Union requires unanimity.)

Still, economic liberals do not despair of direct democracy. They favour citizens' initiative for referenda (which Switzerland has). These restrictions on majoritarianism have in no way harmed the political units involved. Economic liberals view preferences as given and as more or less immutable. Certainly they are unlikely to be altered by the endless debate implied in the theory of DELIBERATIVE DEMOC-RACY (Dryzek 2000). Indeed, they would go along with Schumpeter's view that knowledge and reason decline as soon as the citizen leaves the market and enters the political arena (although they would argue that ignorance and APATHY are actually features of rationality). In DIRECT DEMOCRACY, preferences are registered immediately, at little cost, and are not subject to manipulation by representatives operating under lax constitutional rules.

Liberalism and redistribution

Social liberals are not interested in the complex public choice issues that perplex economic liberals. However, there is some agreement about the need to protect liberal values from potential depredation by unrestrained majority rule. Although there is considerable dissent about what these values are, there is a consensus that they have something to do with individualism, choice and the preservation of a private sphere immune from the state. But for social liberals, that realm does not include economic matters such as property and contract. Private holdings are available for apparently costless reallocation. However, some versions of egalitarian liberalism proceeds in a manner not radically unlike that of classical liberalism. In John Rawls's *A Theory of Justice*, abstract individuals (ignorant of their talents and other information relevant to any future economic ordering) are placed behind a veil of ignorance and asked to deliberate on rules to govern society. In addition to the familiar liberal principles, they come up with a heavily redistributive rule (the 'difference' principle) which validates inequality only if the worst off in society benefit from it. Rawls's individuals are risk averse and ignorant, so to opt for the rule might be thought rational. In the Buchanan and Tullock demonstration, individuals are fully informed of the current distribution of assets and talents; any redistribution here would be based on power, not moral principles.

There is a further justification for egalitarian redistribution which has a rationale derived from classical economics, though this source is never acknowledged by social liberals. This is the idea that we do not own our natural talents and the income we secure from them is a form of economic rent (equivalent to that derived from land ownership). There is no notion of 'desert' in this view of social justice since our income advantages from possessing the talents and owes nothing to our efforts. Natural abilities are available for redistribution at little social cost. This has the added theoretical advantage that since the talent has much less value in an alternative use its possessors will still have an incentive to use it to maximum efficiency. Dworkin (2000) makes an important modification to this view by distinguishing between brute luck, on which we are not morally entitled to any return, and those efforts and choices which determine our futures. Desert would be relevant here, and the inequalities which effort generates are permissible. What we have to do is to buy back natural talents, to which we are not entitled, at some kind of auction.

However, most contemporary social liberals do not speculate in this highly abstract way. Even Rawls's later (1993) demonstration of liberalism makes little or no use of the earlier contractarian method. Although he retains the redistributive criteria, they now seem to be derived from (radicalised) Anglo-American practice rather than rational choice under uncertainty. He is concerned to protect an overlapping consensus, a pluralistic state of affairs that recognises fundamental disagreement about the good amongst the competing groups in society but which allows each to pursue its own value structure in its own way within a social order that tolerates considerable diversity. This is not a tame commitment to compromise, or a *modus vivendi*, but a forthright defence of a philosophical position of some autonomy and integrity. What it does require, however, is regular public affirmation of the basic structure. In this sense, it is veering towards the deliberative democracy mentioned earlier. Whatever its ultimate philosophical founding, it is some way from the complex economic, philosophical, and rational choice reasoning which is such a feature of *A Theory of Justice*.

Today, social liberals tend to make assertions about social justice derived from notions such as desert or need and argue that liberty is seriously incomplete if it is visible only in market relationships; it is vulnerable to the contingencies of the exchange system and the arbitrary inheritances that characterise liberal capitalist society. But there is a detectable movement away from economics in any case. Contemporary social liberals are more interested in human rights, free speech, secularism, a strident separation between church and state and an enthusiastic promotion of minority rights. In these areas, there is a real dissidence between liberals and communitarians, for the latter seek to escape the subjectivism of some aspects of liberalism by appealing to the objective values of the community. In this context, communitarianism ought to support the claims of local communities over things like abortion, free speech and pornography. For social liberals, the rights that we ought to have here derive from hypothetically universal moral principles. Dworkin (1977, 2000) derives his egalitarianism and welfarism from his right to 'equal concern and respect'.

What is especially significant is that social liberals do not spend any time devising constitutional schemes embodying qualified majority voting, or some other constitutional impediment to the will of the (not necessarily liberal) people, but rely on the judiciary. Of course, in a country with a written constitution and extensive judicial review, like the United States, the judiciary will have extensive authority to make law and reshape society in a liberal direction. It is noticeable that many of the liberal advances in that country, for example over abortion, free speech and AFFIRMATIVE ACTION in the workplace, have come not from legislatures but from courts. Indeed, the social liberal strategy is to make certain issues 'rights' matters so that they become virtually immune from interference by elected politicians. Part of the communitarian objection (Barber 1988) to almost any form of liberalism produced by law, is that it bypasses the political process with all the citizen participation and intensity of values which that promotes.

Further reading

Arrow, K. (1963) *Social Choice and Individual Values*, 2nd edn, New York: Wiley.

Barber, B. (1988) *The Conquest of Politics*, Princeton, NJ: Princeton University Press.

Barry, N. (2000) *An Introduction to Modern Political Theory*, 4th edn, London: Macmillan.

Bellamy, R. (2000) *Rethinking Liberalism*, London: Pinter.

Buchanan, J.M. and Tullock, G. (1962) *The Calculus of Consent: Logical Foundations of Constitutional Democracy*, Ann Arbor, MI: University of Michigan Press.

Dryzek, J. (2000) *Deliberative Democracy and Beyond*, London: Oxford University Press.

Dworkin, R. (1977) *Taking Rights Seriously*, London: Duckworth.

—— (2000) *Sovereign Virtue*, Cambridge, MA: Harvard University Press.

Freeden, M. (1996) *Ideologies and Political Theory*, Oxford: Clarendon Press.

Hayek, F.A. (1960) *The Constitution of Liberty*, London: Routledge and Kegan Paul.

Le Grand, J. (1982) *The Strategy of Equality*, London: Allen and Unwin.

Mueller, D. (1996) *Constitutional Democracy*, London: Oxford University Press.

Rawls, J. (1972) *A Theory of Justice*, Cambridge, MA: Harvard University Press.

—— (1993) *Political Liberalism*, New York: Columbia University Press.

Raz, J. (1986) *The Morality of Freedom*, Oxford: Clarendon Press.

NORMAN BARRY

liberation theology

The crucible of liberation theology was the decade of the 1960s. Just as in the first century of the Conquest of the Americas, foundational debates for international law and for the concept of the rights of peoples took place in Spain between Suarez, Victoria, Soto and Las Casas, so now the social doctrine which the (Catholic) Church developed throughout the twentieth century, the revolution in Catholicism unleashed by the Second Vatican Council (1961–3) and an engagement with Marxism contributed to a new worldwide debate about divine salvation and this-worldly justice. To this should be added the growing significance of the non-European world in Catholicism and Christianity in general.

The Council opened a period of unprecedented debate within the Catholic Church at a time when the word 'liberation' was coming into common political usage. On the basis of their interpretation of the Council's injunction to listen to 'the People of God' and 'read the signs of the times' (Mt. 16,3) some theologians began to use the method of Marxism, which they carefully distinguished from Marxism as a creed. The Peruvian theologian Gustavo Gutierrez coined the term with his landmark book challengingly entitled *A Theology of Liberation* (first published in Spanish in 1972, but originating in lectures and papers dating from 1968). The book sets out what was at the time a standard Marxist interpretation of the plight of Latin America, but then proceeds to a highly original theological interpretation of what salvation means in countries where poverty, exploitation and violence are rife. This contextualisation of the question – as distinct from the abstract formulation based on salvation of 'man' ahistorically conceived – was the starting point. The concepts of sin and salvation are shifted away from a 'moralistic' notion (Gutierrez 1973: 196 (in the Spanish edition)) whereby life on earth is lived – and sin on earth avoided – in pursuit of salvation in 'the next world', towards a concept of salvation as communion of all men with God and with one another (Gutierrez 1973: 197) because all people – whatever their religious obeisance – have within themselves the possibility of God's grace. Sin, likewise, is thereby defined as a twofold rupture, of men with God and of the human community. This, and not the more intuitive idea of politically 'progressive' theology, is the core of liberation theology, even if it has evident implications for political action.

A further major departure was liberation theology's critique of the social doctrine of the church as it had been developed by postwar Christian Democracy and Catholic evangelising movements in France, Italy and Latin America. This originated in the revolutionary encyclical *Rerum Novarum* (1891) which distanced the church from excessive CAPITALISM by enshrining the 'social function of property' and opened the way for Catholic encouragement of trade unionism as a counterweight to the influence of socialism. Gutierrez and others were dissenting from the politically conserva-

tive evolution of this tradition, which in the postwar period propagated a misguided separation of religion from politics, which was in its turn used to disqualify more radical interpretations of the social doctrine. The 'distinction of planes' between the church and the temporal world, between the sacred and the profane, between the tasks of faith and of life, as formulated by the philosopher Jacques Maritain, was discarded, but in favour of an explicitly religiously inspired politics, not of a politics under the control of the institutions of the church. This, together with the idea of the universality of God's grace, shows that liberation theology aspires to be more than just a Christian, let alone a Catholic, theology, and although it is widely regarded as a distinctively Latin American contribution, it has indeed been highly influential among Protestants, especially in South Africa.

Although initially, liberation theology shared in the quasi-Protestant post-Conciliar Catholic hostility to 'superstition', its leading figures soon changed their position on the basis that theirs was a fundamentally new approach in which theology is not a purely academic matter, but rather an 'ecclesial function' (Gutierrez 1996: 332) which, though not subject to hierarchical authority, originates from the word of God to all human beings, 'especially the disinherited of the world'. On this basis 'popular religiosity' should be instrumentalised neither in the service of the preservation of the social order nor in that of secular modernisation, nor should it be naively idealised, but the 'liberating', evangelising and even 'theologising' potential of 'the people', and especially of the disinherited gathered in base communities, should be recognised (1996: 330).

This perspective emerges with visible political effect in the grassroots activism of people linked to and protected by the church, which made a major contribution to the proliferation of SOCIAL MOVEMENTS in various parts of Latin America borne along by secular activists as well as radical priests and nuns, many of whom were subsequently sanctioned by the hierarchy.

If Gutierrez can be seen as the spiritual and academic voice of liberation theology, there is another much more activist and 'political' voice coming from the Brazilian theologian Leonardo Boff (1985), who takes up the themes of CEBs (the Spanish and Portuguese acronym for Base Christian Communities) and power within the church. Gutierrez himself had warmly espoused the cause of the CEBs but held back from politicising the issue, whereas for Boff they are the basis of a 'people's church' in which the people of God would hold the power and the hierarchy would be at their service. This has inspired social movements in Brazil and Central America, though it has also generated much controversy, and the concept of a 'people's church' was denounced by Pope John Paul II during his visit to Nicaragua in 1984.

In the 1990s Gutierrez, in reaction to what he seemed to regard as excessively political interpretations of his early work and probably also to the disappointments of socialism, especially the violent abuses of Peruvian 'Maoists', shifted the basis of liberation theology. In his scholarly study of Bartolomé de las Casas (1993) there is not a single reference to Marxism or socialism, and instead human RIGHTS and the oppression of indigenous peoples are brought to the forefront (see RIGHTS, MINORITY AND INDIGENOUS). In a renewal of the emphasis on popular religiosity, Las Casas' defence and illustration of human sacrifice is evoked as an argument for the right to be different and his concept of human rights is distinguished from the liberal concept because it expresses a preference for the most oppressed as opposed to the liberal individualist approach.

See also:

capitalism; social movements; state, relations of church to

Further reading

Boff, L. (1985) *Church, Charisma and Power*, London: SPCK.
Gutierrez, G. (1973) *A Theology of Liberation:*
History, Politics, Salvation, Maryknoll, NY: Orbis Books.
—— (1993) *Las Casas: in Search of the Poor of Jesus Christ*, trans. R.R. Barr, Maryknoll, NY: Orbis Books.
—— (1996) 'Quehacer teológico y experiencia eclesial', in G. Gutierrez, *Densidad del Presente*, Lima: Instituto Bartolomé de las Casas-CEP.
Maritain, J. (1936) *Integral Humanism: Freedom in the Modern World*, trans. O. Bird, J. Evans and R. O'Sullivan, Notre Dame, IN: University of Notre Dame Press, 1996.

DAVID LEHMANN

log-rolling

Log-rolling refers to the exchange of political support, particularly in the LEGISLATIVE PROCESS. The term arose, with disreputable connotations, within the discourse of (extremely) practical American politics. In recent decades the term has entered the vocabulary of academic political science, and some political theorists have argued that log-rolling can promote the efficient and equitable satisfaction of political interests and values.

The term 'log-rolling' evidently arose on the early American frontier. When trees were cut to clear land for farming and to build log houses, heavy logs had to be rolled out of clearings and to building sites, a task beyond the strength of a single person or family. Hence reciprocity arose among neighbours: 'I'll help roll your logs if you'll help roll mine.' By 1809, the term was applied by commentators and editorialists to characterise – but also, to condemn as immoral – assorted instances of political trading in the early American republic (see Safire 1993; Sperber and Trittschuh 1962).

The negative connotations associated with log-rolling might seem puzzling. After all, the frontier practice after which it is named was surely constructive and praiseworthy. And log-rolling may appear to be analogous to voluntary economic exchange, the desirability of which is supported by a massive edifice of theory and evidence. Indeed, the earliest use of the term in academic social science did not condemn it. While conceding that it is 'a term of opprobrium', Arthur Bentley asserted that 'log-rolling, or give and take, appears as the very nature of the [legislative] process. It is compromise... in the practical form with which every legislator who gets results through government is acquainted. It is trading. It is the adjustment of interests' (1908: 370–8).

By the late 1950s and early 1960s, some economists (notably James Buchanan and Gordon Tullock (1962)) and political scientists drew an explicit analogy between economic and political exchange, from which they often drew positive normative implications as well. Since then, the phenomenon of log-rolling has received considerable attention in political science and political theory. Focus on the WELFARE implications of log-rolling has raised a number of analytical problems. These include the prevalence of log-rolling as a function of the nature of DECISION-RULES, ELECTORAL SYSTEMS and PARTY SYSTEMS; the extent to which log-rolling takes account of preference 'intensities'; whether log-rolling avoids or generates the 'cyclical majority' problem; and whether log-rolling produces stable and predictable outcomes.

Let us consider some of these issues by means of stylised examples. First, we have the case of ordinary economic exchange. Suppose A grows nothing but apples and B nothing but oranges, so A controls the allocation of apples between them and B the allocation of oranges. Since each actor prefers more fruit to less, neither would unilaterally transfer fruit to the other. But if A and B each prefers a mixed diet, they can both benefit by trading fruit. We may note three points. First, the fact of mutually beneficial trade depends on 'finer' aspects of the actors' preferences (their 'marginal rates of substitution') that are otherwise irrelevant. Second, since the trade is in private goods, no one else is affected and mutually advantageous trade unambiguously increases social welfare. Third, if (say) apples come in season before oranges, B would have to be able to make a credible promise (for example, by means of an

enforceable contract) to A for the gains from trade to be realised.

Second, let us consider political exchange in a non-legislative (bureaucratic) context. Suppose that A and B are political actors who unilaterally control 'issues' X and Y respectively. Each issue can be resolved in one of two ways: $x1$, $x2$ and $y1$, $y2$ respectively. A prefers $x1$ to $x2$ and $y2$ to $y1$, while B has the opposite preference on each issue. Thus if A and B act unilaterally, the outcome is $(x1, y1)$. But if both prefer $(x2, y2)$ to $(x1, y1)$, they can benefit from a 'log-rolling agreement' such that each trades his preference on the issue he controls (but cares less about) for his preference on the issue he does not control (but cares more about).

We can draw the following conclusions. First, while log-rolling (like economic exchange) depends on finer preference information, it does not depend on interpersonal comparison of preference 'intensities'. Second, a log-rolling agreement is unambiguously welfare increasing if no other actors are affected by issues X and Y or if A and B are perfect representative agents of the affected groups. But neither proviso is likely to be realised in a political context, so the welfare implications are uncertain. Third, non-legislative log-rolling agreements cannot be upset by other actors.

Next, let us suppose that A and B are legislators, each endowed with a single vote on each of two legislative issues X and Y, on which their preferences are the same as those specified above. 'Pork-barrel' (or 'distributive') politics, which arises when the central government finances the construction of public works projects whose benefits are received locally, may give rise to such preferences, especially if legislators are elected from small districts that approximate the catchment area for benefits.

Suppose further that A and B are each in the minority with respect to the issue they care more about (for example, their own projects), but that the support of the other legislator would convert each minority into a majority. Then A and B can engage in a log-roll (or 'vote trade'), each agreeing to vote contrary to his preference on the issue he cares less about, thereby switching the legislative outcome from (x1, y1) to (x2, y2) in the manner they both prefer.

But in legislative context, the actors are trading only votes on issues – not unilateral control – so the preferences and actions of other legislators are relevant. Even if A and B are perfect representative agents of their constituents, the (potential) switch from (x1, y1) to (x2, y2) clearly affects other legislators and their constituents, and other legislators with opposite preferences between (x1, y1) and (x2, y2) may be in position to 'counter-log-roll', neutralising the potential effect of the vote trade between A and B.

However, if the coalition of A and B constitutes a majority of the legislature (if the body has only three members or if A and B are sufficiently large blocs with identical relevant preferences), their log-rolling agreement cannot be upset by the residual minority. The term 'log-rolling' is often reserved to describe the formation of such a majority-sized 'coalition of minorities' (of course, a coalition encompassing many issues may be needed), while 'vote trading' is applied to the kind of pairwise trading described above.

While such majoritarian log-rolling cannot be upset by the minority outside the supporting coalition, excluded legislators can try to break apart the log-rolling coalition by offering proposals to knock out one or a few projects. Any such proposal advantages everyone except the few beneficiaries, which implies that log-rolling agreements are intrinsically unstable. (This also implies that log-rolling is feasible only in the presence of 'cyclical majority' preference over the possible outcomes, a point discovered independently and more or less simultaneously by many different researchers in the early 1970s; see Miller (1977) for a general review.)

It is generally believed that this kind of 'explicit' log-rolling is especially prevalent and visible in the US Congress; prevalent because of its single-member district system and because a 'checks and balances' structure requires broad-based coalitions and visible because

weak party discipline allows members to cut their own deals. But 'implicit' log-rolling engineered by political entrepreneurs attempting to assemble winning coalitions is undoubtedly even more widespread, occurring in the construction of legislative programs and party platforms or manifestos, within one-party cabinets, and in inter-party negotiations leading to coalition governments.

Finally, let us reconsider the welfare implications of legislative log-rolling, using the example of pork-barrel politics. We have two possibilities: (1) the proposed projects are (on average) efficient, as their benefits exceed their costs; or (2) they are (on average) inefficient, as their costs exceed their benefits. The virtue of log-rolling is that even efficient projects cannot command anything like majority support as stand-alone proposals, so log-rolling (of some type) is necessary to assemble the support needed to authorise them. The defect of log-rolling is that even somewhat inefficient projects can be packaged together to secure majority support. Indeed, if a log-rolling coalition is built up sequentially, something like an n-person prisoner's dilemma may result: at every stage, each legislator has a strong incentive to see his own project included in the log-rolling agreement but, as more other projects are included as well, the net advantage to each member of the expanding log-rolling coalition diminishes and may become negative, with the result the everyone would be better off if the log-rolling process had never started. (This is essentially the story told by E.E. Schattschneider (1935), concerning the Smoot–Hawley Tariff passed by the US Congress in 1930, and this scenario is explored formally by Riker and Brams (1973).) Thus we cannot make a conclusive normative judgement concerning log-rolling. But the widespread condemnation of the practice appears to be based on largely unexamined presuppositions rather than analysis. Most students of politics are probably inclined to endorse Bentley's assessment and to be sceptical of proposals (for example, to use new technologies to set up a referendum democracy) that would wholly preclude log-rolling.

See also:

coalitions; electoral systems; majoritarianism; referendums; representation, models of

Further reading

Bentley, A. (1908) *The Process of Government*, Chicago: University of Chicago Press.

Buchanan, J.M. and Tullock, G. (1962) *The Calculus of Consent: The Logical Foundations of Constitutional Democracy*, Ann Arbor, MI: University Of Michigan Press.

Miller, N.R. (1977) 'Log-rolling, Vote Trading, and the Paradox of Voting: A Game-Theoretical Overview', *Public Choice* 30: 52–75.

Riker, W.H. and Brams, S.J. (1973) 'The Paradox of Vote Trading', *American Political Science Review* 62(4): 1235–47.

Safire, W. (1993) *Safire's New Political Dictionary*, New York: Random House.

Schattschneider, E.E. (1935) *Politics, Pressures and the Tariff*, Englewood Cliffs, NJ: Prentice-Hall.

Sperber, H., and Trittschuh, T. (1962) *American Political Terms: An Historical Dictionary*, Detroit: Wayne State University Press.

NICHOLAS R. MILLER

lustration

Lustration re-emerged following the fall of the communist regimes in 1989–90, when its original connotations of religious purification were adapted to the political processes of post-communism. In its modern sense, lustration constituted a subset of the wider notion of decommunisation, itself a concept derived by analogy from the processes of de-Nazification following the Second World War. Decommunisation referred generally to the process of ridding these newly democratising systems of the fundamentals of the old regime. It came rapidly to embrace three analytically distinct but interdependent elements. The first was lustration as a general term for processes of screening or vetting former communist officials and their networks of informers and 'collaborators'. This became entangled with a second issue, that of whether, when and to whom the files of the communist security services should be revealed. The third, the most widely endorsed if difficult to achieve (Moran 1994), concerned the bringing to JUSTICE of the unpunished perpetrators of politically motivated crimes committed during the communist period: cases of torture, political murder, rigged trials and persecution.

Lustration played little role in the newly independent states of the former Soviet Union, where there was considerable elite continuity and thus little interest in opening a potential Pandora's box of revelations. It achieved particular salience in Czechoslovakia and Poland. After the Czechoslovak 'velvet divorce' (1993) Vladimir Meciar's Slovak government announced that the Czechoslovak Lustration Law had ceased to apply; but after Meciar's electoral defeat in autumn 1998 the new coalition returned to the issue. In Hungary, Romania and Bulgaria, early decisions to seal communist files for several decades were also subsequently reopened. 'File wars' continued throughout Central and Eastern Europe.

Lustration aroused heated passions. Advocates stressed the notion of a moral rejection of the previous regime, with lustration in particular (and decommunisation in general) seen as the symbol of a new democratic beginning. Only 'democrats' of sound moral character should hold key positions in the new democratic state. 'Communists' could not be trusted to hold public office, both because of their undemocratic proclivities and their pro-Russian sympathies. Similarly, those who had cooperated with the communist secret police had demonstrated their lack of moral quality. Advocates of opening the files, as happened in East Germany (Engelbrekt 1994), argued that thoroughgoing lustration required such full public reckoning. Society must know and understand the truth of its past in order to lay it to rest. Yet if explicit arguments were based largely on morality and justice, retribution and vengeance were also a factor.

Arguments against lustration were often indistinguishable from those against specific decommunisation programmes. These were encapsulated by Tadeusz Mazowiecki, the first modern non-communist prime minister in Eastern Europe (Poland, 1989–90). Opposing lustration, Mazowiecki argued that the process of democratisation would of itself constitute the most effective mechanism of decommunisation. Both Mazowiecki and Czechoslovak President Vaclav Havel stressed the imputation of collective guilt inherent in the lustration of particular categories of people. Havel also drew attention to the absence of moral gradation in the process: lustration would place a young man beaten into signing an agreement to co-operate on the same moral plane as the policeman who beat him. Moreover, using communist files as evidence raised grave problems of DUE PROCESS and individual RIGHTS. Files were often fabricated, partial, missing or destroyed; they were not always easy to decode, and mistaken identity was a serious risk. Often those registered as sources of INFORMATION did not realise that they were conversing with secret police agents. Again the East German experience was adduced, now to argue the bitter, divisive consequences of learning that family, friends and colleagues had served the communist regime.

In Eastern Germany and Czechoslovakia (and then the Czech Republic), any form of collaboration was sufficient to exclude former functionaries from public office. The Czechoslovak Lustration Law of 1991 barred former senior Communist Party officials, members of its (now disbanded) paramilitary force, students at Party Schools, communist-era secret police and 'collaborators' from holding high office in government, universities and state-owned enterprises for five years. Its opponents, including Havel, who signed it under protest, argued that there was no presumption of innocence and no redress for the accused: an 'agent' or 'informer' was guilty if listed as such in the files (which were falsely assumed to be accurate).

The Czech experience was controversial not least because of the case of former dissident Jan Kavan, who was caught by the inclusion of 'category C collaborators'; these were not in fact collaborators, but persons identified by the secret police as possible 'candidates for collaboration'. Subsequently this provision was removed, but Kavan took five years to clear his name and the law remained contentious (Siklova 1996). However, in 1995 lustration was extended to the year 2000.

In 1999 Lithuania moved to adopt similar provisions, but generally elsewhere the scope of lustration was less than in the Czech Republic and displayed national variations. The 1994 Hungarian law required screening of high-ranking officials not only for collaboration with the secret police but also for participation in the anti-communist revolution of 1956. A Bulgarian law banning former senior communists from holding senior positions in universities and research institutes was annulled in 1995. In Poland, lustration remained a permanent issue on the political agenda after 1989. The implementation of a mild version in 1998 did not end the controversy. The law required public officials to swear an affidavit confirming or denying co-operation with the security services. It provided sanctions only for false witness; however, the Solidarity-led government dismissed numerous public officials who acknowledged their links with the old regime.

Nowhere did lustration provide the anticipated cleansing or expunging of guilt, and no Central or East European country escaped scandal, controversy and false accusation. Lustration did not disappear quickly, as some had anticipated (Holmes 1994; Brown 1997). It remained a tool used by competing elites in their struggle for power. Though it did not assume the savagery potentially associated with retribution, lustration continued to raise profound issues of human rights in democratising societies.

See also:

democratic transition; revisionary justice

Further reading

Brown, J.F. (1997) 'Goodbye (and Good

Riddance?) to De-Communization', *Transitions* 4(2): 28–34.

Engelbrekt, K. (1994) 'Germany's Experience with the Stasi Archives', *RFE/RL Research Report* 3(18): 11–13.

Holmes, S. (1994) 'The End of Decommunization', *East European Constitutional Review* 3(3/4): 33–6.

Moran, J. (1994), 'The Communist Torturers of Eastern Europe: Prosecute and Punish or Forgive and Forget?', *Communist and Post-Communist Studies* 27(1): 95–109.

Siklova, J. (1996) 'Lustration or the Czech Way of Screening', *East European Constitutional Review* 5(1): 57–62.

Welsh, H. (1996), 'Dealing with the Communist Past: Central and East European Experience after 1990', *Europe-Asia Studies* 48(3): 413–28.

FRANCES MILLARD

M

majoritarianism

Majoritarianism is the doctrine or philosophy that majority rule should prevail in democratic DECISION-MAKING. Majoritarianism can also mean a democratic system of government in which power is concentrated as much as possible in the hands of the majority. The two meanings are closely related. Majoritarians tend to think of majoritarian democracy as the only legitimate form of democracy, and to virtually equate democracy with majority rule.

The most basic and literal definition of democracy is government by the people (or, in representative democracy, by the representatives of the people) and government for the people, that is, government in accordance with the people's preferences. The justification of majoritarian democracy arises from the dilemma that this definition poses: who will do the governing and to whose interests should the government be responsive when the people are in disagreement and have divergent preferences? The majoritarian answer to this dilemma is: the majority of the people. Majority rule obviously comes closer to the democratic ideal of 'government by and for the people' than minority rule.

Most majoritarians, however, do not advocate absolute and unlimited majority rule, and they allow that restraints on majorities and minority rights (see RIGHTS, MINORITY AND INDIGENOUS) have a legitimate place under democratic government. Restraints on majorities do not seriously conflict with the principle of majority rule when they are informal – ethical, cultural and social – because such restraints are self-imposed and can therefore also be removed by the majority. Formal – legal and constitutional – restraints do entail a fundamental contradiction with majority rule, because they mean that on certain matters the minority can decide in the sense of preventing decisions favoured by the majority. Moreover, who is to decide to which areas of policy-making minority rights and restraints on the majority should apply? For majoritarians, it is very difficult to accept any other answer than that, in the final analysis, majorities rather than minorities should prevail. Therefore, even when majoritarians do not explicitly reject formal restraints on majority rule, they tend to be extremely reluctant and ambivalent on this issue (Spitz 1984).

What are the implications of majoritarianism for the organisation of democratic government; that is, which political forms, institutions, rules and practices are optimal for concentrating power in the majority's hands? Ten characteristics of government can be derived from the majoritarian principle, on the assumption that democracy is representative (rather than direct) and that representation takes place primarily via political PARTIES (Lijphart 1999). First of all, majority rule is maximised in a parliamentary system if one political party, supported by a majority in the legislature, controls the cabinet. In the case of PRESIDENTIALISM, majority rule is maximised if the president's party also has a legislative majority, and if the president appoints only members of his or her own party to the cabinet. Second, these executives – cabinet or president – should predominate over the legislature, in which one or more other parties will also be represented. Third, single-party dominance is most likely in a two-party system. Fourth, such two-party systems are enhanced by first-past-the-post (plurality) ELECTORAL SYSTEMS.

Fifth, the legislature should be unicameral in order to ensure that there is only one clear majority and to avoid the possibility of competing majorities that may occur when there are two chambers. Sixth, the governmental system should be unitary and centralised in order to ensure that there are no geographical or functional areas, which the cabinet and the parliamentary majority – or the president in a presidential system – fail to control. Seventh, the central bank should not be an independent institution because monetary policy should also be firmly controlled by the cabinet or president. Eighth, the interest group system should be pluralist with free-for-all competition among groups instead of a corporatist system in which the peak organisations of employers and labour can become independent centres of power that can challenge the executive's HEGEMONY (see CORPORATISM). Ninth, the executive and legislature should not be constrained by constitutional limitations: the constitution should be either 'unwritten' or written but subject to amendment by simple majority vote. Tenth, the courts should not have the power to limit the majority's power by exercising JUDICIAL REVIEW.

No contemporary democracy exhibits all of the above ten majoritarian characteristics, but one – the United Kingdom – is a very close approximation. Its main deviation from the majority rule model is its bicameral parliament, but, because the power of the House of Lords is extremely limited, this represents only a slight deviation. New Zealand also came close to the pure majoritarian model until 1996 when it adopted proportional representation, which resulted in a multiparty system and coalition or minority cabinets (see REPRESENTATION, MODELS OF).

The other contemporary democracies are in most respects more non-majoritarian – that is, CONSENSUS DEMOCRACY – than majoritarian. Let us examine the twenty-eight stable democracies with populations larger than two million in the late 1990s, stability being defined in terms of continuous democratic rule for at least twenty years. This set of democracies includes sixteen European countries (Austria, Belgium, Denmark, Finland, France, Germany, Greece, Ireland, Italy, the Netherlands, Norway, Portugal, Spain, Sweden, Switzerland and the United Kingdom), six countries in the Western hemisphere (Canada, Colombia, Costa Rica, Jamaica, the United States and Venezuela), and six countries in the rest of the world (Australia, India, Israel, Japan, New Zealand and Papua New Guinea).

Of these twenty-eight countries, only four parliamentary democracies – Australia, Canada, Jamaica and the United Kingdom – normally have one-party majority cabinets; the other parliamentary systems tend to have coalition or minority cabinets, and the presidential systems frequently experience divided government. In this respect, therefore, twenty-four out of twenty-eight are not majoritarian. Only the same four parliamentary systems, plus presidential France, have clearly predominant executives and subservient legislatures, and twenty-three deviate from the majoritarian norm. Two-party systems occur more frequently – in Australia, Colombia, Costa Rica, Jamaica, the United Kingdom and the United States – but only if we count the tight Liberal-National coalition in Australia as one party and if we count the factionalised and uncohesive American and Colombian parties as real parties instead of mere coalitions of factions. Even so, twenty-two democracies have mainly multiparty systems. Twenty democracies elect their legislatures by proportional representation or a combination of proportional representation and first past the post; only six use pure first past the post (Canada, India, Jamaica, Papua New Guinea, the United Kingdom and the United States) and two use other majoritarian electoral methods (Australia and France).

Only nine of the legislatures are unicameral (Costa Rica, Denmark, Finland, Greece, Israel, New Zealand, Papua New Guinea, Portugal and Sweden), and eighteen are bicameral: Norway's legislature has an unusual one-and-a-half chamber arrangement. Twenty-five have written constitutions that cannot be amended by ordinary parliamentary majorities;

the only exceptions are Israel, New Zealand and the United Kingdom. Twenty-two have judicial review, all except Finland, Israel, the Netherlands, New Zealand, Switzerland and the United Kingdom. The majority of the twenty-eight can be said to have fairly independent central banks and interest group systems that are more corporatist than pluralist, although these two characteristics cannot easily be dichotomised into majoritarian and non-majoritarian categories. The only characteristic on which majoritarianism appears to be the winner is unitary government. Only nine countries are formally federal: Australia, Austria, Belgium, Canada, Germany, India, Switzerland, the United States and Venezuela. On the other hand, several of the formally unitary states – notably Japan, Spain and the Nordic countries – are in fact quite decentralised (see DECENTRALISATION).

In spite of the relative rarity of majoritarian institutions and rules in contemporary democracies, many analysts continue to define democracy in majoritarian terms. For instance, parties that alternate in government and opposition – implying a two-party or two-bloc system – are often regarded as the *sine qua non* of democracy (Lawson 1993: 192–3). This view ignores the many democratic multiparty systems and coalition governments in which a change in the government usually means only a partial change in the party composition instead of the opposition replacing the government. The frequent use of the 'turnover' test to determine whether a democracy has become consolidated – have the party or parties in the government turned over power to the opposition party or parties – betrays the same majoritarian assumption (Przeworski *et al.* 1996: 50–2). Samuel P. Huntington (1991: 266–7) proposes a similar but more stringent two-turnover test. Of the twenty-eight long-term and clearly consolidated democracies listed above, three – Germany, the Netherlands and Switzerland – fail the one-turnover test in the period from the late 1940s to 1996; and no fewer than seven – the same three countries plus Belgium, Finland, Israel and Italy – fail the two-turnover test.

Majoritarianism may therefore be regarded as a Kuhnian paradigm, a basic concept that is widely accepted in spite of major discrepancies between facts and theory (Kuhn 1970). These deviations from the majoritarian paradigm are either ignored altogether, or are explained away as slight exceptions to the majoritarian interpretation of democracy, which is not seriously questioned.

See also:

coalitions; consensus democracy; parliamentary models

Further reading

Huntington, S.P. (1991) *The Third Wave: Democratization in the Late Twentieth Century*, Norman, OK: University of Oklahoma Press.

Kuhn, T.S. (1970) *The Structure of Scientific Revolutions*, Chicago: University of Chicago Press.

Lawson, S. (1993) 'Conceptual Issues in the Comparative Study of Regime Change and Democratization', *Comparative Politics* 25(2): 183–205.

Lijphart, A. (1999) *Patterns of Democracy: Government Forms and Performance in Thirty-Six Countries*, New Haven, CT: Yale University Press.

Przeworski, A., Alvarez, M., Cheibub, J.A. and Limongi, F. (1996) 'What Makes Democracies Endure?', *Journal of Democracy* 7(1): 39–55.

Spitz, E. (1984) *Majority Rule*, Chatham, NJ: Chatham House.

AREND LIJPHART

market forces

Markets of various kinds have a long history, but 'market forces' are a distinctively modern or, more precisely, a distinctively capitalist phenomenon. They operate fully only where there is a generalised economic exchange of goods and services for money and where market relations have been extended to land and natural resources, the capacity to labour, the circulation of stateless money and knowledge as intellectual property.

Barter and trade relations in ancient and medieval markets were typically shaped by customary prices, administrative controls and norms of fairness that limited pure market relations by embedding them in broader social contexts. Market forces were also limited in twentieth-century planned, state socialist economies through the top-down allocation of scarce resources and administered prices. In contrast, CAPITALISM, with its tendential global expansion, is said to maximise the scope for formally free and equal exchange among those who can participate in market relations.

Defenders of the market mechanism regard it as an 'invisible hand' in and through which market forces secure the most efficient and fairest allocation of scarce resources to competing ends. They see it as the most flexible and least disastrous co-ordinating and adaptive mechanism for economic activity, and regard it as far superior to top-down planning. It works best when all economic agents are systematically oriented to opportunities for monetary reward (profit, wage, interest, rent and so on) and consumers calculate rationally how different goods and service may best satisfy their particular material and/or symbolic wants. In these conditions, market forces generate profits for those who provide goods and services for which there is effective (monetary) demand; and they also discourage rational economic agents from undertaking activities they expect to be unprofitable or from purchasing commodities they expect to be unrewarding. The market mechanism thereby equilibrates demand and supply and so ensures that scarce resources are allocated to satisfy consumers' wants. Thus the rational pursuit of self-interest in competitive markets is also said to serve the public interest and, indeed, to do so more effectively than the state. Defenders of market forces further argue that any inequalities that arise from competitive markets are fair and just and that governments (even if

democratically elected and mandated to intervene) should not attempt to 'second guess' the market or correct market-generated inequalities. They claim that such intervention threatens to lead from the market economy via the mixed economy to the servile society. It follows that the response to market failure should be 'more market, not less'. For market forces are a self-correcting learning mechanism, and it makes sense to extend them as far as possible. Paradoxically, this could require state action to promote popular capitalism, develop an enterprise culture and enterprising subjects, and make CIVIL SOCIETY more market-friendly.

Against such an idealisation of market forces, however, we should note that even many liberal economists doubt whether perfect markets, were they actually to exist, could eliminate all forms of market failure. For they may not adequately capture the full social benefits or impose the full social costs of market activity, thereby leading to serious gaps between private profit and loss and social costs and benefits. For liberal economists, this justifies limited forms of juridico-political intervention to correct market imperfections and to promote public WELFARE. Critics of market forces take these arguments much further. One theme that unifies many different lines of criticism is that markets are particularly prone to failure regarding goods and services produced outside a profit-oriented labour process that is subject to the rationalising-competitive pressures of market forces. There are four important categories of such 'fictitious commodities': land and other gifts of nature; labour power as a generic human capacity; money as a medium of exchange; and social knowledge. In each case, market forces are said to be destructive and therefore need to be contained or even excluded from transactions concerning these categories.

Thus political ecologists argue that unfettered market forces lead to the despoliation of the environment and unsustainable development (see GREEN DEMOCRATIC THOUGHT; DEMOCRACY AND SUSTAINABILITY). Marxists argue that capitalism is distinctive, not for markets as such, but their extension to labour power. It is market-mediated exploitation of wage labour that drives 'economic growth' – not the inherent efficiency of markets – and this leads to CLASS antagonisms, recurrent economic crises and the privileging of private profit over social JUSTICE. Theorists on the right as well as the left argue that *laissez faire* capitalism, the dominance of the cash nexus in social relations and the all-pervasive power of money lead to unregulated competition, generate inequality and social exclusion, and corrode social and political order. Other critics see modern markets as a primitive world of predatory capitalism based more on the primacy of politics (whether in the form of private monopoly power or state support for particular capitalist firms) than on the liberal myth of free and equal exchange. Such criticisms are said to apply not only to traditional IMPERIALISM with its military-political division of the world market, but also to hold for the most profitable firms and sectors in today's global capitalism. Finally, recent criticisms have been directed at the extension of market forces into the realm of social knowledge as tribal and vernacular knowledge get commodified, professional expertise is digitised, the human genome is patented, and so on. Nonetheless, another unifying theme across these different lines of criticism is that society – either in general or through specific class or non-class movements – tends to resist the operation of market forces in favour of other values, interests, institutional logics and identities. Indeed, however persuasive the libertarian or liberal defence of market forces regarding simple commodities, such fictitious commodities pose a different order of problems that require social as well as market solutions. This opens a space for DEMOCRATIC DEBATE that libertarians seek to close down and liberals to limit.

The role of market forces has been variously integrated into democratic thought. The most significant dispute concerns the extent to which market forces either promote economic and political FREEDOM or else generate economic and political inequalities inimical to such freedoms. Libertarian defenders of markets argue for the maximum possible extension of market forces in the name of freedom. Liberal theorists generally support the role of markets but also call for social or political action to correct market failures. Cold War liberals have distinguished authoritarian capitalist regimes (such as military dictatorships) from totalitarian regimes (such as communist one-party states) on the grounds that only the former preserve individual property rights and hence the possibilities of a spontaneous regeneration of economic and political freedom (see PRIVATE PROPERTY). Conservative theorists see market forces as eroding traditional institutions and social relations, promoting an excessive INDIVIDUALISM, disrespect for AUTHORITY and secularism. They respond by calling for paternalistic controls over the market, state CORPORATISM, or other limitations on the market. Some industrial democrats and other radical critics argue that political democracy remains incomplete unless complemented by economic democracy or other forms of ACCOUNTABILITY to a wide range of economic and social stakeholders. Finally, Marxists see bourgeois democracy as an ideological complement to capitalist markets on the grounds that, where exploitation takes the form of exchange, dictatorship can take the form of democracy. They argue that the full realisation of democracy therefore depends on the abolition of capitalist economic relations.

A common thread running through criticisms of the market mechanism is that it is always socially constructed and that *homo economicus* is best understood as a specific type of individual rather than a transhistorical human essence. An important illustration of this principle is the current dispute over the treatment of 'GLOBALISATION' as an inevitable product of market forces and the consequent need for states to accept the inevitable by embracing neo-liberalism. Once one accepts that markets are historically specific social institutions, however, market forces lose their appearance as 'forces of nature'. This opens a large space for normative judgement, market regulation, and the search for alternatives or supplements to markets as a co-ordination mechanism for economic, political and social life.

See also:

capitalism; corporatism; economic requirements of democracy; radical democracy; social democracy

Further reading

Altvater, E. (1993) *The Future of the Market: On the Regulation of Money and Nature after the Collapse of Real Socialism*, London: Verso.

Hayek, F. (1944) *The Road to Serfdom*, London: Routledge.

Polanyi, K. (1944) *The Great Transformation: the Political and Economic Origins of our Time*, New York: Rinehart and Company.

Shiva, V. (1997) *Biopiracy: the Plunder of Nature and Knowledge*, Boston: South End Press.

Smith, A. (1910) *An Inquiry into the Nature and Causes of the Wealth of Nations*, London: J.M. Dent.

Swedberg, R. (2000) *Max Weber and the Idea of Economic Sociology*, Princeton, NJ: Princeton University Press.

Thompson, G., Frances, J., Levacic, R. and Mitchell, J. (eds) (1991) *Markets, Hierarchies, Networks: the Coordination of Social Life*, London: Sage.

BOB JESSOP

media

The term media refers to the main forms of large-scale public COMMUNICATION in contemporary society, especially the so-called 'mass media' of press, television and radio. These now extend to embrace a range of 'new media' based on computers and telecommunications, especially the internet. This entry is primarily focused on the national level of political life, although democracy and media are also interconnected at regional and local levels and in other contexts. Although political life and the media have their separate institutional existence, there is now an intimate and even inextricable interdependence between the two. The relationship is also a strained and contested one, and negative as well as positive ideas about the impact of mass media on democracy are to be found in about equal measure. We need to look at both sets of ideas.

The beginnings of modern democracy are associated almost by definition with FREEDOM of the press to report and comment on proceedings of parliament and acts of government. The rise of modern political PARTIES depended on polemical journalism and the wide dissemination of competing claims and visions as well as of INFORMATION. A polity could not claim to be a democracy without realisable rights to free publication and to access to media and this remains true. Aside from fundamental political RIGHTS (such as those of speech, assembly and belief) the working conditions of a democracy, irrespective of different forms and models, cannot be met without diverse and extensive channels of public communication. The main condition is that all citizens have information and an awareness of alternative points of view sufficient to make rational choices between policies, candidates and parties. There is more to it than this, since political democracy is a collective enterprise and depends on the existence of *publics* and of PUBLIC OPINION, both of which are in turn dependent on media for their formation and continuity. The media provide platforms for the expression of opinion by the politically active and give publicity to the issues around which political debate centres. In doing this, even without actually taking a partisan stand, they indicate the range of options for forming opinion and also their relative strength. We have come to rely on the media to make 'visible' the diversity of interests and views in any society. The media also enable less active and involved citizens to participate in a minimal way as audiences for political communication and spectators of political events. Furthermore, editorials and political journalism can provide governments with one quite effective form of 'feedback' to their actions.

Despite the wide currency of these ideas, there is still no fully formed or agreed theory of the role of the media in a democracy. One trend in media theory refers to ideas about a 'public sphere' that have their primary origin in the work of Habermas (1962). As later developed, this version of social theory envisages a 'space' somewhere 'in between' the sphere of private and public life and that of the state and government (see PUBLIC–PRIVATE DISTINC-TION). This notional space is occupied by many voluntary associations and activities, including discussion, debate and opinion for-mation. The media are considered a primary institution of the public sphere.

The negative view of the influence of mass media on politics also has several strands. While freedom to publish was a necessary condition for early democratic movements, by the late nineteenth century, the growing con-centration of a commercialised press in the hands of powerful owners was already seen as a threat to democracy. The power of the press was thought to be mainly on the side of bourgeois governments and conservative or nationalistic ideologies and generally against labour and any form of dissidence. Subsequent developments have not greatly changed this perception, although media commercialisation now seems to go hand in hand with depoliti-cisation rather than with right wing ideology.

However, this trend has posed another kind of danger to democratic politics. The contem-porary media have been accused, variously, of neglecting and trivializing politics, bringing it into disrepute by concentrating on scandals and conflict and failing in their informative role as described above. The general decline of the party press has led politicians and parties to feel that they are denied access to the channels of public communication except on terms that are unacceptable. In free societies, the dangers of undue political bias in the media or simply neglect of politics cannot really be countered, without unduly limiting press free-dom. Nevertheless, a common thread in democratic theory and practice has been the desirability of limiting undue media concentra-tion, either by using anti-monopoly legislation or other forms of economic or political influence. The institution of public broadcast-ing can also be seen as a significant response to the dangers of private monopoly and a guarantee of fulfilling essential public commu-nication tasks.

Despite the lack of agreed theory of 'demo-cratic media', we can assemble a broad picture of what is expected from mass media in a democracy from observation of actual media practice and declared purpose, as well as from certain constitutional, legal and regulatory provisions. First of all, the basic constitutional guarantee of freedom from CENSORSHIP and the various privileges of an economic and legal kind that are enjoyed by media in different ways and degrees in many countries are a witness to the significance of the media for public life. The fact that the claims and expectations of society are not formulated in a specific way is due only to the wide degree of media freedom, which extends to the right to choose *not* to publish and *not* to serve public purposes.

In practice, it is the regulations for public broadcasting (especially in Europe) that have made most explicit what the political role of media should be. These generally require broadcasting to provide full, diverse and balanced information, to give direct access to political parties and candidates, especially during election campaigns (see ELECTORAL CAMPAIGNING) and to reflect the diversity of political views and interests in a society.

Another source of ideas about the political RESPONSIBILITIES of the media is provided by commissions and public enquiries into the performance of the media. Examples can be found in the British Royal Commissions on the Press of 1949 and 1977. Accordingly, a more complete version of the relevant media roles and services to democracy can be put summa-rily as follows:

- to provide full and reliable information about the political environment;
- to provide platforms for the expression of

alternative points of view and a forum for public discussion;

- to provide independent explanations and background commentary on the news;
- to facilitate in various ways the working of the political process, especially at election times;
- to act as independent critic of government, politicians and policies (the watchdog or adversarial role);
- to mobilise political opinion and PARTICIPA-TION, whether or not in the service of the official opposition.

This sets out the norm or ideal view of the role of media in a democracy. In reality, as noted above, with the partial exception of public broadcasting, there is no obligation on any media to perform all or even any of these tasks. Most media systems are organised primarily to make profits and to fulfil a range of tasks, of which service to the political system is only one and one which may be declining in significance. It is certainly the case that in many European countries the specifically partisan (or party aligned) press has declined greatly since the Second World War. Nevertheless, in most countries, certain newspapers do consciously seek to play an active part in political life by reporting or by advocacy, and current political news is relatively privileged, given more prominence than may be deserved on grounds of audience interest alone.

The link between the media and political life has to be understood not only or primarily as an adversarial relationship or an extension of partisanship, but also as a co-operative enterprise. Political figures are of interest to news media, and political news is a staple ingredient of news. In turn, governments and politicians seek media access, especially publicity on their own terms in political news and commentary. More and more attention is given to news management and public relations. This generally involves supplying inside information in return for news attention. Although this can lead to tension with the media, it is not necessarily problematic for democratic theory, since it oils the wheels of information flow.

However, it does tend to give more advantage to the powerful who are more likely either to possess the inside information, or the superior information management resources to engage in this kind of exchange.

As the media have become a more powerful and politically independent industry as well as an institution, fears of neglect of the democratic political role have increased. Public broadcasting is relatively weaker and political parties no longer have very effective means of communication of their own. In general, 'infotainment' is seen as replacing serious political news and comment. However, there are more optimistic interpretations of new television formats of 'political' content, including talk shows 'reality television' and audience participation programming. These are claimed to have a potential for popularising politics, making it more relevant and encouraging participation. Optimism has also been expressed about the potential of new media (for example, the Internet) to reconnect citizens with political leaders, even if, as yet, the great majority do not benefit from this. Other solutions to problems in political communication are found in the rise of new information channels and greater professionalisation of journalists. In the United States in particular, there has been a movement towards what is called 'public journalism', which involves increased attention to the needs of citizens and greater public responsibility. However, the problems perceived to be affecting the media–politics relationship and democracy itself – stem not only from failings of the media, but also from the sometimes cynical use of media by politicians for their own short-term goals without regard for the general 'public good'. There are likely to be causes more fundamental than the doings and failings of the media itself.

See also:

accountability; censorship; citizenship; communication; electoral campaigning; information; public opinion

Further reading

Blumler, J. and Gurevitch, M. (1995) *The Crisis of Public Communication*, London: Routledge.

Dahlgren, P. (1995) *Television and the Public Sphere*, London: Sage.

Habermas, J. (1962) *The Structural Transformation of the Public Sphere*, Cambridge: Polity Press.

Glasser, T.L. (ed.) (1999) *The Idea of Public Journalism*, New York: Guilford Press.

Lichtenberg, J. (ed.) (1990) *Democracy and Mass Media*, Cambridge: Cambridge University Press.

Nerone, J.C. (ed.) (1995) *Last Right: Revisiting Four Theories of the Press*, Urbana IL: Illinois University Press.

Picard, R.G. (1985) *The Press and the Decline of Democracy,* Westport, CT: Greenwood Press.

Royal Commission on the Press 1949, Report Cmd 7700, London: HMSO.

Royal Commission on the Press 1977, Report Cmd 6810, London: HMSO.

Swanson, D. and Mancini, P. (eds) (1996) *Politics, Media and Modern Democracy*, Westport, CT: Praeger.

DENIS MCQUAIL

military constitutionalism

Military constitutionalism refers to the legal status and role of military institutions in the design and practice of constitutional government. From antiquity, military service and citizenship were intertwined; medieval militaries were often contractual, with 'officers' exchanging military service for privileges extended by the prince or king. Medieval towns provided soldiers to monarchs in exchange for tax exemptions, certain degrees of local AUTONOMY and other favours and immunities. Many theorists locate the origins of modern democracy in these medieval restrictions on monarchical AUTHORITY, that is, on medieval CONSTITUTIONALISM and the extent to which it resisted the rise of various forms of centralising absolutism.

The erosion of medieval constitutionalism by centralising national monarchies, followed by the French Revolution and the rise of modern nation-states and national armies, made the issue of civil–military relations a fundamental dilemma for national politics. What would be the role of the armed forces in the constitutional regimes of modernising nation-states? What patterns of civil–military relations could be made compatible with constitutional democracy? To what extent would the armed forces themselves determine the answers to these questions?

Two great political REVOLUTIONS against absolute monarchy and colonialism in the late eighteenth century marked the beginning of a new era. In the former British colonies that became the United States of America, and also in France, the new era was demarcated by constitutions that sought to limit government authority and to guarantee to citizens' basic civil liberties and RIGHTS. These two constitutional traditions were distinctive; on the continent the French version prevailed, and with it a number of anomalous features, especially the tradition of constitutional regimes of exception, dating from the Roman tradition of temporary 'constitutional dictatorship' to meet emergencies, and extensive legislation to protect the 'internal security of the state'. Spain emulated the French model in the Constitution of 1812. In the Spanish colonies in the Western Hemisphere, independence movements in the early nineteenth century also brought a wave of constitution making and efforts to establish republican forms of government. The Spanish Americans borrowed from both the French and Spanish models and from the US constitution, but in practice followed more closely the institutional practices of Bourbon and post-1812 Spain, albeit with presidents rather than monarchs. Constitutional government, in its different versions, thus became the legal foundation for politics in Europe and most of the Western Hemisphere. Only in Britain did the tradition of unwritten 'constitutional' government prevail, leaving no apparent role for military constitutionalism.

Armed forces and military institutions played variable roles in creating and consolidating modern political systems in Europe, North America and Latin America, and, after the Second World War, in the ex-colonial nations of Africa and Asia. In most cases, citizen armies, militias and guerrilla forces made revolutions and anti-colonial movements successful. The role and impact of professional or mercenary armed forces was generally limited to defending the old order, though defectors from royalist or colonial armies everywhere provided leadership to revolutionary and anti-colonial movements. In the aftermath of revolution, military leaders were initially at the forefront in establishing new nations and new institutions, whether in Napoleonic Europe, the United States, the former Spanish colonies in the nineteenth century or former European colonies in the twentieth century.

Thus the constitutional traditions of modern democracies often reflect the concerns of military leaders during and after revolutionary and anti-colonial wars. Nation-building, in part, depended on military force to re-establish political order and to impose the institutions and policies of new governments. Many constitutions and much new legislation assigned military institutions both internal order and external defence missions. In the later nineteenth century, the rise of militant labour movements, the 'social question' and challenges to the liberal-capitalist state pitted the armed forces in much of Europe and Spanish America against labour organisations and leftist parties. In the United States this was also the case, though shortly after the Civil War (1860–5), with the exception of wars against Indian tribes, federal legislation limited the internal police functions of the armed forces. In all cases, however, the constitutional and political role of the armed forces, and more generally the character of civil–military relations, became a central dilemma of constitutional government and of the pressure for more democratic political regimes.

The political consequences of the identification of military institutions with the creation of modern nation-states and defence of their institutions and territory varies greatly. In Spain after 1823, military *pronunciamientos* (coups) were permanent features of political life. In France and Germany the armed forces played significant roles in nineteenth and twentieth-century politics, despite constitutional efforts to limit 'deliberation', beginning with France's 1791 Constitution that declared: 'the armed forces are essentially obedient, no armed force may deliberate' (Title IV, Art. 12). This French restriction – the military was not to enact laws, policies, and regulations for governing society (*deliberer*) but to act (*agir*) subject to civil authority – became commonplace in nineteenth-century Spanish American constitutions. But Spanish Americans gave a different meaning to *deliberer*. In the words of Peru's most important nineteenth-century military president, Ramón Castilla: 'The slow working of civilian law can never be appropriate for suppressing rebellions, since the crime is committed in battle, and the perpetrators identify themselves with the clamorous sound of cannon. All later inquiry [investigation into the matter] is useless.'

Added to this constitutional role for the armed forces, the use of constitutional regimes of exception, such as those first introduced in France (*état de troubles*, 1799; *état de siege*, 1815) to combat 'conspiracies against the security of the Republic', enhanced the constitutional and legal authority of the armed forces. French and subsequent continental constitutionalism (with the notable exception of Belgium's 1830 constitution) permitted total or partial suspension of constitutional rights to protect the internal SECURITY of the state and to suppress internal disorder. In Imperial Germany the *kriegszustand*, or state of war, served the same purpose as the French state of siege. Article 68 of the imperial constitution stipulated: 'The Kaiser can, if the public safety in the federal territory is threatened, declare the state of war in any part thereof.' Under this provision, civilians were subjected to military courts and military officers assumed substantial government authority. Unlike its French and Spanish counterparts, this German 'state of war' was used sparingly in the nineteenth century, but it served as a legal antecedent of Article 48 of the Weimar Constitution. This foundation for constitutional dictatorship was the juridical stepping-stone for Adolph Hitler.

In Latin America, the combination of military constitutionalism, regimes of exception, fusion of military and civilian authority for territorial administration, and military jurisdiction over civilians for crimes against internal security became routine in the nineteenth century. This pattern persisted in most countries to the end of the twentieth century, making 'democratisation' a much more complex issue than suggested by the conventional notion of 'DEMOCRATIC TRANSITION' from authoritarian governments to elected presidents and legislatures. The underlying features of military constitutionalism and constitutional regimes of exception generally constrain 'deep democratisation' and even make respect for civil liberties and rights permanently tenuous. Some of this authoritarian constitutionalism persists also in Europe, though outside of Portugal, Spain, France and Greece, threats of military coups 'to save the fatherland' have not been prevalent after 1945. In contrast, the pattern is common in former French and other European colonies in Africa and Asia, where military governments and dictatorships reigned in more than fifty nations from 1960 to 1990 and significant military influence in everyday politics and POLICY-MAKING is routine.

In most of Latin America, Africa and Asia, the armed forces continue to identify themselves as the 'ultimate guardians' of national interests and the most important interpreters of those interests. In the Latin American case, this tendency is enshrined not only in the history of civil–military relations, but also in the constitutional tradition itself. Over 80 per cent of the 103 national constitutions adopted in the nineteenth century explicitly defined the constitutional functions of the armed forces as permanent institutions of the state. The military was tasked with upholding the laws and maintaining internal order; often these constitutions (or military codes of justice) assigned civilians to military tribunals for 'crimes' against internal security. Officers were constitutionally granted exemptions (*fueros*) from normal criminal and civil jurisdiction.

Thus military constitutionalism established the armed forces as a branch of government, assigned functions much in the same way that functions were assigned to the executive, legislature and judiciary; they became virtually a fourth branch of government with the power of 'judicial review with bayonets'. In some cases the constitutions (or subsequent legislation) assigned the military responsibility for supervising elections, protecting the nation against 'usurpation of authority' by presidents and even by legislatures. These aspects of nineteenth-century military constitutionalism in Latin America have had long-term consequences. In the words of the Supreme Commander of the Armed Forces in El Salvador in 1961 (and in similar statements by thousands of officers before and after): 'Disassociative forces mobilised throughout the republic in a program of agitation designed to undermine and destroy the institutions of the Fatherland'. He stated further that the armed forces 'could do nothing less than confront the emergency and fulfil their constitutional mandate to guarantee public order and respect for law'.

Military constitutionalism is a persistent challenge to democracy and increased democratisation. Democratic politics means, at a minimum (1) selection of political leaders through free and fair elections; (2) open competition and political PLURALISM; and (3) the ability of elected leaders to govern, without veto or threat of veto from the armed forces or other supra-constitutional powers. Yet in most societies the armed forces have a relative monopoly on firepower and capacity for organised, sustained COERCION. Indeed, a major challenge of modern democracy has been how local communities, private associations, diverse social strata and intermediate institutions resist the aggrandisement of the nation-state, and how the elected leaders of the nation-state themselves guarantee the rule of law (see LAW, RULE OF) against centralising and authoritarian tendencies to the contrary. Modern military institutions made possible the victory of the nation-state over feudalism but in turn, partly as a result of military constitutionalism, sometimes became the agents and instruments for modern despotisms.

See also:

coercion; constitutionalism; democratic transition; nations and nationalism; security

Further reading

Clusellas, G. (1987) *Estado de sitio y la armonía en la relación individuo-estado*, Buenos Aires: Ediciones DePalma.

Cruz Villalón, P. (1980) *El estado de sitio y la constitución. La constitucionalización de la protección extraordinaria del Estado (1789–1878)*, Madrid: Centro de Estudios Constitucionales.

Downing, B.M. (1992) *The Military Revolution and Political Change: Origins of Democracy in Early Modern Europe*, Princeton, NJ: Princeton University Press.

Loveman, B. (1993) *The Constitution of Tyranny: Regimes of Exception in Spanish America*, Pittsburgh, PA: University of Pittsburgh Press.

—— (1999) *For la Patria: Politics and the Armed Forces in Latin America*, Wilmington, DE: Scholarly Resources.

Porter, B.D. (1994) *War and the Rise of the State: The Military Foundations of Modern Politics*, New York: The Free Press.

Pinkney, R. (1990) *Right-Wing Military Government*, Boston: Twayne.

Rossiter, C.L. (1948) *Constitutional Dictatorship: Crisis Government in the Modern Democracies*, Princeton, NJ: Princeton University Press.

BRIAN E. LOVEMAN

minorities

The existence of minorities has always posed a significant problem for democratic theory. While democratic political systems are frequently based on an underlying assumption of the rule of the people, who precisely 'the people' are has been subject to many definitions. Athenian democracy was for citizens, not slaves, in much the same way that the formulation of democratic rights by George Washington and Thomas Jefferson excluded most of the individuals living on their family estates at Mount Vernon and Monticello, as well as female members of their households (see DEMOCRATIC ORIGINS). Writing his classic study on *Democracy in America* (1835–40), Alexis de Tocqueville was as much concerned with the 'tyranny of the majority' as with the exclusion of the minorities. That women, blacks and native Americans had no voting rights in this first modern mass democracy was less salient to him than the undeniable fact that majority rule, even within a restricted electorate, was no guarantee of minority rights (see RIGHTS, MINORITY AND INDIGENOUS). As democratic theory and practice in the last two centuries has sought to include an ever wider definition of legitimate participants, the problem of minorities has become an increasingly complex challenge for the advocates of universal democratisation.

Ethnic, racial and national minorities remained an unresolved problem for nineteenth-century LIBERALISM. John Stuart Mill, for example, argued that democracy could never thrive in a multi-ethnic or multi-racial setting. Colonised nations had better mix with the politically dominant Europeans if they were to escape the despotism of custom. According to the same logic, the Scots, Welsh and Irish should also throw in their lot with the English. Mill's position was blatantly ethnocentric, but he cannot be accused of the crude racism of many of his nineteenth-century contemporaries. All groups had the potential for democratic self-government; the problem was how to generate the individual AUTONOMY that was its essential foundation. However, his association of progress with individuality led him along a path that provided a legitimising ideology for colonialism. As a result, he avoided any serious discussion of the types of political structures that would be necessary to permit democracy to coexist with diversity in such pluralistic societies as India, Canada or throughout the African continent.

In the twentieth century, two major non-democratic ideologies – communism and fascism – dealt with diversity in their own particular manner. Marxists, with a few exceptions, largely ignored diversity, or saw it as a force dividing the proletariat from its historic mission. In general, the place of minorities in society became irrelevant after the revolution, a matter of folk dancing and national dress. Fascists sought to eliminate diversity by the ruthless pursuit of genocidal struggle and the promotion of their spurious notions of 'racial' purity. The defeat of both these political ideologies that were so fundamentally hostile to all minorities – fascism in the late 1940s and communism by the end of the 1980s – together with the successes of decolonisation and the civil rights movements, have thrown the minority ball right back into the democratic court.

There have been several attempts to reconcile democratic principles with the existence of diverse ethnic, racial and national minorities within the same political structures. Before considering these, it is important to find a definition of minority that has a reasonably universal application. Most scholars start with Louis Wirth's classic definition that a minority is 'a group of people distinguished by physical or cultural characteristics subject to differential and unequal treatment by the society in which they live and who regard themselves as victims of collective discrimination' (1945: 347; in Stone 1985: 42). This definition raises many of the salient features of minority status stressing a lack of power – a minority need not be a numerical minority – and a sense of grievance at systematic group discrimination. Once this powerful force of racial, ethnic or national resentment (whether based on real or

imagined wrongs) is mobilised in a political arena, it is likely to generate bitter conflicts and intense struggles. As van Amersfoort has pointed out, situations where majority aims and minority aspirations coincide are the exception rather than the rule. Thus resolving such minority tensions is likely to prove a more complex and potentially explosive challenge to democracy than accommodating minorities based on non-ethnic or racial criteria.

A number of strategies have been proposed in order to reconcile the conundrum of democracy and diversity. Some are thinly disguised variants on the old tactic of the dominant majority defining minorities as outside the pale of CITIZENSHIP. Pierre van den Berghe described the *apartheid* regime as an example of '*herrenvolk* democracy': a transparent attempt to justify a system that excluded the overwhelming majority of the population from any serious political PARTICIPATION. In reality, it was a racial dictatorship barely covered by a fig leaf of democratic verbiage. A far more plausible attempt to address the fundamental problems at issue within diverse democracies is what Arend Lijphart has termed 'CONSOCIATIONALISM'. This model has been based on the historical experience of Dutch society, in which competing religious groups have come to a compromise in which a cartel of ethnic elites rule by consensus (see CONSENSUS DEMOCRACY). Claims that this unusual political pattern might hold the key to solving the problems of other, particularly post-colonial, societies has been the subject of considerable debate. Elaborate power-sharing constitutions have been hailed as providing the necessary modifications and safeguards to majoritarian democracy to accommodate the legitimate fears and demands of ethnic minorities. The collapse of societies like Lebanon, once described as the 'Switzerland of the Middle East', into civil war suggests that the extent of internal shared values and, even more crucially, the degree of NEUTRALITY of external political actors, are critical preconditions for the success of any consociational arrangement. The post-colonial African experience, sometimes caricatured by the sarcastic formula, 'one man, one vote, one time', encapsulates the tension between ethnic politics and sustainable democracy. It would appear that the Swiss case is, unfortunately, the exception that proves the rule.

Other strategies devised to resolve the dilemma of democracy and diversity involve varying sets of minority rights and safeguards. Separate constitutional arrangements and treaty guarantees have been particularly salient in the case of indigenous peoples. A difficult problem emerges where 'tribal' or communal societies, whose cultures simply do not define individual rights as being separate from a wider sense of community membership and obligation, come into contact with modern democratic states. As democratic theory has been so permeated by Enlightenment assumptions, based on Western concepts of INDIVIDUALISM, trying to reconcile 'group rights' and communal responsibilities with this form of political system has exposed essentially contested differences of cultural meaning and interpretation. Democracy by consensus lies at the other end of the continuum from democracy by majority vote. Debates on 'African socialism' and 'ASIAN MODELS OF DEMOCRACY', as well as the issues raised by separatist and independence movements around the world, are all linked to varying definitions of the right to self-determination as the cornerstone of any democratic response to diversity. The problem remains that within a single political system one group's self-determination is often another group's exclusion and oppression. Without elaborate mechanisms of devolution, decentralised DECISION-MAKING and entrenched minority rights, self-determination remains a zero-sum game.

The situation is made even more complicated by the ever-changing migratory movements of the modern world working in a milieu of shifting political BOUNDARIES and differential demographic forces. New minorities are constantly being generated and old majorities, and minorities can find themselves trading places. This is a volatile political mixture, which can frequently result in a rejection of democratic processes. Finding democratic solutions

to the so-called 'double minority' situations can be especially difficult. Protestants in Northern Ireland, Arabs in Israel and Russians in the successor states of the former Soviet Union, are all minorities according to one set of political boundaries, and majorities depending on others. These can have a variety of different impacts, but such 'enclave' minorities have been shown to react in fairly consistent, and often hostile ways, as in much of Bosnia, Croatia and Serbia after the break-up of the former Yugoslavia.

Modern forms of civic nationalism have been contrasted with the ethnic nationalist model to provide a possible solution to the multi-national state. One such version is exemplified by the French pattern of consigning all forms of distinct minority political and cultural expression to the private sphere, while reserving the public arena for a secularised majority politics. In the wake of protests from its Islamic minorities, France has been under increasing pressure to find a more flexible formula. Minority groups from North Africa have often felt under cultural siege and have attacked the 'universalistic' principles of civic nationalism as an indirect form of majoritarian hegemony.

A second model of civic nationalism is that of the United States, whose motto, *e pluribus unum*, reflects another attempt to create sufficient unity out of great diversity. This is congruent with America's self-perception as a 'nation of immigrants' although the status of minorities has varied significantly over the past two centuries. The strong assimilative tendencies of the nineteenth and early twentieth centuries have impacted all those minorities who were not marked out by distinctions of colour (see ASSIMILATION). These have subsequently given way to a more pluralistic vision of what it means to be an American. During the final decades of the twentieth century, the politics of ethnicity and policies like AFFIRMATIVE ACTION – which have explicitly recognised claims to special group treatment and compensatory justice – have played a significant part in reshaping the American democratic system. Minorities have definitely come of age in the current phase of American political democracy, but the contested nature of minority demands suggests that there are no simple solutions to these complex relationships. How to truly reconcile highly diverse racial, ethnic and national groups within the same overarching democratic structure remains one of the critical challenges of modern times. An era that claims to have established democracy as a universal human ideal has yet to solve the problem of minorities.

See also:

assimilation; citizenship; individualism; liberalism; rights, minority and indigenous; separatism

Further reading

Brubaker, R. (1992) *Citizenship and Nationhood in France and Germany*, Cambridge, MA: Harvard University Press.

Connor, W. (1984) *The National Question in Marxist-Leninist Theory and Strategy*, Princeton, NJ: Princeton University Press.

Lijphart, A. (1977) *Democracy in Plural Societies*, New Haven, CT: Yale University Press.

Lipset, S. (1994) 'The Social Requisites of Democracy Revisited', *American Sociological Review* 59(1): 1–22.

Parekh, B. (1994) 'Superior People: The Narrowness of Liberalism from Mill to Rawls', *Times Literary Supplement*, 25 February.

Sekulic, D., Massey, G. and Hodson, R. (1999) 'Ethnic Enclaves and Intolerance: The Case of Yugoslavia', *Social Forces* 78(2).

Stone, J. (1985) *Racial Conflict in Contemporary Society*, Cambridge, MA: Harvard University Press.

Stone, J. and Mennell, S. (1980) *Alexis de Tocqueville on Democracy, Revolution and Society*, Chicago: Chicago University Press.

van Amersfoort, H. (1978) '"Minority" as a Sociological Concept', *Ethnic and Racial Studies* 1(2): 218–34.

van den Berghe, P. (1965) *South Africa: A Study in Conflict*, Middletown, VT: Wesleyan University Press.

JOHN STONE

modernisation

A powerful thesis within political science links the emergence and persistence of democracy with the process of (social and economic) modernisation. The thesis was particularly influential in the 1950s and 1960s, then tended to fall out of favour but subsequently enjoyed a partial and qualified revival.

'Modernization' can be understood in different ways. The sociological concept of 'modernisation' builds on nineteenth-century notions of evolution. Closely modelled on the Western experience of continuing social change associated in the first instance with the Industrial Revolution, it describes the process of transformation from a 'traditional' to a 'modern' society. At a more empirical level, the process of social and economic modernisation has been identified in terms of income growth, nationally and per head, urbanisation, expansion of transport and MEDIA communications, increased access to EDUCATION and especially literacy, and so forth.

The thesis elaborated in the 1950s

As most obviously demonstrated by the experience of ancient Greece, forms of democracy have existed in pre-modern times (see DEMOCRATIC ORIGINS). But in the 1950s the argument was developed that in larger, more complex societies, democracy has been closely associated with modernisation, as a prerequisite or even as a cause. An early and influential exponent of this position was Seymour Martin Lipset. Lipset acknowledged there were cases like Nazi Germany where modernisation had been accompanied by extreme authoritarianism and warned against simple determinism. He nonetheless maintained that: 'In the modern world... economic development involving industrialisation, urbanisation, high educational standards, and a steady increase in the overall wealth of society, is a basic condition sustaining democracy' (Lipset 1959: 86).

Lipset (and this has tended to be true of subsequent authors) pursued two convergent lines of argument. On the one hand he observed a strong apparent empirical correlation between a country's level of modernisation and the likelihood of democratic politics. This was most obvious in the case of the western liberal democracies. The emergence and certainly the consolidation of (liberal) democracy had been closely associated in time with industrialisation and economic growth, the spread of cities, rising levels of education and development of the print media. But Lipset sought empirical verification of this association and its pertinence beyond the Western world, in Latin America. As empirical INDICATORS OF DEMOCRACY in Western countries, he used the duration of political democracy and absence of major anti-democratic forces, while for Latin America he used the rather less demanding criterion of regularly held, more or less free ELECTIONS. The indicators of economic development included per capita incomes, number of persons per motor vehicle and per physician, and number of radios, telephones and newspapers per thousand of the population. In addition, industrialisation was gauged by the rate of male employment in agriculture and per capita energy consumption and there were further measures of education and urbanisation. On this basis, he claimed to show a strong statistical association between measures of democracy and of modernisation.

On the other hand, Lipset speculated on the relationships underlying these statistical associations. He suggested that the process of economic development – or modernisation – tended to create a more plural distribution of power and to mitigate the all-or-nothing character of politics in resource-poor societies (see ECONOMIC REQUIREMENTS OF DEMOCRACY). Power was no longer so concentrated in government, and governments were more willing and able to contemplate some redistribution, as through social welfare programmes, to poorer social classes. Modernisation

fostered the growth of the middle CLASS, which acted as a buffer reducing conflict between those at the polar ends of the class system. Education, especially higher education, enabled people to develop longer time horizons and a more complex and gradualist view of politics. Overall, he concluded that modernisation was a prerequisite, though by no means a guarantee, of democracy.

Lipset's argument was echoed in a succession of studies. Many, such as Cutright (1963) similarly aimed to demonstrate a statistical relationship between measures of modernisation, or economic development, and measures of political democracy. The broader literature on 'political development' to an extent incorporated the modernisation and democracy thesis, although some exponents (with the Soviet Union particularly in mind) took care to point out that a modern political system was not necessarily a democratic one.

The thesis in abeyance

But the thesis, and its implied corollary that with further development, or modernisation, the newly emerging nation states of the 'Third World' would become increasingly democratic, was falling out of favour by the late 1960s (although curiously enough it enjoyed a new vogue in the rather insulated sphere of communist studies: adherents of the convergence thesis held that with increasing modernisation communist societies and eventually politics would increasingly resemble those of the capitalist West). There was firstly criticism of the very concept of 'modernisation'. It was argued that the distinction between modernity and tradition tended to ignore vital differences between 'traditional' societies and moreover to present them as static rather than dynamic and changing. It also relied on an unsatisfactory conceptualisation of modernity, largely in terms of the absence of tradition. In addition this whole approach was criticised for its ethnocentric assumptions, that is, its excessive reliance on the historical experience of the west, and its failure to recognise the degree to which economic and political dependence on the Western economies limited the possibilities of autonomous development in Third World countries.

At the same time, and to the extent that such countries could be said to be modernising, the expected strengthening of democracy failed to materialise. On the one hand the few countries – most notably India but also a number of Caribbean states – where democracy after a fashion survived were relatively poor. On the other, there was little democracy to be found in the oil-rich states of the Middle East, while in a series of Latin American countries economic development appeared to be coinciding with the reassertion of harsh military regimes.

In these circumstances, Huntington (1968) called into question the entire modernisation and democracy thesis. Drawing on the work of the economist Mancur Olsen (1963), he argued that rapid economic growth, from a relatively low baseline, could lead to social instability by tending to dissolve traditional sources of social cohesion and raising expectations. This in turn could put excessive pressure on weak political institutions and rather than promoting democracy could lead to political instability and coercive rule. In Latin America, Guillermo O'Donnell (1973) argued that the new trend towards 'bureaucratic authoritarianism' was driven by the logic of the developing capitalist economy: again, the implication was that modernisation could be positively harmful to democracy.

Partial rehabilitation in the era of democratisation

Democracy's 'third wave', from the 1970s, has seen a partial rehabilitation of the thesis. Admittedly the actual term 'modernisation' has been less in use. This is partly because of the narrower emphasis on economic growth favoured in neo-liberal economics. It also reflects a tendency to subsume the process of modernisation in wider theories of 'GLOBALISATION'. Still paradoxically, with the decline of dependency critiques, the underlying conception of a modernisation process has regained some of its former intellectual legitimacy. Indeed, as Roxborough (1988) has argued, and despite all the problems in the way that the traditional–modernity dichotomy has been elaborated, it is difficult to see how any 'sensible theory of historical change' can entirely dispense with the notion of modernisation understood in its core sense, of an increase in the capacity for social transformation or of rationality in human action.

At a more empirical level, this third wave of transition originated in parts of the world – Portugal, Spain and Greece in the southern Mediterranean and Brazil in Latin America – that were relatively advanced in terms of standard modernisation criteria. It is true that thereafter the process caught up a succession of countries comprising not only those like Taiwan and South Korea undergoing rapid modernisation, but many in the poorest regions of Africa. Moreover, some of the more advanced countries such as the Gulf States or Indonesia still managed to resist the tide. Even so, there has been growing agreement amongst observers about the relevance of levels of modernisation to the prospects, in the longer term, for DEMOCRATIC CONSOLIDATION.

A distinctive feature of much of the 'third wave' literature has been its tendency to emphasise agency, or the 'genetic model' of democratic transition (see WAVES OF DEMOCRACY). The judgement and actions of (usually elite) individuals and groups have been stressed and with them the extent to which each transition has followed its own unique and path-dependent trajectory. Even so, there has been recognition that the decisions of actors have been constrained, and the consequences of these decisions have been shaped by wider contextual factors. And it is generally expected that a country's degree of modernisation will be one of the most important. Modernisation here is variously understood or represented. It may be largely equated with development, but at other times its contribution is depicted as more indirect, through the growth of CIVIL SOCIETY, for instance, or a more democratic POLITICAL CULTURE.

The thesis refined

A number of studies have gone further and foregrounded the relationship between modernisation and democracy, often seeming to take up the discussion where it was left off in the 1960s. As in the earlier period, much of the literature focuses on the strength and interpretation of a range of statistical relationships. Not all these studies conclude that the relationship is an important one. For instance Hadenius, who collects and analyses data for the great majority of Third World countries, finds that 'differences in terms of socio-economic development in this part of the world are, although not inconsiderable, far from crucial for democracy' (Hadenius 1992: 147) (see CORRELATES OF DEMOCRACY; DEMOCRATIC DEVELOPMENT). Other studies have offered more support for the relationship but have also sought to establish much more clearly the specific character of the relationship. On the one hand, they have tried to pin down the situations in which the relationship does or does not hold, and on the other hand they have considered which aspects of the very broad process of modernisation are most relevant.

Early writers like Lipset had generally assumed the relationship between modernisation and democracy to be a *positive linear* one, meaning that an increase in modernisation would be accompanied by an increase in democracy. One suggested modification of this position has been that the relationship holds truer for some historical periods than others. It may be that the association was clearer for those countries which began to modernise earliest: in those cases democracy was more of a home-grown product rather than an alien imposition. Latecomers to modernisation faced more demanding and politicised publics placing excessive pressures on incipient democratic institutions, pressures often compounded by dramatic population growth, and were constrained in their policy options by relations of economic and political dependency. Alternatively, the effects of cultural diffusion, accelerated by the revolution in communications technology, could mean that the later a

country has begun to modernise the more irresistible are likely to be the pressures for democratisation. Bollen (1979) sought to test these contrasting hypotheses statistically although he concluded that neither was sustained and that the strongest finding remained the association between modernisation *tout court* and democracy. Writing in 1993, however, Lipset *et al.* found that the relationship in the wake of the third wave was stronger than it had been in the 1960s (although they expected the continuing extension of democratising trends in poorer parts of Africa and elsewhere to modify this difference) when testing the linearity of the association within individual countries. Does the association persist at different levels of modernisation? Back in 1961, Karl Deutsch had suggested that the relationship was more likely to obtain above a certain level of modernisation, while others argued to the contrary that it only held *up* to a certain 'threshold' and was much less in evidence in highly developed countries (Jackman 1975). The implication of O'Donnell's thesis of 'bureaucratic authoritarianism' was of a curvilinear relationship, with variation becoming inverse after a certain point of development. Kurth (1979) argued for an N-shaped relationship, in which the capital goods phase of industrialisation was associated with an inverse association between modernisation and democracy but the subsequent durable consumer good phase was associated with a resumption of positive linearity. Lipset *et al.* modified this yet further to suggest an N with the second upturn flattening off, as an upper threshold of development was reached.

But the concept of modernisation is also extremely broad. It may be that there is indeed some necessary and systematic link between its component features that require us to think of it as a single analytic unit, but the suspicion remains that one or more particular aspects of modernisation are of greatest consequence for democracy. Many of the empirical and statistical studies focus on wealth, generally income per head. Hadenius, in contrast, while unconvinced of the overall thesis and confirming considerable statistical association between different indicators of modernisation, none-theless finds that of these modernisation indicators, literacy is the best predictor.

Discussion

Despite their increasing sophistication, statistical analyses continue to produce conflicting conclusions. This is because there are so many different ways in which the thesis can be tested. Variations in the measures used for democracy, how many and which indicators are used to measure modernisation, the time period covered and the number and range of countries (do micro-states have an inherent greater tendency towards democracy?) can all effect the outcome. Nonetheless, at an intuitive level, the thesis that there is an important association between modernisation and democracy remains strongly persuasive.

For the kinds of reasons originally enunciated by Lipset, the social and cultural changes associated with modernisation, in the longer run at least, are likely to provide the most secure underpinning for democratic transition. The relationship is scarcely a causal one (still less can we infer that democracy in some way promotes economic development or modernisation). As the important case of India underlines, modernisation is not even an unavoidable prerequisite, but its presence enormously strengthens the chances of democracy taking secure root and this conclusion is likely to be confirmed by the experience of consolidation in the 'new democracies'.

See also:

democratic consolidation; democratic development; democratic performance; economic requirements of democracy; social democracy; waves of democracy

Further reading

Bollen, K.A. (1979) 'Political Democracy and the Timing of Development', *American Sociological Review* 44(4): 572–87.
Cutright, P. (1963) 'National Political Devel-opment', *American Sociological Review* 28: 253–64.
Deutsch, K.W. (1961) 'Social Mobilization and Political Development', *American Political Science Review* 55: 493–511.
Hadenius, A. (1992) *Democracy and Development*, Cambridge: Cambridge University Press.
Huntington, S.P. (1968) *Political Order in Changing Societies*, New Haven, CT: Yale University Press.
Jackman, R.W. (1975) *Politics and Social Equality: A Comparative Analysis*, New York: John Wiley and Sons.
Kurth, J.R. (1979) 'Industrial Change and Political Change: A European Perspective', in D. Collier (ed.), *The New Authoritarianism in Latin America*, Princeton, NJ: Princeton University Press.
Lipset, S.M. (1959) 'Some Social Requisites of Democracy: Economic Development and Political Legitimacy', *American Political Science Review* 53(1): 69–105.
Lipset, S.M., Seong, K. and Torres, J.C. (1993) 'A Comparative Analyses of the Social Requisites of Democracy', *International Social Science Journal* 45(2): 155–75.
O'Donnell, G. (1973) *Modernization and Bureaucratic Authoritarianism*, Berkeley, CA: University of California Press.
Olsen, M. (1963) 'Rapid Growth as a Destabilizing Force', *Journal of Economic History* 23: 529–52.
Roxborough, I. (1988) 'Modernisation Theory Revisited', *Comparative Studies in Society and History* 30: 753–61.
Vanhanen, T. (1990) *The Process of Democratization: A Comparative Study of 147 States, 1980–1988* New York: Crane Russak.

VICKY RANDALL

moral improvement

Whether or not democracy provides more technically proficient government than its rivals in terms of formulating policies and taking/implementing decisions, many of its defenders contend that its real strengths – and its decisive justifications – lie in its moral qualities. Some might think that the requirements of morality (in particular EQUALITY) demand the establishment of a democratic regime but assume that, once its institutions have become operational, morality's concerns have been satisfied. It can be contended, though, that the moral case is more extensive, proposing that, after its establishment, democracy continues to promote the ongoing moral *improvement* of citizens and society. Such improvement could accrue to citizens not just in their interactions with the democratic state, but also through PARTICIPATION in a democratised CIVIL SOCIETY. In this way, a 'moral improvement' defence of democracy could posit ideals for social organisations well beyond its institutionalised political relationships.

The daunting variety in characterisations of morality immediately indicates that agreement upon a definition will be extremely hard to obtain and we should therefore expect moral improvement arguments to support a variety in conceptions of democracy. Nevertheless, these can be roughly grouped into two basic categories (though it is important to stress that they are by no means mutually exclusive). The first comprises moralities, which hold that democracy brings what can be termed 'self-regarding' moral improvement, placing justificatory emphasis on those moral benefits, which primarily redound to the individual self. The second category holds that moral benefits are achieved in the relationships between democratic citizens, shifting attention towards the moral well-being of the democratic community as a whole. Some theories hold the moral benefits of democracy to be 'intrinsic', in which these benefits and the outcomes of democratic politics are equated by definition. These will generally yield 'strong' versions of the moral-improvement case, which insist that moral improvement *requires* democracy. Other theories will offer 'instrumental' cases, in which 'morality' is defined independently of 'democracy' and it is contented that democracy is contingently able to promote moral causes.

These, too, can offer 'strong' claims: even if morality and democracy are not the same, the latter may still be absolutely necessary for moral improvement. But they may also be weaker in that they propose democracy to be the preferable option from a range of possible forms of social organisation that share some potential for promoting moral improvement.

Self-regarding moral improvement

Autonomy-based accounts of democratic moral improvement claim that democratic politics promotes the skills of deliberation and choosing that are central to the possibility of competent individual autonomy. Rousseau provides one of the most influential 'intrinsic' definitions of this type, characterising autonomy, or self-mastery, in a manner that morally necessitates the DIRECT DEMOCRACY of the social contractarian polity. For him, if one does not actively will the law to rule oneself, self-mastery is not being realised (Rousseau 1973: 186, 191–3). The perpetually activist life of CITIZENSHIP this type of theory seems to entail might lead one to fear that this is an overly stringent conception of autonomy; perhaps autonomy is wholly reconcilable with less PARTICIPATION in governance. Nevertheless, if one has an autonomy-based morality, one can still argue that *some* degree of democratic EMPOWERMENT is desirable to strengthen the degree of autonomy that citizens possess, even if it is not necessary or desirable to opt for a totally activist direct democracy.

Part of what it means to be fully empowered is that one is a capable chooser. Hence, moral improvement is also promoted in the idea that the skills of democratic deliberation, whether exercised *vis-à-vis* the state or within organisations in CIVIL SOCIETY, promote an appetite for, and competence in, autonomous agency. Participation, as J.S. Mill stressed, can have an educative function in that one learns to reflect upon one's choices in democratic deliberation and DECISION-MAKING such that, ideally, one should become a better chooser (Mill 1972: chaps 2–3, 5–6).

Often featuring 'autonomy' as one of its constitutive concerns but supplementing it substantially, the *self-realizationist* version holds that democracy's value lies in its development of valuable potentials, characteristics or 'essential natures' of individuals. Central to this strand of democratic thought is the idea of 'man' [sic] as a 'political animal', famously postulated by Aristotle (Aristotle 1988: 3). Here it is held to be in one's very nature to be engaged in politics, such that one is not being true to oneself – not flourishing as a human being – if one is unwilling or unable to take an active part in the life of a political community. Democratic participation thus enables the realisation of one's own essence.

Again, this theory is vulnerable to doubt due to the specificity of its intrinsic conceptual link between democracy and what is held to be good for individuals. Echoing the view that modernity is distinguishable from Aristotle's world by the shift of the good life's locus from the public realm to the private, one might indeed wonder what would necessarily be wrong, un-self-realising, with a life that does not involve democratic participation, for there are surely other forms of human activity that could be just as amenable to human flourishing (even Aristotle himself is arguably unclear as to whether active political participation is always required to achieve the good (Mulgan 1990)). Couching the self-realisationist argument in weaker 'instrumental' terms can help to salvage this case, however, for one could still maintain that participation often adds to human flourishing even when it is not deemed to be its necessary central component. This point has some considerable empirical support. In a classic study, Carole Pateman demonstrates that job satisfaction and general spiritual well-being improve markedly for workers who are given substantive control over their immediate working conditions and environment. She suggests a clear analogous possibility in localised participatory political democracy to help overcome citizens' social and political alienation. Given that the research she studied revealed employees to be less concerned to participate extensively in decision-making beyond their immediate environment, the analogy bolsters the contention that democratic participation need not be all-encompassing for self-realisationist purposes (Pateman 1970: chaps 3, 4).

Moral benefits of democratic community

The second, communitarian strand of 'moral improvement' argument can be approached by focusing upon the claim that democracy promotes, and perhaps even requires, citizens to develop specific virtues in order to function well. This idea is certainly present in some 'self-realisationist' arguments, but it can also be categorised separately due to the emphasis given to the development of characteristics which govern citizens' relations with each other, in order to enhance the moral quality of the community as a whole. Among the central virtues familiarly listed in this regard are those based upon respect for others: recognition of their equal status, tolerance, empathy and care, altruism, as well as the dispositions for self-control, sociability and cooperativeness (see CIVIC VIRTUE). Typically, this set of virtues will be complemented by an account of the DUTIES citizens consequently owe to each other. Together these help to facilitate a harmonious, just community characterised by relationships of equality between its members (and greater democratisation will bring the moral improvement of greater equalisation in terms of influence and stake in society).

The 'intrinsic' version of this argument is a variant of the self-realisationist strand and also claims descent from Aristotle; it is often labelled 'civic humanism'. Here, active virtuous citizenship defines the good for individuals (to be a good person is to be a good citizen) and for society (the good society is the society of active, virtuous citizens). As citizens become ever more engaged in participation and ever more disposed to virtue, so the moral condition of each, and of society as a whole, is said to be heightened. The instrumental version of this argument often takes the form of civic REPUBLICANISM which emphasises the need for citizens to acquire specific virtues and discharge certain obligations in order to maintain the type of community that sustains the possibility of individual FREEDOM. If citizens are not appropriately respectful of others, the society loses its civil character and the conditions for peaceful co-existence break down, thus undermining the possibility of individuals formulating and pursuing their own good. This version suggests that virtues can attach to democracy not just when the focus is upon the development of a harmoniously ordered community governed by solidarity and co-operation. For this kind of moral improvement is also available, in an attenuated form, to a democratic AGONISM, where the need for accommodation among inevitably divergent groups disciplines the citizens into peaceful rather than conflictual behaviour without pretending that SOLIDARITY over the pursuit of a wider common good can be achieved.

Democracy versus moral improvement

Two criticisms of the idea that 'moral improvement' arguments have any place in democracy's defence should be considered. The first, forwarded by Elster, need not deny that democracy brings morally improving benefits, but contends that theories which urge us to engage in democracy because of what are essentially *by-products* of its operation are likely to be self-defeating (Elster 1986). If we engage in democratic practices to acquire moral benefits rather than to obtain political decisions, Elster believes we are likely to become so involved in the pursuit of the by-product that we will not achieve the actual purpose of democracy: decision-making itself. Thus, 'moral improvement' considerations should play no role in the reasons we give to justify democracy (see DEMOCRACY, JUSTIFICATIONS FOR). It is unlikely, however, that 'moral improvement' democrats need think that we should engage in democracy *only* for its moral benefits. Of course they will want it to produce decisions, but the 'moral improvement' considerations can come into play as secondary justifications, to help one pick which form of *effective* regime it is best to choose.

Far more serious are the direct challenges to democracy's claims to promote moral improvement. From its very origins, democracy's critics have urged that it lacks any guarantee that it will not produce morally repugnant outcomes (Nazism in Germany is a frequently cited example). The ends to which the self-regarding benefits of democracy are put could be bad as well as good, one might fear, whilst the activity of participation does not automatically promote virtue and a just society. Alternatively, 'disenchanted' democrats oppose its moral aspirations on the grounds that moral PLURALISM disables us from uncontroversially evaluating its moral effects and, further, hold that the opportunities for meaningful democratic participation are now so limited that no such benefit could be realistically achieved anyway. Shorn of such moral justifications, democracy becomes defensible (and defeasible) only on the grounds of its effectiveness as a method for selecting political leaders (Held 1996: ch. 5).

Undoubtedly these arguments gain sustenance from the practical constraints, which really do exist upon the extent and depth of democratic politics in modern states. Yet even if we concede the instrumentalist version of the argument and admit that democracy is only one (and not necessarily the most efficacious) of numerous ways in which moral improvement could be achieved, we can still hold that there remain significant choices to make between democratic and non-democratic regimes, no matter how limited democratic possibilities are. Such choices require criteria and, if whatever participation is possible provides some moral improvement, this remains a powerful and perhaps overridingly unique consideration in democracy's favour.

See also:

citizenship; civic virtue; civil society; duties; education; equality

Further reading

Aristotle (1988) *The Politics*, ed. S. Everson, Cambridge: Cambridge University Press.

Dagger, R. (1997) *Civic Virtues*, Oxford: Oxford University Press.

Elster, J. (1986) 'Self-Realisation in Work and Politics', in E.F. Paul, F.D. Miller Jr, J. Paul and J. Ahrens (eds), *Marxism and Liberalism*, Oxford: Blackwell.

Held, D. (1996) *Models of Democracy*, Cambridge: Polity Press.

Mill, J.S. (1972) 'Considerations on Representative Government', in J.S. Mill, *Utilitarianism, On Liberty and Considerations on Representative Government*, London: Dent.

Mulgan, R. (1990) 'Aristotle and the Value of Political Participation', *Political Theory* 18(2): 195–215.

Pateman, C. (1970) *Participation and Democratic Theory*, Cambridge, Cambridge University Press.

Rousseau, J.-J. (1973) *The Social Contract and Discourses*, trans. G.D.H. Cole, London: Dent.

MARK EVANS

mortgaged democracy

The idea of a mortgage – from the French 'dead pledge' – has existed for at least five hundred years. In legal terms, it refers to the transfer of property from a debtor (the mortgagor) to a creditor (the mortgagee) as security for a money debt, with the proviso that the property shall be reconveyed upon payment to the mortgagee of the sum secured within a certain period. In *The Eighteenth Brumaire* (1869), Karl Marx recognised the importance of the mortgage in the development of capitalist democracy: 'The feudal obligation that went with the land was replaced by the mortgage', and the bourgeois order 'has become a vampire that sucks [the smallholders'] blood and brains and throws them into the alchemist's cauldron of capital' (Marx 1954: 109). The mortgage, for Marx, is an unequal relationship of dependence contributing to poverty and exploitation.

Democracies express two forms of mortgage relationship, which are like agreements for a monetary loan with debtors and creditors. On the one hand, states can be mortgaged to entities such as large corporations or international financial institutions. On the other, individuals mortgage their FREEDOM to the state and financial creditors. What is the nature of these 'mortgages'? What is the form of interest? What happens when the conditions of the loan are not fulfilled? These questions may provide a way of thinking critically about the model of representative government in which the people are deemed sovereign.

Mortgaged states

A democracy is mortgaged when its 'deeds' are held by particular groups or institutions. If the democracy does not fulfil the needs or desires of these groups – that is, repay the loan and interest – then the state, like a mortgaged house, may be claimed or conveyed. The 1954 coup in Guatemala, ending ten years of elected reformist government, demonstrates how a democratic state can be claimed by its creditors. Land reform and labour rights threatened the interests of the Guatemalan business sector, the military and the US-owned United Fruit Company (UFCO). Under pressure from UFCO, and fearing the spread of communism in the region, the USA helped engineer the coup. The United States continues to be an important creditor in the region. Extensive US funding for the Colombian military and the 'war on drugs' shifts government ACCOUNTABILITY from its own citizens to a foreign power. Accountability is complicated by the Colombian state also being mortgaged to drug cartels and the local oligarchy.

The idea of mortgaged democracy can be extended beyond Latin America to the rich established democracies. In exchange for supporting governments, often by financing political PARTIES or keeping investment within the country, large corporations receive innumerable benefits which represent debt repayments. These include state contracts for arms manufacturers and scientific research funding for pharmaceutical and biotechnology companies, low-interest government loans and cheap insurance for firms involved in international trade, state promotion of exports, provision of transport infrastructure, privileged access to decision makers concerning interest rate and exchange rate policy, and state financial backing of stock markets, currencies and banks in times of economic crisis. The US government provides direct subsidies to business of $51 billion a year, with $53 billion in corporate tax breaks; which exceeds WELFARE spending to the poor by around $30 billion (Chomsky 1997: 102–5, 107). When such benefits are not forthcoming, business threatens to take its money elsewhere, or to support an alternative party. In this way, established democracies remain mortgaged, and citizens are made responsible for paying the 'interest' through taxation and social spending cuts.

Poor democracies are frequently mortgaged to international financial institutions (IFIs) and the industrialised nations, which support and control them. The International Monetary Fund and World Bank provide loans to relieve state debts, but on condition that countries accept structural adjustment packages which force PRIVATISATION and the removal of trade barriers to foreign capital. Nicaragua became dependent upon IFIs in this way in the 1990s. In particular instances the 'property' may be deemed worthless and debt repayments cancelled. Russia's mortgaged status was revealed at the end of the 1990s when the US used IFI loans to bolster the ailing Yeltsin regime. Mortgage relationships are being created and enforced through the World Trade Organisation, with developed countries attempting to legislate unimpeded global capital movements to their benefit. The threat of international economic isolation or trade sanctions keeps economically weaker democracies dependent, although the social protest at the WTO meeting in Seattle in November 1999 showed that the mortgage terms are subject to some negotiation. Developed nations can also be caught in a mortgage relationship with the amorphous 'global capital': in 1992 currency speculation forced the United Kingdom to withdraw from the European Exchange Rate Mechanism.

Mortgaged citizens

Like the democratic state, individuals can also be mortgaged. Frequently we give up our freedom to a relationship of dependence in which we make 'payments' to both financial creditors and the state, often with little prospect of regaining liberty.

Mortgaged individuals are a characteristic of nominally democratic states in which debt bondage still exists. In Brazil in the 1990s, for example, an estimated 60,000 people were in forced labour on some 300 agricultural estates. Unable to pay off debts, workers are often surrounded by armed guards to prevent escape, threatened with death and sometimes killed. In conditions of poverty lives are mortgaged at the cost of individual freedom.

Individuals are mortgaged in more subtle ways in the established democracies. Liberal democracies promote the protection of PRIVATE PROPERTY, and there is strong cultural pressure to own such property, particularly a home. In *Walden*, Thoreau writes that in Concord, Massachusetts in the 1840s, it took labourers ten to fifteen years of work to pay off the mortgage for an average house. The situation is little different today. Yet the burden of debt is not simply financial: 'the cost of a thing is the amount of what I will call life which is required to be exchanged for it'. Thoreau realises that the burden of civilisation is the loss of years of life in paying off debt; the Indians, with their wigwams, do not face this prospect. When mortgages are not repaid property can be repossessed, and individuals may face charges of bankruptcy, fines and even incarceration by the state. In the 1980s in the UK, the Thatcher government's sale of council houses encouraged people into the private property and mortgage market. Citizens were given the ambiguous freedom to be in debt. Thoreau also observes that the ownership of a house and other possessions ties people down geographically. The 'need' in modern societies to own a home and the social, psychological and financial pressure to pay off the mortgage promotes a sedentary lifestyle which effectively acts as a limit on freedom of movement for most people. In this sense private property in the mortgaged democracy is at odds with an individual freedom fundamental in liberal thought.

Individuals are mortgaged to the state, incurring certain obligations in exchange for the privileges of CITIZENSHIP (or right of abode). This relationship is generally mediated by taxation – a compulsory levy on individual work or consumption – which acts as a form of interest payment. When income tax is not paid the result can be fines or prison, particularly for the poor. With the shift in recent decades from direct income tax to indirect sales taxes, individuals have less prospect of 'paying off' this debt through reaching retirement age. Since even the elderly and unemployed must be consumers until the ends of their lives, nobody can come fully to possess citizenship without financial obligations to the state. Inequality in the tax relationship is partly generated because individuals do not have control over the use of taxes, except (in general) in the most indirect fashion through ELECTIONS every few years. Individuals may not agree that their taxes are used to finance particular aspects of criminal justice systems, or to embark on wars or to subsidise those groups to whom the state is mortgaged, but have negligible influence over such matters. (Nor do we have much control over what a bank does with the profits from its mortgage lending.) This gap between individuals and the state is not a function of which party is in power. The problem is more with the representative system itself and the existence of an inaccessible, centralised state.

In democracies in which there is forced military service or the possibility of conscription at times of war, individuals mortgage their lives to the state. In these situations the state can call in the ultimate debt. Non-compliance usually results in incarceration or forced labour. The connection between citizenship and war is not surprising given that extension of the franchise in established democracies has been closely associated with the need to mobilise men for war and to integrate women into the war economy.

More broadly, the mortgaged democracy uses the rule of law (see LAW, RULE OF) to place limits on the freedom of individuals as the price of citizenship or the right to live in a country, supposedly for their own or the general good. People may be banned from smoking cannabis or forced to do jury service, and children may be prevented from directing their own EDUCATION. Individual freedom, or individual sovereignty, is mortgaged to the state. The loan of citizenship can never be repaid. And while it is easy for some individuals to choose between a range of house mortgages, it is less easy to select between citizenships with different mortgage terms. Acceptance of these limitations has become so ingrained that it is commonplace to talk about living in a 'free society'. Yet what bank would extend a free mortgage, without any repayment obligations?

While all democratic states and their citizens are mortgaged in some form, not all nominally democratic states express mortgage relationships in the same way or to the same degree. Colombia's politicians are indebted to criminal gangs to an extent not evident in Australia or Denmark. While a number of countries do not enforce their legislation against debt bondage, others largely do so. The referendum system in Switzerland permits citizens greater control of the state than in many countries, providing a mortgage on less severe terms. In New Zealand, Canada and Israel for example, the state tolerates and even encourages 'free schools' where children can opt to attend classes or to take examinations. Governments in some countries appear more responsive to citizen demands than in others and are more likely to adhere to election manifestos. In practice, however, this responsiveness is a complex interaction of PUBLIC OPINION, government manipulation and MEDIA influence which can result in a 'war on crime' or other populist policies.

Alternatives

We might think about alternatives to the mortgaged democracy by returning to the original meaning of mortgage, as a contractual relationship used to purchase property. Community or tenant-run housing co-operatives and self-build housing schemes are methods by which some of the problems of traditional housing have been overcome in modern societies. Housing is frequently cheaper than in the private sector, which reduces the debt burden, and of better quality than that provided by the state. Funding or loans often come from non-profit making institutions, similar to the microcredit schemes found in poor neighbourhoods around the world. Their participatory forms involve people in making decisions about their own lives, the results of which are experienced at the local level. All of this helps provide people with a sense of individual freedom (Ward 1989; Ravetz 1999).

Extending this idea, if the decisions that affect people's everyday lives were made by themselves at a more local and participatory level, without the intermediaries and citizenship debts of the representative system, and the interests to which this system is beholden, then the problems of the mortgaged democracy might be avoided. The distance between state and individual could give way to something like a system of decentralised federated co-operative banks, a horizontal network of social, political and economic organisations managed by the very people they serve, which enable the pursuit of individuality. Individuals would hold the deeds to their own lives.

Metaphors for the state often treat it as a living object that can grow or decay, or a mechanical structure that can be replaced or redesigned. To describe a democracy as 'mortgaged' is to shift our thinking about the state. It becomes a condition, or the expression of a relationship. In one sense there is a mortgage relationship with particular interests such as big business, in another there is a mortgage relationship with citizens. These relationships involve human beings, some of whom are debtors, some of whom are creditors and some, like government bureaucrats or politicians with company directorships, may be both. As such, modern representative democracy cannot be an expression of individual freedom. Colin Ward quotes the German anarchist Gustav Landauer: 'The state is not something that can be destroyed by a revolution, but is a condition, a certain relationship between human beings, a mode of human behaviour; we destroy it by contracting other relationships, by behaving differently' (Ward 1996: 23). The challenge to the political mortgage system will come from establishing forms of contract or association that are local, voluntary, non-hierarchical and based on mutual aid.

See also:

capitalism; freedom; globalisation; individualism

Further reading

Chomsky, N. (1997) *World Orders, Old and New*, London: Pluto Press.

Marx, K. (1954) *The Eighteenth Brumaire of Louis Bonaparte*, Moscow: Progress Publishers.

McMurtry, J. (1999) *The Cancer Stage of Capitalism*, London: Pluto Press.

Ravetz, A. (1999) 'Looking Forward and Looking Back: State Provision and Self-Help in Housing Policy', in K. Warpole (ed.), *Richer Futures: Fashioning a New Politics*, London: Earthscan.

Ward, C. (1989) *Welcome, Thinner City: Urban Survival in the 1990s*, London: Bedford Square Press.

—— (1996) *Anarchy in Action*, London: Freedom Press.

ROMAN KRZNARIC

N

nations and nationalism

The nation is usually defined as a political and/or cultural community. In English, French and Spanish, 'nation' is widely used as a synonym for 'state' (for example, the United Nations), in German and Slavic languages its meaning tends to be closer to 'people' (*Volk* in German), and is often used to describe an ethnic, linguistic or cultural community, or even a race. Nationalism is defined as a state of mind, ideology and/or movement defending and/or enhancing the IDENTITY and the value of a particular nation. Nationalists want their nation at least to be equal to others, and put national identity and loyalty before other group identities and loyalties. To justify their claim, they may invoke the subjective will of individuals to form a nation, the daily plebiscite. In this case, they often deny being nationalists. Or they may appeal to 'objective' facts like a common language, culture, customs, history, economy, a national spirit or character, or a combination of several objective facts and/or the subjective will of their community.

Origins and history

The word nation is of Latin origin. In its original meaning, it signified the geographical origin of persons, their birthplace. In medieval universities, students were organised according to their homelands, and these units were called nations and their territorial extension varied. The use of the term has proliferated since the French Revolution. The revolutionaries used it to designate the body of associated citizens who were ruled by the same laws and represented in the same legislature. Reciprocal bonds of loyalty were seen to exist between the nation and the citizen. This concept was based on popular SOVEREIGNTY. But a concurrent understanding emerged which stressed the existence of traditions and a common language. For German romantics like J.G. Herder, a people was a genuine community, not an artificial association; it existed independently of the state. Every people/nation was a branch of the trunk of humanity, united by bonds of 'tongue and ear', and marked by its own collective soul, its national spirit or character (*Volksgeist*). Herder introduced the term 'nationalism', although he abominated it as foolish and arrogant. However, contrary to his view of all nations as equal in value, the German resistance to Napoleon introduced the notion of a particular mission of the German nation, enhancing German singularity. Some of Fichte's followers started to equate singularity with superiority and based the national community on biological descendance or excluded persons of a particular 'blood'. In many organisations of the rising German national movement, inner unity and equality became more important than individual liberties.

Defence of individual rights and liberties and national independence marched together in the *risorgimento*-nationalism of the first half of the nineteenth century, against the reactionary Holy Alliance of the territorial states. For nationalists like Mazzini, nations were tools to improve mankind. The problem of the delimitation of national BOUNDARIES became relevant, because cultural and/or linguistic coherence was seen as an advantage for the creation and functioning of a liberal state. But not all possible nations were equal. Even Marx and Engels used the Hegelian category of history-less people, who – counter-revolutionary by nature – were condemned to the dustbin of history, and true socialists had to help to send them to their destiny. Marxist classics did not formulate any systematic theory of the nation. Their concept of history as a result of class struggles contributed to this. By the same token, Marxists supported particular national movements and nation-states tactically.

The unification of Italy and Germany was achieved by existing territorial states, not by national movements. From then on, the values of individual rights and liberties and of national sovereignty and strength were in open conflict. In the age of imperialist struggle, the absolute maintenance of national unity seemed essential. 'Integral' nationalists attacked the liberal tradition, and saw the nation as an end in itself. This 'sacred' national egoism reached its apex in fascism. On the other hand, liberals and communists, Wilson as well as Lenin, allied with nationalist movements against the multinational Austro-Hungarian, Russian and Ottoman empires, under the banner of national self-determination. The Treaty of Versailles proved the unviability of the principle of giving every nation its own state. However, this principle was obviously attractive to any national movement, and became a key part of the anti-colonial movements in the Third World (see IMPERIALISM).

At the same time, a certain shift in communism from CLASS CONFLICT within particular societies to economic conflict between societies brought about anti-colonial alliances under the national banner. The range of Marxist positions on the question of nation included the Austro-Marxists, who saw nations as communities of COMMUNICATION and destiny, shaped by history. The favoured solution of this school was non-territorial cultural AUTONOMY. Leninism and Stalinism, which fought against this current, accepted territorial national self-determination as part of their revolutionary strategy. A third position rejected this as economic nonsense and denounced the artificial resurgence of nations and mini-nations. All three arguments, economic viability, political strategy and cultural

non-territorial autonomy, are still discussed in current approaches to the issue. The last concept may even be seen as a precursor for actual propositions to separate cultural membership and territoriality, in order to accommodate multicultural situations by differentiated CITIZENSHIP.

Different approaches

Social scientists began to study nationalism under the influence of the world wars. This section summarises the main currents of interpretation up to the 1980s in chronological order.

The first task was to define and classify. After the Second World War, analysis of nationalist deeds and writings produced typologies which were used to distinguish between 'good' and 'bad' nationalism. In the first case, the nation was seen as a product of the free will of individuals, with citizenship as the base of its membership. This type was characterised as progressive, open and facilitating democratic opinion. The opposite of this civic and political 'nationalism' (often called patriotism) was cultural nationalism, based on the *Volk*, an exclusive, anti-liberal identity, not open to individual decision on membership, and characterised by an irrational rejection of the liberal state and an inferiority complex in relation to the 'rational cosmopolitanism' of the Western nations. This second type was to be found in Germany and eastward (Kohn 1945). This dichotomy still lingers.

After the Second World War political science centred on the importance of the nation-state for modernisation, democratisation and the WELFARE state. Modernisation theorists did not care much for nationalist writers and literature; they analysed the nation-state as a result of the process of social mobilisation. Membership of a nation, nationality, was functionally defined as wide complementarity of social communication, which enabled the members to communicate more effectively among themselves than with outsiders. According to Deutsch (1953), nationalism is a response to the opportunities and insecurities that the lift pump effect of economic growth and social mobilisation brought with it. On the one hand, the nation-state was seen as functional and efficient. On the other, contesting regional nationalism was widely seen as anti-modern, only to be explained by resistance to assimilation of traditional elites which had failed to progress.

In the 1960s and 1970s, political scientists like Moore, Eisenstadt and Rokkan developed research on the origins of the nation-state. State formation meant above all the creation of a centre and administrative penetration of a territory. It was widely seen as preliminary to the nation-building process, which meant the building of the external cultural boundary and internal cultural standardisation. The fit of these two processes was nowhere complete and depended on a number of preconditions. Moreover, the success of the establishment of the nation-state was important for the later move towards mass democracy, and the expansion of the state's administrative apparatus for social redistribution. The achievement of mass democracy and the welfare state further consolidated the nation-state. But in any of these four processes, crises may occur and territorial conflicts may break out. Over-penetration and over-standardisation may produce de-legitimising ideologies in the peripheries, which have their own opportunity structures for political action. This approach corrected the bias towards ASSIMILATION and diffusion of modernity which had been characteristic of older modernisation theories. The multidimensionality of this territorial approach corresponded with a recognition of incongruities of cultural, economic, and political roles and culminated in a normative recognition of the right to roots and the right to options, and a positive view of double or multiple identities. Actual users of the concept of nation-building introduce activist elements like the role of leaders, and arrive at different conclusions, advocating states that no longer aspire to be nation-states, and nations that renounce exclusivity and the obtainment of nation-statehood.

The attempts to correct the assimilationist bias of early modernisation theories may be related to the appearance of national movements in seemingly consolidated nation-states of the West in the 1960s and 1970s. This phenomenon spurred the debate on whether ethnic ties are necessary for the existence of a nation and for nationalism. Defenders of ethnicist and ethno-symbolic approaches criticise modernisation theories as instrumentalist, Western-biased and wrongly focused on the economy. Instead, they give importance to the 'mythomoteurs' of the past and/or the continuing importance of the myth of common descent, the intuitive sense of kinship which is seen as the glue of the nation. It is argued that even today, nations are in need of common myths, memories and symbols, as much as the ethnic groups which underpin them. In this approach, nation is still basically an ethnos, but an ethnos with a territory and citizenship RIGHTS for all inhabitants.

The opposite position holds that nationalism comes first and creates the nation. Structuralists like Gellner (1983) continue the work of modernisation theorists in various respects. They interpret the nation as a purely modern phenomenon. Cultural continuity and national myths are not essential. Congruence of state and high culture is essential, but both are instruments. Nationalism holds that cultural and political boundaries should coincide. This suits the transition from agrarian to industrial society and especially the demand of the latter for a homogenised and literate workforce, which only a state controlled EDUCATION system with a common high culture can provide. Nationalism, in this sense, is the consequence, and the price 'we' have paid for industrialisation.

Finally, the failings in the formation of nations, then, are not rooted in ethnic differences, but result from the uneven diffusion of industrial society. Under the influence of Marxism in the 1970s this was usually labelled internal colonialism. Called sometimes regionalism, minority nationalism or neo-nationalism, contesting movements came to be seen as politically creative and anti-repressive. Nationalism was classified as the precondition for true internationalism. However, some Marxists saw those nationalisms as unhealthy and morally dubious because of their egoism, and a threat to plurality which was better guaranteed by multinational states (see Beiner 1999a). This second group insisted on classifying national symbols as 'invented traditions', engineered by their creators. The injection of ethnicity and linguistic culture into the once revolutionary concept of the nation-state symbolises the end of its progressive character and led to the 'illusory' principle of national self-determination, to the attempts of many nation-states to assimilate, expel, kill or separate permanently those parts of the population which were not seen as members of the dominant ethnos. Small nations may succumb to the charms and pressures of multinational enterprises. If at all, Marxists should ally with particular movements and treat the question pragmatically, rejecting an alliance with nationalism as such.

Current debates

The 1980s and 1990s have added more approaches to the discussion between ethnicists, structuralists and Marxists. These innovative contributions will be summarised shortly. A description of the current debates on the future of the nation-state and the reconsideration of the relation between LIBERALISM and nationalism follows.

In the 1980s, postmodernism brought a refocusing on the elements of nationalist discourse which create the nation as an 'imagined community' (Anderson 1983) in the head of its members. A nation, then, exists when people believe it to exist. Postmodernists are modernists to the point that they despise primordialist or other ethnicist interpretations. Without print or capitalism, for example, no massive imagination of the nation is possible. For postmodernists, a nation can be narrated or read as a text; it has to be deconstructed for its power to be grasped.

As well as ethnicism or even structuralism, postmodernism can be criticised because of its neglect of the political framework. For Breuilly (1982), Anderson's 'imagined communities' only explain the development of nationalist consciousness at the elite level, but not how popular support and effective political activity of nationalists develop. Instead, one should see nationalism as a form of modern politics which is particularly successful, and this can only be explained by the characteristics of the modern state such as possession of sovereignty, territoriality and the separation of the public and the private sphere (see PUBLIC–PRIVATE DISTINCTION) which, according to Breuilly, the nationalists want to overcome in the name of the nation. Nationalism is the tool of opposing elites who want to capture state power, against the ruling classes. This approach, which is modernist but anti-functionalist, tries to introduce more activist elements and the intentions of the actors.

All the approaches described above have been active in the debate of the 1990s. Among its recurrent topics, there is still the question of the primogeniture of nation or modern state. Greenfeld (1992) turned the sequence on its head by insisting that nationalism is not defined by its modernity, but modernity is defined by nationalism, which had made its appearance some centuries earlier in England. But the relationship of state and nation gained current interest with the independence of the successor states of the Soviet Union and Yugoslavia, which may have taken place due to nationalist strength, but also to the weakness of the former states, the duration of the ethnic bonds, or to short-term elite manipulation. However, even if new states continue to appear, many observers argue that the nation-state is in crisis. Regions on one side and international agencies and corporations on the other may draw power away from it. This interpretation is questioned by other authors who argue that nations and ethnic identities are deeply rooted and changes in technology, economics and politics will not ensure that nations and nationalism are in a terminal phase. Ethnicists hold that even the Maastricht Treaty can not wean away the European people from their deeply felt allegiances to nations, but structuralists think that the imperatives of industrialisation and mass education may have begun to operate against nationalism. Some hold that medieval forms of governance may come back when the sovereign and territorial nation-state falls victim to economic and cultural GLOBALISATION. Public–private partnerships may corrode the separation between the public and private spheres, but will that strengthen or weaken the nationalist argument of congruence of society and polity? However, even if the nation-state is in decline, how does that affect nationalism? Maybe this chameleonic phenomenon will, once again, adapt. Perhaps in a watered-down version that does not imply any absolute priority of the nation over other identities, and which will look for non-sovereign realisations of nationalist demands.

Sociological explanatory interpretations of nationalism like Gellner's may argue that normative philosophical inquiries into nationalism are of no use. However, the current debate on the limits of traditional liberalism which has questioned the universality of liberal values has brought with it a new debate on the relations between liberalism and nationalism (see Beiner 1999b). The cultural neutrality of a liberal state has been qualified as a liberal myth. In an increasingly globalised world, demands for recognition made by national and other groups proliferate. Canovan (1996) stresses that contract theories assume given boundaries, and that liberal political thought in general presupposes nationhood, which, as some authors affirm, is necessary to achieve social justice, democracy and political stability (see POPULISM). Against the doubts if nationhood is really needed for those purposes, or in any case is too high a price to pay for the mentioned goods, many authors now accept that liberal political theory has a hidden agenda. Discussed consequences include the proposition to accept the non-universality of liberalism (national liberalism), to separate, finally, politics and culture (Tamir's 'liberal nationalism' (1993)), or to accept nationhood as a universal value (Miller 1995).

Many liberals now accept that the individual cannot be understood outside its socio-cultural context. As a consequence, the discussion of the right to self-determination is still on the agenda. It is discussed whether this is a collective right, and who has this right: any groups of individuals, only authentic groups (Taylor 1992), only encompassing groups, or only nations. Proposed liberal solutions to national questions include FEDERALISM or asymmetrical or plural federalism (Requejo 1999) (see FEDERALISM), rights of MINORITIES and multiculturalism, or secession.

See also:

assimilation; boundaries; citizenship; identity, political; liberalism; minorities; rights, minority and indigenous

Further reading

Anderson, B. (1983) *Imagined Communities*, London: Verso.

Beiner, R. (1999a) '1989: Nationalism, Internationalism, and the Nairn-Hobsbawm Debate', *European Journal of Sociology* 50(1): 171–84.

—— (1999b) *Theorizing Nationalism*, Albany, NY: State University of New York Press.

Breuilly, J. (1982) *Nationalism and the State*, Manchester: Manchester University Press.

Canovan, M. (1996) *Nationhood and Political Theory*, Cheltenham/Brookfield: Edward Elgar.

Deutsch, K.W. (1953) *Nationalism and Social Communication*, Cambridge, MA: Harvard University Press.

Gellner, E. (1983) *Nations and Nationalism*, Oxford: Blackwell.

Greenfeld, L. (1992) *Nationalism: Five Roads to Modernity*, Cambridge, MA: Harvard University Press.

Kohn, H. (1945) *The Idea of Nationalism*, New York: Macmillan.

Miller, D. (1995) *On Nationality*, Oxford: Clarendon Press.

Requejo, F. (1999) 'Cultural Pluralism, Nationalism and Federalism: A Revision of Democratic Citizenship in Plurinational States', *European Journal of Political Research* 35(2): 255–86.

Tamir, Y. (1993) *Liberal Nationalism*, Princeton, NJ: Princeton University Press..

Taylor, C. (1992) 'The Politics of Recognition', in A. Gutmann (ed.), *Multiculturalism and the 'Politics of Recognition'*, Princeton, NJ: Princeton University Press.

KLAUS-JÜRGEN NAGEL

FERRAN REQUEJO

neutrality

The idea of neutrality has been deployed in many political contexts. It has been regarded as an important ideal by some, while others have held that the ideal is at best utopian (because it is unachievable) and at worst dishonest (because it ignores or obscures the true power relations in society). Notions of neutrality applied to a (democratic) polity draw upon and exemplify the use of the concept in 'other' contexts. The 'otherness' of these contexts is, however, part of the dispute about the possibility of neutrality, as we shall see.

The concern with neutrality is a good illustration of the difficulties of combining moral concern and commitment with political realism. This is because the disputes concern the meaning and desirability of neutrality, on one side, and an analysis of whether it is achieved, or achievable, on the other. And, of course, these two sides of the issue need to be brought together in any compelling theory.

The conceptual issue (what is 'neutrality'?) immediately involves three subsidiary questions, all of which relate to consideration of its desirability. These subsidiary questions are: who or what is to be neutral? Between whom or what is that neutrality to be displayed? With respect to what is it to be neutral? For example, a referee is to be neutral between the teams with respect to the impartial application of the rules of the game – and neutrality is desirable because the rules are designed to elicit desired levels of performance and achievement by agreed standards of fair play and settled procedures. This simple example illustrates

wider points about the interpretation of neutrality in any rule-governed activity.

There is first the question of 'the rules' and more particularly of the point of the rules. In some instances, the rules themselves aim to be neutral with respect to persons. They attempt to exclude unfair advantage, to neutralise the impact of factors which are not relevant to the pursuit of the rule-governed activity. Obviously, disputes may arise about the neutrality of a set of rules precisely because of disagreement about which factors are relevant and which irrelevant. Secondly, even a simple set of rules needs interpretation. So a neutral referee is one who interprets the rules in an unbiased way, in a consistent way, in a justified way. And thirdly, rules need to be applied. Here again, lack of favour, consistency and justifiability in DECISION-MAKING are taken as hallmarks. Neutrality is also thought necessary both in interpreting the rules and in applying them, to require lack of a direct interest in the outcome of the activity; so a neutral referee is not a supporter of either team, nor has he placed bets on the outcome of the game. To the extent that democratic politics is a rule-governed activity, all these elements of the idea of neutrality have application to it, often in several specific ways. Neutrality as a virtue of rules, in the interpretation of rules, in the application of rules, and as a characteristic of decision makers all arise.

Apart from the most general questions that arise when we consider neutrality in rule-governed activities, we may also consider some of the particular contexts in which the idea has been invoked. This attention to the general questions and particular contexts will help to explain the multiple applications of the idea of neutrality with reference to a democratic polity.

International law attempts to provide a set of rules to govern relations between states in time of peace and war. 'Neutrality' is a legal status of a non-combatant state if others are engaged in warfare. The interpretation of this status as a matter of law is of course subject to normative criticism. For example, is a truly neutral state one that stands aside completely, cutting of all previous relations with the combatants (for example, no oil for either side)? Or one that does no more and no less for either side than it did before hostilities broke out (as much oil for both as previously supplied)? Or one that is even-handed (equal amounts of oil for both)? Or one that redresses any imbalance between the combatatants (more oil for the side that has greater need for it)? These possible interpretations of the idea of neutrality alert us to similar possible interpretations with respect to a democratic polity. To be neutral may be (a) not to have any involvement with any 'side', (b) not to alter previously existing relations with disputants when controversy arises, (c) to provide equal support to all disputants, irrespective of the previous situation, or (d) to redress imbalances between disputants, to put them in an equal position with respect to some resource.

A second context in which the idea has been specifically applied, and one immediately relevant to the democratic polity, is the neutrality of the civil service. Of course, not all political systems – including those claiming to be democratic – have either valued this or understood it in the same way. The essential idea has been that the civil service should act independently of party considerations, offering its advice with equal loyalty and attention to whomever are their political masters at the time. (In this way the independence of the BUREAUCRACY has been linked to its capacity to pursue the public interest.) The political system of the United States has allowed more political appointments to the civil service than is traditionally the case in the United Kingdom. Worries have nevertheless been raised about the practices of recent prime ministers. With respect to appointments and promotions in the civil service, a concern has arisen that the political disposition of public servants was being taken into consideration, or that the appointment of political advisers was altering the relationship between the partisanship of politicians and the 'independence' of the civil service. The influence of the impartial bureaucracy, it has been claimed, has been diluted or, worse for those who value 'neutrality', undermined.

'Neutrality' has also been invoked in liberal political discourse in the context of theories of JUSTICE. Here the state is required to be neutral towards citizens' conception of the good: their understandings of what constitutes a good life *for them*. In the corresponding debate about whether this sort of neutrality is desirable, and whether it can be achieved, a distinction has been drawn. This distinction isolates two understandings of neutrality applied to conceptions of the good. The first understanding holds that neutrality requires that legislators are debarred from appealing to the intrinsic superiority of one conception of the good over another in their decision-making. It rules out certain sorts of argument. The other understanding refers to the impact of decisions on the conceptions that the good citizens happen to have: neutrality would require an equal effect on their ability or opportunity to follow those conceptions. The second is not a plausible ambition, and may not even be a desirable one. But the distinction between neutrality with respect to relevant considerations, and neutrality with respect to impact, recurs in other aspects of the democratic polity.

Apart from the neutrality of states with respect to war, the neutrality of civil servants with respect to governments and the neutrality of the state towards citizens' notions of the good, we should consider arguments about market neutrality and arguments about the relation between economic power and political power. Whether or not markets *are* neutral, claims about that neutrality can be referred to three issues: the treatment of preferences (markets are neutral with respect to the preferences individuals happen to have, and treat them 'equally'); to power relations (competitive markets diffuse power and competition neutralises the undesirable tendency to monopoly power); and to the identity of persons (the market has no view about the status or identity of participants, and increasingly no concern with location or political allegiance) (see MARKET FORCES). To the extent that democratic politics can be understood analogously to market competition, these ideas have a general application. They have a more particular application with reference to voting systems.

One school of political thought has maintained that the separation of 'the market' or 'the economy' from 'the state' or 'the polity' is misguided. Marxists deny that the polity can be neutral between the interests of different classes in a capitalist system. An exception is made for the – allegedly empirically rare – circumstances in which the balance of class power in CIVIL SOCIETY leads to the 'relative autonomy of the state'. This 'relative autonomy' may be interpreted in the language of neutrality. The claim is that, whereas it is generally impossible for the state to be neutral with respect to the class interests that exist in civil society, there are peculiar conditions in which that possibility arises. The 'general impossibility' has been given a number of explanations, of varying degrees of complexity and sophistication. The explanation which seems most relevant to contemporary conditions is that the mobility and fluidity of capital make it impossible for whatever political grouping has control of government to abolish CAPITALISM, or to significantly hamper its operations.

We turn now to consider the implications of this exploration of 'neutrality' – in terms of the general theoretical issues, and the application of the term in particular contexts – for the debate about 'neutrality' in the context of a democratic political system. If we consider the idea of neutrality in relation to a rule-governed system, the ideal suggest that the political process should be neutral towards the legitimate interests of citizens. The restriction to 'legitimate' interests is, of course, both significant and controversial, since it raises some fundamental issues about the understanding of democracy itself. In particular, three considerations arise. First, if we consider the neutrality of the political process in this way, what conditions are required for it to be achievable? This thought would lead to the consideration of the conditions of democracy, such as freedom of association and freedom of speech. Second, and following from the idea of neutrality with respect to conceptions of the

good, some interests may be especially highly regarded. This is because they might be treated as 'fundamental' or 'especially weighted'. Examples of sources of such important interests that have been proposed include religious affiliation and sexual orientation. Third, the filtering involved with the identification of legitimate interests will (at least) concern the aspirations of anti-democratic political movements and separatists' ambitions.

If we take the neutralist ideal to be that the political process *as a whole* should exhibit the virtues of neutrality previously discussed, we are confronted with a question about the relationship between 'the whole' and 'the parts'. We might hope that each 'part' of the system displayed neutrality. Alternatively, we might have reason to acknowledge that particular components of the political system are incapable of neutrality, but hope to counteract that incapacity by other compensating political arrangements. For example, we might hold that the neutrality of the political process requires elected representatives to give equal attention to the problems and concerns of their constituents, irrespective of the citizens' political affiliation. The hope would be that this 'part' of the political process could be neutral, alongside other elements, to produce a neutral system. On the other hand, we might think that any system that gives space for extensive pressure group activity privileges those who can afford to pay for the lobbying and self-promotion involved, and aspire to neutralise this by countervailing measures.

Taking the political process as a whole, and bearing in mind the rule-governed nature of the activity discussed above, our attention first turns to 'the rules of the game'. We saw that 'neutrality' could be invoked as an objective of the rules, in their interpretation, in their application, and in the desirable characteristics of those involved in these activities. Clearly, the constitution is the political analogue. If our aim is that the political system be neutral between the legitimate interests of citizens, then the rules are critically important. The freedoms of speech and association have already been mentioned in this context. Interpretation of those rules is within the remit of different bodies in different systems. The United States Supreme Court provides an example. The neutrality of the judges raises exactly the problem of the relation of 'the whole' to the 'parts' already mentioned: should each judge be neutral in the relevant senses, or should the panel of judges be neutral 'overall'? Again, is such a court independent, standing aside with impartial, consistent and even-handed interpretation of the rules, or is it subject to political pressures, influences and prejudices that make such ambitions incapable of achievement? Even if, as in the United Kingdom, the absence of a written constitution poses the problem differently, there are similar concerns.

To consider neutrality in a representative democracy, and in a constitutional context, it is helpful to invoke the position of G.W.F. Hegel. Hegel famously proposed that a constitutional representative democracy was the political form that realised FREEDOM (as he understood it). In Hegel's theory of the state, it is recognised that there are many different interests in civil society (roughly, the economy) as a consequence of division of labour. He thought that a representative assembly allowed for the expression of these various interests, and indeed of various classes, while the constitutional monarch expressed the unity of political society (see CONSTITUTIONAL MONARCHY). He elevated the bureaucracy to a position in which they were the bearers of the general interest, nominating them as the universal CLASS in consequence. They stood outside the ordinary division of labour; they had access to the expressions of interest in civil society in the representative assembly; and they were charged to produce (what we might call) the public interest. They were to take account of all legitimate interests in society. Perhaps Hegel's theory of the state provides the most elaborate defence both of the value of neutrality and of the bureaucracy, as its custodian, in constitutional representative government.

Hegel's defence of the desirability and possibility of this sort of neutrality is of course open to many objections. First, there is conceptual scepticism about whether there is any such thing as the public interest. More than one judge in the United Kingdom has held that the public interest is whatever the government of the day says it is, thus denying any basis for its independent evaluation. Political scientists who have denied the conceptual adequacy of the notion of the public interest have been led to identify it with the outcome of interest group interaction. Second, the notion that the bureaucracy could provide the neutrality required to pursue the public interest has been attacked by those who deny that the bureaucracy in any sense stands above the rest of society; they have their own interests, careers, and rewards to pursue.

If bureaucracy is discounted as the locus of impartiality and neutrality, there are other actors in the political process to consider in a democratic system. Another candidate has been the representative assembly itself. Here there are two contrasting views. One holds that representatives express the interests of the electors. Their interaction to produce legislation and policy will produce outcomes that are all that can be hoped for as 'neutral'. Provided there is a fair ELECTORAL SYSTEM, the absence of corruption, appropriate rules of procedure and so on, the outcomes will be neutral in a relevant sense of fairness, even though they will have differential impact on particular interests. The second view supposes that elected representatives are themselves the custodians of the public interest, and that neutrality consists in pursuing it. The hope is that such representatives take a conscientious view of the best outcome for everyone, not a narrow view of asserting the interests of those whom they represent. This view, if plausible at all, seems most appropriate to the activity of specialised committees, like the Select Committees of the House of Commons.

Mention has just been made of a 'fair' electoral system. We also discussed above a possible analogy between market neutrality and the neutrality of the polity. This raises the important question of the design of a neutral electoral system, one that treats the preferences of voters equally. Some of the arguments reported above clearly depend on the neutrality of the electoral system in that sense. Equally, they depend upon the accuracy of the analogy between the political process and the market. Hence questions surround whether the electoral system gives each voter equal power, and on whether the identity of individuals in the process is irrelevant (and, in particular, whether geographical location is irrelevant).

If some have hoped for neutrality from the bureaucracy, others have from the representative assembly. Others have placed their hopes on the voter. If we suppose that voters use their votes to express their own interests (as the economic model proposes) then the representative assembly becomes a sort of scoreboard which (depending on the theory in question) allows the government or bureaucracy to produce a neutral outcome. But we might suppose, as both J.S. Mill and Jean-Jacques Rousseau in their very different ways did suppose, that the voter is capable of the impartiality required by a neutral concern for legitimate interests. The contexts were of course very different: Mill was concerned with representative government, Rousseau with participation in public decision-making by a sovereign community. Nevertheless, both hoped that the citizen was capable of an enlightened use of his share of political power. In Mill's case, the voter was to choose a representative who would be best able to pursue (not the citizen's private but) the public interest. In Rousseau's case, the citizen was to embrace in his vote what was for the general good, not was good for him. Be it indirect DIRECT DEMOCRACY, the voter was himself to be neutral towards the legitimate interests of his fellows.

The ideal of neutrality has, then, been pursued in a number of different ways with respect to a democratic polity. The desirability and possibility of these different ways has been hotly disputed. This is not surprising, since the ideal makes reference in different forms to very general considerations – the constitution, the rules of the game – and to very specific ones – such as whether a representative should have no outside interests, or whether declared interests are effectively 'neutralised', or whether an assembly made up of persons with diverse interests in outcomes suffices. To decide about the value and possibility of a neutral political system requires engagement with both philosophical reflection and the findings of empirical political science. To determine whether it is a noble and realisable aspiration or a dangerous illusion and impossible pipe dream will continue to engage us.

See also:

class; freedom; interest groups

ANDREW REEVE

new institutionalism

In the broadest sense, institutions are simply rules. As such, they are the foundation of all political behaviour. Some are formal (as in constitutional rules), some are informal (as in cultural norms), but without institutions there could be no organised politics. Simply attempt to consider a world in which there were no rules governing social or political behaviour. In this Hobbesian hell there could be no political organisation, indeed no social organisation at all (North 1990). 'Institutionalists' are those that think theoretically about institutions and their impact on behaviour and outcomes. Institutions 'structure' politics because they (1) define who is able to participate in the particular political arena, (2) shape the various actors' political strategies, and (more controversially) (3) influence what these actors believe to be both possible and desirable (that is, their preferences).

Rational versus historical institutionalism

There are two contending research/theoretical approaches within political science which identify themselves as 'institutionalist' today: rational choice institutionalists and historical institutionalists. The role institutions play in these two analytic traditions overlaps in many ways (Hall and Taylor 1996; Thelen 1999). At the same time, the theoretical, indeed epistemological, goals of scholars in these two schools separates them in some rather fundamental ways. In both schools, institutions are important for politics because they structure political behaviour. Perhaps surprisingly the core difference is not over whether people are 'rational' or not. Historical institutionalists do not argue with the observation that most people act 'rationally' most of the time. Nor do rationalists necessarily believe that all action is motivated exclusively by short-term economic self-interest (Fiorina 1995; Immergut 1998). Rather, the key difference between these analytic traditions is found in their approach to the very 'science' of politics.

Historical institutionalists are primarily interested in understanding and explaining specific real world political outcomes. Building on the earlier work of Peter Katzenstein and his colleagues in *Between Power and Plenty*, and then Theda Skocpol and her colleagues in *Bringing the State Back In*, a group of younger scholars embarked upon a variety of studies of specific historical events in widely different places and across large spans of time. They 'discovered' that they could not explain these variations without specifically examining the ways in which the political institutions had shaped or structured the political process and ultimately the political outcomes (Steinmo *et al*. 1992). These historical institutionalists came about their 'institutional' arguments inductively after testing a variety of alternative theories (Marxist, structural functionalist, culturalist and rationalist) against the outcomes they observed. In other words, historical institutionalists are first interested in explaining an outcome (for example, why France and Britain have pursued such different styles of industrial policy or why some welfare states generate more popular support than others). They then proceed to explore alternative explanations for the outcomes they observe.

Because theirs is not a theory in search of evidence, historical institutionalists do not argue that institutions are the only important variables for understanding political outcomes.

On the contrary, these scholars generally see institutions as intervening variables (or structuring variables) through which battles over interest, ideas and power are fought. Institutions are important both because they are the focal points of much political activity and because they provide incentives and constraints for political actors and thus structure that activity. Rather than being neutral boxes in which political fights take place, institutions actually structure the political struggle itself. Institutions can thus also be seen as the points of critical juncture in an historical path analysis because political battles are fought inside institutions *and* over the design of future institutions (see INSTITUTIONAL DESIGN). In either case, the historical institutionalist is interested in developing a deep and contextualised understanding of the politics.

The goal for rational choice institutionalism is different. For rationalist scholars, the central goal is to uncover the laws of political behaviour and action. Scholars in this tradition generally believe that once these laws are discovered, models can be constructed that will help us understand and predict political behaviour. In their deductive model, rational choice scholars look to the real world to see if their model is right rather than look to the real world and then search for plausible explanations for the phenomena they observe. For these scholars, understanding real outcomes is not the first point; rather, it is creating, elaborating and refining a theory of politics.

The implications of this scientific orientation are substantial. Morris Fiorina, a highly regarded scholar at Harvard, put the issue in the following way: 'The most important thing to remember when reading examples of PTI [Positive Theory of Institutions, i.e. 'rational choice'] is that, at heart, most PTI scholars are theorists'. This means, first 'that most PTI scholars are not as interested in a comprehensive understanding of some real institution or historical phenomenon, so much as in a deeper understanding of some theoretical principle or logic'. Second, 'then [rationalists] do not demand a complete understanding of an historical or institutional phenomenon'. You may be quite satisfied with a partial understanding, 'an understanding of those parts of the phenomenon that illuminate the operation of the theoretical principle of interests'. Finally, 'for most PTI scholars breadth trumps depth; understanding 90 per cent of the variance in one case is not as significant an achievement as understanding 10 per cent of each of nine cases, especially if the cases vary across time and place' (Fiorina 1995: 110–11).

At root, then, these two approaches suggest very different understandings of social science. Historical institutionalists apply inductive scientific method. Rational choice institutionalists, in contrast, apply a deductive model of science. In rational choice institutionalism, general principles or 'logics' are invoked in terms of games ('settlers', 'prisoner dilemma', 'tit-for-tat' and so on) which may (or may not) be then applied to particular historical events. These scholars, in short, are interested in the game and its design: institutions are simply the rules of the game(s). Rational choice institutionalists try to understand 'what is the game and how is it played'. Historical institutionalists, in contrast, want to answer more traditional questions such as 'who wins, who loses and why'.

Institutional stability and change

One of the features noted about institutions – no matter what the analytic perspective – is that institutions do not change easily. Rational choice institutionalists view institutional equilibrium as the norm. They argue that the normal state of politics is one in which the rules of the game are stable and actors maximise their utilities (usually self-interest) given these rules. As actors learn the rules, their strategies adjust and thus an institutional equilibrium sets in. Though not everyone is necessarily happy with the current institutional structure, a significant coalition is, or else it would not be stable. Once stabilised, it becomes very difficult to change the rules because no one can be certain what the outcomes of the new structure would be: this is because institutions shape strategies, new institutional rules imply new

strategies throughout the system. Change thus implies enormous uncertainty; it becomes very difficult to calculate the sum effects of the rule changes. In short, the amount of uncertainty implied by a new institutional structures makes actors unwilling to change the structure. In somewhat simpler terms, people are afraid of changing the rules because it is difficult to know what will happen after the rules are changed.

In the rational choice view, there may be many different alternative equilibriums, but the theory itself has no means of explaining why political systems move from one equilibrium to another. 'The greatest achievement of rational choice theory has been to provide tools for studying political outcomes in stable institutional settings... Political transitions seem to defy rational forms of analysis' (Bates *et al.* 1998: 604–5). This is unfortunate, because we know that human history is replete with change. A theory whose goal is to predict, but which cannot explain change has some difficulties.

The most powerful explanation offered by institutionalist scholars draws on the work of Steven Gold's 'punctuated equilibriums' explanation for evolutionary change. In other words, change in any system is a product of external shocks to the system (Thelen and Steinmo 1992). Historical institutionalists, much like most evolutionary biologists, are sceptical of the 'punctuated equilibrium' model if offered up as the sole explanation for change. Indeed in both cases, change seems to be one of the few constants in world history. Historical institutionalism scholars do not deny that dramatic shocks to the system can invoke massive changes; this point seems rather obvious to anyone who studies history. But, historical institutionalist scholars tend to understand outcomes at any one point in time as the product of the convergence of a number of factors (Oren and Skowronek 1994). Indeed, rather than searching for specific equilibria and their consequences, historical institutionalists see their inquiry as one of *path analysis* and/or *process tracing*. To continue with the analogy to evolutionary biology, the scientist in this view is engaged in a process of understanding how and why certain organisms (institutions) have evolved, why some flourish in some contexts and/or why some die out in others. The answers to these questions (in both biology and political science) are discovered through careful historical analysis which examines the ways in which a number of factors have intersected and affected one another over time.

See also:

democratic stability; institutional design

Further reading

Bates, R. *et al.* (1998) 'The Politics of Interpretation: Rationality, Culture, and Transition', *Politics and Society* 26(4): 603–38.

Fiorina, M. (1995) 'Rational Choice and the New "Institutionalism"', *Polity* 38(1): 107–15.

Golden, M. (1997) *Heroic Defeats*, New York: Cambridge University Press.

Hall, P. and Taylor, R. (1996) 'Political Science and the Three New Institutionalisms', *Political Studies* 44: 936–57.

Immergut, E. (1998) 'The Theoretical Core of the New Institutionalism', *Politics and Society* 26(1): 5–34.

Levi, M. (1997) *Consent, Dissent and Patriotism*, New York: Cambridge University Press.

North, D. (1990) *Economic Development in Historical Perspective: The Western World*, conference on 'The Wealth of Nations in the 20th Century'.

Orren, K. and Skowronek, S. (1994) 'Beyond the Iconography of Order: Notes for a "New" Institutionalism', in L. Dodd and C. Jillson (eds), *Dynamics of American Politics*, Boulder, CO: Westview Press.

Rothstein, B. (1996) 'Political Institutions: An Overview', in H.-D. Klingemann and R.E. Goodin (eds), *A New Handbook of Political Science*, Oxford: Oxford University Press: 133–66.

Steinmo, S. *et al.* (eds) (1992) *Structuring Politics: Historical Institutionalism in Comparative Analysis*, New York: Cambridge University Press.

Thelen, K. (1999) 'Historical Institutionalism in Comparative Politics', *Annual Review of Political Science* 2: 369–404.

Thelen, K. and Steinmo, S. (1992) 'Historical Institutionalism in Comparative Politics: State, Society and Economy', in S. Steinmo, K. Thelen and F. Longstreth (eds), *Structuring Politics: Historical Institutionalism in Comparative Analysis*, New York: Cambridge University Press.

SVEN STEINMO

non-governmental organisations

Non-governmental organisations (NGOs) have been defined by various UN agencies as organisations independent of governments, and which have humanitarian or co-operative rather than commercial objectives. More restrictively, Howes (1997) defines NGOs as professionally staffed non-governmental agencies which seek to aid constituencies external to themselves and are not directly accountable to their intended beneficiaries. More generally, NGO has become a shorthand for the diversity of lobbying or INTEREST GROUPS and associations which perform advocacy or service functions and which have been increasingly frequent observers at and participants in international negotiations.

International NGOs are no novelty. Their numbers increased steadily from the mid-nineteenth century. The League of Nations gave added impetus, but their great proliferation began with the formation of the United Nations and with the extension of rights of consultation and, in some cases, representation in the councils of UN agencies. Data from the Yearbook of International Organisations suggests that in the forty years to 1993, the number of international NGOs rose roughly sixfold, the fastest and most recent rise being in the numbers of environmental NGOs.

The growth of international NGOs has

broadly paralleled the development of the global economy and means of COMMUNICA-TION. As states and peoples have become ever more effectively interconnected, and as more of the world's people have enjoyed the benefits of higher EDUCATION, so international NGOs have become more possible and have seemed more necessary. Now, when pervasive economic GLOBALISATION has eroded the AUTON-OMY of states and the capacity of governments to govern, increasing consciousness of the globally shared interests of humankind demands more effective global governance. NGOs are increasingly seen both as a means of articulating that demand and as contributors to meeting it.

For this reason, the proliferation of international NGOs has accelerated. Then UN Secretary General Boutros Ghali, addressing the 47th annual conference of NGOs in 1994, described NGOs as 'a basic form of popular representation in the present-day world', and their participation in international organisations as 'a guarantee of the political legitimacy of those international organisations' (Willetts 1996: 311). The problems of international governance are those of national governance writ large. Just as national governments are increasingly led by growing awareness of the limitations of their competence to draw upon the expertise of NGOs in complex policy areas such as the environment, so international organisations concerned to bolster their legitimacy enter relationships with NGOs which they presume to represent interests otherwise excluded from their councils.

Although NGOs are, by definition, formally independent of governments and of international organisations, it is by no means the case that they have always arisen as a result of popular pressure. From the outset, scientific and cultural NGOs were regarded as suspiciously 'mandarin'. They prospered and stimulated the formation of other NGOs chiefly because emerging international organisations and national governments found them useful (as sources of expert knowledge and advice) and more flexible than formal intergovernmental organisations. Because they were useful,

international organisations and some national governments considered it worthwhile to provide NGOs with facilities, to fund them, and sometimes even to create them. Several early international NGOs thus formed were hybrids representing governments, governmental agencies, inter-governmental agencies and other NGOs. In one significant instance, the 'hybrid' NGO, the IUCN, in 1961 established WWF (originally World Wildlife Fund, latterly World Wide Fund for Nature) as a fund-raiser for and populariser of the IUCN's conservationist mission.

The chief difficulty in discussing NGOs is the increasing vagueness and inclusivity of the term and the difficulty of distinguishing NGOs from other forms of association. Even within a single policy field, NGOs vary greatly in their forms of organisation and their degree of ACCOUNTABILITY to their members. An environmental NGO such as Greenpeace is deliberately elitist: it has no mass membership, and its self-perpetuating boards of directors retain maximum autonomy and forbid the use of the Greenpeace name in independent actions by local support groups. By contrast, Friends of the Earth is a loose federation of self-governing mass membership organisations operating locally as well as nationally (see GREEN DEMOCRATIC THOUGHT). NGOs vary too in the forms of action they prefer, some specialising in the largely publicly invisible provision of services based upon accumulated knowledge and expertise, some specialising in advocacy pursued by a variety of direct forms of highly visible action, and many combining or shifting between the two.

Some NGOs were created or funded by governments (hence the acronym GONGOs) in order to act as agencies to deliver services to or to establish communication with constituencies beyond the normal reach of government. Thus, at the international level, governments and intergovernmental agencies facilitate the activities of NGOs representing the interests of ethnic minorities, stateless peoples and the economically deprived and socially and politically marginalised peoples of the Third World. At both international and national levels, environmental NGOs have been encouraged by governments and international agencies concerned to ensure that debates and policy on environmental matters are not dominated by powerful economic interests. On the other hand, some NGOs have been created by corporations, sometimes apparently as a smoke screen for controversial actions, sometimes in order to ensure the more effective articulation of corporate policy.

The term 'NGO' appears to have made its way into wider social science discourse from international relations. Useful though it has been in diplomatic parlance, its increasing use in discussions of domestic politics is more problematic. 'NGOs' is increasingly used to refer to what used to be called 'pressure groups', 'interest groups' or 'social movement organisations' (SMOs). This is unfortunate, because NGO is a term which is narrower in its compass than 'social movement' and, in principle, broader than 'SMO'.

The relationship between NGOs and SOCIAL MOVEMENTS is problematic. Social movements are usually held to be characterised by mass participation in collective action and by informality of organisation, whereas most NGOs are semi-formal, often semi-institutionalised organisations operating at elite level as negotiators or advocates, and sometimes as service organisations, for interests and constituencies which may be otherwise relatively unrepresented in political processes.

It is often said of NGOs that their freedom from formal constitutional constraints gives them flexibility to act as mediators and to reach where governments cannot, thus adding to the PLURALISM that is an essential characteristic of CIVIL SOCIETY. Indeed it may, but along with that go problems of LEGITIMACY and a relationship with democracy that is at best ambiguous. NGOs which lack formal democratic structures of internal organisation are vulnerable to charges by the governments and corporations whose policies and practices they challenge that they lack democratic legitimacy. At least in liberal democratic states, governments and political PARTIES, it is argued, derive their legitimacy from the ballot box,

while corporations derive theirs from the market. NGOs quite reasonably retort that insofar as they are dependent upon the flow of donations and subscriptions from supporters, they are at least as accountable as corporations.

That defence might be considered satisfactory in the case of mass membership organisations or of massively supported organisations such as Greenpeace. It is not so satisfactory in the case of those NGOs summoned into existence by governments or corporations in order to mediate or 'represent' (sections of) 'PUBLIC OPINION' in those places or under those conditions where efficient democratic mechanisms of the aggregation and representation of popular interests do not already exist. These problems are especially acute in countries where the development of civil society is at best fragile or embryonic, as it is in many parts of the Third World and the post-socialist states of central and eastern Europe.

In these circumstances, local NGOs, whether supported by foreign governments or corporations, by international organisations, or by NGOs based in Western/Northern industrialised states, often are perceived to be heavily dependent upon their sponsors or funders. This tends to undermine local NGOs' legitimacy, limit their effectiveness and diminish their capacity to contribute to the development of democracy through the enrichment of civil society. There is some evidence of the development of a new wave of populist NGOs which refuse such dependency and which increasingly seek to form transnational COALITIONS, such as the Peoples' Global Alliance, but it remains to be seen how well they will manage the consequences of their self-exclusion from the resources of the international organisations. It is said that at the Rio Earth Summit, such organisations spent more time networking than in negotiations. That, however, may be precisely what is required if NGOs are to be the bases of the global civil society to which many aspire.

See also:

associational democracy

Further reading

Howes, M. (1997) 'NGOs and the Institutional Development of Membership Organisations', *Journal of Development Studies* 33(6): 821.

Princen, T. and Finger, M. (1994) *Environmental NGOs in World Politics*, London: Routledge.

Rootes, C. (ed.) (1999) *Environmental Movements: Local, National and Global*, London: Frank Cass.

Willetts, P. (ed.) (1996) *'The Conscience of the World': The Influence of Non-Governmental Organisations in the U.N. System*, London: Hurst.

CHRISTOPHER A. ROOTES

normative approaches to democracy

'Democracy', as it is used in current political discourse, is a thick evaluative term. It serves a descriptive purpose, so far as people use it to mark off some systems of government from others. But it also serves an evaluative purpose, as people use it to express their approval of the systems that they describe as democratic and to express their disapproval of the systems that they characterise as undemocratic.

This feature of the term means that the normative theory of democracy divides into two quite different enterprises. One starts from an independently detailed, descriptive sense of the actual sort of system that counts as democratic – the description might be taken, for example, from history or political science – and asks about why that type of system should be preferred to other, actual alternatives. The second starts from the assumption that the democratic type of system – very loosely understood as one in which ordinary people are sovereign – is indeed to be preferred, outlines reasons for why it is preferable, and then sketches a descriptive characterisation of the ideal system that would be best supported by those reasons.

The first normative approach to democracy

might be described as evaluative analysis, the second as evaluative construction. Both have a role to play, but in practice they are not well distinguished. And the result is that neither exercise is as well conducted as it might be. This entry details that claim in three separate charges:

1 normative democratic theorists tend to run the evaluative analysis of actual democracy into an evaluative construction of the democratic ideal;

2 as a result of that assimilation they often fail to say anything worthwhile in analysis of the value of actual democracy; and

3 almost certainly as another result of that assimiliation, they overlook an important theme in construction of an evaluative ideal of democracy.

First charge

By 'actual democracy' is meant the sort of system that we find in those countries that we are more or less happy, as things stand, to describe as democratic. Such countries differ enormously among themselves. Some are constitutional monarchies, some are republics. Some have directly elected administrations, others conform to the Westminster system. Some are very strict on the RULE OF LAW, the SEPARATION OF POWERS and the limitation of the government sphere; others are less committed to these constraints. Some see recourse to REFERENDUM or plebiscite as a regular instrument of government, even one that citizens themselves may trigger; others place little or no reliance on such direct democratic appeals.

If countries as various as this can all count as democratic, then what does the democracy which they share in common amount to? It involves a system whereby the collective people have a certain direct or indirect control over who shall govern, and by what rules. More specifically, it involves a system that satisfies two broad conditions. First, the occupants of certain key positions in government are determined by periodic elections that have a popular character: ideally, no competent adult is arbitrarily excluded from participating in them – no one is arbitrarily prevented from standing or voting in the ELECTIONS, for example, or from speaking about election issues – and no one's vote is arbitrarily weighted more than anyone else's. And second, the rules whereby those in government operate – and are periodically and popularly elected – are themselves subject to popular control: they can generally be altered by popular referendum or by the determination of the popularly elected representatives.

This definition does not import into the characterisation of democracy many specifications as to how government is practised. It associates democracy with the basis on which governors are selected and constrained rather than with the precise details of how they are constrained or of how they operate. That is one reason why the sort of democracy envisaged can be found in otherwise very different sorts of regimes (For a defence of such a characterisation of democracy, see Przeworksi (2000)).

The conditions involved in the definition given will not be fully satisfied by any existing system of government and in that sense it is somewhat idealised. But this idealisation is the sort that we find in almost any empirical inquiry that seeks to abstract from detail and look to general patterns; it is not the kind that directs our attention away from real world systems and towards purely ideal ones. Thus the idealisation to which Dahl (1998) confesses in his more or less equivalent characterisation of democracy does not direct us to other worlds than our own; it merely serves to reveal a commonality among certain systems of government that might otherwise be invisible. That the idealisation we allow in defining democracy is of this kind will come out in the fact that we can take the definition to present democracy, not as the system that fully satisfies the conditions given, but as the system that satisfies those conditions beyond certain contextually given thresholds: the system that comes 'close enough' to satisfying the conditions.

The question of evaluative analysis in normative democratic theory is, what makes actual democracy in the sense defined desirable, if indeed it is desirable: what makes it the system of choice, as most of us believe it is. This is a pressing question, particularly for countries such as those in the post-communist and the Islamic world, where democracy has failed to establish itself as a stable norm.

But there is a second, related question that we must also expect normative democratic theory to address, and the first charge here is that this is often allowed to absorb the question about the desirability of actual democracy. The second question bears on which, among all the conceivable systems of government that might be described as democratic, best deserves our allegiance. This is a question of evaluative construction, not evaluative analysis. It raises a challenge for the conceptual and the institutional imagination, requiring democratic theorists to try and elaborate a vision of democratic government. It is extremely interesting in itself, but it is quite a different question from the analytical one about what makes actual democracy preferable to actual alternatives.

The charge against much democratic theory is that as it apparently sets out to debate the question about actual or common democracy, it often makes a move that runs that question together with the ideal or visionary issue. The move that leads to the assimilation of the questions comes at the point where we are offered a definition of democracy. For what often happens is that democracy is defined at that point, not in the common sense of the term, but only in one or another constructive or visionary sense. And consequently the question as to what makes democracy desirable becomes a question as to what is desirable about the democratic vision that is represented in the definition.

An example of this slippage can be seen in a recent, in many ways excellent, book by Tom Christiano (1996) on *The Rule of the Many*. Christiano begins with a question that appears to bear on actual democracy, asking: 'Who has the right to define the terms of association for a society?' He asks if the rules should be made by a 'royal family', 'by a body of experts' or by the wealthiest, or 'does the whole of the people have a right to choose?' (1996: 2). The question that Christiano has in mind here is the analytical issue as to what, if anything, makes actual democracy more desirable than monarchy or oligarchy, or a rule of experts, or any such elitist regime. But as the book develops, this question becomes indistinguishable from the constructive question as to what would best satisfy the democratic ideal. Christiano characterises a democracy as a system that incorporates three ideas. The first, popular SOVEREIGNTY, corresponds closely to our definition. 'Each citizen has a vote in the processes by which the decisions are made and each has the opportunity to participate in the deliberations over what courses of action are followed' (Christiano 1996: 3). And the other two, on the face of it, look equally unobjectionable: 'equality among citizens in the process of decision-making', and an arrangement under which 'each has a right, and a duty to participate in open and fair discussion' (1996: 3). But these two ideas are unobjectionably associated with actual democracy, only in the sense in which the notion of popular sovereignty already incorporates them: in this sense EQUALITY is ensured so far as each has a vote and may stand for election, fair discussion so far as no one can be arbitrarily prevented from speaking about election issues. And Christiano, it turns out, does not restrict them in that way. He suggests, without noticing the slippage, that a proper characterisation of democracy would require such ideas to be fulfilled in a far higher degree than under existing systems. Where economic inequalities affect a voter's capacity to understand or participate in decision-making, for example, he says that the system will not display a full democratic profile. 'A society that permits this kind of inequality... does not live up to the democratic ideals of political equality and participation in rational social deliberation' (Christiano 1996: 4). Instead of continuing to address himself to actual democracy, then, he begins to contemplate an ideal system where there is the fullest equality and the fullest access to fair discussion.

Christiano is merely taken as an example. The shift that occurs at this point in his discussion is typical of what happens in many normative theories of democracy. When we ask what if anything makes actual democracy desirable, these theories invite us to think instead about what is desirable in one or another visionary version of democracy. The visionary version may be an egalitarian ideal, as in Christiano's case, or a participatory ideal, or an ideal in which people enjoy a collective identity and AUTONOMY, or an ideal in which everything is governed by deliberative consensus, or.... Whatever particular ideal is involved, the effect is that we are denied the possibility of discussing the analytical question of why actual democracy – democracy as we see it realised or approximated in the actual world – is preferable to actually available alternatives. We are directed to a question of evaluative construction, not analysis.

Second charge

But it is one thing to run the question about actual democracy together with the question about the visionary. It is quite another thing to fail to say anything that bears on the desirability of actual democracy. And the second charge here is that normative democratic theory fails in this way also.

This charge may seem entirely implausible. Suppose that a visionary version of democracy is presented as the most desirable system of government on the grounds of having this or that feature. Does not that imply that whatever else is true about the best available system of government, it must adumbrate the ideal of such a visionary democracy: in effect, it must be democratic in at least the actual sense? It is likely that many democratic theorists believe this is so, and for that reason are unbothered about running together the two issues distinguished in the last section. They may think that there is no problem about concentrating on the desirability of their particular vision of democracy, because a proof that it is the most desirable system possible will yield an argument for why the best alternative among feasible systems must be democratic in at least the minimal, actual world sense.

But it is a fallacy to think that we can move in this way between questions of visionary desirability and questions of real world desirability. Suppose we argue that a certain version of visionary democracy is the most desirable system possible, on the grounds that it best satisfies certain considerations. It may be tempting to think that having answered that question, we also have a reason for thinking that the best feasible alternative must be at least minimally democratic: that that alternative will take us some way, if not the whole way, towards satisfaction of the same considerations. But that would be a serious mistake. Although the considerations are wholly satisfied under the visionary ideal, they may be worse served by actual democracy than by some available non-democratic alternative: notoriously, the second-best option is not always the intuitively closest alternative to the first-best (Brennan 1993: 128).

The possibility can be illustrated, once again, with reference to Christiano's argument. Suppose that what makes Christiano's visionary democracy the best possible political system is, as he believes, that under such a regime each individual has the same political resources and is guaranteed that his or her interests are equally well considered in governmental decision-making (1996: ch. 2). It does not follow that the same consideration argues that among available alternatives the best system must be democratic in the actual world sense. Consider the alternative where each ruler selects his or her predecessor from among a cohort of relevantly trained experts, in the way that the US administration selects the Chief Justice of the Supreme Court. Such a system might do better in ensuring equal consideration of interests than any of the varieties of democracy available in the actual world. Under all such available varieties, it might be much easier for a certain elite to develop a hidden financial and political hold over the governors – most actual practices of campaign financing facilitate this – and to bend government to the grain of their particular interests.

The thrust of our first two charges can be summed up as follows. When philosophers discuss the merits of democracy, they tend immediately to go for a soft, visionary focus and to argue for the advantages of an idealised system that is probably nowhere to be found. In this failing, they resemble those economists who argue for the greater and greater expansion of the market on the assumption – the manifestly false assumption – that the expanded market will be the perfectly open, informed and competitive arrangement that is described in their models (see MARKET FORCES). We are familiar with the observation that the economist's argument does not establish that the best real world alternative, say in the provision of medical services, is to neglect real world constraints and to go willy-nilly for market deregulation. And for similar reasons, we should back away from any suggestion that the philosopher's argument about idealised democracy carries lessons for the superiority of common or minimal democracy.

But the fact that visionary arguments cannot provide effective support for actual world democracy does not mean that no arguments can be provided. It may be useful to illustrate one way in which the superiority of actual world democracy might be argued. The reason this may be useful is that the sort of argument required is very different from anything that is to be found in philosophical defences of democracy and this underlines the extent to which such defences are obsessed with visionary versions of the ideal.

Two observations are fundamental to any argument about what system of government should prevail in the world as we know it:

A Every polity has to have an ultimate controller on matters to do with who is appointed to government and with how those in government should be constrained.
B The circumstances of real-world politics, as Jeremy Waldron (1996) puts it, involve the possibility and indeed the likelihood of deep and irresoluble disagreement between people of different backgrounds; this point is emphasised by Christiano also.

If there has to be an ultimate controller in political life, and if the circumstances of politics involve deep disagreement, then we should look for a political controller who satisfies certain desiderata. Here are some more or less obvious candidates:

1 No capture. The ultimate controller should not be capable of capture by any of the contending parties in the political sphere.
2 No challenge. The controller should represent a final court of appeal and should not be capable of ready challenge, say on the grounds of lacking proper AUTHORITY.
3 No pre-emption. The controller should not be able to intrude easily into the political process, pre-empting deliberation and threatening the integrity and coherence of governmental DECISION-MAKING.
4 No domination. The controller should not represent a personal, arbitrary will such that those controlled have to see themselves as subject to that will: it represents the presence of a master or *dominus* in their lives.
5 No alienation. The controller should be such that individuals do not have to see its decisions as the blind workings of an alien force: they do not have to see it, for example, as blind chance or *fortuna*.

The ultimate controller in a political system may involve a wholly impersonal process, as in resort to a lottery; it may involve an impersonal procedure – say, a certain voting system – that derives a social choice from personal preferences; or the controlling role may be directly implemented by a certain personal agent, or a group of personal agents. The obvious way to choose amongst these is to look for the system of ultimate control under which desiderata such as those listed are best satisfied. And on the face of it, those desiderata would seem to support a democratic system under which the collective or aggregate people are enfranchised and given the role of ultimate controller.

The people are not an agent proper of the kind that can be captured, or at least reliably captured, by any of the rival sides in politics; thus they satisfy the first desideratum on our list. If the people pass a certain verdict on who should be in government, or on any other matter, then it is both institutionally and rhetorically difficult for anyone to challenge that decision: how to argue that the people should be governed contrary to what can be described as the people's wishes? Thus the second desideratum will be satisfied too. And, to take up the third desideratum, the fact that the people are not an agent proper means that it is going to be reasonably easy, short of an unusual level of access to referenda, to keep them out of day-to-day political debates and to preserve the integrity and coherence of governmental decision-making.

The final two desiderata look equally likely to be fulfilled under actual world democracy. The people, as they are empowered under such democracy, satisfy or are capable of satisfying both the no-domination and no-alienation constraints. Unless they are subject to an oppressive, unified majority, those who disagree with the people's verdict do not have to see themselves as living under the arbitrary will of another. Yet neither do they have to see the verdict as the blind dictate of fate; they can see it as a decision that expresses the views of others with whom they share a social identity.

This sketch of a case for actual world democracy does not presuppose that democracy works in a particularly ideal fashion in securing goals such as the full equality of citizens and the ideal of fair discussion. It does not even presuppose that the conditions mentioned in definition of actual world democracy are perfectly fulfilled. In short, the argument does not rely on tendentious, soft focus description of democracy as it might be but takes democracy just as it is in the world today. I do not mean to defend the particular case made. I use it only by way of illustrating a sort of argument that might serve in the evaluative analysis of actual democracy, as distinct from the evaluative construction of democratic ideals. (For another such argument see Dahl 1998: ch. 5).

Third charge

One more charge can be laid against normative

democratic theory as it is commonly practised. This is that the failure to distinguish the analytical and constructive questions of evaluation may also account for the failure in most constructive theory to take into account the non-electoral modes as well as the electoral modes in which government can be controlled by ordinary people.

The oversight is easily presented. Consider the two ways in which a text may be controlled. One mode of control is that of the author who produces the text in draft. But another is that of the editor who, without having any power to produce text, can amend or reject the author's offerings at will. The authorial mode of control is historical, in the sense that text originates only with the author. The editorial mode of control is counterfactual, in the sense that should the editor not like some text, then it will not be published.

The common notion of democracy interprets popular control of government and law in purely authorial terms. The collective people are the direct authors of the law in the case of referenda and in other cases they are the indirect authors: they select those who write the law. It is a striking feature of most of the visionary versions of the democratic ideal that they remain faithful to this pattern. While they develop inspiring images of how voters should be informed and involved in democratic decision-making, while they hold out for strict constraints on how far electoral candidates may depend on private financing, and while they enthuse about various ways of giving a more deliberative character to public life, they continue to interpret the idea of democratic control in purely authorial terms.

But it is obvious that democratic control might also be given an editorial interpretation and I find it surprising that this is almost never remarked upon among democratic theorists (see Pettit 1999, 2000; Shapiro 1996: chaps 5–6). One extreme editorial interpretation would give every elector a veto over any law or decision that the government proposes to make. Another would give this power to certain representatives of the electors, whether acting together or individually. In republican Rome, the tribunes of the plebs had this power on an individual basis and in the utopia imagined by the great seventeenth-century republican James Harrington, the power was given in a collective way to the people's assembly.

Such vetoing possibilities aside, however, we can also see another, less dramatic way in which ordinary people, whether individually or in groups, might be given a sort of editorial control over government. Suppose it is generally agreed that government laws and decisions are unobjectionable if they are well-supported by certain sorts of considerations. Suppose that it is possible for individuals to contest laws and decisions for whether they are suitably supported in a forum that is sufficiently independent of government to command their confidence. And suppose that that forum can force a reversal or an amendment of government policy in the event of the CONTESTATION being upheld. Under such a regime, it is clear that ordinary people would have an editorial control over government that is not ensured just by the fact of living under an electoral democracy. Where electoral democracy gives them a collective authorship of government policy – or something approaching it – this contestatory sort of arrangement would offer them a possibility of individual, editorial control.

One way in which democracy might be given an editorial, contestatory dimension – I say nothing on how successful the measure is likely to be (Waldron 1999) – is by means of JUDICIAL REVIEW. The idea of judicial review is not particularly radical or visionary in itself, but it is a telling comment about democratic theory that even in its most visionary moments it fails to see in judicial review a possible way of extending popular control over government. It represents judicial review, however desirable it is taken to be on other grounds, as a constraint on democracy, not as democracy by other means.

But in any case, it should be clear that arranging for a form of judicial review is not the only way of giving democracy an editorial, contestatory dimension. There is room for a whole variety of appellate bodies, apart from the courts, to serve in a contestatory way.

Think of the administrative appeals tribunals or the ombudsman institutions that have become such a part of contemporary government. And there is room for a range of channels of consultation, whereby people have the opportunity to contest likely government action in an *ex ante* as well as an *ex post* way. Think here of the many provisions now in force in many countries for advisory, community-based bodies that administrative agencies have to consult; for the setting up of public hearings and inquiries relevant to this or that proposed venture of government; for the publication of proposals – say, in 'green' or 'white' papers – and the eliciting of responses from members of the public; and for the conduct of focus group research, or research of a related kind – say, the deliberative poll or the CITIZENS' JURY – into PUBLIC OPINION on issues where the government intends to take action.

It is a striking feature of the constructive versions of normative democratic theory that there is little or no investigation of the ways in which the democratic ideal – the ideal of popular control of government – might be advanced on these contestatory or non-electoral lines. Why does constructive theory limit itself in this way? One plausible explanation is this. Because it does not distinguish itself clearly from the evaluative analysis of actual democracy – in effect, actual electoral regimes – it does not allow itself to venture far away from that sort of dispensation in exploring the best way to institute control of government by ordinary people. In particular, because it shies away from the exploration of any institutions of control that, like judicial review, may seem to work against the sovereignty of the electoral people that distinguishes actual-world democracy.

To return to the main theme, then, there are two distinct questions that normative theory ought to raise about democracy. One, what features of actual world democracy make it preferable to available alternatives? Two, what sort of system would best satisfy the ideal of democracy? These questions are not often clearly distinguished and the result impacts negatively on both the enterprise of evaluative analysis and that of evaluative construction. It means that evaluative analysis often argues for the superiority, not of actual world democracy, but only of some ideal version of democracy. And it means that evaluative construction may tie itself too easily to the image of actual democracy, as it explores ideal ways in which the control of government by ordinary people might be achieved.

See also:

autonomy; contestation; democracy, justifications for; representation, concept of; sovereignty

Further reading

Brennan, G. (1993) 'Economics', in R.E. Goodin and P. Pettit (eds), *A Companion to Contemporary Political Philosophy*, Oxford: Blackwell.

Christiano, T. (1996) *The Rule of the Many: Fundamental Issues in Democratic Theory*, Boulder, CO: Westview Press.

Dahl, R.A. (1998) *On Democracy*, New Haven, CT: Yale University Press.

Pettit, P. (1999) 'Republican Liberty, Contestatory Democracy', in C. Hacker-Cordon and I. Shapiro (eds), *Democracy's Value*, Cambridge: Cambridge University Press.

—— (2000) 'Democracy, Contestatory and Electoral', *Nomos* 42: 105–44.

Przeworksi, A. (2000) 'A Minimalist Conception of Democracy: A Defense', in C. Hacker-Cordon and I. Shapiro (eds), *Democracy's Value*, Cambridge: Cambridge University Press, 23–55.

Shapiro, I. (1996) *Democracy's Place*, Ithaca, NY: Cornell University Press.

Waldron, J. (1996) 'Legislation, Authority, and Voting', *The Georgetown Law Journal* 84: 2185–2214.

—— (1999) *Law and Disagreement*, Oxford: Oxford University Press.

PHILIP PETTIT

O

oligarchic crisis

Aristotle cautioned against too narrow a definition of oligarchy. Although his characterisation of oligarchic rule, as that of the few in their own interest, has enjoyed widespread recognition, he allowed for a variety of forms and means, including a mixture with democracy that he called a 'polity' (Aristotle 1992: 244–63). Such an approach was adopted for the modern era by Pareto, who, like C.W. Mills, employed the more modern and limited term 'elite'; by Mosca, who focused on a minoritarian 'ruling class'; and by Michels, whose 'iron law of oligarchy' was derived from a study of the emergent aristocracy in the labour movement of the early twentieth century.

In this last case, the concentration of social power as a result of massification and organisational complexity was deemed to have subverted the goals of the rank and file although the BUREAUCRACY necessarily continued to avow those goals even as they pursued their own objectives. Any significant weakening in the plausibility of bureaucratic claims would presage a crisis of LEGITIMACY, as occurred with the Second International in 1914, when the working classes of Europe fought each other as national citizens rather than allying as proletarian internationalists. A similar crisis of a very different type of oligarchy can be seen in El Salvador in 1930–2, when the cluster of coffee landlords who dominated the economy were obliged by peasant radicalism to hand over government to the military, which certainly did not conduct policy to the exclusive advantage of the local capitalist class.

It would be misleading to identify as oligarchic every political crisis for which a democratic solution is available. As Aristotle inferred, oligarchies are essentially undemocratic, but they are not innately anti-democratic. Moreover, oligarchic crises are systemic in nature and related to regimes rather than specific governments. The 1832 Reform Act in Britain is often depicted as a crisis of such a type, but it is better understood in tandem with the 1846 reform of the Corn Laws, which did far more to prejudice the interests of the landed oligarchy. Both measures blunted the challenge of Chartism, extended SUFFRAGE and introduced the secret ballot in 1872. These extensions were far less radically democratic than they might otherwise have been (as for example in France in 1848, when Guizot's constitutionalist oligarchy was overthrown).

In a different vein, the US Civil War stemmed from a crisis within a union constituted upon compromise between the free states and a multi-class white southern oligarchy, which was bonded almost solely by the 'peculiar institution' of slavery. The war was not in itself an oligarchic crisis, but it was one of a polity in which, as Aristotle allowed, oligarchic and democratic elements co-mingled in tension. Equally, over the following century the black population of the postbellum South experienced very little socioeconomic or political progress despite the elimination of slavery, while the core values of the white elite were not subjected to serious challenge.

The chameleon and promethean qualities of oligarchies pose a constant challenge to the practice and study of democracy. The tenacity of elements of the *nomenklatura* after the collapse of the USSR, and the capacity of Indonesian 'crony capitalism' to survive the fall of the Suharto government and severe economic crisis in 1997, reflect the prevalence of economic interest over political form in the modern era. In the case of China, the generational passage of oligarchic power was certainly protected by the use of arms at Tiananmen Square in 1989, but it was also ensured by the successful introduction of capitalist economic measures into the political forms of communism. This has not been sought to the same degree in Vietnam, but there the persistence of oligarchic COMMUNITARIANISM is equally founded on a POLITICAL CULTURE where there is a much less dichotomous formulation of democracy and dictatorship than in western LIBERALISM.

Despite the internationalisation of world politics and the proliferation of global institutions – many themselves of quite oligarchic constitution and disposition, as in the European Commission – there is little sign of a lessened variegation of oligarchies and so of the crises which they create for themselves or are driven into.

See also:

capitalism; class; globalisation; market forces

Further reading

Aristotle (1992) *The Politics*, Harmondsworth: Penguin.

Michels, R. (1962) *Political Parties: A Sociological Study of the Oligarchic Tendencies of Modern Democracy*, New York: The Free Press.

Mills, C.W. (1956) *The Power Elite*, New York: Simon and Schuster.

Mosca, G. (1939) *The Ruling Class*, New York: McGraw-Hill.

Pareto, V. (1973) *The Mind and Society*, New York: Dover.

JAMES DUNKERLEY

opposition, loyal

Loyal opposition is a sophisticated and subtle notion. It implies a distinction, one of extreme importance, between the interests of the state and the interests of the government of the day. Paradoxically, it presupposes the temporary and conditional character of the office held by government ministers. The term 'loyal opposition' is derived from British constitutional practice, and originates from the time when politicians were beginning to outgrow the idea that opposition to the executive power was disloyal, indeed quasi-treasonable. Until the eighteenth century, the executive power in Britain was lodged in the king; ministers were his servants, and criticism of these ministers could be construed as an attack upon the monarch. Moreover, kings were exempt from public criticism, and the only way that their ministers could be called to account was by the device of impeachment. The king himself could not be removed constitutionally (the example of James II notwithstanding), and the only way that the royal power could be constrained was by impeaching his ministers. Thus Charles I's hated minister Stratford was impeached and put to death by act of Parliament.

It took two centuries for the notion of loyal opposition to mature in Britain. Vestiges of the old doctrine can be found as late as the mid-twentieth century. Even as late as 1937, one backbencher, speaking on the bill to provide a salary for the leader of the opposition, commented on the absurdity of paying someone to criticise and hinder the work of the king's government (Punnett 1973: 398). The change was made possible by the growth of the party system, and the gradual transformation of the office of monarch from a political but irresponsible role to a formal and ceremonial function. The executive power was gradually transferred from the king to his ministers; they remained in name the king's ministers, but in fact were the leaders of the majority party in Parliament, essentially answerable not to the king but to the elected House of Commons, and to the electorate itself. The political neutrality of the crown is an essential element in the development of the idea of loyal opposition.

The term 'His Majesty's Opposition' was first used in the early nineteenth century. What such a term did was to proclaim that opposition was neither disloyal nor treasonable; the opposition had a public function to perform, and its task of criticism of the executive was one which needed to be discharged in the public interest. Gradually, the leader of the biggest non-government party in the Commons became recognised as the Leader of His (Her) Majesty's Opposition. He was accorded an official title and, from 1937, a salary paid from public funds. The latter symbolises the public nature of his office. He is expected to lead his party in the scrutiny and criticism of the government's legislative programme and of its executive actions. Behind the government, a group of amateur politicians unified by party with only a temporary commission to govern, lies the permanent BUREAUCRACY, a corps of civil servants, professional, independent and anonymous.

To some extent, the opposition–government relationship supplanted, and to some degree overlaps, the traditional division between parliament and government, between legislature and executive. In the past, the tasks of criticising the executive, of censuring its actions, were seen as the functions of the House of Commons as a whole. Thus, ministers were said to be individually responsible to Parliament (effectively the Commons) for the conduct of their departments, and the government as a whole collectively responsible to Parliament for policy. The individual responsibility of ministers emphasises the minister's AC-COUNTABILITY for all the actions of his or her department, including instances of incompetence, blunders and maladministration. However, an institution as heavily dominated by party as Parliament is was unlikely to fulfil the role of a dispassionate, fair-minded jury envisaged by the doctrine. Thus, Finer's pathbreaking article, 'The Individual Responsibility of Ministers', observes: 'Most charges never reach the stage of individualisation at all: they are stifled under the blanket of party solidarity' (Finer 1956: 377–96). While the House of Commons has never lost its position as a place where backbenchers of all parties, government as well as opposition, take the government of

the day to task for its mistakes and misconduct, the main burden falls on the official opposition, now defined as the party not in government, which holds the largest number of seats in the House of Commons. The opposition is led by its elected leader, who chairs a shadow cabinet which formulates day-to-day policy for the party and draws up the priorities for attack.

The loyal opposition in Britain, however, is more than a spearhead for criticism and a searchlight for scrutiny. Today, governments are responsible for legislative policy, the preparation of bills and the delineation of priorities. The opposition is regarded as the alternative government: as such, it is expected to articulate its own legislative programme and to define its stand on the great public issues of the day. That oppositions may soon come to power helps to inhibit reckless criticism or rash promises. 'An Opposition, on coming into power', wrote Walter Bagehot (1963: 160) 'is often like a speculative merchant whose bills become due.' Critics of Britain's political arrangements would argue that, even so, oppositions tend to be irresponsible in their judgements and thoughtless in their pledges. Nevertheless, in the last half-century oppositions have tended to become more circumspect. Up until the Second World War, at least, oppositions tended to be negative in their strictures on government policy; since then, increasingly, oppositions have been expected to relate their critique to a positive expression of their own policies. More and more, the nation seems to expect oppositions to proclaim a policy, which at one and the same time gives force to the opposition attack, but also contains and controls that criticism. That an opposition should be expected to say what it would do if it were in power is an idea which took shape in the mid-twentieth century.

The actions of the opposition are in one sense centred upon the House of Commons, and in another geared towards the campaign in the country. In the Commons, the audience is not so much the party's own MPs as the commentators from press, radio and television. The opposition rarely converts many MPs from the government party to their way of thinking; debate does not change votes. Within the chamber, the most opposition spokesmen can do is to sow a sense of uneasiness among the members opposite, to impair the morale of the government forces. Favourable comment from MEDIA commentators may help the opposition in its campaign amongst the electors.

In Britain, the task of opposing the government of the day is concentrated, perhaps uniquely, in the official opposition; in other countries the performance of this function is more diffused. British parliamentary politics is known as adversary politics, a term derived from the adversarial model of the law courts. Thus just as a good lawyer will do his utmost to ensure the acquittal of a client whom he believes to be guilty, so an opposition spokesman may censure a minister for action which he or she might perform himself, were he or she a minister. Adversary politics reaches its apogee in Prime Minister's Question Time, held for half an hour each Wednesday; the lead in questioning is taken by the leader of the opposition. Some critics would argue that this weekly half-hour sees adversary politics at its worst. It tends to take the form of a dialectical duel between the prime minister of the day and the person who seeks to replace them. It lends itself to point-scoring, the real audience being the journalists in the press gallery and the backbenchers on each side. The aim of each leader is to convince his or her own party colleagues, and the representatives of the press, that he or she has had the better of the argument. At its worst, it has been dubbed 'Yah-boo politics'. On the other hand, there is little doubt that some prime ministers find these regular interrogations an acute strain. 'Even at the end of seven years of Premiership', wrote Harold Macmillan, prime minister from 1957–63, 'I had the same painful anticipation about Parliamentary Questions as men feel before a race or a battle. I always made it a rule on Question Days, Tuesdays and Thursdays, [when Prime Minister's Question Time then took place] to lunch alone' (Macmillan 1966: 41). Some observers see this weekly inquisition

as a salutary way of holding the highest in the land to regular account.

In discharging its functions, the opposition is accorded certain rights. Thus, in debate, the opposition spokesman will follow the minister who has opened for the government, and at the end another opposition spokesman will sum up for his side just before a minister gives the final speech. If, as is normal, the government has a clear majority in the House, the government will win the ensuing division.

The practice of the House confers other rights upon the opposition. Twenty days in the year are set aside for the opposition PARTIES to choose the subject of debate; some of these days are allocated to the smaller opposition parties, but most days are allotted to the official opposition, which therefore has the opportunity to choose topics which will reflect the opposition's propaganda concerns. The Public Accounts Committee, which examines public expenditure, is chaired by a senior opposition figure. Moreover, the Speaker and his deputies, who preside over the House of Commons in debate, will ensure that while the majority party will ultimately have its way, the right of the opposition to oppose will, within limits, be enforced. So, for instance, if the government moves the closure of debate to allow an immediate vote to be taken, the Speaker may refuse to accept the motion on the grounds that the matter has not yet been fully discussed.

The institutionalisation of opposition at its best simplifies and dramatises popular choice. The opposition provides an alternative LEADERSHIP, and a focus for popular discontent. The unremitting criticism of the government of the day which it offers is only one side of its work; not less important is its role in aggregating the often diffuse opinions of the electorate and providing an alternative programme of legislation.

This commentary has so far dwelt on British practice; not surprisingly, because the concept derives largely from Britain and the notion of a loyal opposition has developed most clearly in British constitutional development. Yet though the arrangements may take a different form overseas, the essential features are widespread throughout the democratic world. There are important differences but these largely reflect the form rather than the substance of the constitutional provisions. One obvious difference lies in the separation of executive and legislature, found at its highest pitch in the United States, and polities which have copied that country. Thus, in the USA the President does not sit in either House of Congress, nor do his cabinet officers. Many West European countries elect their parliaments by proportional representation, so ensuring that no single party has an overall majority. In some countries – the USA, Canada, Australia and Germany, for example – SOVEREIGNTY is divided between a central or general government, and regional governments which wield AUTHORITY in their own respective territories, so providing opposition with a territorial base. In all three types of polity, opposition is less concentrated, despite the recent adoption of devolution for Scotland and Wales, than it is in Britain. Opposition abroad is often highly dispersed, and the existence of multi-party government, itself fostered by proportional representation, tends to preclude the development of the British form of adversary politics, whose emergence rests on a two-party system.

What is crucial about loyal opposition is not so much the particular form it may take, or the extent to which it is concentrated or diffused, but that the legitimacy of opposition as such is accepted. In short, what matters is that the status of opposition is recognised. Loyal opposition, therefore, presupposes a pluralistic style of government. That government of some kind is necessary is accepted by all except anarchists. The need for government is one which is easy to grasp. Less obvious, and less simple, is that opposition affords a service to a society scarcely less significant than that rendered by government.

See also:

contestation; leadership; parliamentary models; parties; state, models of

Further reading

Bagehot, W. (1963) *The English Constitution*, Glasgow: Fontana.

Barker, R. (ed.) (1971) *Studies in Opposition*, London and Basingstoke: Macmillan and St Martin's Press.

Dahl, R.A. (ed.) (1966) *Political Oppositions in Western Democracies*, New Haven, CT: Yale University Press.

Finer, S.E. (1956) 'The Individual Responsibility of Ministers', *Public Administration* (Winter): 377–96.

Macmillan, H. (1966) *Winds of Change*, London: Macmillan.

Punnett, R.M. (1973) *Front-Bench Opposition*, London: Heinemann.

HUGH BERRINGTON

P

parliamentary models

Parliamentary government is representative government. In the pure form of the term, the executive rests on the support of the elected legislature, or parliament. The government stays in office as long as it has the confidence of the legislature. When that confidence is withdrawn it resigns, making way for a new government which can command such support, or else dissolves the legislature and faces the electorate at a general election.

Parliamentary government, however, does not come in a single simple form. In the British model, ministers do not merely depend on the backing of the House of Commons; they sit in that House, or the House of Lords, speak and try to sway votes in the chamber. In some countries, ministers are not allowed to be members of the legislature, creating a de facto separation, even though their government only holds office as long as it receives the endorsement of the parliament. That is true, for instance, of France, the Netherlands and Norway.

Parliamentary and presidential government

Parliamentary government, following a distinction made by James Bryce, is sometimes contrasted with presidential government. To avoid possible confusion, let us make clear that the distinguishing features of a presidential form of government have nothing to do with whether the country has a president or a monarch as head of state. In some countries, where the office of president, like that of the monarch in Britain, is largely titular, the regime

may well be parliamentary. The crucial feature of a presidential system is that the executive is chosen separately from the legislature, and holds office regardless of the legislature (see PRESIDENTIALISM). So, in the United States, Congress and president are elected separately. The Congress cannot dismiss the president except by impeachment, and the president cannot dissolve the Congress and call for fresh ELECTIONS to get rid of a refractory legislature. The Fifth French Republic affords yet another variation. The president is elected separately from the legislature, as in the United States. However, the executive power is divided between the president and the government (led by the prime minister); the president can dismiss the prime minister, but cannot impose on the national assembly a government and prime minister that the assembly does not want.

Such examples lead us to question whether there is a sharp distinction between parliamentary and presidential systems. Perhaps it is more helpful to see the two types as models on a continuum, rather than as opposites, with pure parliamentary government at one pole and pure presidentialism at the other. As we have seen, there are countries where, though the regime is normally regarded as parliamentary, the executive does not form part of the legislature.

The diversity of parliamentary regimes: three variants

The relationship between executive and legislature is usually taken as the touchstone of the distinction between pure parliamentary and pure presidential regimes. It also helps us to classify parliamentary systems in a more subtle

481

way, bringing out the differences among them. Thus, the term parliamentary regime can apply to both the French Fourth Republic (1946–58) and the United Kingdom, but the differences between them were acute. There are, however, other ways of distinguishing the various forms of parliamentary system. Thus one distinction focuses on the place of committees in the formulation of policy. In some parliamentary regimes, committees are weak, as in Britain; in others, as in the French Fourth Republic, they are strong. (The United States affords the best instance of a polity with strong committees.) In some, as in Britain, politics is adversarial, a term derived from the English law courts, with a single party government confronted by an opposition largely drawn from one party. In others, where proportional representation is used to elect the legislature, politics is coalition-oriented, and a more consensual style of government is usually found (see CONSENSUS DEMOCRACY).

We can therefore identify three distinct subtypes of parliamentary government. The first, and historically the most important, focuses on the relationship between legislature and executive. The next emphasises the role of committees in legislation and in scrutiny of the executive. The third looks at the character of politics: is the pattern adversarial, or consensual?

The legislature–executive relationship

Britain affords the earliest, and in some ways the simplest, form of parliamentary government and offers a striking illustration of the executive-dominated regime. Normally, there is an automatic tie between the legislature and the executive. At a general election, one party is usually returned with an overall majority in the House of Commons. The leader of that party forms a government, which can normally count on the support of its party to carry through its programme without serious impediment; moreover, the majority party is likely to stay in office for the lifetime of the parliament.

The strength of the executive in countries such as Britain derives largely from the party

system (see PARTY SYSTEMS). Party provides an automatic link between legislature and government; the executive can rely on the majority in the legislature to ratify the bills it introduces. In contrast, there are countries where the legislature is the dominant partner. Here there are frequent changes of government, without fresh elections, and government legislation may be heavily amended or rejected. We may describe these as assembly-dominated parliamentary regimes. In between these two extreme forms we can point to a third class of parliamentary regime which we may call 'balanced regimes'.

In Britain, in form the legislature is supreme, but in practice the executive is on top. Only twice in the last century was a government in peacetime defeated on an issue of confidence, in 1924 and again in 1979. In both cases, the government had no overall majority. A little more often, governments which have not been defeated on the floor of the House have resigned.

The normal pattern in Britain, therefore, is for a single party to win an overall majority at a general election, and for the leader of that party to become prime minister. The government introduces nearly all the important bills, which will nearly always be approved by the House. It will take the major part of the House's time for its own legislation; bills will be amended sometimes in important ways but party discipline will ensure that the government normally has its way on matters of both principle and detail. The maximum life of a parliament is fixed by law at five years; within that period, the prime minister can call a general election at the time which suits him or her or his/her party best.

In contrast, the French Third and Fourth Republics (1871–1940 and 1946–58) and Italy up to 1922, and from 1946 to 1994, provide clear examples of assembly-dominated regimes. No single party was likely to have an overall majority, and in some parties discipline was weak. Governments came and went; the Fourth Republic saw no fewer than 25 governments in 12 years, and in Italy there have been, up to the year 2000, 57 governments since the end of the Second World War. These governments had an uncertain and short tenure, and it was hard for them to push through coherent programmes of legislation. At their worst, such regimes were accused of *immobilisme*; change was hard to enact. Yet the defects have been exaggerated. The much-bruited instability was arguably superficial. Changes of government meant a change in the premiership but some offices were held by the same individual for years on end, itself a source of vexation to some critics. Indeed, the contrary charge is sometimes made, that it was hard for the electors to signal their wish for a change of direction.

The number of assembly-dominated regimes has been falling for at least a century. 'The decline of legislatures' is almost a cliché of political science. The growing complexity of legislation, the greater range of governmental functions, have led to greater concentration of power in the executive. Thus, in Switzerland, the late nineteenth and early twentieth centuries saw a weakening of the parliament and a stronger role for the executive.

A third type of model is to be found in the balanced regime. In the Netherlands, governments are coalitions, formed after perhaps weeks of hard bargaining but remarkably durable once formed. Executive dominance is hardly a term that can be levelled against the Dutch political system, but neither can it be described as rule by the assembly. German governments are also coalitions, but lean somewhat more towards the British example.

Committees in parliamentary government

The importance of committees in parliamentary government can be best gauged by looking at the British model of executive dominance. It is not the prominence of legislative committees in the British system, but the reverse that makes Britain such a useful example. 'But of all the oddest forms of government', wrote Walter Bagehot (1963: 155) more than a century ago, 'the oddest really is government by a public meeting'. Britain stood out among democratic countries for the narrowness of scope, and the powerlessness, of its parliamentary committees. An assembly that wishes to exercise meaningful scrutiny of the executive and to make a palpable contribution to the passage of legislation must be organised to do so. Such organisation requires the devolution of tasks to bodies smaller, more expert and more specialised than the whole. For long, however, the British House of Commons lived up to the description of 'government by public meeting' and gloried in its tendency to take business, however detailed, however esoteric in its appeal, on the floor of the House. The consequence of that was that most members had no knowledge of the clause or amendment under discussion. Indeed the chamber might be almost empty for the debate, but members would appear as if by magic when the vote was called and the division bells were rung. Not surprisingly, members who had not heard a word of the debate and would have been little wiser if they had, would turn to their party whips for guidance. 'Which is our lobby?' members would ask. The first standing committees, the bodies which examine the detail of legislation, were not appointed until 1883. Since then, though the system has grown and become more complex, the narrow remit of these committees remains and membership of any one committee is transitory. The committee effectively disbands as soon as it has completed work on the bill for which it is appointed. The system of select committees, whose task is to investigate and to scrutinise the work of the departments, was established and institutionalised in 1979 after a long struggle. These committees are now accepted and do valuable work, but they do not concern themselves with legislation. In contrast, the committees of the US Congress are specialised, permanent and play a major role in law-making. The Agriculture Committee of the Senate for instance considers both the detailed provisions and the general policy of agriculture bills; its members, appointed for a year at a time and often serving continuously for many years, develop a sense of corporate identity which may well cut across party allegiance.

Thus, where committees on the American pattern are widely used, the legislature has a LEADERSHIP, informed and independent of the executive. A body which, like the House of Commons, fails to throw up an alternative leadership from its own ranks is likely, almost by default, to abdicate its powers to the executive. Thus legislatures may be graded according to the purposes for, and the extent to, which they use committees. Not surprisingly, there are at least two views on the role of legislative committees. Some see them as a way of strengthening the independence of members individually, and of the chamber as a whole. Others see them as a rival to the executive and as making it difficult to achieve coherence of legislation. The drafters of the constitution of the French Fifth Republic saw in the powers of the specialised committees of the Fourth Republic a contributory source of executive weakness. Accordingly, they set out to emasculate the committees; for instance, by reducing the number of committees to six, and so extending the range of each committee and thereby diluting its expertise. The two largest committees each had a membership of 120, recalling once again Bagehot's reference to government by public meeting.

Adversary politics versus consensualism

British parliamentary politics is adversary politics. Two large and disciplined parties confront each other across the dispatch box in the House of Commons. The government spokesman, the appropriate minister, puts his case: the shadow minister then rises to criticise, to expose and to denounce the government's plans. Members from both sides then rise, to make speeches usually supportive of their own party. At the end of the debate members divide, usually joined by those who have not heard a word of the debate. Occasionally members will rebel, either abstaining or voting with the opposite party, but though this behaviour has increased since the 1960s, it remains uncommon. The highly focused debate has certain benefits: it goes far to ensure that errors, blunders, mistaken policies and dishonesty are illuminated by the relentless searchlight of opposition attack. The system makes it easy to hold governments accountable for their

failures. That, at least, is the establishment doctrine. At times, though, the performance has an air of ritual. Shadow spokesmen search desperately for reasons why a policy that they resorted to when last in office is now folly. Government ministers seek justification for measures that they denounced a few years back while in opposition. In the 1960s Labour embraced a statutory incomes policy, to be attacked by the Conservative opposition. When the parties changed places in 1970, they did more than move from one side to the other; after little more than two years, the Conservatives embraced a rigorous statutory incomes policy which Labour opposed in government. Again, in 1975, Labour adopted an incomes policy that fell a little short of being statutory, to be opposed by the Conservative opposition now led by Mrs Thatcher.

'Adversary politics', as practised in Britain, is a 'winner-take-all' type of politics. A single party takes office and seeks to carry out the programme on which it fought the election. Its spokesmen, and no other, share in the distribution of ministerial posts. The 'first past the post' electoral formula not only normally exaggerates the representation of the party which wins most votes, it manufactures a majority where none exists in the electorate. Thus Labour, elected in 1997, had an overall majority of 178 seats yet only 44 per cent of those voting actually supported Labour. In the same way, in 1983 the Conservatives under Margaret Thatcher had an overall majority of 144, but only 42 per cent of the total votes cast. The electoral system heavily penalises minor parties, unless, as with the Ulster Unionists, their support is heavily concentrated geographically.

The term 'adversary politics' is derived from the law courts. A party spokesman acts like a prosecuting counsel or a defending barrister, putting the most powerful case that he or she can, irrespective of private beliefs about the guilt or innocence of the accused. Note that the spirit of adversary politics does not necessarily carry with it the connotation that the parties are divided by a deep ideological gulf. They may be: but adversary politics is as compatible with parties whose differences are shallow and transitory as it is with parties separated by acute doctrinal cleavages. Hence the charge, sometimes made, that the differences between the parties are insubstantial, even unreal, that the conflict is a sham fight, the parliamentary skirmishes mock battles.

On the continent of Europe, coalition politics is common. Most countries there use proportional representation, which ensures that no one party is likely to have an overall majority. Governments are usually coalitions, sometimes of two parties, sometimes of several. After a general election, the character of the new government will not usually be known until there have been negotiations between the parties. Thus, the single party programme, which British electors take for granted, is a document that on the continent hardly outlives the election campaign. Parties that seek to ally in government will have to agree on a programme of legislation, and how many offices, and which, the partners will have. The coalitions will sometimes be fluid, and parties excluded from one coalition may form part of another, sometimes during the same parliament.

Such a process puts considerable weight on negotiation between parties, on a willingness to work together, on a consensual style of government. Critics argue that the lack of a single locus of responsibility blurs accountability. Moreover, the atmosphere of coalition, it is said, lends itself to excessive compromise, to an unwillingness to confront divisive issues and sometimes even to CORRUPTION. Another charge is that it is difficult for the electorate to dismiss an unpopular government. The same politicians who shared in government in the last coalition may surface with new partners in the next.

Consociational regimes are a special form of these consensual polities (see CONSOCIATIONALISM). Some societies are deeply divided by religion, language and ethnic identity and consist in effect of separate communities within the framework of the same state. Such groups have learned, over the years, to live together; their leaders negotiate with one another, sometimes outside the formal structure of parliament and can, if need be, deliver the acquiescence of their followers. In principle, consociational regimes can be found outside the democratic world, but the best examples are to be found in the smaller democracies of Western Europe such as Switzerland and the Netherlands.

Broadly, the British form of adversary politics prevails in the Old Commonwealth – in Canada and with some differences in Australia, and decreasingly in New Zealand. Coalition politics is the norm in continental Europe. The United States, whose title to be called a parliamentary regime would be controverted by some purists, defies classification. Its politics are too decentralised, its parties too loose, to qualify as adversarial; indeed, in practice, it often seems nearer the continental coalition model than to the Anglo-Saxon adversary pattern.

The models discussed here have focused on the status and character of the central legislature. It should go without saying that a country following any one model may share other characteristics with countries adopting a different model. Thus, an executive dominated country may like Britain be unitary, or like Canada federal. The highly centralised French Fourth Republic, and nineteenth-century federal Switzerland, both furnished examples of assembly dominated polities. Nor, indeed, need a parliamentary regime have a wide SUFFRAGE. Before 1867 Britain was hardly democratic; but the system of government was indubitably parliamentary.

It must also be emphasised that though the criteria used to distinguish the different models have been largely institutional, stressing such matters as the relationship between legislature and executive, or the electoral system, a nation's POLITICAL CULTURE, or its social divisions may often account for a country's choice of a particular model. Constitution makers may propose, but all too often their citizens dispose.

See also:

coalitions; electoral systems; majoritarianism; representation, models of

Further reading

Bagehot, W. (1963) *The English Constitution*, London: Fontana.

Bryce, J. (1923) *Modern Democracies*, revised edn, London: Macmillan.

Lijphart, A. (1984) *Democracies: Patterns of Majoritarian and Consensus Government in Twenty-One Countries*, New Haven, CT: Yale University Press.

—— (ed.) (1992) *Parliamentary Versus Presidential Government*, Oxford: Oxford University Press.

Norton, P. (ed.) (1998) *Parliaments and Governments in Western Europe*, London: Frank Cass.

Smith, G. (1989) *Politics in Western Europe*, 5th edn, Aldershot: Gower.

HUGH BERRINGTON

participation

The very idea of democracy implies participation by the citizenry in their own government. In a very small society, all citizens might participate in governance through DIRECT DEMOCRACY. In larger and more complex contemporary nations, participation in governance is necessarily indirect for most citizens, and government is typically representative. Representatives might be chosen by lot or might be elected by constituencies somehow defined. In the latter case, citizen participation typically takes the forms of voting, demonstrating, lobbying and running for office. One might organise a discussion of democratic participation by these forms of participation. Here it will be organised by explanatory aspects of participation as forms of collective action that are influenced by incentives and knowledge. These discussions will then be applied to recent visions of deliberative and participatory democracy and to the problem of ACCOUNTABILITY of officials. Forms of participation will be brought in as they fit into the explanatory context, especially of forms of collective action.

Democratic theory for a large, complex society must inherently be two-stage rather than direct because government of such a society requires intervening institutions, such as a representative legislature. We use popular majoritarian procedures to choose a government that then works without the use of popular majoritarian procedures in handling legislative and other problems. Political theory has long been treated as institutionalist and therefore as indirect or two-stage, as for example in the works of Thomas Hobbes, David Hume, Montesquieu and the less philosophical but more pragmatic James Madison. The entire tradition of contractarianism, despite its general incoherence, is grounded in two-stage argument. First, we supposedly agree on the idea or the general form of government, and then we let government work its wonders without constantly requiring our agreement on its actions and policies. Political participation may nevertheless enter into institutional DECISION-MAKING through lobbying and through holding officials accountable with the threat of voting them out of office.

Collective action

Collective action typically takes one of two strategically distinct forms. One form is essentially acting together, as in a mob, in co-ordination on some purpose, which may not be defined in detail or readily changed. The other is contributing together in co-operation or exchange to generate resources that then may be used for collective purposes (although they may also be misused). These two forms of activity differ strategically in that few people have an interest in doing the latter. Such contribution is subject to Mancur Olson's logic of collective action, which says that if I cannot gain at least as much *from my contribution* to a collective purpose as that contribution costs, then I have no interest in contributing. Typically, this condition must be met for most citizens for virtually every political collective good in a large polity.

Co-ordination does not generally face this problem. We all co-ordinate in driving on one side of the highway rather than the other: on the right in North America, on the left in the United Kingdom. In this case, I directly benefit from following the co-ordination. Co-ordinating on participation in a political movement by, for example, showing up for a demonstration might not so directly serve my interest. But if it is a pleasing day and friends are likely to be along for the event, I might actually prefer to go along as well. In some contexts, political participation is more costly if, for example, the authorities or an opposing group is likely to attack or punish us for our demonstration. In such cases, the costs might decline precipitously if enough of us act, so that the opposing force cannot expect to handle us. Hence, group or mob action can tip from being individually costly to being individually almost costless as the numbers increase.

Historically, much of the most important collective action was acting together; much of recent reformist politics in advanced democratic nations has been based in contributing together. There seem also to be distinctive differences across groups, especially across economic classes, in the forms of collective action they adopt. Most obviously, acting together is the resort of those, such as the poor and the young, who lack resources for contributing together, and of those who are excluded from normal political participation, as women have been even in many otherwise democratic societies. Student movements, poor people's movements and ethnic minority movements are all made up of people whose resources and institutional power are limited but whose numbers can be impressive. The rise of contributing together has accompanied the rise of a large and prosperous middle CLASS. The decline of violent forms of acting together in the advanced democracies has accompanied the increasing wealth and WELFARE stakes of those who might lose from sanctions against such action. This fits the thesis of embourgeoisement that, with prosperity, the working class will have too much to lose from revolution and will therefore turn to more pacific forms of political participation.

It is one of the great achievements of democracy that, under it, acting together has been transformed from violent mob and militia action into a relatively sanguine activity: voting. A well-organised and meaningful system of voting seems to reduce recourse to violence to effect outcomes. Contributing together is commonly bifurcated into contributions for campaigning and for lobbying. In some nations contributing together has, moreover, been transformed into a major activity that is massively biased in favour of corporate groups that have substantial resources to invest in supporting particular policies that clearly benefit them more than the campaign or lobbying contributions cost them. Many European democracies have managed to keep corporate money largely out of politics, so that co-ordination on voting is the major activity of popular politics. In presidential election years in the United States, campaign costs run into the hundreds of millions of dollars and campaigns on state-level referenda on fairly narrowly defined issues regularly cost many millions of dollars, with a very large share of the funds coming from corporate rather than popular sources (see ELECTORAL CAMPAIGNING).

Incentives

In the argument of Anthony Downs's economic theory of democracy, a citizen typically does not have very much interest in voting (Downs 1957). One vote has a minuscule chance of making a difference, so minuscule that, even if the voter has a strong preference for one candidate or party or result over another, when the value of that outcome is multiplied by the chance of making a difference and getting one's preferred candidate or policy, the *expected value* of the vote *to the voter alone* is minuscule. Hence, if there is any real cost involved in casting a vote, that cost swamps the expected value to the voter of voting. Hence, it is no surprise that voting turnouts fall in foul weather, in jurisdictions in which it is hard to vote because, for example, there are too few polling places, where some voters, such as minority voters, are harassed for voting, where, as in the United States, ELECTIONS are very frequent, or where there is a tax placed on voting. In the Netherlands, turnouts declined noticeably when the fine for not voting was rescinded. In practice, therefore, although costs matter, they do not fully determine turnouts even though the expected value of a vote is arguably very small.

Of course, voters might have reasons for voting other than merely concern for how the outcome would serve their personal interests. For example, a voter might wish to express solidarity with other liberals or conservatives, with Catholics or immigrants, with women or blacks. If voting is organised by small local precincts, one might even wish to express one's solidarity with friends and neighbours, who are likely to see whether one votes, as in small towns and in Philadelphia in those precincts that have polling places in virtually every block and every apartment building. Some voters must also vote not merely for their own interests but for the good of the society as they see it. For example, many voters might vote for fiscal policies that would harm them or for welfare policies that would benefit others. In such cases, the incentives against voting may be outweighed by these commitments.

Knowledge

Most normative theories and even much of the predictive discussion of democracy makes sense only if citizens have the knowledge to act as democratic theorists commonly suppose they will. In particular, they must have enough knowledge about candidates and policies to assess how these will affect their interests or the causes to which they are committed. The knowledge that people have about politics is not different in kind from the knowledge they have about anything else. Hence, the quality of knowledge that people have will depend, as in other areas, on the incentive they have to acquire it and on the costs of obtaining it. If we make the effort to know something in large part because it serves our interest to know it, then we cannot generally expect people to know very much about what their representa-

tives do. Some of them might know very much, but if so they will not know it for the reason that they need that knowledge in order to vote well.

As stated, this is a pragmatic claim about the nature of ordinary knowledge, but one can elevate it also to a normative claim. It is implausible that people can be said to have an obligation to know things that they cannot expect to be of use if taking the time to learn those things subtracts from the time they might have available for other activities in which they can have genuine effect.

Editorial writers and many academic observers have commented on the dismal level of knowledge of typical voters who, in the United States for example, commonly do not know the names of their senators even in an election year and who could not begin to explain the implications of a referendum (see REFERENDUMS) that might have massive impact on their lives. This ignorance is well documented in many surveys (see several contributions to *Critical Review* (1998)). It is so massive that there are numerous efforts to show that, despite such ignorance, voters somehow manage to get it right in the sense that they vote their interests and their causes. These efforts are generally ad hoc and so far unconvincing (there are many critical accounts of these claims, such as Bartels 1996). Consider an example of voter ignorance. Repeated surveys of American voters show that they believe that American expenditures on foreign aid are staggeringly high at, on the average estimate, about 15–17 per cent of the federal budget. The true figure is less than 1 per cent. Because of this woeful mismatch between beliefs and facts, the average voter thinks both that the level of foreign aid should be substantially more than 1 per cent and also that the actual level is far too high.

In the face of such evidence of ignorance, many commentators think that we should expect our fellow citizens to be very well informed or to hold their political opinions in abeyance until they are. The first half of this expectation is hopelessly implausible. Ordinary knowledge about foreign aid and other important issues of public policy is unlikely to be very good, and for compelling reasons. Those who are well informed spend many hours each week reading about political and policy issues. Many of these people spend so much time not because they wish to improve the fit of their votes with their interests or their commitments but because they have some other interest to serve, such as teaching the issues, writing about them in the press, or merely being entertained from knowing and keeping up with politics.

In a sense, the second half is also hopelessly implausible, because representative democracy virtually demands that people vote and that they vote according to their actual views, even though these are unlikely to be very well formed. John Stuart Mill recognised the intellectual limits of citizens and the limits of their incentives to overcome these limits and therefore did not much care for completely egalitarian popular participation. Walter Lippmann wrote that, in their quest for popular approval, democratic politicians follow the ignorant will of the people, and thereby cause the 'devitalisation of the governing power'. He called this the malady of democratic states (Lippmann 1955: 29). His point is partly well taken but his vocabulary is wrong. If we have a malady, we perform or prosper less well in some respect than we normally should. But the ignorant will of the people that Lippmann deplored is the *normal* state of a large polity, much and maybe most of the time. It is almost logically deducible from the nature of knowledge and its role in democracy. It is individually healthy not to squander much of one's time learning things that are useless.

If the citizen has no interest in voting, then the citizen has no interest in making the effort to learn enough to vote well. Something that is not worth doing is typically not worth doing well. If the problem of knowing enough to judge government officials is already hard, the lack of incentive to correct that problem is devastating. Indeed, the costs of knowing enough about government to be able to vote intelligently in one's own interest surely swamp the modest costs, for most people in contemporary major democracies, of actually casting a vote. A pragmatic theory of knowledge therefore weighs against knowing enough to vote well because of the incentives cut against investing in the relevant knowledge. The typical voter will not be able to put the relevant knowledge to beneficial use.

The conclusion that we have no incentive to learn enough to vote well was part of Downs's argument, but most of the subsequent research has focused primarily on the incentive to vote rather than the incentive to know enough to vote intelligently. Because many people do vote anyway, despite the absence of a personal benefit from doing so, the knowledge problem may well be the more fundamentally serious issue in democratic theory. Just because my vote has minuscule causal effect on democratically determined outcomes, there is no compelling reason for me to determine how to vote by its causal effect on such outcomes.

In smaller democracies in which there is fairly intense politics, as in Israel, typical voters may have extensive knowledge about the centrally divisive issues. In newly democratising states, such as South Africa, there might be particularly important issues that voters can readily identify. In the era of ideological parties of the left and right, voters might have had a relatively consistent sense of which party served them best. And in times of great crisis in any democratic state, we might expect that knowledge on central issues will be widespread. But in contemporary workaday politics, the shortage of political knowledge is often astonishing.

Deliberative and participatory democracy

A substantial current movement in democratic theory is the defence of deliberation or political discourse as perhaps the most important role of democratic CITIZENSHIP. Deliberation leads ostensibly to better understanding of politics and, in the view of some, such as Jürgen Habermas, to better policies that serve all citizens better (Gutmann and Thompson 1996) (see DELIBERATIVE DEMOCRACY). Against this possibility, critics note that if citizens have little incentive even to vote and therefore still less incentive to acquire sound political knowledge, they cannot be expected either to care to enter very seriously into political discourse or to be able to contribute to debates.

An earlier movement focused on participatory democracy. Examples of citizen participation include mass SOCIAL MOVEMENTS, such as peace movements, anti-government movements and, in the United States and some other nations, the Civil Rights movement and analogues of it. In actual fact only a small percentage of people participated in such movements and few participated more than a modest amount, such as joining a single demonstration, perhaps on a lovely day at a public common. Advocates of participatory democracy often focus on local politics, such as the location of traffic signs in areas where children are walking to school or the commitment to environmental protection of local green spaces. At that level, one can well imagine that the incentive arguments that tell against participation in national politics might not have much bite. Participation can be mobilised around such issues both because individuals might actually expect to make a difference that outweighs their contribution to the effort and because they can express solidarity in a context in which their expression will be noticed.

In Czechoslovakia and other nations in 1989, one might have turned out for demonstrations against moribund communist regimes with several motivations. One could express solidarity with friends, neighbours and fellow citizens, and one could live though a moment of such potential import and excitement that it actually attracted foreigners who had no stake beyond the pleasures of being participant-spectators. Such people typically had no material incentive from any interest they might have in the outcome of the demonstrations. In those heady days when regimes lacked the will to suppress such actions, however, they also faced no costs other than the usual costs of going to, and spending time on, events that were likely to be memorable moments in their own or the collective history. Peaceful demonstrations in many nations are plausibly larger than they would be if only adherents to the

relevant causes showed up, because spectators and those who want to experience the great moments add to the crowds. Acting together in such cases can be a wonderful experience with immediate personal benefits from the action itself that outweigh any of the costs, just as going to watch or be in a public spectacle of any other kind can be. Tens of thousands of people, for example, suffer severe cold in many years to join crowd who wish to be within sight of Times Square in New York City to watch the essentially meaningless event of ushering in the New Year.

The events of 1989 and such events as New Year's Eve celebrations in many places are not typical of politics, in which there may seldom be opportunities for even such nominal participation. Hence participatory democracy seems more a hope and a normative theory, rather than an actuality or an explanatory theory (see NORMATIVE APPROACHES TO DEMOCRACY).

Against the sanguine vision of deliberative democracy, consider two objections from the side of citizens. First, deliberative democracy clearly has the problem that Oscar Wilde saw in socialism: it would require too many evenings, evenings that are in short supply and that are in demand for other worthy activities, such as living. The gloriously politicised society of 1989 Czechoslovakia came as close to being the real world equivalent of the ideal type of deliberative democracy. Should we regret the passing of the participatory and deliberative politics of 1989? No. If 1989 had been kept alive for many years, it would have turned into a nightmare of overzealous politics, indeed of useless politics for the sake of nothing but politics. At some point citizens want to get on with their lives, and their lives are not primarily the lives of citizenship. Anyone looking back over the twentieth century to assess the merits of various political claims for participation must find a relatively anti-participatory stance appealing. In a decent world, living our lives would be our main concern and it would not often be trumped by politics.

It is interesting that the decline of deliberation within the US Congress, if there was much before, is largely a response to the demands of electoral politics, or popular democracy. Popular democracy in a large society with representative government often subverts deliberation. In the United States, the subversion results from two related facts. First, posturing is virtually demanded by the effort to reach a large public audience who, rightly, have other things to occupy their time and thoughts and who deal with politics more through catchphrases and slogans than through analysis. It is analysis that requires deliberation. Being mobilised in support of a candidate or a policy requires no analysis. Second, posturing is an inherent part of the unquenchable demand for money for American electoral politics. For raising money from large public INTEREST GROUPS such as those that support or oppose abortion or immigration, this follows from the nature of mass politics. But even for raising money from concentrated special interests, posturing is often necessary to protect against attacks from larger publics.

Because of the sheer size of the polity, citizens have little interest in participating and, given this fact, even less interest in being well enough informed to participate well. Joseph Schumpeter's (1950) strictures on democracy are devastating for any claim that citizens should deliberate or enter into deliberative discussions. This is not merely a matter of Wilde's complaint against socialism or the implausibility of the continuation of Czech politics much beyond 1989, but also of the intellectual demands that deliberation exacts. As noted above, most people cannot be strongly motivated to understand something that they cannot affect or make use of in their lives, especially something as complex and variegated as public policy over most matters.

To hope, expect, or wish for citizens to do much deliberating is unreasonable and forlorn. Yet if citizens are not chief among the deliberators, how can we speak of deliberative democracy? Deliberation is very important in politics, but it cannot typically be very democratic. Indeed, if deliberation is primarily within government or within smaller critical communities that might be taken as advisory to

government, it can serve as well in a non-democratic society.

Accountability

If there are serious problems of incentives against knowing enough to vote well, the very idea of accountability for democratically elected officials is clouded. If many people do not vote and many do not vote knowledgeably, it may be very difficult in principle for the electorate to hold representatives accountable when we cannot even judge whether they have served our interests. Without some notion of accountability, representation makes little sense in a democratic system. Yet, office holders must often choose in a state of ignorance of what the interests of their constituents are, because it is often beyond practical knowing what are the interests or commitments of an electorate on some issues. This might especially be true for issues which individual members of the electorate have never faced before. How much should our national government spend on airports, research on disease, fighter planes, foreign aid and the alleviation of domestic poverty? Most citizens have dismal knowledge of the scale of expenditure on such things, and yet legislatures regularly make decisions about them.

Because popular participation is highly constrained, official accountability is relatively limited. Citizens do not know enough either to instruct or to judge government. In the democratic vision, government and governors are the agents of the citizens, but in fact our agents are peculiarly our rulers. Hence, our fundamental problem, if participation must be as constrained as it is and seems likely to be, is to structure government institutions in ways that make them responsive to the interests of citizens. For all its flaws, representative democratic government, with officials subject to electoral sanction, seems to be the best device we have yet discovered for doing this. The scale of modern states, the complexity of many issues in them, and the extent of political ignorance in them threaten this device.

See also:

electoral volatility; political culture; public opinion; representation, concept of

Further reading

Bartels, L.M. (1996) 'Uninformed Votes: Information Effects in Presidential Elections', *American Journal of Political Science* 40 (February): 194–230.

Critical Review (1998) special issue (Fall) on 'Public Ignorance'.

Downs, A. (1957) *An Economic Theory of Democracy*, New York: Harper.

Gutmann, A. and Thompson, D. (1996) *Democracy and Disagreement*, Cambridge, MA: Harvard University Press.

Hardin, R. (1991) 'Acting Together, Contributing Together', *Rationality and Society* 3 (July): 365–80.

—— (1999) *Liberalism, Constitutionalism, and Democracy*, Oxford: Oxford University Press.

Lippmann, W. (1955) *The Public Philosophy*, Boston: Little, Brown.

Pateman, C. (1970) *Participation and Democratic Theory*, Cambridge: Cambridge University Press.

Schumpeter, J.A. (1950) *Capitalism, Socialism and Democracy*, 3rd edn, New York: Harper.

RUSSELL HARDIN

parties

Parties are inextricably bound up with democratic politics. Parties can be found in non-democratic regimes, but only in democratic regimes is politics structured by, and around, political parties; and only in democratic regimes is the direction of public policy shaped by the outcome of ELECTIONS in which parties are the principal protagonists. Well before the appearance of modern parties, Edmund Burke (1770) urged the recognition of party – 'a body of men united for promoting by their joint endeavours the national interest upon some particular principle in which they are all

agreed' – and party oppositions as organised competition for power with beneficent effects. Prior to the mid-twentieth century, however, the development of democratic politics as party politics was widely deprecated. Moreover, the stream of normative political theory underpinning the emergence of modern – that is, representative – forms of democratic governance, had little to say about parties. Democratic theory caught up with the practice of party politics only with the emergence of elite and pluralist theorising about democratic practices.

The emergence of political parties, largely during the late nineteenth century, was predicated on two conditions, both consequent on the advance of liberal concepts of CONSTITUTIONALISM and representation (see REPRESENTATION, CONCEPT OF). First, executive power in the national state had become subject to institutional CONSTRAINT, residing in both a written constitution (such as that of the United States), or statutes with constitutional import (such as in Britain), and a representative assembly which supplied the power base of governments. Constitutionalism subjected state power to the rule of law; representation recognised that legitimate government rests on consent and rendered governments accountable. Secondly, as a function of ACCOUNTABILITY, party-structured opposition to incumbent governments had become accepted practice, declared by Robert Dahl (1966) to be 'one of the greatest and most unexpected social discoveries that man has ever stumbled into'. That political opposition came to be regarded as integral to party politics entailed distinguishing, if only implicitly, between, on the one hand, the state as a regime form embodying a political community, and, on the other hand, government as a body of (temporary) occupants of state offices. With these developments secured, further democratisation entailed struggles over the enfranchisement of progressively larger sections of the national community. The arrival of mass electorates provided the final stimulus to the appearance of parties in their modern form and purpose (see SUFFRAGE).

Parties in democratic polities are too various to allow a definition that is comprehensive yet analytically decisive. Most parties share certain characteristics, however. They constitute organisations, varying widely in size and reach, in which activity is focused on mobilising electoral support with the objective of shaping public policy, either by occupying state offices or by influencing incumbents. To this end, parties – more correctly, party elites – advance political agendas, grounded in beliefs about society and economy; endeavour to recruit members, as electoral candidates and potential office-holders, party officials, and as mobilisation activists; seek funds to finance organisation and electoral campaigns; and concern themselves with the conduct of government and 'the rules of the game' in democratic polities. Many activities typical of parties are undertaken by other organisations in CIVIL SOCIETY, such as TRADES UNIONS, business lobbies and reform groups, but parties are distinctive in seeking elective public office in order to lay claim to the legitimate exercise of public power. In short, and uniquely, according to Weber (1922), 'parties live in a house of power'.

Democratic politics is commonly portrayed as competitive politics, implying that parties are essentially competitive organisations, serving democracy by presenting citizens with alternative policy agendas. Party politics is ambivalently competitive, however. PARTY SYSTEMS underpinned by a simple cleavage structure tend to be dominated by two major parties which, propelled by the logic of one-dimensional competition, tend to be weakly differentiated on policy issues. The premium on votes undermines policy competition. In highly fragmented multi-party systems rooted in a complex cleavage structure, with seldom an outright winning party, the competitive logic encourages policy differentiation; the priority is to mobilise a party's 'natural constituency' to ensure the party's presence in the legislature. The premium on mobilisation undermines competition for votes. Electoral mobilisation – not competition – is, then, the more definitive attribute of parties in democratic polities. In this respect, parties in democratic and non-democratic polities are not unalike; their differences arise from whether or not the political system allows for competitive mobilisations.

Despite pioneering studies by Ostrogorski in 1902 and Michels in 1911, systematic examination of democratic institutions largely overlooked parties prior to Maurice Duverger's *Political Parties* in 1954. The study was seminal in marking out a field of systematic investigation and in urging recognition of parties as the prime agents of democratic governance: 'the rise of parties...has alone made possible any real and active co-operation by the whole people in political affairs' (1954: 353) The first wave of empirical studies focused on the internal life of parties as organisations and their external life in relation to the wider society (for example, Epstein 1967). In a second wave, the focus expanded to examine the place of parties in government formation, coalition bargaining and POLICY-MAKING (for example, Castles 1982; Budge and Keman 1990). A third wave of studies centres around claims that parties are fading as dominant political actors (Lawson and Merkl 1988; Dalton and Küchler 1990). A great deal is now known about parties in each of these respects, but by-case variations – in organisational structure, membership numbers or coalition behaviour, for example – make comprehensive generalisations hard to come by. A common theme emerging from the plethora of studies, however, is the shifting place of party, and the dynamics of such shifts, in modern democratic states.

Parties are generally represented as intermediaries between state and civil society, supplying connections between citizens' preferences and government activity. This perspective highlights the relationship between three 'domains' in democratic polities: civil society, party, state. The domains are bounded in that actors in each domain enjoy considerable AUTONOMY, but shifts within one domain impact on the other domains, creating varying balances in the relationship. The civil society–party–state nexus is thus inherently dynamic; and domain boundaries flex as actors in each domain respond to new stimuli. For example, electoral laws and party funding rules cut across the state–party boundary; centralised candidate selection hardens the civil society–party boundary; that parties might recast their ideological position in response to opinion shifts in the electorate indicates permeability in the civil society–party boundary. More tortuously, a party in office might pursue policies resulting in a sea-change in public preferences to the long-term disadvantage of a major competitor (Dunleavy and Ward 1981), impelling the latter to revise fundamentally its organisation and/or ideological orientation; thereby introducing an enduring shift in the agenda alternatives offered to the electorate. Here, boundaries between the three domains become particularly fluid.

In these terms, three broad phases, or ideal types, of party formation can be identified, most evident in the evolution of parties in Western Europe and reflecting evolving conceptions of representation. In the first phase, and not uncommon in pre-democratic politics, parties originated within the legislature. These were principally liberal and conservative parties, founded by parliamentary elites to mobilise newly enfranchised property holders. The party consisted of a group of notables, or caucus, primarily concerned with the election of caucus members. These parties lacked formal organisation and members in the modern sense, and portrayed themselves as trustees of the public interest. With such notables connected, by family or interest, to dominant state actors, caucus parties can be characterised as bridgeheads reaching out from the state into civil society, the fount of LEGITIMACY.

In the second, sometimes coterminous, phase, parties formed outside parliament to secure parliamentary representation for unenfranchised groups and advanced explicitly sectional interests. Most typical were socialist parties, but some religious parties also originated in extra-parliamentary organisation. These parties usually sprang from concerted action amongst organisations in civil society, such as trade unions and confessional associa-

tions, were formally structured, and sought to recruit a large membership, usually 'indirect' via affiliated organisations, to provide financial and organisational resources. This mass party form constituted mobilisations within civil society to break through the boundedness of the state: party organisation provided their power base and electoral support the legitimacy to command access to state institutions. By the 1920s, mass parties of the left were well-established in most democratic states.

The third phase, characterised by the catch-all party, developed out of inter-party dynamics and shifts in state–civil society relations. The arrival of universal SUFFRAGE and the mass party challenged caucus parties to extend their appeal beyond narrow sectors of the electorate and to develop matching mobilisation capacity. This process of 'contagion from the left' led to the mass party emerging as the standard form – for parties of democratic intent – by the mid-twentieth century, encapsulating large swathes of national electorates around sectional interests. The very success, however, of mass politics in settling the most bitter conflicts over political and social rights, especially evident in the emergence of welfare states, led major parties to prioritise electoral objectives rather than the 'encadrement of the masses' (Kirchheimer 1972: 184). The 'catch-all' strategy entailed a distancing between party and civil society: muting ideological appeals, strengthening leadership control over organisation and policy, establishing bureaucracies to manage intra-party relations and electioneering, with membership a measure of party vitality rather than communal encapsulation. Initially a development amongst Christian democratic and conservative parties (never comfortable with the mass party form) the catch-all form was subsequently imitated by social democratic parties, a process of 'contagion from the right'.

The emergence of 'catch-all' parties also presaged shifts in party–state relationships. With the major parties more ready to compete for votes and most lesser parties having some experience of government as coalition partners, parties became primarily 'brokers' between state and civil society. Rather than emphasising sectional interests, major parties in particular came to present themselves as effective managers of state power. In parallel, public office became a resource for sustaining parties: by exercising patronage beyond the offices of government, parties extended their reach into the state; by instituting public subventions, parties became less reliant on civil society for resources; by controlling electoral rules, established parties could deter 'intruder' parties. In short, greater dependence on state resources accompanied, and assisted, the distancing of parties from civil society.

Such developments appear to be encouraging further shifts in party formation, suggesting that a fourth phase is underway: the emergence of the cartel (Katz and Mair 1995) or electoral-professional party (Panebianco 1988). With their enhanced autonomy, parties can nurture professional politicians and employ campaign specialists, further weakening links with civil society; by exploiting the mass MEDIA, especially television, parties can appeal directly to the electorate, vitiating the role of activists; by instituting direct membership, party members are atomised, enhancing elite control of the party; with party penetration of the state, the state–party boundary becomes blurred. Taken together with the emergence of coalition government as 'normal politics' in most Western European countries, such potentialities point, again, to survival rather than competition for office becoming dominant party objectives. In this sense, the cartel party is not unlike the original caucus parties: elite groups seeking legitimation but not active engagement among citizens.

Few parties can yet be identified as cartel parties, just as not all parties fitted the ideal types outlined, nor have undergone evolution from one type to another. Moreover, challenges to the major parties, with their roots in cleavage politics, may impede their development as cartel parties. New parties of the extreme left and the extreme right share a common purpose of 'breaking the mould' of established politics. New SOCIAL MOVEMENTS, especially environmental, feminist and 'gay'

mobilisations, undermine party control of political agendas. With distancing from civil society, established parties risk undermining traditional loyalties, rendering parties more vulnerable to electoral punishment. Evidence of declining party membership and electoral turnout, albeit patchy, suggest that established parties may be losing mobilisation capacity.

Established parties, however, possess resources enabling them to adapt to challenges. The roots of the major established parties lie in the nineteenth century, but in the early twenty-first century they are very different parties in terms of organisation and ideology; even so, they have retained their lead in terms of votes over the period despite considerably enlarged electorates. Much the same parties, conservative, Christian democratic, social democratic, remain dominant governing parties; and in many instances have co-opted the agendas of new social movements. Membership has become less crucial to party, yet membership numbers tend to be broadly stable. Compared to the first two decades after 1945, aggregate-level electoral instability shows some increase, but over the century of democratic politics and compared to the interwar period there has been a steady trend towards aggregate-level stability, albeit with some sharp, short-term turbulence.

Claims made for 'party decline' thus invite scepticism. The interpenetration of party and state has shifted the balance in the civil society–party–state relationship away from civil society as an organisational resource but has not undermined civil society as the prime site of political mobilisation and the locus of political legitimacy. Absent of parties, it remains unclear how democratic polities might resolve the tensions between mass PARTICIPATION and the decision taking expected of parties in office. Nor is it evident what kinds of agents other than parties have the capacity, if not always the incentives, to deliver competitive mobilisations.

See also:

coalitions; elections; party systems; pluralism; political financing; representation, models of

Further reading

Budge, I. and Keman, H. (1990) *Parties and Democracy: Coalition Formation and Government Functioning in Twenty States*, Oxford: Oxford University Press.

Burke, E. (1770) 'Thoughts on the Causes of the Present Discontents', in *The Works of Edmund Burke*, Boston: Little, Brown, 1839.

Castles, F. (ed.) (1982) *The Impact of Parties*, London: Sage.

Dahl, R. (1966) *Political Oppositions in Western Democracies*, New Haven, CT: Yale University Press.

Dalton, R. (2000) 'The Decline of Party Identifications', in R. Dalton and M. Wattenberg (eds), *Parties Without Partisans: Political Change in Advanced Industrial Democracies*, Oxford: Oxford University Press.

Dalton, R. and Küchler. M. (1990) *Challenging the Political Order: New Social and Political Movements in Western Democracies*, Cambridge: Polity Press.

Dunleavy, P. and Ward, H. (1981) 'Exogenous Voter Preferences and Parties with State Power: Some Internal Problems with Economic Theories of Party Competition', *British Journal of Political Science* 11: 351–80.

Duverger, M. (1954) *Political Parties: Their Organisation and Activities in the Modern State*, London: Methuen.

Epstein, L. (1967) *Political Parties in Western Democracies*, New York: Praeger.

Katz, R. and Mair, P. (1995) 'Changing Models of Party Organisation and Party Democracy: The Emergence of the Cartel Party', *Party Politics* 1: 5–28.

Kirchheimer, O. (1972) 'The Transformation of the West European Party System', in J. LaPalombara and M. Weiner (eds), *Political Parties and Political Development*, Princeton, NJ: Princeton University Press.

Lawson, K. and Merkl, P. (eds) (1988) *When Parties Fail: Emerging Alternative Organisations*, Princeton, NJ: Princeton University Press.

Panebianco, A. (1988) *Political Parties: Organisation and Power*, Cambridge: Cambridge University Press.

Weber, M. (1922) 'Wirtschaft und Gesellschaft', in H. Gerth and C. Wright Mills (eds), *From Max Weber: Essays in Sociology*, London: Routledge, 1974

ELINOR SCARBROUGH

partition

Partition refers to the division of a sovereign territory into two or more autonomous states. As a means of conflict resolution, it is a mechanism designed to allow self-government to minority groups who, because of persecution, economic exploitation or the threat of cultural ASSIMILATION, are demanding statehood. The earliest examples of partition coincide with the end of the First World War and the determination of the League of Nations to oversee the breakup of the Austro-Hungarian and Ottoman empires. Following the Second World War, decolonisation led to a second wave of partitions including those of India and Palestine. Although the cause of most partitions is ethnic division or nationalism, this is not always the most important causal factor. The postwar partitions of Germany and Korea, for example, can be understood entirely in a realist context of two major powers, the United States and the Soviet Union, dividing a homogeneous people for territorial and strategic gain. But such examples are the exceptions. In the cases of India (1947), Ireland (1921), Cyprus (1973), Palestine (1948), the Soviet Union (1989) and Yugoslavia (1991), the primary motivation to secession was ethnicity. More specifically, in most of these countries, the immediate cause of partition was a form of ethnic hatred so deeply embedded that any federal, confederal or consociational solution was deemed, rightly or wrongly, to be unworkable.

In most of these examples, partition was widely understood to be the most effective way of resolving or reducing conflict. It was also regarded as a necessary condition for democratisation; a justifiable claim if democracy is understood to include the right to self-determination. Yet the matter is not nearly so simple. International law is widely understood to interpret the right to self-determination as applying to states and not to peoples, although a degree of ambivalence continues to surround this question. What is clear, however, is that the international community, despite these legal ambiguities, consistently advocates the integrity of the existing nation-state system. However, denying a people, itself an ambiguous term, an automatic, legally enforceable right to secession leaves open the question of the appropriate response of the international community in the event of a people seeking or declaring partition. Unsurprisingly, disagreement within the international community concerning particular situations often results from considerations of *realpolitik*. However, the more important reason why this issue is generally so divisive is because the relationship between partition and democracy is itself so deeply complex. The following deceptively simple question is central to the debate: can civic nationalism or democratisation resolve competing nationalisms or, in situations of profound ethnic conflict, is partition/secession a necessary condition for democratisation? There is no definitive answer to this question that does not run the double risk of assuming that what may be appropriate for one conflict situation is necessarily the best for all others or that there is a conception of democracy to which all can agree. Nevertheless, two broad responses can be identified. The first argues that democracy requires the existence of national unity. The second holds to the view that partition is inimical to democracy and that democratisation is a far better strategy to resolve ethnic conflict.

Rustow has argued that the vast majority of citizens in any democracy must have no doubts or mental reservations as to which political community they belong to, and that it is best when this sense of belonging is understood unthinkingly. It is also argued that national unity is a necessary condition for democracy to emerge in the first place. Therefore, in the event

of two competing nationalisms sharing a territory, it is much more likely that secession rather than democracy will result (Rustow 1970: 350–60). A similar argument is made by Beran, who pointed out that democratisation simply cannot deal with societies that are structurally or deeply divided (Beran 1987: 38–42). There is little doubt that these arguments have considerable force both intuitively and empirically. However, Spencer is deeply sceptical about the claim that partition can promote democracy. Her argument is that secession invariably causes far more problems than it solves. This concurs with the analysis of former UN Secretary-General Boutros Boutros Ghali who, when asked whether everyone who asked for a state should get one, replied: 'Certainly not. If every ethnic, linguistic or religious group would ask for a statehood, we would have 2000 states at the end of the century. It is not in the interests of the international community' (Spencer 1998: 14) (see SEPARATISM). In his 1992 document *Agenda for Peace*, Boutros Ghali made a similar point outlining the integrity of the existing international state system and stipulated that the way to resolve rival claims of SOVEREIGNTY was through respect for minority RIGHTS and democratisation (Mayall 1999: 475). In other words, there is not, nor should there be in law, any automatic right to secession.

Spencer argues that separatist wars, even when successful, have disastrous practical effects. That is, they have rarely been successful in preventing further bloodshed, economic dislocation or massive disruption in terms of forced migration (a recent exception to this would be the partition of Czechoslovakia in 1991). She also argues that partition has rarely been successful in promoting democratic change by alleviating existing ethnic tensions. In fact, what partition has tended to do is entrench identity and ethnicity to the severe detriment of the new MINORITIES that it creates. For example, the collapse of the Soviet Union has resulted in disgruntled Russian minorities in most of the newly created states of the CIS. In support of this interpretation, one could cite the example of the Catholic minority in Northern Ireland after the partition of Ireland in 1921. It was not until the state was reformed in the 1970s and 1980s that the DEMOCRATIC DEFICIT inherent in this part of Ireland was acknowledged. In this context, Ireland remains an interesting example. Implicit in the current peace process is the assumption that a fully transparent democratic society will allow the two communities to share power in an atmosphere of trust and reconciliation. Yet, for the moment at least, it is far from clear that this is a realistic expectation.

Although the two positions outlined above are not mutually exclusive, they serve to identify the two ways to approach this question. Rustow argues that if there is not a deeply embedded sense of political community already in place, then there is no possibility of democracy either taking hold or sustaining itself. Implicit in Spencer's argument is the conviction that, because the 'cure of partition' is worse that the condition it is designed to alleviate, it is right that the international community seek to encourage democratisation as a means of resolving ethnic conflict. I would argue that it is right that the international community should oppose any automatic right to partition or secession that can be claimed by any group for whatever reason, and it is right that this refusal be reflected in international law. This is not to confer false LEGITIMACY on the existing state system, or in any way to underestimate the intractability of many ethnic conflicts, but it is to recognise that the international community should not be used as the vehicle for promoting a world order based on separatism and the myth of blood purity.

It is important to recognise, however, the profound tensions that reside in this position. Four in particular require our attention. The first is that, although it may seem reasonable to grant to groups the right to self-determination and secession, especially in circumstances in which human rights are being abused, such a right, if widely claimed, could be inimical to democracy in two distinct ways other than those identified above. The first comes from

what we might call a postmodern or radical democratic perspective (see RADICAL DEMOCRACY). If it is accepted that citizens have multiple identities, and that it is right that these should not be suffocated by an all-encompassing sense of ethnicity or nationalism, then the objective must be to challenge the conventional, territorial conceptions of democracy implicit in the politics of partition (see IDENTITY, POLITICAL). The second is that such a form of politics could lead to a 'logic of fragmentation' in which attention becomes increasingly focused on issues such as identity and difference at the expense of constructing a responsible global CITIZENSHIP capable of confronting what may be seen as some of the more glaring abuses of democracy in the world, for example, disease, poverty and inequality.

Yet, within the position stipulating the dangers of partition, a second tension resides. Although it must be recognised that JUSTICE requires law, it is also true that the universal application of law will often fail to deliver justice. For what of those particular instances where law and justice do not coincide, where it seems clear that partition is a *sine qua non* for democratisation, justice and peace? At what point, and according to what or whose criteria, does the international community suspend its support for national sovereignty and demand that the rights of a separate people to statehood be respected? This difficult tension is mirrored in a number of very different contexts. An interesting analogy would be that of euthanasia. Although in many individual instances it seems indefensible to deny a suffering patient the right to die, this does not, and nor should it, entail that the practice of euthanasia be legalised. Furthermore, although we have to recognise that the policies based on these assumptions are often anomalous, they may, nevertheless, represent the least worst option under the circumstances.

This recognition leads to a third tension. It is important to acknowledge that the international community, while rightly resisting widespread changes to the law on secession, *does* sometimes support partition and the creation of new jurisdictions. One thinks here of the example of the Kurds in Iraq and the encouragement that was given to them at the time of the Kuwait crisis. However, what happens under circumstances when the international community supports the end of partition but cannot endorse the means for its realisation or condone its likely effects? A recent example of this was the Croatian declaration of independence from Yugoslavia. Although widely acknowledged as necessary for long term peace in the area, this partition led to the ethnic cleansing of tens of thousands of Serbs from the Krajina, a situation which has of course been repeated over much of the Balkans. It would seem that, in such circumstances, the ends are normally understood to justify the means.

Situations like that of Yugoslavia lead to the identification of a fourth tension implicit in this question. This refers to the possibility that the creation of ethnically homogeneous states may, *pace* Spencer, sometimes be necessary in order for ethnicity to become a *less* salient feature of the politics of a region. The reason for this is that ethnicity requires the oxygen of conflict in order for it to flourish. In situations where there is little realistic prospect of civic nationalism diluting a poisonous ethnic conflict it may well be best, where possible, to remove that which allows it to thrive. In such circumstances, the emergence of separate nation-states would remove one of ethnicity's most potent constitutive lifelines. In these environments it is important, therefore, that we realise the limitations of politics and democracy. The hope is that from within such newly found states a stronger democracy can emerge that is able to encourage a more benign ethnicity able to live with difference across its borders.

See also:

nations and nationalism; rights, minority and indigenous; separatism; sovereignty

Further reading

Beran, H. (1987) *The Consent Theory of Political Obligation*, London: Croom Helm.

Mayall, J. (1999) 'Sovereignty, Nationalism and Self-Determination', *Political Studies* 47: 474–502.

Spencer, M. (ed.) (1998) *Separatism: Democracy and Disintegration*, Lanham, MD: Rowman and Littlefield.

Rustow, D. (1970) 'Transitions to Democracy', *Comparative Politics* 3: 337–39.

ANTHONY M. CLOHESY

party systems

In liberal democracies, political PARTIES, competing in free and fair elections, are the principal mechanism through which citizens can hold those who govern accountable for their actions. The number and kind of political parties shape the choices voters confront, as well as the decisiveness with which they can express their views. As such, party systems act as filtering mechanisms, bringing some issues forward while excluding others. In parliamentary systems, the number of parties and relationships among them influence cabinet formation and the duration of governments. In presidential systems, party systems shape relationships between the executive and the legislature, particularly the difficulty or ease with which the executive can secure passage of its programme.

A party system is more than the sum total of parties contesting ELECTIONS. 'System' implies regularity and interaction, or that in recruiting candidates, campaigning for office, forming governments, and participating in POLICY-MAKING, parties influence and are influenced by each other. However, what parties do is influenced not only by other parties but also the larger system of which they are a part. This includes not only the party system, defined as the recurring pattern of interaction among parties competing for power, but also the broader political system. Placed between citizens and their governments, parties influence and are influenced by the actual and anticipated behaviour of their competitors, the electorate whose support they seek, and the formal institutional environment in which they operate.

Interest in party systems is almost as old as the study of political parties. Objects of concern include the number of parties, the ways in which they interact, patterns of continuity and change, and the causes and consequences of party systems. Among the former are the degree to which party systems shape or are shaped by the societies in which they operate or the ELEC-TORAL SYSTEMS under which parties compete. Among the latter are fundamental issues of representation, democratic control, political stability and governance.

Classification

Distinguishing among party systems is a necessary step in their analysis. This can be done either by counting parties or constructing typologies. Neither is simple. Before we can count parties, we must decide whether all parties are equally relevant. A party which wins 20 per cent of the vote has more impact than one which has won 2 per cent. Political scientists take account of this by using counting rules, such as those specified by Giovanni Sartori (1976: 121–24), or weighted formulas, such as that proposed by Laakso and Taagepera (1979). Sartori excludes parties with less than 5 per cent of the vote unless they are included in COALITIONS or exert 'blackmail' potential, measured by their ability, directly or indirectly, to influence coalition formation. Laakso and Taagepera (1979) provide us with an indicator of the effective number of political parties and an alternative measure of fragmentation different from Rae's fractionalisation index (Fe).

Typologies take account of the most salient features of party systems. Although the most familiar distinction is between two party and multiparty systems, political scientists have found it useful to distinguish among different patterns of multiparty competition. Blondel (1968) uses the number and relative size of parties to distinguish among two party systems, two and a half-party systems (systems with two larger and one smaller party), and

multiparty systems with or without a predominant party (see DEMOCRATIC EXECUTIVES). Doing so distinguishes among patterns of government formation.

Sartori (1976: 125–29) uses both the number of political parties and the ideological distance among them to build a two-dimensional typology. His categories include predominant party systems, two party systems, moderate PLURALISM, segmented systems and polarised pluralism. The most important distinction is between moderate and polarised pluralism. Moderately plural systems typically have three to five parties and the direction of competition is centripetal. Because parties converge toward the centre, the pattern of competition is similar to two party systems. In contrast, polarised systems typically have six or more parties, including bilateral oppositions (anti-system parties) at each pole. Because the centre is occupied, parties move toward the extremes. Thus, the dynamic is centrifugal rather than centripetal, making it difficult to form or sustain cabinets (Sartori 1976: 131–39ff).

Causes

Accounting for differences among party systems has been an important facet of research. Two views predominate: one argues that party systems are rooted in cleavage structures while the other emphasises the impact of institutions and electoral systems. According to the first, the number of parties reflects societal cleavages and the ways in which they are mobilised. Multiparty competition is more likely in divided than in homogeneous societies. According to the second, the number of parties reflects electoral systems and extent to which they encourage parties to amalgamate (Duverger 1954: 203–5ff). Some, such as single member district systems, force potentially divided factions to stay together in order to defeat opponents. Others, such as proportional representation, allow smaller parties to compete separately without risking their exclusion from the legislature.

Neither view is complete: party systems do reflect societal divisions, but are rarely a direct mirror of them. Some cleavages are mobilised while others are not, and parties may be constructed in ways which either reinforce or bridge lines of cleavage. However, once parties are established they may be difficult to displace, both because they have influence over the choice of electoral system and because parties, by competing in elections and mobilising support, channel portions of electorate and perpetuate earlier divisions. There is a correlation between proportional representation and the number of political parties represented in the legislature (Lijphart 1994) (see CONSENSUS DEMOCRACY). However, the relationship is neither simple nor necessarily causal. The impact of electoral systems depends on both the depth of cleavage and the extent to which the electorate is deeply attached to political parties.

Once consolidated, party systems have remarkable staying power. Although Lipset and Rokkan's (1967) observation that most Western European party systems had been frozen since the completion of SUFFRAGE extension some forty years before exaggerates electoral stability, most Western European party systems continue to be organised around the CLASS and religious cleavages on which they were originally mobilised. However, the salience and intensity of these cleavages has declined, allowing (and in some instances, encouraging) established parties to modify their positions, for example, by recasting themselves as broadly based people's parties. New parties have also emerged. In many countries, Green and new right protest parties have crowded into party spectra. Nevertheless, even though ELECTORAL VOLATILITY has increased and party strengths have changed, established parties have proved to be remarkably resilient. Typically, parties which defined the system and formed its core in previous decades continue to do so. Among Western European party systems, only the Italian party system in the 1990s – buffeted by multiple shocks including societal changes, the fall of Communism in eastern Europe, scandals discrediting of Christian Democracy and the Socialists and changes in the electoral law –

has changed dramatically. Elsewhere, few established parties have disappeared. Although weakening of voter attachments to parties has created opportunities for more substantial changes, in most countries these have yet to occur.

Consequences of multiparty competition

Concern with continuity and change reflects questions about the representation of popular views. Party systems are the principal (though by no means the exclusive) mechanism through which the public can exercise popular control over those who govern. However, voters' ability to do so depends on the alternatives presented to them. If only two, or perhaps a few, parties contest elections, then the public will have greater opportunity to express a clear and decisive choice, but there is also a risk that positions considered important by some segments of the electorate will be ignored. Increasing the number of political parties increases not only the choice available to the public, but also the chance that no one party will gain a majority. There is also a risk that party positions may rigidify.

Political scientists believe that party competition provides a solution for these problems. Proponents of two-party systems argue that competition between two broadly based parties ensures that politicians will be responsive to the public. Parties striving for majorities will take account of the concerns of divergent groups, aggregating them into overlapping alternatives reflecting the views of broad majorities. However, the process of aggregation and pursuit of a 'middle majority' may narrow the scope of conflict and block the presentation of points of view which others might choose. Others argue that multiparty competition and lower electoral thresholds enhance democracy. However, even here there are obstacles. Although voters in established multiparty systems are capable of placing parties on a left–right spectrum, parties do not necessarily address the same issues. Studies of party programmes indicate that parties talk past each other, highlighting the issues or themes which they feel will benefit them while ignoring those which other parties address (Budge 1994) (see ELECTORAL COMPETITION).

The number of parties contesting elections and winning seats affects not only the choices available to voters, but also governability and political stability. Two-party competition produces automatic majorities, but in multiparty systems majorities are less common. Cabinets must be crafted by assembling coalitions or recourse to minority governments. Fears that this could not be accomplished led some political scientists to associate multiparty competition with *immobilisme*, cabinet instability and regime collapse. However, this view is based on a small number of cases (interwar Germany, Spain in the 1930s, Fourth Republic France and postwar Italy), which provided the basis for Sartori's notion of polarised pluralism. Here, centrifugal dynamics weaken not only the cabinet but also the regime itself.

Multiparty regimes are more stable than earlier scholars anticipated. Politicians have recourse to a number of devices to ensure governability. In Scandinavia, minority government provides an alternative to coalitions. Elsewhere, party leaders negotiate coalitions alone or with the help of a mediator appointed by the head of state, as in the Netherlands. Sometimes coalitions are cemented by detailed governing agreements. Both minimum winning and ideologically connected coalitions have proved durable. Problems are likely to occur only when deep divisions divide coalitions or extreme fragmentation gives smaller parties blackmail potential because their support is needed to sustain a cabinet (see CHAOS AND COALITIONS). This has been the case in both Israel and India. However, it can be argued that this reflects not multipartyism *per se*, but rather deep societal divisions, which might in any case be problematic. Instances of polarised pluralism are exceedingly rare. Whether this will continue to be the case remains to be seen.

Conclusion

Would-be constitutional engineers can influence but not necessarily determine the shape of a party system. Prescribing an optimal format is difficult. Choosing involves trade-offs among values such as representation, clear choice, and the decisiveness of electoral decisions (see DEMOCRATIC TRADE-OFFS). Choices depend on the kind of system one desires. If the aim is adversarial politics, the choice should be for two party rather than multiparty systems. If the aim is a more consensual system, then it is crucial to ensure that all significant groups are represented. This is more likely in a multiparty system.

Multipartyism broadens the choices available to voters but makes it difficult to render decisive judgements on public policy. In any case, such sensitivity may be too much to expect of either two party or multiparty systems. There is no guarantee that an enlightened debate will take place in either instance. Except in highly polarised elections, it is difficult to discern just what voters have chosen in either two party or multiparty elections. Victory allows leaders to impute mandates which the majority of voters might not have offered had they been asked directly. Multiparty competition gives voters more choice and requires office-holders to seek consent for what they want to do. Nevertheless, multiparty systems can end up with an excessive number of parties. Optimal party systems force those who govern to be responsive to the electorate. This can occur either in a two-party system in which the opposition calls the government to account or in a multiparty system in which competitors generate similar pressures. However, this depends more on voters being willing to switch parties than on a particular party configuration. What is clear is that a well-developed party system is needed if those who govern are to be held accountable at all. Without a party system in which the same parties compete regularly from election to election, it becomes impossible for voters to render retrospective judgements. Voters who want to be able to assign credit or blame require some means of discerning which groups of leaders were responsible. Parties and the identifiable labels which they provide to teams of leaders serve this minimal purpose.

See also:

cleavages; consensus democracy; constitutional design; democratic breakdown; democratic performance; ideological polarisation; institutional design; majoritarianism; parties

Further reading

Blondel, J. (1968) 'Party Systems and Patterns of Government in Western Democracies', *Canadian Journal of Political Science* 1: 180–203.

Budge, I. (1994) 'A New Spatial Theory of Party Competition: Uncertainty, Ideology and Policy Equilibria Views Comparatively and Temporarily', *British Journal of Political Science*, 24: 443–67.

Daalder, H. (1983) 'The Comparative Study of European Parties and Party Systems: An Overview', in H. Daalder and P. Mair (eds), *Western European Party Systems: Continuity and Change*, London: Sage, 1–28.

Dahl, R.A. (1966) *Political Oppositions in Western Democracies*, New Haven, CT: Yale University Press.

Duverger, M. (1954) *Political Parties: Their Organisation and Activities in the Modern State*, trans. B. North and R. North, New York: John Wiley.

Laakso, M. and Taagepera, R. (1979) 'Effective Number of Political Parties: A Measure with Application to Western Europe', *Comparative Political Studies* 12: 3–27.

Lijphart, A. (1994) *Electoral Systems and Party Systems: A Study of Twenty-Seven Democracies, 1945–1990*, Oxford: Oxford University Press.

Lipset, S.M. and Rokkan, S. (1967) 'Cleavage Structures, Party Systems and Voter Alignments: An Introduction', in S.M. Lipset and S. Rokkan (eds), *Party Systems and Voter Alignments*, New York: The Free Press, 1–64.

Sartori, G. (1976) *Parties and Party Systems: A Framework for Analysis*, vol. I, Cambridge: Cambridge University Press.

Ware, A. (1966) *Political Parties and Party Systems*, Oxford: Oxford University Press.

STEVEN B. WOLINETZ

patriarchy

Interestingly, the terms patriarchy and democracy are not discussed together as much as might be expected, principally because democracy only became a topic for second-wave feminist theorists when 'patriarchy' had lost its attraction as an analytic concept. Although there are feminist democratic theorists who see the issues in terms of the overarching systematic subordination of women associated with the term 'patriarchy', for the most part, contemporary feminist theorists are as much concerned with differences between women as they are with women's oppression by men, so that the term 'patriarchy' is no longer seen as appropriate.

Patriarchy has in fact long been a highly controversial term for feminists. For other social scientists, following Max Weber, it means 'rule of the father', and in this sense it is undoubtedly descriptive of particular times and places where the modern state did not exist. However, for feminists it has the more general meaning of 'subordination of women by men'. Those who oppose the feminist use of the term have argued that it is too monolithic, obscuring women's resistance to male power, co-operation between the sexes, and the way in which CLASS, 'race' and ethnicity cut across sex and gender in such a way that in some situations some women may have power over some men. Patriarchy may also be seen as misleading since it inclines feminists to look for a reductive explanation of the source of male power in biological reproduction (Rowbotham 1982). Others have argued, however, that despite the undoubted subtleties of relations between the sexes, feminists need a theory which helps identify a general structure of women's oppression and the mechanisms by which it is reproduced (Alexander and Taylor 1982). Although the debate remains unresolved, it is certainly the case that 'patriarchy' has been relatively little used by feminists as the general theories of women's oppression formulated in the 1970s – notably those of Marxist and radical feminists – have been discredited. Nevertheless, insofar as feminism necessarily involves a commitment to the belief that women have historically been subordinated to men, arguably a view of patriarchy is implicit in all feminist work.

The question of democracy has been far less controversial, no doubt because it has been less central to feminism. In fact, relatively little was written on the topic in feminist theory until the late 1980s. While first-wave feminism was, of course, concerned with democracy insofar as the vote was the focus of the many different demands made by the movement, the validity of the institutions of liberal democracy itself were not really questioned. In contrast, second-wave feminists tended to be highly suspicious of the political structures of the liberal state and the impoverished model of democracy they embody, taking them – explicitly or implicitly – to be inherently patriarchal. In the 1960s and 1970s, groups affiliated with the women's liberation movement were more concerned with democratising practices in CIVIL SOCIETY, both within women's groups and in everyday life. It is only following disillusionment with more radical ideals in the 1980s and 1990s that a feminist perspective on the politics of more formal democratic institutions has been developed.

The most influential work on patriarchy and democracy in second wave feminism is undoubtedly that of Carole Pateman. She argues that, although women now have formal democratic RIGHTS in Western liberal democracies, substantive inequalities between the sexes remain fundamental to the political system. Pateman argues that, as it is conventionally understood, democracy consolidates the distinction between public and private so that women's 'naturally' subordinate status in the domestic sphere is never challenged. Furthermore, this unequal status is taken up into the public sphere insofar as women *as* women find themselves positioned in civil society and political institutions in relation to their domestic responsibilities. They are therefore at a disadvantage in comparison with men who more closely approximate the ideal individual of democratic theory. In fact, democracy may even be seen in this way as *contributing* to

patriarchy in that women's oppression is obscured by their possession of ostensibly equal rights with men. Pateman also questions the premises of radical participatory democracy, of which she was previously a prominent advocate, arguing that, insofar as it envisions the extension of democracy to the workplace, it again neglects the subordination of women in the home and the different position of women and men in relation to paid employment (Pateman 1989).

Pateman's work stresses the difficulties of achieving genuine EQUALITY through supposedly gender-neutral political institutions and the need to recognise the differences between the sexes if women's full participation in a democratic society is to be realised. This emphasis on sexual difference has been more fully elaborated by feminist democratic theorists oriented towards a 'maternalist ethics', in which it is envisaged that the specificities of women's position as women might provide a more nurturing and less individualist public realm (Elshtain 1981). Seyla Benhabib, for example, argues that women's concerns with care and the basic interdependence of human beings are excluded from the public sphere in democracy because they are assumed to be natural to the female sex. She argues that they should become matters of public concern so that both sexes will be understood in more rounded terms, as constituted by emotions and needs, as well as by the capacity for rational self-determination on which traditional, 'masculinist' accounts of democracy depend (Benhabib 1987).

Although the maternalist ideal of democracy has been influential, particularly in the United States, there is also considerable feminist opposition to this type of 'essentialist' analysis which defines women principally in terms of their traditional roles as wives and mothers. Most importantly, it is argued that it ignores differences between women. Black and white women, for example, have very different experiences in relation to the PUBLIC–PRIVATE DISTINCTION of Western liberal democracies, since historically black women in the USA and Afro-Caribbean women in Britain have been more likely to be positioned as heads of households. The analysis of democracy as patriarchal marginalises other dimensions of women's oppression: those engendered by racism, racialised ethnic or religious differences, heterosexism and so on. Furthermore, as Mary Dietz argues against a 'maternalist ethics', to suggest that women have access to a superior morality as a result of their position in the private domestic sphere is fundamentally at odds with ideals of democratic pluralism (Dietz 1992).

The difficulty which results from the anti-essentialist position, however, is that if we take the argument to its logical conclusion, the feminist project would seem to be lost. If differences between women are to be considered as important as commonalities, then theories and claims made on behalf of women become impossible. This problem has been addressed in two rather different ways by anti-essentialist feminists. Firstly, from a post-structuralist perspective, Chantal Mouffe argues that democracy requires the deconstruction of essentialist identities. It is only if each individual is seen as the site of a multiplicity of identities that the complexity of oppressive social relations may be understood. Furthermore, it is only insofar as such collectivities as 'women', 'men', 'blacks' and 'whites' are seen as discursively constructed that it is possible to create alliances between and across such apparently disparate and even opposed unities. In this way, Mouffe argues, a more genuinely democratic polity may be realised (Mouffe 1993). Mouffe describes her work as post-Marxist and we should note that her vision of RADICAL DEMOCRACY is in some ways closer to that of the socialist tradition than it is to that of liberal-democracy *tout court*. While she does see PROCEDURAL DEMOCRACY and the defence of individual liberties as important, the emphasis of Mouffe's theory is on extending equality and FREEDOM to create the conditions for individual self-determination.

Secondly, Iris Marion Young has developed a republican theory of democracy in which she argues for the representation of differences in the democratic political process. In her view,

although she is otherwise sympathetic to this tradition, the republican ideal of democracy as transcending differences in order to realise the common good is flawed in that if policies and laws do not recognise differences between citizens, they will inevitably favour the more powerful. She suggests that marginalised and oppressed groups should have mechanisms to put forward their views, propose policies and veto those they consider would contribute to their disadvantage. Young argues against essentialism, stating that a group should be seen as the fluid and contextual product of historically specific social relations, made up of individuals with multiple identities, rather than as an essence or nature. Women are not to count as such a group because they all possess a fixed set of attributes as women; the decision that a particular group should be represented cannot be made outside the political process itself (Young 1990). Nevertheless, it is difficult to see how group representation could avoid essentialising differences in practice. Young supposes that all women, at least in the US, share certain experiences, interests and values in common such that they should be represented as a group. It is, however, just this assumption that is questioned by anti-essentialists like Chantal Mouffe.

Anne Phillips has criticised and developed Young's republican ideas. She argues that although it is indeed undemocratic that there should be so few women in the political process of advanced liberal democracies, group representation is not the answer. The most important reason she gives from the point of view of feminist democratic theory again returns us to the anti-essentialist theme of difference. Phillips points out that if it is the case that individuals have multiple identities, it is not possible to know in which capacity they are exercising choice when they act as the member of a group: if a woman votes in a group of women, is she voting as a woman, or as some other aspect of her identity; a Moslem, or an environmentalist, for example? Writing in the British context, Phillips proposes a system of quotas at the level of the selection of party candidates for election in order to approximate more closely the composition of the population, for the sake of equality of participation between the sexes in politics and because, although she explicitly says that women do not all share the same experiences, having women present in policy negotiation makes it possible for concerns specific to women which were not on the political agenda to be incorporated into policies as they are made (Phillips 1991, 1995). Given, however, that, as we have seen, *any* delineation of groups risks essentialism, Phillips's proposals must also be subject to criticisms along these lines: firstly, quotas may contribute to freezing identities which might otherwise be historically transitory such that, arguably, they therefore limit actual possibilities; and secondly, they accentuate one aspect of multiple identities – gender – potentially at the expense of those aspects which are even more marginalised in contemporary Western societies.

In contemporary feminist theory, despite their differences, maternalists, post-structuralists and republicans nevertheless all take seriously the view that formal political institutions are important for the extension of genuine democracy. In this respect, they differ from earlier second-wave feminists for whom the practices of civil society were of far greater importance to women's equality, autonomy and full participation in society (Rowbotham 1986). In this respect, feminists find themselves united in a common project with other political theorists who are drawn to rethinking democracy following the fall of former Communist societies. However, it should be noted that there are dangers as well as opportunities for feminists in the emphasis on women's representation in state elites where it is accompanied by a turn away from the more radical participatory understanding of democracy which accompanied the early second-wave slogan, 'the personal is political'. In fact, it is arguable that insofar as the power of the nation-state is declining as a result of processes of GLOBALISATION, women may gain a voice at this level just as it loses its importance. The discussion in feminist democratic theory concerning women's differences and how they might be accommodated in the context of a common struggle against subordination makes important contributions to the understanding of democracy in general, in particular to the difficulty of combining JUSTICE and PLURALISM. At the same time, however, it is important to remember that if the women's movement has been one of the most successful social movements of the twentieth century, this is due less to political activities oriented towards the state and more to politics in civil society: the contestation of subordinate identities, the politicisation of cultural representations of women, the questioning of lifestyle choices and so on. It is clear that democratisation requires a vibrant civil society oriented towards greater equality and freedom for all as well as political representation. It seems that the former is somewhat in danger of being neglected at the expense of the latter in contemporary feminist democratic theory.

See also:

affirmative action; gendering democracy; identity, political; inclusion/exclusion; suffrage

Further reading

Alexander, S. and Taylor, B. (1982) 'In Defence of Patriarchy', in M. Evans (ed.), *The Woman Question*, London: Fontana.

Benhabib, S. (1987) 'The Generalized and the Concrete Other', in E.F. Kittay and D.T. Meyers (eds), *Women and Moral Theory*, Totowa, NJ: Rowman and Littlefield.

Dietz, M. (1992) 'Context is All: Feminism and Theories of Citizenship', in C. Mouffe (ed.), *Dimensions of Radical Democracy*, London: Verso.

Elshtain, J.-B. (1981) *Public Man/Private Woman*, Oxford: Martin Robertson.

Mouffe, C. (1993) 'Feminism, Citizenship and Radical Democratic Politics', in C. Mouffe, *The Return of the Political*, London: Verso.

Pateman, C. (1989) 'Feminism and Democracy', in *The Disorder of Women*, Cambridge: Polity Press.

Phillips, A. (1991) *Engendering Democracy*, Cambridge: Polity.

—— (1995) *The Politics of Presence*, Oxford: Clarendon Press.

Rowbotham, S. (1982) 'The Trouble with Patriarchy', in M. Evans (ed.), *The Woman Question* London: Fontana.

—— (1986) 'Feminism and Democracy', in D. Held and C. Pollitt (eds), *New Forms of Democracy*, London: Sage.

Young, I.M. (1990) 'Impartiality and the Civic Public: Some Implications of Feminist Critiques of Moral and Political Theory', in I.M. Young, *Throwing Like a Girl and Other Essays in Feminist Philosophy and Social Theory*, Bloomington, IN: Indiana University Press.

KATE NASH

peace, democratic

The term 'democratic peace' was coined in the early 1990s to characterise the phenomenon that stable democracies rarely, if ever, fight wars against each other (Russett 1993; Weart 1998). In the contemporary era, 'democracy' denotes a country where nearly everyone can vote, elections are freely contested, the chief executive is chosen by popular vote or by an elected parliament, and civil rights and liberties are substantially guaranteed. If wars are defined as conflicts with 1,000 or more battle deaths between internationally recognised states, then established democracies fought no wars against one another during the entire twentieth century. Furthermore, democracies were quite unlikely to engage in any kind of militarised disputes with each other. Since 1950, democracies have been only one-eighth as likely as other kinds of states to threaten to use force against each other, and only one-tenth as likely actually to fight.

Scholars and policy makers have long invoked a vision of a peace among democratically governed states as part of a larger structure of institutions and practices to promote peace among nation-states. In his 1795 essay *Perpetual Peace*, Immanuel Kant urged that peace could be based partially upon states sharing 'republican constitutions'. As the components of such a constitution he identified FREEDOM, legal EQUALITY of subjects, representative government and SEPARATION OF POWERS. The other key elements of his 'perpetual peace' were 'cosmopolitan law' embodying ties of international commerce and free trade, and a 'pacific union' established by treaty in among republics. In the twentieth century, the principal founders of what became the European Union expressed a similar vision.

Much research in the 1990s, focusing on pairs of states or 'dyads' as the unit of analysis, supports this perspective. Countries behave differently toward some countries than toward others, and the interaction of two governments is typically required to make a quarrel or establish a peaceful relationship. The more democratic each state in the pair is, the more peaceful their relations are likely to be. Democracies more often employ 'democratic' means of peaceful conflict resolution. They are readier to reciprocate each other's behaviour, and to accept third party mediation, arbitration and adjudication in settling disputes. Careful statistical analyses show that democracies' relatively peaceful relations toward each other are not spuriously caused by other influences such as rapid growth, high levels of wealth or trade, or alliances. The phenomenon of peace between democracies is not limited just to the rich industrialised states, nor was it simply enforced by pressure from a common adversary during the cold war.

Numerous puzzles about the causes and consequences of democratic peace remain. Understanding the causal processes is less complete than is the empirical generalisation. One view is that peace between democracies derives from normative restraints on conflict. That explanation posits that democracies extend to the international arena the cultural norms of peaceful conflict resolution that operate within them. Democracies expect, in relations with each other, that norms of negotiation and mutual respect in domestic politics will carry over into their international behaviour. By contrast, democracies do not expect authoritarian leaders to follow such norms, but instead to act aggressively and to use force. The free press of democracies may improve TRANSPARENCY of intention by both parties in negotiation.

Political institutions also impose constraints on democracies' decisions to go to war. They insure that any two democracies in a conflict of interest can expect ample time for conflict resolution processes to be effective. Moreover, the general population frequently stands to gain fewer of the spoils of war, and to pay more of its costs, than does the political LEADERSHIP. In democracies, the ability of the populace to hold the leadership accountable at election times provides a strong incentive for leaders not to engage in wars, particularly costly ones. Dictators are better able to resist being deposed from office, and so are less restrained by fear of popular reprisal. Finally, democratic institutions may give their leaders superior ability to signal threats and commitments credibly during international negotiations, if the political opposition can be seen as supporting the government. If the opposition disagrees, it will be harder for the government to commit itself credibly to fight, and hence it will be less likely to escalate the conflict by bluffing (Fearon 1994).

These influences reinforce one another. Where normative constraints are weak, democratic institutions may provide the necessary additional constraints on the use of violence against other democratic states. There is not yet agreement among scholars as to which influences are strongest. Each may be important under certain circumstances.

Another puzzle concerns whether democracies are more peaceful in general; with all states, not just in their relations with each other. This question shifts the focus from dyads to individual states. Democracies do engage in many military disputes and wars with autocratic states. This might suggest that democracies are not more peaceful in general than are autocracies. Also, the history of colonialism and IMPERIALISM by Western democracies, and their sometimes militaristic behaviour toward weaker states and peoples, would argue that they are not especially peaceful. Nevertheless, there is reason to be cautious in reaching such a conclusion.

Many instances of imperialism by democracies involve states that, while democratic by the standards of their time, would not be considered very democratic by contemporary standards. They had very restricted voting franchises: women, certain ethnic and racial groups, and people without much property were often denied the vote. Since the evidence is that the more democratic both states in a pair are, the more peaceful they will be with each other, it should not be surprising if only moderately democratic states in the nineteenth century were less peaceful in general than were their more democratic successors in the twentieth century. This difference could also explain why more alleged exceptions or near-exceptions to the 'democracies don't fight each other' generalisation arose in the earlier era.

Another reason is that states may go to war despite their wishes to avoid conflict. If democracies' norms and institutions make them reluctant to fight, autocratic states may try to take advantage of their pacifism, and try to force democracies to make heavy concessions (appeasement) to avoid war (Bueno de Mesquita and Lalman 1992). The people may then become persuaded to resist such pressure, which they would not feel so intensely from another democratic country. If war ultimately does result when a democracy refuses to make any more concessions, the democracy may well have been provoked into fighting. Democracies are much less likely to initiate crises in the first place. But once a military or severe diplomatic crisis arises, democracies are in general – though not with one another – as likely as autocracies to escalate the conflict up to full-scale war (Rousseau *et al.* 1997). Further research is needed not just on who takes part in a dispute or war, but on who initiates or escalates it. Making such judgements is often difficult, however, since a country may escalate a conflict in self-defence.

Increasingly, scholars are concluding that modern democracies are somewhat more peaceful in general than are autocracies (Rummel

1997). Consensus, however, is not as great as that democracies are more peaceful with each other. The statistical generalisation is fairly weak, with numerous exceptions. It is the interaction between two democratic states – both constrained by their norms and institutions to prefer peaceful conflict resolution – which makes the effect of those constraints powerful.

If democracies are more peaceful, especially with each other, one might expect less war in the world if democracies increase as a proportion of all states. The road to greater peace may not be especially smooth, however. The three kinds of dyads behave very differently. Pairs of autocracies are more likely to fight each other than are democratic pairs. But also likely to fight each other are dyads composed of a democracy and an autocracy; their norms and institutions clash. In a world comprised solely of democracies, peaceful conflict resolution should usually prevail. Near the other extreme, a world comprised mostly of autocracies would exhibit much violent conflict. (This is a reasonable characterisation of international relations in earlier centuries.) Wars between autocracies would be fairly frequent, and whereas the few democracies would not fight each other they would often fight autocracies. The most conflict-prone international system could be one with roughly equal numbers of democracies and autocracies: a system marked by a large number of conflicts among the autocracies, and very many conflicts between democracies and autocracies.

This picture seems consistent with what we find in particular regions of the world. This is instructive because most wars arise between countries that are geographically proximate: neighbours can fight each other easily, and often have issues (borders, ethnic conflicts, control of natural resources) that provoke conflict. In regions composed almost entirely of democracies (like Western Europe since the Second World War, or Latin America more recently) there is little fighting between neighbours or within the region in general, but in regions like the Middle East where democracy is rare, war is more common. A similar phenomenon arises for the few countries that count as major powers, with global interests and military capabilities. In every international system, these major powers, democracies included, have been more involved in war than have most smaller states. Overall, peace would become more common only as a solid majority of countries in each region, as well as in the global system, became democratic.

One further puzzle arises from the contention that, whereas stable democracies do not go to war with each other, states in transition from autocratic regimes to democratic ones may be more war-prone (Mansfield and Snyder 1995). If correct, this would raise serious doubts about whether, at least in the short run, creating more democratic states in the world would make the world more peaceful. Nonetheless, the accuracy of this observation is hotly contested; it depends heavily upon exactly how the transition is measured (see DEMOCRATIC TRANSITION). Moreover, war may be equally common, or more so, under transitions from democratic to autocratic regimes; political instability and transition in general, not democratisation in particular, would be the culprit (Ward and Gleditsch 1998). Finally, one must look not just at the general behaviour of democratising states, but at their relations with particular kinds of neighbours. Newly democratising states surrounded by established democracies or other democratising states (for instance, much of Central Europe since 1989) may fight much less often than do those with authoritarian neighbours. Here too one must ask whether the democracy or its autocratic neighbour initiates the conflict; dictators may feel their own security in office threatened by the example of successful democracy nearby.

Thus, beyond the simple statement that pairs of democracies are likely to live in peace, a wide variety of related propositions can be derived and tested. Some of these suggest that democracy and the expectation of international peace feed on each other. Democracies win their wars much more often than do authoritarian states. Perhaps they are more prudent about what wars they get into, or once in war they are more effective in marshalling their resources. Free speech and debate make them more accurate and efficient information processors. Authoritarian governments who lose wars may be often replaced by democratic regimes. As democracies' politically relevant international environment becomes composed of more democratic and internally stable states, democracies tend to reduce their military allocations and conflict involvement.

A less menacing international system can permit the emergence and consolidation of democratic governments (see DEMOCRATIC CONSOLIDATION). Protracted international threats – real or perceived – strengthen the forces of secrecy and authoritarianism. Relaxation of international threats to peace and security reduces the need, and the excuse, for repressing democratic dissent.

The theory about why democracies behave peacefully needs to be carefully developed, attending to their patterns of strategic interaction with other states. Research needs to be done both at the 'macro' level to identify broad patterns of behaviour in large-scale statistical studies, and at the 'micro' level to identify, in carefully constructed case studies, the processes and mechanisms by which countries' leaders, and their peoples, perceive and behave toward other countries.

The relationship of all elements of Kant's vision – democracy, trade, and international organisations (IGOs) – among each other, and each with conflict – needs to be examined thoroughly. Trade and IGOs also reduce conflict between states, and perhaps vice versa; democracies may trade more with each other than with autocracies; democracies and trading partners appear more likely to join IGOs (Russett and Oneal 2001). A Kantian system – an international society as well as a collection of sovereign states – would be sustained by a complex set of mutually supporting relationships.

See also:

democratic transition; globalisation; imperialism; neutrality; revolutions; security; toleration

Further reading

Bueno de Mesquita, B. and Lalman, D. (1992) *War and Reason*, New Haven, CT: Yale University Press.

Dixon, W. (1994) 'Democracy and the Peaceful Settlement of International Disputes', *American Political Science Review* 88(1): 14–32.

Fearon, J. (1994) 'Domestic Political Audiences and the Escalation of International Disputes', *American Political Science Review* 88(3): 577–92.

Mansfield, E. and Snyder, J. (1995) 'Democratization and the Danger of War', *International Security* 20(1): 1–38.

Rousseau, D., Gelpi, C., Reiter, D. and Huth, P. (1996) 'Assessing the Dyadic Nature of the Democratic Peace, 1918–88', *American Political Science Review* 90(3): 512–33.

Rummel, R. (1997) *Power Kills: Democracy as a Method of Non-Violence*, New Brunswick, NJ: Transaction Publishers.

Russett, B. (1993) *Grasping The Democratic Peace: Principles for a Post-Cold War World*, Princeton, NJ: Princeton University Press.

Russett, B. and Oneal, J. (2001) *Triangulating Peace: Democracy, Interdependence and International Organizations*, New York: W.W. Norton.

Ward, M. and Gleditsch, K. (1998) 'Democratising for Peace', *American Political Science Review* 92(2): 51–62.

Weart, S. (1998) *Never at War: Why Democracies Will Not Fight One Another*, New Haven, CT: Yale University Press.

BRUCE M. RUSSETT

perfectionism

Perfectionism is one of the oldest doctrines in moral and political philosophy. It has several versions. In one version it has as its goal the maximisation of intrinsic value. Intrinsic value here is understood objectively as something that is of value independently of human desires or choices. Things such as knowledge or beauty are not intrinsically valuable because human beings desire them or choose them. Rather, human beings should choose such things because they are intrinsically valuable. On a weaker version of perfectionism, advocated by Aristotle in the *Nicomachean Ethics*, human beings should pursue excellences such as knowledge and artistic achievements because by doing so they develop their true nature. Such a view involves a sort of conditional perfectionism. Assuming that we need to pursue human excellences in order to fulfil our nature and flourish; we should set as our goal the promotion of human excellences. If, however, it turns out that human nature requires something quite different, such as the pursuit of SECURITY or SOLIDARITY, then we should pursue these other activities in order to flourish, even if this involves an abandonment of the pursuit of activities which have greater intrinsic value.

Another important distinction is between perfectionism as the single ultimate moral and political principle and perfectionism as one of the ultimate moral and political principles. The most uncompromising teleological version says that the only ultimate principle is the one that involves the maximisation of intrinsic value. Such a view is difficult to reconcile with ideas of liberty or EQUALITY. Thus Nietzsche said in *Beyond Good and Evil* that we must work continually to produce individual great human beings like Napoleon; the rest of us can, when necessary, be sacrificed for the sake of the great achievements of the super-individuals.

Most modern perfectionists tend to be less uncompromising than Nietzsche. Some of them advocate a moderate version which is not obviously at odds with ideas of liberty or equality. Joseph Raz (1986) a liberal perfectionist, claims that in modern societies a good life or a life of well-being must be an autonomous life; he derives the value of liberty from that of AUTONOMY and well-being.

Critics of perfectionism sometimes assume that perfectionism as a political principle is inherently illiberal and anti-egalitarian; it would involve imposing our ideas of the good on others by force. The predominant liberal political philosophy since Rawls has com-mended state NEUTRALITY with regard to the good. This involves a rejection of perfectionism as a political principle. Rawls argues that perfectionist criteria tend to be controversial and often vary from group to group. He allows individuals to pursue perfectionist goals in their private life and also to form associations with like minded people to promote their conceptions of the good. But they must not use the coercive devices of the state to impose their ideas of the good life on others.

The later Rawls (1993) confines neutrality to the basic principles of the constitution and to the basic principles of justice. In less basic areas he allows people to use their comprehensive doctrines in influencing political decisions. Some liberals, such as the early Rawls (1971), reject perfectionism as a political principle at all levels.

Some people reject perfectionism as a political principle because they think that the doctrine of equal respect of all human beings requires the state to be neutral with regard to the good life. Modern perfectionists tend to reject this contention in turn. They claim that the view that some forms of life are inherently superior to others is consistent with the view that all human beings have equal worth. A perfectionist state could subsidise universities and operas and the continued existence of different species and their habitat on the grounds that they involve intrinsically valuable activities or states of affairs; and it could discourage activities on the grounds that they are inherently degrading.

Critics of this view see this as unjustifiable paternalism. To use COERCION against certain sexual practices on the grounds that they are inherently degrading involves an unjust interference in the liberties of those who practice such forms of life without harming others. But perfectionists can reply that the main justification of giving preference to the better forms of life is for the sake of society, not for those who are being coerced. For instance, children and future generations will benefit morally and spiritually if inferior activities, such as bestiality, sado-masochism and pornography, are given lower status. Moreover, the state can give lower status to such forms of life without banning their practice in private. TOLERATION does not imply equal status.

One alleged problem is that we lack knowledge about the good, and so the state should not enter into areas where there is no rational way of resolving disputes. It is argued that, particularly in multicultural societies, there is no one conception of the good; in practice, perfectionism in politics will result in the imposition of the dominant conception of the good life on the disadvantaged. Perfectionists reply that similar problems exist in the case of justice, yet neutralists do not urge the state to be neutral between different conceptions of justice. Rawls does say that the liberal state should only impose views of justice which contain an overlapping consensus across different reasonable alternatives. Perfectionists could point out that there is an equally strong case for implementing, through state action, an overlapping consensus regarding the good life. On this view one would give lower status to forms of life such as bestiality which are regarded as inferior amongst reasonable people. Such discrimination could be combined with equal status to several of the more reasonable forms of life. The problem of how to distinguish reasonable from unreasonable forms of life is of course a real one, but such problems occur at least as much in the case of justice as they do with the good.

Perfectionism as a single principle teleological theory is indeed difficult to reconcile with egalitarian ideas. The sum of intrinsic value might be best increased by very unequal rights and opportunities favouring a few. But another possibility is to adopt moral PLURALISM and commend egalitarianism and perfectionism as two ultimate principles. Yet another alternative would be to construct an egalitarian theory and use perfectionists' considerations to work out the implications of egalitarianism. On one interpretation, this is what Amartya Sen (1992) has done by incorporating Aristotelian views of the good life and human functioning within an egalitarian framework. All human beings are equally entitled to human functioning and human flourishing. True, some have inherently

less capabilities than others but the state should strive for equality of attainment, with the proviso that too much value is not sacrificed. Some, such as Sen, think that the ideal of egalitarian justice is to give every one an equal chance to attain the same absolute level of human functioning. Others such as Frankena (1976) think that egalitarian justice requires that every one has the same chance to enjoy the best life he or she is capable of. On this less extreme view, the state should make the same proportionate contribution to the best life of everyone.

Non-perfectionist egalitarians would insist that we should construct an egalitarian theory without appealing to ideals of the good life. We should give people an equal opportunity to pursue whatever plan of life they choose provided these plans are not anti-social. Perfectionists complain that choices are not made in a vacuum, the preferences we have are largely a result of various kinds of social conditionings. It is the duty of a good state to educate its citizens in such a way that they are less likely to get tempted into degrading forms of life.

Communitarians, like Charles Taylor, have stressed that our choices about the good life are made against a background of social practices and the pursuit of the good of the community. Without such a background, individual choices and activities become empty and lack significance. It is the job of a state to implement and defend the shared sense of the common good, which sustains our lives. Taylor insists that that the good life of individuals within marginalised and disadvantaged groups should be understood by an appeal to the social practices and shared understanding of these groups rather than by those of the dominant community. But not all perfectionists are communitarians. Some such as Sher (1997) and Hurka (1993) think that perfectionist values should be implemented by the state without being ratified by social practices and by shared understanding. Advocates of state neutrality contend that their view is consistent with the importance of the community; only the state is forbidden from implementing the ideals of the good life, whether individual or communitarian.

See also:

communitarianism; equality; liberalism; justice

Further reading

Frankena, W. (1976) 'Some Beliefs About Justice', in K. Goodpaster (ed.), *Perspectives on Morality*, London: University of Notre Dame Press.

Haksar, V. (1979) *Equality, Liberty and Perfectionism*, Oxford: Oxford University Press.

Hurka, T. (1993) *Perfectionism*, Oxford: Oxford University Press.

Rawls, J. (1971) *A Theory of Justice*, Harvard: Harvard University Press.

—— (1993) *Political Liberalism*, New York: Columbia University Press.

Raz, J. (1986) *The Morality of Freedom*, Oxford: Clarendon Press.

Sen, A. (1992) *Inequality Re-examined*, Oxford: Clarendon Press.

Sher, G. (1997) *Beyond Neutrality*, Cambridge: Cambridge University Press.

Taylor, C. (1985) *Philosophy and the Human Sciences*, Cambridge: Cambridge University Press.

Wall, S. (1998) *Liberalism, Perfectionism and Restraint*, Cambridge: Cambridge University Press.

VINIT HAKSAR

pluralism

The first distinction which needs to be established is that between the pluralism prior to the democratic revolution of the end of the eighteenth century (linked to a hierarchical conception of society and a particularistic defence of intermediate corporations and organisations) and that which emerges within the horizon of the democratic revolution. The 'old' pluralism was linked to an insufficient development of the notion of SOVEREIGNTY and to the defence of the RIGHTS of traditional strata and bodies which mediated between the absolute power of the kings and the individuals. Montesquieu can be seen, from this perspective, not only as a theoretician of the division of powers, but also as a defender of a diffusion of power within society on the basis of the recognition of the rights of the intermediate corporations. This traditional pluralism was decisively undermined by the development of absolutism in the first place, and by the emergence of the doctrine of popular sovereignty in the second place, the latter involving the constitution of a unified public space where all particularistic privileges had been abolished and where EQUALITY among citizens was considered to be the very principle of organisation of the political community.

The second type of pluralism was shaped within the horizon of the 'democratic revolution'. The concept of the latter, initially formulated by Alexis de Tocqueville, has been contemporarily developed by Claude Lefort. It is centred on the idea of a radical break in the Western political imaginary, by which the notion of equality (which previously had just been a religious notion: all men are equal before God) becomes a positive principle shaping political relations. Against the hierarchical principles of the *ancien regime*, the democratic revolution institutes, according to Lefort, the place of power as essentially empty; no social force being predetermined, as a result of its specific particularity. The generalisation of the democratic revolution, however, only takes place at the moment in which equality overflows the narrow limits of the public sphere of CITIZENSHIP and becomes the principle underlying a large variety of social demands. As Tocqueville asserted, once men accept being equal in some areas, they will not stop there and will want to be equal in all. Thus Mary Wollstonecraft, a forerunner of contemporary feminism, showed the inconsequence of proclaiming the Rights of Man and Citizen without extending its equalitarian principles to the relations between the sexes. We can see the arch of the democratic revolution, from this respect, as an extension of the principle of equality to wider areas of social relations: to the economic sphere, in the social discourses of the nineteenth century, and to a plurality of social, ethnic and sexual identities in the contemporary world. The important point is that this extension involved the introduction of a pluralist perspective, as far as the new demands were not formulated in the name of the abstract individual or of the community unified in a general will (as in the versions of democracy to be found in its Rousseauian or Jacobine varieties) but in the name of particular sections of the population which reclaim equality in their specific spheres.

As far as the contemporary history of pluralist theories is concerned, McClure (1992) has distinguished between three waves of pluralism. The first generation of pluralists – in the first quarter of the twentieth century – reacted to the Statist orientation of an earlier LIBERALISM epitomised in Austrian jurisprudence and in the British Hegelian School, and presented the state as one association among many. The notion of a 'distributive sovereignty' and the emphasis on functional AUTONOMY at the expense of both a centralised state and the isolated individuals are the central tenets of this approach. Within the socialist tradition, pluralism goes back to Saint-Simonian 'association' and Proudhon's reversal of the relation between state and society through privileging the latter. More strictly connected with the Anglo-Saxon plurality of the writers previously mentioned, we have to refer to the 'guild socialism' of G.D.H. Cole and S.G. Hobson. The principles of functional and territorial DECENTRALISATION leads them to the conception of a 'pluralist state', to an equilibrium between politics and the economy, and to the distinction between three types of organisation (those linked to the consumers, those linked to the producers, and those having civic and cultural aims). The first wave of pluralist thinkers – many of them closely linked to the labour movement – tended to emphasise the self-organisation of CIVIL SOCIETY and to limit the centrality of the state.

The second wave of pluralism, which flourished in America in the decades after the Second World War, is associated with the anti-elitist approach most clearly expressed in the works of Robert Dahl and David Truman. Against sociological theories based on the notion of a 'power elite' – most clearly articulated in the work of C. Wright Mills – pluralists of this generation present a picture of democratic societies as based on the interaction of a plurality of INTEREST GROUPS, whose result is a balance which prevents the exclusive concentration of power in any of them. This multiplicity of power centres would be the very condition of a democratic society. This new discourse presupposes a set of significant displacements *vis-à-vis* the pluralism of the previous generation to which we referred earlier. In the first place, the emphasis is no longer on the state and on the PUBLIC–PRIVATE DISTINCTION, but in the 'social' as an area of constitution of interest groups and in 'government' as a plurality of apparatuses in the process of DECISION-MAKING. In the second place, the pluralist logic is extended from groups articulating a variety of interests in society (such as the TRADES UNIONS) to less organised and more issue oriented ones. These group interests are less stable and social actors can be associated with many of them. Thus, the degree of their mutual coherence requires the constant process of renegotiation. Finally, the reference to the economy, which had been central to the first generation of pluralists and one of the bases of their discrimination between various types of association, loses its centrality in American pluralism. We can say, on the whole, that if the work of Dahl, Truman and others with a similar approach has helped to make our understanding of the distribution of power in contemporary societies more complex, it has however been marred by a myth of an opposite sign from the one they criticise: they have substituted the myth of an absolutely dominant centre of power with that of a balance, which at the very limit, would do away with *any* concentration of power.

Finally, the third wave of pluralist theory is the one that, in McClure's view, covers a large variety of approaches, ranging from Michael Walzer's discrimination between 'spheres of justice' to Laclau and Mouffe's conception of 'hegemonic logics' (see Laclau's HEGEMONY), passing through different kinds of feminist, post-structuralist, post-colonial and multicultural theories. Common features of most of these approaches would be: (1) mechanisms of power are seen as not only explaining the relations between negotiating or antagonistic subjects but the constitution of subjects themselves – that is, power is *productive* and not a simple zero-sum game between pre-constituted social agents; (2) politics does not consist in either the *negotiation* or the *competition* between group interests, but in the displacement of the BOUNDARIES between the groups entering into those relations and, as a result, in the social construction of the very interests which are supposed to constitute those groups; and (3) the relations of representation which organise both competition and negotiations are not a transparent medium through which the will of a group is expressed but they have, instead, a decisive role in constituting the groups which are represented. These approaches are definitely pluralist as they put into question the notion of *a priori* unified subjects and insist, on the contract, on the dispersion of subject positions out of which both demands and interests are constituted, but they differ, however, from the second wave of pluralism, as they do not conceive of power as an entity to be done away with in a balancing process. They assert, on the contrary, the political productivity of power relations. The latter, without being ultimately unified around a centre (as in the theories of the ruling class or the ruling elite), would have pragmatic and changing forms of partial unification which would be at the root of the constitution of political relations and political subjectivities.

As far as the relation between pluralism and democracy is concerned, Giovanni Sartori (1976, 1987) has traced the history of the imbrication between both concepts and has diversified the notion of pluralism by pointing out its various dimensions and species. Thus, he relates a possible definition of pluralism to three levels: the cultural, the societal and the political. The first is the level of beliefs and involves the privilege given to difference at the expense of uniformity; the second tries to differentiate pluralism from mere social complexity (as far as the latter does not imply that an increasing institutional and social differentiation will necessarily move in a pluralist direction); the third level requires an analysis of the relation between pluralism and a set of terms with which it has traditionally been associated, such as the notions of tolerance, consensus and conflict. By tolerance, according to Sartori, we should not understand either indifference or relativism, but the recognition that others have opinions different from ours. Conceived in this sense, however, tolerance cannot be unlimited. Consensus presents various levels and Sartori, following Easton, distinguishes between (a) a basic consensus, or consensus at the level of the community, (b) procedural consensus and (c) political consensus, or consensus at the level of political action. The first is the condition of a homogeneous political culture and, although it is not a *sine qua non* requisite for democracy, contributes to make the latter more solid. The second relates to the rules for conflict resolution. Without agreement about them there is no possibility of a democratic organisation. The third involves the consensus about dissenting and is linked to the value of discussion and the crucial role of the opposition (see OPPOSITION, LOYAL). This institutionalisation of the role of dissensus is the reason for Sartori's reservations concerning the term 'conflict' – which evokes the idea of war – and for his preference for other concepts such as 'dissent' or 'discrepancy' which are more compatible with a pluralist ethos.

In recent years debates on pluralism have developed in new directions as a result of the concerns of multiculturalism in USA and Western Europe and of the proliferation of ethnically oriented movements in Eastern Europe and the countries of the ex-Soviet Union. Translated into the theoretico-philosophical terrain, the main issue has been whether it is possible to construct a communitarian consensus starting from a situation of extreme particularism, or whether the latter involves such a radical incommensurability between cultures that it is not possible to construct a stronger communitarian link. The first position can be found, in its most developed form, in Jürgen Habermas and his school, who have argued for purely procedural agreements which would make it possible to reach, through a dialogical process, some form of communal consensus. The most extreme formulation of a particularistic perspective can be found in the work of Jean-François Lyotard, who conceived society as a plurality of language games in Wittgenstein's sense, each with their own rules which are irreducible to any common denominator. In such a situation, it is impossible to arbitrate in the clashes between language games: as they are strictly incommensurable, the arbitration can only consist in the imposition of a rule by one language game over the other. This imposition constitutes, for Lyotard, a tort, and the absence of common rules between the two language games is at the root of what he calls a 'differand' (as different from a simple litigation). Other authors have tried to find solutions to the tension between pluralistic tendencies and unification of the communitarian spaces, which attempt to avoid extremes such as Habermasian universalism and Lyotard's extreme particularism. We can mention, in this connection, the works of Will Kymlicka and James Tully.

See also:

hegemony; identity, political; inclusion/exclusion; radical democracy

Further reading

Dahl, R. (1967) *Pluralistic Democracy in the United States*, Chicago: University of Chicago Press.

Habermas, J. (1984) *The Theory of Communicative Action*, London: Polity.

Laclau, E. and Mouffe, C. (1985) *Hegemony and Socialist Strategy*, London: Verso.

Lefort, C. (1986) *The Political Forms of Modern Society*, Cambridge, MA: Harvard University Press.

Lyotard, J.-F. (1984) *The Postmodern Condition: A Report on Knowledge*, Manchester: Manchester University Press.

—— (1988) *The Differend: Phrases in Dispute*, Manchester: Manchester University Press.

McClure, K. (1992) 'On the Subject of Right; pluralism, plurality and identity', in Mouffe, C. (ed) *Dimensions of Radical Democracy*, London: Verso.

Sartori, G. (1976) *Parties and Party Systems: A Framework for Analysis*, Cambridge: Cambridge University Press.

—— (1987) *The Theory of Democracy Revisited*, Chatham, NJ: Chatham House.

Walzer, M. (1983) *Spheres of Justice: A Defence of Pluralism and Equality*, Oxford: Oxford University Press.

ERNESTO LACLAU

policy-making

Few concepts in the political world have been more widely agreed upon (and seemingly implemented) than 'democracy'; and, by extension, 'democratic policy-making'. Governments as ideologically diverse as the former East Germany (officially known as the German Democratic Republic) and the United Kingdom all lay claim to a democratic garment, but surely even the most naive observer can see vast differences between the two in terms of a moral justification. Although both propose that they govern 'for the people', the first argues for efficiency and centralised control, the latter for equity and a more decentralised control. One might well posit that when any word – in this case, an adjective – is so widely used, there is something suspicious about its definition. Even in Western countries, which generally trace their democratic thinking back to the classic Athenian polity, citizens are reluctant to recognise that the fabled Athenian democracy – one that basically excluded slaves and women, more than half the population of eligible voters – would have been characterised as sorely 'political incorrect' by current democratic mavens (see DEMOCRATIC ORIGINS). Yet 'democracy' lies at the heart of the Western political ethos, and democratic policy-making is equally central.

Let us arbitrarily offer a definition of democracy, given by Philippe Schmitter and Terry Lynn Karl (1991: 75) who state that modern democracy is 'a system of governance in which rulers are held accountable for their actions in the public realm by citizens acting indirectly though the competition and co-operation of their elected representatives'. For Schmitter and Karl, 'citizens are the most distinctive element in democracies'. It follows, then, that if governments are created to set (and enforce) policy – that is, if policy-making falls within the natural purview of governments – then they are only media for its citizens. In short, 'policy-making' must fundamentally be 'democratic policy-making', and must involve, in some manner or degree, citizen involvement.

Benjamin Barber (1984) has written at length that citizen PARTICIPATION in the United States can be (in his words) either 'weak' or 'strong' democracy (see Barber's DEMOCRACY, JUSTIFICATIONS FOR). Others, drawing upon the Madisonian or Tocquevillian models, would characterise these with a 'indirect' (or representative) versus a 'direct' label, the principal distinction being the degree of citizen participation in their governance (see de Leon 1997). For many reasons – only one of which is the present size of the citizenry that would render complete citizen involvement or participation virtually impossible – Western democracy has come to mean a representative democracy. Similarly, policy-making has come to be viewed by many in government as a complicated, often technical exercise that by its very complexity insulates the policy-maker and administrator from popular sentiment (barring an occasional election). A welter of administrative emphases – ranging from Weberian BUREAUCRACY to scientific management to the 'new' public management – seemingly have conspired to continue these trends, increasingly distancing citizens from their own government and its governance. To draw upon US President Abraham Lincoln's classic definition of democracy, it scarcely appears that democracy

has defined a polity 'of the people, by the people, and for the people'.

It should not be surprising, then, that in recent years a school of thought has emerged within the policy sciences community that holds that if democratic policy-making was meant intrinsically to be 'democratic', something was indeed amiss. Repeated surveys found that Americans no longer trusted their government (see Nye *et al.* 1997), that they were reluctant to join in civic associations and were voting in decreasing numbers, even (or especially, if one likes) in local ELECTIONS whose candidates and issues were often the most known and, more importantly, most likely to affect them directly. It is therefore fair to inquire: What do these trends portend for democratic policy-making?

There is, of course, no easy answer. Nye and his Harvard colleagues (1997) ask these types of questions and come with a wide array of answers, ranging to 'not much' to 'debilitating to the American democracy'. Many economists would agree, suggesting that the market system was more central to the American way of life than a voting system; indeed, a good public choice economist would find little incentive for a single voter to exercise his or her ballot-casting prerogative.

Policy scientists see this condition quite differently, as dangerous in the extreme. The policy sciences were originally established quite explicitly as 'the policy sciences of democracy', and were 'directed towards knowledge to improve the practice of democracy' (Lasswell 1951: 14). Yet as democracy atrophies in the overall policy-making calculus, it would seem that administrative efficiency (perhaps as best symbolised by the use of benefit–cost analyses) has taken its stead. The possibilities have the potential to be disastrous for a citizen-participating democratic system. John Dryzek, taking the phenomenon of increased bureaucratisation of present-day policy-making to its worrisome end, complained clearly about the possibility of the 'policy sciences of tyranny' (Dryzek 1989). Frank Fischer is of a similar bent, as he cautions, 'the role of policy planning organisations and the reform strategy...

raises serious questions for democratic government and their traditional understandings of the public role in it' (Fischer 1993: 33–4).

Robert Dahl (1999), as fine a scholar of democracy as one is likely to find, has gone so far as to suggest that the two totems of Western politics – democracy and capitalism – might well be in opposition to one another, with no sure bets as to the ultimate victor. (A possible harbinger: US foreign policy has long supported governments with complementary trade and economic policies, hardly paying any attention to their ideology positions. President Franklin Roosevelt was said to have commented when he was told that an American ally was a dictator, 'Yes, perhaps so, but he is our dictator.')

There is little reason to doubt these views, but there is less reason to declare a 'crisis' in democratic policy-making. By and large, in Western democracies governments are attentive to PUBLIC OPINION; indeed, many have suggested that with the constant use of surveys and focus groups, that these governments are overly beholden to popular opinion and one might well wonder aloud if what we have is not a crisis in democracy but a crisis in democratic leadership. I contend that we have a crisis in democratic participation, a reluctance to engage in democratic policy-making for the simplest of reasons: first, extant public administrators and policy-makers might want public approval but they are loathe to ask for permission, which they view as generally more troubling than promising; second, citizens see political decisions being made without their contributions – even on issues that concern or affect them directly – and ask, in effect, 'why should I bother?' It is problem of both demand (policy-makers wishing to minimise citizen input) and supply (disenfranchised citizens have to reason to contribute), but certainly the individual citizen is more likely to be left out.

There is an abundant of evidence supporting both sides of this political demand/supply metaphor. On the demand side, a persuasive case has been made by Irving Janis (1980) regarding 'groupthink', that is, virtually all political decisions have been made by a relatively small group of policy-makers and their immediate assistants, with scant attention to the public at large; if public hearings are conducted, they are usually seen as garnering support for a decision already made, or being dominated by interest groups to the exclusion of the affected but nevertheless excluded individual citizen. Only a tremendous organising effort by citizens can overcome this slant; environmental politics has been the most successful, and even here we find that many of the 'eco-successes' have been championed by the courts rather than politicians or public administrators.

On the supply side, many commentators (Greider 1992; Dionne 1991) have written how very focused interest groups effectively pre-empt most political debates, each arguing for its own issues in a manner that generally treats the public interest as relevant only when it coincides with its own particular interest. Dionne (1991: 10) explains the disheartening consequences. He argues that in a period when the citizens of countries such as Poland, Hungary and Czechoslovakia are 'excited' by self-government, 'Americans view politics with boredom and detachment. For most of us, politics is increasingly abstract, a spectator sport barely worth watching... Our system has become one long-running advertisement against self-government'. Greider (1992: 11) is even more forceful in his analysis of the 'decaying condition' of democracy in America. He states that: 'the facts are everywhere... The things that Americans were taught and still wish to believe about self-government – the articles of faith we loosely call democracy – no longer seem to fit the present reality'. For Greider, American democracy is in 'much deeper trouble than most people wish to acknowledge. What exists behind the formal shell is a systemic breakdown of the shared civic values we call democracy' (1992 :11).

If this is the problem, then the solution should be relatively straightforward: everybody, from policy-maker to citizen, should become more active in the daily business of governing. But as Dahl (1999) and others tell us, this solution is one without any credibility.

Issues of simple magnitude would overwhelm the body politic: how would, say, the United States federal government involve well over one hundred million voters in its deliberations and still manage to function on virtually any policy or programmatic level (daily, strategic, whatever)? Or if the citizens could not come to an agreement, or some felt that their participation was somehow being discriminated against)? Or what if there were an emergency that demanded a rapid response, such as a hurricane or a nuclear disaster?

Scholars such as Dahl (1999) and Barber (1984) have proposed a much greater degree of citizen participation, loosely akin to the Athenian forum, or what Dahl refers to as a 'mini-populous' (see POLYARCHY). Others (see Fishkin 1991) have proposed a series of 'CITIZENS' JURIES'. These panels, unlike their counterparts in legal proceedings (whose decisions are confidential and binding on the judicial system), would have the responsibility of becoming knowledgeable in the areas they are debating, and then advising the public policy-makers as to their logic and consensus. These 'juries' can be convened when the government is not under great time pressures to act, and they could sit for upwards to a year; moreover, like their legal counterparts, they could be paid for their time and deliberations.

Naturally, there are some problems with a system of citizens' juries. But if they begin to staunch the erosion of the democratic ethos and the attendant democratic policy-making, one should at least be willing to entertain their establishment, as has been the case in some local communities. Failing this, the risks to democratic policy-making are quite frankly too great to leave possible alternatives unexplored.

See also:

democracy, future of; democracy, justifications for

Further reading

Barber, B. (1984) *Strong Democracy: Partici-patory Politics for a New Age*, Berkeley, CA: University of California Press.

Dahl, R.A. (1999) *On Democracy*, New Haven, CT: Yale University Press.

de Leon, P. (1997) *Democracy and the Policy Sciences*, Albany, NY: State University of New York Press.

Dionne, E.J. (1991) *Why Americans Hate Politics*, New York: Simon & Schuster.

Dryzek, J.S. (1989) 'The Policy Sciences of Democracy', *Polity* 22(1): 97–118.

Fischer, F. (1993) 'Policy Discourse and the Politics of Washington Think Tanks', in F. Fischer and J. Forester (eds), *The Argumentative Turn in Policy Analysis and Planning*, Durham, NC: Duke University Press, 33–4.

Fishkin, J.S. (1991) *Democracy and Deliberation*, New Haven, CT: Yale University Press.

Greider, W. (1992) *Who Will Tell the People: The Betrayal of American Democracy*, New York: Simon & Schuster.

Janis, I. (1980) *Groupthink*, Boston: Houghton Mifflin.

Lasswell, H.D. (1951) 'The Policy Orientation', in D. Lerner and H.D. Lasswell, *The Policy Sciences*, Palo Alto, CA: Stanford University Press.

Nye, J.S. Jr., Zelinkow, P.D. and King, D.C. (eds) (1997) *Why People Don't Trust Government*, Cambridge, MA: Harvard University Press.

Schmitter, P.C. and Karl, T.L. (1991) 'What Democracy Is…and Is Not', *Journal of Democracy* 3(3): 75–88.

PETER DELEON

political action committees

Political action committee (PAC) is the general name given to organisations set up by corporations, labour unions and other groups to advance their interests through the political process. The term PAC is used exclusively in the context of the American political system, although broadly similar organisations do exist in other countries.

Until the 1970s, few commented on PAC activities. One of the first PACs was the

American Federation of Labour/Congress of Industrial Organisation's (AFL/CIO) Committee on Political Education (COPE), which was created in 1948 to channel union money to pro-labour candidates. However, the modern usage of the term PAC was not established until after the passage of the Federal Election Campaign Act (FECA) of 1974. The purpose of this law was to regulate the activities of the large contributors to election campaigns. Until 1974 INTEREST GROUPS, and especially corporations and unions, donated large amounts directly to the main political parties and to particular candidates. In spite of new disclosure rules introduced in 1971, considerable public disquiet existed at what was seen as the exercise of undue political influence by big business and big unions.

With the passage of FECA, however, organised interests were limited to donating $5,000 to each federal candidate per election and $15,000 to each national committee per year. The law also limited contributions by individuals and political PARTIES to just $1,000 to each candidate per year. At a stroke, therefore, the law placed greater limits on party contributions than on contributions by PACs. Moreover, as there was no limit on total contributions per year, the law gave to PACs an incentive to contribute to as many candidates as possible.

As a result, PACs proliferated in number and size. In 1974 just 608 PACs were registered with the Federal Election Commission (FEC). By 1989 this figure had risen to over 4,200, although it fell back slightly to 3,798 at the end of 1998. Of this number, around 1,500 are corporate, 320 labour union, 800 trade association and health connected, and the remainder unconnected to existing associations. PACs have become the leading source of campaign finance contributing more than $400 million to all candidates in 1994/5.

From the very beginning, PACs have been criticised for undermining the democratic process. There are a number of strands to this critique. First, as PACs have partly replaced political parties as the main source of campaign finance so this vital function has been taken one step away from the democratic process (see POLITICAL FINANCING). Whatever the faults of the old system, parties were at the centre of the fundraising system. Even though they often relied on large contributions from 'fat cat' corporate and union donors, the parties remained mass-based local organisations. Moreover, they, rather than the contributors, controlled the nomination of candidates. Today, PAC power can bypass local political parties and instead focus directly on voter decisions. In addition, organised interests, and especially big business, are now discerning about backing winners. As a result, incumbents benefit much more from PAC support than do challengers. In 1995/6, the ratio in the elections for the House of Representatives was 1:6 ($120 million to incumbents and only $22 million to challengers). PACs may, therefore, have reduced the competitiveness of elections (see ELECTORAL COMPETITION).

A related criticism is the rise of single-issue PACs, whose purpose is to promote a particular cause or position. Hence some of the most active PACs can be found in such areas as abortion, gun control, the environment and the use of prayers in public schools. Paradoxically, however, the most telling criticism of PACs is not that they have weakened political parties, but that they nationalised campaign contributions in ways which have *increased* party reliance on the 'big interests'. This is because the laws leaves what is called 'soft money' completely unregulated. Soft money consists of all those contributions which go not to individual candidates or party organisations but instead go towards advancing the interests of a particular party or to promoting a particular issue. In 1996, for example the top 50 PACs contributed some $64 million in soft money to the two major presidential candidates, Bob Dole and Bill Clinton. Much of this money was given to the Republican and Democratic National Committees, who then spent it on advertising the merits of their respective candidates and the faults of the opposition. Large corporate and trade association PACs dominate here. Unlike the contributions of old, which were channelled to local parties and candidates, these monies bypass local organisations and thus give the impression to many voters that a Washington-based elite dominates campaign finance in the United States. The soft money grand total in 1996 came to $260 million, with the tobacco giant RJR Nabisco contributing the largest single amount ($3 million). Fears that the system is dominated by the rich have been reinforced by the creation of special clubs for donors who give more than $100,000 (labelled trustees by the Democrats and Team 100 by the Republicans).

A final criticism of PAC power is that many state and local elections today consist of two sorts of television advertising, one financed by the candidates' organisations and one by soft money special interests. Often the soft money advertisements portray the candidates as much more extreme than they actually are on such issues as abortion, law and order and gun control. Sometimes this backfires and the PACs actually hurt the candidate they are purporting to endorse. Clearly these efforts can distort the democratic process by exaggerating the policy differences between candidates and arousing unjustified fears among the electorate.

Most of the attempts to reform PACs are aimed at closing the soft money loophole, and both President Clinton and members of Congress have supported bills to this end. As of mid-1999, however, these reform attempts had come to nothing, mainly because too many legislators are wary of supporting a reform which would cut off the very contributions that were responsible for their election.

See also:

corporatism; interest groups; political financing; trades unions

Further reading

Ansolabehere, S. and Shanto, I. (1996) *Going Negative: How Political Advertisements Shrink and Polarize the Electorate*, New York: The Free Press.
Biersack, R., Herrnson, P.S. and Wilcox, C.

(eds) (1994) *Risky Business? PAC Decision-making in Congressional Elections*, New York: Sharpe.
Clawson, D., Neustadl, A. and Scott, D. (1992) *Money Talks: Corporate PACs and Political Influence*, New York: Basic Books.
Eismeier, T.J. and Pollock, P.H. (1988) *Business, Money and the Rise of Corporate PACs in American Elections*, New York: Quorum Books.
Gais, T. (1998) *Improper Influence: Campaign Finance Law, Political Interest Groups, and the Problem of Equality*, Ann Arbor, MI: University of Michigan Press.

DAVID H. MCKAY

political culture

The concept of political culture implies that the values, beliefs and skills of mass publics have an important impact on politics in general and on democratic institutions in particular. These orientations are learned, not genetic, but they are relatively central and enduring so they change slowly, largely through inter-generational population replacement. Political culture is transmitted from generation to generation through the socialisation process, but it is also shaped by the first-hand experience of given generations, so it can vary from one generation to another as well as from one society to another.

The thesis that cultural factors play an important role in the emergence and survival of democratic institutions has had a chequered history. Lipset's (1959) seminal discussion of the social requisites of democracy focused primarily on economic factors, but pointed out that the reason why rich countries were far more likely to be democracies than poor ones was probably linked with the fact that prosperity gives rise to social and cultural changes such as increasing trust, moderation and willingness to compromise, that make it possible for democratic institutions to function. But in the absence of the cross-national empirical data that would enable one to test that thesis, little more was said about cultural factors.

Almond and Verba in 1963 (*The Civic Culture*) carried out an empirical test of the linkage between political culture and democracy, finding that the Anglo-Saxon democracies were indeed characterised by a number of cultural traits, such as relatively high levels of trust and subjective political competence, that theoretically were conducive to democracy. Their sample was limited to five countries, which made it impossible to carry out statistically significant analyses of the linkages between individual-level orientations and system-level democracy; but the fact that they *did* have comparable survey data from five societies represented a major advance over previous work. Their study was immensely influential. But in the 1970s and 1980s, political culture research fell out of favour. Writers of the dependency school argued that the emergence of democracy was determined by international factors: global CAPITALISM prevented its spread to peripheral nations, keeping them in a dependent position; neither economic development nor democratisation could take place in any developing society that was enmeshed in the predatory network of global capitalism.

Subsequent developments have largely discredited the dependency school. During the past few decades, those societies that were *most* involved in international trade and investment showed the highest rates of economic growth and democratisation. Growing numbers of East Asian and Latin American societies moved toward democracy, while societies that remained aloof from global capitalism, such as North Korea and Burma, remained impoverished and authoritarian. Although the implications of the dependency thesis were wrong, its stigmatisation of political culture as ethnocentric is still widely accepted.

More recently, the transitions to the democracy school have downplayed the role of political culture for different reasons. This time, the focus is on elite bargaining (O'Donnell and Schmitter 1986; Przeworski 1992). Although this school emphasises the importance of factors within given societies, it deals almost exclusively with the role of elites, arguing that once democratic institutions are installed, they will automatically create a democratic political culture. Ironically, this analysis of democracy assumes that mass publics play no important role in the emergence and survival of democracy. This interpretation also faces a major empirical problem: the fact that one observes an extremely strong correlation between democracy and economic development (see ECONOMIC REQUIREMENTS OF DEMOCRACY). Do rich countries almost always have clever elites who negotiate skilfully, while the elites from poor countries are almost always incompetent negotiators? Or is it possible that underlying internal factors make it more difficult to establish democracy in some settings than in others? Burkhart and Lewis-Beck (1994) demonstrated that economic development is conducive to democracy, but democratic institutions do not necessarily bring economic development. But *why* is economic development conducive to democracy? It is not simply the result of wealth itself; if it were, Kuwait would be a model democracy. Growing empirical evidence that internal cultural factors play an important role has stimulated a renaissance of research on political culture in recent years (Clark and Hoffmann-Martinot 1998; Diamond 1993; Diamond *et al.* 1995; Inglehart 1988, 1990, 1997; Klingemann and Fuchs 1995; Van Deth and Scarbrough 1995).

It seems clear that international developments play an important role in the emergence of democracy: for example, Gorbachev's decision that the Red Army would no longer intervene to prop up beleaguered communist regimes in Eastern Europe was a major factor in the collapse of those regimes, opening up the way for their replacement by liberalising regimes. Elite bargaining also plays an important role: skilful bargaining between Solidarity's leaders and Poland's military government helped that country become the first Eastern European society to attain a non-communist government. But it seems equally clear that these proximate causes of liberalisation reflected deeper underlying causes, including cultural changes that made the population as a whole, and the younger generations in particular, in both Poland and the USSR, increasingly likely to demand democratisation. The effectiveness of Solidarity's leaders in bargaining for shared power ultimately depended on the fact that they had overwhelming support among the Polish public; and when hardliners in the Soviet Union attempted to reverse the reforms launched by Gorbachev through a coup in 1991, they found that the streets of Moscow were blocked by hundreds of thousands of citizens who had come out to demonstrate their support for liberalisation. The hardliners were surprised at this huge outpouring of mass resistance: it would not have happened a decade or two earlier. It reflected underlying changes in the political culture. A society's culture reflects its entire historical heritage, with institutional factors playing an important role; but with economic development and major historical factors (such as the rise and fall of communism, or victory/defeat in the Second World War) also playing major roles.

Inglehart (1997) analysed aggregated national-level data from the forty-three societies included in the 1990–1 World Values Survey, finding large and coherent cross-cultural differences. The worldviews of the peoples of rich societies differ systematically from those of low-income societies across a wide range of political, social and religious norms and beliefs. Factor analysis revealed two main dimensions that tapped scores of variables and reflect cross-national polarisation between traditional versus secular-rational orientations toward AUTHORITY and survival versus self-expression values. The latter dimension taps mass feelings of interpersonal trust, tolerance, participatory values and a sense of well-being that seem conducive to democracy, and a society's position on the survival/self-expression dimension index is strongly correlated with its level of democracy, as indicated by its scores on the Freedom House ratings of political rights and civil liberties from 1972 through 1998. This relationship is remarkably powerful and it is not a methodological artefact, since the two variables are measured at different levels by completely different sources. Virtually all of the societies that rank high on survival/self-expression values are stable democracies (see DEMOCRATIC STABILITY). Virtually all of the societies that rank low on this dimension have authoritarian governments. The overall correlation of 0.87 is significant at an extremely high level, and almost certainly reflects a causal linkage.

One interpretation would be that democratic institutions give rise to the self-expression values that are so closely linked with them. In other words, democracy makes people happy, healthy, tolerant and trusting, and instils post-materialist values (at least in the younger generation). This interpretation is appealing and seems to provide a strong argument for democracy: adopt democratic institutions and live happily ever after.

Unfortunately, the experience of the people of the former Soviet Union does not support this interpretation. Since their dramatic move toward democracy in 1991, they have not become happier, healthier, more trusting, more tolerant or more post-materialist: for the most part, they have moved in exactly the opposite direction (Inglehart and Baker 2000). Similarly, many new democracies were established after the First World War, but most of them did not survive the stresses of the interwar era. The most tragic and fateful case was that of Germany, where democratic institutions were widely seen as a foreign element that had been forced on the society by defeat in the First World War. Authoritarian elites still held influential positions, and the underlying mass political culture was not congruent with democratic institutions. The Weimar Republic collapsed under the stress of the Great Depression: democracy had failed to develop deep-rooted allegiances among the public that might have enabled it to weather difficult times. But culture is a variable, not a constant. After the Second World War, democratic institutions gradually won acceptance among the German public, aided by the postwar economic miracle. The 1959 Civic Culture survey by Almond and Verba showed that while many British and American citizens expressed pride in their political institutions, few Germans did; but Germans did take pride in their economic success. Moreover, the institutions of the Federal Republic (unlike those of Weimar) maintained domestic order and provided for a peaceful transfer of political power from a hegemonic party to the opposition in the 1960s. By the late 1970s, the German public was more apt to express satisfaction with the way their political system was functioning than were most other West European peoples, including the British. Democracy had finally taken root in German society.

Economic development tends to bring social and cultural changes that make democratic institutions increasingly likely to survive and flourish. That is why mass democracy did not emerge until relatively recently in history, and why even now it is most likely to be found in economically more developed countries; in particular, those that emphasise self-expression values rather than survival values. But democratisation does not automatically occur when a society's people attain certain values and attitudes. The process can be blocked or triggered by societal events. For Eastern Europe, Gorbachev's accession to power was important: he made it clear that the Red Army would no longer be used to veto liberalization in these countries. This, together with economic failure, was a triggering event that explains why liberalization suddenly took place throughout the region in 1989–91, rather than a decade earlier or later. But this catalyst would not have worked if underlying societal preconditions had not developed that were not present earlier: apart from Czechoslovakia (the most developed society), none of the Eastern European countries were stable democracies before the Second World War.

Ironically, an unintended consequence of the relative security and rising educational levels provided by four decades of communist rule was to make Eastern European publics less willing to accept authoritarian rule and increasingly adept at resisting it. Such cultural changes can be repressed by domestic elites or by external military force. But by the 1980s, such countries as Poland, Czechoslovakia and Hungary were ripe for democratisation (Huntington 1984). Once it became clear that the threat of Soviet military intervention was no longer present, mass pressures for democracy surfaced almost overnight.

Mass pressures interact with the elites in control of a given society. The generational transition that brought Gorbachev to power could conceivably have brought some other less flexible leader to the top. This might have delayed the process of reform for a number of years, but it would not have held back the clock forever.

The impact of changing values on mass potential for unconventional political action is not limited to Western societies. East Asian societies show the same phenomenon; indeed, it began to manifest itself in South Korea *before* the recent surge of democratisation in Eastern Europe. In 1987 an unprecedented wave of mass demonstrations swept South Korea, demanding direct election of the president. The government yielded, and the ensuing elections were the fairest in South Korean history, with the opposition actually winning a clear majority of the vote. Only the fact that the two main opposition candidates split their vote almost evenly enabled the governing party's candidate to win. In the early 1990s, Taiwan, facing similar pressures from an increasingly educated and articulate populace, also adopted freely contested elections.

China went through a somewhat similar crisis in 1989, but it ended with bloody repression of the dissidents. This illustrates an important point: democratisation is never automatic. It reflects the interaction of underlying social changes and specific historical events and leaders. A resolute authoritarian elite can respond to demands for reform by slaughtering the citizens involved. But in choosing this course, one pays a price: the loss of legitimacy and citizen co-operation. In part, the Chinese leadership's choice of this option was feasible because China was still at a considerably less advanced level of development than the other nations we have discussed. Its per capita income was only a fraction of that in South Korea, Taiwan or most of

Eastern Europe. China's pro-democracy movement, in 1989, was mainly based on the younger and better educated strata in the urban centres. Its repression had little repercussion for China's vast rural masses, which still comprise the great majority of the population.

The evolution of industrial society brings gradual cultural changes that make mass publics increasingly likely to want democratic institutions and more supportive of them once they are in place. This transformation does not come easily or automatically. Determined elites, in control of the army and police, can resist pressures for democratisation. But the emergence of prosperous WELFARE states leads to long-term changes in which mass publics give an increasingly high priority to AUTONOMY and self-expression in all spheres of life including politics. And as they mature, industrial societies develop increasingly specialised and educated labour forces, which become increasingly adept at exerting political pressure. It becomes more difficult and costly to repress demands for political liberalization. Moreover, economic development is also linked with relatively high levels of subjective well-being and interpersonal trust, which also seem to play a crucial role in democracy. With rising levels of economic development, cultural patterns emerge that are increasingly supportive of democracy, making mass publics more likely to *want* democracy, and more skilful at *getting* it.

See also:

citizenship; civic virtue; civil society; hegemony; identity, political; inclusion/exclusion

Further reading

Almond, G. and Verba, S. (1963) *The Civic Culture: Political Attitudes and Democracy in Five Nations*, Princeton, NJ: Princeton University Press.

Burkhart, R.E. and Lewis-Beck, M.S. (1994) 'Comparative Democracy: The Economic Development Thesis', *American Political Science Review* 88(December): 903–10.

Clark, T.N. and Hoffmann-Martinot, V. (1998) *The New Political Culture*, Boulder, CO: Westview.

Diamond, L. (ed.) (1993) *Political Culture and Democracy in Developing Countries*, Boulder, CO: Lynne Rienner.

Diamond, L., Linz, J. and Lipset, S.M. (1995) *Politics in Developing Countries*, Boulder, CO: Lynne Rienner.

Huntington, S.P. (1984) 'Will More Countries Become Democratic?', *Political Science Quarterly* 99(2): 193–218.

Inglehart, R. (1988) 'The Renaissance of Political Culture', *American Political Science Review* 82(4): 1203–30.

—— (1990) *Culture Shift in Advanced Industrial Society*, Princeton, NJ: Princeton University Press.

—— (1997) *Modernization and Postmodernization: Cultural, Economic and Political Change in 43 Societies*, Princeton, NJ: Princeton University Press.

Inglehart, R. and Baker, W. (2000) 'Modernization, Cultural Change and the Persistence of Traditional Values', *American Sociological Review* February: 19–51.

Inglehart, R. and Klingemann, H.-D. (2000) 'Genes, Culture, Democracy and Happiness', in E. Diener and E.M. Suh (eds), *Subjective Well-Being Across Cultures*, Cambridge, MA: MIT Press.

Klingemann, H.-D. and Fuchs, D. (eds) (1995) *Citizens and the State*, Oxford: Oxford University Press.

Lipset, S.M. (1959) 'Some Social Requisites of Democracy: Economic Development and Political Legitimacy', *American Political Science Review* 53(March): 69–105.

O'Donnell, G. and Schmitter, P.C. (1986) 'Tentative Conclusions about Uncertain Democracies', in G. O'Donnell, P.C. Schmitter and L. Whitehead (eds), *Transitions from Authoritarian Rule*, Baltimore: Johns Hopkins University Press, vol. 4, 1–78.

Przeworski, A. (1992) 'The Games of Transition', in S. Mainwaring, G. O'Donnell, and J.S. Valenzuela (eds), *Issues in Democratic Consolidation: The New South American Democracies in Comparative Perspective*,

Notre Dame, IN: University of Notre Dame Press, 105–52.

Van Deth, J. and Scarbrough, E. (eds) (1995) *The Impact of Values*, Oxford: Oxford University Press.

RONALD F. INGLEHART

political financing

In democratic and authoritarian regimes alike, politicians need money to sustain their public activities nearly as much as they require food to nourish their bodies. In democracies, election campaigns could not take place without funds, candidates could not convey their messages to the voters, and political parties could not operate. Political finance is not an evil in itself: it is the opposite. If political contributions are raised and spent properly, the democratic process will be healthy and vigorous. But it is possible to poison politics with undesirable monies; overfinancing and unfair uses of political money have consequences comparable to those of overeating and of an unbalanced or poisonous regimen.

The basic problem is that while democracy involves 'one person, one vote', it is hard to ensure that every voter has the same influence. While there exist huge variations in individual and institutional wealth and access to resources, a rich voter will remain more powerful than a poor one. A millionaire can plug his or her views in countless ways: by contributing generously to a political party or candidate, by financing pamphlets, newspapers or television stations, by paying for politically-relevant research, by lobbying legislators, by bribing officials, or by financing actions before the law courts on matters pertaining to human RIGHTS or other public struggles.

It is not surprising that critics of democracy of both Left and Right have for a long time pointed to the role of money as an Achilles heel of democracy. Friedrich Engels, Vilfredo Pareto and Roberto Michels all pointed to ways in which money undermined democratic assumptions. Nevertheless, it is possible to take seriously many of the arguments presented by anti-democrats about the potential damage money may inflict without accepting their extreme conclusions.

The role of political money

Financial inequalities and abuses involving the political uses of money arguably have a number of consequences:

1 Those able to pay for major MEDIA are able to affect the underlying assumptions and agendas of ordinary members of the public. This influence crosses international boundaries.
2 Lack of money limits political recruitment. Among the poor and among disadvantaged groups such as women, material need may prevent all but the most ambitious from considering a career in politics. To stand for election to the national legislature may be as much a pastime for the prosperous as owning yachts.
3 In some countries such as the United States, academic studies have demonstrated that a candidate with superior resources has an improved chance of success at the polls. Money, as demonstrated by Gary Jacobson (1980), wins votes in legislative campaigns. According to his sophisticated study, the size of the campaign budget has a vital effect on results of contests for the US House of Representatives. In particular, a candidate who wishes to gain victory against an incumbent member of Congress has little chance without a large campaign budget. In 1972 and 1974, candidates who challenged sitting Congressmen gained an extra 1 per cent of the vote for every $10,000 they spent on their campaigns. In view of the large sums spent in the elections, these results are striking.
4 Control over money affects the internal structure of power within political parties.
5 Once a candidate has been elected, cash will start playing a role in his or her political life in other ways. Lobbying on issues before the legislature involves financial muscle, even

when it is honest and legal. Then there are the darker channels of bribery and corruption of elected officials, administrators and law enforcement officers.

Some limitations of money in political life

Not everything or everybody can be bought. It is easy to find examples of candidates who have spent stupendous sums on an election campaign but have failed to win. In Britain, the billionaire businessman Sir James Goldsmith – who knew at the time that he had terminal cancer – was prepared to pay £20 million in the general election of 1997 to put forward a slate of candidates opposed to Britain's INTEGRATION into the European Union. This was a huge sum for one donor, but made hardly a dent in his wealth. It also made only a minor impact on the political scene. Goldsmith's Referendum Party was an irritant to the Conservative Party but proved a small factor in the Conservatives' defeat by New Labour.

In Poland in 1989, the popular revulsion against the ruling communist regime was so strong that the Communist Party's possession of a huge apparatus and almost limitless resources had no impact. At the height of its popularity, the Solidarity Movement had some 10 million supporters. They were glad to do for free the tasks which members of the communist *nomenklatura* did out of duty: Solidarity supporters were keen to place volunteers outside the polling stations as an insurance against electoral fraud, and they performed with gusto the other mundane tasks of campaigning. Its candidates swept the board in the ELECTIONS of May and June of 1989. In the referendum on Zimbabwe's proposed new constitution, held in February 2000, the massive machine of President Robert Mugabe went down to defeat against a sparsely organised opposition.

For all its importance, money is only one of several political resources. The Marxist line is not persuasive in assigning a predominance to material factors. It is not necessary to explain virtually everything, ranging from religious feelings to personal passions, in terms of money. Other approaches stress the independent significance of the psychological urge for power, and factors such as ideology, religion, race and sex drive.

Arguments concerning the relative importance of money and of other forces tend to be highly general and hard to resolve. Broad questions such as, 'how important is money in politics?' and 'is money the most important force in political life?' are almost impossible to resolve scientifically. The frequency with which there are prominent scandals in different parts of the world relating to political financing certainly suggests that funding plays a key role. But that does not mean that money is the only major impulse. Nor does it involve any implicit comparison between the role of money and that of any number of other political motivations and forces.

The study of political money

There were several forays into the study of political money in the period between the two World Wars. The American political scientist James K. Pollock produced what was probably the first systematic book on the subject in 1926, a study of campaign financing in America. In 1932 he published a comparative volume. After the Second World War Pollock acted as an adviser to the US military authorities in West Germany. In 1963, Richard Rose and Arnold Heidenheimer organised a comparative, multi-author study under the auspices of the International Political Science Association (IPSA). From then on, under the leadership of Herbert E. Alexander (director of the Citizens' Research Foundation), the IPSA's research committee on political finance and political corruption became the focal point of international studies on the topic.

Research into political funding has until very recently concentrated on a limited number of advanced Western democracies, especially the United States (see Nassmacher *et al.* 1992a; Alexander and Shiratori 1994.) The first steps on the ladder of research into the financing of politics in developing nations are only now being taken. A 1998 book on political financing in Latin America, edited by Pilar del

Castillo and Daniel Zovatto, is a pioneering example.

Modern scandals concerning political financing

Public interest in problems of political money has been stimulated by a succession of scandals. Scandals and realities are, of course, not always the same. CORRUPTION involving the funding of parties and election campaigns may at some periods pass almost unnoticed or, if noticed, may give rise to little public concern. At some points in his presidency of the United States in the 1980s, Ronald Reagan was dubbed 'Teflon coated'. He was like a non-stick frying-pan: the grease of scandal would not stick on him. President William Clinton too has survived scandals involving campaign funding alongside those concerning his private life.

Scandals tend to arise when a sense of mistrust is already present. Behaviour which would be acceptable when voters have strong faith in the government of the day becomes intolerable when the economy is going wrong or when the party in power seems weak and ineffective. If scandal stems from existing mistrust, it can have the effect of leading to profound disillusionment with politicians and politics. Much of the discontent with democracy which, paradoxically, has gripped the advanced industrialised nations in the 1990s (the decade of democracy's triumph over communism and authoritarianism) has stemmed from problems of political financing.

Major scandals include those which came to attention in the course of the Watergate Affair in America from 1972 onwards. Though 'Watergate' primarily involved questions of abuse of power (the illegal break-in to the offices of the Democratic National Committee by agents associated with President Richard Nixon), political money became an important side issue. Major US corporations, such as American Airlines, were shown to have made illegal contributions to Nixon's re-election fund by means so devious that they came to be known as 'money laundering'. When it became clear that the Lockheed Corporation had been involved in the large-scale, undeclared funding of politics and politicians in Japan and Italy, those countries too found themselves engulfed by the Watergate Affair.

In 1981, it was the turn of West Germany's political parties to face revelations about the massive, undeclared contributions (amounting to some DM 26 million) of the Flick Concern. This large privately owned conglomerate, based on the fortune of the war criminal Friedrich Flick, had indulged in the apparent bribery of Christian Democrats, Free Democrats and Social Democrats alike. Moreover, no fewer than 1,800 separate cases of alleged contraventions of West Germany's political financing laws were pursued by the law enforcement authorities and then dropped under political pressure. The Flick Affair led to important changes in the Parties Law and it appeared that political financing had been cleaned up. The emergence of a serious new scandal in 2000, the so-called 'Kohlgate', showed that this optimism had been unfounded. The former Christian Democrat chancellor Helmut Kohl was shown to have collected a large, illegal political fund which had been kept separate from the party's regular, publicly disclosed finances.

Meanwhile, there has been a prolonged crisis in India, where the Bofors Affair of 1987 involved alleged kickbacks to politicians close to Rajiv Gandhi in return for a contact for the Swedish arms manufacturer for 155m FH-778 guns. In Spain the Social Democrats were damaged by the Filesa scandal, which broke in 1991 and which involved large payments to the party during the 1989 elections disguised as 'consultancy' contracts. In Colombia, there was the affair of the 'narco-tapes'. In June 1994, shortly after the presidential elections, it became known that there existed a set of tapes whose contents suggested that money from drug trafficking had financed the presidential election campaign. Police raids a week or so later yielded documentary evidence linking the Cali drugs cartel with a significant number of politicians. The director of Ernesto Samper's presidential election campaign was jailed together with other senior campaign officials. In Italy, the long-ruling Christian Democrats were engulfed after the end of the Cold War by a torrent of allegations and by the investigations known as 'Operation Clean Hands'. In Belgium, a veteran Socialist leader and Secretary-general of NATO has been convicted on charges involving major political finance abuses. In Britain, the Formula One scandal of 1997 led to an enquiry into the funding of political parties which has resulted in the most fundamental reforms since 1883.

It is easier to describe political funding scandals than to analyse their causes. Among trends in the financing of politics which may possibly have a bearing has been the widely reported increase in campaign costs. Conclusive evidence about changes in the costs of politics is still wanting. It is clear that not only are the forms of campaigning changing, but also that in many countries voluntary participation in the work of political parties has been declining. Possibly, voluntary politics has been giving way to money politics.

'Old style' campaigning relied largely on human contact on the doorstep or on meetings and debates held by candidates and leading party personalities. In some parts of the world – much of Africa and parts of Asia – election campaigns still conform to this pattern. A major item of political spending in Africa is the vehicles needed to transport candidates and party workers to meetings in areas which lack public transport. Newspapers, television and even radio reach a small percentage of the electors in these countries. In the rest of the world (including the emerging democracies of the former Soviet Union and Eastern Europe) television is the main medium of political COMMUNICATION. Therefore, as often commentators have frequently pointed out, professional political mechanics – experts at opinion polling, television presentation and film production – have become vital, expensive components of the modern campaign team. Especially in countries where costly television, newspaper and billboard advertisements are the norm, access to money becomes essential.

The changing style of political campaigning is not wholly convincing as an explanation of continuing corruption and scandal relating to campaign fundraising. The simple fact is that political money is scandal-ridden in technologically backward and technologically advanced nations alike. The fact that the power stakes at issue in competitive elections are so high makes the temptation to corrupt or dodgy fundraising great in all countries. Wrongdoing by politicians and their managers should not be a matter of surprise.

Reforms

Scandal often is the impetus for reform. The public demands measures which will avoid a repetition of recent wrong-doings. Frequently reforms do not work. As fast as legislators close old loopholes, political managers find new ones. Moreover, infringements are difficult to prove and political finance regulations are hard to enforce. The following are among the main types of reform.

Controls. These may consist of (a) regulations requiring parties, candidates or donors to disclose their finances or to list their donations, (b) limits on the size of gifts which a donor is permitted to make, (c) prohibitions against particular kinds of donation (bans against foreign donations are the most common, while bans against political payments from governmental contractors are also found in a number of countries), and (d) limits on the total a party or candidate may spend in an election campaign.

Public funding of political parties, candidates and legislators. Since the 1950s, country after country has introduced schemes of public financing. In Western Europe, countries where there is now direct funding of political parties from the public purse include Austria, Belgium, Denmark, Finland, Germany, Greece, the Netherlands, Norway, Spain and Sweden. In France, there are subventions for presidential and parliamentary campaigns. Other countries with public funding schemes include the United States (for presidential campaigns), Canada (for parliamentary elections), Japan, Russia and most of Latin America. State aid is less common in Africa.

Tax reliefs on political contributions. Scholars

such as Karl-Heinz Nassmacher *et al.* (1992b) have argued that tax reliefs are preferable to direct subventions for parties and candidates. If state money is handed to political professionals on a platter, they will have a reduced incentive to appeal for money to ordinary party members and supporters. Since it is better from a democratic point of view to raise £1 million from a series of small contributions than from one large one, public funding should be tied – according to this argument – to participation by supporters who need not be rich. Tax reliefs on small donations mean that parties do not receive public funds unless they manage at the same time to recruit supporters.

Tax reliefs may take several forms. The most common is income tax relief on political contributions. This exists, for example, in Belgium, France, Germany, Italy and Japan. A more powerful but less common incentive for small contributions is the method of tax credits, which is found in Canada and Germany. Matching grants, used at state and federal levels in the United States, are another variation.

Subsidies in kind. In countries where television and radio are the most important channels of political informations, the most crucial form of in-kind subsidy to parties and candidates is the provision of free air time to parties and candidates. These provisions are widespread. Countries like the United States, where there are no free party political broadcasts, are the exception. Free newspaper advertising for candidates (as in Japan), free poster sites and free or subsidised postage for electoral communications are other forms of subsidies in kind.

See also:

corruption; electoral campaigning; parties

Further reading

Alexander, H.E. and Shiratori, R. (eds) (1994). *Political Finance among the Democracies*, Boulder, CO: Westview Press.
del Castillo, P. and Zovatto, D. (eds) (1998) *La Financiación de la Politica en Iberoamérica*, San José, Costa Rica: Instituto Interamericano de Derechos Humanos/ Centro de Asesoria y Promoción Electoral.
Jacobson, G.C. (1980) *Money in Congressional Elections*, New Haven, CT: Yale University Press.
Nassmacher, K.-H. *et al.* (1992a) 'Comparing Party and Campaign Finances in Western Democracies', in A.B. Gunlicks (ed.), *Campaign and Party Finance in North America and Western Europe*, Boulder, CO: Westview.
—— (1992b) *Burger finanzieren Wahlkämpfe: Anregungen aus Nordamerika für die Parteifinanzierung in Deutschland*, Baden-Baden: Nomos.
Pinto-Duschinsky, M. (1998) 'Parties and Candidates', in ACE Electronic Handbook, www.aceproject.org, United Nations Department of Development Support and Management Services, International Foundation for Election Systems, and International IDEA, New York, Washington, DC and Stockholm.
Pollock, J.K. (1926) *Party Campaign Funds*, New York: Alfred A. Knopf.
—— (1932) *Money and Politics Abroad*, New York: Alfred A. Knopf.
Rose, R. and Heidenheimer, A.J. (eds) (1963) 'Comparative Political Finance: A Symposium', *Journal of Politics* 25.

MICHAEL PINTO-DUSCHINSKY

political frontiers

A good deal of contemporary politics revolves around the construction of political frontiers between individuals, groups, parties or states. Whether it be traditional disputes between states over territory, demands for greater ethnic, regional or national AUTONOMY within states, struggles between social classes over the distribution of material resources, or radical assertions of gendered, sexual or racial identity, which culminate in demands for cultural recognition and the right to be different, politics involves the establishment of divisions and BOUNDARIES between an 'us' and a 'them'.

This has led a number of critical political theorists to conclude that 'there is only politics where there are frontiers' (Laclau 1990: 160), and to inquire into the theoretical and empirical dimensions of their construction and operation (see Bennington 1994; Howarth *et al.* 2000; Wolin 1996).

In so doing, proponents of RADICAL DEMOCRACY and critical theorists more generally question older assumptions about the givenness and naturalness of frontiers, stressing instead their symbolically and politically negotiated character. As a consequence the problem of political frontiers unfolds a rich agenda of issues and topics in contemporary political theory. In normative democratic theory (see NORMATIVE APPROACHES TO DEMOCRACY), it raises questions about the nature of boundaries between states, the constitution and character of liberal democratic orders, as well as urgent practical issues regarding the justification and critique of distinctions between 'insiders' and 'outsiders'. On an explanatory level, the concept of political frontiers raises questions about their constitution and functioning in different historical contexts. In other words, it concerns the different logics of frontier formation with a view to examining their effects on political identities and social orders. This article concentrates on the latter set of issues, though inevitably normative questions intrude, and begins by clarifying various dimensions and usages of the term.

Conceptualising frontiers

In modern thought, the concept of frontiers signifies a complex nexus of issues. For instance, in one of modernity's founding gestures, Kant seeks to establish sharp conceptual and philosophical boundaries between subject and object, and between different types of knowledge, even though this desire sits uneasily with his equally powerful urge to abolish political frontiers through a commitment to universal cosmopolitanism (see Bennington 1994: 262). It is this dialectic of division and reconciliation, particularity and universality, self and other, which lies at the heart of many current debates about modernity and democracy (see Habermas 1998). Moreover, as has been suggested, these concerns about frontiers and boundaries arise not only in philosophical reflection about the limits of reason or knowledge, but are evident in the full immediacy and urgency of practical politics. Politically the question of frontiers is intimately bound up with the establishment of distinctions between, for example, citizens and noncitizens, citizens and refugees, men and women, humans and non-humans.

Indeed, what is at stake in approaching the question of frontiers is precisely the theoretical and political problems of separation, distinction and differentiation (rather than separateness, distinctness and difference), which simultaneously raise questions concerning belonging, holding together and solidarity. As Wolin (1996: 32) argues, boundaries both proclaim identity and signify exclusion: as 'container and excluder, boundaries work to foster the impression of a circumscribed political space in which likeness dwells, the likeness of natives... or of a nationality, or of citizens with equal rights'. Such likeness also acts as an indicator that facilitates the exclusion of those who are not alike (see INCLUSION/EXCLUSION).

This brings us to the heart of contemporary conceptualisations of the character of political frontiers. Its specificity is to be found in the contrast that can be drawn with the earlier conceptualisation of identity, whether it relates to the people, 'DEMOS', nation, ethnic group or citizen. During the nineteenth-century boundaries were associated with collective identities understood in historical and cultural terms, and identified with the nation (Wolin 1996: 32). However, as Weale points out, boundaries only became an issue when one needed to delimit the set of persons who constituted a people 'entitled to govern itself'; a problem that need not have arisen if nineteenth-century assumptions of nationalism were true. That is to say, 'if humanity were divided naturally into territorially discreet social groups, easily identifiable by reference to features such as language or culture', then the boundaries that define the citizens of a polity could be drawn by reference to those characteristics. By contrast, where the legitimacy of historical boundaries are called into question, the issue of boundaries emerges as a problem (Weale 1996: 150).

During the twentieth century, the preoccupation with boundaries has intensified, not least because of the issues raised by the new politics of cultural recognition. This has raised a concomitant problem about how to conceptualise political frontiers anew, taking into consideration the increased politicisation of identities. Whereas in the past, for writers like Hobbes, Kant, Hegel and Weber, the theorisation of boundaries concerned the organisation of power that guarantees domestic peace and SECURITY (Wolin 1996: 33), in current political thinking the concern has been with contingent, multiple and overdetermined identities, which have undergone greater politicisation. Hence even a brief survey of literature in this field reveals a strong preoccupation with questions concerning the theorisation of political identity (see IDENTITY, POLITICAL) in terms of the permeability of boundaries between and around identities, and the relation of identities to the construction and CONTESTATION of larger social imaginaries.

Theorising political frontiers

In order to clarify further the nature of political frontiers, this piece focuses on the writings of Laclau and Mouffe, as they represent one of the few systematic attempts to conceptualise and analyse the construction and deconstruction of frontiers (Laclau 1990; Laclau and Mouffe 1985). Like Weale, the question of limits and frontiers in Laclau and Mouffe's work arises only when identity is no longer conceived in naturalistic terms. Given their post-Marxist approach, they emphasise the absence of necessary laws of history and argue that political and social identities can no longer be analysed simply on the basis of their insertion into relations of production. Thus the manner in which identities are forged and the way societies are unified has to be addressed anew. It is on this terrain that the problematic of frontiers arises.

In brief, their argument suggests that if any political identity and, by extension, society is no longer a given and immutable datum, and if its character cannot be determined in a naturalistic fashion, then it can no longer be individuated on the grounds of positively attributed characteristics. In other words, political identity cannot be determined by reference simply to objectively given CLASS, 'racial' or ethnic factors, as if they were primordial and immutable datum. Instead, attention has to be focused on how these indicators of social division come to be naturalised and accepted as the basis for identity, and how they are dependent on political processes of inclusion and exclusion. In other words, analysis must be focused on how social division is politically produced. To grasp this process, Laclau and Mouffe argue that it is through the consolidation or dissolution of political frontiers that discursive formations in general, and social and political identities more specifically, are constructed or fragmented.

The identities of political subjects are the products of contingent social practices of articulation and disarticulation, rather than a priori givens. In brief, this anti-essentialist account of identity formation does not concentrate on the positive features of identity, but on the relations they establish with other identities, in which any particular identity depends on its differentiation from that which it is not. An example may be useful here. Linda Colley (1996: 6) argues that this was the case with British identity after 1707. The British came to define themselves as a single people, 'not because of any political or cultural consensus at home, but rather in reaction to the Other beyond their shores'. Once confronted with an alien 'them', an otherwise diverse community could become an 'us'. It is this centrality of confrontation, and the role of an 'other' to the constitution of identity, that the idea of political frontiers most crucially captures. Generalising this logic by drawing on Carl Schmitt, Mouffe (1992: 379) argues that 'every definition of a "we" implies the delimitation of a "frontier" and the designation of a "them"'.

Analysing political frontiers

In order to facilitate the analysis of the production of frontier effects, Laclau and Mouffe introduce two logics. They are the logics of equivalence and of difference, and are developed by drawing upon Ferdinand de Saussure's structuralist theory of language. As is suggested above, frontier effects are produced by systems of equivalence in which the construction of identities presuppose the positing of an external 'other'. By contrast, wherever identities are constructed in terms of the logic of difference, there is an attempt to fix relations between social agents as a set of 'mere differences' and, therefore, as a system of stable differences in which each social identity is constructed in positive terms. However, as systems of difference only partially define relational identities, the logic of difference never manages to constitute a fully sutured space. The contingency of these systems of difference is revealed in the unfixity which equivalence introduces. An example can help to explicate these rather abstract logics.

Consider for instance the constitution of black identity in the discourse of the Black Consciousness Movement (BCM) in South Africa during the late 1960s and early 1970s. Three key moments can be discerned in the articulation of Black Consciousness ideology by those organic intellectuals opposed to the apartheid discourse of ethnic and national differentiation (Howarth 1997). These comprise the identification of an enemy to be opposed, the definition of a friend, and a reversal of what they perceived to be the dominant white/black hierarchy. For our purposes it is only necessary to concentrate on the former two processes. The BCM's leader Steve Biko singled out the problem of white racism as the one major force against which the energies of resistance had to be mobilised. Given this, he argued that any collusion with apartheid institutions was fraught with political danger, even though several black political organisations participated in 'separate development' institutions, which formed part of the 'grand apartheid' design. Biko argued that these organisations

could not represent the black community in South Africa, for they worked with the forces of oppression. Foremost among these were white liberals and their discourse of 'non-racialism', which reproduced paternalistic thinking and the prevailing racial hierarchy. Thus the enemy camp was defined in such a manner as to include all those blacks and whites who participated in the existing political system. Defining the friends of the BCM made these lines of division even clearer. In addressing himself to black South Africans, Biko argued that the term 'black' referred only to those members of the African, coloured and Indian people who actively opposed apartheid, while the term 'non-white' was used in a derogatory sense to refer to 'sell-outs', collaborators' and 'lackeys' of the white system. Hence being black was not a matter of pigmentation, but of mental attitude. In terms of the logics outlined earlier, it is clear that the 'enemy' included all those who were opposed to the values and practices of the BCM, and white liberals and 'non-white' collaborators were equivalent in their status as enemies of the movement. By contrast, the category of 'friends' included Africans, coloureds, and Indian South Africans, all differentially defined insofar as they subscribed to the philosophy of Black Consciousness. However, these differentially defined groups gained their identity as members of the BCM only by excluding those liberals and non-whites opposed to its philosophy.

In addition, it is important to note that political frontiers serve not only to individuate identity, but also to organise political space. The simultaneous operation of the logics of equivalence and difference in the construction of political frontiers may be elucidated with reference to the Gramscian idea of transformism. Transformism is a process that involves a gradual but continuous absorption of 'the active elements produced by allied groups – and even of those which came from antagonistic groups and seemed irreconcilably hostile' (Gramsci 1971: 58–9). A transformist project, expressed in terms of the operation of the logics of equivalence and difference, will consist of efforts to expand the systems of difference defining a dominant bloc, and if such a project is successful, will result in a lessening of the antagonistic potential of the remaining excluded elements. A failure of transformism, on the other hand, may lead to the expansion of the logic of equivalence, the construction of clearcut political frontiers and a proliferation and deepening, rather than a limitation, of antagonistic relations. In short, the logic of difference leads to a complexification of social spaces, whereas the logic of equivalence leads to its simplification and division into diametrically opposite camps. An understanding of the operation of these logics is therefore crucial to a proper analysis of the political strategies of movements and political parties.

The frontiers of democracy

On an explanatory level, the concept of political frontiers makes an important contribution to the understanding and explanation of contemporary political phenomena, ranging from the constitution of social and political identities to strategies of containment and resistance. In theoretical terms, theorists of the concept have drawn upon developments in linguistics and post-structuralism to account for the symbolic and discursive dimensions of political practices. Nonetheless, a good deal of normative work is still required for these insights to be deepened, especially with reference to democratic theory. Attention needs to be paid to the complexity of frontier formation and its impact on the production of political identities, as well as to the systematisation of typologies of relations to the 'other' constituted in and through the deployment of frontiers (Derrida 1997; Norval 1996).

More specifically, with respect to democratic theory two related issues spring to mind. In the first place, there are questions of inclusion/exclusion, a question which in turn raises issues about where the boundaries of a democratic form of government ought to be drawn, as well as the character of the instituted boundaries. In other words, with regard to the first aspect, who ought to qualify as a citizen of a democracy, and with what justification? Can

certain individuals and groups be excluded in order to preserve democratic systems? How porous should the instituted boundaries of a democratic government be? In a world of multiple and overlapping identities, should CITIZENSHIP rights be confined to membership of singular 'nation-states', or extended across territorial boundaries?

A related set of problems arises from the theorisation of political frontiers presented above. If, following Laclau and Mouffe, one accepts the ontological centrality of antagonism and exclusion in the construction of political identities – indeed, if one predicates politics on such division and conflict – how is this to be reconciled with the demands and constraints of democratic governance? The difficulty is how to preserve the charge of conflict and the jostling contestation of identities within mutually acceptable rules of the democratic game. In this respect, theorists of agonistic democracy such as William Connolly and James Tully, drawing *inter alia* on the writings of Michel Foucault and Friederich Nietzsche, seek to transform antagonistic relations between mutually exclusive groups and identities into contestations that both acknowledge, respect and cultivate their differences without abandoning altogether the rules of liberal and pluralist democracy. In addition, they offer variety of strategies to displace the politics of exclusion and *ressentiment* into one of agonistic respect. They range from proposals to cultivate a new democratic ethos based on the recognition of the plurality and contingency of the postmodern world to new procedures for the establishment of constitutional and institutional forms.

See also:

agonism; hegemony; identity, political; inclusion/exclusion

Further reading

Bennington, G. (1994) *Legislations: The Politics of Deconstruction*, London: Verso.

Colley, L. (1996) *The Britons: Forging the Nation 1707–1837*, London: Vintage.

Derrida, J. (1997) *The Politics of Friendship*, London: Verso.

Gramsci, A. (1971) *Selections from Prison Notebooks*, London: Lawrence and Wishart.

Habermas, J. (1998) *The Inclusion of the Other: Studies in Political Theory*, Cambridge: MIT Press.

Howarth, D. (1997) 'Complexities of Identity/Difference: Black Consciousness Ideology in South Africa', *Journal of Political Ideologies* 2(1): 51–78.

Howarth, D, Norval, A.J. and Stavrakakis, Y. (eds) (2000) *Discourse Theory and Political Analysis: Identities, Hegemonies and Social Change*, Manchester: Manchester University Press.

Laclau, E. (1990) *New Reflections on the Revolution of our Time*, London: Verso.

Laclau, E. and Mouffe, C. (1985) *Hegemony and Socialist Strategy: Towards a Radical Democratic Politics*, London: Verso.

Mouffe, C. (1992) 'Feminism, Citizenship and Radical Democratic Politics', in J. Butler and J.W. Scott (eds), *Feminists Theorise the Political*, London: Routledge.

Norval, A.J. (1996) *Deconstructing Apartheid Discourse*, London: Verso.

—— (1997) 'Frontiers in Question', *Acta Philosophica* 2: 51–76.

Weale, A. (1996) *Democracy*, Basingstoke: Macmillan.

Wolin, S. (1996) 'Fugitive Democracy', in S. Benhabib (ed.), *Democracy and Difference. Contesting the Boundaries of the Political*, Princeton, NJ: Princeton University Press, 31–45.

DAVID HOWARTH
ALETTA NORVAL

political obligation

Broadly understood, political obligation concerns the specific obligations people have as members of a particular polity. The precise term 'political obligation' has little currency outside of academic political theory; and even there it appears to have been first used only in the late nineteenth century by the English philosopher T.H. Green (1986). The expression itself remains a term of art, but the issues it identifies have a longevity and centrality in political theory and practice which belie its recent origin.

There are three principal dimensions of political obligation. First, there is the object of the obligation: to whom or what is political obligation owed? Secondly, there is the content and extent of the obligation: to do what and how far is one obligated? Third, there is the justification of political obligation: why, or on what grounds, is one obligated? Answers to the first question, about to whom or what obligation is owed, largely reduce to one of four possibilities: directly to government, to the law, to the constitution, or to other members of the polity. The most common answer to the second question about the content of political obligation has been obedience to the law or the legitimate political AUTHORITY, although some have thought this specification too narrow. Most disagreement, however, has been about the limits of political obligation, and when, if ever, revolution, rebellion or CIVIL DISOBEDIENCE are permitted or required. The differing answers given to the first two questions are often explained by differing answers to the third question: the justification of political obligation. It is arguments about moral justification which, above all other aspects of political obligation, have been fundamental.

The 'problem of political obligation' has been a central question within political theory at least from the sixteenth century onwards, but concern with it can be identified as far back as Plato's dialogue, the *Crito*. There Socrates considers several reasons why it would be wrong for him to seek to escape imprisonment and avoid the death penalty to which he had been sentenced. In that remarkable short work can be found the seeds of many later arguments – social contract, consent, gratitude and fairness – about the grounds of political obligation. Subsequent theorising about political obligation prior to the seventeenth century is subtle and complex but, simplifying greatly, justification was mostly construed in naturalistic terms, often Aristotelian in inspiration, or theologically. In the post-classical period, theorising particularly concerned the relationship between spiritual and temporal authority, and included natural law theories (for example, Aquinas), proto-popular SOVEREIGNTY theories (for example, Marsilius), a rich array of arguments in terms of Biblical authority, and patriarchal theories (for example, Filmer).

It is in seventeenth-century Europe, especially in England, in circumstances of religious conflict and civil war, that the problem of political obligation came to dominate political theorising. The social contract theories of Thomas Hobbes and John Locke, conceived in a context of immense political instability, attempted to find a basis for legitimate political order in a country apparently on the edge of disintegration. The feature of such social contract theories which marked a distinct shift in thinking about political obligation that still continues to have enormous influence is the idea that if political authority is to be legitimate it must be created through an act of individual will on the part of those subject to it. In Hobbes's *Leviathan*, the social contract is a hypothetical agreement between people based on rational prudence, through which they can escape from a wretched state of nature by establishing an absolute political authority. This involves the renunciation of the natural right to whatever we want in return for the protection of an all-powerful sovereign. One is obligated to obey the sovereign, who is not party to the contract, whatever he commands, subject only to the residual right to protect one's own life.

Unsurprisingly, many thinkers regarded Hobbes's cure as worse than the disease it is supposed to remedy. Hence subsequent social contract thinking has been concerned to soften Hobbes's unpalatable defence of the absolute authority of the sovereign and the (almost) unlimited obligation of the subject. Locke, for instance, argues that political authority arises in two stages: first through a unanimous contract to form political society, and then by a majority decision to establish a government. Throughout this process people retain their natural rights to life, liberty and property which it is the purpose of government to uphold. The obligation to government is limited, and in some circumstances tyrannical governments may be legitimately resisted. Moreover Locke, in *Two Treatises of Government*, introduces the notion of consent as the explanation of the obligations of people not party to the supposed original contract. Later generations acquire their political obligations either through explicit expressions of allegiance or, more commonly, through 'tacit consent', given for instance when making use of property under the jurisdiction of the state.

Despite powerful criticism the social contract tradition remained vibrant, most notably in the work of Rousseau in *The Social Contract*. He gave the social contract a potentially radically democratic emphasis by locating the basis of political authority and, hence the source of political obligation, in the idea of a general will. Through this notion Rousseau presented political authority as the expression of a genuinely popular will embodying a collective interest shared by all citizens. Although Rousseau's own political ideals were essentially premodern, he foreshadows participatory conceptions of democratic authority and common good theories of political obligation. The latter in some respects marks a significant shift away from the assumptions of the social contract tradition; denying the importance of putative actions by subjects and placing the emphasis firmly on what governments do.

On this view, people have political obligations not because they contracted or consented but because of the benefits of government. One version of this view, utilitarianism, is most closely associated with Jeremy Bentham. In his account, the duty to obey a government obtains whenever the likely benefits of obedience are greater than the harms of disobedience. While modern utilitarian theories have become more sophisticated (Flathman 1972), what exactly is meant by benefits and harms, how they are determined and the best interpretation of the principle of utility have all been matters of continuing debate, both within utilitarianism and (along with other issues) between utilitarians and their critics. One persistent difficulty for utilitarianism is to explain why people have a particular obligation to their own government.

A very different version of this kind of approach is to be found in common good theories associated with thinkers like T.H. Green (1986). On Green's account, obligations are owed to a state when it provides the essential conditions for individuals to pursue their self-realisation. The concept of the common good reconciles the interests of the individual and the collectivity and therefore grounds political obligation in an individual's own interests. One difficulty here is giving acceptable content to the conception of the common good. A second is to do so in a way that renders convincing the claim that it serves everyone's interests. Green's own account, primarily in terms of a specific structure of social and political RIGHTS, inevitably rests on a controversial interpretation of those rights. More importantly, however, he fails to show that there can be no conflict between the common good on the one hand, and competing moral values and personal interests on the other. Generally, such theories are viewed with the suspicion that critics showed towards Rousseau's general will which, like the common good, is regarded as a sinister attempt to render the individual subservient to the collective.

The nineteenth century saw a flowering of views fundamentally antagonistic to all ideas of political obligation associated with the state or coercive political authority. Anarchism rejects the claims of any state to the obligations of its members. Whether in the strongly individualist form in which primacy is given to rights, or in the more social variants in which voluntary co-operation is natural and the only legitimate basis of social order, anarchism rejects the state and government as necessarily oppressive (Miller 1984). How far anarchists accept political obligations to other, non state-like entities varies and is often unclear: one of the persistent difficulties they face is the tendency for supposedly alternative forms of social organisation to acquire the coercive properties to which anarchists object. Moreover, the conception of human nature informing most anarchist theories is widely viewed as overly optimistic and the social forms advocated as unrealistic, at least under modern conditions.

Theorising about political obligation in modern liberal democratic societies mostly centres on its grounds and limits. Although various arguments have been deployed, including considerations of gratitude, neo-Aristotelian theories and attempts to utilise the techniques of rational choice theory, the two most widely canvassed approaches to finding a convincing moral justification of political obligation consistent with the basic values of liberal democracy are in terms of consent and of a principle of fairness. Much effort has also been directed towards the question of when it is morally legitimate to disobey the law, under the rubric of civil disobedience (Singer 1973). Many theorists, however, have concluded that there is no satisfactory moral justification of specifically political obligations; with some arguing further that this lack does not present any serious problems for liberal democracies.

Modern consent theory usually adopts one of two approaches. The first seeks in some institutional process the elusive sign of consent. The most popular candidate for this role is voting in democratic ELECTIONS. It is argued that voting in an election is an expression or sign of consent to accept the outcome (Plamenatz 1968). Of course this could only explain the political obligation of citizens who actually do vote, and the voluntary requirement would be undermined where voting is legally obligatory. Furthermore, even where voting is not compulsory, it remains doubtful that the conditions of genuine voluntariness really are met, given that most people have little realistic opportunity to exit their state. In any case, it appears quite possible for people to participate in elections in an instrumental spirit, without being morally bound by the outcome. It is not valid simply to infer from the fact that people vote in an election that they are therefore under any political obligations.

By contrast, the reformist version of consent theory concedes that existing states fail to meet the conditions for consent to be truly voluntary. However, on this view, liberal democratic states could be reformed to make genuinely voluntary consent possible. On a 'moderate' interpretation, the crucial requirements would be formal opportunities for people to accept or decline membership of a state; the legal right of emigration and, possibly, of secession; and the creation of a dissenter's territory for those who do not find any existing states acceptable (Beran 1987). These reforms would make for greater voluntariness, but they would entail much more far-reaching changes than their proponents admit. Additionally, it is unlikely that the dissenter's territory will be either a viable or attractive option for people united only by their refusal to consent to existing states. The 'radical' interpretation of this view accepts that wholesale social changes are necessary, including dramatic reductions in economic and social inequality, industrial democracy and a genuinely participatory political system (Pateman 1985). However, if these are the conditions for authentically consent based political obligations then it is difficult to see any realistic prospect of them coming about. More fundamentally, it is doubtful whether the model of a state as a voluntary association really is the most appropriate.

Justifications of political obligation in terms of a principle of fairness seek to show that it is an instance of a general requirement that people should contribute their share to supporting co-operative arrangements from which they receive worthwhile benefits. Failure to do so would make one a free rider. The key elements of this account are that the goods arising from a co-operative system must indeed be beneficial; must be worth the burdens of co-operation; and both the benefits and burdens should be fairly distributed (Klosko 1992). With regard to modern democratic states, two difficulties face this view. First, in the absence of any uncontroversial test it may be disputed whether overall benefits do outweigh burdens. Second, there is no widespread agreement about what is a fair distribution of the benefits and burdens. While the principle of fairness does explain obligations arising from some schemes of co-operation, it is questionable whether it can be convincingly applied to even a democratic state.

The perceived failure of attempts to justify political obligation has led some theorists to espouse philosophical anarchism. By contrast with political anarchism, this view denies only the moral authority of a state qua state, and hence of distinctively political obligations. It does not regard the state as necessarily evil or as something which must be opposed. In its strongest form this view maintains that the fundamental irreconcilability of political authority with personal AUTONOMY (except where decisions are unanimous) means that the former can never be morally justified. In its weaker form it is essentially a default position, the view we are left with once all justifications of political obligation have failed. It does not establish that political obligation cannot be justified; only that it has not been and, perhaps, is unlikely to be. On this view, although there are no distinctively political obligations, there may be other valid reasons to obey the law. Good laws should still be obeyed; but only because they are good, not because of a general political obligation (Simmons 1979).

While philosophical anarchism, the fairness theory and various attempts to reconstruct voluntarism, dominate current theorising about political obligation within liberal democracies, there has also emerged a rather different approach. This understands political obligations as essentially associative obligations, expressive of a shared political identity arising from membership of a community of fate rather than choice (Horton 1992). Whether this approach or one of the others can be satisfactorily developed remains to be seen. As yet, however, there is something of a theoretical impasse in discussions of political obligation. Moreover, if, as some GLOBALISATION theorists maintain, we are entering an era in which the state will no longer be the basic unit of political allegiance – a claim which is certainly controversial – then ideas about political obligation will also need to be significantly re-thought.

See also:

civic virtue; civil disobedience; individualism; legitimacy; moral improvement; public service; responsibilities; sovereignty

Further reading

Beran, H. (1987) *The Consent Theory of Political Obligation*, London: Croom Helm.

Flathman, R. (1972) *Political Obligation*, New York: Atheneum.

Green, T.H. (1986) *Lectures on the Principles of Political Obligation and Other Writings*, ed. P Harris and J. Morrow, Cambridge: Cambridge University Press.

Horton, J. (1992) *Political Obligation*, London: Macmillan.

Klosko, G. (1992) *The Principle of Fairness and Political Obligation*, Lanham, MD: Rowman and Littlefield.

Miller, D. (1984) *Anarchism*, London: Dent.

Pateman, C. (1985) *The Problem of Political Obligation: A Critique of Liberal Theory*, Oxford: Polity Press.

Plamenatz, J.P. (1968) *Consent, Freedom and Political Obligation*, Oxford: Oxford University Press.

Simmons, A.J. (1979) *Moral Principles and Political Obligations*, Princeton, NJ: Princeton University Press.

Singer, P. (1973) *Democracy and Disobedience*, Oxford: Oxford University Press.

JOHN HORTON

political order

> In politics, again, it is almost a common-place, that a party of order or stability, and a party of progress or reform, are both necessary elements of a healthy state of political life; until the one or the other shall have so enlarged its mental grasp as to be a party equally of order and of progress, knowing and distinguishing what is fit to be preserved from what ought to be swept away.
>
> (J.S. Mill, *On Liberty*, ch. 2)

Late in the fifteenth century, in the *Oration on the Dignity of Man*, Pico della Mirandola wrote that we must understand human beings as protean: they have no fixed form and repeatedly reinvent themselves and their world. Such a judgement marks the beginning of the modern understanding that humans are to be understood as constantly changing, constantly in motion. Such motility is cause for both celebration and concern. It is cause for celebration as it opens the door to unlimited achievement. On the other hand, if by definition nothing human is fixed, then the primary problem of politics is no longer what kind of life one should live in common with others, but one of establishing the possibility of living together at all. Hence the very motility that Pico and others celebrated in the early Renaissance gives the question of political order centre stage.

Machiavelli is the first great political thinker to make change the centre of his thought. His concern therefore is how to produce the appearance of stability in the midst of constant change. He writes in the preface to the *Discourses* that 'since human affairs are always in motion, either they rise or they fall. So a city or a region can be organised for well planned government...' One might think that Machiavelli's concerns (and those of other Renaissance humanists) were consequent to secularism. However, not only were Machiavelli's judgements themselves shaped by religious concerns (see de Grazia 1989) but they were paralleled by developments in the religious sphere. When Luther was interrogated on his ninety-five theses at the Diet of Worms, he chose famously to end his defence with the proclamation that he could do no other than he was doing, as it was never permissible to go against conscience. This claim, however, drew a sharp response from the interrogating secretary, who pointed out that if all stood on their conscience then collective order, and indeed the existence of a church itself, became impossible. While Luther sought a solution in a semi-separation of the social and the religious (see Wolin 1961: chaps 5–6), his legacy was to require that political society be founded on the FREEDOM and AUTONOMY of each of its members.

What the interrogating secretary recognised is that if one thought that society constituted by autonomous free individuals, choosing by themselves for themselves, all common values suddenly became contingent. What could then be the foundation for a church: how was order to be achieved? That a conflict of values was a fundamental quality of the modern age became the basis of the thought of social theorists as diverse as Max Weber, Isaiah Berlin and John Rawls. If, however, an irreconcilable conflict of values is the bedrock of human political and moral existence, then the achieving of some form of political order becomes the central political question.

Paradoxically then, political order is thought to be a problem when one finds human freedom to be central. Machiavelli's solution to this was to show that the condition of the populace should and could correspond to that of the prince: the estate of the prince was the state of the subjects (Hexter 1957: 113–38).

Machiavelli's approach to the problem of political order suffered, however, from over-reliance on the ability and will of political leaders. Should a prince be inadequate to the twists and turns of fortune, or, being mortal, should he perish at the wrong time, the wheel of fortune might come crashing down (Gilbert 1965, vol. 2: 747). Shakespeare brings these two flaws together in the 'to be or not to be' soliloquy in Hamlet (Strong 1981). It is only with Hobbes that the first truly modern solution to the problem of political order was elaborated.

In Chapter 13, para. 9 of the *Leviathan*, Hobbes paints a portrait of the state of nature as without coherence in either time or space. Famously, life there is made up of negatives, with:

> no place for industry, because the fruit thereof is uncertain, and consequently, no culture of the earth, no navigation, nor use of the commodities that may be imported by sea, no commodious building, no instruments of moving and removing such things as require much force, no knowledge of the face of the earth, no account of time, no arts, no letters, no society, and which is worst of all, continual fear and danger of violent death, and the life of man solitary, poor, nasty, brutish and short.

With this formulation, Hobbes shows that the problem of political order is in fact double. The first problem is to establish stability. The second problem derives from the recognition that stability will only be attainable when it appears to be to the advantage of each. Machiavelli's prince depended on an unsure combination of fear and love on the part of the populace. Hobbes seeks to show that order can in fact be in each individual's interest. If one represents the state of nature as a prisoner's dilemma game, one finds that in the state of nature the *prima facie* rational choice that each player makes – the attempt to minimise personal danger – leads to a collective situation in which each is worse off then they were before interaction with others. We are thus faced with not simply a problem of creating order but of creating an order that is to the advantage of each.

Hobbes's solution to this second problem involves an elaboration of a theory of repre-sentation. In Chapter 16 of *Leviathan*, each individual is to participate in the creation of an 'artificial person', the sum of whose actions will be determined by the covenant that creates him (or it). This artificial person – the sovereign – can only act in our interest since it is our interest in avoiding the state of nature that creates him. Being artificial, the sovereign has no will of his own, no possessions (and thus no interests) of his own, and is not subject to the dangers of mortality. (In Chapter 24, Hobbes notes that when William the Conqueror reserved certain lands for his own hunting forays, he did so 'not in his public . . . but in his natural capacity'.)

Hobbes's solution has been criticised for attributing too much power to the central authority, or producing order at the expense of right and liberty. This is, however, misleading. In fact, Hobbes gives us a theory that allows and encourages most individuals to avoid political engagement and to attend to their own private pursuits. For Hobbes, the Leviathan was minimal because it was our own.

All liberal approaches to political order are in debt to Hobbes. In the centuries that followed his writing, his insights were elaborated by joining them to a theory of constitution that originated in the early middle ages. The Hobbesian understanding of political order slowly came to shape the question of CONSTITUTIONALISM. In the period loosely from Hobbes to Hume, constitution tends to retain the sense of the natural shape order that a given entity has. Thus Locke in the *Second Treatise on Government* (II, vii, 86) will think to differentiate the 'constitution of a family from that of a commonwealth' and Hume in *A Treatise of Human Nature* (Book II, I, 5) will refer to the 'constitution of the mind'. Hobbes had spoken, however, of the 'constitution of sovereign power' (*Leviathan,* II, 18), leaving ambiguous whether he was referring to the making of sovereign power or the quality that such power must have. It is with Rousseau that the making quality comes to the front and the question of political order becomes joined with that of a constitution.

In the preface to his play *Narcisse*, Rousseau suggests that in 'un état bien constitué' – a well-constituted state – each citizen will have tasks to fulfil. (Tellingly, Maurizio Viroli (1986) gives this as a 'well-ordered society'.) In the *Social Contract*, Rousseau sets out what human beings have to do to constitute themselves as a human society (see Affeldt 1999). His claim is that most, if not all, social orders are not the result of reasoned human choice but of accidents and frauds that have been regularised as necessary. Rousseau formulates the conditions of a human society as a problem: 'Find a form of association in which each defends with all the common force the person and goods of each associate and by which each person in joining him or herself to all nevertheless obeys

only him or herself and remains as free as before' (*Social Contract*, Bk 1, ch. 6).

Here political order and a just constitution are co-terminously defined as obedience to oneself when and only when the rule one gives oneself is the same as each gives himself or herself. Rousseau makes the legislating individual the basis of political order when, and only when, the imperatives one gives to oneself are the same as those that each gives. Rousseau refers to the self which so acts as the 'common self', and he means by that action on the basis of the way in which each person is, as human (see Strong 1994: chaps 2–3), exactly the same as each other.

We may think of this as a secularisation of Calvin's argument about religious belief. Rousseau's argument reconceptualises the problem of political order along two dimensions. First, since what is important is that the choices made be the same in each, a proper *procedure* becomes central. Secondly, since what is important is that each individual choose, what becomes important is the element of decision. Kant was to develop a moral philosophy based upon the combination of both of these elements: the development of a *political* philosophy proved more difficult.

In the political realm, the combination of procedure and substance proved difficult to maintain. Over the course of the nineteenth and twentieth centuries, thinking about political order develops separately along each of these dimensions. In turn, this opens a space for a critique of the very idea of political order. We may first identify the two poles.

The first pole derives from thought that starts from Rousseau and Kant and then passes selectively through Hegel and Sidgwick, culminating in John Rawls. In *A Theory of Justice*, Rawls sets the problem of a 'well-ordered society'. (Rawls derives the idea of a social union from Hegel and that of equality of opportunity from Sidgwick.) Justice, he writes, is about 'the basic structure of society, or, more exactly, the way in which the major social institutions distribute fundamental rights and duties and determine the division of advantages from social co-operation' (1971: 7). Rawls argues that individuals choosing from behind a 'veil of ignorance' (1971: 136ff) will choose two principles of JUSTICE. When behind the veil, individuals do not know their place in society, their CLASS or status position, their race, sex and religion, their natural assets, their intelligence or their conception of the good. They *do* know that society has or will have institutions such as those familiar to us in the West, that they will need a conception of justice, that they will prefer to have more rather than less of what there may be to have, and they have some basic knowledge of political affairs and economic theory.

Given these conditions, Rawls argues that, given shared ideas of reasonableness (themselves historically acquired), individuals will rationally choose, first, that each person have a right to an adequate scheme of basic RIGHTS and liberties that is compatible with a similar scheme for all and, second, that any inequalities must both be attached to offices and positions open to all under conditions of equal opportunity and must work to the benefit of the least advantaged members of society.

Rawls's elaboration of a well-ordered society thus rests on the delineation of conditions that must pertain to *allow* rationality to be the basis of social order. Order is here achieved in a manner that is apparently fundamentally separate from conflict. Rawls has resolved the problem of incompatible values by confining to a private, non-political realm all that is not susceptible to rational choice in the public realm.

The second pole draws upon the decisionist and volitional elements in Hobbes and Rousseau, passes, again selectively, through Hegel, Nietzsche and Weber to appear most famously in Carl Schmitt's *The Concept of the Political* (1938). If the problem of political order is a problem of the political, Schmitt inquires into what the qualities of the political are. We are, according to Schmitt, in confrontation with 'the political' when the situation calls for a distinction between friends and enemies. The essence of political order consists in a correct alignment of friends and enemies (Schmitt 1996: 37). What distresses him is that the

historical conjunction of LIBERALISM and politics has obscured this conception such that we are in danger of losing the experience of the political. He dates this loss loosely from the French revolution but finds elements of it already present in seventeenth-century doctrines such as those of Cardinal Bellarmine, whose theory of indirect powers Hobbes was tellingly at pains to refute in the chapter forty-one of *Leviathan* (see foreword to Schmitt 1996).

Instead of procedure, Schmitt found conflict and struggle. Solutions to political problems must be decisive and not matters for compromise. The enemy is liberalism. If a liberal is a person who cannot take his own side in an argument, he is also a person who, as Schmitt notes, if asked 'Christ or Barrabas' responds with a 'proposal to adjourn or appoint a committee of investigation' (Schmitt 1985: 62). Here the achievement of political order rests on a necessity for choice. Order consists in determining that which stands with us and that which is not of us. Such a resolution cannot be made on the basis of a procedural choice for there is no common measure. As Max Weber wrote in *Politics as a Vocation*: 'We are placed into different life spheres, each of which is governed by different laws' (1958: 123). Given such an historical-existential condition, Schmitt and Weber argue that political order requires first and foremost that one accept responsibility for one's choices. One is what one chooses to be: the attainment of political order is here identical to the establishment of identity.

Both of these perspectives capture something important about the attainment of political order. In recent years, the primacy of political order as a goal has come under question, often by thinkers who realise that the two poles of procedures and choice are not incompatible. Michel Foucault argued that the consolidation of power and knowledge in the modern state *produced* rationality as the central quality of that state (Foucault 1988: 73ff). Rather than being irrational or non-rational (as in Schmitt's conception of the political) or resting on rationality (as with Rawls), political order combines the choice of power and rationality.

In this understanding, the only move against the modern state is, as William Connolly has written (1991: 159ff), to 'politicise the ambiguity in human being'. The ambiguity is obscured and made unavailable, Connolly continues, by the association of order with the constitutional structure of the modern state. He has in mind such matters as 'the appeals to national interest or national security, the immunisation of state officials from ordinary procedures of law and penalty, and the routine classification of state documents otherwise susceptible to publicity and accountability' (Connolly 1991: 202).

With this we have come back to the starting point. If the modern problematic of political order is initiated by the need to deal with value PLURALISM, positions such as those of Foucault and Connolly hold that that pluralism is precisely to be upheld and encouraged, even if that means celebrating ambiguity and conflict. How far this goes is hard to say. Connolly defends 'agonistic respect'. We are back here to a pre-modern (though not therefore undesirable) conception of order such as that found in Homer. The difficulty is that (as these thinkers do know) Homer was no democrat. The problem of political order thus forces us to rethink the meaning of democracy.

See also:

agonism; civic virtue; moral improvement; responsibilities

Further reading

Affeldt, S. (1999) 'The Force of Freedom: Rousseau on Forcing to be Free', *Political Theory*, June: 299–333.

Connolly, W. (1991) *Identity/Difference*, Cornell: Cornell University Press.

De Grazia, S. (1989) *Machiavelli in Hell*, Princeton, NJ: Princeton University Press.

Foucault, M. (1988) 'Politics and Reason', in L.D. Kritzman (ed.), *Michel Foucault: Inter-*
views and Other Writings, New York: Routledge.

Gilbert, A. (1965) *Machiavelli: The Chief Works and Others*, Durham, NC: Duke University Press.

Hexter, J.H. (1957) 'Il principe et lo stato', *Studies in the Renaissance* 4: 113–38.

Rawls, J. (1971) *A Theory of Justice*, Cambridge, MA: Harvard University Press.

Schmitt, C. (1985) *The Crisis of Parliamentary Democracy*, Cambridge, MA: MIT Press.

—— (1996) *The Concept of the Political*, Chicago: Chicago University Press.

Strong, T. (1981) 'Shakespeare: Elizabethan Statecraft and Machiavellianism', in B. Barber and M. McGrath (eds) *The Artist and Political Vision*, New Brunswick, NJ: Transaction Books, 193–220.

—— (1994) *Jean-Jacques Rousseau and the Politics of the Ordinary*, Thousand Oaks, CA: Sage.

Viroli, M. (1986) *Jean-Jacques Rousseau and the Well-Ordered Society*, Cambridge: Cambridge University Press.

Weber, M. (1958) 'Politics as a Vocation', in H. Gerth and C.W. Mills (eds), *From Max Weber*, Oxford: Oxford University Press.

Wolin, S. (1961) *Politics and Vision*, Boston: Little, Brown.

TRACY B. STRONG

polyarchy

The term 'polyarchy' or 'polyarchal democracy' refers to the processes and institutions of representative democracy in a large-scale political unit (typically a nation-state or country) where most adults are entitled to the right to vote and possess other basic RIGHTS necessary to effective political PARTICIPATION. The term, rarely used before 1953, was deliberately reintroduced into the vocabulary of political science by Robert A. Dahl and Charles E. Lindblom in *Politics, Economics, and Welfare* (1963).

As a type of democracy, polyarchy is unique because its political institutions, *taken as a whole*, distinguish it from earlier democracies and republics such as the Athenian democracy and the republics of medieval and Renaissance Italy. Although some of the political institutions of polyarchy emerged in several countries during the nineteenth century or earlier, until the twentieth century universal adult SUFFRAGE had existed only in New Zealand. Consequently, as a form of democracy polyarchy is essentially a creation of the twentieth century.

The political institutions of polyarchy

At the most general level, polyarchy is a political order marked by two broad characteristics: CITIZENSHIP is extended to most adults, and the rights of citizenship include the opportunity to oppose and vote out the highest officials in the government of the state. The first characteristic distinguishes polyarchy from more exclusive systems of rule in which, though opposition is permitted, governments and their legal oppositions are restricted to a small group, as was the case in Britain, Belgium, Italy and other countries before mass suffrage was introduced. The second characteristic distinguishes polyarchy from authoritarian regimes in which, though most adults are citizens, citizenship does not include the right to oppose and vote out the government.

More specifically, polyarchy is a political order identifiable by the presence of seven political institutions, *all* of which must be present:

1 Control over government decisions about policy is constitutionally vested in *elected officials*.
2 Elected officials are chosen in frequent and fairly conducted ELECTIONS in which COERCION is comparatively uncommon.
3 Practically all adults have the *right to vote* in the election of officials. As mentioned, the inclusiveness of polyarchies is a twentieth-century practice. Even in countries where the other institutions of polyarchy were mainly in place, women were denied the franchise. In many male polyarchies, restrictions based on property or EDUCATION also deprived

some men of the vote. The first country to grant women the suffrage in national elections was New Zealand (then a British colony) in 1893. Many more countries enacted universal adult suffrage during the first three decades of the twentieth century, though France and Belgium continued to deny women the franchise in national elections until after the Second World War and Switzerland did not guarantee the vote to all women until 1971. In the United States, most blacks were prevented from participating in politics in many southern states until civil rights legislation was passed and enforced in the 1960s.
4 *Right to run for office.* Practically all adults have the right to run for elective offices in the government, though age limits may be higher for holding office than for the suffrage.
5 *Freedom of expression.* Citizens have the right to express themselves, without the danger of severe punishment, on political matters broadly defined, including criticism of officials, the government, the regime, the socioeconomic order, and the prevailing ideology.
6 *Alternative information.* Citizens have a right to seek out alternative sources of information. Moreover, alternative sources of information exist that are not under the control of the government and are protected by laws guaranteeing freedom of expression, as just mentioned.
7 *Associational autonomy.* To achieve their rights, including those listed above, citizens also have a right to form relatively independent associations or organisations, including independent political parties and INTEREST GROUPS.

These seven institutions insure that governments will follow certain fundamental procedures; thus polyarchy is sometimes referred to as PROCEDURAL DEMOCRACY. More than that, however, they guarantee a very broad set of rights that are necessary to each of the institutions; to this extent, then, polyarchy is also a form of substantive democracy.

These statements characterise actual and not merely nominal rights, institutions and processes. With some amplification they can be specified concretely enough, as research has shown, to permit independent observers to rank most countries according to the extent to which each of the institutions of polyarchy is present, in a realistic sense. The rankings can be combined to provide a measure, or scale, of polyarchy that runs from the extreme authoritarian end of the scale, at which none of the institutions exist, to the opposite end at which all of them exist; that is, countries with a polyarchal form of government. Measuring polyarchy in this way is useful in several ways. Among other things, the rankings can be used to investigate the conditions that generally favour or harm the chances for the development and stability of polyarchy in a country.

Democracy and polyarchy

Polyarchy, as defined above, is thus a distinctive form of government. But it is more than just a form of government, it is also a form of democracy, probably the most important and certainly the most widespread form that democracy has taken during its long and fitful history in ideas and practices.

What then is the relationship between polyarchy and democracy? Although many people today who are accustomed to the institutions of polyarchy might say that polyarchy and democracy are identical, there are good reasons for viewing polyarchy as only one form that democracy can take.

In earlier times, and even in the twentieth century, political systems have existed which lack some of the institutions of polyarchy and yet appear to be just as 'democratic' as polyarchies, if not more so. After all, the word democracy was first used in classical antiquity as a name for systems of popular rule that the Greeks introduced in many of their city states, as they did, for example, in Athens around 500 BC (see DEMOCRATIC ORIGINS). To deny the term democracy to its inventors would be an abuse of language. Moreover, we have no hesitation today in calling associations 'demo-cratic' even though they lack some of the institutions of polyarchy: for example, we may judge a committee, a club, a trade union, or some other association to be highly democratic though it does not contain within it smaller autonomous associations like political parties (see ASSOCIATIONAL DEMOCRACY). We can reasonably conceive of 'democracy', then, as something other than 'polyarchy'. A further reason for treating polyarchy as only one historical form of democracy is that we can readily imagine that a specific polyarchal government – that of Italy, say, or the United States – could be *more* democratic than it is.

What these and other implicit conceptions of democracy seem to have in common is a vision of a body of persons governing themselves as political equals, a DEMOS ruling itself, an association making collective decisions that its members are obligated to obey: in short, citizens governing themselves through a *democratic process*. In the sense implied by such a vision of human possibilities, what criteria would a fully democratic process have to meet? Five criteria appear to be necessary and sufficient for a fully democratic process of government among political equals. In a somewhat simplified listing, they are:

1 *Effective participation*. When a fully democratic political system makes decisions that are obligatory for its citizens, the citizens should have an adequate opportunity, and an equal opportunity, for expressing their preferences as to what the final decision should be. They ought to have adequate and equal opportunities for placing questions on the agenda and for expressing reasons for endorsing one outcome rather than another.
2 *Voting equality*. When collective decisions are made in a fully democratic political system, each citizen ought to be offered an equal opportunity to express a choice – to cast a vote – that will be counted as equal to the vote of any other citizen.
3 *Opportunities for enlightened understanding*. Each citizen should have adequate and equal opportunities for discovering which of the possible choices on the matter to be decided

would best serve the goals, values or interests of the citizen, of others, and of the collectivity.

4 *Final control of the agenda.* The citizens should have the exclusive opportunity to decide what matters are to be placed on the agenda of questions that are to be decided according to the three previous criteria.

5 *Inclusive citizenship.* The citizen body should include all adult members of the association with the possible exceptions of short-term transients, such as tourists and persons who are severely handicapped in their learning abilities. As mentioned, this criterion is strictly a product of twentieth-century thinking about citizenship and democracy. Until then, inclusive citizenship was not only rejected in practice, as we have seen, but in democratic and republican ideas and ideals as well.

These criteria prescribe an *ideal* government among politically equal citizens, an ideal of which all actual democracies have fallen short. Thus they suggest a question for which settled answers have not yet appeared: can polyarchal democracies be made *more* democratic and if so, how?

See also:

associational democracy; citizenship; decision-making; interest groups; participation; procedural democracy

Further reading

Dahl, R.A. (1971) *Polyarchy: Participation and Opposition*, New Haven, CT: Yale University Press.
Dahl, R.A. and Lindblom, C.E. (1963) *Politics, Economics, and Welfare*, New York: Harper and Row.

ROBERT DAHL

populism

There is little agreement on the meaning of this term or on the significance for democracy of the phenomena to which it refers. Often used to stigmatise demagoguery or crude MAJORITARIANISM, it has more favourable connotations for some theorists of grassroots PARTICIPATION in politics. It may be provisionally defined as an appeal to 'the people', variously understood, against the established structure of power and the dominant ideas and values within a polity that is formally democratic.

Origins

The term came into common use in the USA in the 1890s to describe the principles and activities of the People's Party, which had emerged out of rural discontent in the West and South of the republic. After attracting enough support to cause alarm in the established PARTIES, the movement faded away, leaving behind a complex legacy. Several aspects of this paradigm case of populism are related to the diverse later uses of the term. Contrary to traditional assumptions about left and right in politics, this was a radical movement with an overwhelmingly rural constituency, but with a platform calling for government intervention in economic affairs, notably for inflation of the currency. Its political style was revivalist and crusading, featuring grassroots campaigning by inflammatory orators. Above all, it made its appeal to the people: not, that is, to a specific CLASS or interest, but to the ultimate political authority of the United States, promising to restore to 'the plain people' the power stolen from them by party politicians and plutocrats on Wall Street. Subsequent uses of the term 'populism' vary widely, having tenuous connections with one or another of these aspects.

For many analysts 'populism' became a convenient general term to cover any kind of radicalism based on or aimed at rural rather than urban populations. This usage owes something to the translation as 'populist' of the Russian *narodnik*, the title given in the late nineteenth century to radical intellectuals who idealised the Russian peasantry, and who went 'to the people' in the 1870s in the vain hope of setting off revolution at the grassroots. There have subsequently been many cases of radical or revolutionary movements based on rural constituencies, whether peasants or farmers, and these have been lumped together and explained as responses to the stresses of modernisation on the part of populations in peripheral or underdeveloped areas. Within that predominantly sociological literature connections between populism and democracy have not been much considered.

A separate tradition of analysis identifies as 'populist' phenomena that represent threats to democracy arising perversely out of the political EMANCIPATION of the masses. Populism seen in this light may subvert democracy by generating charismatic dictatorship, or may distort it into a tyranny of the reactionary majority. Students of Latin American politics use the term to refer to the recurrent phenomenon of a manipulative movement directed by a charismatic leader who mobilises recently urbanised masses with promises of inflationary public spending, seasoned by rhetorical attacks on the power of the local elite and of foreign corporations (Di Tella 1997). Populism, in this sense, recalls the ancient demagoguery that made Greek and Roman democracy seem a short cut to tyranny. The themes of inflationary economics and inflammatory rhetoric are close enough to some aspects of US populism to have allowed hostile critics to cast doubt on the latter's democratic credentials (Shils 1956).

Populism versus liberalism

More sympathetic historians have pointed out that the American populists of the 1890s were not uprooted peasants and were not drawn into politics by a charismatic leader. Instead, as citizens of a country where 'We, the People' form the AUTHORITY on which the constitution is based, their aim was to regain popular control over political power. Populism in this sense means power in the hands of the electorate, to be exercised directly by voting in REFERENDUMS triggered by popular initiative. Devices of this sort, which were advocated by the People's Party and introduced in a number of American states under Populist

influence, are generally known within the literature of political science as 'DIRECT DEMOCRACY' (Budge 1996), terminology which seems to imply that in this respect the populist cause is the cause of democracy.

But this equation of democracy with unmediated electoral decision has been challenged by many theorists. Robert Dahl criticised 'populistic democracy' for offering a model of political EQUALITY, popular SOVEREIGNTY and majority rule that was too simple to have much application to the real world of politics (Dahl 1956). William Riker used social choice theory to show that (because of incoherence in the aggregation of preferences) the process of voting can never deliver a verdict recognisable as the collective will of the sovereign people. Since we can never know what the people as a whole actually want, populism as a programme for government is empty and voting makes sense only on the negative, 'liberal' account, as an opportunity to reject candidates who have offended too many of the electorate. Once the illusions of populism are dispelled, in other words, all democracy can actually mean in practice is that officials (not the people) rule, subject to periodic electoral veto. Though vacuous, the populist ideal of popular sovereignty seemed to Riker to be dangerous because as long as it is believed it helps rulers armed with what is believed to be a popular mandate to erode constitutional limits on their power (Riker 1982).

Most contemporary democratic theory stresses the open and discursive nature of democratic politics rather than popular will and decision. For theorists of DELIBERATIVE DEMOCRACY, unconsidered individual opinions of the sort counted in referendums form the starting point of the democratic process rather than its conclusion, and need to be refined and transformed through deliberation into contributions to a rational consensus. Others stress democratic diversity and mutual tolerance against what is seen as the monolithic model of popular sovereignty, which poses dangers to unpopular MINORITIES.

Long-standing liberal fears of the tyranny of the majority have been fuelled by recurrent episodes in many democratic countries of 'populism' in a further sense: grassroots mobilisation in defence of what are seen as reactionary causes. The liberal dilemma is that democratic SUFFRAGE gives votes to the ignorant and prejudiced as well as to those who feel themselves to be in the vanguard of humane enlightenment. Western democracies are characteristically dominated by a large educated political class, subscribing to a liberal consensus that is not shared by less articulate sections of the population. Topics that highlight this ideological gap include race and nationalism, immigration, law and order, gender and sexuality, offering opportunities for the political mobilisation of 'ordinary people' against the establishment. Movements identified as 'populist' in Western democracies are usually of this kind, challenging the established parties and the elite consensus in the name of the democratic people. Clustered round some individual leader, such movements rise and fall quite rapidly, though some (like the French *Front Nationale*) may manage to become more long-lasting features of the political landscape.

These populist movements regularly call for voters to be allowed to determine policy on issues close to their hearts through wider use of popular initiative and referendum, complicating debates about the virtues and dangers of direct democracy. Advocates of these methods argue that their adoption is a logical extension of universal suffrage in the new context of opportunities offered by INFORMATION technology. They also point out that to object on the grounds that most voters are ill-qualified to judge is in effect to argue against democracy as such (Budge 1996). One way of answering this challenge is to develop more elaborate ways of consulting the electorate, such as 'deliberative opinion polls' or 'CITIZENS' JURIES' which allow a representative sample of citizens to arrive at their conclusion after hearing and discussing evidence, making them representative of what the people would want if they were better informed (Fishkin 1991). Schemes of this kind may be seen either as constructive solutions to the problems posed by populism, or else (from a populist point of view) as devices to keep power away from the grassroots

by making sure that voters deliver the politically correct verdict.

Populism as participatory democracy

Debates about the interpretation of populism in general, and of US populism in particular, have always reflected changes in the prevailing political climate and intellectual mood. Just as fear of McCarthyism in the USA in the 1950s and of popular hostility to immigration in Western Europe in the 1990s have at different times given populism a bad name, so the radical upsurge of the 1960s prompted a different view, particularly in the USA. The intellectual generation inspired by the Civil Rights Movement and the anti-Vietnam War demonstrations sympathised with most cases of grassroots political mobilisation, and from their point of view the emergence of the People's Party could be seen as a classic case of participatory democracy in action, an illustration of the way in which apparently helpless people can join together to generate political power, at least for a time. A study by Lawrence Goodwyn (who later studied the emergence of the Solidarity movement in Poland from a similar perspective) combined historical reinterpretation with theoretical analysis of grassroots democracy. Populism seen from this angle appears not as a betrayal or deformation of democracy, but as its practical realisation, promising power and dignity to the helpless and despised (Goodwyn 1976).

A similar analysis of populism as a general phenomenon was generated in the 1990s by post-Marxist intellectuals gathered around the journal *Telos*. In a move perhaps reminiscent of the Russian *narodniks*' pilgrimage to the people a century earlier, populism was theorised as a democratic alternative to rule by the 'New Class', the centralising elite of liberal intellectuals and policy makers who had high-handedly imposed supposedly enlightened policies toward race, crime and other issues upon the less articulate masses without allowing them any say in matters that directly affected them, and had dismissed as 'populist' all consequent protests. Drawing on postmodern scepticism toward belief in progress and universal values, *Telos* in 1991 defended the view that genuine (populist) democracy means the devolution of real power to local communities, and challenged democrats to allow such communities to work out their own solutions to problems that directly affected them, even if they adopted policies that contravened the norms of the liberal elite.

Populism and democratic theory

Despite the occasional venture by intellectuals into its territory, populism in general cannot profitably be treated as a theory or an ideology. Since the only feature common to all the phenomena variously recognised as 'populist' is an appeal to 'the people', there is scope instead for the analysis of populism as a discourse available to many different groups who find themselves in opposition to the power-holders and dominant intellectual consensus of a society, especially a society formally committed to democracy (Kazin 1995). But this discourse does raise some important issues for democratic theory, precisely because it shines a spotlight on democracy's central symbol, the sovereign people. Several regular features of the populist appeal to the people are worthy of note.

Firstly, this appeal is a characteristically integrative claim to stand for a united people rather than for a specific class, a special interest or a mere collection of individuals. The people feature in the populist imagination as a collective body with a common (public) interest, in common possession of the polity. Secondly, the manner in which the people are invoked is exclusive, characterised by a strong sense of the BOUNDARIES between 'our people' and others (see INCLUSION/EXCLUSION). Two boundaries in particular figure largely in populist rhetoric, that between the people and outsiders (often foreigners or immigrants) and that between 'ordinary people' and the elite. Thirdly, populist invocations of the people rely upon an unreflective faith in the symbols of democracy. Manipulative use of such rhetoric is made possible by the existence of authentic democratic faith. Resisting the temptation to ignore populist discourse as unworthy of consideration, democratic theorists might reflect on its implications, of which three stand out.

The first concerns the presuppositions of democracy. Theorists critical of notions such as the sovereign people argue that these can refer to nothing other than perpetually contending alliances within the open arena that is democracy. Democratic politics cannot even begin, however, unless that arena is defined by boundaries, and it is unlikely to function for long unless the polity enclosed by those boundaries contains a population with enough belief in their lasting collective identity to be able to recognise the polity as theirs and to be bound by the commitments made in their name. The political significance of collective identity is underlined by studies of the barriers to democracy in divided societies, and the ingenuity and commitment to consociational arrangements needed to have any chance of overcoming them (see CONSOCIATIONALISM). Despite their naivety, therefore, populist invocations of the people as a collective body point to an important issue overlooked by democratic theories that take for granted the existence of bounded and stable polities.

Besides directing attention to the hidden foundations of democracy, populism also confronts theorists with a paradox, which is that democracy as conceived by its analysts is far too sophisticated to be understood by most of its citizens. Although political equality and inclusion in political participation remain fundamental principles, there is a wide gulf between the terms in which democracy is theorised and the discourse in which democratic politics is actually carried on. Debates about rational choice, deliberation, AGONISM and presence soar above the heads of politicians and electorate, who continue in their unself-conscious use of the old discourse of 'government by the people', 'majority rule', 'the popular mandate' and so on. Perhaps this should be seen as a further illustration of persistent ambiguities within a liberal democratic elite torn between commitment to political equality and fear of its outcome, ambiguities that can themselves provoke populist reactions on the part of voters treated with disrespect.

The suspicion that democracy is beyond the understanding of most of those supposed to be empowered by it is linked with a further observation prompted by populism, which concerns the significance of democratic faith. Like many political phenomena, modern democratic practice can be analysed as an uneasy mixture of the politics of faith and the politics of scepticism (Oakeshott 1996). In pragmatic, sceptical terms, democracy is above all a political alternative to repression and civil war in conditions of mass mobilisation, offering institutions and practices that allocate power peacefully despite conflicting interests and views. But it is doubtful whether such institutions could work in practice without the LEGITIMACY conferred by democratic faith: faith in salvation through popular power, and particularly in the brave new world to be found on the other side of electoral victory. Without this energising belief that we, the people, can act to make a better world by taking part in the ritual of elections, democratic practices easily fall prey to cynicism and corruption and cease to perform their pragmatic function. But if faith is needed to lubricate the machinery of democracy, then the continuing use of the incantatory discourse of popular sovereignty must be seen as a structural feature, not as a temporary concession to the ignorance of the electorate.

It follows that democratic politics cannot avoid raising expectations that it cannot fulfil. Populations must believe that democratic institutions will empower them and express their will, and must inexorably continue to be disappointed, offering scope for mobilisation by populists better placed than established politicians to make use of the redemptive discourse of popular sovereignty.

Conclusion

Populism has been seen by its supporters as authentic democratic participation, and by its more numerous critics as an infantile disease characteristic of unmodernised societies and immature democracies, to be cured by further doses of development and education. But if populism springs from tensions inherent in democratic practice, and if its characteristic discourse is one that democratic politics cannot do without, then it seems likely to persist as long as democracy itself.

See also:

citizens' juries; empowerment; majoritarianism; referendums

Further reading

Budge, I. (1996) *The New Challenge of Direct Democracy*, Cambridge: Polity.

Butler, D. and Ranney, A. (eds) (1994) *Referendums Around the World*, Houndmills: Macmillan.

Canovan, M. (1981) *Populism*, New York: Harcourt Brace Jovanovich.

—— (1999) 'Trust the People! Populism and the Two Faces of Democracy', *Political Studies* 47(1): 2–16.

Dahl, R.A. (1956) *A Preface to Democratic Theory*, Chicago: University of Chicago Press.

Di Tella, T.S. (1997) 'Populism into the Twenty-First Century', *Government and Opposition* 32: 187–200.

Fishkin, J. (1991) *Democracy and Deliberation*, New Haven, CT: Yale University Press.

Goodwyn, L. (1976) *Democratic Promise: The Populist Moment in America*, New York: Oxford University Press.

Kazin, M. (1995) *The Populist Persuasion*, New York: Basic Books.

Oakeshott, M. (1996) *The Politics of Faith and the Politics of Scepticism*, New Haven: Yale University Press.

Riker, W.H. (1982) *Liberalism Against Populism*, San Francisco: Freeman.

Shils, E. (1956) *The Torment of Secrecy*, London: Heinemann.

MARGARET CANOVAN

presidentialism

Presidentialism is a type of democratic regime in which a popularly elected official, the president, performs executive functions. Often the term refers narrowly to a specific type of regime with an elected president, while other times the term is applied more broadly. When applied narrowly, and sometimes modified as 'pure presidentialism', it refers to the political regime used in the United States, most Latin American countries, and some countries elsewhere in which the president simultaneously holds the constitutional positions of head of state and head of government. When applied more broadly, it refers to any system in which an elected president is at least head of state, although typically with some constitutional powers that make the president more than a mere figurehead. In either its narrow or its broad definition, presidentialism is taken to be distinct from the other primary democratic regime type, parliamentarism (see PARLIAMEN-TARY MODELS).

Constitutions are commonly divided into two broad categories: presidential and parliamentary. That dichotomy, however, defines only one of four variables that affect formal executive–legislative relations: cabinet AC-COUNTABILITY to either the parliamentary majority or to a popularly elected president. The other variables are whether there is a popularly elected president (even if that person is not the head of government), whether terms of office for the president (if any) and assembly are fixed, and whether a presidency functions as a 'veto gate', meaning that its consent is required to pass laws.

A 'pure' parliamentary system has a cabinet accountable to the assembly majority, no president or one who is neither popularly elected nor more than ceremonial, no fixed term for the executive (because of the possibility of votes of no confidence and often the possibility of early dissolution of the assembly), and no 'veto gate' besides the lower (or sole) house of parliament (meaning no other actor whose consent is required to pass laws).

A 'pure' presidential system combines a cabinet accountable to a president who is popularly elected, sits for a fixed term, cannot dissolve the legislature and usually holds veto power or other legislative authority that makes the president a player in shaping legislation. Thus, presidentialism, in its pure type, provides for both full separation of origin (through separate ELECTIONS) and separation of survival (through fixed terms). It is often defined alternatively as a SEPARATION OF POWERS system, but such a term is somewhat misleading, for the two branches share powers over legislative formation through the president's veto (and, sometimes, decree) power.

When the term, presidentialism, is applied more broadly than just to the pure type it encompasses a number of hybrid regimes that combine a popularly elected presidency with a cabinet that is accountable, fully or partially, to the assembly majority. These regimes are often called semi-presidential, although that term too encompasses a range of regime types that differ from one another, as well as from pure presidential, in significant ways.

Origins of presidentialism

The earliest regime that would be identified as presidential was the one that was devised by the Founding Fathers of the American Constitution of 1789. While the American Constitution was the first to define a republican executive with separate origin and survival, the original document did not clearly define a regime that would meet the definition of presidentialism given above. The President was to be elected by an Electoral College made up of electors chosen by each state, and not necessarily via popular election in the state. The founders did not foresee the day when presidential candidates would be supported by political parties with national scope such that the selection of electors would generally reflect popular preferences over competing presidential candidates; rather, they foresaw a large number of presidential candidates being promoted by various regional factions. If no candidate received a majority in the Electoral

College, it would fall to the House of Representatives to make the final selection of the president, thereby violating the criterion of separate origin. However, the House has selected the President in the absence of a majority in the Electoral College only twice in US history, most recently in 1824. The early emergence of national political parties ensured that the procedure for choosing the president was *de facto* a popular election, albeit an indirect one.

Subsequent constitutions, mostly in Latin America, adopted a presidential form of government in which there is direct, popular election of the president, who is constitutionally defined as both head of state and head of government. Many Latin American countries initially provided for election by electoral colleges or by congress itself, but throughout the twentieth century the trend has been towards direct election. Probably there has been no new presidential system established anywhere in the world since the First World War that has provided for an electoral college. Assembly selection of fixed-term presidents remains the reserve of parliamentary regimes with only occasional exceptions to the rule.

While the progenitor of the pure presidential regime type was the American Constitutional Convention of the 1780s, hybrid forms of presidentialism find their roots in Europe. One of the first was the Weimar Republic constitution of Germany after the First World War. Here a directly elected presidency existed alongside a cabinet that was dependent upon parliamentary confidence. The president held the power to dissolve parliament, and also had the right to dismiss the government. Yet the president had no veto power. Thus this constitution provided for a president who was far more than just a head of state, but he could not be assured of heading the government – because of the constant threat of no-confidence votes – and he could not prevent legislation from being passed without his consent. This hybrid form – neither parliamentary nor presidential – generated difficult to resolve conflicts between the president and the parliament. While the collapse of the Weimar Republic and the rise of Nazism cannot be blamed on the constitutional provisions, those provisions did not promote stable government either.

Another early example of a hybrid system (see HYBRID SYSTEMS) with a separately elected presidency is the Finnish system. There the presidency was elected by an electoral college until 1996, when a constitutional amendment provided for fully direct election. In Finland, however, unlike in Weimar Germany, the cabinet is fully and exclusively accountable to the parliamentary majority. The presidency has always been an important institution in Finnish politics, but the logic of government formation and the process of POLICY-MAKING depend on the bargaining between parties in parliament. Likewise, the constitution of the French Fifth Republic, adopted in 1958, and amended in 1962 to provide for direct election of the president, requires that the cabinet have the exclusive confidence of parliament. As in Finland, the French presidency is an important institution, but cabinet formation depends on the outcome of parliamentary elections.

Variation in regime types

The best way to perceive the difference among regimes with elected presidents is to visualise them in a two-dimensional space. In order to do that, a simple method of scoring various aspects of these regimes can be devised. Such a method results in the two-dimensional space depicted in Figure 3. The first dimension, the vertical axis in Figure 3, defines how much constitutional power a president has over the cabinet. That power may range from zero, in which case the choice of the prime minister and other ministers is left entirely to parliament (whether or not there is indeed a popularly elected president), to a maximum, in which the president may appoint whomever he or she wants to the cabinet and may dismiss ministers at any time. Intermediate steps are identified beneath the diagram in Figure 3.

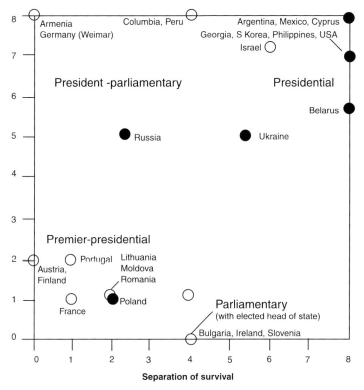

Solid symbols indicate a president who has
a veto that requires an extraordinary majority to override

The placement of each constitution shown is based on the following scoring system:

Powers over cabinet

Cabinet formation
4 President appoints ministers without need for assembly confirmation
3 President appoints ministers with consent of assembly
2 President appoints ministers who need confidence of assembly
1 President nominates prime minister who needs confidence of assembly; prime
   minister appoints other ministers (possibly with consent of president)
0 President cannot name ministers except on recommendation of assembly

Cabinet dismissal
4 President dismisses ministers at will
3 President dismisses ministers with consent of assembly
1 President dismisses ministers, but only under certain restrictions
0 Ministers (or whole cabinet) may be removed only by assembly on vote of censure

Separation of survival in office (scored for both assembly and executive)
4 No provisions compromising separation of survival (i.e. fixed terms)
3 Survival can be attacked, but only attacker must stand for reelection
2 Survival can be attacked only in situation of mutual jeopardy
1 Survival can be attacked, except at specified times
0 Survival can be attacked at any time (i.e., unrestricted censure or dissolution)

Figure 3 Presidential cabinet authority and separation of survival: the property space of regimes
with elected presidencies

The second dimension defines the degree of each branch's separation of survival in office *vis-à-vis* the other; that is, whether terms are fixed, or whether one branch can 'attack' the survival of the other and thereby shorten its term. At the minimum degree of separation (zero on the horizontal axis), the assembly can oust the cabinet at any time on a vote of no confidence and the popularly elected president can dissolve parliament at any time. At the maximum (score of four on separated survival for both the assembly and the executive), neither branch can shorten the mandate of the other, as both have fixed terms.

The scores for individual countries shown in Figure 3 are based on the scoring methodology displayed beneath the figure. A score of 1 is given when survival in office of the other branch can be jeopardised only at specified times. An example is France, where the assembly's survival in office is subject to a presidential dissolution power that can be exercised only once a year. The score is 2 when the term of the cabinet or parliament may be shortened only in the context of 'mutual jeopardy'. For instance, the Polish and Russian presidents' dissolution power may be exercised only in response to censures (votes of no confidence) of the cabinet by the assembly. There is, therefore, more separation of survival in Russia than in France because the Russian parliament can avoid dissolution by not exercising censure. In Poland, parliament can avoid dissolution by 'constructively' electing a new government on the same vote by which it expresses its lack of confidence in the incumbent one.

Finally, either or both branches' separation of survival from the other is scored 3 when the term of office can be shortened only if the branch initiating the shortening of the other branch's term also stands for re-election. For instance, in the post-1996 Israeli system, a parliamentary censure of the executive (including the directly elected chief executive as well as the rest of the cabinet) necessitates a new parliamentary election, and an executive order to dissolve parliament means there must be a new election for the head of government as well as for parliament.

The upper right region contains presidential regimes, in which cabinets are accountable only to the popularly elected president and the term of office for the assembly as well as the presidency is fixed. Moreover, presidents in these countries have vetoes that require more than a majority to override. Most countries of Latin America would be represented at the far upper-right corner as the 'purest' of the presidential systems, though for reasons of space, only Argentina and Mexico are identified in the figure. The figure, which depicts most countries that have been democratic since at least around 1990, shows that few (pure) presidential systems are found outside Latin America and some other areas of the less developed world. None are in Europe, except for Cyprus.

The most common variants of presidential systems in Europe, both west and east, are actually not pure presidential systems at all, but rather various hybrids. The entire left side of the figure contains regimes that are sometimes called semi-presidential or are said to follow the 'French model' of combining an elected president with cabinet accountability before parliament. But many of those regimes are not in fact following a crucial feature of the French model, whereby in a conflict between the president and the assembly over the composition of the government, the parliament has the upper hand constitutionally. The importance of that feature has been revealed already in both Moldova and Poland. In the former country, President Mercea Snegur attempted to dismiss the defence minister but was forced to reinstate him when the parliament argued (and the Constitutional Court agreed) that ministers needed only the parliament's and not the president's confidence. Similarly, in Poland, President Lech Walesa found he had to accede to the opposition majority's preferences for cabinet positions after the opposition won the 1993 parliamentary elections.

Only those regimes in the lower left region, including Moldova and Poland, are in fact close cousins of the French system, wherein the assembly majority rather than the president has the ultimate authority over the composition of the cabinet. It is these regimes that are most frequently meant when the term 'semi-presidential' is used. However, if the prime minister (premier) and cabinet are not exclusively accountable to the assembly majority, the president may prove to be the dominant political figure even in those cases in which the president does not enjoy majority backing in the assembly. Countries in the lower left corner of Figure 3 may be alternatively known as premier-presidential regimes, to signify that the premier – and the assembly majority on which the premier depends to remain in office – is the primary locus of executive power. In premier presidential systems the president is the dominant political figure only informally, and only when his or her party or coalition controls the assembly majority and thus can determine who is the premier. This is the case in France, and French presidents have indeed often appeared all-powerful. However, their powers recede into the background in most day-to-day aspects of governance and policy-making whenever the assembly majority falls into the hands of the president's opposition.

In the upper left region of Figure 3, on the other hand, we find regimes in which the president retains the constitutional power to appoint and dismiss cabinet officials even when the president's party or coalition is not in the majority of the assembly. These cases thus provide for presidents with far more tools of governance and policy-making even when they lack support in the legislative branch. Thus these cases can be called president-parliamentary, in order to signify that the president remains the dominant political figure over the executive branch, though not as dominant as in those regimes that are simply called presidential.

In the far upper left, a full president-parliamentary regime gives the president discretion to dissolve parliament at any time as well as the right to appoint and dismiss cabinets freely. That form of regime is probably inherently unstable because the president can-not keep in office a cabinet of his liking against the wishes of the parliamentary majority, but he can always respond to a vote of no confidence by appointing another cabinet of his own choosing or dissolving parliament. That is exactly the situation that bred repeated parliamentary elections in the latter years of the Weimar Republic in Germany, until Adolf Hitler was finally appointed prime minister in a tragically ill-fated attempt to create a cabinet that could maintain parliamentary confidence.

Unfortunately, there are some newer constitutions, including some in post-communist Europe, that exhibit such dual responsibility of the cabinet. Armenia has full president-parliamentarism, and Russia and Ukraine have important elements of it. In both Russia and Ukraine, presidents have somewhat less authority over the appointment of cabinet ministers, because, unlike in Armenia, the president may appoint the prime minister only with the consent of the assembly and then indirectly appoints the other ministers through the prime minister. The fundamental point about those constitutions is that the president may freely dismiss any minister, and the cabinet may be dismissed by the assembly majority. Thus there is no clear line of authority over cabinets. For this reason, these president-parliamentary systems may be institutionally less well equipped to settle conflicts that might arise between the president and the assembly majority over the composition of cabinets.

Another type of hybrid is Israel's new system. Although terms can be shortened in Israel and hence that country violates the fixed-term component of the definition of presidentialism, neither branch can attack the survival of the other without shortening its own term as well. Thus it is fundamentally different from those other regimes with non-separated survival shown in the left half of the figure, and Israel can be classed as a hybrid variant of presidentialism.

Finally, the presidencies of three countries are so weak that the systems there are effectively parliamentary: Bulgaria, Ireland and Slovenia. Macedonia is almost in that category as well, although there the president has some discretion in the choice of a prime minister.

Multiple veto gates

Figure 3 also depicts those presidents who have veto powers, found in Belarus, Cyprus, Poland, Russia, Ukraine and USA. The Polish presidency stands out in Figure 3 as being unique in having a veto while having only limited authority over the cabinet. (In Armenia, Lithuania and Portugal, vetoes of most types of legislation can be overridden by a majority of all members, meaning a unified majority can prevail, though some vetoes may be sustained.) Not depicted in Figure 3, the Russian president has another important source of legislative power: he can issue decrees that establish new laws in areas where there is no current law; and in the process of establishing a new market economy, there are many such areas. Moreover, because of his veto, the president's decrees are difficult to rescind. With the support of only one-third of the legislators in either house of the assembly, the Russian president can be assured that his decrees stand as law regardless of the preferences of legislative majorities. That kind of decree power is unprecedented in democratic constitutions; elsewhere, for example Brazil and Colombia, presidential decree laws are subject to rescission by a majority of the legislature, meaning that presidents must negotiate with the assembly majority.

If the presidency is a veto gate – and even more obviously if it holds decree powers – the assembly majority cannot always prevail in the legislative process. The give-and-take can be an advantage in that it increases the range of interests represented in policy-making. Both the interests of the president and of the assembly must be accommodated, implying a more consensual form of law making and less hasty DECISION-MAKING (except, as noted, in Russia). On the other hand, it can be a disadvantage in the sense that conflict sometimes erupts over whose conception of voter preferences is more valid. In the extreme, the president, especially if he has supporters in the courts, the military or the police, may be tempted to flout the constitution. At a minimum, policy stalemate may prevail, which is not necessarily a bad thing, but may lead to pressing problems going unresolved.

Partisan support in the assembly and the kinds of powers that the president holds in reserve are important factors determining whether compromise or dangerous interbranch conflict is the most likely outcome. ELECTORAL SYSTEMS that promote numerous or factionalised parties (such as Georgia, Russia and, to a lesser degree, Poland), or where there is no nationalised party system (such as Russia and Ukraine) are likely to have presidents with minimal legislative support. Where the terms of the two branches are of different lengths (for example, in Armenia, Georgia, Poland and Ukraine, but not Romania), elections will sometimes occur in the latter portion of the president's term. Such elections frequently result in a sharp reduction in the president's co-partisan legislative contingent, as in France in 1986 and 1993 and Poland in 1993. If the constitution clearly requires the president to cede authority over the cabinet in the event he lacks legislative support, such situations are less likely to be crisis-producing. If the president has a veto, he is unlikely to be marginalised in the policy process and thereby be tempted to resort to unconstitutional measures. However, worst of all is a situation of little partisan support but an ability to issue decree laws. Then a 'war of laws' may result, with each side attempting to overturn the others' actions, with deleterious consequences for policy – and, perhaps, regime – stability.

Conclusion

Regimes with elected presidencies come in many variations. The term 'presidential system' should be reserved for those systems that have full separation of origin and survival of executive and legislative powers. By this definition, either of the following features remove a regime from the category of (pure) presidentialism: a requirement that the cabinet maintain the confidence of the parliamentary majority, or a provision permitting the president to dissolve parliament. The fact of popular election of the presidency is not enough to make a regime 'presidential'. However, it is enough to give the voters two 'agents' of representation (or three, if the assembly is bicameral). Thus, for good or for ill, in all cases aside from those constitutions that provide for very weak presidencies, a politician who can claim a direct connection to the electorate adds his or her preferences to those of the assembly in the process of forming governments and, often, passing legislation.

See also:

hybrid systems; leadership; parliamentary models

Further reading

Lijphart, A. (1992) *Presidential versus Parliamentary Government*, Oxford: Oxford University Press.

Linz, J.J. and Valenzuela, A. (eds) (1993) *The Failure of Presidential Democracy: Comparative Perspectives*, Baltimore: Johns Hopkins University Press.

Shugart, M.S. and Carey, J.M. (1992) *Presidents and Assemblies: Constitutional Design and Electoral Dynamics*, New York: Cambridge University Press.

MATTHEW S. SHUGART

private property

Definition and principal ideas

Private property is a complex concept and is not easily captured in a concise and precise definition. This is borne out if we consider what has become the standard characterisation of it, namely that given by A.M. Honoré. Honoré argues that private property has ten features (what he terms 'incidents') (1961: 113–24). These include the following reasonably self-explanatory properties: the 'right to possess', the 'right to use', the 'right to manage', the 'right to the income' and the 'right to the capital'. They also include: the 'right to security', by which Honoré means the right to secure long-term use; and the 'incident of transmissibility', by which Honoré means the right to pass a good on. An additional feature of private property is what Honoré terms the 'incident of absence of term'; this means that there is no fixed term at which the owner must relinquish a good. Private property also involves the 'prohibition of harmful use' and, finally, what Honoré terms 'liability to execution' (where this states that an owner's property may be removed from them in certain circumstances, such as to pay debts). These ten properties, then, provide an account of private property. It is crucial to record, however, that Honoré does not claim that they must all always be present for an object to be privately owned. He makes explicit that these properties are 'not individually necessary, though they may be together sufficient' (1961: 112). The concept of private property is thus a highly complicated one.

When analysing private property it is helpful to bear two further points in mind. The first is that to have a full understanding of private property it is helpful to compare it with alternative property relationships. It is common here to distinguish between two alternatives, what Jeremy Waldron terms 'collective ownership' and 'common ownership' (1990: 40–2). The former refers to a state of affairs in which a number of people constitute a group and that group (for example, a state) owns an object. The latter refers to a state of affairs in which an object is not the private property of anyone and each may use it as a common resource: a village common might be an example. Both thus constitute alternatives to private property.

A second important point is also noted by Waldron. Waldron distinguishes between two different accounts of the right to private property. Employing H.L.A. Hart's famous distinction between special and general rights (Hart 1984: 84–8), Waldron contrasts the special right to private property with the general right to private property. The former maintains that an individual may have a right to private property because of some feature about him or herself (for example, that they have been given it or they have worked for it). The general right to private property, by contrast, maintains that all persons have a right to private property (Waldron 1990: 106–24). As we shall see later, this distinction is of considerable importance.

History and evaluation

As even a brief examination illustrates, disputes about the merits of private property are a recurring feature of the history of political thought. Aristotle, for example, criticised Plato's defence of common ownership. In Book Two, Chapter 5 of *The Politics* he argues that common ownership leads to strife and maintains that private property is more efficient. Much later John Locke, as we shall see shortly, also defended private property. Jean-Jacques Rousseau, however, once wrote, in *A Discourse on the Origin of Inequality*, that the creation of private property was one of the defining evils of civil society (1986: 84). A hostile view was also taken by Marx and Engels who famously wrote in *The Communist Manifesto* that 'the theory of the Communists may be summed up in the single sentence: Abolition of private property' (1982: 96).

It is helpful to identify four distinct arguments for private property (for comprehensive discussions see Becker (1977); Carter (1989); Reeve (1986); Ryan (1984); Waldron (1990)). One of the most important and influential arguments is that presented by Locke in his second *Treatise of Government*. Locke argues that if a person mixes their labour with an object that is not privately owned, he is entitled to it. He does, however, add a qualification, namely that this appropriation is legitimate only if there is 'enough, and as good left in common for others' (Bk II, 5: 27). If this proviso is met, mixing one's labour represents a legitimate way of acquiring private property.

This argument has been subject to a number of criticisms. Robert Nozick, who is highly sympathetic to Locke's position, asks why mixing one's labour with an unowned object creates property rights in that object (1974: 174–5). This probing question notwithstanding, Nozick affirms a fairly Lockean approach and seeks to revise and defend Locke's broad outlook.

Others are more critical. G.A. Cohen, for example, criticises Nozick's revised account of Locke's proviso which states that appropriation is justified if it does not worsen the condition of others (Nozick 1974: 175–82). As Cohen points out, this constraint permits someone to appropriate an object for himself even if there are other possible property relationships in which he and everyone else are better off (1995: 78–83). As such it is unduly undemanding. Nozick is thus wrong to allow private property when the latter is better than a state of common ownership if there are other arrangements that are even better for the participants.

A second distinct approach to defending private property argues that the latter is defensible because it has desirable consequences such as promoting efficiency. This idea can be developed in a number of different ways. Since Aristotle, for example, many have argued that the private ownership of resources is superior to other property arrangements because under it people look after resources more assiduously (Bk II, 5: 1263a21). Others argue that private property is justified as an incentive to induce people to work hard (Reeve 1986: 116–22). These efficiency-based defences are vulnerable to counter-examples. Against the second line of reasoning, for example, it is far from clear why there can not be other sorts of inducements to work hard. Against the first, it is a moot point whether private ownership of resources is an effective and efficient way of protecting environmental resources: what is to prevent the owner from using up all the good of the land with no benefit to future generations (Carter 1989: 74)? We can, moreover, ask, at a more general level, whether efficiency is the most important social value (Carter 1989: 64–77)?

A third approach to defending private property invokes the importance of liberty, arguing that liberty requires a system of private property. Abrogations of private property, it is claimed, constitute restrictions of FREEDOM and are therefore wrong. Those who adopt this approach are commonly termed 'libertarians'. A clear and emphatic example of this approach is Robert Nozick's *Anarchy, State, and Utopia* (1974).

Again, this approach is criticised by socialists like G.A. Cohen. Cohen makes at least two distinct types of point. His first is that, contra the claims of libertarians, private property involves restrictions on people's negative liberty. If one person owns an object, then others are accordingly unfree to use it without that person's permission. Private property thus includes unfreedoms (1988: 291–6, 1991: 166–72). Cohen also makes a second more ambitious criticism, arguing that private property includes more restrictions on liberty than do versions of common ownership. To substantiate this claim, he imagines two persons who both privately own some tools. He then asks us to consider a 'communising rule' (1991: 173) which states that if one person is not using a tool then the other may do so without his or her permission. Under such an arrangement each has the same freedoms as before plus the freedom to use someone else's tools if they are not using them themselves. Thus, a shift away from private property increases freedom (1991: 173–4).

A fourth, distinct, argument for private property is given by G.W.F. Hegel in *The Philosophy of Right*. Hegel argues that people have a need to express themselves and he argues, moreover, that private property enables people to do this and is, as such, justified. The Hegelian approach thus invokes the importance of self-realisation and self-expression rather than values like efficiency or negative liberty (Hegel 1967, part 1, 1: 41, 44–6, 51: on which see Reeve 1986: 136–43). As Waldron points out, Hegel's argument, if valid, is best construed as supporting a general right to private property. Unlike Locke and Nozick's arguments, it entails that all persons have a right to private property in order to express themselves (Waldron 1990: 343–89).

Summary

One important point that emerges from analyses of the merits and demerits of private property is that the conventional assumption that those committed to redistribution reject private property is too crude. What they tend to reject is the special right to private property, which may leave many impoverished and others fabulously rich. What they need not reject is the idea of private property, for one may endorse redistribution to bring about a system whereby everyone enjoys a general right to private property (Waldron 1990) or even a general right to an equal (privately owned) proportion of the Earth's resources (Steiner 1994).

See also:

capitalism; equality; rights

Further reading

Becker, L. (1977) *Property Rights: Philosophic Foundations*, Boston: Routledge and Kegan Paul.

Carter, A. (1989) *The Philosophical Foundations of Property Rights*, London: Harvester Wheatsheaf.

Cohen, G. (1988) 'Freedom, Justice, and Capitalism', in *History, Labour, and Freedom: Themes from Marx*, Oxford: Clarendon Press.

—— (1991) 'Capitalism, Freedom, and the Proletariat', in D. Miller (ed.), *Liberty*, Oxford: Oxford University Press.

—— (1995) *Self-Ownership, Freedom, and Equality*, Cambridge: Cambridge University Press.

Hart, H.L.A. (1984) 'Are There any Natural Rights?', in J. Waldron (ed.), *Theories of Rights*, Oxford: Oxford University Press.

Hegel, G. (1967) *The Philosophy of Right*, trans. T.M. Knox, Oxford: Oxford University Press.

Honoré, A. (1961) 'Ownership', in A. Guest (ed.), *Oxford Essays in Jurisprudence: A*

Collaborative Work, Oxford: Oxford University Press.

Locke, J. (1986) *Two Treatises of Government*, London: Dent.

Marx, K. and Engels, F. (1982) *The Communist Manifesto*, Middlesex: Penguin.

Nozick, R. (1974) *Anarchy, State, and Utopia*, Oxford: Blackwell.

Reeve, A. (1986) *Property*, Basingstoke: Macmillan.

Rousseau, J.-J. (1986) 'A Discourse on the Origin of Inequality', in *The Social Contract and Discourses*, trans. G.D.H. Cole, London and Melbourne: Dent.

Ryan, A. (1984) *Property and Political Theory*, Oxford: Blackwell.

Steiner, H. (1994) *An Essay on Rights*, Oxford: Blackwell.

Waldron, J. (1990) *The Right to Private Property*, Oxford: Clarendon Press.

SIMON CANEY

privatisation

Although there was sporadic *ad hoc* privatisation in various Western European countries during the 1960s and 1970s, it was during the 1980s and 1990s that the policy acquired an intellectual and ideological credence which fostered its pursuit on a systematic and comprehensive basis. Furthermore, privatisation became a truly global phenomenon, pursued far beyond Western Europe, and by governments of virtually all political complexions.

Privatisation has been described as 'an umbrella term for many different policies loosely linked by the way in which they are taken to mean a strengthening of the market at the expense of the State' (Heald 1983: 298), but it is most commonly used to refer to the selling of nationalised or publicly owned industries and enterprises to the private sector and individuals (Wright 1994: 8–9). However, more limited forms of privatisation have also been pursued, such as 'hiving off' or 'contracting out' segments of the public sector to private

enterprise, or inviting the private sector to participate in joint ventures with public services, as evinced by the Private Finance Initiative pursued in Britain during the 1990s (Ascher 1987).

Whatever its precise form, the lineage of privatisation can ultimately be traced back to the Enlightenment and the emergence of modernity, when ownership of PRIVATE PROPERTY became a defining feature of individual liberty and, subsequently, of liberal democracy. Indeed, many political theorists from John Locke onwards have adduced that the primary role of the state is the protection of 'life, liberty and estate [property], and that its very legitimacy depends in large part on its success in fulfilling this core function' (*Two Treatises on Government*).

Privatisation has also reflected a particular view of the operation and alleged virtues of the market originally expounded by Adam Smith. Indeed, in Britain during the 1980s and 1990s, the case for privatisation was often articulated with particular vigour by the Adam Smith Institute, which was highly respected by the Conservative governments of Margaret Thatcher and John Major. Furthermore, many Conservative politicians themselves cited Adam Smith with great reverence when presenting the case for private enterprise and the market over public ownership.

The privatisation which was pursued during the 1980s and 1990s reflected a widespread disillusionment with the drift towards *dirigisme*, CORPORATISM and economic intervention which had characterised much of the twentieth century (Vickers and Wright 1989: 2). The New Right articulated a neo-liberal critique of Keynesianism and state regulation of the economy which asserted that a range of problems afflicting Western economies during the 1970s were derived from excessive political interference and constant attempts by government to supplant 'the market'. Thus, whereas the Keynesian or social democratic paradigm had viewed economic problems largely in terms of 'market failure' which could best be ameliorated by government intervention of some kind, the New Right insisted the converse, namely that economic problems invariably reflected political or governmental failure which could only be rectified by reviving 'the market' and restoring the role of private enterprise. As such: 'The selling of state assets to the private sector...[became] the palliative for the economic ills of many countries' (McAllister and Studlar 1989: 155).

This critique held that private enterprise is inherently superior to public ownership, and voluntaristic private endeavour invariably more productive than top-down initiatives pursued by the state. Privatisation thus became central to the goal of reversing collectivism and reviving INDIVIDUALISM. Indeed, it often reflects an assumption about human nature, namely that individuals are inherently acquisitive and motivated by the instinctive desire to obtain greater wealth or material possessions. Privatisation has therefore been portrayed as a means of satisfying a natural human trait by enabling individuals to obtain property or shares which were previously state owned or controlled.

Privatisation also reflects the determination to promote consumer and purchaser interests over those of producers and providers. In this respect, privatisation seeks to supplant SOCIAL DEMOCRACY, whose emphasis is on the RIGHTS of citizens or CITIZENSHIP guaranteed by the state, with a mode of economic democracy, whereby the rights of consumers are promoted through the choice and competition provided by the market. Hence the neo-liberal and New Right emphasis on 'consumer sovereignty' and the reference to customers rather than citizens.

The proponents of privatisation have thus insisted that only a thriving market economy, based on ceaseless competition between a plethora of privately owned companies and industries, can empower individuals as consumers and provide them with the choice, and freedom to choose, which public ownership denies. This perspective holds that nationalised industries and public sector services enjoy both a monopoly position and government subsidies, such that they are not exposed to the competition which would compel them to become more efficient, cost-effective, profitable

and responsive to consumer demand (see MARKET FORCES).

It is here especially that Adam Smith is invoked by proponents of privatisation, for it was he who originally identified the market's apparently benign, self-regulating character and its immutable laws of supply and demand, both of which ensured that the market provided the most effective means of wealth creation and the most efficient mechanism for the allocation of resources. As such, privatisation is presented as a vital means of revitalising this market system by returning state-owned enterprises and nationalised industries to the private sector. Thereafter, the state's economic role is primarily concerned with upholding the framework within which the market functions, only intervening to remove any subsequent obstacles to its effective operation.

At the same time, privatisation is equated with the rolling back of the frontiers of the state, and renewing the demarcation between the economic and political spheres, and between the state and CIVIL SOCIETY, as posited by classic LIBERALISM. It also reflects the application of public choice theory, whereby public employees and government bureaucrats are portrayed as ultimately self-serving and budget-maximising actors with their own goals and agendas, and thus unable to serve the wider interests of civil society or the economy. As such, advocates of privatisation have sought to invoke a populist backlash against nationalised industries and certain public sector employees, urging that they too be exposed to market forces, greater competition, payment by results and consumer SOVEREIGNTY.

Yet privatisation has also been viewed as a means of restoring the AUTHORITY of the state, and enabling it to function more effectively. Not only was state intervention deemed to be a cause of, not a remedy for, a range of economic problems, it was held that attempts by government to exercise ever greater control over economic activity would ultimately render the state a target of growing contempt and hostility. The more the state attempted to regulate the economy and direct the activities of individuals, the greater the 'overload' it would experience, leading ultimately to a crisis of legitimacy. By returning the bulk of economic activity to the private sector and restoring the primacy of the market, privatisation has also been concerned to limit the role and functions of the state to defence, law and order, and removing obstacles to the smooth operation of market forces. The state would have far fewer responsibilities, but would henceforth be able to perform them much more effectively than hitherto, thereby restoring its authority and legitimacy.

Yet the intellectual and ideological rationale presented by the proponents of privatisation has often not been borne out by the actual experience of such policies. In many cases, public monopolies have merely been transferred to the private sector, with little, if any, increase in competition or consumer choice. This has resulted in a plethora of state-appointed regulatory bodies being established to monitor the policies of the privatised industries, and to ensure some protection for customers (Moran and Prosser 1994). Yet in some instances, especially the sphere of public transport, the primacy of the profit motive has actually resulted in a diminution of consumer choice, as privatised enterprises dispensed with less profitable activities (such as rural bus or trains services) in order to focus on those which are most financially lucrative.

By the end of the 1990s, it was becoming increasingly apparent that privatisation was not always a panacea for the economic problems attributed to government regulation or state intervention. On the contrary, increasing attention has been focused on 'market failure' and the lack of ACCOUNTABILITY of privatised industries to consumers and civil society. With public ownership having been discredited, and privatisation engendering its own problems, it is perhaps not surprising that many politicians have begun searching for a 'third way'.

See also:

legitimacy; liberalism; private property; rights; state, models of

Further reading

Ascher, K. (1987) *The Politics of Privatisation: Contracting Out Public Services*, Basingstoke: Macmillan.
Glade, W.P. (ed.) (1986) *State Shrinking: A Comparative Enquiry into Privatisation*, Austin, TX: Institute of Latin American Studies.
Graham, C. and Prosser, T. (1991) *Privatizing Public Enterprises*, Oxford: Clarendon Press.
Heald, D. (1983) *Public Expenditure: Its Defence and Reform*, Oxford: Martin Robertson.
Hennig, J., Hamnett, C. and Feigenbaum, H. (1988) 'The Politics of Privatisation: A Comparative Perspective', *Governance* 1(4): 442–68.
McAllister, I. and Studlar, D.T. (1989) 'Popular versus Elite Views of Privatisation: The Case of Britain', *Journal of Public Policy* 9(2): 155–78.
Moran, M. and Prosser, T. (eds) (1994) *Privatization and Regulatory Change in Europe*, Buckingham: Open University Press.
OECD (1992) *Regulatory Reform, Privatisation and Competition Policy*, Paris: OECD.
Richardson, J. J. (ed.) (1990) *Privatization and Deregulation in Canada and Britain*, Aldershot: Dartmouth Publishing Company.
Vickers, J. and Wright, V. (eds) (1989) *The Politics of Privatisation in Western Europe*, London: Frank Cass.
Wright, V. (ed.) (1994) *Privatization in Western Europe*, London: Pinter.

PETER DOREY

procedural democracy

One prominent position in democratic theory identifies democracy with the presence of certain procedures for popular DECISION-MAKING: what makes a democracy a democracy is that there are regular elections which determine access to political office, wide rights to vote in ELECTIONS, recognised procedures for determining CITIZENSHIP and the scope of public decision-making, and recognised protections for democratic PARTICIPATION in the formation of political agendas, such as freedom of association, freedom of expression and freedom of the press. This position offers what may fairly be called a procedural definition of democracy.

It is also possible to provide a procedural justification for democracy. A procedural justification should be distinguished from both an 'input' and an 'output' justification. An input justification says that democracy is a valuable political system because, and only insofar as, either uniquely or maximally, it institutionalises a respect for certain individuals rights, or delivers an EQUALITY of standing or respect, and that this honouring of rights or respect is, in itself, a fundamental good. The input account justifies the use of democratic procedures by reference to the way those procedures respect certain claims or principles. An 'output' justification says that democracy is to be valued because it produces good outcomes, or the least bad outcomes relative to other systems. In contrast to the input account, it justifies the use of the procedures by their consequences. A procedural justification takes the view that what gives value to the outcomes of democratic decision procedures is that they are the outcomes of those procedures. Similarly, on a procedural view, the 'inputs' to the democratic process may be seen as concomitants or requirements of those procedures, rather than being based on some antecedently specified conception of individual rights. Unlike input and output accounts, procedural justifications do not justify the use of the procedure, so much as justify the result of the procedure when that procedure is used. This asymmetry in what it is that is being justified complicates the classification of theories of democracy. Moreover, theories of democracy often combine elements of more than one of these perspectives, and procedural accounts are not always clearly distinguishable from certain types of input justifications. However, the fullest procedural theory of democracy is that which gives greatest weight to this type of justification.

Procedural definitions of democracy are not necessarily accompanied by procedural justifications. Joseph Schumpeter, for example, argued resolutely against a (largely imagined) classical model of democracy as rule by the general will, in favour of what he called a 'realist' model, in which democracy is defined as no more than 'that institutional arrangement for arriving at political decisions in which individuals acquire the power to decide by means of a competitive struggle for the people's vote' (1943: 269). Schumpeter's account owes much to Max Weber and other turn of the century élite theorists who recognised the inevitability of mass democratic participation but saw little reason to be enthusiastic about it and sought to limit the impact of democratic participation on the political process. In these accounts the procedural definition is not accompanied by a procedural justification; rather, democratic procedures tend to be valued wholly for their consequences. There is no appeal to the intrinsic merits of certain aspects of democratic procedures such as the equal value of each person's vote, the fact that those bound by the rules of the political system contribute to the making of those rules, or that the fairness of the democratic procedures in itself gives some moral weight to their outcomes.

We have seen that procedural justifications justify the result of the procedure when that procedure is used, rather than justifying the use of procedure. Although the use of the procedure might be justified on input or output grounds, there might also be something intrinsic to the character of democratic decision-making which gives further weight to a procedural justification. We can see this by contrasting (following the work of John Rawls) perfect, imperfect and pure procedures. A perfect procedure is one for which there is a right outcome, such as the equal division of a cake, and where we have a procedure which always delivers that outcome. In cases where there is a right answer but where our procedures cannot guarantee that the right answer will be found, we have an imperfect procedure. The jury system is an imperfect procedure.

There is a right and a wrong judgement with respect to someone's guilt, and the jury system is the best we can do to deliver that result. If juries were infallible they would provide a perfect procedure. In contrast, in a pure procedure, there is no right result beyond that which the procedure delivers. A lottery, insulated from fraud and corrupt practices, determines results entirely through the play of chance, so that whatever result it produces is the right answer. Similarly, the race goes to the person who runs it fastest. That it can be obscure as to exactly which type of procedure we are dealing with can be seen in the case of cake-dividing, since it is moot whether the mechanism (in the two-person case) of A cuts/ B chooses is an imperfect procedure to produce equal shares, or a pure procedure in which each person gets what he/she chose or cut. Is democracy a perfect, imperfect or pure procedure?

As an imperfect or perfect procedure, democracy would be seeking to produce decisions which approximate to some externally specifiable standard. The analogue to guilt and innocence in the jury case might be the general will, the common good or the interests of the people. This identifies an end or state of affairs which the specified procedures, perfectly or imperfectly, secure. In both cases, the value of the procedures (whether perfect or imperfect) derives from their 'output'. We value a perfect procedure because it always produces the right outcome. We value imperfect procedures because of their ability to approximate a certain outcome. In both cases, the value of the outcome may be outweighed by other values. Thus, if questioning by torture were a perfect procedure for ascertaining guilt, we might still reject it because we value the kind of society which does not torture its citizens more than we value the ascertaining of guilt or innocence.

If the choice were between regarding democracy as a perfect or as an imperfect procedure, it is clear it would be the latter. Imperfect procedural accounts may take more or less complex forms. For example, rather than specifying the outcome in terms of some positive value (such as the common good), an imperfect account might do so either negatively or by a 'satisficing' requirement. A negative account might argue that there is no independently specifiable right answer which democratic procedures track, but there are a number of outcomes which it must exclude, and which it is more likely to exclude than other political decision-making procedures. Thus Riker starts from a belief in the value of certain liberal principles and provides a reading of the democratic process which (imperfectly but largely) excludes certain non-liberal outcomes. A satisficing account takes the view that a fully rational, democratic order is too costly to achieve and that we should regard democratic procedures as acceptable insofar as their results are good enough, rather than optimal. More generally, liberal proponents of democracy tend to think that the couplet 'liberal democracy' means that liberal values come first and must be taken as constraints on the range of acceptable outcomes of the democratic process; hence the preference for constitutional arrangements and systems of entrenched individual rights. In this preference, however, they reveal the continuing legacy of distrust towards democracy which was refuelled for the nineteenth century by the French Revolution, and for the twentieth century by the European experience of mass democracy in the 1930s.

The alternative to the view that democracy is a good but imperfect procedure is to see it as a pure procedure. On this view, the outcomes of democratic procedures are acceptable so long as they flow from and respect the procedures themselves. Just as in a lottery we attempt to specify the procedure such that the outcome is wholly a function of chance (because we take chance to be definitional of a lottery), so with democracy we design the procedure to express what we take to be definitional of the democratic process. In the broadest terms this concerns the existence of a sovereign decision-making mechanism. However, our more detailed understanding of this mechanism might invoke other elements. Thus, we might take the principle of each to count for one as the key principle, and accordingly propose a way of ensuring that all binding decisions are the result of a majoritarian choice between two options. Equally, if we take something like *isegoria* to be central – the equal right to be heard in the sovereign assembly of the state before public decisions are taken (Dunn 1979: 17) – then a procedure which entrenches protections for 'voice' would be essential. Similarly, if we see democracy as crucially concerned with collective processes of negotiation, deliberation and compromise, then we would design the decision procedure to facilitate those processes. In each case, it is the procedure which justifies the outcome, and it is the fact that we are dealing with cases where we need a sovereign decision procedure and where the decisions concern matters for which there are no external standards, that justifies the use of this procedure.

One reason for thinking that democracy is a pure procedure is the view that, as a preference-aggregating mechanism, it is subject to various public choice problems which ensure that there is no determinate common good, such as Arrow's General Impossibility Theorem, or Condorcet's cycling problem. Although these accounts can be taken as indicating the imperfection of democratic procedures, they might also be taken to show that there simply cannot be an external standard for evaluating their outcomes.

Theorists have also looked to procedural justifications of democratic outcomes with the aim of ensuring that there is no gap between a person's involvement in the procedure and his or her acceptance of the outcome as legitimate and binding, even when that outcome adversely affects his or her interests. As we have seen, many liberal theorists stipulate a range of rights-preserving constraints on democratic outcomes, so that democratic procedures are acceptable if, but only if, the outcomes preserve our basic rights. Others add that the procedure must also be fair, in the sense no group or individual is systematically in the minority and the terms of their participation are preserved (for example, Singer 1974). Where a procedure meets these criteria we should, on this account, accept it as producing decisions which are binding on all participants (the ideal being

that, although they are enforceable, members will also recognise that they have an obligation to abide by the outcomes of the procedures). There are two possible components of such an account: we might follow liberal accounts in specifying a range of outcomes which are, a priori, illegitimate, and/or we might make a number of background assumptions which define the conditions under which the procedure operates so that certain results become impossible, or extremely unlikely. Such background conditions can include equal rationality, the absence of major social, ethnic or religious divisions within the community, or (with Rousseau) proximate material equality. The most ambitious procedural theory aims to generate binding decisions without specifying independent constraints, and by using the least restrictive set of assumptions about the necessary background conditions for the procedure.

For example, Robert Dahl's model of procedural democracy starts from a number of basic conditions: he assumes that a number of persons need a mechanism for producing binding decisions, that a two-stage process exists with agenda-setting preceding the decision-making stage, that decisions are made only by members, that members accept the principles of equal shares for equally valid claims, and that they also accept that no member's claim to determine the binding decisions is superior or overriding in relation to the claims of others. If these background conditions are present, the members of the society will be in a position to ensure that their decision-making could meet certain criteria for procedural democracy. They could meet the criteria of political equality by taking equally into account the expressed preferences of each member, and they can do this by each having an equal vote. In fact, which particular decision procedure or method of apportionment meets this criteria is open to debate; but the debate is dominated by the concern to ensure equal voice, on the basis of the principle of fair shares and the absence of overriding claims. Procedures must also be evaluated to ensure that there are adequate and equal opportunities for effective participation. A system which meets these two criteria will be procedurally democratic in a narrow sense.

Dahl, however, aims higher than this. He wants the procedures to ensure, optimally, that citizens have the opportunity to discover and validate their preferences in relation to the issue to be decided. Achieving this would ensure that both the agenda setting and the decision-making are procedurally democratic, but it would leave open the scope of the decision-making (that is, over what issues the decision-making process is sovereign), and the breadth of the DEMOS (that is, what degree of congruence exists between those who participate in the decision procedure and those subject to the outcomes of that procedure). That is, it falls short of the sovereignty of democracy over all matters relevant to the demos, whereas a system of full procedural democracy implies final collective control of which matters do or do not require binding decisions and over who should be included and what limits there can be on the demos.

There is a tension between the principle that those subject to the law should have a say in the processes which determine it, and the principle that only those with the appropriate competence should participate in the democratic process. The second principle is generally persuasive in the case of children, but that leaves it unclear where the line is to be drawn. Dahl suggests the procedure must ensure equal consideration and that in the absence of compelling proof to the contrary each is assumed to be the best judge of his/her interests, which justifies distributing membership to all adults, except transients. This principle also brings into play a further constraint on the demos, namely that in each case where the demos rules (and thereby overrides individuals' preferences) its capacity to judge must be demonstrably superior to those of its individual members. (Although we can imagine cases where the demos is in error over the need for a binding decision which trumps a set of strongly held individual preferences, it is important that this JUDGEMENT is itself open to question and the constraint of the burden of proof is a serious one. Indeed, it is sufficiently

serious to imply something like a doctrine of political NEUTRALITY, even if this is not worked out in detail in Dahl's account.) When a decision procedure meets these criteria then it is said to instantiate full procedural democracy. Moreover, using the classification developed here, Dahl's account of democracy is clearly a pure procedural account. He does not hold that there are objectively right answers to be had from the procedure. Moreover, unlike several liberal accounts, he does not place substantive external constraints on the decision procedure. Rather, he follows through the condition inherent in the idea of a rule-based procedure that interests be accorded equal weight, and he then shows how this principle can become operative within an ideal democratic process (see POLYARCHY).

Dahl's account rests on the reasonableness of the various criteria he adduces for the democratic procedure. We should accept political equality, effective participation and so on as necessary components of a procedural democracy. Yet many writers have doubted that the 'in principle' reasonableness of such considerations could issue in an 'in-practice' acceptance of them. Clearly, the formal specification of the criteria for a procedural democracy must be distinguished from the mechanisms by which these criteria are realised in practice. Thus, competence is clearly a crucial consideration, even if we have to recognise that this criterion is poorly met in many societies and requires investment in educational and citizenship programmes to increase the level of democratic functioning of members of the demos. However, one major set of doubts as to the viability of procedural democracy comes from those influenced by republican political thought who believe that one critical condition for a stable democratic order is the existence of a civic order in which citizens are active participants and have come to see their interests in terms of the broader interests of the state or community as a whole. Indeed, writers such as Michael Sandel have suggested that what Dahl describes as a procedural republic is simply not viable as a stable political form within the modern world.

The procedural republic is seen as exemplified in the modern American state, whose early twentieth-century project was to create and sustain a national community, 'not as a neutral framework for the play of competing interests, but rather as a formative community, concerned to shape a common life suited to the scale of modern social and economic forms' (Sandel 1984: 93). Sandel believes that that project has failed and that the nation has proved too vast an entity within which to cultivate the shared understandings which are necessary to community. The result has been the move from a politics of the common good, to one which emphasises the rights of the individual and the procedural character of the democratic process. But in this shift, the constitutive attachments of community are further undermined both by the emphasis on individual rights and by the continuing presence of a powerful, centralised nation state which implicates us in an array of dependencies and expectations which we do not recognise as freely chosen and which we frequently reject. The broader picture which this argument indicates, is one in which, in the absence of constitutive attachments to the political community, the modern nation-state is seen as increasingly detached from our concerns, and its decisions become increasingly illegitimate. More generally, in modern versions of classical republicanism, the democratic process is seen as requiring a degree of commitment and attachment to the political community which is extremely difficult to motivate.

We could understand these criticisms of procedural democracy as insisting that democratic procedures must be designed to be compatible with certain outcomes, such as the common good, or a 'thick' conception of civic culture. But it is equally possible to see them as demanding more in the way of background conditions for procedural democracy. The first reading is the more common, and is often coupled with a rather blithe dismissal of procedural accounts, on the assumption that democracy is of value only insofar as it is secures a substantive end, understood as a particular type of society. This can be couched

in terms either of an input or of an output justification, but the procedure continues to be conceived as a more or less imperfect one, with the corresponding difficulty that such accounts must both specify and justify the nature of the standard which democracies should seek to attain. On the second reading, which is rather rarer, we can retain a procedural justification for democracy, but emphasise the importance of certain background conditions (such as some degree of homogeneity in the population) to ensure that the procedure is able to generate results which its participants will find legitimate. The contrast between these two ways of responding can be seen in two contrasting ways of reading Rousseau's *Social Contract*. On the republican reading, Rousseau is seen as having a prior conception of the common good, which, for all the contractualist language he deploys, acts as the substantive end which the general will wills perfectly, even if the particular decisions of the people fall short of this ideal. Moreover, the appeal to a civic religion and public festivals, and the rough equality between citizens are all seen as part of this ideal order. On the alternative reading, these features are simply background conditions which are necessary for the achievement of an entirely procedural democracy; one in which, through our willingness as citizens, we are enabled to live according to laws we prescribe for ourselves and, in surrendering ourselves equally to the direction of all, remain as free as before. Civic religion, public festivals and equality of property are then background conditions for such a state, but they are not integral components of the ideal, nor are they distinct ideals. On such a reading, equality in Rousseau is a necessary condition for the willing of the general will, but it is not a substantive ideal or end in itself.

A further complication is whether those who will the results of the procedure must also be able to will both the procedure and the background conditions for the procedure. Clearly, a central part of procedural accounts of democracy concerns the way that the procedure produces a result with which the participants identify. To identify with the results participants must also be able to accept the constraints which the procedures place upon them. If we add that certain background conditions are required for that procedure to produce results with which all participants can identify, we have to consider whether these background conditions serve as brute facts which shape the participants' attitudes and expectations, or whether these conditions can themselves be willed. Rousseau's solution to this problem, which invokes the legislator, assumes that the people cannot will the background conditions. In contrast, theorists of DELIBERATIVE DEMOCRACY seem to suggest that deliberation not only 'launders' people's preferences, but also educates them so that brute background conditions become reflectively endorsed background conditions.

Although deliberative accounts of democracy might be thought as in contrast to procedural accounts, they are not necessarily disjoint. In Jürgen Habermas's work, democratic deliberation is understood as a means to agreement, where the conditions of agreement are characterised as approximating an 'ideal speech situation' which ensures that deliberation tracks truth. While this makes deliberation an imperfect procedure, Joshua Cohen's account is closer to a pure procedure, since deliberation aims, through 'a free and reasoned assessment of alternatives by equals', to establish a consensus, and relies on each participant being committed to acting only on that basis (Cohen 1989: 23).

Procedural democracy offers a plausible definition of democracy, but it might be thought to be less compelling as a justification for democracy, and still less so as an ideal. But that assessment dramatically underestimates the force of more sophisticated procedural accounts. Procedural democracy gives substance to the idea that democracy is, by its nature, open-ended; that it is best understood, not as an attempt to secure certain given ends or to instantiate certain values, but as a pure procedure; that is, as a decision-making process which, under certain constraints, such as political equality, the burden of proof, and free and reasoned assessment of alternatives, can produce forms of decision-making which the participants can accept as binding. They accept it as binding not because of the outcome, nor simply because it respects certain input rights, but because the procedure is itself one which they can recognise as imposing reasonable constraints upon them in their decision-making.

See also:

civic virtue; deliberative democracy; democracy, justifications for

Further reading

Cohen, J. (1989) 'Deliberation and Democratic Legitimacy', in A. Hamlin and P. Pettit, *The Good Polity*, Oxford: Blackwell, 17–34.

Dahl, R. (1979) 'Procedural Democracy', in P. Laslett and J.S. Fishkin (eds), *Philosophy, Politics and Society*, 5th Series, Oxford: Blackwell, 97–133.

Dunn, J. (1979) *Western Political Theory in the Face of the Future*, Cambridge: Cambridge University Press.

Habermas, J. (1990) *Moral Consciousness and Communicative Action* Cambridge: Polity Press.

Nelson, W.N. (1980) *On Justifying Democracy*, London: Routledge.

Rawls, J. (1972) *A Theory of Justice*, Oxford: Oxford University Press.

Riker, W.H. (1982) *Liberalism against Populism: A Confrontation Between the Theory of Democracy and the Theory of Social Choice*, San Francisco: W.H. Freeman.

Sandel, M. (1984) 'The Procedural Republic and the Unencumbered Self', *Political Theory* 12(1): 81–96.

Schumpeter, J. (1943) *Capitalism, Socialism and Democracy*, London: George Allen and Unwin.

Singer, P. (1974) *Democracy and Disobedience*, Oxford: Oxford University Press.

MARK PHILP

proportionality

In broad terms, proportionality relates to a comparison between two states of affairs and denotes the idea of a correspondence between them. Proportionality is a central feature of the law, requiring that there should be a reasonable relationship between the objectives sought and the means employed to achieve them. In politics, the principle of proportionality arises in many situations where resources have to be shared. It is a guiding principle – though scarcely ever the only determinant – of the way in which seats in parliament are allocated at ELECTIONS, for example. Ministries in coalition governments are usually shared among the political PARTIES that make up the government, in proportion to the number of parliamentary seats held by each party; likewise, in a very factionalised party such as the Liberal Democratic Party of Japan, each faction receives its proportionate share of ministries.

How desirable is proportionality?

Proportionality seems an eminently fair principle, but there may be situations in which, in the name of equity, another principle is preferred (Young 1994: 16–17). When governments decide how to spend public funds, they do not necessarily allocate resources to different parts of the country in proportion to the number of people in each locality; areas of socioeconomic deprivation may receive a disproportionate allocation. Similarly, income in most countries is taxed in what is described as a progressive rather than proportionate manner; those earning higher incomes can expect to be taxed at a higher rate than those on lower incomes.

In practical politics, the principle of proportionality emerges most visibly in the allocation of seats in parliament. Other than in countries – such as Israel and the Netherlands – that are not divided into sub-national constituencies, seat allocation is a two-stage process. The first stage consists of awarding seats to different parts of the country, and this operation is usually performed on the basis of strict proportionality. Even here, though, there are occasional breaches of the principle, out of the belief that in some circumstances equity is not necessarily maximised by proportionality; for example, sparsely populated rural areas may receive a higher degree of representation per capita than urban areas. The American Constitution stipulates that seats in the House of Representatives 'shall be apportioned among the several States . . . according to their respective Numbers', but it further prescribes that each state, no matter how small, shall have at least one representative, as a result of which over the long term the smallest states, such as Wyoming, receive more than their proportionate share of seats. In the Senate, of course, the proportionality principle is abandoned completely; each state, regardless of size, has two representatives.

When it comes to the second stage, the allocation of seats to candidates or political parties, proportionality is not always a sacrosanct principle. ELECTORAL SYSTEMS are the means by which votes cast at elections are converted into seats in parliament, and in their design proportionality is usually only one consideration. While it is of course accepted that the seats won by a party should bear some positive relation to the votes that it wins – any electoral system that did not embody this principle in the broadest terms would be either random or perverse – other considerations may significantly qualify the priority given to proportionality.

This is most apparent in regimes that employ the single-member plurality electoral system, in which the country is divided into single-member constituencies (districts) and the seat in each is awarded to the candidate who receives most votes, whether or not this amounts to a majority. As is well known, the application of such a system to a nation's votes can produce an outcome that does not bring about anything close to proportionality at the national level. For example, in Britain's 1992 election, the Liberal Democrats won 18 per cent of the votes and only 3 per cent of the seats; in Canada in 1993 the Progressive

Conservatives won 16 per cent of the votes and fewer than 1 per cent of the seats. Electoral systems based on single-member constituencies are employed also in Australia, France, India and the United States, and most of these countries have experienced similar cases of disproportionality at elections.

It is important to note, though, that election outcomes in such countries fall so far short of perfect proportionality not because the system has malfunctioned but because it prioritises other criteria. In particular, supporters of such systems argue that proportionality *per se* is no great virtue, since if every party receives close to the same share of the seats in parliament as it won of the votes, the result may be a highly fragmented parliament in which it is difficult to form a stable, effective government. In this perception, sacrificing some degree of proportionality, particularly at the expense of smaller parties, in order to overrepresent larger parties and make it easier for one of them to form a single-party government, is well worth while. Another argument used in favour of such electoral systems is that they fix responsibility for representation unambiguously upon one member of parliament, whereas in electoral systems based upon multi-member constituencies links between citizens and parliamentarians might potentially be less clear.

Despite these considerations, most democratic states use electoral systems that give higher priority than this to the concept of proportionality. Indeed, most countries use an electoral system based on proportional representation (see REPRESENTATION, MODELS OF) with variation only in the precise method by which proportionality is achieved; by means of a list system, as in most European countries such as Germany, Spain and Sweden, or by the single transferable vote, as in Ireland and Malta. However, even though such systems are often grouped together under the heading 'proportional representation', most of them do not in fact set out to achieve or maximise proportional representation at all costs. Proportionality, in the eyes of policy makers, seems to be best when experienced in moderation.

There are several devices that can be employed to attenuate the degree of proportionality that the name 'proportional representation' might seem to imply. Each of them is motivated by one or other of the considerations that we mentioned earlier. One device is to set a threshold that parties must attain before they qualify for any seats in parliament. For example, in Sweden a party needs to win 4 per cent of the votes nationally (or, alternatively, attain a certain level of support in any one region of the country) in order to take part in the share-out of seats. The result is that small parties are not proportionally represented, and the seats that they must forfeit are taken up by larger parties. The rationale, as in single-member plurality systems, is to prevent excessive parliamentary fragmentation and facilitate government formation.

A second device is the adoption of small constituencies. Proportionality is easier to achieve when there is a large number of seats to share out; thus, when the whole country is one large constituency, as in the case of the Netherlands with 150 members, it is possible to award every party something very close to its 'fair share' of seats. In contrast, if a country is divided into a large number of relatively small constituencies – such as Spain, with around fifty constituencies each returning on average about seven members of parliament – proportionality is harder to attain, but citizens may feel that they have a closer link with a representative than is likely in the Netherlands and, again, the construction of a stable, albeit less representative, government may be made easier.

Proportionality and disproportionality

Thus far, we have discussed proportionality as if the concept itself was fairly unproblematic. In one sense, this is true; we can all agree on what constitutes complete or pure proportionality when we see it. If, still discussing the matter in an electoral context, every political party receives exactly the same share of the seats as it won of the votes, then complete proportionality has been attained. Matters become more complex when it is impossible to achieve complete proportionality; that is, when some degree of disproportionality is inevitable, as is usually the case. The goods to be apportioned are not endlessly divisible, and parties' vote shares rarely come in neat quantities. Whereas an individual's income is calibrated in such small units that we can calculate a given proportion of it for tax purposes to everyone's satisfaction, this is not the case with parliamentary seats. If a party wins 26.3 per cent of the votes and there are 200 seats to share out, or 40 per cent of the votes with 659 seats to apportion, exactly how many seats should it receive?

The fairest answer seems to be that for this party, and all other parties, we should devise an allocation that is as close to complete proportionality as is possible, but this apparently simple response glosses over the central question: which of two seat allocations, both of which are to some degree disproportional, is closer to complete proportionality? To give a specific example: if three parties win votes in the proportions 60–28–12, and there are 5 seats to share among them, which allocation comes closest to complete proportionality: is it 3–1–1, 3–2–0 or 4–1–0?

In practice, different, and perfectly defensible, allocation methods will often lead to different outcomes. In the example given in the previous paragraph, the most widely used proportional representation formula in Europe, devised by Victor d'Hondt (and by Thomas Jefferson in America), regards 4–1–0 as the outcome that is closest to full proportionality; in contrast, the equal proportions allocation method, used to award Representatives to states in the USA, sees 3–1–1 as the most proportional.

The maximisation of proportionality can be conceived of in a variety of ways: in terms of equalising, as far as possible, either the 'cost' in votes that each party must pay for a seat or the 'share' that each voter has of a member of parliament, or, alternatively, in terms of mini- mising the overrepresentation of the most over- represented party or the under-representation of the most under-represented party. The notion of 'equalising as far as possible' is itself contested territory, for there is more than one way of judging this. Whether 2 is more different from 3 than 20 is from 25 depends on whether we take the absolute difference (subtracting the smaller number from the larger) or the relative difference (dividing the larger number by the smaller). It need hardly be said that there can be no definitive resolution of the questions as to which of these conceptions of proportion- ality is best; different methods are based on different conceptions, and, as Balinski and Young (1982: 60) put it, each 'has its own seductive logic'.

Although these may seem to be abstruse points, they can be of practical political import, given that seats in parliament may be determined by which particular notion of measuring the degree of proportionality under- pins the electoral system. In the USA, math- ematical arguments about the merits of one conception of proportionality versus another as the basis for awarding Representatives to states were aired extensively in the early decades of the twentieth century, and this resulted in the House changing in 1941 from a method based on absolute differences to one that sees the relative difference as the correct measure of difference – motivated, it is true, not so much by a concern for mathematical correctness as by an awareness on the part of the Democrat majority House that the new method, known as 'equal proportions', would result in a gain of one seat for the Democrats compared with the existing method (Balinski and Young 1982: 58–9).

Conclusion

Proportionality is a concept underpinning decision-making in a variety of areas of political life. Nevertheless, despite its ready association with concepts such as fairness and equity, there may be circumstances in which the maximisation of proportionality is not unam- biguously the best way of maximising equity. In the context of electoral systems, the desire to maximise proportionality is almost invariably qualified by concern that this might make the achievement of effective government more difficult because of the perception that some trade-off between stable government and proportionality is unavoidable; or, perhaps, by the fact that the dominant voices in electoral system design are usually the major political parties, who tend to be the beneficiaries when proportionality is less than perfect.

See also:

decision-making; elections; electoral systems; equality; parties; representation, models of

Further reading

Balinski, M.L. and Young, H.P. (1982) *Fair Representation: Meeting the Ideal of One Man, One Vote*, New Haven, CT: Yale University Press.

Gallagher, M. (1991) 'Proportionality, Disproportionality and Electoral Systems', *Electoral Studies* 10(1): 33–51.

Lijphart, A. (1994) *Electoral Systems and Party Systems: A Study of Twenty-seven Democracies, 1945–1990*, Oxford and New York: Oxford University Press.

Monroe, B.L. (1994) 'Disproportionality and Malapportionment: Measuring Electoral Inequity', *Electoral Studies* 13(2): 132–49.

Pennisi, A. (1998) 'Disproportionality Indexes and Robustness of Proportional Allocation Methods', *Electoral Studies* 17(1): 3–20.

Taagepera, R. and Shugart, M.S. (1989) *Seats and Votes: The Effects and Determinants of Electoral Systems*, New Haven, CT: Yale University Press.

Young, H.P. (1994) *Equity in Theory and Practice*, Princeton, NJ: Princeton University Press.

MICHAEL GALLAGHER

psephology

Psephology is the study of ELECTIONS and voting by means of statistical analysis. The term was coined in 1952 by the Oxford electoral historian R.B. McCallum. It derives from the Greek *psephos*, the pebble thrown into one or another urn to cast a vote in democratic Athens. The related term psephologist is sometimes used with a hint of irony to denote someone so fascinated with electoral statistics that they ignore politics.

Psephology broadly takes two forms, defined by the character of the evidence studied. Geographical psephology analyses election results at ward, constituency and regional level and examines their correlation with census and other official data available for the same geographic units. This was the only psephology undertaken before the development of sample surveys in the 1940s. It produced a quite sophisticated sociology of elections in the Third Republic (Siegfried 1913) and in the United States prior to the Second World War (Merriam and Gosnell 1919).

Geographical psephology has been largely but not entirely superseded by survey-based psephology, which analyses the ELECTORAL BEHAVIOUR and attitudes of representative samples of individual citizens. National 'panel' surveys, in which the same respondents are re-interviewed after and between successive elections, offer the richest source of evidence because they allow for causal as well as correlational multivariate analysis. They are now the preferred method for studying electoral behaviour and explaining election results. Valuable supplementary information is provided by non-panel (cross-sectional) surveys, sub-national surveys and surveys of particular social groups.

Geographical psephology suffers from various drawbacks. It is restricted to those social and demographic variables collected by official agencies with objectives very different from electoral analysis in mind. Statistics on key factors in voters' choice – their wealth, religion or ethnic identity, for example – are often not collected. It excludes data on attitudes and perceptions, which may be crucial for understanding voting behaviour. Most seriously, data for geographical units are subject to the 'ecological fallacy', an exceptionally stubborn problem of spurious correlation, which infers individual-level relationships from aggregate-level data. If, for example, an electoral swing to the Conservative Party correlates strongly with the proportion of farmers in a constituency, it cannot be deduced that it is the farmers who have swung disproportionately. Many other explanations are consistent with the correlation: perhaps the swing has occurred among the elderly retired, who tend to live in rural areas, or perhaps Conservative-inclined voters have moved to country areas in larger numbers than Labour-inclined voters. The impossibility of calculating the combination of straight conversions, differential turnout and abstention, and switches to and from minor parties that underlies the aggregate-level two-party 'swing' (that is, the net shift in the two parties' vote shares) is the same kind of problem. To discover the pattern of individual-level behaviour that produced the aggregate result, a sample survey is needed.

Although survey-based psephology overcomes most of these problems it suffers from others of its own. Non-response can make samples unrepresentative, particularly of the socially and politically disengaged. Such problems are accentuated by sample attrition in successive waves of panel surveys. Respondents' recall of past behaviour, even if it occurred only a few weeks previously, is unreliable and their reports of current attitudes are biased by their perception of what is socially approved. Representative samples generally comprise too few numbers from minority groups for analytic purposes. They are also subject to the 'individualist' fallacy that voters' behaviour can be explained entirely in terms of their individual characteristics and attitudes and they are poor at measuring the influence of voters' local milieux.

Geographical psephology therefore continues to hold some advantages over exclusive reliance on surveys. It is valuable for exploring the electoral behaviour of residentially concentrated groups such as linguistic minorities or occupational communities. The accumulation of long time-series of geographical data allows for a historical depth in voting research that surveys can rarely provide. For the detection of regional variations, of the growth and decay of national uniformities in voting, of long-term glacial changes in electoral cleavages and historical junctures in party fortunes, geographical data are crucial. In addition, ward and constituency-level data are ideally suited to the analytic use of such communal characteristics as racial composition, occupational structure, social CLASS polarisation and local social change. The statistical appendix in the 'Nuffield' series of studies of British general elections skilfully exploits this potential in geographical psephology to analyse the operation of the electoral system, electoral PARTICIPATION, tactical voting and the socio-geographic basis of British voting from a historical perspective (for example, Curtice and Steed 1997).

A free and fair election is the defining institution of a democracy. By explaining the outcome of an election, or series of elections, psephology has contributed to democratic thought and practice in four ways. Firstly, it provides a counterweight to popular (and usually self-serving) interpretations placed on election results by winners and losers. The winner typically claims a popular mandate for the party's entire programme. Survey-based psephology can reveal the varying level of popular support for each main element of a party's programme and the role played by party policy in influencing the shift in votes that was decisive for the result. It is in fact, unusual for a specific policy proposal, as distinct from a party's overall record, image or values, to influence significant numbers of voters. For example, psephology can demonstrate that, contrary to popular belief, the Falklands War did not win the 1983 election for the Conservatives and the issue of tax did not lose the Labour party the election of 1992.

Secondly, survey-based psephology's findings about the social psychology of voters have undermined traditional assumptions about the democratic citizen. The liberal ideal of informed and alert citizens, attentive to the public debate, who cast their vote after careful consideration of the alternative record and prospectuses of the parties, turns out to be far from reality. Psephology shows that the majority of voters in all democracies are relatively uninterested and uninformed about politics – in particular about party policies – and vote on a habitual or hereditary basis. 'Floating' voters, whose vote switching has disproportionate impact on an election result, tend to be the least well-informed and interested of all. Election surveys consistently find that in established party systems most voters' opinions follow from, rather than lead to, their party preferences (Campbell *et al.* 1966). In the interchange of influence between parties and voters, party mobilisation of supporters is considerably stronger than voters' impact on parties. The main causal flow in democracies is top-down and producer-led, not bottom-up and customer-led.

Thirdly, geographical psephology has significantly enhanced our understanding of the operation of electoral systems, in particular the single-member, simple plurality system (SMSP). It can explain why some parties gain more seats than others for any given share of the popular vote and how the national distribution of safe and marginal seats relates to the well-known capacity for SMSP to convert the leading party's plurality of the vote into a majority of seats in the legislature. It can also analyse the sources of partisan bias in SMSP systems in terms of the relative contribution made by the differential size, turnout and marginality in the seats held by the different parties.

Fourthly, psephological analysis is used by parties and politicians to shape their ELECTORAL CAMPAIGNING strategies. Evidence about the demographic and attitudinal make-up of loyal, prospective and alienated party supporters is eagerly seized upon by party tacticians. This contributes to the democratic process if it encourages parties to adapt their agendas and policies to the real concerns of citizens or leads to clearer communication of party messages to the electorate. It can also distort the democratic process if it is used to create manipulative or destructive forms of electoral campaigning. The growth in the late 1990s of virulently negative and personal attacks on opponents in election campaigns in the United States is a case in point.

In their coverage of election campaigns and results, the mass MEDIA make use of psephology. They tend to focus on the 'horse race' element of elections and call upon psephologists to forecast the result on the basis of opinion polls and early declaring constituencies on the night of the election. They also rely on the academic credibility of psephologists to offer authoritative judgements on the electoral performance of the parties, and their leaders. Because elections excite more public interest than most other aspects of politics, psephology can, via the mass media, make a contribution of some intellectual rigour to the ordinary citizen's understanding of the electoral and thus democratic process.

See also:

elections; electoral behaviour; electoral campaigning; electoral systems; party systems

Further reading

Campbell, A., Converse, P. Miller, W. and Stokes, D. (1966) *The American Voter*, New York: John Wiley.

Curtice, J. and Steed, M. (1997) 'Appendix 2: The Results Analysed', in D. Butler and D. Kavanagh (eds), *The British General Election of 1997*, London: Macmillan.

Merriam, C.E. and Gosnell, H. (1919) *The American Party System*, New York: Macmillan.

Siegfried, A. (1913) *Tableau Politique de la France de l'Ouest sous la Troisieme Republique*, Paris: Librairie Armand Colin.

IVOR CREWE

public opinion

In one sense, democracy can be defined as government by public opinion. Forms of government that use non-democratic political principles, like selection for political office by heredity or caste, may pay attention to public opinion but are not dependent upon it for their existence. It was once said of government in eighteenth-century Britain that it was 'despotism tempered by riot'. In one sense, this is government responsive to public opinion, but it is not democratic government.

Democratic governments depend for their existence on public opinion through formal and regularised institutional devices like ELECTIONS, perhaps supplemented by the ability of pressure groups and other organisations claiming to represent opinion to influence public policy. The exact form this dependence takes varies. It may be close, with frequent elections where the fate of a government depends upon the popular vote. It may be remote, with infrequent elections for a variety of bodies that share governing powers among themselves. Yet, wherever governments rest upon popular choice at some point for their continued existence, they thereby rest upon public opinion.

It was precisely this feature of democratic government to which ancient Greek thinkers like Plato and Thucydides objected. They held that the populace was fickle, ignorant and manipulable, and therefore that public opinion was a weak basis upon which to rest political AUTHORITY. In Book VI of *The Republic*, Plato maintained that, just as someone with knowledge of navigation ought to steer a ship at sea, so only someone with moral knowledge was able to steer the ship of state, and this ought to preclude the holding of office by those who merely pandered to the prejudices of public opinion. In Book 6 of *The Peloponnesian War*, Thucydides thought the disastrous and misjudged military expedition to Sicily in 415 BC voted for by the Athenian assembly was the fault of those like Alcibiades who manipulated the popular debate for their own ends to the detriment of virtuous citizens like Nicias. Controversies about the proper role and status of public opinion today pick up at many points these ancient concerns.

Public opinion and representative democracy

When democratic institutions first began to make their appearance in the modern world,

they were accompanied by disputes among political theorists about the role that public opinion ought to play in government. Rousseau's account of the general will in *The Social Contract* (1762) can be seen as an attempt to provide a theoretical justification for the view that the decisions of a government should be in accordance with public opinion provided the conditions existed to ensure that expressed opinion is consistent with the interest of all citizens. By contrast, among founders of the American constitution such as James Madison, there was a conscious attempt to insulate political representatives from the day to day fluctuations and intensity of public opinion by various means. Within the US Constitution, the Senate and the Electoral College, as well as the SEPARATION OF POWERS, were devices by which public opinion could be refined and sifted as political representatives deliberated with one another about the public interest. As Madison said in *Federalist Paper* 62, the necessity of a bicameral legislature is suggested 'by the propensity of all single and numerous assemblies to yield to the impulse of sudden and violent passions, and to be seduced by factious leaders into intemperate and pernicious resolutions'.

Madisonian scepticism about the beneficial effects of making political decisions depend upon the fluctuating movements of public opinion was intensified in the twentieth century by the experience of the rise of fascism to power. Theories of 'totalitarian democracy' (Talmon 1955), for example, highly influential in the middle of the century, can be read as a warning of what would happen if the attempt was made to apply Rousseauian ideas of democratic decision-making to the circumstances of a modern society. At best one would expect plebiscitary democracy, and at worst totalitarianism. In reaction to this analysis, radical democrats from the 1960s onwards started to revive the Rousseauian critique of government divorced from the people and to highlight the extent to which active CITIZENSHIP was the antidote to the flattening and homogenising of popular attitudes in what

Marcuse (1972) called a 'one-dimensional' society.

In modern political theory, therefore, the debate has become one between those who favour a strong and definitive role for public opinion in the making of public and political choices and those who favour a weak or more constrained role. Those who advocate a strong role follow the dictum in *On Representative Government* by John Stuart Mill, himself often ambivalent about the influence of public opinion, that there 'is no difficulty in showing that the ideally best form of government is that in which the sovereignty, or supreme controlling power in the last resort, is vested in the entire aggregate of the community' (Mill 1861: 244). By contrast, sceptics take the view of Joseph Schumpeter (1943: 262) who thought that citizens dropped down to a lower level of mental performance when they reasoned about politics and the fundamental lesson that the public needed to learn in a modern democracy was not to engage in political back-seat driving.

This division of approach finds expression in competing views about the form that institutions responsible for making decisions on public policy should take in a democracy. Those inclined to the Rousseauian populist view favour practices that enable public opinion to have a direct effect upon public policy. These include such devices as the extensive use of referendums in the making of public decisions, as in Switzerland, or the right of citizens to initiate legislation or policy, as in some states of the USA. Sceptics about the role of public opinion in a democracy favour checks and balances and other forms of constitutional CONSTRAINT provided by the institutions of representative democracy.

To understand the considerations at issue in these debates, it is useful to look at three questions: the meaning of the term 'public opinion'; the rationality of public opinion; and the ways in which governments can be responsive to public opinion.

The meaning of public opinion

In understanding the role that public opinion does and ought to play in a democracy, much depends on what the term 'public opinion' is taken to mean, and in particular on what is meant by the term 'public'. Walter Bagehot thought that parliament and government in nineteenth-century England ought to be responsive to public opinion, but he also held to a view of the political public in which some views, those of a social elite, would have more influence than others, so that, as he put it, 'happy nations weigh votes as well as count them' (Bagehot 1867: 171). By contrast, a theorist might assign only a limited role to public opinion in the making of policy, but hold that the relevant public should be broadly defined so that it includes as many citizens as possible on equal terms. Practices of widespread public consultation in the making of public policies are quite compatible with a commitment to the view that representative democratic institutions are preferable to ones resting on a Rousseauian POPULISM.

Before the advent of mass sampling, public opinion had to be defined in terms of expressions of view at public assemblies or the sort informal assessment that Bagehot identified in nineteenth-century England. However, the invention of the random sample survey picking on a set of respondents small enough to be interviewed but from which reliable inferences could be made about the views of the whole population fundamentally changed the picture. Henceforth, public opinion did not need to be understood in terms of a popular assembly as it was no longer feasible in a large scale society. Nor did it have to be understood in terms of a restricted salon set of the people whose views were thought to matter. Instead, it could be seen as the views volunteered in response to standardised prompts extrapolated from a random sample and taking the form of a frequency distribution across the range of responses. Proponents of the survey method, like George Gallup, thought that scientific sampling would restore citizen influence to the making of public policy.

An important feature of the survey method of ascertaining public opinion is that the results are always statistical in form. That is to say, public opinion by this method takes the form of a frequency distribution of views in response to questions that are asked. In older views of public opinion, resting on ideas like the sense of the meeting or an hypothesised Rousseauian general will, the view could often, if not always, plausibly, be maintained that there was an underlying social consensus to which policy should conform. Indeed, in some writings on DELIBERATIVE DEMOCRACY influenced by the work of Habermas (1996), this notion of public opinion as a consensus to be discovered or achieved is still influential. By contrast, mass sampling shows how much disagreement over a particular question might exist in a community.

The rationality of public opinion

If the opinion poll view of public opinion is now the predominant one, new twists on familiar questions immediately come to the fore. The issue that arose in ancient Athens was whether the populace could be trusted with power, given that when it met in assembly it was prone to fickleness and manipulation. In modern opinion poll terms, the parallel questions concern the quality of the public's understanding of political issues that opinion polls reveal. Thus, where knowledge can be measured in a reasonably objective way, large proportions of respondents make mistakes on matters to do with basic political facts. In addition, they often mistake the policy positions of political PARTIES on important issues. Moreover, respondents' replies about their own policy positions appear to change when sampled over time in a way that appears to be random. Fluctuations of response to small changes in question wording are a further symptom of instability. Schumpeter's claim that the average citizens drops down to a lower level of mental performance when thinking about politics seems to be justified by these findings.

However, against this interpretation, there are those who argue that aggregate patterns of public opinion are far more stable than those at the level of the individual. These aggregate patterns are also correlated with obvious measures of citizen well-being such as the state of the economy. In other words, individual irrationality is offset by collective rationality. It is, of course, a nice question of political theory whether this aggregate rationality, which presumably arises as the result of a large number of mutually self-cancelling errors, is a sufficient basis on which to rest the claims of LEGITI-MACY that democratic governments claim.

Understanding of this issue promises to be further enhanced by the invention of delibera-tive polling, the practice of bringing a statisti-cally representative sample of the population together to discuss and debate a particular issue (Fishkin 1995: 161–76). This method of polling public opinion still keeps individual variety in response but enables respondents to talk to one another about the merits of different views. The assumption in such an approach is that deliberative polling can compensate for the discursive deficit inherent in modern mass democracies by providing an opportunity for a group of citizens to reflect upon their own preferences in the light of evidence, INFORMATION and discussion with others. It is too early to say exactly what light the practice of deliberative polling will shed on the ancient question of the rationality of public opinion in a democracy. One possibility, however, is that it will show that the defects of expressed public opinion are likely to be due less to the intrinsic shortcomings of citizens themselves and more to the settings within which preferences are formed and matured. In other words, Schumpeter was not wrong to assert that people drop down to a lower level of mental performance when they think about politics, but ignored the possibility that their performance could be enhanced by placing citizens in a setting that fostered responsible deliberation.

Responsiveness

The ancient dispute about the role of public opinion turned on the perception by anti-democrats that public opinion was ignorant and fickle and therefore manipulable by demagogues. Modern social choice theory has detached the question of manipulation from assumptions about the ignorance and instability that might underlie preferences. In a series of results stemming from Arrow (1963), but going back further to Condorcet, it has been shown that manipulation by political actors can occur even when popular preferences are well-formed and stable. For example, those in a position to influence the order in which votes are taken or the sequence of issues that are to appear on the agenda can sometimes achieve outcomes that they favour. In other words, even with a stable public opinion – one that is not fickle – there can still be instability in policy choice depending on the way in which the aggregation of diverse opinions is handled.

An example of how this can arise is given in instances where there are three possible choices. When there are three or more alternatives over which choice has to be made, it can sometimes happen that there is a majority against any one of them. We can thus observe majority rule cycles, in which public opinion favours alternative X over Y, Y over Z but Z over X. In these cases, it is argued, the notion of a popular will expressing public opinion becomes meaningless. From these results, political theorists like the late William Riker (1982) have drawn pessimistic conclusions about the value of a democracy resting on a Rousseauian general will, arguing for example that those who control the political agenda can effectively manipulate public opinion as much as any classical demagogue.

The question about exactly what the results of social choice theory mean for our understanding of the place of public opinion within a democracy is not one that is easy to resolve, however. Cycles may be no more than bare logical possibilities, difficult to observe in practice and failing to emerge by the constraints of individuals feeling the need to conform to a pattern of beliefs. Even if they are present in the structure of public opinion, they may be very difficult for elite political actors to manipulate in the way that demagogues like Alcibiades were said to manipulate the crowds of the Athenian assembly.

If, despite the possibility of majority rule cycles, democratic governments are capable of being responsive to public opinion without manipulation, what do we know about the conditions under which responsiveness is enhanced or reduced? The two main competing models of representative government are the responsible party model, associated with Westminster systems, in which a plurality of votes determines the outcome, and a more consensual view of democracy in which systems of proportional representation in election give rise to coalitional bargaining among parliamentary parties which in turn determines the government (Lijphart 1984) (see CONSENSUS DEMOCRACY). At first sight it would look as though the WESTMINSTER MODEL was superior of the two in terms of its responsiveness to public opinion, since the electorate can unambiguously express its opinion of a party by removing it from office and installing its opponents. In this way, it can be argued, there is a direct dependence of the government on the state of public opinion. By contrast, consensual systems remove the formation of governments from the direct control of the electorate by fractioning party systems and producing results in which governments typically have to be made and unmade through parliamentary bargaining.

Despite these initial intuitions, it looks as though coalition governments emerging from consensual systems are likely to pursue policies that approximate to the views of the median voter as well as allowing the expressing of opinions that cannot be easily accommodated within a two-party system. So long as parties whose policy positions coincide with that of the median voter are central to governing coalitions in such systems, they can facilitate responsiveness to popular opinion at least as much as the first past the post, simple plurality system. The Madisonian can, of course, always reply that the virtues of responsible government are at least as important as those of responsive government, at which point the argument shifts to other ground.

Whatever the relative merits of ELECTORAL SYSTEMS in terms of their ability to translate public opinion into political choice, it is clear that no electoral mechanism is sufficient to the task. In all representative democracies elaborate systems of interest articulation have grown up to put the point of view of MINORITIES who feel particularly affected or moved by a policy. These systems of interest group representation open up further important issues in the principles of democracy, again reflecting the division between Rousseau and Madison. Is public opinion to be conceived as the averaging of the opinions of all citizens in society, as Rousseau thought, or is it better thought of as the balance of opinion that emerges through the clash of competing interest groups, as Madison asserted? Theoretical descendants of Rousseau, as well as of Bentham, would argue that the expression of public opinion is distorted if 'partial' or 'sinister' interests are allowed to influence policy. Theoretical descendants of Madison think that the balancing of opinion among a plurality of irreducibly plural interests is the only way to avoid the tyranny of the majority.

Conclusion: new problems

In addition to those problems with classical roots, new political issues suggest new challenges for the analysis of public opinion. There is a line of argument asserting that the understanding of public opinion is especially important in relation to those issues that involve controlling the technology of a 'risk society' (Beck 1992), that is to say, a society in which new production processes impose large-scale risks on populations. With this view goes the idea that new methods are required for gauging the strength of public opinion towards environmental and health risks, because existing representative institutions have failed in their mandate to cope with such issues. Yet, though representative democracies may be inadequate, no one has to date invented the institutional forms that are capable of reliably and sensitively capturing the public's view on such matters.

In a way, discussion about the adequacy of the institutions of representative government goes to the heart of competing conceptions of democracy. If democratic government is defined as government by public opinion, the means by which this might be achieved and its dangers averted over many important policy questions still have to be discovered.

See also:

communication; democratic debate; electoral campaigning; information; interest groups; media; political obligation; psephology; representation, concept of

Further reading

Arrow, K.J. (1963) *Social Choice and Individual Values*, 2nd edn, New Haven, CT: Yale University Press.

Bagehot, W. (1963) *The English Constitution*, ed. R.H.S. Crossman, London: Fontana/ Collins.

Beck, U. (1992) *Risk Society*, London: Sage.

Converse, P.E. (1964) 'The Nature of Belief Systems in Mass Publics', in D.E. Apter (ed.), *Ideology and Discontent*, New York: The Free Press, 206–61.

The Federalist Papers (1961), ed. C. Rossiter, New York: New American Library.

Fishkin, J.S. (1995) *The Voice of the People: Public Opinion and Democracy*, New Haven, CT: Yale University Press.

Habermas, J. (1996) *Between Facts and Norms*, Cambridge: Polity Press.

Lijphart, A. (1984) *Democracies*, New Haven, CT: Yale University Press.

Marcuse, H. (1972) *One Dimensional Man*, London: Sphere Books.

Mill, J.S. (1991) 'Considerations on Representative Government', repr. in J. Gray (ed.), *John Stuart Mill On Liberty and Other Essays*, Oxford: Oxford University Press.

Page, B. and Shapiro, R.Y. (1992) *The Rational Public: Fifty Years of Trends in Americans' Policy Preferences*, Chicago: University of Chicago Press.

Riker, W.H. (1982) *Liberalism against Populism*, San Francisco: Freeman and Co.

Schumpeter, J.A. (1954) *Capitalism, Socialism and Democracy*, London: Allen and Unwin.

Talmon, J.L. (1955) *The Origins of Totalitarian Democracy*, London: Secker and Warburg.

Zaller, J.R. (1992) *The Nature and Origins of Mass Opinion*, New York: Cambridge University Press.

ALBERT WEALE

public–private distinction

There are two different conceptions of the public–private distinction in liberalism: the state–civil society distinction and the social–personal distinction. In the first, CIVIL SOCIETY is private in the sense that it is not governed by the public power of the state. In the second, which arises later than the first and in some ways may be viewed as a response to it, the personal is private in that it represents a sphere of intimacy to which one might retreat in face of the pressures to conform within society. This creates a tripartite, rather than dual, division of social relations: the state, civil society and the personal. It is clear that the state is always cast as public. It is equally clear that the personal (when considered within political theory) is cast as private. Confusingly, civil society is cast as private when opposed to the state, and public when opposed to the personal.

With the rise of feminist theory, a third public–private distinction is delineated. Neither of the first two distinctions explicitly invokes the family. In contrast, the third form of the public–private distinction contrasts the public, comprising both the state and civil society, with the private, defined institutionally as the relations and activities of domestic life. The intriguing, and politically significant, issue that feminist theory draws attention to is the fact that contemporary liberal theory nowhere explicitly theorises the relation between this third articulation of the public–private dichotomy and either of the other two. For some feminist theorists, this neglect renders the entire liberal project suspect; had the family been viewed as a part of civil society, liberal theorists would surely have been compelled to oppose its hierarchical form and argue for its

organisation on the basis of EQUALITY and consent as they did with all other forms of civil co-operation.

One can distinguish three general orders of feminist critique of the liberal characterisation of the public–private distinction: the first addresses the premises of LIBERALISM itself (especially its conception of the self), the second addresses liberalism's historical origins in social contract theory, and the third addresses the historical practice of liberal regimes. Let us consider each in turn. The first critique focuses on the question of subjectivity, claiming the liberal discourse of individual AUTONOMY to be prescriptive rather than descriptive, structuring rather than simply reflecting social relations. Recognition of this fact leads to two further insights. The first is that very particular social structures and institutions are needed to shape individuals into this mould; the second is that this conception of subjectivity may not apply equally to everyone. The first insight leads to a concern with the processes of reproduction, nurturance and socialisation. The second to an exploration of the extent to which women have been understood as subordinate, dependent and emotional, and so excluded from the category of 'individuals' within liberal theorising. These two issues are linked in women's status as primary carers. Neither the process of caring and nurturing nor the status of carers and nurturers are theorised in liberal theory. The concern of feminist theorists is that, as a result of this omission, not only have women been denied the RIGHTS and privileges granted to the 'rational individuals' of liberal societies, but also that a crucial aspect of life, associated with the caring performed by women, has been glossed over. This insight has implications not only for the role of caring as a practice, but also for its role as a perspective. The significance of caring, as both practice and perspective, has generated a large feminist literature on the 'ethic of care' (Bubeck 1995; Elshtain 1981; Tronto 1993).

This critique of the public–private distinction is complemented by the second, which focuses on contract. Here the object of concern is not the rational liberal individual, but liberalism's origins in social contract theory. This contract-based critique places the subjectivity-based critique in historical context. The focus here is the particular social and political forces that created the situation in which women were confined to a private, domestic, care-taking role while men were presumed to be able to move freely between the private (domestic) and the public (civil society and state) spheres. The most influential theorist here is Carole Pateman. She claims that the social contract that generates liberal politics and establishes the political FREEDOM of individuals simultaneously entails the sexual subordination of women in marriage (Pateman 1983). The social contract that is required to create both civil society and the state requires a sexual contract to accommodate the patriarchalism that predates liberalism. The liberal social contact therefore represents the reorganisation, but not the abolition, of patriarchy. Patriarchy was relocated into the private domain and reformulated as complementary to civil society. In this way gender is given a highly specific and structuring role within liberal theory at the same time as liberal theory presents itself as gender-neutral.

The third critique of the public/private dichotomy focuses on the historical practice of liberal regimes. The charge here is that, notwithstanding the abstract commitment to the importance of a prohibition on state intervention in the private sphere, liberal states have in practice regulated and controlled the family (Okin 1998). Not only has this practice been contrary to the fundamental principle of liberalism, it has been adopted in pursuit of a profoundly illiberal end: the perpetuation of patriarchy. Whilst the state adopted this directly non-neutral relation to personal and domestic life, it also upheld practices within the marketplace which presumed that those engaged in waged work could rely on the support and care of someone at home. To add to the insult, from the perspective of women, the principle of non-intervention in the private sphere has been used by the state to justify inaction regarding cases of child-abuse, marital rape and domestic violence. In short, liberal states have actually enforced patriarchal power relations within the family, while formally denying their responsibility to intervene in familial disputes on the grounds that it is essential to limit state intervention in civil society and personal relations. This tension, arising from the very formulation of liberalism itself, is the inevitable conclusion of the ambivalent role of the family in relation to the private sphere.

These three feminist critiques of the public–private distinction have received varying receptions even within feminist theory, but together they have generated a widespread suspicion of discourses of public and private, which is only recently giving way to attempts to positively re-theorise a public–private distinction in more gender-neutral ways. This re-theorisation characteristically entails three main elements: the de-sexualisation of the values associated with the public and the private, the exploration of the ways in which the public and the private are interconnected and mutually constitutive, and a recognition of the changing nature of the boundary between the two spheres (Lister 1997: 120–1). The public–private distinction is viewed, in this current literature, as a contested construct which can be revised rather than simply rejected. In contrast to the early feminist slogan that 'the personal is political', theorists holding quite diverse theoretical perspectives are fairly unified in their endorsement of the importance of maintaining some form of distinction between the public and the private (Elshtain 1981; Young 1990).

The precise formulation of these new visions vary. Elshtain depicts the private sphere as a potential sphere of intimate human relations protected from the influence of the political (1981). Young proposes a definition of the private as: 'that aspect of his or her life and activity that any person has the right to exclude from others' (Young 1990: 119). Okin accepts the threefold traditional liberal definition of the private as a place for intimate relations with others, a space where one can temporarily shed one's public roles and as a means of securing the time alone to develop one's creativity (Okin

1998: 136). Despite the variations, there is a shared commitment to maintaining a private sphere which is equally realisable for both men and women and a clear acknowledgement that any such sphere will be socially constituted and historically and culturally contingent.

Various new articulations of the public have also emerged of late. Many of these have been influenced by Jürgen Habermas's work on the public sphere. His major contribution was to isolate the public sphere as a structure within civil society in which he locates 'the political', which is distinguished from both the narrow conception of politics as the state and a wider notion of the political as power relations (Habermas 1989). This conception of a public sphere is characterised by the institutionalisation of the ideal of equality, the existence of rational COMMUNICATION and the deliberation on issues of general significance. Many feminist theorists have criticised this model for being overly universalistic and so suppressing concrete difference, which has the effect of marginalising women from the public (Benhabib 1992; Yeatman 1994; Fraser 1990). Yet several nonetheless aim to revise and 'feminise' this vision of the public sphere rather than reject it (Benhabib 1992; Fraser 1990). Perhaps the most significant alternative vision of public life is offered by Iris Young, who proposes a more heterogeneous public, open to 'bodily and affective particularity' (Young 1998: 443). Her suggestion is that the public should be open and accessible, which will require the rejection of the tradition of Enlightenment republicanism that, in aspiring to the 'common good', inevitably submerges particularity. If public spaces are to be inclusive, Young maintains, they must promote the positive recognition of differences of perspective, experience and affiliation. The distinction between public and private is maintained, but its association with distinct institutions or human attributes is firmly rejected (Young 1990: 166–121).

See also:

gendering democracy

Further reading

Benhabib, S. (1992) *Situating the Self: Gender, Community and Postmodernism in Contemporary Ethics*, Cambridge: Polity Press.

Bubeck, D. (1995) *Care, Gender and Justice*, Oxford: Clarendon Press.

Elshtain, J.B. (1981) *Public Man, Private Woman: Women in Social and Political Thought*, Oxford: Martin Robertson.

Fraser, N. (1990) 'Rethinking the Public Sphere', in *Social Text*, 25–6.

Habermas, J. (1989) *The Structural Transformation of the Public Sphere*, trans. T. Burger, Cambridge, MA: MIT Press.

Lister, R. (1997) *Citizenship: Feminist Perspectives*, Basingstoke: Macmillan.

Okin, S.M. (1998) 'Gender, the Public and the Private', in A. Phillips (ed.), *Feminism and Politics*, Oxford: Oxford University Press, 116–41.

Pateman, C. (1983) 'Feminist Critiques of the Public/Private Dichotomy', in S. Benn and G. Gaus (eds), *Public and Private in Social Life*, London: Croom Helm, 281–303.

Tronto, J. (1993) *Moral Boundaries: The Political Argument for an Ethic of Care*, New York: Routledge.

Yeatman, A. (1994) *Postmodern Revisionings of the Political*, New York: Routledge.

Young, I.M. (1990) *Justice and the Politics of Difference*, Princeton, NJ: Princeton University Press.

—— (1998) 'Impartiality and the Civic Public', in J. Landes (ed.), *Feminism, The Public and the Private*, Oxford: Oxford University Press, 135–63.

JUDITH SQUIRES

public service

Good democratic practice relies heavily on an ethos of public service. This ethos refers to the willingness of citizens, elected officials and public administrators to contribute to the governance of society and the protection of the public interest through service to the state.

This encompasses those formally engaged in the public sector as well as those voluntarily contributing their time, skills and energy to public goals. Public service is an essential aspect of democratic government, one guided by normative ideals that are shaped by different cultural settings. As such, the INSTITUTIONAL DESIGN and actual practice of public service can vary significantly over time and place.

The contemporary notion of public service is a product of the Enlightenment in that it presumes that social and political orders are constructed by human will, political actors and secular institutions rather than divinely preordained and governed by immutable laws (March and Olsen 1995). Ideals of the early seventeenth-century Enlightenment period continue to shape our understanding of democratic practice and public service: the belief that, individually and collectively, citizens can shape events and steer political institutions and, optimistically, that such interventions can solve public problems and improve community well-being. Norms of obligation encourage this engagement; they correspond to a sense of community and shared purpose, a notion of protecting the common good even as citizens continue to pursue individual interests.

When citizens engage in public service, they often are providing public goods. From an economic viewpoint, public goods offer benefits that generally are not supplied by the marketplace but are important and necessary to community well-being. From this perspective, public goods, the activities of the public sector and public service itself can not easily be assigned precise market values. In addition, public service incorporates altruism when the full benefits do not accrue to the individual engaged in service. This is the heart of the democratic community praised by CIVIL SOCIETY theorists: a dense web of informal relations, a spirit of voluntarism, and a sense of trust and reciprocity mark a healthy civil society. In this climate, individuals do not expect to gain the full benefits of each act of public service but anticipate that they and their community will be better off in the long-run for individual voluntary acts – recycling, election watches, community gardens – that serve public goals. In many countries, services previously provided by the public sector are often now 'co-produced' by the voluntary contributions of citizens. Public service through co-production ranges from mundane services such as garbage collection to involvement in citizen crime watch activities.

But to most people, public service centres on more formal service to the state. In the nineteenth and early twentieth century, Britain and the United States began to institutionalise avenues for public service. Such paths continue to be more or less formal; some individuals give advice and expertise to elected officials on an *ad hoc* basis where others provide public service through electoral office or administrative service. Indeed, references to 'the public service' often include the mix of political and career officials engaged in making and carrying out public policies. Elected officials often refer to themselves as 'public servants' to underscore their commitment to put aside personal interests and individual gain to serve the public interest. Their decisions and activities are intended to benefit the community rather than the individual officials or those who helped them to win office. Of course, few public decisions could match this ideal standard; nevertheless, few public officials would argue explicitly that public service is a means of personal enrichment and patronage for supporters even though others may judge them as acting as if this were so (see CIVIL SERVICE).

Public service also encompasses carrying out the decisions and laws made by elected officials. In contrast to *ad hoc* advisors selected on the basis of trust and expertise and officials elected on their promise to represent citizen interests and concerns, civil servants entrusted with the implementation of public policies are selected on merit. Again, this normative ideal for public service is not always attained. The belief, however, is that those selected to serve the public interest as civil servants should be those with the skills, knowledge, experience, and aptitudes needed for particular tasks. Public AUTHORITY is delegated to civil servants on the basis on this expertise and knowledge; they are held accountable for their actions through a hierarchy of control and rules exemplified by bureaucratic organisational arrangements.

Although considered managers and administrators, civil servants often are directly involved in initiating and drafting legislation and programme guidelines. These RESPONSI-BILITIES stem from the greater expertise and technical knowledge within the civil service and the inclination of elected officials to sign off on vaguely worded legislative compromises. It is a necessary co-operation but one fraught with tensions. Civil servants charged with crafting and managing public policies must act in accordance with the priorities set out by elected officials; they are accountable to the legal authority and political power of elected representatives. But those in public service must also remain ready to present 'principled opposition to actions' they consider unlawful, inappropriate, or unwise (Peters and Rockman 1996). On occasion, these tensions over protecting the public interest erupt in disputes that lead to the resignation or firing of civil servants who can not, in conscience, support the acts of the elected officials to whom they are accountable. Such events tend to be more frequent, visible and celebrated in parliamentary systems (United Kingdom, France, Germany) than in those with other legislative systems (such as the United States).

The Enlightenment ideals of confidence in citizen capacities, of faith in the political system to protect public interests, and of trust that political leaders would serve the larger community according to norms of duty, JUSTICE and reason are shaken by the experiences of contemporary democratic societies (March and Olsen 1995). The very notion of 'a common good' or 'public interest' is open to challenge. After all, there are recurrent appeals to such ideals to justify undemocratic processes and unethical regimes. Furthermore, the proliferation of different social identities and communities of interests makes any agreement on what this common good might be seem an increasingly impossible goal. In some instances,

those involved in public service are criticised as a political elite unrepresentative of and unresponsive to ethnic, religious, sexual, CLASS and other identities. In this context, to speak of public service and the public interest becomes problematic and contested.

Although rarely addressed directly, the role and value of public service is subject to continuing debate in democratic societies. Nowadays there are frequent exhortations to greater voluntary public service as a means to enhance civil society and recover a sense of community. But those fearing that these calls to voluntarism mask and rationalise cuts in public sector responsibilities remain sceptical; they point out that public service depends on a vibrant state and is intended to support and complement public goals, not substitute for them. When citizen efforts are used to replace public sector services and regulatory activities, ACCOUNTABILITY, fairness and TRANSPARENCY issues rise in new forms that have yet to be addressed adequately.

The notion of providing public service through elected office garners even greater cynicism. Independent of elections and the occasional investigation of the ethical behaviour of individual politicians, there are few means of assessing the quality of public service contributed by elected officials. The growing weight of campaign finance in the United States and of MEDIA influence in all democracies makes corruption of the ethos of public service easier, more likely and more possible to obscure (see POLITICAL FINANCING).

The civil service, only one aspect of public service, is an easier and more frequent target of reform movements. Reforms historically aimed at protecting civil servants from political intervention through regulations, sanctions and explicit ethical standards governing their activities. More recent civil service reforms centre on internal improvements in the quality of management, reinventing public administration in ways congruent with private sector management, and downsizing of the public sector itself. Although these initiatives champion public service as the catalyst for community problem-solving and more collaborative

DECISION-MAKING, they rarely emphasise the citizen EDUCATION and organisational structures that would ensure these democratic outcomes. As these new reform initiatives spread across the globe, concerns about the accountability, transparency and legitimacy of public service in these new arrangements are likely to expand as well.

Three trends will require rethinking the role of public service in democratic societies: GLOBALISATION, marketisation, and the reliance on third sector organisations for public policy needs. Globalisation trends undermine the very nature of our understanding of public service. When we speak of service to the state, we now are referring to nation-states that are more permeable, less sovereign political units. Rather than reducing the need for public service, globalisation trends suggest we need to think of public service at different scales. For many individuals, salient interests and identities are increasingly defined by communities and issues that cross national BOUNDARIES. Thanks to new COMMUNICATION technologies, citizens can think of public service in terms of international non-state organisations advocating such global concerns as environmentalism, human RIGHTS and gender EQUALITY. In the future, public service increasingly may be in the form of contributions to global civil societies rather than to nation-states; whether this will result in displacement of public service in a national context or in an overall enhancement of civil society is not yet clear.

Although the core value of public service in a democracy remains intact, challenges to its current institutional design and practice are increasing. Throughout the world, there are strong pressures for PRIVATISATION and marketisation of previously public responsibilities. Using franchises and contracting arrangements with private firms to provide services is often advocated as more efficient and effective than direct public provision. In shrinking the public arena, fewer are directly engaged in public service and their roles and responsibilities often shift to managing contracts with public providers and public–private partnerships. This blurred line between public and private sectors

complicates the rationale for public service. It also raises further concerns about accountability and transparency. Whereas public service provided through a bureaucratic structure could be held to formal rules and ethical strictures ascribing accountability, providing services more indirectly, through contracts and partnerships, removes those accountability structures. When services are provided indirectly, both the processes and outcomes are less transparent. In the absence of accountability and transparent practice, CORRUPTION becomes a real threat to any form of public service.

Reliance on a third sector of non-profit and non-governmental organisations to formulate and carry out public policies complicates current notions of public service. Non-public, non-market organisations are increasingly active in addressing community needs, especially in education and research, health, social services, and culture and recreation sectors (Salamon and Anheir 1996). These non-state organisations may enhance the capacity, vitality and flexibility of the state by providing services in ways that circumvent bureaucratic structures without abandoning community values. They even offer a 'third way' to some, a political strategy that hews to social concerns but in a more flexible and cost-efficient way than might be possible through traditional channels. Despite a tendency to romanticise the roles of non-governmental organisations, they depend substantially on the state for revenue support and often on volunteers and modest staffs for operations. While these organisations may open up new opportunities for public service, they also remind us of the difficulties of holding such organisations accountable and of evaluating the quality of the services they provide.

Many are concerned that these trends, along with the downsizing rhetoric of privatisation and flexibility, will undermine the LEGITIMACY of the public sector and those serving it (Peters and Rockman 1996). One potential consequence would be that those hoping to serve the public would turn away from elected office or the civil service. A weakened and ineffective public sector is in no one's interest; in the absence of a vibrant civil service, democratic societies would fail the fundamental test of providing for the well-being of their citizens.

Making a case for supporting and enhancing public service in a democracy does not entail advocating for a large public sector. Rather, it requires rethinking of the normative and ethical values underlying contemporary opportunities for public service and adapting to the changing character of public order. The case for public service also recognises that the rules and institutions that embody and encourage public service as a duty and obligation of citizenship significantly shape democratic political identities (March and Olsen 1995). In this broader view of citizenship and public service, civic identity becomes critical to democratic practice; engagement in public service becomes more than a matter of personal preference for a few, but a matter of meaningful human identity for many.

See also:

affirmative action; civic virtue; non-governmental organisations; public–private distinction; standards of conduct in public life

Further reading

March, J.G. and Olsen, J.P. (1995) *Democratic Governance*, New York: The Free Press.

Peters, B.G. and Rockman, B.A. (eds) (1996) *Administering the State*, Pittsburgh, PA: University of Pittsburgh.

Salamon, L.A. and Anheir, H.K. (1996) *Defining the Nonprofit Sector: A Cross-National Analysis*, Manchester: Manchester University Press.

SUSAN E. CLARKE

R

radical democracy

There are several different strands of thinking that make up contemporary radical democratic theory. These include participatory, gendered, discursive, deliberative and pluralist conceptions of radical democracy. All of them take as their starting point analyses of the limits and critique of liberal democracy and are committed to its radicalisation and deepening. First formulated by Macpherson (1977), the basic question inspiring radical democratic models is whether liberal democratic government can be made more democratic, and if so, how? In the 1960s and early 1970s, Macpherson's question was answered by developing a participatory model of democracy. His own work was particularly important in this respect, since it contextualised the discussion of democracy by showing the contingent articulation between LIBERALISM and democracy. Far from rejecting this, he argued that democracy had to be extended, while the basic liberal principle of equal RIGHTS be retained. Drawing on these ideas, he argued for a conception of participatory democracy that combined DIRECT DEMOCRACY at the lowest level with delegate democracy at every level above that.

During the 1970s and 1980s, the critique of liberal democracy has been deepened by gendered, ethnic and other identity-based perspectives. In contrast to the politics of the nineteenth and first half of the twentieth century, dominated as it was by struggles over wealth, late-modern politics is increasingly structured around struggles over ecology, gay rights, issues of racial, ethnic and gender identity, and brings new actors to the centre stage of politics. Contemporary radical democratic theory may be understood as an attempt to come to terms with these features of contemporary politics without sacrificing its roots in classical conceptions of radical democracy. In short, two features in particular shape contemporary conceptions of radical democracy: first, a commitment to a critique of liberal democracy, and, second, an attempt to retain dimensions of the liberal tradition while attempting to further democratise it. Both of these have their roots in earlier conceptions of radical democracy.

Classical radical democracy

Central to the radical democratic tradition is a particular critique of liberalism, one that can be traced back to the writings of Rousseau and Marx. Rousseau's account of democracy is important for contemporary theorists of radical democracy, not so much for its distinctive view of the general will, which is found wanting in much contemporary thought, but for its particular criticisms of the liberal tradition. His critique of representative democracy and understanding of self-government challenge the key assumptions of liberal democracy, especially the notion that democracy can be reduced to the periodic selection of deputies through the ballot box. His conception of self-rule – the active giving of consent to rules by citizens – means that a political order providing opportunities for such PARTICIPATION in public affairs must be more than a mere form of government. For contemporary radical democrats, this is an article of faith. Rousseau also develops his theory of democracy in relation to a critique of economic dependency. Freed from economic dependence, citizens are able to make autonomous judgements. Both of these themes are continued in the work of Marx. Like Rousseau, Marx tried to recover a radical heritage against the tide of the liberal tradition. For Marx, participation confined to the periodic election of deputies was an expression of the separation between civil and political spheres, which could only be overcome in communist society. Exposing the political character of liberal rights, he argued for a deepening of popular control over wider areas of life, as well as the need to develop the conditions of economic equality.

Both Rousseau and Marx, however, conceived of politics in negative terms as something to be overcome in favour of a self-regulating, transparent society. This desire to transcend politics and to institute a non-political transparent social order is problematised as undemocratic by contemporary radical democrats. As Macpherson's early writings make clear, it is no longer a question of rejecting liberal democracy *tout court*. Rather, a more nuanced, deconstructive critique of liberal democracy has been articulated, which recognises that some liberal norms are crucial to the development and deepening of democracy.

The Marxist conception of democracy, with its anti-individualistic goal of the EMANCIPATION of self-creating humanity, is extended in the tradition of critical theory that sets out to correct its normative deficits. Like Marx, critical theorists such as Habermas seek to replace liberal possessive INDIVIDUALISM as the basis of a democratic polity. However, while orthodox Marxism turned this into a complete negation of liberalism, critical theory offers a more balanced critique of liberalism, while accepting some liberal ideals such as the ideal of universal FREEDOM and equality as constitutive of genuine political consensus. Democratic institutions are no longer regarded as merely aggregative or based on rational self-interest; they are transformative in nature, aiming at a rational consensual social whole to replace the fragmented and anonymous order of the market in CIVIL SOCIETY.

Post-structuralist inspired conceptions of radical democracy echo many of these concerns. They also regard modern democracy as a specific form of political human coexistence that results from an articulation of two different traditions. These include, on the one side, that of political liberalism (the rule of law (see LAW, RULE OF), SEPARATION OF POWERS and individual rights), and on the other hand, the democratic tradition of popular SOVEREIGNTY (Mouffe 1996: 246). However, given the hostility of the classical radical tradition to PLURALISM, the idea of popular control over public decisions is substantively reworked. Rousseau feared the threat of particular interests leading to the inability to discern the common good, and opted for the 'solidarity-oriented bonds' of a small-scale community instead of the partially shared identities that citizens of a complex post-industrial polity can only construct through democratic public life. Similarly, Marx was suspicious of the value of diversity and plurality in modern society. He held them to be antithetical to the kind of closely integrated community he envisaged, one which would obliterate the artificial and corrupt barrier between 'public' and 'private' (see PUBLIC–PRIVATE DISTINCTION). In contrast to the classical tradition, post-structuralist accounts of a radical democratic politics aim to deepen the moment of pluralism, difference and dissensus.

In sum, contemporary radical democratic theory retains the earlier critique of liberal democracy. However, against the classical radical tradition, contemporary radical democrats deconstruct rather than reject the liberal tradition. They retain the need to deepen democratic participation through an extension of the domains in which it may be exercised. However, they are critical of an emphasis on a homogenising conception of popular sovereignty and its desire to transcend politics through the institution of a non-political, transparent social order.

Towards a definition

Radical democracy may be characterised as an ethos of radicalisation. This ethos is constitutive of agonistic, antagonistic and discursive, as well as deliberative models of democracy, all of which form part of contemporary radical democratic theory. If defined in this manner, two questions immediately spring to mind. What are the conditions of possibility for such radicalisation? What precisely is meant by 'radicalisation'? To answer the first, it is appropriate to turn to the concise answer provided by Lefort. He argues that the basic feature of the modern democratic order is that the place of power is, by the necessity of its structure, an 'empty place'. In a democratic order, sovereignty lies in the people. However, because the people cannot immediately govern themselves, the place of power must always remain an empty place and any person or group occupying it can do so only temporarily (Lefort 1986: 279). The condition of possibility for radicalisation is to be found in what facilitates the emptying out of the place of power, namely, the absence of a world-transcending principle of political ordering. Alongside modernity comes the recognition that principles of ordering are immanent and, therefore, political (subject to struggle) and contingent (historically articulated).

Post-Marxist radical democrats, such as Laclau and Mouffe, offer a distinctive answer to the second question. They emphasise that we must not be 'radical' in the sense of aiming at a radical solution, a solution that can once and for all settle questions of political ordering. Rather, in a democracy every solution is provisional and temporary. The radicalisation of democracy is thus precisely not 'radical' in the sense of pure, true democracy. Its radical character implies, on the contrary, that we can save democracy only by taking into account its own radical impossibility. As Slavoj Zizek (1989: 6) points out, this implies that we have reached the opposite extreme of the traditional Marxist standpoint. In traditional Marxism, revolution is the universal resolution of all particular problems. For contemporary radical democrats, such a desire for ultimate solutions is undemocratic and metaphysical.

Principal ideas

The principal ideas of radical democracy may be related back, on the one hand, to the liberalisation of radical tradition (while holding onto the latter's insights into the inequalities of power) and, on the other hand, to the democratisation of liberal tradition. Contemporary radical democrats reject both the instrumental character of liberalism and the anti-political reductionism of much of the Marxist and socialist traditions. However, beyond these broad statements, differences amongst radical democrats start to emerge. I will begin by drawing out some of these key differences. This will be done with specific reference to conceptions of radical democracy that are inspired by critical theory and post-structuralist thought respectively.

Three principal ideas characterise contemporary conceptions of radical democracy. The first concerns the claim of the permanence and centrality of the political. In contrast to the anti-political position of Rousseau and Marx, radical democrats now argue that the political is an ineradicable part of society. This is not something to be regretted since it is the condition of possibility for democratic politics. The ordering of society is viewed not as a necessary, determined structure, but as a contingent result of political CONTESTATION. This places politics at the heart of society. For politics to be democratic, both the everyday aspects of politics, and the very principles ordering a polity must be open to contestation. The second concerns the characterisation of democracy. In contrast to modern liberals, for whom democracy is a process through which pre-given interests are aggregated, radical democrats shift attention to the construction and articulation of interests and identities. Thus, radical democrats view democracy as something more than a form of government; they view it as a mode of being, a regime instituting the ordering principles of society. The third characteristic follows from this conception of democracy. If democracy is more than a procedure for aggregating interests, attention has to be given to the process of subject formation in general, and the constitution of democratic identities in particular. Working with a relational conception of identity, radical democrats argue that there is no essentially given and no historically privileged subject. Homogeneous conceptions of subjectivity, such as the 'people', 'nation' and 'class', are put into question. Instead, emphasis is placed upon difference and pluralism, not as a regrettable feature of late modern life, but as an ontological condition (see IDENTITY, POLITICAL).

There are also three key areas in which radical democratic theorists differ quite markedly from one another. The first concerns the goal of democratic activity. For those radical democrats inspired by critical theory with its emphasis on deliberation, the goal of democratic activity is the reaching of a rational consensus. This stands in sharp contrast to radical democrats starting from a post-structuralist perspective who are concerned with the disruptive and dislocatory potential of democracy. Second, while deliberative conceptions of democracy proceed from a model of unconstrained dialogue, devoid of power and of 'distortions', post-structuralists argue that power relations are ineliminable from their account of democracy. Finally, in contrast to the Habermasian project, post-structuralists make no attempt to specify normative preconditions and foundations for democratic discourse. Thus, whereas deliberative democratic politics, in its strong procedural form as defended by Habermas, immunises politics against the forces of cultural and ethical life, theorists of agonistic and antagonistic politics view democracy as the incessant contestation over such ethical and cultural questions (Benhabib 1996: 9).

Main contemporary exponents

In what follows, I will concentrate on elaborating the agonistic and antagonistic conceptions of radical democracy as outlined in the works of Connolly, and Laclau and Mouffe. While they take their inspiration from different intellectual sources, both agonistic and antagonistic conceptions of radical democracy agree on the centrality of difference, dislocation and destabilisation to democratic politics. These theor-

ists, and others, all start from post-structuralist premises and eschew any commitment to an ontologically fixed conception of human identity and interests. Their focus is on the destabilising presence of difference and the role it plays in conceptualising a radical conception of democracy. As Honig (1996: 258) argues, to take difference – and not just identity – seriously in democratic theory is to affirm the inescapability of conflict. It is to free ourselves from the dream of a place free of power, conflict and struggle, and of a form of life not riven by difference.

Post-structuralist conceptions of radical democracy also hold distinctive views on the theoretical status of pluralism and its significance for political practice. Pluralism is treated not merely as an empirical fact; it is regarded as constitutive of the very nature of modern democracy. For instance, Mouffe (1996: 246) argues that all understandings of pluralism which depend on a logic of the social that regards objectivity as belonging to the things themselves, necessarily lead to a reduction of plurality. This is the case with liberal pluralism which starts from the 'fact of pluralism' and then seeks procedural solutions to deal with differences. The objective in this case is actually to make those differences irrelevant and to relegate pluralism to the private sphere. As with Mouffe, Connolly argues against conventional forms of pluralism that treat the 'congealed results' of past struggles as if they constituted essential standards. Instead, he argues for 'an ethos of pluralisation' that translates 'the pluralist appreciation of established diversity' into an active cultivation of difference (Connolly 1995: xv). Such acceptance of pluralism implies a profound transformation of the symbolic ordering of social relations. While in broad agreement on the question of pluralism and the nature of the subject, agonistic and antagonistic conceptions of radical democracy do differ in emphasis. The former emphasises agonistic respect and ethical responsiveness, while the latter tends to focus on the need to construct antagonisms and POLITICAL FRONTIERS, which make ethical considerations subservient to politics. These divergences are the product of differences in intellectual trajectory. Connolly's work is greatly influenced by his readings of Nietzsche and Foucault, while Laclau and Mouffe draw their inspiration from the Marxist tradition, Lacanian psychoanalysis and a Schmittian conception of the political.

Connolly's characterisation of 'agonistic democracy' contains three main components: normalisation, depoliticisation and politicisation (Connolly 1993: 202–7). Influenced by Foucault, he argues that modern societies are normalising societies. In order to develop a radical and pluralising conception of democracy, it is crucial that one understands the impact, the limits and possibilities that this poses for politics. To call a society 'normalising' is to draw attention to the violence within it from the point of a critical assumption concerning identity, namely, one of a decentred, split subject, intrinsically unable to be unified and reconciled to itself. This stands in marked contrast to both communitarian and Habermasian conceptions of the self, which hold out the possibility of collectivity achieving an 'unconstrained consensus' binding it together as a community. In normalising societies, difference is subjugated in the name of individual self-fulfilment and/or common realisation. While individualist and communitarian ideologies diverge in where they locate the site of normalisation – in the individual or the community – Connolly argues that they both deploy strategies of normalisation. Normalising societies give institutional priority to a limited set of identities, and those identities are established as the norms against which a variety of modes of 'otherness' are defined. Those who differ from these norms are treated as 'abnormal', 'perverse' or 'deviant'. Thus, the conception advanced is wary of postulates about true identity and a fully achieved community. The objection is not simply against the projection of an ideal against which actuality is appraised, but against the suggestion that the ideal stands above problematisation.

Connolly proposes that one might problematise one's own ideals, for instance, by treating them as inherently contestable projections to which one is devoted. Alternatively one may strive to legitimise the claims of those whose contingent formation of self differs from dominant norms (Connolly 1993: 207). Following Foucault, he thus regards democratic politics as 'the site of a tension or productive ambiguity between governance and disturbance of naturalised identities. It thrives only while this tension is kept alive' (Connolly 1993: 208). Central to this account is an attempt to overcome the false dichotomy between consensus and contestation. Connolly argues that it is possible to construct a democratic theory appropriate to late modern states that combines 'a critique of consent and consensus when they are absent with a critical engagement of both when they are present' (Connolly 1993: 213). To do so, one must explore the implications of normalisation and politicisation for democratic theory.

Politicisation defamiliarises internalised standards of normality and is a key component of an agonistic ideal of democracy in which practices of politicisation 'subject established identities, norms, conventions, and ideals to denaturalisation'. Democracy itself, Connolly argues, is ambiguous on this score. If, on the one hand, sedimented identities and norms present themselves as deep truths through the definition of that which deviates from them, then democratic contestation can attenuate these tendencies. On the other hand, democratic contestation can unsettle naturalised settlements and disturb customary assignments of abnormality. Since democracy contains the possibility of heightening the experience of CONTINGENCY, the ethos of democracy, is a disruptive and denaturalising one. However, democracy also acts as the medium in which general purposes become crystallised and enacted. For Connolly, it is only when democracy maintains the tension between these interdependent antinomies that it can function 'as the perfection of politics' (Connolly 1993: 210). Adherence to this ambiguous practice of democracy would be achieved where criticism of the politics of non-consensualism is fostered, while the comforts of a stable consensus are periodically disturbed (Connolly 1993: 214). As Connolly recognises, this is a difficult task in a world in which such disturbances more often than not evoke anti-democratic, re-naturalising responses.

The antagonistic conception of democracy developed in the work of Laclau and Mouffe places greater emphasis on the discursive mechanisms through which radical democracy may be articulated, and is less concerned than agonistic accounts of democracy with the tension between sedimentation and denaturalisation. The emphasis is almost exclusively on the latter. In large measure this can be accounted for by their particular understanding of the distinction between the political and politics. 'The political' refers to the ineradicable presence of antagonism in social relations, a presence that cannot ever be domesticated, while 'politics' refers to the ensemble of institutions and practices whose objective is to organise human co-existence in a conflictual context. Politics, in this sense, always entails the establishment of political frontiers and the formation of an 'us' as opposed to a 'them'. From the point of view of democratic politics, the aim is not to overcome the 'us/them' division, but to institute it in a manner that would leave open the possibility of disagreeing about the interpretation and implementation of democratic principles. It is important to emphasise that this does not mean that democratic politics should aim to eradicate all power relations. This was the dream of perfect harmony which inspired both Rousseau and Marx. To negate the ineradicable character of antagonism, and aim at a universal rational consensus would threaten democracy (Mouffe 1996: 248). Thus, radical and plural democracy rejects the very possibility of a public sphere of rational argument where a non-coercive consensus could be attained. Rather, the democratic character of politics, they argue, can only be achieved once it is recognised that no limited social actor can attribute to itself the representation of the totality (the general will in Rousseau; the proletariat in Marx). Thus, the thesis is that relations between social agents become more democratic only insofar as they accept the particularity and limitation of their claims.

This thesis is based upon a non-unitary conception of the subject. As against the rationalist and liberal conception of the human being as a homogenous subject, contemporary philosophical stances informed by post-structuralist and psychoanalytic thought have come to regard the subject as a decentred agent. This agent is constituted at the point of intersection of a multiplicity of subject-positions in which there is no a priori or necessary relation between them, and whose articulation is the result of hegemonic practices. Like Connolly, Laclau and Mouffe argue that the fragmentation of the unitary subject is, as in Foucault, both a source of the experience of subjugation and a precondition of the democratisation of the contemporary social world.

This project depends upon the construction of a new common sense or HEGEMONY that alters the identities of the different subject positions so that the claims and demands of each are articulated in an equivalential fashion. In contrast to a conception of instrumental political alliances, the project of radical and plural democracy requires integrative equivalences, and the creation of political frontiers on the one hand and the autonomisation of political spaces on the other, to further radical pluralism. Through hegemonic practices, subject positions could be articulated together so that their symbolisation would be seen by social agents as equivalent and mutually supportive. These equivalential constructions, far from enforcing a violent suppression of the differences, open the very space for the autonomisation of particular struggles. For instance, the feminist struggle is made possible only through reference to democratic–egalitarian political discourse. Where such articulation takes place around the nodal point of democracy, one would speak of the expansion of democratic equivalences. The expansion of such 'webs of equivalence', as Yanarella (1993: 90) calls them, across diverse social movements and other antagonistic relations, holds the promise of strengthening specific democratic struggles and potentially consolidating them into a new historical bloc whilst the logic of difference mitigates against full integration. For Laclau and Mouffe, such expansion could be conceived as the gradual radicalisation and extension of the democratic project to new domains. Simultaneously, it contains a reconceptualisation of the relation between universality and particularity. In contrast to the universalism espoused in critical theory, post-structuralist inspired accounts of radical democracy regard the universal as a receding horizon resulting from the expansion of an indefinite chain of equivalential terms. In other words, the universal does not have a concrete content of its own, but neither can it exist apart from particularity. Following Lefort, Laclau (1996: 35) argues that this paradox is the very precondition of democracy: 'If democracy is possible, it is because the universal has no necessary body and no necessary content; different groups, instead, compete between themselves to temporarily give to their particularisms a function of universal representation.'

Critical conclusion

Much criticism of radical democracy emerges amongst the different traditions of radical democratic argumentation. These criticisms throw light on areas of divergence between these different interpretative traditions, while simultaneously highlighting their respective strengths. There are two points in particular around which debate tends to coalesce. They concern, firstly, the question of critique and the resources for its development and, secondly, the question of the *raison d'être* of democratic activity. These areas of argumentation are, of course, intimately related to one another. The first area of debate relates to the question of the possibility of critique. For those radical democrats writing from within the tradition of critical theory this does not arise as a problem since critique is grounded, from the outset, in a theory of communicative action. This theory, which also informs deliberative accounts of democracy, is based upon the idea that there is an ideal of mutual understanding inherent in language that allows for the identification of the structures and forces that hinder undis-

torted communication. As Forst (1996: 139) reminds us, a critical theory of this kind does not just criticise society by its own standards, but draws upon a set of normative standards that transcend any such particularistic limits. From this perspective, radical democrats of a post-structuralist persuasion seem to lack the resources for critique. Their anti-foundationalism seemingly cuts them off from any recourse to universal and context-transcending viewpoints. However, it is clear that this oversimplified picture misses the point.

If critique is defined in the sense used by Forst, then post-structuralist radical democrats do not have any grounds from which it could be developed, and they would indeed fall foul of the criticism emanating from a critical theory perspective. Post-structuralist radical democrats argue that they do not need to have access to such context-transcendent principles in order to develop a critical perspective. This is done differently in agonistic and antagonistic accounts of radical democracy. The former, inspired by Nietzsche, Foucault and Heidegger, does so through the development of the idea of a critical ethos of problematisation. That is to say, through an ethos which discloses the contingent limits of our modes of being. Such disclosure opens the space for the valuing of diversity. As Connolly (1995: 40) puts it, since nothing is fundamental, almost everything counts for something.

A similar argument informs the antagonistic conception of radical democracy. Drawing more on the resources of deconstruction and Lacanian psychoanalysis, this opening is couched in terms of undecidability and lack, making visible the contingency of any of our political imaginaries and identities. According to Laclau and Mouffe, this impossibility of closure is what keeps open the space that enables one to distance oneself from dogmatic, naturalistic foundationalism. For their critics, however, this simply shifts the problem to another point. Benhabib's criticisms exemplify this position. She asks whether agonistic visions of democratic politics inevitably invite questions about how we can be sure that 'the contest of pluralisms that cannot be adjudicated at the higher levels, will all be instances of good and just democratic politics as opposed to being instances of fascism, xenophobic nationalism, rightwing populism?' (Benhabib 1996: 8). What underlies this demand is a quest for a safeguarding of freedom and JUSTICE, which transcends characteristic political contests, and echoes the classical radical democratic desire to transcend the political.

This brings us to the second area of debate, namely the question concerning the *raison d'être* of radical democratic politics. For deliberative radical democrats, the aim of political activity is most centrally to reach a rational consensus. This centrality of consensus is questioned by post-structuralist radical democratic theorists who take problematisation to be central to a democratic politics. This fundamental difference in approach, as indicated earlier, arises from the divergent conceptions of language and of the self informing each of these approaches to radical democracy: the one desiring a resting place where the self could be fully reconciled with itself and with others, and where debate always proceeds from within the limits of a narrowly conceived rationality, while the other cultivates a restless, homeless struggle where debate is always potentially marked by an irreducible conflict.

Acknowledgement

I am grateful to the Leverhulme Trust for funding the research upon which this contribution is based.

Further reading

Benhabib, S. (1996) 'The Democratic Moment and the Problem of Difference', in S. Benhabib (ed.), *Democracy and Difference*, Princeton, NJ: Princeton University Press.

Connolly, W.E. (1993) 'Democracy and Contingency', in J.H. Carens (ed.), *Democracy and Possessive Individualism. The Intellectual Legacy of C.B. Macpherson*, Albany, NY: State University of New York Press.

—— (1995) *The Ethos of Pluralization*, Minneapolis, MN: University of Minnesota Press.

Forst, R. (1996) 'Justice, Reason, and Critique: Basic Concepts of Critical Theory', in D. Rasmussen (ed.), *Handbook of Critical Theory*, Oxford: Blackwell.

Honig, B. (1996) 'Difference, Dilemmas, and the Politics of Home', in S. Benhabib (ed.), *Democracy and Difference*, Princeton, NJ: Princeton University Press.

Laclau, E. (1993) 'The Signifiers of Democracy', in J.H. Carens (ed.), *Democracy and Possessive Individualism. The Intellectual Legacy of C.B. Macpherson*, Albany, NY: State University of New York Press.

—— (1996) *Emancipation(s)*, London, Verso.

Laclau, E. and Mouffe, C. (1985) *Hegemony and Socialist Strategy: Towards a Radical Democratic Politics*, London: Verso.

Lefort, C. (1986) *The Political Forms of Modern Society*, Cambridge, MA: Harvard University Press.

Macpherson, C.B. (1977) *The Life and Times of Liberal Democracy*, Oxford: Oxford University Press.

Mouffe, C. (1996) 'Democracy, Power, and the "Political"', in S. Benhabib (ed.), *Democracy and Difference*, Princeton, NJ: Princeton University Press.

Schwartz, J.M. (1995) *The Permanence of the Political. A Democratic Critique of the Radical Impulse to Transcend Politics*, Princeton, NJ: Princeton University Press.

Yanarella, E.J. (1993) 'Whither Hegemony?: Between Gramsci and Derrida', in J.P. Jones III, W. Natter and T.R. Schatzki (eds), *Postmodern Contentions: Epochs, Politics, Space*, New York: Guilford Press.

Zizek, S. (1989) *The Sublime Object of Ideology*, London: Verso.

ALETTA NORVAL

referendums

Referendum is now accepted as the general term used to describe a direct vote by an electorate on an issue or policy. Referendums can be advisory or, more usually, mandatory. They can be used to enact laws, approve decisions taken by legislatures or executives, or to approve constitutional changes. They can be *ad hoc* in nature such as the British votes on devolution to Scotland, Wales and Northern Ireland, or required in constitutions for specific policy changes such as increases in taxation. In addition referendums derive from one of two main sources: governments may present them to the electorate (sometimes called *plebiscites*), or, on the presentation of a prescribed number of signatures, the people themselves may present a proposal direct to the electorate (usually called *initiatives*). One final variation is the *recall* where on the presentation of a minimum number of signatures, a vote can be put to the electorate proposing that an official be removed from office. Referendums can be exercised at the local or state/provincial levels (as in the USA and Switzerland), or at the national level (as in a wide variety of countries). Referendum devices are often called instruments of DIRECT DEMOCRACY, and much of the debate in this area relates to the respective merits of direct democracy as opposed to traditional political party democracy.

The Swiss have a special place in the history of referendums for the very first direct vote took place in the Swiss canton of Schwyz in 1294. By the fourteenth century the device was well-established as a DECISION-MAKING tool in the German-speaking mountain cantons, and by the sixteenth century almost all of the cantons had adopted the referendum. As Kobach observes, this development is remarkable. While the rest of Europe languished under feudalism or absolutist rule, mass participatory democracy (at least for adult males) was a fact of life in many parts of Switzerland (Kobach 1994). This tradition continues to this day so that in the modern world Switzerland remains the only country where the referendum is used as the main means of taking political decisions at the local, state and national levels (for a review, see Linder (1998)).

The first national referendums were instituted in post-revolutionary France, first to approve new constitutions and subsequently to approve the Napoleonic HEGEMONY. Napoleon also initiated referendums in a number of other European countries including Switzerland, all of which were designed to win approval for new constitutions. Use of the referendum at the national level gradually spread during the nineteenth and early twentieth centuries, but the device was often employed to legitimise authoritarian regimes, or to win approval for unpopular measures. The most notorious use of the measure was, of course, in Nazi Germany, where Hitler won overwhelming public approval for his regime and the suspension of democratic institutions. (For a comprehensive list of national referendums down to 1994, see Butler and Ranney 1994, Appendix A.)

During the twentieth century there have been three major developments in the use of the referendum. First, the spread of populist political ideas has encouraged the spread of direct democracy. This has been most notable in the American states where (mainly in the West and South) the initiative had been used with increasing frequency. As Magleby notes, between 1898 and 1992 over 1700 initiative measures were placed before voters in the American states (Magleby 1994: 231). Populist impulse has also been responsible for the use of the referendum at the national level, notably in New Zealand, Ireland and Italy; although only in Italy can voters bypass legislatures by directly using the initiative. Second, governments of all types ranging from authoritarian to parliamentary, have found the referendum a convenient device for winning approval of diverse measures. Often these votes involve the approval of new constitutional arrangements. In a number of cases referendums have been used to facilitate the transition to democracy. Such was the case with measures passed in Greece, Hungary, Poland, Romania, Russia, Spain, South Africa, the Philippines and a number of Latin American states. In Europe, the referendum is also increasingly employed as a device to aid the legitimisation of controversial policies including issues linked to the extension of European Union (EU) powers and the legalisation of abortion.

Third, referendums have been employed in a number of contexts to determine the status of subordinate territories. The earliest of these votes involved a vote by the citizens of Metz, Toul and Verdun in 1552 to decide whether they would remain in France. After the First World War, populations in Schleswig, Silesia and elsewhere voted on their territorial status under the aegis of the League of Nations. More recently, the status of particular territories in Africa and the Pacific has been subject to referendum votes in the process of decolonisation. And the granting of more autonomy (or independence) to regions of Spain, the United Kingdom, Denmark and Canada have been facilitated by referendums.

The relationship between referendums and democracy has long been a source of political debate. Down to the outbreak of the Second World War, many scholars of democracy regarded the referendum with a combination of contempt and suspicion. Referendums were associated with the efforts of Napoleon and Hitler to legitimise authoritarian regimes. As such, they appeared to pander to the will of uninformed masses and thus to encourage demagoguery and, in the worst possible cases, the suspension of democracy itself. In addition, many at the time viewed democracy primarily in distributional terms. Only mass-based political PARTIES operating with majorities in national legislatures could facilitate the redistribution of resources from the haves to have-nots in society. CLASS-based programmatic politics were the order of the day. Referendums undermined programmatic political parties and advantaged those with the power and resources – usually the better off – to organise support on particular issues. Commentators pointed to the experience of Switzerland and the American states to support their view that referendums were essentially a conservative, anti-party influence. In Switzerland, for example, a referendum held as late as 1959 voted down women's SUFFRAGE and it was not until 1971 that a positive vote was passed.

Recently, however, the referendum device has enjoyed something of a revival among supporters of democracy and democratic in-stitutions. There are a number of reasons for this. As democratic institutions and processes spread, so referendums are viewed increasingly not as an alternative to party democracy but as devices that can complement and enrich democracy. This can apply in two distinct ways. First, referendums can be used by parties in government to determine the public's position on controversial issues. In the EU context, for example, fifteen referendums have been held in Ireland, Norway, France, Denmark, the United Kingdom, Austria, Sweden and Finland. Few argue that these votes on EU membership, enlargement and approval of the Single European Act and the Treaty of Maastricht have undermined party democracy. Indeed, they may have even strengthened the position of parties in government because governments rather than the people have determined the wording and timing of votes. In addition, governments have often been advantaged by being able to orchestrate referendum campaigns.

Second, research has shown that it is not easy to demonstrate that referendums as such have undermined party democracy in Switzerland, Italy and the states of the USA. Very often what looks like a close link between weak political parties and the use of referendums is muddied by the concomitant presence of institutional devices such as the SEPARATION OF POWERS, annual ELECTIONS and proportional representation all of which can have the effect of weakening parties (see Budge 1996: chaps 4–6) (see ELECTORAL COMPETITION). Moreover, even when referendums are deeply embedded in the DECISION-MAKING process, as they are at all levels of government in Switzerland, parties continue to play a major role in the political system. Budge argues that without a doubt, parties have the ability 'to guide popular voting and discussion . . . even when it takes the form of more complex, two way electronic interactions on individual issues'. Parties 'can improve popular debate and decision-making so that it contributes constructively to the government of society – which will, for the foreseeable future, remain in the hands of political parties' (Budge 1996: 132).

Some scholars have gone so far as to argue that a truly democratic society can *only* be achieved through a combination of traditional party democracy and direct democracy. Benjamin Barber, the most influential of these writers, calls this 'deep democracy', where the individual citizen will constantly be involved in decision-making, preferably by electronic means (Barber 1984, 1988) (see DEMOCRACY, JUSTIFICATIONS FOR).

Another reason for the intellectual revival of the referendum idea is that the alleged link between referendums and incompetent – and often conservative – decision-making is not always easy to demonstrate empirically. The most extensive analysis of the use of initiatives in the states of the USA concludes that although they do have a conservative impact in fiscal terms (taxes are typically reduced rather than increased), the rights of MINORITIES (see RIGHTS, MINORITY AND INDIGENOUS) are not unambiguously threatened by direct democracy (Bowler *et al.* 1998). In some instances, including the medical use of marijuana, state-wide initiatives have produced liberal rather than conservative outcomes. Anti-gay measures have typically failed at the state-wide level but passed at the local level. But local assemblies in these same communities may also pass such measures. The authors claim, therefore, that the problem is not direct democracy as such, but the intolerance of many small homogeneous communities (1998: ch. 12). Liberal communities such as San Francisco, have, of course, used democratic institutions to protect the rights of minorities.

Defenders of referendums also point to the fact that when incompetent or unjust decisions are taken, their effects are usually ameliorated by other institutions in the political system, and especially the courts. Hence the 'three strikes and you're out' initiatives (a third felony offence leads to a mandatory life sentence) were much criticised as insensitive to the particulars of individual cases. But judges have found ways to bypass the law. In other cases, including some anti-gay and anti-civil rights

initiatives, the courts have simply declared the new laws unconstitutional.

In sum, the extensive use of direct democracy in the states of the USA and in Switzerland has not led to the sort of policy disasters which many of the opponents of direct democracy have long predicted. In combination with the organisational advantages enjoyed by the better-off, the use of referendums has almost certainly had fiscally conservative outcomes. In addition, rash and ill considered policies have been passed, but their effects have usually been modified or reversed by other political institutions. Of course, the institutions of traditional party democracy also sometimes produce perverse and incompetent decisions.

Two final points need to be stressed. First, although the referendum device has returned to favour, its use remains very limited. Only in Switzerland, Italy and less than half of the states of the USA is its use extensive, and only in Switzerland is it a regular part of decision-making at all levels. Modern states increasingly use referendums on an ad hoc basis to win approval for controversial measures; they have not employed the device as a normal part of democratic decision-making. Second, it has never been suggested that referendums and other measures of direct democracy should *replace* party democracy. Instead, scholars have argued that referendums should be more widely employed as complements to traditional party politics. Neither can it be argued that the use of referendums by authoritarian regimes in any way advances democracy. The use of direct democracy in such contexts usually serves to manipulate the population and strengthen the regime. A clear link between democracy and referendums can only be established when the device is initiated by the people or is reserved by provisions within democratic constitutions for the expression of the will of the people.

See also:

direct democracy; participation; representation, concept of

Further reading

Barber B. (1984) *Strong Democracy: Participatory Politics for a New Age*, Berkeley, CA: University of California Press.

—— (1988) *The Conquest of Politics*, Princeton, NJ: Princeton University Press.

Bowler, S., Donovan T. and Tolbert C. (eds) (1998) *Citizens as Legislators: Direct Democracy in the United States*, Columbus, OH: State University Press.

Budge, I. (1996) *The New Challenge of Direct Democracy*, London and Cambridge, MA: Blackwell.

Butler D. and Ranney A. (1994) *Referendums Around the World: The Growing Use of Direct Democracy*, Washington, DC: American Enterprise Institute Press.

Fishkin, J.S. (1993) *Democracy and Deliberation*, New Haven, CT: Yale University Press.

Gallagher, M. and Uleri, P.V. (eds.) (1996) *The Referendum Experience in Europe*, Basingstoke: Macmillan, and New York: St. Martin's Press.

Linder, W. (1998) *Swiss Democracy*, 2nd edn, Basingstoke: Macmillan, and New York: St. Martin's Press.

Kobach, K.W. (1994) 'Switzerland,' in D. Butler and A. Ranney (eds), *Referendums Around the World: The Growing Use of Direct Democracy*, Washington, DC: American Enterprise Institute Press.

Magleby, D.B. (1994) 'Direct Legislation in the American States,' in D. Butler and A. Ranney (eds), *Referendums Around the World: The Growing Use of Direct Democracy*, Washington, DC: American Enterprise Institute Press.

DAVID H. MCKAY

representation, concept of

The term 'representation' is derived from the Latin *representare*. In its modern sense, it entered European language in the Middle Ages both as a term and as a distinct political idea. The notion of representation has undergone several radical transformations from its inception. It can be applied in a number of distinct ways, and has been used as the basis of postmodern, feminist and minority attempts to deconstruct contemporary political systems. As democratic theory and practice in the conditions of mass society requires some degree of representation, these challenges call upon the concept of representation to be dealt with in some fundamental way. This entry will deal with the fundamental and foundational problems of representation.

Responses to the fundamental challenges arising out of the very idea of representation can be made in a number of ways. One has been to increase the degree to which representative systems are responsive to variations in that which they purport to represent. This frequently involves a variety of trade-offs between the responsiveness, stability and ACCOUNTABILITY of government. A second has been to challenge and deconstruct the entire basis of representation. A third has been to deal with these challenges by shifting the balance between representation and accountability in favour of the latter. When accountability is favoured accuracy of representation is traded off against responsibility for political actions (see DEMOCRATIC TRADE-OFFS). It is far from clear that such a shift to accountability can entirely deal with all the issues arising from the problems of representation. It is likely that problems surrounding the problem of representation will continue to bedevil democratic theory and practice.

Origins

The idea of political representation is distinctly modern. Pitkin, for example, places it as late as Hobbes (Pitkin 1984), but it is found in embryonic form in the earliest known expressions of human experience. Carl Schmitt (1985) has argued forcefully that there is no major political concept that has not been transformed from a theological concept. Representation is no exception, and was imported into western political experience through a religious and political transformation rooted in the idea of the pope as Christ's representative. The break between church and state left political theory bereft of the context of the *polis*. With no immediately available and autonomous political language, the emerging modern state drew initially on numerous ecclesiastical formulations (see STATE, RELATIONS OF CHURCH TO).

The origins of the idea of representation, however, precede both the modern state and Christianity. In one of the earliest and most beautiful extant poems, *The Lament of Ur*, Ningal, the goddess and protector of the city of Ur, unsuccessfully represented a case for sparing the city of Ur to the assembled gods. The very first kingships of the early Mediterranean city states (*c.* 3000 BC) appear to have been held with a quasi-representative function. Even claims to absolute kingship were justified by an appeal to the abstract ideal of the king as the bearer or representative of higher ideals. *Potestas* was then, as now, not *sui generis*, but always subject to further justification. To introduce a principle: there is no *potestas* that is *sui generis*. The *fons et origens of potestas*, stems from *representare*.

In the ancient world, the mythical condition of representing a city was well understood. For example, Pallas Athene, the daughter of Zeus, represented the city of Athens to the gods. Solon, Archon of Athens *c.* 594 BC, cultivated the foundation of political representation across a variety of interests, persons and concerns. Solon declared that he would protect the weak while preserving the sensibilities of the strong (Clarke 1994: 37). This formula can, with some justification, be reasonably said to begin the self-conscious political tradition (see DEMOCRATIC ORIGINS).

This general ideal of representing an entire city or peoples has been revitalised in the twentieth century by Eric Voegelin (1952), who has argued that there is a sense in which even otherwise non-representative totalitarian regimes may be represented to others. Representation has come to be closely associated with models of voting, but the connection between these two dimensions is not necessary. Indeed, voting is a latecomer in the history of representation.

Development

It is from a combination of mythopoesis, early political formation and later Christian universalism that the modern doctrine of representation is based and from which many of its contemporary difficulties arise. Its modern formulation was, however, set against the growth of mass society and, more particularly, the relations between the emerging modern categories of individual, CIVIL SOCIETY and the state.

The discovery and translation of Aristotle's *Ta Politika* in the twelfth and thirteenth century introduced the idea of a political mode of life, a *bios*, which was distinct from the church and contained its own imperatives. It was on this basis, among others, that church and state divided. Once the split occurred, the logical demand was that the people be involved in government. Two major changes in understanding are worth mention. Dante, in *De Monarchia* (1309–13), invented the modern concept of humanity (*humanitas*) as an inclusive concept. Marsilius of Padua, in *Defensor Pacis*, published in 1324, was one of the first champions of the separation of church and state and made it clear that the decisions of state were to be made by the greater part of the people affected by those decisions.

These two conditions, inclusiveness and PARTICIPATION, could not be met within the burgeoning conditions of mass society. With a few exceptions, such as some early medieval German cities and the city-states of the Italian quattrocentro, popular or direct participation or direct forms of civic REPUBLICANISM were short lived. This required re-presencing or representation. That representation could take several forms. A significant solution was to make one person stand as the representative of all. The doctrine of the 'divine right of kings' attempted to deal with this problem by making the king the representative of God on earth. What was being represented is God, not the people, but the people must be treated justly, and so even in its extreme form the doctrine was always subject to some clear challenges. Even before it was fully developed, Aquinas made it clear that a kingship that led to tyranny had no justification in natural law.

This formulation limited the legitimate power of the king by containing within it the idea that the king represented the people in the larger sense of keeping their behaviour and his own actions within the confines of natural law. In *The Second Treatise* (1690), Locke carried this natural law view to its conclusion when he placed the people as the foundation of *potestas*, of power. Prior to Locke, Hobbes had developed the idea of representation as authorisation, and so is frequently regarded (as with Pitkin above) as the founder of the modern doctrine of representation. That modern doctrine was presaged in the shift of power from God or king to people in Marsilius with the doctrine of the separation of church and state. The idea that power ascended rather than descended is expressly claimed by Starkey. In an imaginary dialogue between Pole and Lupset (1535), Starkey dealt with representation within the context of the first growth of modern civil society (Clarke 1994: 83–6). After three millennia, Starkey finally banished the gods and put the problem of representation in its modern context: from the bottom up rather than from top down. The doctrine was completed with Hobbes.

Hobbes placed the source of representation in authorisation, but regarded it as possible that a person could be represented (Hobbes 1968: 223–8). This was a significant development, for it took it that persons rather than gods or God could be re-presented, that persons were the foundation of authority, and that representation was a form of authorised presentation. Such ideas fed into various representations of the people's act as they found their way into the development of democracy and into different models of representation. A significant question that arose centred on what it was, or whom it was, that was being represented.

Models of representation

Representation may take many different forms. Sargon in 1850 BC claimed to represent JUSTICE; kings and popes claimed to represent God or Christ. The AUTHORITY in these cases, while not blind to the people, was not derived from them. The inversion of the doctrine of representation, characteristic of early modernity, placed the source of representation with human individuals. Human individuals and the community affairs in which they participate could be understood in a variety of ways. Hobbes, for instance, was quite clear that a multitude of men even of differing interests could be represented for 'it is the unity of the "representer"' (1968: 239–51) that is both possible and significant. This formulation is quite telling for on examination it turns out that this is possible only because the multitude so represented is united: is homogenous. This solution, whatever its other problems might be, is not appropriate to the plural societies of contemporary, late modern times and postmodern times.

Edmund Burke offered a more mystical approach to representation. Burke argued that the duty of a representative was to act for the entire nation and not to be concerned with particular interests. There are dangers in this kind of notion. In the wrong hands, it might be, for instance, that a *Führer* could claim to represent an imaginary, mystical, mythical and dangerous *Volk*. Such ideas contain clear dangers. In extremis, they may be anti-democratic, reducing genuine participation to mystical representations of 'Imaginary Communities' (Anderson 1983). Not surprisingly, the antithesis of this kind of representation has been to emphasise more formalistic and transparent ways of bringing representation and responsibility together.

These twin requirements, of relating representation and TRANSPARENCY, can be met in a variety of ways. The need of representation, however, is driven primarily by the necessity to permit popular participation, and senses of stakeholding in situations that inhibit, or even prohibit, DIRECT DEMOCRACY. This is the position taken in *The Federalist Papers* (1787) whose authors, especially Madison, argued that representative government was a means of incorporating large numbers of the population in the affairs of government. While Madison felt that it was important to preserve the sense of a political community within government, he feared that the representation of interests might turn out to be divisive (Clarke 1994: 128).

The potential divisiveness of this kind of particularity is well recognised. Rousseau's famous distinction between particular wills and the general will drew specific attention to the evils of particularity. His device of the general will, while seeming unusual, has a long lineage (Riley 1988) and his broad notion, that particularity might undermine the political community, has been a source of concern from Solon, to Pericles, Bruni and into Arendt and contemporary civic republicanism.

The issue of representation in late modernity has divided into a distinction between persons and interests. Formally, neither of these alternatives are exclusively included nor precluded in any model of representation. However, the civic republican bias is, on the whole, toward the representation of persons, while the liberal bias is, on the whole, toward the representation of interests.

The representation of interests lies at the foundation of LIBERALISM, for that model permitted an attempt to resolve particularities within a domain rather than making the domain the source of the resolution of particularities. This shift, indeed the inversion, of the traditional model, is critical, for it permitted a model of representation that broke with the tradition that had characterised Western politics from Solon onwards. The original model had sought to regard political actions as contributing towards the public domain and substituted instead a model of intersecting private interests.

The liberal model deals with this conflict in a decisive manner. It downplays the possibility of civic republicanism and argues that what is crucial in human being is subjectivity. What can be represented, therefore, are subjects who have interests, rather than persons who are participants. Utilitarian philosophers, by virtue of their conception of subjectivity, were able to present this view well. John Stuart Mill, while not denying the importance of an incidental

collective, put forward a view that what was represented was not merely peoples, but interests. The importance of individuals in civil society and the need for those individuals to provide a countervailing power against the state was a significant part of democracy.

But, if it is not people that are being represented then it is not people, however indirectly, that are participating in government. If interests are re-presented then, qua Madison, aspects are being administered. Put another way, it is qua Rousseau's *Social Contract* that particular rather than general concerns are being addressed. In either case, there is no *res publica*; no public thing or domain to which one can directly belong. In such a case, representation has removed politics from the life of the people: a position far removed from the ideas of Thucydides, Bruni, Rousseau and the other masters who claimed the advantages of civic republicanism.

The effective response to this has been the development of liberalism with its focus on an effective life in civil society. Liberalism tends to regard the polity as a means of protecting civil society rather than regarding the polity as a mode of life. The liberal tradition, which finds its foundation in Hobbes, places the subjective qualities of people above their communal setting. The effect of this shift in focus is to place interests rather than people at the forefront of the theory of representation. This makes the state an administrator of things rather than of persons. When Engels, in what seemed to be a radical challenge to liberalism, was to talk of the state 'withering away', leaving behind it only the 'administration of things', he not so much challenged liberal orthodoxy as expressed it at it fullest. Engels, in many respects, was a fine classical liberal.

Challenges and foundations

Representation can stand for many things: authorisation, delegation, advocation and mandate are but a few. It can be of persons, or of interests, and each of these alternatives present difficult problems and at different levels. The most fundamental philosophical problem concerns the coherence of the notion of representation itself. On some (particularly postmodern) accounts, it is held that it is difficult to understand how something once present can be re-presented. It is rather presented again and, hence, becomes something else or not re-presented at all and is, therefore, absent. It is always the case that acting for another, in whatever way, contains within it the possibility of denying that original voice and substituting another voice in its place.

The most significant challenge, however, is that regardless of how representation is expressed, the very idea of representation is an expression of male Christian supremacy. This is a potentially serious charge, for if correct, it undercuts the entire egalitarian basis of the democratic enterprise. Making present that which is absent is, it is argued, a sign of the logocentric bias in Western philosophy. This bias is significant for it assumes a white, male and even patriarchal ascendancy that excludes significant minorities, female, black and so on. It does this not merely by surface practice, but through a deep perspective that builds into its outlook an assumption of a presence and an agent/subject. Such an assumption and such a representation is itself open to challenge, for it assumes that there are subjects, and/or that there be presence which can be re-presented. (The broad issues are well rehearsed in Cadava *et al.* 1991.) That assumption is contestable (see AGONISM).

The source of the difficulty with presence is frequently traced back to Plato and his preference of speech over writing. Speech, it is argued, assumes a presence and therefore an agent, whereas writing assumes a text in which the agent, the presence, is subservient. The Platonic emphasis on speech over writing is supported in the Hebraic–Christian tradition in the Gospel of St John. The statement that, 'In the beginning was the word' (John 1:1) places presence with God. 'Man' is made in the image of God, so he also has a presence.

The notion of presence and re-presencing was further developed in the theology of the early patristic fathers. This gradually converged upon the idea that a person, an entity having an essential core, was present in every Christian 'man'. (The logocentric bias emphasised men, even men who were slaves, rather than women.) A major transformation occurred in Descartes, Hobbes, Hume and Mill, when the theological underpinnings to presence and representation were secularised. Presencing became tied to subjectivity rather than to divinity. The cognitive idea of subjectivity and its related external and relational state, the subject, permitted the notion of re-presencing the person as a subject. This shift from person to subject is significant for it implied that representation was possible: that some one could re-present a distorted picture of a person as an aspect rather than the entire personage of another.

The converse of this kind of argument is that there is no presence *per se*. It is rather that the world consists of a single substance with apparent changes (Parmenides); that it has attributes (Spinoza); structures, or processes without agency (Althusser in the continental tradition); or is primarily systemic (Easton, in the Anglo-American tradition). This kind of general claim is, perhaps, best represented in the postmodern dictum that, 'in the beginning was the text'. This dictum inverts subjectivity, individuality and presence. It throws out Plato's foundations, sets aside John's presencing claim, sets aside the patristic fathers, throws out the Church Fathers, sets aside Descartes and dispenses with patriarchy and male white supremacy all in one go.

To put this another way, presence becomes the dependable variable rather than the independent variable, re-presencing is thus doubly dependent. On the face of it this insight and this inversion ought to diminish individual demands and voices. To some extent that occurred with the growth of structuralist theories, post-structuralist theories, systems theories, cybernetics theories, process theories and so on. Where are the people? This is a question that has often been asked of this kind of theorising.

The answer is that the people were finding a variety of differing voices of varying, yet equally self-regarded, legitimacy. They were learning how to express these voices, seeking to open the world to their variety, yet their demand was for presence; not re-presence.

The source of the twist in the tale is clear enough. It takes two principal forms. The first is the breakdown of homogenous societies and the generation of heterogeneous societies. The second, more philosophical reason is that the logocentric tradition might well have been thrown out, but so were all the constraints on individuality. The logocentric tradition, patriarchy and authority, turned out to have been held in deep tension. Vanquishing Plato and the Church Fathers might have, but did not, reveal structuralism, cybernetics or whatever. The actual social heterogeneity was too deep for that, so instead it revealed voices, particularities and presences. In this case, at least, shifts in social structure dominated mere tensions in thought. Sociality here overcame ideality; this is not a general principle but one that appears to hold in this particular case.

It is, however, a general principle that there can be no presence without some degree of substance and without some degree of particularity (Clarke 1988). In consequence, the distinctness of presence has latterly come to be understood as a presence with particular qualities, which have become interpreted in particular terms. Potentially such terms are infinitely variable. In practice, however, they have turned out to be expressed primarily in terms of a limited range of possibilities. In effect, the bias in representation has been often taken to relate one particular kind of story or voice, while precluding other possible stories and voices. So feminine, black, Hispanic, Chinese, Malaysian and other voices are potentially present in a pluralistic society.

This variation and variety of voices all seeking representation undercuts the universalistic and logocentric bias of the standard model of universal representation in favour of the particularity of differential voices. If correct, these perspectives undercut a major egalitarian and universalistic premise of representation and suggest that a universal and logocentric concept of representation requires rethinking, if it is to remain ethically sustainable and practically enabling.

The resolution to the deep problem of re-presencing rests on a fundamental contradiction, for what could be re-presented was only that which was general and universal. Yet, that which appeared was that which was local and particular. Moreover, that which was local and particular could not faithfully be re-presented under the doctrine of universality. That which is particular can be re-presented, that which is particular cannot, however, be represented in universal terms without serious distortion or loss. This is precisely the point made by women, by blacks, by gays and others. Representation, in its very foundations implies universalism, but latterly what has been required as represented is particular and local. It is frequently highly vocal, noisy, demanding and of sufficient variety and variation that it is not capable of being represented alongside all the other demands. Presentable it may be, re-presentable with a view to forming some part of a universalism it may not readily be.

As a theoretical point, it is clearly difficult enough to convey presentation and presence. Nevertheless, the problem has to be dealt with in a practical manner and whatever putative solutions are offered are tentative, subject to modification, fungible and part of the ineliminable and ongoing dynamic of democracy. A democracy that determinedly avoids answers to questions of this sort ceases to be democracy at all.

Practical representation

More practically, representation forms part of most indirect democracies where elective representatives are expected to represent the views of their constituents. An issue arises at this point as to whether the representation provides direct instructions (delegation), or whether it contains a degree of autonomous JUDGEMENT (genuine representation). The distinction between delegation and representation is crucial here. Delegates merely communicate the views of their clients with the minimal interpretation, whereas representatives attempt to stand for the views and interests of their constituents while making their own views, particularly on matters of conscience, paramount. Such representation becomes more problematic if the diversity of peoples and views to be re-presented becomes extremely diverse or divergent, for it highlights fragmentation. Such fragmentation draws out a distinction between persons taken as a whole and the representation of the views and interests of the constituents in a way that reflects their narrow needs. When the latter is emphasised the ways in which their views and needs fit into the common good taken as a whole is ignored or undercut.

These problems indicate two serious types of challenge to the very idea of representation. The first lies in the deep questions of the kind referred to above. The second admits that some sort of representation is possible, but that there are institutional barriers to its success. Such institutional barriers may take many forms but can, with care, be overcome.

Whatever their inadequacies, taken together these models permit, if not full democratic representation, what might fairly be regarded as democratic accountability. Each model may be imperfect, yet, if sensitively applied, they might offer some means by which diverse viewpoints can be honourably and reasonably brought together and some means by which they might be brought to account.

Given the necessity that modern democracies be indirect, there is a serious set of questions about the relation between the representative and the constituents. The standard solution is to treat the representative as one who re-presents universal, or at least general, features of the constituents rather than particular interests. Representatives are not delegates and are therefore free to act within broad limits, according to belief, conscience and broad mandate. On this model, they would rarely need to consult and to act on the particular concerns of constituents. This model works reasonably well providing some universalistic assumptions are made: namely, that whatever the differences between particular constituents might be, their common ground outweighs these differences.

An alternative but not wholly exclusive model is to treat representatives as dealing with interests rather than persons. This model has a number of attractions: it bypasses the problem of what is involved in re-presenting a person, and it bypasses the problems of universality. However, it raises particularities rather than persons to the centre stage of democracy. It can, therefore, be said to be attentive to interests above persons, *ipso facto* leading to the disenfranchisement of persons. This is such a serious shortcoming that it may fail the central task of representation completely: that representation should be of peoples, and ultimately that can be achieved only through the representation of persons.

Modes of representation

The institutional practice of representation is highly varied. The different technical methods used to exact a working balance between wider and more substantive democratic representation and effective government all exhibit clear strengths and weaknesses. Every type of system reveals different sets of trade-offs between the ideals of true representation of the DEMOS and the practicalities of strong and unified government. The particular socioeconomic and demographic circumstances and POLITICAL CULTURE and traditions of different nations, therefore, provide the most basic reasons why one system is chosen over another.

The most central modern democratic representative institutions clearly pertain to choosing the representatives who will compose state and local government by voting in local, parliamentary or presidential ELECTIONS. Other essential modes of representation may concern, for example, procedures such as voting through plebiscites or REFERENDUMS on proposed legislation. Alternatively, they may concern politico-economic relations such as corporatist organisations that attempt to create a more equal representation of interests between the state, employers and workers (Held 1996: ch. 6) (see Held's COSMOPOLITAN DEMOCRACY).

The spectrum of representative electoral institutions range from simple majority or 'first past the post' systems at one extreme to pure proportional representation at the other. The former usually comprises of single-member constituencies and tends to emphasise the importance of strong government. Such systems, examples of which are found in the USA, UK, India and Canada, make it difficult for more than a few main political parties to have any effective strength in parliament. Government is, therefore, more likely to be unified, at least along party lines if not within the PARTIES themselves. However, the trade-off in the simple majority system lies in that it fails to represent those members of the electorate who did not vote for the winning candidate in their constituency.

Proportional representation (PR) attempts to counter this particular problem by allocating a percentage of party seats corresponding directly to the percentage of actual votes cast for that party. In this way, minority votes are not wasted as in the single majority system. However, the trade-off is reversed in this model and coalition governments, with all their problems of plurality, particular interests and constantly shifting patterns of bargaining, are not uncommon in PR systems (see CHAOS AND COALITIONS; COALITIONS).

A variety of models falling within these two extremes attempt to capture a more sensitive balance between their strengths and weaknesses. Tending toward PR, 'party list systems' (PLS or 'additional member systems') allocate three-quarters of the available seats to single-member constituencies while the remaining seats are secured by the 'best runners-up' according to the number of votes won. Since the Hansard Society recommended PLS in 1976, there has been some discussion as to whether it should be adopted within the UK. However, current debate suggests that a radical shift from the British first past the post tradition seems unlikely in the near future unless the Liberal Democrats manage to secure either office or a balance of power. Variations on the PLS are utilised in Belgium, Israel, Spain, Italy, the Netherlands, Luxembourg, in several Latin American countries and in Germany's 'additional member system'.

The alternative vote method, where the voters rank candidates in order of preference, is used for example in the Australian House of Representatives. A variant of this is the single transferable vote (STV) as practised in the Republic of Ireland and Malta, which transfers any superfluous votes over and above the number required to win to the voter's second-preference. The Japanese version of PR is by 'limited vote'. Finally, the second ballot system is used in Egypt and France, where a limited number of qualifying candidates proceed to a second round.

The success of democratic representation in these models rests on an assumption of relative social, economic, ethnic and political homogeneity. However, as postmodern society becomes more heterogeneous, so these systems are discovering that re-presenting diverse interests, views and needs is increasingly difficult. It seems that democratic political systems have two fundamental options at their disposal in attempting to deal with the diversification of the postmodern condition. The first is obviously the introduction of wider and more effective forms of representation to quell public dissatisfaction over failing to be (or feel) adequately represented. The public demonstrations in Scotland and Britain over the introduction of the 'poll tax' would be a particular case in point, where the government might have responded more sensitively. Instead, when the poll tax became law, it actually reduced the eligible electorate by 2.5 per cent; that is, by over one million individuals. Perhaps an even more distressing example is belied in the incredibly poor voting turnout in US presidential elections. Consistently, 50 per cent or more of the American public do not feel represented enough to make the effort to vote, a state of affairs that enabled George Bush to be elected president in 1988 on the basis of only 27 per cent of the American population.

That the bastion of Western democracy has the lowest turnout in the industrialised world is indeed cause for concern. However, the democratic representatives themselves seem unable or unwilling to deal with that concern through widening public representation. The other option open to them is, of course, attempting to provide a stronger, more authoritarian approach to democratic rule. This strategy certainly appeared to influence the recent Conservative government in Britain which, notwithstanding the public disapproval of the poll tax in 1989–90 that lead to Margaret Thatcher's downfall, quickly pushed through the Civil Rights Bill in spite of wide public outcry. Once it became an Act of Parliament this statute, *inter alia*, severely curtailed the rights of persons engaging in public demonstrations. It also radically increased the authorities of the police in attempting to deal with them; an authority sorely felt by those active in the recent spate of environmental demonstrations and occupations throughout Britain.

Nevertheless, while the pluralisms and diversifications of postmodern societies provide a serious challenge to the idea of representation and the spirit of representative, as opposed to merely accountable, democracy, new arenas of homogeneity are being forged. Perhaps the best example is the European Union, for despite the difficulties in co-ordinating a body to represent a multiplicity of not only nationally, but internationally diverse interests and views, the EU does seem to somehow capture and/or symbolise a broad European need for unity represented by MEPs. Here it is felt that it is less a parliamentary body with sovereign powers that is being voted for than a European-wide voice. It is interesting that voting models for the European Parliament from UK constituencies have since 1999 been based on proportional representation. The justification for this is based on the view that the Strasbourg parliament provides a variety of voices but does not provide an executive. It can, therefore, be wholly representative without any significant engagement in the executive.

Best practice

It is clear that representation challenges the foundation of democracy in a variety of ways. It is also clear that it is necessary that democracies respond in certain ways. Most crucial is that the breakdown of the logocentric tradition has produced a variety of voices that need to be directly heard rather than indirectly re-presented. Ideally, this would be attained via the route of direct democracy. That route is not attainable. Additionally, the structural shift in societies has produced western societies that are heterogeneous rather than homogenous. Again, this increases and diversifies the number of voices that demand to be heard.

This places a dual tension on modes of representation. On the one hand they must attempt to incorporate and express that which is common, general and universal within peoples and humanity respectively. On the other hand they must reduce the degree of representation to an absolute minimum so that presencing, rather than re-presencing is maximally permitted. Universality must be set against a variety of voices and must be done in such a way that viable government is permitted. The task is almost impossible, and involves a variety of trade-offs that leaves no one happy or satisfied yet which, for all that, may be necessary for a stable government that permits some voices to emerge. Inevitably, someone is bound to be unhappy. The trick, it seems, is to make enough people happy for enough of the time so that the system can cope for the time being.

See also:

accountability; autonomy; citizenship; democratic origins; direct democracy; electoral systems; liberalism; representation, models of; state, relations of church to; suffrage

Further reading

Anderson, B. (1983) *Imagined Communities*, London: Verso.

Cadava, E. *et al.* (eds) (1991) *Who Comes After the Subject?*, New York and London: Routledge.

Clarke, P.B. (1988) *The Autonomy of Politics*, Aldershot and Brookfield: Avebury.

—— (1994) *Citizenship*, London and Boulder, CO: Pluto Press.

Held, D. (1996) *Models of Democracy*, Cambridge: Polity Press.

Hirst, P.Q. (1990) *Representative Democracy and its Limits*, Cambridge: Polity Press.

Hobbes, T. (1968) *Leviathan*, ed. Macpherson, Harmondsworth: Penguin.

Madison, J. (1952) 'Federalist Paper No. 10', in R.D. Heffner (ed.), *A Documentary History of the United States*, New York: New American Library.

Pitkin, H. (1984) *The Concept of Representation*, Berkeley and Los Angeles: University of California Press

Plant, R. (1993) *Report of the Working Party on Electoral Systems*, London: Labour Party.

Riley, P. (1988) *The General Will Before Rousseau: the Transformation of the Divine into the Civic*, Princeton, NJ: Princeton University Press.

Schmitt, C. (1985) *Political Theology*, trans. G. Schwab, Cambridge, MA and London: MIT Press.

Voegelin, E. (1952) *The New Science of Politics*, Chicago: University of Chicago Press.

PAUL BARRY CLARKE

representation, models of

Representation is a central concept within liberal democracy, as it provides the link between the people and the decision makers. The key components are that the people choose representatives and that those representatives then make the decisions and are accountable to the people for those decisions. Thus there are two important groups of people within the representative framework: voters and MPs (Members of Parliament). Voters are being represented and need to hold MPs accountable through ELECTIONS. So for voters the important question is how to choose a representative or what it is about yourself that you want to be represented in parliament. For the MPs, representation is an important part of their job and their perspective is on the ways in which they might be expected to fulfil the wishes of the people. The important question for MPs is who they represent and how this impacts on their behaviour in parliament. The two perspectives cast very different lights upon the question of representation in practice and each is the subject of a distinct academic literature. The other crucial component needed for an understanding of how representation happens is the impact of political institutions, particularly ELECTORAL SYSTEMS.

Norms of representation at the beginning of the twenty-first century are very different from a century earlier. At the most basic level, far more people are now entitled to vote, for instance in most countries women received the vote after the First World War and the voting age was lowered to eighteen in the 1960s. Changes in SUFFRAGE have had a major impact on representation: parliament and government are now chosen by, and accountable to, a higher proportion of the total population of the country. Another crucial factor is that in the nineteenth century there were few political PARTIES, and those that existed tended to be loose groupings rather than the disciplined units of modern politics. Prior to the electoral domination of political parties, MPs were chosen for their integrity and perceived ability to make good decisions, or because they were from one of the key economic groups, such as landowners or industrialists. The people who entered politics were also different: there were greater restrictions on who could stand for election or become an MP in terms of gender or religion; and usually MPs were not paid, so only those with an alternative income could enter politics.

How does a voter choose a representative, and what is it that the voter wants to be represented within parliament? From PSEPHOLOGY, the study of ELECTORAL BEHAVIOUR, it is clear that the most common answer is the party. However, voters may also want to elect people who share another political identity (see IDENTITY, POLITICAL) such as ethnicity, language, gender or CLASS. Another aspect in the voters' choice of a representative is between a delegate and a trustee. Delegates follow the instructions of those they represent while trustees are expected to make their own decisions.

Delegation requires MPs to follow instructions. In modern politics, with large populations and fast political decision-making, direct instruction of MPs is rare at the government level. However assumed delegation occurs when MPs are chosen based on an assumption about how they will behave. If voters want an MP who they predict will act in a certain way then they can base that choice upon the party label or some characteristic of the person that will shape their political views.

In the British Commonwealth countries, single member districts are generally used and historically there was a strong idea that the MP was to speak for local interests. If this assumption translates into the MP being a local delegate, then the MP needs to know what the local constituents think. Such information is hard to acquire, although some MPs use the results of local PUBLIC OPINION polls. Another problem is the expectation that there is one view from the constituency. Electorate BOUNDARIES are supposed to encompass local communities, but just because people live in the same area such as an inner city or small tourist town, it does not mean that they share the same views. In some cases, the assumption is that the local delegate's instruction is to secure benefits for the local area, such as legislation useful to the local industry or more spending on hospitals in that area. This behaviour is often called CLIENTELISM.

Delegation is most common through the responsible party model. If voters select a candidate or party because of the party's programme and election promises, then the expectation is that they want the party to carry out that programme. The voters are instructing the MPs to deliver on these policies. Therefore the party must follow that line and thus must ensure that the MPs are disciplined and adhere to the party line rather than following their own ideas and opinions. So, under the responsible party model, the MPs are delegates for the party programme. The voter selects a candidate or party based upon their programme and

expects it to be followed: the party, not personal traits, are what wins the vote. PSEPHOLOGY shows that most voting in Western democracies is for the party rather than the person, making partisan delegation the most common form of representation.

Another approximation of delegation is when as a voter, I choose someone who I expect will behave as I would want them to if I were to give them instructions on every issue. My best guess at finding such a person is to select someone who shares those characteristics which I feel shape my political opinions: voting based on political identity. So a farmer may want another farmer as the MP, or a member of an ethnic minority someone from the same ethnic group. Early studies of electoral behaviour suggested that most people's party choice correlated with some socioeconomic factor. The impact of different identities varied depending upon major CLEAVAGES in the country: class was paramount in most places, such as Britain and Australia, religiosity in France and region in Italy. One problem for the voter, however, is that there may not be a candidate available who shares their political identity. The candidate selection process within each political party acts as a filter on the type of people that voters can choose between. So it is the people choosing candidates, rather than the voters, who have the greatest impact on the type of people in parliament.

With a trustee, the voters select someone they feel will make good decisions. A trustee is expected to look at the evidence and then reach a decision based either upon their idea of what would be best for the locality or country or on purely personal views. So a voter may look at the past record of the candidates and assess their ability to make good decisions: a retrospective decision. Or the voter may assess the personal integrity of the candidates and choose the one most likely to make good decisions. Again, when deciding who I think will be a good decision maker, I may be interested in the candidates' political identity and ideology as well as their record of policy decisions. Debate rather than decisions may be the most important focus of the trustee model, with MPs selected to express a particular perspective in parliament. If voters decide that the MPs are there to contribute to debate, then it is important to have a range of views present within parliament. Thus the election is to choose a whole parliament rather than one individual MP. These ideas are behind the increasingly frequent and vehement demands that parliaments should reflect the society they govern. Many of these demands are from MINORITIES, but the proportion of women in decision-making bodies is also at issue. So the Inter-Parliamentary Union, amongst others, calls for each parliament to be composed equally of men and women, as is society. Likewise Native Americans in the USA decry the absence of one of their people in Congress and African-Americans the small number of blacks.

If the intent is to ensure that each sizeable group within society has their views heard within parliament, then the aim is to have one person from each group. When the presence of a group is guaranteed, then this is called symbolic representation and is akin to the virtual representation practised in Britain in the nineteenth century. There are not many examples of guaranteed places for particular groups, but in New Zealand there are MPs elected just by voters from the indigenous Maori, and the Irish Republic's upper house has members elected by distinct interests such as graduates and farmers. Calls for half of MPs to be women moves argument into the realms of proportionate presence: the idea that the proportions within society be reflected in parliaments because the size of the voting bloc matters.

Trustee models of representation assume the election of a group of people who will make decisions for the country, so arguments about the socioeconomic composition of parliament relate to this idea and the need for the full range of interests to be heard during debate. In part, voters can choose a candidate because of what they are, but also parties will choose a range of candidates to cover the main groups within society and a voter may look at this mix of people when assessing the parties. Much

depends upon the type of choice that the voters have in the electoral system used in that country (see ELECTORAL SYSTEMS).

Different electoral systems were designed with different forms of representation in mind. The party list, used in the majority of democracies, is based on the idea of the responsible party model. Voters choose between parties and the PROPORTIONALITY formulae, used to assign seats to parties, assures that the parties are as strong as the size of their voter base. The multi-member electorates mean that there is no concept of the local representative. In open list systems, the voters can indicate a preference for certain candidates within the slate proposed by the party they vote for and thus representation based upon political identity is also possible. In a closed list system the voter must assess the entire slate.

Under STV (single transferable vote), voters indicate a preference for the candidates and can cross party lines, So voters can choose to base their decisions primarily upon party or personal traits. For instance, a socialist woman who sees her ideology as paramount would vote for the socialist women, then the socialist men, then the women from another centre–left party, then the men from that party and so on moving through the parties. The same voter, but with an emphasis upon wanting women elected, would vote for the socialist women, then the women from other acceptable parties, then the socialist men and then the men from other acceptable parties. STV was designed to allow choice between people and the hope of some of its inventors, such as J.S. Mill, was that the use of STV would lead to the decline of parties. So the original idea was very strongly upon MPs being elected by a group of like-minded voters with the MP then free to act on issues as they arose. This situation lends itself to delegation based upon the MPs responding to the people who elected them. In all of the systems using multi-member electorates, there is an acceptance that in any geographic area people are not all the same and thus there should be a representative for each sizeable group.

Under electoral systems using single-member electorates, the choice is of a person to represent all in the locality. Voters are free to make that choice based upon the candidates' party or upon some other character trait. The use of the plurality system, 'first past the post', predates the creation of disciplined parties, having been used in Britain since early in the nineteenth century. The majority system, used in Australia and France, allows voters to indicate some preferences but there is no choice between candidates from the same party. The top-up systems used in Germany, New Zealand, Scotland and Wales provides a mix of representative roles. Voters elect a local MP using 'first past the post' and also choose a party using the party list method. Allocation of MPs to parties is based upon the party vote, so a voter can choose a local MP from a party other than their favourite without damaging the strength of that party in parliament. In 1996, a third of New Zealand voters split their two votes between two parties, indicating in some cases a desire to make different types of representative choices with the two votes.

Who does a representative represent and how does this role fit with other components of the MP's job? The distinction between the trustee and delegate is again important. If the MPs are there as delegates, then their primary role is to do as instructed. If the MPs are trustees, then they are expected to listen to debate and to reach good decisions. However, most MPs play a mix of the two roles. Even in those countries with strong party discipline, known as whipping in the Westminster system, some issues are designated as conscience votes. For instance, votes on abortion law and capital punishment are often left to the personal views of the MP. In these circumstances, some MPs will seek to determine the views of their constituents, while others make a purely personal choice. So in voting on legislation in parliament, the MPs must decide if they should heed the party, their electorate, their own conscience or the popular will. Of course, under the party list systems MPs do not have a local electorate and thus this consideration is not part of the problem. However, some MPs will see themselves as representative of a non-geographic constituency of interest, such as

farmers or indigenous peoples or mothers. Some MPs also seek to follow the views of the voters, either in their constituency or the country, by following trends in opinion polls. Such behaviour is another part of the delegate role, as the intent is to follow the wishes of the voters.

While there are a number of choices for the MP when deciding who to heed when voting, the casting of votes is only one part of the job of an MP. The vote on legislation is only the final and most visible part of the process with the detailed work done in committees. If the key representative ideal is that the people elect an assembly that will debate and so hear all views and thus reach a decision for the good of all then an important representative role is to be part of debate and committee discussion and express the views of the group you were elected to represent. MPs also have a number of other roles that are vital for democracy but not directly related to representation. Elections are a time to create a government as well as a parliament (an executive and a legislature), so some MPs will also be running a government department. MPs from other parties have an important role of scrutiny so as to keep the government accountable, which is why many countries call the largest party not in government the opposition. MPs also have a role in assisting the people in their interactions with the political system. So while the idea of representation is vital for voters when deciding how to vote, a great deal of the job of an MP is not directly related to the role of making decisions on behalf of the people.

In the LEGISLATIVE PROCESS, party discipline is the dominant force in most votes in all democracies except the USA. So representation is mostly following the responsible party model. In countries using a party list system, then the norms within parliament match the type of choice that voters are offered. However there are high levels of discontent within some such democracies over the extent to which the parties detail what they will do if they become a government and the extent to which they then keep those promises. If parties give few details of their intended actions then voters cannot deliver a detailed mandate. If voters cannot trust the parties to do what they said during the election campaign, then there is also no basis for any idea of a mandate or delegation. Often parties explain the breaking of election promises by the need to meet changing circumstances, like a drop in exchange rates caused by the international economic situation. When MPs make this argument, they are in effect saying that they are elected as trustees: people who will make a good decision based on the situation at hand. But all of the electoral behaviour evidence is that voters expect a greater delegate component and that the government will at least behave in line with their general ideology.

When a government is expected to follow the election mandate, then one role of non-government MPs is to question the government and so make it accountable to parliament and thus the people. In the Westminster system, the tradition of the mandate is that the party with the most MPs has been instructed by the voters to carry out their manifesto policies. In this situation, the role of MPs from other parties is to ensure that the government carries out those promises. However, in Australia there is a debate on the idea of 'competitive mandates'. Some parties argue that they were instructed by their voters to follow their promises and so must argue their case through the legislative process and in some cases defeat part of the government's legislative programme. The issue of competing mandates is most relevant where there is a COALITON or minority government or where the government does not control the second chamber and therefore a minor party may be able to defeat government legislation. The question is about interpreting the will of the people: follow government promises or a minority party's promise to oppose such policies.

There may also be confusion between voters and MPs over the role of MPs from distinct groups. Is a black MP for the British Labour Party supposed to have primary concern for the views of Labour or blacks? In this case the MP was elected for a distinct geographic constituency, probably with a large number of black voters, and so the primary concern may be for the views of the people in that electorate. In multi-member district electoral systems, the same problem is still present. Does a Maori MP elected from the party list of the New Zealand Labour Party owe allegiance primarily to the party, or to the views of Maori voters? Women MPs may face a similar dilemma: are they expected to speak for woman as well as follow the party line?

What is starkly clear is that the electoral system has the major impact upon representation. The choices that voters can make are determined by the system: is the choice of party paramount, or can they select on the basis of personal characteristics? The ease with which parties can work towards having MPs from across the range of groups within society also depends upon the electoral system. When parties select a slate then they can ensure there is balance, but when they are selecting a series of individuals then it is very hard to influence the overall composition of the group of candidates. The extent to which party label dominates election choice will also impact upon the MPs' decisions regarding voting the party line and thus their representative role.

See also:

accountability; boundaries; class; cleavages; clientelism; electoral behaviour; identity, political; legislative process; liberalism; minorities; opposition, loyal; Westminster model

Further reading

Birch, A.H. (1971) *Representation*, London: Pall Mall.

Bogdanor, V. (ed.) (1985) *Representatives of the People?*, Cambridge: Gower.

Bowler, S. and Farrell, D. (1991) 'Party Loyalties in Complex Settings: STV and Party Identification', *Political Studies* 39: 350–62.

Catt, H. (1999) *Democracy in Practice*, London: Routledge.

Grofman, B. and Davidson, C. (eds) (1992)

Controversies in Minority Voting, Washington, DC: The Brookings Institute.

Harrop, M. and Miller, W.L. (1987) *Elections and Voters*, London: Macmillan.

Norris, P. (ed.) (1997) *Passages to Power*, Cambridge: Cambridge University Press.

Peterson, P.E. (ed.) (1995) *Classifying by Race*, Princeton, NJ: Princeton University Press.

Phillips, A. (1995) *The Politics of Presence*, Oxford: Clarendon Press.

Pitkin, H.F. (1967) *The Concept of Representation*, Los Angeles: University of California Press.

Studlar, D. and McAllister, I. (1996) 'Constituency Activity and Representational Roles among Australian Legislators', *Journal of Politics* 58: 69–90.

HELENA CATT

republicanism

Republicanism broadly refers to a tradition of political theory that advocates an active role in the political process for the different elements within a republic. The word 'republic' is Roman in origin, with Cicero's *De Re Publica* being perhaps the most famous work of republican theory from this period, yet speculation concerning the nature of the *res publica* or the public thing may be traced beyond the formal etymology to ancient Athens. The purpose of the early republic was to act as a safeguard for the people or DEMOS, maintaining their freedom from the corruption of tyrants and, in the words of Aristotle, to provide a situation where citizens could rule and be ruled in turn.

While there is not a simple definition of republicanism, there are a number of different principles that make it distinct from competing theories such as LIBERALISM which has tended in recent history to overshadow its much older predecessor. It is best understood as a tradition of political thought that has undergone, and is undergoing, differing degrees of conceptual change. However, common to most, if not all, historical variations is a measure of exclusion and a concern with political stability, a concern that is to some degree appeased by the notion of CIVIC VIRTUE or active public involvement of citizens or other interested parties in the politics and defence of the republic. The form this involvement may take varies, but has often included military training and adherence to a civic religion as well the rotation of political office.

These features have resulted in republicanism's democratic credentials often being challenged. It is certainly the case that by twentieth-century standards, many historical republics and much republican theory fails the criteria by which contemporary democratic practice is judged; universal SUFFRAGE and racial and sexual EQUALITY. As the classical historian Moses Finley pointed out on numerous occasions, the unquestioned premises of the Greek *polis* were such that human flourishing was possible only within a *polis*, that the good man and the citizen were virtually synonymous, and that slaves and women were excluded from the right to *politeuesthai*, to engage in the activities of the political sphere. Moreover, as one would expect of a saga culture, ancient Greek republicanism supported the manly virtues of courage and military glory and had little time for the concerns of the private, economic and predominantly female sphere.

However, it is important to note that while there are 'anti-democratic' tendencies within the tradition, broadly speaking, republicanism shares many common and central themes with democracy, and furthermore has actually been used to challenge some of the central assumptions of the liberalised form of democracy that currently prevails. While it is clear that there are no true republics in the modern political environment, it is equally clear that there are no true democracies. Indeed, the few opportunities that citizens have for active involvement in the modern play of politics within contemporary society would have been regarded by classical authors as most undemocratic.

History and development

The works of the early philosophers, particularly Aristotle's *Nichomachean Ethics* and

Politics, while somewhat ambiguous towards the desirability of democracy, discussed in some detail the nature of political life and of human fulfilment within the *polis* or free-state of Athens. However, after the demise of the Greek *polis* the notion of the *vita activa*, or citizen involvement in political affairs, failed to retain its hold as a political idea. Republicanism resurfaced within the extended republic of Rome, but in changed form. The notion of a small city-state, the precise composition of which was a subject that had occupied Aristotle and a theme that was set to recur in later republican writing notably with Rousseau, seemed simply unfeasible and an unsustainable political ideal. The Roman solution was perhaps the first attempt at the reconceptualisation of the political space of republicanism by attempting to accommodate politics to the expansion of its regions. The changing space of politics rendered the Greek notions, such as *eudaemonia* (human flourishing) and moral education (*paedia*), inappropriate to the vastness of an empire whose 'citizens' now identified with the emperor through his insignia on a common currency.

After a millennium of silence, the rediscovery and translation in the west of Aristotle's *Politics* in the mid-thirteenth century marked a renewed interest in republican thought. Thomas Aquinas made significant efforts to reconcile Aristotle's *homo politicus* with Augustine's *homo credens*, but it was not until theorists such as Marsilius of Padua, who argued for popular SOVEREIGNTY in his *Defensor Pacis*, Leonardo Bruni and most famously, Niccolò Machiavelli in his *Discourses on Livy*, seized upon and to some degree transformed republican ideas for the city-states of the Italian Renaissance that a republican revival can properly be said to have taken place.

Machiavelli's own brand of theory, in particular, defined a republicanism specifically suited to the tenor of the period in which he was writing; albeit one that shared with classical commentators a concern with the problem of political instability and the threat from external force. Yet unlike Aristotelian

'republicanism', which concentrated on the intrinsic value of political PARTICIPATION for citizens *qua* human beings, Machiavelli's 'civic humanism' focused on the instrumental aims of republican theory. Active CITIZENSHIP was required if people were to safeguard their own particular ends and not because it signified the 'supreme human good'. In this sense, Machiavelli was closer to the aspirations of Rome than Athens.

In Machiavelli's Florentine republic, politics was a tool, a means by which greatness and glory for the city might be achieved and corruption overcome while securing the individual liberty of the citizenry. For Bruni, writing in the same period, the priority of the city-state was to allow access to political office rather than participation in a general assembly. This suited the requirements of the dominant merchant oligarchy, but it meant that popular participation was translated into a form of indirect democracy with an emphasis upon the ACCOUNTABILITY of rulers. However, for Marsilius and for Machiavelli, the disunity that was a fact of life for the city-state demanded a commitment to public duty that was a necessary element in securing one's liberty and in overcoming class conflict between the magnates and the people.

The place of democracy during this 'Italian revival' is significant. A large number of citizens participated in the political organisation of a city state either as *podesta* (ruling officials), or members of a council ultimately accountable to the wider body of citizens. This act of self-government was also significant given the ecclesiastical dominance of the period and the almost constant threat of invasion from abroad. Yet how an individual was granted the possibility of involvement depended upon seemingly undemocratic stipulations; one was required to be a resident of long standing, a property owner and, above all, male.

The development of republican thought continued into the modern period with James Harrington's *The Commonwealth of Oceana*, Montesquieu's *Spirit of the Laws* and Jean-Jacques Rousseau's *Social Contract*. Significantly, all three recognised the limitations of the republican heritage yet proceeded to address that issue in different ways. Harrington and Rousseau wrote of utopias and appealed to classical sentiments and classical citizens within their ideal republics. Montesquieu, and those that followed him, notably Alexis de Tocqueville and the authors of the *Federalist Papers*, adopted a slightly different approach marking a second important transition in the development of republican thought, a transition made all the easier by the debate that surrounded the precise meaning of the term 'republic'. They recognised that when applied to the thirteen colonies of America, existing republican models simply made no provision for the size and diversity of a modern state. Under such conditions, a shared sense of duty and responsibility would have to be replaced by other, more appropriate sentiments. Furthermore, the face-to-face contact available to members of a *polis* and perhaps an Italian city-state was no longer possible.

The authors of the *Federalist Papers*, Alexander Hamilton, James Madison and John Jay, collectively and synonymously known as Publius, borrowed directly from Montesquieu the notion of a 'confederate republic'. According to Hamilton, the modern extended republic, which used the new political science now available to the moderns, could construct a self-correcting, representative federal government which preserved both vitality and FREEDOM. However, while representation was clearly a novel way of coping with the changed circumstances and perceived possibilities for and of republicanism, a leading contemporary commentator has noted that the demos or people were, as a result, 'left in so monistic a condition that it mattered little what characteristics it was thought of as possessing' (Pocock 1975: 517).

This feature of the new government was examined by de Tocqueville's *Democracy in America*. His ideas complemented the modern representational institutions of an extended republic, recognising and advocating an active dynamic between large and small political associations. Writing from the perspective of one who saw democracy as a practice that was

eroding citizenship in France by its broad egalitarianism, he considered intermediary or secondary institutions in the public sphere, which incorporated more than the exclusive political concerns of national government, to be of first importance. He allowed himself, when writing about America, to imagine the possibilities of a democratic republic, one that he hoped would be transferred to France.

Along with religion, de Tocqueville thought that the local association or township played an integral role in the republic, a place where citizens might learn about the practice of politics. It was important to multiply the points where citizens could exercise their independence and autonomous JUDGEMENT. Government could be divided between those concerns that only a national legislature could decide. But many other 'administrative' functions, de Tocqueville believed, could be handed down to the townships. Centralisation of these activities he wrote, 'only serves to enervate the peoples that submit to it, because it constantly tends to diminish their civic spirit' (de Tocqueville 1994: 88).

The failure to preserve this buffer against the centralising tendencies of central government led de Tocqueville to analyse democratic society in terms that are reminiscent of recent communitarian critiques. Without the possibility of active citizen involvement, each person 'grew like the rest', 'lost in the crowd' with only 'the great imposing image of the people' remaining (de Tocqueville 1994: 669). The seeds of tyranny were being sown, for without an interest in public business, citizens voluntarily gave up their rights and even the smallest party could become the master of public affairs. The choice, de Tocqueville wrote at the end of the *Democracy in America*, was plain. Equality could not be halted. It was, however, 'up to the nations of the day to prevent the spread of servitude, barbarism and wretchedness and to champion the cause of freedom, knowledge and prosperity' (de Tocqueville 1994: 705).

De Tocqueville provides a good illustration of the tensions between republicanism and democracy, and moreover, between republicanism and liberalism. The exact political colours of the American founding fathers, liberal or republican, have been hotly debated by historians. J.G.A. Pocock, for example, sees a continuum between the renaissance in Italy and the American Constitution, one that 'provide[s] an important key to the paradoxes of modern tensions between individual self awareness on the one hand and the consciousness of society, property and history on the other' (Pocock 1975: 462). This is an issue that has also been widely debated within the fields of political theory and philosophy and within legal theory largely as a result of the liberal communitarian debate of the last two decades. As a consequence, republicanism in various forms is now enjoying something of a theoretical revival.

Political theorists concerned with this issue have identified with the writing of particular republicans like Aristotle, Marsilius or Machiavelli and have sought to redefine liberalism by focusing on the similarities it shares with republicanism, and have even thrown into question the very distinction between liberalism and republicanism. Legal theorists of similar persuasions, notably Frank Michelman (1988) and Cass Sunstein (1988), have attempted to introduce republican notions within the American legal system itself. Michelman suggests a new role for courts within the legal establishment, as semi autonomous institutions designed to effect change with the capacity for critical self reflection. Sunstein conceives republican thought in more broadly Tocquevillian terms, as requiring constitutional theory to be rewritten so that subordinate groups within society may have access to political and legal powers through the creation of intermediate organisations. Interestingly, the major criticisms of these and other authors who share similar aspirations have been that the liberal republican vision they have created lacks substance, and that while advocating the protection of individual rights, these authors are unwilling to impose a theory of value on the political community.

Indeed, few authors have attempted to address the problems created by the 'liberal republican' symbiosis. Of those that have, the republican concern with civic EDUCATION has resurfaced. A preferable educational system is said to encourage, on the one hand, critical thinking and cultural literacy while at the same time encouraging individuals to be responsible citizens. The definitely and somewhat ominous republican issue of the 'love of country' hangs over these attempts, however, such that meaningful forms of DECENTRALISATION and increased opportunities to practice citizenship have been emphasised over republicanism's less desirable aspects.

The precise nature of these theoretical measures requires development. Yet, it seems relatively clear that there are two approaches to the concept of a political education, approaches that are mutually supportive. The first argues that individuals have to be socialised into behaving in the appropriate manner and respecting the demands and RESPONSIBILITIES that go along with active participation in political life. The second argues that politics contains an educative component that is intrinsic to the activity of politics itself, which if defined broadly enough, may arise spontaneously outside the formal institutions of government. Whatever the case, this still leaves the question open as to what kind of political education would be included on a national curriculum, what would be excluded from it and what would be tolerated.

Conclusion

Republicanism, at the very least, poses a challenge to the shallow liberalisms that have dominated much political theory during recent times. Republicans of a Classical or Renaissance persuasion continue to raise important issues that are relevant to citizens of democratic states. Yet, by far the most interesting and perhaps important development arising from the discussion to date has been as a result of the attempt to reconcile liberals and republicans in order to produce a theory with real theoretical force and vigour. It seems clear that if shallow liberalisms are to be deepened by elements from the republican tradition, then that same tradition must in some way be transformed again. The imaginative capacity to reshape republican thought historically is, however, an encouraging precedent. As a result, factors such as the size and complexity of states together with citizen mobility, factors that have been used as negative constraints upon republican aspirations in the past, may well turn out to be strengths. Much depends upon how much faith one places in new technologies to provide links that tie and bind. Equally important is the imaginative challenge one faces as a result, how far, for example, one is prepared to reconceive the forms of political community, the elements that constitute political action and, perhaps, even what is understood by politics itself.

Overcoming problems of participation within the size of modern communities dictated historically either a political community of limited size or a political community of representative government. On the one hand, alternatives to representation, in their bid to have the citizenry actively involved in politics, demand the physical building of assemblies where people might gather. On the other hand, the extension of current representational institutions or the recognition that instances of action not formerly considered political do contain political elements are positive steps in a slightly different direction. Yet, these alternatives fall somewhat short of the mark if they remain undeveloped as a theory or unachieved as a policy. That said, it is not automatically clear that the conditions of mass society preclude political participation. The complexity and scale of modern societies does not automatically exclude the possibilities of genuinely political action. It remains up to political actors themselves to decide the best means of securing their liberty.

See also:

democratic origins; moral improvement; representation, concept of

Further reading

De Tocqueville, A. (1994) *Democracy in America*, ed. J.P. Mayer, trans. G. Lawrence, London: Fontana Press.

Hamilton, A., Madison, J. and Jay, J. (1975) *The Federalist Papers*, New York: Mentor Books.

Harrington, J. (1992) *The Commonwealth of Oceana, and A System of Politics*, ed. J.G.A. Pocock, Cambridge: Cambridge University Press.

Michelman, F. (1988) 'Law's Republic', *The Yale Law Journal* 97(8).

Montesquieu, C.L. de S. (1989) *The Spirit of the Laws*, trans. A.M. Cohler, ed. B.C. Miller and H.S. Stone, Cambridge and New York: Cambridge University Press.

Pocock, J.G.A. (1975) *The Machiavellian Moment: Florentine Political Thought and the Atlantic Republican Tradition*, Princeton, NJ: Princeton University Press.

Sunstein, C.R. (1988) 'Beyond the Republican Revival', *The Yale Law Journal* 97(8): 1539–90.

LAWRENCE QUILL

responsibilities

Democratic politics can be said to be 'responsible' politics in at least three distinct senses, all of which suggest behavioural ideals both for the democratic state (its administrative officials as well as its elected politicians) and its citizens (both as individuals and as organised groups in CIVIL SOCIETY). The first holds that those who exercise power are responsible to those whom they represent for the decisions they take and the way in which they are implemented. In some substantive sense, they have to act in the interests of the people according to the accepted democratic procedures, and they are liable to censure or removal from office if they do not do so. The second sense is that everyone who belongs to a democratic system, citizens and governors, has 'responsibilities to act' in certain ways which uphold the democratic order. This idea leads into the third sense, in which people can be said to be 'responsible citizens' if they actually do behave in a particular, praiseworthy way. The nature of such conduct will be at least partly informed by the responsibilities identified in the second sense, though it is important not to conflate the two as it is quite possible to have responsibilities without actually being a responsible person.

Responsibilities in the democratic exercise of power

Although not necessarily exclusive to it, the first sense highlights a crucial pillar of representative democracy in particular. The idea that politicians have responsibilities to the electorate for the actions performed in their name is designed to embody the democratic insistence that power should not be exercised arbitrarily as it is granted as a revocable trust from the citizens. If continuous direct PARTI-CIPATION from the citizens themselves cannot be practised, the democratic notion of power's responsibilities to them helps meaningfully to preserve the commitment to popular SOVER-EIGNTY: democratic politicians are expected to be able to justify their actions before the people and should rightfully suffer censure or even removal from office if they fail to do so. A democratic polity should therefore devise institutions and practices by which such ACCOUNTABILITY can be exercised. Ultimately, regular ELECTIONS perform this function but other institutional mechanisms – typically for legislatures to scrutinise the activities of executives – are needed between polls. This scrutiny is important not just to monitor and validate or challenge the policies being implemented, but also to guard against general misuses of power either by the politicians who take the decisions or their staff who administer them.

A paradigm of this norm in practice is the widespread parliamentary convention of 'ministerial responsibility', holding that the senior elected officials in ministries are responsible for the activities of their departments, including those of unelected bureaucrats, and should resign where errors have been made at that level even when they are not themselves directly to blame (Marshall 1989). Techniques and practices of modern governance have, however, posed problems for the maintenance of this convention. In Britain, for example, the extent of ministerial responsibility has become blurred. A devolution and concomitant increase in the nominal AUTONOMY of large sections of the state's administrative apparatus has in some cases prompted ministers to attempt an avoidance of responsibility by blaming policy failures on their supposedly inadequate execution by unelected bureaucrats. The increasing complexity of modern governance makes the practice of responsible politics in this sense more difficult (Lewis and Longley 1996).

The 'second-sense' responsibilities of democratic government obviously include the requirement to be responsive to the preferences of the citizens but – again for representative democracy in particular – to be a responsible government (in the third sense) does not mean that it should always follow their whims. Responsible government requires prudence, careful consideration and wisdom in its DECISION-MAKING, the process and outcome of which might well frustrate the majority. Representative democracy's defenders often claim that direct democracy's failings lie in its ability to guarantee this kind of responsible governance, and they claim that theirs is still a democratic system insofar as it produces decisions which are in the public interest, that which is best for the public overall even if they do not immediately appreciate it as such. However, insofar as it is crucial to a genuine democracy that the public themselves have a large role in determining the 'public interest', this tension between democracy and responsible government may not be wholly eradicable in practice, for the electorate remain free to re-elect or reject their representatives according to their own JUDGE-MENT of how they have been ruled. It has been claimed that herein lies democracy's central weakness: the impetus to win votes encourages the taking of irresponsible decisions that buy short-term electoral popularity, but which are not in the longer term public interest. As examples, one could point to democratic governments' frequent inflation of their economies in the run-up to elections, when such policies may incur longer-term economic costs. Here, democracy's best defence may well be to admit this as a flaw, but urge that no one has yet been able to practise alternatives that come even close to matching democracy's imperfectly responsible rule.

Responsibilities of citizens

Responsibilities in the second and third senses can be borne by individual citizens and the organisations which they form for political ends in civil society, particularly political parties. These responsibilities may well be akin to the DUTIES that are sometimes postulated to be central to democratic CITIZENSHIP, although calling them 'responsibilities' rather than 'duties' perhaps removes something of the impression that they are compulsory. Nevertheless, a strong case can be made for the claim that the well-being of a democratic order is critically dependent upon the discharge of responsibilities by responsible citizens.

Political parties, for example, could be said to have responsibilities to campaign for and hold office in ways that support rather than undermine the democratic process. 'Responsible behaviour' might include the avoidance of 'dirty campaigning' and the various forms of political CORRUPTION, obedience of the laws and conventions which govern political campaigning, and supporting policies and causes for sincere rather than disingenuous, manipulative reasons. The irresponsibility of parties in this regard fuels citizens' cynicism and disillusionment about politics which can devastatingly diminish respect for the democratic order as a whole.

The possibility of individual citizens acquiring and maintaining a sense of democratic responsibility, a willingness to behave in those ways which support democratic practices, must therefore rest in part on the perceived respect for democratic responsibilities displayed by political leaders themselves. Studies of the problems in developing this sense in post-communist countries have also suggested other factors (Hankiss 1990). The motivation to behave responsibly may also depend upon a wider sense of community to which people can feel more generally responsible and in which they feel themselves to have a meaningful stake and role to play (something which Hankiss believes was undermined by the lack of fully developed civil societies under communism). Citizens also require the ability to act responsibly (arguably undermined under communism by the state's restrictions on liberty and attack on human dignity) and, of course, the possibility: avenues for meaningful activity in which they can really can act responsibly.

Perhaps the most perplexing possible democratic responsibility raises the prospect that the state–citizen relationship cuts both ways in this regard: can citizens of a democracy be held responsible for the actions of their government, even when they themselves had no direct role in making and executing the decision to act, and may indeed have opposed it? Karl Jaspers conceives of a category of moral liability which 'results in my having to bear the consequences of the deeds of the state whose power governs me and under whose order I live. Everyone is co-responsible for the way he is governed' (Jaspers 1947: 31). He seems to suggest that a citizen of any state has some degree of liability for the nature of that state. Although Jaspers was writing about the German people's responsibility for Nazism, it could well be that such liability should fall even more heavily upon the shoulders of democratic citizens, for if they have allowed a regime capable of wrongdoing in their midst, they must surely have some direct responsibility for it.

Ironically, 'elite' theorists of democracy might rescue the moral standing of citizens from this troubling proposition by arguing that, as there is so little chance of ordinary citizens being able meaningfully to participate, it is unfair to level a disproportionately large responsibility for their state's actions on them (Schumpeter 1952: ch. 21). The challenge for those who harbour more generous accounts of citizens' potentials must be to consider whether

Jaspers's proposition can or should be resisted. Perhaps we should recognise that, when the democratic state transgresses morality's boundary, citizens have not only a right but a responsibility – to themselves as much as anything – to campaign against it, insofar as they too bear some of the moral liability for its injustices.

See also:

citizenship; civic virtue; moral improvement; political obligation; self and politics; standards of conduct in public life

Further reading

Hankiss, E. (1990) 'The Loss of Responsibility', in *The Political Responsibility of Intellectuals*, Cambridge: Cambridge University Press.

Jaspers, K. (1947) *The Question of German Guilt*, trans. E.B. Ashton, New York: Dial Press.

Lewis, N. and Longley, D. (1996) 'Ministerial Responsibility: The Next Steps', *Public Law* (Autumn): 490–507.

Marshall, G. (ed.) (1989) *Ministerial Responsibility*, Oxford: Oxford University Press.

Schumpeter, J. (1952) *Capitalism, Socialism and Democracy*, 5th edn, London: Unwin.

MARK EVANS

revisionary justice

Many democracies have come into being by replacing deeply authoritarian, dictatorial governments: ones which ignored all human RIGHTS, tortured and killed their political opponents, and considered democracy to be an unpleasant irrelevance. Such new democratic governments are immediately faced with the problem of what to do with the leaders of the old regime and its many supporters. That is the issue of revisionary (or transitional) justice. A wide variety of different solutions have been tried, ranging from doing nothing (as in Spain) to sentencing the old LEADERSHIP to death (as after the Second World War).

Two objectives must be considered: the practical one that the new (and often weak) democracy has to preserve itself and make sure that it is not overthrown by another authoritarian dictator; and the moral one that it must act (and be seen to act) in accordance with democratic values, and not those of its authoritarian predecessors. Often these two objectives reinforce each other, so that acting in accordance with democratic values strengthens the new democracy. But, unfortunately, sometimes they are in tension and then the scope of action of the new democracy is constrained. This can occur when the old regime leaves office with its power base intact and can threaten to overthrow the democracy if it is too displeased: many military regimes, for instance, retained the loyalty of the army when they handed power over to civilians, so that the new government dared not confront the military (as occurred in Chile, Greece and South Korea). Conversely, there may be such hatred of the old regime that the new government would not survive if it did not turn on its predecessors (for example, after the fall of Vichy France or Quisling Norway at the end of the Second World War). Such practical constraints on the FREEDOM of action of the new democracy might severely limit its choices.

If there is no such CONSTRAINT, the new government will be free to choose how to demonstrate that its rule will be very different from its predecessor. One apparently plausible way for the new government to distance itself from the abhorrent conduct of the previous regime is by putting the leaders (and lackeys) of the old regime on trial, thus both symbolising the abhorrence that is felt for what they did, and demonstrating that there is a clear break with the past.

But democratic theory has several very powerful objections to such a move. One is that to put one's political opponents on trial is, in fact, usually not a break with the past at all: the old regime would, by staging elaborate show trials, have thought it normal to use the legal system as a political weapon against its opponents. A democracy cannot do this. Whatever else it does, it cannot simply take revenge on its hated predecessors in the way they revenged themselves on their opponents. While the victims of the oppression might be crying out for vengeance, they must be ignored (if that is politically possible), for almost all theorists agree that vengeance cannot be an acceptable basis for punishment in a democratic state.

There are several different views on what *does* provide a satisfactory justification of punishment (see Ten (1987) for a survey). One suggestion, often invoked in this context, is deterrence: that punishing someone is justified if it deters others from doing the same thing, because they fear that they will also be punished. Philosophers have found difficulties with this as a general justification of punishment (Ten 1987: ch. 2), but here it faces the more uncontentious drawback that deterrence only justifies punishments that actually do deter. It is, however, extremely naive to imagine that a brutal dictator will be encouraged to be less brutal by the thought that *if* he is overthrown (and *if* he survives, yet does not escape abroad) and *if* he is put on trial, then he might well be jailed for a few years. Rather, the prospect of a trial will have the effect of encouraging dictators not to risk punishment by handing power to democratic governments – which is precisely the reverse of what is wanted. Deterrence theory, then, provides little justification for punishing leaders of the old regime.

Further, liberal jurisprudence emphasises that states must adhere to due legal process. Dictatorships invariably pay no respect to DUE PROCESS, and that is part of what is wrong with them; a democratic state, by contrast, is a law-respecting state (*Rechtsstaat*). This limits the state's freedom of action. Specifically prevented is retrospective legislation: the state can only punish those who have broken laws that were clearly in force at the time they acted. Most tyrannical regimes, however, are careful to make sure they pass laws making legal whatever they want to do. (See Adams (1993) on the difficulties of punishing East German border

guards who killed escapees.) If the new regime cannot override these laws retrospectively, it can only punish people for acts of brutality done under the old regime if it can somehow magic the old regime's laws away (see Hart 1958; Fuller 1958; Fuller 1969). Some states have felt unable to do this, and so have decided that the legal system cannot touch the previous regime (as in Hungary). Others have strained to find laws of the old regime that the rulers of that regime have broken, such as embezzling funds (as in Bulgaria).

The new democracy can try to ignore, as invalid, the laws of the old regime by relying on theories of natural law or international law. The theory of natural law is that laws are not made by states but discovered by reason. If the old regime passed a 'law' permitting the torture of opponents, this 'law' would not really be a law at all, because it runs counter to our knowledge of what a law should be. This sort of thinking was part of the justification of the Nuremberg War Crimes process, whereby German leaders were tried (and punished) for acts that were legal by German law but completely abhorrent to the Allies. More recently – to escape the charge that Nuremberg was merely 'victor's justice' – there have been attempts to find and codify such conclusions of natural law and embody them in international law, which the governments of all states are expected to respect; these international laws override, some claim, a state's domestic laws. Unfortunately, while there have been many developments in international law in the 1990s, these laws are still very vague and of disputed validity.

Legal theory, then, provides good reasons why the new democracy should not punish members of the previous regime. Sometimes such punishments may nevertheless be the best course of action: they state firmly and dramatically that prevalent past abuses such as torture will no longer be tolerated. But it must always be borne in mind that using the courts to make such political statements is to violate the central legal principles that the democratic regime should be trying to establish. In short, the values that the new democracy stands for include both substantive beliefs that certain actions are unacceptable, and procedural norms as to how these beliefs can be enforced. In periods of transition, the substantive beliefs and the procedural norms are often in conflict; it may well be unwise to underestimate the importance of procedures.

Even if it rejects the legal process, the new democratic state can consider other approaches. Two such are LUSTRATION and Truth Commissions. Lustration (which means 'purification') involves preventing those implicated with the old regime from occupying senior and sensitive offices under the new one. There are strong reasons why members of the intelligence services, the military or the judiciary, for instance, should not be kept on in their jobs. (Sometimes, though, the lack of suitably qualified replacements means that in practice they have to be retained.) But it must always be made clear that the motivation here must involve neither revenge nor nepotism; neither attempting to remove previous enemies from lucrative jobs, nor rewarding one's supporters with them. Rather, it is justified only insofar as those who worked under the old regime cannot be expected to be able to work properly in the very different requirements of a democracy. This requires that the range of jobs involved is interpreted narrowly. Even then, the worry when any policy of lustration is applied strenuously (as, at first, in the Czech Republic) is that the standards of proof are lower than that required in a legal process, so that people can be dismissed – and ruined – on mere suspicion of having been associated with the old regime. Indeed, it can involve denying employment to people simply on the basis of their past political views (such as membership of political parties), which is rightly condemned by international covenants. Therefore, while some policy of lustration is invariably necessary, it must be clearly and narrowly drawn, with adequate safeguards to ensure that the only people barred are those who demonstrably cannot be trusted to work within a democracy.

Truth Commissions have been held alongside prosecutions and lustration, but the essential idea is different: that it is important

in itself that the truth about the old regime be known. The truth can have the effect of purging the old regime, by exposing its horrors (as the evidence produced at Nuremberg did for Nazi Germany). It can also allow a psychological line to be drawn under the old regime: by allowing victims to tell their stories, and the society to produce an authoritative account of the past, people – both individually and collectively – can put the past behind them and turn to the future. Importantly, the Commission can act in the name of the society, so that the society can then not merely *find* the truth (a truth the victims might know all too well), but *acknowledge* the truth. This acknowledgement of the truth is a necessary precondition for the reconciliation that is essential if the society is to be governable peacefully.

However, such Commissions can be double-edged swords, for revealing abuses that are indeed horrendous may increase the popular desire that the perpetrators receive some form of punishment. This is particularly the case if the Commission both names names and grants amnesties or pardons to people so named. Yet, insofar as one can assess the evidence to date, Truth Commissions seem to have rarely made the situation worse, and sometimes have been beneficial in reducing tension and increasing national reconciliation.

In conclusion, there is no blueprint that can be applied to all cases of democratisation. Each situation will be different, and will require handling with sensitivity to its uniqueness. What may secure reconciliation in one country might heighten tensions in another. What is likely to be common to all situations is that the new democratic government will be faced with significant numbers of people who have strongly held and divergent views on what should be done about the past. But there is nothing unusual in that: all democracies are likely, at some time or other, to be faced with deep divisions of opinion. Democratic leaders have to be able to evolve ways of limiting such divisions; and also – and possibly more importantly – the people have to realise that, if they want a democracy, they will have to live in peace with those with whom they deeply disagree.

See also:

corruption; democratic transition; lustration

Further reading

Adams, K.A. (1993) 'What is Just? The Rule of Law and Natural Law in the Trials of Former East German Border Guards', *Stanford Journal of International Law* 29: 271–314.

Elster, J. (1998) 'Coming to Terms with the Past', *Archives Européennes de Sociologie* 39: 7–48.

Fuller, L.L. (1958) 'Positivism and Fidelity to Law', *Harvard Law Review* 71: 630–72.

—— (1969) *The Morality of Law*, New Haven, CT: Yale University Press.

Hart, H.L.A. (1958) 'Positivism and the Separation of Law and Morals', *Harvard Law Review* 71: 593–629.

Koh, H.H. and Slye, R.C. (eds) (1999) *Deliberative Democracy and Human Rights*, New Haven, CT: Yale University Press.

Kritz, N.J. (ed.) (1995) *Transitional Justice: How Emerging Democracies Reckon with Former Regimes*, 3 vols, Washington: US Institute of Peace Press

McAdams, A.J. (ed.) (1997) *Transitional Justice and the Rule of Law in New Democracies*, Notre Dame, IN: University of Notre Dame Press.

Ten, C.L. (1987) *Crime, Guilt, and Punishment*, Oxford: Oxford University Press.

The Truth and Reconciliation Commission [of South Africa] (1998) *Report*, http://www.truth.org.za.

PETER MORRISS

revolutions

Concepts and issues

The term 'democratic revolutions' implies a set of events consisting of three parts: (1) an undemocratic old regime; (2) a revolution; and (3) a democratic new regime. This idea raises three initial problems, two conceptual and one empirical. What conception of 'democracy' should we use? What is a 'revolution'? What role, if any, have 'revolutions' played in the establishment of democratic regimes?

The conceptual problems are difficult for at least two reasons. First the term 'democratic revolutions' applies to the long historical period from classical Athens to the present, in which conceptions of both 'democracy' and 'revolution' have changed fundamentally. Second, the designation of particular events as 'revolutions' can be controversial, since different definitions of 'revolution' are favoured by different authors on scientific and/or ideological grounds.

The simplest definition of 'democracy' is that it is rule by the people. This rule can be direct or indirect. In an indirect democracy the rulers are elites who are accountable to the people. The forms and degrees of ACCOUNTABILITY are extremely variable. Since indirect or 'representative' democracy is the most common form in modern societies, there are today many forms and degrees of democracy.

'Revolution' is a special form of social change, but its special characteristics are difficult to specify uncontroversially. For Marxists, 'revolutions' are social, structural and radical. Others distinguish between political and social revolutions or conceive of revolutions as a form of political change. Some include violence in the definition of 'revolution', but this is unsatisfactory, since it would exclude by definition such events as the 'Velvet Revolution' of 1989 in Czechoslovakia. Many writers require that 'revolutions' be, by definition, 'sudden', in order to exclude such long-term changes as 'the industrial revolution'. This requirement is, however, very problematic for the analysis of 'democratic revolutions', for most famous 'sudden' revolutions – such as the French Revolution of 1789 – did not have immediate democratic outcomes, and most contemporary stable democracies were not established by 'sudden' revolutions. The understanding of 'democratic revolutions', therefore, requires us both to analyse the role of 'sudden' revolutions in the development of democratic societies, and to elucidate the complex, and often long-term processes by which undemocratic regimes are replaced by democracies.

A theoretical link between democracy and revolution was forged by the liberal tradition from Locke to Paine. This version of liberal theory held that all human beings were naturally free, and consequently could be ruled legitimately only with their consent. It followed that the people might change their government or form of government whenever they chose. This doctrine could, however, be interpreted conservatively, as it was by Locke, who held the right of the people to revolution should be constrained by a prudent concern for stability, or more radically, as it was by Paine, who emphasised the right to overthrow unjust regimes. The radical version was adopted by the very influential Jacobin–Marxist conception of revolution. Jacobinism, the ideology of the radical democrats in the French Revolution, represents revolutions as uprisings of the people to replace tyrannies with democracies. Marxism replaces 'the people' with the proletarian class and 'democracy' with communism. Although Jacobin–Marxist interpretations of the French Revolution in particular and of revolution in general are now widely rejected, they have been replaced by little consensus about how to understand the concept of 'democratic revolutions'. The failure of Jacobin–Marxist projects and the complex ways in which authoritarian regimes have been replaced recently by democracies has led to a terminological shift from 'democratic revolutions' to 'democratisation' and 'DEMOCRATIC TRANSITION' (Linz and Stepan 1996).

A brief history

We usually trace democracy back to ancient Athens. The origins of Athenian democracy are obscure, but they are now usually attributed to reform from above by Kleisthenes. Democratic revolution was known to the Greek city-states as conflicts arose between oligarchic and democratic factions. Plato argued in *The Republic* that democratic revolutions were caused primarily by the corruption and oppression of oligarchies, but that their causes might be either wholly internal or a combination of internal and external conflicts. Aristotle in *The Politics* also held that non-democratic constitutions were vulnerable to democratic revolution if the people were unjustly treated.

Modern democracy had origins in the development of urban self-government in northern Italy from the eleventh to the thirteenth centuries. The Italian city-states of the Renaissance were characterised by intense conflicts, often between oligarchic and popular factions. These led Machiavelli to analyse revolutions, democratic and anti-democratic, in a way that recalls the 'class analysis' of Plato and Aristotle (Held 1996: 51). Skinner argues that, although these city-republics did not regard themselves as 'democratic', since the concept of 'democracy' carried Aristotelian connotations of unjust and unstable government, they made an important contribution to democratic thought in advocating both the principle of popular SOVEREIGNTY and the institution of elected government. Marsilius of Padua in 1324 inferred from the principle of popular sovereignty the conclusion that, if the rulers betrayed their trust and failed to govern in the public interest, the people had the right to remove them from office (Skinner 1993).

Another source of modern democracy was feudal resistance to monarchy and the concomitant idea that authority rests upon contract. As states made greater demands on their peoples for the sake of more effective warmaking, appeals to ancient popular rights gradually evolved from conservative measures of defence to embryonic claims to CITIZENSHIP. The Reformation invigorated movements of popular resistance, particularly during the Netherlands revolt against Spain, which combined democratic, nationalist and revolutionary elements.

Both Italian republicanism and Dutch Protestantism influenced the parliamentary party during the English Civil War (Skinner 1993: 67). Wootton has argued that the Levellers were the first modern political movement committed to popular sovereignty. They were, he maintains, the first democrats who thought, not in terms of the self-governing city-state, but of representative government in the nation-state. They claimed a number of fundamental civil and political RIGHTS, including the right to vote and the right to resist tyranny by revolution. The political theory of John Locke repeated a number of basic Leveller themes, especially those of natural rights and revolution, but Locke did not clearly endorse democracy. Seventeenth-century Puritanism led to democracy neither in England nor in America (Huntington 1991: 13). Yet the English Revolution did strengthen the power of Parliament, and thus contributed to the evolution of British democracy. After the Glorious Revolution of 1689, the English state proved strong enough to prevent further revolution while allowing the evolution of democracy.

English resistance to royal authority was reproduced in America, where it was intensified by the conflict between metropolis and colonies. The burdens of taxation were material causes of grievance, but monarchical oppression was also interpreted in terms of Protestant conceptions of popular sovereignty. In 1776 the American Declaration of Independence declared that the people had the right to alter or abolish any form of government that had become destructive of life, liberty or the pursuit of happiness. The American Revolution has been acclaimed as the first modern democratic revolution. The Founding Fathers, however, retained traditional reservations about democracy. They consequently established a mixed form of government, with a separation of powers and a bill of rights. Yet the terms 'republic', 'democracy' and 'representative democracy' were all applied to the early USA (Wood 1993). It was nevertheless a very imperfect democracy, excluding women, slaves and indigenous peoples.

The French Revolution was seen by contemporaries, and has been considered by later activists and scholars, as a new type of revolution that changed and came to dominate the very meaning of 'revolution' as a transformative social upheaval. It was thought at the time, both by its supporters and its critics, to be a democratic revolution. *The Declaration of the Rights of Man and of the Citizen* (1789) affirmed the sovereignty of the people. Yet the ideology of the Revolution was a mixture of ancient Greek democracy, REPUBLICANISM and representative government. In the face of practical difficulties at home and abroad, revolutionary elites suppressed the liberal democratic ideals of 1789 in the name of republican virtue. The revolution was a traumatic event in the difficult evolution from the classical idea of DIRECT DEMOCRACY to the modern idea of representative government. Notwithstanding its degeneration into Terror and its completion in the Napoleonic dictatorship and the restoration of the monarchy, the ideas of universal rights and democratic citizenship that were proclaimed in the French Revolution deeply influenced later democratic thought (Fontana 1993).

The American and French revolutions placed democracy on the agenda of world history without establishing democratic regimes in the short run. Huntington has referred to the period 1828–1926 as the 'first, long wave of democratisation', in which thirty countries established 'minimal national democratic institutions' (Huntington 1991: 16–17). After the French Revolution, liberals and democrats viewed each other with suspicion. Liberals sought to protect individual FREEDOM and minorities from 'the tyranny of the majority'. Democrats held liberalism to be a defence of bourgeois property rights against popular interests. The French Revolution, with its democratic ideology and imperialist practice, generated nationalist reactions throughout Europe, and eventually beyond, that were often revolutionary and sometimes, but by no means always, democratic in ideology. The failed revolutions that took place in several European countries in 1848 had (partially) democratic and nationalist elements.

Marx's theory of revolution combined the democratic, 'Jacobin' elements of French revolutionary thought with the idea that class conflict was the locomotive of history. This 'Jacobin' conception of revolutionary democracy was adopted by Lenin, although the relations between the views of Marx and Lenin are controversial (Harding 1993). The apparently democratic ideology of Lenin was transformed into the extreme authoritarian regime of Stalin in the USSR. Various explanations of this transformation have been advanced, including the proposition that revolution itself may be incompatible with democracy. The argument underlying this proposition is that revolution creates a power vacuum, which must be filled by an authoritarian power. Explanations of Stalinism in particular, and of revolutionary authoritarianism in general, must however be complex, although we now know that revolutions with democratic ideologies often have authoritarian outcomes.

The weakening of the European imperial powers by the Second World War led to a wave of anti-colonial revolutions in the 1950s and 1960s. Many of these revolutions appeared to be motivated by democratic ideologies, and some led initially to the establishment of democratic regimes. Most of these regimes, however, soon collapsed into authoritarian rule. Postwar regimes established by anti-colonial revolution were mostly characterised by a national variant of Marxism-Leninism, more or less unstable 'Western style' democracy, or developmental authoritarianism. In 1979 the Iranian Revolution challenged the French revolutionary tradition of secular, democratic revolution by combining a Jacobin-style popular uprising with the institution of an authoritarian Islamic regime.

The end of 'revolution'? Democracy's third wave

Jacobin–Marxist theory held revolution to be the way to democracy. Empirically, revolutions have rarely led directly to democracy, although some revolutions have played an important role in advancing democratisation and/or diffusing democratic ideas. In the last quarter of the twentieth century, a number of events have taken place that may be called 'democratic revolutions', but which have called into question earlier theories of revolution. They have

sometimes been analysed under the heading of what Huntington has called 'democracy's third wave' (Huntington 1991, 1996). The first wave of democratisation, according to Huntington, covered the century from the 1820s to the 1920s. The second took place after the Second World War in the years 1945–62. The third wave began in 1974, and has perhaps not yet ended (Huntington 1996: 3–4) (see WAVES OF DEMOCRACY).

Whether the democratisation of the 'third wave' has consisted of 'democratic revolutions' raises complex empirical and conceptual problems. Viewed as a whole, the 'third wave' was remarkable: between 1974 and 1995, more than sixty authoritarian regimes became at least formally democratic. The collapse of the USSR not only discredited Marxism-Leninism as a political theory and as a developmental ideology, it called into question all forms of developmental authoritarianism, and thus considerably boosted the prestige of democracy worldwide (Diamond and Plattner 1996: ix). In one sense, the 'third wave' of democratisation constitutes a 'revolution' in world politics, but it has largely taken the form of peaceful, negotiated transitions rather than mass, violent uprisings, although the form of these transitions – slow or sudden, peaceful or violent, elitist or mass mobilising – has varied considerably (Plattner 1996: 38).

The complexity of third wave democratic transitions can be illustrated by the Portuguese revolution of 1974. This began with a military *coup d'état*, which generated a large popular mobilisation, which in turn led to the establishment of a stable liberal democratic regime. In Spain, the death of the dictator Franco opened the way to a transition to democracy through a combination of reform from above led by King Juan Carlos and popular mobilisation. The success of these transitions has been explained by three factors: the weakness of anti-democratic forces, the unity of pro-democratic forces, and a strongly pro-democratic international environment (Huntington 1991: 3–5; Goldblatt 1997: 107–13). The democratic transitions in Latin America have been interpreted as, in most cases, predominantly elitist, although in Nicaragua, exceptionally, a Jacobin–Marxist revolution had eventually a liberal democratic outcome. In East Asia, South Korea and Taiwan made transitions from authoritarianism to democracy by a combination of elite strategies, popular pressures and international political and economic changes. The democratic transition in South Africa had similar general features. Although popular resistance to and international pressure on the apartheid regime were strong, the South African process of democratisation took the form primarily of elite negotiation. The perceived need to conform with the requirements of global capitalism dominated the Jacobin–Marxist tendencies that were present in the South African 'revolution'. In explaining the 'third wave' of democratisation, Huntington has employed the concept of 'snowballing' to suggest that, once the wave was in motion, it had its own causal force: unpopular and unstable authoritarian regimes were undermined further by the fall of authoritarian regimes elsewhere. Both the stability and the depth of democracy in societies that have recently made the transition are uncertain, but certainly variable (Diamond and Plattner 1996: x, xxxi; Huntington 1996: 7).

Almost all the varieties of democratic transition followed the collapse of communism in Eastern Europe. This was proximately caused by the economic and military weakness of the USSR. Most other European communist societies were also experiencing severe economic difficulties. The apparent weakness of the USSR produced 'snowballing' throughout Eastern Europe, and indeed beyond, as the end of the Cold War undermined both communist and anti-communist authoritarian regimes in the Third World. As in Latin America, elite economic and political liberalisation sometimes preceded democratisation. This made space for 'CIVIL SOCIETY' to exert pressure for democratic change (Lewis 1997). The collapse of authoritarian multinational societies in the USSR and Yugoslavia led to violent ethno-nationalist conflicts. The ability of civil society to sustain democracy in the post-communist era is uncertain, but certainly variable from one society to another (Ascherson 1993: 234–5). However, there is a strong correlation between the relative economic success of communist societies and the success of their transition to stable, liberal democracy (Lewis 1997: 410). Whether or not Eastern European democratisation was 'revolutionary' depends on one's definition of 'revolution'. None of the transitions was much like the French Revolution, but each had revolutionary features, even though each was in significant respects unique in its causes, processes and outcomes.

Conclusions

Revolutions have played an important role in the evolution of democracy, and revolutions have recently played an important role in the transition from authoritarian to democratic regimes. There is some truth in the Jacobin view that popular uprisings can play a part in democratic revolutions, although they do not always lead to democracy, and when they do, other important factors are usually at work. There is also some truth in the Marxist view that class struggles are sometimes part of democratic revolutions, but again, they do not necessarily lead to democracy, and when they do, other important factors are at work. The history of democracy has been strongly influenced by three great factors – revolution, CAPITALISM and war – but the relations among these factors have been contingent upon complex historical specificities.

Transitions from authoritarianism to democracy, in order to become stable, must meet the economic expectations of both elites and the people. This explains the complex relations among democracy, revolution and capitalism. Capitalism sometimes produces a pro-democratic, and even revolutionary bourgeois class, and it may also produce the economic and social development supportive of democracy. It may, however, produce social inequalities that undermine democracy. Economic problems of democratic transition are often combined with problems of managing ethnic divisions. Civil society is commonly said to be necessary to democracy, but this proposition needs at least two qualifications: (1) not all elements in civil society are necessarily pro-democratic, and (2) the stabilisation of democracy may require moderately strong states (Diamond and Plattner 1996: xxiii–iv; Schmitter 1996: 87–8). The stability of democracy depends also on its international economic and political environment. 'The new democracies of the third wave', Diamond and Plattner write, 'are, to varying degrees, hollow, fragile, and insecure' (Diamond and Plattner 1996: xxviii–xxxiii) (see Diamond's DEMOCRACY, FUTURE OF). Leftwich (1997) has identified the paradox of 'democratic revolution' in the difficult balance that democracy has to strike between radicalism and conservatism. On the one hand, democracy has over the long haul of history been the outcome of heroic, violent and often tragic struggles of millions of human beings for dignity and JUSTICE. On the other hand, democracy requires moderation, toleration and compromise. This difficult struggle continues.

See also:

Asian models of democracy; civil society; democratic transition; lustration; republicanism

Further reading

Ascherson, N. (1993) '1989 in Eastern Europe: Constitutional Representative Democracy as a "Return to Normality"?', in J. Dunn (ed.), *Democracy: The Unfinished Journey 508 BC to AD 1993*, Oxford: Oxford University Press, 221–37.

Diamond, L. and Plattner, M.F. (1996) 'Introduction' in L. Diamond and M.F. Plattner (eds), *The Global Resurgence of Democracy*, 2nd edn, Baltimore: The Johns Hopkins University Press, ix–xxxiii.

Fontana, B. (1993) 'Democracy and the French Revolution', in J. Dunn (ed.), *Democracy: The Unfinished Journey 508 BC to AD 1993*, Oxford: Oxford University Press, 107–24.

Goldblatt, D. (1997) 'The Democratic Revolutions in Southern Europe', in D. Potter, D. Goldblatt, M. Kiloh and P. Lewis (eds), *Democratization*, Cambridge: Polity Press, 107–14.

Harding, N. (1993) 'The Marxist-Leninist Detour', in J. Dunn (ed.), *Democracy: The Unfinished Journey 508 BC to AD 1993*, Oxford: Oxford University Press, 155–87.

Held, D. (1996) *Models of Democracy*, 2nd edn, Cambridge: Polity Press.

Huntington, S.P. (1991) *The Third Wave: Democratization in the Late Twentieth Century*, Norman, OK: University of Oklahoma Press.

—— (1996) 'Democracy's Third Wave', in L. Diamond and M.F. Plattner (eds), *The Global Resurgence of Democracy*, 2nd edn, Baltimore: The Johns Hopkins University Press.

Leftwich, A. (1997) 'From Democratization to Democratic Consolidation', in D. Potter, D. Goldblatt, M. Kiloh and P. Lewis (eds), *Democratization*, Cambridge: Polity Press, 517–36.

Lewis, P. (1997) 'Democratization in Eastern Europe', in D. Potter, D. Goldblatt, M. Kiloh and P. Lewis (eds), *Democratization*, Cambridge: Polity Press, 399–419.

Linz, J.J. and Stepan, A. (1996) *Problems of Democratic Transition and Consolidation: Southern Europe, South America and Post-communist Europe*, Baltimore: Johns Hopkins University Press.

Plattner, M.F. (1996) 'The Democratic Moment', in L. Diamond and M.F. Plattner (eds), *The Global Resurgence of Democracy*, 2nd edn, Baltimore: The Johns Hopkins University Press, 36–48.

Potter, D., Goldblatt, D., Kiloh, M. and Lewis, P. (eds) (1997) *Democratization*, Cambridge: Polity Press.

Schmitter, P.C. (1996) 'Dangers and Dilemmas of Democracy', in L. Diamond and M.F. Plattner (eds), *The Global Resurgence of Democracy*, 2nd edn, Baltimore: The Johns Hopkins University Press, 76–93.

Skinner, Q. (1993) 'The Italian City-Republics', in J. Dunn (ed.), *Democracy: The Unfinished Journey 508 BC to AD 1993*, Oxford: Oxford University Press, 57–69.

Wood, G. S. (1993) 'Democracy and the

American Revolution', in J. Dunn (ed.), *Democracy: The Unfinished Journey 508 BC to AD 1993*, Oxford: Oxford University Press, 91–105.

MICHAEL FREEMAN

rights

The concepts of 'rights' and 'democracy' are closely associated in theory and practice. Theories of democracy normally accord an important place to rights. In much contemporary political discourse, 'democracy' is defined to include respect for rights. Yet the logic and history of rights and democracy are different, and the conceptual and empirical relations between rights and democracy are complex and problematic.

Rights are entitlements of individuals or collectivities derived from rules. These rules can be legal, socio-political and/or moral. Many rights are created and changed by ordinary legal processes. Other legal rights are 'entrenched' in constitutions, are considered more fundamental, and are harder to change. Certain rights derive from international law. Socio-political rights are those generally recognised in a society on the basis of custom and/or political struggle. Some socio-political rights may not be legally recognised, and some legal rights may not have general social approval. Moral rights are those entailed by moral principles, and they may or may not be legally or socially recognised. For example, many people believe that women have the right to be treated as the moral equals of men, whether or not this right is recognised by the law or customs of their societies.

Political theorists have identified two main conceptions of rights: the interest conception and the choice conception. The interest conception, which is the more influential, grounds rights in human interests. Since interests can conflict, rights in this conception can conflict, and democracy can be endorsed as a fair method of resolving such conflicts, although some rights theorists hold that certain interests are so important that they should be protected from even democratic DECISION-MAKING. The choice conception grounds rights in the SOVEREIGNTY or 'self-ownership' of the individual. This conception accords no LEGITIMACY to democracy unless it is based on the consent of sovereign rights-holders.

The concept of 'rights' has four elements: (1) the subjects or bearers of rights; (2) the objects or scopes of rights (what subjects have rights to); (3) the correlative duties of others in respect of rights; and (4) the reasons for, or grounds of, rights. Thus, every citizen of a democracy as a rights-bearer has the right to freedom of speech subject to certain limitations; every citizen and state agent has the correlative duty not to interfere with the exercise of that right; and the reasons for this are that all citizens have a legitimate interest in expressing their opinions and democracy requires the free exchange of ideas.

The concept of 'democracy' has its origins in classical Athens, and means rule by the people (see DEMOCRATIC ORIGINS) It does not refer explicitly to rights at all. It may imply that citizens have certain rights, but the Athenians appear to have considered that democracy entailed DUTIES rather than rights, and classical democratic thought completely lacked the concept of human rights. The modern concept of 'rights', by contrast, originates in the seventeenth century, and is particularly associated with the liberal theory of John Locke. Locke held that every human being had certain natural rights; that government was necessary to protect those rights; and that such protection was a necessary condition of governmental legitimacy. However, although Locke also held that government should be accountable to the people, he did not explicitly require that it be democratic.

The concepts of 'democracy' and 'rights' have, therefore, been used to answer different questions. The concept of 'democracy' answers the questions 'who rules?' or 'who should rule?' by saying 'the people', whereas the concept of 'rights' identifies certain fundamental interests that it attributes to all human beings, and that it requires all governments, democratic or not, to respect. The concept of 'democracy' refers to the distribution of power. The concept of 'rights' refers to the limits of legitimate power. Democrats can endorse rights, but are necessarily committed only to those rights that are necessary to democracy. Rights liberals can (and today usually do) support democracy, but only insofar as it respects rights. For democrats, rights are political; for liberals, rights are pre-political. Thus liberal democracy must, in theory and practice, reconcile two concepts that pull in different directions.

The distinction between the rights of citizens and human rights is important but often confused, because, although their rationale is different, their content may be similar. The rights of citizens govern the relations between citizens and their states, and are typically outcomes of political struggles within particular societies. The concept of 'human rights' has played an important role in international law and politics and in the national politics of many societies since it was made a principal aim of the United Nations in response to the atrocities of fascism. Many international legal texts set out human rights, ranging from the prohibition of torture, racial and gender discrimination to the rights of children. The idea of the universality of human rights was re-affirmed by a special UN conference in 1993. Almost all governments pay lip service to this idea, but gross violations of human rights are common, and many governments express reservations about human rights either on practical grounds (claiming, for example, that they must be limited for the sake of national SECURITY or economic development) or by appeal to cultural differences.

The idea of human rights has inspired an international, non-governmental movement, and many national movements which combine claims for human and citizens' rights. However, the idea of human rights has been subjected to criticism on various grounds: for example, that it is unrealistic, and perhaps dangerous, to impose such ethical restraints on governments; that the very idea of 'rights' is culturally specific to the West and to 'impose' it on other cultures is an example of 'cultural imperialism';

that the human rights of individuals cannot properly claim priority over the good of society; and that there is not, and perhaps cannot be, any secure theoretical foundation for the idea. The idea of 'human rights' has received surprising little attention from political theorists, and there is no consensus on its theoretical foundations. Such consensus may be unattainable because of the 'essentially contested' nature of political theory. If this is so, it is not necessarily regrettable, since, if the idea of human rights deserves global support, it must in practice be derivable from various philosophies and religions. The concept of 'human rights' differs from, and has a moral advantage over, that of 'citizens' rights' in that democratic citizens may deny rights to non-citizens (for example, refugees or migrant workers) who may be legally and/or morally entitled to the protection of their human rights.

The idea of human or pre-political rights has, however, also been challenged on the ground that it is inconsistent with democracy, which ought to take priority over rights. Rights, it is said, are subject to different interpretations and to reasonable disagreement. Democracy is the fairest method to resolve such disagreements, since it gives equal status to each citizen. Property rights are particularly controversial, in theory and practice (see PRIVATE PROPERTY). Some theorists have held that property rights are pre-political, and no government, democratic or not, may legitimately violate them. Some defenders of property rights have been anti-democratic because they have believed that democracies are particularly likely to violate these rights. Other theorists have argued that society not only has the right to regulate property for the common good or for the good of its citizens, but may have an obligation to do so. The concept of universal human rights recognises certain social and economic rights that clearly require governmental regulation and redistribution of property.

Even where rights are not generally controversial, their particular interpretation and application may be so. For example, all actual liberal democracies place some limitations on freedom of speech (by laws prohibiting incitement to racial hatred, for instance). Such laws are commonly controversial, and some democrats say that such controversies can be fairly resolved only by democratic procedures. It follows from this argument that democracy has priority over rights, and that rights are political, not natural.

This tension between pre-political rights and democracy raises important questions about the role of politics and the rule of law (see LAW, RULE OF), the place of constitutions, and the roles of legislatures and judiciaries in democratic polities. Waldron has questioned the constitutional entrenchment of rights by appealing to the basic theory of rights (Waldron 1993). The concept of rights, he argues, is based on respect for individual AUTONOMY, that is, the capacity of individuals to make morally responsible judgements about matters that concern their well-being. Given unavoidable controversies about different conceptions of rights, the theory of rights requires that these controversies be settled on the basis of respect for the right of each individual to participate in collective decision-making, that is, through democratic processes. The constitutionalisation of rights, and the EMPOWERMENT of judges to decide constitutional disputes about rights, is undemocratic and manifests a distrust of ordinary citizens that is inconsistent with the reasons that they are held to have rights. Thus, the constitutionalisation of rights is inconsistent with the rationale of rights. Whereas Waldron proposes a rights-based critique of constitutional rights, Dahl makes a similar argument on democratic grounds. The principal alternative to democracy, he argues, is some version of Plato's 'guardians', who, according to this anti-democratic theory, should rule because only they know what justice is. Dahl objects to the rule of 'guardians' on two main grounds. Firstly, there are strong philosophical reasons for scepticism about the existence of a truth about justice that could be known by such 'guardians'. Secondly, even if there were such a truth, and 'guardians' were the only ones who could know it, such political elites would be less likely to be motivated to pursue

justice than their own interests. The case for democracy, according to Dahl, rests on this scepticism about 'guardians' of justice, and the belief that ordinary people are best able to know, and best motivated to seek their own interests, and that 'justice' is the outcome of agreement among free and equal citizens, that is, of democratic processes (Dahl 1989) (see POLYARCHY). On this view, democracies may be unjust according to some reasonable theory of justice, but democrats believe that they are less likely to be so than rule by even wise, virtuous and benevolent 'guardians'. Dahl's argument converges with Waldron's in that both see the judicial protection of rights from democratic politics as a form of 'guardianship' by an elite of legal, moral and political experts. Both consequently consider the constitutional protection of rights to be inconsistent with democracy.

There are liberal and democratic responses to these arguments. Liberals fear abuse of power, and consequently oppose unlimited power. They do not cease to oppose unlimited power because it is democratic. They have developed two main institutional devices to limit democratic power. The first is the 'SEPARATION OF POWERS', which distributes power in democracies among different institutions, which exert 'checks and balances' against each other. The second is the constitutional entrenchment of fundamental rights under the protection of a judiciary that is guaranteed independence from the other institutions of power. This liberal limitation of democracy is known as 'constitutional democracy', which seeks to balance respect for democracy with the rule of law and the protection of rights. Dworkin has proposed a democratic argument for the constitutionalisation of liberal rights by distinguishing between two conceptions of democracy: majoritarian and egalitarian (Dworkin 1978, 1996). Majoritarian democracy, he argues, is not legitimate because it can exclude MINORITIES from the equal rights of CITIZENSHIP. Egalitarian democracy, by contrast, guarantees the equal rights of all citizens. The best way to do this is to entrench them in a constitution that is difficult to amend, and to entrust its interpretation to a group of constitutional experts who are guaranteed independence from pressures by the majority. This is not undemocratic, Dworkin argues, because it protects the equal rights of all citizens and does so by the use of 'public reason' in a forum to which the people have access, and which is subject to public scrutiny; and, if its decisions prove unacceptable to the people in the long run, to being overruled (see MAJOR-ITARIANISM).

There is, therefore, considerable theoretical tension between rights and democracy. Democracy rests on the principle of the sovereignty of the people, which can in turn be based on the principle of respect for individual persons. LIBERALISM rests on concern for the freedom and/or well-being of each individual and the distrust of power. Thus, the principles of respect and concern for every human individual can support a conception of rights as the outcomes of democratic politics or a rival conception of rights as defences against abuses of democratic (and, of course, also of non-democratic) politics. Some theorists distinguish between rights that are constitutive of democracy, such as freedom of speech, association and voting, rights necessary to democracy, such as minimally adequate standards of living, health and EDUCATION, and rights unrelated to democracy, such as freedom of religion (Ely 1980; Dahl 1989; Weale 1999). These distinctions help to clarify the relations between rights and democracy, but they are themselves contestable and do not definitively resolve disputes about CONSTITUTIONALISM. Empirically, most liberal democracies entrench rights in one way or another. The outcomes of this entrenchment are controversial, both in general theory and in particular applications (Alexander 1998). There is, however, a consensus among supporters and critics of the constitutional protection of rights that both courts and legislatures can violate fundamental rights, and that they have done so historically.

Refined debates about the relations between democracy and constitutionalism may seem to have little relevance to the vast numbers of the most deprived and oppressed people of the world, who are struggling for 'rights and democracy', and whose concern is with physical security, an adequate standard of living and access to such basic goods as health and education, rather than with subtle distinctions in political theory. For such people, the conventional thesis that rights and democracy are mutually necessary may be as much empirical truth as they need. There is a consensus among political scientists that, empirically, democracies have a much better record in respecting human rights than other forms of government, and that, while some rights may be constitutive of democracy, a general respect for human rights is necessary for a flourishing democratic polity.

There are, however, at least two reasons why analysis of the conceptual and empirical relations between rights and democracy may have practical importance beyond the shores of those countries in which respect for both individual rights and democratic institutions is well-established, and controversy, though important, is secondary. The first reason is that, in the transition from authoritarian to democratic regimes in societies with relatively weak traditions of respect for rights and democracy, getting the balance right between the political and the judicial protection of rights may be extremely important. Democrats may argue that, in cases of doubt, democracy should determine rights, but the best way to defend democracy and rights is partly an empirical question, and the empirical record of legislatures and courts in 'new' democracies, as in the older ones, is mixed. The second reason for careful thought about the relation between rights and democracy in non-Western societies is that several commentators have argued that, because such societies have 'collectivist' rather than 'individualist' cultures, the democratic idea of popular sovereignty has more appeal than that of individual rights. Thus, it is said, we have, and are likely to have in the foreseeable future, several 'illiberal democracies' in what used to be called 'the Third World' (Whitehead 1993; Aidoo 1993; Bell et al. 1995). The empirical picture in these societies is very complex. On the one hand, vigorous human rights movements are active in many of them. On the other hand, democratisation has not only not improved the protection of human rights in the short run, but it has in a number of cases, especially when it has been combined (as it usually has been) with 'neo-liberal' economic policies, led to a worsening of human rights protection. The empirical relation between democratisation and human rights is even more problematic than that between democracy and rights. There is no reason to believe that there is a general institutional solution to the problems of stabilising democracy and protecting rights in transitional societies (see DEMOCRATIC TRANSITION). Neither dogmatic rejection of nor blind faith in the efficacy of constitutional democracy is justified.

The relation between rights and democracy is complex in theory because the deep moral grounds of rights and democracy are both similar and different. They are similar in that both rights and democracy rest on respect for individual persons and their autonomy. They are different because the concept of rights belongs both to the liberal tradition that accords priority to the need to protect individuals from abuses of power and to the democratic tradition that accords priority to the sovereignty of the people. The relation between rights and democracy is complex in practice because the best way to defend the values inherent in both rights and democracy is contingent upon historical traditions and circumstances. Enlightened, undemocratic 'guardians' may protect rights quite well, but, empirically, they rarely do so, and, even if they do, their successors may be less enlightened. Democracies may perpetrate gross violations of the rights of unpopular minorities. Liberals tend to look to judges to protect the rights of individuals and minorities against abuses of power by democratic majorities or their representatives. Democrats argue not only that this is undemocratic but also that, where the people is hell-bent on the violation of rights, courts are likely to be weak and unreliable guardians: if the people cannot be trusted, neither can the judges. This has led some theorists to conclude that the safest repository for rights is in the POLITICAL CULTURE and the institutions and practices of 'civil society'. There can be no absolute guarantees for rights. Too much should not be made of the incompatibilities between rights and democracy. Morally and politically, they are close and generally mutually supportive relatives, even if from time to time they can be quarrelsome and contentious.

See also:

autonomy; citizenship; justice; law, rule of; rights, minority and indigenous

Further reading

Aidoo, A. (1993) 'Africa: Democracy without Human Rights?', *Human Rights Quarterly* 15(4): 703–15.

Alexander, L. (ed.) (1998) *Constitutionalism: Philosophical Foundations*, Cambridge: Cambridge University Press.

Bell, D.A., Brown, D., Jayasuriya, K. and Jones, D.M. (1995) *Towards Illiberal Democracy in Pacific Asia*, New York: St. Martin's Press.

Dahl, R.A. (1989) *Democracy and its Critics*, New Haven, CT: Yale University Press.

Dworkin, R. (1978) *Taking Rights Seriously*, London: Duckworth.

—— (1996) *Freedom's Law: The Moral Reading of the American Constitution*, Cambridge, MA: Harvard University Press.

Ely, J.H. (1980) *Democracy and Distrust: A Theory of Judicial Review*, Cambridge, MA: Harvard University Press.

Waldron, J. (1993) 'A Rights-Based Critique of Constitutional Rights', *Oxford Journal of Legal Studies* 13(1): 18–51.

Weale, A. (1999) *Democracy*, Basingstoke: Macmillan.

Whitehead, L. (1993) 'The Alternatives to "Liberal Democracy": A Latin American Perspective', in D. Held (ed.), *Prospects for Democracy: North, South, East, West*, Cambridge: Polity Press, 312–29.

MICHAEL FREEMAN

rights, minority and indigenous

There is no universally accepted definition of minority and indigenous rights. However, the main criteria for defining 'minority' are implied in the title of the 1992 United Nations Declaration on the Rights of Persons Belonging to National or Ethnic, Religious and Linguistic Minorities. In this context, a minority may be defined as a group which is numerically inferior to the rest of a state's population, occupies a non-dominant position, possesses distinctive national, ethnic, religious or linguistic characteristics, and seeks to ensure its survival and development as a culturally distinct population. In addition to these general criteria, indigenous peoples are defined as the descendants of the population of a country or region which underwent conquest and colonisation, and who seek to maintain indigenous cultural institutions as well as achieve EQUALITY with the dominant groups in society.

The history of minority and indigenous rights can only be understood, on the one hand, in the context of the formation and development of nation-states and, on the other, in terms of the impact of colonialism and GLOBALISATION. In Europe, struggles against religious orthodoxy led to the first type of minority right, the FREEDOM of religious expression. This was followed by the creation of independent states in which a culturally distinct group, or 'nation', claimed the right to self-determination. This right became that of a centralised state rather than the right of all peoples residing within its borders. As a result, modern European nation states attempted to centralise political AUTHORITY and create a sense of cultural homogeneity. Members of minority groups were protected only by laws that were equally applicable to all individuals. Minority groups as such were denied collective rights. This liberal, individualistic model was also used to deny the existence of national minorities in the United States.

Theorists of liberal democracy have been divided over the extent to which individual and group rights are compatible. John Stuart Mill firmly believed that only a homogeneous population could understand and uphold the principles of representative government, implying the forced ASSIMILATION of national MINORITIES in Great Britain. In this case, Mill believed that the effective extension of individual rights would be sufficient to protect minorities from the will of the majority. On the other hand, Lord Acton argued that some degree of autonomous control by national minorities provided a check against the abuse of centralised state power. For this reason, individual rights needed to be supplemented by recognition of group rights if they were to be meaningful. This latter argument led to the creation of a minority rights regime within the League of Nations. However, this regime was manipulated by the Nazis, who mobilised ethnic Germans in Poland and Czechoslovakia against their governments. As a result, the concept of minority rights fell into disfavour after the Second World War, being replaced by an almost exclusive focus on individual rights, which was most clearly enshrined in the United Nations Declaration on Human Rights of 1948 (Kymlicka 1995).

Whereas in Europe minority rights have evolved in the context of NATIONS AND NATIONALISM, in developing countries minorities and indigenous groups have had to respond to the legacies of colonialism and IMPERIALISM. In Africa, one of the most salient legacies is the rivalry between ethnic groups for control of state resources. Through 'divide and rule' tactics, colonial powers pitted one group against another in order to maintain political control. In addition, the colonial administration of territories bore no relation to ethnic identities. When African states gained political independence after 1945, existing borders were retained, creating an artificial sense of nationhood which was determined by territorial demarcation rather than by social composition. As a result, those ethnic groups which claim a majority have tended to hold state power and use it to exclude rival minority groups.

Most African and Asian states have sought to constitute themselves as unified nations through the centralisation of control over

EDUCATION, religious practices and economic development, accompanied on occasion by the massive expulsion of minority populations and the systematic discrimination toward nomadic, peripheral and mountain peoples. Whereas in Asia many of these efforts have enforced a significant degree of national conformity, in Africa they have usually failed, leading to almost permanent conflict between ethnically defined factions and a collapse of state authority amid civil war.

In Latin America, minorities and indigenous peoples have not traditionally been seen as a significant factor in national politics. This is due to the marked decline of the native population after the European conquest and the subsequent policies of forced assimilation that occurred under liberal, conservative and nationalist elites. Since the 1970s, however, indigenous peoples have become more active in demanding autonomy in the areas of development, education and land rights (Van Cott 1994). This has paralleled similar movements of indigenous peoples and minorities in the United States and Canada.

Struggles for minority and indigenous rights have been compounded by economic globalisation and increasing competition for scarce resources. Minorities are particularly affected as they make up much of the migrant labour force that faces discrimination in the receiving countries. The livelihoods of indigenous farmers are also affected by structural adjustment policies, which aim to privatise land holdings and promote transnational agribusiness. Scarcity of land and depletion of natural resources are often at the root of political upheavals involving ethnic minorities and dominant national and global elites.

In the 1990s, the importance of minority and indigenous rights has gained international recognition. Several European states have moved away from centralism to a greater formal recognition of group rights. The Council of Europe has also developed the European Charter for Regional or Minority Languages (1992), and the Framework Convention for the Protection of Minorities (1994). The latter explicitly seeks to end assimilationist policies,

especially in the states of Eastern Europe. In 1992 the United Nations Declaration on the Rights of Persons Belonging to National or Ethnic, Religious and Linguistic Minorities was also adopted by the General Assembly. Although this document still avoids recognition of collective rights, it goes beyond earlier UN documents by obliging states to not only tolerate but also actively promote minority cultures (Minority Rights Group 1997: 755).

With regard to indigenous rights, the main international documents have been developed by the UN International Labour Organization (ILO) in Conventions 107 (1957) and 169 (1989). The former was assimilationist in its intent and reflected the post-war rejection of minority rights in favour of national integration. Convention 169 is more supportive of the rights of indigenous peoples as peoples, obliging states to allow for greater PARTICIPATION by indigenous peoples in decision-making with regard to social, cultural and economic development. A draft declaration of the UN Working Group on Indigenous Populations in 1995 went further, calling for the right of indigenous peoples to self-determination. The main obstacle facing acceptance and implementation of these instruments is state sovereignty over matters of 'domestic jurisdiction' (Thornberry 1991a: 31).

While recognising the great diversity of experiences, it is possible to identify several factors that appear to facilitate GOOD PRACTICE in this area. These include the decentralisation of power to democratic and accountable units of local and regional government, security of access to land and other necessary resources for the maintenance of distinct cultural traditions, a sufficient degree of national consensus on the value of cultural diversity, and the supporting role of international law. Given the nature of the international state system, it is unlikely that secessionist movements will be successful in gaining recognition for new states. Minorities and indigenous peoples will therefore have to seek accommodation with their current states through a variety of possibilities, including new models of FEDERALISM, autonomy and representation. In their favour is the international legitimacy of democracy and human rights. In their way are the legacies of nation building and colonialism, combined with the effects of economic globalisation. Their struggles will help shape the future content of democratic thought and practice, promoting either a multicultural renewal of PLURALISM, or succumbing once more to the centralisation of institutional power.

See also:

assimilation; autonomy; decentralisation; education; equality; globalisation; imperialism; nations and nationalism; representation, models of; rights; sovereignty

Further reading

Hannum, H. (1996) *Autonomy, Sovereignty and Self-Determination*, Philadelphia: University of Pennsylvania Press.
International Work Group for Indigenous Affairs (1996) *The Indigenous World, 1995–6*, Copenhagen: IWGIA.
Kymlicka, W. (1995) *Multicultural Citizenship*, Oxford: Oxford University Press.
Miller, M.S. and Cultural Survival (eds) (1993) *State of the Peoples: A Global Human Rights Report on Societies in Danger*, Boston: Beacon Press.
Minority Rights Group (ed.) (1997) *World Directory of Minorities*, London: Minority Rights Group International.
Palley, C. *et al.* (1991) *Minorities and Autonomy in Western Europe*, London: Minority Rights Group International.
Thornberry, P. (1991a) *Minorities and Human Rights Law*, London: Minority Rights Group International.
—— (1991b) *International Law and the Rights of Minorities*, Oxford: Clarendon Press.
Van Cott, D.L. (1994) *Indigenous Peoples and Democracy in Latin America*, New York: St. Martin's Press.

NEIL HARVEY

S

security

'Security may not be the highest political end but it is the necessary basis for the achievement of any other political end; and therefore the first claim on government' (Mabbott 1947: 21). This generally accepted proposition fairly conveys the importance of security as a condition for the maintenance of political and social life. For security (Latin: *securitas*) is literally freedom from care, and thus, in a political context, freedom from those anxieties which would, were they to dominate people's lives, prevent them from engaging in the relationships regulated by government to safeguard life and property. By extension, then, security consists in the state of affairs that renders people free from such anxieties; a general state of safety. The former is sometimes designated the subjective and the latter the objective sense of the term (Bull 1977: 18). However, it is the former sense which is the more illuminating in bringing out what it is at which government should aim in its objective of maintaining security, namely to provide the conditions for a well regulated social life by countering threats that undermine public confidence in a reliance on such a life.

Here it is important to distinguish between security and order as aims of government. Sometimes it is claimed that there are two kinds of security at which government aims, external and internal, internal security being achieved by the maintenance of public order through the administration of JUSTICE (Raphael 1976: 46). It is true that the maintenance of order is sometimes referred to as the preservation of 'public security', but this usage, like 'social security', blurs the distinction between threats to personal safety within a generally well regulated social order and threats to that order itself. It is against the latter that the maintenance of security, properly speaking, is directed, so that external and internal, or 'domestic', security provisions counter, respectively, threats from without, such as foreign aggression, and threats from within, such as insurgency and communal strife.

Threats of both sorts are a recurrent feature of political life. It is the state's duty to deal with these because the state may plausibly be viewed as that political organisation which is charged with maintaining order through making and enforcing laws. It follows from its having this constitutive function that the state must act to ensure that the conditions exist for order to be maintained, that is to say, it must preserve security. This will normally involve protecting the state's frontiers from violation and ensuring that its law enforcement agencies can operate effectively. The former is a special case of the latter, since what foreign invasion does is to deprive the state of the power to administer its laws in the occupied area, a deprivation of powers that can be brought about as much by insurgency as by foreign aggression (Gilbert 1994). Either kind of threat can arise from a challenge to the state's LEGITIMACY, that is to say, from a challenge to its claim to be the rightful political organisation for maintaining order. This claim may be challenged either because the borders of the state are disputed or because its very existence as a polity is contested. Within the context of democratic theory, such challenges may represent a denial that the state in question properly represents the people over which it rules, either in some portion of its territory or in the whole of it.

And such challenges may be based on the nationalist view, whether democratically founded or not, that state BOUNDARIES should correspond to nations. The belief that they do explains the common use of the expression 'national security' to connote the security of the state.

On democratic principles only a political organisation appropriately controlled by its people will be entitled to discharge the security functions of a state. Any state, however, whether democratic or not, has a general duty to protect the people in its care against the hazards of strife and disorder. But sometimes this duty may be best fulfilled by conceding the claims of insurgents or neighbouring states, rather than resisting them by force. This distinction between protecting people and preserving the state, as currently configured, roughly corresponds to one often drawn between individual centred and state-centric notions of security (Buzan 1991). Yet, properly understood, this is not a contrast between the security of individuals on the one hand, and of their political organisation on the other. The contrast in question is between the continuance in some form or other of relationships regulated by law and their continuance in just the form determined by the boundaries and institutions of the existing state. People have a vital interest in security of the first sort; whether they have an interest in security of the latter sort will depend, on democratic principles, on whether the existing state is a state appropriately controlled by them, a threat to which significantly reduces their power to determine their own social lives.

This last point enables us to note a connection between security and democracy which is of both historical and contemporary importance. The people of a democratic state have an interest in preserving its security because they have an interest in their relationships being regulated by laws to which they have themselves agreed. In this case they have a responsibility for maintaining their security against external aggression or internal faction, if necessary by taking up arms themselves. This was recognised in Athenian democracy by excluding from membership of the DEMOS various categories of people unable or unwilling to bear arms; women, those too poor to arm themselves, slaves and foreigners. In modern states, it has been suggested, 'the incorporation of the workers into parliamentary democracy was itself largely a trade-off for universal military service' (Shaw 1994: 145).

The Hobbesian nightmare

Two diametrically opposed models of what is required to ensure security have dominated political thinking at least since Saint Augustine's attack on the classical orthodoxy of Ciceronian humanism. But the claim that human beings are not essentially social animals and instead require the imposition of government to live together in peace is particularly associated in modern times with Thomas Hobbes's nightmare vision of a 'warre of everyman against everyman' outside of the security provided by the state (Hobbes 1651: I 13). This vision generates a model of the requirements of security which still influences theorists, particularly those of the so-called realist school in international relations (Morgenthau 1948). Its principal features are as follows. First, it is not merely a contingent fact that the security of human communities is often threatened, so that they require political organisation to protect them. Rather, it is the *raison d'être* of sovereign states to preserve security, for in their absence there can be no communities governed by law, but only a general condition of insecurity arising from the rationality of unfettered competition for resources in the absence of coercive restraints. A second feature of the model follows immediately, namely that it is in states that people must put their faith to ensure the continuance of an orderly social life. Thirdly, indeed, it is their states in which they have vested or acknowledged this power, so that their political obligations depend upon the state carrying out this security function satisfactorily. If states fail in this, then they lose political authority because people are returned to a situation of having to rely upon their own devices for survival.

Hobbes preferred a monarchical state to a democratic one simply because he thought a monarchy better suited 'to produce the Peace, and Security of the people' (Hobbes 1651: II 19). But this is no essential feature of the model which Hobbes's vision generates, for it could instead be argued that non-democratic states are inherently unstable, lacking the social cohesion which adherence to democratically agreed rules can provide and thus prone to internal disturbances that threaten security. On the Hobbesian model, though, security considerations must be of crucial relevance to determining the proper shape and constitutional form of states.

The three features of the Hobbesian model just mentioned concern the state's internal aspect: others concern its external ones. The first is that the condition of states is analogous to that of people outside of society, namely that they have to rely upon their own resources for their survival and protection. Since the chief end of the state is the security of its people this means, secondly, that there are no limits on what it may do to ensure this. It follows, thirdly, that states are in a constant condition of what Hobbes terms war, by which he means competition for power in which, outside of a framework of enforceable rules, each state will be uncertain of what another will do to gain strategic advantage. Fourthly, then, open war may be a necessary move in such a power struggle, so that, apparently paradoxically, security may be better achieved by war than by peace.

The Hobbesian model is clearly a state-centric one, to the extent of making it impossible for states to concede that they may have a duty to ensure the protection of those in their care otherwise than by preserving the state with its current boundaries and institutions. For on this model, the preservation of the existing state is the way that security is maintained. This approach is exemplified in the way that separatist movements and the like are characteristically dealt with as inevitable threats to security rather than as possible bases

for a new security order (Gilbert 1994) (see SEPARATISM). The tendency is manifest in democratic states where such movements will usually represent the aspirations of MINORITIES but where, it can be argued, the security of the state's people taken as a whole may be reduced by any secession. However, the minority population may feel that its own security would be better served by secession, particularly if the armed forces of the state themselves become a threat to the orderly continuance of the minority's social life.

Externally, the Hobbesian model requires states to maintain their security through retaining and developing the power to counter threats militarily. Even though the aim of gaining such power is only security, the result may be the threat of war from other states which fear this power, and thus a reduction rather than the desired increase in security. This is the celebrated 'security dilemma' (Buzan 1991). Open war may be prevented in these circumstances if a balance of power (Bull 1977) can be achieved in which it will not be in the interests of one state to attack another since it will lack any confidence in victory. A balance of power can be achieved by the formation of military alliances. However, while on the one hand these will work effectively only if the mutual obligations they invoke are honoured, on the other, the Hobbesian model prescribes that once the alliance ceases to act in the interests of a given state it is permissible, indeed imperative, for that state to renege on its undertakings. Similar considerations apply to the international obligations incurred by membership of bodies such as the United Nations.

Some, like Hedley Bull (1977), have argued that the Hobbesian picture of the international state system is over-gloomy in failing to accommodate the understandings between states which make an international *society* possible without any overarching authority. This has been dubbed the Grotian model in view of its supposed origins in the thought of Hugo Grotius. Arguably, however, the Hobbesian model can accommodate such interstate understandings, adding only that they are always provisional, dispensable should necessity so require. The problem with the Hobbesian model is, indeed, that while security is maintained internally through the preservation of a social order, which the state has the power to establish the conditions for, the result overall is that the threat of war from without constantly menaces the security enjoyed within the social order. This is a consequence of the unlimited sovereignty of states in conditions of competition and uncertainty. But this reflects, in democratic states, the fact that no enforceable limits are placed upon the political decisions made in the name of the people. It has been suggested (Doyle 1983) that democratic states do not usually go to war with each other, but this 'democratic peace' hypothesis lacks any firm theoretical grounding (see PEACE, DEMOCRATIC).

The Kantian dream

An alternative to the Hobbesian model offers an account of how security might be assured which aims to eliminate the threats posed by wars between states. It is essentially a cosmopolitan theory, originating in classical Stoic thought but given its most influential modern expression by Immanuel Kant (Reiss 1970; Bohman and Lutz-Bachmann 1997) and contributing to the so-called idealist school of international relations. The model is founded on a denial of two fundamental Hobbesian presuppositions, that outside of the political order it is rational for human beings simply to maximise their competitive advantage, and that the state is the only political organisation which can deliver security as a condition of well-regulated social relations. The Kantian model postulates instead, firstly, that it is rational for persons to respect others as ends in themselves and thus to act in the interests of others as well as of themselves. Insecurity is thus not an endemic aspect of the human condition but a contingent consequence of human failure which it is an important purpose of politics to prevent. Insecurity can, furthermore, spring from a wider range of threats, economic and environmental for instance, than the violence Hobbes envisaged (Booth 1991;

Lynn-Jones and Miller 1995). Secondly, however, there is no reason to pick out sovereign states as those organisations best fitted to preserve security. For states are organised to defend the security of particular collectivities, while, on the Kantian model, the security of all people is something in which everyone should acknowledge a common interest. It follows, thirdly, that people should recognise obligations not just to the states of which they happen to be members, but to whatever political institutions foster security and, indeed, the good of mankind generally (see POLITICAL OBLIGATION).

Evidently the Kantian model is not a state-centric one, and in this respect it goes beyond the Grotian as well as the Hobbesian alternatives. It holds that states often act in ways not best suited to fulfil the security requirement of their peoples precisely because they aim to serve their interests too exclusively. But political organisations, like individuals, ought to act in ways that serve wider moral ends. This is the first feature of the Kantian model which differentiates its conception of international relations from that of the Hobbesian one. The second consequential feature is that there should be limits, enshrined in international law, on the behaviour of political units. Thirdly, the avoidance of war should be an overriding objective of policy since, fourthly, it can never be in the security interests of people to resort to war, in which they become means to others' ends or are forced to treat others so. Peace and security thus cannot come apart in the Kantian model, as they can in the Hobbesian one.

There are various different ways in which the model can be developed, Kant himself moving from an earlier espousal of world government to the idea of a league of republican states. It is however worth noting that, far from being an inevitable consequence of the application of the model to ideal circumstances, world government would be necessary only on Hobbesian assumptions that a supreme power is required to enforce a moral order, which Kantians reject. The Kantian model prescribes instead whatever agencies might be needed to ensure peace and justice, and there may be no a priori way of telling in particular circumstances what these are. What is clear is that such political institutions should be under broadly democratic control. This follows from the equal value, as ends, that all persons enjoy and their equal capacity as rational beings to contribute to deciding how their common good, including their mutual security, is to be assured. The difficulty is to see how such democratic aspirations can be realised globally, rather than just within the state.

It is this difficulty on which democratic theorists will concentrate in evaluating the practical consequences for contemporary world politics of adopting the Kantian model. Some theorists, most notably David Held (Held 1995), have advocated support for developments that seek to preserve security transnationally through institutions which administer a system of international law with, in the last resort, powers to intervene in the affairs of states and to force compliance. This position goes beyond the idea of 'collective security' maintained by states that remain sovereign, as in the United Nations. It envisages, instead, 'a democratic cosmopolitan community' (Bohman and Lutz-Bachmann 1997: 244), given concrete expression through regional parliaments and an international democratic assembly, in addition to lower level structures, so that there is no single locus of political obligation as in the state system (see COSMOPOLITAN DEMOCRACY). Democratic theorists will need to consider whether such an alternative world order would actually extend people's control over their own lives at which democracy aims or rather threatens the tyranny of majorities (Dahl 1989).

See also:

authority; coercion; globalisation; identity, political; irredentism; neutrality; state, models of

Further reading

Bohman, J. and Lutz-Bachmann, M. (eds) (1997) *Perpetual Peace: Essays on Kant's Cosmopolitan Ideal*, Cambridge, MA: MIT Press

Booth, K. (ed.) (1991) *New Thinking about Security and International Relations*, London: HarperCollins.

Bull, H. (1977) *The Anarchical Society*, London: Macmillan.

Buzan, B. (1991) *People, States and Fear*, London: Harvester Wheatsheaf.

Dahl, R. (1989) *Democracy and its Critics*, New Haven, CT: Yale University Press.

Doyle, M. (1983) 'Kant, Liberal Legacies and Foreign Policy', *Philosophy and Public Affairs* 12: 205–35, 323–53.

Gilbert, P. (1994) *Terrorism, Security and Nationality*, London: Routledge.

Held, D. (1995) *Democracy and the Global Order*, Cambridge: Polity Press.

Hobbes, T. (1651) *Leviathan*, ed. J.C.A. Gaskin, Oxford: Oxford University Press, 1996.

Lynn-Jones, S.M. and Miller, S. (eds) (1995) *Global Dangers: Changing Dimensions of International Security*, Cambridge, MA: MIT Press.

Mabbott, J.D. (1947) *The State and the Citizen*, London: Hutchinson.

Morgenthau, H.J. (1948) *Politics among Nations*, New York: Alfred P. Knopf.

Raphael, D.D. (1976) *Problems of Political Philosophy*, London: Macmillan.

Reiss, H. (ed.) (1970) *Kant's Political Writings*, Cambridge: Cambridge University Press.

Shaw, M. (1994) *Global Society and International Relations*, Cambridge: Polity Press.

PAUL GILBERT

self and politics

How to understand the relation of the self and politics is necessarily a central concern of anyone who asks after the nature and possibility of JUSTICE. As such, the question of the relation of the self and the political realm is not a new one. It has been with Western thought at least since Sophocles wrote *Oedipus Tyrannus* and raised the question of the relation between the question 'who am I' and the achievement of the common good.

In recent times, however, two general accounts of the relation of the self to the political order and to politics dominate discussion (Strong 1992). The first holds the self, or the most important attributes of the self, to be morally and epistemologically privileged. The 'I' comes before the 'We'. In this vision, politics tends to be thought of as a mechanism required to regulate properly the interaction between individual human beings. Such an understanding is at the basis of most of what is taken to be social contract theory and appears in Hobbes, Locke, Rousseau and with some variations in modern contractarians such as John Rawls. It also is central to a rights-based INDIVIDUALISM such as that which one finds in Robert Nozick, as it is to so-called 'rational choice' approaches to political science. What is central is a 'thinly' conceived self.

The second understanding is the mirror image. Here the 'We' is prior to the 'I'. Such an understanding holds that what it means to be a self has no important meaning, epistemologically or morally, other than the result of the interactions that occur over time between individuals. In such an understanding, society pre-exists individuals and politics becomes the human determination to live in a particular chosen manner, an invention that teaches what it means to belong and to be involved one with another. Here CITIZENSHIP becomes the model for the fulfilment of human nature. Such a teaching appears in the thought of Aristotle, of Rousseau (who makes a second appearance), in Hegel and Marx. In modern times we find it in the work of Alasdair MacIntyre, Michael Sandel and Charles Taylor, among others. The self must be understood here as 'thick'.

Both of these theories tend to construe the problem of justice as the problem of the relation between the self and the political realm. This opposition has become known as that between 'liberals' and 'communitarians'. If one looks at experience it appears, however, that this dichotomy is misleading in that the insistence that either the self or politics are prior one to the other leaves us without

resources in the face of certain salient facts. Two examples, admittedly extreme. Starting in 1962, Stanley Milgram, a research psychologist at Yale University, undertook a series of experiments to investigate the compliance of subjects to commands that he had expected them to find morally repugnant. He found that 62 per cent of those he tested were willing, while thinking themselves engaged in a laboratory experiment to determine the relation between pain and learning, to inflict what they thought was a shock of 450 volts on another human being, despite the fact that the subject complained and was apparently in great pain. No shocks were actually being inflicted, but the testee thought he was hurting the 'learner'. The results generally held irrespective of socio-economic status, ethnicity, gender and educational or cultural/national backgrounds.

A second example: in a classic article in 1943, 'Individual and Mass Behavior in Extreme Situations', the psychologist Bruno Bettelheim described his experiences in two Nazi concentration camps during the late 1930s. He found that unless an inmate was able to draw a line beyond which he or she would not go (yet not so strait that he or she would refuse all commands), he or she would eventually succumb totally to the moral structure of the camp and lose all sense of self.

These cases raise two anxieties, and they tell against both the liberal and the communitarian views. The first is that the self is not strong enough to resist society; the second is that society is dangerously protean, subject to moulding. Liberals and communitarians tend to focus on only one of these. If you are a liberal, you will say that precisely because society can be so awful, we must rest our hopes for justice on the rational individuals and procedures. If you are a communitarian, you will say that the isolated or 'procedural' self is a dangerous reed on which to rest justice and is in the end incapable of resisting the forces of society (Sandel 1984b: 81–96). Therefore one must make societies better.

A better conclusion is one which states that the dichotomy misses something important, namely that one can neither think of a self independently of a political realm, nor of a political realm independently of a self. This was, indeed, the teaching of the first great book in political theory, *The Republic*. Plato notably does not pose the question of justice in terms of the relation between the individual and the state, but in terms of the mutual and interactive constitution of each (see Books 8 and 9). In Michel Foucault's term, the self and the political realm 'codify' in different manners a similar pattern of relations (Foucault 1980: 122). Thus there is for Plato a competitive honour-oriented timocratic society and a timocratic self that goes along with it. However, the fit is not perfect. The courageous soul of the timocracy, Plato argues, slowly turns his activity, especially in old age, to the making of money. And thus the competitive man becomes a wealthy one, commercially rather than honourably oriented. So also does the society change.

What is important here is the realisation that Plato argued as he did about the relation of self to the political realm because he thought that both were composed of several elements, never in harmony with each other. These elements – knowledge, spirit and appetite for Plato – can stand in different possible relations to each other. This points at an important fact. As Amelie Rorty has argued, precisely the qualities that make human beings capable of political life are also qualities consequent to the fact that that human beings are multiply constituted (Rorty 1986: 115–32). Jean-Jacques Rousseau had made this the centre of his political thought, arguing that 'we are not precisely double, but composite' (Rousseau 1964: 57). In this vision, there is no single entity that constitutes the core of either the individual or political society.

Against this, both liberals and communitarians share the idea that a just society must start from a vision of coherence (either individual or social) and move from there to plurality. Yet the idea of coherence as a necessary starting point is not obvious. Already in 1738 Hume had argued, in *A Treatise of Human Nature* (Bk 1, vi), that 'the mind was a kind of a theatre' and that personal identity ('which', he notes,

'has become so great a question in philosophy, especially in late years in England') is merely a fictitious creation of the mind from appearances. Hume rather finds the right metaphor for the self in a comparison to the political order. He compares (the idea of) a person to a 'commonwealth', the 'identity' of which depends on no single factor. Hume's argument has been intensified and radicalised in our century by Derek Parfit. For Parfit, 'a person is like a nation' (Parfit 1984: 216–17). This means that the idea of the self comprises simply the manner in which experiences are connected (or not connected) over time. Selves have no more and no less identity then do polities. Hume and Parfit thus challenge the premise of coherence as the basis for understanding the relation between the self and the political realm. Stretching this point, the feminist anthropologist and theorist Donna Haraway has asked, 'Why should our bodies end at our skin or include at best other beings encapsulated by skin?' (Strong 1992: 250).

The effect of the Hume/Parfit/Haraway challenge of the understanding of the relation between our conception of the self and our conception of the political order is to introduce a much more nuanced understanding of that relation (see also Mosher 1991). Let us look first at the different kinds of relations that can be thought to occur between political entities, be these selves or political communities.

Theorists can conceive of the self and of the political realm either as requiring sharp and clear-cut borders between entities, or else as allowing those borders to be permeable. Some like them hard. Thus political thinkers like Locke and Nozick share with thinkers like Sandel and Taylor the idea that boundaries (for the first around the self, for the second boundaries around the community) are to be thought of as sharp. They serve to distinguish us from them.

The Sandel/Nozick positions share a central concern with that which separates humans one from another. For Nozick, this separation takes place on the level of the individual. I am to be concerned with what I have a right to, and my rights are mine, in the sense that my arms and legs are mine. For Sandel, the separation takes place on the level of communities. Who I am is tied up with those and to a great degree only with those whom I can acknowledge as sharing my 'way of life'. For both the Nozickian liberal and the Sandelian communitarian, however, I am defined by what is mine, by what constitutes the basis of my separation from others. The basis of separation differs – rights for Nozick, identity for Sandel – but separation is essential.

In opposition to this, other theorists have thought of the boundaries between selves and/or communities as porous rather than hard: some like them soft. What is important to Rawls (or Kant, or to some degree Rousseau) is not so much how separate we are one from another but rather what we share with each other. This is why questions of distribution are so central to Rawls's conception of justice (in a manner in which they are neither to Nozick nor to Sandel). What Rawls calls the 'difference principle' is his attempt at resolving the questions of distribution. Interestingly, Rawls here sides with thinkers like Parfit and Hume. For Rawls, given that that which differentiates you from me ('social contingencies or natural chance') cannot be the basis of a public understanding of justice, one must be concerned not with selves, but with the structure of society. And that means to be concerned with the manner in which human beings are connected to each other (Rawls 1971: 74–5).

For Hume and Parfit, questions of distributive justice likewise come to the fore. Given that there is no 'natural' singular definition of either self or society, Parfit argues that the door is open if not for utilitarianism at least for utilitarian concerns as, for instance, 'when we are trying to relieve suffering, neither persons nor lives are the morally significant unit' (1984: 341). Relieving the maximum amount of suffering overall, however, might be. This, however, implies that the lines between each of us are not fixed and hard but protean and changeable over time.

The above is concerned with the nature of the BOUNDARIES that theorists see between the entities that are central to their conception of justice. There is additionally another way of looking at the relations between these theorists. Instead of being concerned with the nature of the boundaries (between selves, between communities), one may also differentiate between theories that see agents (be these individuals or communities) as unitary and ones that see them as multiple. (It is the consequence of the Hume/Parfit challenge that we must make such a distinction.) Here the categories line up differently: this is a more familiar distinction. Some think of the self as unitary. A self is defined in terms of its own interests and choices Thus for Rawls, Nozick, Locke, Hobbes and others, the self is singular. For others, the agent is complex or multiple, without a separable singularity. The agent is, as Sandel puts it, 'thick', an accretion of historically developed qualities that it shares to a greater or lesser degree with others of a similar genealogy. Aside from Michael Sandel, this group includes Charles Taylor and Alasdair MacIntyre. It also includes, however, theorists like Parfit and Hume, who see the agent as composed of a changing and changeable set of relations in time and space. There is more activity in the constituting of the self in Parfit and Hume, but we have again a 'thick' self.

Instead of the simple liberal-communitarian opposition, we thus have four categories for understanding the relation of the self to the political realm. One can first, view the self as singular and emphasise that which is shared with others (Rawls and Rousseau). In this case, the pursuit of justice will consist in concern with the elaboration of what Rousseau called a 'well-constituted society'. Politics is concerned with each person's respective share of that which we share.

Secondly, one can view the self as singular and emphasise that which separates individuals from each other. Such is the position of Locke and Nozick. Here, the central concern will be with the degree and kind of boundary maintenance between that which is private and inviolable and that in which one must allow collective regulation (the 'public'). Thus, for Locke, the central concerns of politics are with the establishing of a proper understanding of the limits of the self, a concern that he phrases as that of property. 'Property' here does not simply mean possessions, but a concern with the extent to that with which I have mixed myself can count as 'me'.

Thirdly, one can view the self as multiple and insist on the centrality of its relation to others: this, we have seen, is the position of Parfit and Hume, and to some degree that of Plato. Here the possibility of justice and the relation of the self to political society is centrally concerned with either what one can say about oneself (the problem of self-knowledge) or with what others will say about oneself (the problem of shame). In Plato, the prerequisite for justice is that one be able to mean what one says. Thus Socrates finds the sources of injustice in the discrepancy between the assumption that one understands the meaning of one's actions and the actual meaning they carry. Self-knowledge is the remedy here. For Hume, Parfit and, one might add, Homer and Haraway, justice has to do with how one acts in the sight of others. It is that judgement that is central. Shame takes the place of self-knowledge as the kinetic power of justice.

Lastly, one can view the self as multiple and insist on the importance of differentiation and separateness between selves: as noted above, this is the position of Sandel and Taylor. Here the central prerequisite for justice is that the self not be disengaged from its community. A concern with rights (Nozick and Locke) or with the beneficence (in the manner of utilitarians, or Hume or Parfit) is of a much lesser value (see Mosher 1991; Taylor 1989: 88–9). The PUBLIC–PRIVATE DISTINCTION becomes a focus of suspicion.

From this, one can conclude that the liberal-communitarian dichotomisation of the relations between self and the political realm oversimplifies both the world we encounter and the sense we make of it. One can ask, however, in conclusion, which of the above manners of conceiving of the relation between the self and the political order is the most conducive to a democratic politics.

To some degree the answer will be, 'that depends on what you mean by democracy'.

Nonetheless, it seems that Plato caught something important about the democratic self and democratic politics when he wrote, 'Like a variegated cloak splashed with every colour, democracy is embellished with every personality' (*The Republic*, Book VIII). One need not draw the negative conclusions that Plato does, but instead celebrate the fact that the glory of a democratic polity is that, as George Kateb has written about Whitman, 'all the personalities that I encounter, I already am: that is to say, I could become or could have become something like what others are; and this that necessarily means, in turn, that all of us are always indefinitely more than we actually are' (Kateb 1990). This position, with its links to Hume and Parfit rather than to Rawls and Nozick, was foreseen by Tocqueville. Tocqueville, in his discussion of the possibility of democratic poetry, makes clear that what democracy makes available is the human species as and in itself.

In *Democracy in America* (Book 2), Tocqueville argues that in 'democratic ages, the extreme mobility of people and their impatient desires lead them to move from one place to another without pause, and the inhabitants of different countries to mix together, see each other, listen to each other'. For Tocqueville, it is not just the people of the same nation that 'come to resemble each other; nations assimilate themselves one to another and all together. They constitute for the eye of the spectator only a vast democracy of which each citizen is a people'. Tocqueville's discussion goes on to suggest that it is only in a democratic society that 'one can form a picture . . . in which a nation counts as a single citizen'. Thus, he concludes, '*for the first time this places in clear daylight the figure of the human species*' (*Democracy in America*, Bk 2, 1: 17; my italics).

Democratic poetry, it would appear, makes available the understanding of the human. What, one might ask, does it mean to see the world as a democratic poet would see it? For Tocqueville, the discussion of poetry serves to bring out several claims about the nature of democracy. The first is the necessity for a new

self and politics

grounding of human activity in a new age. 'The spread of equality of the earth', he writes, 'dries up the old springs of poetry. We must try to show how other springs are revealed' (*Democracy in America*, Bk 2, 1: 17). Some of these new sources will have to do with what the democracy of belief has done to that which can serve as subject for poetry. Importantly, poetry is, as Tocqueville argues, the depiction and portrayal of the 'ideal' (Strong 1996). Poetry, he continues, presents to the spirit a 'superior image'. In aristocratic and past times, the vision of the poet was directed, as it were, upwards but now, 'doubt brings...the imagination of [democratic] poets back to earth and closes them into the visible and real world'. Democracy thus allows – although it does not require – a new focus for poetry as it does for politics. This focus will be this earth, the human itself. Whereas in aristocratic societies past individuals are idealised as the exaltation of the present, in democratic ones no 'individual in particular can be subject for portrayal'. Thus: 'I am convinced that, in the end, democracy turns the imagination away from all that is external to humans, to fix it only on the human' (*Democracy in America*, Bk 2, 1: 17).

The ideal of democratic society is the human, understood by Tocqueville (as by Rousseau) as that which is the same in me as it is in you. The subject of poetry in democratic societies is not the superior man, nor nature; it is certainly not community, and not even properly the depiction of the self. What does it give its reader? Tocqueville answers, 'In democratic societies, where all are very small (*très petits*) and much alike, each, in considering himself, sees at that moment all the others' (*Democracy in America*, Bk 2, 1: 17)

I think Tocqueville means here exactly what he says. It is not that I see a great community in the vista of democratic poetry, but that I see, as I see myself, every other as myself. This is not identity but commonalty as a topic. This vision holds that from the point of view of democratic politics (and poetry) anything that can happen to anyone can happen to me. Anything that anyone can be, I can be. In principle, at least, no identity is foreclosed on the basis of race,

colour, creed, ethnicity, gender: anything. And likewise, no identity of self can claim any privilege over any other. We are nothing. In fact, Tocqueville is careful to say, this is an historically notable achievement (or will be when Whitman starts publishing) for 'the most profound and greatest geniuses of Greece and Rome never arrived at this idea, at once so general and so simple, of the likeness of human beings and the equal right to liberty that each of them brings by birth' (*Democracy in America*, Bk 2, 1: 3). Democratic poetry thus introduces an idea which Tocqueville finds to be at least on a par, and probably greater than anything achieved by Plato, Aristotle or Cicero. Democracy makes the human possible. He writes: 'All that has to do with the existence of the human species taken as a whole, to its vicissitudes, its future, becomes a very productive (*féconde*) mine for poetry' (*Democracy in America*, Bk 2, 1: 17).

Tocqueville goes on to argue that precisely the quality of democratic societies focusing on 'the human species itself' produces a transformation in the status of religion. Although religious faith is often precarious in democratic societies (in part because the belief in 'intermediary powers' such as saints, priests, cardinals and popes is weakened), humans become increasingly disposed to develop a more extensive idea of the divinity itself, as co-extensive with all that which is, for now the entire human species appears to be following the same path. Tocqueville here anticipates Emerson's recovery and sacralisation of the ordinary. Emerson writes: 'Other world! there is no other world. God is one and omnipresent; here or nowhere is the whole fact' (Emerson 1883: 199).

It is the case, then, that both Tocqueville's conception of the 'human' as that which is the common share to all human beings is central to his conception of democratic politics. For Tocqueville, insofar as a democratic society is capable of idealisation, it will focus on the human. For him, the human is a condition which is prior to all definition of self: it is in fact that which resists definition as limiting and as engendering a false concrete. It is for this

reason that it would seem that the understanding of the relation of self and polity most
compatible with democracy would appear to be
a variant on the line of argument advanced by
writers like Plato, Hume, Parfit, Tocqueville
and Kateb.

See also:

citizenship; civic virtue; hegemony; identity,
political; political culture; rights

Further reading

Bettleheim, B. (1943) 'Individual and Mass
Behaviour in Extreme Situations', *Journal of
Abnormal and Social Psychology* 38(4):
417–52.

Emerson, R.W. (1883) 'Sovereignty of Ethics',
in *Lectures and Biographical Sketches; The
Complete Works*, Vol. 10, Boston: Houghton
Mifflin.

Foucault, M. (1980) 'Truth and Power', in C.
Gordon (ed.), *Power/Knowledge*, New York:
Pantheon.

Kateb, G. (1990) 'Walt Whitman and the
Culture of Democracy', *Political Theory*
18(4): 545–71.

Milgram, S. (1974) *Obedience to Authority*,
New York: Harper and Row.

Mosher, M. (1991) 'The Deconstruction of
Moral Personality in Rawls, Nozick, Sandel
and Parfit', *Political Studies* 34: 287–302

Parfit, D. (1984) *Reasons and Persons*, Oxford:
Oxford University Press.

Rawls, J. (1971) *A Theory of Justice*, Cambridge, MA: Harvard University Press.

Rorty, A.O. (1986) 'Self-Deception, Akrasia
and Irrationality' in J. Elster (ed.), *The
Multiple Self*, Cambridge: Cambridge University Press.

Rousseau, J.J. (1964) 'Manuscript Favre de
l'Emile', *Oeuvres Complètes*, vol. 3, Paris:
Gallimard.

Sandel, M. (1984a) *Liberalism and the Limits of
Justice*, Cambridge: Cambridge University
Press.

—— (1984b) 'The Procedural Republic and the
Unencumbered Self', *Political Theory* 12:
81–96.

Strong, T. (1992) *The Self and Political Order*,
Oxford: Blackwell.

—— (1996) 'Politics and Transparency', in A.
Sarat and D. Villa (eds), *Liberal Modernism
and Democratic Individuality; Essays on the
Work and Thought of George Kateb*, Princeton, NJ: Princeton University Press.

Taylor, C. (1989) *Sources of the Self; The
Making of Modern Identity*, Cambridge, MA:
Harvard University Press.

TRACY B. STRONG

separation of powers

Governments perform three functions: executive, legislative and judicial. In a political
system with a strict separation of powers, these
functions or powers are each allocated to a
distinct institution of government. The major
premise underlying the separation of powers is
that individuals have the potential to harm
others, and potential can become reality when
power is concentrated in one person, faction or
institution. Thus, in separating powers, the
major aim is to prevent tyranny and safeguard
liberty by ensuring that no one can accumulate
despotic powers. A further related aim is to
ensure that laws are made in the interests of all
by giving the law-making power to the people's
representatives in parliament. Another is to
ensure the ACCOUNTABILITY of government.
For example, the legislature is accountable to
the people for the laws it makes and the
executive to the people and/or the legislature
for the execution of those laws. A final aim is to
ensure that government operates effectively
and efficiently. The rationale is that different
types of institution perform different functions
better than others. For example, it is often
argued that putting laws into effect requires a
strong, unified hand. Thus, a legislature
composed of many individuals with many ideas
representing many interests could not effectively execute the laws; a chief executive or
president best performs the task.

Writing in the mid-eighteenth century, Montesquieu is usually regarded as the first to identify and argue for a separation of powers. While this is not strictly true – others such as George Buchanan, John Locke, and the English Levellers all previously proposed something resembling his formulation – Montesquieu provided a more profound and systematic synthesis (Gwyn 1965). He developed his argument in Book 11 of *Spirit of the Laws* (1748) after studying the constitution of England. He saw there a distinction, albeit not strict, between making laws and putting them into effect. He applauded the division between the executive (the monarch) and the legislature (parliament), which itself was divided between the House of Lords (the aristocracy) and the House of Commons (the people). Such a division of powers should, in theory, prevent a concentration of power and promote liberty because the making and enforcing of laws are separated and inexpedient laws or dangerous actions are prevented. Montesquieu had his greatest influence on the founding fathers of the USA, and in particular on James Madison. Madison famously noted in *The Federalist* 47 that 'the accumulation of all powers, legislative, executive, and judiciary, in the same hands, whether of one, a few, or many, and whether hereditary, self-appointed, or elective, may justly be pronounced the very definition of tyranny'.

While Montesquieu's analysis was certainly influential, there is a dispute among scholars over whether he was correct to describe England's constitution as separated. The answer is that he rightly recognised the existence of a separation of powers in England (although not in the form it is generally understood today), *and* he recognised it was one of several important features of its government. It is worth examining these other features and distinguishing them from the separation of powers because this will facilitate a better understanding of the theory of separation and a deeper knowledge of how it works in practice. Briefly stated, for the separation of powers to work in practise, its theory must be violated.

In addition to a separation of powers,

Montesquieu identified in England a mixed constitution, a balanced constitution, and checks and balances (Richter 1977: 86). William Blackstone, writing at the end of the eighteenth century, analysed and described the mixed constitution more succinctly than Montesquieu. He argued that the English system was different from others. It was not a democracy, aristocracy, or monarchy; it was, rather, a mix of all three. For Blackstone, democracies are virtuous and thus best in determining what the end shall be; aristocracies are wise and thus best at determining the means to reach the end; and monarchies are powerful and thus best at executing the means. In combining the three in separate institutions (the Commons, Lords and Crown respectively), the English constitution provides all that is necessary for good government.

Another feature of the English system was a balanced constitution, which is related to but subtly different from a mixed one. Mixed refers to the combining in government of different classes or estates, but it says little or nothing about the distribution of power other than that it should be shared. In a balanced constitution as in a mixed one, power is divided, but it is done so in an equal way. Each independent institution's power is balanced against that of the other. And because each institution represents a different social CLASS or estate, neither can become subservient to the other/s. In these ways, tyranny is prevented and public liberty safeguarded.

The final feature of the English system was checks and balances. Montesquieu, Blackstone and Madison, among others, recognised that dividing and separating power between classes and institutions may not on its own prevent tyranny. The powerful will always desire more power. It is possible, both theoretically and practically even in a separated system, that they may appropriate the powers of others if controls are not in place to prevent them doing so. Madison argued in *The Federalist* 47 and 48 that delineating the separation on paper, even in a written constitution that was difficult to amend, would be a futile gesture. He quotes at length Thomas Jefferson's experience in

Virginia where the legislature usurped the powers of the other branches, despite an unequivocal statement in its constitution that there should be no sharing of powers. To maintain a separation of powers, then, checks and balances between institutions are necessary to prevent usurpation. What would such checks look like? On a practical level, the executive may have the power to veto legislation, especially if its passage would result in the legislature assuming the powers of others. Likewise, the legislature should be able to prevent the executive appropriating others' prerogatives, perhaps through the impeachment of executive officers. On a theoretical level, however, introducing checks and balances to guard the separation of powers actually produces a diminution of the separation. In effect, what checks and balances do is allocate some legislative power to the executive and some executive power to the legislature. Thus, the theory of separation is violated to save it in practice.

The question, which is as important today as it was during the battle over the ratification of the US Constitution, is to what extent must the theory be violated? Too few checks and the separation can be violated; too many and the separation expires. Madison sought to tackle this question, and did so with clarity and sense. He argued that executive, legislative and judicial powers need to 'be so far connected and blended as to give each a constitutional control over the others' (*The Federalist* 48). There must therefore be encroachment of each upon the others, but each should maintain its own will and powers, and each should never be allowed completely to administer, appoint or overrule another. As famously stated in *The Federalist* 51, 'defense must . . . be made commensurate to the danger of attack. Ambition must be made to counteract ambition'.

In the US, on the vertical dimension, the governments of the states check the national government, and vice versa. The constitution's supremacy clause gives federal laws primacy over state laws, but the tenth amendment reserves to the states all powers not enumerated in the constitution. On the horizontal dimen-

sion, the executive, legislature and judiciary check each other. For example, the president nominates members of the Supreme Court, but Congress appoints. Congress declares war, but the president is commander-in-chief of the armed forces. The president can veto bills passed by Congress, Congress can override the veto with a two-thirds majority in both chambers, and the Supreme Court can declare legislation unconstitutional. There are a multitude of other checks too numerous to list here. However, despite the impressive list, Madison was pessimistic that his ambition dictum would work in the legislature's case; its potential for encroachment was too great. To prevent its self-aggrandisement, the legislature was made bicameral, with each chamber responsive to different passions (electorates) at different times (ELECTIONS). Thus, checks and balances operate between different levels of government (federal versus state), between different branches of government (executive versus legislature versus judiciary), and between different institutions within a branch of government (House versus Senate).

The discussion began with a strict definition of the separation of powers. By now, however, it should be clear that a strict theory of separation is unworkable in practise. The example of the USA showed that the checks and balances required to maintain the separation necessarily result in its violation. Richard Neustadt was right when he argued that the US system should not be described as a separation of powers. Rather, checks and balances between institutions create a system best described as 'separated institutions *sharing* powers' (1990: 29).

Such sharing, as the founding fathers intended, promotes inaction because it curtails power to change. It does not, however, prevent all change. Indeed, Madison would be surprised, perhaps disturbed, by the rise in presidential power (see PRESIDENTIALISM). (Hamilton would not.) The federal government has also seen its power increase at the expense of the states. The centralisation of power is a twentieth-century phenomenon, a result of depressions, world wars and advances in communication technologies. It is also a phenomenon not specific to the USA. What it shows, though, is that there is flexibility within separated systems to adapt and change. Perhaps nowhere is this more clear than in the United Kingdom. The limited separation of powers identified by Montesquieu in the uncodified English constitution no longer exists. The executive in the form of the prime minister and the cabinet is drawn from the largest party in parliament, where strong political PARTIES and non-proportional electoral systems encourage artificially large majorities. The JUDICIARY, too, is not independent of the legislature or executive. The senior judicial officer, the Lord Chancellor, is appointed by the prime minister, sits in the cabinet and presides over the House of Lords, where the most senior judges, the law lords, also sit.

While the UK moved slowly away from separation over many years, the crucial question facing many emerging nations is whether the separation of powers, defined strictly or otherwise, works. Should they adopt it? A definitive answer is, of course, impossible. First, it depends what 'works' means; what criteria should be used in judgement? Second, even assuming a satisfactory answer to the first question, there are many independent variables, both exogenous and endogenous to constitutional structures, confusing the picture. The structure of government is far from the only factor influencing governmental success. Ceaser (1986: 169) identifies several other potential factors: informal structures, such as political parties and INTEREST GROUPS; social structures, such as class, race and ethnicity; and POLITICAL CULTURE, including attitudes towards liberty, leadership and democracy. The cases of the USA and Mexico illustrate the importance of these other factors. Both have very similar constitutional structures, with a separation of powers, checks and balances and a federal system. In practice, however, Mexico's political culture and its informal and social structures are more important in defining its political system than its formal constitutional structures. In sum, the USA and Mexico are

formally similar, but practically very different. This is not to say, though, that formal structures do not matter. The case of France after 1958 demonstrates they do.

Keeping in mind Ceaser's warning that it is not only government structures that structure governments, it seems sensible to judge the separation of powers by its own aims. Does it prevent tyranny and safeguard liberty? Does it ensure that laws are made in the interest of all? Does it promote accountability? And does it result in effective and efficient government?

In response to the first question, the answer appears to be no; a separation of powers cannot on its own guarantee liberty. Even in the case of the USA, it is difficult to argue all Americans across history have had their liberty protected. African Americans, first as slaves and later subject to segregation, Japanese Americans interned during the Second World War, communists, homosexuals and immigrants, whether documented or not, have all had their freedom violated. It is also difficult to argue that Americans enjoy greater liberty than citizens of, say, the UK or Germany, where there is no separation of powers. While these examples demonstrate that MINORITIES have at times suffered what legitimately may be labelled tyranny, does the separation of powers protect the majority against tyrannical rule? The answer at first glance is more positive; majorities have not, at least in the USA, suffered at the hands of despotic rulers. However, this has less to do with the separation of powers specifically than with democratic elections generally. Rarely do majorities endure tyranny in countries with free and fair elections; majorities are less fortunate in countries without free and fair elections, even with the constitutional safeguard of separated powers. This analysis also goes some way to answering the second question. Laws cannot be made in the interests of all if some have their liberty abridged.

Regarding the third question, the answer again appears to be no; separating powers does not appear to promote accountability. This negative, though, may have less to do with the separation itself and more to do with the structure necessary to maintain the separation; that is, checks and balances. If the legislature wields some executive power and the executive some legislative power, which is to be held accountable for the failed passage of a good law or the successful passage of a bad law? Put simply, accountability requires the identification of responsibility; when powers are shared, this is problematic. Who or what is the government? Even under a strict separation of powers where there is no sharing, accountability may still prove a problem. Is poor public policy the result of the law-making process or of its implementation? As Hardin put it, 'Power must be concentrated to be held accountable' (1986: 114). One solution to these problems is to link institutions to each other and to the people through intermediate institutions, such as political parties. If the party in power does poorly in the eyes of the electorate, it is held responsible for its actions and may lose power at the next election. The problem, though, is that in a separated system it is possible (probable in the USA) that different parties will control different institutions. The phenomenon of divided government produces a reformulation of an earlier question: which party is the government? Without this knowledge, accountability is difficult. Even under unified government, parties are so weak in the USA as to make any talk of party accountability meaningless. As Neustadt eloquently put it, 'What the constitution separates our political parties do not combine' (1990: 29).

The final question of the four has produced the most research, and the most disagreement. How efficacious can government be when power is separated? While DEMOCRATIC PERFORMANCE is inherently difficult to quantify, many scholars have argued that separated powers encourage stalemate, GRIDLOCK, fragmentation, inefficiency, weak LEADERSHIP and poor public policy among other things. A cursory glance at the gun control, healthcare and national debt problems in the USA would seem to demonstrate these arguments' validity. However, are weak political parties, strong interest groups, the committee system in Congress or hyper-democracy the real culprits?

The answer is that they are probable contributors, along with the separation of powers. All democracies, even those with strong parties and leaders and no separation of powers, face similar problems to the USA. What the separation of powers most likely does, *ceteris paribus*, is prolong the policy formulation process and exacerbate the tensions within it, making it slow and deliberative especially during times of normal politics. This was, after all, what the Founding Fathers intended, and may be no bad thing. Those US scholars who look longingly at Europe's governments and those involved in establishing new constitutions around the world should remember that strong does not always equal good, and efficient does not always mean effective. They should also remember that during abnormal or crisis periods in US history the political system has proved responsive, and that effective policy solutions have been formulated; as evidenced by the growth in executive power in the Cold War period, by Roosevelt's response to the depression in the 1930s, and by Johnson's response to race and poverty in the 1960s. Finally, they should also remember the US's economic, military and cultural power; have these been achieved in spite of its governmental structures? Political scientists would hope not.

See also:

accountability; constitutional design; judiciary; legislative process; parties; presidentialism; separatism

Further reading

Blackstone, W. (1803) *Commentaries on the Laws of England*, 14th edn, London: Cadell and Davis.

Ceaser, J.W. (1986) 'In Defense of Separation of Powers', in R.A. Goldwin and A. Kaufman (eds), *Separation of Powers – Does it Still Work?*, Washington, DC: American Enterprise Institute.

Fisher, L. (1993) *The Politics of Shared Power: Congress and the Executive*, Washington, DC: CQ Press.

Goldwin, R.A. and Kaufman, A. (1986) *Separation of Powers – Does it Still Work?*, Washington, DC: American Enterprise Institute.

Gwyn, W.B. (1965) *The Meaning of the Separation of Powers: An Analysis of the Doctrine from its Origin to the Adoption of the United States Constitution*, New Orleans: Tulane University Press.

Hardin, C.M. (1986) 'The Separation of Powers Needs Major Revision', in R.A. Goldwin and A. Kaufman (eds), *Separation of Powers – Does it Still Work?*, Washington, DC: American Enterprise Institute.

Merry, H.J. (1980) *Five-Branch Government: The Full Measure of Constitutional Checks and Balances*, Chicago: University of Illinois Press.

Montesquieu, C. de S. (1748) *Spirit of the Laws*, trans. A.M. Cohler, B.C. Miller and H. Stone, Cambridge: Cambridge University Press, 1989.

Neustadt, R.E. (1990) *Presidential Power and the Modern Presidents: The Politics of Leadership from Roosevelt to Reagan*, New York: The Free Press.

Richter, M. (1977) *The Political Theory of Montesquieu*, Cambridge: Cambridge University Press.

Smith, P.H. (1979) *Labyrinths of Power*, Princeton, NJ: Princeton University Press.

Vanderbilt, A.T. (1963) *The Doctrine of the Separation of Powers and Its Present-Day Significance*, Lincoln, NB: University of Nebraska Press.

Weaver, R.K. and Rockman, B.A. (eds) (1993) *Do Institutions Matter? Government Capabilities in the United States and Abroad*, Washington, DC: The Brookings Institution.

ANDREW J. WROE

separatism

Separatism is the project of a social movement aiming to secede from a sovereign state and create another independent, sovereign country. Such movements usually are based on nationalism, 'a principle which holds that the political and national unit should be congruent' (Gellner 1993: 1) and that each person's highest political duty is to the polity that encompasses and represents his or her 'nation (Hobsbawm 1990: 9)'.

Since each nationalist movement promotes the political primacy of a particular 'nation', much depends on the clarity with which nations can be identified. This is not a simple matter. One common definition is Joseph Stalin's: 'A *nation* is a historically evolved, stable community of language, territory, economic life and psychological make-up manifested in a community of culture' (Stalin 1936: 8). While this definition is conceptually clear, ambiguities always arise when applying it to judge whether a particular separatist movement is speaking on behalf of an authentic 'nation'. For example, in almost any given territory there co-exist more than one linguistic community, and those inhabitants who do speak the same language may not be unified in terms of their economic interests, nor in terms of other psychological and cultural attributes, such as religious affiliation. There may be many intergroup marriages whose partners and offspring do not define their identity in terms of ethnicity, religion, language or nationality. Moreover, many inhabitants have migrated to or become refugees in territories where they lack historical roots. Thus in objective terms the very existence of nations is problematic, albeit with some nationalist movements appearing more questionable than others.

Despite its ambiguous underpinnings, the notion of 'self-determination' has gained considerable legitimacy in separatist rhetoric and even in the charters of globally influential bodies such as the United Nations. Self-determination is the controversial doctrine that each 'people' or 'nation' has the right to determine its own political future, including whether to be part of a multicultural state or to claim SOVEREIGNTY over its own territory. Acceptance of this principle is a *sine qua non* for any separatist movement basing its aspirations on an assertion of nationhood.

At any one time, there are several separatist movements agitating for their causes, though these campaigns ordinarily fail to achieve secession. However, during certain historical periods there are 'waves' of separatism when claims of AUTONOMY become especially numerous. At such times, several movements may complete the PARTITION of their states and gain recognition by the other nations of the world as newly sovereign, independent countries, entitled to membership in all international bodies.

Rarely, however, is the partition of a state accomplished painlessly; in most cases the secession is accompanied by warfare and civil strife. In each year of the 1990s, for example, between 40 and 50 per cent of all the wars going on were wars of secession (Spencer 1998: 18). Since the end of the Second World War, probably more than 20 million persons have been killed in wars fought over separatism. Nor is there much prospect of reducing separatist violence in the twenty-first century. For this reason the prevalence of separatist movements is among the more serious, but less recognized, social problems of our day.

Separatism in history

Throughout world history most great empires have been multicultural, with the populations of capital cities especially diverse in ethnicity. It used to be assumed that only the backward or 'barbarian' parts of an empire were composed of single cultural groups, whereas 'civilised' persons preferred the stimulation of heterogeneous urban life.

Nationalism did not become a truly potent political force in Europe until the nineteenth century, when in many respects it was a liberalising and unifying impulse. For example, Italy and Germany were created, not by separatism but by merging a number of smaller political units. The citizens of the new and enlarged states often had to learn a common language and system of writing so as to be able interact with all their countrymen. To be sure, the new nation-states of Europe often made war against each other, but there were fewer internal separatist wars than in today's world. When a state was partitioned it was usually after a war, when the victors distributed parts of their enemies' territory among themselves.

The first great upsurge in partitions came after the First World War, when the British divided Ireland into two states, north and south, and the Allies created a number of smaller new states from what had been the Ottoman and the Austro-Hungarian empires. Although there were political and ethnic tensions throughout the Middle East and East–Central Europe, the break-ups of the two empires did not really result from popular demands on the part of separatists, but more from the political decisions of Allied leaders at Versailles.

Oddly, both Woodrow Wilson and V.I. Lenin endorsed the principle of national self-determination. They were probably motivated by the same objective: to foster the break-up of European empires, especially the British and Russian Empires respectively. Neither the United States nor the Soviet Union allowed its own territories to become independent, though they both demanded that the older empires do so. Even so, the victorious powers were not attempting to fragment European territories so much as to unify them; for example, Yugoslavia was created during that period in the hopeful expectation that Croats and Serbs would live together in one new state.

Another wave of partitions took place after the Second World War, when Britain divided India and Palestine and the great powers divided Germany, Korea, China and Vietnam. In Palestine, India and Ireland the divisions were made in terms of ethnic-religious social CLEAVAGES, but Korea, Germany, China and Vietnam were split along secular, ideological lines – communist versus capitalist– rather than ethnic lines.

A third wave of separatism has been taking place during the 1990s, chiefly on the basis of popular demands for autonomy led by nationalists. Most of those movements have taken place in the formerly socialist countries, where, despite Lenin's declared policy of self-determination, nationalism had been firmly suppressed for half a century. However, there also have been separatist movements all over the world, including in Scotland, Brittany, the Basque part of Spain, Quebec, Sri Lanka and Ethiopia; some have won independence, while others (so far) have not.

Consequences of separatism

The costs of attempting secession are generally high because of the widespread bloodshed and, as Robert K. Schaeffer and others have shown, the consequences of successfully accomplishing secession are also negative. Violence has generally followed the partition and millions of refugees have fled or have become MINORITIES in their ancestral homelands (Schaeffer 1990). Millions crossed the borders of the newly partitioned China, Korea, India, Vietnam, Germany, Chechnya, Moldova and Yugoslavia.

Each new state represented a nationality that had become a majority in its own separate country and that had little incentive to grant its old rival community, which now constituted a minority in the new state, the right to select its own political leaders or use its own language or religious traditions. The majorities tried to accumulate power at the expense of their enemies who were now minorities; those who protested were told to cross over to the 'sibling' states where their group now was a majority and was acting in an equally oppressive way. Almost always, human RIGHTS and democracy have become more vulnerable after the partition of a state than before.

Moreover, the newly divided states have been less able to function as full members of the international system than the predecessor states. For two decades Communist China was not admitted to the United Nations, and then Taiwan was unseated to make room for its rival. Neither North Korea nor South Korea has been admitted, nor was Vietnam until it had been reunited after a war (Schaeffer 1995: 13).

The partitioning of a state initiates a chain of events that frequently leads to further partitioning. For example, when the Ottoman, Austro-Hungarian and Soviet Empires were broken up, numerous new states were formed (such as Czechoslovakia, Palestine, Yugoslavia, Georgia, Azerbaijan and Ukraine), that have subsequently confronted new separatist movements of their own. Often the leaders of partitioned states have not liked the way they were divided. For example, the South Vietnamese and North Vietnamese constitutions both claim some of the same territory, as did the constitutions of the Irish, Germans, Chinese and Taiwanese. This and other unresolved issues prolonged the conflicts that had preceded the partitions, but now as major international rather than civil wars. The new states obtained tanks, airplanes and other weapons, escalating the intensity of warfare.

During the Cold War, each sibling state tended to become allied with one of the superpowers and their wars sometimes led to superpower intervention. The United States became involved in Korea, Vietnam, China and, without sending troops, the Middle East and India/Pakistan. The superpowers also tended to make nuclear threats, as the United States did against China during the Korean War. Out of fear, China decided to develop nuclear weapons of its own, which frightened India into developing nuclear weapons in turn. Next India's nuclear buildup frightened Pakistan into following suit and calling its weaponry the 'Islamic bomb', which made Israel nervous. And so it went; separatism has been one indirect cause of the horizontal proliferation of nuclear weapons (Schaeffer 1995: 13).

Many economic changes are required in the aftermath of partitioning a state, and not all secessionist regions of the world have the same resources, international support or managerial expertise. Obviously a new country that won its independence without a war has far more favourable economic prospects than one devastated by civil war (Bookman 1998: 85). For this and other reasons, some of the newly divided states may fare considerably better than their siblings. For example, the post-Czechoslovak Czech Republic is better off economically than Slovakia; post-Yugoslav Slovenia is better off than Bosnia, Serbia or Kosovo; and post-Soviet Estonia is better off than Tajikistan. In general, however, secession sets back the economies of each state for many years: in part because smaller states tend to be less efficient, in part because of the economically destructive fighting associated with partition, but mostly because trade relationships and other complex financial transactions are inevitably disrupted by the very process of partitioning sovereign states (Bookman 1998: 89).

The future of separatism

The test of whether a separatist movement has attained its objective is simple: is the would-be country recognised by other countries as a sovereign state, entitled to join such international bodies as the United Nations, and to exchange diplomats with other countries?

The separatists themselves cannot answer this question; the other sovereign states provide that answer. If no other country extends diplomatic recognition to a would-be state, the separatists cannot overcome this obstacle. If all secessionist groups knew that no other country would ever recognise their proposed new states, claims for independence would diminish sharply. However, this degree of certainty is unattainable, since the leaders of existing states jealously protect their prerogative to recognise or not recognise other states as they please. The most promising strategy by which to diminish the probability of diplomatic recognition is to seek clarification from the International Court of Justice (ICJ) as to the minimum conditions that should be met before any state should recognise a secessionist state. Should the ICJ discourage such acceptance, one effect would be to perpetuate injustice in cases where separatists are motivated by real human rights violations.

At present, international law is ambiguous regarding the right to secede. Some documents assert that self-determination is a fundamental right, but in practice the United Nations and other international organisations have very rarely recognized breakaway states, and the trend at the turn of the millennium seems to be toward increasing the opposition to separatism, largely as a result of the grave effects

observable in most cases where it has been attempted. One ICJ judge, Rosalyn Higgins, has written that there is no legal right of secession where there is representative government (Higgins 1994: 117). However, some other experts disagree, adding that self-determination is justifiable where there is representative government but the minority nevertheless faces severe human rights violations.

Most authorities at least agree that if the legitimacy of separatism is curtailed, new means should be created by which the international community can protect the rights of persecuted minorities within existing states, despite all restrictions against interfering in the domestic politics of sovereign countries. In any case, the ICJ does not offer opinions unless it is requested to do so by a body (such as the United Nations General Assembly) with sufficient standing to bring the matter to its attention. Whether that will happen may depend on the climate of PUBLIC OPINION in the great powers, though until now popular views concerning this subject have remained mixed.

See also:

assimilation; boundaries; identity, political; inclusion/exclusion; minorities; nations and nationalism; partition; political frontiers; statelessness

Further reading

Bookman, M. (1998) 'The Economics of Secession', in M. Spencer (ed.), *Separatism: Democracy and Disintegration*, Lanham, MD: Rowman and Littlefield.

Gellner, E. (1993) *Nations and Nationalism*, Oxford: Blackwell.

Higgins, R. (1994) *Problems and Process: International Law and How We Use It*, Oxford: Clarendon Press.

Hobsbawm, E.J. (1990) *Nations and Nationalism Since 1780: Programme, Myth, Reality*, Cambridge: Cambridge University Press.

Schaeffer, R.K. (1990) *Warpaths: The Politics of Partition*, New York: Hill and Wang.

—— (1995) 'Secession and its Outcomes', *Peace Magazine* May/June: 13.

Spencer, M. (1998) 'When States Divide', in M. Spencer (ed.), *Separatism: Democracy and Disintegration*, Lanham, MD: Rowman and Littlefield.

Stalin, J. (1936) *Marxism and the National and Colonial Question*, London: Left Book Club.

METTA SPENCER

social capital

Social capital is a recent and potentially powerful development in the long and classical line of social science research that tries to establish the relations between social and economic conditions, on the one hand, and DEMOCRATIC DEVELOPMENT and political stability on the other. In essence the theory argues that strongly developed social norms of trust, reciprocity and co-operation are typically accompanied by dense networks of voluntary organisations. These in turn are associated with high levels of civic activity and political PARTICIPATION, which help to promote social INTEGRATION and co-ordination, create an awareness of the common good, and help society overcome some of the problems of producing public goods and achieving common goals. Consequently, a good stock of social capital – that is, well-developed norms of CIVIC VIRTUE among citizens, and a dense network of social relations and organisations – is a necessary foundation for social co-operation, peaceful politics, democratic government and effective public institutions. Societies that are not well-endowed with social capital will find it difficult, if not impossible, to create the social foundations of peaceful politics and stable democracy. Similarly, societies that are suffering a marked decline of social capital will show signs of democratic malaise: declining levels of political trust and confidence in public institutions, lower levels of voting turnout and political activity, and higher levels of political cynicism, alienation and dissatisfaction.

Social capital is therefore analogous to physical and human capital, in that it helps society to achieve certain goals that otherwise could not be attained. However, social capital is less tangible than the other two forms because it is not owned or identified with individuals, but is a property of social relations that is not easy to identify or measure. Nor are the products of social capital, like social integration, stable democracy, or social co-ordination as easily identified or measured as, say, gross national product or productivity or educational qualifications.

Although social capital theory is relatively new in the social sciences, it has much in common with some strands of classical social and political theory. Most notably, it follows Alexis de Tocqueville and John Stuart Mill in arguing that voluntary associations are important breeding grounds of democratic values and practices among citizens. It also reflects the theories of earlier sociologists (especially Émile Durkheim and Georg Simmel) that social integration in modern society is based upon overlapping and interlocking networks of intermediary organisations, which link individuals into the wider society, and create an elaborate set of cross-cutting CLEAVAGES that tie society together by its own internal divisions. Social capital theory also echoes the central theme of mass society theory (Kornhauser 1960), which claims that social integration and political stability in modern society rests fundamentally on a closely woven social fabric of voluntary organisations and intermediary associations.

In spite of its much-discussed and refined classical antecedents, it is difficult to write concisely or with any great certainty about social capital theory at present. The theory is still new and unsettled, the concept is not yet clearly defined, and the literature around both the theory and the concept is currently developing and changing fast. Moreover, social capital has attracted the interest of researchers in all major branches of the social sciences – sociology, anthropology, political science, economics, and psychology – and each tends to have its own approach. It is also difficult to come to grips with the theory because it focuses on an extremely complex set of social and political relations between subjective attitudes and values (norms of trust, reciprocity, respect for others), objective social conditions (networks of individuals and voluntary organisations of all kinds), and the possible outcome of these (democratic stability, social integration, efficiency). Each of these may be a cause, an effect or a symptom of another, and it may take many years of research to sort out their roles in an explanatory theory.

In political science, the term 'social capital' is closely linked with the work of Robert Putnam on Italy and the United States. Putnam (1993: 167) defines social capital as referring to 'features of social organisation, such as trust, norms, networks, that can improve the efficiency of society by facilitating co-ordinated actions'. The norms of reciprocity and trust are an essential aspect of social capital since it enables individuals in society to co-operate peacefully with one another, to take risks and short cuts in social relations, and to achieve social goals collectively that could not be achieved individually. According to Simmel (1950: 326), trust is 'one of the most important synthetic forces within society'. In some research trust is treated as the best single indicator of social capital, or as a synonym for it.

Networks of voluntary organisations are the second essential component of social capital because they help to develop and sustain relations of trust and reciprocity between individuals. Putnam uses the example of a choir to capture this aspect of social capital. By practising together, the members of a choir – men and women, young and old, rich and poor, Catholics, Jews and Protestants, left and right – produce a musical harmony that is beyond the power of any individual. In doing so, they may also generate social harmony because choirs teach the skills of social co-operation, understanding and tolerance.

It is clear that not all voluntary organisations promote harmony or the common interest. The social consequences of exclusive organisations, such as the Mafia or extremist political or sectarian religious groups, are entirely different from organisations with a broad social base. For this reason, social capital theory distinguishes carefully between exclusive organisations that reinforce social differences and divisions, and bridging associations that bring together different social types and help to transcend social divisions. Moreover, it is important that voluntary organisations involve social interaction between individual members, not merely the act of writing a membership cheque each year. Even so, one piece of historical research suggests that the Nazi drive for power in Germany in the 1930s was actually facilitated by the presence of a dense network of voluntary organisations that was used to infiltrate and control CIVIL SOCIETY. One branch of social capital research, therefore, tries to identify the different consequences for social capital of different types of groups and voluntary organisations.

On the basis of his research on Italian regions, Putnam (1993) argues that government effectiveness and democratic development depends upon the stock of social capital. He argues that the regions of northern Italy, which have relatively good stocks of social capital and high levels of civic engagement, are comparatively efficient and effective both economically and politically. In the south, where social capital, civic awareness and community activity are relatively low, the regions are poorer and their governments less effective, more corrupt and held in lower public regard.

Similarly Putnam's (1995a, 1995b, 2000) later work on the USA argues that the country is experiencing a progressive decline in voting turnout, membership of political parties, trust in political leaders and confidence in political institutions. This, he argues, is caused by a loss of social capital as shown in many different ways, from membership of bridging associations to the frequency that families eat together, and from a decline of ten-pin bowling leagues to a decline in greeting card sales. He assembles a huge amount of information to show that civic engagement and communal activity of many different kinds has declined in the United States over the past few decades. This shows up most clearly in the generation of

Americans born since the 1960s. In the phrase which has now become famous, Putnam claims, that Americans are now 'bowling alone', not in teams and clubs but more usually as isolated individuals, which does little to foster the civic virtues of co-operation, reciprocity, respect and trust.

There are said to be many causes of this decay of social capital in America: increased pressure of work, an increased proportion of working women (housewives typically run many voluntary organisations), geographical mobility, the breakdown of the family, racial integration, the immigration of non-English-speaking people, loss of religious beliefs and the secularisation of society, the growing strength of American INDIVIDUALISM, the fragmentation of post-modern society. Although all of these may contribute something to the 'bowling alone' syndrome, none of them can take the main responsibility because the timing is not right; the trends start well before or some time after the decline of social capital. The one factor to have exactly the right timing is television. Television ownership in the United States spread within the single decade of the 1950s: at the start, television ownership was comparatively rare, but by 1960 it was virtually universal. And it is the generation that came of age with television that shows the largest decline in the indicators of social capital.

Television has two main effects. First, it pulls people out of the community and its civic associations and activities, and isolates them in their homes. Second, it is said to generate social attitudes and values that undermine social capital. Entertainment television (films, game shows, soap operas and situation comedies) presents increasing amounts of sex and violence, and emphasises individualism and materialism. Television news with all its 'bad news' (crime, corruption, incompetence, scandal, war, famine and natural disasters) is said to encourage a mood of political alienation, APATHY, incomprehension and hopelessness. Television news not only encourages distrust of political leaders, but also promotes a lack of confidence in the core institutions of American society. Television news is said to have a particularly unfortunate effect on the relatively

large numbers who 'fall into the news'; those who watch the news because the television is on, rather than turning on the television in order to watch the news. The 'media malaise' hypothesis is strongly supported by many social scientists, especially in the United States, but contested by others (see for example Norris 1996; Newton 1999b). At present, however, rather little research has been done, and this remains an important and open question.

One attraction of social capital theory is that it can be formulated in many different ways and used for many different purposes. Originally developed by sociologists and anthropologists, it has attracted the interests of philosophers, economists, psychologists and many political scientists. The concept of trust alone has three books devoted to it (Misztal 1996; Seligman 1997; Levi and Braithwaite 1998). Social capital theory, or component parts of it, particularly trust, have been used in cultural theory, institutional theory, social choice theory and rational choice theory. Indeed, Putnam has deliberately cast the theory so that it can be formulated in cultural, institutional or rational choice frameworks. Social capital, or component parts of it, has also been used to explain economic growth and development, democratic development and stability, social integration, social participation, tax paying and right-wing extremism. It is not difficult to elaborate theories connecting social capital with such diverse things as school achievement, community crime rates, illegitimate birth rates, election turnout, life happiness and even illness and longevity.

At the same time, one of the weaknesses of the theory may be the way in which it combines many important aspects of social and political life into a single whole, when each part has a complex cause and effect relationship with each of the others. Do people join organisations because they are trusting, or do they learn trust in the organisations, or is it a bit of both? Does social capital facilitate economic growth, or is it the growth which tends to make people happy and trusting? Do people trust their governments because they are trusting people, or is it governments that perform well that elicit trust from their citizens? Is democracy founded on trust and social networks, or do effective and efficient governments facilitate citizen co-operation and create the conditions of a vibrant civic life? The relationship between each component part of social capital is likely to occupy sociologists and political scientists for some time to come (see, for example, Brehm and Rahn 1997; Newton 1999a). This work has already established that socially trusting individuals are not necessarily politically trusting as well, but there is some indication that socially trusting nations tend to be politically trusting (Newton and Norris 2000). That is, social capital, true to its nature as a concept, is an emergent or systemic property of social and political systems, not a property or characteristic of individual citizens.

Another problem for social capital theory is its cross-national application. Relatively little research on social capital has been done outside OECD countries, so it is not clear how well the concept will travel. However, the small amount of research done on Western democracies has produced mixed results. For example Hall (1999) finds that some of the symptoms of declining social capital in the USA are repeated in Britain in the last two decades or so: declining election turnout, some loss of trust in politicians, loss of confidence in public institutions. On the other hand, there are few signs that a decay of social capital is responsible for these trends. On the contrary, membership of voluntary associations is fairly constant, and there are no strong indications of generational variation as there are, according to Putnam, in the USA. Similarly Pharr (2000) finds many of the American symptoms of democratic malaise in Japan, especially a steep decline of trust in politicians and confidence in public institutions, but few indications of decaying social capital. She concludes that it is not social capital, but rather a realistic public reaction to corruption, that underlies democratic malaise in Japan.

Research on social capital is still highly controversial. The theory has a great potential, but there is the danger that something so broad can be used to explain everything and therefore nothing. Perhaps the only certain conclusion at present is that it is likely to provoke an even larger body of research than is presently under way, and that the theory will continue to be fiercely debated for some years to come.

See also:

apathy; civic virtue; civil society; interest groups; non-governmental organisations; political obligation; public service

Further reading

Brehm, J. and Rahn, W. (1997) 'Individual Evidence for the Causes and Consequences of Social Capital', *American Journal of Political Science* 41(3): 999–1023.

Hall, P. (1999) 'Social Capital in Britain', *British Journal of Political Science* 29: 417–59.

Kornhauser, W. (1960) *The Politics of Mass Society*, London: Routledge and Kegan Paul.

Levi, M. and Braithwaite, V. (1998) *Trust and Governance*, New York: Russell Sage Foundation.

Misztal, B.A. (1996) *Trust in Modern Societies*, Oxford: Blackwell.

Newton, K. (1997) 'Social Capital and Democracy', *American Behavioral Scientist* 40(5): 575–86.

—— (1999a) 'Social and Political Trust', in P. Norris (ed.), *Critical Citizens: Global Support for Democratic Government*, Oxford: Oxford University Press.

—— (1999b) 'Politics and the Mass Media: Media-Malaise, Moblisation and Social Capital', *British Journal of Political Science* 29: 25–47.

Newton, K. and Norris, P. (2000) 'Confidence in Public Institutions: Faith, Culture, or Performance?', in S. Pharr and R. Putnam (eds), *Disaffected Democracies*, Princeton, NJ: Princeton University Press.

Norris, P. (1996) 'Does Television Erode Social Capital? A Reply to Putnam', *PS: Politics and Political Science*, September: 1–7.

Pharr, S. (2000) 'Official's Misconduct and Public Distrust: Japan and the Trilateral

Democracies', in S. Pharr and R. Putnam (eds), *Disaffected Democracies*, Princeton, NJ: Princeton University Press, 173–201.

Putnam, R. (1993) *Making Democracy Work: Civic Traditions in Modern Italy*, Princeton, NJ: Princeton University Press.

—— (1995a) 'Bowling Alone: America's Decline of Social Capital', *Journal of Democracy* 6(1): 65–78.

—— (1995b) 'Tuning In, Tuning Out: The Strange Disappearance of Social Capital in America', *PS: Politics and Political Science* 28(4): 664–83.

—— (2000) *Bowling Alone: The Collapse and Revival of American Community*, New York: Simon & Schuster.

Seligman, A.B. (1997) *The Problem of Trust*, Princeton, NJ: Princeton University Press.

KEN NEWTON

social democracy

Social democracy has often been described as a movement rather than a doctrine or programme. Thus, after insisting that it could not be identified even with an unchanging set of values, the editors of *The New Social Democracy* go on to claim that the only constant feature of social democracy is the attempt 'to build and sustain political majorities for reforms of economic and social institutions which counter injustice and reduce inequality' (Gamble and Wright 1999: 2). This definition may be extremely broad, but it nevertheless serves to identify social democracy's outer limits: the aim of combating injustice and inequality distinguishes it from *laissez faire* programmes of government, while its commitment to pursuing this objective through the construction of political majorities distinguishes it from revolutionary and authoritarian programmes of social change. As the pursuit of socialist objectives by democratic means, social democracy stands between unbridled CAPITALISM on the one hand and state socialism on the other: it is, at least on this understanding of the term, the original third way of modern politics.

Social democracy has not always been identified with such an intermediary position. During the nineteenth century and the early part of the twentieth century, the terms 'socialism' and 'social democracy' were more or less interchangeable: they referred to a radical transformation of social life with the aim of curbing the more destructive effects of unfettered economic activity. Its supporters saw socialism as transcending national BOUNDARIES and as serving the interests of the working class and other oppressed and disadvantaged groups wherever they might be. The largest and most successful socialist party of this period, the German Social Democratic Party (SPD), was heavily influenced by Marxism, which took the view that the socialist transformation of society would be brought about by the political action of the working class. Socialists debated whether their objectives could be achieved by legal and peaceful means – essentially by building and sustaining political majorities – or whether more radical political action, a revolution, might also be required. The SPD strongly supported the former view, as did the majority faction (the Mensheviks) of the much smaller Russian Social Democratic Party. Significant minorities, including the Bolshevik faction of the Russian Party, argued to the contrary, that the state must be overthrown if socialist objectives were to be secured and that their pursuit by legal and peaceful means alone was doomed to disappointment. These disputes were further compounded by bitter divisions within socialist parties over whether to support the war aims of their respective national governments during the First World War, and again over how to respond to the Bolshevik seizure of power in 1917. The Bolshevik success effectively settled the socialist dispute over the need for revolution by forcing supporters of conflicting views on this issue into distinct and implacably opposed camps. Thereafter, socialism was divided between communist and other revolutionary organisations on the one side and social democracy on the other.

Thus social democracy in its predominant modern sense is constituted by its rejection of the revolutionary path, and consequently by its commitment to a politics that largely respected the boundaries of established states. Something of the earlier internationalism remained, especially in the anti-fascist movements of the interwar years and in campaigns for colonial freedom, but the primary focus of social democratic concern was to win political support for its reforms within established Western states. The split in socialism had the effect of identifying social democracy with a relatively novel, liberal understanding of democracy – as a system of representative government – which first appeared in the early nineteenth century following the American and French revolutions. Before that time, democracy had been seen as a matter of government directly by the people themselves rather than by a system of elected representatives and bureaucratic state agencies which claimed to act in the people's name. While the latter understanding of democracy has since come to predominate, the earlier meaning has nevertheless persisted, surviving now as a basis for 'democratic' critique of the failings of modern democracy. Many socialists, for example, have favoured the introduction of industrial democracy, in which enterprises are managed by the workers themselves, and substantially greater popular involvement in the organisation of government, the social democrats among them arguing that such reforms should supplement representative government, not replace it, and that they must be brought about only by democratic (parliamentary) means. Marxists have taken the radical democratic critique of representative government further, insisting that the liberal democratic state is in fact a form of CLASS rule. Thus Lenin argued that representative government was a form of bourgeois democracy which must be overthrown and replaced by a system of popular or proletarian democracy in which the people were able to govern themselves directly. This rejection of bourgeois democracy encouraged many communist states to identify themselves as 'people's democracies', at least in aspiration. Karl Kautsky, one of the leading figures in nineteenth- and early twentieth-century German social democracy, drew rather different conclusions from the Marxist analysis of the state: of course, he argued, modern representative government was a form of capitalist rule but in the long run, guided by a social democratic party and learning from the experience of political struggle, the working class could use its electoral strength to take control of the state by legal and peaceful means and transform it into an instrument of popular rule.

Kautsky's argument presents a Marxist version of reformist social democracy. Reformists maintain both that the pursuit of socialist objectives requires radical social change, and that such a change can and should be brought about by a process of reform, not by revolution. They have taken different views of what actual changes are required, with Kautsky insisting on the overthrow of capitalism through the socialisation of economic activity and others, less influenced by Marxist theory, settling for an accommodation with capitalism involving arrangements such as a mixed economy with substantial private and public sectors, a significant degree of industrial democracy, government regulation of overall economic activity through fiscal and other policy instruments, and a redistributive WELFARE state. They have taken different views, too, of how the necessary reforms are to be achieved, with Kautsky relying on the strength of the organised working class and others arguing that support must also be obtained from other quarters. But in all cases they have insisted on the need 'to build and sustain political majorities' as the only way to secure their preferred reforms.

In social democratic politics, reformism has always had to live with two competing perspectives on the pursuit of socialist objectives by democratic means. For convenience we can call them labourism and revisionism: the one identifying socialist objectives with the interests of the labour movement, the other aiming to go beyond class-based politics by defining those objectives in terms of socialist values. Like Marxist versions of reformism, labourism equates social democratic politics with the pursuit of class interests but, unlike reformism, its concerns lie primarily in the achievement of short term gains for the organised working class. Revisionism, on the other hand, regards a political focus on class politics as limited and ultimately self-defeating. Eduard Bernstein, the most important revisionist thinker in the early years of German social democracy, argued against Kautsky's vision of social democratic politics on two grounds: first, that the working class alone would never be sufficiently large to provide a political majority for social democracy, and therefore that support must also be secured from other quarters; secondly and more fundamentally, that class and other material interests were becoming less pressing as people became more prosperous, and that social democracy must therefore aim to secure support for its programmes on the basis of socialist values. If the revisionist focus on values suggests an alternative to class politics, it also implies that social democracy should not be identified too closely with any particular set of institutional arrangements; for example, with extensive public ownership or a seriously redistributive welfare state. What matters on this view are the values themselves, and the decision as to how best to implement them is one that should be made in the light of conditions prevailing at the time. Thus, Anthony Crosland, the leading British revisionist of the 1950s and 1960s, argued that extensive public ownership was no longer needed for the implementation of EQUALITY and other socialist values since, given the development of Keynesian techniques of national economic management, governments could now rely on fiscal and other policy instruments both to determine the overall distribution of income and to fund egalitarian social policy reform.

The coexistence of these three perspectives, usually in a number of competing versions, has produced a variety of disparate forms of social democracy, each regarding the others as somewhat unreliable allies, as actual or potential opponents and often as electoral liabilities. From the perspective of labourism, both the reformist pursuit of long-term change and the revisionist focus on the implementation of distinctly socialist values appear as examples of impractical dreaming, and therefore as electoral liabilities and distractions from the serious business of pursuing political power. Reformists and revisionists tend to regard labourism not so much as a form of social democracy as an unfortunate but necessary evil: it is the perpetual temptation of any politics closely associated with the labour movement. Because it focuses on the interests of a limited portion of the electorate, it too can be seen as an obstacle to electoral success. Those who identify social democracy with extensive public ownership or a seriously redistributive welfare state see the revisionist emphasis on adapting socialist values to prevailing conditions as a betrayal of social democracy proper, while the revisionists in turn tend to see reformist positions as doctrinaire and often simply outdated and, for these reasons, as electoral liabilities. The skirmishes provoked in the late 1990s by proposals associated with the Labour Government in Britain, President Clinton in the United States and the Social Democratic leadership in Germany for a new 'third way' in Western politics – one that would adapt social democracy to the demands of neo-liberal economic and social policy agendas – are merely the latest round in these disputes.

In the second half of the twentieth century, social democracy was favoured neither by the internal politics of newly independent states nor by the effects on these and other states of both the Cold War and the pro-market social and economic policy regimes imposed on their beneficiaries by the World Bank and International Monetary Fund. By the end of the century, social democracy was effectively confined to its original European heartland and a few other Western states, and the complicity of the larger social democratic parties in the management of the international financial system had seriously compromised the socialist character of their internationalism. Elements of socialism's earlier internationalism remain, especially in the comparatively generous aid programmes of the Scandinavian states, but the primary focus of social democratic politics is now on domestic and European issues. The concern for oppressed and disadvantaged groups wherever they might be has been left for other movements to take up and social democracy has developed into an inward-looking, largely European movement promoting the living conditions of citizens in some of the world's most prosperous states.

See also:

capitalism; class; direct democracy; liberalism; representation, concept of; representation, models of; state, models of; trades unions

Further reading

Bernstein, E. (1961) *Evolutionary Socialism*, New York: Schocken.
Crosland, C.A.R. (1956) *The Future of Socialism*, London: Cape.
Gamble, A. and Wright, T. (eds) (1999) *The New Social Democracy*, Oxford: Blackwell.
Giddens, A. (1998) *The Third Way: The Renewal of Social Democracy*, Oxford: Polity Press.
Low, D.A. (1996) *The Egalitarian Moment: Asia and Africa, 1950–1980*, Cambridge: Cambridge University Press.
Padgett, S. and Paterson (1991) *A History of Social Democracy in Postwar Europe*, London: Longman.
Przeworski, A. and Sprague, J. (1986) *Paper Stones: A History of Electoral Socialism*, Chicago: University of Chicago Press.
Schorske, C.E. (1955) *German Social Democracy 1905–1917: The Development of the Great Schism*, Cambridge, MA: Harvard University Press.

BARRY HINDESS

social movements

Social movements and individual rights

A social movement has been defined as 'a sustained series of interactions between power holders and persons successfully claiming to speak on behalf of a constituency lacking formal representation, in the course of which those persons make publicly visible demands for changes in the distribution or exercise of power, and back those demands with public demonstrations of support' (Tilly 1984: 306). This definition is more comprehensive than most because it focuses on political activity rather than organisation, and on political demands rather than outcomes. In the modern era, social movements begin to matter to democracy once their demands are stated as RIGHTS, or have a potential impact on the extension or exercise of rights. In sum, social movements influence the development of democratic government through struggles for individual rights and the genesis of CITIZENSHIP.

There is a broad degree of academic consensus that the individual rights of citizenship are won by social struggles 'from below'. If the poor, oppressed and excluded are only willing to fight, they will be able to win their rights and redress the injustices they suffer. This picture is simple, comforting but incomplete. For rights are not always granted easily or willingly, and struggles 'from below' may provoke more repression not rights. Both the dominant classes and the state will often resist the demands for rights, or at least insist on deciding the timing and form of their delivery. Consequently, it is only collective action and sometimes collective violence that can overcome this resistance, so it is not the protests of individuals but the 'collective struggles of the dispossessed' (Bowles and Gintis 1987: x) that have won the rights of citizenship. Almost paradoxically, the individual rights of citizenship can only be achieved by collective struggle in the form of social movements.

Traditionally, these collective struggles have been understood to express CLASS conflict, and especially the rise of the working class. The English school of social history, for example the work of E.P. Thompson, has shown that poor and working people began early to speak the language of rights, and successfully defended the FREEDOM of association as part of the lexicon of rights. Across nineteenth and early twentieth-century Europe, the biggest working-class struggles were spurred by the prospect of electoral reform, and the labour movement has played a central role in the conquest of citizenship rights in this century (Rueschemeyer *et al.* 1992). The movement is important both because it is often bigger than all other movements combined, and because it has a unique capacity to hit capitalist economy where it hurts through strike action. It therefore gains leverage wherever government LE-GITIMACY depends closely on economic performance. Yet only rarely has the movement been able to win rights by itself; it has had to wait for political allies, splits in ruling-class COALITIONS or incursions by conquering foreign armies.

The main body of social movement theory is today so far distracted by the proliferation of 'new social movements' since the 1960s (Foweraker 1995: ch. 3) that there is a clear need to 'bring labour back in'. But the labour movement is just one of many social movements to fight for the rights of freedom of speech, expression, belief and INFORMATION, as well as the freedom for women in relation to marriage and property. On the one hand, these movements have sought AUTONOMY and self-determination in the face of hierarchy and political oppression. On the other, they have sought social inclusion and political PARTICI-PATION. Early forms of legal citizenship were often elitist in constitution and restricted in scope (even, or especially, in the United States), and even where citizens were equal under the law, the law was silent on their ability to use it. Thus, the different movements had different objectives, but their struggles usually converged on equal rights under the law or the effective exercise of these rights. In this way, the universal rights of citizenship are partly an historical result of specific social movement struggles.

Thus social movements took their place alongside political parties as one of the main forms of associational and autonomous activity in CIVIL SOCIETY. They therefore contribute to mediating the relationship between the individual and the state (Hegel), and protect the individual from state oppression by defending his or her rights (Durkheim). In other words, the effective enjoyment of individual rights requires active associations, not just legal guarantees. Thus for modern theorists like Dahl, a full sense of citizenship combines the two dimensions of participation and (sufficient organisational resources and rights to achieve) public CONTESTATION. It may be possible to construe higher levels of participation in the modern polity as a passive result of urban society and the process of MODERNISATION writ large. But active contestation inevitably involves social mobilisation and political struggles to vindicate individual rights in more or less adverse political circumstances. Although it is unusual for the social movements themselves to be fighting 'for democracy', or even be capable of imagining it, the historical result may be some degree of democratic advance.

Social movements and the national state

The rise of modern social movements coincided with the formation of the national and 'nationalising state' in the late eighteenth and early nineteenth centuries. The state became a 'target for claims' as the movements took advantage of the political space created by the state to press for political rights. At the same time the movements developed a new 'repertoire of contention' (Tilly 1978) that sharpened their strategic response to the new political context and prepared them for sustained campaigns of collective action. Local, communal and reactive struggles became national, thematic and proactive, as many social groups combined to fight for the rights to vote, hold office and make policy. This does not mean that no social movement any longer has a communal identity (many do) or that reactive claims are not typical of many modern movements, including the labour movement (they are). It is rather that most movements came to recognise a 'modular' repertoire of action that could be used by very distinct groups for a wide variety of purposes and goals. The repertoire included protest meetings, electoral rallies, demonstrations, strikes and barricades.

The new forms of collective action made it easier to form coalitions across localities to press general demands on the state. For its part, the state developed standardised procedures for dealing with its citizens, so providing a framework for political action and contributing to shape the trajectory of social movement activity. Long waves of protest firmed up the conventions governing the interaction of social movement and state, and prepared the ground for the fully national social movements of the twentieth century. In this perspective, there is a close historical coincidence between the increase in state administrative power and the popular EMPOWERMENT implicit in social movement activity. But, to balance the record, this rather benign account of the role of the state should be tempered by a more Weberian and sceptical view of the growth of legal and bureaucratic AUTHORITY. In this view, the state is mainly preoccupied with raising taxes and waging war, and citizenship is imagined as a modulated form of subjection. It may occur that state intrusion into the daily lives of ordinary people provokes the kind of social mobilisation that is successful in claiming rights. But it is argued that it was the early bourgeois revolutions of the late eighteenth and early nineteenth centuries that promoted liberal rule and legal citizenship. Later revolutions that set out to achieve capitalist industrialisation 'from above' were far less favourable to civil and political freedoms. In the latter cases, citizenship could appear in the guise of forcible conformity, with social movements mainly motivated by xenophobia and racism.

Two immediate conclusions can be drawn. First, social movements are not always 'good' movements, and do not necessarily act to advance or defend democratic values. Second, the state apparatus and state actors will always shape the relationship between social mobilisation and citizenship rights. It is therefore argued that modern social movements must develop a strategic appreciation of their political constraints, or what the current theory calls the 'political opportunity structure' (Kitschelt 1986). In any one time and place, this structure may include, variously, possible political alliances, political party programmes (where parties exist), the effects of political discourse, divisions or 'openings' within the legal-bureaucratic apparatus of the state, and the presence of sympathetic elite reformers.

Social movements and the language of rights

Thus in the modern period, rights demands are spread across a wide range of social movements, and their political centre of gravity shifts towards these demands. In this way the specific demands (communal, class, sectoral) of particular movements are translated into a common language of rights that facilitates political alliances and movement networks. This language is like a set of tools used to assemble the components of social struggle, and has served the strategic purposes of different movements in widely different cultures, since strategic economy favours the adoption and adaptation of a language that appears universally effective. In fact, it is a perfect example of the kind of 'master frame' that underpins effective social mobilisation. Furthermore, just as more 'modular' forms of mobilisation serve to diffuse rights demands, so the language of rights raises the rhythm of citizenship struggles. To illustrate, the core notion of 'equality of opportunity' sustained the civil rights movement in the US South by binding the southern black middle class to the white liberal 'conscience constituents' whose external support was essential to the movement's success. A traditional rhetoric of rights was adapted to a new 'repertoire of action' that included sit-ins and staged media events.

Although vested in individuals civil and political rights are a 'form of power' which are used to create 'movements of every kind' (Marshall 1965: 142). Since this common language is indeed about rights, not goods, it has only limited distributive implications; and this contributes to make it such a powerful political instrument. But it soon became apparent that legal EQUALITY did not prevent and might even deepen social inequality, and the combination of the two tended to spawn social disruption and broaden the base of political struggle. These were matters either for the police or for social policy; but over the long term the state tended to respond with a range of measures designed to assuage the inequalities of market outcomes and provide basic social security for the mass of the population. These measures correspond to the era of what Marshall called social citizenship, comprised of so-called social rights. But while civil and political rights define freedoms the state must not invade, and so are rights against the state, social rights on the contrary are claims to benefits guaranteed by the state and provided by the administrative apparatus of the state. Consequently, social rights can reduce citizens to passivity and lead to the 'clientelisation' of the citizen's role, so constricting the possibilities of social mobilisation.

Yet the distinction between the mobilising power of civil and political rights on the one hand and social rights on the other does not describe the real process of social mobilisation and democratic struggle outside of the confines of the WELFARE capitalist states. Under both authoritarian governments and fiscally poor democratic governments, most social movements are initially motivated by immediate, concrete and material demands. But these demands usually precede and are frequently transformed into claims for civil and political rights (Foweraker 1989). The initial demands can rarely be satisfied in their entirety, and are restricted, repressed, reversed or delayed. The new demands then focus on the civil and political conditions for putting demands and making claims. In this way, mobilisation driven by the material demands of peasants, workers, women, and poor urban residents promotes struggles for universal rights. This conclusion also holds for the labour movement that often fought first for 'economic-corporate' privileges, so tending to trade civil and political rights for social rights. But the restricted form of regulated citizenship achieved through the struggle for social rights provided a political platform for subsequent demands for civil and political rights and eventually made the labour movement into the vanguard of the citizenship struggle.

In liberal democratic contexts social movements may challenge INTEREST GROUPS, TRADES UNIONS, political parties and other actors in civil society to take up their demands. But in authoritarian contexts, demands will almost inevitably be addressed to the regime and will risk an antagonistic and dangerous response from the state. For this reason too, whether the demands are reactive or proactive, expressive or instrumental, material or political, they will tend sooner or later to take the form of rights demands. Yet state repression and especially state CENSORSHIP may curtail the dissemination of these demands so that popular activists remain unaware of their common grievances. In these circumstances, the social movements can act as schools of rights, with the process of organisation and mobilisation creating a popular EDUCATION in rights. Far from being an automatic outcome of social movement activity, however, this education depends on active LEADERSHIP. By speaking the language of rights to both people and state, the leaders define and delimit a field of political action, which is then confirmed by the iteration and reiteration of rights in assemblies, meetings, marches and demonstrations, as well as in petitions and broadsheets.

There is a sense here in which individuals make themselves citizens of the political community by asserting their own claims on that community through collective action in the specialist demand-making of social movements. This is not to deny that a shared experience of oppression and manipulation may provide a basis for social SOLIDARITY. But it suggests that common circumstance is not a sufficient basis for collective action, and that leadership, COMMUNICATION, organisation and strategic choice are all essential to the shaping of social movement activity. Moreover, for such activity to be effective, the movement must have acquired proper knowledge of the 'political opportunity structure' and the balance of political forces in the society at large. These are exacting requirements, so it is no surprise that social movement successes –

especially under authoritarian regimes – are partial and reversible, with democratic advance occurring piecemeal and against the odds.

Social movements and democratic transitions

Nonetheless, social movements have played crucial roles in processes of DEMOCRATIC TRANSITION. These transitions tend to be seen as discrete moments in historical time. But in his seminal article, Rustow argued that most transitions are 'set off by a prolonged and inconclusive political struggle' (Rustow 1970: 352) and suggested that one generation is usually the minimum period required to achieve such transitions. It is therefore helpful to distinguish between democratic transition *per se* and the period of democratic transformation that precedes it and creates the political conditions for it (Foweraker 1989). In this perspective, democratic transition refers to the change of political regime and the legal-constitutional norms governing the new regime, while democratic transformation encompasses the social movement activity within civil society that prepares the political ground for these changes. The labour movement may play a key role in the latter process both by asserting a sense of rights and by forging a tradition of free collective bargaining that can underpin the new democratic arrangements. Mainstream political science has begun to recognise that, although democracies may be brought down by elite conspiracies, the liberalisation and eventual fall of authoritarian regimes requires the 'crucial component' of large-scale mobilisation, amounting to a 'resurrection of civil society' (O'Donnell and Schmitter 1986: 26).

Despite these salutary observations, most studies of democratic transitions still focus on elite actors and derive their typologies of transition from the *ex post* modelling of elite DECISION-MAKING. Some consider the choices made by different attitudinal groups of elite actors (liberalisers and hardliners). Other examine the elite pacts and settlements made at the moment of transition. In short, it is the short-term manoeuvring of elites that remains central to the analysis, with little or no consideration of the links to mass publics or popular organisations. By ignoring the question of popular agency, and the role of social movements in particular, these studies miss an important dimension of democratic transition, and so may misunderstand the making of democracy. A social movement perspective is an essential complement to the accounts that concentrate exclusively on elite and state actors.

Yet it must also be recognised that, with the transition to democracy, the struggle for citizenship rights will move to the constitutional sphere, and so social movements may lose their pre-eminent role as defenders and promoters of civil and political rights. Every state administration that is organised through bureaucratic power relations will seek to institutionalise positive law and so create 'subjects capable of political obligation, and later the rights of citizens' (Cohen and Arato 1992: 439); and a newly democratic regime will seek to build legitimacy by insisting on these rights. In other words, citizenship becomes an identity that is defended and disseminated by the state against all class and regional differences, and against the specific identities and claims of social movements. During the period of democratic transformation it was social movements that had demanded citizenship rights and had challenged the regime to put these rights into practice. Insofar as this occurs through democratic transition, many of these demands have been met, and the political impetus of the movements begins to decline. Successful social movements may begin to lose their reason for being.

This social movement perspective on democratic achievement offers a direct challenge to the claims of Robert Putnam in *Making Democracy Work* (Putnam 1993) where democracy is seen to be the result of good behaviour in the form of the civic community. But to the dismay of those peoples still aspiring to achieve or improve democracy, Putnam's 'civicness' may take centuries to accumulate (nine centuries in the case of Northern Italy, the focus of his study). This leaves democracy as a distant hope on a far horizon, and seems to condemn large swathes of humankind to a savage and uncertain life under capricious authoritarian governments. Putnam is forced inexorably into this reactionary stance because he insists on searching for the functional prerequisites of democracy rather than exploring the popular agency that may achieve it. (His version of 'civicness' includes neither popular political struggle nor individual rights.) A focus on social movement activity, in contrast, suggests that 'bad behaviour' in the form of the fight for rights can achieve democracy in the space of one or two generations.

Social movements and liberal democracy

The role of social movements in democratic transitions raises the question of the political context. In particular, does the relationship of social movements and democracy vary significantly between secure liberal democratic regimes and authoritarian or 'democratising' regimes? The question is rarely addressed directly, in part because of the increasing separation of the sites of theoretical production on the one hand, and collective action on the other. Over the past twenty years, social movement theory has mainly flourished in Western Europe and North America. But the social movements themselves have been most numerous and active in Latin America, South Africa, Eastern Europe, China and Southeast Asia; that is, in regions of the world where the struggle for universal rights is still high or foremost on the popular political agenda. Social movements are therefore still mainly engaged in struggles for the individual rights of citizenship, and their struggles are clearly centred on the authoritarian state or the exclusionary democratic regime.

But it is argued that in Europe and the United States, social movements no longer struggle for universal rights but for specific protections, particular privileges or special prerogatives like regional autonomy. Furthermore, it is the diversity of social movements and the multiplication and variety of their sites of struggle that constructs the postmodern

form of decentred democratic struggle. Historically, social movements have frequently involved culturally, regionally or ethnically specific actors. Their initial demands have often been particular, restricted and even idiosyncratic. They may even have aspired to rights that were not universal but professional or corporate. Yet the historical encounter with the language of rights meant that specific struggles could contribute, purposively or contingently, to the achievement of universal rights. But once the universal rights of citizenship are inscribed in the constitution and protected in law, real tensions may arise between the specific demands deriving from specific identities and the universal content of liberal citizenship. Citizenship comprises rights that apply equally to everyone and so abstracts from the differences of identity. It also constructs a status that is common to everyone rather than differentiated, and so may suppress these differences. This may create further tensions between the heterogeneity of social movements based on gender, race, community or region and the homogeneity of citizenship, and eventually between the autonomy of social movements and heteronomy of citizenship rights as upheld by the liberal state.

If this is true, how will social movements affect the longer-term legitimacy and effectiveness of liberal democratic regimes that still depend on universal and equalising forms of political mediation? In other words, are the movements necessarily beneficial to continuing democratic advance? These questions are posed most acutely by those social movements that appear not so much 'new' as frighteningly dated, with the resurgence of right-wing movements in France, and equally right-wing xenophobic and irredentist movements in Germany and Italy (see IRREDENTISM). The labour movement, on the other hand, historically a strong protagonist of the struggle for universal rights, is now weaker than it has been for several decades. These developments may not create but certainly do not alleviate the present crisis of confidence in democratic institutions, both at national level and within the European Union. Advocates of reform call for constitutional change. Conservatives of different hues seek salvation in retrenchment. It is currently unclear whether social movements will contribute to more open and plural democratic government or will precipitate more exclusionary forms of democracy.

In the early 'mass society' versions of social movement theory, social movements were understood to express the rage and disorientation of anomic social actors whose traditional social contexts had been destroyed by processes of modernisation. Social movements were dangerous to the institutional order of liberal society, and were therefore a 'bad thing'. (The historical examples they had in mind were the national socialist movement and, to a lesser degree, the communist movement.) Later theories of 'new social movements' saw social movements as raising new issues and extending the political agenda. They mobilised constituencies that would otherwise go unrepresented, creating an important source of political renewal in liberal society, and were therefore a 'good thing'. Currently, one view of social movements sees them as destabilising incipient democracies in Eastern Europe and the former Soviet Union, or as threatening the institutional supports and political freedoms of established democracies in the West. Another and contrary view sees them as a crucial protagonist in struggles for democratic rights in South Africa, China, Southeast Asia and Latin America. Social movements are therefore both a 'good thing' and a 'bad thing', depending on the political context where the social movement activity takes place. But it is apparent that the context serves as a metaphor for whether social movements appear to promote or threaten the development of liberal democratic government founded on the universal rights of citizenship and the rule of law.

See also:

autonomy; capitalism; civil society; class; coalitions; contestation; democratic transition; equality; interest groups; legitimacy; modernisation; participation; radical democracy; rights; trades unions; welfare

Further reading

Bowles, S. and Gintis, H. (1987) *Democracy and Capitalism: Property, Community and the Contradictions of Modern Social Thought*, New York: Basic Books.

Cohen, J. and Arato, A. (1992) *Civil Society and Political Theory*, Cambridge, MA: MIT Press.

Foweraker, J. (1989) *Making Democracy in Spain: Grass-Roots Struggle in the South, 1955–1975*, Cambridge: Cambridge University Press.

—— (1995) *Theorizing Social Movements*, London: Pluto Press.

Kitschelt, H. (1986) 'Political Opportunity Structures and Political Protest: Anti-Nuclear Movements in Four Democracies,' *British Journal of Political Science* 16: 58–95.

Marshall, T. H. (1965) *Class, Citizenship and Social Development*, Garden City, NY: Anchor Books.

O'Donnell, G. and Schmitter, P.C. (1986) *Transitions from Authoritarian Rule: Tentative Conclusions about Uncertain Democracies*, Baltimore: Johns Hopkins University Press.

Putnam, R. (1993) *Making Democracy Work: Civic Traditions in Modern Italy*, Princeton, NJ: Princeton University Press.

Rueschemeyer, D., Stephens, E.H. and Stephens, J. (1992) *Capitalist Development and Democracy*, Cambridge: Polity Press.

Rustow, D.A. (1970) 'Transitions to Democracy: Toward a Dynamic Model', *Comparative Politics* 2: 337–63.

Tilly, C. (1978) *From Mobilisation to Revolution*, Reading, MA: Addison-Wesley.

—— (1984) 'Social Movements and National Politics', in W. Bright and S. Harding (eds), *State Building and Social Movements*, Ann Arbor, MI: University of Michigan Press.

JOE FOWERAKER

solidarity

The term 'solidarity', broadly construed, connotes that quality of human association or social cohesion that holds the individual members of a group together in some commonality (of purpose, interests, values, mutual trust and so on) such that they are willing to act on one another's behalf (May 1996: ch. 2). The term itself entered the English language from the French only in the mid-nineteenth century, and the more influential theoretical elaborations of solidarity did not appear until the late nineteenth and early twentieth centuries. Nonetheless, conceptual equivalents and other closely related ideas have enjoyed a long history in Western thought. These ideas include Plato's organic conception of the just polity and the Aristotelian–Thomistic conceptions of friendship and the common good. Specifically modern equivalents and precursors of the notion of solidarity can already be discerned in the early modern period (for example, the writings of the Scottish moralists). However, it is only in the nineteenth century, with the new forms of association and SOCIAL MOVEMENTS developed in response to urbanisation, industrialisation and abuses of *laissez faire* CAPITALISM that the term itself enters into widespread usage. Across a number of traditions – from the Jewish nationalism of the *Alliance Israélite Universelle* to Harlem Renaissance philosopher Alain Locke's cosmopolitan approach to race, from socialist analyses of CLASS to Christian social doctrine – one begins to find not only the term itself but in many cases mature theories of solidarity or its conceptual equivalent.

The best-known theoretical developments of the term itself begin to appear in the late nineteenth century. As a descriptive sociological concept, solidarity is associated above all with the name of Émile Durkheim. Rejecting interest-based accounts, Durkheim argues that the solidarity exhibited by a given social order arises from its 'collective conscience', the sentiments, beliefs and values shared by the members and expressed in the legal institutions of that society. Durkheim distinguishes two basic forms of solidarity. In premodern kinship-based societies, the predominant source of social cohesion is the substantive similarities of a 'mechanical solidarity' that directly subordinates the individual to the collective, as part to whole. In modern societies, with their developed division of labour and emphasis on individual AUTONOMY, solidarity becomes increasingly 'organic', based on the interdependence of individual agents to whom are imputed moral commitments binding on all persons as such.

Marxist and socialist thought provides the spur to the moral-political theories of solidarity – that is, solidarity as a prescriptive concept – that emerge at the end of the century. Drawing on G.W.F. Hegel's socialised conception of labour, Karl Marx argued that capitalist forms of industry, though alienating, also foster an association of workers with revolutionary potential. From their association in the workplace and awareness of the immiseration they share in virtue of their class position, a class consciousness should emerge that unites the proletariat as the revolutionary class. Christian thinkers made some of the earliest attempts to elaborate a conception of solidarity in response to the socialist challenge. Working out of the Protestant social gospel movement, Baptist theologian Walter Rauschenbusch developed a version of 'Christian Socialism' centred around a conception of social solidarity that attempted to reconcile Christian commitments with socialist ideas of collective ownership. In the tradition of Catholic social teaching, perhaps the most influential early analysis was that of moral philosopher and social theorist Heinrich Pesch, whose 'Christian Solidarism' proposed a middle way between socialist collectivism, with its perceived devaluation of the dignity of the individual person, and liberal INDIVIDUALISM, with its atomistic, contractualist understanding of social relations. The concept of solidarity has continued to play an important role in Catholic thought (including papal encyclicals) and, more generally, in political theology (Doran 1996; Metz and Moltmann 1995).

Discussions of solidarity in moral-political theory in the latter half of the twentieth century tend to track the broad constellation of debates involving liberal proceduralists, communitarians and civic republicans, feminists and postmodernists. In the liberal-communitarian debate, proceduralists such as John Rawls and Jürgen Habermas champion neo-Kantian conceptions of JUSTICE defined in terms of an impartiality achieved through formal procedures. Drawing on such thinkers as Aristotle and Hegel, the communitarians in effect maintain that the liberal model of politics provides an inadequate account of the solidarity required for its theory of political justice to work: either because the model presupposes a self stripped of identity-constitutive communal attachments, because it engenders value scepticism and social fragmentation, or because it remains blind to its own substantive assumptions about the good life (see COMMUNITARIANISM).

Communitarian criticisms tend to be aligned with civic REPUBLICANISM, which draws upon the tradition of political thought running from the Greeks through Machiavelli, Harrington, Rousseau and Arendt. For civic republicans, human beings achieve their telos or highest good precisely as citizens engaged in political activity. The theoretical elaboration of such activity prioritises substantive conceptions of CIVIC VIRTUE, community traditions and shared values over neutral procedures, in some cases to the point where collective solidarity overwhelms individual liberty. Thus communitarian and civic republican models face the charge that their strong conceptions of community and ascribed identities assume an implausible degree of social homogeneity and lead to an authoritarianism incompatible with individual autonomy.

On both sides of the debate, one finds attempts at a middle path. Habermas, who provides one of the more developed accounts, conceives solidarity as the flip-side of his proceduralist conception of justice. That is, one can respond to individuals in a just manner – show them equal concern and respect – only if one also exhibits a solidaristic concern for the integrity of that web of social relationships in which individuals alone can achieve and stabilise their unique identities. Solidarity acquires a universalistic character, on his view, insofar as norms of justice can be validated only through a rational discourse involving all those affected. Thus moral autonomy presupposes a kind of rational solidarity with the community of moral inquirers – the 'ideal communication community' – that extends beyond the confines of one's particular group.

In his political theory, Habermas distinguishes two levels of INTEGRATION within a given polity. At a subcultural level, particularistic group solidarities are essential for the identity-formation of members. A legal system based on individual rights, rather than undermining such solidarities as critics claim, integrates them at the political level: legitimate law accords an equal right to coexistence to any group that accepts constitutional democracy. Habermas realises that such political integration presupposes loyalty to a POLITICAL CULTURE, a 'constitutional patriotism' able to motivate civic engagement not only on behalf of the polity but for immigrants and foreigners as well.

Although this political culture feeds off a particular national consciousness, the universalistic tenor of Habermas's conception of solidarity points beyond the nation-state to a cosmopolitan legal order. His idea of a global human solidarity gains some empirical support from such interventions as international relief efforts, humanitarian peacekeeping missions and boycotts of corporations. Nonetheless, theorists who conceive solidarity in more concrete and group-specific terms doubt the efficacy of global solidarity. Richard Rorty, for example, holds that solidarity always takes as its object the fellow members of a concrete 'we' rather than a universal humanity. Indeed, his postmodern interpretation of American pragmatism eschews all reliance on transcultural universals or metaphysical conceptions of a common human nature to ground the solidaristic commitments of democratic institutions. Emphasising the radical historical contingency of democracy and its ideals, Rorty advocates instead the attitude of the 'liberal ironist' for whom an aesthetic sensibility for suffering – in particular the cruelty that institutions and individuals inflict – suffices for solidarity.

At a pragmatic political level, however,

Rorty's model retains universalist aspirations, inasmuch as good liberals strive to develop their ability to notice and respond to the suffering of ever wider circles of strangers. This project presupposes an acceptance of democracy inasmuch as its institutions, better than any alternative to date, have promoted such solidarity while giving individuals greater chances for autonomous self-creation. However, most citizens today are not ironists, as Rorty admits. Thus the question remains whether a solidarity lacking standards of rational debate can supply democratic institutions with sufficient resources for adjudicating conflicts and responding to criticism.

Feminists have also been in the forefront of reflection on solidarity, and their views cover a broad spectrum. Indeed, Habermas's conception of solidarity is also intended to respond to the criticism, raised notably by feminists working in moral theory and moral psychology, that an emphasis on justice as impartiality ignores those aspects of morality displayed in a solidaristic care for the 'concrete other' with his or her unique identity and needs. In political theory, feminists have drawn on critical social theory and poststructuralist analyses to criticise the binary oppositions – reason/emotion, public/private, and the like – that have traditionally legitimated constitutional democracies. Such categories, while pretending to universality, have in fact masked existing power structures that exclude subordinate groups such as women and other MINORITIES. However, in reasserting the group-specific differences that universal categories ignore, the feminist critique of power runs the risk of falling into a divisive identity politics that reinforces the mutual separation of subcultural groups, thereby promoting social fragmentation (see GENDERING DEMOCRACY; PUBLIC–PRIVATE DISTINCTION). As in the liberal-communitarian debate, the problem arises of how one can conceive a wider solidarity that allows for the recognition of particular identities and differences. One can also ask whether the feminist critique of universalist categories must not itself rely on universalisms of some sort.

These problems have led some feminist theorists to seek out alternative models that do not dispense altogether with universalist aspirations. Emphasising the constructed, fluid and pluralistic character of identities, such theorists have proposed models of solidarity based more on the acknowledgement of difference than on the assertion of sameness. For example, according to Jodi Dean's conception of 'reflective solidarity', members of groups and social movements should go beyond identity politics by practising an ongoing self-criticism and attentiveness to the exclusions suffered by strangers. The practice of such open communication fosters a broader, more inclusive solidarity inasmuch as group boundaries remain porous to one another and exclusionary practices become more difficult to maintain. Although such approaches often draw upon Habermas, they shift the focus from consensus to contest, from argument over principles to inclusion in an ongoing conversation.

In summary, across a variety of approaches one finds a very broad agreement on the key elements in a wider, more universalistic conception of solidarity that acknowledges the importance of particularity and difference: that is, a conception adequate to today's pluralistic democratic societies. These elements include a democratic institutional framework, commitment to dialogue, openness to alternative perspectives and a willingness to question one's own assumptions. Beyond such broad agreement, theorists differ in how they understand and accentuate these elements. For proceduralists such as Habermas and Rawls, wider solidarity is achieved precisely through justice as defined by fair democratic procedures that approximate certain transcultural idealisations. For feminists, the accent shifts to solidarity as the road to justice, understood primarily as less exclusionary social relations and institutions. Finally, on a postmodernist view such as Rorty's, a philosophically unjustifiable affective solidarity is the only effective means of securing justice as the reduction of cruelty. Behind these divergences lie different assessments of two central tensions in the concept of solidarity: the relation between concrete communal bonds and more abstract, institutional forms of association, on the one hand, and on the other, the tension between a cohesion based on shared identities and the moral demand for inclusion of the other.

See also:

communication; democratic debate; inclusion/exclusion; political culture

Further reading

Dean, J. (1996) *Solidarity of Strangers: Feminism after Identity Politics*, Berkeley, CA: University of California Press.

Doran, K.P. (1996) *Solidarity: A Synthesis of Personalism and Communication in the Thought of Karol Wojtyla/Pope John Paul II*, New York: Peter Lang.

Habermas, J. (1998) *The Inclusion of the Other*, ed. C. Cronin and P. DeGreiff, Cambridge, MA: MIT Press.

May, L. (1996) *The Socially Responsive Self: Social Theory and Professional Ethics*, Chicago: University of Chicago Press.

Metz, J.-B., and Moltmann, J. (1995) *Faith and the Future: Essays on Theology, Solidarity, and Modernity*, Maryknoll, NY: Orbis.

Peitz, D.A. (1992) *Solidarity as Hermeneutic: A Revisionist Reading of the Theology of Walter Rauschenbusch*, New York: Peter Lang.

Phillips, A. (1993) *Democracy and Difference*, University Park, PA: State University of Pennsylvania.

Rehg, W. (1994) *Insight and Solidarity: A Study in the Discourse Ethics of Jürgen Habermas*, Berkeley, CA: University of California Press.

Rorty, R. (1989) *Contingency, Irony, and Solidarity*, Cambridge: Cambridge University Press.

Seligman, A.B. (1997) *The Problem of Trust*, Princeton, NJ: Princeton University Press.

Troen, S.I. and Pinkus, B. (eds) (1992) *Organizing Rescue: National Jewish Solidarity in the Modern Period*, London: Frank Cass.

Washington, J. (1986) *Alain Locke and Philosophy: A Quest for Cultural Pluralism*, New York: Greenwood.

WILLIAM REHG

sovereignty

The concept of sovereignty is of central importance to modern politics, and especially to several influential conceptions of democracy. It is, however, a complex concept, difficult to characterise in an uncontroversial manner. The core idea of sovereignty is the notion of the ultimate source of political AUTHORITY within a realm. In contemporary political thought it is customary to distinguish between 'internal' and 'external' sovereignty, the first pertaining to the structure or constitution of a state, the second to the relations between states. Internal sovereignty thus conceived has to do with the state's authority over its subjects, while the second notion refers to the independence or AUTONOMY of states. The two conceptions are closely linked in early modern conceptions of sovereignty. In the writings of Jean Bodin (1530–96), Thomas Hobbes (1588–1679) and Jean-Jacques Rousseau (1712–78), internal and external sovereignty are tightly connected. These thinkers thought sovereignty to be absolute (legally unconstrained or unlimited), indivisible (unique and undivided) and inalienable (cannot be delegated or 'represented'). If absolute sovereignty is attributed to states, then their authority cannot be constrained by international law or possibly even by the RIGHTS of individuals. Conceiving of sovereignty as absolute thus requires granting states a certain autonomy or liberty in their 'international relations'.

To understand the notion of sovereignty, it is important to keep in mind aspects of the history of the emergence of the state in early modern Europe. Medieval rule was, broadly speaking, feudal, imperial and/or theocratic. The early modern competitors of what we now think of as the state were numerous: city-republics, leagues of cities, empires, the Church and various remnants of feudalism. Two features of modern governance were relatively absent in all of these earlier forms of rule: exclusivity of rule (a 'closed' system of governance) and territoriality. The modern state emerges only when its claim (or that of its head, the monarch) to govern alone exclusively is recognized. A determinate realm, with relatively unambiguous geographical BOUNDARIES, is a prerequisite of the modern state and is largely missing in early forms of political organisation. A 'sovereign' in this sense is the unique ruler of a realm, whose sphere of authority encompasses the whole realm without overlapping that of any other ruler. It – initially the monarch, later the state, then 'the people' – rules without superiors. As the historian F.H. Hinsley says, 'at the beginning, the idea of sovereignty was the idea that there is a final and absolute political authority in the political community...*and no final and absolute authority exists elsewhere*' (Hinsley 1986: 25–6). With the development of the concept of sovereignty, we have the main elements of what is now called 'the state system': independent states and 'international relations' (and international law).

The core idea of sovereignty is that of the ultimate source of political authority within a realm. This is the power that monarchs claimed in their battles against lords and princes, and against popes. Their realm or kingdom was theirs, and their authority over it was to be shared with no one. The history is very complex, but it is useful to emphasise the appeal of this conception of political governance as territorial, unitary and absolute. In the ferocious battles fought by European monarchs against the limits imposed on them by imperial and papal authorities and against the independent powers of feudal lords, self-governing towns and autonomous guilds, a modern ideal of unitary and absolute political power emerges and finds expression in the notion of sovereignty.

The core notion of sovereignty – the ultimate source of political authority within a realm – requires unpacking. Sovereignty is associated with modern kingdoms and states; the 'realms' in question are the well-defined territories of such states. The relevant notion of political

authority is more controversial. Some social theorists think of authority as something attributed or conferred to leaders or institutions. But these sorts of accounts often leave unanalysed that which is conferred. (Something has authority if people treat it as authoritative. But what is it to treat it thus?) The primary meaning here is normative, though not necessarily moral: something is an authority, in the sense relevant here, only if its directives are (and are intended to be) action-guiding. For instance, consider the law. It forbids us from doing certain things, and it intends these prohibitions to guide our behaviour; specifically, these prohibitions are reason-providing. Authorities, then, mean to guide behaviour by providing reasons for action to their subjects. On this view, political authority is not to be understood simply as justified force; something is a genuine authority only insofar as its directives are reasons for action. Sanctions or force may frequently be necessary as a means to make effective this authority, but the two are not to be conflated.

The key to the notion of sovereignty lies in the idea of ultimate authority. What is required for a source of authority to be ultimate? An authority may be ultimate if it is the highest in a hierarchy of authorities. Such an authority may also be final: there is no further appeal after it has spoken (it has 'the last word'). Lastly, an ultimate authority may be one which is supreme in a particular sense: it has authority over all other authorities in its realm. The state's authority is sovereign in this sense; it takes precedence over competing authorities (corporate, syndicate, church, conscience). In sum, then, sovereignty is the highest, final and supreme political authority within a modern territorial realm.

Today, few wish to understand sovereignty as absolute or unconstrained; it is now widely thought that sovereignty can and should be limited. We now also think that one of the most effective institutional means of limiting the authority and power of states is to divide sovereignty amongst a plurality of agents or institutions. *Contra* Hobbes and others, republican and democratic theorists have stressed the value and importance of divisions of power within states; indivisibility is no longer assumed to be essential to sovereignty. Our notion tends to be one of divisible, limited sovereignty. But to attribute even limited sovereignty to a monarch or state is to grant it considerable power. For the sovereign retains the power to judge the nature of the limits to its authority, and its judgement here is final and supreme. Even if sovereignty is not absolute, it remains formidable.

While sovereignty is now often understood to be a defining attribute of states, it was initially attributed to, or claimed by, monarchs. In Britain it became customary to attribute sovereignty to the trinity of 'the monarch in Parliament'. Rousseau and some of the founders of the American system attributed sovereignty to the people, and the French *Declaration des droits de l'homme et du citoyen* of 1789 claims sovereignty for the 'nation'. The doctrine of 'popular sovereignty' – the idea that peoples are the rightful bearers of sovereignty – is especially influential in the American and French political traditions and is held by many to be the foundation of modern democracy.

The identity of 'the people' who are thought to be sovereign is not altogether clear. The radical idea of the French Revolution was that the members of the non-aristocratic (and non-clerical) classes of society or their representatives had the right to rule, *contra* the claim of all of the European aristocracies. But gradually 'the people' comes to be more inclusive, covering all members of the polity and sometimes all subject to its governance (including, for example, non-citizen residents). This notion of 'the people' echoes classical Roman ideas, as does its associated notion of CITIZENSHIP.

It is not clear, however, that we should wish to attribute limited sovereignty either to states or to peoples. Many have agreed with Blackstone in thinking that, 'there is and must be in all of [the several forms of government] a supreme, irresistible, absolute, uncontrolled authority, in which the *jura summi imperii*, or the rights of sovereignty, reside' (Blackstone 1973: 36). But it is arguable that the authority, for instance, of conscience, church, community

or international law is not always pre-empted by that of the state (or the people) when the two conflict. JUSTICE, and in particular the rights of humans or persons, may be thought to be standards that have supremacy over others, contrary to the claims of sovereign states or peoples. It is not easy to adapt this complex early modern concept to our contemporary conceptions of politics. Many have thus thought that it might be best to do without the notion of sovereignty, however important it has been to the development of modern politics. Certainly, its usefulness in contemporary legal theory or jurisprudence is doubtful (Hart 1994: chaps 2–4, 10). Adapting our constitutional states and democratic institutions to new forms of international co-operation and law may perhaps best be done without the notion of sovereignty.

See also:

democracy, justifications for; judicial review; law, rule of; legitimacy; parliamentary models; representation, concept of; state, models of

Further reading

Beitz, C. (1991) 'Sovereignty and Morality in International Affairs', in D. Held (ed.), *Political Theory Today*, Stanford, CA: Stanford University Press.

Blackstone, W. (1973) *The Sovereignty of the Law, Selections from Blackstone's Commentaries on the Laws of England*, ed. G. Jones, Toronto: University of Toronto Press.

Bodin, J. (1962) *The Six Bookes of a Commonweale*, trans. R. Knolles, ed. K.D. McRae, Cambridge, MA: Harvard University Press.

Hart, H.L.A. (1994) *The Concept of Law*, 2nd edn, Oxford: Clarendon Press.

Hinsley, F.H. (1966) *Sovereignty*, 2nd edn, Cambridge: Cambridge University Press.

Lyons, G. and Mastanduno, M. (eds) (1995) *Beyond Westphalia? State Sovereignty and International Intervention*, Baltimore: Johns Hopkins University Press.

Morgan, E. (1988) *Inventing the People: the*

Rise of Popular Sovereignty in England and America, New York: W.W. Norton.

Morris, C. (1998) *An Essay on the Modern State*, Cambridge: Cambridge University Press.

—— (2000) 'The Very idea of Popular Sovereignty: "We the People" Reconsidered', *Social Philosophy and Policy* 17(1): 1–26.

Pogge, T. (1992) 'Cosmopolitanism and Sovereignty', *Ethics* 103(1): 48–75.

CHRISTOPHER MORRIS

standards of conduct in public life

From October 1994 to November 1997 I served as the first Chairman of the Committee on Standards in Public Life, a body set up by the prime minister with the support of the opposition parties. Our task was to make a report and recommendations on a perceived crisis of confidence in the integrity of the political and administrative systems of the United Kingdom. In the opinion of many, this was the worst such crisis since the Profumo affair some thirty years previously. Our report and recommendations were framed in the context of the situation in the United Kingdom, but we learned much from the experiences of other advanced democracies, especially those with political systems based upon our own. We found that their problems were remarkably similar to ours. In particular, we encountered an almost universal distrust of politicians as a class. We concluded that each country, including our own, must work out its own salvation in accordance with its individual character, its constitution and the gravity of its plight. Thus in our first report we made recommendations some of which – such as the creation of a Parliamentary Commissioner for Standards and a Public Commissioner for Appointments – were radical in nature. All could be achieved by Parliamentary resolution, by executive action under the royal prerogative or simply by consent, without recourse to the delay and inflexibility of the sort of legislation that other

countries have found it necessary to adopt. But we also concluded that, whatever form the solutions to the common problems of advanced democracies might take in particular countries, those solutions must be based upon the same fundamental principles.

A statement of principles is nothing more than empty words unless endorsed wholeheartedly by those to whom it applies. As stated in the foreword to the first Issues and Questions paper put out by the Committee, 'A Committee, or a set of rules, can only do so much. In the end, high standards depend upon the beliefs, philosophy, and self-discipline of individuals.' This statement can be seen to reflect the views expressed by an earlier law lord, Lord Moulton, some eighty years previously. The unlikely occasion was an impromptu speech to the Authors' Club, a private speech that subsequently won widespread public acclaim. He spoke of self-discipline as obedience to the unenforceable. Thus:

> Mere obedience to law does not measure the greatness of a nation. It can easily be obtained by a strong executive, and most easily of all from a timorous people. Nor is the licence of behaviour which so often accompanies the absence of law, and which is miscalled liberty, a proof of greatness. The true test is the extent to which the individuals composing the nation can be trusted to obey.

But how do you deal with a situation where many of the individuals composing the nation are doubtful about the content of the law that should be self-imposed? One of our earliest lessons on the Committee was that there was great uncertainty and confusion about what was right and what was wrong in the sphere of ethical conduct, both in this country and abroad. We therefore set out seven principles or criteria which seemed to us to form the basis of propriety in public life, and which we felt that everyone would understand and accept. The seven principles are selflessness, integrity, objectivity, ACCOUNTABILITY, openness, honesty and LEADERSHIP. At the risk of insisting too much, we added a few words describing what we meant by each of these terms. For example, by selflessness we meant that 'holders of public office should take decisions solely in terms of the public interest. They should not do so in order to gain financial or other material benefits for themselves, their family or their friends.'

The number could easily have been greater or smaller than seven. It might be argued that the last three principles of openness, honesty and leadership are alone enough to cover the whole subject. Or the list might have included courage, such as the courage required of a junior official to blow the whistle at wrongdoing by his or her superiors, at the risk of jeopardising his or her career. Or it might have embraced humility – this does not come easily to the British – as a necessary antidote to arrogance and pomposity, a realisation of one's own unimportance, a sense of proportion, or even, more simply, a sense of humour. But we thought that our seven was about right for the brief of the Committee.

We put them forward with some diffidence because they seemed so obvious. To anyone brought up in a religious faith, or indeed to any rational agnostic or atheist, they are elementary rules of private as well as of public behaviour. We were therefore relieved as well as encouraged to learn that they were widely welcomed, both here and abroad. It was particularly encouraging to find that the seven principles, complete with explanations, were adopted verbatim by the House of Commons in its new code of conduct, as well as by many other institutions.

Codes of conduct, long common in the professions, have now become the norm not only in the various departments of the government and public life generally but also in many commercial organisations. They are an essential means of expression of the self-imposed law, but they need to be backed up by an appropriate form of independent scrutiny, such as auditors, ombudsmen, regulators and the like. The introduction by the House of Commons of its first ever code of conduct, incorporating the seven principles and accom-

panied by the creation of the office of Parliamentary Commissioner for Standards, was by far the most important consequence of the Committee's first report. The Commissioner is an official appointed by and answerable to the House, but totally independent of any political party. The House of Commons is the centre of our democracy. As long as the people have confidence in the House of Commons, nothing much can go wrong. Without that confidence, nothing much can go right.

The Committee was first formed in response to a series of scandals concerning the behaviour of members of parliament. These included the cash-for-questions affair and various allegations about the financial relationships between members of parliament and ministers and important figures in the private sector. There were also suspicions that government appointments to well-paid and influential jobs on quangos (quasi-autonomous NON-GOVERNMENTAL ORGANISATIONS) were being made on the basis of political or personal association rather than merit, and that ex-ministers were moving to the boardrooms of companies with which they had dealings while in office.

The background to these individual scandals, allegations and suspicions was the distrust of politicians generally, consistently reflected in opinion poll results. Three examples will be enough. Sixty-four per cent of respondents agreed that 'most MPs make a lot of money by using public office improperly'. No less than 87 per cent agreed that 'most MPs will tell lies if they feel the truth will hurt them politically'. And when asked about categories of people who could generally be trusted to tell the truth, only 14 per cent were prepared to say 'yes' in the case of politicians. In the case of government ministers, the score was an appalling 11 per cent. All of these results were not only damning in themselves, but much more damning when compared to the results of similar questions asked by the pollsters some nine or ten years previously. The inevitable conclusion was that the faith in the elected MPs and ministers upon which our democracy depends was giving way to disillusion and cynicism. It was scant consolation to find that the same disillusion and distrust was experienced by our fellow democracies.

Why has this decline in confidence occurred? There are three main reasons. The first is that even the best politicians are sometimes guilty of such faults as economy with the truth, making promises without being sure that they will be able to carry them out, and denigration of their political opponents, accusing them of dishonesty, especially at election times. It is hardly surprising that the public tend to take them at their own valuation, thinking that they ought to know. Secondly, their faults are exaggerated by MEDIA coverage, much of which is superficial and concentrates on failings rather than virtues. Thirdly, most of the blame lies with us, the public, the armchair cynics, who like reading bad things about other people and who would soon become bored with the virtuous truth.

For the truth is that, in this country at least, the majority of politicians are honest and decent people who are offended by the allegations of sleaze generated by the behaviour of a small minority. Typical of this majority were the leading figures from the three main political parties on the Committee itself. Moreover, the House of Commons accepted the Committee's recommendations almost in their entirety, and successfully implemented them in the subsequent years. This offers grounds for hope that future opinion polls will show faith in the House of Commons to have been restored in some degree, or the downward spiral in confidence to have been arrested. Yet scandals, allegations and suspicions are still with us. They always will be so long as we are represented and governed by fallible human beings. The difference is that the means are now there to identify, expose and punish the wrongdoers promptly and effectively. There has been at least one case where the House adopted procedures that departed fundamentally from the recommendations of the Committee, and the House has yet to achieve a full reform of its procedures. If a proper code of conduct cannot be agreed by the House itself, then there can be no alternative to the creation by statute of an external body to adjudicate upon the conduct of members (as envisaged in the Committee's first report). The issue is too important to be shelved or fudged.

The main focus here has been on the House of Commons and its members because they and they alone bear the ultimate responsibility for the health of our democracy and the maintenance of high standards. But certain conditions must be satisfied at all levels of public life if proper standards of conduct are to be maintained. These conditions are conviction, commitment and clarity. There must be conviction about what is right and agreement on the broad principles of proper behaviour. These should be set out in individual codes adopted by each organisation in the public sector, using the seven general principles as a guideline. When every organisation has responsibility for developing its own code there can be no excuse for anyone to believe that the rules do not apply to him or her.

There must be a strong public commitment at all levels to the highest standards of conduct. There must be an expectation by those who work in the public service that their leaders will devote themselves to ensuring the highest ethical standards. There is always a risk that standards will be seen as necessary to keep the junior staff in line but as irrelevant to managers. If standards are to be maintained, they must permeate the organisation from top to bottom and back again.

Finally, there must be clarity, not just in the formulation of the rules but in their communication, by means of both induction training and continuing training. The Committee's first report to the prime minister highlighted 'confusion over what is and what is not acceptable behaviour' and 'a certain slackness in the observance and enforcement of high standards by those concerned'. In a relatively corruption-free society such as ours, confusion and slackness are much more widespread than dishonesty, and they can be equally destructive of public confidence. Constant vigilance by a wholly impartial and independent body is the only safeguard. There should be a long and busy future for the Committee on Standards in Public Life.

See also:

corruption; elections; electoral behaviour; electoral campaigning; parties; political financing

LORD NOLAN

state, models of

The state is hard to define and describe. Although the word 'state' is used freely and un-self-consciously in everyday discourse, as a concept in normative and empirical democratic theory it is essentially and often hotly contested. Theorists disagree over whether the state is best defined by its legal form, its coercive capacities, its institutional composition and boundaries, its modes of political representation and intervention, its internal operations and modes of calculation, its declared aims, its functions for the broader society, or its sovereign place in the international system. There are also disputes over the relationship between the state and law, the state and politics, the state and CIVIL SOCIETY, the public and the private, state managers and citizens, top-down state power and micropower relations. And there are disagreements over the essentially benign or malign character of the state, the substantive as opposed to formal differences between democracy and dictatorship, the possibility of control over state managers in representative democracies, the feasibility of DIRECT DEMOCRACY, the scope for a COSMOPOLITAN DEMOCRACY in a global world, or the scope for a stateless society in an increasingly complex and interdependent world. This contribution addresses some, but not all, of these issues.

The classic definition of the modern state in political science comes from the German social scientist, Max Weber. He argued against defining the state in terms of its self-declared goals or its actual tasks on the grounds that there is no core set of such goals or functions that all states have always undertaken and that there is practically no goal that states have not at some time proclaimed and practically no task they have not undertaken. Instead, Weber defined the state in terms of its distinctive means of political control. Thus he analysed the modern state as a compulsory association that has successfully monopolised the legitimate use of physical force as a means of domination within a given territory (Weber 1948). Its defining features were an administrative staff, means of organised COERCION, an effective claim to the legitimate exercise of that coercion, a distinct territory within which this coercion was exercised and subjects over whom it was exercised. Weber distinguished four forms of state in terms of the bases on which their LEGITIMACY claims rested: tradition (for example, inheritance), a rational-legal constitution, charismatic personal AUTHORITY and the value-rational (*wertrational*) promise to achieve a specific future objective (for example, to establish communism). Weber's definition is quite consistent with standard definitions of the state as an apparatus that makes decisions that are collectively binding on members of a given society and justified in the name of the public interest or common good. It is also easily combined with orthodox approaches in international relations, for which a state is said to exercise legitimate authority insofar as its claim to SOVEREIGNTY within its territory is recognized by other states. The same basic features of sovereignty, coercion and territoriality are also emphasised in the recent North American social scientific movement to 'bring the state back in' (Evans *et al.* 1985).

None of this implies, of course, that the modern state need be democratic, however this is defined. On the contrary, there are still many authoritarian and totalitarian regimes that claim a legitimate monopoly of coercion within their territories and are accepted as full members of the community of states. The problems with such a Weberian definition are that states tend to infringe their own legality and/or legitimacy (there is always a seamy, shadowy side to the state); that the exercise of coercion, legitimate or otherwise, is not the most obvious and immediate feature of contemporary democratic WELFARE states; and that there is now much talk about the crisis of the sovereign state organised around a given national territory.

One might expect the most radical alternative to the classic Weberian view to come from anarchists. But they accept that such modern states exist, reject their legitimacy (even if this is accepted by the state's subjects or citizens), argue that such states involve the domination of rulers over the ruled, and work for the eventual abolition of the separation between state and people through the introduction of some form of direct democracy. In this sense they depart from orthodox accounts of the state primarily in their negative evaluation of state power rather than in their description of its defining institutional features. The most radical challenge to orthodox accounts of the state actually comes from recent work in discourse analysis. This regards the state as an illusory and polyvalent phenomenon, a product of the 'political imaginary'. Refusing to treat the state as a thing or as a rational subject, such work claims that the state (like God) exists only to the extent that people act as if it existed. It originates in political discourses that establish an internal boundary within the political system that defines some institutions, organisations, and actors as belonging to the 'state' and others as lying beyond it in the wider political system and its public sphere, in civil society, or in systems defined for the time being as beyond politics (such as the operation of the market economy in classical liberalism) (Mitchell 1991; Bartelson 1995). In this way state discourses orient political action, provide a vocabulary of motives and grounds for political action, and contribute to the production of an illusory 'state effect' that unifies what is essentially a heterogeneous ensemble of institutions, organisations and actors. There is no common discourse of the state, however: at best we find a dominant or hegemonic discourse. It follows that the demarcations between the state and the public sphere, state and economy, state and civil society and so on, are variable and open to

CONTESTATION. Different boundary lines are drawn for different purposes and, indeed, the division between state and non-state is itself an important resource in political struggles. It enables issues to be defined as political or not, it enables state managers to deny responsibility for some issues but not others and to establish quangos for some purposes or involve its 'social partners' in managing others, it provides a basis for defenders of 'PRIVATE PROPERTY' or 'civil society' to resist state encroachment into the economy or civil society, and so forth. Despite (and because of) this variability, state discourses nonetheless serve to reproduce the distinction between state and society. Thereby they have a key role in shaping the state as a complex ensemble of political relations linked to society as a whole.

Whereas the origins of the state from a Weberian perspective coincide with the centralisation of legitimate control over organised coercion, for a discourse-theoretical analysis its origins are coeval with the political imaginary of the state. Yet both approaches tend to locate the rise of the modern Western state in the same period, one that links a consolidated absolutism and the rise of the constitutional state based on the rule of law. For Weberians, absolutism marks the centralisation of state power within a given territory at the expense of the estates system (*Ständestaat*) and/or autonomous cities; for discourse theorists, absolutism is linked to the distinction of an abstract, impersonal, sovereign state from other parts of society (notably the church, economy, and civil associations) and the distinction between man (initially in the gendered sense) in his capacity as private individual and as political citizen.

Locating the origins of the modern state in this period does, of course, pose problems about the premodern state. Are we justified in talking about the state before the semantics of the state emerged? This question can be answered affirmatively if we accept a minimum definition of the state as the institution involved in the effective territorialisation of political domination (Luhmann 1989). In this sense, the state can be contrasted with nomadic stateless societies (whether simple hunter and gatherer tribes or more complex nomadic herding and/or war-making societies); it develops with settled, territorially-rooted communities with state power being binding on all residents of that territory. This requires new forms of political organisation that go beyond household management and palace administration. In primitive or premodern political systems, such state power was typically identified with a specific personage, agency or institution (the *polis, communitas, civitas, regnum*, etc.). With the modern state, however, the state is regarded as an impersonal authority distinct both from the rulers in charge of the state for the time being (themselves subject to constitutions and state authority) and the ruled (who are distinct from the rulers and subject to state authority even where they have some say in choosing these rulers).

Models of state and democracy

Knowing how to define the state is only a first step in relating it to democratic thought. There are four main issues here. The first is whether any state could be said to be democratic. The second concerns typologies of the state, including its democratic and non-democratic forms. The third concerns the relationship between formal democratic institutions and the actual extent of democratic representation (see RE-PRESENTATION, CONCEPT OF) and ACCOUNT-ABILITY. The fourth concerns the future of democracy in the face of contemporary challenges both to its forms and its substance as organised at the level of the national sovereign state (see DEMOCRACY, FUTURE OF).

First, it is hard (if not impossible) to establish the democratic nature of the state when the latter is institutionally separated from the wider society and thus involves a division of labour between rulers and ruled. This poses a series of problems concerning the proper relationship between the logics of the political and other orders (for example, reasons of state and electoral logics versus the profit and loss logic of the market economy) and the nature and validity of political representation when this is unavoidably mediated through specific but highly variable forms of political organisation. In the absence of an unambiguous criterion for comparing the popular will and state policies, it is always problematic to know whether any state (in)action can be adjudged democratic. The normal response to this problem is to define democracy in formal procedural terms, that is, in terms of free and fair ELECTORAL COMPETITION among alternative political elites to control the state apparatus (Schumpeter 1943). Yet this solution simply provides a basis for conflicts over the democratic constitution and its associated procedures of election, representation and accountability.

Second, assuming that the modern state is at least a constitutional state based on the rule of law and has adopted democratic procedures, the next question concerns the forms of democratic state in an era of mass politics. An initial step is to distinguish 'normal' and 'exceptional' states. A normal state is one in which legitimacy is premised on a formally free competitive electoral principle and in which the sovereign DECISION-MAKING authority in the state is accountable to the electorate. In these cases the moment of popular consent predominates over the moment of state coercion. Conversely, an exceptional state is one that suspends both the electoral principle (apart from plebiscites and referendums controlled from above) and its associated plural party system, either during a state of emergency or indefinitely. The legitimacy of democratic principles in the modern era generally requires that any such suspension be declared temporary and attributed to a national emergency or threats to national SECURITY. The right to declare a state of emergency has also been used to define the locus of sovereignty (Schmitt 1985). A second step is to distinguish different types of normal and exceptional state according to which particular branch of the state apparatus is dominant and the forms of accountability, if any, that are involved. Thus democratic states might comprise (a) parliamentary systems (where the elected legislature is the dominant branch of the state); (b) executive systems (where the executive branch is dominant); and (c) constitutional systems (an ideal typical liberal nightwatchman state heavily constrained by a constitutional court). Exceptional states can be distinguished in turn in terms of the particular branch of the state apparatus that is dominant: examples include military dictatorships, political police states, one-party regimes, theocracies (dominated by a fundamentalist religious organisation) and Bonapartist regimes (dominated by the bureaucracy). But all exceptional states tend to share three further features besides the suspension of the electoral principle: a lack of constitutional or legal controls over the reorganisation of political institutions and the state's role in restructuring the wider society; close state control over the media, EDUCATION and other organs of opinion formation; and limitations on the separation of powers. Nonetheless, their legitimacy and longevity depend on the extent to which they can still mobilise and channel mass support, promote an ideology that unifies the rulers with a significant part of the ruled, and encourage limited forms of PLURALISM within the state apparatus so that competing interests and public opinion find some expression within them (see Poulantzas 1976).

Third, the distinction between normal and exceptional states is still rather formal. Thus we should also consider how power is exercised in these different regimes. Several competing empirical and/or normative models of state power are relevant here. If the state is seen largely as a simple, neutral instrument of government that is equally accessible to any political force and can be used for any purpose, it can be linked with elitist, pluralist and class perspectives on state power. Elitism regards all state power as organised around the basic political distinction between rulers and ruled. All forms of state entail the exercise of power by an elite over non-elites. At best, democracy would involve competition between elites for the right to rule. Pluralism denies that a single elite can monopolise political power and argues that power is inevitably dispersed and circulates among competing interests. It also suggests that an excessive concentration of power will trigger countervailing power and mobilisation.

This implies that the concentration of power is ultimately self-limiting and self-defeating because power provokes resistance. Pluralists also propose specific constitutional and institutional designs for the architecture of the state to secure most effective pluralist pressure on the state. In contrast, class analysts tend to argue against elitists that the ruling elite tends to be recruited from the class that controls the means of production or, at least, tends to represent its interests; and against pluralists, that it is the development of political class struggle that is the most important influence over state policies.

In contrast to these different versions of instrumentalism, the structural model argues that it is largely irrelevant which particular forces control the state. For the exercise of state power is heavily constrained by external forces and is more or less obliged to respect their interests. Some Marxist theorists, for example, argue that no state in a capitalist society could survive if it did not protect the profitability of capital, since economic growth is the source of its tax revenues and its legitimacy. Likewise, some feminist theorists argue that the state is inherently patriarchal because it is structurally rooted in a division between public and private that typically oppresses women (see PATRIARCHY AND DEMOCRACY).

An alternative to simple instrumentalism and crude structuralism is the view that the state comprises a strategically selective institutional ensemble, a set of institutions that may privilege some actors, some identities, some strategies, some spatial and temporal horizons and some actions over others (Jessop 1990), but one that is nonetheless open to different forces and different purposes to a limited, but changing and changeable, extent. This suggests that the exercise of state power always involves certain forms of bias (something inherent in the institutional architecture of the state) but that the nature and extent of these biases are shaped by the changing balance of political forces in struggle. It also allows for the influence of struggles to redesign the state (and its biases) and for the impact of struggles at a distance from the state that nonetheless indirectly influence the political calculations of state managers and other explicitly political forces.

Finally, many analyses of the democratic state in contemporary conditions take the nation-state (or national state) as their unit of analysis. Since the late 1980s, however, there has been growing interest in the crisis of this state form in an era of GLOBALISATION. This is associated in turn with calls to relocate democracy: either upward towards supranational bodies such as the European Union or even to the global level with a subsidiaritarian cosmopolitan democracy, downwards to local or regional communities (perhaps linked together in horizontal co-operation networks), or even into another dimension, that of cyberspace through virtual democratic communities. Although there are many proposals circulating for de-nationalisation of democracy, it is likely that the national territorial state (not to be confused with the nation-state) will continue to be the primary locus of democratic organisation for some years yet.

See also:

capitalism; civil society; cosmopolitan democracy; institutional design; nations and nationalism; security

Further reading

Bartelson, J. (1995) *A Genealogy of Sovereignty*, Cambridge: Cambridge University Press.

Evans, P.B., Rueschemeyer, D. and Skocpol, T. (eds) (1985) *Bringing the State Back In*, Cambridge: Cambridge University Press.

Jessop, B. (1990) *State Theory: Putting Capitalist States in Their Place*, Cambridge: Polity.

Luhmann, N. (1989) 'Staat und Staatsräson im Übergang von traditioneller Herrschaft zu moderner Politik', in N. Luhmann, *Gesellschaft und Semantik*, Frankfurt: Suhrkamp, Band 3, 65–148.

Mitchell, T.C. (1991) 'The Limits of the State: Beyond Statist Approaches and their Critics', *American Political Science Review* 85(1): 77–96.

Poulantzas, N. (1976) *Crisis of the Dictatorships*, London: New Left Books.

Schmitt, C. (1985) *Political Theology: Four Chapters on the Concept of Sovereignty*, trans. G. Schwab, Cambridge, MA: MIT Press.

Schumpeter, J.A. (1943) *Capitalism, Socialism, and Democracy*, London: Unwin.

Weber, M. (1948) 'Politics as a Vocation', in *From Max Weber: Essays in Sociology*, ed. H.H. Gerth and C.W. Mills, London: Routledge.

BOB JESSOP

state, relations of church to

Christianity, by contrast with Islam, offers no detailed political blueprint. Its founder envisaged perennial tension between the demands of God and Caesar but provided no unambiguous guidance as to how the problem might be tackled. Christian scriptures variously recommend political conformity and resistance. In practice, the Church's prevailing response has been politically conservative though a socially critical dimension never wholly disappeared. A decisive watershed was the Roman Empire's adoption of Christianity as its official religion. The Church then became a legitimator of political power within a hierarchical social order claiming divine sanction.

A still relevant divide emerged following the Empire's collapse. To the west, the Papacy developed as an autonomous institution presiding over a centralised Church supplying cultural unity to post-imperial kingdoms. It consequently became involved in sustained jurisdictional conflicts with rulers significantly dependent upon ecclesiastical legitimation. Eastern Byzantine emperors, claiming supreme divinely ordained power, presided over localised Orthodox churches lacking the institutional or theological resources needed effectively to challenge imperial rule. Subsequent experience of Islamic and, recently, of communist rule did not substantially alter this picture. Rather, Orthodox churches assumed the guardianship of distinctive Russian, Serb, Greek and other identities.

The Reformation shattered Western Christendom's unity and provisionally resolved Church–state disputes in the latter's favour. Where the Reformation triumphed, state-controlled churches supplanted the Catholic Church. Where Catholicism remained entrenched, monarchs asserted new controls over ecclesiastical institutions. The prevailing model (exported to the Spanish and Portuguese empires) envisaged co-terminous political and ecclesiastical communities in which subjects adopted the ruler's religion.

Monarchical AUTHORITY was now at least partially legitimated by appeals to the essentially secular concept of SOVEREIGNTY. The aim was to make claims for rulers overriding the potentially competing claims of religion. It was especially associated with absolute monarchies where the Catholic Church remained so linked to established authority that opposition acquired anti-clerical dimensions. Equally, following the French Revolution, partially secularised understandings of monarchical authority yielded to wholly secularised notions of popular sovereignty. The outcome in the ensuing era of European (and Latin American) mass politics was a fundamental anti-clerical versus clerical divide where Church–state disputes were part of wider disputes concerning the political order. Centre–left proponents of change advocated a religiously neutral state and the diminution of clerical influence. The Papacy initially repudiated all French Revolution-inspired ideologies and the Catholic Church, where it had been dominant, remained allied to conservative and sometimes anti-democratic elites.

Lutheran Protestantism long remained similarly conservative. Luther's own theology generally favoured political obedience. The outcome, notably in Germany, was legitimation of authoritarianism. Calvin's theocratic Geneva was also authoritarian but his theology was compatible with alternative possibilities. The concept of a divinely ordained lay 'elect' could, as in the South Africa of apartheid, underwrite political repression. But, as in mid-seventeenth-

century England and Scotland, it could inspire protest movements pointing ultimately to modern liberal understandings. British and North American LIBERALISM, associated with Locke, owed something to Renaissance humanism but also stemmed from reassessed Christian traditions emphasising personal RIGHTS, FREEDOM of conscience and hence ultimately facilitating acceptance of religious TOLERATION and political PLURALISM.

An initial twentieth-century outcome of Catholic responses was, as in Fascist Italy and Franco's Spain, support for right-wing dictatorships. Church–state concordats granted the Church a legally protected status in return for recognition of existing power holders. In Germany, the Catholic Church joined many Protestants in initially accepting Nazi rule.

Since the Second World War, Church–state relationships have been the subject of sometimes unprecedented reassessments. Three explanatory factors are discernible. First, and especially in Europe, has been the impact of long-term secularising processes tending to erode traditional solidarities and to undermine institutionalised religion's socio-political significance. To varying degrees, and across the erstwhile 'Cold War' divide, religious practice has declined together with the authority of religious leaders. The consequent loosening of ties to established secular elites could facilitate an enhanced freedom to espouse socially and politically critical attitudes.

Second, Europe's experience of fascism facilitated new democratic forms of political engagement which, amidst secularisation processes, had long-term and often unforeseen consequences for religious authority. Franco's and Salazar's initially Catholic supported dictatorships remained (within Europe) as anachronisms. Elsewhere, in countries with large Catholic communities, the Church encouraged Christian Democratic Parties. West Germany's Christian Democratic Union purposefully embraced Protestants.

Such PARTIES signified lay EMANCIPATION from clerical tutelage. In Italy, for example, clerical leadership was eventually repudiated by many even in such ecclesiastically sensitive matters as divorce. In post-communist Poland, the Catholic hierarchy has faced similar difficulties despite close links between Church and nation during anti-communist resistance. Italian Christian Democracy's final collapse signals a further step in the elimination of traditional forms of political engagement.

Third, wartime experiences plus the emergence of post-colonial Churches, frequently in non-privileged minority positions, fostered an embryonic cross-confessional and international ecclesiastical consensus concerning socio-political matters that, in secular terms, is of a new left-leaning kind. The World Council of Churches, most notably, adopted radical socio-economic positions. It similarly promoted internationalist attitudes and the questioning of traditional nationalistic claims. A major Roman Catholic watershed was the Second Vatican Council (1962–5), which legitimated new radical Catholic political movements sometimes open to collaboration with the secular left. Portions of some Catholic hierarchies have embraced similarly radical attitudes. The most radical outcomes have been in Latin American and other 'Third World' contexts. Catholic leaders and activists have there sometimes been in the vanguard of opposition to military authoritarianism (see MILITARY CONSTITUTIONALISM).

Pope John Paul II has presided over a period of ecclesiastical reaction. Some post-Vatican trends, however, seem irreversible and the Papacy itself has emerged as an obviously global institution officially committed to human rights, democratic governance and radical critiques of CAPITALISM. Such changes represent both institutional adjustments to a changing environment and a major reappraisal of inherited practices. They have found expression in a reassertion of the Church's public role as critic of established elites and structures. At the level of formal Church–state relations they are expressed in an international cross-confessional tendency to reduce ecclesiastical reliance on state protection and correspondingly to increase Church autonomy. The Catholic Church in, for example, Spain has abandoned traditional concordats. Swedish Lutheran

moves toward disestablishment and the Church of England's evolving synodical system point in the same direction. Greece provides an example of an Orthodox church beginning to query conventional ties.

Enhanced ecclesiastical autonomy generally coexists with continuing, though re-defined preferences, for political consensus conducive to liberal democracy's maintenance. The bridging of old clerical versus anti-clerical divides and the depoliticisation of old confessional differences have clearly tended to strengthen democratic institutions. Equally, the general presumption in established liberal democracies is that governments will no longer obviously favour particular belief systems in ways likely to promote destabilising conflicts. The detailed arrangements regulating Church–state relationships vary, however, according to local historical, constitutional, legal and political circumstances. The one common factor is that Church and state can, in reality, never be wholly indifferent to each other's existence. Thus the United States maintains a theoretically rigid Church–state separation that, in practice and given widespread religiosity, can discriminate against believers in such a sensitive matter as EDUCATION. Similarly, France has a formal Church–state separation, reflected in a strongly secular public educational system, but which allows for municipal care of Church buildings and the religious commemoration of a deceased socialist president. Germany, by partial contrast, though lacking a state church, officially recognises both Catholic and Protestant communities and relies heavily on state funded but Church-provided educational and social services. Non-Christian believers, however, lack such levels of public recognition. The Dutch state is similarly related to churches while deliberately offering equal support to non-Christian and secular bodies. Denmark, by further contrast and despite notably advanced secularisation processes, raises taxes to support a single state church whose clergy are classified as civil servants, which registers the births of all citizens, irrespective of belief and which, in the absence of its own national governmental institutions, answers to parliament via a ministerial department. Yet again, England has an established Church that receives no direct state financial assistance, has its own synods but has retained episcopal representatives in the House of Lords.

Outstanding questions arise out of politically relevant divisions now cutting across the boundaries separating not only Christian churches but also the other great world religions. One concerns the division between those who view religion as an individualistic private affair and those seeing it as retaining a legitimate public role, helping to define the terms of democratic debate, to nurture democratically oriented civil societies, to reassess traditional national identities and even to foster transnational political linkages. Another concerns the tension between believers disposed to accept the demands of democratic pluralism or debate and those religious conservatives or fundamentalists disposed, to varying degrees, to use state power to impose a single moral vision. Orthodox religious groups in Israel and the 'religious right' in the USA keep this issue on the agenda of well-established non-European democracies. Postcolonial immigration by Islamic and other non-Christian groups puts it firmly onto the agenda of European democracies. The issue, in often acute form, is faced by many emergent 'Third World' and especially African or Asian democracies. The outcome of the relevant debates has implications for democracy's long-term viability. The persistence of the debates underlines the perennially significant character of the tensions between religious and POLITICAL OBLIGATION.

See also:

authority; Christian democracy; nations and nationalism; pluralism; state, models of

Further reading

Buchanan, T. and Conway, M. (eds) (1996) *Political Catholicism in Europe, 1918–1965*, Oxford: Clarendon Press.
Casonova, J. (1994) *Public Religions in the Modern World*, Chicago: University of Chicago Press.
DeGruchy, J.W. (1995) *Christianity and Democracy*, Cambridge: Cambridge University Press.
Monsma, S.V. and Sopa, J.C. (1997) *The Challenge of Pluralism: Church and State in Five Democracies*, Oxford: Rowman and Littlefield.
Moyser, G.H. (ed.) (1991) *Religion and Politics in the Modern World*, London: Routledge.
Skinner, Q. (1978) *The Foundations of Modern Political Thought*, 2 vols, Cambridge, Cambridge University Press.

KENNETH MEDHURST

statelessness

People who are forced to live outside the state of their origin and are restricted from transferring their CITIZENSHIP, or are born in a state which does not recognise their identity on an equal footing with all other members of that society, are often referred to as being stateless. Exiles, refugees, asylum seekers, migrants and even indigenous peoples are often placed under this category. What they all have in common is the painful and unjust experience of being exposed to discrimination and exploitation.

Statelessness has been often defined as a diminished form of existence. Poets and politicians representing stateless people stress that being stateless is like being stripped of the most vital qualities of your culture and identity (Said 1993). It refers to not just the physical displacement from the homeland but also the cultural, political, economic and personal RIGHTS that are attached with belonging to a nation-state. Being cut off from their homeland and forced to speak in a foreign language can inspire both nostalgic and critical thoughts about the relationship between identity and culture. Assumptions and everyday values which are 'taken for granted' in their homeland are always challenged by the condition of statelessness. Thus the condition of statelessness is defined by the physical and cultural separation from the homeland. It is one of the most profound paradoxes of the modern period that the strongest artistic expressions has come from people who have become stateless or who have chosen to leave their homeland (Bhabha 1995).

The modern use for the word homeland is predicated on the existence of a nation-state. However, for every state that is recognised by the United Nations there are countless more ethnic groups whose homeland has no formal recognition. Vast numbers of people are stateless not only because they have taken flight from their own nation but because their homeland was never constituted as a nation. For instance, the historical homeland of the Kurdish people is now spread across the boundaries of at least three other nations. The indigenous peoples of Australia have also struggled to maintain their own sense of homeland in a context of ongoing displacement by the invading presence of European settlers. While the Australian state eventually recognised the indigenous peoples as citizens, this has not erased the trauma of the past nor altered the structural inequalities that prevent them from feeling at home in their own homeland.

As the territory of the world has been completely divided into the discrete spaces of various nation-states it is now impossible to live outside of a state (Giddens 1985). However, the entry to states and the access to rights within states are not universally defined in terms of human rights. States discriminate between citizens and strangers. Some states confer citizenship in relation to ethnicity rather than to birthplace, and all states distinguish between wanted and unwanted strangers. Tourists and foreign corporate representatives who travel relatively freely across national borders cannot be described as living in a condition of statelessness.

However different the degrees of suffering experienced in this condition, it is important to identify the scale of the problem. The number of people living outside of their homeland increased dramatically throughout the twentieth century. In 1990, according to the International Organisation for Migration, there were 80 million people who were defined as international migrants. In 1995 the United Nations High Commission on Refugees also estimated that there were 27 million refugees. For the last twenty years the number of refugees has quadrupled every decade. By 1997 the number of refugees worldwide had increased by another 4 million to stand at 31 million. These calculations do not include the estimated 24 million people displaced by violence and persecution and who have become homeless within their own countries. Some commentators consider these statistics as being too limited, for they fail to capture the full numbers of displaced people and are unable to record the ongoing consequences for families and communities (Castles and Miller 1993). In historical terms, the condition of statelessness has never been as widespread, and as consistently worsening, as it is at present.

The trajectory of GLOBALISATION is often outlined in terms of a borderless world. New COMMUNICATION technologies, the restructuring of patterns of economic production and the turbulent patterns of global migration are seen as indicators of the reduced effectiveness of the nation-state. Despite the uneven history of the nation-state in defining and defending the rights of all its members to enjoy common rights of belonging, there are still no supranational institutions of governance which offer more effective forms of protection and association (Held 1995). Nation-states still regulate movement across the BOUNDARIES of their territory, organise armies to defend their territory and police conduct within their territory. Globalisation may have diminished the AUTONOMY of the nation-states to control these activities, but it has not rendered the nation-state an obsolete geo-political unit. The condition of statelessness has not been diminished with the advent of globalisation; on the contrary, due to the growing illegal forms of migration and the disruption of traditional communities, it has both proliferated and made the edges of its experience more jagged (Papastergiadis 2000).

See also:

assimilation; identity, political; inclusion/exclusion; partition; political frontiers

Further reading

Bhabha, H. (1995) *The Location of Culture*, London: Routledge.

Castles, S. and Miller, M. (1993) *The Age of Migration*, London: Macmillan.

Giddens, A. (1985) *The Nation-State and Violence*, Cambridge: Polity Press.

Held, D. (1995) *Democracy and the Global Order: From the Modern State to Cosmopolitan Governance*, Cambridge: Polity Press.

Papastergiadis, N. (2000) *The Turbulence of Migration*, Cambridge: Polity Press.

Said, E. (1993) *Culture and Imperialism*, London: Chatto and Windus.

NIKOS PAPASTERGIADIS

subsidiarity

Definition

Subsidiarity espouses two interrelated aspects of social and political life. One concerns the relationship between man and society, stressing the growth of the individual in society, with the aim of protecting the individual against an excessively corporate state structure or assistance from the state for those in need. The second aspect relates to a sharing of power between different levels of government. Here subsidiarity implies a need to determine the DECISION-MAKING tier at which each problem can be most effectively or appropriately tackled, the possibility ranging from local, regional, national or European levels.

Subsidiarity is connected with the Latin term of *subsidium* or *subsidiarius*, which initially meant something in reserve and later acquired the sense of assistance or aid to those in trouble. As this derivation of the word indicates, the notion of subsidiarity can contain positive connotations, as it envisaged the intervention of forces for the benefit of those in trouble (Endo 1994: 632).

The principle of subsidiarity has its philosophical roots in natural and positive law, central to which is the idea that the nature and character of human beings is achieved through their individual and social drive (Wilke and Wallace 1990: 13). The foundations of subsidiarity can thus be located in the relationship of subsidiarity with human dignity, CORPORATISM, liberty and personalism.

History

In historical terms, the notion of subsidiarity can be traced back to Aristotle and Thomas Aquinas in their writings on justice (Millon-Delsol 1990). Between the seventeenth and nineteenth centuries, concerns with the extent of state power led Althusisus (a Dutch Calvinist), John Locke, Montesquieu and J.S. Mill to stress the need for the sharing of power between national and local levels. In the early twentieth century, it was the Roman Catholic Church which, in seeking to protect the individual and the family against the omnipresent state, enhanced the meaning and application of subsidiarity in social and political life. More recently, the principle of subsidiarity has provoked an intense debate about the centralising or decentralising nature of the European Union.

Suprisingly few books exist on the subject, and of those the majority date back to the 1950s; the use of articles becomes more common in the 1970s. However, whereas the earlier books deal mostly with socio-philosophical or legal aspects, the articles nearly exclusively focus attention upon EU matters (Endo 1994: 648).

Principal ideas

Subsidiarity, as used by Locke, Montesquieu and Mill, encapsulated both the idea that the state should not intervene unless it was necessary and the idea that the state should intervene when it was necessary, raising issues of efficiency and general well-being. Many tasks of government ought not to be controlled by central authorities alone and should be shared between central and local bodies. Mill (1861) saw local government as often better informed about what electors want, and as more accountable.

For the Roman Catholic Church, the principle of subsidiarity is linked to the well-being of individuals and families. Particularly privileged rights are given by nature to the individual or the family and when these rights have priority over state law, it is the principle of subsidiarity which is to ensure these rights. Subsequently, certain domains of initiative and action should not be subject to interference from either state or society.

Subsidarity in the European Union context is enshrined in the core ideas of peace, democracy, prosperity and supranationalism. However, initially it was based heavily on the concept of FEDERALISM, and only in the 1990s developed as a concern with citizen PARTICIPA- TION and support.

Development

Subsidiarity as it originated with the Roman Catholic Church was primarily concerned with the ordering of relationships between the public authorities and civil societies (Endo 1994: 614). However, the limitation of the activities of the higher organisation was stressed more than its duty of intervention, that is, emphasising the negative rather than the positive interventions of the state. The importance of the positive implication is more fully developed by Jacques Delors (1991: 9), who argued that subsidiarity is not simply a limit to intervention by a higher authority *vis-à-vis* a person or a community in a position to act itself, it is also an obligation for this AUTHORITY to act *vis-à-vis* this person or this group to see that it is given the means to achieve its ends.

While the Catholic Church was primarily concerned with its own AUTONOMY and that of occupational groups (for example, guilds) and the family, the conceptual focus of subsidiarity began gradually to shift after the Second World

War from this non-territorial scheme to the territorial one or the context of federalism, i.e. the division of powers among several levels such as the EU, the state, the region and the local authority. The German Basic Law of 1949 became one of the first important expressions of this fusion between subsidiary and federalism. However, it is interesting to note that the German constitution never explicitly used the term.

With the expansion of central government policy tasks during the late 1960s and early 1970s, subsidiarity temporarily lost its importance (Genesko 1986). With the rise of neoliberalism in the 1970s, this trend was reversed. It was also during this period that, implicitly and explicitly, subsidiarity began to figure in the debate with the EU, linked with questions about the appropriate competencies of the EU and the criteria for the allocation of powers to different levels of government, supranational, national and regional. Most prominent among the early debating initiatives were the Spinelli Draft Treaty on European Union, the Mac-Dougall Report (analysis of fiscal federalism), and the Tindemans Report on European Union.

Evaluation

What counts as GOOD PRACTICE? There are two dimensions to the subsidiarity principle in the EU context. First, the Treaty of European Union (Articles B and 3b) provides for action by the EU outside areas of its exclusive competence only if and insofar as the objective cannot be achieved by the member states and can therefore, by reason of scale or effects of the proposed action, be better achieved by the EU. The common policies (agriculture, external trade and so on) provided for in the Treaty of Rome, the creation of a frontier-free area and the flanking policies provided for in the Single European Act; all these initiatives have been fully justified by the imperatives of European INTEGRATION.

However, the dividing line between exclusive and concurrent competencies is blurred. The area of exclusive competence continues to be a problem, particularly because it is not laid down in the Treaties by reference to specific fields, but by means of functional description. The question of whether a matter is outside the limits of EU competence cannot be answered without touching upon essential political questions concerning what the scope of Community Law should be and who should exercise power in a particular field (de Burca 1998: 220). Legislative or executive bodies would therefore have to be in charge of judging the necessity of EU action.

Second, by ensuring that the level of decision-making and action is commensurate with the objective pursued, the subsidiarity principle enables the member states to avoid EU interventionism where EU legislation is not necessary. Accordingly, each proposal, whether in an area of exclusive or shared competence, must be put to the so-called PROPORTIONALITY test; that is, whether rules and regulations go into excessive detail and could be dealt with by a more flexible instrument such as a recommendation or code of conduct, instead of a binding legal instrument. This is most visible in the completion of the internal market, in which national legislation will not be replaced but framed in a way that respects minimum EU requirements (mutual recognition). Other examples involve economic and monetary union, where reference is made to a European system of central banks as distinct from a single, by implication centralised, European Central Bank, and the reference to subsidiarity in the Charter for Fundamental Social Rights.

The application of subsidiarity in the EU context has expanded over time not only with regard to proportionality, but can also be seen in the establishment of the Committee of the Regions in the 1990s. Similarly, it can be noted that in Germany, in response to the EU Internal Market programme, the principle has been effectively strengthened, enabling the states, through an amendment of the German Constitution, to participate at the EU Council of Ministers level in matters (for example, environment, media broadcasting and so on) where the states have exclusive competencies. Because of reunification, the principle of subsidiarity was also put to new task in inner German relations, especially with regard to the working of fiscal federalism. It will be interesting to see whether similar features will be adopted both in Belgium and the United Kingdom after the introduction of devolution.

Summary

There is fundamental disagreement about the very nature of the concept of subsidiarity and consequently, not only about what it means but, as importantly, how it can be applied in practice (Hearl 1996: 4). The principle is politically complex and legally uncertain (de Burca 1998: 218). Part of the complex nature relates to the fact that subsidiarity is not a stand-alone principle. It has been linked both in theory and practice to notions of SOLIDARITY and JUSTICE, and in the EU context to democracy, TRANSPARENCY and openness. Subsequently, these linkages require a broad definition. However, when attempting such a definition, problems in the operationalisation occur. This is particularly evident with regard to the legal status of subsidiarity. Should the subsidiarity principle be 'pinned down' or rather be debatable and negotiable? Marc Wilke and Helen Wallace (1990: 5) provide a plausible answer by suggesting that in essence subsidiarity is a socio-political term, not a constitutional principle. In other words, they see it is a guideline to be applied in combination with other relevant principles of social action, such as stewardship or justice.

Another issue over which there is much confusion is whether subsidiarity has centralising or decentralising tendencies. Clearly, it can be identified with both (Schwartz 1990). Centralisation can deal with externalities (costs or benefits not taken account of by trade, such as the effect of lax environmental rules in one country on pollution in another) (CEPR 1993). However, most references to subsidiarity by either national, regional or local governments intend to seek guarantees against perceived encroachments on SOVEREIGNTY from the EU. These somewhat excessive endeavours have even resulted in attempts for derogation on internal market rules which, if granted by the European Commission, would clearly undermine the core philosophy of the single market.

It is important in this context to differentiate between a priori or *ad hoc* procedures. As Andrew Cox (1994: 137) correctly points out, the real test of whether the EU institutions or member states should be the competent body to make and implement policy rests, not on any a priori assumption about rights, but on whether or not agreed aims of policy are best achieved by supranational rather than national action. In his view, the failure of subsidiarity in policy-making occurs when either the aims of policy are overtaken by the desire to defend constitutional rights about sovereignty, or supranational and national institutions are used to maintain discriminatory national behaviour against other member states. This suggests that decisions about subsidiarity need to be made on a case-by-case basis about the levels at which policy may be devised and implemented most effectively. However, while subsidiarity rests on the EU's diversity, it also presupposes a sufficient convergence of values and it would be unrealistic to expect it to solve intractable political conflicts. It is only where basic objectives are defined that subsidiarity can give clear guidance as to the allocation of competence.

Further reading

CEPR (1993) *Making Sense of Subsidiarity: How Much Centralisation for Europe?*, Monitoring European Integration 4, A CEPR Annual Report.

Cox, A. (1994) 'Derogation, Subsidiarity and the Single Market', *Journal of Common Market Studies* 32(2): 127–48.

De Burca, G. (1998) 'The Principle of Subsidiarity and the Court of Justice as an Institutional Actor', *Journal of Common Market Studies* 36(2): 217–36.

Delors, J. (1991) 'The Principle of Subsidiarity: Contribution to the Debate', in J. Delors *et al.* (eds), *Subsidiarity: The Challenges of Change (Proceedings of the Jacques Delors Colloquium 1991)*, Maastricht: European Institute for Public Administration.

Endo, K. (1994) 'The Principle of Subsidiarity: From Johannes Altusius to Jacques Delors', *The Hokkaido Law Review* 44(6): 553–652.

Genesko, J. (1986) *Der wechselnde Einfluss des Subsidiaritaetsprinzip auf die wirtschafts und sozialpolitische Praxis in der Bundesrepublik Deutschland*, Stuttgart: G. Fischer Verlag.

Hearl, D. (1996) 'Crisis or Opportunity? Subsidiarity, The Public and the Credibility Gap' a discussion paper of the Jean Monnet Group of Experts, Hull, Centre for European Union Studies, University of Hull.

Mill, J.S. (1861) *Representative Government*, London: Parker Son and Bourn.

Millon-Delsol, C. (1990) 'Le principe de subsidiarité: origines et fondements', Institut La Boetie, No. 4.

Schwartz, P. (1990) 'Is the Principle of Subsidiarity a Solution?', in F. Goguel *et al.*, *A Europe for Europeans*, London: The Bruges Group.

Stadler, H. (1951) *Subsidiaritaetsprinzip und Foederalismus*, Freiburg: Universitätsbuchhandlung.

Wilke, M. and Wallace, H. (1990) 'Subsidiarity: Approaches to Power-sharing in the European Community', RIIA Discussion Papers, No. 27.

EMIL KIRCHNER

suffrage

The suffrage (also called 'franchise') is the right to vote. Since voting is the main method by which ordinary citizens exercise power in democracies, a central question in democratic theory and practice has always been how extensive should the suffrage be.

The central meaning of the word 'franchise' is a privilege granted to the few; the word is used for the right to vote because until recently, even within democracies, the vote was seen as a privilege to be restricted to an appropriate elite. Athens in the fifth century BC and the USA in 1860 are normally described as democracies, yet probably less than 20 per cent of the adult population had votes. In the mid-nineteenth century, the only people with votes in 'democracies' were adult (usually white) property-owning males; the franchise has since been gradually extended to incorporate propertyless males, women, and relevant racial and religious MINORITIES.

Surprisingly, perhaps, there are no major works of democratic theory that advocate universal suffrage; indeed, most of them take pains to exclude a considerable proportion of the population (for example, Mill (1820) and Mill (1861)). Universal suffrage did not come about as an application of settled democratic theory. Instead, the franchise was extended piecemeal, as the result of successful agitation for inclusion by specific excluded groups: thus the suffragettes achieved votes for women in Britain early in the twentieth century, and in the 1960s the civil rights movement won votes for blacks in the southern USA. Cynics allege that extensions of the franchise usually occurred for electoral gain: PARTIES would enfranchise their natural supporters, or hope that the new voters would, from gratitude, vote for whoever had enfranchised them. The public rhetoric offered was that groups could have the privilege of the vote because they had somehow earned it (often by participation in a war); or because they were no longer perceived as a threat to the established order; or because they were thought of as more of a threat if unenfranchised.

Yet it is now usually thought that democracy requires universal suffrage. New democracies assume that universal suffrage is a requirement of being democratic, and that it must follow from some principle of democratic theory. The usual candidate for such a principle is that everybody affected by political decisions should have a say in those decisions (or, in a representative democracy, should have a say in choosing those who make the decisions). In other words, it is undemocratic – indeed, tyrannical – for a decision that vitally affects some people to be made without those people having a say in it.

Unfortunately, there are currently a number of important ways in which all democracies infringe this principle, without apparent concern. Perhaps the most blatant follows from the fact that the effects of political decisions are not neatly contained within the BOUNDARIES of a state: thus, if my democratic state has to decide whether to build a power station that will poison the air in your neighbouring democratic state, you will not have a vote on the decision even though the effects will be felt more by you than by me. Similarly, the effects of the foreign policy of the USA are felt more by the rest of the world than by the American electorate; and yet the rest of the world has no vote to help determine American foreign policy. Further, the suffrage is necessarily restricted to people currently alive, and yet the resulting decisions could have huge effects on future generations: to decide, for instance, to adopt technology that gave us cheap energy but produced lethal levels of nuclear radiation in 100 years time would simply be inter-generational tyranny.

Even if we make the clearly unrealistic assumption that the effects of political decisions are restricted in both time and space, there are still several ways in which the principle is still widely flouted. One is that all children are disenfranchised, and yet children are certainly affected by state decisions. Indeed, they are expressly prohibited from doing many things that adults can do, without themselves having any say in the matter: this exactly fits the definition of tyranny given above. Also many adults who are clearly affected by state decisions are disenfranchised in most states: both some categories of citizens (for instance, the insane, criminals, and ex-criminals) and most non-citizens (however long they have lived in the country). Conversely, non-resident citizens, who are not affected by domestic decisions, are often allowed a vote; it has even recently been proposed (in, for instance, Ireland and South Korea) that the franchise should be extended to non-resident non-citizens who are descended from emigrants.

So, the principle of universal suffrage is less obvious and less respected than many think. We need therefore to investigate what reasons can be given for universal suffrage, or whether there are reasons for awarding the vote to some and denying it to others.

The most obvious argument for universal suffrage would seem to be that the right to vote is a natural right that needs no further defence. This, however, cannot work. First, invoking a natural right does not provide an *argument*; it is simply an assertion, and one that will not persuade anyone disinclined to agree with the assertion: natural rights can be denied as easily as they are claimed. Second, any supposedly 'self-evident' natural right cannot help in resolving the borderline cases mentioned above; these need more careful argumentation. But in any case, the right to vote is not the sort of thing that can sensibly be a natural right at all. As Mill (1861) amongst many others has pointed out, to vote in an election is necessarily to attempt to exercise power over others, for it is an attempt to gain control of the state; and the state claims the right to tax people (against their will) and even conscript them into the army (against their will) and send them to fight and be killed. No natural rights theorist has claimed that anyone has the natural right to force someone else to die on their behalf. The right to vote cannot be a natural right.

The main alternative to a natural rights view is utilitarianism. On this view democracy is to be preferred because (and insofar as) it produces outcomes that are the best for all concerned. If we are favouring democracy because it produces desirable outcomes, then obviously the franchise should be limited to those who will use it wisely. Since the vote can be a means of coercing others, there are reasons for restricting it to those who will not misuse it; just as we require a licence to drive a car or own a gun – and this licence can be withdrawn if we are thought likely to use the car or gun to damage others – so there should be limits on those who can vote. Thus it has been suggested that only the literate (and maybe numerate) should be allowed to vote. It has also been argued that anyone who is clearly unable to run their own life (such as a child, or a claimant of poor relief) should not be given the power to make decisions affecting other people's lives. That is, there should be some test of competence, and only those who pass it should have the vote. Arguments of this form are the normal basis for denying the vote to young teenagers: reject the idea of limiting the franchise to the competent, and it would seem that we have to extend the franchise to include very young children indeed.

The main objections to such tests are not objections of principle, but of practice. It is very difficult (and contentious) to determine exactly what is an unacceptable use of a vote; a problem less marked with cars and guns. (For this reason, the US Supreme Court has declared it constitutionally impermissible to 'fence out' a sector of the population because of the way they may vote.) It is also difficult to establish what competencies are required in order to use the vote satisfactorily.

That few now accept the idea of a competence requirement (apart from for children) is in large part because it was consistently misapplied. A fundamental error was that it was used to disenfranchise general categories of people (such as blacks or women). This was easily discredited: advocates of women's suffrage could rightly argue that it was inconsistent to deem a woman with a university degree incompetent, while declaring the stupidest man competent. The right way to use a competence test is, on the analogy with gun and car licences, to test all adults (and any children who care to apply) on an individual basis, and all (and only) those who pass the test have the vote. But when there has been an attempt to do this (as with the literacy test in the American south) it has invariably been misused by those in power to exclude those they disliked or disagreed with. Although in principle some sort of competence test might be defensible, if impartially applied, the practice has been so deplorable that the idea has been discredited.

A lesson can be learned from this: that those who have the vote are always likely to succumb to the temptation to exploit those from whom it is withheld. This is a powerful argument for having as wide a franchise as possible. The vote can be seen not as implicitly coercive, but rather as necessary to defend oneself, to give oneself a voice. Those who do not have the vote can be all too easily ignored by those who exercise power; and if they are ignored their interests will not be taken into account (Thomson 1825; Mill 1861). This is not an argument of principle for a wide franchise, but one based on the empirical belief that those who *can* be ignored all too often *will* be ignored.

There is a further important aspect to the franchise. This is that to deny the vote to someone when most people have it is demeaning to that person: to be singled out as unfit to have a vote, in the absence of good reason, is unacceptably insulting. This was well put by Frederick Douglass, a black opponent of slavery who argued that if he was in a 'monarchical government... where the few... ruled and the many were subject, there would be no special stigma resting upon me, because I did not exercise the elective franchise'. However, he goes on to state that in the USA where universal suffrage is an idea that is fundamental to the government, 'to rule us out is to make us an exception, to brand us with the stigma of inferiority'. The vote is, then, an emblem of public recognition and respect even more than it is an instrument for exercising political power; and disenfranchisement is a symbol of rejection (Shklar 1991).

This idea helps explain the gradual extension of the franchise in the nineteenth and twentieth centuries: as more became enfranchised, it became more insulting to be excluded. The exclusion of teenagers is less insulting, because it is only for a few years: no statement is being made about the lack of worth of the persons themselves. However, it is indefensible to exclude resident aliens, guest workers and ex-convicts. Conversely, the desire to give the franchise to non-resident citizens (and ethnically related non-citizens) is done (when not done simply for political gain) out of a desire to include these people within the body politic.

Near-universal suffrage is now an accepted part of the definition of democracy, but unfortunately there is no simple argument of principle in its favour. Rather, it is now taken for granted because limitations of the franchise were so blatantly abused in the past. If we cannot construct a fair and impartial competence test, then we must extend the franchise to every person who is significantly affected by political decisions.

See also:

citizenship; elections; empowerment; inclusion/exclusion; rights; rights, minority and indigenous; statelessness

Further reading

Dahl, R.A. (1979) 'Procedural Democracy', in P. Laslett and J.S. Fishkin (eds), *Philosophy, Politics and Society*, fifth series, Oxford: Blackwell.

Goodin, R.E. (1992) *Motivating Political Morality*, Oxford: Blackwell.

Mayo, H.B. (1960) *An Introduction to Democratic Theory*, Oxford: Oxford University Press.

Mill, J. (1820) 'Essay on Government', in J. Mill, *Political Writings*, Cambridge: Cambridge University Press.

Mill, J.S. (1861) *Considerations on Representative Government*, New York: Prometheus Books, 1991.

Note (1989) 'The Disenfranchisement of Ex-Felons', *Harvard Law Review* 102: 1300–17.

Raskin, J.B. (1993) 'Legal Aliens, Local Citizens: The Historical, Constitutional and Theoretical Meanings of Alien Suffrage', *University of Pennsylvania Law Review* 141: 1391–1470.

Shklar, J. (1991) *American Citizenship: The Quest for Inclusion*, Cambridge, MA: Harvard University Press.

Thomson, W. (1825) *Appeal of One-Half the Human Race, Women*, London: Virago, 1983.

Walzer, M. (1983) *Spheres of Justice*, Oxford: Blackwell, ch. 2.

Weale, A. (1999) *Democracy*, London: Macmillan, ch. 8.

PETER MORRISS

T

toleration

Toleration consists in allowing, or refraining from interfering with, actions and opinions which one dislikes or disapproves of. The presence of dislike or disapproval is crucial for distinguishing between toleration on the one hand, and indifference or licence on the other. Toleration also implies that the person tolerating has the power to interfere, but refrains from using that power. Politics frequently provides contexts in which toleration is prudent or expedient: for instance, in some circumstances, it might be the only alternative to civil unrest and strife. However, in liberal political theory, toleration is often held to be not merely expedient but morally right. This claim is problematic, for it is difficult to see how it can be morally right to permit what is (or is believed to be) morally wrong. The problem of toleration, then, is the problem of explaining when and why things thought to be wrong ought nevertheless to be permitted. It is the problem of showing how it can be right to allow what is wrong.

Although the problem of toleration arises over many kinds of disagreement, it has its historical origins in the context of specifically religious disagreement. One of the first and most influential discussions of toleration is to be found in John Locke's seventeenth-century work, *Epistola de Tolerantia* (Letter Concerning Toleration). The *Letter*, which was first published anonymously in 1689, was written while Locke was in exile in the Netherlands, and it is an attempt, born partly of Locke's own experience of religious persecution, to defend toleration in principle and as something more than a political expedient in the interests of

civil harmony. Locke's discussion is confined to the toleration of religious difference, and he argues that since religion is essentially a matter of individual belief; since political power cannot effect a change in belief, the persecution or intolerance of religious dissenters is fundamentally irrational. The persecutor employs means inappropriate to his end when he attempts, via threats and force, to induce others to change their religious beliefs, for belief is not subject to the will, nor is it amenable to threat. Although the *Letter* is a very significant contribution to the literature on toleration, the argument it presents is restricted in three ways: firstly, it focuses exclusively on religious intolerance and says nothing about other forms of intolerance; secondly, it is designed to display the irrationality of persecution, not its moral wrongness; thirdly, it says nothing about the positive value of diversity.

John Stuart Mill's nineteenth-century essay *On Liberty* is more wide-ranging in all three respects. Mill is concerned with toleration in general and does not restrict himself to religious toleration. He also differs from Locke in being concerned with the moral wrong inherent in intolerance, not merely its alleged irrationality. And he emphasises the positive value of diversity and insists that it is good that there should be different ways of life and a variety of 'experiments in living'. Although (as its title implies) Mill's work focuses on liberty in general not toleration in particular, its arguments have set the agenda for modern discussions of toleration, and it is in *On Liberty* that we find the seeds of the most powerful defences of toleration as a virtue of liberal societies, not merely a pragmatic response to the facts of diversity and conflict. These defences are of three main kinds: the argument from scepticism, the argument from NEUTRAL-ITY and the argument from AUTONOMY.

The argument from scepticism

It is often thought that toleration is a concomitant of moral scepticism. The fact that we cannot know, or at least cannot be sure, what is morally right suggests that toleration is the appropriate response to diversity and conflict. However, historically speaking, scepticism has not always been closely allied to toleration, nor certainty to intolerance. Thus, Locke's defence of toleration was mounted against a background of moral and religious certainty, and similarly Mill argues that a commitment to toleration is compatible with commitment to moral and religious truth. Indeed, for Mill, one of the main arguments in favour of toleration is that it will encourage the discovery of truth and will also sustain truth, once discovered, as a lively belief and not merely as dead dogma. By contrast, sceptics have often been intolerant, or committed to toleration only on the pragmatic grounds that it promotes civil peace. Where those pragmatic grounds falter, scepticism will dictate intolerance. Thus, the argument from scepticism can provide, at best, only a limited and pragmatic defence of toleration. It cannot show why toleration is morally required.

The argument from neutrality

A second defence of toleration is to be found in the concept of neutrality. The guiding thought here is that modern democratic societies contain people who subscribe to a variety of diverse and conflicting 'conceptions of the good'. They are societies in which different people have very different religious, moral and philosophical beliefs. This variety is not something to be despised or lamented, but is natural and inevitable, and the role of the liberal state is to provide a neutral arena in which people may, so far as possible, pursue their conceptions of the good unhindered by others.

This commitment to diversity is manifest in Mill's *On Liberty* and is also a characteristic of many modern defences of toleration. For example, John Rawls takes the fact of PLURALISM as the initial premise of his defence of political LIBERALISM, where he notes that democratic societies are marked by a diversity of opposing and irreconcilable religious, philosophical and moral doctrines. Moreover, since many of these doctrines are reasonable, the democratic state must be tolerant of them and must aspire to neutrality between them.

Though influential, this defence of toleration is problematic in a number of ways. Firstly, it is limited in scope: it is a defence of toleration with respect to conceptions of the good, not with respect to conceptions of right, and it is not clear that a stable and uncontroversial distinction can be drawn between conceptions of the good and conceptions of the right. Thus, different religious beliefs (different conceptions of the good) might imply different understandings of JUSTICE (different conceptions of the right), but the argument from neutrality will not support toleration of diverse conceptions of justice. On the contrary, different conceptions of the good must flourish within a state which subscribes to a distinctively liberal understanding of the right in general, and of justice in particular.

Secondly, it is far from clear what exactly neutrality requires of a government: is it simply a matter of standing back and allowing people to pursue the kind of life they think best (of neutrality in intention) or is it a matter of assisting people in their pursuit of their conception of the good (of neutrality in outcome)? If the former, then a policy of neutrality will allow some ways of life to wither away and die. For example, speakers of minority languages will need government support if their language is to flourish: toleration as non-interference will not suffice to protect the language. On the other hand, if neutrality requires ensuring that every group has an equal chance of flourishing, then the call upon government resources will be vast and unsustainable. Additionally, and yet more problematically, the requirement of neutrality, if understood in this way, may be impossible in principle, for it is arguable that, in some cases, state policy must favour some ways of life over others. Thus, a society which has laws governing trading on the sabbath might be said to favour religious believers (sometimes members of a specific religious group, such as Christians) over others, but a society which has no laws governing trading on the sabbath might equally be said to favour atheists. Either way, the aspiration to neutrality in outcome is jeopardised.

The argument from autonomy

The difficulties inherent in defining neutrality and understanding what its requirements are prompt us to consider a third defence of toleration, the defence in terms of autonomy. It is sometimes argued that both toleration in general, and the neutral state in particular, are to be justified by reference to the importance of individual autonomy. The state should tolerate diversity and aspire to neutrality between competing conceptions of the good, primarily because of the importance of each individual leading the life which he or she thinks best. The fact of pluralism dictates that different people will have different conceptions of the good, and considerations of autonomy dictate that government refrain from imposing any conception of the good on its citizens. Even if people are mistaken about the way of life which is best for them, it is better that they should be master of their own fate than that they should lead a life dictated by government edict.

However, the autonomy-based defence of toleration is also problematic, for if values are both plural and conflicting, then there may be cases in which one person's autonomy can only be purchased at cost to another person's autonomy. This problem is sometimes thought to arise in disputes about legislation governing pornography. It is often argued that restrictions on the availability of pornography threaten the autonomy of those who wish to read it. A liberal state, committed to toleration, must acknowledge that some people wish to read this material, and legislation restricting or prohibiting it is undermining of their autonomy. In reply, however, some feminists have

argued that the availability of pornographic material also serves to undermine autonomy: the autonomy of women. A society in which pornographic material is freely and widely available is, it is said, one where women are made to feel inferior and thus denied the conditions necessary for the development of autonomy.

It seems, therefore, that each of the three major justifications of toleration in liberal democratic societies is fraught with difficulty. The argument from scepticism can provide, at best, a pragmatic defence; the argument from neutrality suffers from ambiguity of meaning; the argument from autonomy fails to deliver clear prescriptions.

Against this background, Joseph Raz has argued that the moral value of toleration flows from the fact that conflicting conceptions of the good foster conflicting, and incompatible, virtues. These virtues have concomitant defects, but we should note that the defects are not thereby simple vices: they are, often, limitations without which the virtues could not exist. Thus, the life of contemplation fosters virtues of patience and forbearance. In some contexts these qualities may appear to be defects, for example where instant decision and action are required. What we must remember is that no single conception of the good can incorporate all virtues, and also that even those virtues which are incorporated may, depending on context, appear to be limitations. The acknowledgement that not all valuable qualities can be realised in a single way of life or conception of the good, when coupled with a commitment to the importance of individual autonomy, can therefore serve to justify commitment to toleration as a moral ideal in liberal democratic societies.

Raz's argument shows why diversity is a good and toleration a moral virtue, but it also raises questions about the limits of toleration. Not all defects are simply limitations on virtue; some are straightforward evils and not all can be tolerated in the name of autonomy. There remains, therefore, a set of intransigent problems associated with the defensible limits of toleration, even when diversity is deemed to be a good.

See also:

civic virtue; justice; liberalism; pluralism; rights, minority and indigenous

Further reading

Locke, J. (1983) *A Letter Concerning Toleration*, Indianapolis: Hackett.

Mendus, S. (1989) *Toleration and the Limits of Liberalism*, London: Macmillan.

Mill, J.S. (1977) *The Collected Works of John Stuart Mill: Essays on Politics and Society*, Vol. 18, London and Toronto: Routledge and University of Toronto Press.

Rawls, J. (1993) *Political Liberalism*, Columbia: Columbia University Press.

Raz, J. (1985) *The Morality of Freedom*, Oxford: Clarendon.

SUSAN MENDUS

TRADE-OFFS see democratic trade-offs

trades unions

According to Sidney and Beatrice Webb's (1920: 1) classic definition, a trades union 'is a continuous association of wage earners for the purpose of maintaining or improving the conditions of their working lives'. This definition is relatively narrow and does not fully account for the political role trades unions have played beyond such 'pure and simple' unionism in many democratic states. In liberal democracies, trades unions frequently act as INTEREST GROUPS articulating and promoting their constituents' demands *vis-à-vis* government institutions (parliament, executives, BUREAUCRACY, courts), influencing PUBLIC OPINION and forming alliances with sympathetic political PARTIES. Between 1945 and the 1970s, many liberal democratic governments involved trades unions and employers' peak organisations directly in key areas of economic and social policy (neo-corporatism).

The first trades unions can be traced in Britain in the late sixteenth century. These early craft unions, largely representing skilled workers in small-scale handicraft production, grew out of medieval guilds. Early trade unionism in Britain and the United States of America was localised and highly fragmented along occupational lines. In the eighteenth and nineteenth century, the growth of the mining, iron and steel industries led to the establishment of larger industrial unions, which organised workers in a particular industry, often operating at the national level. Especially in Britain, the new industrial (and later the general unions) did not replace the old crafts unions completely, however. A large number of craft unions have survived to the present day. Unlike in Britain and the United States, union organisation in continental Western Europe was less fragmented along occupational lines, but often more politicised and fragmented along party political lines. Trades unions have often been part of a socio-political milieu, and served as the industrial wing of communist, socialist, social democratic, Christian democratic or nationalist parties. The expansion of the service sector after the Second World War led to the growing importance of white-collar unions in all advanced industrial societies, many of which were occupational in character. In most European countries, the postwar period expansion of WELFARE states also contributed to the growth of public sector unionism. In other countries such as Japan, there has been a strong tradition of enterprise unions.

Trades unions vary greatly in the size of their membership, the extent of hierarchical (vertical) centralisation of power within the organisation and the extent of (horizontal) dispersal of power at the same level of the organisational hierarchy. The extent of trades union organisation in a state or particular industrial sector is commonly measured by the union density statistic. 'Union density is the number of union members expressed as percentage of the number of people who could potentially be union members. This potential constituency is called the dependent labour force. It is often defined to include all wage-earners plus the unemployed' (Western

1997: 15). There are considerable cross-national, inter-sectoral and diachronic variations in union density. In 1985, union density in the OECD countries varied between 94 per cent in Sweden and 18 per cent in the United States of America (Visser 1991). With a few exceptions, trades union density has fallen in all OECD countries since the early 1980s. To some extent, trades unions have attempted to compensate for such losses by merging and forming more encompassing organisations (Chaison 1996). Larger size often allows unions to make economies of scale and allows intra-organisational specialisation. Intra-organisational (vertical and horizontal) centralisation may also increase a trades union's clout in collective bargaining and reduce its vulnerability *vis-à-vis* environmental uncertainties such as those dealt with below. Yet larger size and stronger intra-organisational centralisation are often seen as inhibiting PARTICIPATION and democracy as well as the individual member's ability to influence union policies.

Most explanations of cross-national, inter-sectoral or diachronic variations in trades union density focus on the organisational 'environment' within which trades unions operate. One of the most influential schools of thought emphasises the importance of the structure of the economy as the most important causal factor. The growth of the industrial sector in most advanced industrial economies during the late nineteenth and the first half of the twentieth century is believed to have favoured trades union organisation. Its contraction since the 1960s is often seen to have affected trades union density negatively. Although there are considerable cross-national differences, the level of socio-economic development, the structure of the economies and the large size of the 'informal sector' in the developing world is often believed to be one of the main causes of low union density in developing countries. Another economic factor that is often referred to is the business cycle. Phases of economic boom are believed to favour trades union organisation, while periods of recession are said to have a negative impact.

A second set of factors refers to the legitimacy of trades unions in the realm of collective bargaining and in politics. Union recognition by employers and the state is believed to provide favourable conditions for trades union organisation. The third factor that is often believed to strengthen union organisation is the *extent of labour market centralisation*, that is, the level at which collective bargaining is commonly conducted. In some countries (such as Scandinavia and the Netherlands), collective bargaining has been centralised at the national level. Where trades union leaders act as national CLASS representatives, employers have often been less resistant to union organisations and the relations between unions were characterised by co-ordination rather than competition. A fourth factor is the extent to which trades unions are directly involved in the management of unemployment funds. Where trades unions are directly involved (the so-called 'Ghent system' as currently practised in Belgium, Denmark, Finland and Sweden), unions have been better able to organise those out of work. In countries with public unemployment insurance, by contrast, 'exit from the labor movement usually follows exit from the labor market' (Western 1997: 9). A fifth important factor is economic GLOBALISATION, which is believed to have had a negative impact on trades union organisation. Globalised economic competition and the high international mobility of capital and goods have limited the capacity of national institutions to regulate the effect of MARKET FORCES.

Finally, it is often held that the political opportunity structure, within which trades unions operate, matters. The most fundamental variable in this context is the extent to which a political system offers freedom of association and tolerates trades unions as legitimate actors in the process of collective bargaining. In some non-democratic states, union activity (including the right to strike) is suppressed or curtailed. In many dictatorial or totalitarian regimes such as National Socialism in Germany, fascism in Italy, Peronism in Argentina, Stalinism and real socialism in the former Soviet Union and its former satellites, unions existed and had a large number of members, but were interlocked with management, government and party organs, losing their independent function. In liberal democracies, the presence or absence of allies in the respective country's party system is often believed to be a crucial element of the political opportunity structure. Social democratic governments, for example, reformed industrial relations institutions to support union organising and expand union power. The strength of trades union organisation in between the 1940s and 1970s is often believed to reflect the growing power of social democratic parties in advanced industrial democracies in this period. Their weakness since the 1980s partly reflects the general weakness or ideological change of SOCIAL DEMOCRACY throughout in this period. Unsympathetic governments such as the Thatcher government in the United Kingdom (1979–90) enhanced employers' ability to resist union organisation.

Despite a number of adverse developments such as globalisation and the decentralisation of collective bargaining, trades unions in some OECD countries have also discovered some new opportunities. In countries such as Germany or Sweden, where elected works councils represent employees on the boards of companies, trades unions have begun to find an important micro-institutional role with a potential to contribute not only to 'industrial democracy' but also to increased flexibility and productivity at the plant level.

See also:

Christian democracy; cleavages; consensus democracy; equality; freedom; interest groups; revolutions; social movements; solidarity; welfare

Further reading

Chaison, G.N. (1996) *Union Mergers in Hard Times: The View From Five Countries*, Ithaca, NY: Cornell University Press.
Cohen, R., Gutkind, P.C.W. and Brazier, P. (eds) (1979) *Peasants and Proletarians: The Struggles of Third World Workers*, London: Hutchinson.
Crouch, C. (1993) *Industrial Relations and European State Traditions*, Oxford: Oxford University Press.
Triska, J.S. and Gati, C. (eds) (1981) *Blue-Collar Workers in Eastern Europe*, London: Allen and Unwin.
Visser, J. (1989) *European Trade Unions in Figures*, Deventer: Kluwer.
—— (1990) 'In Search of Inclusive Unionism', *Bulletin of Comparative Labour Relations* 18 (special issue): i–ix, 1–278.
—— (1991) 'Trends in Union Membership', *OECD Employment Outlook* 97–134.
Visser, J. and Waddington, J. (1996) 'Industrialisation and Politics: A Century of Union Structural Development in Three European Countries', *European Journal of Industrial Relations* 2(1): 21–53.
Webb, S. and Webb, B. (1920) *The History of Trade Unionism*, 2nd edn, London: Longmans.
Western, B. (1997) *Between Class and Market: Postwar Unionization in the Capitalist Democracies*, Princeton, NJ: Princeton University Press.

THOMAS SAALFELD

transparency

The term transparency is heavily used in contemporary discussion of institutions and public policy, in law, economics and political science. It has figured large over the last decade in recipes for 'good governance' in the development literature (with good governance becoming part of loan conditionality by the World Bank in the early 1990s, and transparency later becoming part of good governance). Indeed, there is now a non-governmental organisation called Transparency International operating as an information exchange on regime CORRUPTION and openness (http://www.gwdg.de/~uwvw/icr.htm). Transparency is likewise a key element in econocratic doctrines for public policy to minimise transaction costs in the economy and in visions of open executive government as a necessary entailment of democracy and legality. Transparency is central to contemporary discussions of both democratic governance and PUBLIC SERVICE reform, since open access to INFORMATION and elimination of secrecy is taken to be a condition for prevention of corruption and promoting public ACCOUNTABILITY. The term also appears in Habermasian ideals of generalised COMMUNICATION in society and prophecies of a techno-future embracing open information from cameras and computers (Brin 1998).

Ironically, however, the exact meaning of this much-used word is hard to determine. In fact, it is commonly used to mean a number of different things, such as disclosure, policy clarity, consistency or a culture of candour. There is no classic modern treatise that embraces all those meanings. Even the authoritative *New Palgrave Dictionary of Law and Economics* (1998) has no entry for this widely used term.

In perhaps its commonest usage, transparency denotes government according to fixed and published rules, on the basis of information and procedures that are accessible to the public, and (in some usages) within clearly demarcated fields of activity. Within that umbrella meaning, there are at least two general streams of thought about transparency. One comes from jurisprudential and political theory doctrines, and the other comes from institutional economics ideas.

For lawyers, transparency is an entailment of rule of law ideas, and its minimum meaning is that government should operate according to fixed, published and predictable rules. That position (contrasting with Jacobin notions of democracy or Confucian ideals of discreet paternalism by morally superior state officials) has a long history in developed systems of government (as reflected for instance in the publication of gazettes and official journals). It was further emphasised in Western jurisprudence after the Nazi era, and received an additional fillip after the collapse of communism in the former USSR and Eastern Europe. Transparency in this sense can include requirements for public DECISION-MAKING to operate on a known timescale, for decisions to be communicated to affected parties, to be based on verifiable statements of reasons and for affected parties to be told of the remedies available to them and the period within which such remedies can be exercised.

One of the classic twentieth-century expositions of that doctrine (albeit not using the specific term 'transparency') is Lon Fuller's (1964) *The Morality of Law*. Fuller proposed eight standards of legal excellence by which to assess any system of rules, and all eight incorporate some element of transparency. They are generality, promulgation, non-retroactivity, clarity, consistency, avoidance of requirements that are beyond the power of the affected party, stability, and congruence between published rules and their administration (Fuller 1964: 39ff). Fuller saw these eight tests as representing a rising scale of difficulty for a political system to achieve, in the order they are set out above.

Two further extended entailments of the rule of law meaning of transparency are the notion of FREEDOM of official information and the notion of decision-making in open fora. The freedom of information doctrine, reflected in the Swedish state tradition, holds that the rule of law can only be effective if information on which government decisions are based is available for public inspection. Brin (1998) has extended this doctrine, arguing that contemporary developments in information technology and camera surveillance make it all the more important that collective information-sharing takes precedence over privacy arguments if dominance by a small information-rich elite is to be avoided. The notion of decision-making in open fora holds that government should be conducted through 'open covenants... openly arrived at' (in Woodrow Wilson's famous phrase, the first of his 'Fourteen Points' for the peace settlement after the First World War) or 'government in the sunshine', in more recent US parlance. Such doctrines are reflected in the widespread adoption of freedom of information legislation (on some more or less watered-down version of Swedish practice) across the developed countries in recent decades and more selective adoption of public hearing or decision forum practices, notably in regulatory practices in some countries.

Like most good government doctrines, transparency in this sense is not a new idea. The utilitarian philosopher Jeremy Bentham expounded the doctrine in detail in the late eighteenth and early nineteenth century, making 'transparent management or publicity' one of his central and recurring principles for public management (see Hume 1981: 161). He saw the principle as a prerequisite for the rule of law in organisations as well as in government more generally, and for exposing corruption or mismanagement. For example, in his proposals for a National Charity Company for welfare services, every decision and every act of management was to be recorded, no decisions were to be secret and all 'official acts' were to be exercised in a common room. Similar doctrines are embedded in the formal procedures of some contemporary public organisations, such as US regulatory commissions, with their norms of decision-making on the basis of public hearings and prohibitions on private meetings among commissioners under the Government in the Sunshine Act. Transparency for Bentham also entailed full publication of fees for office and government accounts in as accessible a form as possible – a key feature of his famous *Constitutional Code* (Bentham 1983: 265). The aim of publishing fees, salaries and accounts was to open up public management to wide public scrutiny, even and perhaps particularly from the vindictive or disappointed. As Bentham (1931: 410) put it, in a famous phrase, transparency can work effectively as a remedy for misgovernment because 'the worst principles have their use as well as the best; envy, hatred, malice, perform the task of public spirit'. That idea links to contemporary pluralist ideas in which widespread dissemination of official information is seen as the basis for effective monitoring of government by INTEREST GROUPS. An application of that principle is the doctrine of open public disclosure of each legislator's expense claims, adopted for the US Congress, but not by many other legislatures (see Holdich 1989: 12–13). An extension of it (at the edge of the mainstream meaning of transparency) is to adopt legal protection for 'whistleblowers'; individuals seeking to expose wrong-doing in government and private organisations.

In addition to these classic doctrines of transparency in political theory and jurisprudence, there is a different, albeit related set of ideas about transparency associated more with economics and accounting, and reflected in rules about the conduct of economic activities in the European Union and elsewhere. Within this stream of thought 'transparency' relates to the ease with which an organisation's 'principals' (shareholders or the public at large) can monitor 'agents' (managers or bureaucrats) or overseers (like auditors or regulators) can monitor those they regulate, and the degree of difficulty economic agents face in ascertaining the rules that apply to them. Such ideas have developed in accountancy-sourced doctrines of greater disclosure as a recipe for better corporate governance (rediscovering Benthamite principles), and in institutional economics. Transparency in this sense is achieved when activities are readily auditable (through being able to relate results to plans or aims and activities to responsible units or individuals), when different organisational elements are kept separate and those being monitored are forced to make their trade-offs publicly.

Following this theme, there is a long history of advocacy by economists of institutional arrangements that prevent hidden cross-subsidisation of one activity or set of consumers by another by making any such transfers readily visible. An example of this sort of reasoning dating back to Australian (Victorian) railways in the nineteenth century is the 'recoup' concept (Wettenhall 1966). The recoup concept is the doctrine that subsidies for provision of uneconomic services to particular groups of beneficiaries by public enterprises should be explicit, costed, and funded from general taxation rather than implicit and funded at the expense of profitable services. Disclosure rules are also conventionally seen as a way of lowering transaction costs through information asymmetries, for instance in making property vendors reveal the past flood history of the area instead of leaving it up to buyers to find out. A clear statement of the doctrine of transparency in this sense and its rationale comes from the New Zealand Treasury (1987: 48), arguing that the degree of clarity and openness about government's objectives and instruments, together with the degree of policy consistency, can link to overall economic performance through levels of transaction costs:

> the complex government interventions such as taxes, regulations and subsidies increase the information problems facing private actors. This complexity may discourage economic activity. For example complex regulations... may reduce value maximizing transactions owing to the uncertainty they create. The source of this uncertainty is the information costs of discovering rights and obligations, and the potential for policy changes....
> (New Zealand Treasury 1987: 40)

The same argument has been advanced in doctrines for reshaping government in developing countries and in recent debate about the role of high transaction costs in the Asian economic slump of the late 1990s (see Fons 1998).

The latter approach is prominent in the EU's usage of the word 'transparency', which is applied both to markets (for example in requiring published tariffs rather than ad hoc pricing) and to regulatory interventions. Here the preoccupation is with segmentation of different parts of member-state governments or regulated firms such that outside monitoring of any discrimination in favour of national firms or interests is easier to achieve. That usage is reflected in the title of the EU's 1980 'Transparency of Undertakings' Directive (Commission Directive 80/723/EEC, amended by Directive 85/413/EEC (2) and 93/84/EEC). It also appears in its directive requiring transparency of gas and electricity prices (Council Directive 90/377/EEC) and its directive on the transparency of medical products regulation (Council Directive 89/105/EEC). Key to 'transparency' in this sense are cost accounting systems that separate different aspects of both government and regulated business, requirements for certain information to be obtained and/or retained by governments or firms, and to be supplied to EU regulators,

users or applicants. But the EU's requirements for transparency vary from one context to another, and the EU's own practices are far from achieving the 'transparency' it advocates for decision-making in its member-states. EU opacity derives from practices such as the secrecy of its Council of Ministers proceedings, the common resort to category-blurring to paper over differences and its widespread use of the so-called 'comitology' approach (that is, institutionalised system of addressing member states' interests through committees clearing legislation).

One of the reasons why 'transparency' so often appears in arguments about better government is that the word combines the rhetorical advantages of ambiguity and positive associations (for who, apart from those with guilty secrets to hide or dubious interests to protect, could possibly be against 'transparency?). But transparency presents at least four unresolved problems as a recipe for institutional reform in government.

First, at the instrumental level, attempts to create more transparency will not necessarily do so, and if they do may create severe side-effects. This problem, pervasive in public policy, may be especially salient for transparency, because of the power issues at stake. Institutional responses to freedom of information or 'government in the sunshine' measures, for example, commonly involve substantial game-playing, including the familiar tactics of delay, substitution behaviour and classification politics. And when transparency is achievable, it may as a side-effect destroy the conditions for agreement or brokerage. Sociologists have long been aware of 'the social functions of ignorance' (Moore and Tumin 1949), for example in upholding institutions like marriage, and transparency requirements, if successful, may disrupt those functions. Several students of budgetary reform have argued that the management accounting notion of transparency cuts across some basic features of political behaviour, notably the possibility of forming political COALITIONS around particular measures even if the parties are diametrically opposed on the goals they wish to pursue. The 'fudge', as in the EU's own practice, is a universal means of achieving political agreement when consensus is not readily forthcoming.

The other three problems with transparency go beyond these familiar (if often severe) instrumental difficulties. One is the difficulty of establishing exactly when a 'transparency' requirement is satisfied. For example, the EU's transparency requirements are met in some cases by publication, while in others transparency requires specific transmission of information to affected parties (see Nihoul 1998: 15ff). A second is a dilemma inherent in most 'principles' of INSTITUTIONAL DESIGN, namely that transparency must be traded against other contradictory values, including security and privacy. One person's transparency (for instance in making government information about convicted sex offenders available to parents or teachers) may be another person's privacy or commercial confidentiality. Which of these rival desiderata is to have primacy? No major state (including Sweden) has been able to do without official secrecy for some of its activities, and transparency invariably runs up against rival policy goals.

A final problem is that transparency may itself incorporate elements that are incompatible with one another. Fuller (1964: 45) noted this point in commenting on his eight transparency-related tests of legal excellence discussed earlier. For instance, making laws or legal documents clear to citizens or consumers may make application of the law by the courts less predictable or consistent, by removing the arcane language the latter understand. Breaking government up into hundreds of separate accounting units or contracts to make covert cross-subsidisation harder to conceal may, at the same time, make the public accounts or public administration too complicated for most people to understand. Requiring all public decisions to be made in public fora may mean endless deadlock, such that chronic uncertainty ensues. In such circumstances, which – or whose – transparency is to have precedence? To make such points is not to deny the value of transparency as a remedy for misgovernment, only to note that like most

institutional design principles it has its limits and internal contradictions, and can conflict with rival design principles.

See also:

accountability; civil service; corruption; legitimacy; secrecy

Further reading

Bentham, J. (1931) *The Theory of Legislation*, trans. R. Hildreth, London: Routledge.

—— (1983) *Constitutional Code*, Oxford: Clarendon.

Brin, D. (1998) *The Transparent Society*, Reading, MA: Addison-Wesley.

Fons, J.S. (1998) 'Improving Transparency in Asian Banking Systems', paper presented to Federal Reserve Bank of Chicago/IMF sponsored conference, 'Asia: An Analysis of Financial Crises', 9 October, published at http://www.gwdg.de/~uwvw/icr.htm.

Fuller, L. (1964) *The Morality of Law*, New Haven, CT: Yale University Press.

Holdich, R. (1989) *Fair Enough: Possible Changes in the Way in Which Salaries and Allowances for Australian Parliamentarians are Set and Administered*, Canberra: Australian Government Publishing Service.

Hume, L. (1981) *Bentham on Bureaucracy*, Cambridge: Cambridge University Press.

Moore, W.E. and Tumin, M.M. (1949) 'Some Social Functions of Ignorance', *American Sociological Review* 14: 787–95.

New Zealand Treasury (1987) *Government Management*, Vol. 1, Wellington: New Zealand Treasury.

Nihoul, P. (1998) 'Convergence in European Telecommunications' *International Journal of Telecoms Law and Policy* 2: 1–33.

Wettenhall, R.L. (1966) 'The Recoup Concept in Public Enterprise', *Public Administration* 44: 391–414.

CHRISTOPHER C. HOOD

VOTING *see* elections

W

waves of democracy

Waves of democracy have been defined as a group of democratic transitions 'that occur within a specified period of time and that significantly outnumber transitions in the opposite direction during that period' (Huntington 1991: 15). It is broadly agreed that there have been three such waves in world history. The first long wave from 1828 to 1926 saw some thirty countries achieve minimal democratic institutions. The second wave from 1943 to 1962 was driven by anti-colonial struggles that in some cases led to new democratic regimes. The third wave began with the Portuguese revolution of 1974 and has continued to the present. Each of the first two waves ended with a reverse wave of democratic breakdowns, from 1922 to 1942 and 1961 to 1975, when some but far from all the democratic governments of the time collapsed.

The third wave began in southern Europe in the mid-1970s, spread to South America by the late 1970s and early 1980s, entered East, Southeast and South Asia by the mid to late 1980s, accelerated with the surge of transitions in Eastern Europe and former Soviet Union at the end of the 1980s, and reached Central America and Africa by the beginning of the 1990s. The number of democracies in the world grew from 39 at the beginning of the wave in 1974 to 117 in 1998 (Diamond 1999: 1). Consequently, although the number of independent states grew by more than a third over this period, the proportion of democracies expanded from 27 per cent to over 60 per cent. Moreover, a systematic investigation of the democratic and autocratic elements both within and across regimes concluded that by 1990, for the first time, 'the degree of democracy in the international system surpassed the degree of autocracy' (Jaggers and Gurr 1995: 476). Whether expressed in absolute or relative terms, this growth of democratic government is unprecedented in world history. There has been no third reverse wave (yet), but the third wave has been punctuated by occasional democratic breakdowns.

Why did the third wave happen? Huntington states five possible reasons (Huntington 1991: 61–3): the crises of LEGITIMACY in authoritarian regimes; the high levels of growth of the 1960s; the changes in the doctrine and practice of the Catholic Church; the changes in the policies of important external actors such as the European Union and United States; and the operation of demonstration effects or 'snowballing'. He finds that 90 per cent of all countries that liberalise or undergo democratic transitions are in the 'middle range' of world per capita GDP, and uses arguments from modernisation theory – new values, EDUCATION, trade liberalisation, expansion of the middle class – to provide the causal links between economic growth and democratic outcomes. He also emphasises the role of the progressive Catholic Church in the 75 per cent of all third wave democracies (until 1990) that are Catholic.

The idea of 'snowballing' suggests that the third wave carries its own causal force, with unstable authoritarian regimes being undermined by the fall of similar regimes elsewhere, and especially nearby. But Diamond suggests that the demonstration effects do not occur naturally, but require institutional support in the form of, first, the US government, and, second, international agencies such as the United Nations and Organisation of American

States, as well as the myriad NON-GOVERN-MENTAL ORGANISATIONS or NGOs (Diamond 1999: 56–8). He recognises the importance of the cross-cultural diffusion of values and models, and, in particular, of an increasingly global sense of entitlement to democratic governance (that was already present in the Universal Declaration of Human Rights of 1948). But he believes that the future of democracy depends in no small degree on the power and will of the United States (see Diamond's DEMOCRACY, FUTURE OF).

It appears that the third wave has wrought a democratic revolution, and so transformed the political universe. Not only do democratic governments now outnumber all others, but liberal democracy also serves to legitimate state AUTHORITY nearly everywhere. It was this 'remarkable consensus concerning the legitimacy of liberal democracy' that served as the premise of Fukuyama's thesis on 'the end of history' (Fukuyama 1992: xi) and the global triumph of liberal democracy. Yet this triumphalism may be premature. Its truth turns first on a minimal and procedural definition of liberal democracy as a political system where multiple political PARTIES compete for control of government through relatively free and fair ELECTIONS. Secondly, it depends on a focus on governments rather than on populations. It is not simply that some of the most populous states are not democracies (China, Iran, Indonesia), but that the populations of many democratic states may not enjoy liberal democratic freedoms. This is the recurrent problem of the potential gap between formal rules and political realities. In short, constitutions may enshrine full liberal democratic principles that fail to operate in practice.

The minimal and procedural definition of democracy has been termed 'electoral democracy' to distinguish it from a more fully liberal democracy defined by the rule of law, freedom of INFORMATION, civil liberties and horizontal ACCOUNTABILITY between different branches of government. Liberal democracy is therefore constitutional democracy, where individual and group rights are protected and where autonomous spheres of civil and private life flourish free from state control (Diamond 1999: 12). Thus electoral democracy falls a long way short of liberal democracy, but different political parties still compete in an open fashion, and elections serve to make and unmake governments. Both liberal and electoral democracy can be further distinguished from pseudo democracy where elections do nothing but mask the true authoritarian character of the regime. About half of the forty or so pseudo-democracies in the world today can be found in sub-Saharan Africa.

The current total of 117 democracies in the world includes all the electoral democracies, irrespective of their liberal content. According to the measures of Freedom House (1997), 29 of the 57 electoral democracies with a population of over one million born during the third wave fall short of the liberal threshold (Diamond 1999: 61). Moreover, the gap between liberal and electoral democracy tends to widen over the course of the third wave, and never more so than in recent years. In other words, the quality of democracy – as measured by civil and minority rights for example – is declining, even or especially in some of the most influential democracies of the third wave like Russia, Turkey, Brazil and Pakistan. Democracy may not have expired altogether in a reverse wave, but it is being progressively hollowed out (Diamond 1999: 19) leaving a shell of multiparty electoralism. Yet this remains sufficient to secure international legitimacy and assistance, so long as the 'international community' continues to set low democratic standards that emphasise free elections to the exclusion of almost everything else.

This hollow and poorly institutionalised democracy is therefore characteristic of the third wave. Thus just four of the fifteen third wave democracies studied by Linz and Stepan fulfil the criteria for liberal democracy, and one of these was still 'low quality' (Greece) and another 'risk prone' (Uruguay) (Linz and Stepan 1996: 457). Electoral politics persist in the absence of civil and minority rights. The armed forces and the police remain unaccountable to elected civilian government. The

JUDICIARY is ineffective or corrupt. Elites, especially landed elites, frequently resort to violence to protect their PRIVATE PROPERTY. So the privileged few are free to pursue political power through competitive party politics, but the poor, the powerless and the MINORITIES remain unprotected and subject to abuse.

What is at issue here is the rule of law. In most instances it is not the law itself that is at fault, although many third wave democratic constitutions do accord special immunities or protections to the military and the police that may contribute to damage the integrity of civil and minority rights. But if the corporate privileges of the military and police do encourage an abuse of rights it is because of a lack of horizontal accountability that might hold this abuse in check. The most common symptom of this lack of accountability is an overweening executive that is able to ride roughshod over both legislature and judiciary, frequently legislating by decree. It is a symptom made chronic by the often long-term suspension of constitutional guarantees in conditions of domestic strife or national emergency, especially in states with deep ethnic or religious divides (see DEMOCRATIC BREAKDOWN).

Where there is no rule of law because the law is routinely bypassed or subverted, there is no liberal democracy but only illiberal democracy. The governments of illiberal democracies may be freely, universally and fairly elected, but they 'either do not respect or do not maintain the state based on the rule of law' (Merkel 1999: 10). Since these governments enjoy the legitimacy of popular election and remain vertically accountable through constitutionally scheduled elections, it is the violation of the rule of law, not of the democratic principle of popular SOVEREIGNTY, that makes them defective. Most of the third-wave democratic regimes are plainly illiberal in this sense, and frequently act to repress minorities, restrict civil rights, manipulate the MEDIA and undermine the autonomy of the judiciary or hinder its work.

It is perhaps too easy to suggest that it is the POLITICAL CULTURE that explains the illiberalism of third wave democracies. But there is a case for arguing that it is the pervasive presence of CLIENTELISM, in particular, that creates the conditions that underpin this illiberalism. Clientelism in this context may include the regional oligarchies that retain their traditional powers through deeply embedded systems of patronage, the political machines and political families in national government and national congress that protect military autonomy or Mafia commerce, or the bossism of electoral politics that constrains the reach of political parties and political representation. Such clientelism has two major political effects. First, it underpins a patrimonial pattern of politics, where there is no clear and enduring distinction between the private and public spheres, and therefore no cultural defence of a *res publica* that requires the rule of law. Second, it assumes and promotes a particularistic style of politics that produces and reproduces power through particular relationships of favour and loyalty that are inimical to the general claims of individual rights. If individual rights are not well respected in third wave democracies it is frequently because this 'particularism vigorously inhabits most formal political institutions' (O'Donnell 1997: 49).

According to the most comprehensive study of the phenomenon, the third wave may now be drawing to a close. The proportion of electoral democracies is no longer expanding, and many of the most powerful authoritarian states (China, Iran, Saudi Arabia) show little or no sign of democratising. The DEMOCRATIC PERFORMANCE of many third wave democracies is deteriorating. The best prognosis for the third wave is that its fifty or so electoral democracies can begin to consolidate (Diamond 1999: 60–63). The assumption here, and in the mainstream literature, is that democracies will consolidate if they become sufficiently liberal (see DEMOCRATIC CONSOLIDATION). Thus, the third of Linz and Stepan's five arenas of a consolidated democracy is the 'rule of law to ensure legal guarantees for citizens' freedoms and independent associational life' (Linz and Stepan 1996: 7). Furthermore, it is clear that the rule of law is essential to the autonomy and independence of civil and political societies (arenas one and two), and to a useable state bureaucracy and regulated economic society (arenas four and five).

This approach to *democratic consolidation* assumes that the presence of these five arenas will have specific effects on political attitudes and political behaviour. This is the route that leads to the shorthand definition of the conditions of consolidation, which is said to occur when the routine and deeply ingrained expectations of all political actors make democracy the 'only game in town' (Linz and Stepan 1996: 15–16). Sufficient consensus and active consent will enable new democracies to endure. But these conditions will only obtain if these democracies are successful in establishing a liberal constitutional state and defending the integrity of the rule of law. In sum, in this perspective, democratic consolidation requires 'a reasonably close fit between formal rules and actual behaviour' (O'Donnell 1997: 47).

But the historical fact of the third wave and the increasing longevity of many third-wave democracies cast considerable doubt on this assumption. The evidence suggests, on the contrary, that an increasing number of illiberal democracies are becoming consolidated. Democracies may therefore be consolidated without being liberal, and liberal without being consolidated. Self-evidently, it is not the rule of law that either consolidates or is consolidated, but the informal rules that coalesce in clientelism and patrimonialism. The result is not the rule of law but the rule of informal rules that favour the powerful and discriminate systematically against the powerless. In this perspective, third wave democracies may well be consolidated, but what is consolidated is very different from the model of liberal democracy that preceded them.

The one exception to this institutionalised informality (partial or complete depending on the country in question) is the electoral arena, which remains 'ring-fenced' (O'Donnell 1997: 49). This 'ring-fencing' may be achieved through the measure of accountability implicit in political party competition. It may also be buttressed by international monitoring, and motivated by the requirements of international legitimacy and finance. After all, membership of the 'democratic club' brings privileges and serves to assuage sanctions, and democratic governments can only claim membership 'so long as elections are institutionalised' (O'Donnell 1997: 45). The consolidation of illiberal democracies maintains the dramatic divide between ring-fenced electoral politics and the fragility of civil rights and liberties. Whether the electoral principle alone is sufficient to sustain the subsequent 'liberalisation' of the third wave democracies is an open question, and one that will no doubt receive different answers in different political contexts and different historical moments.

See also:

clientelism; democratic breakdown; economic requirements of democracy; information; judiciary; law, rule of; legitimacy; minorities; parties; political culture; rights

Further reading

Diamond, L. (1999) *Developing Democracy: Toward Consolidation*, London and Baltimore: Johns Hopkins University Press.

Freedom House (1997) *Freedom in the World: the Annual Survey of Political Rights and Civil Liberties, 1996–97*, New York: Freedom House.

Fukuyama, F. (1992) *The End of History and the Last Man*, Harmondsworth: Penguin.

Huntington, S. (1991) *The Third Wave: Democratisation in the Late Twentieth Century*, Norman, OK: University of Oklahoma Press.

Jaggers, K. and Gurr, T.R. (1995) 'Tracking Democracy's Third Wave with the Polity III data', *Journal of Peace Research* 32(4): 469–82.

Linz, J.J. and Stepan, A. (1996) *Problems of Democratic Transition and Consolidation: Southern Europe, South America, and Post-Communist Europe*, Baltimore: Johns Hopkins University Press.

Merkel, W. (1999) *Defective Democracies*, Working Paper 1999/132, Madrid: Instituto Juan March de Estudios y Investigaciones.

O'Donnell, G. (1997) 'Illusions About Consolidation', in L. Diamond, M.F. Plattner, Yun-han Chu and Hung-mao Tien (1997) *Consolidating the Third Wave Democracies: Themes and Perspectives*, Baltimore: John Hopkins University Press.

JOE FOWERAKER

welfare

The concept of 'welfare' is derived from an old English term *wel-faran* (well-get along), whose origin can be traced to 1303. The modern term welfare was first recorded in 1904, following late nineteenth century movements such as Fabianism in England and Bismarckian Social Policy in Germany. Coincidentally, the Fabian society was born in London in 1884, the same year that the first social welfare legislation, insurance against injury for factory workers, was passed by the Reichstag in Berlin. Many of the welfare policies that will be traced below, had their beginning with these two movements. Although Fabian and Bismarckian approaches to social policy were both a response to industrialisation, they were founded on very different underlying philosophical premises.

Fabianism was articulated by a small group in London who sought to reconstruct society 'in accordance with the highest moral possibilities', but by democratic and evolutionary means rather than by revolutionary means. It advocated a non-Marxian, moderate and gradual approach to social and political change. Nevertheless, in the context of the times, a volume of essays published in 1889, *Fabian Essays in Socialism*, caused a stir in London, for revolutionary Marxism was the recognized socialist doctrine of that period. The Fabians did not themselves seek political power, and they argued that their socialist principles could be pursued by already existing governments and political parties; this led to an affiliation of their followers with the new Independent Labour Party. The Fabians then encouraged and co-operated with the TRADES UNIONS in founding the British Labour Party in 1906. This party's stated purpose was to pursue policy in the direct interest of labour, and with its active PARTICIPATION. In the election of 1906, it was apparent that the moderate brand of socialism represented by the Fabians and the nascent Labour party had a very broad appeal, and would prove to be an important factor in British politics.

In Germany, Otto Von Bismarck contemplated the implications of the enormous increase of the CLASS of factory workers that occurred as Germany developed into an industrial state. He recognized the growth in socialistic and radical doctrines among the working class and the threat that this incipient militancy held for the stability of the state. His response was to seek state guaranteed insurance for workers against sickness, accidents, old age and disability, thus demonstrating to them that they too could realise advantages from the existing organisation of the state. Bismarck's early efforts to introduce universal workmen's insurance were thwarted by Germany's liberal parties, who argued that any form of compulsory insurance was an infringement of civil liberties. They shared his suspicion of socialism, and they supported him in the passage of legislation in 1878 that gave the government new powers to control those identified as 'socialist agitators'. In 1884, Bismarck's government was finally able to pass a weakened insurance bill; insurance was to be funded by the contributions of employers and employees. This was a disappointing result, for Bismarck had wanted the workers to identify their benefits as coming through the largesse of the state. A patchwork of acts followed, instituting sick funds and insurance for old age and disability. Bismarck's objective was clearly to mollify the workers, and his efforts were responsible for developing a view of the state that perceived it to be in a tactical struggle with societal forces to achieve social peace and social control. The underlying principle was that the people were to be governed in a way that would ensure the continued stability of the state (and economic) apparatus.

The history of the development of welfare programs is suffused with the tension between these two approaches. On the one hand, the

Fabians endeavoured to realise EQUALITY and JUSTICE by seeking the redistribution of resources in the name of the 'common good'. On the other hand, the Bismarckian approach sought to sustain existing state structures by advocating welfare programs that appeased the working class, thus attaining social acquiescence and political stability. These two approaches result in very different forms of welfare state transfers.

The evolution of the welfare state

The term 'welfare state' was apparently first used in the English language by William Temple, Archbishop of York, in 1941. Although often used pejoratively in its early development, it became, in the third quarter of the twentieth century, to be understood as the use of state power to ameliorate the negative effects of MARKET FORCES in a modern, industrialised, capitalist state. That is, in all the states where industrial capital became the economic motor, it was accompanied by varied attempts to introduce social reforms. In this sense, the term 'welfare state' denotes more than a type of state, but also a type of society, if not an ideology.

Asa Briggs in 1967 identified three types of welfare state activities: the provision of minimum income, provision for the reduction of economic insecurity as the result of sickness, accident, unemployment or old age, and the universal provision of a range of social services (such as health care). It has also been suggested by Richard Titmuss (1958) that a broader conception of the welfare state should include the range of services provided by other societal institutions such as churches, trade unions and non-profit organisations funded by a combination of state and private sources. This is a more problematic conception, but in the 1990s all liberal democracies encouraged the participation of NON-GOVERNMENTAL ORGANISATIONS in social service provision.

The expansion and entrenchment of welfare programs is predicated on the expectation of the reduction of inequality, the expansion of FREEDOM, and the promotion of democracy

(Beveridge 1942). Modern exponents of social welfare (social democrats) argue that political democracy must also include social and economic democracy, or equal rights to EDUCATION, medical care, pensions, employment and safety in the workplace (see SOCIAL DEMOCRACY). This requires an activist, interventionist state that uses its power to meaningfully redistribute society's wealth. There is a continuing dichotomy between those who adhere to this view of the purpose and effects of welfare policies and those who perceive social welfare policy in Bismarckian terms: its purpose is to maintain social peace and political and economic stability. Neo-Marxists refer to this latter purpose as the legitimation function of the modern liberal democratic state.

James O'Connor (1973) suggested that the liberal democratic (and therefore capitalist) state had two functions to perform, and to keep in balance: accumulation and legitimation. By this he meant that a major function of the state was to create and maintain the conditions for capitalist accumulation, while preserving social harmony and political stability by providing welfare policies that involve a degree of redistribution of income and resources. It is this role of the state – liberal democracy, rather than social democracy – that has prevailed in most late twentieth-century Western nations. Tension between the two roles is evident in the evolution and historical development of welfare policy.

Social reform was a necessary accompaniment of the industrial revolution, which created a new capitalist labour market, or working class. Industrialisation precipitated rapid urbanisation and a consequent breakdown of traditional social institutions and community support systems. The early response of the state to the changing needs was largely regulatory in nature, and social welfare consisted of programs to address immediate need: relief for the indigent and care for the insane, handicapped and neglected. By the late nineteenth and early twentieth century, all industrialised countries had working-class parties and trade unions familiar with socialist thought, and determined to pursue social reform. Social unrest was widespread, with general strikes and revolutionary movements in several states. The success of the Bolshevik revolution in 1917, declaring the Soviet Union a 'workers' state', was a catalyst for social reform in the West.

In an incremental, ad hoc and piecemeal fashion, social reforms (sometimes called 'concessions' by capital) occurred in different countries. Old age pensions, industrial accident schemes, industrial relations legislation, public education and some hospital insurance were introduced in the early years of the twentieth century. Programs were mostly sporadic, fragmented and totally inadequate to ameliorate the deprivations that accompanied the downturns of the capitalist business cycle, particularly the serious depression of the 1930s. During this decade, the seminal work of John Maynard Keynes appeared, virtually establishing a new approach to economics in the western world. Keynesian economics refuted the 'invisible hand' of Adam Smith's nineteenth-century economic theory, and argued for manipulation of the economy to reduce the destabilisations inherent in market-based systems. This required active use of fiscal and monetary policy to stimulate domestic output and employment. Keynesian economics advocated discretionary government measures, or interventions, to promote economic growth, stability of employment and an increased standard of living. With a growing acceptance of government intervention, income maintenance programs and social policy development were also harnessed to improve economic management.

In 1942, another influential document appeared in Britain – the Beveridge Report – that outlined a new direction for social insurance. It received international attention and acclaim, with its farsighted and innovative concepts and its comprehensive review of social welfare. Beveridge emphasised that the objective of his report was to achieve social progress by attacking the five 'giant evils': Want, Disease, Ignorance, Squalor and Idleness. Views such as this, in conjunction with forms of economic manipulation espoused by Keynes, led to a new

social/economic/political paradigm. The welfare state that emerged from this new paradigm in the 1940s and 1950s did little to alter existing market structures, but because it increased the legitimation role of the state, it has been suggested that Keynesian policies amounted to a 'third alternative' between orthodox CAPITALISM and Marxian theory. Certainly in the economic sense, Keynesian policy was revolutionary, but in the social sense, the welfare policies that emerged were evolutionary and limited, only an adjunct to capitalism.

In any event, Keynesian policy and the expanding welfare state were seriously reconsidered in the 1970s and subsequently abandoned in the 1980s. Eroding economic growth and increased government expenditures, in conjunction with broader social and economic changes and an ideological shift towards neoliberalism during the 1980s brought moves towards retrenchment and reform of social welfare systems.

Modern welfare and democratic theory

The area of contemporary social welfare in the industrialised nations continues to be characterised by a struggle between the perception of social equity as a democratic right of CITIZENSHIP and the belief that social policy is a residual area of policy, essential to protect the truly dependent and to maintain social harmony. In many ways, the debate parallels the debate over 'classical' democratic theory. On the one hand, it is argued that 'classical' democratic theory is based on an assumption of broad participation in DECISION-MAKING (Pateman 1970). On the other hand, there is the contention that 'classical' democratic theory rests on institutional arrangements and elected representatives who govern (Schumpeter 1943; Dahl 1970). The former captures the expectation of fulfilling the implicit promise of democratic society. It is based on Rousseau's political theory which argued that individual participation in decision-making is essential, and economic equality and independence are necessary to attain a truly participatory democracy (Pateman 1970: 22–4) and political equality (although, as is well known, Rousseau envisioned small communal societies, or city-states). The latter theory emphasises the effective operation of the machinery of government (see DEMOCRATIC PERFORMANCE) and ELECTORAL BEHAVIOUR, and has little of the normative content implicit in theories of democratic participation: welfare policy follows the *noblesse oblige* approach. It has even been suggested by some adherents of this theory that the stability of modern mass society is dependent upon low participation in electoral politics, to avoid emotional extremism (Lipset 1960, in Fetscher, 1994: 83).

The defining characteristic of democracy is self-governance, clearly requiring participation in the institutions, processes and norms devised to effect democratic rule. In his classical study of democracy, de Toqueville described democracy as a society in which distinctions of rank had been abolished; an egalitarian society, at least in the political and social sense, although certain restrictions (such as gender-based) were deemed appropriate. He also exhibited an aristocrat's fear of the majority – what he called the tyranny of the majority, exemplified in permitting the many, an irrational, unintelligent and uneducated mob – to participate in governing. This attitude – or fear – has permeated democratic theory, creating an uneasiness over the implications of the self-governance principle. Dahl (1970: 64–67), for example, developed his 'Principle of Affected Interests' to include the right to participation for all who would be affected by a government's decision – and then argued his Principle must be curbed by the criteria of Competence and Economy. Yet, if there is to be a realisation of the normative aspects implicit in democratic theory – equality, justice, popular rule and inclusive citizenship – participation is necessary. And if social transformation is to occur, democracy is 'at least the prior if not also [the] fundamental requirement' (Letgers *et al.* 1994: iv), although in 'actually existing democracies' it has not yet fulfilled this potential. Liberal democracy continues to rest on the 'liberal' values of property rights, stability, institutional structure and electoral process rather than the

'democratic' values of equal concern and respect for persons, the values of communal citizenship and the satisfaction of human interests (Letgers *et al.* 1994: xvii). The latter values are the deepest justification for the struggle often required to realise the former.

Gosta Esping-Andersen examines international variations in social rights and welfare state stratification, and identifies three existing models of capitalist (and democratic) welfare states (1990: 26–28). These are the liberal, the conservative (corporatist-statist), and the social democratic. Each has distinguishing features, although in reality, there are many overlaps.

The 'liberal' welfare state relies on means-testing income assistance and 'modest universal transfers or modest social insurance'. This model caters mainly to the low-income working class, and progress in social welfare development has been encumbered by traditional, liberal work ethic norms. Entitlement rules are strict, and associated with social stigma. In such a welfare state, welfare is a residual category of public policy; it focuses on improving the relative position of the very poor. Basically, the purpose of this welfare state ideology is to enable the able-bodied poor to reintegrate into the formal labour market (a 'hand up', not a 'hand out'). These states have a tendency to treat social services such as health care, child care, housing and home care as commodities, requiring the participation of the private sector. Anglo-Saxon nations are predominantly liberal democratic welfare states, although Britain, for example, is far more advanced than is the United States.

The second model of capitalist welfare state identified by Esping-Andersen is the cluster of conservative or historically corporatist-statist welfare states. Essentially, these are the European states that have mostly been shaped by the authoritarian Catholic Church. They place less emphasis on market efficiency and 'commodification' than do the liberal welfare states, and programs typically preserve existing status and class differentials. The state is the primary provider of welfare in these regimes, and occupational fringe benefits based on private insurance play a very minimal role. However, the emphasis is on upholding existing class and status differences and this means that the real redistributive and social equality impacts of the programs are minimal. Furthermore, these regimes are strongly committed to traditional family values preservation; the benefits for non-working wives are typically tied to their husbands' earnings, and generous child benefits and underdeveloped child care programs encourage women to remain out of the workforce.

Finally, Esping-Andersen identifies the characteristics of the social democratic states that are primarily Scandinavian. This cluster of states is smaller than the previous two, and programs are based on the universalism of social rights; programs have been extended to the middle class, ensuring their support for the programs, and especially for the level of taxation needed to sustain them. There has been emphasis in these regimes on the 'decommodification' of services such as health care and child care. Promoted by social democratic governments, these regimes have been committed to reducing the dichotomy between state and market and between working class and middle class. The intent of the social democrats is to achieve services of high rather than minimal standards and they have upgraded them to levels 'commensurate with even the most discriminating tastes of the new middle classes' (Esping-Andersen 1990: 27). This also implies that the workers have been guaranteed full participation in the quality of rights that are enjoyed by the better-off.

As 'neo-liberal' ideology gained strength in the 1990s, all three clusters of welfare state models attempted retrenchment and reform of social programs, but the erosion of programs proved to be more difficult than most anticipated. Entitlements once given are very resistant to withdrawal, and no government has had the courage to submit questions regarding the future of social welfare programs to the electorate in a plebiscite or referendum; that is, to embrace DIRECT DEMOCRACY. Erosion did occur, however, and evidence grew in the 1990s of an increasing disjunction between the accumulation and legitimation functions of the state, as the distance between the wealthy and the working class/poor surged.

Conclusion

In the normative sense, there is clearly more than a tenuous link between welfare and democracy. In addition to the promise of institutional efficacy, procedural fairness, and ELECTORAL COMPETITION, the promise and substance of democratic theory encompass a way of life that values equality, justice, an inclusive conception of citizenship and personal freedom. Existing democracies fall short of this ideal. Human welfare, in the sense of 'getting along well' embodies a broader idea of democratic purpose than sporadic, legitimising and minimal social policy and a *noblesse oblige* approach to inequalities. Indeed, if 'the lasting worth of democracy is in its moral objectives, not just in its decision-making machinery' (Qualter 1986: 260), then democratic theory and practice must seek to encourage the realisation of moral as well as political values.

See also:

democracy, future of; democracy, justifications for; electoral behaviour; inclusion/exclusion; legitimacy; liberalism; participation; procedural democracy; referendums

Further reading

Beveridge, W. (1942) *Social Insurance and Allied Services*, New York: Macmillan.

Briggs, A. (1961) 'The Welfare State in Historical Perspective', *European Journal of Sociology* 2.

Dahl, R.A. (1970) *After the Revolution?*, New Haven, CT: Yale University Press.

Esping-Andersen, G. (1990)*The Three Worlds of Welfare Capitalism*, Cambridge: Polity Press.

Fetscher, I. (1994) 'Democracy and the Majority Principle', in L. Letgers, J. Burke and A. Diquantro (eds), *Critical Perspectives on Democracy*, Boston: Rowman and Littlefield.

Letgers, L., Burke, J. and Diquantro, A. (eds)

(1994) *Critical Perspectives on Democracy*, Boston: Rowman and Littlefield.

Lipset, S. (1960) *Political Man*, London: Heinemann.

O'Brien, M. and Penna, S. (eds) (1998) *Theorizing Welfare: Enlightenment and Modern Society*, London: Sage.

O'Connor, J. (1973) *The Fiscal Crisis of the State*, New York: St. Martin's Press.

Pateman, C. (1970) *Participation and Democratic Theory*, Cambridge: Cambridge University Press.

Perrin, R. (1994) 'Rehabilitating Democratic Theory: The Prospects and the Need', in L. Letgers, J. Burke and A. Diquantro (eds), *Critical Perspectives on Democracy*, Boston: Rowman and Littlefield.

Qualter, T. (1986) *Conflicting Political Ideas in Liberal Democracies*, Toronto: Methuen.

Schumpeter, J. (1943) *Capitalism, Socialism and Democracy*, London: George Allen and Unwin.

Titmuss, R. (1958) *Essays on 'The Welfare State'*, London: Allen and Unwin.

JOAN PRICE BOASE

Westminster model

The system of institutions and procedures for democratic legislation which evolved in England and was widely adopted by the states of the former British Empire, where it mutated into variants of the original model (Low 1918). It was almost universally admired by democrats until the middle of the twentieth century as the only pre-democratic system to have adapted to democratic changes without major political unrest. An ideal typification is difficult and subject to continuing modification because of Westminster's ad hoc and piecemeal development over seven centuries. It is best understood through its history. Nevertheless, among its salient structural characteristics are: (1) a democratically elected parliament which makes the laws; (2) the subordination of the JUDICIARY, the administration and the executive to that parliament which, as the only elected body

in the polity, is sovereign; and (3) an executive or cabinet which cannot act without the support of the majority of members of the parliament. The practical relationships between these institutions have been worked out over centuries and changed and adapted to new circumstances. Their operation is now laid down in a labyrinth of written laws and in long-established unwritten 'conventions'. In the United Kingdom, there is no written constitution. In other Westminster systems, there are written constitutions. In neither is it stated what democracy is.

Unlike other democratic systems the people are not made formally sovereign, in law the 'monarch (executive) in parliament' is sovereign. Moreover, many of its procedures, like that of Cabinet secrecy, conflict with the democratic principle of open government with transparent decisions. The rule of law which governs the operation of a Westminster system and the relations between citizens and the state is a complex of 'common law' decisions and interpretation of legislation by the courts. This common law is seen as the defender of individual rights and the cornerstone of democracy in the system (Dicey 1908; Menzies 1964) (see LAW, RULE OF).

The strength of the Westminster model has been its practical adaptability and capacity for building consensus and compromise. Its weakness is the relatively weak formal place for democracy in its overall structure. Both became obvious as the mutation of the original began when the model was adopted after 1839 in the 'settler' Commonwealth: Canada, Australia, New Zealand and South Africa. The contradictions were compounded when it was further developed in the Indian subcontinent in the first half of the twentieth century and finally in tiny colonies like Fiji and the Cook Islands after the 1960s.

The mutations started because of the British principle of the exclusive SOVEREIGNTY of 'the monarch in Parliament'. This meant that even when it was assumed that emigrants of 'British stock' would inherit the traditions of Westminster, their institutions and procedures could only be created by a British Act of Parliament.

Emigrants therefore had written Constitutions whose powers were necessarily subject to judicial control. Moreover, these new states were vast territories comprising many ethnicities with different value systems. The unitary system established in Britain could only at first be established in limited areas. The existing states are artificial amalgamations by British parliamentary Act of such pre-existing structures in the limited areas of former colonies. Thus Australia was made up of the colonies of New South Wales, Tasmania, Western Australia, South Australia, Queensland and Victoria.

Canada, Australia, South Africa, India (and it was mooted for New Zealand) were therefore established as federations, a complete novelty for the Westminster model. Inspiration was sought above all from the United States' example. Thus there began the 'Washminster' mutation (Thompson 1980, 1994). This created a written federal constitution which restricted sovereignty by its terms. Usually, the governors were the monarch's representatives and had reserved powers to protect the latter's interests (until recently the governors were usually not nationals and were appointed by the Crown); the Cabinet was neither fully sovereign nor fully responsible to Parliament and the Parliament was composed of an Upper House designed to control the excesses of the Lower House by a rigid constitution which was almost impossible to change. The virtue of the Westminster model, its flexibility and adaptability, was completely lost.

On the other hand, its practical democratic dimension was also lost. The federal constitutions of the British imperial dominions were – unlike the US or Swiss model – instrumental documents designed to preserve pre-existing rights in accord with the notion of the sovereignty (albeit limited) of the pre-existing colonial constitutions (*Harris* v. *South Africa* (1952) AC). For example, their power ended at their borders; Britain made all foreign policy. As technical legal documents, read as such for their powers by the judiciary, they did not contain positive contents about the rights of citizens against the state or dramatic statements about popular sovereignty and democracy but left those matters to be worked out by 'convention', which in the Dominions became something on which the judiciary pronounced. The judiciary became very powerful as an institution of government, without being accountable either to Parliament or the electorate (Davidson 1991; Fraser 1990). The result of the absence of bills of rights was a strong, relatively unaccountable, executive and state machinery. The dangers of this were first felt in countries of different ethnicities: India and South Africa, where demands by the local population for Westminster rules provoked repressive state action. They led the critique of the Westminster model before 1945, but they were rapidly joined when the 'white' Commonwealth became multi-ethnic through European migration after 1945. Then newcomers, who had experienced continental European democracy, identified an 'Axminster' mutation, where the population was walked all over by the state because of the absence of grounded rights, particularly a constitution which made clear that the people are sovereign in a democracy.

The critique of the Westminster model in such places came home to the mother of all Parliaments in the 1980s when the vaunted cornerstone of the system, the capacity of the common law to defend citizens against a tyrannical state, was discredited. Statistics made clear that the UK was the worst offender against the European Convention on Human Rights, whose standards it was enjoined to observe by adopting that document domestically. Overall, the model is again in crisis. It remains to be seen if it has the flexibility to adjust again without adopting a written constitution embodying democratic and human rights as law.

History and development

The Westminster model grew out of already existing institutions of a feudal and absolute monarchy which claimed to rule practically at whim according to the 'prerogative'. Starting with the Magna Carta (1215), the monarch's lords subordinated this power to a rule of law. Within its rules, Parliament asserted the right in the next four centuries, especially in the seventeenth century, to share in making all laws, above all to control taxation. The sovereignty of the king in Parliament was finally established as a practical reality by the 1830s. The extension of the franchise in the period 1832–84 gave elected members new power to compel the Executive or Cabinet to be accountable to them alone. This principle of Cabinet responsibility became the linchpin of the claim to democracy at Westminster. It was reinforced in 1911 when the hereditary House of Lords was compelled to accept that it could not block legislation which forced ELECTIONS. With women being given the vote in 1928, Britain could claim to be democratic in fact.

As this progress had been exacted piecemeal and without any overall Constitution being drawn up, the original unaccountable power in the monarch remained as the foundation of legal relations, like a gigantic gruyère cheese, most of which was holes and the prerogative was only the rind. As the monarch remained sovereign, albeit together with Parliament, the people remained formally his subjects and the law his commands to them. A Westminster system leaves the democratic citizen out.

The difference from the French and American Constitutions of the eighteenth century was striking. These stated that the people as citizens were sovereign, and that their rights could not be taken away. It was a canon of political theory that FREEDOM was living under laws which one made for oneself to be a subject was inconsistent with democracy. Moreover, any submission to received wisdom like the common law was regarded as acceptance of patriarchal authority and a refusal of the individual's ability to think (Burke 1774; Kant 1784). Yet, both before and after 1789, Europeans regarded Westminster as a model because they mistakenly attributed to it a separation and balance of powers together with a rule of common law which prevented any popular tyranny arising from the political assertion of universal rights (Montesquieu 1964; Gauchet 1989). It did adapt without the frequent political revolutions and bloodshed of nineteenth-century Europe. This view had

some validity until the middle of the nineteenth century, but it was undermined by the development of complex societies. In fact, the protection of democracy in a Westminster model always lay in the strength of responsible government which was built up in the nineteenth century. It was the only way that power 'from below' could be guaranteed.

The vices and virtues identified by Europeans became stronger as the state grew and had to cope with the crises of the twentieth century. There was an incremental development of administrative rule resting on the formal sovereign power really vested in Cabinet, a secret council. Party discipline ensured that no member would challenge its decisions without sanction. While its power had been offset by the extension of the franchise in 1832, 1867, 1884, 1918 and 1928, that enfranchising legislation could be repealed or ignored by a sovereign Parliament. The central debate from the 1930s onward was how and what limits could be posed to the tendency towards irresponsible Cabinet government (Ivor Jennings 1947). The rights of individuals against a state which could do no wrong were inadequately protected by incoherent extensions of the common law into rules of natural justice in an invented administrative law based on continental principles. While the need for a Bill of Rights became ever clearer, it faced centuries of received wisdom that rights were nonsense on stilts.

Nowhere was this clearer than in the 'white' Empire which inherited the 'six hundred year patrimony' of Westminster. Durham's Report (1839) proposed responsible government for Canada, and by the 1850s it was catch-cry in Australia and New Zealand as well. By the 1890s the colonies' Westminsters had outstripped Britain by introducing adult SUFFRAGE. All the forms, down to the mace, were reduplicated. But the hidden defects were magnified greatly. The judiciary decided the extent of power under the Constitution and whether legislation was beyond power (Davidson 1991; Fraser 1990). Where the principle was that the monarch in Parliament could do no wrong and so no legislation could be reviewed in Britain, the converse was the rule in the Dominions. The judgements significantly reduced the democratic and human rights ingredient in the original model. Loss of belief in the common law as the defence of the people was already clear in India and Africa in the 1940s, where, for example, Gandhi, Nehru and Mandela all started as believers in its efficacy.

While each Dominion developed its own jurisprudence, particularly after 1931 when Westminster declared that the Dominions could make their own foreign policy, common themes emerged. All highlighted how undemocratic the system was in new contexts.

Summary

Chief among these themes was the failure of the common law to defend the individual citizen against the State. Starting with the constitution of newly independent India (1948), Bills of Rights were written into such documents. The Canadian Charter (1982) came next in a peaceful transition. It was followed by South Africa and New Zealand, leaving Australia and Britain as the only states not to adopt such documents, considered essential to democracy after the Universal Declaration of Human Rights of the UN. In both it has been mooted constantly in the last decade. British resistance to its obligations under the equivalent European Convention seems finally overcome in 1998. The decision to eliminate the House of Lords – a last vestige of undemocratic power – also augurs a recognition of popular sovereignty in law there. Australia is most reluctant to reform its system.

See also:

constitutional design; constitutional monarchy; constitutionalism; imperialism; judiciary; law, rule of; legitimacy; parliamentary models

Further reading

Burke, E. (1774) 'Speech to the Electors of Bristol', in *Speeches and Letters on American Affairs*, London: Everyman.

Davidson, A. (1991) *The Invisible State The Formation of the Australian State 1788–1901*, Cambridge: Cambridge University Press.

Dicey, A. (1908) *Introduction to the Study of the Law of the Constitution*, London: Macmillan.

Fraser, A. (1990) *The Spirit of the Laws: Republicanism and the Unfinished Project of Modernity*, Toronto: University of Toronto Press.

Gauchet, M. (1989) *La Revolution des droits de l'homme*, Paris: Gallimard.

Ivor Jennings, W. (1947) *Cabinet Government*, Cambridge: Cambridge University Press.

Kant, I. (1784) 'What is Enlightenment?', in C. Friedrichs (ed.), *The Philosophy of Kant: Immanuel Kant's Moral and Political Writings*, New York: Modern Library.

Low, D. (1918) *The Governance of England*, London: Fisher Unwin.

Menzies, R. (1964) *Central Power in the Australian Commonwealth*, Melbourne: Cassell.

Montesquieu, C. (1964) *Oeuvres complètes*, Paris: Seuil.

Thompson, E. (1980) 'The Washminster Mutation', in D. Jaensch and P. Weller (eds), *Responsible Government in Australia*, Sydney: Drummond.

—— (1994) 'The Washminster Republic', in G. Winterton (ed.), *We, the People: Australian Republican Government*, Sydney: Allen and Unwin.

ALASTAIR DAVIDSON

NAME INDEX

Name index

Name index

Gilbert, A. 540
Gilbert, P. 284–7, 637–41
Gilligan, C. 303
Gintis, H. 663
Gleditsch, K. 509
Godwin, W. 161, 162
Goldblatt, D. 308, 625, 626
Goodin, R.E. 147–8, 315–6, 319–20, 363
Goodwin-Gill, G.S. 248
Goodwyn, L. 548
Gordon, M. 16
Gosnell, H. 572
Gottman, E. 323
Gramsci, A. 67–8; hegemony 327–9; transformism 533–4
Grant, W. 114
Gray, J. 8, 239, 307, 349
Green, L. 21
Green, S. 402
Green, T.H. 535
Greenfeld, L. 456
Greenstein, F.I. 398
Greider, W. 518
Grotius, H. 639
Gump, J. 63
Gunderson, A. 144, 146
Gunther, R. 175
Gurr, T.R. 351, 353, 354, 705
Gutenberg, J. 84, 85
Gutierrez, G. 420–1
Gutmann, A. 489
Gwyn, W.B. 648

Haas, P. 184, 370
Habermas, J. 130, 179, 180, 270–1, 329, 402, 531, 591; deliberative democracy 89, 138, 193, 287, 489, 568, 577, 516; ideal speech situation 50, 271; public sphere 68, 433, 582; solidarity 671–2
Hadenius, A. 115–7, 185–8, 444–5
Haksar, V. 510–3
Halifax, Lord 285–6
Hall, P. 463, 659
Hall, S. 284
Hamburger, J. 286
Hamilton, A. 45, 289, 649
Hankiss, E. 618
Hannaford, I. 281
Haraway, D. 643, 645
Hardin, C.M. 651
Hardin, R. 80–3, 337–40, 486–92
Harding, N. 625
Hare, R.M. 286
Harrington, J. 473, 613–4, 671
Harris, J. 392
Harrop, M. 246
Hart, H.L.A. 340–2, 392, 620, 675; special/general rights 557–8
Hart, R.P. 83–6
Hartsock, N. 275–6, 303

Harvey, N. 633–5
Haurion, M. 363
Havel, V. 425
Hayek, F. 164, 191, 415
Heald, D. 560
Hearl, D. 690
Heclo, H. 190, 373
Hegel, G.W.F. 26, 67, 87, 107, 327, 328, 461, 532, 541, 542, 559; civil society 327, 664, 670
Heidegger, M. 593
Heidenheimer, A.J. 116, 117, 527
Heilbroner, R. 314, 315, 318
Held, D. 9, 604, 623; cosmopolitan democracy 120–3, 310; globalisation 306–11, 641, 687
Helliwell, J. 116, 202, 235
Herder, J.G. 453
Herodotus 194, 197
Herz, J.J. 34
Hexter, J.H. 540
Higgins, R. 655
Highley, J. 175
Hindess, B. 660–3
Hindley, J. 280–4
Hinsley, F.H. 274
Hipparchus 197
Hirschmann, N. 303–4
Hirst, P. 307, 308; associational democracy 18–29, 299–300
Hitler, A. 43, 85, 172
Hix, S. 370
Hobbes, T. 21, 25, 81, 105, 106, 117, 163, 281, 365, 367, 486, 532, 600, 601, 673, 674; *Leviathan* 21, 46, 540–1, 542; social contract theory 536, 638–40; state of nature 82, 363
Hobson, J.A. 222, 344
Hobson, S.G. 514
Hofferbert, R. 313
Hoffman, S. 370
Hoffman-Martinot, V. 522
Hohfeld, W. 340–1
Holdich, R. 702
Hollinger, D. 17
Holmes, O.W. 43
Holmes, S. 425
Holt, J. 243
Holyoake, G.J. 18
Homer 543, 645
Honig, B. 590
Honoré, A.M. 557
Hood, C. 700–4
Horkheimer, M. 270
Horton, J. 535–9
Howarth, D. 191–4, 346–51, 530–5
Howes, M. 465
Huber, J.D. 90, 331
Hume, D. 110, 285, 359, 486, 541, 643, 644
Hume, L. 702
Hunt, A. 402, 403

Name index

Locke, A. 670
Locke, J. 21, 105, 110, 163–4, 281, 333, 396, 536, 558, 559, 623, 624, 642, 644, 688, 695, 696; natural rights theory 81, 628; *Second Treatise of Government* 21, 248–9, 411, 541, 558, 560, 600
Long, H. 77
Longley, D. 617
Loomis, B.A. 374
Lorwin, V. 92
Lovemann, B.E. 435–8
Low, D. 714
Lowe, A.V. 33
Lukes, S. 107
Lupia, A. 212
Luther, K.R. 91–3
Luther, M. 84, 539–40, 684
Lutz-Bachmann, M. 640
Lybeck, J. 76
Lyotard, J.-F. 329, 516

Mabbot, J.B. 637
McAllister, I. 561
McCallum R.B. 572
McClosky, H. 44
McClure, K. 514–5
McCubbins, M.D. 212, 323–4
McDowell, J. 377
Machiavelli, N. 25, 27, 58, 221, 365–6, 539, 540, 613, 623, 671
MacIntyre, A. 87, 348, 587–8
McIver, S. 51
McKay, D. 519–21, 594–8
McKelvey, R. 44, 79
McKenzie, E. 34
MacKenzie, W.J.M. 333
Macmillan, H. 478
MacPherson, C.B. 280
McQuail, D. 432–5
McRae, K.D. 92
Madison, J. 45, 129, 289, 321, 322, 324, 372, 486, 575, 579, 600–1, 648–9
Magleby, D.B. 595
Mainwaring, S. 171, 203, 210, 267
Mair, P. 76, 266, 267, 495
Mandela, N. 306, 717
Mann, M. 31, 307
Manor, J. 128
Mansbridge, J. 231
March, J.G. 202, 363, 583, 584, 586
Marcuse, H. 270, 271, 579
Maritain, J. 377
Marks, G. 369
Marshall, T. 11, 52, 54, 617, 665; social citizenship 54, 55, 271, 666
Marsilius of Padua 110, 536, 599, 600, 613, 623
Marx, K. 12, 37, 39, 67, 87, 328, 339, 449, 587–9; class 72–3, 109, 327, 454, 670; critique of democracy 587–8, 589, 592; emancipation 269–71
Mawhood, P. 127

May, L. 670
Mayall, J. 497
Mazowiecki, T. 425
Mazzini, G. 453
Mead, G.H. 333
Meadowcroft, J. 316, 318
Meciar, V. 424
Medhurst, K. 683–6
Meighan, R. 239–44
Mendus, S. 695–8
Merkl, P. 493
Merriam, C. 78, 572
Méry, Y. 190
Metz, J.B. 670
Meyer, D.S. 60–4
Michelman, F. 615
Michels, R. 475, 493, 526
Midlarsky, M.I. 142
Milgram, S. 642
Mill, J. 11, 163, 692
Mill, J.S. 42–3, 58, 67, 126–7, 138, 163, 164–5, 281, 291, 295, 348, 380, 438, 446, 462, 489, 539, 576, 609, 633, 656, 688–9, 692, 693, 694; *On Liberty* 695–6; utilitarianism 318, 601
Millard, F. 424–6
Miller, D. 457, 537
Miller, N.R. 421–3
Miller, W.L. 246
Millon-Delsol, C. 688
Mills, C.W. 281, 475
Milward, A. 370
Minoves-Triquell, J. 98–100
Misra, B.D. 345
Mitchell, T.C. 680
Mitrany, D. 369
Mohammed, M. 157
Moltmann, J. 670
Montaigne, M. 333
Montesquieu, C.L. 104, 321, 366, 368, 372, 486, 613, 614, 648, 650, 688, 716
Moore, B. Jr. 172, 214, 235, 237–8
Moore, W.E. 703
Moran, J. 424
Moran, M. 562
Morgenthau, H.J. 638
Morris, C. 673–6
Morris, I. 195
Morris, W. 87
Morriss, P. 619–22, 691–4
Mosca, G. 475
Moscovici, S. 221
Mosher, M. 643, 645
Mouffe, C. 193, 329, 336, 337, 350, 505, 532–3, 534, 588, 589, 590, 591; antagonistic conception of democracy 592–4
Mueller, D. 417
Mulgan, R. 447
Muller, M. 687
Munck, G. 175–8, 207–11

Name index

Renn, D. 50
Requejo, F. 289–93, 453–7
Rhodes, R.A.W. 125–9
Rich, P. 370
Richardson, J.J. 372, 373
Richter, M. 648
Rief, K.-H. 254
Riefenstahl, L. 85
Riker, W. 44, 45, 46, 130, 212, 423, 547, 564, 578; coalitions 79
Riley, P. 601
Roberts, J.M. 411
Robertson, D. 380–4, 384–7, 395–7
Robinson, N. 35–8
Rockman, B.A. 584, 585
Rogers, C. 241
Rogers, J. 299, 300
Rokkan, S. 75–6, 250, 267, 455, 501
Rondinelli, A. 125, 126, 127
Roosevelt, F. 85, 399, 518
Rootes, C. 465–7
Rorty, A. 643
Rorty, R. 193, 640, 671–2; 'final vocabulary' 107
Rose, R. 527
Rosenberg, M. 11
Ross, A. 138
Rousseau, D. 508
Rousseau, J.-J. 6, 11, 26, 54, 57, 58, 178, 249, 365, 372, 408, 410, 411, 446, 462, 519, 587–8, 592, 599, 613, 642, 643; democracy, theory of 587–8; general will 44, 162–3, 224, 296–8, 537, 567–8, 575–6, 673; political order 541–2; social contract 280, 281, 536, 541, 567, 601, 613–4
Rowbotham, S. 503, 505
Roxborough, I. 443
Rueschemeyer, D. 172, 173, 202, 216, 235, 236, 238
Rummel, R. 508–9
Russell, B. 165
Russett, B. 116, 507–10
Rustow, D. 208, 497, 498, 667
Ryan, A. 558

Saalfeld, T. 698–700
Sack, R.D. 32
Said, E. 686
Saidman, S. 336
Saint-Simon, C.H. 514
Salamon, L.A. 585
Sandel, M. 147, 566–7, 642, 643–4, 645
Sani, G. 203
Sartori, G. 203, 500
Saussure, F. 28, 533
Saxonhouse, A.W. 194–202, 217–20
Scarbrough, E. 74–6, 248–53, 492–6, 522
Schadler, A. 175
Schaeffer, R.K. 654
Schattschneider, E.E. 372, 423
Schick, A. 323

Schmitt, C. 591, 598; concept of the political 6, 542, 681; political theology 25, 532
Schmitt, H. 254
Schmitter, P. 369, 517, 522, 667
Schofield, N. 44–7, 79, 80
Schumpeter, J.A. 13, 150, 163, 351, 417, 491, 576, 577, 618, 681, 711; realist model of democracy 563
Schutz, A. 28
Schwartz, P. 690
Scully, T.R. 267
Seigfried, A. 572
Selbourne, D. 230, 232
Sen, A. 312
Seneca 10
Sened, I. 79–80
Shakespeare, W. 25
Shanks, J.M. 250
Shapiro, I. 473
Sharp, G. 223
Shaw, M. 638
Shepsle, K. 44, 79, 212
Sher, G. 512
Shils, E. 100, 286, 547
Shklar, J. 151, 694
Shugart, M. 210, 264, 321, 322, 551–7
Siculus, D. 24
Sidgwick, H. 541
Silbey, S. 402
Simmel, G. 656, 657
Simmons, A.J. 538
Singer, P. 537, 565
Sinnott, R. 253–7
Siraj-Blatchford, I. 242, 244
Skinner, Q. 623
Skocpol, T. 463
Skowronek, S. 464
Smith, A. 355–6, 357, 367, 560–1
Smith, B.C. 126, 127
Socrates 53, 161–2, 201, 219
Solon 24, 53, 194, 196–7, 365, 599, 601
Sophocles 61, 200
Sørensen, E. 129
Spencer, M. 497–8, 499, 652–6
Spinoza, B. 602
Spitz, E. 427
Squires, J. 273–7, 302, 580–2
Stalin, J. 652
Starkey, T. 25, 600
Stavrakakis, Y. 333–7
Steed, M. 315, 316, 317, 318
Steiner, J. 92, 130–2
Steinmo, S. 462–5
Stepan, A. 151, 155, 156, 172, 173, 177, 208, 210 216; democratic transition 623, 706, 707–8
Stewart, J. 50
Stokes, G. 128
Stone, J. 438–41
Strawson, P.F. 355
Strong, T.B. 539–43, 641–7

Name index

SUBJECT INDEX

Subject index

community, political 272, 498; recovery of 584; Sandel's critique 566–7

computers, effects on democracy *see* communication; electronic democracy; information

confederalism 291; *see also* federalism

Congo-Brazzaville 187

Congo-Kinshasa (Zaire) 187

Congress Party 13

conscription, military 541

consensus democracy **90–1**, 180, 428, 439, 482, 484–5, 501; coercion and 82; decision-making in 131; non-consensualism 591; responsiveness to public opinion 578

consent theory 81, 162–3

conservatism 338–9

consociationalism 90, **91–3**, 281, 439, 485, 549; cleavages and 93; minority rights and 283; sub-cultures, role of 92, 349, 413

consolidation *see* democratic consolidation

constitutional courts 103, 382–4

constitutional design **94–7**; balance with democracy 97; democratic transition and 216; immunities and protections **340–2**; power-concentration 97; power-diffusion 97

constitutional monarchy 46, 98, **98–100**, 461, 715–16; non-democratic 99; Westminster model and 715–16

constitutional review 380–2

constitutional rights 630

constitutionalism 93, 94, **100–3**, 104; authoritarian 437; civil society 71, 435–6; medieval 435; military *see* military constitutionalism; negative 100, 102; origins of 541; positive 101, 102; tension with democracy 102–3, 630–1

constitutions: immunities 340–2; protections 341; purpose of 100, 492; nominal 101–2; stable democracies with written constitutions 428

constraint **103–6**; decision-rules and 134–5; exclusion, use of 104–5; role in democracy 105–6; state constitutional 100

consumerism, promotion of 561

contestation 8, 10, **106–8**, 164, 473; agonism and 106; cleavages 74–5

continental philosophy 357

contingency **108–13**, 193, 591; ethos of 193

contract law 81–2

contractarianism 281, 418, 446, 457, 486; *see also* social contract theory

Cook Islands 714

corporatism **113–14**, 299, 560; associationalism 19; consensus democracy 90; eco-corporatism 143–4; interest groups and 372, 519–21; neo-corporatism 113–14; third way, the 113

correlates of democracy **115–17**; economic development 215–16, 235–6; industrial development 115; wealth 116, 235–6; *see also* indicators of democracy

corruption **117–20**; civil service 66; clientelism 77–8; codes of political conduct 677; future of democracy and 156; good practice and 312, 313; institutional 118–19; legislation and 119; market centered 118;

politicians and 676–9; political 117–18, 119, 155–6, 618; political financing and 528–9; state 100, 117; transparency and 702–3

cosmopolitan democracy **120–3**, 641; citizenship 84; globalisation as a major force for 120–3

Costa Rica 203, 428

Council of Europe 60, 413, 634

crime, political: justice and 424; lustration and 424–5

crises of democracy *see* democratic breakdown

critical theory 270, 589; democracy, concept of 588; radical democracy and 593

Croatia 440, 499

Cuba 172–3, 174

culture: acculturation 16; assimilation 15–17; bureaucratic 35–6; civic 56, 522, 523–4; contingency and 109, 111; legitimacy 12; multiculturalism 17; *see also* identity, political; political culture

Cyprus 554, 556

Czechoslovakia 169, 170, 185, 497, 518, 633, 654; deliberative democratisation in 490, 491, 521; lustration 424–5, 621; Velvet Revolution 622

debt: bondage of 450–1; international finance institutions and 450; mortgaged democracies 447–52

decentralisation **125–9**, 290, 429; advantages of 127; associational democracy 19–20; democracy and 127; environmental politics and 146, 318; functional/territorial 514; local government and 126–7; managerial 128–9; mutualist socialism 18; problems of 126–7; state 34; subsidiarity and 690

decision-making 44, **130–2**; cabinet governments 189–90; capital mobility 40–1; chaos and coalitions **44–7**; consensus democracy 91; cosmopolitan democracy 121; factionalism 323; indecision and 322–4; by interpretation 131; majoritarianism 91; perfect/imperfect procedures of 563–5; procedural democracy 562–8; referendums and effects on 597; trade-offs and 211–13; veto power 322–3 *see also* policy-making

decision-rules 130, **132–7**; log-rolling and 422; monetary policy 171–4

Declaration of the Rights of Man and the Citizen 26, 101, 105, 241, 249, 411, 513, 675

decommunisation 424–6; *see also* lustration

deconcentration 125–6

deconstruction, theory of 107, 532–4; ethnicity 533; feminist political thought and 302–3, 505; political identity and 532–4; radical democracy 588, 591–4; *see also* difference; discourse analysis; structuralism/post structuralism

defence: civic virtue 58

delegates and delegation 603–4, 607–8; trustees and 610

deliberative democracy 23, 50–1, **137–41**, 179, 547; Czechoslovakia and 490; communitarianism 88, 89; information and 360, 361; procedural democracy and 568; public opinion, role of 577; radical democracy and 590, 593

deliberative polling 160, 577

254; determining strategies of 574; funding 254, 256–7, 373, 487, 519–21, 526–30; interest groups and their effect on 373–4; political action committees 519–21; use of media and technology 255–7
electoral competition 149, **257–60**; median voter preference 212, 258–9; modes of 258–9; party organisation and 258–9, 501–2; salience theory 259–60; unconstrained 133
electoral culture 246; *see also* political culture
electoral rules *see* electoral systems
electoral systems 79–80, 246, 247–8, **260–5**; alternative vote 262; design of 260; effects of on party systems 264–5; double ballot 262; fair and neutral 461–2; geographical psephology 574, 608; good practice and 312; hybrid systems 263–4, 330–1; logrolling and 422; majoritarianism and 428, 610; multi-member systems 262–3; proportionality principle and 569–72, 609; ring-fencing and 708; single-member systems 261–2, 264, 569–70, 574; single-transferable vote 263, 570, 605, 609–10; suffrage and 245–6; types of 261–4; *see also* party systems; representation, models of
electoral volatility **266–8**, 501; gross/net 266–7; measurement of 266; Pedersen Index 266; party systems and 267–8
electoralism, fallacy of 150–1, 152–3
electronic democracy 12, 85–6, 159–60; *see also* information; internet
elites 14, 475; accommodation of in democracy 92; anti-elitism 514; bargaining and 522–3; democratic transition, role of 667; good practice and 313; political control of 93; political culture and 522; theory 563, 618–19
emancipation **268–73**, 588; autonomy and 270; communication theory (Habermas) 271; critical theory and 270–1; as the extension of democratic politics and rights 271–3; feminism and 269, 302 (*see also* patriarchy); Marx's theory of 269–71
employment: capitalism 40
empowerment **273–7**; bureaucracy 37; class 73; democracy as promoting 446; and differing conceptions of power 274–5; feminism and 273, 274, 275–6; as the quest for social equality 279–80; theories of 274–6
enfranchisement *see* suffrage
environmentalism 314–21; deep ecology 147; democracy and 141–9, 316–21 (*see also* green democratic thought); direct action and 222–3; ethics of 143; global impact 122, 145, 148; NGO's 466–7; political theory and 141–9, 314–21; public opinion and 579; resource scarcity 141
equality 162, **277–80**, 511–13; accountability 3; affirmative action 3–5; authority 23; capitalism 40; and citizenship 52, 278, 280, 302; concept of justice and 388; 'democratic equality' (Rawls) 280; democratic revolution and (Lefort) 513–14; different conceptions of 277–8; direct democracy and 280; feminist theory 279, 302–3, 304; gender equality 302–3, 304; history of the concept 277; intrinsic equality (Dahl)

277; juridical equality 278–9; as a justification for democracy 162–3, 411, 446, 470; patriarchy and 504; perfectionism and 511–12; political participation and 278–9; polyarchy and 545–6; procedural 181; separation of powers and 95; social democracy and 660; social equality 279–80; struggle for by social movements 665–6; *see also* proportionality
equivalences, relations of 329, 592–4; *see also* radical democracy
eschatology 110; apocalyptic turn 111
essentialism and identity 334–5
Estonia 170, 185, 291, 654
Ethiopia 654
ethnic cleansing 33, 282, 379, 499
ethnicity **280–4**; assimilation 15; boundaries 32–3, 281, 282, 377–6; conflict and 496–8, 499; differentiation and 533; ethno-nationalisms 282; partition and 496–7; statelessness and 686–8; theoretical approaches 282–3; *see also* minorities; nations and nationalism; rights, minority and indigenous
Europe, Eastern 155, 157, 169, 185, 267, 376, 509; feudalism 72; revolutions of 1989 46, 343, 424–6, 490, 522, 524, 626
Europe, Western 157, 185; cleavage model of politics 75; electoral behaviour, study of 250–1; electoral volatility in 267; trade unionism 698
European Parliament 182; cosmopolitan democracy 122
European Union (EU) 155, 369–71, 417, 606, 688–91; central bank and monetary union 41, 135–6, 182–3, 206, 370, 450, 690; citizenship 54, 55–6, 58, 60; Council of Ministers 182, 206, 703; decision-making in 130, 182–3; democratic deficit and 9, 11, 182–4; elections 11; history of 369–70; human rights, missions of 413–14; integration and 368, 369–71, 689; Maastricht Treaty 54, 182, 183, 370, 456, 596; membership conditions of 413; minority and indigenous rights 634; nationalism and 456–7; referendums 596–7; Single European Act 1986 182, 596, 689; subsidiarity and 688–91; theory of federalism and 370–1; transparency and 703–4
evil, problem of 108
exclusion *see* inclusion/exclusion
Exclusive Economic Zone 33
executive orders 393
executives, democratic **188–91**; functions of 188–9; irredentism 376; relationship with legislature 482–3; *see also* leadership, democratic
experts, rule of 59–60
extremism **284–7**; democratic policy and 286–7; terrorism 286

factionalism: Asia 14; gridlock and 322–4
fascism 86, 88, 170, 171–2, 222; church/state relations and 684
federalism 90, 104, **289–93**, 429, 457, 715; confederations 291; decentralisation and 126; federal agreements 289–91; history of 289; integration, theory of

Subject index

Subject index